HANDBOOK OF RISK AND CRISIS COMMUNICATION

The *Handbook of Risk and Crisis Communication* explores the scope and purpose of risk, and its counterpart, crisis, to facilitate the understanding of these issues from conceptual and strategic perspectives. Recognizing that risk is a central feature of our daily lives, found in relationships, organizations, governments, the environment, and a wide variety of interactions, contributors to this volume explore such questions as "What is likely to happen, to whom, and with what consequences?" "To what extent can science and vigilance prevent or mitigate negative outcomes?" and "What obligation do some segments of local, national, and global populations have to help other segments manage risks?", shedding light on the issues in the quest for definitive answers.

The *Handbook* offers a broad approach to the study of risk and crisis as joint concerns. Chapters explore the reach of crisis and risk communication, define and examine key constructs, and parse the contexts of these vital areas. As a whole, the volume presents a comprehensive array of studies that highlight the standard principles and theories on both topics, serving as the largest effort to date focused on engaging risk communication discussions in a comprehensive manner.

With perspectives from psychology, sociology, anthropology, political science, economics, and communication, the *Handbook of Risk and Crisis Communication* enlarges the approach to defining and recognizing risk and how should it best be managed. It provides vital insights for all disciplines studying risk, including communication, public relations, business, and psychology, and will be required reading for scholars and researchers investigating risk and crisis in various contexts.

Robert L. Heath, Ph.D., is a retired Professor of Communication at the University of Houston. He has engaged in risk communication studies since the early 1990s, primarily related to the relationship between chemical manufacturing complexes and near neighbors. Dr. Heath's numerous publications include encyclopedias, handbooks, textbooks, edited volumes, and journal articles.

H. Dan O'Hair, Ph.D., is Professor of Communication and Director of Advanced Programs in the Department of Communication at the University of Oklahoma. He is the immediate past editor of the *Journal of Applied Communication Research*, and has served as an associate editor for over a dozen scholarly journals. Dr. O'Hair has authored and co-authored research articles and scholarly book chapters in the fields of communication, health, medicine, and business.

ROUTLEDGE COMMUNICATION SERIES

Jennings Bryant/Dolf Zillman, General Editors

Selected titles in Public Relations (James Grunig, Advisory Editor) include:

Aula/Mantere – *Strategic Reputation Management: Towards Company of Good*

Austin/Pinkleton – *Strategic Public Relations Management: Planning and Managing Effective Communication Programs, Second Edition*

Botan/Hazleton – *Public Relations Theory II*

Fearn-Banks – *Crisis Communications: A Casebook Approach, Second Edition*

Hearit – *Crisis Management by Apology: Corporate Response to Allegations of Wrongdoing*

Lamb/McKee – *Applied Public Relations: Cases in Stakeholder Management*

Lerbinger – *The Crisis Manager: Facing Risk and Responsibility*

Millar/Heath – *Responding to Crisis: A Rhetorical Approach to Crisis Communication*

Van Ruler/Tkalac Vercic/Vercic – *Public Relations Metrics: Research and Evaluation*

HANDBOOK OF RISK AND CRISIS COMMUNICATION

Edited by

Robert L. Heath

H. Dan O'Hair

Routledge
Taylor & Francis Group
NEW YORK AND LONDON

First published 2009
by Routledge
270 Madison Ave, New York, NY 10016

Simultaneously published in the UK
by Routledge
2 Park Square, Milton Park, Abingdon, Oxon OX14 4RN

Routledge is an imprint of the Taylor & Francis Group, an informa business

Typeset in Times and Helvetica by EvS Communication Networx, Inc.
Printed and bound in the United States of America on acid-free paper by Edwards Brothers, Inc.

Library of Congress Cataloging in Publication Data
Handbook of risk and crisis communication / Robert L. Heath and H. Dan O'Hair, editors. — 1st ed.
p. cm.
1. Risk management—Handbooks, manuals, etc. 2. Crisis management—Handbooks, manuals, etc. 3. Emergency management—Handbooks, manuals, etc. 4. Communication in management—Handbooks, manuals, etc. I. Heath, Robert L. (Robert Lawrence), 1941- II. O'Hair, Dan.
HD61.H325 2008
658.4'5—dc22
2008003266

ISBN10: 0-8058-5777-X (hbk)
ISBN10: 0-203-89162-7 (ebk)

ISBN13: 978-0-8058-5777-1 (hbk)
ISBN13: 978-0-203-89162-9 (ebk)

Contents

Contributors

Linda Aldoory
University of Maryland

Matthew T. Allen
University of Oklahoma

Peter A. Andersen
San Diego State University

Amanda D. Angie
University of Oklahoma

Joseph Arvai
Michigan State University and Decision Research

Cindi Atkinson
University of Oklahoma

Elizabeth Johnson Avery
University of Tennessee–Knoxville

Kevin J. Ayotte
California State University, Fresno

Daniel Rex Bernard
University of Oklahoma

John C. Besley
University of South Carolina

Carl H. Botan
George Mason University

Shannon A. Bowen
Syracuse University

Michael D. Bruce
University of Oklahoma

Cristina L. Byrne
University of Oklahoma

Caron Chess
Rutgers University

Shane Connelly
University of Oklahoma

W. Timothy Coombs
Eastern Illinois University

Vincent T. Covello
Center for Risk Communication

Josh L. Davis
University of Oklahoma

Wändi Bruine de Bruin
Carnegie Mellon University

Julie S. Downs
Carnegie Mellon University

Jaye Ellis
McGill University

Karen Farnsworth
George Mason University

Baruch Fischhoff
Carnegie Mellon University

Christopher Galloway
Swinburne University of Technology

Catherine E. Goodall
The Ohio State University

Kirk Hallahan
Colorado State University

Robert L. Heath
University of Houston

Keith Michael Hearit
Western Michigan University

Bradford Hesse
National Cancer Institute's Health Communication and Informatics Research Branch

Gary L. Kreps
George Mason University

Branden Johnson
Rutgers University

Shirley Leitch
University of Wollongong

Katherine A. McComas
Cornell University

Steve Maguire
McGill University

Ed Maibach
George Mason University

David McKie
University of Waikato

Judy Motion
University of Wollongong

Michael D. Mumford
University of Oklahoma

Kurt Neuwirth
University of Cincinnati

H. Dan O'Hair
University of Oklahoma

Michael J. Palenchar
University of Tennessee

Ingar Palmlund
Independent Scholar

Tarla Rai Peterson
Texas A&M University

Stephanie Proutheau
CELSA, Paris IV – Sorbonne University

Steve Rayner
Oxford University

Ortwin Renn
University of Stuttgart

Barbara Reynolds
Centers For Disease Control and Prevention

Kasie Mitchell Roberson
Miami University

Anthony J. Roberto
Arizona State University

Katherine E. Rowan
George Mason University

Michael Ryan
University of Houston

Lynne M. Sallot
University of Georgia

Sergei Samoilenko
George Mason University

Matthew W. Seeger
Wayne State University

Timothy L. Sellnow
University of Kentucky

Brian H. Spitzberg
San Diego State University

Jeffrey K. Springston
University of Georgia

James Tansey
University of British Columbia

Jessica Leigh Thompson
Colorado State University

Robert R. Ulmer
University of Arkansas at Little Rock

Jami VanCamp
Oklahoma City University

Courtney Vaughn
University of Oklahoma

Kim Witte
Michigan State University

Introduction

Risk is an amazing concept. It has lingered on the fringe of academics for years, but only in the past three decades has its broad application and examination become adopted. It becomes more widely adopted, in large part because it is so relevant to management and communication themes.

It's a bird's nest on the ground. It can help to explain interpersonal relationships, and the communication used to create, maintain, and terminate them. People put themselves at risk of not being seen as interpersonally attractive. We risk not being seen as a worthy friend, family member, or romantic partner. As we engage with others, good and bad outcomes can occur and with various degrees of predictability and consequence. Risk arises as individuals work to become romantic partners. And, risks occur as they are romantic partners, and if either decides to terminate such relationships.

Likewise, risk is a central feature of organizational communication, and strategic business management. Organizations put capital at risk, regardless of whether they are for profit, non-profit, or governmental. They work on the simple, but actually daunting logic, if this expenditure under X risks, then Y outcome. Some companies, government agencies, and non-profits explicitly are in the risk management business. Banks and insurance companies, as well as regulatory agencies (such as those that oversee worker or consumer safety), and non-profits such as American Heart Association or American Cancer Society work to understand and help targeted individuals manage risks. Management works to help employees manage risks of employment. Organizations are variously risk takers, the definition of the entrepreneurial organization, as opposed to the risk averse bureaucratic organization. Advertising is essentially predicated on risk management as its rationale for communication. Ad after ad advises people how they can manage various risks in life, ranging from the best purchase for a child or spouse at Christmas or other holiday, to matters of personal grooming, hygiene, and health.

News is all about risk. It features bad outcomes because a fatal automobile accident provides a kind of useful information for those who seem interested in knowing why a fatality occurred so they can manage such matters for themselves and others. Political discussion centers on risk management: Risks of higher taxes, unfunded projects, bad trade agreements, wars, terrorism, epidemics, storms, and fires6an endless list. Even TV sit-coms deal with risks. The risks of being caught in a lie or not being prepared to engage effectively with someone, especially someone who is ruthless or devious (the basis of soap operas?).

This volume tries to embrace the scope and purpose of risk and its counterpart crisis to better understand them conceptually and strategically. Such matters are not trivial. The essence of sound risk and crisis management are matters of safety, security, happiness, good health, sound financial future, and other matters that variously have individual or public consequences for positive and negative outcomes of various magnitudes. What is likely to happen, to whom, and with what consequences? To what extent can sound science and vigilance prevent or mitigate negative outcomes? Is the occurrence and outcome fairly and equally distributed, or does some factor such as power or money skew the risks? Is risk management something for elites, or is it truly the essence of democracy, thus the concept of risk democracy? Is the rationale of society the collective management of risk? Are those individuals, groups, and society's "best" which can more successfully manage the risks they encounter? What obligations do some segments of local, national, and global populations have to help other segments manage risks? How does discourse help, and hinder this process? These questions arise in various ways in this book, which often helps to shed light, but does not provide definitive answers on such matters.

The book constitutes, as far as we know, the first broad approach to risk and crisis as joint concerns. It also presents the most comprehensive array of studies in one place that brings out the standard principles and theories on both topics. It is the most major effort on the part of communication academics to engage in risk communication discussions in some comprehensive manner. Previous risk studies have been individual statements or collections of works by academics who are not necessarily informed by the principles and findings that have been the stock and trade of communication scholars for more than 50 years. The communication scholars are late to the party, and they have to run to keep or catch up. But, we believe they have special insights and shared knowledge that will help them offer insights to crisis and risk. These topics were led by management academics, scientists, and other social scientists who engaged early on with real events in the scope of community security and harmony.

In some ways, crisis is less multidisciplinary than is risk. However, if we approach crisis from a risk perspective (rather than the opposite), we think we gain useful insights. Such matters are often a case of science, social science, and humanities. The perspectives brought by psychology, sociology, anthropology, political science, economics, and communication enlarge the sense of what is a risk and how should it best be managed. We also see the many faceted reality that risk can be the purview of no social science or humanity. If we believe that effective risk management is the rationale for society (including comparative views of societies), we then realize how essential this topic is to the human experience.

It is this theme that gives coherence and purpose to this book, and to the academics and professional efforts of the individuals who so willingly contributed to the dialogue.

I

EXPLORING THE REACH OF CRISIS AND RISK COMMUNICATION

Beginning as a relatively innocent way of expanding the scope and purpose of applied communication theory and research, interest in crisis management and communication has grown into a practitioner and academic cottage industry. Although not receiving as many interested discussants and practitioners, risk management and communication has experienced a similar surge in popularity. Over the years, risk is likely to surpass crisis in volume of discussion merely because it is foundational to crisis.

Crisis is a niche discipline that lends itself well to discussions and application of communication to any event in the history of an organization or individual (such as professional athlete or entertainer) that someone else might deem a crisis. That generous interpretation of crisis is ready made for consulting proposals as well as case studies. To advance the interest in crisis, we have had long lists of responses proposed. That approach to crisis has been a sort of mix and match rules logic: If type y crisis occurs, then push buttons 2, 5, and 13 for the appropriate response to achieve Z outcome. Fortunately, the discipline of crisis management and communication has progressed beyond such simplistic responses and academic pursuits. More work is needed, and it is being conducted.

Sometimes these two areas of practice and research—risk and crisis—come together. What informs one is likely to be relevant to the other. In fact, for this discussion, we prefer to think of crises as risks that are manifested. For instance, we know that a major storm is likely to hit populous areas along the Gulf Coast or savage storms are likely to hit the upper regions of the United States. We prepare both the infrastructures (levees and pumps, and snow removal, for instance) as well as emergency response protocols. Then, as field commanders say, once the battle begins planning is put to use, but operations often, and even soon, require adaptations not well understood during the quiet of the planning period.

Section One opens with a chapter by Heath and O'Hair that discuses not only major underpinning themes of crisis and risk, but demonstrates in more detail the point made above that they are interrelated, rather than independent matters of practice and research. Although risk and crisis are likely to evoke emotional responses, they both are at heart matters of sound science—fact based. We can know and interpret facts relevant to planning and response, and to the evaluation of the actions of others in those circumstances, even the conditions of the crisis. For instance, we can ascertain whether major league athletes took performance enhancing substances. But violations of scientific methodology occur all of the time, as do failures to understand and agree with the findings of science. Therein lies one of the theoretical and practical themes of risk communication, often summarized as the mental models approach. Whether taking a cultural approach to risk and crisis or merely realizing that in various ways risk management is a collective activity, we realize that community standards are imposed, and evaluations are made of what scientists and other officials think and say. "We're in this together" is a theme featured in chapter 1 and carried throughout the book.

Although chapter 1 gives historical insights, chapter 2, by Palenchar, details the historical trends of risk and crisis communication. This foundation helps us understand and appreciate how these disciplines have developed, how they endure, and are refined. That discussion is essential to what follows which often demonstrates the challenges and advances that shape current discussions and build toward a future of great prospect. It's probable that risks and crises are timeless. Surely it was a topic of discussion that occurred around camp fires by roaming bands and more stationary ancestors of the current citizens of the world. What has changed? Without doubt technological advances have brought humans to a new awareness of the kinds of crises and risks they suffer. But we often marvel at the acuity of our ancestors, such as the ability to navigate the oceans by reading currents—the foundation of Polynesian migration and trade. It also suggests how personal, private, and public practice is devoted to the wise management of risks. Companies, activists, and government agencies around the world are not only assessing but also seeking to manage risks, as well as preventing, mitigating, and commenting on crises. And, some of these entities are working to make risks the kind and magnitude of which humans have never witnessed. For instance, discussions of the creation of nuclear weaponry used during World War II always include assessment of the number of lives of military and civilian populations saved by the violent atomic destruction of the lives of others. With all of this effort, the *Handbook* uses this chapter to ask whether society is getting better at crisis response and risk management.

As mentioned above, risk and crisis require a sound science underpinning. Having said that, the cultural theorists then ask: Whose science and whose scientists will get to decide what is a risk and when is it tolerable? If humans were all scientists of the same training, or even robots programmed to read data the same way, discussions of risk and crisis would be substantially different. But people are not and therefore neither are risks and crises straight forward matters. One timeless principle that runs throughout this book is that science and culture may be friends or enemies but neither is benign in such matters. Chapter 3 offers an excellent discussion of the perils of avoiding culture in matters of risk. It also suggests how a simplistic approach to some matter that ignores the human element is fraught with functional and ethical disaster. Some matters have their institutional life. Cultural theory offers analytical approaches as well as a clearer lens through which to see how people can, do, and should respond to risks. Cultural theory, Tansy and Rayner stress, helps explain the playing area various disciplines work to navigate as players seek to thrust and parry (block and tackle?) through debates over meaning. The struggle for shared sense making is fraught with nuance and subtlety.

Renn begins chapter 4 with a telling opening line: "The ultimate goal of risk communication is to assist stakeholders and the public at large in understanding the rationale for a risk-based decision, and to arrive at a balanced judgment that reflects the factual evidence about the matter at hand in relation to their own interests and values." In a few words, that's the breadth and depth of the discipline. Renn, as do Tansey and Rayner, brings the perspective of European scholars who often have exceptional insights into the socio-political role of risks and risk decisions. Renn introduces the concept of legitimacy into the discussion and examines the structures and functions of a sociopolitical arena where risks are subjected to scientific and cultural interpretations. Society simply is not of one mind on such matters. How it discusses risks entails many types of discourse and the political arrangements that facilitate and frustrate such discourse. The matter of risk assessment and accommodation requires multiple voices, perceptual biases, understanding, and agreement. The challenge is to foster public venues where people come to trust and work with rather than oppose regulatory bodies, which in turn need to be sensitive to the perils of risk assessment and policy implementation.

Chapter 5 presents Coombs' interpretation of the status and conceptualization of crisis communication. The paradigm of crisis, Coombs argues, is a dialectic between what an ostensibly offending organization does and says and the reaction various stakeholders have to that action (inaction) and statement (lack of statement). Coombs has been one of the innovators to explain and justify a three phased sense of crisis: pre-crisis, crisis, and post-crisis. What occurs or does not occur at each stage can affect ultimately the efforts of the organization and its stakeholders to prepare for, understand

and evaluate, and put the event behind them. How all of this is accomplished, or why and how it fails, constitutes the foundation for conceptualizing crisis communication. Effective crisis management begins with prevention and event mitigation. As the event occurs and unfolds, various attributions result as stakeholders work to make an account of what happens, who or what is responsible, and what may need to be done to patch things up. This chapter provides a solid overview of this topic drawing together key themes that have developed over the past two decades that define ethical and effective crisis management and communication. As Renn suggests that trust is a key variable to risk, it also is an underpinning of crisis. It is a test of what an organization can do, do well and badly, and how that can affect the well being of others. It also looks at how they can respond in kind.

However local or isolated some matter of risk or crisis might be, it eventually entails others—their interests and judgments. How we make decisions regarding the risk and whether it is tolerable is never simple. Over the years, various decision heuristics have been developed to assist in the socio-political discussion and decision making regarding risk. One of those is the precautionary principle. The first section of this book ends with a discussion of what the principle is and how it can advance and frustrate such discussions. In chapter 6, McGuire and Ellis offer a glimpse into the daunting effort to invoke precaution as a wise means for making a soundly scientific and culturally responsible decision. As we invoke caution, some argue that we miss opportunity which in and of itself is a matter of wise or unwise risk management. It is the essential form and substance (process and content) of dialogic risk decision making. It requires many voices that have a focal point to guide the discussion and inform and advance the debate. It is both hope and challenge, frustration and doubt. As these authors conclude, this principle is neither utopic nor dystropic. But it offers a goal and a system.

1

The Significance of Crisis and Risk Communication

Robert L. Heath
University of Houston

H. Dan O'Hair
University of Oklahoma

Get a credible spokesperson who can deliver a knowledgeable message in a clear manner. Communicate in ways—dress, manner, and posture—that encourage audiences to identify with risk communicators. Be clear to be understood. Be sensitive to the audience members' outrage and concerns. Time was, when this kind of advice captured the essence of risk and crisis communication. Let experts determine the probabilities of risks, hold a public meeting, share this expertise with those who attend, and move on with the project. Or, just do the project and wait until the protests occur and let public relations experts handle the problem. **Know the risk, frame the risk with a fear appeal (of varying degrees), report the risk, and gain the advantage of behavioral change to alter targeted audiences' health related behavior. Do your best with risk communication, but only become truly serious if protesters raise challenges that achieve crisis level**. This kind of reasoning once was, and even today often seems to be, a compelling logic underpinning risk communication in the community relations and public health tradition.

What's beyond that starting point, or perhaps what precedes it? One answer to that question is that we can only understand crisis and risk communication by first examining the nature of people and the society they build. To understand this topic requires insight into society as a foundation. Over the years more and more attention has focused, both through best practices and academic research, on the best ways to communicate about crisis and risk. Along the way, substantial conversation and counseling have also made these management challenges along with communication responsibilities.

Much of the literature, especially in public relations as an academic study and professional practice, relevant to crisis communication got its start with the notoriety created by Johnson & Johnson Company's successful handling of the Tylenol scare in 1982. Bracketed against that ostensibly paradigm case was the oil spill that resulted when the Exxon *Valdez* grounded on Bligh Reef in Prince William Sound on March 24, 1989. In one sense, both cases help us to understand crisis as a risk manifested. Any product manufacturer suffers the risk of product tampering. All of the trips carrying oil across Prince William Sound are variously risky, but only one was a risk manifested to crisis proportion. Such experiences initiated the era of crisis response with advice such as "keep the media informed with details. Be heavy on details, and what ever you do don't acknowledge any responsibility. Otherwise you will face the wrath of general counsel."

Crisis management experts, Berg and Robb (1992) observed that by the date of their publication the Valdez "case had become, in the minds of the experts, a paradigm for how not to handle a corporate crisis" (p. 97). In contrast to Exxon's handling of the Valdez spill, Johnson & Johnson's "image rescue project was quickly judged by most commentators as an unqualified success" (Berg & Robb, 1992, p. 100). Other experts looking at either crisis may hold different or conflicting opinions. So, how an organization should assess and manage risk and respond to crisis is a strategic problematic. How well each organization meets its challenge is a strategic problematic. Experts, professional and academic, will disagree, but nevertheless engage in healthy controversy to help others understand the challenges and evaluative measures for success or failure in such endeavors. Risks surround us every day; how they occur and how the relevant individuals respond has a lot to do with risk and crisis management and communication. We know, for instance, that hurricanes are a predictable part of the life of those who live along the Gulf and East Coasts of the United States. But Rita, for instance, posed different risks than Katrina. One took on crisis proportion that in fact affected how people responded in risk management ways to the other—including a highly visible and eventually fairly dysfunctional evacuation of the Houston, Texas area. A mass evacuation occurred in the Houston area and around Texas driven by what people had seen on television during Katrina. Then, the hurricane did not hit Houston, but the evacuation killed people and hundreds of animals transported in the Texas heat.

The logics driving the practice and study of crisis management and communication have tended to focus on company reputation prior to the crisis, the way the organization responded during the crisis, facts of the case, effect of the facts on the reputation of the organization, and the success or failure of the organization to redeem itself and repair or restore its image. Some crisis response analysis tends to feature the image or reputational nature of the response too much, ignoring the facts of the case. For instance, the greatest advantage Wendy's had in 2005 was not its crisis response team, but the fact that the gang of extortionists who had put the finger in the chili was apprehended and the plot revealed. But, such analysis and probing discloses that people, practitioners, experts, and the public believe that crisis management and response can be evaluated qualitatively. Some responses are better than others. So too is the case for risk communication. This is a paradigm of the communication discipline—to be knowledgeable of the strategic challenges and measures for success within the limits of each rhetorical problem.

Two themes seem to ground crisis and risk management and communication. One is that they are counterparts (See for instance, Heath, 1997; Reynolds & Seeger, 2005). Accordingly, we become interested in how performance of organizations is judged by many critics who hold court in public with potentially high performance stakes at risk; any risk that is manifested can constitute a crisis which requires one or more organizations to stand before its community and issue statements relevant to the occurrence. And, featuring the concept that society is organized for the collective management of risk, the key to crisis and risk management is the effect such matters have on society—as judged by members of that society. These companion disciplines do not occur under placid circumstances, but engage when difficult societal, organizational, and personal choices need and deserve enlightenment. They are often engaged in contention, reluctance to agree, preferences to oppose rather than support, and unwillingness to comply even with expert judgment and prescriptions.

Thus, we not only see crisis and risk as challenges that are intertwined but also understand that each of the processes occurs in the context of society and to some benefit or harm for the society where it occurs. As the modern history of crisis communication was spawned by Johnson & Johnson's Tylenol tragedy, the parallel history of risk management and communication resulted from or was accelerated by the MIC release from a Union Carbide plant in Bhopal, India, in 1984. That release spawned legislation, Superfund Amendments and Reauthorization Act of 1986 (SARA Title III) and conferences on risk communication challenges and protocols. Out of this crisis of risk management arose the Emergency Planning and Community Right-to-Know Act of 1986. Industry responses included the formation of the then-named Chemical Manufacturers' Association (now called the American Chemistry Council) Responsible Care Program. This confluence of events and policy development set the foundation for the concepts of community right to know and risk democracy. Thus, we have the discipline of risk communication, accompanied with risk perception, analysis, and management. The latitude of this discussion has also embraced crisis communication as occurring in stages: Pre-crisis, crisis response, and post-crisis. Thus, for instance, pre-crisis communication can be quite relevant to risk management. At this point, an organization may communicate to create awareness, supply information to augment knowledge, suggest appropriate attitudes, and recommend actions to reduce the likelihood that a risk might manifest. For instance, weather prediction engages in pre-crisis communication to reduce the potential harms of a hurricane.

Most recently, the federal government has ushered in a new form of preparedness action steps in the guise of the National Response Framework (NRF), replacing the National Response Plan. The goal behind of the *National Response Framework* is to develop a comprehensive, all-hazards approach to national incident response. The national response doctrine identifies five principles from which to operate: (1) engaged partnership; (2) tiered response; (3) scalable, flexible and adaptable operational capabilities; (4) unity of effort through unified command; and (5) readiness to act (*National Response Framework*, 2007, p. 8). Based on a local response paradigm (response should be handled at the lowest, jurisdictional level possible), the NRF prescribes a process of capability building through three phases of incident management: prepare, respond, and recover. Inherent within the NRF's incident management plan is a common organizational structure to which all jurisdictions and organizations should adhere: the National Incident Management System (NIMS). *NIMS* requires "standard command and management structures that apply to incident response" (NRP, 2007, p. 27). Pursuant to the promulgation of these statutes, a number of agencies and organizations who pursue grants for preparedness and recovery purposes must adhere strictly to these guidelines, often restricting the level of improvisation and flexibility some feel are necessary during times of crisis.

Focusing on matters of health and other aspects of well being, these companion disciplines offer substantial promise for enhancing the quality of society. The quality of crisis and risk communication indicates the responsiveness of community to individual needs and concerns. As Fischhoff (1995; see also Morgan, Fischhoff, Bostrom, & Atman, 2002) modeled the developmental and multidisciplinary character of the risk communication process: getting the numbers regarding risks correct, putting those numbers into a community at risk, explaining what is meant by them, showing that members of the community have accepted similar risks, showing the benefits of risks, treating the public with respect, and creating partnerships to understand and properly control risks which includes giving lay publics a seat at the table and an opportunity to voice their concerns. Perspectives taken in the risk and crisis literature argue that the strongest component of this progression is the creation of meaningful partnerships that respond to the concerns and needs of community members for information and to bring collective wisdom and judgment to bear on that problem. This stress on "we" gives a community grounding for two-way communication and partnership development (Chess, Salomone, Hance, & Saville, 1995). Here is the rationale for collaborative decision making that includes risk bearers, including those who can be affected by a crisis. This logic suggests that infrastructures within a society arise or are specifically created to discuss, challenge, and make decisions relevant to risk and crisis tolerance, mitigation, and communication.

In very broad terms, the challenge of crisis and risk communication is to base judgments on sound science, responsible values, and reasonable policy which challenges convention and even puts obstacles in the way of those who work to make the system responsive to lay publics' concerns and their often limited ability to engage with, understand, and appreciate complex messages. In this balance, science, policy, management philosophy and culture meet, collide, and reinforce one another in what can be an unhappy confluence. This view allows us to instantiate the role of science without denying the cultural critique which reasons that people's subjective assessments of risk and crisis must be accommodated in various ways in any model of risk and crisis communication which advances beyond the purely functional, linear (expert to lay audience) approach which can actually marginalize those who deserve a major role in the process. Scientific assessments are neither trivial nor invincible. They must be sustained in community infrastructures where dialogue privileges various views and concerns. Rarely is this a symphony, but it need not be a cacophonous wrangle.

As crisis and risk become a topic for conversation and media attention, concerns, values, facts, and policies circulate throughout relevant parts of society. This process has been called the social amplification of risk (Kasperson, 1992). As a foundational discussion for the social amplification of risk, Renn (1992) posed a model that pitted an actuarial approach and toxicological/epidemiological approach against those which featured the psychology of risk, social theories of risk, and cultural theories of risk. The logics of this model and the concept of social amplification focus attention on that variety of players who can address risks and crises by playing up or playing down the facts, causes, outcomes, and affects of the matter under consideration.

This chapter lays a foundation for the companion chapters that follow. It explores the significance of crisis and risk communication as a foundation for the chapters and thoughts compiled into this *Handbook*. A central theme appears to be worth exploring.

BRACKETING CRISIS AND RISK MANAGEMENT AND COMMUNICATION

Risk and crisis management and communication have become topics of increased interest in the past 30 years. In one sense, they have fairly common origins, but they also tend at times to take quite different trajectories. Legend has it that people, especially in management and the practice of public relations became concerned about crisis planning and response following the Johnson & Johnson Tylenol case, not because J&J failed, but because it was a legendary success in responding to the crisis caused by product tampering. Other managements seriously worked to enhance their crisis management, prevention, and response capabilities. They feared embarrassment as well as litigation, but also knew that they would be compared to the J&J response team. Management likes to be seen as effective and not wanting. Fear of embarrassment and failure to perform at the highest levels can be a serious motivator. Likewise, management teams seeking to defend or propose some operation learned over the recent decades that the best laid management strategic planning can be derailed by community outrage and resistance. Science may not save the day for such efforts. Costs of operations can sour if risk averse community groups protest and even litigate the start or continuation of industrial activities.

These circumstances offer professional opportunities. Consultants love the opportunity to bill managements solve these problems. In this way, best practice professionals help to foster a new discipline and academics think themselves lacking if they do not sieze this opportunity for curriculum, research, and consulting. Public relations firms started a bandwagon loaded with crisis planning and response client based services.. It even became fashionable to proclaim expertise in crisis and risk management and communication. In this way, crisis communication became a cottage industry for the public relations industry. Plans were developed and media training occurred. Billings soared. Academics and practitioners have created a substantial body of literature on the strategies and phases of crisis planning, training, response, and evaluation.

As this trend continued, anything and everything became a "crisis." Managements were challenged to consider all of the "risks" that might not be manageable in ways that would allow them to achieve return on investment. Whereas most savvy thinkers realized that a crisis was a big moment in the life of an organization, the term, at least in some circles, became associated with any occurrence where operations were not absolutely smooth and media attention (unfavorable publicity) resulted. Irate airline customers inconvenienced by long lines, unscheduled changes, and even prolonged delays on the tarmac could be counted as a "crisis." Any media inquiry might be lumped into the crisis response category. Such glosses of crisis, however, tended to leave management more frustrated than satisfied with their advisors' and consultants' insights. They were asked to prepare for everything, which might in fact lead them to realize they were then not prepared to respond properly to much at all.

Given the tendency by some to be overly inclusive in terms of what events are put into the crisis or risk management basket, companies and other organizations quite savvy in the challenges of crisis even abandon the term and prefer emergency response as an alternative term, for instance. They reserve the term crisis for those "emergencies" that are so much more daunting than normal that they require extraordinary personnel, technical, and messaging responses. For many thinkers, in fact, crisis is reserved for moments where the turning of events and interpretations could affect the organization's ability to accomplish its mission and business plan. That standard, for instance, underpinned the definition of crisis by Lerbinger (1997): "an event that brings, or has the potential for bringing, an organization into disrepute and imperils its future profitability" (p. 4). By featuring profitability, Lerbinger may seem to ignore government agencies or non-profits, but that would be unfortunate. They too can be materially affected, either by a drying of tax allocation or donation.

Furthering the relevance of Lerbinger's observation to the work in this *Handbook* is the subtitle of his book: *Facing Risk and Responsibility*. A crisis, then, is a risk manifested. How it is handled and whom it affects becomes relevant to how it is judged and what kind of response is required. (For a summary of definitions of crisis, see Heath & Millar, 2004).

Despite Lerbinger's sensitivity to the connection of risk and crisis, much of the crisis literature pays little attention to their interconnectedness. The risk literature has often tended to feature communication efforts by experts to lay people, who have a right to know they work and live in proximity to some hazardous product or process. Union Carbide's "crisis" with MIC release in Bhopal, India became a poster child harbinger for refined approaches to risk management and communication. Starting with lawsuit decisions on asbestos, the concepts of "failure to warn" and "right to know" came to define risk communication. Immediately after the Bhopal tragedy, Rosenblatt (1984) observed, "If the world felt especially close to Bhopal last week, it may be because the world is Bhopal, a place where the occupational hazard is modern life" (p. 20). He and others were aware that the chemical and processes at the heart of the Bhopal disaster were manufactured and used at various locations in the United States. His concern was that felt by neighbors and employees of these facilities.

Risk communication was largely created as a discipline whereby experts could be brought together with lay audiences to explain and compare risks. Once the lay audiences understood the science (scientists' perspectives) and compared the risk to other acceptable risks, their concern should be put into "proper perspective." By this approach, risks believed to be intolerable (at least questionable) could become acceptable, especially if benefits could be weighed in balance. Concerned neighbors and employees should understand and appreciate the balance of risk to benefit. One of the undercurrent themes behind the scientific hegemony of risk management and communication builds on the cultural archetype: You can't make an omelet without breaking an egg. This archetype might serve as the guiding principle to lead people to know that economic progress could not be achieved without some risks, which were knowable (especially in probabilistic terms), comparable, and manageable to a tolerable degree. Many persons in the risk discipline have cautioned against a "science" only view of risk communication (Ayotte, Bernard, & O'Hair, this volume). Covello, Sandman, and Slovic, as long ago as 1988, reasoned against a science only paradigm: An expansive, community oriented view suggests that decisions regarding what level of risk exposure is acceptable "*is not a technical question but a value question*" (p. 6).

Over time practitioners and academics have realized that the broad and elaborated topics of crisis and risk overlap in significant and complementary ways. If a risk occurs and is not well managed, it can become a crisis. A badly handled crisis can reduce trust for the offending organization (or chemical, technology, or process). A crisis may reveal the lack of effective risk management and communication. People may fail to recognize risks in an appropriate light. They may know the risks and not manage them properly. They may fail to communicate effectively. People may come to believe they are asked to bear what appear to be, but actually are not undue or intolerable, risks. Conceived in this way, crisis can be defined as a risk manifested.

During the summer of 2005, two hurricanes strained (federal, state, and local) governments' capacity to understand, mitigate, communicate about, and otherwise manage risk. The levies in New Orleans failed for what occurred to be lots of attributed reasons. Blame became the name of the game. All of that blaming and naming evidenced to the objective spectator that there was enough blame to go around. Even how people communicated about the risk—and encouraged evacuation—failed. Thus, Katrina created a crisis, or many crises, largely because the response was predicated on evacuation without realizing that was impossible for a large, vulnerable, and visible segment of the population. So, did Rita. The evacuation of Houston and surrounding areas became an orderly debacle as resources were strained. New risks appeared for which people were not warned. For instance, since people had been reluctant to evacuate New Orleans and leave pets behind, pets were allowed to evacuate in the face of Rita. Thus, a risk occurred or manifested itself in the form of hundreds of dogs dying from heat. Caged in the back of pickup trucks and other vehicles, many were overcome by heat and/or dehydration.

One of the standard definitions of risk is that each one is the product of probability of occurrence and intensity or magnitude of harm. One major approach to risk features probability assessment which in its simplest form is the result of the number of people who could suffer a risk divided by the number of persons who actually suffer the risk. In this way, infant mortality can be calculated by the number of births in a population by the number of children who die before a specified age. What such probability assessments misses is the value motivated definition of what level of infant mortality is acceptable and whether it is evenly distributed regardless of race, class, or other salient variables.

Whereas we often think in terms of risks associated with chemicals or radiation, we also need to realize the potency of public health risks as a topic of concern. And, it well may be industrial processes rather than the science of specific hazardous materials that poses risk. People may realize the danger of exposure to chemicals, but know that the real harm results from industrial processes, such a pipeline leaks, overturned trucks transporting chemicals, sudden releases of health threatening amounts of the chemical, or slowly developing health problems that result from extended dose response to certain chemicals that lead to cancer or lung dysfunction. So, the substance of the risk communication may not merely be scientific assessment of the toxicology, but faith on an organization's willingness and ability to operate at an appropriate level of safety. This will certainly be the case of nanotechnology where risks will remain unknown for years (it is also ironic that scientists perceive more risks for nanotechnology than do the public).

Predicated on this view of risk, a crisis can be defined as the manifestation of a risk. We know, for instance, that some number of all senior managements of publicly traded organizations will cook the books and go to jail. So, we can estimate the probability of that risk occurring.

In both concepts, we address the likelihood of and reaction to the occurrence of some small set of events. What attracts attention and therefore deserves academic and professional attention is the way risks and crises occur, how they originate, who or what they effect, and to what magnitude.

THE NATURE OF THESE BEASTS

Early efforts to meet the challenges of communicating about risks responded to an incentive to both lay a rationale for the practice and to codify the strategies that should be used. The National Research Council was one of the first bodies to forge the spear point for this discipline. Published in 1989, *Improving Risk Communication* acknowledged in its preface, "a major element in risk management in a democratic society is communication about risk" (p. ix). Such is the case, the preface continued, "because the issues are scientific and technical in content;" "in addition to being critically important, (they) are complex, difficult, and laden with political controversy" (p. ix). The scope of risk communication ranged from social or societal choices (such as regulation of chemical manufacturing processes) to personal choices, "such as whether to change eating habits to avoid cancer or sexual habits to avoid AIDS" (p. xi).

From the start of the discipline, thoughtful innovators realized that science and scientific judgment had to be a foundational part of effective risk assessment, policy development, and communication. However, many of these assessments were political, requiring sensitivity to the interests of and relationships between all of the affected parties. What was the broad scope of successful risk communication, as established during the National Research Council (1989) project? The report made this distinction:

> Some take the position that risk communication is successful when recipients accept the views or arguments of the communicator. We construe risk communication to be successful to the extent that it raises the level of understanding of relevant issues or actions for those involved and satisfies them that they are adequately informed within the limits of available knowledge. (p. 3)

Even superficial analysis suggests the limits of this view. Scientific understanding is only one of many cognitive variables leading to behavioral outcomes. It also assumes a rational, objective approach to risk, even though the study acknowledged the emotionality and even irrationality that often plague efforts to communicate about risks. Easily summarized, people may acknowledge the probability of risk, but certainly not wish to be or welcome being that part of the equation that suffers the risk manifested. Outcomes of a social kind would include support or opposition for the organization creating and responding to the risk. People in a community, for instance, may protest (not support) a manufacturing facility they believe to be a harmful neighbor. In the case of risk campaign outcomes in a public health context, the potentially affected people (those at heightened risk because of their health care patterns) may be asked to take a personal response to risk that would include compliance and noncompliance. They might, for instance, be encouraged to engage in safe sex, reduce alcohol consumption, drive safely, or adopt healthier eating habits.

In discussions of crisis and risk assessment, response, and communication, credibility is one of several problems identified. Those who should be credible—viewed as having credibility—may not enjoy that status, whereas persons who do not deserve to be viewed as credible on such matters, obviously may be highly credible. Is not the peer who offers a cigarette more "credible" in the mind of an adolescent than a public health official with a string of titles? Is not some risk intolerant neighbor more likely to be credible than a third-party toxicologist or epidemiologist?

Trust, as a sub-variable or counterpart of credibility, has long been theorized and studied to better understand its role in this equation. Covello and Peters (1996; see also Palenchar & Heath, 2007), among others, have noted the decline in institutional trust and credibility, perhaps at a time when it is needed most. What factors lead to improved trust and credibility? Knowledge and expertise pay a role in connection with concern and care. Either the perception that a source is knowledgeable and expert increases the perception that they are caring and concerned, or the opposite relationship exists as community members are asked to think about industry and government. For both of those sources of risk information and advice, they are more trusted and credible if they are perceived to be concerned and caring about the interest of those at risk. Such is also true for citizens groups. Openness and honesty play a minor role in the equation. If people concerned about a risk don't think that either government or industry is caring and concerned, they are likely to trust citizens groups which are often seen as exhibiting more care and concern. Thus, in crisis and risk contexts, facts count, but the character of each source (its care and concern) is likely to give life to facts rather than the other way around. We can well imagine that such dynamics have a lot to do with the perception of whose interest is being represented. If the people, the risk bearers, think that their interest is treated as less important than that of industry or government, they are likely to trust citizens groups more and the other sources of information and advice less.

Puzzling these myriad problems and other challenges to define the nature and socially responsible approaches to risk communication, the National Research Council (1989) undoubtedly achieved more uncertainty than certainty. Nevertheless, the NRC raised questions and fostered discussion. One great achievement of this project to better understand risk communication was to leave many questions unanswered and people thirsting to understand this beast.

One additional theme in this study is worth noting. The National Research Council (1989) noted the connection between risk and crisis. The report focused on crises as emergencies. It raised concerns and offered advice on how to communicate about risks during emergencies. Participants in either risk or crisis venues realize, even if they don't often make the case specifically, that the two disciplines are interconnected.

The upshot of the early efforts to define and shape risk communication was many relatively glib observations, some reasonably sound guidelines, lots of cautions, and some thought provoking suggestions. Those persons working in the 1980s were to find their ideas and prescriptions supported or confounded by work conducted through the National Research Council project (1989) which defined risk communication as a matter of "democratic dialogue": "*An interactive process of exchange of information and opinion among individuals, groups, and institutions. It involves multiple messages about the nature of risk and other messages, not strictly about risk, that express concerns, opinions, or reactions to risk messages or to legal and institutional arrangements for risk management*" (p. 322; emphasis in original).

What culminated as the essence of this discipline during the late 1980s and 1990s was a reliance on prescriptive and formulaic guidelines. One such set was issued by the Environmental Protection Agency (1988) as the "seven cardinal rules of risk communication." These rules advised communicators to use "simple, non-technical language. Be sensitive to local norms, such as speech and dress. Use vivid, concrete images that communicate on a personal level. Use examples and anecdotes that make technical risk data come alive. Avoid distant, abstract, unfeeling language about deaths, injuries, and illnesses" (p. 4). This advice assumes that "If people are sufficiently motivated, they are quite capable of understanding complex information, even if they may not agree with you" (p. 5).

The Chemical Manufacturers Association (1989) added four items to the EPA's cardinal rules list. One called for refined strategic business planning, "Run a safe operation," whereas another demanded a higher operating standard, "Reduce [toxic chemical] releases." Improved issue monitoring is required to "Find out the concerns of the community so you can decide what kinds of community outreach activities will be successful." One recommended better external communication: "Get involved in the community; establish a speakers bureau and join service organizations to make industry's presence known and to 'de-mystify' the chemical industry for local citizens." These additions acknowledge the need to be open and demonstrate concern and caring as a way of demonstrating the willingness and ability to solve problems and meet community standards. This guideline revealed how much the CMA believed that an ongoing process would be needed, a strategic option that demonstrates the profound limitation of any single calming, soothing messages

From some obscure moment of inception to today, risk communication has been in a learning curve. Crucial differences distinguish what Hadden (1989) called "old" and "new" versions of risk communication. In the old approach, "experts tried to persuade laymen of the validity of their risk assessments or risk decisions." This option is "impeded by lay risk perception, difficulties in understanding probabilities, and the sheer technical difficulty of the subject matter" (p. 301). In contrast, the new approach is based on "dialog among parties and participation in the choices among activities whose risks are being discussed" (p. 301). The new form of risk communication is impeded when institutions are unresponsive to the needs, interests, and level of understanding of the publics affected by the potential or ostensible risk. Institutional barriers stand in the way of meaningful dialogue in communities where people experience risks that they worry are intolerable.

The early 1990s was a time of turmoil in the evolution and development of sound risk communication protocols. Heath and Nathan (1990–1991) observed "a revolution in environmentalism and personal health is requiring that reasonable and responsible communication be employed to change personal and collective behaviors and to create and promulgate legislation and regulation" (p. 15).

Prescriptive guidelines such as those by the Environmental Protection Agency and the Chemical Manufacturers Association seemed to feature what the source in the risk communication process wanted to say rather than what the receivers wanted to know and say. As did many others, Heath and Nathan emphasized that risk communication is political, not merely scientific. Persons who bear or think they bear risks want to reduce uncertainty; they want control exerted over the risk by themselves or responsible parties (broadly industry, government, or citizens groups). Risk communication is not purely scientific but contains, often by implication, values that need to be made part of the dialogue and relevant decision processes. These values often focus on interests at play in risk situations.

Heath and Nathan (1990–1991) agreed with a central theme of the National Research Council (1989): "To remain democratic, a society must find ways to put specialized knowledge into the service of public choice and keep it from becoming the basis of power for an elite" (p. 15). That guideline is daunting. Controversy, however disrupting, is not a weakness of the process, but its strength. The most sound paradigm, Heath and Nathan argued was rhetorical, the wrangle of ideas, facts, policies, and values, instead of something that could be narrowly called, sharing or exchanging information.

By the early 1990's academics and professionals saw the weakness of glib prescriptions. These were not bad guidelines, but would they suffice under the pressure of agencies and companies having to respond to community concerns? A national symposium of risk communication practitioners and researchers noted and spawned trends that have shaped the growing discipline. In the abstract summarizing the conference, Chess et al. (1995) observed "a shift from simply communicating risk to forging partnerships with communities" (p. 115). Such observations demonstrated that a linear, sender->receiver model, expert to lay audience model was in decline. The symposium also noted that audience diversity was becoming a recognized challenge. These developments were touted as advances beyond the foundation established during the 1986 which had featured risk democracy and the leadership of William Ruckleshaus, the former administrator of the EPA. Despite growth, Chess et al. (1995) believed that "the definition of successful risk communication also continues to be in dispute" (p. 115). And, so, they asked:

> Is successful risk communication persuasion, transfer of information, public participation, or empowerment of citizens to make decisions? Should it produce an informed citizenry, a compliant citizenry, an alert citizenry, or an empowered citizenry? Should the goal be better decisions, fairer decisions, more consistent decisions, or, in the throes of environmental gridlock, any decisions at all? Or are there "different motivating forces" and therefore different risk communication goals, for every "group, person, agency administrator, and middle manager"? These questions, in turn, have raised others about the ethics, and evaluation of risk communication. (p. 115)

A decade later, we may still not have sound answers and consensus for major answers in the literature or practice.

In this era, Fischhoff (1995) argued for ending a transfer of information model and for adopting one that facilitated a commitment to community partnerships. He argued that risk analysis, management and communication progress through seven stages:

Getting the numbers right
Telling key publics what the numbers are
Explaining what the numbers mean
Showing these publics that they have accepted similar risks before
Explaining how the risk benefits outweigh the costs
Treating people with respect; being nice to them
Making them partners

Knowledge, analysis, comparisons, cost/benefit analysis, and empowerment became important themes.

Still, Rowan (1994) asked, what strategies beyond guidelines of the kind offered by EPA and CMA can advance the discipline? Instead of a rules based approach, she challenged practitioners and academics to explore and adopt the possibilities of strategic, problem solving approaches to risk communication. To that end, each challenge might be idiosyncratic but could be approached in terms of the logic of "(1) identifying communication goals, (b) determining principal obstacles to those goals, and (c) selecting research-based methods for overcoming or minimizing these difficulties and achieving communication objectives" (p. 365). She raised questions about the complexity of the communication process and challenge that offered much fruit for thought. Along with these cutting points, she offered a societal challenge. Risk communication must be "accompanied by knowledge and a commitment to justice. The more we can recognize the understandability of people's concern and the power their concerns provide in solving challenging problems, the more we can work together to create rational and fair procedures for the management of hazardous substances and situations" (p. 373).

Questions raised about the pragmatic effectiveness and ethics of risk communication were never irrelevant to persons interested in defining and advancing the practice of crisis prevention, management and response—including communication. Often the concerns and motives overlap. Medication, for instance, helps society manage risks of disease. Once the harmful side effects of a medication, for instance, become a matter of scientific and media news concern, we have a risk manifested and expect crisis response. As experts work vigilantly to reduce the risks associated with industrial processes, we know that even the best plans can fail, leading to crisis. Hurricanes pose risks; they create crisis. Epidemics pose risk; they create crisis. So goes an endless list of daunting associations between crisis and risk.

PROBABILITIES, CULTURE, AND SOCIETY

Two dominant views are at play in the perception/recognition, analysis, management, and communication about risks. One relies heavily on scientific methodologies and probabilistic predictions. The other, characterized as risk society and cultural interpretations, invests evaluation into the process in many profound ways beyond the mere efforts to affect probabilities of occurrence, harms, and magnitudes.

The first of these perspectives seeks to know what risks occur, what their probability is, who they are most likely to affect, under which circumstances are these people to be most likely affected, and with what positive or negative outcomes given the possibility of interventions in the chain of risk. A chain of risk model or a fault tree model (see National Research Council, 1989) assumes that events and choices (however random, probabilistic or causal) occur in some recognizable and manageable sequence. For instance, weather conditions create the possibility, then probability, and eventually the certainty, of a hurricane which will take a track of least resistance striking some points with different amounts of impact and incurring varying amounts of damage on people, nature, and property. In this sequence, people can take measures before hurricanes (such as building codes, construction standards, levies, and evacuation plans) to minimize damage. So many variables need to be understood in such predictions and the emergency response to them.

Persons, nevertheless, who study risks do so by featuring probabilities, correlations, and causal modeling. Science is brought to apply its sound methodologies to understand and respond to some problem. Scientists are typically satisfied by their ability to understand and predict events at various degrees of probability. These fall short of certainty. Lay audiences often are concerned by uncertainties, some of which are quite tolerable by science. They often make evaluative attributions about risks and their cause (the source) by focusing first on their fears or apprehensions and then looking for and interpreting information to confirm their evaluations. For instance, traffic scientists can predict how many people will die or be injured in automobile accidents. They simply do not know at the start of each year who these people will be or how severe their injuries will be. Lay audiences tend to treat automobile travel as a familiar risk (as opposed to a terrorist attack). And they have comfortable attribution processes that place blame for the risk occurrence on others rather than themselves.

The logic of this scientific (actuarial or epidemiological) approach is that as people understand the causes, randomness/predictability of, and effects of risks certain measures can be taken on a personal and societal level to alter the occurrence, impact, and magnitude of the damage. For instance, to counter the probability of thousands of deaths and injuries by automobile accident cars can be made safer, drivers can be taught to operate more safety, and highways and streets can be properly maintained and more safely designed. The logic is that the more that can be understood about the risk in a scientific and management sense the more likely that something constructive can be done, including communicating about the risk. Those in chemical manufacturing know they cannot operate without incidents as well as ambient release of materials into the environment. Does the design and operation of the facility produce health conditions that violate the predictions for total populations based on statistical study? What designs and operations might alter, if any, the predictions of health or quality of life impact?

Thus, in one sense, the crisis counterpart of risk occurs when people did not act properly who could have known and taken proper steps to perceive the potential of crisis, to prevent the occurrence of the crisis as a manifestation of a risk, to know and implement measures needed to prevent or mitigate the crisis and its impact, and to know and communicate in a pre-crisis plan the best response options by emergency responders as well as affected or potentially affected individuals. By this logic, a crisis is a risk manifested. So, appropriate risk analysis and crisis management are partners. They are connected by similar challenges of science, management, and communication.

Without doubt, scientific investigation is essential to understanding and mitigating risks. Morgan et al. (2002) have proposed that first scientific knowledge needs to be assembled so that the science, however sound, complete, and uncontroversial, can be used as a perspective against which the knowledge, beliefs, and concerns of various publics is compared. The strategic logic prescribes ways to increase the extent to which the key public's views come to be similar to that of the scientists who have studies and made recommendations based on risk assessment and mitigation. Scientists often are more comfortable with probabilistic assessment, as a process and conclusion, than are lay audiences, especially if they fear they will fall into the population known by probabilistic assessment to be at risk.

So, one view of risk features scientific probabilistic estimations and neutral predictions and recommendations. At the other end of the continuum are social and cultural theories of risk (Renn, 1992). The risk society approach to risk perception, analysis, management and communication takes a sociological view that offers means for evaluating and judging the distribution of risk occurrence and magnitude throughout society. This societal or cultural view postulates that risk analysis becomes sensitive to prevailing institutions, sometime featuring the role of science and diminishing the importance of community engagement and evaluation. Analysis is most solid if it begins with a foundational examination of the nexus between people, culture, society, risk, and crisis. Because they are such a routine part of persons' lives, crises and risk perception, analysis, management, and communication are often obscured as taken for granted. But, history is a drama of people perceiving, assessing, communicating about, and creatively preventing or adapting to risks (Plough & Krimsky, 1987).

Ancients predicted hazards and risk outcomes. They used myths, metaphors, and rituals to communicate knowledge needed to accommodate to or avoid hazards. These interpretative processes became institutionalized and in some instances have changed little to today. One of the more daunting of these assessments has pitted against one another two competitive conservative religious perspectives. One, the one that acknowledges global warming, features the part of the Book of Genesis that says that God gave humans dominion over the earth and expects them to care for their planetary home. In contrast, a competing religious interpretation reasons that if the globe is warming it is the will of God and totally beyond human control or influence.

Today, techniques for assessing and responding to risks may have matured little beyond those of the ancients (Douglas, 1992). The issue to be managed is how to understand and control risks, as well as gain acceptance for these measures in ways that foster the wisest outcomes in any community of interests (Freudenberg, 1984). In their struggle to control risks, people seek and contest facts, evaluative premises, and conclusions to be derived from those facts and premises. They argue over what level of safe is safe enough. Addressing this conundrum, Fishhoff, et al. (1978) compared a psychometric model to the economic model of Star (1972) based on perceptions of risk/benefit tradeoffs. Fischhoff et al.'s analysis suggested that perceived benefit was not a reliable predictor of risk tolerance, people want risks to be lowered, and are concerned when they are involuntary victims in a risk manifestation model.

One reality of risk is its cultural dimension. As we often say about beauty, which is in the eye of the beholder, such is also true of crisis and risk. Thus, interpretative frames or cognitive constructions are a vital dimension of crisis and risk magnitude and the quality of the preparation for, prevention or minimization of, and response to such occurrences. At a rhetorical level, such analysis makes substantial sense on the premise that no fact reveals itself. It must be perceived, interpreted, assessed, weighed, and used or discarded as the case might be. Writing on rhetorical theory and criticism, Campbell (1996) concluded that rhetoric is "the study of what is persuasive. The issues it examines are social truths, addressed to others, justified by reasons that reflect cultural values. It is a humanistic study that examines all the symbolic means by which influence occurs" (p. 8). Campbell (1996) compared scientists for whom "the most important concern is the discovery and testing of certain kinds of truths" whereas "rhetoricians (who study rhetoric and take a rhetorical perspective) would say, 'Truths cannot walk on their own legs. They must be carried by people to other people. They must be explained, defended, and spread through language, argument, and appeal'" (p. 3). From this foundation, Campbell reasoned, rhetoricians take the position "that unacknowledged and unaccepted truths are of no use at all" (p. 3).

Parallel analysis is provided in the construction tradition. To this point, Beck (2004) reasoned, "Risk statements are neither purely factual claims nor exclusively value claims. Instead, they are either both at the same time or something in between, a 'mathematicized morality' as it were" (p. 215). As Adam and Van Loon (2000) reasoned,

> The essence of risk is not that it *is* happening, but that it *might be* happening. Risks are manufactured, not only through the application of technologies, but also in the making of sense and by the technological sensibility of a potential harm, danger or threat. One cannot, therefore, observe a risk as a thing-out-there—risks are necessarily constructed. (p. 2)

The construction of risk requires definitions of risk. As such, "all interpretation is inherently a matter of perspective and hence political (p. 4).

It appears then that the risk management community has come to two conclusions about risk and community perceptions: "(1) Individual and community concerns and ideas about risk are multidimensional, and (2) the task of incorporating these varied perspectives is complex, if not difficult. Public judgments about risk, as evidenced by risk-perception research utilizing the psychometric and cultural approaches, have shown that lay judgments do not correspond with those of experts who manage hazards based on their quantitative assessments of risk" (Scherer & Juanillo, 2003, p. 226). When you couple complexity of community perceptions of risk with an overall decline in public trust in scientists, experts, government officials, and other sources of authority, the prospect of managing community risk perceptions and crisis response becomes challenging.

In risk society, tensions exist between and within disciplines regarding risks, their perception, analysis, management, and communication. Disciplines introduce perspectives and hence politics. Language, as the means for creating and sharing meaning, is vital to this analysis. It influences what people perceive, how they perceive it, and how they respond to it. Relevant to the problematic of the risk society is the reality that terms can ossify. As perspectives of one time become embedded in language, they can frustrate attempts to change perceptions of and responses to risks, as well as the morality of the persons or entities that create, intervene, and bear risk. Some see risk as inherent to industrialism whereas others will reason that industrialism is the antidote to risk. By implication, such analysis instantiates a cost/benefit balance into discussions of risk even though both cost and benefit may be viewed and described differently by various parties in context.

Adam and Van Loon (2000) advanced this analysis by reasoning: "Risk society has already taken us beyond the security of mathematics; we have to acknowledge that in this sense of constituting a new sort of reality, risk is not reducible to the product of occurrence multiplied with the intensity and scope of potential harm. Instead, reflexivity requires us to be meditative, that is, looking back upon that which allows us to reflect in the first place" (p. 7). Risk and technology are by this analysis teleological. Any solution to a risk may and often does pose new and potentially greater risks. Change and solution are often implied in the political perspectives that drive the logics of the technologies as related to the risks attendant. This line of reasoning leads to a sharp criticism of the hegemony of "Big Science" (p. 12).

Capturing the essence of the risk society, Adam and Van Loon (2004) observed, "risk culture is better conceived as a loose ensemble of sense-making and sensibilities, that constitute a reflexive-ethics of contextualization, challenging disclosure, and politicization. Risk cultures in (Ulrich) Beck's work are reflexively transgressive, situated, pragmatic and responsive" (p. 30). Many focal points can be extracted from that conclusion, but two are essential: contextualization and reflexivity. Both are ways to make explicit the politicization of science on matters of risk and crisis. The critique introduces politics in science, which the objectivity advocates, can miss. It asks why patterns exist, and wonders whether the answer rests with key aspects of culture basic to each risk society.

As a proponent of the risk society interpretation, Beck (2004) pointed to the focal point: "The discourse of risk begins where trust in our security and belief in progress end" (p. 213). He continued his critique, "The concept of risk thus characterizes a peculiar, intermediate state between security and destruction, where the *perception* of threatening risks determines thought and action" (p. 213). Such analysis focuses attention on the distribution of risks, fears, risk consciousness, and the utopian outcome of reduced or eliminated risk. It requires a reflexive society: "A society that perceives itself as a risk society becomes *reflexive*, that is to say, the foundations of its activity and its objectives become the object of public scientific and political controversies" (Beck, 2004, pp. 221–221). Such examination forces us to realize that purely probabilistic or epidemiological analysis does not adequately address the larger questions concerning who decides what risks exist, who must bear these risks, and whether mitigation is needed and proper to reduce the likelihood of the risk, its magnitude, or the likelihood of affecting the persons who are vulnerable. What knowledge needs to be put into play? How will the knowledge be generated and put into play? Will this occur? Who is responsible? Are they responsible enough?

On one end of the continuum, then, is the scientist who scrupulously recognizes, records, and conducts probabilistic analysis of risk events. This sort of person serves a vital role, but one that is incomplete. For instance, industrial accidents were frequent and often horrific in the later decades of the 19th Century in the United States. As the industrial mass production revolution progressed it did so at the pain of workers. The railroad industry, the steel industry, and the mining industry were particularly hazardous. Deaths and dismemberment could be tallied and predicted across a population of workers. One realizes however that the story of risk recognition and management did not stop there, with probabilities and epidemiological assessment. Scientists working with responsible managers sought safer working conditions because they realized that those conditions their investigations found were not optimal. The concept of the optimal introduces the logics of the risk society and cultural interpretations. In this analysis of change, however, we cannot forget or slight the role of citizens groups (such as labor unions), activism, social movement, responsible business interests, and government. (For insights into such reforms, see for instance Raucher, 1968; Weibe, 1968.)

For these reasons, risk communication and crisis communication are best thought of as strategic processes designed to respond to various rhetorical problems in ways that can be evaluated by standards of empirical success, value, and ethics. These are multidisciplinary disciplines. They demand a blending of many talents and soundly responsible judgments. This *Handbook* seeks to draw into perspective many of these judgments to see if they are adequate or could be improved. To improve them is to make society more fully functional in its collective management of risk.

CULTURAL THEORY AND RISK COMMUNICATION

Advances toward an optimal sense of risk responsiveness have been made through the efforts of many disciplines. Worth noting, advances in risk analysis also augment our understanding of the requirements to observing, mitigating, and responding to crisis. As one looks for a potential crisis, focus centers on various risks and the consequences of their occurrences and the potential managerial and communication responses. How a risk or crisis is interpreted depends on the meaning embedded in one or more salient cultures relevant to the event.

Anthropologist Mary Douglas (1992) established an anthropological rationale for studying risk as a cultural phenomenon. She built her critique on the status quo's "concerns for the purity of the risk analysis profession and the danger of moving out of the favoured paradigm of individual rational choice" (p. 11). Such analysis tended to focus on the problematic of benefit/cost ratios—who benefits from a risks and who suffers cost. She also realized that risks and crises are political events, as well as scientific ones. Facts blend with values and policy preferences.

Douglas saw a battle line drawn between purely objective assessment of risk, as in epidemiological studies, that have not been "polluted by interests and ideology" (p. 11) and a side that is much more qualitative in its evaluation of risk. She argued that attempts to achieve purity of objective assessment obscure the reality that ideology is not a contaminant but the essential ingredient in risk perception, management, mitigation, and response. This clash of perspectives may well lead risk experts, issue advocates, and members of the lay public to see and address risks in quite different ways.

Being able to bridge or avoid these differences challenges risk experts to make risk identification, assessment, management, and communication less a purely scientific project and more vital to the societal and individual experience. Based on her awareness of this breach in relationship, she then wondered how people could "know how consensus is reached. Placing all the focus on individual cognition excludes the problem. The risk perception analysts say practically nothing about intersubjectivity, consensus making, or social influences on decisions" (p. 12). Early efforts to address risks gave substantial power to the scientists who could and were expected to make relevant, fact-based decisions. This power tends to exclude other parties, especially concerned publics, who want to know how decisions were made. They are likely to press for such information as a means for gaining control or forcing others to bring control to risks and their manifestation.

Given the origins of risk assessment and management, it is not surprising that once scholars and practitioners of various disciplines saw the diversity of risk assessments based on cultural factors, they were prone to factor the role of culture into their analysis. In fact, they realized that statistical assessment was cultural and political, but often did not recognize those brackets in their work.

One factor of cultural bias is the need to find someone to blame for a risk—or crisis. Those participants in this analysis who possess a "rational individual" bias in their analysis prefer to blame the person, the individual, who willfully and knowingly undertook a risky activity. By scientific standards, such behavior seems irrational—a violation of the rational individual paradigm featuring benefits and costs. Or, conversely, some scientific assessments feature the randomness of risk events. According to the rational individual paradigm, one can blame an automobile accident on the reckless (irrational) driver who careens into a carload of people and does substantial damage. Blaming that event on the carelessness of the driver does not account for the randomness of the damage to that specific carload of people who happened to be at that exact point in time and space. What if some persons in the vehicle die or are seriously injured and others sustain minimal injury? Who then is particularly at blame? Who is irrational? And, is the ability to place blame on one or more individual who is responsible at some point of assessment a sound approach? Perhaps some mythic explanation is applied to rationalize the event and outcomes? Would that not argue that individuals are irrational if they work in or live near what is thought to be high risk industries? Are other factors at play, including the balance of reward/costs from taking risks, the limited choices people have where they work or live, and the ability to force sources that create risk to be accountable to employees and neighbors?

At the pure statistical level, risk is a matter of probability, as Douglas reflected: "*Risk* then meant the probability of an event occurring combined with the magnitude of the losses or gains that would be entailed" (p. 23). To mitigate risk occurrence and magnitude, the logic follows, individuals would be better able to manage risks if they were more aware of and knowledgeable of them. This line of reasoning blurs many of the identifiable elements of the risk perception, management, mitigation, and communication equation. For instance awareness of a risk does not equate with knowledge of the risk as a risk or the consequences of the risk. Nor does it necessarily involve an attitude formed about the risk or the behavioral response which is a part of the logic of this model. It does not assume or evaluate whether the source of the risk can think and operate in ways that reduce the risk or its impact.

A major contribution by cultural theory is its rationale for holding members of society accountable for risks. As Douglas reasoned, "Cultural theory starts by assuming that a culture is a system of persons holding one another mutually accountable. A person tries to live at some level of being held accountable which is bearable and which matches the level at which that person wants to hold others accountable. From this angle, culture is fraught with the political implications of mutual accountability" (p. 31). Thus, various parties become responsible for risks, their assessment, management, mitigation, and communication. This logic, however, does not leave the individual immune to responsibility. But, it suggests that by specialty, certain individuals' roles in society make them more responsible for certain risks. For instance, the medical community has its regime of risks, as does a police force, or a fire department, or accountants. In this way, society is organized on the rationale of collective risk management.

Sensitive to the problems of getting, interpreting, and communicating risk data, Susan Hadden (1989) worried that institutional barriers stand in the way of meaningful dialogue in communities where people experience risks that they think are intolerable. Such barriers result, at least in part, from statutes that do not specify what technical data are crucial and, therefore, should be collected. Required to provide information, those who are responsible may merely engage in data dumps. Thus, substantial databases may be created, but the important or most important data may not be interpreted and used for policy decisions. Statutes and professional protocols may not recognize the need for community involvement and clarity of presentation. Collection may not include a sense of how the data are to be communicated. Even when data have been collected by industry or governmental agencies, institutional barriers prevent citizens from gaining access to them. People may encounter a maze of agencies, do not know where and how to acquire information, and suffer data dumps that provide huge amounts of information in ways that make it difficult to access (see Heath, Palenchar, & O'Hair, this volume).

Encountering such barriers, people may become frustrated or unsure that they have the data they need or want. They may doubt the accuracy and value of the information given various uncertainties and controversies about its accuracy and relevance. Even when information is obtained, people run into barriers as they seek to exert changes they hope will mitigate the risks they believe they have discovered. A related barrier is the failure on the part of governmental agencies, as well as industrial groups, to agree on what data interpreted by which standards truly give meaningful insights. The institutions related to this process refuse--for various reasons, some of which are completely ethical and honest—to be precise in the report, use, and interpretation of data.

As she worried about the dysfunction of data dumps, Hadden (1989) was also frustrated by one-way—expert to lay audience—communication. This, she called the "old" version of risk communication that gave power to the experts who were the source of data, while often disempowering the persons who had a right to the information in useful form because they worried that some risk might be intolerable. Hadden was one of many who observed that "information alone is not adequate; because of the inevitable gaps and uncertainties about how to evaluate risks, risk communication depends upon trust among all parties to the communication" (p. 307).

Cultural theorists believe that the technicality of data can frustrate communication efforts because the experts believe that lay publics cannot understand, appreciate, and make correct choices from the data. So, the experts tend to take a "trust us" persona in such communication efforts which essentially evolve as efforts to persuade others of the rightness of their research and conclusions. In fact, they may be incapable of creating trust for their analysis no matter how accurate and appropriate it might be. They have not been able to demonstrate their accountability. Key publics who worry about risks—or may be unaware of them—can encounter elitist experts who cannot engage in dialogue. Also, they may believe their responsibility ends with the gathering or analysis of data. They may not see communication as their responsibility. They may lack the necessary temperament and communication skills.

Cultural theory very much supported the dialogic approach to risk communication. The balance, according to cultural theory, rests with each and every party being accountable and being held accountable. As Douglas (1992) reasoned, each "person is assumed to be sifting possible information through a collectively constructed censor set to a given standard of accountability" (p. 31). An essential part of this accountability is the varying balance between reward or benefits and costs as perceived by the various individuals who comprise the culture. Different people see various risks as being more or less worth taking or bearing. How well the people of each culture share an intersubjective filter and how well the filter operates to understand, manage, and communicate risk is another focal point of concern. Each filter is a perspective that by its nature gives credence to some information as more important and relevant than other information. Such interpretations cannot be understood and reconciled without seeing differences as honest but conflicting perspectives.

For this reason, risk analysis is inherently moral and political. It is not strictly objective. "Risk analysis that tries to exclude moral ideas and politics from its calculations is putting professional integrity before sense" (Douglas, 1992, p. 44). "The political question is always about acceptable risk" (p. 44). Viewed this way, cultural theory acknowledges the value of epidemiological assessments, but reasons that many moral dimensions lead to complex decisions that often require inclusive rather than exclusive frames of interpretation and modes of communication. Can every risk be lowered to make it more acceptable? Is it unjustly borne by some to the unjust advantage of others? Should those more at risk ethically be expected to bear the risk? And, reflective of the essential theme of risk democracy and community right to know legislation that grew up in the 1980s in the United States, we can ask how can the dialogue regarding risk sufficiently includes all interested parties and deals productively with their concerns and suggestions? How and why does the community have a right to know? Who has that right? Who does not have that right? Cultural theory gave substantial support for discussing such questions as they came to be asked, particularly after chemical releases such as occurred in Bhopal, India.

Answers to these questions and the policy decisions that arise from them and guide them are not easy to acquire. As Douglas (1992) continued, "Each culture is designed to use dangers as a bargaining weapon, but different types of culture select different kinds of dangers for their self-maintaining purposes" (p. 47). Out of this perspective comes a wholeness that embraces all that constitutes a community: "This analysis of attitudes to risk treats the system of society as one: The community, its political behavior, its theory of how the world is, the strengths and weaknesses of its forms of solidarity" (Douglas, 1992, p. 48). Viewed in this way, risk perception, analysis, management, and communication are not trivial or incidental parts of each community. They are the essential elements of community. Community serves as a rationale and infrastructural means for the collective management of risk.

So, instead of ignoring or eliminating politics and morality from probability analysis, culture theory sees any scientific assessment as only a part, and perhaps a smaller than larger part of the analysis. Thus, the role of scientist is politicized. "Scientists are being pressed to take the role of ultimate arbiter in political contests when there is no hope of ultimate arbiter in political contests when there is no hope of diehard adversaries coming to agreement" (Douglas, 1992, p. 49). In an optimal world, some arbiter—perhaps scientists—might be able and therefore are empowered to make assessments and final decisions on risks. To do so, however, is likely to give them a role greater than their ability to accomplish, especially if their role includes convincing others of the accuracy and evaluative soundness of their conclusions. They may be adept at perceiving and assessing, but any attempt at management, which includes allocating and/or gaining acceptance for risks, becomes instantly political. It brings communication challenges similar to that of clearing a minefield. It is the business of more than the scientists, especially if they work for some vested interest. That interest can be at odds with and a biasing aspect of the collective efforts to assess and manage risks. There is no place for apolitical analysis in matters of risk.

Decisions of this kind, cultural theorists argue, are confounded by value judgments. "The rational chooser's definition of a situation is not to be taken as given: The selective elements are the outcomes of psychological and sociological processes, including the chooser's own activities and the activities of others in his environment" (Douglas, 1992, p. 56). No interpreter of risk, especially those with "professional" status can be conceptualized as being free standing or independent of the society where they operate. They are part of various institutions and the total culture. The roles of such institutions are based on accountabilities to the larger society and to other institutions. It is exactly the word risk and its implications for this dialogue that challenges the players to see themselves as part of a larger community with its characteristic values, goals, and responsibilities. In such infrastructures, scientists can be asked and even assigned the role of final arbiter. Scientists, Douglas (1992) probed, come to have status because of the institutions, and "individuals transfer their decision-making to the institutions in which they live" (p. 78). Such institutions must acknowledge that individuals are variously risk averse and self-interested. Rather than some absolute standard, the nexus of such tendencies, Douglas (1992) reasoned, rests with the individual's relationship to such institutions: "the self is risk-taking or risk-averse according to a predictable pattern of dealings between the person and others in the community. Both emerge, the community and the person's self, as ready for particular risks or as averse to them, in the course of their interactions" (p. 102).

Tensions arise from situations of conflicting interest and differing levels of risk taking and aversion. Such shared experience not only translates into language but also into institutions. Rituals and history of community activities bring to each set of risk decisions a legacy that is political in every sense of the word. Thus, public debate is oriented to the future. "In the public debate the future form of the society is at stake; the contenders define the options" (Douglas, 1992, p. 134). This debate centers on tensions between individual and collective interests. Out of this tension can arise a sense of collective support or intractable opposition. The debate centers on normative decisions: What is done? What should be done? Whose rights are promoted, protected, and compromised? Dichotomous choices arise that yield in various ways to discourse and are the essence of the norms built into and expressed by culture.

Here then arises the logic of risk discourse, and by the same logic crisis discourse. At issue is a contest over what is (logics of factual analysis) and what ought to be (logics of policy and value). The rhetorical dynamics of society focus on three kinds of broad choices:

(a) "whole systems of relations for bonding insiders together against outsiders"
(b) "the trust necessary for exchange between individuals"
(c) the legitimacy of "up-down hierarchical bonding of individuals" (Douglas, 1992, p. 137).

In such dialogue occur discussions of exchange. The culture of risk not only poses risk loss against benefits, but the logics of who gain or lose from various risk assessments and responses. Who gains and who loses? Is this fair? Are those who can or will lose part of the dialogue?

At one level, the collective interest translates into the public good. But as Douglas (1992) observed, "the question of public good arises in different forms in each kind of community, and the different definitions proffered reflect the different social forms which frame the debate" (p. 146). Such dialogue integrates and battles the integration and compatibility of individual and community beliefs. "The community equivalent of individual beliefs are collectively held beliefs, public knowledge, and generally accepted theories, or culture. Self-perception of a community will correspond to what its members think proper, and likewise, the knowledge of the self that is available to members will be limited by the forensic process" (p. 222). Decisions are collective even if they do not arise easily or at all from the compatible and disparate voices of the members of each community.

Because risk and crisis are inherently matters of choice, Douglas helps us comprehend the dynamics of the dialogue and the challenges involved in integrating interests, as well as distributing risk and reward. "Culture is the point at which claims and counter-claims come to rest and where authority is attributed to theories about the world" (p. 223). And, in sum, she asked "What is culture?" To this she answered, "I take it to be an ongoing, never resolved argument about the rightness of choice" (p. 260).

This cultural view underpins a communicative and rhetorical rationale for risk dialogue. It sees analysis and decision as being best when it leads to enlightened choice, Nichols' (1963) rationale for rhetoric in society. It is a matter of many choices, variously individual but ultimately always collective. How and what one gains can affect what and why another loses. Such decisions require input from many disciplines. To this end, collective processes focusing on risk and crisis can reflect each culture's (individual, organizational, community, etc) sense of what they are and how they can be managed.

NEW HORIZONS AND OLD PROBLEMS

One of the challenges facing a project such as this *Handbook* is to track key trends that have brought some subject (here is it is crisis and risk) to its current state and to look to its future to see advances that are likely and those that are needed. One contributor to such thinking has recently reaffirmed the need for a multidisciplinary approach to risk. Althaus (2005) reasoned that "risk is an ordered application of knowledge to the unknown" (p. 567). Such problems, she demonstrated, are relevant to many disciplines, each of which offers insights worthy to the task, but none are definitive. She stressed the distinction between "risk defined as a reality that exists in its own right in the world (e.g., objective risk and real risk) and risk defined as a reality by virtue of a judgment made by a person or the application of some knowledge to uncertainty (e.g., subjective risk, observed risk, perceived risk)" (pp. 567–568). The former is metaphysical, whereas the latter centers on epistemology. "Taken as an epistemological reality, risk comes to exist by virtue of judgments made under conditions of uncertainty" (p. 569). Another of the splitting points is this: "The idea is that risk and uncertainty both relate to the unknown, but that risk is an attempt to 'control' the unknown by applying knowledge based on the orderliness of the world. Uncertainty, on the other hand, represents the totally random unknown and thus cannot be controlled or predicted" (p. 569).

Science, logic, and mathematics, Althaus (2005) reasoned, focus on calculable phenomenon and objective reality. The other disciplines tend to center on subjective reality. She did not list communication per se, but did include other social sciences and humanities. Is communication, as linguistics, interested in terminology and meaning as terministic screens (Burke 19698) or identification (Burke 1968)? Like history and the humanities, does it deal with narratives by which people live (Fisher, 1958)? Is it something else, as Campbell (1996) synthesized, that gives life to facts, voice to evaluations, and reason to policy debates? Can scientists convince others of the rightness of their investigation and conclusions without communicating? Can the policy makers and the concerned citizens engage in debate and dialogue without applying the knowable strategies of communication? As Rowan (1994) reasoned, communication can be more or less effective, merely the application of prescriptive guidelines or the cautiously and ethically developed strategies of propositional discourse.

Althaus (2005) rightly observed five kinds of risk: Subjective, objective, real, observed, and perceived. A communication perspective would suggest that each of these in various ways constitutes not only an analytical perspective but also a rhetorical problem. The problem results from the need to engage others, to bring discourse to bear on shared subjectivity, the probative force of analysis of the objective and real, to give effective voice to the concerns that arise from observed and perceived uncertainties. Finally, one can argue that communication is a vital part of the means by which people in society, as well as each community, work together and set themselves at odds with one another in the attempt to bring control to risk. A communication perspective assumes the roles and responsibilities to engage in discord and achieve harmony as people collaborate and compete in the definition of risk, its analysis and management, as well as its allocation. In this way, communication is foundational to efforts to create that partnership sought by Fischhoff (1995).

Treatises on crisis and risk communication range from the highly theoretical, to the research based, and the totally practical. The latter is often characterized by guidelines tested through experience by professional communicators and offered as best practices.

One fairly recent book offers practical advice predicated on a mental models approach (Morgan et al., 2002). It is a self-proclaimed do-it-yourself book aimed at helping communicators know how to "provide information that people need to make informed decisions about risks to health, safety, and the environment" (p. ix). The tack of this book is to blend "the natural science of how risks are created and controlled and the social science of how people comprehend and respond to such risks" (pp. ix–x). Such advice is valued because "the stakes riding on public understanding are high for those who create risks, as well as for the public that bears them" (p. 3). Done poorly, risk communication is corporate propaganda seeking falsely deserved understanding and support by important publics. Done properly it brings sound scientific knowledge to be the servant of the public interest. It requires "authoritative and trustworthy sources" (p. 4). It must meet the needs of one or more key public hoping to make enlightened choices. Those who engage in this endeavor need to realize that they can and will meet opposition from scientists who doubt the goal of making an informed public, which is "mostly a waste of time," they think (p. 7).

One of the key challenges is to recognize the useful communication outcome to be accomplished with decisions about risks that are variously controllable as well as variously observable. To solve such problems, the mental models approach (MMA) "offers a way to ensure that, if they choose to, laypeople can understand how the risks they face are created and controlled, how well science understands those risks, and how great they seem to be" (Morgan et al., 2002, p. 14). The success of this process rests with "its ability to improve the understanding of those who attend to the communications that it produces" (p. 14).

MMA assumes as an underpinning the seven stages of developing analysis, message and partnership outlined by Fischhoff (1995, discussed above). Once basic analysis by experts has developed sufficiently so that a scientifically sound risk assessment can be achieved, the risk communicators are ready to start developing messages and partnerships by applying the MMA. This approach recognizes the value of what the experts want to tell lay audiences, but also knows that messages need to respect and address those publics' concerns. The message in the risk communication cannot successfully and ethically be only what the experts want to say. Expects are unwise to blame the public for thoughts and beliefs that appear to be stupid, irrational, or hysterical.

Thus, the MMA process begins with the development of an expert decision model which features what is known and what needs to be known to make appropriate risk decisions. This model must reflect what is known and where gaps exist in expert knowledge. The second step is to conduct general, open-ended interviews to ascertain what people believe about hazards. The third step requires getting even more insights through surveys to determine what is on the mind of the public. Knowing the scientific decision model and the concerns as well as beliefs of the public, the risk communicators are now ready to compare the expert model and the lay model to determine where agreement and disagreement exist. It's time to determine where knowledge gaps exist and what beliefs need to be corrected. With this information at hand, a tentative risk message can be drafted. This is tested by getting reactions from members of the lay audience. With this information as feedback, the message is evaluated and refined. After the message has been refined, it is put into play. It needs to be presented by a single spokesperson. The voice should be respectful and neutral. The content needs to feature the information the lay public needs to make the correct decisions and the way best to interpret such information and to make decisions about each specific hazard.

Messages relevant to risks that others seem to control, such as a nuclear generating facility or a chemical plant, need to be objective. Public health risk communication messages, so the MMA logic goes, can be more persuasive because compliance is essential in this context. People, in this situation, need information and persuasive motivation to take control of their health. In facility-based contexts, source neutrality and decision guidance are intended to help people understand the specific risk and approach it with the appropriate level of risk tolerance—or intolerance.

One of the early contributors to the effort to understand and refine the risk communication process, Rowan (1995) advanced the CAUSE approach which features five steps: Credibility, awareness, understanding, satisfaction, and enactment. Step one calls on leaders to establish *credibility* with key publics. Second, they need to create or recognize the target audience's *awareness* of the likely occurrence of the risk and its severity as well as measures for constructive response to it. Third, achieve sufficient scientific *understanding* of the risk and its consequences. The expert-based model of risk communication (scientific-positivistic) assumes that scientists become satisfied by the assessment and management of a risk and seek public concurrence. According to Rowan's scheme of things, the fourth step requires that *satisfaction* must be community based; it depends on the decisions the concerned public feel comfortable to make given the data they know and believe and the heuristics they apply to interpret the data and make decisions regarding the hazard. The last step, *enactment*, requires that appropriate measures—by key individuals, by the risk entity, or by a government agency—be put into place based on the decision derived through community dialogue.

Such community dialogue can occur in many venues, including the use of public meetings, public hearings, protests, and citizens advisory committees (CACs or citizens advisory panels, CAPs). Such infrastructures can succeed or fail; the design and management of CACs seems predictive of success (Lynn & Busenberg, 1995). Infrastructures are best when they bring together company representatives (management, scientific, and communication), government (elected officials and emergency response and environmental monitoring personnel), and interested citizens (Heath, Bradshaw, & Lee, 2002).

The community partnership, infrastructural approach builds on the assumption that sound science and informatics as well as emergency response protocols must be vetted collectively so that members, risk bearers, of the community come to an appropriate level of risk tolerance. The scientific and emergency response parts of the message are either reinforced or frustrated by the quality of the process leading members of the community to support or oppose the inter-organizational collaborative process as well as the organizations and individuals in the process. Such analysis features at least the following concepts: Benefits/harms associated with the risk, support/opposition, uncertainty, control (personal, organizational, and community), trust, cognitive involvement, risk tolerance, proximity, and knowledge (Heath, 1997).

The logic of this approach squares with Rayner's (1992) observation, "risk behavior is a function of how human beings, individually and in groups, perceive their place in the world and the things that threaten it" (p. 113). More than a simple communication process, effective risk communication reflects the wholeness of the communities where it occurs. Guidelines help us understand what makes the community whole and strengthens the process which often counts for more than the content—from the lay perspective. Experts need to acknowledge the desire of the public to exert influence over factors they feel put them at risk. To this end, a collaborative approach occurs when experts, managers, politicians, community experts, and the general public work together to find facts and put appropriate emergency response protocols into place (O'Hair, Heath, & Becker, 2005). The public must be empowered, rather than marginalized. Their value-laden judgments should be acknowledged and appreciated as such. Trust needs to develop over time through relationship development and mutual regard. Scientists need to recognize their uncertainty and that of the community. It may well be a strength, not a weakness, to acknowledge knowledge gaps and conflicting opinions. Benefits and harms need to be weighed as part of the total decision model. Responsive strategic business planning and high standards of corporate responsibility can earn trust and help people to be appropriately risk tolerant. People need to come to believe in the decision making process which can sustain them, as risk bearers, as well as the risk creators and risk arbiters. Proaction is likely to be more successful in such situations than reaction (Heath, 1997).

In the public health arena, many powerful approaches to risk communication have been proposed, tested, and refined. One, Witte's (1994) extended parallel process model (EPPM), acknowledged the role of fear as a factor in risk assessment, management, decision making, and communication. This model assumes that messages, external stimuli, can point to and arouse feelings of self-efficacy, response efficacy, susceptibility, and severity. These factors can be built into public health messages. How, the theory asks, do people respond to and process such messages? The answer predicts that some people will not perceive a threat to themselves or others and therefore will make no response to the message. Otherwise they may focus on the perceived efficacy or the perceived threat. If they do the former, they are likely to progress toward the hazard as danger control applying protective motivation and accepting the public health message. If they respond with fear, they are likely to become defensive and reject the message. This leads to fear control.

Such logics have been used in many public health contexts, such as AIDS-protective behaviors (Murray-Johnson, Witte, Liu, & Hubbell, 2001). If targets of public health messages believe or can be brought to believe they have the self-efficacy to manage the fear their decision can lead to, dread control which includes response efficacy adds a vital dimension to the content of the risk message. By extension, one could argue that a similar model is likely to predict how people in a community at risk would respond to emergency response measures such as shelter in place. They need to believe they can successfully follow that advice and that the advice is sound for them to fully appreciate and appropriately respond to the message.

Reviewing accomplishments achieved from 1995 to 2005, McComas (2006) concluded that notable achievements had occurred in understanding the role of mass media, social trust, science, and affect. She pointed to advances in strategically designing messages by using risk comparison, narratives, and visualization. She reasoned that key advances were continuing in the understanding of risk severity, social norms and response efficacy as foundations for improve risk communication can lead to productive outcomes for the benefit of society and those concerned about and affected by risks. She believed that one of the major communication contexts, public outreach, was also improving in design and execution. In all, risk communication advances best in practice and through research when it is seen as multidisciplinary and multidimensional, and when trust is emphasized in risk management.

Throughout this section, we have featured risk communication but have not been unmindful of crisis response preparedness. A crisis is a risk manifested. Excellence in risk communication can both reduce the likelihood of a crisis, but serve as the knowledge, evaluative, infrastructural, and risk tolerance foundation for crisis response. As is true of risks, people seek control. A crisis can suggest that some one or some organization has not been willing or able to exert the appropriate control to respond appropriately to protect the interests of some risk bearers. Thus, crisis assessment and management begins with sound approaches to risk management.

PRECAUTIONARY PRINCIPLE

In the midst of the debates over degrees of risk and risk management policy, the precautionary principle has enlivened and frustrated the dialogue. This concept was introduced into the risk literature to foster restraint against risks. It was intended to insert a principle and a procedure into such debates to maximize the visibility of the intolerance some advocates have for certain risks. It was intended to focus the controversy. It became itself a centerpiece for controversy, especially as it has been interjected into discussions of the tolerability of biotechnology risks.

The logic of this principle is that if the consequences of an action are not well known and the subject of substantial controversy regarding the potentiality of irreversible consequences, then actions and decisions should err on the side of caution. As such this principle was advocated to slow the approval or even deny it for those risks which are not yet well known and the consequences of which can in fact be of great magnitude (nanotechnology for instance).

This principle has often been captured in various cultural truisms. "Look before you leap." "Two wrongs do not make a right." "Better safe than sorry." "An ounce of prevention is worth a pound of cure." Colloquialisms such as these can be challenged by other familiar sayings. "The early bird gets the worm" suggests that the bird willing to judge the risks of daylight or spring time is more likely to get the reward than will the more cautious one. We might add this one, "nothing ventured, nothing gained."

These ordinary expressions suggest not only the boundaries but the essence of contention regarding this concept. If we are too cautious, goes the argument of certain biotechnologies that could increase crop production, people will die of famine while we are worrying about the consequences of new crops. The likelihood of death by famine, so these advocates would say, is starkly demonstrable, whereas the uncertainty about the long-term effects of the new technology are merely or essentially only potential and perhaps risk. They may be nothing more than politically motivated caution to throw a cold blanket over the fire of innovation.

Rather than reducing the uncertainty of risk decisions, the precautionary principle may in fact raise the level of uncertainty. Some scientific premises can only be tested through implementation. If they are kept from being tested, the degree to which they increase or decrease risk may not be known. Critics of the principle suggest that outcome is contradictory to the desires of the advocates of the principle. If, for instance, science knows the hazards of lead pipes, should the precautionary principle reduce the implementation of an alternative, such as vinyl pipe, until the health hazard of that technology is determined? If public health specialists know that X percent of the population will die or suffer severe consequences from small pox inoculation, what then would be the advisability of inoculating health care workers on the assumption that one or the many potential means of bioterrorism is small pox?

Such conundrums are the essential themes of contention in risk communication. The objective is to reduce the likelihood that a risk becomes manifested and a crisis occurs. Without doubt both (or the various) sides of a risk controversy opt for manageable caution. The problematic is the full understanding of manageable caution and enlightened choice. Those who favor the role of science in such discussions may be either more or less cautious accordingly. Science does not necessarily predict caution or high levels of risk tolerance. These parameters are necessary ingredients in such debates and their politics. Until some better system results, and perhaps none will, part of risk communication's mission then is to give voice to the competing perspectives (factual and evaluative) and provide platforms for contentious but constructive and honest dialogue. The precautionary principle is not irrelevant in such discussions, nor is it inherently the clarity that ends controversy. It does demonstrate one important principle of risk management however; that is the cultural dimension that surrounds the role of science and seeks to constrain and guide it.

PROSPECTS AND PROBLEMS

Obligation is a fundamental assumption guiding crisis management and response, as well as risk assessments, management and communication. Those on whom focus centers during what may or may not be a crisis have an obligation to society, key publics, to answer concerns relevant to the nature, magnitude, cause, responsibility, severity, and lessons learned. A starting point in crisis response is a vigilance for the kinds of risks that might manifest themselves and the persons who could be affected by such occurrence. A crisis, in this sense, can be foreseen as occurring; the moment and magnitude of such occurrence, however, may be difficult and even impossible to predict. Various individuals and organizations are variously obligated to risk and crisis management. How they respond has societal implications.

As we project this base of intellectual inquiry into the chapters that follow, we recognize that some universal and recurring questions seem worth raising. The framework for these questions results from the intersection of issues to be managed, crises to be managed, and risks to be managed. (For a typical list of questions relevant to risk management and communication, see Golding 1992, p. 28). To that end, we ask:

1. What is a crisis? What makes it a crisis? What risk was basic to the crisis?
2. What can be done to mitigate each kind of crisis through planning, prevention, and pre-crisis communication?
3. What makes some organizations crisis prone?
4. What responses to a crisis are demanded by various exigencies that prescribe and limit the available responses?
5. What ethical challenges drive crisis preparation, planning and response?
6. What is a risk? Is a crisis a risk manifested?
7. Why is the "risk" actually so?
8. How safe is safe enough? Who decides how safe is safe enough?
9. How good is the knowledge base for risk analysis, management, and communication? How can social informatics be leveraged for better community response?
10. How well do the participants in risk decision making handle uncertainty—and the locus of control and blame?
11. Do the institutions engaged have a positive or negative affect on the dialogue—its nature, trajectory, and outcome?
12. Do the motives of the communicators lead to aligned or divergent interests?
13. What factors influence perceptions of risk and benefit?
14. What perceptions are integrated in each policy position? How well are the perceptions so integrated?
15. How does society manage and communicate about risks that are unacceptable to some segment of society?
16. How are the normative considerations such as equity and social justice integrated into risk policy?
17. What criteria guide risk management and crisis response policies? Are the NRF and NIMS platforms sufficient?
18. How well do participants share meaning and interpretive heuristics of risks?
19. What are the dynamic connections between issues, crisis, and risk?
20. How can media and technology be leveraged more effectively for community response?

CONCLUSION

The last decade witnessed an explosion of risk communication research focusing primarily on natural and man-made disasters, preventable diseases, and health hazards. During the same period, advances in communication sciences reached levels of proliferation unmatched in the history of the discipline (O'Hair, 2004). A dramatic emphasis on homeland security creates unprecedented opportunities to integrate risk communication research with new theories of communication science resulting in confluent models of community risk communication. A recent NSF report argues for greater interdisciplinary cooperation among basic natural sciences, human decision processes, economists, engineers, and communication scholars (NSF, 2002). The Government Accounting Office reported to Congress last year that risk communication theory and protocol must assume a greater role in threat mitigation plans (GAO-04-682, 2004). In numerous government reports, the authors highlight the important role of communication in mitigating, preventing, and responding to terrorist acts. Just about every GAO report on public response organizations and agencies places communication at the top of the list.

Regardless of the content of the various arguments advanced in this volume, despite differences of perspective and philosophy, we think the authors are united in one central theme. They believe that risks, and related crises, should be understood, managed, and communicated so that people can lead a more healthy and happy existence. On matters of crisis, the holding line is that the literature must never forget that those who violate the public trust should not be judged to manage crises so well as to unfairly benefit from them but must be found wanting because of their transgressions. This is the blending of science, management, social responsibility, public policy, and cultural morality. These are the ingredients of an infrastructure that must operate to abate risk and ferret out the violator in crisis.

Aside from companion disciplines that are intimately engaged in crisis and risk communication problematics, the communication discipline boils down to process and meaning. It needs to understand and bring in the voice of science and the decisions of management. It must accept and foster communication infrastructures that weave through the fabric of society teetering between monologue and dialogue. The past is not irrelevant as a point of comparison and as a foundation, but it is not an hegemony dictating risk acceptance and crisis response. In this sense, progress becomes an objective and a peril. People cannot be trod on in its name, nor can we forget its lure as the essence of perfection, and, as Burke (1968) said, humans are rotten with perfection.

For this reason, we are obliged to acknowledge that "risk statements are by nature statements that can be deciphered only in an interdisciplinary (competitive) relationship, because they assume in equal measure insight into technical know-how and familiarity with cultural perceptions and norms" (Beck, 2004, p. 215). Here is the logic of control. The concern is the nature and locus of control.

On the one hand, society can be enriched by the control of risks to its advantage. The other hand suggests that the peril is the loss of dialogue and the instantiation of an hegemony of control that privileges some and marginalizes others. Now, if risk manifested into crisis occurs because the offending party did not exercise control in the public interest (preferring partisanship qua partisanship) we see that control is distorted. That can threaten the viability of society which can be conceptualized as the collective management of risk.

Such concerns, at a societal level, are matters of degree not binary decisions. To ask whether people are risk tolerant or risk intolerant can mask that this is an interval judgment, one that is contextualized. To ask whether some one violated public trust during a crisis is not binary, but embraces a range of expectation violations, in type and degree. Such decisions blend, rather than deny, the interaction or reality and interpretation. To that degree, then, they are the fodder of communication, especially dialogue rather than monologue.

REFERENCES

Adam, B., & Van Loon, J. (2000). Introduction: Repositioning risk; the challenge for social theory. In B. Adam, U. Beck, & J. Van Loon (Eds). *The risk society: Critical issues for social theory* (pp. 1–31). Thousand Oaks, CA: Sage.

Althaus, C. E. (2005). A disciplinary perspective on the epistemological status of risk. *Risk Analysis*, 25, 567–588.

Beck, U. (2004). Risk society revisited: Theory, politics, and research programmes. In B. Adam, U. Beck, & J. Van Loon (Eds). *The risk society: Critical issues for social theory* (pp. 211–229). Thousand Oaks, CA: Sage.

Berg, D. M., & Robb, S. (1992). Crisis management and the "paradigm case." In E. L. Toth & R. L. Heath (Eds.), *Rhetorical and critical approaches to public relations* (pp. 93–109). Hillsdale, NJ: Erlbaum.

Burke, K. (1968). *Language as symbolic action: Essays on life, literature, and method.* Berkeley: University of California Press.

Burke, K. (1969). *A rhetoric of motives.* Berkeley: University of California Press.

Campbell, K. K. (1996). *The rhetorical act* (2nd ed.). Belmont, CA: Wadsworth.

Chemical Manufacturers Association (1989). *Title III: One year later.* Washington, DC: Chemical Manufacturers Association.

Chess, C., Salomone, K. L., Hance, B. J., & Saville, A. (1995). Results of a National Symposium On Risk Communication: Next steps for government agencies. *Risk Analysis, 15,* 115–125.

Covello, V. T., & Peters, R. G. (1996), The determinants of trust and credibility in environmental risk communication: An empirical study. In V. H. Sublet, V. T. Covello, & T. L. Tinker (Eds.). *Scientific uncertainty and its influence on the public communication process* (pp. 33–63). Dordrecht: Kluwer Academic.

Covello, V. T., Sandman, P. M., & Slovic, P. (1988). *Risk communication, risk statistics, and risk comparisons: A manual for plant managers.* Washington, DC: Chemical Manufacturers Association.

Douglas, M. (1992). *Risk and blame.* London: Routledge.

Environmental Protection Agency (1988, April). *Seven cardinal rules of risk communication.* Washington, DC: Author.

Fischhoff, B. (1995). Risk perception and communication unplugged: Twenty years of process. *Risk Analysis, 15,* 137–145.

Fischhoff, B., Slovic, P., Lichtenstein, S., Read, S., & Combs, B. (1978). How safe is safe enough? A psychometric study of attitudes towards technological risks and benefits. *Policy Sciences,* 9, 127–152.

Fisher, W. R. (1987). Human communication as narration: Toward a philosophy of reason, value, and action. Columbia, SC: University of South Carolina Press.

Freudenberg, N. (1984). *Not in our backyards! Community action for health and the environment.* New York: Monthly Review Press.

Golding, D. (1992), A social and programmatic history of risk research. In S. Krimsky & D. Golding (Eds.). *Social theories of risk* (pp. 23–52). Westport, CT: Praeger.

Hadden, S.G. (1989). Institutional barriers to risk communication. *Risk Analysis, 9,* 301–308.

Heath, R. L. (1997). *Strategic issues management: Organizations and public policy challenges.* Thousand Oaks, CA: Sage.

Heath, R. L., Bradshaw, J., & Lee, J. (2002). Community relationship building: Local leadership in the risk communication infrastructure. *Journal of Public Relations Research,* 14, 317–353.

Heath, R. L., & Millar, D. P. (2004). A rhetorical approach to crisis communication: Management, communication processes, and strategic responses. In D. P. Millar & R. L. Heath (Eds.). *Responding to crisis: A rhetorical approach to crisis communication* (pp. 1–17). Mahwah, NJ: Erlbaum.

Heath, R. L., & Nathan, K. (1991). Public relations' role in risk communication: Information, rhetoric and power. *Public Relations Quarterly, 35*(4), 15–22.

Kasperson, R. E. (1992). The social amplification of risk: Progress in developing an integrative framework. In S. Krimsky & D. Golding (Eds.), *Social theories of risk* (pp. 153–178). Westport, CT: Praeger.

Krimsky, S. (1992). The role of theory in risk studies. In S. Krimsky & D. Golding (Eds.), *Social theories of risk* (pp. 3–22). Westport, CT: Praeger.

Lerbinger, O. (1997). *The crisis manager: Facing risk and responsibility.* Mahwah, NJ: Erlbaum.

Lynn, F. M., & Busenberg, G. J. (1995). Citizen advisory committees and environmental policy: What we know, what's left to discover. *Risk Analysis,* 15, 147–162.

McComas, K. A. (2006). Defining moments in risk communication research: 1995–2005. *Journal of Health Communication,* 11, 75–91.

Morgan, M. G., Fischhoff, B., Bostrom, A., & Atman, C. J. (2002). *Risk communication: A mental models approach.* Cambridge: Cambridge University Press.

Murray–Johnson, L., Witte, K., Liu, W. L., & Hubbell, A. P. (2110). Addressing cultural orientations in fear appeals: Promoting AIDS–protective behaviors among Mexican immigrant and African American adolescents, American and Taiwanese college students. *Journal of Health Communication,* 6, 335–358.

National Research Council (1989). *Improving risk communication.* Washington DC: National Academy Press.

National Response Framework. (2007). Washington, DC: Department of Homeland Security.

Nichols, M. H. (1963). *Rhetoric and criticism.* Baton Rouge: Louisiana State University Press.

Palenchar, M. J., & Heath, R. L. (2007). Strategic risk communication: Adding value to society. Public Relations Review, 33, 120–129.

O'Hair, D., Heath, R., & Becker, J. (2005). Toward a paradigm of managing communication and terrorism. In D. O'Hair, R. Heath, & J. Ledlow (Eds.), *Community preparedness, deterrence, and response to terrorism: Communication and terrorism* (pp. 307–327). Westport, CT: Praeger.

O'Hair, D. (2004). *Measuring risk/crisis communication: Taking strategic assessment and program evaluation to the next level. Risk and crisis communication: Building trust and explaining complexities when emergencies arise* (pp. 5–10). Washington, DC: Consortium of Social Science Associations.

Plough, A., & Krimsky, S. (1987). The emergence of risk communication studies: Social and political context. *Science, Technology, & Human Values*, *12*(3–4), 4–10.

Raucher, A. R. (1968). *Public relations and business: 1900–1929*. Baltimore: Johns Hopkins University Press.

Rayner, S. (1992). Cultural theory and risk analysis. In S. Krimsky & D. Golding (Eds.), *Social theories of risk* (pp. 83–115). Westport, CT: Praeger.

Renn, O. (1992). Concepts of risk: A classification. In S. Krimsky & D. Golding (Eds.). *Social theories of risk* (pp. 53–79). Westport, CT: Praeger.

Reynolds, B., & Seeger, M. W. (2005). Crisis and emergency risk communication as an integrative model. *Journal of Health Communication*, 10, 43–55.

Rosenblatt, R. (1984, December 17). All the world gasped. *Time*, *124*, p. 20.

Rowen, K. E. (1994). Why rules for risk communication are not enough: A problem–solving approach to risk communication. *Risk Analysis*, 14, 365–374.

Rowan, K. E. (1995). What risk communicators need to know: An agenda for research. In B. R. Burleson (Ed.), *Communication yearbook 18* (pp. 300–319). Thousand Oaks, CA: Sage.

Starr, C. (1972). Benefit–cost studies in sociotechnical systems. In Committee on Public Engineering Policy, *Perspective on Benefit–Risk Decision Making. Washington*, DC: National Academic of Engineering.

Wiebe, R. H. (1968). *Businessmen and reform: A study of the progressive movement*. Chicago: Quadrangle Books.

Witte, K. (1994). Fear control and danger control: A test of the extended parallel process model. *Communication Monographs*, 61, 113–134.

2

Historical Trends of Risk and Crisis Communication

Michael J. Palenchar
University of Tennessee

The industrial and information ages have created a whole new range of risks and crises, while advances in communication and information technologies have increased people's awareness of these risks as well as increasing the opportunities for dialogue and shared decision making based on risk assessment and associated political and social discussions. As the factors that have a propensity to increase risk and crises proliferate and as headlines shout out newsworthy crises such as increasing population density, increased settlement in high-risk areas, increased technological risk, aging U. S. population, emerging infectious diseases and antimicrobial resistance, increased international travel and increased terrorism (Auf def Heida, 1996), risk and crisis communications will play a larger role in Quintilian's (1951) principle of the good person communicating well as a foundation for fostering enlightened choices through dialogue in the public sphere.

Technological developments also led to the advancement of new tactics for terrorism that require risk and crisis communication initiatives. For example, the American Council on Science and Health's (2003) manual *A Citizens' Guide to Terrorism Preparedness and Response: Chemical, Biological, Radiological, and Nuclear* extended its worst-case scenario developments to include among others: chemical weapons such as lewisite, mustard, arsine, cyanide, phosgene, sarin, tabin and VX, including related risk and crisis communication elements. The council's communication goal with the manual was to educate the public about the health hazards of these weapons and to offer suggestions as to how people might protect themselves.

As Erikson (1994) adeptly stated, modern disasters challenge humans with a "new species of trouble," and risk, crises and ultimately disasters are the definitive challenge to communication and public relations scholars and practitioners. With this new species of trouble as a center point, this chapter explores the historical trends of risk and crisis communication research, unraveling the rapid growth and evolution of both fields while noting similarities and differences between them, and reviews the development of academic research centers related to advancing the study and practice of risk and crisis communication.

RAPID GROWTH OF RISK COMMUNICATION

Identifying or pointing to a specific date or event that launched risk communication or crisis communication is impossible, as both movements grew organically out of a variety of perspectives and initiatives, whether they are community-based activism, government response or industry initiated. Certain incidents, events and research streams, however, loom large in the history of both these fields of communication study.

The history of risk management and risk assessment can be traced back beyond Greek and Roman times (Covello & Mumpower, 1985). The origins of risk analysis have been traced to the Babylonians in 3200 BC where myths, metaphors, and rituals were used to predict risks and to communicate knowledge about avoiding hazards; risk communication was embedded in folk discourse (Krimsky & Plough, 1988).

Modern risk analysis was developed in the early part of the 20th century by engineers, epidemiologists, actuaries, and industrial hygienists, among others, who looked at hazards associated with technology that was rapidly developing from and during the industrial revolution (Kates & J. Kasperson, 1983). The development of probability theory during the 17th century in Europe brought explicit formulations of risk concepts. U.S. federal legislation in the 1970s, including the formation of the Environmental Protection Agency (EPA), elevated the role of formal risk assessment.

Explicit, modern-era interest in risk communication can be traced back to the 1950s and the "Atoms for Peace" campaign. The later development of the anti-nuclear movement in the 1970s helped bring risk communication to the limelight (R. Kasperson & Stallen, 1991). Interest in risk communication was considered "quite recent" during the late 1980s (Krimsky & Plough, 1988). According to the National Research Council (NRC, 1989), the motivating sources and goals for this direction in risk communication was a requirement for or desire by government and industry officials to inform, to overcome opposition to decisions, to share decision-making power, and to develop effective alternatives to direct regulatory control. Overall, according to Krimsky and Golding (1992), the field of risk studies, including risk communication, developed from the practical needs of industrialized societies to regulate technology and to protect its citizens from natural and man-made, technological hazards.

The modern age of environmental risk communication in the United States, with its focus on health and environmental issues, also can be traced to the second term (1983–1985) of William Ruckelshaus as EPA Administrator (Peters, Covello, & McCallum, 1997). According to Ruckelshaus (1983), he advocated the Jeffersonian goals of informing and involving the public as foundation principles in environmental risk management.

Citizen participation in environmental regulation is a relatively new development, although since the mid-1970s, it has been viewed as a standard feature of public policy (Szasz, 1994). The legacy of today's philosophy of community-right-to-know began to change dramatically in the mid-1980s. One of the most horrific modern industrial crisis events occurred on December 3, 1984, by the release of methyl isocyanate (MIC) at the Union Carbide plant at Bhopal, India, which caused more than 3,000 deaths and over 200,000 major injuries (Shrivastava, 1987). According to Union Carbide (2004), the release caused more than 3,800 deaths while several other thousand suffered permanent or partial disabilities.[1]

Within two years of the disaster, after 145 law suits against Union Carbide, and after the occurrence of other incidents on American soil—among smaller incidents, a Union Carbide's plant in West Virginia leaked a different toxic gas in 1985, injuring 135 people (*New York Times*, 1985)—the U.S. Congress heeded advice from a federal government-sponsored research project that showed more than 7,000 accidents of the kind between 1980 and 1985 (Falkenberry, 1995), and numerous provisions and legislations were developed and passed. Most notably the Comprehensive Environmental Response, Compensation, and Liability Act (CERCLA), or Superfund, and its reauthorization (Superfund Amendment and Reauthorization Act (SARA)) of 1986 requires that specific procedures be implemented to assess the release of hazardous substances. Specifically focused on risk communication, SARA requires public participation provision and the community right-to-know requirements of the Emergency Planning and Community Right-To-Know Act of 1986 (EPCRA). SARA requires companies to provide public information concerning chemical emissions; in so doing this act gave a new scope and purpose to risk communication.[2] According to Peters et al. (1997), "In a period of barely ten years, environmental risk communication has evolved from a management concept to codified legislation" (p. 43).

For risk communication, the key part of SARA is EPCRA, which gives the EPA oversight of risk communication efforts related to the formation of local emergency planning committees (LEPC). SARA also mandated each state's governor to appoint members to a State Emergency Response Commission (SERC), which in turn created LEPCs. Each SERC is responsible for implementing EPCRA provisions within each state, including the 3,500 local emergency planning districts and appointed LEPCs for each district. By 1986, 30 states or cities had some form of community-right-to-know pollution requirements (Hearne, 1996).

Codifying environmental risk communication, SARA and other federal policies require companies to inform citizens regarding the kinds and quantities of chemicals that are manufactured, stored, transported and emitted in each community. SARA's underpinning assumption is that as companies report the toxicity about the materials they produce, transport and store people could become more informed of the level of risk in their neighborhood. Among other outcomes, this federal initiative was intended to increase the flow of various kinds of technical information from experts to community residents and to open channels of commentary between them. It is also likely that some of the motives for the legislation was to pressure the industry to adopt and implement even higher standards of community and employee safety.

According to Hadden (1989a), the regulation by itself is useful, but not enough to avoid accidents like the one in Bhopal. Crude technical information about the proximity of hazardous materials alone does not empower citizens to control or prevent disasters in industrial facilities. Few states had right-to-know laws before the federal regulation was passed. Hadden determined that the number of citizens who were actively using those laws for any practical reasons were very low, mostly due to the fact that people in the communities ignored the existence of the law and that local governments and companies were not making an effort to educate them about it.

Although the right to know as an approach to the policymaking process took an important transformational step with EPCRA, it has its roots in the first U. S. constitutional convention. James Wilson, an influential lawyer among the American Founding Founders (National Archives, 2007), argued that the right to know should be used as a way for the public to have some control over their elected officials. Later on, the press argued for the public's right to know against censorship during World War II, but only in the mid-1980s did the right to know become an established federal law (Hadden, 1989a). Jacobson (2003) identified the Freedom of Information Act of 1966 (FOIA), an amendment to the Administrative Procedure Act (APA) signed by President Lyndon Baines Johnson, as the first statutory regulation that included the right to know principle. However, as Jacobson (2003) noted, FOIA "was not an environmental statute, but a broader effort" (p. 344) to establish a statutory right to access government information.

Numerous other events highlight the development of both the research and practice of risk communication science. The 1979 National Governor's Association Emergency Management Project helped conceptualize emergency management and related literature into four interrelated phases that are still used to guide much of the risk and crisis communication research today: mitigation, preparedness, response and recovery (Lindell & Perry, 2004).

Also in 1979 the U. S. House Committee on Science and Technology urged the National Science Foundation to develop a research program to evaluate comparative risks of alternative technical solutions related to areas such as energy and the environment and promote education related to risk assessment (U.S. Congress, 1979). With the formation of the Technology Assessment and Risk Analysis (TARA) group as a result of Congress' urging and the efforts of the National Science Foundation, this put risk analysis at the forefront of the National Science Foundation efforts (Golding, 1992).

Another turning point in the study and practice of risk communication was the founding of the Society for Risk Analysis in 1980. The multidisciplinary and international membership group had 300 members within the first year, 1,500 members by 1987 (Golding, 1992) and has a current membership of approximately 2,000. Their focus on risk analysis includes risk assessment, characterization, communication, management and policy (Society for Risk Analysis, 1993).

Lindell and Perry (2004) suggested that the current era in risk communication also can be traced back to a risk communication conference held in Washington D.C. in 1986 that brought more than 500 scholars, government officials and industry representatives from an eclectic range of private and public organizations and academic and professional disciplines. Another of the key moments in the development of risk communication within the United States was the formation by the NRC of their Commission on Risk Perception and Communication, which met six times from May 1987 through June 1988. The NRC formed this new committee after completing a 1983 study entitled *Risk Assessment in the Federal Government: Managing the Process*, which focused on improving risk assessment and risk decisions within the government, but failed to adequately address and thus importantly pointed out that "a major element in risk management in a democratic society is communication about risk" (NRC, 1989, p. ix).

Another milestone in the development of risk communication was the *Emerging Paradigms of Risk and Risk Communication: A Cultural Synthesis* project, headed by Krimsky and Golding under an agreement of the Center for Environmental Management at Tufts University and the EPA, whose culminating work was their 1992 edited book *Social Theories of Risk*, which was the first systematic effort to highlight the contributions of social sciences to the theory of risk (Krimsky & Golding, 1992).

Similar academic and professional conferences and workshops have been held throughout the United States and the rest of the world. One of the more recent was a 2006 symposium sponsored by the Society for Risk Analysis and the National Science Foundation, entitled *Strategies for Risk Communication: Evolution, Evidence and Experience*, which explored practical methods and theories of risk communication arising from recent research in risk perception, neuroscience, and evolutionary social science focusing on how humans process and perceive uncertainty and risks, and to synthesize the findings from the multidisciplinary fields and develop practical risk communication strategies.

Recently, the Food and Drug Administration announced a new advisory committee designed to counsel the agency on how to strengthen the communication of risks and benefits of FDA-regulated products to the public. The Risk Communication Advisory Committee advises the FDA on strategic plans to communicate product risks and benefits and how to most effectively communicate specific product information to vulnerable audiences. The Institute of Medicine's 2006 report, *The Future of Drug Safety: Promoting and Protecting the Health of the Public,* recommended that Congress enact legislation establishing this new advisory committee.

If exposure to risk is not new, then why was there a renaissance in risk communication research and communication? Peters et al. (1997) suggested that there has been a long-term decline in public confidence and trust in traditional social institutions, especially government and industry that has paralleled the growth in environmental risk communication legislation. At the same time, as noted by Laird (1989) more than two decades ago, there has been a dramatic growth in the rise of citizen environmental groups, which is a major institutional shift in society moving from trust in public institutions to trust in citizens groups. Fischhoff (1990) argued a similar perspective, that stakeholders and other publics have insisted on a role in deciding how health, safety and environmental risks will be managed. According to Macauley (2006), "Perhaps what is different today is the widespread attention throughout all echelons of modern society—the public at large; governments at the federal, state and local levels; industry; and universities and other nongovernmental organizations—to questioning the limits and applications of risk analyses" (p. 1).

Evolution of Risk Communication Research

It has been approximately two decades since risk communication was identified as a new and emerging area of public health communication research and considered to be one of the fastest growing parts of public health education literature (Covello, von Winterfeldt, & Slovic, 1987; NRC, 1989). Krimsky and Golding (1992) argued that the field of risk studies and in particular risk communication matured in the 1970s and 1980s as evidenced by the appearance of distinct paradigms, models and conceptual frameworks that provided structure and coherence through scientific investigation, case studies and empirical findings, as well as the emergence of professional risk societies that focus on risk communication, specialized journals and academic programs of study. Many of fundamental concepts of risk communication have a long history, but the identification of risk communication as a distinct subject matter has only occurred since the early 1980s (Lindell & Perry, 2004). The past 30-plus years have seen a continued maturation of the field of risk communication as indicated by not just the evidence but the explosion of research in this field.

Leiss' (1996) historical analysis of risk communication determined that the term "risk communication" was coined in 1984, according to references listed in Rohrmann, Wiedemann and Stegelmann's *Risk Communication: An Interdisciplinary Bibliography* (4th edition). According to Leiss (1996), risk communication has from the onset had a practical intent based off the differences between risk assessments by experts and how they are perceived and understood by those who are affected.

Beyond systems and regulatory standards, however, risk communication grew out of risk assessment and risk perception studies. While some suggest that these streams developed separately, risk assessment and risk management research have never been separate streams of the risk research branch. A 1983 NRC report, known as the Red Book and entitled *Improving Risk Communication,* as well as other early risk research by the EPA, argued risk assessment and management including communication was a common theme. Goldstein's (2005) review of advances in risk assessment and communication suggested "a common theme by those involved in assessing and managing risks has been the need to integrate risk assessment and risk communication" (p. 142).

The EPA established risk communication as a means to open, responsible, informed, and reasonable scientific and value-laden discussion of risks associated with personal health and safety practices involved in living and working in proximity to harmful activities and toxic substances (NRC, 1989). Defined this way, risk management, including communication, is successful to the extent that people who fear that they may be or are demonstrably harmed by a risk can become more knowledgeable about and confident that sufficient control is imposed by the sources of the risk and by government or other external sources that are responsible for monitoring the risk generators.

At its inception, risk communication took on a source-oriented, linear approach that privileged the expert as the key participant in the process. Leiss (1996) called this the technical risk assessment period. In this period, industrial spokespersons were advised to appease or assuage the publics' apprehension by being credible and clear; it featured the role and work of experts who conducted epidemiological studies to ascertain whether risks exist. Typical of this view was the establishment of the EPA's (1988) seven cardinal rules of risk communication that advised communicators to tailor their messages to audiences and to use simple language and other basic, linear communication approaches. Part of the technical risk assessment period was the original work done by the NRC (1989) that emphasized the dissemination of information and featured potential outcomes. It treated risk communication as successful only to the extent that it raises the level of understanding and satisfies those involved that they are adequately informed within the limits of available knowledge.

Risk communication progressed through a period during which experts advised organizations that pose health, safety, or environmental risks to assuage employees and community members' apprehensions by being credible and telling the truth. The truth was to be based on the known likelihood of each risk's occurrence and the magnitude of its effect. The second phase of risk communication featured a more interactive approach: "We see risk communication as the interactive process of exchange of information and opinion among individuals, groups, and institutions" (NRC, 1989, p. 2).

Previous models of risk communication predicted that if people receive credible and clear information regarding scientifically assessed risk levels, they will accept the conclusions and policy recommendations of risk assessors. These models over-assume the power of information and do not acknowledge the power resources that concerned publics employ to exert political pressure in their effort to impose higher operating standards on the source of the ostensibly intolerable risk. Liu and Smith (1990) suggested that the view assumes that "if people are given the facts their subjective perceptions will begin to align with scientific judgments" (p. 332). That perspective reasons that if laypeople understand the company or government's side of the story, then confidence about risk would increase and complaints would go away (Gaudino, Fritsch, & Haynes 1989).

Continuing his summary of the discipline's history, Leiss (1996) identified a third phase, the current version of risk communication that features social relations. Risk communication based on a shared, social relations, community infrastructural approach works to achieve a level of discourse that can treat the content issues of the risk—technical assessment—and the quality of the relationships along with the political dynamics of the participants.

Hadden (1989b) observed crucial differences between what she defined as the old and new versions of risk communication. In the old approach "experts tried to persuade laymen of the validity of their risk assessments or risk decisions." This option is "impeded by lay risk perception, difficulties in understanding probabilities, and the sheer technical difficulty of the subject matter" (p. 301). In contrast, the new approach is based on dialogue and participation. According to Otway (1992), "Risk communication requirements are a political response to popular demands.... The main product of risk communication is not information, but the quality of the social relationship it supports. Risk communication is not an end in itself; it is an enabling agent to facilitate the continual evolution of relationships" (p. 227). This and other more recent approaches to risk communication highlight the importance of a dialogic, relationship-building approach to dealing with the concerns and perceptions of community residents and employees.

The new form of risk communication, however, is often impeded by the lack of institutions that are responsive to the needs, interests, and level of understanding of the publics affected by the potential or ostensible risk. Hadden (1989b) found that institutional barriers stand in the way of meaningful dialogue in communities where people experience risks that they worry are intolerable. Such barriers result, at least in part, from statutes that do not specify what technical data are crucial and, therefore, should be collected. People often encounter a maze of agencies, do not know where to acquire information, and suffer data dumps that provide huge amounts of information in ways that make it difficult to interpret.

Within these three eras of risk communication history are numerous research streams advanced by leading scholars from a multitude of fields. Concerned that residents rely on invalid assumptions, Fischhoff, Slovic, Lichtenstein, Read, and Combs (1978; Covello, 1983; Slovic, 1987) initiated "expressed preference" research, which involves measuring a wider array of attitudes than benefits to ascertain tolerable risk levels. These researchers found laypeople's risk ratings, unlike those of experts, are not just influenced by fatality estimates but also by their judgments of several qualitative factors such as involuntary, unfamiliar, unknown, uncontrollable, controlled by others, unfair, memorable, dreaded, acute, focused in time and space, fatal, delayed, artificial, and undetectable, as well as if individual mitigation is impossible.

Another important line of research is the mental models approach to risk communication that is based on the concept of how people understand and view various phenomena grounded in cognitive psychology and artificial intelligence research (Geuter & Stevens, 1983). The mental modes approach as applied to risk communication is built on the researchers from Carnegie Mellon University, including Baruch Fischhoff, Granger Morgan, Ann Bostrom, and associates (Morgan, Fischhoff, Bostrom, & Atman, 2002).

Other risk communication approaches that have led to the development of risk communication as a rich field of study and practice include convergence communication approach (Rogers & Kincaid, 1981), which is a theory that communication is an interactive, long-term process in which the values of the risk generating organization and the audience affect the process of communication. Hazard plus outrage approach, originally developed by Fischhoff and Slovic, has been extended and advanced in much of the work of Peter Sandman (e.g., 1987). From this research perspective, the risk bearer's view of the risk reflects the danger (hazard) and also just as importantly how they feel about the risk and their related emotions about the action (outrage). Finally, another major approach is the mental noise approach, championed by Covello (e.g., 1983, 1992), is that when people perceive themselves to be at risk is when communication is the most challenging and thus needs to carefully constructed, particularly in crisis situations.

One of the leading frameworks within risk communication studies that has been widely debated among sociologists and public relations among others during the past 20 years is "risk society." In his seminal book of the same name, Ulrich Beck (1992) argued that evolution of Western societies is more and more characterized by the pervasiveness of risk—uncertainties, insecurities and hazards. Central elements to risk society include uncertain personal identity that are subject to flux and choice, environmental hazards posed by new technologies, "self-endangerment" of industrial societies as their environmental choices and consequences become increasingly large and uncontrollable.

According to Beck (1992), one of the unique differences with Chernobyl in respect to risk is that the accident destroyed any concept of geographical boundaries for risk. The risk was not tied to a local community, physical location, and governmental boundary. Hazardous materials and their effects not only effected citizens in Belarus and the Ukraine, but went beyond borders, including no temporal limitations, with unknown long-term effects (Beck, 1992; Wynne, 1996). "The injured of Chernobyl are today, years after the catastrophe, not even all born yet" (Beck, 1996, p. 31). According to Beck (1995), incidents such as Chernobyl reformulate social understanding of risk.

While the study of risk and crisis communication, strategies, models and theories are important and helpful, we are reminded that these fields of study also have human implications and a critical examination must be included in the research stream. For example, McKie and Munshi (2007), in a critical reflection on the Union Carbide factory in Bhopal, India, crisis in 1984, suggested that post-crisis research in public relations publications "continue to treat Bhopal as a source of data to help frame guidelines for Western centres, without much concern for the fate of the victims of the tragedy" (p. 67).

Numerous other risk communication scholars, in their review of the literature, have suggested various typologies or evolutions of the field. Rowan (1994) suggested that risk communication literature contains three kinds of work that could provide a foundation for future risk communication. These include a technical versus democratic research perspective, with comparing and contrasting a more organizational management perspective that tends to privilege scientific and technical information to persuade the lay public, in contrast with a more democratic perspective that are concerned more with matters of justice and fairness. The second perspective are phenomenological analyses of people's everyday experience and notions of environmental risk, and the third perspective builds on broad philosophical principles for what constitutes good risk communication.

Fischhoff (1995) summarized the first 20 years of risk communication research into the developmental stages in risk management, moving through the various developmental stages characterized by the primary communication strategy: all we have to do is get the numbers right, all we have to do is tell them the numbers, all we have to do is explain what we mean by the numbers, all we have to do is show them they've accepted similar risks before, all we have to do is show them that it's a good deal for them, all we have to do is treat them nice, all we have to do is make them partners, and finally, all we have to do is all of the above.

More recently, Krimsky (2007) suggested three stages to the evolution of risk communication. Stage one was a linear communication process of delivering messages to a potentially unrealistic and irrational lay audience. Stage two was founded on the scientific uncertainty, subjective and cultural aspects of risk, while the last stage is tied to post modernist and social constructionist views of risk.

Witte, Meyer and Martel (2000) noted that risk communication is most closely aligned with research focused on fear appeals as persuasive models, presenting a threat and then subsequently providing and describing a behavior that may alleviate the threat. Sandman's (e.g., 1993) work on risk as a function of hazard (technical assessment) and outrage (cultural, personal view) has provided a framework and reference for much of the work in risk communication and health communication.

As one could easily argue from the variety of risk communication orientations and models and typologies that have developed over the past three-plus decades, there has been a tremendous and eclectic growth in risk communication research. Pidgeon, R. Kasperson and Slovic (2003) charged that despite substantial progress the risk perception and risk communication literature remain "seriously fragmented: between the psychometric paradigm and cultural theories of risk perception; between post-modernist and discourse-centered approaches and behavioral studies of risk; between economic/utility-maximization and economic-justice approaches; and between communications and empowerment strategies for risk communication" (p. 2).

McComas (2006), however, suggested that making a clear distinction between public health risk communication and environmental risk communication may be unnecessary, basing at least part of her opinion on research by Gurabardhi, Gutteling and Kuttschreuter (2004) that identified some of the most prolific researchers publishing in the area of environmental risk communication and also publishing in the journals on health risk communication. McComas (2006) review of a decade of research between 1996 and 2005 showed a growth of research in the areas of public reaction to health risks, including the continued study of risk perceptions and advances made to the affective dimensions of risk-related behaviors; research analyzing media's influence on risk perceptions; developing health risk messages; and communicating health risk messages. She suggested that while a strength of risk communication is the interdisciplinary nature of the research, the knowledge is not centralized, that "risk communication research presently is characterized by many, sometimes overlapping, variable analytic studies but few integrative theoretical frameworks" (p. 85), noting exceptions such as social amplification of risk (R. Kasperson, Renn, Slovic, et al., 1988) and risk information seeking and processing model (Griffin, Dunwoody, & Neuwirth, 1999).

Academic Risk Communication Research Centers

Along with the Society for Risk Analysis, which was mentioned earlier as a pivotal moment in the development of risk communication, numerous social science academic centers began to focus on the study of risk. Beginning in 1963 with the Disaster Research Center at the University of Delaware, through the development of the Center for Risk Analysis in 1989 at the Harvard School for Public Health, to one of the newest, the Center for Health and Risk Communications at the University of Georgia, these academic programs have focused on risk not only from a risk management perspective but also from social science and communication.

A review of major centers for risk research in the social sciences field developed by Golding (1992) outlined several important institutions. One of the first centers for risk research was the Disaster Research Center established in 1963 at Ohio State University and, in 1985, was moved to the University of Delaware, with a focus on group and organizational aspects of disaster. According to the Disaster Research Center (2002), it is the first social science research center in the world devoted to the study of disasters, conducts field and survey research on group, organizational and community preparation for, response to, and recovery from natural and technological disasters and other community-wide crises.

Other risk centers,[3] with their founding dates, include: Center for Technology, Environment, and Development, George Perkins Marsh Institute, Clark University (1975); Decision Research, Eugene Oregon (1976); National Hazards Center, University of Colorado at Boulder (1976); Environment and Policy Institute, East-West Center, Honolulu, Hawaii (1977); Institute for Risk Analysis, American University (1978): NRC, National Academies of Science (1979, originally established in 1916); Department of Engineering and Public Policy, Carnegie Mellon University (1970s); Institute for Safety and Systems Management, University of Southern California (1970s); Institute for Philosophy and Public Policy, University of Maryland (1980, originally established in 1976); Energy, Environment and Resources Center, University of Tennessee (1982, presently the Institute for a Secure and Sustainable Environment); Center for Environmental Management, Tufts University (1984); and the Risk Management and Decision Processes Center, Wharton, University of Pennsylvania (1985).

For example, Decision Research was founded in 1976 by Sarah Lichtenstein, Baruch Fischhoff, and Paul Slovic, all of whom were part of the Oregon Research Institute. Originally a branch of the consulting group Perceptronics, Decision Research became an independent non-profit group in 1986 (Golding, 1992) and is a non-profit research organization investigating human judgment and decision-making based on the premise that decisions should be guided by an understanding of how people think and how they value the potential outcomes—good and bad—of their decisions (Decision Research, 2007). Golding (1992) has suggested that "perhaps no other center has had a more profound influence on the nature of the risk debate. Slovic, Fischhoff, and Lichtenstein and their colleagues were largely responsible for developing the psychometric paradigm, which seeks to explain the discrepancy between public and expert perceptions of risk... This work on perceived risk has spawned several other themes that have dominated the field at different times, most notably the notion of acceptable risk and the more recent interest in risk communication" (p. 43).

Developed from some of the early centers for risk analysis, a growing interest in risk communication was responsible for the creation of the next generation of risk centers in the United States such as the Environment Communication Research Program at Rutgers University that was the Center for Environmental Communication (Golding, 1992), founded by Peter Sandman in 1986. Other next generation research centers for risk communication include but are not limited to: Carnegie Mellon University Engineering and Public Policy Program; Center for Health and Risk Communication, Department of Communication, George Mason University; Center for Health and Risk Communication, Department of Communication Arts and Sciences, Pennsylvania State University; Center for Law and Technology, Boston University; Center for Risk Communication, Division of Environmental Sciences, Columbia University; Center for Risk Communication, New York University; Center for Risk Management, Resources for the Future, Washington, D.C.; Center for Risk Management of Engineering Systems, University of Virginia; Center for Risk Perception and Communication, Carnegie Mellon University; Center for Risk Science and Communication, School of Public Health, University of Michigan; Center for Risk Communication Research, Department of Communication, University of Maryland; Centers for Public Health Education and Outreach, School of Public Health, University of Minnesota; Consortium for Risk Evaluation with Stakeholder Participation that includes Vanderbilt University, Howard University, New York University School of Law, Oregon State University, Robert Wood Johnson Medical School, Rutgers, The State University of New Jersey, University of Arizona, University of Pittsburgh; Duke University Center for Environmental Solutions and Nicholas School of the Environment and Earth Sciences: Harvard Center for Risk Analysis, Harvard School of Public Health, Harvard University; Health and Risk Communication Center, College of Communication Arts and Sciences, Michigan State University; Johns Hopkins University School of Public Health Risk Sciences and Public Policy Institute; University of Maryland, Food Safety Risk Analysis and Center for Risk Communication: University of North Carolina at Chapel Hill Institute for the Environment; University of Washington, Institute for Risk Analysis & Risk Communication; Vanderbilt

Institute for Environmental Risk and Resource Management as well as the Center for Environmental Management Studies, both at Vanderbilt University; Western Institute for Social and Organizational Resources, Department of Psychology, Western Washington University; and Yale Center for Public Health Preparedness, Yale School of Public Health, Yale University.

RAPID GROWTH OF CRISIS COMMUNICATION

Perrow's (1984) research suggested that serious accidents are inevitable no matter how hard organizations try to avoid them, especially those related to hazardous systems such as commercial airlines, nuclear power plants, shipping and transportation, and the petrochemical industry. From the genome project to the International Space Station, organizations are increasingly operating in a complex and intimately linked society. According to Lerbinger (1997), "The incidence and severity of crisis is rising with the complexity of technology and society. Fewer crises remain unpublicized as the number of society's watchdogs increases" (p. 16). Overall, the increasing media coverage of hazardous incidents and related risks (Lichtenberg & MacLean, 1991) has increased the prominence of crisis management.

From an American perspective, crisis communication was originally applied to political situations, following the Cuban missile conflict in the early 1960s, using a series of hypothetical situations with strategic applications measuring the cost and or benefits of preventing crises. When Tylenol capsules were replaced with cyanide capsules in the 1980s, it sparked the beginning of research in organizational crisis communication. The *Exxon Valdez* oil spill in 1989 furthered this practice by lending validity to corporate crisis communication and helping to serve as the foundation for wide-spread research in the 1990s (Fishman, 1999). For the environmental community, the 1962 release of Rachael Carson's *Silent Spring* was an iconic publishing event that alerted scientific, emerging environmentalists and the general public to the prospect that chemicals and nature were on a collision course, making people think about the environment in a way they had never done before (Smith, 2001).

Probably more than any other incident and federal response to a crisis, the September 11, 2001, terrorist attacks on the United States spurred the creation of the Department of Homeland Security (DHS)[4] and put crisis management and communication to the front of the line for federal government resources and research dollars. Based on the Homeland Security Act of 2002, the new department was tasked with providing federal assistance to state and local governments who responded to natural or accidental disastrous events. The Federal Emergency Management Agency (FEMA), the department that coordinates all federal assistance to natural and non-natural crisis events, became the central component of the DHS. The new department was charged with the development of an all-hazards approach to crisis response (Abbott & Hetzel, 2005).

Large, eclectic arrays of federal agencies play a role in risk and crisis communication in the United States. Centers for Disease Control and Prevention (CDC) is the lead federal agency for protecting the health and safety of people and providing credible information to enhance health decisions. The Federal Bureau of Investigation (FBI), on the other hand, has final authority over the release of information about an incident related to terrorism and bioterrorism. The Department of Justice, along with the FBI, have principle objectives to ensure that health information be promptly and accurately provided during a terrorist or suspected terrorist incident.

Other federal agencies that are involved with crisis communication include the Central Intelligence Agency; Department of Agriculture; Department of Defense; Department of Energy; Department of Health and Human Services (DHHS), including the National Institutes of Health; DHS, which oversees many of these other agencies; Department of Interior; Department of Justice's Office for Domestic Preparedness; Department of Labor, and specifically the Occupational Safety and Health Administration; Department of State; Department of Transportation, including their Federal Aviation Administration and Federal Railroad Administration; Department of Treasury; Environmental Protection Agency, including the Chemical Emergency Preparedness and Prevention Office; Federal Emergency Management Agency; National Domestic Preparedness Office; Nuclear Regulatory Commission; and the Transportation Security Administration, which is a new federal agency developed in 2001 in response to 9/11 to protect the nations various transportation systems.

Within each of these agencies are numerous organizations that have various roles in risk and crisis management and communication. For example, the Agency for Toxic Substances and Disease Registry, part of DHS, provides health information to prevent harmful exposures and diseases related to toxic substances. The Joint Information Center (JIC) was established by the federal agency that is leading the risk and crisis response, under the operational control of the FBI or FEMA public information officer, as the coordinated point for information to the public and media about the federal response to an emergency. The JIC is a physical location where public affairs professionals from agencies and organizations involved in incident management work together to provide emergency information, crisis communications and public affairs support (DHS, 2007b). Many other parts of the federal government also play a role in risk and crisis communication management and research, including federal labs such as the Environmental Science Division at the Argonne National Laboratory, the Center for Advanced Modeling and Simulation at the Idaho National Laboratory, and the Risk Assessment Information System at Oak Ridge National Laboratory.

A central component of the preparedness efforts include specific, detailed plans such as the National Response Plan, which was developed in 2004 and is the core plan for national incident management and provides guidelines, coordination and stability for the federal government's role in emergency events (Abbott & Hetzel, 2005). According to the National Information Management System, an element of the National Response Plan, all emergency preparedness units must ensure their communication process comply with the interoperable communication standards and guidelines (Abbott & Hetzel, 2005). Similarly, the Public Affairs Support Annex (2007) is responsible for forming the message content, which addresses the facts, health risks, pre-crisis and post-crisis preparedness recommendations and any other appropriate warning information. Additionally, Emergency Support Function 15, External Affairs Annex (DHS, 2007b), ensures that "sufficient Federal assets are deployed to the field during incidents requiring a coordinated, timely Federal response to provide accurate, coordinated, and timely information to affected audiences" (p. 1).

Within the National Response Plan are emergency support functions (ESF), including two focused on communication. ESF #2 is entitled "Communications," which is responsible for the coordination with the telecommunications industry; restoration, repair and temporary provisioning of communications infrastructure; and the protection, restoration and sustainment of national cyber and information technology resources. ESF #15, entitled "External Affairs." addresses emergency public information and protective action guidance, media and community relations, congressional and international affairs, and tribal and insular affairs (DHS, 2004).

The DHS (2007a) released during the fall 2007 the National Response Framework, successor to the National Response Plan. This plan focuses on response and short-term recovery, articulates the doctrine, principles and architecture by which our nation prepares for and responds to all-hazard disasters across all levels of government and all sectors of communities. The Framework is responsive to repeated federal, state and local requests for a streamlined document that is shorter, less bureaucratic and more user-friendly (DHS, 2004).

Of special interest for risk and crisis communicators is the advent of the Uniting and Strengthening America by Providing Appropriate Tools Required to Intercept and Obstruct Terrorism Act of 2001 (PATRIOT Act). The terrorist attacks of September 11, 2001, led to heavy reassessments of whether information about potential targets for terrorists should be disclosed in any way. Babcock (2007) affirmed that that the events of 9/11 brought into "sharp focus" the clash between safety and other values like the right to healthy environment. With the introduction of the USA PATRIOT ACT in October 2001 and the Critical Infrastructure Information Act of 2002 many corporations used the excuse of protecting sensitive targets from terrorist attacks to stop providing information about hazardous materials to communities under the EPCRA (Cheroukas, 2007). Babcock (2007) described how the PATRIOT Act undermined many provisions of FOIA and EPCRA, among many other environmental laws, about right to know and access to information.

Evolution of Crisis Communication Research

Similar to the concept of risk, defining the term "crisis" is a challenge. Lerbinger (1997) defined a crisis as "an event that brings, or has the potential for bringing, an organization into disrepute and imperils its future profitability, growth, and possibly, its very survival" (p. 4), while noting three classes of crises—of the physical world, of the human climate, and of management failure. Coombs (1999) included technical breakdowns in his typology of crisis types.

Fearn-Banks (2001) incorporated threat in her latter definition of crisis when she defined it as a "major occurrence with a potentially negative outcome affecting an organization as well as its publics, services, products, and/or good name. It interrupts normal business transactions and can, at its worst, threaten the existence of the organization" (p. 480). Similarly, Pearson and Clair (1998) addressed the frequency and impact of the event as they defined a crisis as "a low-probability, high-impact event that threatens the viability of the organization and is characterized by ambiguity of cause, effect, and means of resolution, as well as by a belief that decisions must be made swiftly" (p. 60). Coombs (2007) synthesized common traits others have used to define and describe a crisis including that a crisis is perceptual, unpredictable but not unexpected, violates expectations of stakeholders about how organizations should act, serious impact, potential to create negative or undesirable outcomes, and finally environmental damage as an outcome of the accident.

Crisis is often recognized in the literature to be a perception of events rather than the events themselves; what constitutes a crisis differs from person to person (Aguilera, 1998; Janosik, 1994; Penrose, 2000). Penrose (2000) suggested that the perception of crisis can ultimately affect the outcome of the crisis. He noted that although most perceive crises as bad; when viewed as an opportunity it may have significant implications. Such implications may include the emergence of new leaders and an accelerated change in business processes (2000). Other literature supports this idea that crises have the potential to produce opportunities (e.g., Brock, Sandoval, & Lewis, 2001).

A clear, denotative definition of crisis may be easier to come by than the connotative meanings held by researchers, journalists and other stakeholders. According to Fishman (1999), the term "crisis" is field or context dependent; "one individual's crisis may be another's incident… with no attempt to delineate the scope or severity of a given problem" (p. 347).

Much of the early research on crisis communication developed from the speech communication field, such as the seminal article in the *Quarterly Journal of Speech Quarterly Journal of Speech* by Ware and Linkugel (1973), who were one of the first to examine crisis response strategies as communication used to defend one's reputation from public attack. Their article demonstrated the focus of speech communication scholars on communication coming from an individual or organization that is faced with a crisis; typically descriptive.

Much of this early research, especially by rhetoricians, focused on persuasion when communicating in the aftermath of a personal or organizational crisis. According to Heath and Millar (2004), when applying rhetoric to crisis, one must move past simply defining crisis by its potential to create damage or actual damage inflicted on an organization or its possible effects on stakeholder relationships and organizational reputation. As such, a rhetorical approach to crisis communication places focus on the responsibility, severity, and duration of a crisis while acknowledging each is questionable.

Heath (2004) suggested that "a crisis event constitutes a rhetorical exigency that requires one or more responsible parties to enact control in the face of uncertainty in an effort to win key public's confidence and meet their ethical standards" and "it challenges the ability of the organization to enact the narrative of continuity through constructive change to control the organization's destiny" (p. 167). He added that when a narrative rationale is applied to crisis situations, crisis communicators and managers are able to systematically apply cultural and rhetorical narratives in order to assist in their planning and management. As a result, they are better prepared to predict possible organizational threats and to suggest ways to control them.

Other communication and public relations scholars have focused much more on the organizational perspective of the crisis. Dionisopolous and Vibbert (1988) extended Ware and Linkugel's (1973) examination to the use of apologia to defend reputations. In the event that an organization's image cannot be protected from crisis, Benoit (1997) provided an argument for using image restoration theory as an attempt to repair it. He focused on message options, or what an organization can say when faced with a reputational crisis. The image repair line of research, builds upon apologia, includes five primary aspects of image restoration: denials as a course of action, evading responsibility, reduce the perceived offensiveness of that act, corrective action, and finally mortification.

When crisis is assessed from an organizational perspective one of the primary goals is to decrease damage inflicted by the crisis. Seeger, Sellnow and Ulmer's (1998) work is comprised of several phases including a pre-crisis stage, before the crisis actually begins; an acute crisis stage, immediately following a dramatic event; and a post-crisis stage, when an organization must respond to the crisis.

Coombs (2007) has argued that apologia offered a limited number of crisis response strategies and developed the situational crisis communication theory (SCCT) as part of a growing body of research built from attribution theory to crisis management (e.g., Ahluwalia, Burnkrant, & Unnava, 2000; Coombs, 2007; Dean, 2004). Coombs (1998) symbolic approach perspective emphasizes how communication can be used as a symbolic resource to protect the organization's image. Crisis communication provides attributes of responsibility, and in turn these attributes shape how a stakeholder feels and behaves toward an organization. According to Coombs (2007), "SCCT utilizes attribution theory to evaluate the reputation threat posed by the crisis situation and then recommends crisis response strategies based upon the reputational threat level" (p. 138). SCCT's 11 major crisis response strategies are centered around four major postures: denial (attacking the accuser, denial, scapegoating), diminishing (excusing, justification), rebuilding (compensation, apology), and bolstering (reminding, ingratiation, victimage). Three factors used by SCCT to evaluate reputational threat include crisis type, crisis history and prior reputation.

According to Wan and Pfau (2004), both Coombs (1998) and Benoit's (1997) approaches center on post-crisis communication skills that are helpful for organizations after crises have occurred. However, the need for proactive strategy focusing on the prevention of crisis in the first place is stated as their ideal orientation to crisis communication. Their results revealed that "inoculation, as well as the traditional bolstering approach, work to protect people's attitude slippage when encountering a negative occurrence" (p. 324). Their recommendation is to be well prepared in advance for organizations that have maintained positive images (and no prior crises) to consider both supportive and inoculation approaches into their crisis communication plans.

In a review of crisis management literature, Coombs (2007) identified three influential approaches to crisis management that has guided a preponderance of the literature. These three are Fink's (1986) four-stage model, Mitroff's (1994) five-stage model, and a general three-stage model that has no identifiable creator but has been used by numerous researchers as a meta-model.

Fink's (1986) four-stage model is one of the earliest models based on stages in the crisis life cycle, including: (1) prodromal stage that hints that a potential crisis is emerging, (2) acute triggering crisis event stage, (3) chronic stage based on the lingering effects of the crisis event, and (4) resolution stage. Mitroff (1994) suggested five crisis management stages, including signal detection, probing and prevention, damage containment, recovery, and learning and evaluation.

Meyers (1986) suggested three categories of crisis—pre-crisis, crisis, and post-crisis—each of which is influenced by crisis elements such as surprise, threat, and available response time. Similar to Fink's prodromal phase, Meyer's pre-crisis phase includes perceiving signs of the crisis. The second stage, crisis, includes the actual crisis event. Recovery from the crisis and assessment of crisis activities take place during the post-crisis phase.

Mitroff (1994) went a step further by addressing what steps should be taken during each phase in a crisis. He divided crisis management into five stages: signal detection, when an organization detects new crisis by identifying and acting to prevent it; probing and prevention, working to reduce the potential for harm; damage containment, attempt to prevent the spread of a crisis once it has occurred; recovery, attempting to return to normal business operations; and learning, evaluating crisis response and use of information gained to improve future plans. Mitroff organized crises responses, placing primary emphasis on containing the effects of the crisis, based upon the best preventive actions for each phase.

Within the organizational perspective lies a large area of research dominated by the development and analysis of crisis communication plans. Much of the traditional crisis management literature descriptively highlights the value of developing, implementing and maintaining a crisis management plan (Penrose, 2000). Crisis management plans are advocated to guide organizations during times of crisis. The crisis management plan (CMP) or crisis communication plan (CCP) are both considered primary tools of the field, to prepare for or follow when a crisis occurs. Fearn-Banks (1996) described a CCP as "providing a functionally collective brain for all persons involved in a crisis, persons who may not operate at normal capacity due to the shock or emotions or the crisis event" (p. 7).

A common theme among crisis communication literature is the need for a crisis management plan (Quarantelli, 1988), including clear, tested, crisis communication. Penrose (2000) posited the four most common elements of a crisis plan include: the plan, the management team, communication and post-crisis evaluation. However, an unlimited amount and variety of crisis situations make a specific or paradigmatic guiding principle of crisis management nearly impossible (Burnett, 1998). Several problems persist in the development of these manuals, including providing a false sense of security, rarely a living document that is updated, lack of a temporal context and filled with irrelevant information (Pearson, Clair, Misra, & Mitroff, 1997). Ostrow (1991) presented a negative side of crisis planning as he claimed that as organization prepare for crisis they begin to "assume that crises will evolve to defined scenarios" (p. 24).

Marra (2004) also found crisis plan shortcomings when he questioned the usefulness of simply creating instructions, suggestions, and checklists. He claimed the value of crisis communication plans may be overrated as organizations with comprehensive plans often manage crises poorly while those with no plan often manage crises well. Marra argued this is a result of crisis communication research primarily focusing in the technical aspect of managing crisis.

The organizational perspective, though dominate, is not the only crisis communication perspective. Martin and Boynton (2005) pointed out that now the focus of crisis communication has shifted from the organization to those with an interest in the organization, reflecting stakeholder theory literature. At the core of stakeholder theory is that stakeholders are affected by corporations and other organizations, but also that these organizations are affected by stakeholders (2005).

Other researchers have moved away from quantitative, categorized, prediction-oriented research in their study of crisis communication. For example, Streifel, Beebe, Veil, and Sellnow (2006) looked at ethical aspects of crisis communication decision-making from a social constructivist perspective. Tyler (2005) suggested that crisis communication should be explored from a postmodern perspective. She used postmodern theory to criticize the emphasis on current research on crisis plans and regaining order and control. Tyler wrote that instead of focusing on the impossibility of crisis control and protecting those in power, crisis communication should be used to alleviate stakeholder suffering—that the voices of management should not be the only one heard and that postmodern perspectives to crisis communication are a more humane way to communicate.

There have been a few research streams related to postmodernism and crisis communication. However, numerous elements of postmodern research are starting to be discussed in relationship to risk and crisis communication, including but not limited to concepts such as resistance to positivism and certainty, realization of chaos, resistance to meta-narratives, and differences in power disparities in relationships. For example, chaos theory looks at the underlying reasons for a system to appear to be in a chaotic state. According to Sellnow, Seeger, and Ulmer (2002), "chaos theory may elucidate how communicators characterize the behavior of such systems in their descriptions and predictions of outcomes. It may also point to the ways in which communication processes relate to systems moving in and out of chaos and order" (p. 269).

Lee (2005) suggested several challenges in current crisis communication research and writings, including: lack of a shared definition, conceptual framework not yet developed, audience-orientation not been addressed, current case studies lack contextualization, and that most of the research is from a Western-based perspective. Shrivastava (1993) and Coombs (2007) expressed similar concerns that the cross-disciplinary nature of organizational crises has contributed to the lack of integration in crisis communication research, a similar complaint of the risk communication literature.

Academic Crisis Communication Research Centers

Similar to risk communication but not as well developed, numerous crisis communication research centers located at or in coordination with American universities are guiding crisis communication research. For example, one of the newest research centers, as of August 2007, that has a crisis communication component is the George Mason University's new Center of Excellence in Climate Change Communication Research, the nation's first research center devoted exclusively to addressing the communication challenges associated with global climate change.

One relatively new center in crisis communication is The National Center for Food Protection and Defense (NCFPD, 2006) was officially launched as a Homeland Security Center of Excellence in July 2004. Developed as a multidisciplinary and action-oriented research consortium, NCFPD addresses the vulnerability of the nation's food system to attack through intentional contamination with biological or chemical agents. NCFPD's research program is organized thematically into three primary areas—systems (supply chain, public health response, economic analysis, and security), agents (detection, inactivation, and decontamination), and training (risk communication and education). Preparedness is a major component of the training theme, with an emphasis on pre-crisis communication planning, message development, communication with under-represented populations, media relations, and risk communicator training for a variety of audiences, including subject matter experts, government officials, food industry representatives, and extension educators. The Risk Crisis Communication Project History, which began at North Dakota State University in 2000 and now has a satellite campus at the University of Kentucky, is part of this effort and seeks to unify a series of research opportunities to develop best practices in risk and crisis communication.

The Oak Ridge Institute for Science and Education helps prepare the emergency response assets of the U.S. Department of Energy and other federal and state agencies by managing and conducting programs, studies, research, exercises, and training in the response to incidents involving weapons of mass destruction and improvised explosive devices, the readiness of our nation's security assets, and emergency preparedness and response.

Using technology, the Food Safety Information Center (FSIC) develops solutions that disseminate information on a variety of food safety topics to educators, industry, researchers and the general public.. The center was established at the USDA's National Agricultural Library in 2003 to efficiently use library resources, develop stronger collaborations among the library's food safety programs, and ultimately deliver the best possible services to the food safety community.

Drawing on the research capacity in each of New York University's 14 schools, the Center for Catastrophe Preparedness and Response facilitates research projects that address issues ranging from medical capacity during crises, to legal issues relating to security, to first-responder trauma response, to state-of-the-art training for first-responders. At the academic association level, the National Communication Association's Risk and Crisis Communication Working Group recently conducted two crisis and risk preconferences that explored the common research elements among crisis, risk, and health communication and identified common research areas to advance a strategic research agenda.

COMMON ELEMENTS OF RISK AND CRISIS COMMUNICATION

There are an eclectic range of common intersections to risk and crisis, and risk and crisis communication. Both risk and crisis have to the potential to disrupt your organization's survival, and more importantly the health, safety and environment of stakeholders. No individual, community or organization, whether private, public, nongovernmental or informal is immune from risk or crisis. Not intrinsically negative elements of society, both risk or crisis offer opportunities for learning, developing and improving. Failure in a risk or crisis situation tends to make the organization weaker to address future risk or crisis events, and damages organization reputation.

From a research standpoint, both fields have evolved from a linear progression of communication to a more interactive, dialogic perspective that takes into account the social construction of risk and crisis. Both fields include researchers from a wide variety of disciplines, which has led to often fragmented research streams.

Risk and crisis communication both deal and address intentional as well as unintentional risks or crises. Reviewing, Ulmer, Sellnow, and Seeger's (2007) list of types of crises include terrorism, sabotage, workplace violence, poor employee relationships, poor risk management, hostile takeovers, unethical leadership, natural disasters, disease outbreak, unforeseeable technical interactions, product failure and downturns in the economy, all of which are studied within the rubrics of risk and crisis communication.

Seeger (2005) created a best practices in risk and crisis communication typology, including: risk and crisis communication is an ongoing process, conduct pre-event planning, foster partnerships with publics, collaborate and coordinate with credible sources, good media relations, including meeting the needs of media and remaining accessible, listen to publics' concerns and understand audiences, communicate with compassion, concern and empathy, demonstrate honesty, candor and openness, accept uncertainty and ambiguity, and provide messages that foster self-efficacy.

Sandman (2006) saw crisis communication as a part of three distinct risk communication customs. He described these three areas as: precautionary management—warning people who are insufficiently concerned about a serious risk; outrage management—reassuring people who are excessively concerned about a small risk; and crisis communication—helping and guiding people who are appropriately concerned about a serious risk.

Within health communication researchers and practitioners, severe public health concerns are often discussed and framed as risk communication (e.g., Covello, 1992; Witte, Meyer, & Martel, 2000). At the same time, these similar risks are viewed as crisis communication from an organization perspective (e.g., Barton, 2001; Seeger, Sellnow & Ulmer, 1998, 2003).

Reynolds and Seeger (2005), while focusing on the numerous differences, also acknowledged that risk and crisis communication have much in common and intersect at multiple points. These include: production of messages designed to create specific responses by the public, messages are largely mediated through mass communication channels, rely on credibility as a fundamental element of persuasion, and both share a fundamental purpose of seeking to mitigate and reduce harm to public health and safety. Both forms of communication involve the production of public messages designed to create specific responses by the public (Reynolds & Seeger, 2005). Lundgren (1994) suggested that crisis communication is a more limited form of risk communication, suggesting that risk communication is the larger communication paradigm and that crisis communication is part of or a more limited form of risk communication.

Merged Definitions

Recently efforts have been made to combine risk and crisis communication into an area of research and practice defined as *crisis and emergency risk communication* (Reynolds, 2002). According to Reynolds (2002) in conjunction with the Centers for Disease Control and Prevention (CDC), crisis and emergency risk communication merge the urgency of disaster communication with the necessity to communicate risks and benefits to stakeholders and the public, especially in response to an era of global health threats. "Crisis and emergency risk communication is the effort by experts to provide information to allow an individual, stakeholder, or an entire community to make the best possible decisions about their well-being within nearly impossible time constraints and help people ultimately to accept the imperfect nature of choices during the crisis" (p. 6). According to the authors, this type of communication differs from risk communication because of the narrow time constraint, decisions may be irreversible, decision outcomes are uncertain and often made with incomplete or imperfect information, while this type of communication differs from crisis communication because the communicator is not perceived as a participant in the crisis or disaster except as an agent to resolve the situation.

According to Reynold's (2002) work, within this framework risk communication is seen within the developmental stages of a crisis. This combination of perspectives is demonstrated in their crisis and emergency risk communication model in five stages: pre-crisis (risk messages, warnings, preparations), initial event (uncertainty reduction, self-efficacy, reassurance), maintenance (ongoing uncertainty reduction, self-efficacy; reassurance), resolution (updates regarding resolution, discussions about cause and new risks/new understandings of risk), and evaluation (discussions of adequacy of response; consensus about lessons and new understandings of risks).

Environmental risk communication is another perspective and definition that has gained attention in recent years. According to Lindell and Perry (2004), environmental risk communication as an accurate term to describe risk communication related to technological risks of hazardous facilities and transportation, as well as natural hazards. Abkowitz (2002) described environmental risk as man-made or natural incidents or trends that have the potential to harm human health and ecosystems, including physical assets of organizations or the economy in a broader scale, and suggested that environmental risk communication addresses such incidents or trends in two distinct categories, which are events that might occur in the future where prevention is the focus and emergency situations that require immediate notification and deployment of mitigation and other response actions.

Oepen (2000) defined *environmental communication* as the "planned and strategic use of communication processes and media products to support effective policy-making, public participation and project implementation geared towards environmental sustainability" (p. 41). According to Oepen, then, to influence the policy-making process is constitutive of environmental communication, as much as to guarantee the implementation of projects that envision the protection of the natural environment through public participation.

Oepen (2000) saw the role of environmental communication as an educative and engaging social interaction process that enables people to "understand key environmental factors and their interdependencies, and to act upon related problems in a competent way" (p. 41). Hence, environmental communication is not only—not even mainly—a tool for disseminating information, but a process that aims at producing "a shared vision of a sustainable future and at capacity-building in social groups to solve or prevent environmental problems" (p. 41).

For Cox (2006), a well-informed public is fundamental for good governance and environmental communication is the right tool for the job for "[i]t educates, alerts, persuades, mobilizes, and helps us to solve environmental problems" (p. 12). Moreover, according to him, it also "helps to compose representations of nature and environmental problems as subjects for our understanding" (p. 12).

CONCLUSION

Epictetus (1983), the Greek Stoic philosopher, suggested that people are disturbed not by the things themselves but by the view they take of them. As such, risks are embedded within and shaped by social relations and the continual tacit negotiation of our social identities (Wynne, 1992). Such an orientation toward risk and crisis communication adds value to society by increasing organizations' sensitivities regarding how stakeholders create and manage interpretative frames related to issues that define, affect, and ultimately support or oppose organizational activities, such as supporting or imposing limits on business activities that can either be beneficial or harmful.

As this chapter has demonstrated through the intertwined developments and rapid expansion of both fields, two unfailing philosophies that should guide risk and crisis communication have developed, whether located in the academy, private practice, governmental agencies or nongovernmental organizations, is that that better managed risks and crises are likely to result in less financial and social capital damage, and that risk and crisis generating organizations are required, by regulation, law or community standards, to demonstrate how and why they are responsible for events that can harm themselves, their employees and the interests of humans. Underlying these two concepts and running at the core of risk and crisis communication research and practice is that a crisis can be defined as risk manifested (Heath, 2006). When a risk is manifested, such as a hurricane (e.g., Katrina and Rita in 2005), it is likely to create a crisis and lead to the creation of multiple issues that must be addressed or the continuation of the risk cycle would result.

At the core of a decade of lessons learned from developing and analyzing risk communication campaigns, Palenchar and Heath (2007) argued that each organization should strive to be moral and to communicate to satisfy the interests of key markets, audiences and publics that strive to manage personal and public resources, make personal and sociopolitical decisions, and form strong and beneficial relationships. A good organization can and should utilize risk communication and crisis communication to empower relevant publics by helping them to develop and use emergency responses that can mitigate the severe outcomes of a risk event.

NOTES

1. Arguments over what really happened in Bhopal more than 20 years ago continue. The exact injury and death toll remains under debate, with some estimates reaching more than 20,000 people killed and multi-systemic injuries to over 500,000 people (The International Campaign for Justice in Bhopal, n.d.). Some consider this the world's worst industrial accident (Greenpeace International n.d.).
2. Additional U. S. federal acts and regulations will be discussed in more detail in later sections of this chapter.
3. Most of these centers include risk communication research projects. Most of the list is developed from Golding's (1992) thorough review of risk centers, including their founding date; most though not all centers are still active though a few have changed their name and the new name is noted.
4. There are numerous other federal agencies involved in crisis communication, such as the Centers for Disease Control and Prevention, which will be discussed in more detail later in the chapter.

BIBLIOGRAPHY

Abbott, E., & Hetzel, O. (2005). *A legal guide to homeland security and emergency management for state and local governments.* Chicago: American Bar Association.

Abkowitz, M. D. (2002, March). *Environmental risk communication: What is it and how can it work?* Environmental Risk Communication Summit, Vanderbilt University, TN.

Aguilera, D. C. (1998). *Crisis intervention: Theory and methodology* (8th ed.). St. Louis: Mosby.

Ahluwalia, R., Burnkrant, R. E., & Unnava, H. R. (2000). Consumer response to negative publicity: The moderating role of commitment. *Journal of Marketing Research, 27,* 203–214.

American Council on Science and Heatlh. (2003). *A citizens' guide to terrorism preparedness and response: Chemical, biological, radiological, and nuclear.* New York: Author..

Auf der Heide, E. (1996, May). Disaster planning, part II: Disaster problems, issues and challenges identified in the research literature. *Emergency Medical Clinics of North America, 14*(2), 453–480.

Babcock, H. (2007). National security and environmental laws: A clear and present danger? *Virginia Environmental Law Journal, 25*(2), 105–158.

Barton, L. (2001). *Crisis in organizations* (2nd ed.). Cincinnati, OH: South-Western College.

Beck, U. (1992). *Risk society: Towards a new modernity.* London: Sage.

Beck, U. (1995, fall). Freedom from technology. *Dissent,* 503–507.

Beck, U. (1996). Risk society and the provident state. In S. Lash, B. Szerszynski & B. Wynne (Eds.), *Risk, environment and modernity: Towards a new ecology* (pp. 27–43). London: Sage.
Benoit, W. L. (1997). Image repair discourse and crisis communication. *Public Relations Review, 23*(2), 177–186.
Benoit, W. L. (2000). Another visit to the theory of image restoration strategies. *Communication Quarterly, 48*(1), 40–44.
Brock, S. E., Sandoval, J., & Lewis, S. (2001). *Preparing for crisis in the schools: A manual for building school crisis response teams* (2nd ed.). New York: Wiley & Sons.
Burnett, J. J. (1998). A strategic approach to managing crises. Public Relations Review, 24, 475–488.
Cheroukas, K. (2007). Balancing national security with a community's right to know: maintaining public access to environmental information through EPCRA's non-preemption clause. *Boston College Environmental Affairs Law Review 34*, 107. Retrieved on June 28, 2007, from Lexis Nexis.
Coombs, W. T. (1998). An analytic framework for crisis situations: Better responses from a better understanding of the situation. *Journal of Public Relations Research, 10*(3), 177–191.
Coombs, W. T. (1999). *Ongoing crisis communication: Planning, managing, and responding*.Thousand Oaks, CA: Sage.
Coombs, W. T. (2007). *Ongoing crisis communication: Planning, managing, and responding* (2nd ed.). Thousand Oaks, CA: Sage.
Covello, V. T. (1983). The perception of technological risks: A literature review. *Technological Forecasting and Social Change, 23*, 285–297.
Covello, V. T. (1992). Risk communication: An emerging area of health communication research. In S. A. Deetz (Ed), *Communication yearbook* (Vol. 15, pp. 359–373). Newbury Park, CA: Sage.
Covello, V. T., & Mumpower, J. (1985). Risk analysis and risk management: An historical perspective. *Risk Analysis, 5*(2), 103–119.
Covello, V., & Sandman, P. M. (2001). Risk communication: Evolution and revolution. In A Wolbarst (Ed.), *Solutions to an environment in peril* (pp. 164–178). Baltimore, MD: John Hopkins University Press.
Covello, V. T., von Winterfeldt, D., & Slovic, P. (1987). Communicating scientific information about health and environmental risks: Problems and opportunities from a social and behavioral perspective. In V. T. Covello, L. B. Lave, A. Moghissi & V. R. Uppuluri (Eds.), *Uncertainty in risk assessment, risk management and decision making* (pp. 221–239). New York: Plenum.
Cox, R. (2006). *Environmental communication and the public sphere.* Thousand Oaks, CA: Sage.
Dean, D. H. (2004). Consumer reaction to negative publicity: Effects of corporate reputation, response, and responsibility for a crisis event. Journal of Business Communication, 41, 192–211.
Decision Research. (2007). About decision research. Retrieved October 27, 2007, from http://www.decision-research.org/
Department of Homeland Security. (2004, December). National response plan. Retrieved March 3, 2006, from http://www.dhs.gov/xlibrary/assets/NRP_FullText.pdf
Department of Homeland Security. (2007a, Sept. 10). Draft national response framework released for public comment. Retrieved October 17, 2007, from http://www.dhs.gov/ xnews/ releases/ pr_1189450382144.shtm
Department of Homeland Security (2007b). Emergency Support Function 2. Communication Annex. National Response Plan. Retrieved July 28, 2007, from http: www.dhs.gov.xlibrary/assets/NRP_FullText.pdf
Disaster Research Center (2002). Mission statement. Retrieved October 27, 2007, from http://www.udel.edu/DRC/mission.html
Dionisopolous, G. N., & Vibert, S. L. (1988). CBS vs Mobil Oil: Charges of creative bookkeeping. In H. R. Ryan (Ed.), *Oratorical encounters: Selected studies and sources of 20th century political accusation and apologies* (pp. 214–252). Westport, CT: Greenwood.
Douglas, M. (1992). *Risk and blame: Essays in cultural theory*. London: Routledge.
Environmental Protection Agency. (1988). *Title III fact sheet emergency planning and community-right-to-know.* Washington, DC: U.S. Government Printing Office.
EPCRA. (1986). 42 U.S.C. 11001 et seq.
Epictetus. (1983). *Epictetus: The handbook.* (N. P. White, Trans.), Indianapolis, IN: Hackett.
Erikson, K. (1994). *A new species of trouble: The human experience of modern disasters.* New York: W. W. Norton.
Falkenberry, E. M. (1995). The Emergency Planning and Community Right-to-Know Act: A tool for toxic release reduction in the 90's. *Buffalo Environmental Law Journal, 3*(1), 2–36.
Fearn-Banks, K. (1996). *Crisis communications: A casebook approach.* Mahwah, NJ: Erlbaum.
Fearn-Banks, K. (2001). Crisis communication: A review of some best practices. In R. L. Heath & G. Vasquez (Eds.), *Handbook of public relations* (pp. 479–486). Thousand Oaks, CA: Sage.
Fink, S. (1986). *Crisis management: Planning for the inevitable.* New York: American Management Association.

Fischhoff, B. (1995). Risk perception and communication unplugged: Twenty years of process. *Risk Analysis, 15*(2), 137–145.

Fischhoff, B. (1990). *Risk issues in the news: Why experts and laymen disagree.* Pasadena, CAA: The Foundation for American Communities.

Fischhoff, B., Slovic, P., Lichtenstein, S., Read, S., & Combs, B. (1978). How safe is safe enough? A psychometric study of attitudes toward technological risks and benefits. *Policy Sciences, 9*(3), 127–152.

Fishman, D. A. (1999). Valujet Flight 592: Crisis communication theory blended and extended. *Communication Quarterly, 47,* 345–375.

Gaudino, J. L., Fritsch, J., & Haynes, B. (1989). If you knew what I knew, you'd make the same decision: A common misconception underlying public relations campaigns? In C. H. Botan & V. Hazelton, Jr., (Eds.), *Public relations theory* (pp. 299–308). Hillsdale, NJ: Erlbaum.

Geuter, G., & Stevens, A. L. (1983). *Mental modes.* Hillsdale, NJ: Erlbaum.

Golding, D. (1992). A social and programmatic history of risk research. In S. Krimsky & D. Golding (Eds.), *Social theories of risk* (pp. 23–52). Westport, CT: Praeger.

Goldstein, B. D. (2005). Advances in risk assessment and communication. *Annual Review of Public Health, 26,* 141–163.

Greenpeace International. (n.d.). *Bhopal—The world's worst industrial accident.* Retrieved December 19, 2006, from http://www.greenpeace.org/international/

Griffin, R. J., Dunwoody, S., & Neuwirth, K. (1999). Proposed model of the relationship of risk information seeking and processing to the development of preventive behaviors. *Environmental Research, 80*(2), 230–245.

Gurabardhi, Z., Gutteling, J. M., & Kuttschreuter, M. (2004). The development of risk communication. *Science Communication, 25*(4), 323–349.

Hadden, S. (1989a). *A citizen's right to know: Risk communication and public policy.* Boulder, CO: Westview Press.

Hadden, S. (1989b). Institutional barriers to risk communication. *Risk Analysis, 9*(3), 301–308.

Hearne, S. A. (1996). Tracking toxics: Chemical use and the public's "right-to-know." *Environment, 38*(6), 1–11.

Heath, R. L. (1997). *Strategic issues management: Organizations and public policy challenges.* Thousand Oaks, CA: Sage.

Heath, R. L. (2004). Telling a story: A narrative approach to communication during crisis. In D. P. Millar & R. L. Heath (Eds.), *Responding to crisis: A rhetorical approach to crisis communication* (pp. 167–187). Mahwah, NJ: Erlbaum.

Heath, R. L. (2006). Best practices in crisis communication: Evolution of practice through research. *Journal of Applied Communication Research, 34*(3), 245–248.

Heath, R. L., & Millar, D. P. (2004). A rhetorical approach to crisis communication: Management, communication processes, and strategic responses. In D. P. Millar & R. L. Heath (Eds.), *Responding to crisis: A rhetorical approach to crisis communication* (pp. 1–17). Mahwah, NJ: Erlbaum.

International Campaign for Justice in Bhopal, The. (n.d.). *What happened in Bhopahl?* Retrieved January 13, 2007, from http://www.bhopal.org/whathappened.html

Jacobson, J. D. (2003). Safeguarding national security through public release of environmental information: moving the debate to the next level. *Environmental Law 9,* 327–397.

Janosik, E. H. (1994). *Crisis counseling: A contemporary approach.* Boston: Jones Bartlett.

Kasperson, R. E., Renn, O., Slovic, P., Brown, H. S., Emel, J., Goble, R., Kasperson, J. X., & Ratick, S. (1988). The social amplification of risk: A conceptual framework. *Risk Analysis, 8*(2), 177–187.

Kasperson, R. E., & Stallen, P. J. M. (1991). Risk communication: The evolution of attempts. In R. E. Kasperson & P. J. M. Stallen (Eds.), *Communicating risks to the public* (pp. 1–14). Boston: Kluwer.

Kates, R. W., & Kasperson, J. X. (1983). Comparative risk analysis of technological hazards (A review). *Proceedings, National Academy of Sciences, 80,* 7027–7038.

Krimsky, S. (2007). Risk communication in the internet age: The rise of disorganized skepticism. *Environmental Hazards, 7,* 157–164.

Krimsky, S., & Golding, D. (1992). Preface. In S. Krimsky & D. Golding (Eds.), *Social theories of risk* (pp. xiii–xvii). Westport, CT: Praeger.

Krimsky, S., & Plough, A. (1988). *Environmental hazards: Communicating risks as a social process.* Dover, MA: Auburn House.

Laird, F. N. (1989). The decline of deference: The political context of risk communication. *Risk Analysis, 9*(2), 543–550.

Lee, B. K. (2005). Crisis, cullture, community. In P. J. Kalbfeisch (Ed.), *Communication Yearbook* (Vol. 29, pp. 275–309). Mahwah, NJ: Erlbaum.

Leiss, W. (1996). Three phases in the evolution of risk communication practice: *Annals of the American Academy of Political and Social Science, 545,* 85–94.

Lerbinger, O. (1997). *The crisis manager: Facing risk and responsibility.* Mahwah, NJ: Erlbaum.

Lichtenberg, J., & MacLean, D. (1991). The role of the media in risk communication. In R. E. Kasperson & P. J. M. Stallen (Eds.), *Communicating risks to the public* (pp. 157–173). Dordrecht, Netherlands: Kluwer.

Lind, N. C. (1987). Is risk analysis an emerging profession? *Risk Abstracts, 4*(4), 167–169.

Lindell, M. K., & Perry, R. W. (2004). *Communicating environmental risk in multiethnic communities*. Thousand Oaks, CA: Sage.

Liu, J. T., & Smith, V. K. (1990). Risk communication and attitude change: Taiwan's national debate over nuclear power. *Journal of Risk and Uncertainty, 3,* 331–349.

Lundgren, R. E. (1994). *Risk communication: A handbook for communicating environmental, safety and health risks*. Columbus, OH: Battelle Press.

Macauley, M. K. (2006, January). *Issues at the forefront of public policy for environmental risk*. Paper presented at the American Meteorological Society's Annual Policy Colloquium, Washington, DC.

Marra, F. J. (1998). Crisis communications plans: Poor predictors of excellent crisis public relations. *Public Relations Review, 24*(4), 461–474.

Marra, F. J. (2004). Excellent crisis communication: Beyond crisis plans. In R. L. Heath & D. P. Millar (Eds.), *Responding to crisis: A rhetorical approach to crisis communication* (pp. 311–325). Hillsdale, NJ: Erlbaum.

Martin, R. H., & Boynton, L. A. (2005). From liftoff to landing: NASA's crisis communication and resulting media coverage following the Challenger and Columbia tragedies. *Public Relations Review, 31,* 253–261.

Marra, F. (2004). Excellent crisis communication: Beyond crisis plans. In D. P. Millar & R. L. Heath (Eds.), *Responding to crisis: A rhetorical approach to crisis communication* (pp. 311–325). Mahwah, NJ: Erlbaum.

McComas, K. A. (2006). Defining moments in risk communication research: 1996–2005. *Journal of Health Communication, 11,* 75–91.

McKie, D., & Munshi, D. (2007). *Reconfiguring public relations: Ecology, equity, and enterprise*. Abindgon, Oxon: Routledge.

Meyers, G. C. (1986). *When it hits the fan: Managing the nine crises of business*. New York: Mentor.

Mitroff, I. I. (1994). Crisis management and environmentalism: A natural fit. *California Management Board, 36*(2), 101–113.

Morgan, M. G., Fischhoff, B., Bostrom, A., & Atman, C. J. (2002). *Risk communication: A mental modes approach*. New York: Cambridge University Press.

National Archives. (2007). *Charters of freedom: A new world is at hand*. Retrieved November 1, 2007, from http://www.archives.gov/national-archives-experience/charters/constitution_ founding_fathers_pennsylvania.html

National Center for Food Protection and Defense. (2006, Jan. 25). *2005 Annual Report*. Minneapolis, MN: Author.

National Governors' Association. (1987). *Comprehensive emergency management*. Washington, DC: National Governors' Association Emergency Preparedness Project.

National Research Council. (1989). *Improving risk communication*. Washington, DC: National Academy Press.

New York Times. (1985, December 4). Averting more chemical tragedies, p. A30.

Oepen, M. (2000). Environmental communication in a context. In M. Oepen & W. Hamacher (Eds.), *Communicating the environment: Environmental communication for sustainable development* (pp. 41–61). New York: Peter Lang.

Otway, H. (1992). Public wisdom, expert fallibility: Toward a contextual theory of risk. In S. Krimsky & D. Golding (Eds.), *Social theories of risk* (pp. 215–228). Westport, CT: Praeger.

Ostrow, S. D. (1991). It will happen here. *Bank Marketing, 23*(7), 24–27.

Palenchar, M. J., & Heath, R. L. (2007). Strategic risk communication: Adding value to society. *Public Relations Review, 33*, 120–129.

Pearson, C. M., & Clair, J. A. (1998). Reframing crisis management. *The Academy of Management Review, 32*(1), 59–76.

Pearson, C. M., Clair, J. A., Misra, S. K., & Mitroff, I. I. (1997). Managing the unthinkable. *Organizational Dynamics, 26*(2), 51–64.

Penrose, J. M. (2000). The role of perception in crisis planning. *Public Relations Review*, *26*(2), 155–171.

Perrow, C. (1977). Three types of effectiveness studies. In P. S. Goodman & J. M. Pennings (Eds.), *New perspectives on organizational effectiveness*. San Francisco: Jossey-Bass.

Perrow, C. (1984). *Normal accidents: Living with high risk technologies*. New York: Basic Books.

Peters, R. G., Covello, V. T., & McCallum D. B. (1997). The determinants of trust and credibility in environmental risk communication: An empirical study. *Risk Analysis, 17*(1), 43–54.

Pidgeon, N., Kasperson, R. E., & Slovic, P. (2003). Introduction. In N. Pidgeon, R. E. Kasperson & P. Slovic (Eds.), *The social amplification of risk* (pp. 1–11). New York: Cambridge University Press.

Public Affairs Support Annex. (2007). *National Response Plan*. Retrieved July 27, 2007, from http: www.dhs.gov.xlibrary/assets/NRP_FullText.pdf

Quarantelli, E. L. (1988). Disaster crisis management: A summary of research findings. *Journal of Management Studies, 25*(4), 373–385.

Quintilian, M. F. (1951). *The institutio oratorio of Marcus Fabius Quintilianus* (C. E. Little, Trans.) Nashville, TN: George Peabody College for Teachers.
Reynolds, B. (2002, October). *Crisis and emergency risk communication.* Atlanta, GA: Centers for Disease Control and Prevention.
Reynolds, B., & Seeger, M. W. (2005). Crisis and emergency risk communication as an integrative framework. *Journal of Health Communication, 10,* 43–55.
Ruckelshaus, W. D. (1983). Science, risk, and public policy. *Science, 221,* 1026–1028.
Rogers, E. M., & Kincaid, D. L. (1981). *Communications networks: Toward a new paradigm for research.* New York: The Free Press.
Rowan, K. E. (1994). What risk communicators need to know: An agenda for research. In B. R. Burleson (Ed.), *Communication Yearbook 18* (pp. 300–319). Thousand Oaks, CA: Sage.
Sandman, P. M. (1987, Nov.). Risk communication: Facing public outrage. *EPA Journal,* 21–22.
Sandman, P. M. (1993). *Responding to community outrage: Strategies for effective risk communication.* Fairfax, VA: American Industrial Hygiene Association.
Sandman, P. M. (2006). Crisis communication best practices: Some quibbles and additions. *Journal of Applied Communication Research, 34*(3), 257–262.
SARA: Superfund Amendments and Reauthorization Act of 1986 (SARA), U.S. Code, vol. 42, sec. 9601, et seq. (1995).
Szasz, A. (1994). *Ecopopulism.* Minneapolis: University of Minnesota Press.
Seeger, M. W. (2005). Best practices of risk and crisis communication: An expert panel process. *Journal of Applied Communication Research, 43*(3), 323–244.
Seeger, M. W., Sellnow, T. L., & Ulmer, R. R. (1998). Communication, organization, and crisis. In Michael Roloff (Ed.) *Communication Yearbook 21* (pp. 230–275). Thousand Oaks, CA: Sage.
Seeger, M. W., Sellnow, T. L, & Ulmer, R. R. (2003). *Communication and organizational crisis.* Westport, CT: Praeger.
Sellnow, T. L., Seeger, M. W., & Ulmer, R. R. (2002). Chaos theory, informational needs, and natural disasters. *Journal of Applied Communication Research, 30,* 269–292.
Shrivastava, P. (1987). *Bhopal: Anatomy of a crisis.* Cambridge, MA: Ballinger.
Shrivastava, P. (1993). Crisis theory/practice: Towards a sustainable future. *Industrial and Environmental Crisis Quarterly, 7,* 23–42.
Slovic, P. (1987). Perception of risk. *Science, 230,* 280–285.
Smith, M. B. (2001). 'Silence, Miss Carson!' Science, gender, and the reception of Silent Spring. *Feminist Studies, 27*(3), 733–752.
Society for Risk Analysis (1993). *Vision statement.* Retrieved October 27, 2007, from http://www.sra.org/about_vision.php
Streifel, R. A., Beebe, B. L., Veil, S. R., & Sellnow, T. L. (2006). Significant choice and crisis decision making: MeritCare's public communication in the Fen-Phen case. *Journal of Business Ethics, 69*(4), 389–397. Szasz, A. (1994). *Ecopopulism.* Minneapolis: University of Minnesota Press.
Tyler, L. (2005). Towards a postmodern understanding of crisis communication. *Public Relations Review, 31,* 566–571.
Ulmer, R. R., Sellnow, T. L., & Seeger, M. W. (2007). *Effective crisis communication: Moving from crisis to opportunity.* Thousand Oaks, CA: Sage.
Union Carbide (2004, October). *Chronology of key events related to the Bhopal Incident.* Retrieved February 28, 2007, from: http://bhopal.net/bhopal.con/chronology
U.S. Congress. House Committee on Science and Technology. (1979). *Authorizing appropriations to the National Science Foundation.* House Report 96-61. Washington, DC: Government Printing Office.
U.S. Food and Drug Administration. (2007, June 4). *FDA announces new advisory committee to address risk communication* (Press Release). Retrieved October 29, 2007, from: http://www.fda.gov/bbs/topics/NEWS/2007/NEW01648.html
U.S. National Response Team. (1987). *Hazardous materials emergency planning guide.* Washington, DC: Author.
Wan, H., & Pfau, M. (2004). The relative effectiveness of inoculation, bolstering, and combined approaches in crisis communication. *Journal of Public Relations Research,* 16(3), 301–328.
Ware, B. L., & Linkugel, W. A. (1973). They spoke in defense of themselves: On the generic criticism of apologia. *Quarterly Journal of Speech, 59,* 273–283.
Witte, K., Meyer, G., & Martel, D. (2000). *Effective health risk messages.* Thousand Oaks, CA: Sage.
Wynne, B. (1992). Risk and social learning: Refinement to engagement. In S. Krimsky & D. Golding (Eds.), *Social theories of risk* (pp. 275–300). Westport, CT: Praeger.
Wynne, B. (1996). May the sheep safely graze? A reflexive view of the expert-lay knowledge divide. In S. Lash, B. Szerszynski, & B. Wynne (Eds.), *Risk, environment and modernity: Towards a new ecology* (pp. 44–83). London: Sage.

3

Cultural Theory and Risk

James Tansey
University of British Columbia

Steve Rayner
Oxford University

Cultural theory was first applied to risk and environmental problems in the early seventies, although it builds on a lineage that can be traced back over a century through the work of Mary Douglas and Edward Evans-Pritchard to the work of Emile Durkheim. By focusing on the inherently political character of risk controversies, it offers an approach to the interpretation of risk issues that contrasts starkly with atomistic economic, engineering and psychometric approaches. While many have come to know the theory through the grid-group typology of institutional forms, we spend the first part of this chapter describing the broader theoretical foundations of the theory. This context is essential to the correct interpretation of the typology. In the second part of the chapter, we describe the typology in more detail and show both how it can be used as a descriptive tool to predict patterns of risk and policy responses associated with specific institutional forms.

The typology itself is a heuristic device that describes four archetypal cultures or as they are now often called, solidarities, and was developed from a wide range of sociological and anthropological studies. It can only be properly understood in the context of the wider theory from which it is derived and with the caveats that were originally attached to it. Over the last decade it has been taken out of this context in a number of studies and commentaries, most recently Boholm (1996), Rosa, (1998), Sjöberg, (1997), Sjöberg, (1998)[1] and has been distorted beyond recognition. The first purpose of this chapter is to set the record straight by setting out a brief sketch of the much broader body of literature from which Douglas' expeditions into the field of risk were mounted. The typology is presented in the second half of this chapter in the context of this wider literature. But it is not enough to show that cultural theory has been misunderstood. It is crucial to show how and where this approach remains relevant to current risk research, relative to the recognised clusters of risk theories.

In the third section of the chapter, we discuss some of the contemporary applications of cultural theory to issues of trust, pluralism, democratization and risks associated with new and emerging technologies.

The disjunctures between social theories of risk (Krimsky & Golding, 1992; Renn, 1998) reflect both ontological differences (addressed here) and epistemological differences. The ontological differences are most apparent, and typically one can distinguish between two approaches. One is agent-centered and derived from rational utility approaches that focus on the capacity of individuals to conduct a complex calculus of costs and benefits, under the unconscious influence of pervasive heuristics such as 'dread' and 'familiarity'. In order to compare risks systematically across all the areas in which society might intervene in matters of life and death, the first school needs a model of individual rationality that is fixed and invariant. This is necessary in order to make the social production of safety subject to traditional scientific methods and standards. Socio-cultural approaches emphasize that social institutions exert a deterministic influence both on the perception of risks and on social action. Socio-cultural approaches recognise that societies cannot function with the mechanical efficiency of a well-oiled machine, producing outcomes that systematically identify, characterize and reduce the hazards to which the population is exposed. Moreover, as we show below, risk issues are inextricably linked to the never-ending conflict over the legitimacy of power relations in society.

In seeking to demonstrate the relevance of Douglas' work, it is worth considering the popular risk amplification framework. This framework suggests that social institutions alter the risk signal and amplify or attenuate the perception of dangers. This general macroscopic framework tells us what happens but not why. The untapped value of cultural theory is that it contains a thoroughly institutional theory of social action, which could be employed to populate and explore this framework. While many cultural accounts either leave culture unexplained, or reduce the individual to the status of automaton, Douglas' political sociology starts from the assumption that collective social action is hard to generate and sustain and that struggles over the legitimacy of power and authority are constant. Change, in this analysis is easier to account for than stability.

NEO-DURKHEIMIAN EXPLANATION

Cultural theory finds it origins in the work of Durkheim (1995) and Fleck (1935) but has been modified over the past century by a number of contributors, most notably Evan-Pritchard (1937). Durkheim's contribution to social theory was to argue that the values and beliefs that individuals hold must be interpreted in the social context in which they are actively employed, since he considered that culture exerts a strong or mechanical influence over cognition. Giddens (1984) described the functional form of explanation that emerged from Durkheim's work as distinctly different from Cartesian explanations where subject and object are separated. In place of a linear causal model that is the result of giving either agency or structure deterministic qualities, functional explanations identify feedback loops in order to account for the unintentional production and maintenance of social institutions. Douglas continued this functionalist tradition by exploring the beliefs of individuals in a particular social context relative to how they act. What matters is not what people believe, but what they do with those beliefs. At the heart of her work is a dual concept of culture as classification and contention (Fardon, 1999); the remainder of this section is organized around these inseparable themes.

Pursuing Durkheim's interest in the social factors controlling cognition, Douglas focused on the social institutions that produce the classifications deployed in the most fundamental of human activities: that of sense making. Social classifications impose order on the complex and unpredictable flux of human experience and enable collective social action. Douglas' theory focuses on the importance of ritual action in this process of sense making and hence argues that:

> As a social animal, man is a ritual animal. If ritual is suppressed in one form it crops up in others ... Without the letters of condolence, telegrams of congratulations and even occasional postcards, the friendship of a separated friend is not a social reality. It has no existence without the rites of friendship. Social rituals create a reality, which would be nothing without them. It is not too much to say that ritual is more to society than words are to thought. (Douglas, 1984, p. 63)

The implications of the social construction of reality debate have preoccupied scientists for many years. In the Durkheimian tradition, institutions supply the metaphors and analogies of which mental models are constructed:

> All knowledge and everything we talk about is collectively constructed. Language is no private invention. Words are a collective product, and so are meanings. There could not be risks, illnesses, dangers, or any reality, knowledge of which is not constructed. It might be better if the word "social construal" were used instead of "construction", because all evidence has to be construed. (Douglas, 1997, p. 123)

Durkheim's approach sometimes suggests that society is the individual mind writ large. This aspect of his work has been criticized for its mechanical determinism, since it implies that social institutions map exactly on patterns of cognition (Douglas, 1986, p. 6, 1999). Boholm (1996) wrongly accused cultural theory of the same error even though Douglas described culture as dynamic, "an ongoing, never resolved argument about the rightness of choices" (Douglas, 1992, p. 260). Individuals constantly and actively question social classifications and the patterns of authority they represent, indeed the functional role of this process is to ensure that power is legitimated (c.f. Beetham, 1991).

The notion of determinism is misleading and should be replaced with the term "constraint." Institutions constrain what will be taken seriously in a given context and define the conditions under which a statement will be taken seriously and treated with felicity (Haugaard, 1997). No amount of structural determinism prevents us from saying the words "Cats are a sign of good luck," but it will not be met with felicity in a biology class. The same is true at the level of formal social institutions: "individuals negotiating their way through the organizational constraints of actively interpreting, challenging, accepting, and recreating their social environment are limited to a style of discourse consistent with the constitutive premises of that environment" (Rayner, 1992, p. 90). There is nothing to prevent an individual making any statement they choose, but it will only have the power of an utterance if it meets with felicity (Foucault, 1980; Haugaard, 1997). More importantly, there is nothing to prevent an individual from acting in a way that may be deemed inappropriate, but institutions structure the availability of social and economic incentives. As will become clearer below, pollution and taboos are deployed when other incentives are not available and dangers are mobilized to defend moral norms.

Social construal implies the selection of some social facts for special emphasis and some for avoidance. For instance, Douglas (1986, pp. 81–90) suggested that the professional academe of psychology has consistently ignored the effect of sociality on cognition because it is organized around the emancipatory goal of individual liberation from conventions and socialization processes. The notion that cognitive heuristics have social origins is antithetical to the central axiom of the discipline and claims to the contrary are treated with infelicity. The power of the functional form of explanation is that values and beliefs that have power in society are inseparable from the institutions that sustain them—the same institutions that mobilize the benefits of collective action. Hence, Douglas instructed us to treat the processes of classification and contention as inseparable, since the dominant concern in any social context is how to organize together in society.

Focusing on culture as contention, Douglas argued that since individuals are conscious agents, they are aware of the demands being made on them by others that share the same institutional context. The consequence is that that power and authority are always precariously held and are constantly sensitive to change. The essential message of her brand of functionalism is that there is a constant irreconcilable tension between individual agency and power. Douglas (1986) made an elegant case for functional explanations in social science, indicating that it is not functionalism per se that is problematic but bad functionalism. The challenge is to describe the rational foundations for collective action without resorting to a number of alternatives for explaining social solidarity that are considered unsatisfactory. Douglas discounted various forms of social glue that provide essentialist or purely intentional explanations for social solidarity. For instance, Olson (1965) described two special cases where collective action may emerge from latent groups: smallness of scale (individuals are tightly bound by conditions of mutual reciprocation and trust) or coercion (individuals have no choice). Both can be discounted since there are numerous examples in the anthropological literature where either smallness of scale fails to result in collective action or where collective action is evident despite the absence of coercion. The social glue Durkheim employed to explain the strength of mechanical solidarity in pre-modern societies was the emotion produced by religion but as Douglas pointed out, "Religion does not explain, religion has to be explained" (Douglas, 1986, p. 36). Finally, forms of explanation that suggest that collective action is catalyzed by psychological needs for emotional security, acceptance and recursiveness are discounted. This precludes Giddens' argument that social institutions are stabilized by the essential need for "ontological security." Such psychic explanations may explain some effects some of the time, but are insufficiently robust, representing society as conservative and social structures as the product of human emotional fragility.

The feedback loops that maintain institutions in a functional explanation are the unintended consequences of behavioral effects. Elster (1983) set out the logical steps and conditions for a robust functional explanation and suggests that they would almost never be fulfilled. In contrast, Douglas focused on latent groups to demonstrate that a functional explanation is viable even where there are limited individual benefits available as incentives to collective action. The critical variable is the ratio between the cost of membership and the benefits of collective action. Where the ratio is low, this creates an underlying tendency towards fission, since each individual has the threat of withdrawal on hand where the demands of the group become cumbersome. The unintended effect is that only a weak form of leadership can emerge, since individuals are highly cognizant of demands upon them. Secondly, individuals protect their commitment to the group by insisting on equality and full participation. While the intention behind this behavioral effect is to prevent free riding, the unintended consequence is to create a stable boundary around the group defining those classified as insiders and those classified as outsiders. Finally, in the absence of strong consensus for formulating rules or for punishing deviance, mutual accusations of betrayal are the only strategy for ensuring mutual accountability. The model that Douglas and Wildavsky (1983) present fills in the logical steps that were missing in the account of the formation of environmental groups in *Risk and Culture*. The explanation of collective action appears pessimistic and resembles game-theoretic formulations, but it explains the minimal conditions for the appearance of collective action from latency. Thompson, Ellis, and Wildavsky (1990) developed analogous explanations for different contexts and Grimen (1999) has developed this logical approach to functionalism further. Where there are greater benefits of collective action, for instance in hierarchies, there is less of a propensity for fission. Nonetheless, hierarchies must work hard to legitimate the distinctions they create. For example, one can read Hobbes' *Leviathan* as a cultural account constructed to legitimate the authority of sovereign rulers through appeal to the order they create, in contrast to the chaotic state of nature, where life is 'nasty, short and brutish'.

Douglas suggested that conventions are legitimated and reified through analogy with what counts locally as natural. Consider how in western society, competition in the biological theory of natural selection is used to support the 'naturalness' of individualism. Nature is a strategic resource mobilized to support truth claims and categories in nature mirror and reinforce conventions relating to social practices (Douglas, 1999 [1975], pp. 256–260). In this account, and resembling Foucault's assertion that power is pervasive at all levels, "social institutions, classification, thought and ideas are at bottom *political,* because they express, mobilize and trigger patterns of power" (1999, p. 9). Power comes center stage in the never-ending concern with the distribution, organization and exchange of accountability and responsibility (Douglas, 1999 [1975], pp. 284–309). Douglas' central argument is that mishaps, misfortunes and risks are mobilized in the process of holding those wielding power accountable. These mechanisms are present in all societies from the remote pre-industrial societies studied by the anthropologists of the early twentieth century to contemporary western societies and it was from this perspective that Douglas first launched her foray into the risk literature.

A number of caveats must be mentioned at this stage. Firstly, unlike earlier functional explanations, the neo-Durkheimian approach does not apply to whole societies but rather to the multifarious social institutions of which they are composed. There is not only a need for accountability within institutions, but also between institutions as they compete for power and influence and forge settlements in society. The greater popularity of the approach inspired by Douglas in the field of political science is a result of the power of the theory in explaining the political nature of social life (Thompson, Grendstad & Selle, 1999, Thompson et al., 1990, Coyle & Ellis, 1994, Hoppe & Peterse, 1994). Secondly, the emphasis on functionalism in this section does not preclude intentional explanations where individuals deliberately produce collective action (Thompson et al., 1990; 6, 1999), although the constraints on power and authority remain.

The neo-Durkheimian approach has been applied to a number of topics and Douglas has focused on what happens when beliefs and practices meet with infelicity. Contra Rosa (1998) the neo-Durkheimian version of constructionism does not imply a relativistic argument that all knowledge claims are equal. Some beliefs are antithetical to the institutions of power and authority, and every effort is mobilized to exclude them. Hence, when Christian fundamentalists mobilize against abortion, they seek to protect their god's unassailable authority to decide between life and death. Douglas' approach has been to study aversion and identify the rules for what is reprehensible, since this is often much less ambiguous than what an institution supports. Hers is a theory of rejection (Douglas, 1986)—a forensic approach that uses dangers, taboos and risks to reveal the internal structure and systems for accountability and responsibility of cultures.

RISK, DANGER AND TABOO: SIMILAR BUT NOT THE SAME

Douglas' goal in the field of anthropology was to challenge the orthodox interpretation of the pollution myths and taboos of non-industrial societies. Her mission was to challenge the dominant analyses of these societies that suggested some fundamental cognitive disjuncture between "them and us" (Douglas, 1992, p. 3). Her alternative to explanations of witchcraft, taboos and pollution that relied on notions of "primitive mysticism" was to argue that these activities play a role in maintaining particular social institutions. Furthermore, social concerns over purity, dirt and pollution perform analogous social functions in modern secular and religious societies (Douglas, 1984, 1970, 1992). These insights have been summarized and reviewed in a number of accounts (Fardon, 1999; Lupton, 1999; Wuthnow et al., 1984).

For example, during her fieldwork with the Lele of Kasai, Douglas (1963) recognized that a number of animals had particular symbolic and political significance within that society. Everyday food rules in that society were a subtle form of politics, which served to represent and reinforce social distinctions. Social taboos specified which social strata within the tribe were allowed to eat particular animals. The most revered animal was the pangolin, which was deemed poisonous to all except the highest initiates. Douglas argued that the functional role of such cultural practices is to maintain social order and to reproduce a differentiation of roles. The everyday practices of the Hima of Uganda, recounted in *Risk and Culture* perform an equally important function by providing explanations for seemingly independent events. In the case of the Hima people, it was believed that if women come into contact with cattle that the cattle will become sick or die or that if a woman is adulterous that her husband will receive a fatal arrow wound. The function is to attribute an act that transgresses moral norms with foreseeable yet undesired consequences. Douglas (1990) argued that most cultures develop a common term to moralize and politicize dangers. Pollution myths perform a special role in the struggle to maintain a moral order. Amidst the uncertainty, political and economic forces are mobilized on a daily basis and pollution and taboos are mobilized when other sanctions are inadequate (Douglas, 1984, pp. 131, 140).

The concept of sin in Christian societies performs an analogous function by attributing certain actions inconsistent with institutional conventions with the power to cause negative consequences in this life or the next:

> The very name of the sin is often a prophecy, a prediction of trouble ... first comes the temptation to sin, and then the thought of future retribution, then warnings from friends and relations, attacks from

> enemies, and possibly a return to the path of righteousness before the damage is done. (Douglas, 1984, p. 6)

At issue is not the validity of taboos or beliefs in dangers, indeed Douglas pointed out that in the pre-industrial world where life expectancy is short and infant mortality high that "[s]tarvation, blight and famine are perennial threats. It is a bad joke to take this analysis as hinting that the dangers are imaginary" (Douglas, 1984, p. 8). Similarly, the reality of risks is rarely subject to dispute. The conflict is most often over the magnitude of the risks and over who is responsible for them. The process of construal described above implies that social institutions attribute the causes of (real) dangers with behavior that is collectively disapproved of. The conservative function of attribution is only half the story. The act of attribution is also a sense-making activity. The classifications and categories of institutions enable order to be discerned in the stream of events engulfing individuals, filtering out some perceptions and combining others (Rayner, 1991; 6, 1999). The more profound implication of this argument is that institutions generate emotional responses to risk events. Just as the aversion to pollution taboos produces a real physical response in the examples above, so the fear of "perceived" risks produces real emotional reactions upon which individuals act.

In her quest to vindicate pre-industrial societies from subtly racist charges that they had failed to evolve to the sophistication of industrialized societies, Douglas looked for analogous functional mechanisms in the West. While environmental risks were discussed in the first edition of Implicit Meanings (Douglas, 1999 [1975]), more common themes included everyday conventions related to dirt and hygiene (Douglas, 1984). Social norms that define what counts as dirt describe objects that are 'out of place' in the social order. Shoes are not inherently dirty; they become classified as dirty when they are placed on a kitchen table. In a fundamental sense, the functional role of this attribution process is to defend social order as a sense-making activity. Douglas also showed that the moralization of misfortune was common in the west. In the early stages of the AIDS epidemic, there was so often speculation that infection was the result of behavior believed to be immoral—such as homosexuality or promiscuity—that one would have to assume that a virus was capable of moral judgement (Douglas, 1992).

In an essay entitled "Environments at Risk," Douglas drew explicit parallels between the tribal and the modern condition:

> We are far from being the first civilisation to realise that our environment is at risk. Most tribal environments are held to be in danger in much the same way as ours. The dangers are naturally not identical. Here and now we are concerned with overpopulation. Often they are worried by underpopulation. But we pin the responsibility in quite the same way as they do. Always and everywhere it is human folly, hate, and greed which puts the human environment at risk. (Douglas, 1999 [1975], p. 204)

The everyday practices of the Hima of Uganda, recounted in *Risk and Culture* (Douglas, 1983) perform an important function by providing explanations for seemingly independent events. In the case of the Hima people, it was believed that if women come into contact with cattle that the cattle will become sick or die or that if a woman is adulterous that her husband will receive a fatal arrow wound. The function is to attribute an act that transgresses moral norms with foreseeable yet undesired consequences.

> Among the verbal weapons of control, time is one of the four final arbiters. Time, money, God, and nature, usually in that order, are universal trump cards plunked down to win an argument. (Douglas, 1999 [1975], p. 209)

These verbal weapons help to entrench beliefs in ways that reflect the distribution of power in a particular social context. Douglas (1990) argued that most cultures develop a common term to moralize and politicize dangers. Pollution myths perform a special role in the struggle to maintain a moral order. Amidst the uncertainty, political and economic forces are mobilized on a daily basis and pollution and taboos are mobilized when other sanctions are inadequate (Douglas, 1984, pp. 131, 140).

While risks and sins function both to account for past events and to constrain future behavior they must also be distinguished (Douglas, 1990). Sins and taboos bind individuals into institutions and also make collective benefits available. Risk, in contrast, "is invoked to protect individuals against the encroachment of others" (Douglas, 1990, p. 7) and in this sense it is the reciprocal of being in sin.

In industrial societies cultures risks are morally charged, and ecological crises are considered to have emerged because of immoral human action. The fragile state of nature reflects the fragile state of society or as Wuthnow et al. (1984) argued "the sudden appearance of troubled nature reveals troubles in that society" (p. 95). Pervasive and ominous risks are selected and serve to reinforce social solidarity among emergent groups, reinforcing boundaries and assigning blame to what is perceived as a corrupt leadership. In seeking to make claims about the generality of these mechanisms, Douglas (1992) argued that:

> The modern concept of risk ... is part of the system of thought that upholds the type of individualist culture, which sustains an expanding industrial system. The dialogue about risk plays the role equivalent to taboo or sin, but the slope is tilted in the reverse direction, away from protecting the community and in favour of protecting the individual. (p. 28)

This central notion, that the political mechanisms of sense making, accountability and control are continuous and consistent across all human societies and that, essentially, boundary crises are managed through risk controversies, is a central contribution of cultural theory.

CULTURAL THEORY AND THE ENVIRONMENT

The relatively recent emergence of the concept of risk can be traced to the deliberations of merchants over the benefits of financial transactions relative to the costs. While originally couched in neutral terms as incorporating both costs and the benefits, the term has evolved in modern times to refer primarily to negative outcomes. Modernity is characterized by emancipation from the seemingly arbitrary truths of religion and tradition and hence sin and taboo are no longer effective; they no longer mobilize social power. While the concept cannot be reduced to a single definition, one of the common features of the family of definitions (Rayner, 1992) is the commitment to the production of safety: systematic increases in longevity and the taming of natural hazards. The consequence is that the unified self is reified and appears "self evident" (Douglas, 1999 [1975], pp. 252–283):

> The modern concept of risk ... is part of the system of thought that upholds the type of individualist culture, which sustains an expanding industrial system. The dialogue about risk plays the role equivalent to taboo or sin, but the slope is tilted in the reverse direction, away from protecting the community and in favour of protecting the individual. (Douglas, 1992, p. 28)

In other words, the modern concept of risk is the product of the large-scale institutions that characterize modern societies. Individualism as it is commonly understood is the product of the legal system, the medical system, the democratic vote and even conspicuous consumption.

Cultural theory argues that risks are defined, perceived, and managed according to principles that inhere in particular forms of social organization. The cultural theory of risk perception first entered public policy debates with the publication of Michael Thompson's paper "Aesthetics of Risk: Culture or Context" in Schwing and Albers' (1980) landmark volume *Societal Risk Assessment: How Safe is Safe Enough*. Since that time, the theory has been the focus of widespread debate in both scholarly and policy communities.

Cultural theory differs from other approaches to risk perception, risk communication, and risk management in several important ways. Almost without exception, attempts to understand human behavior related to technological risk assume that it is a response which follows from an external event, an activity, or a statement of the probability and consequences of an activity. The conventional order of risk events is assumed to be as follows: The external risk stimulus causes an individual risk perception, which may be the subject of attempts at risk communication, leading to risk management efforts to prevent the unwanted event or ameliorate its consequences.

This ordering is implicit or explicit in both the natural hazards research tradition and in psychometric risk studies, although the histories of these two approaches are quite separate (see Krimsky & Golding, 1992). This model of perception is that of vision or hearing rather than that of touch or taste. The perceiver essentially is the passive recipient of an independent stimulus, rather than an active agent, like a baby, groping with or sucking on the world in the search for information. The risk perception problem in these approaches is to account for the discrepancy between some people's estimates of the risks or potential consequences of certain events and actuarial data or expert assessments.

The dominant model of risk communication essentially is one of information transmission with the goal of educating the recipient to arrive at a rational understanding of the probable risks. The main concern is how to pass quantitative information about the probabilities and consequences of events from one information bearer (the transmitter) to another (the receiver) through a medium (the channel) with the minimum of distortion (Kasperson et al., 1988). In fact, information transmission is only one part of communication which also involves developing shared meaning among individuals, institutions, and communities and establishing relationships of trust (Rayner, 1988).

The concept of management implicit in the conventional conceptualization of risk is both directive and reactive. It is directive in that it actively seeks to achieve specifiable goals of prevention or limitation through explicit procedures. Piecemeal coping, development of tolerance, and implicit avoidance behaviors usually are not considered management strategies in this framework.[2] Conventional risk management also is reactive in that it is the final step in the process. Its role is to solve problems that have been perceived and made the subject of communication, either as a precursor or management response, rather than to seek out issues for attention.

Cultural theory differs from conventional approaches to risk perception in that it assumes an active, rather than passive, perceiver. Furthermore, this perceiver is not an individual, but an institution or organization that is driven by organizational imperatives to select risks for management attention or to suppress them from view (Douglas, 1985). The question is not how individuals think about risk per se, but how institutions think. According to cultural theory, institutional structure is the ultimate cause of risk perception; risk management is the proximate stimulus rather than its outcome. In addition to being proactive, management strategies in cultural theory include various coping and adaptive behaviors that tend to be discounted in conventional approaches. Finally, risk communication in cultural theory emphasizes creation of shared meaning and trust over the transfer of quantitative information (Rayner, 1988). Thus, cultural theory is fundamentally a social theory concerned with dynamic relationships among human beings.

While *Purity and Danger* (1966) won widespread acclaim, Douglas' next book *Natural Symbols* (1970) was more controversial. In this work, Douglas began to systematize her insights from *Purity and Danger* to develop a typology of social structure and views of nature. This was the origin of *grid/group analysis* discussed later in this chapter.

The cosmological focus of *Natural Symbols* was much broader than environmental, technological, or human health risks. Douglas had demonstrated her interest in the cultural aspects of emerging environmentalism in a short paper entitled "Environments at Risk" (1972). However, it was not until 1978 that Michael Thompson authored the first papers explicitly linking grid/group to risk preferences in the West German debate about nuclear energy (Thompson, 1982a) and among Sherpa Buddhists in the Himalayas (Thompson, 1982b). In 1982, the same year that Thompson's papers appeared in the open literature, Mary Douglas and Aaron Wildavsky published *Risk and Culture.*

In *Risk and Culture*, Douglas and Wildavsky attributed concern with cancer risks from industrial pollution in the United States to the growth of an essentially egalitarian environmentalist movement dedicated to the elimination of involuntary exposure to danger. However, *Risk and Culture* reduces the complex societal debate about risk behavior already sketched out by Michael Thompson to a simple conflict between society's center and its border. The even-handed technical application of cultural theory to risk is pushed into the background, while an anti-egalitarian polemic is brought to the fore. The culture theoretic distinctions between markets and hierarchies are blended into the legitimate "center" of modern society, bound together by self-interested resistance to assault from a homogenized egalitarian "border" which Douglas and Wildavsky characterized as *sectarian*. While markets and hierarchies are portrayed as making rational tradeoffs among the benefits and costs of difficult technological choices, so-called border sectarians are delegitimated at the outset by the authors' choice of terminology and subsequently taken to task for employing irrational fears about nature and technology to resolve their own organizational problems. The rich cultural diversity encompassed by cultural theory as a model of social possibilities is, in effect, reduced to a traditional conflict of interests between the hegemonic capitalism of the market and the state on the one hand and its egalitarian critics on the other.

Douglas' response to the difficult reception given *Risk and Culture*, was a slim volume entitled *Risk Acceptability According to the Social Sciences* (Douglas 1985). Although it was not directly a reply to critics, Douglas acknowledged in her introduction that the controversy over *Risk and Culture* provided much of the impetus for the later work.

As in *Risk and Culture*, Douglas initially used two kinds of societies to illustrate her case about the selection of risks by active perceivers. These are the competitive, market-type society, based on contract, and the hierarchical society in which social relationships are constrained by status. While markets and hierarchies together comprise Douglas and Wildavsky's *center* of modern society, here there is more exploration of the differences between them. Rather than a dichotomy between center and border, Douglas creates a triangular space for societal disagreement about risk that includes a third kind of institution, the egalitarian-collectivist type that is frequently represented in industrial society by voluntary groups.[3]

If Douglas's reply to the criticism leveled at *Risk and Culture* was characteristically hierarchist in its attempt at inclusion through technical justification, Wildavsky's was the typically unapologetic response of the individualist. In *Searching for Safety*, Wildavsky (cite) abandoned defense of hierarchy altogether on the basis that it exhibits "monumental" bias towards anticipatory measures to manage risk and has difficulty making piecemeal adjustments to policies and regulations through trial and error learning. In effect, Wildavsky dismissed hierarchy in the contemporary United States as the captive of egalitarian constituencies bent upon greater equality of condition. In contrast, Wildavsky clearly identified societal resilience to unexpected hazards with the cultural strategy of markets, both because they adapt rapidly to new information and because they help to create the wealth that he regarded as the source of health and longevity.

If we allow that the concept of risk has a range of closely associated meanings, then we can use Douglas' work to look for its influence in other areas. Political activity to protect the environment seeks to sustain conventions and norms central to cultures. Burger (1990) suggested that political arguments in defense of such conventions are expressed under the only banner that will rally support—that of individual protection. In the demonstrations prior to the collapse of Soviet rule in Lithuania, the population took to the streets, accusing their communist rulers of environmental destruction. Dawson (1995) suggested that environmental protests focusing on a Soviet-Lithuanian Nuclear Power Station were a surrogate for nationalism in a period where calls for independence would have been taboo. Risk was mobilized as a stick to beat authority (Douglas, 1992, p. 24).

Eliasoph's (1998) detailed insider account of the activities of US environmental groups supported the assertion that risks are mobilized as ace cards in moral conflicts. Employing Goffman's distinction between the backstage and frontstage roles that actors may assume, she identifies the contrast between the complex moral arguments that activists provide in private and their frontstage performances in the context of the group, particularly in front of the media. Individuals simplify their concerns frontstage and seek to give authority to their positions by selecting the features of their concerns that will be treated with felicity: direct harm to themselves or harm to their children. Other distributive or procedural concerns seem to be constrained by the context and the desire to be taken seriously.

Douglas and Wildavsky's (1983) analysis of the politics of environmental groups in the United States has to be set in the context of the wider literature above. Read alone, the text leaves too much for the reader to infer about the meaning of culture and the analysis generalized about environmental groups (Gerlach, 1987). The analysis at the macro scale of a whole society focuses on the way technology risks are deployed by "sectarian" environmental groups associated with a critical border as part of the struggle with the "center." The "center" is composed of a synergistic alliance between bureaucracies of government and the markets. This conflict over meanings is part of a political struggle for influence in society and is deployed to secure the legitimization of power relations inherent to the governance of industrial societies.

While the "border" and "center" are poorly defined, the central point of the analysis as a two-fold struggle still stands. The internal struggle is to mobilize collective action out of latency; the challenge of maintaining solidarity selects certain credible dangers for attention. The purpose of the group is to hold government and industry accountable. In pre-industrial societies, pollution myths are mobilized to defend moral norms in the absence of alternative sanctions. In the west, groups with marginal political or economic power can only exert their influence by appealing to the populace through accusations that those in power are responsible for exposing them to dangers.

Finally, a number of other core themes in Douglas' work have not been elaborated in the risk and environmental literature. Douglas' emphasis on the sociology of rejection has obscured what constitutes purity in modern societies. Wilderness in the environmental literature is often treated as the pure and sanctified ground defiled by development. In addition, research on risk-seeking behavior has received less attention, but could be analyzed through a neo-Durkheimian lens by examining the social function of such behavior. Finally, we should remember that one of the core themes of *Purity and Danger* was to examine the way that different societies deal with anomalies. By definition, one of the goals of gene technology is to create hybrids; species that transgress biological classifications. If we want some help in understanding people's aversion to these activities, then we should look to Douglas' work (Douglas, 1984; Douglas & Hull, 1992).

CONTEMPORARY RRISK ISSUES: BIOTECHNOLOGY

Biotechnology builds upon and extends the work of biologists who have sought for centuries to classify species according to clear and logical phenotypical and morphological taxonomies. As a result of this accumulated knowledge, we have a generally accepted understanding of species as distinct biological types. Much of the controversy surrounding biotechnology focuses on transgenic organisms and by definition these organisms represent hybrids across categories that have been made more distinct by biological research. While the methods for combining genetic material at the cellular level are unprecedented, hybrid species have been present in many cultures including the fanciful creatures of Greek mythology such as the Minotaur and many tribal cultures including those studied by Douglas. Some, but certainly not all, modern genetic hybrids have been the focus of controversies and as the biotechnology industry expands it seems likely that more candidates will emerge. What is already clear is that some hybrid species are more controversial than others. For instance, the vast majority of corn, soy and canola production in North America utilizes genetically modified variants that incorporate genes for herbicide resistance. In stark contrast to European experience, environmental groups have been largely unsuccessful in drawing attention to the introduction by stealth of these variants.

Douglas' work (1963) comparing the food taboos of the Lele with those of the Israelites, as described in Deutronomy may be helpful. Douglas discovered very quickly that the Lele had a wide range of food rules and that their taxonomy of species was based not on phenotype or genotype but rather on the medium the species occupied. Since pigs live on the mud on river margins, they are grouped with fish. Flying squirrels are grouped with birds and secondary classifications distinguish between young and old animals within a species. In most cases, animals were seen as inferior but extremely fecund, while humans were considered superior but chronically infertile. In the case of the Lele, food rules were often not prohibitive but instead assigned species to social strata in ways that assumed they were beneficial for members of that strata to eat. By consuming animals, the beneficial characteristics of that species would be transferred to members of the social group although it would be inappropriate or even dangerous for others to consume the same animals. Of particular interest to Douglas was the pangolin or spiny anteater, eaten only by those men who have demonstrated that they are fertile. The pangolin is considered a hybrid or boundary crosser that has human and animal attributes. It is described by Douglas as a "scaly fish-like tree dweller, it bows its head like a man avoiding his mother-in-law. As a mammal which brings forth its young singly, it evidently does not share the fecundity which distinguishes animals from mankind. This anomaly mediates between humans and spirits and assures fertility" (Douglas, 1999 [1975], p. 272).

The Israelites have much stricter and more prohibitive dietary rules, which were formalised in the Old Testament books of Deutronomy and Leviticus. Douglas analyzed the food rules not simply as doctrines but as products of the historical circumstances in the fourth century BC that the Israelites found themselves in. Species that are hybrids or mixtures and violate the Judaic system of classification are universally classed as abominations, to be avoided at all costs. Jewish dietary classes are based on physiology: animals that chew the cud and have a cloven hoof are deemed acceptable. In contrast, animals that only display one of these characteristics are deemed anomalous. While the pig is the best-known example, the class of animals includes the camel, the hare and the rock badger.

In an argument first set out in *Purity and Danger* and substantially revised in later work, Douglas argued that the explanation for the reaction to anomaly is a political one, grounded in the social context of the group and in the internal struggles to maintain solidarity and credibility.

> Foul monster or good saviour, the judgment has little to do with the physical attributes of the being in question and much to do with the prevailing social pattern of rules and meanings which creates anomaly. (Douglas, 1999 [1975], p. 259)

The Lele, like many small fragmented tribal groups faced real concerns related to depopulation, and the pangolin cult was open to men who returned to the village in which the clan was founded. It attracted sons-in-law back to the village. The pangolin is a boundary crosser and is revered as a hybrid with human and animal characteristics. Drawing membership of the pangolin cult also helps to solve demographic problems within the village and this ability of individuals to cross clan boundaries is also revered.

The view among the Israelites was that no good could come from boundary crossing and from external exchange. The highest goal was to maintain the integrity of the group from foreign incursion. Boundaries are cherished and must be kept strong in a historical context where the Israelites were surrounded by powerful forces, tempting members of the group away through defection. They addressed the fear of the hybridization of their own identity through strong sanctions against anomalous hybrid organisms. Dragging nature in to provide greater credibility in the face of possible defections reinforced social rules governing the behavior of the collective.

These two contrasting views of hybridity contain a number of important lessons, not least of which is that hybrids are not necessarily negative or threatening. Contemporary risk discourse has tended to focus on these negative dimensions (Lupton, 1999),[4] but we need to separate the condition of hybridity from the moral valence. This implies that there may be new explanations for the appeal of boundary spanning organisms or activities in certain cultural settings.

Both examples demonstrate a strong linkage between the real political challenges affecting the viability of distinct cultures and systems of belief about nature. Drawing on the logic of functionalist theory, the insight of cultural theory was to see the human body as, "a conceptual microcosm for the body politic" (Lupton, 1999, p. 40), involved on a daily and mundane ritual basis to mark out, stabilize and reify the classifications that bring order and power. Political struggles, in this account, are struggles for both meaning and power. The body represents a potent symbol in the struggle for social control, and contamination or pollution of a pure interior or past body is easily projected onto the struggles to police the boundaries of the body politic.

A recent study indicates how this mechanism manifests in the context of an emerging technology: genetic biobanks. Biobanks combine genetic information, derived from human tissue, with phenotypic information related to disease manifestation. A number of large-scale biobanks have been established to study patterns of disease within large populations. The application is not primarily for quantifying disease probabilities at the individual level. Simple genetic disorders can be assessed by studying family pedigrees. Instead, these systems are used for studying aggregate associations between genetic variation and the distribution of disease.

The study explored emerging concerns about the implementation of these biobanks within Canada using a series of focus groups. One focus group targeted Canadian First Nations and elicited their response to the proposal to develop biobanks. Two broad findings emerged from this study that exemplify the utility of cultural theory. Firstly, the myth of genetic determinism has penetrated popular culture to a surprising degree and it provided a portable and pervasive resource for the focus group participants. The image of the aboriginal body in genetic disequilibrium with new environmental, chemical and malnutritional insults recurred throughout the discussion. Genetics replaces the clean body maintained by hygienic ritual from outside impurities with a molecular self, poorly prepared for colonial influence. Genetics, in some cases, is a logical trap that sustains the status quo; it both accounts for misfortune and implies that continued disequilibrium is inevitable. The discussion revealed the political struggles within the community to build and maintain solidarity. Boundaries are repeatedly marked on a colonised physical and political territory; the outsider contaminates and pollutes. Against this backdrop, the role of the specific technology is subsumed beneath the need to build and sustain solidarity across First Nations that have suffered enormously as a result of colonization.

The study shows how the institutional context selects and frames a technology in a particular way in order to support an essential political role at the level of the collective. To put it another way, the characteristics of the technology itself, in this case, a biobank, is largely irrelevant the explanation of it apparent dangerousness.

THE TYPOLOGY

While it is often confused with the theory itself, the grid/group typology was developed as a heuristic device, the purpose of which was to "gently push what is known into an explicit typology that captures the wisdom of a hundred years of sociology, anthropology and psychology" (Douglas, 1982, p. 1). Douglas recognized the limitations of typologies and identified a number of caveats to the typology, to which those of Ostrander (1982) are added. The first is that the typology makes no claim to represent the nature of individual free will and hence is not deterministic:

> the grid/group model does not preclude psychological theories of how different personality types might gravitate towards one kind of social context or another. (Gross & Rayner, 1985, p. 18)

Secondly, the typology is a static device, not a causal model designed to illustrate change. According to the framework described above, change is the norm and stability would require a special explanation. Thirdly, the typology is a relative rather than an absolute tool, so it is primarily of heuristic value. Finally, Ostrander (1982) emphasized that the typology should be applied to social institutions rather than to societies and hence is technically incapable of distinguishing whole social systems.

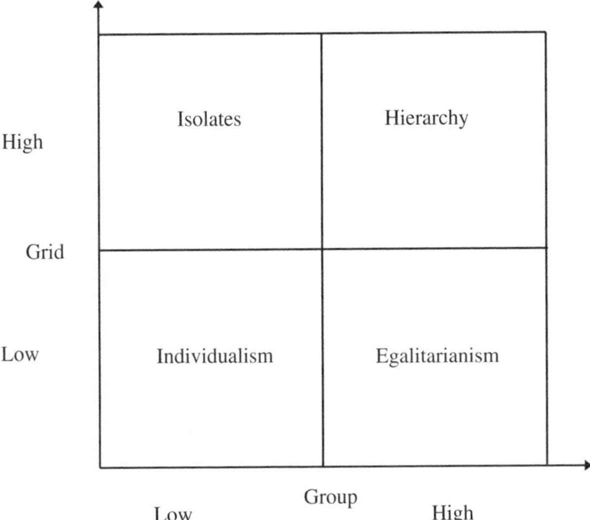

FIGURE 3.1 Grid/group dimensions and solidarities.

Douglas (1982) set out the basic assumptions behind the two axes of the typology. Firstly, she considered the minimum forms of commitment to life in a society postulated by political theory. These are represented in terms of the strength of allegiance to a group and the axis varies from weak to strong. Secondly, she considered the extent of regulation inside or outside of the group-the grid axis. The grid varies from low to high. For instance, a military regiment with its prescriptions for behavior and rigid timetabling represents a high grid social environment. Ostrander (1982) defined the two axes succinctly by arguing that social order limits the freedom of individuals in two spheres: whom one interacts with (group) and how one interacts with them (grid). A more elaborate version suggests that:

> Group refers to the extent to which an individual is incorporated into bounded units. The greater the incorporation, the more individual choice is subject to group determination. Grid denotes the degree to which an individual's life is circumscribed by externally imposed prescriptions. (Thompson et al., 1990, p. 5)

From these two variables, the four possible forms of social environments in Figure 3.1 can be drawn. The labels attached to the four social environments have been a cause of some confusion. While individualism implies atomism, coordinated activity is perfectly feasible in a low group, low grid context, indeed a shared language and shared symbols of value are precursors to even the most rudimentary market. Under these conditions, coordinated activity assumes a predictable form that is distinctly different to that which occurs in a high grid, high group context.

Rayner's (1992) intensive study uses a range of methodologies to explore the different institutional contexts that operate in one complex organisation—a hospital—and the manner in which they mediate the construction of radiological risks. The culture within which surgeons interact was found to be competitive and individualistic and to foster cavalier attitudes towards the risks to which they and their patients were exposed. In contrast, the Radiological Protection Officers were responsible and accountable to the hospital management for the regulation of occupational exposures to radiation. Rayner identifies contexts that corresponded to each of the four quadrants of the typology and describes the manner in which these mediated attitudes to risk. The point was not to demonstrate how individuals were 'hierarchical' or 'individualist' but to demonstrate that the culture within which social actors operate both enables some forms of behavior and constrains others.

Traditional surveys were first used by Dake and Thompson (see Dake, 1992) in a study of households, but this data collection was accompanied by detailed ethnographic research. Dake and Wildavsky (1990) then focused on the use of surveys to examine the relationship between individual values or biases and risk perception. Their quantitative scale employs a series of statements to which the interviewee responds using a Likert scale. The statements are based on predictions from the four idealized types derived from the typology and the scales measure the extent to which interviewees agree or disagree with them. This approach has become the most popular and has ultimately subverted the central message of cultural theory to such an extent that it appears inconsistent and contradictory (Boholm, 1996). The error has been to focus on the grid/group typology at the expense of other elements of the theory in which it is grounded (see, for instance, Grendstad & Selle, 1997). The four institutional forms described by the typology are taken to refer to four idealised personality types of which the world is composed. In one step the theory is converted into a psychological theory of risk perception and the origins of the individual's bias becomes a sacred private affair. A series of studies have reproduced this error including research by cultural theorists, but the work of Sjöberg (1997, 1998) has received the most attention and so is focus of this section.

Sjöberg reproduced the quantitative component of the theory-testing framework developed by Dake and Thompson and his primary aim is to test the explanatory power of the typology. By this Sjöberg means the extent to which the personality types implied in the typology are useful predictors of risk perception; he argues that they perform badly and makes two broad points. Firstly, he distinguishes between proximal and distal variables (Brunswick, 1952). Proximal variables are direct and immediate influences on individual behaviour, whereas distal variables are more abstract. For instance, a study of child poverty in Canada (Trudel & Puentes-Neuman, 2000) suggested that poverty may be a distal variable, while maternal anxiety can be considered a proximal variable. Sjöberg argued that there is a more general problem in social research with the use of distal variables, since these tend to have low explanatory power. He favors the use of proximal variables that are associated with the target behaviour. Secondly, Sjöberg argued that researchers have taken statistical significance to indicate strong predictive power whereas the important item is the correlation co-efficient. Although findings are often statistically significant, they typically explain very little of the variation in the data.

Two levels of critique of Sjöberg's work can be considered. The first criticism maintains an emphasis on the typology but questions his analytic techniques. Slovic and Peters (1998) respond to Sjöberg's critique of their grid/group survey of 1512 Americans. Sjöberg argued that the correlation coefficients in the study must be squared in order to derive the measure of variance and hence the strength of the association. When this is done the explanatory power of the analysis is vastly reduced. In response, Slovic and Peters pointed out that the use of squared correlation coefficients in medical studies is not the norm and that the appropriate measure relates to the percentage change as captured by Binomial Effect Size Display. For instance, the variance measure in a clinical trial of the drug AZT for the treatment of AIDS produced a low r^2 of 0.05 but a reduction in deaths from 61.5% to 38.5% (Rosenthal, 1990). Their own results were much more robust when percentage change measures were used. Secondly, proximal variables are considered more efficient predictors of behaviour. For example, there appears to be a high correlation between attitudes towards nuclear power stations and perceived risk of nuclear waste (Sjöberg & Drottz-Sjöberg, 1993). In contrast, distal variables are defined as dissimilar in content to the variable being explained (Slovic & Peters, 1998, p. 169).

One must question whether the strength of association between proximal variables is simply an effect of autocorrelation, since the two variables may simply reflect the same underlying attitude or belief. The second level of criticism is that the methodologies employed are simply inappropriate to the theoretical framework. The original caveats attached to the typology emphasise that it is not a psychological approach but one that emphasises distal variables. Although cultural theorists have contributed to the confusion by referring to "individualists" and "hierarchists" (for instance, Dake & Wildavsky, 1990), the proposed solution is to:

> desist from methodological and epistemological individualism altogether [and] no longer talk about individuals as "egalitarians", "hierarchists," etc ... The values people express or reveal will depend on whether they are attempting to make or dissolve solidarity with others in one of the respective social contexts. (Rayner, 1998, personal communication)

Sjöberg prefers a strong form of methodological individualism that sees individual attitudes as sovereign in determining risk perceptions. These disjunctures in risk research have been discussed and debated widely (Douglas, 1985; Rayner & Cantor, 1987; Renn, 1998; Tansey & O'Riordan, 1999) and syncretic efforts such as the "social amplification" approach rightly imply that theoretical diversity may be of value (Kasperson et al., 1988).

The deeper disjuncture between these approaches is methodological rather than ontological. For Sjöberg, there is only one tool suitable for the task of testing a theory—the extensive (nomothetic) questionnaire survey—which reveals the expressed values and preferences of random samples of large (typically national) populations. The test of the strength and utility of the theory is whether independent variables derived from it are able to predict the dependent variable, in this case, individual and general risk perception. Sjöberg's detailed paper suggests that surveys using items derived from cultural theory generate only weak correlations and that 'r-squared' values are very low. Guilty as charged. One may hope that Sjöberg's findings affirm what Mary Douglas and many others have been saying for years: the archetypes derived from cultural theory do not work well when used for narrow and heavily scientistic psychological models of risk perception (Douglas, 1985; Douglas, 1992). Sociologists do not expect humans to exhibit the kind of mechanical rule driven behavior that natural scientists expect of the inanimate objects they study and which produce high correlations and high r-squared values. There are many reasons why we would not expect this analysis to produce the high correlations Sjöberg craves, including the weak relationship between attitudes and behavior, biases introduced by power relations in survey implementation, the generality of the risks individuals are asked to rate and fact that every variable in the survey is thrown into the multivariate analysis, regardless of whether it is relevant to the social context of the respondent's daily life.

The most valuable contribution of the neo-Durkheimian approach is to explain why politicised debates over meaning are so central to the field of risk. So called "risk perceptions" that carry the force of social power are neither irrational nor simply psychological in origins. The context within which they are felicitous and hence rational reveals features of social institutions that are normally treated as self evident—risk has a forensic function. Whether they are described as meanings, constructions, symbols or metaphors, classifications are defended because they legitimate the distribution of social power within an institution. Risk becomes politicised not simply because it is a threat to life but because it is a threat to ways of life. Rather than ask how a risk comes to be magnified or how risk perceptions are influenced by heuristics, irrationality or pure emotion, this approach asks indirect questions: At whom is the finger of blame being pointed? Who is being held accountable? What is being rejected and what is being defended in a particular collective social action? This implies that for issues such as genetically modified organisms, research that seeks to demonstrate the safety of the technology will not dissipate political opposition since protest is in defence of a moral boundary. More subtly, cultural theory implies what Kuhn (1977) called a hermeneutic method. In place of an explanation that accuses the institution supporting it of irrationality, this approach asks how the seemingly absurd could be rational.

BROADER APPLICATIONS AND ENHANCEMENTS

While recognizing that the typology is a heuristic device, a number of authors have elaborated on the basic forms to identify patterns typically associated with the four institutional types. Each of the four types frames mundane and extraordinary events in consistent and predictable ways. For instance, drawing again on Rayner's (1992) study of risk in the hospital environment, we can deduce a series

TABLE 3.1
Four Organizational Contexts of Medical Personnel Exposed to Ionizing Radiation

Organizational context	*Competitive individualist*	*Bureaucratic*	*Egalitarian small group*	*Stratified individuals*
Personnel	Radiotherapists, Radiodiagnosticians	Radiotechnicians, Hosptial administrators	Staff of free clinics, Coalition for medical rights for women	Maintenance staff, junior nurses, cleaners
Transactional arena	Ego-based networks	Organic groups	Mechanical groups	Atomized niches
Transactional mode	Competition	Routine procedures	Cooperation	Controlled
Decision making	Individual	Committee	Consensus	Limited by others
Driving values	Expansion	System maintenance	Equality	Survival
Focus of attention	Professional career (cure)	Routinization of procedures (standardization)	Health maintenance (prevention)	Diverse

Source: Rayner, 1992, p. 13

of characteristics of the organizational context and establish hypotheses that can be tested empirically (see Table 3.1).

Other applications have used the typology as the foundation for more theoretical political science. Hood (1994, 1996) for instance, explores the implications of the grid/group typology for understanding the control of bureaucracies. Hood recognised that the categories define each other in opposition to one another and hence, paradoxically, are mutually dependent. In addition, each of the four types is considered to have both strengths and weaknesses, inherent to their internal structures. Some of these have been alluded to above and Hood describes them in terms of mechanisms for control over bureaucracies. In other words, hierarchical institutions have strengths and weaknesses and the other grid/group categories may counteract some of these as "forms of control." Hood explored the four pure forms of control derived from the typology (contrived randomness, mutuality, competition and review) and also six hybrid combinations of the four types. This approach is only indirectly relevant to the issue of risk, but demonstrates the wider relevance of the typology.

Schwarz and Thompson (1993) borrowed the term "regime" from political science to describe organizational frameworks that include a number or institutional forms. This is a similar approach to a study by Gerlach and Rayner (1988) of international regimes. A further synthesis of ideas has occurred in the last few years between this strand of cultural theory and the work of Young (1989) in the field of international relations which places institutions at the centre of the analysis (Jordan & O'Riordan, 1995a; Jordan & O'Riordan, 1997). This synthesis facilitates the application of cultural theory to global environmental risk issues such as climate change. The grid/group typology has been difficult for many theorists to swallow and recent accounts have tended to put less emphasis on the orthogonal axes and more on the competing cultural types. Hence, Thompson and Rayner (1998a, 1998b) identified three kinds of social solidarity—the market, the hierarchy and the egalitarian types—for an institutional analysis of climate change. These are represented as a policy space wherein conflict over policy formulation occurs. The isolate is left out because it tends to be politically bereft. In other words, it lacks the capacity for social power. Several accessible accounts have been produced very recently which seek to advance this approach to cultural theory (Thompson & Rayner, 1998a, 1998b; Ellis & Thompson, 1997). The three active voices identified by Thompson and Rayner (1998a, 1998b) express distinct diagnoses of the underlying causes of climate change and offer very distinct cures to the problem. The egalitarian voice of the activist focuses on profligacy in resource use, while the individualist voice focuses on inefficiency and pricing failures as the underlying causes. The third hierarchical voice emphasises population growth as the main problem.

TABLE 3.2
Climate change discourses

	Hierarchical	*Market*	*Egalitarian*
Myth of Nature	Perverse/tolerant	Benign	Ephemeral
Diagnosis of cause	Population	Pricing	Profligacy
Policy bias	Contractarian	Libertarian	Egalitarian
Distribution	Proportionality	Priority	Parity
Consent	Hypothetical	Revealed	Explicit
Liability	Deep pocket	Loss Spreading	Strict fault
Intergeneration responsibility	Present > future	Present > future	Future > Present
Discounting	Technical standard	Diverse/high	Zero/negative

Source: Thompson and Rayner, 1998, p. 331.

Each diagnosis is attached to a cure: frugality, price reform and population control respectively. Thompson and Rayner elaborated on this analysis to anticipate a range or institutionally deterimined responses to climate change. These are summarised in Table 3.2.

The diagnoses and cures are so distinct that cultural theory applies the term "contradictory certitudes," which suggests that these differences cannot be easily reconciled. Concepts of fairness of process and outcome also vary systematically by solidarity, with each aligning broadly with literatures on egalitarianism, libertarianism and contractarianism. In the context of the climate problem, a range of predictions can be derived capturing these systematic differences (see Table 3.2).

NORMATIVE IMPLICATIONS

Cultural theorists have expended most of their effort on explaining why risks are inherently political. The typology is a useful heuristic device for generalizing about the tendencies inherent to different arrangements of power and authority in social life. Issues relating to methodology in case study research using cultural theory have been neglected with the result that inconsistent approaches which 'test' the typology have prevailed.

The normative implications of cultural theory are also rarely emphasized. They are necessarily procedural because the theory demonstrates that there are fundamentally different representations of nature. This has been referred to as *essential cultural pluralism* (Schwarz & Thompson, 1993, p. 54), and it leaves an unanswered question: Which view should prevail and what does cultural theory offer to inform the policy debate?

First and foremost, cultural theory transcends a number of unhelpful dualisms including the expert-lay dichotomy, which contrasts objective rationality with emotional irrationality. In its place, cultural theory demonstrates that knowledge and social structure are interdependent. In other words, social conflict occurs between competing rationalities.

Douglas and Wildavsky (1983) argued that the plurality of rationalities is a source of strength rather than weakness, hence they advocate the repoliticization of risk. Their view of the sectarian institutions at the borders of US society is as critical arenas that reflect what Habermas (1976) calls a "legitimation crisis." The critical border confronts some of the contradictions generated by the two mainstays of the industrial nation state: the hierarchy and the market. It was a powerful movement in the US because it gained such widespread popular support. In particular, sects act as a counterweight to the centralizing and objectifying tendencies of bureaucracies and force more active debate about power and authority. The advice that Douglas and Wildavsky (1983) offered is that "if the center were to ignore the sayings of shaggy prophets, it would close itself to criticism and lose the power of reform" (p. 189).

The normative procedural recommendations of cultural theory are that "fairness" is of prime importance (Thompson & Rayner, 1998a, 1998b). The cultural biases of different institutions are so fundamental to their reproduction through time that it is pointless to try to reconcile their different representations of nature. Hence, there can be no satisfactory answer for a sectarian organization to the question: "How safe is safe enough"? The fundamental problems of maintaining membership mean that they will continue to evoke dangers:

> Risk ... is immeasurable and its unacceptability is unlimited. The closer the community moves toward sharing their views, the faster the sectarian groups move on to new demands. (Douglas & Wildavsky, 1983, p. 184)

Rayner asks instead "How fair is safe enough?" This procedural emphasis on fairness is important because it means that the issues the legitimacy of power and authority, often obscured by the clashes between contradictory representations of nature, can be addressed. The conventional risk equation (R = PM) is replaced by the equation R = TLC. This changes the emphasis to trust (T), liability (L) and consent (C).

Moving one stage further, Douglas and Wildavsky (1993) borrowed the idea of resilience from ecology. Ecologists found that frequent disturbance enhanced the capacity of systems to change and so they argue that in social systems, change allows learning to occur about how to deal with the unknown (Douglas & Wildavsky, 1983, p. 196). Along similar lines Thompson argued that instead of concentrating on modeling risks we ought to focus on "enhancing security" by "covering all the bases." In other words, it is important to ensure that the full repertoire of management styles is available. This implies that forms of fundamentalism, referred to by Thompson (1997) as "monomania." where all aspects of social life are dominated by one quadrant of the typology are not resilient or desirable. Along similar lines, Haugaard (1997) (not a cultural theorist) argued that: "When one way of life becomes extended to all spheres of social life, people will have to be sacrificed in the attempt to make social practice consistent with the monological world view" (p. 184).

Confronted with an unpredictable world of possible hazards the weak normative strategy of cultural theory is to ensure that there is a portfolio of possible responses. Most recently Rayner and Malone (1997) have taken a similar line with regards the theme of vulnerability to global environmental risk issues. In the light of high levels of scientific uncertainty, they suggest that policy makers ought to concentrate on increasing adaptive capacity (p. 332). In a recent article entitled 'Risk and Governance' the importance of plurality and resilience crops up again:

> the uneasy coexistence of different conceptions of natural vulnerability and societal fairness is a source of resilience and the key to the institutional plurality that actually enables us to apprehend and adapt to our ever-changing circumstances. (Thompson & Rayner, 1998b, p. 143)

An empirical example of this use of cultural theory in practice can be found in the energy sector. The US Department of Energy's Oak Ridge National Laboratory launched its Nuclear Power Options Viability Study in 1984 to explore the possible availability of advanced nuclear power reactor concepts in the 2000–2010 timeframe (Trauger et al., 1986). The project was overwhelmingly dominated by technical assessments of alternative designs, mostly embodying so-called passive safety features. A social science assessment of the issues most likely to influence their market and public acceptability was commissioned (Rayner & Cantor, 1987), especially in the light of widespread concerns about the safety of existing nuclear power reactors. This was a challenging task, not least because of the implausibility of projecting existing electric power industry structures, management and regulatory regimes, political priorities, economic conditions and technical capabilities some 20 years into the future.

The study assumed that there were everyday meanings for risk and rather than anchoring on the technical concept of probability times consequence, the team sought to understand how people actually used the term in everyday speech. This approach revealed concerns about authority and legitimacy, consistent with the language of "Trust, Liability and Consent." Concerns about consent revolved around the question of whether affected parties believed that they had been given the opportunity to accept or reject the technology in a manner that they regarded as legitimate. Issues of liability focused on whether the affected parties were satisfied that costs were appropriately distributed and that appropriate arrangements were in place to make reparation for any unwanted consequences. Trust hinged on whether the affected parties were satisfied that the institutions responsible for the commissioning, design, implementation, management, and regulation of the technology (including arrangements for consent and liability) are appropriate and adequate.

Focusing on the supply side, the utilities viewed the demand for power as a surrogate for consent to capacity addition. This is what social scientists call a "revealed preference" approach, embodying the idea that people vote with their pocket books and reveal their preferences for trade offs through their behavior in the market (Thaler & Rosen, 1975). Following John Rawls (1971), the team characterized the regulators' approach to public consent as "hypothetical," reflecting the idea that the social contract between citizens and government permits agencies to assume consent to specific actions. This hierarchical approach to consent is also consistent with a focus on procedural rationality. In the case of US Public Utility Commissions, power demand forecasts were often regarded as the justification for the administrative determination that a new power station could be built.

The public-interest intervenors took a different approach to consent, often arguing that the granting of a "certificate of convenience and necessity" to build a new power station should be made, or at least ratified, by popular referendum. In so doing they were demonstrating an "explicit preference" approach to consent. Significantly, commitment to explicit consent makes it impossible to impose risks on future generations who, by definition, are not available to give consent.

Looking at liability (see Calabrese, 1970), the utility companies were committed to the idea of spreading risk as broadly as possible away from the company itself. In other words, the cost of the plant, both foreseen and unforeseen, should be transferred to the customers. The utilities also campaigned for the preservation of the Price-Anderson Act that limited liability of nuclear power generators in the event of an accident. Regulators, on the other hand, adopted a deep pocket approach to costs, seeking to make a regulatory allocation of resources where they would have least impact on society—a so-called deep pocket approach. Intervenors took the opposite view from that of the utilities, seeking strict liability that concentrated responsibility for costs, losses, and accidents in the hands of directors and shareholders of utility companies. This position was clearly related to the issue of trust insofar as it was explicitly seen as a way to "keep the bastards honest," by making them liable for failures. With respect to trust as a specific variable, it was clear that the utilities trusted good managers and successful firms.

Consistent with their procedural approach to consent, regulators demonstrated that they trust rules and processes, especially those of longstanding effectiveness. Intervenors, also consistent with their approach to consent, trust the collective wisdom of the people. Overall, the study demonstrated that it is impossible to separate technical assessments of risk from the credibility and trustworthiness of the institutions involved in creating or mediating the risk. To focus on the provision of better science is to miss the point about the ultimate foundation of risk.

The procedural solution lies in recognizing and understanding the different representations of risks and nature and in finding ways of negotiating agreement between them. Whilst there are distinct differences between the approaches to social theories of risk (see for instance, Krimsky & Golding, 1992) there is a reasonable convergence on the normative implications. The theoretical mountaineers have just taken different routes to the same destination. As Thompson and Rayner (1998b) acknowledged, there is much in common with the themes of risk society (Beck, 1992), the ideal speech concept (Habermas, 1981), and ecological modernization (Hajer, 1995). Furthermore, there is a common acknowledgement that the operationalization of these normative commitments is easier said than done.

Risk concerns are employed forensically in an ongoing debate about the legitimacy of power relationships in society and hence concern about risks that are industrial in origin reflect concerns about the uses to which technologies are being applied. The social debate about GMOs is a good example (see Grove-White et al., 1997). Much of the debate focuses on the concerns about the *safety* of genetically modified organisms and conflicts occur between different scientific analyses. Cultural theory suggests that the real problem is not the substantive issue of safety but the wider moral questions regarding the appropriateness of applications of technology and the processes by which decisions are made. The danger comes not so much from the presence of physical hazards but from the transgression of norms that inhere to particular social groups. This suggests that increasing concern in society over environmental threats may be symbolic of wider concerns:

> the uncertainty of environmental risks is paralleled by increasing uncertainty and insecurity among individuals in (mainly Western) society. The interaction of environmental and social risks may pave the way for a shift in social values. (Blowers & Leroy, 1996, p. 259)

Wynne (1996) argued the 'Risk Society' thesis conceives of risks precisely as such external physical threats to person which are identified and arguably caused by science. Wynne also argued that Beck and Giddens (1990) have generally failed to recognize the broader social meaning and embeddedness of risks.

The degree of social insecurity that is *felt* has been shown to be a function of structural factors such as efficacy and trust (Macnaghten et al., 1995). In the absence of these factors, individuals feel alienated and apathetic. Indeed, it has been argued that existence of normative positions within social groups is contingent upon a belief in the possibilities for agency or efficacy:

> the sense of moral obligation was also supported by feelings of efficacy—the sense of individual control over the outcome of their actions, and a demonstration of the worth of what they had done. (Harrison et al., 1996, pp. 217–288 in Eden, 1992)

In terms of the model of power set out in the sections above, social actors feel threatened not only by physical hazards but also by threats to their social resources. The transgression of moral boundaries represents a threat to the social power gained from that social order.

CLUMSINESS BY DESIGN

The normative procedural recommendations emerging out of cultural theory have coalesced into the concept of 'clumsiness' in institutional design. This term, borrowed from Shapiro's concept of clumsy institutions, cautions against making single and final choices between contradictory alternatives. Preserving difference throughout a decision making process is equivalent, on one level at least, to maintaining diversity in an investment portfolios. Cultural theory offers two further enhancements on this metaphor of resilience through diversity. First it explains why contradictory problem frames persist through time: each solidarity or culture reconfigures the problem with itself as the solution. The second refinement, which differs from the disconnected assets in a diverse financial portfolio is that the competing worldviews are locked in endemic conflict and are defined in contradistinction to each other. Each culture needs the other cultures to maintain difference and identity and it is partly for this reason that it is difficult to achieve settlements, let alone consensus. For instance, each of the three active cultures—the individualist, the egalitarian and the hierarchical forms—identifies contrasting causes of and solutions to the climate problem. The diagnosis and cure solve internal problems of social organization, authority and socio-cultural viability. Given the critical role of these beliefs to the viability of each of the organizational forms, it is unlikely that progress can be made on the basis of a reconciliation across competing values. Instead, clumsiness seeks to identify workable compromises.

A recent edited volume captures many of the arguments for and examples of clumsiness in institutional design (Verweij & Thompson, 2006). The volume describes the contribution of the principle of clumsiness in two ways. The first is to identify examples that are striking because of the presence or absence of clumsiness in institutional design. For instance, Intriligator, Wedel, and Lee's (2006) work on the liberalization of the former Soviet Union shows the damage wrought by a monocultural view of the world: rampant individualism in post-Soviet reform fundamentally damaged economic growth in the region, elevated mortality rates and create a fatalistic and skeptical population. Secondly, Verweij and Thompson (2006) suggested that what counts as a preferable form of clumsiness will vary from between culture, just as the meta-concept of justice remains contested across solidarities: "Each of the active ways of organizing lends itself to a particular preference for how clumsy institutions can be arrived at" (p. 21).

These arguments are slightly enigmatic and one is left wondering how clumsiness can be operationalized. The second argument suggests that society is simply competitive field for organizations seeking resources and political influence. While in modern society, some argue that the power of the state has been diminished, it is still the case that the executive and the judiciary are called upon to mediate between conflicting interests and can ultimately impose a solution in law. Clumsiness is an important organizing principle because it suggests that diversity should be sustained and that a process, convened in many, but not all cases, by the state, should seek to identify viable settlements.

Other chapters in the volume provide detailed accounts of experience with or without clumsiness and start to define a procedural framework for its implementation. Intriligator et al. (2006) focus on post-Soviet Russia and argued that, in stark contrast to China, reform failed due to an excess of individualism and a dearth of hierarchy. The storyline reveals, in Hood's (1996) terms, a failure of control systems in the art of the state, on a grand scale. In the case of the USSR, the collapse of communism invited a rapid period of reform as the social infrastructure, industry and state-owned organizations were 'liberalized, stabilized and privatized' in a grand fire sale designed to create a vibrant market out of the remains of an extensive and centralized bureaucracy. The dogmatic form of individualism, made manifest in these reforms, valorized the free market over other cultures and was matched by a degree of myopic decision making on the part of key decision makers that, in some cases, was criminal. It created the conditions for the abuse of positional power throughout the system, the flight of capital from industry and sufficient political risk to deter external investment:

> Translated into the language of clumsiness: the reform programs, being singularly based on an extreme individualistic logic, did not promote any of the ways of organizing, perceiving and justifying social relations (except for fatalism). (Intriligator et al., 2006, p. 114)

In contrast, Chinese reform followed the model, established in Taiwan, Japan and South Korea, of reforming from the centre, under the control of bureaucracy through a settlement that sustained the legal and political institutions that are essential to a functioning market. It reduced political risk and created the stable conditions necessary to attract foreign direct investment and the growth of sectors in manufacturing. What is missing from the current configuration in China are the egalitarian cultures, associated with institutions of democracy and with civil society. While the current settlement appears to be robust, cultural theorists would argue, almost on cybernetic grounds, that all three active solidarities must be present. In the USSR, central control was replaced very rapidly by the democratic institutions that came hand in hand with market reforms, but in the face of the failure of liberalization and the significant financial losses suffered by the middle classes in particular, the project as a whole is at risk.

If Hood's work described the range of organizational forms resulting from hybrid forms of execution and control designed to sustain the tension he considers to be vital to develop robust systems of accountability, Intriligator et al. (2006) described the failure that results from extreme lopsidedness in organization design.

Kahan, Braman, and Gastil (2006) told a detailed story of the conflict over gun control in the United States. They illustrate the inherently political and normative character of risk controversies, expressed in proxy conflicts over risk statistics and safety. The reduction of risk controversies to debates over technical evidence was described by Douglas as the "depoliticisation of risk," over 20 years ago. Kahan et al. argued that the technical framing of moral conflict is a product of liberal norms, which prevent the state from establishing or protecting a strong moral orthodoxy. Instead they argue that:

> the prevention of physical harm seems morally ecumenical in this way. That is why most citizens are moved to speak in the empirical, consequentialist idiom of public safety, even though instrumental arguments conceal the normative foundations of their views towards guns. (Kahan et al., 2006, p. 158)

They argue that the gun control conflict cannot be resolved through this strategy of depoliticization; it cannot be resolved by reducing the evidence base to the purely technical. At the heart of the conflict are competing moral visions, with guns cast as rich political symbols, representing, for one side, the embodiment of individualism and domain of man over nature and for the other side the "elevation of force over reason" (p. 158) and the violent defense of inequalities. Both parties assemble statistical evidence to support their case, focusing on the impact on public safety as a proxy for their moral commitments.

Nina Eliasoph (1998), in *Avoiding Politics*, documents the same phenomenon at the individual level through her observations of environmental activists engaged in conflict. Using Goffman's distinction between backstage and frontstage identity, she illustrates how complex arguments about the acceptability of technologies are condensed into simpler pleas to avoid harm and danger when participants find themselves in the public limelight. The modern secular and rational polity establishes the conditions under which utterances will be treated with felicity and given authority. Discourses of rationality have dominated for so long that openly normative arguments carry less weight.

Jasanoff (2005) made a similar argument about the power of technical risk arguments, using the contrast between the governance of biotechnology in the UK and the US. She argued that because conflict is often settled in an openly adversarial court system in the US, this tends to polarize the debate, which conscripts science as an objective arbitrator or authority. Numbers reign in this highly adversarial setting. The British tradition allows a greater role for expertise and for the judgements of government appointed advisors, leading to more nuanced decision-making.

In the context of gun control, Kahan, Braman, and Gastil (2006) set out a procedural framework that they argue will help to lay bare the normative commitments of the organizations involved in the conflict. Their goal is to repoliticize the process through three principles. The first principle, "social-meaning over-determination" asks the participants to provide a rich account of the meanings that motivate their involvement in the conflict. This deliberate saturation of meaning helps to clarify the values that are defended in the conflict. The second principle, "identity vouching," provides participants with an opportunity to verify that a compromise is acceptable to other members and particularly to authority figures in their own organization; it is a mechanism that lends credibility to compromise. The third principle, "discourse sequencing," recognizes that the first two principles create the conditions for more open and accepting dialogue and suggests that the careful crafting of a decision can ensure that all parties walk away believing that the process has been fair and accountable.

The final example of the efficacy of clumsiness as a procedural principle is Lach, Ingram, and Rayner's (2006) account of institutional innovation in water use management in California. They map out three organizational voices active in a discourse and conflict over the most appropriate solution to the pressing water scarcity facing California. Each of the three separate approaches exemplifies one of the three active quadrants in the typology. The individualist voice emphasizes market solutions through pricing and competition and is resentful of the expensive interventions by bureaucracies. The hierarchy argues that rational planning and management should prevail in the struggle over competitive interactions; hierarchy preserves the long view of water supply and demand. The egalitarian organizations involved in the conflict draw attention to impacts of human activity on the natural environment and to the inequities generated by the current system of distribution. Each position assembles evidence to reinforce its argument and the science contains enough uncertainty to support a range of approaches. In the face of overarching pressure to resolve problems with the system of water allocation and the thinly veiled threat of external intervention, the three groups carved out a settlement. The procedure for establishing the rate, devised with stakeholder input, embodies three competing principles of equity, at least one of which can be seen to appeal to each of the egalitarian, hierarchical, and competitive ways of organizing to be found among the stakeholders. These are principles of parity, proportionality, and priority (Young, 1993; see also, Rayner, 1995a).

First, each household is allocated the same fixed allowance for human consumption, i.e., for drinking, cooking, bathing, etc. thus meeting the requirement of *parity,* which is in turn characteristic of egalitarians, who view water as a basic need and human right rather than as a commodity.

Each household then receives an additional variable allowance for use outside the house—mainly irrigation of lots. This allowance is determined by a formula that includes the area of each lot (obtained from real estate records), the evapotranspiration rates of typical plantings, and records of seasonal temperatures. Thus the allowance varies by lot size and by month to allow for efficient irrigation of gardens. Charts showing usage alongside allocation have proven effective in correcting householders' tendency to over water their yards late in the growing season. This second allowance satisfies hierarchical preferences for *proportionality* in allocation.

Consumers wishing to consume in excess of these allowances are, in principle, subject to an escalating scale of charges, the rate rising more precipitously as consumption increases, although in practice punitive levels of charging have seldom been reached. However, this does allow for individualist householders to assert their *priority* in allocation, should they choose to do so. Individualists are also attracted by the market-like emphasis on establishing prices and property rights.

Hence, egalitarians see a strong instrument that motivates conservation as well as protects everyone's access to sufficient water for basic needs. Hierarchists appreciate the rationality of the strategy and its ability to help in long term planning. Individualists appreciate how the strategy protects the customer's freedom of choice to use as much water as can be afforded.

It is a clumsy solution for all three cultures that demonstrates that a compromise by all parties is preferable to elegant, monocultural but unviable solution.

Author Perri 6 (2006) provided perhaps another extension to the framework for embedding the typology dynamically within social systems as a range of scales. He argued that coexistence in the face of contradictory certitudes requires settlements: institutionalized conciliation between rival imperatives necessary to achieve viability (p. 307). These settlements can be formally designed, as in the case of peace negotiations, or can emerge over time as processes of "muddling through" are institutionalized. The existence of contradictory certitudes suggests that solidarities, occupying a shared organizational field have the capacity to be in an endemic state of conflict. Ashby's concept of "requisite variety," imported into cultural theory, implies that it is difficult for any one of the solidarities to be excluded; in one version of this argument, each solidarity contains the others in some embryonic form. To put it more practically, members of a solidarity may use strategies, arguments and incentives from other contexts in the course of struggles for control and power internally.

Perri 6 provides an acute and detailed account of the phenomenon of settlement, which plays an obvious role in enabling contradictory certitudes to co-exist. He argues that clumsy institutions represent one form of settlement, built on mutual tolerance and conflict management. The goal is to maintain a balance where no solidarity has veto power. There are three other forms that can be arranged into another matrix:

- Separation—settlement into distinct spheres either structurally or sequentially, which effectively keeps difference apart.
- Exchange or mutual dependence—this relies on some service or resource dependence between solidarities.
- Compromise/hybridity: concession and trade-offs between solidarities.

The language of settlement throws light on our earlier question of how clumsiness can be operationalized by offering a typology of types of arrangements suited to the complex organizational and inter-organizational environment in industrial societies. Combined with the underlying typology of solidarities and the dynamics described above, an ambitious framework emerges. Most applications of this framework are partial, but one can discern a larger scaffolding from each site ranging from the detailed account of the workings of the regulation of risk by the UK government (Hood, Rothstein, & Baldwin, 2001) to the complex international relations of climate change.

CONCLUSION

It would be fair to say that cultural theory has evolved significantly in recent years, both through applications to specific to the field and in the broader literature on the politics of collective action and governance (Rayner, 1992; Thompson et al., 1990; Douglas, 1992; Johnson & Covello, 1987; Rayner & Thompson, 1998a, 1998b).

The most valuable contribution of the neo-Durkheimian approach is to explain why politicised debates over meaning are so central to the field of risk. So called "risk perceptions" that carry the force of social power are neither irrational nor simply psychological in origins. The context within which they are felicitous and hence rational reveals features of social institutions that are normally treated as self evident—risk has a forensic function. Whether they are described as meanings, constructions, symbols or metaphors, classifications are defended because they legitimate the distribution of social power within an institution. Risk becomes politicized not simply because it is a threat to life but because it is a threat to ways of life. Rather than ask how a risk comes to be magnified or how risk perceptions are influenced by heuristics, irrationality or pure emotion, this approach asks indirect questions: At whom is the finger of blame being pointed? Who is being held accountable? What is being rejected and what is being defended in a particular collective social action? This implies that for issues such as genetically modified organisms, research that seeks to demonstrate the safety of the technology will not dissipate political opposition since protest is in defense of a moral boundary.

Much of the recent interest in the concept trust in the risk literature uses a heavily individualist framing, which implies that the key task is to convince citizens that risk management organizations are credible and accountable. As governments withdraw from the direct provision of public goods in many areas, deference declines and social movements become professionalized, endemic mistrust may become the norm rather than a temporary problem to be tackled through wider consultation and engagement. Cultural theory anticipated this trend in the eighties and provides a solid foundation for both diagnoses and cures.

On a fundamental level, the functional form of explanation developed by Douglas offers an explanation for the origins of the emotion of fear and hence an avenue for psychological approaches to explore the origins of heuristics and mental models in social institutions. A number of key texts focus on the relationship between classifications and cognition (Douglas, 1999; Douglas & Hull, 1992). It would be a shame if the contribution of cultural theory to risk management were ignored because of a fundamental misrepresentation of the theory.

Finally, it is worth noting the irony inherent in the transformation of the grid-group typology described in above . A crude metaphor for the cultural approach described above is that of a filter, through which knowledge is interpreted using pre-existing classifications in order to make it understandable and to deal with ambiguity. In the act of trying to make sense of cultural theory, researchers have transformed a richly sociological theory into a theory of personality types, despite Douglas' persistent criticism of methodological individualism (Douglas & Ney, 1998). One hopes this chapter has done some justice to the wider literature from which the typology is derived.

NOTES

1. For an earlier discussion see Tansey and O'Riordan (1999).
2. Of course there are important exceptions to this generalization. Natural hazards research has addressed piecemeal adaptation and risk avoidance is addressed in economics, e.g., Calabresi, G., *The Cost of Accidents*, Yale University Press, New Haven, 1977.
3. Both markets and collectives espouse equality, but whereas the market institution focuses on equality of opportunity among individuals, the collectivist institution emphasizes strict equality of condition among members (Rayner 1988b).
4. Lupton examined the modern social experience of pregnancy and draws on Douglas' work to make sense of wider social attitudes towards the pregnant body. In individualist societies, the pregnant form is seen as abject and Lupton argued that the hybrid nature of the pregnant woman is risky in purely and dramatically negative terms "She is a monstrous being, because she has entered a liminal state in being a body with another body inside it, and thus disrupts notions of the ideal body being autonomous and singular" (p. 75).

BIBLIOGRAPHY

6, Perri. (1999). *Neo-Durkheimian institutional theory*. Paper given at the University of Strathclyde conference on 'Institutional Theory in Political Science', Department of Government.

6, Perri. (2006). Viable institutions and scope for incoherence. In L. Daston & C. Engel (Eds.), *Is there value in inconsistency?* (pp. 301–353). Baden-Baden: Nomos.

Beetham, D. (1991). *The legitimation of power.* Hong Kong: Macmillan.

Boholm, A. (1996). Risk perception and social anthropology, *Ethnos*, 61, 1–2, 64–84.

Blowers, A., & Leroy, P. (1996). Environment and society. In A. Blowers & P. Glasbergen (Eds.), *Environmental policy in an international context* (Vol, 3, pp. 255–383). London: Arnold.

Brunswick, E. E. (1952). *The conceptual framework of psychology*. Chicago: University of Chicago Press.

Calabrese, G. (1970). *The cost of accidents*. New Haven, CT: Yale University Press.

Burger, E. J. (1990). Health as a surrogate for the environment, *Daedalus*, 119(4), 133–150.

Coyle, D. J., & Ellis, R. J. (Eds.) (1993). *Politics, policy and culture*. Boulder, CO: Westview Press.

Dake, K. (1992). Myths of nature: Cultural and social construction of risk. *Journal of Social Issues*, 48(4), 21–37.

Dake, K., & Wildavsky, A. (1990). Theories of risk perception: Who fears what and why? *Daedalus,* 119(4), 41–60.

Dawson, J. I. (1995). Anti-nuclear activism in the USSR and its successor states: A surrogate for nationalism. *Environmental Politics*, 4(3), 441–466.

Douglas, M. (1963). *The Lele of Kasai*. London/Ibadan/Accra: Oxford University Press for International African Institute.

Douglas M. (1984 [1966]). *Purity and danger: A study of the concepts of pollution and taboo*. London: Routledge.

Douglas M. (1970). *Natural symbols: Explorations in cosmology*. London: Routledge.

Douglas, M. (1972). Environments at risk. In J. Benthall (Ed.), *Ecology: The shaping enquiry* (pp. 129–145). London: Longman.

Douglas, M. (Ed.) (1982). *Essays in the sociology of perception*. London: Routledge and Kegan Paul.

Douglas, M. (1985). *Risk acceptability according to the social sciences*. New York: Russell Sage Foundation.

Douglas, M. (1986). *How institutions think.* London: Routledge and Kegan Paul.

Douglas, M. (1990). Risk as a forensic resource, *Daedalus,* 119(4), 1–16.

Douglas, M. (1992). *Risk and blame*. London: Routledge.

Douglas, M. (1997). The depoliticisation of risk. In R.J. Ellis & M. Thompson (Eds.), *Culture matters: Essays in honour of Aaron Wildavsky* (pp. 121–132). Boulder, CO: Westview Press.

Douglas, M. (1999 [1975]). *Implicit meanings: Selected essays in anthropology* (2nd ed.) London: Routledge.

Douglas, M., & Hull, D. (1992). *How classification works*. Edinburgh: Edinburgh University Press.

Douglas, M., & Ney, S. (1998). *Missing persons*. London: University of California Press.

Douglas, M., & Wildavsky, A. (1983). *Risk and culture: An essay on the selection of technological and environmental dangers*. Berkeley: University of California Press.

Durkheim, E. (1995). *The elementary forms of religious life.* (trans. K.E. Fields). New York: Free Press.
Eliasoph, N. (1998). *Avoiding politics: How Americans produce apathy in everyday life.* Cambridge: Cambridge University Press.
Elster, J. (1983). *Explaining technical change: A case study in the philosophy of science.* Cambridge: Cambridge University Press.
Evans-Pritchard, E. (1937). *Witchcraft, oracles and magic among the Azande.* Oxford: Clarendon Press.
Fardon, R. (1999). *Mary Douglas: An intellectual biography.* London: Routledge.
Fleck, L. (1935). *The genesis and development of a scientific fact,* Translation, 1979. Chicago: University of Chicago Press.
Foucault, M. (1980). *Power/knowledge: Selected interviews and other writings 1972–1977* (Ed. Colin C. Gordon). Brighton: Harvester Press.
Gerlach, L.P. (1987). Protest movements and the construction of risk. In B. B. Johnson & V. T. Covello (Eds.), *The social and cultural construction of risk* (pp. 103–146). Dordrecht: Kluwer.
Giddens, A. (1984). *The constitution of society: Outline of the theory of structuration.* Cambridge: Polity Press.
Grendstad G., & Selle, P. (1997). Cultural theory, postmaterialism and environmental attitudes. In R. J. Ellis & M. Thompson (Eds.), *Culture matters: Essays in honour of Aaron Wildavsky* (pp. 151–168). Boulder, CO: Westview Press.
Grimen, H. (1999). Sociocultural functionalism. In M. Thompson, G. Grendstad, & P. Selle (Eds.), *Cultural theory as political science* (pp.103–118). London: Routledge.
Gross J. L., & Rayner, S. (1985). *Measuring culture: A paradigm for the analysis of social organization.* New York: Columbia University Press.
Grove-White, R., Macaghten, P., Meyer. S., & Wynne, B. (1997). *Uncertain world: Genetically modified organisms, food and public attitudes in Britain.* Lancaster: CSEC.
Halfpenny, P. (1997). The relation between quantitative and qualitative social research, *Bulletin de Methodologie Sociologique,* 57, 49–64.
Harrison, C. M., Burgess, J., & Filius, P. (1996). Rationalizing environmental responsibilities. *Global Environmental Change*, 6(3), 215–34.
Haugaard, M. (1997). *The constitution of power.* Manchester: Manchester University Press.
Hood, C. (1994). *Explaining economic policy reversals.* Buckingham: Oxford University Press.
Hood, C. (1996). Control over bureaucracy: Cultural theory and institutional variety. *Journal of Public Policy,* 15(3), 207–230.
Hood, C., Rothstein, H., & Baldwin, R. (2000). *The government of risk: Understanding risk regulation regimes,* Oxford University Press.
Hoppe, R., & Peterse, A. (1994). *Handling frozen fire: Political culture and risk management.* Oxford: Westview.
Intriligator, M. D., Wedel, J. R., & Lee, C. H., (2006). What Russia can learn from China in its transition to a market economy. In M. Verweij & M. Thompson (Eds.), *Clumsy solutions for a complex world: Governance, politics and plural perceptions* (pp. 105–131). Basingstoke/New York: Palgrave Macmillan.
Jasanoff, S. (2005). *Designs on nature: Science and democracy in Europe and the United States.* Princeton, NJ: Princeton University Press.
Johnson, B. B., & Covello, V. T. (Eds.) (1987). *The social and cultural construction of risk.* Dordrecht: Kluwer.
Kahan, D. M., Braman, D., & Gastil, J. (2006). Gunfight at the consequentialist corral: The deadlock in the United States over firearms control, and how to break it. In M. Verweij & M. Thompson (Eds.), *Clumsy solutions for a complex world: Governance, politics and plural perceptions* (pp. 157–180). Basingstoke/New York: Palgrave Macmillian.
Kasperson, R. E., Renn, O., Slovic, P., Brown, H. S., Emel, J., Goble, R., Kaperson, J. X., & Ratick, S. (1988). The social amplification of risk: A conceptual framework. *Risk Analysis*, 8(2), 177–187.
Krimsky, S., & Golding. D. (Eds.) (1992). *Social theories of risk.* Westport, CT: Praeger.
Kuhn, T. (1977). *The essential tension: Selected studies in scientific tradition and change.* London: University of Chicago Press.
Lach, D., Ingram, H., & Rayner, S. (2006). You never miss the water till the well runs dry: Crisis and creativity in California. In M. Verweij & M. Thompson (Eds.), *Clumsy solutions for a complex world: Governance, politics and plural perceptions* (pp. 226–240). Basingstoke/New York: Palgrave Macmillan.
Lupton, D. (1999). *Risk.* London: Routledge.
Macnaghten, P., Grove-White, R., Jacobs, M., & Wynne, B. (1995). *Public perceptions and sustainability in Lancashire: Indicators, institutions and participation.* Report for Lancashire County Council, University of Lancaster.
Morrow, R. (1994). *Critical theory and methodology.* Thousand Oaks, CA: Sage.
Olli, E. (1999). Rejection of cultural biases and effects on party preference. In M. Thompson, G. Grendstad, & P. Selle, (Eds.), *Cultural theory as political science* (pp. 59–74). London: Routledge.

Olsun, M. (1965). *The Logic of collective action: Public goods and the theory of groups.* Cambridge, MA: Harvard University Press.
Ostrander, D. (1982). One- and two-dimensional models of the distribution of beliefs. In M. Douglas (Ed.), *Essays in the sociology of perception* (pp. 14–30). London: Routledge and Kegan Paul.
Rawls, J. (1971). *A theory of justice.* Cambridge, MA: Belknap Press.
Rayner, S. (1991). A cultural perspective on the structure and implementation of global environmental agreements. *Evaluation Review*, 15(1) 75–102.
Rayner, S. (1992). Cultural theory and risk analysis. In S. Krimsky & D. Golding (Eds.), *Social theories of risk* (pp. 83–116). Westport, CT: Praeger.
Rayner, S. (1995a). A conceptual map of human values for climate change decision making. In A. Katama (Ed), *Equity and social considerations related to climate change: Papers presented at the IPCC Working Group III Workshop*, Nairobi: ICIPE Science Press.
Rayner, S. (1995b). Governance and the global commons. In M. Desai & P. Redfern (Eds.), *Global governance: Ethics and economics of the world order* (pp. 60–93). New York: Pinter.
Rayner, S., & Cantor, R. (1987). How fair is safe enough? The cultural approach to technology choice. *Risk Analysis*, 7(1) 3–9.
Renn, O. (1998) Three decades of risk research: Accomplishments and new challenges, *Journal of Risk Research*, 11, 49–72.
Rosa, E. A. (1998). Metatheoretical foundations for post-normal risk. *Journal of Risk Research*, 11, 14–44.
Rosenthal, R. (1990). How are we doing in soft psychology? *American Psychologist*, 45, 775–777.
Schwing, R. C., & Albers, W. A. (Eds.). (1980). *Societal risk assessment: How safe is safe enough?* New York: Plenum Press.
Sjöberg, L., & Drottz-Sjöberg, D. (1993). Attitudes toward nuclear waste. *Rhizikon Research Report*, No. 12, August, Sweden, Stockholm School of Economics, Center for Risk Research.
Sjöberg, L. (1997). Explaining risk perception: an empirical evaluation of cultural theory, *Risk, Decision and Policy,* 2(2), 113–130.
Sjöberg, L. (1998). World views, political attitudes and risk perception. *Risk: Health, safety and environment,* 9(2), 137–152.
Slovic, P., & Peters, E. (1998). The importance of worldviews in risk perception. *Risk, Decision and Policy*, 3(2), 165–170.
Tansey, J., & O'Riordan, T. (1999) Cultural theory and risk: A review. *Health, Risk and Society*, 1(1), 71–90.
Thaler, R., & Rosen, S. (1975). The value of saving a life: Evidence from the labor market. In N. E. Terleckyj (Ed.), *Household production and consumption* (pp. 265–297). New York: National Bureau of Economic Research.
Thompson, M. (1982a). A three dimensional model. In M. Douglas (Ed.), *Essays in the sociology of perception* (pp. 31–63). London: Routledge and Kegan Paul.
Thompson, M. (1982b). The problem of the centre: An autonomous cosmology. In M. Douglas, (Ed.). *Essays in the sociology of perception* (pp. 302–327). London: Routledge and Kegan Paul.
Thompson M, Ellis, R. J., & Wildavsky, A. (1990). *Cultural theory.* Boulder, CO: Westview Press.
Thompson, M., Grendstad, G., & Selle, P. (Eds.). (1999). *Cultural theory as political science.* London: Routledge.
Thompson, M., & Rayner, S. (1998). Risk and governance part I: The discourses of climate change. *Government and Opposition,* 35(2), 139–166.
Trauger, D. et al. (16 authors) (1986). *Nuclear power options viability study: Volume III Nuclear discipline topics.* ORNL/TM-9780/V3 Oak Ridge National Laboratory, Oak Ridge TN.
Trudel, M., & Puentes-Neuman, G. (2000). The contemporary concepts of at-risk children: Theoretical models and preventive approaches in the early years. Paper to the Council of Ministers of Education, Canada, Ottawa.
Verweij, M., & Thompson, M. (Eds.) (2006). *Clumsy solutions for a complex world: Governance, politics and plural perceptions.* Basingstoke/New York: Palgrave Macmillan.
Wildavsky, A. 1988. *Searching for Safety.* New Brunswick, Transaction.
Wuthnow, R., Hunter, J. D., Bergesen, A., & Kuzweil, E. (1984). *Cultural analysis.* London: Routledge and Kegan Paul.
Young, P. (1993). *Equity in theory and practice.* Princeton, NJ: Princeton University Press.

4

Risk Communication: Insights and Requirements for Designing Successful Communication Programs on Health and Environmental Hazards

Ortwin Renn
University of Stuttgart

1. INTRODUCTION

The ultimate goal of risk communication is to assist stakeholders and the public at large in understanding the rationale of a risk-based decision, and to arrive at a balanced judgment that reflects the factual evidence about the matter at hand in relation to the interests and values of those making this judgment. In other words, good practices in risk communication are meant to help all affected parties to make informed choices about matters of concern to them. At the same time, the purpose of risk communication should not be seen as an attempt to convince people, such as the consumers of a chemical product, that the communicator (e.g., a government agency that has issued advice concerning the product) has done the right thing. It is rather the purpose of risk communication to provide people with all the insights they need in order to make decisions or judgments that reflect the best available knowledge and their own preferences.

Most people show a distinct sensitivity to risks with respect to health and environment. Comparative cross-cultural studies (Rohrmann & Renn 2000) confirm that people all over the world are concerned about the health risks and the environmental quality. Risks pertaining to complex health threats and environmental changes are difficult to communicate because they are usually effective only over a longer time period, may induce negative impacts only in combination with other risk factors and can hardly be detected by human senses (Peltu 1988; Morgan et al. 2002). Risk communication in the field of health and environment needs to address the following major challenges:

- to explain the concept of probability and stochastic effects;
- to cope with long-term implications;
- to provide an understanding of synergistic effects;
- to improve the credibility of the agencies and institutions that provide risk information (which is crucial in situations in which personal experience is lacking and people depend on neutral and disinterested information).

Given these circumstances, risk communication is a necessary and demanded activity which is partly prescribed by laws and regulations (also pertaining to the European Community), partly required by public pressure and stakeholder demand. Stakeholders are socially organized groups that are or perceive themselves as being affected by decisions made. In the light of new activism by consumer and environmental groups, people expect governmental regulatory agencies and the industry to provide more information and guidelines for consumers, workers and bystanders. This challenge is embedded in a new industrial and political paradigm of openness and "right to know" policy framework (Baram 1984). In addition, globalization and international trade make it mandatory that potentially dangerous products are identified, properly labeled and regulated. All people exposed to risks should have sufficient information to cope with risk situations.

If we turn to the public, the effect of new technologies or substances on public opinion is difficult to assess. Most people simply demand healthy and safe products and like to act on the assumption "better safe than sorry" (Lee 1981; Renn 2004a). This attitude is likely to encourage regulators to err on the safe side and may conflict with the idea of using "real" effects as benchmarks even if these benchmarks are divided by a large safety factor. At the same time, however, people as consumers have an interest in a large variety of products, low prices and opportunities to improve their life. Unless risk information explicitly addresses aspects of potential benefits and social needs, it will not correspond to the expressed and revealed preferences of the people it is supposed to serve. For this reason, it is important to address the issue of how to communicate the complex picture of risks and benefits to stakeholder groups as well as to the public at large. This is the more prevalent as the debate about potential regulatory actions will trigger public attention and make people more aware of potential risks. In this situation proactive communication is essential.

This chapter summarizes the main results of risk communication research. First, it addresses the main context variables which have an impact on the success or failure of any risk communication program. Those refer to (1) levels of the risk debate, (2) different types of audiences, and (3) subcultural prototypes. Second, the chapter deals with the major functions of risk communication: (1) dealing with public perception, (2) changing individual behavior, (3) gaining trust and credibility, (4) involving stakeholders in the communication process. The last section draws some conclusions for improving risk communication practice.

2. CONTEXT MATTERS: RISK COMMUNICATION IN PERSPECTIVE

2.1 The Three Levels of Risk Debates

One of the major goals of all risk communication programs is to reconcile the legitimate intention of the communicator to get a message across with the equally legitimate set of concerns and perceptions that each person associates with the risk agent. It is obvious that technical experts try to communicate the extent of their expertise while most observers are less interested in the technical details but want to communicate about the likely impacts of the exposure to the risk for their health and well-being. Regardless of the intension of the communicator, the first step in any communication effort is to find a common denominator, a common language, on which the communication can proceed and develop.

Finding a common denominator or a common wavelength requires a good understanding of the needs of the audience. Having investigated many different types of audiences and issues, our own research has lead us to a classification of typical communication levels that are normally addressed during a risk debate (based on: Funtowicz & Ravetz 1985, Rayner & Cantor 1987, first published in Renn & Levine 1991; refined in Renn 2001, 2008; OECD 2002). These levels refer to:

- factual evidence and probabilities;
- institutional performance, expertise, and experience;
- conflicts about worldviews and value systems.

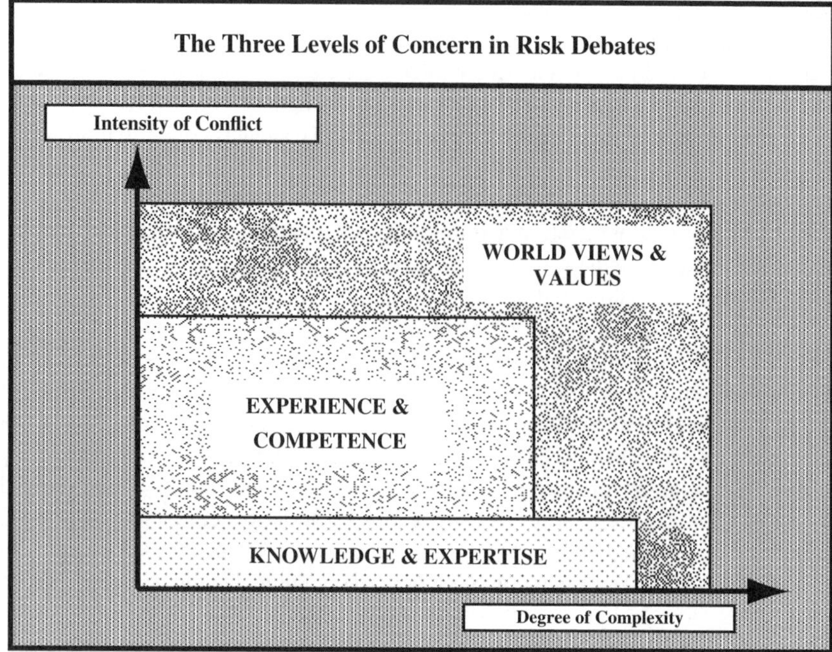

FIGURE 4.1 Levels of concern in risk debates.

Figure 4.1 is a graphical representation of this model using a modified version of the original categories. An overview of the three levels of risk debate and their requirements (including elements for evaluation) is illustrated in Table 4.1. The first level involves factual arguments about probabilities, exposure levels, dose-response-relationships and the extent of potential damage.

The function of communication on the first level is to provide the most accurate picture of factual knowledge including the treatment of remaining uncertainties (how can one interpret confidence intervals?) and ambiguities (are the assumed safety factors sufficient?). Even if the objective here is to transfer knowledge or create a common understanding of the problem, an attempt at two-way-communication is needed to make sure that the message has been understood and that all the technical concerns of the respective audience have been addressed.

TABLE 4.1
The Three Levels of Risk Debate and Their Communication Needs and Evaluation Criteria

Levels	*Issue of Conflict*	*Communication Needs*	*Evaluation Criteria*
1	Technical expertise	Information transfer	– access to audience – comprehensibility – attention to public concerns – acknowledgment of framing problems
2	Experience, trustworthiness	Dialogue	– match between stakeholders and public expectations and agency performance – openness to public demands – regular consultations – commonly agreed procedures for crisis situations
3	Values, Worldviews	Dialogue, Mediation	– fair representation of all affected parties – addressing the concerns of all parties in the debate – involvement of major stakeholders – transparent and inclusive form of decision making

The second, more intense, level of debate concerns the institutional competence to deal with risks. At this level, the focus of the debate is on the distribution of risks and benefits, and the trustworthiness of the risk management institutions. This type of debate does not rely on technical expertise, although reducing scientific uncertainty may help. Risk communication on the second level requires evidence that the risk managers of private institutions as well as public agencies have met their official mandate and that their performance matches public expectations. In a complex and multifaceted society such evidence is difficult to provide.

The second level requires permanent assurance that risk management agencies and the industry are capable and willing to apply the knowledge gained through research and experience to restrict exposure to hazardous substances. Many people may doubt the capability of management institutions to come to the right decisions due to remaining uncertainties and ambiguities in the risk data. They may lack trust in the management performance of the regulator. Gaining institutional trust in such situations requires a continuous dialogue between risk managers, stakeholders, and representatives of the public. In such dialogues, trust can be gained by showing that the risk managers from private industry and public agencies have been and continue to be competent, effective, and open to public demands. This will be a major challenge in today's climate of distrust in "big industry" and regulatory agencies. A constant dialogue between stakeholders, regulatory agencies and the public will help all parties involved to come to a mutually beneficial match between institutional performance and public expectations.

At the third level of debate, the conflict is defined along different social values, cultural lifestyles, and their impact on risk management. In this case, neither technical expertise nor institutional competence and openness are adequate conditions for risk communication. Dealing with values and lifestyles requires a fundamental consensus on the issues that underlie the risk debate. This implies that the communication requirements of the first and second levels, i.e. risk information or involvement in a two-way dialogue, are insufficient to find a solution that is acceptable to all or most parties.

Third level debates require new unconventional forms of stakeholder involvement such as mediation, citizen panels, open forums with special groups and others. The main task of such exercises is to reflect on the relevant values that apply to the situation and to search for solutions that all participants find acceptable or at least tolerable, but also to build an atmosphere of mutual trust and respect.

There is a strong tendency for risk managers to re-frame higher level conflicts into lower level ones. Third level conflicts are presented as first or second level conflicts, and second level conflicts as first level debates. This is an attempt to focus the discussion on technical evidence in which the risk managers are fluent. Stakeholders who participate in the discourse are thus forced to use first level (factual) arguments to rationalize their value concerns. Unfortunately, risk managers often misunderstand this as "irrationality" on the part of the public. Frustrated, the public retreats to direct action and protest rituals. The result is only disillusionment and public distrust in the risk managing institutions.

What is the appropriate level of the debate? Which of the three levels is the most important for the communicator, which for the audience? On the first level, it is wise to document the scientific results of the risk assessments, make them available to the public (for example via the internet), demonstrate transparency and provide easy-to-understand interpretations of the findings. On the second level, it is important to show how industrial or public risk managers continuously monitor the situation, ensure a professional safety culture in the daily operations and invest in quality control. In addition, it may be advisable to forge a close cooperation with public risk management agencies to have an effective and efficient regulatory regime that is based on cooperation among the actors rather than competition. On the third level, it is essential to monitor the political and social climate with respect to the risk in question and initiate a dialogue program as soon as signs of distrust or deep concerns appear on the horizon.

2.2 Different Risk Cultures

For risk communication to be effective, one needs to be aware not only of the levels of risk debates, but also of the various subcultures within a society. It is therefore essential to tailor the content of the communication process to the interests and concerns of the different social and cultural groups within society. Risk communication must refer to the arguments and cognitive maps that the different types of audiences understand and find "acceptable" or "reasonable". Often, only few words inserted in a conversation without much further thought might ignite public outrage, whereas long arguments may not even be followed by those who are interested in the subject. Again, it is futile to find a classification that provides a full representation of all potential types of audience. But is has been helpful to work with a classification that has been labeled as the cultural approach to risk.

A group of distinguished anthropologists and cultural sociologists such as Aaron Wildavsky, Mary Douglas and Michael Thompson have investigated the social response to risk and have identified four or five patterns of value clusters that separate different groups in society from each other (Douglas & Wildavsky 1982; Rayner 1990; Thompson et al. 1990; Wildavsky & Dake 1990; Schwarz & Thompson 1990). These different groups have formed specific positions on risk topics and have developed corresponding attitudes and strategies. They differ in the degree of *group* cohesiveness (the extent to which someone finds identity in a social group), and the degree of *grid* (the extent to which someone accepts and respects a formal system of hierarchy and procedural rules).

These groups are: the entrepreneurs, the egalitarians, the bureaucrats, the stratified individuals, and—added in some publications—the group of the hermits. They can be localized within the group-grid continuum (see Figure 4.2). Organizations or social groups belonging to the *entrepreneurial* prototype perceive risk taking as an opportunity to succeed in a competitive market and to pursue their personal goals. They are characterized by a low degree of hierarchy and a low degree of cohesion. They are less concerned about equity issues and would like the government to refrain from extensive regulation or risk management efforts. This group contrasts most with organizations or

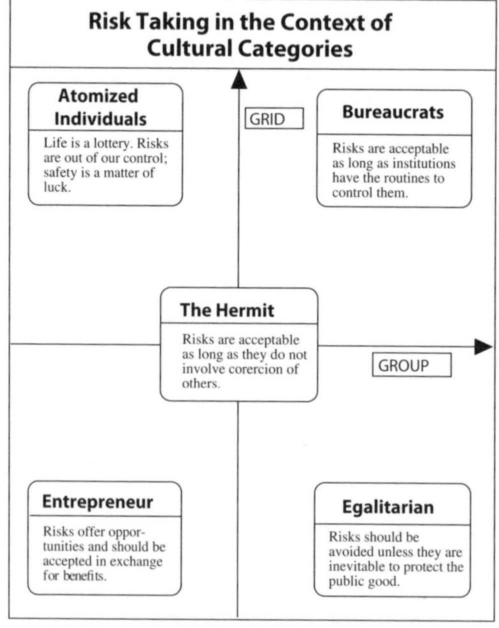

FIGURE 4.2 Cultural categories of risk taking.

groups belonging to the *egalitarian* prototype which emphasize cooperation and equality rather than competition and freedom. Egalitarians are also characterized by low hierarchy, but have developed a strong sense of group cohesiveness and solidarity. When facing risks, they tend to focus on long-term effects of human activities and are more likely to abandon an activity, even if they perceive it as beneficial to them, than to take chances. They are particularly concerned about equity.

The third prototype, i.e. the *bureaucrats,* relies on rules and procedures to cope with uncertainty. Bureaucrats are both, hierarchical and cohesive in their group relations. They find that as long as risks are managed by capable institutions and coping strategies have been provided for all eventualities, there is no need to worry about risks. Bureaucrats believe in the effectiveness of organizational skills and practices and regard a problem as solved when a procedure to deal with its institutional management is in place.

The fourth prototype, the group of *atomized or stratified individuals,* principally believes in hierarchy, but they do not identify with the hierarchy to which they belong. These people trust only themselves, are often confused about risk issues, and are likely to take high risks for themselves, but oppose any risk that they feel is imposed on them. At the same time, however, they see life as a lottery and are often unable to link harm to a concrete cause. In addition to the four prototypes, there is a hybrid group called the *autonomous individuals* or *the hermits* which can be grouped in the center of the group-grid coordinates. Thompson describes autonomous individuals as self-centered hermits and short-term risk evaluators. They may be also referred to as potential mediators in risk conflicts, since they build multiple alliances to the four other groups and believe in hierarchy only if they can relate authority to superior performance or knowledge (Thompson 1980; Thompson et al. 1990).

This theory has been criticized on several grounds (Nelkin 1982; Sjöberg 1997). This is not the place to review the critical remarks and the counter-evidence provided by many scholars. The debate is still proceeding without a clear consensus in sight. Most risk communicators have assured us, however, that this classification has helped them tremendously in preparing communication programs for different audiences. There is sufficient anecdotal evidence that people with an entrepreneurial attitude react very differently to specific arguments compared to people with an egalitarian or bureaucratic attitude. For example, a reference to cost-benefit ratios makes perfect sense when presented to an audience of entrepreneurs but would trigger outrage when being referred to in a group of egalitarians.

2.3 Different Types of Audiences

The last context variable that is important to mention here is the interest of the target audience in the issue. As previously pointed out, the group of the atomized individuals will have little if any interest in the debate on risk assessment methods. For practical purposes of preparing risk communication programs, it is helpful to have a classification of potential audiences at hand, even if each audience is certainly unique. The classification that is offered here refers to two dimensions: the interest of the audience in the subject and the type of arguments that different audiences may find appealing or, at the other end of the spectrum, appalling. For the first classification, i.e. specifying different degrees of interest, our preferred choice is the "elaboration-likelihood model of persuasion", developed by Petty and Cacioppo (1986). The major component of the model is the distinction between the *central or peripheral route of persuasion.* The central route refers to a communication process in which the receiver examines each argument carefully and balances the pros and cons in order to form a well-structured attitude. The peripheral route refers to a faster and less laborious strategy to form an attitude by using specific cues or simple heuristics (Renn, 2008).

When is a receiver likely to take the central route and when the peripheral route? According to the two authors, route selection depends on two factors: *ability and motivation. Ability* refers to the physical availability of the receiver to follow the message without distraction, *motivation* to

TABLE 4.2
Clues Relevant for Peripheral Communication

Type	*Examples*
Source-related	credibility, reputation, social attractiveness, perceived impartiality
Message-related	length, number of arguments, package such as color, paper, graphical appeal, illustrations, layout), presence of highly appreciated symbolic signals
Transmitter-related	perceived neutrality, past performance of transmitter, perceived credibility, reputation
Context-related	crisis situation, conflict situation, dependence on "zeitgeist", social and cultural setting, circumstances of transmission

the readiness and interest of the receiver to process the message. The central route is taken when the receiver is able and highly motivated to listen to the information. The *peripheral route* is taken when the issue is less relevant for the receiver and/or the communication context is inadequate to get the message across. In this case, the receiver is less inclined to deal with each argument, but forms an opinion or even an attitude on the basis of simple cues and heuristics. One can order the cues into four categories: *source-related, message-related, transmitter-related, and context-related cues.* These are illustrated in Table 4.2 (adopted from Renn & Levine 1991).

Within each route, the mental process of forming an attitude follows a different procedure. The central route is characterized by a systematic procedure of selecting arguments, evaluating their content, balancing the pros and cons, and forming an attitude. The peripheral route, however, bypasses the systematic approach and assigns credibility to a message by referring to the presence of cues.

Unfortunately, the communication process is more complex than the model implies. First, the audience of a communicator may be mixed and may consist of persons with central and peripheral interests in the subject. Many cues that are deliberately used to stir peripheral interest (e.g., using advertising methods for risk communication) can be offensive for people with a central interest in the subject. Second, most people are not predisposed to exercise a central or peripheral interest in a subject. It may rather depend on the message itself whether it can trigger central interest or not. Third, and most important, the two routes are prototypes of attitude formation and change, and therefore only analytically separable. In reality, the two routes are interlinked. Persons may tend to respond primarily to the cues or primarily to the arguments presented, but they will not exclusively pursue one route or the other.

An effective risk communication program must therefore contain a sufficient number of peripheral cues to initiate interest in the message, but also enough "rational" argumentation to satisfy the audience with central interest in the subject. The problem is how to avoid anger and rejection by centrally interested persons if they are confronted with "superficial" cues, e.g., the simple assertion that the respective product will remain safe and healthy, and how to sustain the interest of the peripherally interested persons if they are confronted with lengthy arguments. The problem can be resolved if the message eschews "obvious" cues, but includes additional cues that are acceptable to both types of audiences.

3. RESPONDING TO RISK COMMUNICATION NEEDS

3.1 Functions of Risk Communication

The variety of objectives that one can associate with risk communication can be summarized in four general categories (cf. Covello, Slovic, & von Win 1986; National Research Council 1989; Renn 2002, 2008; OECD 2002):

- to foster understanding of risks among different constituencies (customers, workers, consumers, interest groups, environmental groups, and the general public), including risks pertaining to human health and the environment, taking into account the dominant risk perception patterns of the target audiences *(enlightenment function)*;
- to assist people in changing their daily behavior or habits with the purpose to reduce their risks to life and personal health *(behavioral change function)*;
- to promote trust and credibility towards those institutions that handle or regulate risks *(trust-building function)*;
- to provide procedures for dialogue and alternative methods of conflict resolution as well as effective and democratic planning for the management and regulation of risks *(participative function)*.

The first objective relies on a better understanding of peoples' concerns and perceptions of risk. Section 3.2 will deal with this issue. Section 3.3 will cover the communicational means to promote trust and credibility. The last section in this chapter will deal with the possibilities of organizing effective and fair forms of dialogue with the various stakeholders and public representatives. Since the second objective is less relevant for health and environmental risks, we will not pursue this topic any further.

3.2 Function 1: Coping with Risk Perception

Today's society provides an abundance of information, much more than any individual can digest. Most information to which the average person is exposed will be ignored. This is not a malicious act but a sheer necessity in order to reduce the amount of information a person can process in a given time. Once information has been received, common sense mechanisms process the information and help the receiver to draw inferences. These processes are called intuitive heuristics (Kahneman & Tversky 1979; Slovic 1987). They are particularly important for risk perception, since they relate to the mechanisms of processing probabilistic information. One example of an intuitive strategy to evaluate risks is to use the mini-max rule for making decisions, a rule that many consumers and people exposed to human-made hazards prefer to apply (Lopes 1983). This rule implies that people try to minimize post-decisional regret by choosing the option that has the least potential for a disaster regardless of its probability. The use of this rule is not irrational. It has been developed over a long evolution of human behavior as a fairly successful strategy to cope with uncertainty, i.e. better safe than sorry.

This heuristic rule of thumb is probably the most powerful factor for rejecting or downplaying information on risks. If any exposure above zero or above a defined threshold (minus safety factor) is regarded as negative, the simple and intuitively reasonable rule to minimize exposure makes perfect sense. Most regulatory regimes are based on this simple rule (Morgan 1990) ranging from the as low as reasonable achievable principle (ALARA) to the application of the best available control technology (BACT). Such principles imply that any exposure might be negative so that avoidance is the most prudent reaction.

Psychological research has revealed different meanings of risk depending on the context in which the term is used (review in Slovic 1992; Boholm 1998; Rohrmann & Renn 2000; Jaeger et al 2001). Whereas in the technical sciences the term risk denotes the probability of adverse effects, the everyday use of risk has different connotations. With respect to human-induced risks Table 4.3 illustrates the main semantic images (Renn 1990).

Risks associated with substances that can be linked to toxic, carcinogenic or genotoxic effects are mostly to be found in the category of slow agents. This has far-reaching implications. Most agents belonging to this category are regarded as potentially harmful substances that defy human senses and "poison" people without their knowledge. Risks associated with potentially genotoxic substances are mostly undetectable to the person exposed and are always associated with negative

TABLE 4.3
The Four Semantic Images of Risk in Public Perception

1. *Pending Danger*
   - artificial risk source
   - large catastrophic potential
   - inequitable risk-benefit distribution
   - perception of randomness as a threat
2. *Slow Agents*
   - (artificial) ingredient in food, water, or air
   - delayed effects; non-catastrophic
   - contingent on information rather than experience
   - quest for deterministic risk management
   - strong incentive for blame
3. *Cost-benefit Ratio*
   - confined to monetary gains and losses
   - orientation towards variance of distribution rather than expected value
   - asymmetry between risks and gains
   - dominance of probabilistic thinking
4. *Avocational Thrill*
   - personal control over degree of risk
   - personal skills necessary to master danger
   - voluntary activity
   - non-catastrophic consequences

side effects. Along with that image, people tend to believe that toxicity depends less on the dose than on the characteristics of the substance. Hence they demand a deterministic regulatory approach when it comes to controlling potentially carcinogenic substances in food.

Most surveys show that people demand zero-risk-levels, at least as the ideal target line (Sjöberg 2000). Health risks which are characterized by high ubiquity, high persistency and high irreversibility hence trigger responses of avoidance and desires for strict regulatory prohibitions. The former US food regulations—the so-called Delaney clause—reflect this public sentiment. Something that is regarded as truly bad and vicious is almost impossible to link with a consideration of its relative advantages. The only exception may be the exposure to "natural" agents. Most people believe that anything that exists in nature cannot be harmful for people if consumed in modest amounts. That is why "natural" drugs are associated with fewer or even no negative side effects compared to allegedly chemical drugs. The perceptions of natural toxins as benign reflect the modern impression or myth of Mother Nature who offers an invaluable set of beneficial resources to humankind in response for taking good care of her. Pesticide residues and other human-induced substances, however, are associated with artificiality and seen as threats to human health independent of the dose of exposure. Dialogue illustrates the capability of regulatory agencies to deal with these risks adequately.

In addition to the images that are linked to different risk contexts, the type of risk involved and its situational characteristics shape individual risk estimations and evaluations (Slovic, Fischhoff, & Lichtenstein 1981). Psychometric methods have been employed to explore these qualitative characteristics of risks (Slovic 1992). Table 4.4 lists the major qualitative characteristics and their influence on risk perception.

Furthermore, the perception of risk is often part of an attitude that a person holds about the cause of the risk, i.e. consumption, production or use of hazardous materials. Attitudes encompass a series of beliefs about the nature, consequences, history, and justifiability of a risk cause. Due to the tendency to avoid cognitive dissonance, i.e. emotional stress caused by conflicting beliefs, most people are inclined to perceive risks as more serious and threatening if other beliefs contain negative connotations and vice versa. Often risk perception is a product of these underlying beliefs rather than the cause for these beliefs (Renn 1990). This has an effect on, for instance, chemical additives

TABLE 4.4
List of Important Qualitative Risk Characteristics

Qualitative characteristics	*Direction of influence*
1. Personal control	increases risk tolerance
2. Institutional control	depends on confidence in institutional performance
3. Voluntariness	increases risk tolerance
4. Familiarity	increases risk tolerance
5. Dread	decreases risk tolerance
6. Inequitable distribution of risks and benefits	depends on individual utility, strong social incentive for rejecting risks
7. Artificiality of risk source	amplifies attention to risk, often decreases risk tolerance
8. Blame	increases quest for social and political responses

as they are associated with strong negative connotations in contrast to natural ingredients such as acrylamide where people are more willing to assign risk-risk or risk-benefit tradeoffs.

3.3 Function 2: Enhancing Trust and Credibility

With the advent of ever more complex technologies and the progression of scientific methods to detect even smallest quantities of harmful substances, personal experience of risk has been more and more replaced by information about risks and individual control over risks by institutional risk management. As a consequence, people rely more than ever on the credibility and sincerity of those from whom they receive information on risk (Barber 1983). Thus, trust in institutional performance is a major key for risk responses (Earle & Cvetkovich 1995). Trust in control institutions is able to compensate for even a negative risk perception and distrust may lead people to oppose risks even if they are perceived as small. Indeed, some research shows clearly that there is a direct correlation between low perceived risk and public trust and vice versa (Kasperson, Golding, & Tuler 1992).

Trust can be divided in six components (Renn & Levine 1991). These components are listed and explained in Table 4.5. Trust relies on all six components, but a lack of compliance in one attribute can be compensated for by a surplus of goal attainment with another attribute. If objectivity or disinterestedness is impossible to accomplish, fairness of the message and faith in the good intention of the source may serve as substitutes. Competence may also be compensated by faith and vice versa. Consistency is not always essential in gaining trust, but persistent inconsistencies destroy the common expectations and role models for behavioral responses.

In risk debates, issues of trust evolve around institutions and their representatives. People's responses to risk depend, among others, on the confidence they have in risk initiating and control-

TABLE 4.5
Components of Trust

Components	*Description*
Perceived competence	degree of technical expertise in meeting institutional mandate
Objectivity	lack of biases in information and performance as perceived by others
Fairness	acknowledgment and adequate representation of all relevant points of view
Consistency	predictability of arguments and behavior based on past experience and previous communication efforts
Sincerity	honesty and openness
Faith	perception of "good will" in performance and communication

ling institutions (Slovic et al. 1991). Since the notion of risk implies that random events may trigger accidents or losses, risk management institutions are always forced to legitimate their action or inaction when faced with a negative health effect such as cancer or infertility. On the one hand, they can cover up mismanagement by referring to the alleged randomness of the event (labeling it as unpredictable or an act of God). On the other hand, they may be blamed for events against which they could not possibly provide protective actions in advance (Luhmann 1990, 1993). The stochastic nature of risk demands trustful relationships between risk assessors, risk managers and risk bearers since single events do not prove nor disprove assessment mistakes or management failures.

The handling of risk by private corporations and governmental agencies has been crucial for explaining the mobilization rate of individuals for taking actions. The more individuals believe that risks are not properly handled, in addition to being perceived as serious threats, the higher is the likelihood of them becoming politically active. It has been shown that in the case of nuclear power generation, the disillusionment of the US population with the nuclear option as well as the number of people becoming political advocates of antinuclear policies grew simultaneously with the growing distrust in the nuclear regulatory agency (Baum, Gatchel, & Schaeffer 1983). Negative attitudes are a necessary but by far not a sufficient reason for behavioral responses. Public confidence in institutional performance is another and even more important element in triggering behavioral responses.

Establishing and gaining trust is a complex task that cannot be accomplished simply by applying certain operational guidelines (such as declaring empathy) in a mechanical fashion. There is no simple formula for producing trust. *Trust grows with the experience of trustworthiness.* Nobody will read a brochure, attend a lecture, or participate in a dialogue if the purpose is solely to enhance trust in the communicator. Trust is the invisible product of a successful and effective communication of issues and concerns. The less trust is being alluded to in a communication process, the more likely it is either sustained or generated. *There is only one general rule for building trust: listening to public concerns and, if demanded, getting involved in responsive communication.* Information alone will never suffice to build or sustain trust. Without systematic feedback and dialogue there will be no atmosphere in which trust can grow (Morgan et al. 2002).

3.4 Function 3: Communicating with Stakeholders

Stakeholder involvement and public participation in risk assessment and management process help to improve the quality of decision making and to avoid damaging and time-consuming confrontations later on in the decision-making process, although involvement is not a guarantee that such confrontations and challenges will not take place even if consultations with stakeholders have been organized in advance (Yosie & Herbst 1998). The intensity and scope of stakeholder involvement depends on the issue and the extent of controversy. What can risk managers expect from stakeholder participation? Depending on the context and the level of controversy, stakeholder participation can assist risk managers in (Webler & Renn 1995; Renn 2004b):

- providing data for analysis or offering anecdotal evidence;
- providing background information about past experiences with the risk;
- balancing benefits and risks and arriving at a judgment of acceptability;
- providing information on preferences between different types of risks and benefits (tradeoffs);
- commenting on distributional and equity issues; and
- participating in the formulation of outputs, thus enhancing the credibility of the decision-making process.

The timing of stakeholder involvement is a crucial factor in determining whether stakeholders can and will effectively participate in risk management tasks (Connor 1993). Representatives of organized groups such as NGOs should be addressed at an early stage in the risk management process so that they can prepare themselves for the involvement and provide comments and input at an early stage before final decisions are made (this is particularly important for addressing the concerns of the egalitarians). One should be aware that many stakeholder groups meet irregularly and may not have teams in place capable of collecting data and for reviewing documents before the required date. The earlier they are notified the more input they can provide. A slightly different timing strategy is required for including affected individuals or neighborhood groups. Opportunities for public participation need to be scheduled at a time when sufficient interest has been generated but decisions are still pending and open for changes.

In addition, the purpose of the involvement should govern the timing. If the interest is to get more and better knowledge about a risk and its implications, involvement should be organized in the beginning of the process starting with risk characterization and assessment. If the involvement is meant to assist risk managers in setting priorities or determining a tolerable or acceptable level of exposure, the involvement should take place directly after the assessment has been completed. If representatives of groups or individuals who might be affected by the consequences of the decision are targeted for the involvement, timing depends on the intensity of the controversy. If the whole activity is controversial, involvement at an early stage is recommended. If the ambiguities refer to management options, such as accepting low levels of a non-threshold substance, the time of generating and evaluating options is obviously the best opportunity for the participatory exercise.

In addition to timing, the selection of participants is a major task that demands sensitivity to the potential participants' needs and feelings and the right balance between efficiency and openness (Chess, Dietz, & Shannon 1998). For participation to become effective, groups of more than 30 people are not advisable. If more stakeholders want to be included, one can form alliances among groups with similar goals and perspectives or form special subgroups with additional memberships that report to the main body of involvement. The following list proposes potential invitees to assist in risk management decisions:

- people who might bring additional expertise or relevant experience in the respective risk area (experts from other industries, universities, NGOs);
- representatives of those public interest groups that are affected by the outcome of the risk decision (industry, retailers, consumer protection groups, environmental groups, etc.);
- people who might be directly affected by the outcomes of the decision-making process regardless whether they are organized or not (average consumer);
- people who could represent those who are unable to attend or otherwise excluded from the process (such as the next generation or the interests of animals).

A more detailed approach to stakeholder involvement and public participation has been developed by one of the authors with respect to complex or systemic risk management (Renn 2001, 2004b, 2008). The starting point for this approach is the distinction of three phenomenological components of any risk debate. These are the challenges of complexity, uncertainty and ambiguity. Complexity refers to the difficulty of identifying and quantifying causal links between a multitude of potential candidates and specific adverse effects. The nature of this difficulty may be traced back to interactive effects among these candidates (synergism and antagonisms), long delay periods between cause and effect, inter-individual variation, intervening variables, and others. It is precisely these complexities that make sophisticated scientific investigations necessary since the cause-effect relationship is neither obvious nor directly observable. Complexity requires scientific assessment procedures and the incorporation of mathematical settings such as extrapolation, nonlinear regression and/or fuzzy set theory. To communicate complexity, scientific expertise and technical skills are needed.

Uncertainty is different from complexity. It is obvious that probabilities themselves represent only an approximation to predict uncertain events. These predictions are characterized by additional components of uncertainty that have been labeled with a variety of terms in the literature such as ignorance, indeterminacy, incertitude, and others. All these different elements have one feature in common: uncertainty reduces the strength of confidence in the estimated cause and effect chain. If complexity cannot be resolved by scientific methods, uncertainty increases. Even simple relationships, however, may be associated with high uncertainty if either the knowledge base is missing or the effect is stochastic by its own nature. If uncertainty plays a major role, in particular indeterminacy or lack of knowledge, the public becomes concerned about the possible impacts of the risk. These concerns express themselves in the request to be consulted when choosing management options.

The last term in this context is ambiguity or ambivalence. This term denotes the variability of legitimate interpretations based on identical observations or data assessments. Most of the scientific disputes in the fields of risk analysis and management do not refer to differences in methodology, measurements or dose-response functions, but to the question of what all this means for human health and environmental protection. Hazard data is hardly disputed. Most experts debate, however, whether a specific hazard poses a serious threat to the environment or to human health.

In this respect, four different risk classes can be distinguished i.e. simple, complex, uncertain and ambiguous risk problems. These classes demand different forms of participation (Renn 2008; IRGC 2005):

- *Simple risk problems:* For making judgements about simple risk problems, a sophisticated approach to involve all potentially affected parties is not necessary. Most actors would not even seek to participate since the expected results are more or less obvious. In terms of cooperative strategies, an **instrumental discourse** among agency staff, directly affected groups (such as product or activity providers and immediately exposed individuals) as well as enforcement personnel is advisable. One should be aware, however, that often risks that appear simple turn out to be more complex, uncertain or ambiguous as originally assessed. It is therefore essential to revisit these risks regularly and monitor the outcomes carefully.
- *Complex risk problems:* The proper handling of complexity in risk appraisal and risk management requires transparency over the subjective judgements and the inclusion of knowledge elements that have shaped the parameters on both sides of the cost-benefit equation. Resolving complexity necessitates a discursive procedure during the appraisal phase with a direct link to the tolerability and acceptability judgement and risk management. Input for handling complexity could be provided by an **epistemic discourse** aimed at finding the best estimates for characterising the risks under consideration. This discourse should be inspired by different science camps and the participation of experts and knowledge carriers. They may come from academia, government, industry or civil society but their legitimacy to participate is their claim to bring new or additional knowledge to the negotiating table. The goal is to resolve cognitive conflicts. Exercises such as Delphi, Group Delphi and consensus workshops would be most advisable to serve the goals of an epistemic discourse (Webler, Levine, Rakel, & Renn, 1991; Gregory, McDaniels, & Fields 2001).
- *Risk problems due to high unresolved uncertainty:* Characterising risks, evaluating risks and designing options for risk reduction pose special challenges in situations of high uncertainty about the risk estimates. How can one judge the severity of a situation when the potential damage and its probability are unknown or highly uncertain? In this dilemma, risk managers are well advised to include the main stakeholders in the evaluation process and ask them to find a consensus on the extra margin of safety in which they would be willing to invest in exchange for avoiding potentially catastrophic consequences. This type of deliberation called **reflective discourse** relies on a collective reflection about balancing the possibilities of over- and under-protection. If too much protection is sought, innovations may be prevented or stalled. If too little protection is provided, society may experience unpleasant surprises. The classic question of ‘how safe is safe enough’ is replaced by the question of ‘how

much uncertainty and ignorance are the main actors willing to accept in exchange for some given benefit'. It is recommended that policy makers, representatives of major stakeholder groups, and scientists take part in this type of discourse. A reflective discourse can take different forms: round tables, open space forums, negotiated rule-making exercises, mediation or mixed advisory committees including scientists and stakeholders (Amy 1983; Perritt 1986; Rowe & Frewer 2000).

- *Risk problems due to high ambiguity:* If major ambiguities are associated with a risk problem, it is not enough to demonstrate that risk regulators are open to public concerns and address the issues that many people wish them to take care of. In these cases the process of risk evaluation needs to be open to public input and new forms of deliberation. This starts with revisiting the question of proper framing. Is the issue really a risk problem or is it in fact an issue of lifestyle and future vision? The aim is to find consensus on the dimensions of ambiguity that need to be addressed in comparing risks and benefits and balancing the pros and cons. High ambiguities require the most inclusive strategy for participation since not only directly affected groups but also those indirectly affected have something to contribute to this debate. Resolving ambiguities in risk debates requires a **participatory discourse**, a platform where competing arguments, beliefs and values are openly discussed. The opportunity for resolving these conflicting expectations lies in the process of identifying common values, defining options that allow people to live their own vision of a 'good life' without compromising the vision of others, to find equitable and just distribution rules when it comes to common resources and to activate institutional means for reaching common welfare so all can reap the collective benefits (coping with the classic commoners' dilemma). Available sets of deliberative processes include citizen panels, citizen juries, consensus conferences, ombudspersons, citizen advisory commissions, and similar participatory instruments (Dienel 1989; Fiorino 1990; Durant & Joss 1995; Armour 1995; Applegate 1998).

Categorising risks according to the quality and nature of available information on risk may, of course, be contested among the stakeholders. Who decides whether a risk issue can be categorised as simple, complex, uncertain or ambiguous? It is possible that no consensus may be reached as to where to locate a specific risk. It seems prudent to perform a risk screening for assigning each risk issue to the appropriate management and participation channel. The type of discourse required for this task is called **design discourse**. It is aimed at selecting the appropriate risk assessment policy, defining priorities in handling risks, organising the appropriate involvement procedures and specifying the conditions under which the further steps of the risk handling process will be conducted.

Figure 4.3 provides an overview of the different requirements for participation and stakeholder involvement for the four classes of risk problems and the design discourse. As is the case with all classifications, this scheme shows a simplified picture of the involvement process. To conclude these caveats, the purpose of this scheme is to provide general orientation and explain a generic distinction between ideal cases rather than to offer a strict recipe for participation.

It is clear that these different types of discourse need to be combined or even integrated when it comes to highly controversial risks. Our experience, however, has been that it is essential to distinguish the type of discourse that is needed to resolve the issue at question. Cognitive questions such as the right extrapolation method for using animal data should not be resolved in a participatory discourse. Similarly, value conflicts should not be resolved in an epistemic discourse setting. It seems advisable to separate the treatment of complexity, uncertainty and ambiguity in different discourse activities since they need other forms of resolution. Often they need different participants, too.

Stakeholder involvement and public participation require an organizational or institutional setting in which the various procedures for implementing involvement can be embedded and integrated. It is important that the choice of discourse for enhanced participation matches the organizational capabilities of the organizing institution and fits into the socio-political climate in which the issue is

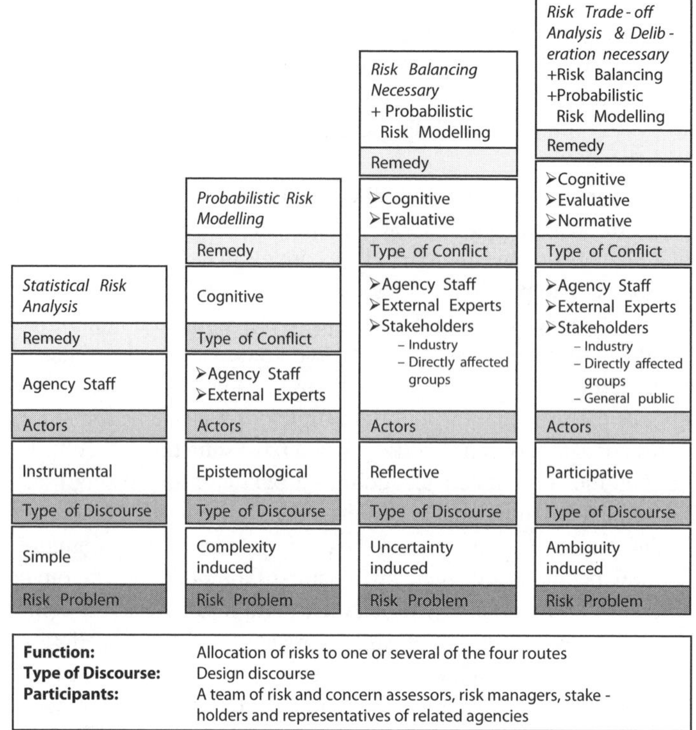

FIGURE 4.3 The risk management escalator and stakeholder involvement (from simple via complex and uncertain to ambiguous phenomena).

debated. It is therefore essential to do a thorough context analysis before deciding on any one of the procedures described below. The most important aspect to keep in mind is that stakeholder involvement is a form of risk communication that is done before the final (regulatory) decision is made. Nobody likes to be involved to approve to something that has been predetermined by the organizer. The timing of involvement is therefore a crucial task.

Epistemic discourses should be organized in the beginning of the process starting with risk characterization and assessment. Reflective discourses should be placed right after the completion of the assessment process when it comes to balancing the pros and cons and choosing the right management options. Participatory discourses are more difficult to fit into the risk assessment and management schedule. Much depends here on the nature of the ambiguity. If the whole activity is controversial—such as the generic decision which safety factor is adequate to call a risk tolerable or acceptable—an early stage of involvement is recommended. If the ambiguity refers to management options, such as labeling products with respect to potential toxic effects, the time of generating and evaluating options is obviously the best opportunity for the participatory exercise.

4. CONCLUSIONS

The objective of this chapter has been twofold: First, it has been aimed at providing the necessary background knowledge in order to understand the needs and concerns of the target audiences when it comes to risk communication. Second, it is designed to provide specific information on the potential problems and barriers for successful risk communication.

The main message of this chapter is that *risk communication goes beyond public information and public relation.* It needs to be seen as a necessary complement to risk assessment and management. Advertisement and packaging of messages can help to improve risk communication, but they will be insufficient to overcome the problems of public distrust in risk assessment and management institutions and to cope with the concerns, worries, or complacency of consumers (Bohnenblust & Slovic 1998). The potential remedies to these two problems lie in a *better performance* of all institutions dealing with or regulating risks and in structuring the risk communication program mainly as a *two-way communication process*. With respect to performance, it is well understood that many risk management institutions complain that their specific task is not well understood and that public expectations do not match the mandate or the scope of management options available to these institutions. This is specifically prevalent for any communication program on possible non-threshold toxic effects. First, the issue at stake, health and environment, tops the concerns of the public of all industrialized countries. So, people are very concerned when confronted with a challenge to their fundamental belief that all exposure to potentially toxic or even carcinogenic material is bad and should be avoided. Second, the probabilistic nature of risk impedes an unambiguous evaluation of management success or failure. If there is a small chance that somebody might experience adverse effects from a low dose that is deemed acceptable by the risk regulators, it will be difficult to justify the decision to set this limit. In spite of these difficulties, careful management, openness to public demands, and continuous effort to communicate are important conditions for gaining trustworthiness and competence. These conditions cannot guarantee success, but they make it more probable.

The second most important message is that risk management and risk communication should be seen as parallel activities that complement each other. Risk communication supports ongoing management efforts as a means to gain credibility and trustworthiness. By carefully reviewing in-house performance, by tailoring the content of the communication to the needs of the final receivers, and by adjusting the messages to the changes in values and preferences, risk communication can convey a basic understanding of the choices and constraints of risk assessment and risk management and thus create the foundations for a trustworthy relationship between the communicator and the audience. Specifically, a sequential organization of different discourse models is required to develop a continuous link between public dialogue and further management decisions.

The third main message is to take risk perception seriously. Any successful risk communication program needs to address the problems faced by risk perception. Risk perception studies can help to anticipate public reaction to new risk sources. Regardless of whether individuals belong to the cultural category of the risk-taking entrepreneur or the rather risk-averse egalitarian, timely information and dialogue are favored by all.

Such a sophisticated risk communication program requires an approach based on multi-channel and multi-actor information tailoring. A communication program needs to be designed to meet the needs of different audiences. In addition, I recommend a dialogue program with the potential stakeholders if the issue becomes a hot topic in the public debate. In the case of a heated debate leading to an intense controversy it is not sufficient to establish round tables of participants and let them voice their opinions and concerns. Since all three levels of a risk debate are then affected at the same time, one needs a more structured approach. First, it is necessary to continue to organize epistemic discourses on the questions of the scientific benefits of this approach, the best benchmarking procedure and the suggested safety factors employed. Once credible answers are provided to these questions, a more reflective discourse is necessary in which stakeholders from industry, NGOs, consumer groups and other influential groups convene and discuss the issue of risk tolerability thresholds and the determination of acceptable regulatory frameworks. As soon as the consumers would be affected by any regulatory changes, a participatory discourse is required. The goal here would be for risk analysts and managers to consult with opinion leaders and get their informed consent or informed rejection.

Risk communication will not perform any miracles. It can help to overcome some of the perception biases that have been outlined above and make people more susceptible to the risks and benefits of the products or activities in question. Information and dialogue are valuable instruments to generate and sustain public trust in regulating agencies and the industry.

BIBLIOGRAPHY

Allen, F. W. (1987), "Towards a holistic appreciation of risk: the challenge for communicators and policymakers", *Science, Technology, and Human Values*, 12, Nos. 3 and 4, 138–143

Amy, D. J. (1983), "Environmental mediation: An alternative approach to policy stalemates," *Policy Sciences*, 15, 345–365.

Applegate, J. (1998), "Beyond the usual suspects: The use of citizens advisory boards in environmental decisionmaking," *Indiana Law Journal*, 73, 903.

Armour, A. (1995), "The citizen's jury model of public participation," in: O. Renn, T. Webler and P. Wiedemann (eds.): *Fairness and competence in citizen participation. Evaluating new models for environmental discourse.* Dordrecht: Kluwer, pp. 175–188.

Baram M. (1984), "The right to know and the duty to disclose hazard information", American *Journal of Public Health*, 74, No. 4, 385–390.

Barber, B. (1983), *The logic and limits of trust.* New Brunswick: Rutgers University Press

Baum, A., Gatchel, R.J. and Schaeffer, M.A. (1983), "Emotional, behavioral, and physiological effects of chronic stress at Three Mile Island", *Journal of Consulting and Psychology*, 51, No. 4, 565–572.

Bohnenblust, H. and Slovic, P. (1998), "Integrating technical analysis and public values in risk-based decision making", *Reliability Engineering and System Safety*, 59, No. 1, 151–159.

Boholm, A. (1998), "Comparative studies of risk perception: A review of twenty years of research", *Journal of Risk Research,* 1, No. 2, 135–163.

Brickman R. S., Jasonoff S., Ilgen T. (1985), *Controlling chemicals: The politics of regulation in Europe and the United States.* Ithaca, NY: Cornell University Press.

Calabrese, E.J. and Baldwin, L.A. (2000), "Radiation hormesis: The demise of a legitimate hypothesis", *Human Experimental Toxicology*, 19, 76–84.

Calabrese, E.J. and Baldwin, L.A. (2001), "The frequency of u-shaped dose responses in the toxicological literature", *Toxicological Sciences*, 61, 330–338.

Calabrese, E.J., Baldwin, L.A. and Holand, C.D. (1999), "Hormesis: A highly generalizable and reproducible phenomenon with important implications for risk assessment", *Risk Analysis*, 19, 261–281.

Cadiou, J.-M. (2001), "The changing relationship between science, technology and governance", *The IPTS Report*, 52, 27–29.

Chaiken, S. and Stangor, C. (1987), "Attitudes and attitude change", Annual Review of Psychology, 38, 575–630.

Chess, C., Dietz, T. and Shannon, M. (1998), "Who should deliberate when?" *Human Ecology Review*, 5, No. 1, 60–68.

Connor, D. (1993), "Generic Design for Public Involvement Programs", *Constructive Citizen Participation*, 21, 1–2.

Covello, V.T., Slovic P. and von Winterfeldt, D. (1986), "Risk communication: A review of the literature", *Risk Abstracts*, 3, No. 4, 172–182.

Dake, K. (1991), "Orienting dispositions in the perceptions of risk: An analysis of contemporary worldviews and cultural biases", *Journal of Cross-Cultural Psychology*, 22, 61–82.

Dienel, P.C. (1989), "Contributing to social decision methodology: Citizen reports on technological projects," in: C. Vlek and G. Cvetkovich (eds.): *Social decision methodology for technological projects*, Dordrecht: Kluwer, pp. 133–151.

Douglas, M. and Wildavsky, A. (1982), *Risk and culture.* Berkeley: University of California Press.

Drottz-Sjöberg, B.-M. (1991), *Perception of risk. Studies of risk attitudes, perceptions, and definitions.* Stockholm: Center for Risk Research.

Durant, J. and Joss, S. (1995), *Public participation in science.*.London: Science Museum.

Earle, T.C. and Cvetkovich, G. (1995), *Social trust: Towards a cosmopolitan society.* Westport, CT: Praeger.

Fiorino, D. J. (1990), "Citizen Participation and Environmental Risk: A Survey of Institutional Mechanisms," *Science, Technology, & Human Values*, 15, No. 2, 226–243.

Fischhoff, B. (1995), "Risk perception and communication unplugged: Twenty years of process", *Risk Analysis*, 15, No. 2, 137–145.

Funtowicz, S. O. and Ravetz, J. R. (1985), "Three types of risk assessment: Methodological analysis", in: C. Whipple and V.T. Covello (eds.), *Risk analysis in the private sector.* New York: Plenum.

Gregory, R., McDaniels, T., and Fields, D. (2001), "Decision Aiding, Not Dispute Resolution: A New Perspective for Environmental Negotiation," *Journal of Policy Analysis and Management,* 20, No. 3, 415–432.

IRGC (International Risk Governance Council) (2005), *Risk governance: Towards an integrative approach.* Author:

Jaeger, C. C.; Renn, O.; Rosa, E. and Webler, T. (2001), *Risk, uncertainty and rational action.* London: Earthscan.

Kahneman, D. and Tversky, A. (1979), "Prospect theory: an analysis of decision under risk", *Econometrica,* 47, 263–291.

Kasperson, R.; Golding, D. and Tuler, S. (1992), "Social distrust as factor in siting hazardous facilities and communicating risks", *Journal of Social Sciences*, 48, 161–187.

Lee, T.R. (1981), "The public perception of risk and the question of irrationality", in: Royal Society of Great Britain (ed.), *Risk perception*, Vol. 376. London: The Royal Society, pp. 5–16.

Leiss, W., "Three phases in risk communication practice", in: Annals of the American Academy of Political and Social Science, Special Issue, H. Kunreuther and P. Slovic (eds.), *Challenges in risk assessment and risk management*. Thousand Oaks, CA: Sage, pp. 85–94.

Lopes, L.L. (1983), "Some thoughts on the psychological concept of risk", *Journal of Experimental Psychology: Human Perception and Performance,* 9, 137–144.

Luhmann, N. (1986), *Ökologische Kommunikation.* Opladen: Westdeutscher Verlag

Luhmann, N., (1990) "Technology, environment, and social risk: a systems perspective", *Industrial Crisis Quarterly,* 4, 223–231.

Luhmann, N. (1993). *Risk: A sociological theory* (R. Barrett, Trans.). New York: Aldine de Grusyter.

Morgan, M. G. (1990), "Choosing and managing technology-induced risk", in: T.S. Glickman und M. Gough (eds.), *Readings in risk*. Washington, D.C.: Resources for the Future, pp. 17–28.

Morgan, M.G., Fishhoff, B., Bostrom, A., and Atmann, C.J. (2002), *Risk communication. A mental model approach.* Cambridge: Cambridge University Press.

Mulligan, J., McCoy, E., and Griffiths, A. (1998), *Principles of communicating risks.* Alberta: The Macleod Institute for Environmental Analysis, University of Calgary.

National Research Council, Committee on the Institutional Means for Assessment of Risks to Public Health (1983), *Risk assessment in the Federal Government: Managing the process.* Washington, D.C: National Academy Press.

National Research Council (1989), *Improving risk communication.* Washington, D.C.: National Academy Press.

Nelkin, D. (1982), "Blunders in the business of risk", *Nature*, 298, 775–776.

OECD (2002), *Guidance document on risk communication for chemical risk management.* Paris: OECD.

O'Riordan, T. and Wynne, B. (1987), "Regulating environmental risks: A comparative perspective", in: P. R. Kleindorfer and H. C. Kunreuther (eds.), *Insuring and managing hazardous risks: from Seveso to Bhopal and beyond.* Berlin: Springer, pp. 389–410.

Peltu, M. (1985), "The role of communications media", in: H. Otway and M. Peltu (eds.), *Regulating industrial risks.* London: Butterworth, pp. 128–148.

Peltu, M (1988), "Media reporting of risk information: Uncertainties and the future", in: H. Jungermann, R. E. Kasperson and P.M. Wiedemann (eds.), *Risk communication.* Jülich: Nuclear Research Center, pp. 11–32.

Perritt, H. H. (1986), "Negotiated Rulemaking in Practice," *Journal of Policy Analysis and Management*, 5, 482–95.

Petty, R.E. and Cacioppo, E. (1986), "The elaboration likelihood model of persuasion", *Advances in Experimental Social Psychology*, 19, 123–205.

Plough, A. and Krimsky, S (1987), "The emergence of risk communication studies: Social and political context", *Science, Technology, and Human Values*, 12 , 78–85.

Rayner, S. and Cantor, R (1987), "How fair is safe enough? The cultural approach to societal technology choice", *Risk Analysis*, 7, 3–13.

Rayner, S. (1990), Risk in cultural perspective: Acting under uncertainty. Dordrecht: Kluwer

Renn, O. (1990), "Risk perception and risk management: a review", *Risk Abstracts*, 7, No.1, 1–9 (Part 1) and No.2, 1–9 (Part 2).

Renn, O. (1992), "Risk communication: Towards a rational dialogue with the public", *Journal of Hazardous Materials,* 29, No. 3, 465–519.

Renn, O (2001), "The role of risk communication and public dialogue for improving risk management", in: S. Gerrard; R. Kerry Turner and I. J. Bateman (eds.): *Environmental risk planning and management.* Cheltenham, UK: Edward Elgar Publishing, pp. 312–337.

Renn, O. (2002), "Hormesis and Risk Communication", *Belle Newsletter. Biological Effects of Low Level Exposures.* Special Edition on Risk Communication and the Challenge of Hormesis, Vol. 11, No. 1, 2–23.

Renn, O. (2004a), "Perception of Risks," *The Geneva Papers on Risk and Insurance*, 29, No. 1, 102–114.

Renn, O. (2004b), "The Challenge of Integrating Deliberation and Expertise: Participation and Discourse in Risk Management," in: T. L. MacDaniels and M.J. Small (eds.), *Risk analysis and society: An interdisciplinary characterization of the field.* Cambridge: University Press: Cambridge, pp. 289–366.

Renn, O. (2008). *Risk governance: Coping with uncertainty in a complex world.* London: Earthsan.

Renn, O. and Levine, D. (1991), "Trust and credibility in risk communication", in: R. Kasperson and P.J. Stallen (eds.), *Communicating risk to the public*. Dordrecht: Kluwer, pp. 175–218.

Renn, O. and Rohrmann, B (2000), "Cross-cultural risk perception research: state and challenges", in: O. Renn and B. Rohrmann (eds.), *Cross-cultural risk perception. A survey of empirical studies.* Dordrecht: Kluwer, pp. 211–233.

Rohrmann, B. and Renn, O (2000). Risk perception research – An introduction", in: O. Renn and B. Rohrmann (eds.), *Cross-cultural risk perception. A survey of empirical studies.* Dordrecht: Kluwer, pp. 11–54.

Rowe, G. and Frewer, L. (2000), "Public participation methods: An evaluative review of the literature," *Science, Technology and Human Values*, 25 (2000), 3–29.

Sandmann, P. M. (1989), "Hazard versus outrage: A conceptual frame for describing public perception of risk", in: H. Jungermann, R. E. Kasperson and P. Wiedemann, (eds.): *Risk communication.* Jülich: Forschungszentrum Jülich, pp. 163–168.

Schwarz, M. and Thompson M. (1990), *Divided we stand: Redefining politics, technology, and social choice.* Philadelphia: University of Pennsylvania Press.

Sjöberg, L. (1997), "Explaining risk perception: An empirical evaluation of cultural theory", *Risk, Decision and Policy*, 2, 113–130.

Sjöberg, L. (2000), "Factors in risk perception", *Risk Analysis*, 20, 1–11.

Slovic, P., Fischhoff, B., and Lichtenstein, S. (1981), "Perceived risk: psychological factors and social implications", in: Royal Society (ed.), *Proceedings of the Royal Society.* A376. London: Royal Society, pp. 17–34.

Slovic, P. (1987), "Perception of risk", *Science,* 236, 280–285.

Slovic, P. (1992), "Perception of risk: Reflections on the psychometric paradigm", in: S. Krimsky and D. Golding (eds.), *Social theories of risk.* Westport, CT: Praeger, pp. 117–152.

Slovic, P. (1993), "Perceived risk, trust and democracy", *Risk Analysis*, 13, 675–682.

Slovic, P.; Layman, M. and Flynn, J. (1991), "Risk perception, trust, and nuclear power: Lessons from Yucca Mountain", *Environment,* 33, 6–11 and 28–30.

Stebbing, A.R.D. (1998), "A theory for growth hormesis", *Mutatlon Research*, 403, 249–258.

Stern, P.C. and Fineberg, V. (1996), *Understanding risk: Informing decisions in a democratic society. National Research Council, Committee on Risk Characterization.* Washington, D.C.: National Academy Press.

Thompson, M. (1980), *An outline of the cultural theory of risk,* Working Paper of the International Institute for Applied Systems Analysis (IIASA), WP-80-177, Laxenburg, Austria: IIASA .

Thompson M., Ellis W. and Wildavsky A. (1990), *Cultural theory.* Boulder, CO: Westview.

Webler, T. (1999), "The Craft and Theory of Public Participation: A Dialectical Process," *Risk Research*, 2, No. 1, 55–71.

Webler, T. and Renn, O. (1995), "A brief primer on participation: Philosophy and practice", in: O. Renn, T. Webler and P. M. Wiedemann (eds.), *Fairness and competence in citizen participation. Evaluating new models for environmental discourse.* Dordrecht: Kluwer, pp.17–34.

Webler, T., Levine, D., Rakel, H., & Renn, O. (1991). "The group Delphi: A novel attempt at reducing uncertainty", *Technological Forecasting and Social Change*, 39, pp. 253–263.

Wildavsky, A. and Dake, K. (1990), "Theories of risk perception: Who fears what and why?" *Daedalus*, 119, 41–60.

Yosie, T.F. and Herbst, T.D. (1998), "Managing and communicating stakeholder-based decision making", *Human and Ecological Risk Assessment,* 4, 643–646.

5

Conceptualizing Crisis Communication

W. Timothy Coombs
Eastern Illinois University

On average, only one-eighth of an iceberg is visible above the water. About the same amount of crisis communication is visible to those outside of an organization in crisis. What we typically see are the public words and actions of an organization, the crisis responses. Perhaps the visibility of the crisis response is why the bulk of crisis communication research is dedicated to examining this topic. That leaves a broad spectrum of crisis communication under researched because crisis communication occurs throughout the crisis management process. Crisis management can be divided into three phases: pre-crisis, crisis response, and post-crisis. Pre-crisis involves efforts to prevent a crisis, the crisis response addresses the crisis, and post-crisis concerns the follow-up actions and learning from the crisis.

To conceptualize crisis communication we must look below the water and examine how communication is used throughout the crisis management process. The primary goal of crisis management is to protect stakeholders from harm and the secondary goals are to protect reputational and financial assets. The number one priority is protecting human life—the stakeholders. The best-managed crisis is the one that is averted. Hence there is the need for crisis prevention. It is imperative that stakeholders exposed to a crisis know what they need to do to protect themselves from harm, a part of the crisis response. The learning from a crisis helps to prevent future crises and to improve future responses.

A crisis can be viewed as the perception of an event that threatens important expectancies of stakeholders and can impact the organization's performance. Crises are largely perceptual. If stakeholders believe there is a crisis, the organization is in a crisis unless it can successfully persuade stakeholders it is not. A crisis violates expectations; an organization has done something stakeholders feel is inappropriate—there is e. coli in a food product or drink, the CEO siphons off millions of dollars, or the organization exploits child labor. In turn, the violated expectations place the organization's performance at risk. Production can be stopped or reduced, sales and stock prices can drop, and/or the organization's reputation can be eroded. Crisis management is a process that "seeks to prevent or lessen the negative outcomes of a crisis and thereby protect the organization, stakeholders, and/or industry from damage" (Coombs, 1999b, p. 4).

Crisis communication is composed of two related communication processes: (1) crisis knowledge management and (2) stakeholder reaction management. Crises create a demand for knowledge. The term knowledge is used to denote the analysis of information. Knowledge is created when information is processed. Managers utilize communication to collect and process information into knowledge. Crisis managers try to achieve what is often called situational awareness. Situational awareness is when managers feel they have enough information to make decisions. Communication provides the knowledge the crisis team needs to make decisions. By understanding the crisis situation the crisis team can make decisions about what actions to take and what messages to communicate—formulate the crisis response. The decision making process itself is communicative. The decisions then must be communicated to the requisite stakeholders.

Part of understanding the situation is appreciating how stakeholders will perceive the crisis and the organization in crisis, especially their attributions of blame for the crisis. By understanding stakeholder perceptions, the crisis team is better prepared to manage stakeholder reactions to the crisis. Stakeholder reactions can deplete both reputational and financial assets. Communication is used in attempts to influence how stakeholders react to the crisis and the organization in crisis. Clearly, communication is woven throughout the entire crisis management process because of the demands to generate and disseminate crisis knowledge and the need to management stakeholder reactions. This chapter considers the application of crisis communication to the entire crisis management process.

The chapter's structure follows the basic crisis management process: pre-crisis, crisis response, and post-crisis. The role of crisis communication at each phase of the crisis management process will be examined. The bulk of the chapter will focus on the crisis response phase because it is the most thoroughly researched phase of crisis management from a communication perspective.

PRE-CRISIS

Pre-crisis is composed of the actions organizations take before a crisis ever occurs. There are two components to the pre-crisis stage: (1) prevention and (2) preparation. Prevention tries to stop a crisis from developing while preparation readies people for the occurrence of a crisis.

Prevention

Crisis prevention is also known as mitigation. Prevention seeks to identify and to reduce risks that can develop into crises. A crisis risk is a weakness that can develop or be exploited into a crisis (Pauchant & Mitroff, 1992). A risk is the potential to cause harm. The risk has a probability of developing into a crisis/negative event. The magnitude of the damage resulting from a risk becoming a crisis is the threat level. Common sources of risk include personnel, products, the production process, facilities, social issues, competitors, regulators, and customers (Barton, 2001). Prevention has strong ties to emergency preparedness and reflects Fink's (1986) belief that all crises have warning signs or prodromes. A warning sign is an indicator that a risk is beginning to manifest itself into a crisis.

The most effective way to manage a crisis is to prevent it. Olaniran and Williams (2001) are among the few communication scholars to address prevention. Their anticipatory model of crisis management focuses on finding and reducing risks. Great crisis managers actively look for these signs and take action to prevent a crisis from materializing. However, prevention is easier said than done. Risks can be difficult to identify especially if people in the organization do not want them to be found. For example, people in organizations will try to hide information that makes them look bad or that is illegal. Enron and WorldCom are but two examples of this unfortunate fact.

Risk is often difficult to prevent. Prevention can take one of three forms: (1) eliminate the risk, (2) reduce the likelihood of a risk manifesting, and (3) reduce the threat of a risk. Eliminating a risk means you completely remove a risk. Many risks, such as those associated with personnel or geographic location, occur naturally and cannot be eliminated. No one can prevent hurricanes. However, an organization may be able to replace a hazardous chemical with a non-hazardous one thereby eliminating a risk. Steps can be taken to reduce the likelihood of a risk manifesting itself. Increased safety training and emphasis can reduce the likelihood of an accident. Finally, the magnitude of the threat from a risk can be reduced. One example would be storing smaller amounts of a hazardous chemical on site or storing the chemical in smaller, separate storage tanks in order to reduce the amount of damage that would occur if containment breech occurred.

Prevention assumes that the mitigation efforts will be effective. Management must determine if they should even attempt mitigation. The question is "Will the prevention efforts produce results?" If the reduction in the magnitude of the threat is small or has a minimal chance of being successful, management may choose not to attempt mitigation. Management needs to be fairly certain that the investment in mitigation will actually produce results. If mitigation is not a viable option, management should continue to monitor the risk carefully for signs of an emerging crisis.

Communication networks are the essential element in the prevention stage. The crisis team must create a vast communication network in order to collect as much risk-related information as possible. I term this the *crisis-sensing network* (Coombs, 1999a). The crisis team is creating what some would call a knowledge network or knowledge management. Wider networks collect more information and make the evaluation of the risk more accurate and effective. Risk information can be found in a variety of sources throughout the organization including production, safety, employee behavior, consumer responses and complaints, insurance risk audits, and regulatory compliance. Risk information is also found in the organization environment including policy concerns, activist hot buttons, and shifting societal values. Interpersonal communication is critical. The crisis team must talk to and cultivate relationships with a variety of internal and external stakeholders to form the crisis-sensing network.

The crisis team must be media savvy as well. The news media and the Internet must be scanned for signs of risks. By and large the Internet is a collection of odd information with little utility to an organization. However, nuggets of prized information can be gleaned from the myriad of web pages, discussion boards, and web logs (blogs). The difficulty is searching for the nuggets. Like miners in a stream, crisis managers must search through the worthless gravel for the pieces of gold. What poses a threat is not always immediately identifiable. Crisis sensing is an active search process. A crisis manager cannot assume the risks will find her or him. More attention should be given to the role of communication in crisis prevention.

Preparation

No organization can prevent all crises. Management must live with the reality that a crisis is a matter of "when" and not "if." The shear number and nature of threats/risks makes it impossible to eliminate them all. The preparation component readies the organization for the crisis. A crisis management plan (CMP) is created and exercises are used to test the CMP and to train the crisis management team. The CMP is a rough guide for how to respond to the crisis. The CMP pre-assigns responsibilities and tasks and that enables a quicker and more effective response. The team does not have to waste time deciding *what* to do and *who* will do it. The core of the CMP is a set of contact information for key people and organizations and set of forms for recording key actions and messages.

The forms serve as reminders of the basic tasks that must be completed and as a means for documenting what the crisis team has done and when those actions were taken. Most crises are likely to breed litigation, thus, documentation of the crisis team's actions is important. Another use of forms is to track requests for information, most coming from the news media, and responses to those requests. Crises move at their own pace. Most crises move rapidly making it difficult to remember and to respond to all the inquiries. When crisis teams fail to response to inquiries they appear to be disconnected from stakeholders or to be stonewalling. The crisis team may not yet have the requested information and promises to deliver said information when it does arrive. Forms documenting information requests make follow-up easier and more accurate. The crisis team will know who still needs to receive what specific pieces of information.

Some team members will also need spokesperson training. Certain team members must be able to answer media questions in a press conference format. Spokesperson training relies heavily on public speaking skills. An effective spokesperson must appear pleasant, have strong eye contact, answer questions effectively, and be able to present information clearly (free of jargon and buzzwords) (Coombs, 1999b).

Exercises simulate the crisis management process by focusing on collecting, analyzing, and disseminating crisis-related information as well as sharpen decision-making skills. Exercises determine if the CMP is effective or needs modification, if the crisis team members have the necessary skills for the task, and allows the crisis team to practice their communication skills. The communication skills of crisis team members include being able to engage in vigilant decision-making (including conflict management), being able to request information clearly, and being able to disseminate knowledge accurately. A real danger during all of this information gathering and exchange is serial reproduction error. Not all messages will be sent in writing, even with the extensive use of e-mail. The greater the number of people a message passes through before reaching its destination, the greater the likelihood the message will become distorted (Daniels, Spiker, & Papa, 1997). Crisis teams must recognize the potential for problems to arise as they collect and share information instead of assuming it a simple and rather error-free process.

A CMP in a binder and names comprising a crisis team roster are of little value if they are never tested through exercises. Exercises serve to simulate the crisis experience. It is an opportunity to learn the crisis management process in the safety of a controlled environment with out organizational resources being placed at risk. Exercises can range from simple tabletop exercises where the team talks through a crisis scenario to full-scale exercises where a crisis is re-created as realistically as possible. A full-scale exercise will involve the deployment of actual equipment to be used, people playing victims, and interactions with the real local emergency responders (Coombs, 2006a). Full-scale exercises are an opportunity to teach local stakeholders about the actions that the organization and they must take during a crisis. During a crisis, community members may be asked to evacuate an area or shelter-in-place (stay inside and try to seal the house from outside air). Community members need to understand when they must evacuate or shelter-in-place and how to enact each of these emergency procedures. In fact, most organizations do involve at least some community members when exercising chemical emergency responses (Kleindorfer, Freeman, & Lowe, 2000)

Preparation is one way that risk communication is tied to crisis communication, a point reinforced by this book. Risk communication is a process or dialogue between organizations and stakeholders. Stakeholders learn about the risks an organization presents and how they try to control those risks. The organization comes to appreciate stakeholder perceptions and concerns about risk (Palenchar, 2005). Crisis management preparation can be an indictor that the organization has taken some responsibility for the risk. Management has taken actions to prevent and be ready to respond to crises (Heath & Coombs, 2006). Research has shown that cooperative efforts to develop and implement emergency warning communication and response systems will generate support for the organization (Heath & Abel, 1996). Heath and Palenchar (2000) found that knowledge of emergency warning systems increased concern over risks while still increasing acceptance for the organization. Knowing about the emergency warning kept community member vigilant rather than lulling them into a false sense of security. Vigilance is preferable to complacency in a crisis. Participating in exercises or news media coverage of exercises can increase perceptions of control. Community members will realize that the organization has emergency plans and that those emergency plans will work.

The Extended Parallel Process Model (EPPM) can help to further explain the positive effect of exercises on community members. Kim Witte's (Witte, Meyer, & Martell, 2001; see also chapter 14 of this volume) EPPM provides a mechanism for understanding how people respond to risk messages. In EPPM, fear can motivate people to action. For fear to motivate, a threat needs to be relevant to people and perceived as significant. For people living near a facility with hazardous materials, the threat can be perceived as relevant and significant. If people believe a threat is real, they then make assessments of efficacy. For people to follow the advice given in a risk message, they must believe that the proposed action will work (response efficacy) and that they can enact the proposed action (self-efficacy). If people do not believe the response will work and/or do not think they can execute the response, they ignore the risk and messages associated with it (Witte et al., 2001). Exercises help community members understand that the organization's emergency plan can work. Moreover, if community members participate in the exercise they can learn that they can enact the actions required in the emergency plan—they can take the steps necessary to evacuate or to shelter-in-place. Crisis managers would be wise to assess efficacy efforts before and after full-scale exercises. This would provide important insights into how the community is reacting to crisis preparation.

An important element in a CMP is the assessment of crisis vulnerability (CV). A crisis team should identify and rate all possible risks that could become crises for the organization, what is termed crisis vulnerability. Each possible risk should be rated on likelihood (L) and impact (I). Likelihood represents the odds a risk will manifest into a crisis will happen and impact is how severely the resulting crisis will affect the organization. Typically a crisis team rates both likelihood and impact on a scale of 1 to 10 with 10 being the highest score. A common formula for evaluating crisis vulnerability is $L \times I = CV$ (Coombs, 2006a). Based on the crisis vulnerability, the crisis team can begin to assemble the supporting materials for the CMP.

Ideally, a CMP is kept brief. Bigger does not mean better with CMPs. Crisis teams should construct a database of supporting materials that is related to the CMP. Call it a crisis appendix. The crisis appendix is a collection of information you anticipate needing during a crisis. For instance, it includes information you will need such as safety/accident records, lists of chemical at a facility, any past recalls, training related to the crisis event, and government inspections. The crisis appendix will be vast so it should be kept in electronic form with backup copies included with other critical data the organization has stored in an off-site storage facility as well as in hard copy format. Part of the crisis plan includes procedures for accessing the crisis appendix.

As with prevention, the role of communication in preparation has been underdeveloped. Applications of ideas from risk communication have a strong potential for expanding our knowledge of crisis communication in the preparation phase.

CRISIS RESPONSE

When a crisis hits, an organization is in the crisis response phase. Management focuses on handling the crisis situation and attempting to return the organization to normal operations. A crisis demands action so an organization should respond in some way. The bulk of the crisis communication writings involve the crisis response: what is said and done after a crisis (Seeger, Sellnow, & Ulmer, 1998, 2001). To be more precise, we can label this *crisis response communication.* Both practitioners and researchers have been fascinated with crisis response communication. This has led to a robust but disjointed literature. Many people representing many different perspectives have written on the subject. I will impose an order on crisis response communication by categorizing the research. The first categories divide crisis response communication into form and content. Form refers to *how* an organization should respond while content refers to *what* an organization says and does.

Form

The first writings on crisis response communication focused on form. Form centers on how an organization should present the response and the general nature of the response. The form recommendations for crisis response communication rely heavily upon early practitioner ideas. This conventional wisdom has been proven to be useful over the years. The four key features of form are: (1) be quick, (2) avoid "no comment," (3) be accurate, and (4) be consistent (speak with one voice).

Being quick means the organization must get its message out fast. Writers frequently mention the "golden hour" meaning an organization should respond in 60 minutes or less. The need for speed has been intensified by the use of the Internet. A crisis creates a knowledge vacuum. Stakeholders need to know what has and is happening with the crisis. The news media needs sources. If the organization does not speak quickly enough with the news media, the media moves on to other sources. If the organization does not tell its story, some one else will tell the story of the crisis. This "other" story can be inaccurate and/or framed such that it makes the organization look bad. Silence is a passive response that allows others to control the discussion of the crisis. An organization must take charge and articulate what has happened and the steps they are taking to address the crisis.

The Internet and the 24-hour news cycle have intensified the need for a quick response. The news media can post stories any time of the day or night. Observers of the crisis and critics of the organization can do the same with comments they post to blogs. Crisis teams are wise to integrate the Internet into their crisis response. A crisis section can be added to a web site or a separate crisis web site created before a crisis. The crisis web site is simply a "dark site," one that is not active. Once a crisis hits, the dark site is customized to the actual crisis and activated. The crisis team can then post real-time updates if need be (Caikin & Dietz, 2002; Holtz, 1999).

Related to being quick to respond is avoiding the "no comment" response. A spokesperson may have to face the news media or other stakeholders before much is known about the crisis. If you do not know an answer to a question, say that you do not have the information and promise to answer the question when you get the relevant information. Research has shown that when a spokesperson says "no comment" the stakeholders hear "I am guilty and trying to hide something" (Kempner, 1995).

It stands to reason that an organization must provide accurate information to stakeholders about the crisis. The problem is that speed and accuracy are not always a good fit. Errors can be made in the rush to deliver information. The very tragic Sago coal mine disaster was a harsh reminder of misinformation during a crisis. In January of 2006, 13 men were trapped in the International Coal Group's mine in Sago, West Virginia. Late on January 3, relatives were told that 11 or 12 men had survived resulting in a massive celebration. Three hours later, friends and families were told by an official spokesperson that only one man had survived. People were told the miners were alive when in fact all but one had perished. This "miscommunication" added to the tragedy and pain. The initial message was that rescuers had found 12 men and were checking them for vital signs. Some how the message became jumbled and was not delivered through official channels. Accuracy is important and it is worth waiting to insure the message is correct.

The emphasis on consistency means the crisis response messages emanating from the organization must not contradict one another. Originally this was known as "speaking with one voice." However, speaking with one voice has two problematic connotations. First, people assume that only one person should speak for an organization. This is an unrealistic expectation. Crises can extend for days making it impractical, if not impossible, for only one person to speak for the organization.

The news media wants to receive information from experts. Hence, the spokespersons are more likely to be employees, such as engineers, with technical expertise than the public relations staff. When I have conducted crisis media training for corporations, I have worked with the technical people. This is not a denigration of the public relations staff. It is simply a realization that a technical expert can answer the types of questions that will be asked about the crisis. As much as you brief a public relations person on the production process, the person who runs that process will know more and provide greater detail. Which is more valuable to have in front of the news media? Because different types of expertise, such as safety or production, may be needed to explain the crisis, multiple voices are demanded.

Finally, it is unrealistic to expect no one outside of the crisis team will talk to the media or other stakeholders. You actually do want employees explaining the crisis to stakeholders they know. As Ketchum, a major public relations firm, notes, employees provide a very credible source for friends, neighbors, and customers (Handsman, 2004). Second, speaking with one voice does not require all employees to spout the "organizational line." Instead, the idea is that all who speak for the organization have the same knowledge from which to draw. The same knowledge will help to create consistent messages. All employees should be kept well informed so they can be a source of accurate crisis-related knowledge for stakeholders. One way to keep employees informed is through computerized phone notification systems. The Internet and organizational Intranet provide additional channels for keeping employees up-to-date on the crisis.

Content

Content delves more deeply into the nature of the response. The focus shifts to the specifics of what the crisis message should communicate. Content has a strategic focus and relates to the goals of crisis response communication. The central goals of crisis response communication reflect those of crisis management: (1) preventing or minimizing damage, (2) maintaining the organization's operations (business continuity), and (3) reputation repair. Damage can include harm to people, reputation, finance, or the environment. The number one priority in damage control is protecting people. Business continuity directly relates to financial harm. Efforts to maintain business operations are known as business continuity. Organizations must return to regular operations as soon as possible after a crisis. The longer a crisis interrupts operations, the more the financial loss for the organization. A crisis also threatens to damage an organization's reputation (Barton, 2001; Dilenschneider, 2000). A reputation is a valued intangible resource that should be monitored and protected (Davies, Chun, de Silva, & Roper, 2003).

Sturges (1994) developed an excellent system for organizing crisis response communication. The post-crisis strategies are divided into three functions: (1) instructing information, (2) adjusting information, and (3) reputation repair. The majority of crisis response communication research examines reputation repair. However, it is important to understand the relevance of instructing and adjusting information to provide a complete picture of crisis response communication.

Instructing Information

Instructing information uses strategies that seek to tell stakeholders what to do to protect themselves from the crisis. Protection can involve physical and/or financial harm. Customers and community stakeholders can be at physical risk. Defective or tampered products can hurt customers. As a result, organizations must warn customers of any dangers. The warning typically involves supplying the necessary recall information such as the product's name, description, and, if relevant, the batch number.

An example of instructing information would be the 2006 recall of dog food by Diamond Pet Food. Some of their dog food products had been contaminated with corn aflatoxin, a corn fungus that is harmful to dogs. Not all products were affected and not all of the products in the recall were a threat, only those in a particular batch. Diamond Pet Food's recall information included the list of states where the product had been sold, the names of its specific brands covered in the recall, the "Best By Date" that identifies the contaminated batch, and symptoms of illness if dogs had consumed the contaminated food (Diamond, 2006). The Federal government has specific requirements for recalls. Table 5.1 lists the main aspects of governmental requirements for information to be given to consumers during recalls.

Threats to the community are another form of instructing information. Accidents that can release hazardous materials threaten the nearby members of the community. Community members must be warned to either evacuate the area or to shelter-in-place. From 1995 to 1999, over 200,000 people were involved in chemical releases that required either evacuation or the need to shelter-in-place. No fatalities to community members occurred (Kleindorfer et al., 2000). The evacuation and shelter-in-place statistics reinforce the need for and value of instructing information.

Instructing information returns us to the Extended Parallel Process Model. Stakeholders at risk must believe there is a threat and that the prescribed actions will protect them from this threat. It is not as simple as disseminating information. Stakeholders must act upon the information in the desired fashion—they must protect themselves. If stakeholders do not act upon the instructing information, the damage will not be prevented or limited.

Crises can threaten to disrupt supply chains. A supply chain follows a product from raw materials to finished goods. Various organizations can be linked by the creation of a product. For instance,

TABLE 5.1
Food and Drug Administration Recall Guidelines for Instructions to Consumers

Product Identification
Include an accurate and complete description of the product and any codes used to identify the product, e.g., lot/unit numbers, expiration dates, serial numbers, catalog numbers, model numbers, and UPC codes.

Consider including a copy of the product label with the recall notification. This could be helpful for wholesalers and retailers in identifying and removing the recalled product.

Your Instructions should be clear. For example:
 Remove product from sale
 Cease distribution
 Subrecall (if appropriate)
 Return Product
 Explain procedures for product correction

Include a RETURN REPSONE card/form. This return response card/form should include all instructions for your from your recall letter. Your customers should be required to indicate that they followed every instruction (Product, n.d.).

producers of apple juice and manufacturers of mobile phones need specialized computer chips. A break in one of these links is problematic for the other members of the chain, especially those immediately tied to the "broken" link for an organization. Suppliers and customers represent the adjacent links. Suppliers and customers require information about business continuity.

The key piece of business continuity information is whether or not the company will maintain production and the level of that production. If production is stopped for a time or continues in a diminished capacity, suppliers and customers must adjust their behavior. If production will be stopped, suppliers and customers need estimates for when it will resume. Suppliers will not send shipments or will send smaller amounts. Customers must find alternative suppliers for key resources or reduce their production. One option for maintaining business operation is to use a hot site. Another is to increase production at a similar facility. A *hot site* is a temporary facility a business can use to provide the same level of products or services. Suppliers need to know if the hot site or another facility is being used to adjust production levels because they must deliver materials to a different address. Suppliers need to know where the hot site is (they should know where your other existing facility is) and how long the alternate arrangements will be in use.

Employees also need to know how the crisis affects their work. Employees must be informed if they will be working and where they will be working. In some cases a hot site or other facility will be a substantial distance away. The organization will have to arrange transportation and perhaps housing for employees. The exact details must be communicated to employees in a timely manner so they can adjust their lives to this shift. If employees are not working, they need to know how the disruption will affect their pay and benefits.

Very little research exists that explores ways to improve the development and delivery of instructing information. As noted in this section, risk communication research can inform instructing information. Crisis communication would benefit from research that addresses specific instructing information concerns. One of those concerns is compliance with recalls. We know that many consumers ignore product recalls. This places them in danger from product harm. What can be done to improve recalls? Are there better communication channels for delivering the message or ways to structure the message to increase compliance?

Adjusting Information

Adjusting information helps stakeholders cope psychologically with the effects of a crisis. The uncertainty surrounding a crisis produces stress for stakeholders. To cope with this psychological stress, stakeholders need to know about what happened and what the organization is doing to address the crisis. Crisis managers should provide a summary of the event and outline of what actions are being taken. Furthermore, stakeholders want to know what is being done to protect them from similar crises in the future—what corrective actions are being taken. Corrective actions reassure stakeholders that they are safe thereby reducing their psychological stress (Sellnow, Ulmer, & Snider, 1998). An organization cannot always be quick in providing corrective action. It often takes weeks or months to discover the cause of many crises (e.g., Ray, 1999). Crisis managers cannot discuss corrective action until the cause of the crisis is known. Crisis managers are warned not to speculate; if the speculation is wrong, the crisis manager looks either incompetent or deceptive. Neither perception is desirable. Talking about corrective action prior to understanding the cause is a form of speculation.

Stakeholders can become victims of the crisis. There are expectations that the organization will acknowledge the victims in some way, typically with an expression of concern (Patel & Reinsch, 2003). The recommendation to express sympathy or concern for victims is born out of the need for adjusting information. Research generally supports using expressions of concern. The legal danger with expressing concern is that it can be construed as accepting responsibility. The feeling is that an expression of sympathy is an indication of accepting responsibility. A number of states now have laws that prevent statements of sympathy from being used as evidence of accepting responsibility in lawsuits (Cohen, 1999; Fuchs-Burnett, 2002).

Reputation Repair

Reputation repair is a study in the use of crisis communication designed to protect an organization's reputation/image/character during a crisis (Seeger, Sellnow, & Ulmer, 2001). The researchers attempt to construct recommendations, offering advice for when crisis managers should utilize particular crisis response strategies (Hearit, 2001). The crisis response strategies are the discourse and actions used to rebuild/repair the organizational reputation.

Value of Reputations. Not that many years ago people were debating the value of "reputation." Reputation is an evaluation of the organization. Thus we can talk of unfavorable and favorable reputations. It refers to how stakeholders perceive the organization (Davies et al., 2003). Reputations are now recognized as a valuable, intangible asset. Reputational assets yield such significant outcomes as attracting customers, generating investment interest, attracting top employee talent, motivating workers, increasing job satisfaction, generating more positive media coverage, and garnering positive comments from financial analysts (Alsop, 2004; Davies et al., 2003; Dowling, 2002; Fombrun & van Riel, 2003). A reputation is built through the organization-stakeholder relationship (Fombrun & van Riel, 2003). Favorable reputations are created through positive interactions while unfavorable reputations are built through negative interactions. Crises present a threat to an organization's reputation and crisis response strategies provide a mechanism for protecting this vital organizational resource.

Corporate Apologia. One of the initial research lines in crisis response communication was corporate apologia. Apologia or self-defense is a concept derived from genre theory in rhetoric. The focus of apologia is on defending one's character following accusations of wrongdoing (Hearit, 2006; see also chapter 27 of this volume). People respond to attacks on character using one of four strategies: denial, bolstering, differentiation, and transcendence. The denial strategy claims there is no wrongdoing or the person is uninvolved in the wrongdoing. Bolstering connects the individual to something the audience would view positively. Differentiation attempts to take the action out of its current, negative context. The idea is that it is the negative context, not the act that creates unfavorable audience reactions. Transcendence attempts to place the action in a new, broader context to make the action seem more favorable (Hobbs, 1995; Ice, 1991).

Dionisopolous and Vibbert (1988) were among the first to argue it was appropriate to examine corporate apologia, self-defense rhetoric created by organizations. The premise was that organizations have a public persona (a reputation) that may be attacked and in need of defense. In other words, organizations can experience and respond to character attacks. Dionisopolous and Vibbert (1988) outlined the parameters of corporate apologia without specific application to crisis management.

Keith Hearit (1994, 1995a, 1995b, 2001, 2006; see also chapter 27 of this volume) developed corporate apologia into a distinct line of research. Corporate apologia is a response to criticism that "seeks to present a compelling, competing account of organizational actions" (Hearit, 2001 p. 502). He developed a vocabulary and unique perspective for integrating corporate apologia into crisis communication. The cornerstone of the perspective is social legitimacy, the consistency between organizational values and stakeholder values. A crisis threatens social legitimacy by making an organization appear incompetent (e.g., a hazardous chemical release) and/or violating stakeholder expectations (e.g., unfair labor practices). Hearit (1994, 1995a) posits that the social legitimacy violation is a form of character attack that calls forth apologia. Hearit (1996, 2001) extended corporate apologia beyond the four rhetorical strategies by addressing the concept of dissociation.

Dissociations involve splitting a single idea into two parts. Through dissociation the organization tries to reduce the threat a crisis poses to its reputation. Hearit (1995b, 2006) identifies three dissociations that are pertinent to reputation management: (1) opinion/knowledge, (2) individual/group, and (3) act/essence. Opinion/knowledge is used to deny a crisis exists. The crisis manager asserts that the claims of a crisis or the organization's involvement in the crisis are just opinion and do not match the facts of the situation. If people look at the facts, they will see there is no crisis or no connection to the organization. If the organization is not involved in a crisis, there can be no damage from the crisis. The individual/group dissociation tries to deflect some responsibility from the organization by blaming only a part of the organization for the crisis. Some person or group of persons were responsible for the crisis, not the entire organization. The crisis was a result of a few bad apples. The organization will then punish those responsible. Overall, the organization has acted responsibly and should not be punished by stakeholders. Finally, the act/essence dissociation accepts responsibility for the crisis but claims the crisis does not represent the "real" organization. The crisis was an anomaly and is not a true reflection of the organization. The organization should be forgiven for this lapse if stakeholders believe the organization is truly good (Hearit, 1996; Ilgen, 2002).

Impression Management. Legitimacy, whether or not an organization conforms to the social rules held by its stakeholders, drives the impression management line of crisis response communication research. A crisis threatens legitimacy by violating the social rules, hence, crisis response strategies are used to rebuild legitimacy. The ideas strongly parallel those in corporate apologia but employ different terminology. Airplanes should not crash and dangerous chemicals should not be released into the environment. Only a small number of studies can be classified as reflecting impression management but the research expanded the number of crisis response strategies beyond those in corporate apologia by drawing strategies from the impression management literature. A set of seven strategies was identified: excuse, avoiding responsibility; justification, accept responsibility for the act but not the consequence of the act; ingratiation, try to build stakeholder support or approval; intimidation, threat of action against a person or group; apology, accept responsibility and accept punishment; denouncement, claim some other party is responsible; and factual distortion, information about the event is untrue or distorted in some fashion (Allen & Caillouet, 1994; Caillouet & Allen, 1996; Massey, 2001). Table 5.2 provides a complete list and definition of the various crisis response strategies.

Image Restoration Theory. Benoit (1995) has developed the widely cited theory of image restoration strategies employed in crisis communication research. Two key assumptions provide the foundation for Benoit's theory of image restoration strategies. First, corporate communication is

TABLE 5.2
Allen and Caillouet's (1994) Impression Management Strategies

Excuse: Try to lessen responsibility for the event
  Denial of Intention: negative effects were accidental or unforeseeable
  Denial of Volition: could not control the trigger event
Denial of Agency: organization did not perform the act leading to the crisis

Justification: try to show the negative consequence were not that bad
  Denial of Injury: no one was hurt so crisis was trivial
  Denial of Victim: the victim deserved the injuries

Condemnation of Condemner: crisis was unimportant because others have had ones that are worse.
  Negative Events Misrepresented: things are not as bad as they seem

Ingratiation: try to gain approval of stakeholders

Self-enhancing Communication: try to persuade stakeholders that organization has positive qualities.
  Role Model: the organization should serve as an example for others
  Social Responsibility: organization claims to accept social responsibility
  Other-enhancing Communication: praise stakeholders to win their approval
  Opinion Conformity: organization expresses values and beliefs similar to
stakeholders

Intimidation: try to convey that the organization is potent and dangerous, may include threats.

Apology: organization admits responsibility and requests punishment

Denouncement: try to blame some external agent for the crisis

Factual Distortion: try to establish that information about the crisis was taken out of context or is incorrect

conceptualized as a goal-directed activity. Second, maintaining a positive reputation for the organization is one of the central goals of this communication. According to Benoit, "communication is best conceptualized as an instrumental activity" (Benoit, 1995, p. 67). Benoit claims, "Communicative acts are intended to attain goals important to the communicators who perform them. These utterances are ones that the communicators believe will help accomplish (with reasonable cost) goals that are salient to the actor at the time they are made" (Benoit, 1995, p. 67).

While not designed specifically for crisis management, Benoit and others have applied image restoration theory to a wide variety of crisis cases including airlines (Benoit & Czerwinski, 1997), entertainment (Benoit, 1997), and the chemical industry (Brinson & Benoit, 1999). Image restoration identified five basic crisis response strategies: denial, claim the actor (organization) is not involved in the crisis; evading responsibility, eliminate or reduce personal (organizational) responsibility for the crisis; reducing offensiveness by making the event (crisis) seem less negative; corrective action, restore the situation to pre-event (pre-crisis) conditions and/or promise to take action to prevent a repeat of the event (crisis); and mortification, accept responsibility for the act (crisis) and ask for forgiveness. Table 5.3 provides a complete list and definition of the image restoration strategies.

The primary recommendation emerging from image restoration theory is for crisis managers to use mortification. It is presumed that publicly accepting responsibility for an act is the one, best way to respond to a crisis (Brinson & Benoit, 1999; Tyler, 1997).

Situational Crisis Communication Theory

As with the other crisis response communication research reviewed thus far, Situational Crisis Communication Theory (SCCT) identifies crisis response strategies. SCCT organizes previously delineated crisis response strategies using Attribution theory as a guiding light. SCCT presumes

TABLE 5.3
Benoit's (1995) Image Restoration Strategies

1. Denial
   Simple Denial: there is no crisis
   Shift the Blame: so other agent is responsible for the crisis, not the organization
2. Evading Responsibility
   Provocation: crisis was a result of response to someone else's actions
   Defeasibility: lack of information about events leading to the crisis situation
   Accidental: lack of control over events leading to the crisis situation
   Good intentions: organization meant to do well
3. Reducing Offensiveness
   Bolstering: remind stakeholders of the organization's positive qualities
   Minimize: try to reduce the perceived offensiveness of crisis by saying it was minor
   Differentiation: try to reduce offensiveness of crisis by comparing act to similar, more serious ones
   Transcendence: place act in a different, more favorable context
   Attack Accuser: attack those who claim a crisis exists
   Compensation: organization offers money or goods to victims
4. Corrective Action: organization tries to restore the situation to pre-act status and/or promise change and prevent a repeat of the act
5. Mortification: organization admits responsibility, asks for forgiveness, and expresses regret

stakeholders will make attributions about the cause of a crisis. Crises vary in terms of whether the stakeholders attribute the cause of the crisis to the organization or external factors. The stronger the attributions of organizational control for the crisis (crisis responsibility), the greater the reputational threat posed by a crisis (Coombs, 1995; Coombs & Holladay, 2002). SCCT holds that crisis managers can use crisis discourse to (1) alter attributions about the crisis, (2) change perceptions of the organization in crisis, or (3) a combination of the two. It was from this attributional perspective that a synthesized list of crisis response strategies was developed (Coombs, 1999a). As Benoit (1995) observed, how strategies are arranged and grouped is a matter of choice. Different organizational schema result in different lists of crisis response strategies.

SCCT organized crisis response strategies based on whether they were used to either alter perceptions of the crisis or the organization in crisis. Four postures or groups of similar crisis response strategies were identified: (1) deny; (2) diminish; (3) rebuild; and (4) bolstering. Deny involves removing any connection between the organization and the crisis. If the organization is not involved, it will suffer no damage from the event. Diminish is connected with reducing the attributions of organizational control for the crisis or the negative impact of the crisis. If crisis managers can lessen the organization's connection to the crisis and/or have people view the crisis less negatively, the harmful effects of the crisis are reduced. Rebuild represents direct efforts to improve the organization's reputation. The crisis managers say and do things to benefit stakeholders and thereby take positive actions to offset the crisis. Finally, bolstering is a supplemental strategy to the other three. Organizations who have had positive relationships with stakeholders can draw upon that goodwill to help protect the organizational reputation or praise stakeholders as a means of improving relationships with them. Table 5.4 provides the lists and definitions of crisis response strategies in each posture.

While SCCT does offer a list of post-crisis response strategies, it diverges sharply from theother reputation repair research in communication. SCCT is developing a theory-based and empirically tested approach to reputation repair. The theory is predictive, rather than descriptive. SCCT does not use the case study method employed by corporate apologia, impression management, and image restoration. Instead, experimental and quasi-experimental designs are used to test the relationships identified in the theory and the guidelines its recommends. The methods are consistent with the roots of SCCT in Attribution theory. The focus of SCCT is on finding the post-crisis response strategy that best fits with the given crisis situation.

TABLE 5.4
SCCT Crisis Response Strategies by Posture

Deny Posture

Attack the accuser: crisis manager confronts the person or group claiming something is wrong with the organization.
"The organization threatened to sue the people who claim a crisis occurred."

Denial: crisis manager asserts that there is no crisis.
"The organization said that no crisis event occurred."

Scapegoat: crisis manager blames some person or group outside of the organization for the crisis.
"The organization blamed the supplier for the crisis."

Diminish Posture

Excuse: crisis manager minimizes organizational responsibility by denying intent to do harm and/or claiming inability to control the events that triggered the crisis.
"The organization said it did not intend for the crisis to occur and that accidents happen as part of the operation of any organization."

Justification: crisis manager minimizes the perceived damage caused by the crisis.
"The organization said the damage and injuries from the crisis were very minor."

Rebuild Posture

Compensation: crisis manager offers money or other gifts to victims.
"The organization offered money and products as compensation."

Apology: crisis manager indicates the organization takes full responsibility for the crisis and asks stakeholders for forgiveness.
"The organization publicly accepted full responsibility for the crisis and asked stakeholders to forgive the mistake."

Bolstering Posture

Reminder: tell stakeholders about the past good works of the organization.
"The organization restated its recent work to improve K-12 education."

Ingratiation: crisis manager praises stakeholders and/or reminds them of past good works by the organization.
"The organization thanked stakeholders for their help and reminded stakeholders of the organization's past effort to help the community and to improve the environment."

Attribution theory serves as the basis in SCCT for determining which crisis response strategies are appropriate for a given crisis situation. Variables from Attribution theory were adapted to the evaluation of crisis situations. Attribution theory holds that people will assign responsibility for negative, unexpected events (Weiner, 1986). Crises fit perfectly into Attribution theory. Even with limited information, stakeholders will determine the degree to which an organization is responsible for a crisis. There is a growing body of research applying Attribution theory to crises in marketing as well as in communication (Ahluwalia, Burnkrant, & Unnava, 2000; Bradford & Garrett, 1995; Dawar & Pillutla, 2000; Dean, 2004; Folkes, Koletsky, & Graham, 1987; Härtel, McColl-Kennedy, & McDonald, 1998). Attribution theory provides a framework for understanding the potential reputational threat posed by a crisis situation.

SCCT utilizes three factors to assess the reputational threat of a crisis: crisis type (frame), crisis history, and prior reputation. Crisis type is the frame used to define the crisis. The literature has identified a set of three crisis types/frames for categorizing crises: (1) victim, (2) accidental, and (3) intentional. Each crisis type/frame has been found to generate predictable amounts of crisis responsibility (Coombs & Holladay, 2002). Table 5.5 identifies the crisis types used in SCCT and level of crisis responsibility associated with each one. Crisis responsibility is a threat to the reputation. The greater the attributions of crisis responsibility, the greater the damage a crisis can inflict on a reputation (Coombs, 2004b; Coombs & Holladay, 1996, 2004). The crisis type/frame provides the initial reputational threat.

Crisis history and prior reputation serve to modify the initial reputational threat. Organizations that have suffered previous crises will find the reputational threat of the current crisis stronger than if they had not had crises (Coombs, 2004a; Coombs & Holladay, 2001, 2004). A history of crises means stakeholders will treat a victim crisis like an accidental crisis and an accidental crisis like an

TABLE 5.5
Crisis Types and Level of Crisis Responsibility

Victim Crises: Minimal Crisis Responsibility
Natural disasters: acts of nature such as tornadoes or earthquakes.
Rumors: false and damaging information being circulated about your organization.
Workplace violence: attack by former or current employee on current employees on-site.
Product Tampering/Malevolence: external agent causes damage to the organization.

Accident Crises: Low Crisis Responsibility
Challenges: stakeholder claims that the organization is operating in an inappropriate manner.
Technical error accidents: equipment or technology failure that cause an industrial accident.
Technical error product harm: equipment or technology failure that cause a product to be defective or potentially harmful.

Preventable Crises: Strong Crisis Responsibility
Human-error accidents: industrial accident caused by human error.
Human-error product harm: product is defective or potentially harmful because of human error.
Organizational misdeed: management actions that put stakeholders at risk and/or violate the law.

intentional crisis (Coombs, 2004a, 2004b). Research on prior reputation has found limited support for the belief that a favorable prior reputation is a halo that protects a reputation during a crisis. Instead, the results strongly indicate that an unfavorable prior reputation makes a crisis more difficult to manage by intensifying the reputational threat. As with crisis history, an unfavorable prior reputation means stakeholders will treat a victim crisis like an accidental crisis and an accidental crisis like an intentional crisis (Coombs, 2006a; Coombs & Holladay, 2002). However, there is little support to demonstrate a favorable prior reputation creates a meaningful halo effect (Coombs & Holladay, 2002; Klein & Dawar, 2004).

Based on the assessment of crisis type/frame, crisis history, and prior reputation, SCCT has generated a list of recommendations for selecting crisis response strategies. The key to protecting the organizational reputation is to select the appropriate crisis response strategy(ies). SCCT argues that as the reputational threat increases, crisis managers must use more accommodative strategies. Accommodation refers to the degree to which the response centers on the victim and takes responsibility for the crisis (Coombs & Holladay, 2004). Rebuild strategies are the most accommodative followed by diminish. Deny strategies are the lease accommodative of all (Coombs, 2006b; Marcus & Goodman, 1991). Table 5.6 summarizes the recommendations offered by SCCT.

TABLE 5.6
Crisis Response Recommendations for Situational Crisis Communication Theory

1. All victims or potential victims should receive instructing information.
2. All victims should be provided adjusting information including an expression of sympathy.
3. For crises with minimal attributions of crisis responsibility and no history of crises or a negative prior reputation, instructing and adjusting information is sufficient.
4. For crises with minimal attributions of crisis responsibility and a history of crises or a negative prior reputation, add diminish strategies to the instructing and adjusting information.
5. For crises with weak attributions of crisis responsibility, and no history of crises or a negative prior reputation, add diminish strategies to the instructing and adjusting information.
6. For crises with weak attributions of crisis responsibility and a history of crises or a negative prior reputation, add rebuild strategies to the instructing and adjusting information.
7. For crises with strong attributions of crisis responsibility and a history of crises or a negative prior reputation, add rebuild strategies to the instructing and adjusting information.
8. Reinforcing strategies can be used to supplement any response.

Deny response strategies are best used only for rumor and challenge crises.

9. Attempt to maintain consistency between post-crisis response strategies by not mixing deny strategies with either rebuild or diminish strategies.

More recently, SCCT has expanded beyond reputation repair to consider the effects of the crisis situation on stakeholder emotion. Of particular interest is the amount of anger generated by a crisis. Anger follows a pattern similar to attributions of crisis responsibility; as crisis responsibility intensifies so too does anger. Anger is important because it can facilitate a negative communication dynamic. Anger will dissipate over time. However, angry stakeholders are more likely to engage in negative word-of-mouth—say bad things about a business or its products (Coombs & Holladay, 2005). Negative word-of-mouth has been shown to reduce purchase intentions, a consequence most organizations would like to avoid (Brown & Reingen, 1987; Herr, Kardes, & Kim, 1991; Laczniak, DeCarlo, & Ramaswami, 2001). By incorporating emotion into SCCT, research may determine ways to reduce the anger generated by a crisis and prevent the negative communication dynamic from developing.

SCCT acknowledges that crisis response strategies are discretionary; crisis managers can choose which, if any, to use in a crisis situation. Financial factors, for example, can pose a constraint for crisis managers. Crisis response strategies become more expensive as they become more accommodative. Apology is a perfect illustration. Apology is a very expensive strategy because it opens the door to payments on lawsuits initiated by victims (Tyler, 1997). Crisis managers may opt not to use apology because of the price tag. SCCT indicates the possible effectiveness of the various crisis response strategies. As a result, crisis managers can decide what the next most viable strategy might be if the recommended strategy is not used.

Summary

Reputation repair is a valuable aspect of crisis response communication. Organizations spend a great deal of time, effort, and money on building a favorable reputation. It is imperative to understand how the words and actions of the organization impact the way stakeholders react to the crisis and how the crisis may alter its reputation. We can never diminish the critical role of instructing and adjusting information. Crisis managers should never attempt to repair a reputation until instructing and adjusting information is provided. Moreover, the instructing and adjusting information can be enough to protect a reputation when crises present a minor reputational threat.

We know more about crisis response communication than any other aspect of crisis communication but there is still much more to explore. The lack of theory-driven research and the emphasis on case studies derived from second-hand sources has limited the development of reputation repair work. Case studies based on media accounts lack the depth and insight provided by cases that collect information from those involved in the crisis management process. Rob Ulmer's (2001) analysis of Mulden Mills is an example of the benefits from studies that tap into first-hand experiences. His article is a rare and insightful insider view of a crisis case. Ulmer's work has evolved into the rhetoric of renewal and this research retains the focus on insider information and insights (Ulmer & Sellnow, 2002; Ulmer, Selnow, & Seeger, 2006). Another problem with second-hand case studies is that the prescriptive advice is really speculation if untested. This is dangerous if the speculation is incorrect. Coombs and Schmidt (2000), for instance, tested "conclusions" from one image restoration case study and found them to be incorrect. In sum, much of the existing reputation repair research has generated more speculation about what should be done rather than testing of actual prescriptive claims. A shift to more theory building and testing and less reliance on case studies will create a more fruitful area of post-crisis communication research.

POST-CRISIS

The transition from crisis response to the post-crisis phase is not always distinct. In the post-crisis phase, the organization is returning to operations as normal and the crisis is now a lower priority. However, there will still be lingering crisis communication concerns and a need to learn from the crisis.

Even when a crisis is "over," people are back to work or the product has been recalled, there are still communication concerns. The post-crisis communication concerns reflect the need for follow-up communication to stakeholders. Follow-up communication includes updates on progress to recover from the crisis, actions taken to prevent a repeat of the crisis, delivery of information promised to stakeholders during the crisis, release of reports about the investigation of the crisis, and providing information to any governmental agencies that are investigating the crisis.

Suppliers, customers, employees, and investors want to know how the recovery is progressing. Suppliers and customers want to know exactly when the supply chain will be fully restored. For suppliers, this includes any changes in shipping addresses as a damaged facility returns to operations. Investors want some idea of how long the crisis might affect their earnings while employees will want to know there are any lingering effects on their jobs. Victims of the crisis want to know the steps the organization has taken to prevent a repeat of the crisis. During a crisis, management may not have certain requested information and promise to provide that information once it is known. The organization builds credibility by delivering all of the promised information.

All crises will involve some investigation of the cause. The investigations will vary in the degree of formality and the parties involved. These investigations can be conducted by government agencies and/or the organization itself. The organization must cooperate by supplying the necessary information to governmental investigations. For very high profile crises, an organization will want to release the findings of its own report. Examples include E.F. Hutton and its check kiting scandal in the 1980s, Mitsubishi and its sexual harassment epidemic in the 1990s, and BP and its Texas City explosion in 2005. Organizational reports often include the corrective actions thereby addressing the prevention concerns of victims. Follow-up communication must be accomplished in a timely manner and be clear to the target audience. It is often a challenge to translate technical information from an investigation into clear information for stakeholders. Communication clarity is a serious challenge for follow-up communication. Research has largely ignored the problems of clearly presenting the technical aspects of follow-up communication to stakeholders.

The final component in crisis management is learning. The discussion of exercises touched briefly on learning. Crisis managers dissect exercises and actual crises to determine what worked and what needs improvement. This dissection is known as a post-mortem. The idea of a crisis post-mortem is to improve the crisis management process. Communication is a critical part of the process. As a result, a key component of a post-mortem is the assessment of various aspects of crisis communication. This is as simple as determining if the contact information is useful in the CMP and as complex as determining the effectiveness of disseminating the various crisis messages to the many stakeholders involved in the crisis management effort.

Learning informs the other phases. A crisis can reveal a risk or threat that had not been high on the organization's list or even on its crisis radar. Like an exercise, a crisis can reveal flaws in a CMP or identify weak crisis team members. A CMP may need to be refined or a crisis team member replaced. Changes in preparation should translate into more effective responses when a crisis hits.

If we dig deeper into the communicative aspect of learning, a danger appears. A post-mortem involves collecting information from people involved in the crisis management effort. If the crisis management effort went poorly, a barrier arises. People can view a post-mortem as a search for blame. As a result, people may withhold important pieces of negative information. In general, people do not like to disclose bad news in an organization, especially if it reflects negatively upon them. The challenge is to create a climate where people know the purpose is improving the crisis response and not trying to pin blame on anyone. Advice on how to specially address such a challenge is beyond the scope of this chapter. However, it is important to recognize that learning from a crisis does have communicative challenges.

CONCLUSION

Crisis communication is much more complex and diverse than the extant literature would suggest. The limited research focus has constrained what we could know about crisis communication. Crisis communication is integral to the pre-crisis, crisis response, and post-crisis stages and can provide value throughout the crisis management process. At every stage communication is the lifeblood that fills the knowledge demands created by a crisis—allows people to make sense of the crisis. Communication enables the collection, analysis, and dissemination of crisis-related knowledge and provides the foundation for decision making.

Research that centers on crisis knowledge management is scant. One reason for this neglect is the assumption that information is easy to collect, analyze, and disseminate. We know the process is not easy and is fraught with potential problems. There are a variety of principles and theories in organizational communication and management that could be applied to the study of crisis knowledge management to illuminate those potential problems. As a result, crisis knowledge management offers great research potential that should be tapped.

Thus far, the vast majority of crisis communication research has centered on stakeholder reaction management through crisis response studies oriented toward reputation repair. This results in a rather narrow knowledge base. What we do not know and still need to know is vast. Instructing and adjusting information have a critical role in the crisis response but have received little attention (e.g., Sturges, 1994; Coombs, 1999a). Even the highly researched reputation repair topic is limited by an emphasis on descriptive case studies built from news media reports and other second-hand accounts. There is room for growth even in the best-understood aspect of crisis communication through the application of first-hand reports about crises and the experimental study of factors that shape the crisis response.

Throughout this chapter I have tried to complicate our thinking about crisis communication. We must expand our scope beyond crisis responses and reputation repair. I do not mean we should abandon crisis communication as reputation repair; instead, we should integrate other topics to the mix. Crisis communication is a growing field whose potential remains far greater than its current yields. It is time to open new fields of study and sharpen our understanding of crisis communication. This book is an important step in that direction as it serves to integrate risk and crisis communication, a much needed step in the evolution of crisis communication.

BIBLIOGRAPHY

Ahluwalia, R., Burnkrant, R. E., & Unnava, H. R. (2000). Consumer response to negative publicity: The moderating role of commitment. *Journal of Marketing Research, 27*, 203–214.

Allen, M. W., & Caillouet, R. H. (1994). Legitimate endeavors: Impression management strategies used by an organization in crisis. *Communication Monographs, 61*, 44–62.

Alsop, R. J. (2004). *The 18 immutable laws of corporate reputation: Creating, protecting, and repairing your most valuable asset*. New York: Free Press.

Balzer, W. K., & Sulsky, L. M. (1992). Halo and performance appraisal research: A critical examination. *Journal of Applied Psychology, 77*, 975–985.

Barton, L. (2001). *Crisis in organizations II* (2nd ed.). Cincinnati, OH: College Divisions South-Western.

Benoit, W. L. (1995). *Accounts, excuses, and apologies: A theory of image restoration*. Albany: State University of New York Press.

Benoit, W. L. (1997). Hugh Grant's image restoration discourse: An actor apologizes. *Communication Quarterly, 45*, 251–267.

Benoit, W. L., & Czerwinski, A. (1997). A critical analysis of USAir's image repair discourse. *Business Communication Quarterly, 60*, 38–57.

Bradford, J. L., & Garrett, D. E. (1995). The effectiveness of corporate communicative responses to accusations of unethical behavior. *Journal of Business Ethics, 14*, 875–892.

Brinson, S. L., & Benoit, W. L. (1999). The tarnished star: Restoring Texaco's damaged Public image. *Management Communication Quarterly, 12*, 483–510.

Brown, J. J., & Reingen, P. H. (1987). Social ties and word-of-mouth referral behavior. *Journal of Consumer Research, 14*, 350–362.

Caillouet, R. H., & Allen, M. W. (1996). Impression management strategies employees use when discussing their organization's public image. *Journal of Public Relations Research, 8,* 211–227.

Caiken, I., & Dietz, S. (2002). The internet's role in crisis management—Part 1. Retreived March 11, 2006, from http://www.efluentials.com/documents/internetroleincrisismanagement.pdf.

Cohen, J. R. (1999). Advising clients to apologize. *S. California Law Review, 72*, 1009–1131.

Coombs, W. T. (1995). Choosing the right words: The development of guidelines for the selection of the "appropriate" crisis response strategies. *Management Communication Quarterly, 8*, 447–476.

Coombs, W. T. (1999a). Information and compassion in crisis responses: A test of their effects. *Journal of Public Relations Research, 11*, 125–142.

Coombs, W. T. (1999b). *Ongoing crisis communication: Planning, managing, and responding*. Thousand Oaks, CA: Sage.

Coombs, W. T. (2004a). A Theoretical frame for post-crisis communication: Situational crisis communication theory. In M. J. Martinko (Ed.), *Attribution theory in the organizational sciences: Theoretical and empirical contributions* (pp. 275–296). Greenwich, CT: Information Age Publishing.

Coombs, W. T. (2004b). Impact of past crises on current crisis communications: Insights from situational crisis communication theory. *Journal of Business Communication, 41*, 265–289.

Coombs, W. T. (2006a). *Code red in the boardroom: Crisis management as organizational DNA*. Westport, CT: Praeger.

Coombs, W. T. (2006b). The protective powers of crisis response strategies: Managing reputational assets during a crisis. *Journal of Promotion Management, 12*, 241–260.

Coombs, W. T., & Holladay, S. J. (1996). Communication and attributions in a crisis: An experimental study of crisis communication. *Journal of Public Relations Research, 8*, 279–295.

Coombs, W. T., & Holladay, S. J. (2001). An extended examination of the crisis situation: A fusion of the relational management and symbolic approaches. *Journal of Public Relations Research, 13*, 321–340.

Coombs, W. T., & Holladay, S. J. (2002). Helping crisis managers protect reputational assets: Initial tests of the situational crisis communication theory. *Management Communication Quarterly, 16*, 165–186.

Coombs, W.T., & Holladay, S.J. (2004). Reasoned action in crisis communication: An attribution theory-based approach to crisis management. In D.P. Millar and R. L. Heath (Eds.), *Responding to crisis: A rhetorical approach to crisis communication* (pp. 95– 115). Mahwah, NJ: Erlbaum.

Coombs, W. T., & Holladay, S. J. (2005). Exploratory study of stakeholder emotions: Affect and crisis. In space N. M. Ashkanasy, W. J. Zerbe, & C. E. J. Hartel (Eds.), *Research on emotion in organizations: Volume 1: The effect of affect in organizational settings* (pp. 271–288). New York: Elsevier.

Coombs, W. T., & Schmidt, L. (2000). An empirical analysis of image restoration: Texaco's racism crisis. *Journal of Public Relations Research, 12*(2), 163–178.

Daniels, T. D., Spiker, B. K., & Papa, M. J. (1997). *Perspectives on organizational Communication* (4th ed.). Dubuque, IA: Brown & Benchmark.

Davies, G., Chun, R., da Silva, R. V., & Roper, S. (2003). *Corporate reputation and competitiveness*. New York: Routledge.

Dawar, N., & Pillutla, M. M. (2000). Impact of product-harm crises on brand equity: The moderating role of consumer expectations. *Journal of Marketing Research, 27*, 215–226.

Dean, D. W. (2004). Consumer reaction to negative publicity: Effects of corporate reputation, response, and responsibility for a crisis event. *Journal of Business Communication, 41*, 192–11.

Diamond Pet Foods statement on detection of aflatoxin in grain prior to recall. (2006). Retrieved April 13, 2006, from http://www.diamondpertrecall.net/updates.php?ID=9.

Dilenschneider, R. L. (2000). *The corporate communications bible: Everything you need to know to become a public relations expert*. Beverly Hills, CA: New Millennium Press.

Dionisopolous, G. N., & Vibbert, S. L. (1988). CBS vs Mobil Oil: Charges of creative bookkeeping. In H. R. Ryan (Ed.), *Oratorical encounters: Selected studies and sources of 20th century political accusation and apologies* (pp. 214–252). Westport, CT: Greenwood Press.

Dowling, G. (2002). *Creating corporate reputations: Identity, image, and performance*. New York: Oxford University Press.

Fink, S. (1986). *Crisis management*. New York: AMACOM.

Fink, S. (2000). *Crisis management: Planning for the inevitable*. Lincoln, NE: iUniverse.com, Inc.

Fombrun, C. J., & van Riel, C. B. M. (2003). *Fame & fortune: How successful companies build winning reputations*. New York: Prentice Hall Financial Times.

Folkes, V. S., Koletsky, S., & Graham, J. L. (1987). A field study of causal inferences And consumer reaction: The view from the airport. *Journal of Consumer Research, 13*, 534–539.

Fuchs-Burnett, T. (2002, May/July). Mass public corporate apology. *Dispute Resolution Journal, 57,* 26–32.

Handsman, J. (2004). Don't neglect employees in times of crisis. Retrieved March 11, 2006, from http://resources.Ketchum.com/web/neglect_eomplyees.pdf.

Härtel, C., McColl-Kennedy, J. R., & McDonald, L. (1998). Incorporating attribution theory and the theory of reasoned action within an affective events theory framework to produce a contingency predictive model of consumer reactions to organizational mishaps. *Advances in Consumer Research, 25*, 428–432.

Hearit, K. M. (1994). Apologies and public relations crises at Chrysler, Toshiba, and Volvo, *Public Relations Review, 20,* 113–125.

Hearit, K. M. (1995a). "Mistakes were made": Organizations, apologia, and crises of social legitimacy. *Communication Studies, 46*, 1–17.

Hearit, K. M. (1995b). From "we didn't it" to "it's not our fault": The use of apologia in public relations crises. In W. N. Elwood (Ed.), *Public relations inquiry as rhetorical criticism: Case studies of corporate discourse and social influence* (pp. 117–131). Westport, CT: Praeger.

Hearit, K. M. (1996, Fall). The use of counter-attack in apologetic public relations crises: The case of General Motors vs. Dateline NBC. *Public Relations Review, 22*(3), 233–248.

Hearit, K. M. (2001). Corporate apologia: When an organization speaks in defense of itself. In R. L. Heath (Ed.), *Handbook of public relations* (pp. 501–511). Thousand Oaks, CA: Sage.

Hearit, K. M. (2006). *Crisis management by apology: Corporate response to allegations of wrongdoing*. Mahwah, NJ: Erlbaum.

Heath, R. L., & Abel, D. D. (1996). Proactive response to citizen risk concerns: Increasing citizens' knowledge of emergency response practices. *Journal of Public Relations Research, 8*, 151–172.

Heath, R. L., & Coombs, W. T. (2006). *Today's public relations: An introduction*. Thousand Oaks, CA: Sage.

Heath, R. L., & Palenchar, M. (2002). Community relations and risk communication: A longitudinal study of the impact of emergency response messages. *Journal of Public Relations Research, 12*, 131–162.

Herr, P. M., Kardes. F. R., & Kim, J. (1991). Effect of word-of-mouth and product attribute information on persuasion: An accessibility-diagnostic perspective. The *Journal of Consumer Research, 17*, 452–462.

Hobbs, J. D. (1995). Treachery by any other name: A case study of the Toshiba public relations crisis. *Management Communication Quarterly, 8*, 323–346.

Holtz, S. (1999). *Public relations on the net: Winning strategies to inform and influence the media, the investment community, the government, the public, and more!* New York: AMACOM.

Ice, R. (1991). Corporate publics and rhetorical strategies: The case of Union Carbide's Bhopal crisis. *Management Communication Quarterly, 4*, 341–362.

Ihlen, O. (2002). Defending the Mercedes a-class: Combining and changing crisis response strategies. *Journal of Public Relations Research, 14*, 185–206.

Kempner, M. W. (1995). Reputation management: How to handle the media during a crisis. *Risk Management, 42*(2), 43–47.

Klein, J., & Dawar, N. (2004). Corporate social responsibility and consumers' attributions and brand evaluations in a product-harm crisis. *International Journal of Marketing, 21*, 203–217.

Kleindorfer, P., Freeman, H., & Lowe, R. (2000). Accident epidemiology and the U.S. chemical industry: Preliminary results from RMP*Info. Retreived March 13, 2006, from http://opim.wharton.upenn.edu/risk/downloads/00-1-15.pdf.

Laczniak, R. N., DeCarlo, T. E., & Ramaswami, S. H. (2001). Consumers' responses to negative word-of-mouth communication: An attribution theory perspective. *Journal of Consumer Psychology, 11*, 57–73.

Marcus, A. A., & Goodman, R. S. (1991). Victims and shareholders: The dilemma of presenting corporate policy during a crisis. *Academy of Management Journal, 34,* 281–305.

Massey, J. E. (2001). Managing organizational legitimacy. *Journal of Business Communication, 38,* 152–182.

Olaniran, B. A., & Williams, D. E. (2001). Anticipatory model of crisis management: A vigilant response to technological crises. In R. L. Heath (Ed.). *Handbook of public relations* (pp. 487–500). Thousand Oaks, CA: Sage.

Palenchar, M. J. (2005). Risk communication. In R. L. Heath (Ed.), *Encyclopedia of public relations* (Vol. 2, pp. 752–755). Thousand Oaks, CA: Sage.

Patel, A., & Reinsch, L. (2003). Companies can apologize: Corporate apologies and legal liability. *Business Communication Quarterly, 66*, 17–26.

Pauchant, T. C., & Mitroff, I. I. (1992). *Transforming the crisis-prone organization:Preventing individual, organizational, and environmental tragedies*. San Francisco: Jossey-Bass.

Product (n.d.) Retrieved March 15, 2006, from http://www.fda.gov/cber/gdlns/prodrecall.pdf.

Ray, S. J. (1999). *Strategic communication in crisis management: Lessons from the airline industry*. Westport, CT: Quorum Books.

Seeger, M. W., Sellnow, T. L., & Ulmer, R. R. (1998). Communication, organization, and crisis. In M. E. Roloff (Ed.), *Communication Yearbook 21* (pp. 231–276). Thousand Oaks, CA: Sage.

Seeger, M. W., Sellnow, T. L., & Ulmer, R. R. (2001). Public relations and crisis communication: Organizing and chaos. In R. L. Heath (Ed.). *Handbook of Public Relations* (pp. 155–166). Thousand Oaks, CA: Sage.

Sellnow, T. L., Ulmer, R. R., & Snider, M. (1998). The compatibility of corrective action in organizational crisis communication. *Communication Quarterly, 46,* 60–74.
Sturges, D. L. (1994). Communicating through crisis: A strategy for organizational survival. *Management Communication Quarterly, 7,* 297–316.
Tyler, L. (1997). Liability means never being able to say you're sorry: Corporate guilt, legal constraints, and defensiveness in corporate communication. *Management Communication Quarterly, 11*, 51–73.
Ulmer, R. R. (2001). Effective crisis management through established stakeholder relationships: Malden Mills as a case study. *Management Communication Quarterly, 11*, 51–73.
Ulmer, R. R., & Sellnow, T. L. (2002). Crisis management and the discourse of renewal: Understanding the potential for positive outcomes of crisis. *Public Relations Review, 28*, 361–365.
Ulmer, R. R., Sellnow, T. L., & Seeger, M. W. (2006). *Effective crisis communication: Moving from crisis to opportunity*. Thousand Oaks, CA: Sage.
Weiner, B. (1986). *An attributional theory of motivation and emotion*. New York: Springer Verlag.
Witte, K., Meyer, G., & Martell, D. (2001). *Effective health risk messages: A step-by-step guide.* Thousand Oaks, CA: Sage.

6

The Precautionary Principle and Risk Communication

Steve Maguire and Jaye Ellis

McGill University

Often described as little more than a formalization of the homilies "better safe than sorry", "look before you leap", and "an ounce of prevention is worth a pound of cure", the precautionary principle is an increasingly prominent feature of contemporary risk management. A guide for decision making about risks—and inevitably, therefore, about risk-generating activities and technologies—in a context of scientific uncertainty, the precautionary principle's conceptual origins have been traced to the *Vorsorgeprinzip*, or "foresight" principle, which emerged in West German environmental law in the 1970s (Freestone, 1991; O'Riordan & Jordan, 1995; Freestone & Hey, 1996; Trouwborst, 2002; de Sadeleer, 2002). Internationally, a recognizable formulation of the principle can be found as early as the 1984 and 1987 Declarations of the International Conferences on the Protection of the North Sea (Freestone, 1991; McIntyre & Mosedale, 1997), and precaution has since been incorporated into numerous international conventions addressing a wide range of environmental risks,[1] as well as into international trade law.[2] Principle 15 of the 1992 Rio Declaration on Environment and Development (UNCED, 1992) represents one of the most commonly cited formulations of precaution:

> In order to protect the environment, the precautionary approach shall be widely applied by States according to their capabilities. Where there are threats of serious or irreversible damage, lack of full scientific certainty shall not be used as a reason for postponing cost-effective measures to prevent environmental degradation.

The precautionary principle's influence ranges from global to local policy contexts. Article 174 of the Treaty establishing the European Community, for instance, stipulates that environmental policy be based on precaution.[3] Some municipalities are also implementing the precautionary principle, such as San Francisco which adopted it as city and county policy in 2003. And even some business organizations have begun to embrace precaution, as with those firms participating in the United Nations' "Global Compact" corporate social responsibility initiative, Principle 7 of which states: "Business should support a precautionary approach to environmental challenges".

Along with its ascendance and increasingly widespread application, however, has been a great deal of contestation—"it would be fair to say that the use of the precautionary principle for regulatory purposes is highly controversial" (Löfstedt, 2002, p. 285)—as well as an extraordinary amount of attention from a wide range of scientific disciplines—"[s]cholarly works on precaution are published at an alarming rate, and have been for more than a decade" (Ellis, 2006, p. 446). The resulting literature is vast and heterogeneous; in addition to risk analysts, precaution has been addressed by scholars of law, international relations, policy studies, ethics, environmental studies, economics and business. Despite—or perhaps because of—this attention, no convergent view has yet emerged; indeed, MacDonald's (1995, p. 276) decade-old observation that "the literature devoted to defining the principle is enormous and divisive" remains true today.

As a result, an exhaustive review of scholarly writing on precaution is beyond the scope of a chapter such as this. Rather, our goal is to establish the central role of the precautionary principle for risk communication scholars by introducing it, summarizing contemporary debates surrounding its role in risk management, and discussing its application in policy and law. To this end, we draw from—and, for readers wishing to pursue topics in more depth, point to—notable works in a range of academic literatures. The review portion of our chapter then serves as the foundation for a concluding section in which we reflect upon the direct implications of the precautionary principle for risk communication.

PRECAUTION AS A CONTINUUM OF CONTESTED FEATURES

In this section, we introduce the precautionary principle and highlight its key contested features by distinguishing between "modest" and "aggressive" precaution (Graham & Hsia, 2002)[4]—two ends of a continuum of perspectives that differ in terms of (a) how the precautionary principle is formulated; (b) when it is invoked; (c) its impact on precautionary deliberations; and (d) its implications for precautionary actions.

Among the precautionary principle's most enthusiastic supporters are environmentalists whose championing of it has contributed significantly to contemporary debates. For instance, the NGO-championed "Wingspread Statement" on the precautionary principle[5] (Raffensperger & Tickner, 1999, p. 353) is widely cited by both proponents and opponents of the principle, especially in North America:

> When an activity raises threats of harm to human health or the environment, precautionary measures should be taken even if some cause and effect relationships are not fully established scientifically. In this context the proponent of the activity, rather than the public, should bear the burden of proof. The process of applying the Precautionary Principle must be open, informed, and democratic and must include potentially affected parties. In must also involve an examination of the full range of alternatives, including no action.

That this formulation differs from Rio Principle 15 is not only obvious but significant: it evidences how the precautionary principle has itself become a site for contestation by holders of different stakes in struggles over risks—a situation that has implications for risk communicators, as we discuss below.

The absence of a single universally agreed formulation, let alone interpretation, of the precautionary principle, both fuels and results from ongoing debates. Sandin (1999), for example, has catalogued 19 different versions. To bring order to this heterogeneity, it is useful to distinguish between "modest" as compared to "aggressive" (Graham & Hsia, 2002) formulations of the precautionary principle. Rio Principle 15 is an example of a modest formulation while the Wingspread Statement illustrates an aggressive one. Whereas the former is "argumentative" or "deliberation-guiding" in that it can be paraphrased as "uncertainty does not justify inaction", the latter is "prescriptive" or "action-guiding" in implying that "uncertainty justifies action" (Dickson, 1999; Sandin et al., 2002; Wiener & Rogers, 2002). By merely restricting a certain form of argumentation, i.e. that uncertainty justifies inaction, argumentative formulations place few positive demands on policy makers charged with risk management, which is why it is to these—and to Rio Principle 15 in particular—that the widest set of interests has publicly subscribed. On the other hand, because environmentalists often advocate stronger, prescriptive formulations, it is towards these that opponents of precaution have targeted much of their criticism. In navigating and appreciating the debates on precaution, it is helpful to keep in mind this paradox: although it is, for the most part, modest precaution that informs and is implemented in policy-making and the law, it is aggressive precaution that fuels much of the polarized debate.

The precautionary principle is invoked to achieve risk management goals in the face of scientific uncertainty. Modest and aggressive precaution differ in terms of goals, relevant risks, as well as the nature and level of uncertainty which justifies invoking the principle. Consider policy goals; whereas the aims of Rio Principle 15 are "to protect the environment" and "to avoid environmental degradation", more aggressive formulations stress environmental protection as a means to broader aims, such as the provision of ecological margins for error or repayment of ecological debts; the recognition of nonhuman interests; or intergenerational equity (Jordan & O'Riordan, 1999). In addition, whereas Rio Principle 15 refers to only those threats to the environment that are serious or irreversible, the Wingspread Statement refers to *all* threats of harm to the environment and, additionally, to human health.

The level of evidence of harm which justifies invoking the precautionary principle continues to be vigourously contested: "clear guidelines are still lacking for the weight of evidence needed to trigger the principle" (Foster, Vecchia & Repacholi, 2000, p. 981). Aggressive precaution is associated with a lower hurdle of evidence at which deliberations are triggered as compared to modest precaution. Additionally, understandings of the nature of the scientific uncertainty justifying the principle differ among advocates of modest and aggressive precaution. The former tend to conceptualize uncertainty in formal terms drawn from the science of risk analysis; it is seen to arise from data unavailability and to make impossible the assignment of probabilities to a defined set of negative outcomes and thus the calculation of "risk", formally defined. Those promoting aggressive precaution, on the other hand, are more likely to interpret uncertainty in broader and less formal terms; in addition to "uncertainty" as formally defined by risk analysts, invoking the principle is also justified in the face of other types of "incertitude" (Stirling, 1999), including indeterminacy (when the system being studied is too complex to permit reliable predictions) as well as ambiguity and ignorance (when the set of negative outcomes is ill defined) (see O'Riordan & Jordan, 1995; Stirling & Mayer, 2001). Importantly, the threat and uncertainty dimensions are not independent, as "some sort of balancing test is implicit…; the greater the possible risk to the environment, the greater the level of scientific uncertainty which may be acceptable for the precautionary principle to become engaged" (Freestone, 1991, p. 33).

Invoking the precautionary principle triggers precautionary deliberations. At this point, key differences between modest and aggressive precaution relate to its impact on the burden of proof and the role of cost-benefit analysis. Because deliberations are triggered before scientific certainty is achieved, even modest precaution necessarily *shifts* the burden towards defenders of risk-generating activities and away from protectors of the environment. This is because, in removing the burden of fully demonstrating risk from those who would regulate an activity for protection of human health or the environment, precaution enhances the impact of scientific evidence pointing to potential harms, which creates an incentive for defenders of risk-generating activities to respond by producing evidence of safety or discrediting evidence of harm. Associated with more aggressive formulations like the Wingspread Statement, however, are claims that the precautionary principle *reverses* the burden of proof, placing the onus of demonstrating safety with defenders of risk-generating activities. The question of whether and how the cost-effectiveness of alternative precautionary actions should be incorporated into deliberations is another where disagreement is common; whereas the requirement that precautionary actions be cost-effective is a prominent feature of Rio Principle 15 (and one attributed to the insistence of U.S. negotiators: see Sand, 2000), it is conspicuously absent from the stronger Wingspread Statement.

It is very important to distinguish precautionary deliberations from precautionary actions. During precautionary deliberations, all sorts of positions for or against particular actions can be advocated by holders of different stakes in risk-generating activities, but the precautionary principle is necessarily silent as to their merits: "a principle such as precaution cannot tell actors precisely what result they are to achieve, make distinctions between legal and illegal behaviour, or identify particular equilibrium points between competing sets of interests" (Ellis, 2001, p. 293). Answers to questions of whether and what measures should be taken are *not* contained in the principle, as these depend upon the specific issue as well as the decision process through which the consequences of possible actions are considered. Ultimately, "what [the precautionary principle] means in practice is a matter of negotiation between the stakeholders involved in deliberations about particular environmental problems" (Adams, 2002, p. 301).

As a result, application of the precautionary principle can result in and legitimize very different forms of action: "it can promote basic research and technological research and development; it can force the setting up of liability and compensation regimes; it can require the immediate investment in cleaner technologies through regulation; it can employ the use of economic measures such as state subsidies or taxation to 'internalize' externalities" (Adams, 2002, p. 303). This is not to say that the precautionary principle provides license for arbitrary action. Even strong advocates contend that precautionary actions should meet a set of criteria associated with general principles of risk management, as summarized in an influential *Communication on the Precautionary Principle* from the European Commission (2000, p. 3):

> Where action is deemed necessary, measures based on the precautionary principle should be, *inter alia*:
>
> - *proportional* to the chosen level of protection,
> - *non-discriminatory* in their application,
> - *consistent* with similar measures already taken,
> - *based on an examination of the potential benefits and costs* of action or lack of action (including, where appropriate and feasible, an economic cost/benefit analysis),
> - *subject to review*, in the light of new scientific data, and
> - *capable of assigning responsibility for the scientific evidence* necessary for a more comprehensive risk assessment.

Importantly, a decision not to act is a valid outcome of all precautionary deliberations, even those triggered by calls for aggressive precaution (see the Wingspread Statement, above). Thus, the direct impact of the precautionary principle is to trigger a deliberative process which *may* result in action. In other words, in situations of scientific uncertainty, the precautionary principle "facilitates and speeds up the process through which the questions of whether and what measures should be taken are put on the policy making agenda" (Maguire & Ellis, 2005, p. 508).

As compared to actions taken in regimes of modest or weak precaution, those in regimes of aggressive or strong precaution tend to be more restrictive of the risk-generating activity, taken earlier, and recommended with greater force—possibly mandated. Capturing well the continuum of precaution, Wiener and Rogers (2002, p. 320) argued that precaution can be conceptualized as a continuous variable where "on the time path over which a risk is forecast to become manifest, a regulation is more precautionary the earlier it takes effect and the more stringently it restricts the suspected source of the risk". Obviously, the broader implications of modest and aggressive precaution differ. In general, the former is compatible with traditional risk management practices and more protective of the status quo whereas the latter predicates greater social and institutional change (O'Riordan & Jordan, 1995).

ASPIRATIONS FOR AND CRITICISMS OF THE PRECAUTIONARY PRINCIPLE

Many environmentalists and other supporters of the precautionary principle see its scope as broad and have high expectations for its impact, including transformation of the relationship between society and the science-technology nexus. For example, Raffensperger, Schettler and Myers (2000,

p. 269) argued that precaution is "an overarching principle" that will "change the way we make decisions about technology"; in their view, not only will it "sit above risk assessment and all other tools in the regulatory tool box" to determine specific tools used, but it will offer "a chance to move precautionary decisions upstream and establish a precautionary, public interest research agenda". Some have even described advocates of precaution as a "social movement" (Myers, 2004), noting that the precautionary principle "has become the repository for a jumble of adventurous beliefs that challenge the status quo of political power, ideology and civil rights", and arguing that its coherence stems from the challenge it poses to "the authority of science, the hegemony of cost-benefit analysis, the powerlessness of victims of environmental abuse, and the unimplemented ethics of intrinsic natural rights and inter-generational equity" (O'Riordan & Jordan, 1995, p. 191). Precaution along with the ideas of sustainable development and global citizenship "have become metaphors for a global power play between the forces of what might be termed 'humanity'—namely caring for the well-being of others and the survival of the Earth via some sort of primordial Gaian urge—and the drive for material acquisition, economic security and efficiency in the conduct of human affairs"; in this way, precaution "is the voice of conscience and care set against strident demands for progress and prosperity" (O'Riordan & Jordan, 1995, p. 209). Popular accounts, at least in North America, generally reinforce this view, characterizing the precautionary principle as disruptive force with major economic consequences. For example, Pollan (2001, p. 92) informs readers of the *New York Times Magazine* that "the precautionary principle poses a radical challenge to business as usual in modern, capitalistic, technological civilization".

Unsurprisingly, then, like other social movements precaution has generated a counter-movement. Because precaution authorizes more government intervention to manage potential as well as demonstrated risks, some of the principle's most vocal critics come from the political right and think-tanks which promote free markets, such as the Cato Institute (see Goklany, 2001), the Competitive Enterprise Institute (see Miller & Conko, 2001) and the Institute of Economic Affairs (see Morris, 2001). Critics of precaution are self-conscious about engaging in struggle and do not mince words in characterizing their opponents; Miller and Conko (2001), for instance, claim that the principle is promoted by activists who are "more antibusiness and antitechnology than pro-safety". The main thrust of their accusations is that precaution results in outcomes that are inefficient in an economic sense. For example, Morris (2001, p. 8) warns that, when applied, "the precautionary principle becomes an excuse for arbitrary restrictions on technology" with "perverse effects". Miller and Conko (2001), writing of the "perils of precaution", argued that: it stifles innovation; it places undue restrictions on consumer options; and, because wealth correlates with health, in wasting scarce resources it endangers health. Precaution, their argument goes, is economically inefficient: "it distracts consumers and policy makers from known, significant threats to human health and diverts limited public health resources from those genuine and far greater risks". As a result, and notwithstanding those firms who have signed onto the United Nations' Global Compact or endorsed precaution in other arenas, when business weighs into the debate it is usually to argue against precaution. In North America, for example, the U.S. Chamber of Commerce,[6] which "has long supported the use of sound science, cost-benefit analysis, and risk assessment when assessing a particular regulatory issue", has among its objectives to "[e]nsure that regulatory decisions are based on scientifically sound and technically rigorous risk assessments, and oppose the adoption of the precautionary principle as the basis for regulation" as, in their view, precaution is something that "radical environmentalists are pushing for".

It is important to note, however, that not all criticism of the precautionary principle originates from these sources; a broad spectrum of scholars of risk analysis, policy and law have criticized precaution, not to mention those actors benefiting from risk-generating activities about which there is scientific uncertainty and which have been called into question as a result of invoking the precautionary principle. In addition to accusations that (1) it is economically inefficient (including stifling useful innovations), other critiques of precaution include: (2) it creates legal (Hickey & Walker, 1995) and business uncertainty (Diriwaechter, 2000); (3) it facilitates protectionism (Charlier &

Rainelli, 2002); and (4) "in practice, the precautionary principle politicizes decisions about risk under uncertainty" (Bernstein, 2002, p. 12).

These are all serious charges. We address them in various places throughout the rest of this chapter, showing that they are inaccurate or, at minimum, require nuancing. We make efforts, however, to ensure an even-handed treatment by addressing the limits of the precautionary principle and cautioning against unrealistic aspirations for it. In our view, although it does represent a political shift, which we discuss below, precaution heralds neither a utopic or dystopic future.

PRECAUTION AS POLICY CONTEXT: HOW THE NEW DISCOURSE OF PRECAUTION AFFECTS RISK MANAGEMENT

We begin by making distinctions between (1) precaution conceptualized broadly as a discourse; (2) precaution as a principle of risk management which triggers and guides deliberations by policy makers facing scientific uncertainty; and (3) precaution as those particular regulations and actions advocated during and/or flowing from deliberations triggered by invoking precaution as a principle. These map, more or less, to the context, process and (advocated and actual) outcomes of risk management decision making.

It is insightful to conceptualize precaution as a new discourse that has emerged among actors with interests in regulatory decisions to manage risks posed by contemporary technologies (Maguire & Hardy, 2006). A growing body of work adopts this frame to address "precautionary discourse" (Litfin, 1994; Litfin, 1995; Stirling, 1999) or "the discourse of precaution" (Andrée, 2005; Maguire & Hardy, 2006)—"a set of linguistic practices informed by this [precautionary] principle and embedded in a social network" (Litfin, 1995, p. 255)—which has at its core, but is not limited to, the precautionary principle.

The discourse of precaution is one that both reflects and reproduces our contemporary "risk society", a notion advanced by Beck (1992) to describe the most recent phase of modernization which, because it increasingly attends to human-produced risks which are by-products of economic development, is reflexive (for work linking precaution and risk society, see: Pieterman, 2001; Stirling, 2001; Richter, Berking & Muller-Schmid, 2006). Whereas the central focus in the governance and study of modern political economies has historically been the production and distribution of wealth, increasingly these concerns have been displaced by "the problems and conflicts that arise from the production, definition and distribution of techno-scientifically produced risks" (Beck, 1992, p. 19). Risks differ essentially from wealth. "One can possess wealth, but one can only be afflicted by risks" which "include systematic and often irreversible harm, generally remain invisible, are based on causal interpretations, and thus initially only exist in terms of the (scientific or anti-scientific) knowledge about them" and, because risks can be constructed and redefined, the mass media and the scientific and legal professions move into key social and political positions (Beck, 1992, p. 23). Social risk positions are formed because risk is not equally distributed in society consistent—a premise underlying the environmental justice movement. Often, in fact, risks generated by a particular activity or technology are not borne by those who invest in or otherwise benefit from it.

A discourse is a structured collection of texts, along with related practices of their production, distribution and consumption that, in accordance with social constructionist assumptions, bring phenomena into being (Fairclough, 1992; Parker, 1992). In other words, discourses—texts and discursive practices—"construct" rather than "reveal" phenomena (Phillips & Hardy, 2002); they "systematically form the object of which they speak" (Foucault 1979, p. 49) by creating the concepts and categories through which actors understand the world (Grant & Hardy, 2004). A given object, e.g. a risk-generating activity or technology, may have an independent material existence but it can only be understood with reference to concepts applied to it through a given discourse (Hardy & Phillips 1999). When actors participate in particular discourses, they are forced to take up one of a limited number of available subject positions (Parker, 1992) which position actors in relationship to each other and give them more or less rights to speak; some individuals "warrant voice" while others do not (Potter & Wetherell, 1987). Discourses also create "conditions of possibility" for different discursive formations—certain things can be said while others cannot—and these have power effects: "[a]s determinants of what can and cannot be thought, discourses define the range of policy options and operate as resources which empower certain actors and exclude others" (Litfin, 1995, p. 253).

This is well illustrated by Maguire and Hardy (2006) who compare the new discourse of precaution with the legacy regulatory discourse of "sound science" with which it is commonly contrasted by defenders of risk-generating activities (see Stirling, 1999; Stirling & Gee, 2002; van den Belt & Gremmen, 2002). They show how the discourses create very different conditions of possibility for what can be said about the risk-generating technologies or activities that are the objects they address, because they link these with different concepts and subject positions, as shown in Table 6.1.

The focal objects of both discourses are risk-generating activities and technologies. The discourse of sound science constructs the meaning of these as safe until it is demonstrated that they pose risks, while the discourse of precaution constructs their meaning as potentially dangerous and warranting attention at a lower threshold of evidence of harm. One reason for this is that the concept of scientific knowledge differs in the two discourses. Whereas the discourse of sound science constructs scientific knowledge as something that experts can state with relative certainty about risk-generating technologies and their impact on the environment, the discourse of precaution constructs scientific knowledge as uncertain and limited, foregrounding and emphasizing these features. Prior to the emergence and ascension of the precautionary principle, the prevailing assumption guiding

TABLE 6.1
Comparing Discourses for Regulating Risk-Generating Technologies*

Element of discourse	*Legacy discourse of sound science*	*New discourse of precaution*
Object	Risk-generating activities and technologies	Risk-generating activities and technologies
Key concepts	Sound scientific knowledge Demonstrated risk Risk assessment, analysis and management	Uncertain, limited scientific knowledge Potential risk Risk avoidance in addition to risk assessment, analysis and management
Key subject positions	Scientific experts supply hard facts to the policy process. Governments are arbiters of demonstrated risks and benefits; they trigger policy conversations and regulate accordingly. Non-government organizations can legitimately voice concerns about demonstrated risks. Business organizations respond to concerns about demonstrated risks.	Scientific experts supply soft, contested claims to the policy process. Governments are arbiters of potential risks and benefits; they trigger policy conversations and regulate accordingly. Non-government organizations can legitimately voice concerns about potential risks Business organizations respond to concerns about potential risks.
Conditions of possibility	*"Scientific uncertainty justifies inaction"* is a valid discursive construction for governments and those seeking to influence them. *"This product is associated with that risk"* is a valid discursive construction for scientific experts, and is more likely to come later rather than earlier.	*"Scientific uncertainty justifies inaction"* is *not* a valid discursive construction for governments or those seeking to influence them. It is explicitly ruled out by the precautionary principle (see Principle 15 of Rio Declaration). *"This product is associated with that risk"* is a valid discursive construction for other actors in addition to scientific experts, and is more likely to come earlier rather than later.

* The table has been adapted from Maguire & Hardy (2006: 15).

regulatory policy making was that the environment was capable of absorbing pollutants, exploitation of resources and other forms of interference up to some knowable assimilative capacity (Hey, 1992). However, the public's and governments' experiences of scientific fallibility in numerous issue areas, from fisheries (mis)management to the (non)regulation of toxic substances, have meant that these assumptions have been shaken. It has become uncomfortably apparent to policy makers and citizens alike that scientists may not be capable of identifying safe levels of resource exploitation or pollution. For example, MacDonald (1995, p. 273) noted that "the emergence of the precautionary principle in fisheries management is in part a response to the increased frustration within the international community at past failures of fisheries management", stating that "perhaps the greatest of these failures was the inability to act in the face of uncertainty." Because it acknowledges and foregrounds the limitations and uncertainty of scientific knowledge, the precautionary concept stands in direct contrast to the assimilative capacity concept which is at the core of the sound science discourse. Hey's (1992, p. 308, footnotes omitted) comparison of the world before and after the emergence and ascendance of the discourse of precaution is instructive:

> The assimilative capacity concept emphasizes: 1) the carrying capacity of the environment; 2) the ability of science to accurately predict threats to the environment and the measures needed to prevent such threats; 3) the availability of technical possibilities to mitigate threats once they have been accurately predicted; and 4) the reliance on short-term economic considerations, while emphasizing the unreliability of long-term economic considerations and the uncertainties involved in determining the present value of future environmental degradation.

This stands in contrast to precaution:

> The precautionary concept advocates a shift away from the primacy of scientific proof and traditional economic analyses that do not account for environmental degradation. Instead, emphasis is placed on: 1) the vulnerability of the environment; 2) the limitations of science to accurately predict threats to the environment, and the measures required to prevent such threats; 3) the availability of alternatives (both methods of production and products) which permit the termination or minimization of inputs into the environment; and 4) the need for long-term, holistic economic considerations, accounting for, among other things, environmental degradation and the costs of waste treatment.

Thus, the discourse of precaution, with the precautionary principle at its core, highlights the limits and shortcomings of science; it "fills the vacuum created by a science that continually searches for certainty but which continually fails to deliver" (Adams, 2002, p. 311).

Related, a second key concept is risk. The discourse of sound science stresses the importance of accurately assessing and demonstrating risk prior to government intervention whereas the discourse of precaution draws attention to potential and uncertain risks and how these also merit societal deliberations about possible government intervention. A third concept for which the discourses differ relates to ways of dealing with risk. Although some advocates of precaution distinguish it from risk management (see Raffensperger, Schettler & Myers, 2000) a conceptual integration of precaution and risk management is increasingly common (for example, see EC, 2000): "viewing the precautionary principle as part of a process for making provisional decisions about risk management under uncertainty would reduce criticism from its more fervent critics or advocates for more extreme interpretations of it" (Foster, Vecchia & Repacholi, 2000, p. 979). Nonetheless, although both discourses are associated with risk management (Maguire & Ellis, 2003), the discourse of precaution is also associated with the more aggressive concept of risk *avoidance* and the associated shift in values that this stance towards risk reflects. Capturing precisely this shift in values, MacDonald (1995) characterized precaution as "ethical evolution" notable for its explicit recognition and incorporation into decision-making of ethical ideals from both utilitarian and natural rights philosophies.

As a result, the discourses are associated with different subject positions, summarized in Table 6.1. Whereas the legacy discourse of sound science privileges scientific experts, seen to deliver hard facts to the policy process, the position of experts is somewhat diminished in the discourse of precaution because the latter foregrounds the uncertainty and limitations of their knowledge and provides for a greater role of the public who can legitimately voice concerns about risk-generating technologies on the basis of a lower threshold of evidence. Governments are also seen differently; with sound science, they manage—and are called upon to arbitrate conflicts over—demonstrated risks but with precaution they must engage in the management and arbitration of *potential* or uncertain risks. As a result, whereas in a regime of sound science business is called upon only infrequently to defend their risk-generating activities and technologies, in a precautionary regime business is called upon to defend its risk-generating activities and technologies more frequently and earlier (Maguire & Hardy, 2006).

Like any discourse, precaution has consequences in terms of power relations but these are often misunderstood, in our view. Whereas critics accuse the precautionary principle of politicizing decision-making, a preferable interpretation is that the discourse of precaution represents, as compared to the legacy discourse of sound science, a loss of "non-decision making power"—a "second face of power" related to agenda-setting and exercised when actors devote energy to "creating or reinforcing social and political values and institutional practices that limit the scope of the political process to public consideration of only those issues which are comparatively innocuous" (Bachrach & Baratz, 1962, p. 948)—by actors who formerly benefited from societal inertia and "nondecision-making" in situations of scientific uncertainty (Maguire & Ellis, 2003). As Maguire and Hardy (2006, p. 17) described, "by foregrounding the limitations of scientific knowledge and emphasizing the concept of potential risk", the discourse of precaution makes it "easier to trigger action at an earlier stage and directly challenge the validity of non-decision making and inaction". Consequently, rather than being seen to politicize decision making, the precautionary principle is more accurately viewed as rendering the inherently political nature of risk management more explicit; it highlights distributive and allocative consequences of action (i.e. decision making) *and* inaction (i.e. nondecision-making in the inertial sense, as well as decision-making that results in a decision not to act) (Maguire & Ellis, 2003). Precaution thus provides resources for those who invoke it in "discursive struggle" (Hardy & Phillips, 1999) over the existence, level and acceptability of a given risk. In this way, precaution is a key feature of resistance in risk society, by those who have or would have uncertain risks imposed upon them (Maguire, 2006).

PRECAUTION AS POLICY PROCESS: HOW THE PRECAUTIONARY PRINCIPLE GENERATES MORE AND ALTERS RISK MANAGEMENT

By lowering the threshold of scientific knowledge required to trigger deliberations about taking actions (or not) to manage risks, the precautionary principle challenges and generates more risk management work for policy makers (Maguire & Ellis, 2003), encouraging them to avoid the "paralysis of uncertainty" (McIntyre & Mosedale, 1997). Because potential in addition to demonstrated risks must be managed when applying the precautionary principle, more risk management work results.

Additionally, the nature of this risk management work is altered: (1) "as compared to risk management contexts with less uncertain science, precautionary deliberations will be associated with more scientific uncertainty and therefore potentially more policy uncertainty" (Maguire & Ellis, 2003, p. 43); (2) precautionary risk management tends to be more participatory and transparent as compared to regulatory decision making prior to precaution (see Bäckstrand, 2004; Löfstedt, 2004; Saltelli & Funtowicz, 2004); and, consequently, (3) more overt political struggle is to be expected, including around cost-benefit analysis (O'Riordan & Jordan, 1995).

All risk management involves acting under conditions of uncertainty, because risk necessarily involves an element of contingency. As Klinke and Renn (2001, p. 159) put it, risk involves "the distinction between reality and possibility", and has both descriptive and normative aspects: descriptive in that risk involves some event that may or may not be realized; and normative in that the occurrence of this event is evaluated negatively, compelling actors to make choices about what type of future they want as well as how they should work to attain it. Generally speaking, an important function of the precautionary principle is the redistribution of the burden of scientific uncertainty (Maguire & Ellis, 2002; Maguire & Ellis, 2005) through the translation of descriptive uncertainties into normative ones. When the precautionary principle is invoked to trigger deliberations, "uncertainty about impacts on human health and the environment is initially *translated* into uncertainty about the value of industrial assets linked to the potential harms that triggered precautionary deliberations"; in other words, scientific uncertainty is translated into policy and economic uncertainty (Maguire & Ellis, 2005, p. 518). Whereas in a non-precautionary regime, the burden of scientific uncertainty it borne by vulnerable populations of humans and/or other species exposed to potential hazards, in a precautionary regime, it is more likely that issue entrepreneurs representing the interests of vulnerable populations can trigger precautionary deliberations because of the lower threshold of evidence of risk required. Because these deliberations are unlikely to be trivial, there will be uncertainty as to their outcomes. But the precautionary principle does not create a new kind of policy uncertainty; rather, it is the kind generated by all risk management decision making, because outcomes depend upon the particular configuration of actors, interests and values brought together during deliberations. Maguire and Ellis (2003) pointed out that this increase in policy and economic uncertainty is perhaps what leads some actors to experience precaution as an injection of politics into the risk management process, a common but unfair criticism of the principle as, strictly speaking, this is not the case: risk management decision making—and, importantly, non-decision making—is inherently political.

In addition to greater uncertainty, Löfstedt (2004) pointed out that the increased levels of stakeholder participation and transparency associated with precautionary deliberations can also pose new challenges for risk managers. Although participation and transparency can lead to stakeholders having more trust in policy processes and more ownership of policy outcomes, they can also lead to more distrust (Lofstedt, 2003). This is because greater participation and transparency make scientific pluralism and dissent more apparent to the public than they might otherwise be (Lofstedt, 2004), and can also create policy vacuums (Powell & Leiss, 1997) in which regulators, without having all information relevant to a policy problem let alone its solution, lose control of an issue and cede the regulatory agenda to other stakeholders advancing their own narrow priorities and interests. The greater scientific uncertainty associated with precautionary policy deliberations aggravates this tendency.

Another challenge of increased transparency and greater participation by stakeholders is managing the clash of interests and perspectives, and this is well illustrated by struggles over cost-benefit analysis, an ostensibly neutral, scientific tool. Answers to the question of whether the benefits of precaution justify its costs are, however, unlikely to generate consensus. (It should be noted that, even if all stakeholders could agree on costs and benefits, it is nonetheless highly unlikely that precautionary deliberations would become depoliticized, technical or so-called rational exercises in decision-making because they deal inevitably with distributive issues (Maguire & Ellis, 2003); in risk conflicts, it is just as or even more likely that the question of an acceptable *distribution* of costs and benefits will not generate consensus as the question of whether benefits exceed costs when comparing alternative precautionary actions.) One reason for this is that, although cost-benefit analysis works relatively well for assessing readily quantifiable factors which can be expressed in comparable units—costs of production, number of jobs lost or created, and so forth—its utility for more qualitative questions such as impacts on human health, the beauty of a landscape or the value of a population of animals or plants is debatable.

When cost-benefit analysis is applied to environmental policy-making, three possible avenues exist for taking into account qualitative factors. The first possibility is simply to exclude them from the analysis on the basis that they cannot be objectively measured. The second is to use proxies to represent their value. Thus, impacts on human health can be rendered in terms of costs of health care, payouts on insurance policies, loss of salaries, days of work lost to illness, etc. Similarly, impacts on the environment could be calculated with reference, for example, to the amount that an individual would be willing to pay to preserve a natural landscape. The third possibility is to introduce both qualitative and quantitative factors into cost-benefit analysis on their own terms without attempting to reduce them to a single metric—an approach that sometimes provokes the objection that it introduces subjective, arbitrary and political considerations into the decision-making process of making trade-offs. However, it must be observed that the first two approaches do not banish political considerations from decision-making; they simply displace them. The decision to exclude certain kinds of costs and benefits from consideration is a political decision, and the various proxies that might be used to impute a monetary value to non-commercial goods such as a beautiful landscape or a species of no commercial interest are necessarily normative judgments. Further complicating matters, the contexts of scientific uncertainty in which precautionary deliberations occur mean that policy makers must arbitrate between competing descriptive claims in addition to competing normative ones as, like the public, they too must reach conclusions within an environment characterized by scientific pluralism and contestation—another political act. A final complication occurs because alternative precautionary actions may themselves be characterized by uncertainty as to their precise consequences or associated with other risks. In other words, to avoid, minimize or otherwise manage the specific risks initially triggering precautionary deliberations may entail the acceptance of other ones which, if policy makers are to be consistent, also need to be addressed with precaution; such "risk tradeoffs" (Graham & Wiener, 1995), challenging in and of themselves, are rendered more difficult by uncertainty, ambiguity and contestation. For all these reasons, as O'Riordan and Jordan (1995, p. 202) underlined, "any cost-benefit decision rule therefore is likely to be intensely political, not purely financial".[7] All in all, therefore, the precautionary principle makes more risk management work for policy makers, and of a more challenging nature.

PRECAUTION AS POLICY OUTCOME: HOW THE PRECAUTIONARY PRINCIPLE HAS AN IMPACT IN LAW

We begin this discussion with some comments on what the precautionary principle, as a general principle, does *not* do in the law. Despite claims to the contrary by promoters of aggressive precaution, application of the precautionary principle does not impose a reversal of the burden of proving that an activity or technology poses no or minimal risks—an impossible burden, since one cannot prove a negative. Interpreted as such, the principle would make it difficult to legally pursue virtually any activity. This is not to say, however, that as an outcome of precautionary deliberations policy makers cannot decide to shift the burden of demonstrating safety in large part or in whole to the defenders of a risk-generating activity in situations, for example, where an activity poses potentially severe risks while yielding insignificant benefits or benefits achievable through alternative means of comparable cost. But precaution as a general principle implies no such reversal of the burden of proof. Nor, indeed, does it impose a positive obligation to take any specific regulatory steps (von Moltke, 1996); invoking the precautionary principle does not obligate regulators to ban risk-generating activities, and precautionary deliberations can result in a wide range of precautionary actions, as discussed above.

As a general principle of law, therefore, precaution is best understood as a procedural rather than a substantive principle. Regulators of risk-generating activities to which the precautionary principle is to be applied are reminded that it is inappropriate to wait until risks manifest themselves before taking action. As a result, almost inevitably this points in the direction of obligations of information-gathering prior to deliberation, debate and decision-making on possible regulatory interventions.

Depending upon how precaution is incorporated into an individual legal regime, as a specific legal rule it can either narrow or broaden the scope of regulatory discretion by (a) creating obligations to take particular types of regulatory action when certain triggering conditions are met; or (b) authorizing decision-makers to make decisions in ways that go beyond mechanistic responses to predetermined thresholds or triggers. An example of the former is the 1995 Agreement for the Implementation of the Provisions of the United Nations Convention on the Law of the Sea of 10

December 1992 relating to the Conservation and Management of Straddling Fish Stocks and Highly Migratory Fish Stocks (Fish Stocks Agreement), which incorporates the precautionary principle into the process through which exploitation limits are established for individual fisheries. The Fish Stocks Agreement applies to high seas fisheries, where the problem of establishing sustainable exploitation levels is an extremely complex one, requiring reference not only to the lifespan, fertility rates and reproductive cycles of individual species but also to myriad other factors in the ecosystems of which these fish are a part, and about which scientific knowledge is often quite limited. The response of the international community in the form of the Fish Stocks Agreement has been to establish population thresholds which, when approached, trigger certain policy responses. The first threshold, known as the target reference point, represents a level of exploitation that, taking into account uncertainties, is deemed sustainable. The second, the limit reference point, represents a point at which the sustainability of the stock is deemed to be threatened. Regulators charged with establishing exploitation levels are to ensure that the target reference point, while approached and perhaps reached in a given season, is never surpassed. If this threshold is approached very near to the beginning of a fishing season, this is an indication that catch quotas were set too high—a situation for which a variety of regulatory interventions can then be justified, such as reductions or suspensions of quotas or early closure of the fishing season. If the target reference point is surpassed and the limit reference point approached, more drastic regulatory responses are authorized such as fisheries moratoria.

An example of the latter is the 2001 Stockholm Convention on Persistent Organic Pollutants (POPs) which contains a provision for adding new chemicals "in a precautionary manner" to its lists of substances to be banned or restricted.[8] Although the Convention specifies precise technical screening criteria meant to assess a chemical's propensity to be persistent and to bio-accumulate into greater concentrations in animals higher up food chains, these are to be applied "in a flexible and transparent way, taking all information provided into account in an integrative and balanced manner", and parties to the Convention, not technical experts, make final decisions. As a result, the listing of additional chemicals is "a process involving 'grey areas' of judgment and negotiation of parties to the Convention rather than 'black and white' calculations by technical experts" (Maguire & Ellis, 2003, p. 40).

One of the best ways to identify the legal implications of the precautionary principle is to examine how it operates when confronted with potentially contradictory rules or principles. Such a situation occurs in the field of international trade law, and most specifically in the interaction between the precautionary principle and the Agreement for Sanitary and Phytosanitary Measures (the SPS Agreement). This agreement, concluded under the auspices of the World Trade Organisation (WTO), applies to domestic environmental and human health measures in WTO member states that have an impact on international flows of goods. Thus, for example, a domestic regulation banning sales of a product containing a particular hazardous substance would fall under the rubric of the SPS Agreement, since the regulation would have implications for importation of such products. The SPS Agreement seeks to establish a balance between (a) the rights of sovereign states, recognized in article 2, to establish for themselves the acceptability of particular risks and to introduce environmental and human health measures accordingly; and (b) the goal of trade liberalization. The SPS Agreement establishes criteria against which environmental and human health measures are to be evaluated in order to determine whether they are necessary to achieve stated ends. The question is whether a precautionary measure, that is, a measure implemented to control a risk about which there is scientific uncertainty, can be deemed necessary and therefore justifiable under the meaning of the Agreement.

This issue has been squarely raised on two occasions, both involving measures adopted by the European Community (EC). The first measure involved a ban on importations of hormone-treated beef from Canada and the United States on the ground of potential risks to human health (GATT 1997; Bohanes 1998; Hurst 1998; McNeil, 1998). The second involved a moratorium on importations of food products containing genetically modified products (GATT 2001; Peel, Nelson & Godden, 2005; Scherzberg 2006). Both measures were found to be incompatible with the EC's obligations under the SPS Agreement, and the EC's argument that precaution should be interpreted to condition and qualify the obligation in the SPS Agreement generally was rejected. Despite these apparent setbacks for precaution, these decisions certainly do not close the door to precautionary measures under the SPS Agreement, and indeed they leave much about the relationship between precaution and the WTO unclear.

Precaution is incorporated into the SPS Agreement, to some extent, in article 5(7), which permits states to adopt provisional measures "in cases where relevant scientific information is insufficient." Furthermore, if domestic measures are compatible with international environment and health standards, they are deemed necessary within the meaning of the agreement. What remains unclear is the scope that states have to adopt precautionary measures on a unilateral basis on the ground that potential risks—risks subject to scientific uncertainty—are deemed by the population and by policy makers to be unacceptable.

One of the key functions of the precautionary principle is to underline the political aspects of decision-making about environmental risks. Science is a fundamentally important part of such decision-making, but, as underlined above, while it *contributes* to this process it cannot *drive* it. The question raised by the SPS Agreement itself, and by WTO decisions relating to the agreement, is whether regulating states are obliged to justify measures on a scientific basis, or whether they can refer as well to assessments by policy makers, informed both by science and by public consultations, that the potential risks are unacceptable and that measures are therefore warranted (Bohanes 1998). The compatibility of precautionary measures with obligations under the SPS Agreement hinges on the meaning to be given to the notion of measures *necessary* to protect environment and health. This could be taken to mean that regulating states would have to demonstrate that environmental and health impacts would *certainly* result in the absence of measures. Alternately, it might mean that states can regulate to prevent risks as well as certain outcomes, but that those risks must be demonstrated based on scientific evidence. A third possible interpretation is that states must demonstrate that the measures are taken in light of real concerns about health or environmental risk for which there is a scientific basis. In line with this third interpretation, Bohanes (1998) argued for a procedural approach to determining the compatibility of a precautionary environmental or health measures with the SPS Agreement, in which regulating states are to demonstrate that scientific evidence was carefully considered and taken into consideration, but would not require the state to await scientific proof of the necessity of the measure before proceeding.

The larger question raised by the debate over precaution and the SPS Agreement is whether precaution and trade liberalization are compatible; whether, in short, the WTO needs to keep the precautionary principle at bay in order to realize its trade objectives. If one concludes that only those policy measures are justifiable that are based on clear scientific evidence of a not insignificant risk of harm (or some higher threshold), then precautionary measures will have at least a whiff of protectionism about them. However, WTO jurisprudence reveals that dispute settlement panels have various ways of distinguishing measures taken for genuine policy purposes and those taken for protectionist measures, without requiring that the regulating state prove the necessity of its measures in light of policy objectives deemed legitimate or acceptable. As a result, the process of reconciling precaution and international trade law is ongoing.

PRECAUTION AND RISK COMMUNICATION: SOME REFLECTIONS

To date, a relatively small amount of research has explicitly explored the implications of the precautionary principle for risk communication (see, for example, Biocca, 2004; Löfstedt, 2004; Goldstein, 2005), although it should be stressed that the larger and rapidly growing literature on whether and how the precautionary principle is compatible with risk management often addresses risk communication issues, if implicitly. In this section, we draw upon this emerging body of work as well as our introduction and discussion of the precautionary principle, above, to reflect upon the implications of precaution for risk communication.

As with risk management policy making, the precautionary principle makes for more risk communication, and of a more challenging nature. First, since under precautionary decision-making uncertain risks are not being ignored, precaution generates additional work for risk communicators: there are simply more risks, actual and potential, that are deemed of interest to members of the public. But, given the goals of precaution, it is possible that this extra work may be compensated by less crisis communication. In other words, if more precautionary risk communication and the taking of precautionary actions are effective, less crisis communication should be required, as serious and irreversible threats will be avoided. Additionally, if somewhat ironically, it appears that risk communicators also have the extra burden of communicating about the precautionary principle itself—what it is, what it is not, when it is to be applied, what its implications are, etc.—as there is a lot of misunderstanding as a result of ongoing contestation around the precautionary concept by holders of different stakes in risk conflicts.

Second, effective communication of a risk that is uncertain, as compared to a well understood risk, is a much more complex and difficult undertaking—one that is subject to misunderstandings that have both pragmatic and ethical aspects (Fong, Rempel, & Hall, 1999). The manner in which one proceeds to communicate information about an uncertain risk will, of course, depend on what the purpose of risk communication is understood to be: risk communication as a persuasion technique aimed at convincing listeners of the correctness of a given point of view, perhaps combined with the aim of having them to change their attitudes or behaviours (Leiss, 1996; Renn, 1998; Biocca, 2004); risk communication as information transmitted, perhaps because stakeholders have a right to it (Biocca, 2004), with the intent of ensuring that receivers understand its meaning and are empowered to act upon it in ways that they themselves judge appropriate (Renn, 1998); and risk communication as a condition for advantageous dialogue (Biocca, 2004) and learning (Leiss, 1996), often serving as a means to resolve risk conflicts (Renn, 1998).

One way to understand the purpose of risk communication is to view it as essentially an exercise in marketing: a policy decision has been reached, and the policy maker wishes not only to inform the public about the decision but also convince them that the decision is sound (Biocca, 2004). This approach is often based on an assumption that not only the data generated by risk assessments but also that the results of risk evaluation and management are objective and incontrovertible. Alternately, another common assumption is that a determination of the acceptability of a risk is a matter for experts as members of the public are not appropriately skilled, knowledgeable or to be trusted to make appropriate or sound determinations (see Jasanoff [1998] on the psychometric paradigm of risk perception). Such an approach is in many respects antithetical to the precautionary principle. Precaution reminds us that decisions about risks, and particularly about uncertain risks, involve processes of interpretation, weighing of alternatives and judgment that are inherently political. The judgment of one person, whether that person is an expert or a lay person, cannot be substituted for that of another. Therefore, the public requires information about risks, uncertain and certain, in a form that permits them to reach their own conclusions about the acceptability of the risk.

Precaution, therefore, appears to be more compatible with the second approach, where risk communication "empowers recipients to make confident risk-relevant decisions" (Fong et al., 1999: 173). With its emphasis on transparency, this approach favors the transmission of as much information as possible, including information about levels of scientific uncertainty, to members of the public. This approach is not paternalistic, but it may go too far in the other direction. Even if we agree that members of the public are entitled to make their own decisions about acceptability of risk and the levels of exposure to risk with which they are comfortable, it is not at all guaranteed that the simple transfer of information will achieve this goal. Despite efforts at ensuring that scientific data is presented in an accessible form, members of the public may nonetheless feel overwhelmed by this mass of information, and may not be equipped to incorporate it into sound decision-making processes. The uncertainty associated with the focal risks of precautionary deliberations acerbates this. As a result, this approach can be complemented by explicit recognition of a need to provide guidance in interpreting and evaluating the information they receive, while seeking to avoid paternalism: the fact that people may struggle with scientific information about actual and potential risks is not a good reason to deprive them of such information, but rather a good reason to devise processes and mechanisms to help members of the public deal with the information.

Continuing in this interactive direction, the precautionary principle appears to be most compatible with the third approach to risk communication—a dialogic approach through which stakeholders, including both experts and lay persons, are brought together in discussions about risk (see Jasanoff [1998] on the constructivist approach to risk perception), typically with the aim of resolving conflicts. Risk communication, intimately connected to processes of discussion, debate, deliberation and decision of risk management, requires discussions among stakeholders; as Maguire and Ellis (2003, p. 45) point out, "precautionary deliberations involving affected stakeholders are essentially conversations about appropriate levels and distributions of risks (and benefits)". The simple transfer of information on risk will not necessarily help members of the public make intelligent and informed decisions: individuals benefit from dialogue with scientists and policy makers as they seek to understand the risk which they may be facing and to make decisions about how to react to those potential risks. But it is also because scientists and policy makers engaged in risk communication benefit from inputs from stakeholders. Precautionary risk communication is therefore usefully seen as a dialogic process which involves two-way communication and not the unidirectional transfer of information (Biocca, 2004).

Finally, building on the theme of interaction, it is possible that the precautionary principle heralds a new era in risk communication—one that goes beyond dialogic and bilateral flows of messages to conceive of risk communication as a highly multilateral process. Precautionary deliberations—"conversations about appropriate levels and distributions of risks (and benefits)" (Maguire & Ellis, 2003, p. 45)—must necessarily include a range of stakeholders in addition to risk-communicating policy makers and the receivers of their messages who presumably bear the burden of uncertain risks, such as those with an interest in the risk-generating activity. Maguire (2006) argued that, because a larger class of risks imposed on vulnerable stakeholders are now, with the precautionary principle, more easily and quickly translated back into business risks for the firms generating them, the application of a risk management logic *within* firms should lead to an increase in importance of the function of stakeholder management; for businesses selling or using or otherwise benefiting from risk-generating technologies, the management of stakeholder relations—including risk communication—becomes a key strategic competence. Others have drawn similar conclusions, arguing that the precautionary principle "provides opportunities for improved relationships and partnerships with a risk-averse public which allows the firm to incorporate public concerns into decision-making processes, thus enhancing corporate image" (Tickner & Raffensperger, 1998, p. 81). We can thus expect more conversations amongst holders of different stakes in risk conflicts. Regardless of whether one is an arbitrator of, a policy maker for, or a holder of stakes in a risk conflict, the precautionary principle makes for more, and more challenging, risk communication.

CONCLUSION

In this chapter, we have drawn from a wide range of academic literature to establish the central role of the precautionary principle for risk communication scholars. More specifically, we have introduced the precautionary principle; summarized contemporary debates surrounding its role in the management of risks about which there is scientific uncertainty; discussed its application in policy making and the law; and reflected upon its implications for risk communication. We have shown that the precautionary principle, which is at the core of the broader discourse of precaution, does indeed herald a political shift—one which has emerged from a more humble conception of science and changed values in respect to the environment, including when and how policies should be made and action taken to protect it. Contradicting a popular accusation against it, however, we have shown that the precautionary principle does not politicize decisions about risk; rather, it renders the inherently political nature of risk management more explicit, highlighting the distributive consequences of both action *and* inaction.

Does invoking the precautionary principle generate policy and business uncertainty? Yes, but we have argued that this sort of uncertainty is not novel and no more undesirable or deserving of additional consideration in moral calculations as to its acceptability than the scientific uncertainty as to the existence, nature and level of risks borne by those vulnerable peoples and species exposed to the unintended consequences of modern technologies that precedes and motivates precaution; the precautionary principle redistributes the burden of scientific uncertainty about risks, triggering and democratizing societal deliberations as to whether and how to respond to it. And, under certain circumstances, the precautionary principle is efficient in an economic sense, although we have also underlined that reaching any conclusion about efficiency is itself a political act, given the uncertainty, ambiguity and other forms of incertitude which characterize contexts in which the principle is invoked. Although it does represent a political gain for those stakeholders who would bear the burden of exposure to uncertain risks in situations of non-decision making, the precautionary principle heralds neither a utopic or dystopic future for any stakeholder or society in general; it does, however, make for more risk management and risk communication challenges.

ACKNOWLEDGMENTS

The authors thankfully acknowledge the financial support of the Social Sciences and Humanities Research Council of Canada, les Fonds pour la Formation des Chercheurs et l'Aide à la Recherche du Québec, the Desautels Faculty of Management, Faculty of Law, and School of Environment at McGill University in carrying out this research.

NOTES

1. Precaution has been incorporated into a range of conventions on marine environmental protection (Convention on the Protection of the Marine Environment of the Baltic Sea Area, 1992, the Convention for the Protection of the Marine Environment of the North-East Atlantic, 1992, and the 1996 Protocol to the Convention on the Prevention of Marine Pollution by Dumping of Wastes and Other Matter, 1972); protection of the global atmosphere (Framework Convention on Climate Change, 1992 and Montréal Protocol on Substances that Deplete the Ozone Layer, 1987); fisheries conservation and management (Agreement for the Implementation of the Provisions of the United Nations Convention on the Law of the Sea of 10 December 1982 relating to the Conservation and Management of Straddling Fish Stocks and Highly Migratory Fish Stocks, 1995, Convention on the Conservation and Management of Fishery Resources in the South-East Atlantic Ocean, 2001 (not yet in force); Convention on the Conservation and Management of Highly Migratory Fish Stocks in the Western and Central Pacific Ocean, 2000 (not yet in force); biological diversity (Convention on Biological Diversity, 1992; Cartagena Protocol on Biosafety, 2000) and global regulation of chemicals (Stockholm Convention on Persistent Organic Pollutants, 2001).
2. Reference to precaution is found at art. 5(7) of the Agreement on Sanitary and Phytosanitary Measures (1994). Precaution has twice been invoked by the European Community in trade disputes litigated within the WTO, in cases relating to bans on hormone-treated beef and genetically modified products.
3. This provision, art. 174 para. 2 of the consolidated text, appears in Title XIX: Environment: "Community policy on the environment shall aim at a high level of protection taking into account the diversity of situations in the various regions of the Community. It shall be based on the precautionary principle and on the principles that preventive action should be taken, that environmental damage should as a priority be rectified at source and that the polluter should pay." See da Cruz Vilaça (2004); Christforou (2003).
4. As an alternative to "modest" and "aggressive", some writers distinguish between "weak" and "strong" precaution (O'Riordan & Jordan, 1995). Because this latter pair of terms lends itself to pejorative interpretations, we have opted to emphasize the former, invoking the latter less frequently and usually in reference to work employing those terms.
5. The name derives from the Wingspread Conference Center in Racine, Wisconsin where the Science and Environmental Health Network, a consortium of North American non-governmental organizations, hosted a 1998 conference whose participants endorsed precaution.

6. See: http://www.uschamber.com/issues/index/regulatory/precautionaryprinciple.htm, accessed 7 November 2006.
7. This is not to say that formal analyses of the economics and, in particular, economic efficiency of precaution are impossible. See Gollier, Jullien & Treich (2000), Gollier (2001), Gollier & Treich (2003) for a discussion of those conditions under which the precautionary principle is an efficient economic guideline. See Mabey (1998) for a critique of the approach. Because other types of incertitude (Stirling, 1999) beyond the formal uncertainty with which economists and risk analysts are comfortable are so integral to applying the precautionary principle in practice—ambiguity, ignorance, etc.—our view is that political issues will tend to overwhelm economic ones.
8. Art. 8(7). of Convention on Persistent Organic Pollutants, 22 May 2001, 40 I.L.M. 532.

REFERENCES

Adams, M.D. (2002) 'The Precautionary Principle and the Rhetoric Behind It', *Journal of Risk Research* 5.4: 301–316.

Andrée, P. (2005) 'The Cartegena Protocol on Biosafety and Shifts in the Discourse of Precaution', *Global Environmental Politics*, 5(4): 25–46.

Bachrach, P., and Baratz, M.S. (1962) 'The Two Faces of Power', *American Political Science Review,* 56: 947–952.

Bäckstrand, K. (2004) 'Scientisation vs. Civic Expertise in Environmental Governance. Ecofeminist, Ecomodernist and Postmodernist Responses' *Environmental Politics,* 13(4): 695–714.

Beck, U. (1992) *Risk Society* (London: Sage).

Bernstein, S. (2002) 'Liberal Environmentalism and Global Environmental Governance', *Global Environmental Politics,* 2(3): 1–16.

Biocca, M. (2004) 'Risk Communication and the Precautionary Principle', *International Journal of Occupational Medicine and Environmental Health,* 17(1): 197–201.

Bohanes, J. (1998) 'Risk Regulation in WTO Law: A Procedure-Based Approach to the Precautionary Principle', *Columbia Journal of Transnational Law,* 40: 323.

Charlier, C. and Rainelli, M. (2002) 'Hormones, Risk Management, Precaution and Protectionism: An Analysis of the Dispute on Hormone-Treated Beef between the European Union and the United States', *European Journal of Law and Economics,* 14(2): 83.

Christforou, T. (2003) 'The Precautionary Principle and Democratizing Expertise: A European Legal Perspective', *Science and Public Policy,* 30(3):205.

da Cruz Vilaça, J.L. (2004) 'The Precautionary Principle in EC Law', *European Public Law,* 10(2):369.

de Sadeleer, N. (2002) *Environmental Principles: From Political Slogans to Legal Rules* (Oxford: Oxford).

Dickson, B. (1999) 'The Precautionary Principle in CITES: A critical assessment', *Natural Resources Journal,* 39(2): 211–228.

Diriwaechter, G. (2000) 'The Precautionary Approach: An Industrial Perspective', *Science in Parliament* 57(4): 6–8.

EC (2000) *Communication from the Commission on the Precautionary Principle* [COM(2000) 1 final: 2.2.2000] (Brussels: European Commission).

Ellis, J. (2001) 'The Straddling Stocks Agreement and the Precautionary Principle as Interpretive Device and Rule of Law', *Ocean Development & International Law,* 32: 289–311.

Ellis, J. (2006) 'Overexploitation of a Valuable Resource? New Literature on the Precautionary Principle', *European Journal of International Law,* 17.2: 445–462.

Fairclough, N. (1992) *Discourse and Social Change* (Cambridge, UK: Polity Press).

Fong, G.T., Rempel, L.A. and Hall, P.A. (1999) 'Challenges to Improving Health Risk Communication in the 21st Century: A Discussion', *Journal of the National Cancer Institute Monographs,* 25: 173–176.

Foster, K.R., Vecchia, P. and Repacholi, M.H. (2000, May 12) 'Science and the Precautionary Principle', *Science* 288: 979–981

Foucault, M. (1979) *Discipline and Punish: The Birth of the Prison* (London, UK: Penguin).

Freestone, D. (1991) 'The Precautionary Principle' in R. Churchill and D. Freestone (eds.) *International Law and Global Climate Change* (London: Graham and Trotman/Martinus Nijhoff): 21–39.

Freestone, D. and Hey, E. (1996) *The Precautionary Principle in International Law: The Challenge of Implementation* (The Hague: Kluwer).

GATT Appellate Body Report (2001) *EC Measures concerning Meat and Meat Products (Hormones),* GATT Doc. WT/DS26AB/USA, WT/DS26/AB/R and WT/DS48/AB/R.

GATT Panel Report (1997) *EC Measures Concerning Meat and Meat Products (Hormones)* WT/DS26/R/USA, WT/DS48/R/CAN, 18 August 1997.

GATT Panel Report (2006) *European Communities - Measures Affecting The Approval And Marketing Of Biotech Products,* WT/DS291/R, WT/DS292/R and WT/DS293/R.

Goklany I.M. (2001) *The Precautionary Principle: A Critical Appraisal of Environmental Risk Assessment* (Washington, DC: CATO Institute).

Goldstein, B.D. (2005) 'Advances in Risk Assessment and Communication', *Annual Review of Public Health,* 26: 141–163.

Gollier C. (2001) 'Should we beware of the precautionary principle?', *Economic Policy,* 16(33): 301–328.

Gollier, C., Jullien, B. and Treich, N. (2000) 'Scientific progress and irreversibility: An economic interpretation of the Precautionary Principle', *Journal of Public Economics,* 75: 229–253.

Gollier, C. and Treich, N. (2003) 'Decision-making under scientific uncertainty: The economics of the precautionary principle', *Journal of Risk and Uncertainty,* 27(1): 77–103.

Graham, J. and Hsia, S. (2002) 'Europe's Precautionary Principle: Promise and Pitfalls', *Journal of Risk Research* 5(4): 371–390.

Graham, J.D. and Wiener, J.B. (1995) *Risk vs. Risk: Tradeoffs in Protecting Public Health and the Environment* (Cambridge, MA: Harvard University Press).

Grant, D. and Hardy, C. (2004) 'Struggles with Organizational Discourse', *Organization Studies,* 25(1): 5–14.

Hardy, C. and Phillips, N. (1999) 'No Joking Matter: Discursive Struggle in the Canadian Refugee System', *Organization Studies* 20(1): 1–24.

Hey, E. (1992) 'The Precautionary Concept in Environmental Law and Policy: Institutionalising Caution', *Georgetown International Environmental Law Review,* 4: 303.

Hickey, J.E. and Walker, V.R. (1995) 'Refining the Precautionary Principle in International Environmental Law' *Virginia Environmental Law Journal,* 14: 423–454.

Hurst, D.R. (1998) 'Hormones – European Communities – Measures Affecting Meat and Meat Products', *European Journal of International Law,* 9: 182.

Jasanoff, S. (1998) 'The Political Science of Risk Perception', *Reliability Engineering and System Safety,* 59: 91–99.

Jordan A. and O'Riordan, T. (1999) 'The Precautionary Principle in Contemporary Environmental Policy and Politics' in C. Raffensperger and J. Tickner (eds.) *Protecting Public Health and the Environment: Implementing the Precautionary Principle* (Washington, DC: Island Press): 15–35.

Klinke, A. and Renn, O. (2001) 'Precautionary Principle and Discursive Strategies: Classifying and Managing Risks', *Journal of Risk Research,* 4(2): 159–173.

Leiss, W. (1996) 'Three Phases in the Evolution of Risk Communication Practice', *The ANNALS of the American Academy of Political and Social Science,* 545(1): 85–94.

Litfin, K. (1994) *Ozone Discourse: Science and Politics in Global Environmental Cooperation* (New York: Columbia University Press).

Litfin, K. (1995) 'Precautionary Discourse and the Ozone Treaties', *Millenium,* 24(2): 251–277.

Löfstedt, R.E. (2002) 'Editorial to Special Issue on the Precautionary Principle: New Insights', *Journal of Risk Research,* 5.4: 285–286.

Lofstedt, R.E. (2003) 'Science Communication and the Swedish Acrylamide Alarm', *Journal of Health Communication,* 8: 407–430.

Löfstedt, R.E. (2004) 'Risk Communication and Management in the Twenty-First Century', *International Public Management Journal,* 7(3): 335–346.

Mabey, N. (1998) *The Economics of Precaution: Strengths and Limitations of an Economic Interpretation of the Precautionary Principle* (London: WWF-UK).

Macdonald, J.M. (1995) 'Appreciating the Precautionary Principle as an Ethical Evolution in Ocean Management', *Ocean Development and International Law,* 26: 255.

Maguire, S. (2006) 'Ignorance Management: Business and the Precautionary Principle' paper presented at the *Business as an Agent of World Benefit Global Forum,* 10/22, Case Western Reserve University, Cleveland, OH.

Maguire, S. and Ellis, J. (2002) 'Uncertainty, Precaution and Global Interdependence: Implications of the Precautionary Principle for State and Non-state Actors' in F. Biermann, R. Brohm, and K. Dingwerth (eds.) *Proceedings of the 2001 Berlin Conference on the Human Dimensions of Global Environmental Change: Global Environmental Change and the Nation State, PIK Report No. 80* (Potsdam: Potsdam Institute for Climate Impact Research): 256–265.

Maguire, S. and Ellis, J. (2003) 'The Precautionary Principle and Global Chemical Risk Management: Some Insights from the Case of Persistent Organic Pollutants', *Greener Management International: The Journal of Corporate Environmental Strategy and Practice,* 41: 33–46.

Maguire, S. and Ellis, J. (2005) 'Redistributing the Burden of Scientific Uncertainty: Implications of the Precautionary Principle for State and Non-state Actors', *Global Governance,* 11(4): 505–526.

Maguire, S. and Hardy, C., 2006, 'The Emergence of New Global Institutions: A Discursive Perspective', *Organization Studies,* 27(1): 7–29.

McIntyre, O. and Mosedale, T. (1997) 'The Precautionary Principle as a Norm of Customary International Law', *Journal of Environmental Law,* 9(2): 221–241.

II

KEY CONSTRUCTS OF CRISIS AND RISK COMMUNICATION

Section One focused attention on the overarching challenges of crisis and risk communication. It serves to give the big picture that frames the remaining chapters of this discussion. Building on what was established there as the reach of the disciplines, the chapters of this section address specific challenges that arise during matters of crisis and risk.

To that end, this part of the *Handbook* adopts a perspective employed decades ago by the iconic persuasion research team led by Hovland, Janis, and Kelly who shed many insights in what has been called the Yale Persuasion Research Project. Those pioneers reasoned that because the SMCR (source, message, channel, and receiver) model was a useful heuristic for conceptualizing the communication process it could help them and other researchers to define the key factors of the learning theory approach to persuasion and persuasive communication. In the same way, the chapters in Section Two focus, however generally, on the SMCR elements of communication. In deference to the pioneers of persuasion theory and with reserve and respect for the simplistic assumptions of that approach, we offer chapters that feature the key elements of the process. We recognize that the communication process can never easily be treated as "parts," but it still seems logical to focus attention on requirements, challenges and frustrations that occur at each point of the process.

Chapter 7 features source and receiver variables, the concerns that should face risk communicators as well as advice born from decades of research and consulting practice. Employing psychological underpinnings of risk perception, Covello offers a practical philosophy of how risk communicators should approach the challenge of addressing perceptual factors that increase or decrease efforts to help interested parties understand risks and make enlightened choices as to their severity and manageability.

Chapter 8 adopts an educational design approach to designing messages addressed to local emergency managers. The centerpiece of this discussion by Rowan, Botan, Kreps, Samoilenko, and Farnsworth, is the CAUSE Model. One of the challenges faced by local emergency managers is to understand risks, plan for their occurrence, and gain community acceptance for the execution of a response plan. In this way, they may and often are expected to bring sound science and relatively technical plans into being in ways that foster trust for the plan and its implementation. In one sense, this challenge seems simple enough until we realize that coordinating a community response can be akin to herding cats, especially ones that are suffering various degrees of fear and denial. The acronym CAUSE stands for Confidence, Awareness, Understanding, Satisfaction, and Enactment. For our understanding of message design challenges, this chapter offers a practical approach developed through research, including case studies. The concern addressed in this chapter is that incorrect message design leads to inaccurate enactment of emergency response.

Using a familiar line from Shakespeare, Palmlund describes a narrative approach to risk communication that takes the view that "all the world's a stage" and humans think and act according to narratives. Chapter 9 addresses the challenge of how risk communicators can use narrative as the design motif for risk messages that connect with the views of the world adopted and enacted by the players, individual citizens as well as others, including emergency managers, for instance. She addresses quandaries from citizens' points of view: What should I know to reduce uncertainty that is inherent to the nature of risk? How should I act, individually and in concert with others in the face of that uncertainty? Various narratives not only define and evaluate risks as variously acceptable, but also consist of a cast of characters including the risk creators/generators, researchers, bearers, risk bearers' advocates, informers, and arbiters. The various narratives that exist throughout society assess risks and offer responses to them. Such taxonomy helps understand the risk messages and the logics that flow from them that define the relationships between individuals in society and their responses to the risks they encounter.

Risk and crisis communication necessarily have a basis in presentation and discussion of fact. In various ways risk, especially, relies on sound science however daunting that challenge is. Chapter 10 looks at this paradox from the point of view of the myths that become part of risk messages, and reactions to them. Recognizing the need for messages that contain accurate information as the basis for competent communication, Anderson and Spitzberg offer an insightful examination of how discourse can fall short of its need to be fact based. Myths cloud the accuracy of many messages and therefore lead away from sound communication in the face of disasters. As a partial antidote for this problem, they offer message design suggestions that if applied can help community members respond more appropriately in response to disasters, crises, and risks.

Continuing the discussion started in chapter 3, Aldoory focuses on the perilous assumption that facts are neutral and free from interpretative frames that may result in quite different interpretations of the same information. Chapter 11 looks at the matter of messages through the frame of social constructionism and key constructs relevant to its challenges. Various cultures bring into risk and crisis communication unique, idiosyncratic sets of interpretive heuristics. Traditional questions raised in risk communication have included how safe is safe, and what are the facts and do we have them straight. Aldoory reminds us that risk communicators also need to ask, what interpretative frames are at work in each community at risk.

Examining what happens to messages once they get into the media, Ryan analyzes the paradox of science as reported and interpreted. However sound the science might be that defines risks and leads to policy recommendations, the reality as constructed depends on how well that discussion survives in public conversation. Media, politicians, and activists play a role in framing messages which are necessarily variations on the theme created by science, which itself may be corrupted by the motives of key players in a risk controversy. Uncertainty is a defining characteristic of risk; key discussants may magnify rather than reduce the amount of uncertainty on some matter more as a political move than a more altruistic effort to put the best science into play to serve risk bearers. In chapter 12, Ryan demonstrates how such distortions can paralyze risk discussion. Scientific literacy and journalism are exploited to the advantage of some discussants.

Discussion of message factors continues in chapter 13 which looks broadly at rhetorical, persuasion, and information theories to help explain how messages are shaped into discourse and how discourse shapes messages. We often hear or read the comment that effective risk communication and crisis response involve open reporting of information, a sort of information sharing model. Section Two, rather, stresses the dynamics at work as facts are put into play. In this chapter, Springston, Avery, and Sallot explain the reality that discourse is designed to influence opinion and action; it is propositional. Thus, as much as risk communication experts would like an informed consent model of risk communication and crisis response they realize that discourse is tailored to be competitively influential. Influence theories feature the molar concepts of knowledge, attitude, and behavior (KAB) as a logic of influence. To understand and enact socially responsible risk communication, practitioners and academics must understand the ways in which people interpret and respond to the dangers in their lives and the messages that discuss those dangers.

Fear and denial not only confound the efficacy of risk communication but offer opportunities for effective message design leading targets of such messages to experience efficacy: Self, expert, and community. This combination of constructs, chapter 14 reasons, offer opportunities to tailor messages in ways that increase their chances for improving individual and public health. This line of argument features the Extended Parallel Process Model as developed by Witte and featured by her colleagues Roberto and White. Uncertainty can manifest itself as fear or dread. In large part which route that takes in the thoughts and decisions of individuals depends on the kinds and degrees of efficacy that can frame it as a manageable response rather than denial.

As risks are manifested into crisis, organizations are expected to respond. Crisis scholars have featured crisis management as consisting of three phases: pre-crisis, crisis, and post-crisis. Chapter 15 features the post-crisis stage as consisting of the need for renewal. Ulmer, Sellnow, and Seeger examine the message challenges that result as crisis communicators work to achieve a new level, perhaps including restoration of the reputation of the organization which suffered the crisis. As much as a crisis poses threats to managements, it can offer an opportunity. Both by improvements achieved through its strategic business plan and by enhanced communication efforts, organizations can not only put a crisis behind them but also emerge from trying times on the prospect of an even better future, an enhanced legitimacy to operate.

Risk communication, as does crisis response, both have a public and private face. Chapter 16 offers insights into the back story, the private aspects of risk analysis and response that influence how the message will be created and put into play. Shifting the focus from public display to organizational practice, Chess and Johnson build from the mental models approach, the desire to get the data right, as the foundation for effective external communication. Power and reflective management are important aspects of ethical risk management. No message is better than the quality of organization that promotes it into the risk dialogue. This is not only a matter of the challenge of organizational legitimacy, but also of the community where the dialogue transpires.

Implied in many of the chapters of this volume, ethical judgment is as important as is sound science. Taking a systems approach to the examination of the relationship between organizations and their publics, chapter 17 gives Bowen the opportunity to examine the ethical implications of risk communication in conjunction with issues management. The essential theme is that ethical challenges arise from the consequences risk assessment and management, as well as communication, have on those affected by the risks, the risk bearers. Those responsible to other members of the community for their role in the creation and mitigation of risk, Bowen reasons, are obligated to engage in discourse that brings parties together in meaningful ways for the betterment of society.

Such challenges take on local and global proportions because risks within communities may cross national boundaries. Through various levels of colonialism, one political economy can create risks for members of other political economies. Messages need, then, to emerge from dialogue rather than merely emanate from some ostensibly credible source. Chapter 18 discusses the challenges of public participation and decision making. McComas, Arvai, and Besley summarize and advance the discussion of public participation, long a principle of risk democracy. Those who have an interest in how risk is analyzed and translated into action should have a constructive role in every phase of the discussion. One parallel of public engagement is a kind of paralysis that results from collective indecision. Through logics that arise for analysis of group dynamics, a science based approach to public participation leads us to believe that effective public engagement not only leads to better decisions, but also ones that people are most likely to enact.

Collective decision making also occurs, or should occur, at the global level with the attendant problems of governmental and corporate colonialism and political dysfunction. One of the most controversial issues of global proportions is global warming. Taking the spirit of "we are all in this together," chapter 19 addresses the kinds of risks that bring people together and pit them against one another across country boundaries. Bringing the problematics of the precautionary principle into global discourse, McKie and Galloway reason that as science unravels mysteries of risks, risk communicators must engage to foster understanding and acceptance. Such dialogue requires a venue that depends on the standards of a civil society in which decisions, based on shared interpretations, can lead to sound, even if demanding sacrifice and appropriate actions.

Chapter 20 addresses the role of media as media. That is in keeping with the overarching theme of Section Two to address all of the components of the SMCR model of communication. Other chapters address media as channels. Some chapters, such as McComas and her colleagues even give us insights into public participation as a "channel" for risk and crisis communication. In this chapter, Neuwirth builds his analysis by introducing key media theories and using that discussion as the foundation for examining how crisis and risk discussions are helped and hindered by mass communication processes. His discussion includes information diffusion as well as agenda setting and framing. He examines research and theory that address the knowledge gap in society, between those who know and understand risks and crises, the problem of those who are attentive to such discussions and those who are not. He also brings our attention to media dependency theory, spiral of silence, and cultivation theory. Neuwirth observes that media in various ways (even some by news and other information sources including entertainment programming) puts information and evaluation out for people to acquire and consider, in varying ways.

The new communication technologies, by this logic, offer additional opportunities for individuals to acquire information. That observation, however, is just the start to understanding the challenges and perils that occur as crises and risks are discussed in Cyberspace. Hallahan expands this topic in chapter 21. He gives a nuts and bolts tour of the communication structure and functions allowed by Cyberspace. The sword cuts two ways. Not only do the new technological options allow organizations more communication channel and message placement options, but they also create opportunities for both bogus crisis and risk claims, as well as those which have merit. Given the openness of the Internet facts and claims can circulate that create crises and raise as well as distort the discussions of risk. For good or bad, this is the new mediated communication environment.

Following the themes raised by Hallahan, chapter 22 examines the role of new media in violent and nonviolent ideological groups. Because the Internet is unregulated, communication activities occur that would be less likely or substantially restrained by conventional media. As described by Allen, Angie, Davis, Byrne, O'Hair, Connelly, and Mumford, crises can be created and risks magnified because ideological voices invite discussions and provide the means for persons of similar mind to come together and identifiy with one another in ways that foster virtual risks for other individuals. A feeding frenzy of ideological outrage can occur as can copy cat acts such as violence against carefully selected or totally random targets.

Section Two ends with chapter 23 which argues that although one organization or individual might be the focal point in the discussion of risks, or crises, the reality is that such matters are best studied, understood, and practiced as something that occurs in an infrastructure, the dynamics of the communication processes and message discourse in each relevant community (local, regional, national, or global). Heath, Palenchar, and O'Hair discuss some of the mandated structures that are required for the discussion of risks. This approach to risk communication is fundamental to what has been called risk democracy, a concept that is not universally practiced in preference to an approach that features one source providing data, analysis and prescription for others who are in various ways the risk bearers. Access to facts, ability to interpret them, sense of concern and uncertainty, and challenges of trust: These factors, only a few of the various determinants of risk acceptance, are best seen as what exists idiosyncratically within a community. Facts and evaluations are only as good as their ability to survive discourse, often conducted by lay members of the public in their living rooms and at the coffee shop.

7

Strategies for Overcoming Challenges to Effective Risk Communication

Vincent T. Covello
Center for Risk Communication

I. INTRODUCTION

Effective risk communication is critical to effective risk management. It establishes public confidence in the ability of an organization to deal with a risk. It is integral to the larger process of information exchange aimed at eliciting trust and promoting understanding.

The National Academy of Sciences has defined risk communication as:

> *...an interactive process of exchange of information and opinion among individuals, groups, and institutions. It involves multiple messages about the nature of risk and other messages, not strictly about risk, that express concerns, opinions, or reactions to risk messages or to legal and institutional arrangements for risk management.* (p. 21; italics in original)

Numerous studies have highlighted the importance of effective risk communication in enabling people to make informed choices and participate in deciding how risks should be managed. Effective risk communication provides people with timely, accurate, clear, objective, consistent and complete risk information. It is the starting point for creating an informed population that is:

- involved, interested, reasonable, thoughtful, solution-oriented, cooperative, and collaborative;
- appropriately concerned about the risk;
- more likely to engage in appropriate behaviors.

While the overarching objective of effective risk communication is always to build, strengthen, or repair trust, its specific objectives vary from situation to situation. In some situations, the objective is to raise awareness of a risk or to provide people with information that allows them to better respond to a risk. In other cases, the purpose is to disseminate information on actions to take before, during, and after a disaster or emergency. In yet other cases, the purpose is to build consensus or engage people in a dialogue about appropriate behaviors and levels of concern.

II. RISK COMMUNICATION MODELS

Effective risk communication is based on several models that describe how risk information is processed, how risk perceptions are formed, and how risk decisions are made. Together, these models provide the intellectual and theoretical foundation for effective risk communication.

a. The Risk Perception Model

One of the most important paradoxes identified in the risk perception literature is that the risks which kill or harm people, and the risks that alarm and upset people, are often very different. For example, there is virtually no correlation between the ranking of hazards according to statistics on expected annual mortality and the ranking of the same hazards by how upsetting they are to people. There are many risks that make people worried and upset many people but cause little harm. At the same time, there are risks that kill or harm many people, but do not make people worried or upset.

This paradox is explained in part by the factors that affect how risks are perceived. Several of the most important are described below..

- Trust. Risks from activities associated with individuals, institutions, or organizations lacking in trust and credibility (e.g., organizations with poor health, safety, or environmental track records) are judged to be greater than risks from activities associated with those that are trustworthy and credible (e.g., regulatory agencies that achieve high levels of compliance among regulated groups).
- Voluntariness. Risks from activities considered to be involuntary or imposed (e.g., exposure to chemicals or radiation from a waste or industrial facility) are judged to be greater, and are therefore less readily accepted, than risks from activities that are seen to be voluntary (e.g., smoking, sunbathing, or mountain climbing).
- Controllability. Risks from activities viewed as under the control of others (e.g., releases of toxic agents by industrial facilities or bioterrorists) are judged to be greater, and are less readily accepted, than those from activities that appear to be under the control of the individual (e.g., driving an automobile or riding a bicycle).
- Familiarity. Risks from activities viewed as unfamiliar (such as from leaks of chemicals or radiation from waste disposal sites) are judged to be greater than risks from activities viewed as familiar (such as household work).
- Fairness. Risks from activities believed to be unfair or to involve unfair processes (e.g., inequities related to the siting of industrial facilities or landfills) are judged to be greater than risks from fair activities (e.g., vaccinations).
- Benefits. Risks from activities that seem to have unclear, questionable, or diffused personal or economic benefits (e.g., nuclear power plants and waste disposal facilities) are judged to be greater than risks from activities that have clear benefits (jobs; monetary benefits; automobile driving).
- Catastrophic potential. Risks from activities viewed as having the potential to cause a significant number of deaths and injuries grouped in time and space (e.g., deaths and injuries resulting from a major industrial accident) are judged to be greater than risks from activities that cause deaths and injuries scattered or random in time and space (e.g., automobile accidents).
- Understanding. Poorly understood risks (such as the health effects of long-term exposure to low doses of toxic chemicals or radiation) are judged to be greater than risks that are well understood or self-explanatory (such as pedestrian accidents or slipping on ice).
- Uncertainty. Risks from activities that are relatively unknown or that pose highly uncertain risks (e.g., risks from biotechnology and genetic engineering) are judged to be greater than risks from activities that appear to be relatively well known to science (e.g., actuarial risk data related to automobile accidents).

- Delayed effects. Risks from activities that may have delayed effects (e.g., long latency periods between exposure and adverse health effects) are judged to be greater than risks from activities viewed as having immediate effects (e.g., poisonings).
- Effects on children. Risks from activities that appear to put children specifically at risk (e.g., milk contaminated with radiation or toxic chemicals; pregnant women exposed to radiation or toxic chemicals) are judged to be greater than risks from activities that do not (e.g., workplace accidents).
- Effects on future generations. Risks from activities that seem to pose a threat to future generations (e.g., adverse genetic effects due to exposure to toxic chemicals or radiation) are judged to be greater than risks from activities that do not (e.g., skiing accidents).
- Victim identity. Risks from activities that produce identifiable victims (e.g., a worker exposed to high levels of toxic chemicals or radiation; a child who falls down a well; a miner trapped in a mine) are judged to be greater than risks from activities that produce statistical victims (e.g., statistical profiles of automobile accident victims).
- Dread. Risks from activities that evoke fear, terror, or anxiety (e.g., exposure to cancer causing agents, AIDS, or exotic diseases) are judged to be greater than risks from activities that do not arouse such feelings or emotions (e.g., common colds and household accidents).
- Media attention. Risks from activities that receive considerable media coverage (e.g., accidents and leaks at nuclear power plants) are judged to be greater than risks from activities that receive little (e.g., on-the-job accidents).
- Accident history. Risks from activities with a history of major accidents or frequent minor accidents (e.g., leaks at waste disposal facilities) are judged to be greater than risks from those with little or no such history (e.g., recombinant DNA experimentation).
- Reversibility. Risks from activities considered to have potentially irreversible adverse effects (e.g., birth defects from exposure to a toxic substance) are judged to be greater than risks from activities considered to have reversible adverse effects (e.g., sports injuries)
- Personal stake. Risks from activities viewed by people to place them (or their families) personally and directly at risk (e.g., living near a waste disposal site) are judged to be greater than risks from activities that appear to pose no direct or personal threat (e.g., disposal of waste in remote areas).
- Ethical/moral nature. Risks from activities believed to be ethically objectionable or morally wrong (e.g., foisting pollution on an economically distressed community) are judged to be greater than risks from ethically neutral activities (e.g., side effects of medication).
- Human vs. natural origin. Risks generated by human action, failure or incompetence (e.g., industrial accidents caused by negligence, inadequate safeguards, or operator error) are judged to be greater than risks believed to be caused by nature or "Acts of God" (e.g., exposure to geological radon or cosmic rays).

These factors determine a person's emotional response to risk information. For example, they affect levels of public fear, worry, anxiety, fear, anger, and outrage. Levels of fear, worry, anxiety, fear, anger, and outrage tend to be greatest and most intense when a risk is perceived to be involuntary, unfair, not beneficial, not under one's personal control, and managed by untrustworthy individuals or organizations.

b. The Mental Noise Model

The mental noise model focuses on how people process information under stress. Mental noise is caused by the stress and strong emotions associated with exposures to risks. When people are stressed and upset, their ability to process information can become severely impaired. In high stress situations, people typically display a substantially reduced ability to hear, understand, and remember information. For example, because of mental noise, when people are stressed and upset they typically can attend to no more than three messages at time. They also typically (1) process information at four or more levels below their educational level; (2) focus their attention on information they hear first and last. Exposure to risks associated with negative psychological attributes (e.g., risks perceived to be involuntary, not under one's control, low in benefits, unfair, or dreaded) contributes greatly to mental noise.

c. The Negative Dominance Model

The negative dominance model describes the processing of negative and positive information in high-concern and emotionally charged situations. In general, the relationship between negative and positive information is asymmetrical in high stress situations, with negative information receiving significantly greater weight. The negative dominance model is consistent with a central theorem of modern psychology that people put greater value on losses (negative outcomes) than on gains (positive outcomes). One practical implication of the negative dominance model is it takes several positive or solution-oriented messages to counterbalance one negative message. On average, in high concern or emotionally charged situations, it takes three or more positive messages to counterbalance a negative message. Another practical implication of negative dominance theory is that communications that contain negatives—e.g., words such as no, not, never, nothing, none, and other words with negative connotations—tend to receive closer attention, are remembered longer, and have greater impact than messages with positive words. As a result, the use of unnecessary negatives in high-concern or emotionally charged situations can have the unintended effect of drowning out positive or solution-oriented information. Risk communications are often most effective when they focus on positive, constructive actions; on what is being done, rather than on what is not being done.

d. The Trust Determination Model

A central theme in the risk communication literature is the importance of trust in effective risk communications. Trust is generally recognized as single most important factor determining perceptions of risk. Only when trust has been established can other risk communication goals, such as consensus-building and dialogue, be achieved.

Trust is typically built over long periods of time. Building trust is a long-term, cumulative process. Trust is easily lost. Once lost, it is difficult to regain.

Because of the importance of trust in effective risk communication, a significant part of the risk communication literature focuses on the determinants of trust. Research indicates that the most important trust determination factors are: (1) listening, caring, empathy, and compassion; (2) competence, expertise, and knowledge; and (3) honesty, openness, and transparency (Figure 7.1). Other factors in trust determination are accountability, perseverance, dedication, commitment, responsiveness, objectivity, fairness and consistency. Trust determinations are often made in as little as 9–30 seconds.

Trust is created in part by a proven track record of caring, honesty, and competence. It is enhanced by endorsements from trustworthy sources.

Trust in individuals varies greatly depending on their perceived attributes and their verbal and non-verbal communication skills. Trust in organizations also varies greatly. For example, surveys indicate that the most trustworthy individuals and organizations in many heath risk controversies are pharmacists, firefighters, safety professionals, nurses, educators, religious leaders, and citizen advisory groups.

III. CHALLENGES TO EFFECTIVE RISK COMMUNICATION

The four models are the backdrop for two of the most important challenges to effective risk communication:

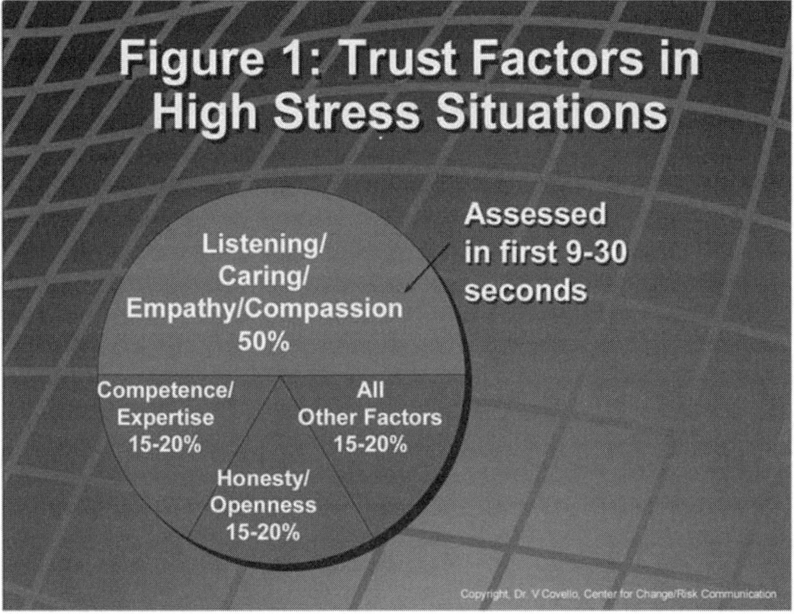

FIGURE 7.1 Trust factors in high stress situations.

- Selectivity and bias in media reporting about risk;
- Psychological, sociological, and cultural factors that create public misperceptions and misunderstandings about risks.

Each challenge is discussed below.

a. Selectivity and Bias in Media Reporting About Risks

The media play a critical role in the delivery of risk information. However, journalists are often highly selective in their reporting about risks. For example, they often focus their attention on:

- controversy
- conflict
- events with high personal drama
- failures
- negligence
- scandals and wrongdoing
- risks or threats to children
- stories about villains, victims, and heroes.

Much of this selectively stems from a host of professional and organizational factors. Several of the most important are described below. Each factor contributes to distortions and inaccuracies in media reporting about risks.

Newsworthiness. Journalists typically look for stories that will attract the largest number of readers, listeners, and readers. Stories that most attract the most attention typically have a high emotional content. They typically involve people in unusual, dramatic, confrontational, conflict, or negative situations (e.g., emotionally charged town hall meetings). Attractive stories about risk typically involve dreaded events (e.g., cancer among children), risks to future generations, involuntariness, unclear benefits, inequitable distribution of risks and benefits, potentially irreversible effects, and incompetent or untrustworthy risk managers. One result of this selectivity process is that many media stories about risk contain substantial omissions, or present oversimplified, distorted, inaccurate information. For example, media reports on cancer risks often fail to provide adequate statistics on general cancer rates for purposes of comparison.

Division of Labor. In many cases, the headline or the lead to a story about a risk is written by a person other than the journalist who covered the story. The headline or lead is often more sensational than the story. One reason for this is there are a wide variety of tasks carried out within a typical media organization. These tasks are often performed by different individuals with different goals. An important goal for the headline writer is to attract readers, listeners, or viewers.

Generalists. Most journalists are generalists rather than specialists, even in large media organizations. As a result, most journalists who cover risk stories lack expertise in the risk sciences, including medicine, engineering, epidemiology, toxicology, ecology, and statistics. In addition, journalists are often shuffled among content areas ("beats"). Shuffling often results in a journalist being assigned to cover a risk story with little experience, background, or specialized knowledge on the issue. Lack of expertise and experience often leads to distortions and inaccuracies in media reporting about risks.

Resources. Most media organizations do not have the resources needed to conduct in depth research on risk stories.

Objectively and Balance. Journalists typically attempt to achieve balance and objectivity by citing multiple sources with diverse viewpoints. However, the sources quoted by journalists quoted are often highly variable in their expertise and objectivity.

Career Advancement. Journalists typically advance their careers by moving from smaller media markets to larger media markets. As a result, there is often high staff turnover. Staff turnover, in turn, often results in stories written by journalists who are unfamiliar with the issue.

Watchdogs. Many journalists see themselves as watchdogs of industry and government and focus their attention on wrongdoing.

Source Dependency. Journalists are highly dependent upon individuals and organizations for a steady and reliable flow of newsworthy information. When a steady flow of information from authoritative sources is not forthcoming, journalists often turn to less authoritative sources. Additionally, journalists often look unfavorably on scientists or decision makers who use overly cautious or hedging language. In such cases, journalists may turn to sources willing to speak with certainty on the risk issue even though these sources are less reputable or less well informed.

Competition. Competition within and among media organizations (as well as among journalists) is often intense. Many news organizations compete zealously against one another for viewers, listeners or readers. Much of this competition is centered on getting the story out first. This in turn can lead to omissions and inaccuracies.

Deadlines. Journalists typically work under short deadlines. Short deadlines limit the ability of journalists to pursue accurate and credible information. Additionally, authoritative sources who do not respond to a journalist within their deadline are often looked upon with disfavor and may be bypassed in the future.

Information Compression. Because of the limited amount of time or space allocated for a story, journalists are limited in their ability to explore the complexities surrounding a risk issue.

b. Psychological, Sociological, and Cultural Factors that Create Public Misperceptions and Misunderstandings about Risks

The second major challenge to effective risk communication are psychological, sociological, and cultural factors that create risk misperceptions and misunderstandings. As a result of these factors, people often make biased judgments, or use only a small amount of available information to make risk decisions.

One of the most important of these factors is called "availability." The availability of an event (one that is accessible or easily remembered) often leads to overestimation of its frequency. Because of availability, people tend to assign greater probability to events of which they are frequently reminded (e.g., in the news media, scientific literature, or discussions among friends or colleagues), or to events that are easy to recall or imagine through concrete examples or dramatic images.

A second factor is conformity. This is the tendency on the part of people to behave in a particular way because everyone else is doing it, or because everyone else believes something.

A third factor is overconfidence in one's ability to avoid harm. A majority of people, for example, consider themselves less likely than average to get cancer, get fired from their job, or get mugged. Overconfidence is most prevalent when high levels of perceived personal control lead to reduced feelings of susceptibility. Many people fail to use seat belts, for example, because of the unfounded belief that they are better or safer than the average driver. In a similar vein, many teenagers often engage in high risk behaviors (e.g., drinking and driving, smoking, unprotected sex) because of perceptions, supported by peers, of invulnerability and overconfidence in their ability to avoid harm.

A fourth factor is called "confirmation bias." What this means is that once a belief about a risk is formed, new evidence is generally made to fit, contrary information is filtered out, ambiguous data is interpreted as confirmation, and consistent information is seen as "proof."

A fifth factor is the public's aversion to uncertainty. This aversion often translates into a marked preference and demand by the pubic for statements of fact over statements of probability—the language of risk assessment. Despite statements by experts that precise information is seldom available, people often want absolute answers. For example, people often demand to know exactly what will happen, not what might happen.

A sixth factor is the reluctance of people to change strongly held beliefs. As a result of this tendency, people often ignore evidence that contradicts their beliefs. Strong beliefs about risks, once formed, change very slowly. They can be extraordinarily persistent in the face of contrary evidence

IV. STRATEGIES FOR OVERCOMING CHALLENGES TO EFFECTIVE RISK COMMUNICATION

a. Strategies for Overcoming Selective and Biased Reporting by the Media about Risks

Risk communicators can use a variety of strategies to enhance the quality of media reporting. For example, if done in advance of a crisis, the following strategies can result in better media stories.

- Informational materials for journalists about risk issues should be prepared in advance.

- A lead spokesperson should be designated who has sufficient seniority, expertise, and experience to establish credibility with the media. The lead spokesperson should be skilled in communicating risk and uncertainty.
- Relationships with local journalists and editors should be developed in advance. This includes educational opportunities for journalists to learn more about the risk issue. It might also include visits with editorial boards.
- A Joint Information Center (JIC) should be established in advance that would function as the hub for media questions and inquiries during a disaster, emergency, or crisis. The JIC should have a room set up for daily media briefings. It should also have work room for public information officers from all partnering organizations.
- A comprehensive risk communication plan should be developed in advance. The basic elements of a comprehensive risk communication plan can be found in Appendix A. In risk communication, time is of the essence. Delay of even a few hours in informing the public is likely to lead to severe criticism. A pre-requisite to effective management of risks is the willingness and ability to share information in a timely manner. A risk communication plan is essential for this purpose. Unfortunately, most public and private sector organizations do not have an approved comprehensive risk communication plan in place. This adversely affects risk communication performance, particularly in crises. Risk communication plans should, at a minimum identify members of the risk communication team and clarify roles and responsibilities.
- A briefing book should be prepared in advance with answers to the most frequently asked questions by reporters. One such list of questions is found in Appendix B.
- Answers to frequently asked questions should be prepared in accordance with the principles of message mapping (see Appendix C).
- Background materials should be prepared for journalists that provides information about the quality of the risk numbers and information (see Appendix D).

In general, journalists typically write better stories about risk when risk communicators provide:

- accurate and truthful information;
- evidence-based information;
- regular updates of information;
- early disclosure of information;
- brief and concise information;
- first-hand information;
- graphics and other visual information (e.g., photographs, pictures, charts, timelines, diagrams, flowcharts, maps, drawings, videos, and animations);
- simple statistics with explanations;
- balanced information;
- human interest stories;
- access to experts and managers;
- information that is provided within media deadlines.

A more comprehensive list of strategies is found in Appendix E. The value of using these strategies derives from the advantages that come from working collaboratively with journalists as partners. For example, journalists can help risk communicators to:

- inform and educate the public;
- get a story out quickly;
- reach major target audiences;
- rally support;

- prevent undue fear and anxiety;
- provide accurate and needed information;
- correct erroneous information;
- encourage appropriate behaviors; and
- calm a nervous public.

b. Strategies for Overcoming the Psychological, Sociological, and Cultural Factors that Create Public Misperceptions and Misunderstandings about Risks

A broad range of strategies can be used to help overcome distortions in risk information caused by psychological, sociological, and cultural factors.

The most important strategy derives from the risk perception model. For example, because risk perception factors such as fairness, familiarity, and voluntariness are as relevant as measures of hazard probability and magnitude in judging the acceptability of a risk, efforts to reduce outrage by making a risk fairer, more familiar, and more voluntary are as significant as efforts to reduce the hazard itself. Similarly, efforts to share power, such as establishing and assisting community advisory committees, or supporting third party research, audits, inspections, and monitoring, can be powerful means for making a risk more acceptable.

Moreover, because risk acceptability depends greatly on perceived control, and because perceived control depends on values and opinions, risks are less likely to be misperceived when:

- organizations are clear about their values and goals;
- there is openness and transparency about decisions;
- the organization is the first to announce bad news;
- early warnings have been provided;
- decisions are clearly grounded in scientific evidence;
- public values, concerns and perceptions are taken into account in decision making;
- people perceive that authorities share their values;
- sufficient information is provided to allow individuals to make balanced, informed judgments;
- mistakes are quickly acknowledged and acted on by authorities;
- actions are consistent with words (judgments about trust often depend more on what is done than on what is said);
- uncertainty is acknowledged;
- excessive reassurance is avoided;
- "trusted voices" are enlisted to support messages;
- outrage and the legitimacy of fear and emotion are acknowledged.

A more detailed list of strategies is presented in Appendix F. Because of institutional and other barriers, strong leadership is often required to implement these strategies. An excellent example of such leadership occurred on September 11, 2001. Mayor Rudolf Giuliani shared the outrage that Americans felt at the terrorist attack on the World Trade Center. He delivered his messages with the perfect mixture of compassion, anger, and reassurance. He displayed virtually all the risk communication skills needed to be effective as a leader in a crisis. These include:

- Listen to, acknowledge and respect the fears, anxieties, and uncertainties of the many public and key stakeholders.
- Remain calm and in control, even in the face of public fear, anxiety, and uncertainty.
- Provide people with ways to participate, protect themselves and gain or regain a sense of personal control.
- Focus on what is known and not known.

- Tell people what follow-up actions will be taken if a question cannot be answered immediately, or tell people where to get additional information.
- Offer authentic statements and actions that communicate compassion, conviction and optimism.
- Be honest, candid, transparent, ethical, frank, and open.
- Take ownership of the issue or problem.
- Remember that first impressions are lasting impressions—they matter.
- Avoid humor because it can be interpreted as uncaring or trivializing the issue.
- Be extremely careful in saying anything that could be interpreted as an unqualified absolute ("never" or "always")—it only takes one exception to disprove an absolute.
- Be the first to share bad or good news.
- Balance bad news with three or more positive, constructive, or solution-oriented messages.
- Avoid mixed or inconsistent verbal and non-verbal messages.
- Be visible or readily available.
- Demonstrate media skills (verbal and non-verbal) including avoidance of major traps and pitfalls—for example, speculating about extreme worst-case scenarios, saying "there are no guarantees," repeating allegations or accusations, or saying "no comment"
- Develop and offer three concise key messages in response to each major concern.
- Continually look for opportunities to repeat the prepared key messages.
- Use clear non-technical language free of jargon and acronyms.
- Make extensive but appropriate use of visual material, personal and human-interest stories, quotes, analogies, and anecdotes.
- Find out who else is being interviewed and make appropriate adjustments.
- Monitor what is being said on the internet as much as other media.
- Take the first day of an emergency very seriously—drop other obligations.
- Avoid guessing—check and double-check the accuracy of facts.
- Ensure facts offered have gone through a clearance process.
- Plan risk and crisis communications programs well in advance using the APP model (anticipate/prepare/practice)—conduct scenario planning, identify important stakeholders, anticipate questions and concerns, train spokespersons, prepare messages, test messages, anticipate follow-up questions and rehearse responses.
- Provide information on a continuous and frequent basis.
- Ensure partners (internal and external) speak with one voice.
- Have a contingency plan for when partners (internal and external) disagree.
- When possible, use research to help determine responses to messages.
- Plan public meetings carefully—unless they are carefully controlled and skillfully implemented they can backfire and result in increased public outrage and frustration.
- Encourage the use of face-to-face communication methods, including expert availability sessions, workshops, and poster-based information exchanges.
- Be able to cite other credible sources of information.
- Admit when mistakes have been made—be accountable and responsible.
- Avoid attacking the credibility of those with higher perceived credibility.
- Acknowledge uncertainty
- Seek, engage, and make extensive use of support from credible third parties.

Mayor Giuliani particularly understood the danger in making unfounded or premature reassuring statements. Unfounded or premature reassuring statements are often motivated by a desire of government officials to calm the public and avoid panic and hysteria. Panic and hysteria describe an intense contagious fear among individuals. However, research indicates that most people respond cooperatively and adaptively in emergencies. Among the risk factors that cause panic and hysteria are:

- The belief that there is a small chance of escape;
- Seeing oneself as being at high risk of being seriously harmed or killed;
- Available but limited resources for assistance;
- Perceptions of a "first come, first served" system;
- A perceived lack of effective management of the disaster;
- Loss of credibility of authorities; and
- The lack of meaningful things for people to do (e.g., tasks that increase group interaction, increase connectedness, and help bind anxiety).

Perhaps the most important risk communication skill demonstrated by Mayor Giuliani was his ability to communicate uncertainty. He recognized the challenge to effective risk communication caused by the complexity, incompleteness, and uncertainty of risk data. In addressing this challenge, Mayor Giuliani drew on risk communication principles for communicating uncertainty:

- Acknowledge—do not hide—uncertainty.
- Explain that data are often uncertain because it is hard to measure many health, safety, and environmental effects.
- Explain how the risk estimate was obtained, and by whom.
- Share risk information promptly, with appropriate reservations about its certainty.
- Tell people what you believe (a) is certain, (b) is nearly certain, (c) is not known, (d) may never be known, (e) is likely, (f) is unlikely, (g) is highly improbable, and (h) will reduce the uncertainty.
- Tell people that what you believe now with certainty may turn out later to be wrong.
- Announce problems promptly.

SELECTED READINGS: STRATEGIES FOR OVERCOMING CHALLENGES TO EFFECTIVE RISK COMMUNICATION

Auf der Heide, E. (2004). Common misconceptions about disasters: Panic, the "Disaster Syndrome," and Looting. In M. O'Leary (Ed.), *The first 72 Hours: A community approach to disaster preparedness* (pp. 340–380). Lincoln, NB: iUniverse Publishing.

Bennett, P., & Calman, K. (1999). (Eds.). *Risk communication and public health.* New York: Oxford University Press.

Bennett, P., Coles, D., & McDonald, A. (1999). Risk communication as a decision process. In P. Bennett & K. Calman (Eds.), *Risk communication and public health.* New York: Oxford University Press.

Blendon, R.J., Benson, J.M., DesRoches, C.M., Raleigh, E., & Taylor-Clark, K. (2004). The public's response to Severe Acute Respiratory Syndrome in Toronto and the United States. *Clinical Infectious Dis*eases, 38, 925–931.

Brunk, D. (2003). Top 10 lessons learned from Toronto SARS outbreak: A model for preparedness. *Internal Medicine News*, 36(21), 4.

Cava, M. Fay, K., Beanlands, H., McCay, E., & Wignall, R. (2005). Risk perception and compliance with quarantine during the SARS outbreak (severe acute respiratory syndrome). *Journal of Nursing Scholarship*, 37(4), 343–348.

Centers for Disease Control and Prevention (2002). *Emergency and risk communication.* Atlanta, GA: CDC

Chess C., Hance B.J., & Sandman P.M. (1986). *Planning dialogue with communities: A risk communication workbook.* New Brunswick, NJ: Rutgers University, Cook College, Environmental Media Communication Research Program.

Covello, V.T. (2003). Best practice in public health risk and crisis communication. *Journal of Health Communication*, 8, Supplement 1, 5–8.

Covello, V.T. (2005) Risk Communication. In H. Frumkin (Ed.), *Environmental health: From global to local* (pp. 988–1008). San Francisco: Jossey-Bass/Wiley.

Covello, V.T. (2006) Risk Communication and message mapping: A new tool for communicating effectively in public health emergencies and disasters. *Journal of Emergency Management*, 4(3), 25–40.

Covello, V.T., & Allen, F. (1988). *Seven cardinal rules of risk communication.* Washington, DC: Environmental Protection Agency.

Covello, V.T., Clayton, K., & Minamyer, S., (2007) Effective Risk and Crisis Communication During Water Security Emergencies: Summary Report of EPA Sponsored Message Mapping Workshops. EPA Report No. EPA600/R-07/027. Cincinnati, OH: National Homeland Security Research Center, Environmental Protection Agency.

Covello, V.T., McCallum, D.B., & Pavlova, M.T. (Eds.) (1989). *Effective risk communication: The role and responsibility of government and nongovernment organizations.* New York: Plenum Press.

Covello, V.T., Peters, R., Wojtecki, J., & Hyde, R. (2001) Risk communication, the West Nile virus epidemic, and bio-terrorism: Responding to the communication challenges posed by the intentional or unintentional release of a pathogen in an urban setting. *Journal of Urban Health*, 78(2), 382–391.

Covello, V.T., & Sandman, P. (2001). Risk communication: Evolution and revolution. In A. Wolbarst (Ed.). *Solutions to an environment in peril* (pp. 164–178). Baltimore, MD: John Hopkins University Press.

Covello, V.T., Slovic, P., & von Winterfeldt, D. (1986) Risk communication: a review of the literature. *Risk Abstracts* 3(4), 171–182.

Cutlip, S.M. Center, A.H., & Broom, G.M. (1985). *Effective public relations* (6th ed.). Upper Saddle River, NJ: Prentice-Hall.

Douglas, M., & Wildavsky, A. (1982). *Risk and culture: An essay on the selections of technological and environmental dangers.* Berkeley: University of California Press.

Embrey, M., & Parkin, R. (2002). Risk communication. In M. Embrey et al. (Eds.). *Handbook of CCL microbes in drinking water.* Denver, CO: American Water Works Association.

Fischhoff, B. (1995) Risk perception and communication unplugged: twenty years of progress. *Risk Analysis*, 15(2), 137–145.

Hance, B.J., Chess, C., & Sandman, P.M. (1990). *Industry risk communication manual.* Boca Raton, FL: CRC Press/Lewis Publishers.

Hyer, R., & Covello, V.T. (2007). *Effective media communication during public health emergencies: A World Health Organization handbook.* Geneva: World Health Organization.

Kahneman, D., Slovic, P., Tversky, A. (Ed). (1982). *Judgment under uncertainty: heuristics and biases.* New York: Cambridge University Press.

Kahneman, D., & Tversky, A. (1979). Prospect theory: An analysis of decision under risk. *Econometrica*, 47(2), 263–291.

Kasperson, R.E., Renn, O., Slovic, P., Brown, H.S., Emel, J., Goble, R., Kasperson, J.X., & Ratick, S. (1987). The social amplification of risk: A conceptual framework. *Risk Analysis*, 8, 177–187.

Lundgren, R., & McKakin, A. (2004). *Risk communication: A handbook for communicating environmental, safety, and health risks* (3rd ed.), Columbus, OH: Batelle Press.

McKechnie, S., & Davies, S. (1999). Consumers and risk. In P. Bennet (Ed.), *Risk communication and public health* (p. 170). Oxford, UK: Oxford University Press.

Morgan, M.G., Fischhoff, B., Bostrom, A., & Atman, C.J. (2001). *Risk communication: A mental models approach.* Cambridge, UK: Cambridge University Press.

National Research Council (1989). *Improving risk communication.* National Academy Press, Washington, DC.

National Research Council (1996). Understanding risk: Informing decisions in a democratic society. Washington, DC: National Academy Press.

Peters, R., McCallum, D., & Covello, V.T. (1997). The determinants of trust and credibility in environmental risk communication: An empirical study. *Risk Analysis*, 17(1), 43–54.

Sandman, P.M. (1989). Hazard versus outrage in the public perception of risk. In: Covello, V.T., McCallum, D.B., Pavlova, & M.T. (Eds.), Effective risk communication: The role and responsibility of government and non-government organizations (pp. 45–49). New York: Plenum Press.

Slovic, P. (Ed.) (2000). The perception of risk. London: Earthscan Publication, Ltd.

Slovic, P. (1987). Perception of risk. *Science*, 236, 280–285.

Stallen, P.J.M, & Tomas, A. (1988). Public concerns about industrial hazards. *Risk Analysis*, 8, 235–245.

Weinstein, N.D. (1987). *Taking care: Understanding and encouraging self-protective behavior.* New York: Cambridge University Press.

APPENDIX A
TWENTY-FIVE ELEMENTS OF A COMPREHENSIVE RISK AND CRISIS COMMUNICATION PLAN

(Adapted from Hyer, R.N. and Covello, V.T., *Effective Media Communication during Public Health Emergencies: A World Health Organization Handbook*, World Health Organization, Geneva, Switzerland, 2007.)

1. Identify all anticipated scenarios for which risk, crisis, and emergency communication plans are needed, including worst cases and low probability, high consequence events
2. Describe and designate staff roles and responsibilities for different risk, crisis, or emergency scenarios
3. Designate who in the organization is responsible and accountable for leading the crisis or emergency response
4. Designate who is responsible and accountable for implementing various crisis and emergency actions
5. Designate who needs to be consulted during the process
6. Designate who needs to be informed about what is taking place
7. Designate who will be the lead communication spokesperson and backup for different scenarios
8. Identify procedures for information verification, clearance, and approval
9. Identify procedures for coordinating with important stakeholders and partners (for example, with other organizations, emergency responders, law enforcement, elected officials, and provincial, and federal government agencies)
10. Identify procedures to secure the required human, financial, logistical, and physical support and resources (such as people, space, equipment, and food) for communication operations during a short, medium and prolonged event (24 hours a day, 7 days a week if needed)
11. Identify agreements on releasing information and on who releases what, when, and how polices and procedures regarding employee contacts from the media
12. Include regularly checked and updated media contact lists (including after-hours news desks)
13. Include regularly checked and updated partner contact lists (day and night)
14. Identify schedule for exercises and drills for testing the communication plan as part of larger preparedness and response training
15. Identify subject-matter experts (for example, university professors) willing to collaborate during an emergency, and develop and test contact lists (day and night); know their perspectives in advance
16. Identify target audiences
17. Identify preferred communication channels (for example, telephone hotlines, radio announcements, news conferences, Web site updates, and faxes) to communicate with the public, key stakeholders and partners
18. Include message maps for core, informational, and challenge questions
19. Include message maps with answers to frequently asked and anticipated questions from key stakeholders, including key internal and external audiences
20. Include holding statements for different anticipated stages of the crisis
21. Include fact sheets, question-and-answer sheets, talking points, maps, charts, graphics, and other supplementary communication materials
22. Include a signed endorsement of the communication plan from the organization's director
23. Include procedures for posting and updating information on the organization's Web site
24. Include communication task checklists for the first 2, 4, 8, 12, 16, 24, 48 hours, and 72 hours

25. Include procedures for evaluating, revising, and updating the risk and crisis communication plan on a regular basis

APPENDIX B
77 QUESTIONS COMMONLY ASKED BY JOURNALISTS DURING AN EMERGENCY OR CRISIS

Journalists are likely to ask six questions in a crisis (who, what, where, when, why, how) that relate to three broad topics: (1) what happened; (2) what caused it to happen;
(3) what does it mean. Specific questions include:

1. What is your name and title?
2. What are you job responsibilities?
3. What are your qualifications?
4. Can you tell us what happened?
5. When did it happen?
6. Where did it happen?
7. Who was harmed?
8. How many people were harmed, injured, or killed?
9. Are those that were harmed getting help?
10. How are those who were harmed getting help?
11. What can others do to help?
12. Is the situation under control?
13. Is there anything good that you can tell us?
14. Is there any immediate danger?
15. What is being done in response to what happened?
16. Who is in charge?
17. What can we expect next?
18. What are you advising people to do?
19. How long will it be before the situation returns to normal?
20. What help has been requested or offered from others?
21. What responses have you received?
22. Can you be specific about the types of harm that occurred?
23. What are the names of those that were harmed?
24. Can we talk to them?
25. How much damage occurred?
26. What other damage may have occurred?
27. How certain are you about damage?
28. How much damage do you expect?
29. What are you doing now?
30. Who else is involved in the response?
31. Why did this happen?
32. What was the cause?
33. Did you have any forewarning that this might happen?
34. Why wasn't this prevented from happening?
35. What else can go wrong?
36. If you are not sure of the cause, what is your best guess?
37. Who caused this to happen?
38. Who is to blame?
39. Could this have been avoided?
40. Do you think those involved handled the situation well enough?

41. When did your response to this begin?
41. When were you notified that something had happened?
43. Who is conducting the investigation?
44. What are you going to do after the investigation?
45. What have you found out so far?
46. Why was more not done to prevent this from happening?
47. What is your personal opinion?
48. What are you telling your own family?
49. Are all those involved in agreement?
50. Are people over reacting?
51. Which laws are applicable?
52. Has anyone broken the law?
53. What challenges are you facing?
54. Has anyone made mistakes?
55. What mistakes have been made?
56. Have you told us everything you know?
57. What are you not telling us?
58. What effects will this have on the people involved?
59. What precautionary measures were taken?
60. Do you accept responsibility for what happened?
61. Has this ever happened before?
62. Can this happen elsewhere?
63. What is the worst case scenario?
64. What lessons were learned?
65. Were those lessons implemented?
66. What can be done to prevent this from happening again?
67. What would you like to say to those that have been harmed and to their families?
68. Is there any continuing the danger?
69. Are people out of danger? Are people safe?
70. Will there be inconvenience to employees or to the public?
71. How much will all this cost?
72. Are you able and willing to pay the costs?
73. Who else will pay the costs?
74. When will we find out more?
75. What steps need to be taken to avoid a similar event?
76. Have these steps already been taken? If not, why not?
77. What does this all mean? Is there anything else you want to tell us?

APPENDIX C
MESSAGE MAPPING

A risk communication message map is an example of a tool utilized for preparing clear and concise messages about risks. It consists of detailed and hierarchically organized information that can be used to respond to anticipated questions or concerns. It is a visual aid that provides, at a glance, the organization's messages on high-concern issues. The message map template enables spokespersons to meet the demands of the media as well as the public and other interested parties for timely, accurate, clear, concise, consistent, credible, and relevant information. The message map can also serve as "a port in a storm" when questioning by journalists or others becomes intense or aggressive. Message maps also allow organizations to develop risk messages in advance. Once developed, the effectiveness of message maps can be tested through focus groups and other empirical studies.

Message Map Template

Stakeholder:
Question or Concern:

Key Message 1	*Key Message 2*	*Key Message 3*
Supporting Information 1-1	Supporting Information 2-1	Supporting Information 3-1
Supporting Information 1-2	Supporting Information 2-2	Supporting Information 3-2
Supporting Information 1-3	Supporting Information 2-3	Supporting Information 3-3

The top section of the message map identifies the stakeholder or audience for whom the messages are intended as well as the specific question or concern being addressed. The next layer of the message map contains the 3 key messages which can function individually or collectively as a response to a stakeholder question or concern. These key messages are intended to address the information needs of a wide variety of audiences.

The three key messages can also serve individually or collectively as a media sound bite—the quote in a media story attributed to a spokesperson. Sound bites are an essential element in effective media communication as short, quotable messages will often be played repeatedly by the media. Speaking in sound bites helps to ensure that prepared key messages are carried in news stories. Reporters and editors almost always cut interview material into sound bites. The final section of the message map contains supporting information arranged in blocks of three under each key message. This supporting information amplifies the key messages by providing additional facts or details. Supporting information can also take the form of visuals, analogies, personal stories, or citations of credible information sources.

Sample Message Map for Smallpox—With Keywords in Italics

Stakeholder: Public
Question or Concern: How contagious is smallpox?

Key Message 1	*Key Message 2*	*Key Message 3*
Smallpox *spreads slowly* compared to many other diseases.	This allows *time to trace* those who have come into contact with the disease.	Those who have been traced *can be vaccinated.*
Supporting Information 1-1	Supporting Information 2-1	Supporting Information 3-1
People are only infectious when the rash appears.	The incubation period for the disease is 10–14 days.	People who have never been vaccinated are the most important to vaccinate.
Supporting Information 1-2	Supporting Information t 2-2	Supporting Information 3-2
Smallpox typically requires hours of face-to-face contact.	Resources are available for tracing contacts.	Adults who were vaccinated as children may still have some immunity.
Supporting Information 1-3	Supporting Information 2-3	Supporting Information 3-3
There are no carriers without Symptoms.	Finding people who have been exposed and vaccinating them has proved successful in the past.	Adequate vaccine is on hand.

As a strategic tool, a message map provides multiple benefits. It provides a handy reference for leaders and spokespersons who must respond swiftly to questions on topics where timeliness and accuracy are crucial. Multiple spokespersons can work from the same message map to ensure the rapid dissemination of consistent and core messages across a wide spectrum of communication outlets. Message maps provide a unifying framework for disseminating information on a wide range of public health issues. Message maps also minimize the chance of "speaker's regret" at saying something inappropriate or not saying something that should have been said. A printed copy of the message map allows spokespersons during interviews to "check off" the talking points they want to make in order of their importance. This helps to prevent omissions of key facts or misstatements that could provoke misunderstandings, controversy, or outrage.

One important lesson learned from message-mapping exercises is that the process of generating message maps can be as important as the end product. Message-mapping exercises involve teams of scientists, communication specialists, and individuals with policy expertise, and often reveal a diversity of viewpoints on the same question, issue or concern. Gaps in message maps often provide early warning that a message is incomplete providing scientists and issue-management teams with an opportunity to focus their efforts on filling the information gaps. Message-mapping exercises also frequently identify changes needed in organizational strategies and policies.

The crucial final step in message-map construction is to conduct systematic message testing using standardized procedures. Message testing should begin by asking subject-matter experts not directly involved in the original message-mapping process to validate the accuracy of the information given. Message testing should then be conducted with individuals or groups who have the characteristics to serve as surrogates for key internal and external target audiences. Finally, sharing and testing messages with partner organizations will promote message consistency and coordination. Once developed, message maps can be brought together to produce a media briefing book. They can also be used individually or collectively for use in news conferences, media interviews, information forums and exchanges, public meetings, Web sites, telephone hotline scripts, and fact sheets or brochures.

APPENDIX D
QUALITY OF RISK NUMBERS AND INFORMATION

Risk numbers are only as good as the studies from which they are derived. As a result, information pertaining to the following questions should be provided to journalists:

1. **General**
   - Have the researchers only found a statistical correlation or a difference that has actual implications?
   - Have the findings been published yet in a peer-reviewed journal?
   - Have the researchers published other research in this area?
   - What are the institutional affiliations of the researcher(s)?
   - Are there any possible conflicts of interest?
2. **Methods**
   - What research methods were used?
   - Are the research methods conventional?
   - Have the results been replicated by other researchers?
   - What do other professionals in the field think about these methods?
   - Is the sample size adequate to make a conclusion?
   - If the research involves a diagnostic test, how often does the test produce a false negative or a false positive?

3. **Conclusions**
   - Have important caveats need to be made? For example, were there important variables that could not be, or were not, controlled?
   - Are the findings preliminary of final?
   - Are there other possible interpretations of the data?
   - Do the findings differ markedly from previous studies?
   - To what extent can the findings be generalized?

APPENDIX E
STRATEGIES FOR EFFECTIVE COMMUNICATION WITH THE MEDIA

Listed below are strategies for effective communication with the media. This summary is adapted from Hyer, R.N. and Covello, V.T., *Effective Media Communication during Public Health Emergencies: A World Health Organization Handbook*, World Health Organization, Geneva, Switzerland, 2007.

1. **Accept the media as a legitimate partner**
   - Recognize that effective media communication in an emergency or crisis:
   - enables the media to play a constructive role in protecting the public's health;
   - enables public health officials to reach a wide range of stakeholders; and
   - enables public health officials, in cooperation with the media, to build trust, calm a nervous public, provide needed information, encourage cooperative behaviors, and save lives.
   - Demonstrate respect for the media by keeping them well informed of decisions and actions.
   - Establish good working relationships with media contacts before an emergency arises.
   - Include journalists in public emergency response planning exercises.
   - Be polite and courteous at all times, even if the reporter is not.
   - Avoid embarrassing reporters.
   - Provide information for on-site reporters on the location of electrical outlets, public telephones, rest rooms, hotels, restaurants, and other amenities.
   - Avoid being defensive or argumentative during interviews.
   - Include elements in interviews that make a story interesting to the media, including examples, stories, and other aspects that influence public perceptions of risk, concern, and outrage.
   - Use a wide range of media communication channels to engage and involve people.
   - Adhere to the highest ethical standards—recognize that people hold you professionally and ethically accountable.
   - Strive to inform editors and reporters of agency preparedness for a public health emergency.
   - Offer to follow-up on questions that cannot be addressed immediately.
   - Strive for "win-win" media outcomes.
   - Involve the media in training exercises and preparedness drills.

2. **Plan thoroughly and carefully for all media interactions**
   - Assess the cultural diversity and socioeconomic level of the target populations.
   - Assess internal media-relations capabilities.
   - Recognize that all communication activities and materials should reflect the diverse nature of societies in a fair, representative, and inclusive manner.
   - Begin all communication planning efforts with clear and explicit goals—such as:
   - informing and educating;
   - improving knowledge and understanding;
   - building, maintaining, or restoring trust;
   - guiding and encouraging appropriate attitudes, decisions, actions, and behaviors; and

- encouraging dialogue, collaboration, and cooperation.
- Develop a written communication plan.
- Develop a partner communication strategy.
- Establish coordination in situations involving multiple agencies.
- Identify important stakeholders and subgroups within the audience as targets for your messages.
- Prepare a limited number of key messages in advance of potential public health emergencies.
- Post the key messages and supporting information on your own well-publicized Web site.
- Pre-test messages before using them during an interview.
- Respect diversity and multiculturalism while developing messages.
- Train key personnel—including technical staff—in basic, intermediate and advanced media communication skills.
- Practice media communication skills regularly.
- Never say anything "off-the-record" that you would not want to see quoted and attributed to you.
- Recruit media spokespersons who have effective presentation and personal interaction skills.
- Provide training for high-ranking government officials who play a major role in communication with the media.
- Provide well-developed talking points for those who play a leading role in communication with the media.
- Recognize and reward spokespersons who are successful in getting their key messages included in media stories.
- Anticipate questions and issues that might be raised during an interview.
- Train spokespersons in how to redirect an interview (or get it back on track) using bridging phrases such as "what is really important to know is...".
- Agree with the reporter in advance on logistics and topic—for example, the length, location, and specific topic of the interview—but realize that the reporter may attempt to stray from the agreed topic.
- Make needed changes in strategy and messages based on monitoring activities, evaluation efforts and feedback.
- Work proactively to frame stories rather than waiting until others have defined the story and then reacting.
- Carefully evaluate media communication efforts and learn from mistakes.
- Share with others what you have learned from working with the media.

3. Meet the functional needs of the media

- Assess the needs of the media.
- Be accessible to reporters.
- Respect their deadlines.
- Accept that news reports will simplify and abbreviate your messages.
- Devise a schedule to brief the media regularly during an emergency, even if updates are not "newsworthy" by their standards—open and regular communication helps to build trust and fill information voids.
- Refer journalists to your Web site for further information.
- Share a limited number of key messages for media interviews.
- Repeat your key messages several times during news conferences and media interviews.
- Provide accurate, appropriate, and useful information tailored to the needs of each type of media, such as sound bites, background videotape, and other visual materials for television.

- Provide background material for reporters on basic and complex issues on your Web site and as part of media information packets and kits.
- Be careful when providing numbers to reporters—these can easily be misinterpreted or misunderstood.
- Stick to the agreed topic during the interview—do not digress.
- If you do not know the answer to a question, focus on what you do know, tell the reporter what actions you will take to get an answer, and follow up in a timely manner.
- If asked for information that is the responsibility of another individual or organization, refer the reporter to that individual or organization.
- Offer reporters the opportunity to do follow-up interviews with subject-matter experts.
- Strive for brevity, but respect the reporter's desire for information.
- Hold media availability sessions where partners in the response effort are available for questioning in one place at one time.
- Remember that it benefits the reporter and the agency when a story is accurate.
- Before an emergency occurs, meet with editors and with reporters who would cover the story.
- Work to establish durable relationships with reporters and editors.
- Promise only that which can be delivered, then follow through.

4. **Be candid and open with reporters**
   - Be first to share bad news about an issue or your organization, but be sure to put it into context.
   - If the answer to a question is unknown or uncertain, and if the reporter is not reporting in real time, express a willingness to get back to the reporter with a response by an agreed deadline.
   - Be first and proactive in disclosing information about an emergency, emphasizing appropriate reservations about data and information reliability.
   - Recognize that most journalists maintain a "healthy skepticism" of sources, and trust by the media is earned—do not ask to be trusted.
   - Ask the reporter to restate a question if you do not understand it.
   - Hold frequent media events to fill information voids.
   - Do not minimize or exaggerate the level of risk.
   - Acknowledge uncertainty.
   - Be careful about comparing the risk of one event to another.
   - Do not offer unreasonable reassurances (i.e., unwarranted by the available information).
   - Make corrections quickly if errors are made or if the facts change.
   - Discuss data and information uncertainties, strengths and weaknesses—including those identified by other credible sources.
   - Cite ranges of risk estimates when appropriate.
   - Support your messages with case studies and data.
   - If credible authorities disagree on the best course of action, be prepared to disclose the rationale for those disagreements, and why your agency has decided to take one particular course of action over another.
   - Be especially careful when asked to speculate or answer extreme or baseless "what if" questions, especially on worst-case scenarios.
   - Avoid speaking in absolutes.
   - Tell the truth.

5. **Listen to the target audience**
   - Do not make assumptions about what viewers, listeners, and readers know, think, or want done about risks.

- If time and resources allow, prior to a media interview, review the available data and information on public perceptions, attitudes, opinions, beliefs, and likely responses regarding an event or risk. Such information may have been obtained through interviews, facilitated discussion groups, information exchanges, expert availability sessions, public hearings, advisory group meetings, hotline call-in logs, and surveys.
- Monitor and analyze information about the event appearing in media outlets, including
- the Internet.
- Identify with the target audience of the media interview, and present information in a format that aids understanding and helps people to act accordingly.
- During interviews and news conferences, acknowledge the validity of people's emotions
- and fears.
- Be empathetic.
- Target media channels that encourage listening, feedback, participation, and dialogue.
- Recognize that competing agendas, symbolic meanings, and broader social, cultural, economic or political considerations often complicate the task of effective media communication.
- Recognize that although public health officials may speak in terms of controlling "morbidity and mortality" rates, more important issues for some audiences may be whether people are being treated fairly in terms of access to care and medical resources.

6. **Coordinate, collaborate, and act in partnership with other credible sources**
   - Develop procedures for coordinating the activities of media spokespersons from multiple agencies and organizations.
   - Establish links to the Web sites of partner organizations.
   - Recognize that every organization has its own culture and this culture impacts upon how and what it tries to communicate.
   - To the extent possible, act in partnership with other organizations in preparing messages in advance of potential emergencies.
   - Share and coordinate messages with partner organizations prior to media interviews or news conferences.
   - Encourage partner organizations to repeat or echo the same key messages—such repetition and echoing by many voices helps to reinforce the key messages for target audiences.
   - In situations involving multiple agencies, determine information clearance and approval procedures in advance when possible.
   - Aim for consistency of key messages across agencies—if real differences in opinion do exist be inclined to disclose the areas of disagreement and explain why your agency is choosing one course of action over another.
   - Develop a contingency plan for when partners cannot engage in consistent messaging—be prepared to make an extra effort to listen to their concerns, understand their point of view, negotiate differences, and apply pressure if required and appropriate.
   - Devote effort and resources to building bridges, partnerships, and alliances with other organizations (including potential or established critics) before an emergency occurs.
   - Consult with internal and external partners to determine which organization should take the lead in responding to media enquiries, and document the agreements reached.
   - Discuss ownership of specific topics or issues in advance to avoid one partner treading upon the perceived territory of another.
   - Identify credible and authoritative sources of information that can be used to support messages in potential emergencies.
   - Develop a plan for using information from other organizations in potential emergencies.
   - Develop contact lists of external subject-matter experts able and willing to speak to the media on issues associated with potential emergencies.

- Cite as part of your message credible and authoritative sources that believe what you believe.
- Issue media communications together with, or through, individuals or organizations believed to be credible and trustworthy by the target audience.

7. **Speak clearly and with compassion**
   - Be aware that people want to know that you care before they care what you know.
   - Use clear, non-technical language.
   - Explain medical or technical terms in clear language when they are used.
   - Use graphics or other pictorial material to clarify and strengthen messages.
   - Respect the unique information needs of special and diverse audiences.
   - Express genuine empathy when responding to questions about loss—acknowledge the tragedy of illness, injury, or death.
   - Personalize risk data by using stories, narratives, examples, and anecdotes that make technical data easier to understand.
   - Avoid distant, abstract and unfeeling language about harm, deaths, injuries, and illnesses.
   - Acknowledge and respond (in words, gestures, and actions) to the emotions people express, such as anxiety, fear, worry, anger, outrage, and helplessness.
   - Acknowledge and respond to the distinctions people view as important in evaluating risks, such as perceived benefits, control, fairness, dread, whether the risk is natural or man-made, and effects on children.
   - Be careful to use risk comparisons only to help put risks in perspective and context, and not to suggest that one risk is like another—avoid comparisons that trivialize the problem, that attempt to minimize anxiety, or that appear to be trying to settle the question of whether a risk is acceptable.
   - Give people a sense of control by identifying specific actions they can take to protect themselves.
   - Identify significant misinformation, being aware that repeating it may give it unwanted attention.
   - Recognize that saying "no comment" without explanation or qualification is often perceived as guilt or hiding something—consider saying instead "I wish I could answer that. However...".
   - Be sensitive to local norms, such as those relating to speech and dress.
   - Always try to include in a media interview a discussion of actions under way by the agency, or actions that can be taken by the public.

APPENDIX F
STRATEGIES FOR OVERCOMING THE PSYCHOLOGICAL, SOCIOLOGICAL, AND CULTURAL FACTORS THAT CAN CREATE RISK MISPERCEPTIONS AND MISUNDERSTANDING

Leaders and risk communicators use a variety of specific tools for overcoming the psychological, sociological, and cultural factors that can create risk misperceptions and misunderstanding. These include:

- Collecting and evaluating empirical information (e.g., through surveys, focus groups, or interviews) about stakeholder judgments of each risk perception factor. To develop effective risk and crisis communication messages, it is necessary to develop a shared understanding of perceptions and expectations.
- Exchanging information with stakeholders on a regular basis about identified areas of concern.

- Developing only a limited number of key messages (ideally three or one key message with three parts) that address underlying concerns or specific questions.
- Developing key messages can also serve individually or collectively as a media sound bite—the quote in a media story attributed to a spokesperson. Sound bites are an essential element in effective media communication as short, quotable messages will often be played repeatedly by the media. They often will also be quoted by other sources of information. Speaking in sound bites helps to ensure that prepared key messages are carried in news stories. Reporters and editors almost always cut interview material into sound bites. The average length of a media sound bite is 27 words for print media and 9 seconds for broadcast media.
- Developing messages that are clearly understandable by the target audience (typically at or below their average reading grade level).
- Adhering to the "primacy/recency" or "first/last" principle in developing information materials. This principle states that the most important messages should occupy the first and last position in lists. In high-stress and emotionally charged situations, listeners tend to focus most on (and remember) information that they hear first and last. Messages that are in the middle of a list are often not heard.
- Citing sources of information that would be perceived as credible by the receiving audience. The greater the extent to which messages are supported and corroborated by credible third party sources, the less likely it is that mental noise will interfere with the ability to comprehend messages.
- Providing information that indicates genuine empathy, listening, caring, and compassion—crucial factors in establishing trust in high-concern and emotionally charged situations. When people are upset, they typically want to know that you care before they care what you know. The greater the extent to which individuals and organizations are perceived to be empathetic, caring, listening, and compassionate, the less likely it is that mental noise will interfere with message comprehension.
- Using graphics, visual aids, analogies, and narratives (such as personal stories) to increase an individual's ability to hear, understand, and recall a message.
- Constructing messages that recognize the dominant role of negative thinking in high-concern and emotionally charged situations. As noted earlier, people tend to focus more on the negative than on the positive in emotionally charged situations, with resulting high levels of anxiety and exaggerated fears. Risk communication strategies related to this principle include:
  - avoiding unnecessary, indefensible or non-productive uses of absolutes, and of the words "no," "not," "never," "nothing," and "none";
  - balancing or countering a negative key message with positive, constructive, or solution-oriented key messages;
  - providing three or more positive points to counter a single negative point or bad news. (It is important to note in this regard that a trust-building message is a positive response in and of itself and can count as one or more of the positives. It is also important to recognize that organizations have very limited control over what messages the media will emphasize. The media control which messages will be cited, what visibility they will be given, and how often they will be repeated. As a result, many positive messages may fall by the wayside. This is especially likely to be the case if the positives are hypothetical or predictive and the negatives are matters of fact.)
- Presenting the full message using the repetitive structure found in the "Tell me, Tell me more, Tell me again model" (the "Triple T Model") namely:
  - Tell people the information in summary form (i.e., the three key messages;
  - Tell them more (i.e., the supporting information)
  - Tell people again what was told in summary form (i.e., repeat the three key messages). (The greater the extent to which messages are repeated and heard through various channels, the less likely it is that mental noise will interfere with the ability to comprehend them.)

- Developing key messages and supporting information that address risk perception, outrage and fear factors such as trust, benefits, control, voluntariness, dread, fairness, reversibility, catastrophic potential, effects on children, morality, origin, and familiarity. Research indicates that the greater the extent to which these factors are addressed in messaging, the less likely it is that mental noise will interfere with the ability to comprehend messages.
- Providing people with understandable, concise, accurate, reliable information at the outset so their first impressions are correct.
- Layering information according to individual needs. One recommendation for information materials is providing multiple levels of information that can be targeted to various audiences. Most importantly, information materials cannot replace the dialogue between stakeholders.
- Motivating people to understand risk information. When people are sufficiently motivated, they can learn even very complex material.
- Using message maps (see Appendix C).
- Having an approved comprehensive risk communication plan (see Appendix A).
- Presenting and using risk comparisons effectively. The goal of risk comparisons is to make a risk number more meaningful by comparing it to other numbers. For example, small probabilities are often difficult to conceptualize (just how small is "1 in 10 million" or "a probability of 0.00015"?). Although risk comparisons can provide a yardstick and are therefore useful for putting numbers in perspective, they can also create their own problems. For example, use of the concentration comparisons can lead to disagreements. The statement "one part per million of a contaminant is equal to one drop in an Olympic-size swimming pool" is typically intended to help people understand how "small" an amount is. However, for some individuals, such comparisons appear to trivialize the problem and to prejudge their acceptability. Furthermore, concentration comparisons can sometimes be misleading since risk agents vary widely in potency—one drop of some biological agents in a community reservoir can kill many people, while one drop of other biological agents will have no effect whatsoever. Comparing the probabilities associated with different risks has many of the same problems. For example, it is often tempting to make the following type of argument:

  > The risk of "a" (breathing polluted air) is lower than the risk of "b" (injury or death caused by an automobile accident). Since you (the target audience) find "b" acceptable, you are obliged to find "a" acceptable.

- This argument has a basic flaw in its logic. Trying to use it can severely damage trust and credibility. Some receivers of the comparison will analyze the argument this way:

  > I do not have to accept the (small) added risk of breathing polluted air just because I accept the (perhaps larger, but voluntary and personally beneficial) risk of driving my car. In deciding about the acceptability of risks, I consider many factors, only one of them being the size of the risk; and I prefer to do my own evaluation.

Probabilities are only one of many kinds of information upon which people base decisions about risk acceptability. Risk numbers cannot pre-empt those decisions. Explanations of risk numbers are unlikely to be successful if the explanation appears to be trying to settle the question of whether a risk is acceptable.

Many variables affect the success of using risk comparisons, including context and the trustworthiness of the source of the comparison. The most effective comparisons appear to be:

- comparisons of the same risk at two different times;
- comparisons with a regulatory standard;

- comparisons with different estimates of the same risk;
- comparisons of the risk of doing something versus not doing it;
- comparisons of alternative solutions to the same problem; and
- comparisons with the same risk as experienced in other places.

The most difficult comparisons to communicate effectively are those that disregard the risk perception factors people consider important in evaluating risks.

8

Risk Communication Education for Local Emergency Managers: Using the CAUSE Model for Research, Education, and Outreach

Katherine E. Rowan, Carl H. Botan, Gary L. Kreps, Sergei Samoilenko, and Karen Farnsworth
George Mason University

Communication skills are integral to emergency management. Local emergency managers working for cities and counties throughout the United States cope with earthquakes, rail, air, and highway incidents, floods, droughts, fires, hurricanes, tornadoes, industrial accidents, cyber-terrorism, and terrorist attacks. They (a) gather information to analyze threats; (b) share information; (c) collaborate with all layers of government, businesses, schools, nonprofits, and residents; (d) coordinate and release alerts and warnings; (e) plan and carry out evacuations, and (f) develop and implement public education programs (Bea, 2005; Drabek & Hoemer, 1991; U.S. DHS, 2006a). Each of these inherently communicative activities requires character, empathy, intelligence, leadership, and considerable communication skill.

But despite the extent to which communication is inherent in emergency management work, the amount of formal communication education accessed by local emergency managers is not extensive. A 2006 survey of county emergency management offices found that "over half of top emergency managers (57 percent) have more than a high school education, but only less than 10 percent hold either a bachelor's or postgraduate degree within the field [of emergency management]" (Clarke, 2006, p. 1). This is a severe problem considering that most emergency managers play important roles in improving public education and eliminating illiteracy regarding health, risk prevention, and safety.

Currently, there are a number of initiatives aimed at supporting local emergency managers through advanced education (e.g., Emergency Management Institute, www.emilms.fema.gov; FEMA Higher Education Project, n.d.; Thomas & Mileti, 2003; USDHS, 2006b). In addition, prominent sociologists, communication scholars, and consultants offer seminars and consulting in risk and emergency communication (see, for example, Covello, www.centerforriskcommunication.com; Heath & Abel, 1996; Sandman, 1993, www.psandman.com). Continuing education is offered through the Centers for Disease Control and Prevention, and other federal and state offices that update emergency managers on new threats such as pandemic flu (www.pandemicflu.gov).

But if one takes seriously the idea that local emergency managers (EMs) need to understand fundamental patterns of human behavior (e.g., why people procrastinate in preparing for emergencies; why they may be more afraid of residents in nearby counties than they are of natural or manmade disasters) and how one communicates to address and overcome these and other powerful human tendencies, then the necessity of developing communication education and training specifically for emergency managers becomes clear. Communication education should prepare emergency managers to (a) build working relationships with community members; (b) develop systematic ways of encouraging local preparedness; (c) respond to anger, fear, outrage and grief in disasters, and (d) assess and refine interpersonal and public communication efforts after emergencies occur.

To meet this need, this chapter (a) describes the number of EMs nationwide and their responsibilities; (b) compares and contrasts EMs in two geographically and economically distinct areas, Southeast Louisiana and Washington, DC, to illustrate these challenges; and (c) presents the CAUSE model as a tool for identifying a predictable set of five communication challenges likely to plague local emergency management. Throughout the chapter, the CAUSE model is used to sketch a research program for understanding and enhancing emergency communication by generating hypotheses about ways of addressing and overcoming frequent risk communication challenges faced by emergency managers. The model is also used to suggest communication courses, training, and outreach that would support local emergency management and preparedness for the long term.

LOCAL EMERGENCY MANAGEMENT IN THE UNITED STATES

Definition

An EM is anyone who supervises response or responds to emergency calls.[1] EMs work for all levels of government. They also work in the private sector and for public schools, universities, parks, and hospitals. In this chapter, we focus on the communication challenges facing local government employees in the United States who are employed in emergency management on a part- or full-time basis. Local emergency management has been particularly affected by the 1986 federal Community Planning and Emergency Right to Know Act, which required "local emergency planning committees" or LEPCs to organize. These groups include emergency management directors, fire chiefs, industry leaders, and interested citizens who meet regularly to identify situations and places in a community that could harm citizens, property, evidence, or the environment. There are 4,145 LEPCs nationwide (Starik, Adams, Berman, & Sudharsan, 2000).

Numbers of County Local Emergency Managers and Their Responsibilities

The number of people engaged in local emergency planning and response is not large. According to Clarke, there is approximately 1 emergency management administrator for every 1,000 U.S. county residents (Clarke, 2006, p. 3), and 77 percent of county emergency management heads have duties other than emergency management, chiefly in law enforcement, emergency medical services, or fire fighting (Clarke, 2006, p. v). That is, in many less populated areas, a local fire chief or paramedic might also function as a county's emergency management director. On top of these duties, local EMs are responsible for communication-intensive tasks such as supplementing their budgets by writing grants and partnering with local businesses and volunteer groups to acquire essential equipment and supplies such as trucks, antibiotics and water (Clarke, 2006, pp. 7–8). One emergency management official in Connecticut said he was most proud of the fact that he had converted an old bread truck into his town's emergency response vehicle (Rowan, Toles-Patkin, Troester, Samoilenko, Penchalapadu, Farnsworth, & Botan, 2006).

Local EMs receive support from state and federal authorities, the American Red Cross, and other charitable and religious organizations (American Red Cross, 2006; US DHS, 2006). However, in a major disaster such as Hurricane Katrina in 2005, all of these organizations may be overwhelmed. As the American Red Cross' assessment of its actions in 2005 noted, "The 'Red Cross' in a community during a disaster may transition from being one paid staff member with a total annual budget of $100,000, to 1,000 employees and volunteers distributing meals and assistance in excess of $25 million. That expansion generally takes less than a week.... Because of the enormity of the 2005 hurricanes ... volunteer and paid staff were stretched beyond their capacity" (ARC, 2006, pp. 7–8). In 2005, the nation watched on television as many Hurricane Katrina victims had to wait at least a week for assistance. While this situation may have seemed attributable to factors distinctive to Hurricane Katrina and Louisiana, it is unlikely that any major metropolitan area in the United States is prepared to care for large numbers of residents if a Katrina-sized disaster were to strike (U.S., DHS, 2006b).

To illustrate the communication challenges facing local EMs, we studied both Southeast Louisiana, which includes New Orleans and its surrounding parishes, and metropolitan Washington, DC. Although the economic and geographic profiles for these areas differ, their emergency communication challenges have many similarities.

COMMUNICATION CHALLENGES IDENTIFIED BY SOUTHEAST LOUISIANA EMERGENCY MANAGERS PRIOR TO HURRICANE KATRINA

In June of 2005, Southeast Louisiana emergency management officials had already done considerable work with state and federal officials to devise plans for evacuating in the event of a major hurricane. Geographically, Southeast Louisiana is a large punchbowl, much of the land being below sea level (Travis, 2005). Because of the area's punchbowl contour, it is quite plausible that even a Category I or II hurricane could cause flooding in some parishes with or without levee failure. A number of systematic efforts had been made to alert residents to the need to evacuate if a hurricane were to strike. For example, residents in many parishes throughout Louisiana had been sent 60-page booklets through the mail describing the need for emergency planning, how to plan, and the contents of household survival kits (e.g., Case, 2005; see also www.trac4la.com,; Louisiana, n.d.). Stories about the vulnerability of the area to hurricane damage had been published in the New Orleans newspaper, *The Times-Picayune,* for years. On the other hand, there were many reasons why large numbers of Southeast Louisiana residents did not evacuate. One is that 27 percent of them live at or below the poverty line, as compared to 10 percent of U.S. residents in the rest of the nation (Fussell, 2005).

The hurricane evacuation plan for Southeast Louisiana assumed that most residents would evacuate on their own initiative, mostly in private vehicles. Even if all residents had their own vehicles, emphasis on private transportation for evacuation is not ideal. Transportation planners generally do not design major roads leading to and from metropolitan areas to accommodate a mass exodus. Consequently, a phased evacuation plan called "contra-flow" had been devised for Southeast Louisiana, and emergency managers were spending considerable time explaining this plan to residents.

Salient Concerns for SE Louisiana Emergency Managers in June 2005

There was concern among emergency managers about the contra-flow plan for evacuating. Residents of relatively in-land parishes were upset that parishes nearer the coast were being allowed to evacuate earlier than they. The order of evacuation was dictated by the need to avoid trapping those in coastal areas from behind massive inland traffic jams. However, it was a source of concern to the inland residents that they would have to wait for others to travel through their parish before they themselves could evacuate. Emergency managers were also worried about residents of their parishes having to use side roads to evacuate. Some were worried about their residents having to evacuate in the middle of the night. Howell (2005, personal communication; Howell & Bonner, 2005) noted that many residents did not know what intersections were near them, which means they were unfamiliar with the roads they had to travel to evacuate.

Second, there was disagreement among emergency managers about whether to mandate evacuation. Officials in Southeast Louisiana were reluctant to make evacuation mandatory for many reasons. One reason is that evacuation is costly. If an evacuation is ordered and turns out to be unnecessary, the official who ordered it would be criticized for imposing substantial financial burdens on citizens and businesses. Another concern is that mandatory evacuation is unenforceable. To deal with these challenges, there were some efforts to create buddy systems that could reach the poor (Shirley Laska, University of New Orleans, personal communication), but, as is well known now, the principal plan for all those who, it was believed, chose not to evacuate, was to tell them to head for shelter in the Superdome. It is now known that people over age 51 accounted for more than 84 percent of the bodies at the St. Gabriel morgue (Louisiana Recovery Authority, 2006). In Louisiana, 50 percent of those 65 and older have disabilities (Fussell, 2005, citing the U.S. 2000 census).

In sum, Southeast Louisiana emergency managers were communicating with the public; however, there was a gap between what they were doing and what was needed. State and local emergency management offices were coordinating mailings, television appearances, and presentations to civic groups about the importance of evacuation in the event of hurricane. These messages were reaching middle- and upper-class Louisiana residents. These activities were probably not communicating to the poor, those not reading daily newspapers, and those who were not members of local civic groups. Additionally, although emergency managers were well aware of the dangers hurricanes could cause, and some of them were issuing strong warnings to everyone they met, other emergency managers were ambivalent about the necessity of mandating evacuation.

Perceptions of Southeast Louisiana Residents About Their Vulnerability to Hurricanes Prior to Katrina. In addition to the ambivalence felt by some emergency managers, residents of Southeast Louisiana were also feeling ambivalent about evacuating in the event of a hurricane. According to a phone survey, conducted prior to Katrina, there were a number of reasons residents gave for their reluctance. As Howell and Bonner (2005) reported, residents said:

- I do not need to evacuate because my home is strong, sturdy brick.
- My home is on high ground, not in the flood zone.
- I am in danger only in a Category 4 or 5 hurricane
- I will be safe if I evacuate by going to my mother's home [a location still in the danger zone].

These perceptions were inaccurate. Depending on the location of people's homes, many could easily have been flooded or subjected to wind damage depending on how close they were to the levees or other bodies of water and the angle with which even a Category 1 storm could hit. However, these perceptions had been apparently validated by the comparative luck Southeast Louisiana residents had for decades. Howell and Bonner's survey showed that the longer residents had lived in that area, the more likely it was that their homes had survived other storms, such as Hurricane Camille in 1969.

Communication Challenges Salient to Washington, DC, Area EMs in 2006

In June 2006, emergency managers in the Washington, DC, metropolitan area were concerned by the gap between awareness and action. One large county had spent $5 million on a campaign to increase residents' awareness of the need for emergency plans and household emergency kits containing water, food, medicine, battery-powered radios, and other necessities if one were forced to shelter in a home, car, or office. Prior to the campaign, 38 percent of the residents were aware of the need for emergency planning and felt it was important. Following a media blitz, distribution of free wallet-sized cards with "what you need to know" information and room for a family's emergency information, the number who felt such planning was important crept from 38 to 43 percent. Unfortunately, even after $5 million was spent, the number of those who said they had made emergency plans and stocked household survival kits did not (Fitzgerald, 2006, personal communication).

A second problem specifically concerning emergency managers on university campuses was ensuring that warnings were heard and understood. In comparison to elementary schools and high schools where there are loudspeakers, large college campuses are difficult contexts in which to create universal awareness that danger is approaching. Some campuses do not have emergency sirens that can be sounded in the event of a tornado or other bad event. One emergency manager on a college campus said that his campus was purchasing a siren, but he worried not everyone would hear it.

A third problem was that of identifying and managing the needs of vulnerable populations. As Hurricane Katrina illustrated too vividly, in all U.S. metropolitan areas there are vulnerable groups likely to need support in emergencies. They include the disabled, elderly, low socio-economic status individuals, and those who do not speak English. Despite the relative wealth and power of the Washington, DC, area, 36 percent of the District's residents are functionally illiterate, compared with 21 percent nationwide (Alexander, 2007). Some of these vulnerable groups are present on college campuses, particularly those with disabilities. Barriers to reaching many vulnerable groups include language and literacy skills, resistance to authority, predispositions and cultural beliefs, and access to communication channels (Kreps, 2005, 2006).

Individual Differences in EMs' "Lay Communication Theories." When discussing these challenges, some frustrated EMs described residents as lazy, selfish, and stupid when they reflect on interactions with the public and ways of managing public communication. Other EMs cast challenging communication tasks less as matters of ignorance or apathy and more as matters of strategy. This apparent difference suggested that one important way to enhance the quality of emergency communication is to help EMs move away from "people are idiots" as an implicit model of communication and toward a "what communication strategy did or should we use" model. The CAUSE model presented next in this chapter fosters this move toward reflective, systematic, and testable thinking.

There are no magic words that miraculously result in safety for all, but the CAUSE model for risk and emergency communication can locate communication barriers frequent in risk and emergency contexts, describe research from many fields on the reasons for these barriers, and direct communicators to research-supported strategies likely to improve their communication efforts.

THE CAUSE MODEL FOR COMMUNICATION IN HEALTH, RISK, AND EMERGENCY CONTEXTS

Communicating about physical hazards of any sort is fraught with a distinctive cluster of challenges. As we have argued elsewhere (Rowan, 1991a, 1994, 2004; Rowan, Kreps, Botan, Bailey, Sparks, & Samoilenko, in press), there are five fundamental tensions. Because communicating about physical risks makes people uneasy and skeptical, risk and emergency communication is plagued by lack of confidence in others and in oneself. Because it often involves information about newly discovered hazards, risk communication is harmed by a lack of awareness about, for example, what pandemic flu is, where a tornado has been sighted, or what some new terrorist tactic involves. Because risk and emergency communication often involves complex scientific and legal matters, it is harmed by lack of understanding about, for example, the difference between tornado watches and tornado warnings or the legal distinctions between quarantine and isolation when these states are used to prevent the spread of disease. Because risk communication frequently deals with phenomena about which even well-informed individuals disagree, it is affected by lack of satisfaction with solutions for managing a pandemic flu, eliminating lead from drinking water, or whether to require weather-related school closings. And, last, because risk communication also involves topics about which nearly all agree but on which there is a lack of enactment (e.g., the importance of having an emergency plan or washing hands frequently), risk and emergency messages sometimes need to move people from states of psychological inertia to action. In sum, these five fundamental tensions suggest five fundamental communicative goals. We list them with the mnemonic, CAUSE, referring to the goals of establishing:

Confidence
Awareness
Understanding
Satisfaction (with proposed solutions), and
Enactment, or moving from agreement to action.

Research is available from many social science fields on the relational patterns and message features associated with hindrance and accomplishment of each of these communication goals. The CAUSE model can be taught in courses on risk and crisis communication, strategic communication, health communication, persuasion, and public relations.

Building Confidence, the C in CAUSE

Local emergency officials face numerous challenges, both in being perceived as credible and in earning the confidence of community members. There are at least three frequent threats to the development of a community's "credibility infrastructure" as Heath and his colleagues have described the local contexts in which risk and emergency preparedness communication occur (Heath, 1995; Heath & Abel, 1996; Heath, Liao, & Douglas, 1995; Heath & Palenchar, 2000; also see Seeger, Sellnow, & Ulmer, 1998; Sellnow, Seeger, & Ulmer, 2005; Trumbo & McComas, 2003). These are: (a) the "Chicken Little" phenomenon; (b) frustrations with emergency personnel arising after disaster strikes, and (c) EMs' own uncertain feelings and prejudices about community members.

First, community members may have ambivalent feelings about the competence of local emergency officials and about the merit of "be prepared" messages. EMs are often fire chiefs, firefighters, and police officers. In large communities, members of the public may not know these individuals well. Some members of the public may have encountered them in unpleasant law enforcement situations. Though research shows that local emergency personnel may be more trusted than industry officials (Heath & Palenchar, 2000), people often are skeptical about those charged with managing any hazard. Another challenge is that the "be prepared" messages that EMs communicate may be perceived as trivial—until some disaster strikes. EMs refer to this latter problem as the "Chicken Little" syndrome: that is, they are continually accused of either unnecessarily panicking the public or not having done enough when disaster strikes. As this chapter is written, the threat of pandemic flu is a "Chicken Little" topic for emergency management. Across the nation, the Centers for Disease Control and Prevention is supporting local government efforts to prepare communities for pandemic flu. Epidemiologists say this threat is serious and likely. It could affect up to 40 percent of the work force with waves of illness in certain locales for as long as two years (Caldwell, n.d., also www.pandemicflu.gov). Local officials who are trying to encourage household preparedness for pandemic flu, severe storms, or power outages must deal with a good deal of un-informed skepticism.

A second more specific threat to local emergency managers' credibility with community members is the doubting process that occurs after a disaster has struck. When emergencies occur, members of the affected community become concerned about the competence and character of those on whom they are now uncomfortably dependent. They know something bad has occurred, so they begin asking, "What's the danger? What are you doing to protect me? What can I do to protect myself?" (Chess, 2000; also Dynes & Rodriguez, 2005; Quarantelli, 1988). Research shows that, ironically, when the need for emergency planning is widely discussed such efforts may *reduce* public confidence in those managing the hazard (Heath & Palenchar, 2000; Trumbo & McComas, 2003). However, this diminished public confidence seems to be associated with increased understanding of local hazards and steps for self-protection (Heath & Palenchar, 2000). That is, after extensive efforts to inform residents about emergency planning, people are less confident in local officials but more informed about local hazards and sometimes about ways to protect themselves.

A third challenge involves emergency managers' own feelings about members of the public. Firefighters, police officers, and emergency managers routinely see people at their worst. They see people struck by disaster who might have prevented their bad luck. Worse, they deal with trivial complaints during emergencies. For example, after Hurricane Isabel, some individuals demanded that ice be delivered to them to preserve refrigerated food. State and local emergency personnel complied in some cases, but soon realized that doing so would divert them from helping individuals with much greater needs and that ice should be used only to preserve essential medical supplies (City, 2004, p. 18). The authors of this chapter have heard EMs complain about inappropriate demands for ice using "people are stupid" theories of human behavior. Unfortunately, these implicit notions may reduce EMs' empathy and communication effectiveness.

Research-Supported Steps for Building Confidence. One approach to supporting emergency managers with credibility challenges is to provide spokesperson training. There are a number of excellent resources on spokesperson training for leadership during crises and emergencies (e.g., the CDC's "Face the Media" training at www.bt.cdc.gov; U.S. DHHS, 2002), and many professionals who provide this service (e.g., www.robin@greatanswers.com). A more comprehensive approach is to view credibility as Heath and his associates do as being less a quality attributed to a single person and more a matter of a community's long-term commitment to ensuring safety and to maintaining its "credibility infrastructure" (Heath, 1995; Heath & Abel, 1996; Heath, Liao, & Douglas, 1995; Heath & Palenchar, 2000; also see Seeger, Sellnow, & Ulmer, 1998; Sellnow, Seeger, & Ulmer, 2005). That is, communities need regular safety audits and recurring communication programs reminding residents about how best to prepare for emergencies.

A potential threat to community credibility may result from the practical need of emergency managers to focus their work on special-needs populations. After Hurricane Katrina, emergency managers in many areas decided that they cannot help everyone (Goodnough, 2006). Instead, they principally assist those with special needs: the disabled, elderly, and those too ill or without resources to evacuate or shelter themselves. The implications of this decision may not be widely known or understood; discussion of this topic in non-urgent contexts is needed. To address this reality, universities could work with area LEPCs to host crisis simulations and tabletop exercises where limited capacity to respond to everyone in an emergency is made clear. In addition, many local areas need support in locating special-needs individuals and encouraging them to register as persons needing assistance in disasters (Goodnough, 2006). Faculty and students in social work and communication could assist these efforts.

A second way local emergency officials can earn community confidence is to reach out, directly or indirectly, to the groups that need their help in emergencies. In large metropolitan areas, EMs need to communicate with ethnically and culturally diverse populations by getting to know community religious, medical, and business leaders in relaxing contexts. When this step is taken, these respected community members can confirm the advisability of emergency recommendations. During Hurricane Isabel, Fairfax County, Virginia, sent uniformed police officers to tell people that tidal flooding in Alexandria would flood their cars, and so it was important to move their cars to higher ground. The officers distributed fliers explaining this situation. Despite this door-to-door communication, some individuals did not heed this advice, and cars were flooded. In hindsight, Fairfax County realized that they needed to have built relationships in advance with community leaders who could vouch for the soundness of the move-your-car-or-it-will-be-flooded message (Bass, personal communication, 2006 [Bass is director of emergency management for Fairfax]). Another effective instance of building credibility through local contacts occurred during Hurricane Katrina. The CDC found that attributing its health guidance to trusted local sources was more effective than attribution to the federal government because many Gulf Coast residents were angry with the federal government for its inadequate response to their plight (Vanderford, Nastoff, Telfer, & Bonzo, 2007).

Steps to earn confidence may be most effective when they take advantage of already established credibility infrastructure. For example, EMs who directly ask members of special-needs populations to register themselves as needing special help when disasters strike may not be successful. In contrast, the same request made through social workers, religious leaders, or other community leaders who are trusted by these individuals may be achieve better results (Cutter, 2005; Dynes & Rodriguez, 2005; Fussell, 2005; Kreps, 2005, 2006).

Research literatures on steps that harm or help the process of earning confidence in connection with physical hazards, emergencies, and disasters, can be found in fields such as social work and communication, and particularly on topics such as risk communication, disaster research, persuasion, trust and public relations, social support, social networks, safety culture, preparedness culture, and intercultural communication (e.g., Drabek, 1986; Heath, 1994; Heath & Abel, 1996; Fischer, Morgan, Fischhoff, Nair, & Lave, 1991; Fischhoff, 1989; Lichtenstein, Slovic, Fischhoff, Layman, & Combs, 1978; Kreps, 2005, 2006; Morgan, Fischhoff, Bostrom, & Atman, 2002; O'Hair, Heath, & Becker, 2005; Quarantelli, 1988; Perry & Mushkatel, 1984; Roberts,1993; Rowan, 1991, 1994, Rowan et al., in press; Weeks & Bagian, 2000). The conceptual framework offered by the Kaspersons, Slovic, and their associates on factors that amplify or dampen perceptions of hazards is particularly relevant to local emergency management (e.g., Kasperson & Kasperson, 1996; Kasperson, Golding, & Tuler, 1992; Kasperson, Kasperson, Pidgeon, & Slovic, 2003; Pidgeon, Kasperson, & Slovic, 2003).

How Universities Can Help with Building Confidence. Faculty can bolster the credibility infrastructure of their communities by talking to local emergency managers and asking how they might help. Universities can create events where groups come together to listen to one another. They can also provide research expertise and facilities for meetings and drills.

Recommended Research. Questions and hypotheses this discussion suggests are:

Questions:

1. What local best practices reduce fear and stigma in coping with outsiders or special populations during natural and man-made emergencies?
2. What practices minimize the "Chicken Little" syndrome which leads many to doubt EMs when they warn of disaster and to blame them for doing too little when disaster strikes?

Hypotheses:

1. EMs educated in behavioral science and communication skills will be less likely to use "people are stupid" accounts to explain community members' behavior than those who lack this education.
2. EMs who contact special-needs individuals indirectly through social workers, ministers, or business leaders who know these individuals well will be more successful at registering them than will those who contact these individuals directly.

Creating Awareness, the A in CAUSE

Research on how people respond to warning signs, sirens, and messages shows that the process is more complex than it might initially appear. Scholars studying disasters, the public's role in spotting severe storms, warnings on consumer products, and human factors psychology have identified patterns in the ways people respond to audio and visual warnings (e.g., Anderson & Spitzberg, chapter 10, this volume; Doswell, 1998; Magat & Viscusi, 1987; Miller, Lehto, & Frantz, 1990; Perry, 1988; Perry & Mushkatel, 1984; Stewart & Martin, 1994; Stanton, 1994; Vanderford, et al., 2007; Viscusi & O'Connor, 1987; Wogalther & Silver, 1995; Wright, Creighton, Thulfall, 1982). Specifically, as Perry (1988) explains, warnings must be *detected, decoded, interpreted,* and *confirmed.* First, a warning must be detected. This is no small feat when one considers what has to occur for everyone in a metropolitan area to detect a warning or prevention message. Even the task of detecting a warning siren on a single college campus is not easy. On a typical afternoon, students, faculty, and staff may be in buildings, between buildings, or in their cars. Some will be talking on cell phones, working on projects, or distracted by music and entertainment programs. Others may be watching direct satellite television from other continents, programming that is unlikely to carry "crawl" messages on the screen alerting viewers to tornadoes or other emergencies in the United States. Still others may be sleeping or may be deaf and not have told colleagues or fellow students about their deafness because of embarrassment. Consequently, emergency managers have substantial challenges designing systems that increase the likelihood that everyone on a campus or community detects warning sirens.

Decoding. Assuming a warning siren is heard, the next challenge is ensuring that everyone "decodes" or deciphers the message correctly. Decoding is hampered if those who hear the siren or read a warning do not have a command of the language in which it is issued or do not believe it is a real emergency. Local emergency planners are testing methods to increase the chances that all residents decode warnings accurately. Universities with warning sirens are considering if they can have loudspeaker, web site, and radio messages that would help the campus community know what to do when they hear the siren sound. One emergency manager said a loudspeaker message such as, "Run like hell. This ain't no damn drill," might work. More seriously, others are recommending educational programs to teach campus community members that a warning siren means "come inside and seek information"; that is, tune in to news programs on the Internet, radio, or television (Callan, 2006, personal communication [Callan is a safety officer at George Mason University]). Mass media are important partners in helping the National Weather Service and government officials convey warning messages. More needs to be done, however, to teach which stations, Internet sites, text messaging services, and other outlets to turn to "decode" a warning siren. Along these lines, many prevention campaigns are aimed at making battery-powered NOAA all-weather radios as ubiquitous as smoke-detectors, and some efforts are under way to ensure that all offices on all university campuses have them (e.g., Campus Security, Northern Illinois University, 2003). Communication scholars are an ideal group to study and support these efforts. Information about ways to receive emergency information is available from local emergency managers, the federal government at www.ready.gov, and the American Red Cross (www.arc.org).

Confirming and Inferring Next Steps for Protection. Perry (1988) said that people do not automatically obey decoded warnings. Instead, once they understand that, for example, a tornado has been sighted, they engage in confirmatory behavior. Said simply, they talk to one another about what they have heard and how others are planning to respond. They also try to alert family members or friends and gather these individuals around them. Initially, confirmatory behavior may seem irrational. If the tornado is near, why don't people seek protection immediately? However, there may be wisdom in people's intuitive responses. It may be that warnings should legitimate confirmatory and family-gathering activities but encourage people to be quick.

Research-Supported Steps for Enhancing Awareness. Research shows that one of the best strategies for enhancing awareness of signage, sirens, and warning messages on consumer products is sheer repetition. That is, if a message is important, it should be repeated many times (O'Keefe, 2002; Petty & Cacioppo, 1986). Another strategy involves repeating the message but doing so in ways that seem fresh or different. Universities post emergency information on signs in buildings (e.g., George Mason, n.d.) and place information on web sites about how to act in case of fire, if a suspicious person appears on campus, or if there is a severe weather threat, but in actual incidents, people may realize they do not know what to do in such contexts. As with all warnings, there should be routine testing of whether this information has been detected. Post-disaster contexts also make message detection difficult. After Katrina, the CDC realized that evacuees in shelters and hotels were unlikely to detect its prevention messages concerning shaken baby syndrome and other hazards for people under stress if these messages were sent through news media. To solve this problem, the CDC developed and distributed "palm cards," or playing card-sized materials with prevention messages on "parenting under stress," "when your baby cries," and "suicide prevention" (Vanderford et al., 2007). Finally, the age-old formula for drawing attention to news by suggesting that one's information is "outrageous if true" is highly effective (Sandman, 1993). However, it is easy for this method of gaining attention to be over-used.

Outreach Efforts to Create Heightened Awareness. Research on the communication of warnings could become part of basic communication courses that, on many campuses, every student is required to take. In addition, communication scholars could study campus activities or organizations that promote safety knowledge. One university safety officer conducts a "Fire Academy" experience for resident hall advisors. Rather than simply listening to 15 minutes of lecture on fire safety, residence hall advisors travel to a firefighters' training site, practice navigating through real smoke in a mock up of a smoked filled building, and then debrief to discuss dangers from candles in dorms, and so forth (Callan, 2006, personal communication). Awareness of fire safety information is apt to be enhanced by those having such an experience. There are probably many other ways to foster a "safety culture" that heightens awareness of safety information among many more campus and community members (see, for example, Roberts, 1993; Weeks & Bagian, 2000). For example, emergency managers say that people learn the most about how to decode emergency warnings when they are in elementary school. Many can repeat the mantra of "stop, drop, and roll" because it was taught to them in elementary school.

Recommended Research on Creating Awareness. Questions and hypotheses this discussion suggests include:

Questions:

1. Across the nation, what communication methods are in use currently to alert university campuses to emergencies such as tornadoes or snipers?
2. To what extent does high personal involvement in emergency drills (where involvement means responsibility for planning and executing the drill) lead to increased awareness of emergency information?

Hypotheses:

1. Warnings that legitimate confirmatory behavior (e.g., talking to others to find out if the warning is real and what to do in response) will increase intentions to engage in protective behavior more than warnings that do not include legitimating components.
2. Repeated emergency messages that vary in their illustrations or media (playing card sized messages vs. public service announcements) but remain the same in substance will be recalled more than messages repeated without variation.

Deepening Understanding, the U in CAUSE

There is an important distinction between *awareness* and *understanding*, the U in CAUSE. Awareness has to do with knowing the latest information about an understood topic; i.e., if a message is sent saying a roadway has been blocked or a sniper sighted, people understand road closures and snipers. They need awareness about where the road closure or sniper is. In contrast, efforts to deepen understanding are needed when people can pronounce the terms in a message and understand the terms' referents, but do not understand intended meanings of key terms, cannot visualize a complex structure or process, or have an intuitive notion inconsistent with that of widely accepted expert knowledge. Research has identified steps to overcome these three sources of confusion (Rowan, 1988, 1995, 1999, 2003; Rowan et al., in press).

Clarifying Confusions Over Terms. Unfamiliar words cue communicators and audiences that they have not understood an important concept in a message. Unfortunately, confusion often surrounds familiar words intended in specific ways. People hear terms such as "tornado watch" and "tornado warning," but do not know the difference between the two. The terms "quarantine" and "isolation" are being discussed in connection with pandemic flu, but the legal distinctions between these two terms are not obvious. The phrase "100-year flood plain" is commonly misunderstood to mean that a flood could only occur once every 100 years, i.e., a period longer than most people will be in their homes. Instead, this statistical term means that there is a 1 in 100 chance of a flood occurring in any single year, which means flood insurance is recommended or mandated (www.floodsmart.gov). To overcome this sort of confusion, elucidating explanations are needed. Elucidating explanations make the essential meaning of key terms clear. Research-supported steps for effective explanation of confusing terms include (a) defining a term by its essential meaning; (b) noting what the term does not mean; (c) giving a range of varying examples showing instances of the term (e.g., if there are several forms of isolation one might use in a pandemic, several would be listed instead of one so that people do not wrongly infer the features of one kind are common to all forms, and (d) explaining a "non-example," an instance one might think is an example but is not (Merrill & Tennyson, 1977; Rowan, 1988, 1995, 2003; Rowan et al., in press; Tennyson & Cochiarella, 1986).

In Washington, DC, many had not heard the phrase "shelter in place" until the September 11, 2001, attacks on New York and the Pentagon. Some thought wrongly that it meant to "drive to a shelter." An effective elucidating explanation of this term could be placed on fliers, buses, subways, explanatory web sites, fact sheets, and given to emergency spokespersons so that people are not confused. It might simply say that shelter-in-place does not mean evacuation. Rather it means to take shelter where one is currently located, at home, at work, at school, or in some other safe place. Giving a range of examples of places where one could shelter would be clarifying. Finally, one might give a "non-example" and explicitly say that "shelter in place" does not mean to drive to a public shelter. Then, the clarity of these messages should be periodically tested.

Visualizing Complex Structures and Processes. Some ideas are hard to understand because they are hard to visualize. Tornado spotters need to know what cloud formations look like just before a tornado forms. Those who give first aid need to know how the heart and lungs work. Effective explanations of structures and processes difficult to visualize are called quasi-scientific explanations (Rowan, 1988, 2003). Research shows that good quasi-scientific explanations contain features such as diagrams, analogies, headings, titles, and preview statements (e.g., the five parts of radar are …) that assist people in seeing the "big picture" and distinguishing main components from minor ones. Research in educational psychology by Mayer and his associates has shown that the more individuals can identify main points about, for example, a storm surge or a lightning strike, the more they are able to use this knowledge to solve problems such as explaining why lying in a ditch would be a better way to avoid lightning strikes than standing next to a lone tree in the middle of a field. Information on effective quasi-scientific explanations is available in educational psychology, particularly in work by Mayer and his associates (e.g., 1983, 1989; Mayer, Bove, Bryman, Mars, & Tapangco, 1996; Rowan, 1999, 2003).

Fischhoff and his associates have developed procedures for interviewing experts and novices to determine discrepancies between each group's "mental models" or visualizations of physical hazards (e.g., chapter 25, this volume; Morgan, Fischhoff, Bostrom, & Atman, 2002). Information about these differences is used to improve explanatory materials such as brochures on radon gas or Lyme disease. Other research on effective explanation suggests that news stories written using the traditional "inverted pyramid" format, which puts the latest information or news first in a story and explanatory material last, may not be the most effective way of explaining complex physical hazards. Yaros (2006) found that stories on scientific topics that were organized in the classic inverted pyramid format were more difficult to comprehend than stories that began with news but also put key explanatory material early in the story. His finding is consistent with work in educational psychology that showed "advance organizers" such as titles, analogies, and previews at the front of a text enhanced comprehension more than when these features appeared at the end of texts (Ausubel, 1960; Mayer, 1983).

Explaining Counter-Intuitive Ideas Using Transformative Explanations. Research shows that people struggle to understand ideas that run counter to deeply held intuitive theories about fundamental aspects of reality such as weather, illness, family relations, and so forth (Anderson & Smith, 1984; Hewson & Hewson, 1983, 1984; Rowan, 1991b). For example, people who live in arid Arizona may find it hard to believe that they could fall victim to a flash flood. In fact, flooding is the most likely natural disaster in the United States, and flash floods—a distinct possibility in Arizona when dry ground cannot absorb sudden rain—are the number one weather-related killer in the United States (www.floodsmart.gov). Further, "almost 25 percent of all flood insurance claims come from areas with minimal flood risk" (www.floodsmart.gov). Each of these ideas is apt to be difficult to understand because it is inconsistent with powerful lay notions about the circumstances where flooding is likely. Another counter-intuitive idea is that one could fall victim to hypothermia while jogging on a beautiful 60-degree (Fahrenheit) day. Everyday notions or "lay theories" may say that it is impossible to become chilled to the point of illness in 60-degree weather (Rowan, 2003). Or, people may have lay theories that say brick homes are safe from hurricanes or that tornados do not touch down in urban areas.

Research has shown that people are best able to question lay theories and overcome them if transformative explanations are used (Anderson & Smith, 1984; Hewson & Hewson, 1983; Rowan, 1988, 1991, 1999, 2003). There are four steps in effective transformative explanations. Specifically, because people struggle to give up a lay theory, good transformative explanations call these theories to people's attention, acknowledge their apparent reasonableness, call attention to inconsistencies between the lay theory and accepted science, and then explain the accepted science. Here's an example of a transformative explanation explaining why someone with a home in Southeast Louisiana is vulnerable to damage even in a Category 1 or 2 hurricane.

State the lay theory and acknowledge its apparent reasonableness. Many assume they are safe in a Category 1 or 2 hurricane. People can often remember storms they "rode out" in their homes where neither they nor their homes were harmed.

Create dissatisfaction with the lay view by noting familiar experiences inconsistent with it. Over the last three decades SE Louisiana has sunk farther below sea level, and the surrounding wetlands that act like sponges to absorb flood water are much smaller now (e.g., Case, 2005, p. 16).

Explain the more accepted view. A relatively low storm surge from a slow Category 2 or 3 hurricane could flood an area that is below sea level. Learn more about the risk for your area of your parish so you are not surprised by flooding.

Elucidating, quasi-scientific, and transformative explanations are best presented in contexts where people are interested in learning. That is, people may find unsolicited explanations insulting or "face" threatening (Goffman, 1959; Metts & Grohskopf, 2003). On the other hand, people seem to enjoy and appreciate advice and explanation they voluntarily seek. Fortunately, many mass media materials are usually voluntary rather than required reading. Feature news stories on emergency management topics may be more compelling and understandable if they use elucidating, quasi-scientific explanations, and transformative explanations (Rowan, 1999, 2003).

How Universities Can Help. Communication scholars and students could use research-supported steps to test and refine the educational materials local EMs use to communicate about floods, hurricanes, storms, terrorist attacks, and other emergencies.

Recommended Research Needed on Deepening Understanding Research questions and hypotheses this discussion suggests include:

Questions:

1. What misperceptions about hurricanes, floods, tornadoes, industrial accidents, accidental chemical releases, and terrorist attacks do local emergency managers routinely face?
2. To what extent do brochures, pamphlets, and other explanatory materials used by local emergency managers incorporate research-supported text features to enhance comprehension?

Hypothesis:

1. Explanatory materials (feature stories, fact sheets, fliers, web sites) with the features of elucidating explanations, quasi-scientific, and transformative explanations will be more fully understood than those that lack these textual components.

Gaining Satisfaction with Solutions, the S in CAUSE

Having confidence, awareness, and understanding about some physical hazard is often not enough. The next step in the CAUSE model involves gaining satisfaction with recommended solutions. There are many predictable sources of disagreement. Some are:

- Doubts about an event's *probability* and *severity* (e.g., how likely is it that pandemic flu would keep me housebound for weeks? How badly would I suffer if I did not have a battery-powered radio during a power outage? (For information on how to influence perceptions of probability and severity, there are many sources. Intriguing ones include Paton & Johnston, 2001; Paton, Smith & Johnston, 2005; Sandman, 1993; Witte et al., 2001.)
- Disagreement about *benefits* and *costs* (e.g., I know I will lose time and money preparing an evacuation plan in case of hurricane. Will the possible benefits outweigh this certain loss? Making a paper copy of key cell phone numbers takes time. Will I ever need it? [See Steel & Konig, 2006, on motivation.])
- Concerns about loss of "*face*" or embarrassment (e.g., Will my friends laugh at me if I seem too worried about emergency preparedness? [See Goffman, 1959; Metts & Grohskopf, 2003.])
- Worries about "*response efficacy*" or whether the recommended action will really work (e.g., Will having a three-day survival kit at home actually come in handy in a power outage, blizzard, industrial accident, or terrorist attack? [See Aldoory & Bonzo, 2005; Chess, 2000; Witte, Meyer, & Martell, 2001, on fostering agreement with messages, particularly messages about safety and preparedness.])

This brief list of factors that can inhibit satisfaction with solutions shows that earning acceptance of a recommendation is a very complex matter. However, one way to consider this challenge is to analyze it through two fundamental and interrelated questions: (a) What relationships do publics believe exists between themselves and those preparing for emergencies and (b) how persuasive or satisfactory is the message itself? People may disagree with officials' judgments that, for example, the pandemic flu is a threat to be taken seriously, or that industrial accidents or terrorist attacks are likely in their community. In short, relationships among people heavily influence the persuasiveness of any message, and message quality, in turn, affects relationships. Steps to enhance relations among EMs and their key publics were discussed earlier in this chapter's account of building a community's credibility infrastructure. We focus here on a quality of these relationships that can seriously hinder community acceptance of emergency managers' recommendations.

Paternalism. Paternalism is the attempt to govern or provide for people's needs based on the assumption that the provider knows best what those people need and that, therefore, their opinions can be ignored. In a communication context such as emergency communication, paternalism is a meta-comment on the relationship between sender and receiver. Regardless of the technical "correctness" of a message from trained EMs, or maybe because the EMs are convinced of the technical content of their messages, any message delivered with paternalistic undertones is more likely to be unsatisfactory in the eyes of publics than a non-paternalistic message.

There are too many factors contributing to a paternalistic tone in messages to discuss them all in this chapter. Two deserve quick mention. First, EMs actually *are* often more knowledgeable about what publics need in emergency situations, and quicker to understand those needs, than the publics themselves. That is how they gained certification as emergency managers. Second, EMs are trained to deal with issues of probability (e.g., flood warnings, accidental chemical releases, pandemic flu risk) and to take precautions based on these probabilities. Such probabilities, however, are both hard to communicate clearly to publics and may not address issues of principle or other probabilities that drive the decision making of some publics. For example, with every hurricane or flood warning some homeowners feel they have to decide between accepting the risk of staying if there is such an event with the risk of theft, looting, and extra expense if they evacuate.

In these cases, while the EMs may be technically correct, their message may not be accepted as satisfactory, and deaths could result. If, on the other hand, the publics perceive EMs as competent individuals who care a great deal about them, messages are likely to be seen as satisfactory. There is one general strategy useful in these day-to-day interactions, and in emergency message situations: two-sided persuasion.

Research supported steps to solutions: Two-sided persuasion Two-sided persuasion (e.g., Hovland, Lumsdaine, & Sheffield, 1949; O'Keefe, 1998; Pfau, 1997) is based on careful listening skills (e.g., Wolvin & Coakley, 1996), and while it is not a perfect approach to every situation, it is a wise default communication mode for emergency communication situations.

In a two-sided approach, the other side, from the speaker's point of view, is always presented *first*, and is presented *objectively*, *fully*, and *fairly*. This means that emergency messages in other than the most time-urgent situations should start *objectively, fully and fairly* acknowledging the counter arguments in the minds of publics. This step demonstrates that the speaker has a clear and fair evaluation of the public's arguments and that after such a full and fair evaluation the EM still believes that certain actions are necessary. The speakers then present their own side of the issue, in effect saying, "I gave your perspective full and fair consideration, and now I ask that you fairly consider what my training and experience tell me." The advantage to this approach is that audiences are less likely to be busy rehearsing their objections or being defensive while listening to the EMs' points of view. Hovland et al. (1949) found two-sided persuasion is vastly more effective than one-sided approaches when the audience is exposed to counter-arguments (see also O'Keefe, 1998, 2002). Recent research on the closely related idea of inoculation theory (e.g., Pfau 1992, 1997; Pfau & Wan, 2006) supports the merits of the two-sided approach. For example, inoculation theory might lead EMs to acknowledge at the start of a message that sometimes government officials or emergency managers over-respond to possible dangers, but that what is being suggested in the current case is a matter of public safety, not-over reaction.

How Universities Can Help. Universities can provide practice in techniques like two-sided persuasion in non-threatening contexts such as classes, workshops, and on-line education. Faculty can assess local EMs' listening, outreach, and presentations skills, and teach EMs to coach one another.

Research Needed on Gaining Satisfaction. There are many research questions and hypotheses to test concerning ways to gain satisfaction with recommended safety solutions:

Questions:

1. Does paternalism exist locally?
2. If so, how aware are EMs of paternalistic communication patterns?
3. Do perceptions of paternalism or over-reaction inhibit the effectiveness of emergency communication efforts in actual practice?

Hypotheses:

1. An emergency message presented in a two-sided approach will be more acceptable to publics than one presented in a traditional approach.
2. An emergency message preceded by an inoculation step will be more accepted by publics in an emergency situation than an emergency message not preceded by an inoculation step.

Motivating Enactment, the E in CAUSE

One of the biggest challenges for emergency management officials is to increase the likelihood that citizens not only agree with preparedness recommendations but actually act on their beliefs. Research by Steel and Konig (2006) showed that people value "today" far more than they value benefits that may accrue to them in the future. Further, they are far more likely to act on their intent to prepare an emergency kit or to develop a family emergency plan if they perceive the need to do so as being very near. In one study, those who perceived an earthquake affecting them within the next 12 months were more likely to secure cabinet doors with latches and bookshelves to walls than were those who anticipated an earthquake affecting them at some point beyond 12 months (Paton, Smith, & Johnston, 2005).

A further challenge is that for most emergency preparedness efforts, the goal is to have people not only take a single step toward preparedness but to integrate preparedness behaviors into their lives for perpetuity. To increase the likelihood that people develop and maintain preparedness routines throughout their lives, it is useful to look at research on adopting good habits. According to Booth-Butterfield (2003), habitual behavior may be viewed as "embedded" or "unembedded." Embedded behaviors are frequent and integral to daily routine. Cigarette smoking and eating are examples. In contrast, unembedded behaviors occur infrequently. Less embedded or unembedded behaviors include visiting a museum occasionally or cleaning the attic once a decade.To increase the embeddedness of a safety behavior, an analysis needs to be conducted of how the new behavior will fit into a routine. As Booth-Butterfield notes, the analyst should ask how often the behavior should occur, with whom, in what setting, and how participants will react and feel. Thoughtful answers can guide efforts to increase citizens' likelihood of having emergency plans and survival kits.

For example, following Booth-Butterfield's (2003) guidelines, one should consider when and how frequently to issue reminders about stocking emergency kits and updating family emergency plans. People may be more likely to adopt and maintain this set of behaviors if they begin to associate them with times when organizing is important such as the beginning of the school year or in connection with sending holiday greeting cards. Or, perhaps this activity could be associated with the start of the calendar year or even Valentine's Day. "Keep connected to those you love" messages could be bundled with new calendars, planners, and cell phones. Booth-Butterfield's analysis also encouraged consideration of the feelings people should associate with these activities. Perhaps feelings of protectiveness or pride in one's identity as a responsible planner should be invoked.

Another factor associated with moving from intention to prepare for emergencies to actually doing so is that of "self-efficacy," or belief that one is capable of carrying out the recommended action. People perceive themselves as capable of enacting a recommended behavior if (a) they have taken the recommended action previously; (b) are physically capable of doing so; (c) receive messages encouraging the recommended behavior; (d) see others enacting the recommended behavior, and (e) identify with groups where the desired behavior is encouraged (Bolam, Murphy, & Gleeson, 2004; Harwood & Sparks, 2003; Witte, et al., 2001). Interestingly, female members of the Church of the Latter Day Saints encourage one another to have well-stocked pantries as a part of their faith. One would assume LDS members who identify strongly with their faith might be more likely to have emergency supplies in their homes than would individuals for whom this identity is less essential. For other groups, there may be ways to help people take pride in preparedness and to become skilled at developing self knowledge about what prevents them from adopting a new habit. According to Steel and Konig (2006), people who maintain a new behavior are skilled at dividing large tasks into easier, smaller steps, and removing distractions from their efforts such as television.

Motivating People to Move from Agreement to Action. Actual preparedness is the "gold standard" of emergency communication. Research by each of the scholars listed above sheds some light on how best to motivate and maintain behavior change. In addition, some steps for increasing the likelihood that people move from agreement to enactment are summarized by Clark (1984). According to Clark, this movement is most likely when the recommended behavior is easy, quick, inexpensive, and more enjoyable to do than not to do. Ease may be enhanced if attractively packaged survival kits were stocked at Wal-Mart, grocery stores, and home centers ready to be grabbed quickly, purchased, and stored. Cell phone manufacturers already make purchasing a new cell phone easy by offering to transfer all stored numbers in an old phone to a new one in minutes. Updating emergency contact lists for storage on one's phone, computer, and in hard copy could be made equally easy with some cleverly marketed software product. One might make updating emergency kits enjoyable by sponsoring "mock crisis" parties where college students, neighbors, religious, or civic groups pretend to be "sheltering in place" or camping indoors for a few hours. Attendees could come home with fresh supplies of canned goods, water, and other essentials to store until the next "crisis" party. The Red Cross, the Department of Homeland Security's web site (www.ready.gov), and many counties throughout the United States have information aimed at preparing local residents for the emergencies most likely to affect them. If people received federal tax credits for receipts associated with updated emergency kits each year, perhaps this emergency kit re-stocking would become widespread.

Finally, one way to move people from saying they will prepare for emergencies to actually doing so is to require emergency preparedness as a condition of employment. Drabek (2001) found that private businesses were effective at ensuring that employees were prepared for emergencies; however, those businesses that mandated emergency preparedness often did so because the nature of the business required that employees remain at work and be separated from the families during emergencies. This separation created considerable stress. Nevertheless, Drabek's finding suggests that local government might increase local emergency preparedness by discussing emergency preparedness challenges with the business community and seeking their expertise. Public relations professionals might donate time planning an emergency preparedness campaign. It may be that motivating local emergency preparedness could help sell local products such as specially packaged toiletries.

How Universities Can Help. Universities can assist emergency managers by doing research on campaigns to increase local emergency preparedness. They can take steps such as sponsoring "mock crisis" parties and other exercises to increase student, faculty, and staff knowledge of proper response to fires, tornadoes, snipers, and other crises. Faculty in public relations and other similar disciplines can encourage students to design and implement safety campaigns aimed at ensuring that students avoid using candles in residence halls, know how to evacuate in case of a fire, and know how to take shelter in case of a tornado, industrial accident, or sniper.

Research Needed on Motivating Enactment. This discussion suggests several questions and hypotheses to address in future work:

Questions:

1. How do key publics respond to efforts to partner safety with "fun" such as having mock crisis parties to increase the number of college students who have "72-hour bags" full of food, water, and other essentials necessary if they were to shelter in place without power for several days?
2. Which segments of the business community are most interested in supporting efforts to encourage individuals to stock emergency kits and have plans for contacting family in case of emergencies?

Hypotheses:

1. Emergency kits labeled "72-hour" bags (a positive, neutral label) will sell in supermarkets and discount stores more quickly than bags labeled "emergency kits."
2. Packaging "72-hour bags" for easy purchase and placing them near check-registers in grocery and discount stores will increase the number of these bags sold over placement of them in less visible parts of stores.

Teaching Risk and Emergency Communication: Cautions Associated with Having Students Convey Risk and Emergency Messages to Publics. In this chapter we encourage communication faculty to integrate units on risk and emergency communication into their communication courses. One way this may be done is to have undergraduate and graduate students work on projects where they actually alert members of their campus or local community to emergency or risk situations. These projects are often very fulfilling for students because they are real. On the other hand, there are some cautions to consider when using projects of this sort in class.

In these cases a sort of two-step-flow of risk communication takes place and the lay communicators upon whom receivers come to depend take on some attributes of what the literature calls "influentials" or, more commonly, "opinion leaders" (Lazersfeld, Berleson, & Gaudet, 1948: Katz, 1957; Katz & Lazarsfeld, 1955). These risk opinion leaders often operate through interpersonal channels rather than more formal and mediated ones typically used by risk communication specialists. Such lay risk communicators can also be understood as diffusers of risk information (Cragan & Shields, 1998; Rogers, 1995). In major catastrophes, where mass media systems and the internet may fail, the vast majority of risk information shared may be that between lay communicators and lay receivers, with no communication specialists involved.

Lay risk communicators are people who, by virtue of seeking out needed information, or simply by chance, possess risk information that others want. They become *de facto* opinion leaders in often dangerous situations. For example, in the case of the aftermath of Katrina in New Orleans with which this chapter started, we all saw instances of survivors who had no mass media, Internet, or qualified experts available for several days. Under such circumstances, people still seek out whatever information is available from the best source available, often others sharing the risk experience.

Research has shown that under such circumstances publics will turn to the most reasonable available source of information. For example, Botan and Taylor (2005) discussed a rare risk communication situation, communicating within Bosnia after the ethnic cleansing campaigns. They concluded that even in extreme risk situations people will place at least some trust in whatever channels of communication are available to them. This finding is consistent with research on behavior in disasters which shows that the victims and the first responders in many disasters are the same individuals (e.g., Dynes & Rodriguez, 2005; Quarantelli, 1988).

Student groups are not, of course, equivalent to the lay risk communicator experience during and after Katrina, during a flu pandemic, or after an earthquake. They do, however, have some characteristics in common with lay risk communication in those situations. First, student groups often communicate about health and safety needs. One author on this paper has had student groups communicate about cancer prevention, community emergency preparedness, dangers of lead-based paint, hygiene for combating a flu pandemic, and heart attack prevention. Second, students are learning to become professional communicators but typically have little or no actual experience at systematically communicating risk information to large audiences. Third, students are often confronted with the need to draw on their own lay backgrounds to figure out ways to communicate information learned from another source (in this case a teacher or client) to lay publics. Finally, student groups often are perceived as having more in common with lay audiences than the teachers or clients from whom they get information.

In our experience, students in these contexts are likely to make two errors. First, they focus unnecessarily on a single aspect of a multi-faceted risk. Second, they "over-reach" or present their own views and opinions as expert.

Focusing on a Single Aspect of Risk. Many risk and emergency situations have complex causes and solutions. Trained emergency communicators are often conversant with each facet and know when focusing on a single aspect is inappropriate. Lay risk communicators and students, on the other hand, often are conversant with only one aspect so they focus on that. For example, one of the authors has had multiple student groups present cancer avoidance or detection campaigns. Upwards of 75 percent of American public relations students are female, which may partially explain why most of those groups have chosen to focus on breast cancer. Information regarding breast examination, both self-examination and mammography, has often been the focus of the resulting campaigns. Statistics or horror stories of breast cancer deaths are typically used to motivate lay receivers to attend to the message and techniques of breast self-examination or professional tests are presented as the appropriate response. There is nothing wrong with these campaigns, but experienced cancer communication specialists know better than to make it sound as if there is just one appropriate response to the threat of breast cancer. Sometimes lay risk communicators are involved in a situation because of a personal or emotional involvement in the disease. In such cases, it is also common for them to focus on one aspect of the risk, often the one that got them involved in the first place. Several of the students mentioned in the last paragraph, for example, have been personally touched by breast cancer, often in their own families. These risk communicators correctly see the disease as deadly, but sometimes focus on that aspect—even to the exclusion of the hope-centered messages that those facing the prospect of breast cancer often also need to hear.

Helping to remedy the tendency for lay communicator to over-focus on a single aspect of a risk or emergency can range from easy to the near impossible. If a student group over-emphasizes the threat from wind during a storm and ignores the threat of flooding, for example, it is easy to refer them to scientific or professional sources. In emergency situations, such as after Katrina, however, there may be no way to get such balancing information to lay communicators so knowing about this tendency and alerting students to it may be the only alternative.

Over-Reaching. According to Coombs (2006), "when a crisis hits, an information vacuum forms" (p. 172). A crisis creates a demand for information (Fearn-Banks, 2002; Hearit, 1994; Heath, 1994) and, as Botan & Taylor (2005) found, publics will tend to accord at least medium levels of trust in all the available channels of strategic communication, even in an extreme risk environment such as Bosnia. The particular kind of information sought has been called *instructing information* (Sturges, 1994). Coombs said that instructing information offers (a) an explanation of what happened and (b) recommendations of how to protect oneself.

Lay communicators may well be called on to fill the vacuum with instructing information during and after an emergency. Nowhere is H.G. Wells' (1913) famous statement "in the country of the blind, the one-eyed man is king" more true than in the case of those in possession of even limited emergency information in the presence of an information vacuum. Inexperienced at being treated as the provider of critical information, lay communicators may be tempted to overreach, attempting to provide more instructing information than they actually possess, or generalizing between situations and solutions.

The student groups we have worked with have not typically responded to actual emergencies, but several have been called on to help plan instructing information to be used during or after an emergency such as a flu pandemic. Our experience, although limited, is consistent with the overreaching hypothesis. Student lay communicators tend to overreach, seeking with the best of intentions to provide needed information in times of crisis, but sometimes going too far.

Remedying the tendency to overreach has taken the form of instructing lay communicators in the dangers of overreaching. It may not be possible for instructors to check the content of instructing information during or even after an emergency, but lay communicators should at least be instructed to disclose whether the advice they are giving is based on confirmed fact or their own opinion. This recommendation is similar advice given to professional risk and emergency communicators in a booklet issued by the U.S. Department of Health and Human Services. It cautioned:

1. First do no harm. Your words have consequence—be sure they're the right ones.
2. Don't babble. Know what you want to say. Say it … then say it again.
3. If you don't know what you are talking about, stop talking.
4. Focus more on informing people than on impressing them. Use everyday language.
5. Never say anything you are not willing to see printed on tomorrow's front page (U.S. DHHS, 2002).

CONCLUSION

The U.S. Department of Homeland Security issued a 2006 report saying that many major cities, including New Orleans, New York, and Washington, DC, were not ready for disasters. If the criteria for readiness included ensuring that all residents have emergency plans, three days' worth of water, food, and other supplies, then few areas in the United Sates are prepared. The process of helping local emergency managers reduce the occurrence and impact of emergencies is challenging. This chapter presented the CAUSE model for meeting this challenge. It argued that in any situation where people must manage a physical hazard, five predictable tensions and psychological barriers emerge. These barriers are absences of confidence, awareness, understanding, satisfaction with solutions, and action. Second, the model directed communication scholars and emergency managers to existing research on effective ways of addressing and overcoming these predictable barriers when interacting with lay audiences.

There is substantial work needed to support local emergency managers. We hope that communication scholars will contact these individuals, listen to their communication challenges, and conduct research, teaching, or outreach efforts to deepen understanding of the communication steps needed to increase emergency preparedness in the communities surrounding universities and colleges.

NOTE

1. This chapter focuses on emergency managers rather than on first responders. Emergency managers are responsible for ensuring that first responders such as firefighters, paramedics, police officers, and those operating equipment for these individuals become involved in the early stages of incidents to protect and preserve life, property, evidence, and the environment (6 United States Code 101). Many emergency managers also work as first responders.

BIBLIOGRAPHY

Aldoory, L., & Bonzo, S. (2005). Using communication theory in injury prevention campaigns. *Injury Prevention, 11*, 260–263.

Alexander, K. L. (2007, March 19). Illiteracy aid found to lag in District. *Washington Post*, p. B1, 2.

American Red Cross (2006, June). *From challenge to action: American Red Cross actions to improve and enhance its disaster response and related capabilities for the 2006 hurricane season and beyond.* Washington, DC: American Red Cross. Retrieved March 19, 2007, from www.redcross.org/hurricanes2006/actionplan

Anderson, C. W., & Smith, E. L. (1984). Children's preconceptions and content-area textbooks. In G. Duffy, L. Roehler, & J. Mason (Eds.), *Comprehension instruction* (pp. 187–201). New York: Longman.

Ausubel, D. P. (1960). The use of advance organizers in learning and retention of meaningful material. *Journal of Educational Psychology, 51*, 267–272.

Bea, K. (2005, March 10). *The national preparedness system: Issues in the 109th Congress.* Washington, DC: Congressional Research Service. Retrieved, Feb. 18, 2007, from www.fas.org/sgp/crs/homesec/RL3283.pdf

Bolam, B., Murphy, S., & Gleeson, K. (2004). Individualization and inequalities in health: A qualitative study of class identity and health. *Social Science & Medicine, 59*, 1355–1365.

Booth-Butterfield, M. (2003). Embedded health behaviors from adolescence to adulthood: The impact of tobacco. *Health Communication, 15*, 171–184.

Botan, C. H., & Taylor, M. (2005). The role of trust in channels of strategic communication for building a civil society. *Journal of Communication, 55,* 685–702.

Campus security and environmental quality committee (2003, Jan. 28.) *Minutes of January 28, 2003.* DeKalb: University of Northern Illinois. Retrieved Jan. 12, 2007, from www.niu.edu/u_council/CSEQ

Caldwell, J. (n.d.). A worldwide epidemic, a local response. *Virginia Town & City*, publication of the Virginia Municipal League.

Case, P. (2005). *Louisiana storm survival guide: St. John the Baptist Parish.* Houma, LA: TRAC, www.trac4la.com

Chess, C. (2000, May). Risk communication. Presentation for the "Risk Communication Superworkshop," sponsored by the Agricultural Communicators in Education and the U.S. Department of Agriculture, Orlando, FL.

City of Alexandria, Va. (2004. May 25). Hurricane Isabel after action report. Retrieved March 17, 2007, from http://www.ci.alexandria .va.us/city/citizencorps/isabelafteraction.pdf

Clark, R. A. (1984). *Persuasive messages.* New York: Harper & Row.

Clarke, W. (2006, August). *Emergency management in county government: A national survey* [prepared for The National Association of Counties]. Athens, GA: University of Georgia's Carl Vinson Institute of Government.

Coombs, W. T. (2006). Crisis management: A communicative approach. In C. Botan & V. Hazleton (Eds.) *Public relations theory II* (pp. 171–197). Mahwah, NJ: Erlbaum.

Cragan, J. F., & Shields, D. C. (1998). *Understanding communication theory: The communicative forces for human action.* Boston: Allyn & Bacon.

Cutter, S. L. (2005). The geography of social vulnerability: Race, class, and catastrophe. In [unknown editors] (eds.). *Understanding Katrina: Perspectives from the social sciences.* New York: Social Science Research Council. Retrieved June 9, 2006, from www.ssrc.org.

Doswell, C. A., Moller, A. R., & Brooks, H. E. (1999). Storm spotting and public awareness since the first tornado forecasts of 1948. *Weather and Forecasting, 14*, 544–557.

Drabek, T. (1986). *Human system responses to disaster: An inventory of sociological findings.* New York: Springer-Verlag.

Drabek, T. (2001). Disaster warning and evacuation responses by private business employees. *Disasters, 25*, 76–94.

Drabek, T., & Hoetmer, G. (1991). (Eds.). *Emergency management: Principles and practices for local government.* Brookfield, CT: Rothstein Associates.

Dynes, R. R., & Rodriguez, H. (2005). Finding and framing Katrina: The social construction of disaster. In [unknown editors] *Understanding Katrina: Perspectives from the social sciences*. New York: Social Science Research Council. Retrieved June 9, 2006, from www.ssrc.org

Fearn-Banks, K. (2002). *Crisis communication*, 2nd ed. Mahwah, NJ: Erlbaum.

Federal Emergency Management Agency (FEMA). (n.d.). *FEMA higher education project*. Retrieved Feb. 18, 2007, from www.training.fema.gov/emiweb.edu

Fischer, G. W., Morgan, M. G., Fischhoff, B., Nair, I., & Lave, L. B. (1991). What risks are people concerned about? *Risk Analysis*, *11*, 303–314.

Fischhoff, B. (1989). Risk: A guide to controversy. In National Research Council (Ed.), *Improving risk communication* (pp. 211–319). Washington, DC: National Academy Press.

Fussell, E. (2005*). Leaving New Orleans: Social stratification, networks, and hurricane evacuation.* In [unknown editors] *Understanding Katrina: Perspectives from the social sciences*. New York: Social Science Research Council. Retrieved June 9, 2006, from www.ssrc.org

George Mason University (n.d.). *Emergency procedures* [poster]. Fairfax, VA: Author.

Goffman, E. (1959). *The presentation of self in everyday life*. Garden City, NY: Doubleday.

Goodnough, A. (2006, May 31). As hurricane season looms, states aim to scare. *New York Times*. Retrievd June 1, 2006, from http://www.nytimes.com

Harwood, J., & Sparks, L. (2003). Social identity and health: An intergroup communication approach to cancer. *Health Communication*, *15*, 145–170.

Hearit, K. M. (1994). Apologies and public relations crisis at Chrysler, Toshiba and Volvo. *Public Relations Review*, *20*, 113–125.

Heath, R. L. (1994). *Management of corporate communication: From interpersonal contacts to external affairs*. Hillsdale, NJ: Erlbaum.

Heath, R. L. (1995). Corporate environmental risk communication: Cases and practices along the Texas Gulf Coast. In B. R. Burleson (Ed.), *Communication yearbook 18* (pp. 255–277). Thousand Oaks, CA: Sage.

Heath, R. L., & Abel, D. D. (1996). Proactive response to citizen risk concerns: Increasing citizens' knowledge of emergency response practices. *Journal of Public Relations Research*, *8*, 151–171.

Heath, R. L., Liao, S., & Douglas, W. (1995). Effects of perceived economic harms and benefits on issue involvement, use of information sources, and actions: A study in risk communication. *Journal of Public Relations Research*, *7*, 89–109.

Heath, R. L., & Palenchar, M. (2000). Community relations and risk communication: A longitudinal study of the impact of emergency response messages. *Journal of Public Relations Research*, *12*, 131–161.

Hewson, M. G., & Hewson, P. W. (1983). Effect of instruction using students' prior knowledge and conceptual change strategies on science learning. *Journal of Research in Science Teaching, 20*, 731–743.

Hewson, P. W., & Hewson, M. G. (1984). The role of conceptual conflict in conceptual change and the design of science instruction. *Instructional Science, 13*, 1–13.

Hovland, C., Lumsdaine, A., & Sheffield, F., (1949). *Experiments in mass communication*. Princeton, NJ: University Press.

Howell, S. E., & Bonner, D. E. (2005). *Citizen hurricane evacuation behavior in southeastern Louisiana: A 12 parish survey*. New Orleans, LA: Center for Hazard Assessment, Response, and Technology (CHART), University of New Orleans. Retrieved July 25, 2005, from http://www.uno.edu/~poli

Katz, E. (1957). The two-step flow of communication. *Public Opinion Quarterly, 21*, 61–78.

Kasperson, R.E. & Kasperson, J.X. (1996). The social amplification and attenuation of risk. *The Annals of the American Academy of Political and Social Science*, *545*, 95–106.

Kasperson, R.E., Golding, D. & Tuler, P. (1992). Social distrust as a factor in siting hazardous facilities and communicating risks. *Journal of Social Issues*, *48*, 161–187.

Kasperson, J. X., Kasperson, R. E., Pidgeon, N., & Slovic, P. (2003). The social amplification of risk: Assessing fifteen years of research and theory. In N. Pidgeon, R. E. Kasperson, & P. Slovic (Eds.). *The social amplification of risk* (pp. 13–46). New York: Cambridge.

Katz, E., & Lazarsfeld, P. (1955). *Personal influence: The part played by people in the flow of mass communication*. New York: Free Press.

Kreps, G. L. (2005). Communication and racial inequities in health care. *American Behavioral Scientist, 49*(6), 1–15.

Kreps, G. L. (2006). One size does not fit all: Adapting communication to the needs and literacy levels of individuals. *Annals of Family Medicine* (online, invited commentary). Retrieved March 31, 2008, from http://www.annfammed.org/cgi/eletters/4/3/2005.

Lazarfeld, P., Berleson, B., & Gaudet, H. (1948). *The people's choice*. New York: Columbia University Press.

Lichtenstein, S., Slovic, P., Fischhoff, B., Layman, M., & Combs, B. (1978). Judged frequency of lethal events. *Journal of Experimental Psychology: Human Learning and Memory*, *4,* 557–578.

Louisiana Recovery Authority (2006). Emergency preparedness. Retrieved June 1, 2006, from http://www.hud.gov/content/releases/pr06-058.pdf

Louisiana, State of. (n.d.) *Louisiana citizen awareness & disaster evacuation guide*. Available from Louisiana State Police. Phone: 800.469.4828.

Magat, W. A., Viscusi, W. K. (1987). Implications for economic behavior. In W. K. Viscusi & W. A. Magat, (Eds.), Learning about risk: *Consumer and worker responses to hazard information* (pp. 125–132). Cambridge, MA: Harvard University Press.

Mayer, R. E. (1983). What have we learned about increasing the meaningfulness of science prose? *Science Education, 67*, 223–237.

Mayer, R. E. (1989). Systematic thinking fostered by illustrations in scientific text. *Journal of Educational Psychology, 81*, 240–246.

Mayer, R. E., Bove, W., Bryman, A. Mars, R., & Tapangco, L. (1996). When less is more: Meaningful learning from visual and verbal summaries of science textbook lessons. *Journal of Educational Psychology, 88*, 64–73.

Merrill, M. D., & Tennyson, R. D. (1977). *Teaching concepts: An instructional design guide.* Englewood Cliffs, NJ: Educational Technology Publications.

Metts, S., & Grohskopf, E. (2003). Impression management: Goals, strategies, and skills. In J. O. Greene & B. R. Burleson (Eds.) *Handbook of communication and social interaction skills* (pp. 357–399). Mahwah, NJ: Erlbaum.

Miller, J. M., Lehto, M. R., & Frantz, J. P. (1990). *Instructions and warnings: The annotated bibliography*. Ann Arbor, MI: Fuller Technical Publications.

Morgan, M. G., Fischhoff, B., Bostrom, A., & Atman, C. J. (2002). *Risk communication: A mental models approach.* Cambridge: Cambridge University Press.

National Research Council. (1989). *Improving risk communication.* Washington, DC: National Academy Press.

O'Hair, H. D., Heath, R. L., & Becker, J. A. H. (2005). Toward a paradigm of managing communication and terrorism. In H. D. O'Hair, R. L. Heath, & G. R. Ledlow (Eds.), *Community preparedness and response to terrorism* (pp. 307–328). Westport, CT: Pager.

O'Keefe, D. J. (1998). How to handle opposing arguments in persuasive messages: A meta-analytic review of the effects of one-sided and two-sided messages. In M. E. Roloff (Ed.), *Communication yearbook 22* (pp. 209–249). Thousand Oaks, CA: Sage.

O'Keefe, D. J. (2002). *Persuasion: Theory and research.* Thousand Oaks, CA: Sage.

Paton, D., & Johnston, D. (2001). Disasters and communities: Vulnerability, resilience, and preparedness. *Disaster Prevention and Management, 10*, 270–277.

Paton, D., Smith, L. M., Johnston, D. (2005). When good intentions turn bad: Promoting natural hazard preparedness. *The Australian Journal of Emergency Management, 20*, 25–30.

Perry, R. W. (1988). *The communication of disaster warnings.* Paper presented at the Symposium on Science Communication. Sponsored by the U.S. Environmental Protection Agency and the Annenberg School of Communications, University of Southern California. Los Angeles, CA.

Perry, R. W., & Mushkatel, A. H. (1984). *Disaster management: Warning response and community relocation.* Westport, CT: Quorum.

Petty, R., & Cacioppo, J. (1986). *Communication and persuasion: The central and peripheral routes to attitude change.* New York: Spring-Verlag.

Pfau, M. (1992). The potential of inoculation in promoting resistance to the effectiveness of comparative advertising messages. *Communication Quarterly, 40*, 26–44.

Pfau, M. (1997). The inoculation model of resistance to influence. In G. A. Barnett & F. J. Boster (Eds.), *Progress in communication sciences: Advances in persuasion, 13* (pp. 133–171). Greenwich, CT: Ablex.

Pfau, M., & Wan, H., (2006). Persuasion: An intrinsic function of public relations. In C. Botan & V. Hazleton (Eds.) *Public relations theory, 2nd ed.* Mahwah, NJ: Erlbaum.

Pidgeon, N., Kasperson, R. E., & Slovic, P. (2003). (Eds.). *The social amplification of risk.* New York: Cambridge.

Quarantelli, E. L. (1988). Disaster crisis management: A summary of research. *Journal of Management Studies, 25*, 373–385.

Roberts, K. H. (1993). Cultural aspects of reliability enhancing organizations. *Journal of Managerial Issues, 5*, 165–281.

Rogers, E. M. (1995). *The diffusion of innovations*. New York: Free Press.

Rowan, K.E. (1988). A contemporary theory of explanatory writing. *Written Communication, 5*, 23–56.

Rowan, K. E. (1991a). Goals, obstacles, and strategies in risk communication: A problem-solving approach to improving communication about risks. *Journal of Applied Communication Research, 19*, 300–329.

Rowan, K. E. (1991b). When simple language fails: Presenting difficult science to the public. *Journal of Technical Writing and Communication, 21*(4), 369–382.

Rowan, K. E. (1994). Why rules for risk communication fail: A problem-solving approach to risk communication, *Risk Analysis, 14*, 365–374.

Rowan, K. E. (1995). A new pedagogy for explanatory speaking: Why arrangement should not substitute for invention. *Communication Education, 44*, 236–250.

Rowan, K. E. (1999). Effective explanation of uncertain and complex science. In S. Friedman, S. Dunwoody, & C. L. Rogers (Eds.), *Communicating new and uncertain science* (pp. 201–223). Mahwah, NJ: Erlbaum.

Rowan, K. E. (2003). Informing and explaining skills: Theory and research on informative communication. In J. O. Greene & B. R. Burleson (Eds.), *The handbook of communication and social interaction skills* (pp. 403–438). Mahwah, NJ: Erlbaum.

Rowan, K. E. (2004). *Risk and crisis communication: Earning trust and productive partnering with media and public during emergencies*. Washington, DC: Consortium of Social Science Associations.

Rowan, K. E., Kreps, G. L., Botan, C., Sparks, L., Bailey, C., & Samoilenko, S. (in press). Communication, crisis management, and the CAUSE model. In H. D. O'Hair, R. L. Heath, K. Ayotte, & G. Ledlow (Eds.), *Terrorism: Communication and rhetorical perspectives*. Cresskill, NJ: Hampton.

Rowan, K. E., Toles-Patkin, T., Troester, R., Samoilenko, S., Penchalapadu, P., Farnsworth, K., & Botan, C. H. (2006, November). *Emergency kits for everyone: Report of interviews with local emergency managers in the East.* Paper presented at the annual meeting of the National Communication Association, San Antonio, TX.

Sandman, P. (1993). *Responding to community outrage: Strategies for effective risk communication*. Fairfax, VA: AIH Association.

Seeger, M. W., Sellnow, T. L., & Ulmer, R. R. (1998). Communication, organization and crisis. In M. E. Roloff (Ed.), *Communication yearbook, 21* (pp. 231–275). Thousand Oaks, CA: Sage.

Sellnow, T. L., Seeger, M. W., & Ulmer, R. R. (2005). Constructing the "new normal" through post-crisis discourse. In H. D. O'Hair, R. L. Heath, & G. R. Ledlow (Eds.), *Community preparedness and response to terrorism* (pp. 167–189). Westport, CT: Praeger.

Stanton, N. (1994). *Human factors of alarm design*. London: Taylor & Francis.

Starik, M., Adams, W. C., Berman, P. A., Sudharsan, K. (2000, May 17). *1999 LEPC survey.* Washington, DC: Center for Environmental Policy and Sustainability Management. Retrieved March 19, 2007, from http://yosemite.epa.gov/oswer/CeppoWeb.nsf/vwResourcesByFilename/lepcsurv.pdf/$File/lepcsurv.pdf

Steel, P., & Konig, C. J. (2006). Integrating theories of motivation. *Academy of Management Review, 31*, 889–913.

Stewart, D. W., & Martin, I. M. (1994). Intended and unintended consequences of warning messages: A review and synthesis of empirical research. *Journal of Public Policy and Marketing, 13*, 1–19.

Sturges, D. (1994). Communicating through crisis: A strategy for organizational survival. *Management Communication Quarterly, 7*(3), 297–316.

Tennyson, R. D., & Cochiarella, M. J. (1986). An empirically based instructional design theory for teaching concepts. *Review of Educational Psychology, 56*, 40–71.

Thomas, D., & Mileti, D. (2003, Oct.). *Designing educational opportunities for the hazards manager of the 21st century: Workshop report.* Boulder, CO: Natural Hazard Center, University of Colorado, Boulder.

Travis, J. (2005, Sept. 9). Scientists' fears come true as hurricane floods New Orleans. *Science*, 309, 1656–1659.

Trumbo, C. W., & McComas, K. A. (2003). The function of credibility in information processing for risk perception. *Risk Analysis, 23*, 343–353.

U.S. Department of Health and Human Services (2002). *Communicating in a crisis: Risk communication guidelines for public officials*. Washington, D.C. Retrieved April 10, 2005, from www.riskcommunication.samhsa.gov

U.S. Department of Homeland Security (2006a). *Emergency management competencies and curricula*. Emmitsburg, MD: Emergency Management Institute. Retrieved February 18, 2007, from www.training.fema.gov

U.S. Department of Homeland Security. (2006b, Dec.) *U.S. Department of Homeland Security Fiscal Year 2006 performance and accountability report.* Washington, DC: Office of the Department of Homeland Security.

Vanderford, M. L., Nastoff, T., Telfer, J. L., & Bonzo, S. E. (2007). Emergency communication challenges in response to Hurricane Katrina: Lessons from the Centers for Disease Control and *Prevention. Journal of Applied Communication Research, 35*, 9–25.

Viscusi, W. K., & O'Connor, C. (1987). Hazard warnings for workplace risks: Effects on risk perceptions, wage rates, and turnover. In W. K. Viscusi & W. A. Magat, (Eds.), *Learning about risk: Consumer and worker responses to hazard information* (pp. 98–124). Cambridge, MA: Harvard University Press.

Yaros, R. (2006). Is it the medium or the message? Structuring complex news to enhance engagement and situational understanding by nonexperts. *Communication Research, 33*, 285–309.

Weeks, W. B., & Bagian, J. P. (2000). Developing a culture of safety in the Veterans Health Administration. *Effective Clinical Practice, 3*, 270–276.

Wells, H. G. (1913). *In the country of the blind.* Retrieved June 13, 2006, from http://www.readbookonline.net/readOnLine/2157/. (T. Nelson and Sons).

Witte, K., Meyer, G., & Martell, D. (2001). *Effective health risk messages*. Thousand Oaks, CA: Sage.

Wogalther, M. S., & Silver, N. C. (1995). Warning signal words: Connoted strength and understandability by children, elders, and non-native English speakers. *Ergonomics*, *38*, 2188–2206.

Wolvin, A. D., & Coakley, C. G. (1996). *Listening*, 5th ed. Dubuque, IA: Brown.

Woods, D. (2005). Behind human error: Human factors research to improve patient safety. *APA Online*, Public Policy Forum. Retrieved January 17, 2005, from http://www.apa.org/ppo/issues/shumfactors.2.

Wright, P., Creighton, P., & Thulfall, S. M. (1982). Some factors determining when instructions will be read. *Ergonomics*, *36*, 172–181.

9

Risk and Social Dramaturgy

Ingar Palmlund
Independent Scholar

> Whether 'tis nobler in the mind to suffer the slings and arrows of outrageous fortune, or to take arms and by opposing end them.
>
> William Shakespeare in *As You Like It*, Act II, Scene 7.

"To be or not to be" says the actor on the stage. "Whether t'is nobler to die than to take arms against a sea of trouble and by opposing end them." This is Hamlet, Prince of Denmark, making a risk/benefit calculation. It is theatre, yes, but remove the theatrical trappings of a production of a Shakespeare play and replace them with a different setting, for instance one with the flag in the corner of the office of a governor or president deciding on whether to go to war. Or replace Hamlet's costume with the grey suit of a business executive, or the helmet and camouflage uniform of a military in a battle field, or the pullover of a researcher at a desk, or the white coat or green scrubs of a doctor, or the T-shirt of an environmental activist, or the outfit a politician has carefully selected for an encounter with his or her constituency. Ask yourself: what, in fact, is different? Fundamentally all are grappling with finding the right balance between action and inaction and with the choice of how to declare what they want people to perceive and believe—above all, they act to make people believe in their act. Trust is at stake—trust in their professional capacity and trust in the institutions they represent. All exist as individuals but constantly adapt appearance, behavior, and words to circumstances, as if personalities and characters were concealed behind the facemasks of a theatrical production. The word 'persona' means exactly that—facemask.

To act or not to act—in many positions the choice means the difference between to be or not to be a business executive, a mutual fund manager, an officer or soldier, a researcher, a physician, an activist in a non-governmental organization, a politician, a public official, or even the president of country. The choice concerns whether and how to participate in a social process around the construction of ideas. For some it means stepping forth, claiming to be a leader with a following, particularly if the situation demands the confrontations or negotiations necessary to reach the agreements that form the fabric of society. Others prefer not acting—although one possible consequence is that they risk losing their role.

Risk, in my vocabulary, means threats to people and what people value. Some writers make a distinction between hazards as threats to people and what they value, and risks as measures of hazards (Kates & Kasperson, 1983). Scientists, economists and engineers, who are trained to measure and assign numerical values and never to express absolute certainty, might prefer to express risk in terms of statistical probabilities and percentages within certain narrow, predefined boundaries. I adhere to the view expressed and discussed by Mary Douglas and Aaron Wildavsky in their book *Risk and Culture* (1982): what is regarded as risk in a specific group or society is essentially the result of a cultural choice, a selection of good and evil that is functional and fits the cultural context.

Risk must be understood as essential uncertainty, with roots in existential anxiety and in the need to exert control over the unknown and uncontrolled. Emotional as well as intellectual experiences are woven into the social interaction over risk. Risk is also code word that alerts society that a change in the social order is being requested. Persons and groups have different attitudes to changes in the prevailing order, be they ever so marginal. Society is a kind of order, more or less firmly structured, which we as individuals are born into and which we participate in defending, reproducing and adjusting. Within that social order, risk issues are used to provide leverage in action to change or to defend the existing pattern. Every reference to risk contains a tacit reference to safety. And our need for safety and security is related to our need for control.

Conflicts over how to handle risks are part of the power plays in social life. Societal evaluation of risk must be seen as a contest—an *agon*, from a Greek word meaning competition—where protagonists and antagonists offer competing views of how reality should be viewed and interpreted, what should be regarded as benefit and what should be feared as risk.

The anecdote about the business executive interviewing candidates for a position as chief financial officer demonstrates a characteristic feature in many discourses over risks. The executive asked each candidate: 'How much is two and two?' The first interviewee confidently replied: 'Four.' He was immediately asked to leave. The second candidate was asked the same question. He suspected a trap and replied 'Twenty-two.' He was also asked to leave. The one remaining candidate did not answer immediately. Instead he rose, tiptoed over to the door to check that it was firmly closed, then walked back and, leaning over the executive's desk, asked in a subdued voice "What would you like it to be?' In the anecdote, the third candidate got the job. This story teaches that in some circumstances and to some audiences appearance may be held to be more important that truth.

If truth rests in the eye of the beholder, there are in a pluralist society—by definition—many claims for truth. The contest is a process over time, a process colored by emotions, created by the action of several participants, some of which represent juxtaposed interests in the outcome. The process moves forward by blaming games and games of celebration. The participants engage because of concerns that matter to them, emotionally or economically. The aim of each one in the competition is to convince an audience about the preferred, 'right' view of reality. It is essential to view the process as one of social dramaturgy in order to understand what really happens when societies evaluate risks, whether the threat is to human life, health, environment, or the social fabric (Palmlund, 1992). These social processes over time are part of the making of history.

Theories developed in philosophy, literary criticism, semiotics, political science, sociology, and anthropology throw light on the dramatism in social communication over risk. The classical theory of drama as a form of universal representation of historical events was formulated by Aristotle. Humanist and literary theorists have since then built a considerable body of knowledge regarding the social uses and importance of theatre and drama. Among social scientists in the twentieth century Guy Debord, Murray Edelman, Clifford Geertz, Erving Goffman, Joseph Gusfield, Helga Nowotny, Victor Turner, and Robin Erica Wagner-Pacifici have added to the development of a theory concerning the function of drama in society.

Theatricality in processes propelled by discourses over risks, the separation between actors and audience, a classification of the roles in the process, the characteristics of the process, and the choice of dramatic genre are the characteristics of social drama that will be discussed in the following.

RISK IN THE SOCIETY OF THEATRICAL SPECTACLE_

In societies, where modern conditions of production prevail, all of life presents itself as an immense accumulation of spectacles. The spectacle appears to encompass society wholly or partially. Spectacle is important as an instrument of unification. It is a social relation mediated by images (Debord, 1967).

Each day, by mass media, we are reconfirmed as social beings by partaking of theatrical spectacles over risks. Even war, the potentially most devastating risk venture engineered by humans, is conducted in theatres—at least that is the term used in strategic and tactic reasoning by invaders and commentators. But to perceive war as played out on the stages of theaters implies a view from afar. Civilians and soldiers, who fall victims to the stark reality of violence, hardly conceive of warfare in that way. Theatricality implies a disjunction, a dis-connect between the reality lived and the reality as presented, described, and played out before an audience in order to amuse, frighten, persuade, placate, and sway that audience into trusting the agents conducting the rhetoric.

The dramatism over risks, be they war ventures, technological risks or natural disasters, is political. These political processes concern the allocation not only of tangible economic values, such as property, markets, and business opportunities, but also of symbolic assets and liabilities. At stake are the control of perceptions of reality and the trust in the elites elected to handle difficult decisions regarding the common weal. Often also at stake are human life and health and quality of life.

An issue, where there is no fear, nor any threat to social elites, would hardly make it to a stage, where public controversies are played out. The dramaturgy in social controversies over risks reveals that emotions such as fear and pity for victims may be as strong a driving force in politics as economic self-interest—or even stronger. Competitive conflicts over the undertaking of a new venture or the use of a specific technology ultimately concern the legitimate view of the world; they concern what is worth producing and the best way of producing it. They are really political conflicts concerning the power to enforce the dominating definition of reality (Bourdieu, 1990).

Consider the language in political commentaries. The following expressions are fished from various articles printed in an issue of *The Economist* (2006):

- "It has been *a great tale, played out* in just the short blaze of publicity…"
- "Unfortunately, real life has not followed the rags-to-riches-to-rags *script*."
- "… every Tokyo financial scandal of the past 20 years has *featured* those arts."
- "His practices were pretty traditional, but he used them with a speed, aggression and *visibility* that were new."
- "… there has been an escalation of the war of *words*..."
- "From this perspective, the most important *scene* was not Mr. Bush holding forth…"
- "This *highlights* the central flaw…"
- "… the health secretary wants a *change of scene*…"
- "Politicians, like television producers, know where the *action* and *glamour* are in medicine."
- "All this is an inevitable *piece of theatre*, you might think."
- "… Hamas has *played the* democratic *game* rather successfully …"

Also in other newspapers and media, events are often presented in theatrical terms. Here are two examples from the *New York Times*. One is a report on the trial of previously admired business executives, who had dealt brazenly with financial risks and lost millions of dollars belonging to others (Barrionuevo, 2006). Trials, of course, in most countries are adversary rituals, dramas conducted in order to establish a viable 'truth' about the nature of events and to re-establish a fair balance between the perpetrators and victims of risky actions.

First, the title: "Who Will Steal The ENRON Show?"

Then, excerpts from the text:

- "How will the trial *play out*?"
- "While there are always unforeseen *twists and turns* in a lengthy criminal trial a review of the most important witnesses summoned to appear at the trial offers some *suggestion* of how the government may *present its case* and how the defendants may try to *rebut* it."
- "Prosecutors will use a variety of witnesses in an effort to *weave a story* for jurors …"
- "… in their zeal to make Enron *appear* to be a profit powerhouse … repeatedly *lied* and *misrepresented* the company's financial situation to investors"
- "The *presentation* is likely to be choppy, with many *scenes out of order* …" (Barrionuevo, 2006)

Another example is an op-ed commentary by columnist David Brooks in *The New York Times* on media presentations of a risk incident, potentially tragic with lethal as well as political consequences. In February 2006, the U. S. Vice President Dick Cheney during a quail hunt accidentally shot an old man, his friend, in the face and chest. One pellet reached the heart, but the old man survived. The Vice President at first kept mum. After a day, the hostess of the hunting party informed a local newspaper about the incident. When national newspapers picked up and began to feature the story, the Vice President complained about their lack of responsibility. Finally, when media worldwide were featuring the story, he engaged in more effective damage control. The Vice President's statement, broadcast across the globe, could have been the line of a sharp-shooting hero in a cowboy film: "It was not Harry's fault. You can't blame anybody else. I'm the guy who pulled the trigger and shot my friend." The victim emerged from hospital. In front of an array of television cameras he apologized for the pain he had caused the Vice President. This was the front. Backstage, hidden from the public's eye, there must have been discussions about how best to save the situation and control potentially damaging discourses in the media. So, unity was demonstrated and nobody was blamed.

Consider the theatrical quality of this risk incident. Significantly, the title of the op-ed piece is: "Places, Everyone. Action!"

- Then the commentary about the rhetoric in the presentations of the incident:
- "One of the most impressive things about us in Washington … is our ability to unfailingly play our assigned roles. History throws unusual circumstances before our gaze, but no matter how strange they may at first appear, we are always able to squeeze them into one of our pre-approved boxes so we may utter our usual clichés."
- "The victim is suffering but gracious. The shooter is anguished in his guilt. … In normal life, people would look at this event and see two decent men caught in a twist of fate. They would feel concern for the victim and sympathy for the man who fired the gun."
- "But we in Washington are able to rise above the normal human reaction. We have our jobs. We have our roles."
- "… we in the regular media … are assigned by the Fates to turn every bad thing into Watergate, to fill the air with dark lamentations about cover-ups and appearances of impropriety and the arrogance of power. We have to follow the money. … We are impelled to … write tales in which the quality of the message management takes precedence over the importance or unimportance of what's being said. Then, rushing to the footlights, come the politicians, with their alchemist's ability to turn reality into spin."
- "But life is a campaign, and they are merely players."
- "… the vice president was compelled to recreate his role as Voldemort, Keeper of the Secrets."
- "We have our roles, dear audience. Ours is not to feel and think. Ours is but to spin or die." (Brooks, 2006)

These are insightful statements about an event on the border between private and public life, a flash in a series of theatrical events, invented, rehearsed and staged, the way we are used to seeing events staged and played out on the television screens in our living rooms. As the satirical film comedy *Wag the Dog* (with original working title *Bite the Bullet*) reminded us (Levinson, 1997), much may be skillfully engineered backstage in order to present a flawless spectacle that does not arouse a complacent audience.

Bread and circus, the Roman emperors knew, had to be provided if the citizenry—the silent crowds as well as the unruly mobs—were to be kept quiescent and under control. Politicians in present day empires likewise know that foods, theatrical storytelling and games are basic necessities for the consumers they cater for. However, risk incidents may break the quiescent acknowledgement of the rulers' right to rule as quickly as the shell breaks of an egg dropped on a stone floor. A nuclear power plant running amok, a scare over the risks of a drug taken by thousands of people and identified as triggering deadly cancer, a hitherto unknown virus that modern medicine is not equipped to prevent and control, a bombing of the World Trade Center on Manhattan resulting in over 2,600 deaths, a tsunami in the Indian ocean hitting beaches full of wealthy tourists and taking some 3,000 lives, a hurricane Katrina wrecking the city of New Orleans, leaving almost 1,500 of its inhabitants dead and disrupting uncountable lives—these are all threats to people and what people value. Such events disturb the calm business as usual and inspire fear of further risks. They prod people to begin to question, to criticize, and to blame their rulers for not providing protection. Charity, as it is often said, begins at home. Distant risks of disaster inspire less empathy with victims. Distance can be social as well as spatial. Dismal reports about hundreds of thousands at risk of starving to death because of drought in Sub-Saharan Africa concern a reality too distant, threats with too few advocates for victims, voices too far away to be heard at the centers of power, where decisions are made. Thus, in each setting, the risk exposure of actors already on stage or moving close to the stage becomes main material in the political dramaturgy over risk.

THE AUDIENCE

Social decisions about risk are always taken with an eye to an audience, at least one audience, sometimes more. If there were no audience, no decision on acceptable risk would be publicly announced. Indeed, the acceptability of risk might not even be an issue worth bothering about. There are specific audiences with the individuals on the stage as their agents. There are target groups for the messages from the agents on the stage. There is also a large, heterogeneous audience, often politely referred to as the general public. To enlist groups out of that audience into political action or to keep that audience quiet are two opposing objectives acted out in social dramas.

The legislative and regulatory history on technological risks is full of evidence that decisions to intervene in the free market to define a level of acceptable risk come about as reactions to political conflicts over risks to human health and environment. They are the legacy of how political leaders and administrators in governmental bureaucracies have responded to situations of distrust and in some cases even social unrest.

The victims—groups under threat and the people who speak and act politically on their behalf—constitute a first audience in discourses over risk. Fear and compassion for victims can be discerned as major driving forces in legislative and regulatory decisions on risk. After all, the experience of risk has to do with fear of loss. People's fear of nuclear energy, fear of potentially toxic chemicals, fear of hazardous waste dumps, and fear of the adverse effects of pharmaceuticals trigger political actions in the same way as the fear of an enemy. If it becomes known that people have come to harm—especially suffering children and women in childbearing age—the risk issue carries a deep emotional appeal with roots in survival instincts.

A second audience for decisions on acceptable risk is the group that produces and uses a technology that gives rise to risks and, perhaps not least, the professionals who base their living on the existence, dissemination, and further development of the technology. These might be the professionals investing their time and money into building and running nuclear power installations. Others could be the producers of chemicals used as pesticides and the professional groups, which base their livelihood on the increased use of these chemical products; or the producers of pharmaceuticals and the professional groups, which base their livelihood on the increased use of these products. The professionalized assumption of needs is a strong driving force defending the existing and future use of the specific technology the professional groups produce and apply (Illich, Zola, McKnight, Caplan, & Shaiken, 1977). A technology or a type of products is celebrated in a competition, where a critique of the underlying assumptions, the *doxa*, about the need for the technology or the products would be an act of self-destruction. To raise issues of risks undermines discourses on benefits. Within a certain setting, as a *modus vivendi*, open conflicts regarding the definition of situations are avoided (Goffman, 1959, p. 10). The fate of many so-called whistle-blowers is a good illustration of the social punishments meted out to those who dare speak out about risks concealed behind the screen of celebrated benefits of a technology or a practice.

A third audience for decisions on acceptable risk is the citizenry at large, mostly complacent or indifferent to what the elites in government and market construct. Keeping that complacency and quiescence is what much political maneuvering is about (Edelman, 1976, pp. 22–41). It is also what markets are about. In the end, it is not what those in power do that is important, but what they can get away with. If the citizenry is aroused, those in power may be thrown out and markets may be lost.

As soon as we introduce the notion of an audience for decisions we have a separation: activity from passivity; actors from spectators; a stage with a fairly limited number of actors elevated above a diffuse multitude of people with a multitude of characteristics; the bright light on the stage in contrast to the darkness where the audience watches; the performance by the visible few in front of the quiescence of the concealed. The action on the stage has to do with the attention of the audience. As theatre director Peter Brook (1988) stated: "The only thing that all forms of theatre have in common is the need for an audience. This is more than a truism: in the theatre the audience completes the steps of creation" (p. 142).

In politics, as well, the audience completes the performance. A statement that is not directed to an audience, nor received by an audience, whether friendly or hostile, is devoid of social function. Groups in the audience perceive a message about risk in different lights, from different sides. That which appears as an expression of distrust or manipulation to some is a manifestation of autonomy and group identity to others. The social function of statements over risk has to do with separation and distance, with bonding and unity. On the surface these statements deal with defining risk and comparing risk, with communicating and persuading. On another level their meaning has to do with changing or preserving the prevailing established social order. When questions are raised about how social elites handle what is entrusted to them, groups in the audience clamor for voice in political processes. In short, they demand an adjustment of the social order. In public discourses over risk, the statements before the audience have a double aim: to demonstrate a rift in the social fabric and to mend that rift so that equilibrium can be restored and practices return to "normal". The rift itself appears when a particular group feels threatened by exposure to a hazard. The experience of feeling unprotected and excluded from the processes, where hazards are defined or controlled, is expressed by distrust and by claims for redressive measures. The degree of outrage has to do with the degree of distrust and refusal to submit to social elites. Authorities, to whom power is entrusted, are looked to for rebuilding social unity, sometimes by integrating dissident opinions, other times by disregarding, or discrediting, or even suppressing the dissidents.

In social drama and political spectacle, the audience has a more powerful role than in the poetical drama. The sociodramatic audience not only considers the messages and ideals of the plot; it also ultimately determines the success of the drama. The public can decide either to applaud the production of political events or to withdraw its attention passively, indifferently, or resentfully. It may threaten to invade the stage. Or, it may decide to deny a particular dramatic resolution and thus deny the legitimacy of the actors. The reaction of the public directly influences the political legitimacy of the actors in a social drama. To arouse the audience or to keep the audience quiet in passive consent—that is part of what the play on the stage is about.

THE ROLES AND THE AGENTS

The moment an individual chooses to appear with a certain front, in a certain way, on a certain stage, with a specific type of message directed to a specific audience persuading it to accept a specific desirable action, he or she engages in political action.

Conventional sociology and anthropology view human beings, singly or in groups, as agents, who by their behavior reveal underlying interests and relationships. Persons are viewed not as individual, unique human beings but as *personae*, as human beings with face masks that may be changed depending on the context where the individual acts (Goffman, 1959; Bourdieu, 1990, p. 52). Viewing social processes as performed by agents, always more or less 'in character', enacting roles—rather than viewing the processes as shaped by particular individuals or particular organizations—facilitates an analysis of structural and causal relationships in social controversies. Moreover, it allows for emotions and attitudes as facts, worthy of the same importance as the results of analytical scientific endeavors.

As human beings we are social creatures, whose personalities, worldviews, and behaviors are molded by the standards of the groups to which we belong (Frank 1974, pp. 5–6). Social construction and search for consensus and approval have a great influence on human perceptions. The behavior of individuals is related to the institutions to which they are linked. Concepts are formed and learning takes place in social settings. Social concerns influence our selective perception of risk (Douglas, 1985, pp. 38–39).

Thus, the behavior of the individual in societal evaluation of risk can, in general terms, be regarded as a coded behavior, a role. That role is to some extent defined by the relationship to the risk(s) in question, but more by the institutional setting in which the individual acts. Both the agents and the audience know, both before and during the performance, that the role has certain demands, which the player must meet in order to be allowed to perform the role and to stay on the stage.

The combination of functional roles in a specific social controversy over a risk characterizes the situation and the succession of events. The individual qualities of the agents may only shift the emphasis in the drama, change the tempo of the action, and engage the emotions of the audience in differing ways. The roles are characterized by a rational search for satisfaction of the interests that define them. The individual agents on different stages may express that interest in different ways, but the basic rationale for their actions remains the same, defined by their roles.

In social controversies over technological risk one important distinction is between those bearing risk and those generating risk. Wars, disasters of nuclear energy, and hazards due to the handling and consumption of toxic and potentially toxic chemicals are good illustrations of how the bearing and the generating of risk are separated in society. The two principal functional roles in a risk conflict—risk bearing and risk generating—are often separate and adversary in nature, seldom congruent. The majority of those who bear risk related to many major threats to life, health and environment in the modern world are not directly engaged in generating these risks. The soldiers and the civil men, women, and children who die in the high-tech wars have little say about why and how the war is conducted. The people living in the neighborhood of industrial plants with hazardous processes have little say about how the hazardous materials and processes should be managed. Innocent bystanders and car drivers have little say, when young men show their prowess in reckless car racing.

The opposed interests between those bearing risk and those generating risk is the pivot for the balancing acts that the dramatic tension generates in conflicts over risk. The agents for these juxtaposed interests act as stakeholders in a conspicuous struggle—the *agon*—in each risk controversy.

Other generic roles can also be identified in social dramas over risk. These roles have a mediating function in the conflict between the two opposed roles of risk bearing and risk generating. They intervene in the conflict by gathering, creating and providing information, both descriptive and normative, about the nature of the risk. One of these roles is performed by those engaged in research, attempting to find and gather evidence of why, how, and under what circumstances a phenomenon may be defined as risk, the extent of exposure to the risk, and in what range it may be regarded as acceptable. They are like the messengers in the classical dramas, who characteristically beg not to be killed because they are about to announce bad news. Those engaged in the arbitration of a conflict, moving to determine the extent to which risk should be accepted, how it should be limited or prevented, and how those exposed to risk should be compensated for running risk and experiencing harm have a different role. Informers in the mass media, engaged in placing issues of risk to human life, health and environment on the public agenda are in a third category. Sometimes independent observers, sometimes co-opted, they assist the players as the chorus in the ancient Greek dramas, commenting and explaining the conflict for the benefit of the general public. They may amplify or attenuate the messages (Kasperson, Renn, Slovic, et al., 1988). Their function as theatrical chorus is to scrutinize the action and to portion out praise and blame.

Thus, six generic roles can be discerned in the societal evaluation of risk—risk bearer, risk bearers' advocate, risk generator, risk researcher, risk arbiter, and risk informer (Palmlund, 1992). They neatly correspond with the universal functions identified in semiotic analysis of dramatic situations (Elam, 1980, pp. 126–134). A person representing risk bearers enters a public stage as a protagonist desiring the Good (truth, justice, prevention of harm), not necessarily on his or her own behalf but for another individual or for the community at large. This protagonist is the incarnated thematic force in a drama. The risk generators are the opponents—rivals or antagonists who present obstacles to the fulfillment of the goal. The risk arbiters have as their role to re-establish an acceptable balance between protagonists or antagonists and thereby resolve the conflict. The risk researchers and risk informers act as helpers to reinforce the action by supporting one or other of the agents in the dramatic process.

The generic roles in the societal evaluation of risk are characterized in the matrix in Table 9.1. For each issue raised in societal risk dramas the specific agents can be sorted into the fields of the matrix, thus revealing the structure of the interests represented in the issue. A division that seems relevant for understanding the positions and acts of the agents is whether they appear as agents for private or public interests. Risk bearing—the suffering of harm and loss—is always in the private realm. All other roles may be performed either in the private or in the public realm, and sometimes in both, depending on the type of society and the type of issue that is investigated. It is easy to attach conventional dramatistic labels to these generic roles defined by their position in social conflicts

TABLE 9.1
Generic Roles in Societal Evaluation of Risk

Example: Controversy over the risks of global climate change

Generic roles	*Dramatistic labels*	*Roles in conflicts over global climate change*
Risk bearers	*Victim*	Communities in low-lying areas prone to flooding. People in areas subject to drought. Humanity at large.
Risk bearers' advocates	*Protagonist* *Hero*	Activists in environmental organizations. Some scientists. Some politicians.
Risk generators	*Antagonist* *Villain*	Stake-holders in industry, agriculture and transport systems emitting large quantities of green-house gases. Consumers not choosing energy efficient housing and transport means.
Risk researchers	*Seer* *Helper* *Servant*	Scientists.
Risk arbiters	*Deus ex machina*	Governments and governmental agencies.
Risk informers	*Chorus* *Messengers*	Producers, journalists, writers etc. in media (newspapers, television, books,films etc.).

over risk. The differentiation of roles in the politics over the risks of global climate change is used as an example in the table.

A role does not necessarily have to be performed by one agent, who is a single person or organization. Even in theatrical drama masks are shifted. A player can act in more than one role, just as one role can be performed by more than one player. An actor may find himself both among risk generators and among risk bearers, having to choose which role to play. A manager of a pharmaceutical company, for instance, may realize that he or someone in his family suffers from the adverse effects of a drug promoted by his company. Or a scientist/risk researcher may, for a while, step out of the role of helper and into the role of protagonist—as many scientists have done with regard to the risks of global climate change. And in the role of, say, risk arbiter many agents may succeed each other within the same social drama. Recurring controversies over the appointments of judges to the U.S. Supreme Court demonstrate that not even the most supreme risk arbiters are regarded as wholly objective. There may even be conflicts between the roles a single player performs. In real life, an agent's appearance in more than one role in an enacted controversy adds to ambiguity—but it also adds to influence and control over events.

Acts and agents are heavily influenced by the scene and the setting, where the action takes place. In principle, the nature of the acts and agents in a social drama is consistent with the nature of the scene (Burke, 1945, pp. 3, 11–20, 77–83). The social structures—laws and institutions—that provide the setting for new dramas are the symbolic monuments erected in previous dramatic acting. Laws and public institutions created to safeguard the public, common interest in a specific issue over technological risk merely reflect how earlier agents, who represented the general, common sense, expected that the risk should be handled in the future. Thus, the national setting in which controversies over technological risk are acted out, conditions the roles as well as the performances that take place.

THE DRAMATIC PROCESS

A drama is representation in universal form of a process of conflict. Awareness of the dramatic form directs participants' and spectators' attention not at singular persons or incidents but at the anatomy of the constituent conflicts as they develop over time. Drama is also a powerful paradigm for social action, conditioning the participation in social processes as well as the interpretation of what the processes are about. One salient example are national elections, where the action presented to the electoral audience is supported by carefully chosen props and prepared sound bytes, which often get more attention than the ideologies or interests that the electoral candidates represent. Another example is the dramatic and adversarial judicial process, characterized by its carefully defined roles and even scripts for the participating persons, played out before an audience. Such processes aim at the production of meaning, but they are also processes, where the produced meaning is explicitly open for interpretation.

Here it is necessary to state a truism: the conflicts over risks are enacted over time. A conflict measured in calendar time may be brief—a few days, or weeks, or months—from initiation to resolution. Some remain unresolved for years, are brought to temporary closure from time to time but then flare up again. The controversy over the major chemical explosion at a Union Carbide chemical plant in Bhopal, India in 1984, for instance, had over twenty years later not yet reached closure.

Some writers on societal risk evaluation have analyzed the processes over time in conflicts over risks. Downs (1972) suggested two alternative sequences for how issues are handled in social controversies over technological risk: a) pre-problem stage, alarmed discovery, risk assessment reflective, decline of public interest, and post problem stage; and b) nascent stage, achieves status of public issue, taken up by public jurisdiction, technocratic analysis, political response, and decline of public interest. Lawless (1977) traced how risk controversies rise in intensity and then peter out. Mazur (1981) also identified peaks of intensity in the social dynamics of technical controversy.

Turner (1974, pp. 37–42) has developed the Aristotelian concept of drama in a way that is pertinent to the study of social coping with conflicts over technological risk. He defines social drama as a unit of a-harmonic or disharmonic process, arising in situations of social conflict. In social drama, Turner identifies four diachronic, typical main phases of public action, accessible to observation. They are *breach*, *crisis*, *redressive action*, and *reintegration* or *irreparable schism*. They largely coincide, in social controversies over technological risk, with the conventionally defined phases *risk identification*, *risk assessment*, and *risk management*. They also largely coincide with the phases *exposition*, *complication*, *crisis*, and *dénouement*, which can be discerned in the construction of dramas produced on stage. The dramatic action of an episode of societal evaluation of technological risk indeed has the shape of a 'well-made' play as it is defined in the drama literature (Styan 1965; Palmlund, 1992).

Each controversy over risk is based on a precipitating event perceived as a representative kind of accident—an event that makes manifest that fears may be warranted—otherwise the social conflict would never get off the ground. A list of criteria for when a risk issue is adopted as a controversial issue on the agenda of public politics might look like this:

1. The risk should be tied to effects that appear familiar and close to people.
2. The effects should be such that they stir up emotions of fright and fear.
3. The risk should concern a large enough group of people or an important enough group of people for politically appointed politicians and senior administrators to worry about their support.
4. Raising the issue of risk in national politics should not obviously threaten fundamental national interests of major importance.
5. The issue should ideally be such that the mass media grasp it and assist politicians in placing it and keeping it on the agenda in national politics so as to satisfy the public's need of spectacular drama. (Palmlund, 1989, p. 613)

A performance is presented to a public—and the public decides whether the offerings are good enough. The position of the general public as audience in plays over risks to life, health, and environment can be interpreted as having to do with the exertion of power by the performing agents. One must assume that the relationship between agents appearing on stage and audiences differs from one country to another, from one field to another, and from one time period to another. That would explain why some conflicts are resolved in one way in one country and in another way in another country. That would also explain why, within a country, conflicts over a technology are resolved in one way at one point in time and in another way at another point in time. An active public makes demands on its agents and makes them accountable for what they do and don't do. A passive public remains quiet, watching the games on political theaters in respectful distance.

THE CHOICE OF DRAMATIC GENRE

Societal evaluation of risk contains the stuff tragedies are made of. It is action and representation of "men's characters as well as what they do and suffer" (Aristotle, 1909, p. 5).

Imagine the script of a comedy played out on a television screen with shouts of laughter inserted at appropriate moments: On a holiday farm, two old men go out to shoot quail. One of them happens to shoot the other, who staggers and falls to the ground. He is in pain and bleeds, but the damage does not seem serious. An ambulance arrives. The victim is taken off to hospital. The failed marksman expresses in various ways that he is in trouble. He searches to find a way to explain to the world what happened. He discovers that he has not even paid the eight dollars for his license to shoot. The woman, who is the hostess of the quail hunt, eventually comes up with a solution: Let's tell the press, but not the big media, only the local press. The article in the local press is picked up by major news-media and journalists besiege the farm. The failed marksman escapes into hiding. The man shot in the face emerges, seemingly safe and sound, in front of the cameras, apologizing that he had caused pain. A final scene shows the two old buddies trudging off into the wilderness for another hunting trip.

Imagine this as an unfunny episode, where the old man, who was shot in the face, blames the failed marksman and accuses him of negligence, perhaps even criminal intent to harm. This might evolve as a melodrama, where many years of close friendship turn into bitter word fights, where the contacts between two former buddies are managed by aggressive, adversary lawyers, and where the litigation after a series of confrontations ends a financial settlement, which is what none of the two old men do not really need. The transfer of money, with a good percentage going to the lawyers, does not heal the rift: the loss is of a human bond. A final scene shows the grief of the two former friends, now lonely and separated forever.

The cunning management of the press in reality sculpted this material for social drama into a non-drama. Why? Because the conflict of interest was defused by declarations of unity and also because laughter released the tension. TV show hosts eagerly competed with caustic comments to bring out the comic element. Here is a sample: "In a post 9/11 world, the American people expect their leaders to be decisive. To not have shot his friend in the face would have sent a message to the quail that America is weak" (Corddry, 2006).

Social dramas over risk are not necessarily conscious or planned social constructs. As after the destruction of the World Trade Center in New York in 2001 or the devastation of New Orleans by hurricane Katrina in 2005, dramatic action seems to be a normal human reaction to disaster. Even in minor controversies over risk there are enough of dramatistic elements to indicate that at least some participants in each controversy are well aware that they are engaged in the social construction of a belief, and that the controversy is a competition over legitimating a dominant view of reality and over social arrangements to provide safety.

Mass media presentations of controversial issues contribute to shaping social controversies in dramatic form. The globe is now extremely well equipped to be used as a global repertory theater with communications technology allowing diverse audiences instantly to plug into whatever crisis is a the top of the public agenda at a specific moment. Media are an important channel for creating global conformity in social behavior, increasingly employed as complements to the more discreet and secretive mechanisms traditionally used for enlisting the support of specific audiences for specific causes.

However, media heavily rely on available material (Friedman, Dunwoody & Rogers, 1986). Any politician or senior administrator, any corporate entity or professional association, any environmental organization—or any journalist or editor for that matter—knows that to get time and space in multimedia is an achievement. Among all efforts to get "good" press coverage only few are successful. Those who already have voice in the media have a better chance than others to make their voices heard.

The editorial media practice of featuring an issue by a succession of entries illustrating juxtaposed interests induces a sense of crisis in the audience. Many major issues are run as an escalating crisis to a peak before the interest quickly tapers off; in some of these issues, after a while, new facts may emerge and a new escalation of crisis takes place, until the issue is abandoned and left as a historical incident not worthy of further interest (Lawless, 1977; Mazur, 1981; Krimsky & Plough, 1988; Palmlund, 1989; Nelkin, 1979; Sapolsky, 1986).

Do the participants in a social controversy with the characteristics of drama consciously choose which type of drama they want to enact on the public stage? Comedy, romance, tragedy, melodrama, or satire? Or the modern Theater of the Absurd where the tragic farce is the mode of choice? Wagner-Pacifici (1986, pp. 20–21, 278–283) argues that generic choices of mode in the theater of politics condition the amount and quality of public participation, as well as do the character richness and psychological complexity. In her own empirical work she makes a distinction between two ends of a generic continuum: tragedy and melodrama.

In societal evaluation of risk we can observe many of the elements characteristic of the classical tragedy. In tragedy, to quote Kenneth Burke (1945, p. 38), "the agent's action involves a corresponding passion, and from the sufferance of the passion there arises an understanding of the act, an understanding that transcends the act. The act, in being an assertion, has called forth a counter-assertion in the elements that compose its context. And when the agent is enabled to see in terms of this counter-assertion, he has transcended the state that characterized him at the start. In this final state of tragic vision, intrinsic and extrinsic motivations are merged."

Tragedy allows for and encourages the audience to identify with the tragic victims and their decisions, dilemmas, weaknesses, and fates, whereas melodrama excludes the audience both from such identification and from engaged participation beyond that of the prescribed booing of the villain and applauding of the hero (Wagner-Pacifici, 1986, pp. 1–21, 40–43, 272–294).

It may well be that the participants in a drama over risk differ in their understanding of what type of drama they participate in. There may be expectations among risk bearers and their representatives that they act in a tragedy, expecting a resolution of the conflict, which permits an integration of the experience of harm and injury as an increased moral awareness in the social consciousness. And there may be cynical interpretations by other participants in the action that the controversy merely is one more round in a game that is much broader than the particular conflict, a game that will continue long after the particular conflict is settled, put aside, or buried.

One important criterion for the choice of mode in tragic social dramas may be embedded in the relationship between the agents on the stage and the audience. The tragic drama allowing for catharsis permits the public real political participation in public decision-making. Tragic dramas, which do not appeal to the audience for emotional involvement, leave the public as a passive, watching audience, permitted to act politically only at times, when formal elections are necessary for the legitimation of political agents. If one views social interaction as merely Darwinian struggles for existence, there is no room for a moral or spiritual meaning in the games that are enacted. The only difference between social tragedy and social melodrama would then be a difference in the control exercised by social elites.

To sum up: the public processes concerning societal evaluation of technological risks to human health and environment can be seen as social dramas. Societies may choose between, on the one hand, open reconciliation, acknowledgement and transcendence of the constituent conflict and, on the other hand, repression of the conflict. The choice reveals something about the sense of morality in society. It also manifests the degree of control exercised by social elites.

The theory of theater and drama provides categories for analysis of social conflicts over risks to life, health and environment. It provides a vocabulary and a critical perspective on the discourses and the symbolic action in societal risk evaluation. It is a summons to introspection and self-criticism: if all the world's a stage and all the men and women merely players—what are the roles we choose to play?

BIBLIOGRAPHY

Aristotle. 1909. *On the Art of Poetry*. A Revised Text with Critical Translation and Commentary by Ingram Bywater. Oxford: Clarendon Press.

Barrionuevo, Alexei. 2006.Who will steal the ENRON show? *The New York Times*. January 29.

Bourdieu, Pierre. 1990. *The Logic of Practice*. Cambridge U.K.: Polity Press.

Brook, Peter. 1988. *The Empty Space*. London: Pelican Books.

Brooks, David. 2006. Places, Everyone. Action! *The New York Times*. February 16.

Burke, Kenneth. 1945. *A Grammar of Motives*. Berkeley: University of California Press.

Corddry, Rob. 2006. In televised The Daily Show as quoted in Shot-in-the-Face. *The Observer*, February 19, 2006.

Debord, Guy. 1967. *La société du spectacle*. Paris: Editions Buchet-Chastel. (Revised English edition 1983. *Society of the Spectacle*. Detroit, MI: Black & Red.)

Douglas, Mary and Aaron Wildavsky. 1983. *Risk and Culture: An Essay on the Selection of Technological and Environmental Dangers*. Berkeley: University of California Press.

Douglas, Mary. 1985. *Risk Acceptability According to the Social Sciences*. New York: Russell Sage Foundation.

Downs, Anthony. 1972. Up and Down with Ecology—The 'Issue-Attention' Cycle. *Public Interest*, 28, 38–50.

The Economist, February 4, 2006.

Edelman, Murray. 1976. *The Symbolic Uses of Politics*. Urbana.: University of Illinois Press.

Edelman, Murray. 1988. *Constructing the Political Spectacle*. Chicago: The University of Chicago Press.

Elam, Keir. 1980. *The Semiotics of Theatre and Drama*. New York: Methuen & Co.

Frank, Jerome D. 1974. *Persuasion and Healing*. New York: Schocken Books.

Friedman, Sharon, L., Dunwood, Sharon, and Rogers, Carol, L. (ed.). 1986. *Scientists and Journalists: Reporting Science as News*. New York: Free Press.

Geertz, Clifford. 1980. *Negara: The Theater State in Nineteenth Century Bali*. Princeton, NJ: Princeton University Press.

Goffman, Erving. 1959. *The Presentation of Self in Everyday* Life. Garden City, NY: Doubleday.

Gusfield, Joseph R. 1975. *Community: A Critical Response*. Oxford: Basil Blackwell.

Illich, Ivan, Irving Kenneth Zola, John McKnight, Jonathan Caplan, and Harley Shaiken. 1977. *Disabling Professions*. London: Marion Boyars.

Kasperson, E. E., Renn, O., Slovic, P., Brown, H. S., Emel, J., Goble, R., et al. 1988. The social amplification of risk: A conceptual framework. *Risk Analysis*, *8*, 177–187.

Kates, Robert W. and Jeanne X. Kasperson. 1983. Comparative Risk Analysis of Technological Hazards (A Review). *Proceedings of the National Academy of Science, U.S.A.*, 80(November),7027–38.

Krimsky, Sheldon and Alonzo Plough. 1988. *Environmental Hazards: Communicating Risks as a Social Process*. Dover, MA: Auburn Publishing Company.

Lawless, Edward M.. 1977. *Technology and Social Shock*. New Brunswick, NJ: Rutgers University Press.

Levinson, Barry. 1997. *Wag the Dog*. New Line Cinema. A Tribeca/Baltimore Pictures/Punch Production. Produced by Jane Rosenthal, Robert de Niro, and Barry Levinson. Screenplay by David Mamet and Hilary Henkin.

Mazur, Allan. 1981. *The Dynamics of Technical Controversy*. Washington, D.C.: Communications Press.

Nelkin, Dorothy (ed.). 1979. *Controversy: Politics of Technical Decisions*. Beverly Hills, CA: Saga Publications.

Nowotny, Helga. 1979. *Kernenergie: Gefahr oder Notwendigkeit*. Frankfurt am Main: Suhrkamp Verlag.

Palmlund, Ingar. 1989. *The Case of Estrogens: An Inquiry into Societal Risk Evaluation*. Doctoral dissertation at Clark University.

Palmlund, Ingar. 1992. Social Drama and Risk Evaluation. In: Sheldon Krimsky and Dominic Golding (eds.). *Social Theories of Risk*. Westport, CT: Praeger.

Sapolsky, Harvey M. (ed.). 1986. *Consuming Fears: The Politics of Product Risks*. New York: Basic Books.

Shakespeare, William. 2000. *As You Like It*. Michael Hattaway (ed.). Cambridge: Cambridge University Press.

Shakespeare, William. 2003. *Prince of Denmark*. Philip Edwards (ed.). Cambridge: Cambridge University Press.

Styan, J.L.. 1965. *The Dramatic Experience*. Cambridge: Cambridge University Press.

Turner, Victor. 1974. *Dramas, Fields, and Metaphors: Symbolic Action in Human Society*. Ithaca, NY: Cornell University Press.

Turner, Victor. 1982. *From Ritual to Theater: The Human Seriousness of Play*. New York: Performing Arts Journal Publication.

Wagner-Pacifici, Robin Erica. 1986. *The Moro Morality Play: Terrorism as Social Drama*. Chicago: The University of Chicago Press.

10

Myths and Maxims of Risk and Crisis Communication

Peter A. Andersen and Brian H. Spitzberg

San Diego State University

A number of misleading myths permeate the literature of risk and crisis communication. Are different types of disasters and crises really unique and different? Is panic a common response to disasters? Does the public heed warnings of disaster? Is a single warning message sufficient in most cases? Is the source of information a key variable? Are public risk assessments accurate? What is the relationship between the frequency of prior messages and compliance? What effect does ethnicity and socioeconomic status have on risk and crisis communication efforts? What is the role of communication with the family and children in disaster communication? Are there generalizable principles or maxims that can guide policy and practice in preparing for and responding to crises? This chapter provides a concise critical and analytic review of the literatures on risk and crisis communication in an attempt to dispel the myths, and formulate the maxims, by which communication functions in these contexts

A CAUTIONARY TALE OF CRISIS COMMUNICATION

In the fall of 2001, anthrax-contaminated letters were sent to the media and congressional representatives, with direct symptomatic effects on 68 persons, resulting in 5 known deaths (Kerkvliet, 2004). "More than 10,000 persons potentially exposed to anthrax in Connecticut, Florida, New Jersey, New York City, and Washington DC were recommended to take postexposure antibiotic prophylaxis" (Fowler et al., 2005, p. 601). The decontamination of the Hart building and the postal plants in Brentwood and Hamilton required many months and over $125 million, yet "the amount of anthrax involved in the contamination of each of these facilities was probably <1 g" (Webb, 2003, p. 4356). According to some estimates, "the costs associated with a real or perceived *B. anthracis* bioterror attack have been estimated at more than $26 billion per 100,000 persons exposed" (Fowler et al., 2005, p. 601).

Since the events of 2001, there have been 20,000 incidents of suspected hazards (e.g., "white powder incidents") sent through the mail, and although 99.9% are determined to be hoaxes or mistakes, 133 evacuations were required, resulting in 18,745 lost work hours and producing 28 arrests and 25 convictions for using the mail system as a mechanism of delivering a threat (United States Postal Inspection Service, 2004, p. 31). The United States is not alone in contending with such threats (e.g., Hagenbourger, 2003).

These experiences with anthrax have represented relatively localized events because of the delivery mechanism: envelopes delivered through the Postal Service. Envelopes are relatively traceable in their routes and areas of exposure. But what if a larger, more diffuse exposure to anthrax occurred in a major metropolitan area, such as San Diego, home to a population of three million? Scaling a recent model to the potential population of 3 million in San Diego County, downwind aerosolized inhalation infection of 393,000 (13%) people by release of approximately 1 kg of anthrax would result in 32,619 deaths, even with rapid prophylactic response (Wein, Craft, & Kaplan, 2003). In this model, "the death count doubles if the detection delay increases from 2 to 4.8 days" (Wein et al., 2003, p. 4350). This scenario could play out in virtually any city in America.

THE CENTRALITY OF COMMUNICATION

"The most basic ingredient in any disaster response is communications" (Herbert, Collins, & Rowland, 2003, p. 23). Disasters link numerous people and agencies creating large and unique communication problems (Omer & Alon, 1994). During a crisis, every segment of the public, visitors, emergency personnel, public employees, and the news media, need competent communication and accurate information (Kapsales, 2004). Interagency communication is essential during a disaster both within and between agencies (Paton & Jackson, 2002). "In the response stages of a terrorist incident, the ability to save lives is directly proportional to the first responders' capability to communicate" (Beauchesne, Shanley, McIlroy, & Lee, 2002, p. 36). During some types of emergencies (e.g., nuclear accident), a jurisdiction has only a few minutes to alert those at risk.

There are numerous reasons communication fails in disasters: (1) People are inclined to deny or rationalize away their actual risk, (2) many people do not take risks seriously, (3) people take many factors into account in considering response (e.g., location of family members, actions of neighbors, etc.), (4) some people are disinclined to follow authority, (5) numerous people will not understand the complexity of the situation or message, (6) the disaster itself may seem too diffuse, abstract, or unavoidable, (7) the population at risk may be highly heterogeneous (i.e., in language, access to media, etc.), making general messages inapplicable to large segments, (8) informal social and personal communication networks sometimes undermine or deflect formal and official communication messages (Handmer, 2000), (9) communication may arrive to the populations in need too late, and (10) the message may go to the wrong medium for the population in need. These are merely some of the causes of communication problems during disasters; there are many more.

PUBLIC COMPLIANCE IN CRISES

Even if the infrastructure and plans were in place to rapidly distribute mass prophylactic antibiotic regimens or to evacuate the entire population of a major city, would "the public" comply? First, the amorphous nature of the public has caused researchers to more carefully consider multiple "publics" and their often disparate responses to events (DeGrazia, 1951; Pool, 1973; Weiss, 1988). Several studies have examined models of optimal public response to mass anthrax exposure. These studies indicate that mass post-exposure prophylactic antibiotic therapy (doxycycline or ciprofloxacin) is likely to yield a cost effective strategy (e.g., Brookmeyer, Johnson, & Bollinger, 2004; Fowler et al., 2005; Wein et al., 2003). However, these models are highly sensitive to changes in parameters. Indeed, the "biggest shortcoming" of such models, "and the most difficult challenge to address" is the "omission of people's behavioral responses to various strategies and the different "publics" with disparate responses. For example, what proportion of people will flee by car, shelter in place with plastic and duct tape, or go to their nearest hospital or pharmacy and belligerently demand antibiotics, how will different groups respond, and how are these proportions affected by the antibiotic distribution approach (PODs vs. postal delivery)?" (Craft, Wein, & Wilkins, 2005, p. 693). In highly controlled populations, such as with military deployments, compliance with immunization regimens is extremely high (e.g., Folio et al., 2004). However, "publics" are diverse, and anything but a captive audience.

Consider some of the potential obstacles to mass prophylactic treatment of the population. Small pox and anthrax manifest entirely distinct profiles of illness contagion and etiology. However, some of the ways in which people respond *psychologically and behaviorally* to one illness may be informative to how they would respond to the other. This is illustrated first by a study of 2,545 randomly selected U.S. adults inquiring about their probable reactions to two disaster scenarios: a smallpox outbreak, and a dirty nuclear bomb (Lasker, 2004). The following are some of the select concerns revealed in this study, focusing primarily on the smallpox scenario:

- "Only two-fifths of the American people would go to the vaccination site in the smallpox outbreak" (p. ii).
- "Three-fifths of the American people would have serious worries about the smallpox vaccine—that's *twice* as many people as would be seriously worried about catching smallpox in the outbreak situation" (p. ii).
- "Worries about vaccine side effects would make one-fifth of the American population afraid to follow instructions to go to the vaccination site" (p. ii).
- "People who are worried *only* about catching smallpox but are not worried about the vaccine, are three times more likely to cooperate as those who are not worried about smallpox. But that increase in cooperation is completely *eliminated* when people are also seriously worried about the vaccine" (p. iii).
- "Going to a public vaccination site *violates* people's inclination toward protective isolation. Two-fifths of the population would be afraid of catching smallpox from other people at the site" (p. iii).
- Reasons people would not seek a vaccination in the event of a smallpox outbreak in their community include: "lack of worry about catching smallpox in this situation [36%]; serious worries about what government officials would say or do [65%]; serious worries about the vaccine [61%]; and conflicting worries about catching smallpox and getting sick from the vaccine (pp. 8–9).
- "16% of the American population believe there is a very high or high chance that government officials in the United States would decide to do something in this situation that they *know* would harm them or people like them in some way (42% of the population believe there is a moderate to very high chance of this happening)" These concerns are higher among people who are Hispanic (61%), African-American (57%), foreign-born (55%), of low income (57%), and non-college educated (51%). "Only 26% of the American population have a lot of trust in official instructions and actions" (pp. 10–11). Obviously, each "public" may have different reasons for trusting or not trusting government.
- "People's cooperation in the smallpox scenario is *not* significantly correlated with their cooperation in the dirty bomb scenario" (p.18).
- "Half of the population (48%)—and two-thirds of African-Americans (68%)—would be extremely or very worried if, when they went to get vaccinated, they were asked to sign a piece of paper saying that the smallpox vaccine is an investigational drug that has not been completely tested....and 32% of the population say this worry would make them decide *not* to get the vaccine" (p. 14).
- "Although current plans are focusing almost exclusively on vaccination to protect the public in a smallpox outbreak, two-thirds of the American population (65%) say they would engage in protective isolation" (p. 24).

An extremely cautionary tale results from this study for any public information officers planning for a potential mass bioterrorist attack: "If three-fifths of the American people were reluctant to follow instructions in a smallpox outbreak, the protection of large-scale vaccination might not be achieved, even if planners worked out all of the challenging logistics involved in dispensing the vaccine" (Lasker, 2004, p. iv). Given the evidence that sizable segments of the population, especially several minority populations, are suspicious of the government's intentions regarding vouchsafing public safety in a bioterrorist scenario, any public information officer will need to attend to the potential that such suspicions will apply to the nature of any public pronouncements and messages intended for public safety.

The fact that the smallpox vaccination scenario is entirely different from an anthrax prophylactic antibiotic regimen may not matter in terms of risk and disaster communication. A study of those who were potentially exposed to the anthrax incidents of late 2001 revealed a variety of similar concerns:

- People were concerned with a "general absence of information" (43%), "lack of clarity/confusing information" (21%), "delay in communication" (19%), and "problems with communication specifically involving hearing impaired" (9%) (Blanchard et al., 2005, p. 491).
- People also experienced "mistrust" (31%), "felt agencies treated them with disrespect" (15%), "treated groups differently based on race/socioeconomic status" (14%), "treated them as experiments" (11%), "did not have the proper knowledge to provide information" (10%), and "felt personal physician/ community medical facilities lacked information or were prevented from giving information" (6%) (Blanchard et al., 2005, p. 491).
- 52% of those exposed to anthrax expressed a need for "better communication," 23% expressed a need for "better leadership" (Blanchard et al., 2005, p. 491).

Due to the numerous psychological and communicative obstacles involved in such a situation, simple, linear, rational models of risk communication are unlikely to work. In short, "informing people what they should do in these terrorist attack situations will *not* be sufficient to garner their timely cooperation" (Lasker, 2004, p. v; see also Kahan, Fogelman, Eliezer, & Shlomo, 2003). Furthermore, "if planners' assumptions about the public are wrong—as they have been in the past—the plans being developed will not work as expected, and a large number of people who should be protected will be unnecessarily harmed" (Lasker, 2004, p. i).

Even when communication planning has occurred, it can still go wrong. The Centers for Disease Control (CDC) is the preeminent national agency equipped to contend with a bioterrorist attack. It had a communication plan in place prior to the anthrax incidents of 2001, but quickly found the plan was obsolete in the throes of an actual bioterrorist attack. Interviews of CDC public communicators revealed that numerous problems were encountered during the anthrax incidents (Robinson & Newstetter, 2003), including: (a) a lack of assigned proximal spaces for communication team members and scientists, (b) excess load on the telephone lines from media, (c) excess load on electronic communication with scientists resulting in wide scale unresponsiveness to e-mail inboxes, (d) excess media demand for "top" scientific spokespersons, (e) a lack of encryption of intra-agency electronic communications to protect such messages from potential media eavesdropping, (f) bottlenecks in the chain of "written approvals" of out-going messages, and (g) a general "loss of control" of the communication process. In the absence of timely and sufficient information, the media searched for other sources, resulting in misinformation and rumor becoming news. "In the wake of the anthrax crisis, as one communication officer noted, 'the paradigm is forever changed' at CDC" (Robinson & Newstetter, 2003). It is not unusual that crises elicit organizational paradigm shifts, but there are obvious advantages to developing paradigms that better anticipate crises rather than merely react to them.

Any barriers, psychological, logistical, or communicative, which delay public compliance with health messages, have severe consequences to the success of an intervention. For example, in various tests and iterations of anthrax release models,

> the fraction of infected people who die is shown to be linear in the length of time it takes to distribute antibiotics and in the efficacy of the antibiotics, both as prophylactic and as treatment; moreover, prophylactic efficacy is approximately three times more effective (on a percentage basis) than treatment efficacy. This fraction is also increasing and concave in the intervention delay, i.e., the delay from the time of the attack until intervention begins. (Craft et al., 2005, p. 692)

Thus, every day, hour, and minute of delay in the distribution availability and public compliance with proximal prevention or crisis response spells the potential for more deaths and injuries. To the extent that better communication response plans can be more effective at achieving public compliance, the more lives can be saved in such an event.

In summary, direct experience with anthrax scenarios, as well as hypothetical scenarios of exposure to a dangerous infectious agent (smallpox) illustrate numerous obstacles to any public communication campaign intending to produce compliance with a prevention or response regimen, even when the risks are salient in a target audience. Under such circumstances, preparation, planning, and performance all become vital to the success of a public health campaign aimed at limiting the catastrophic impact of a terrorist event. This is all the more true to the extent that the media can play both facilitative and obstructive roles during disasters (Payne & Schulte, 2003, p. 124). To better ascertain the types of communication practices that may enhance public response, this analysis begins with general principles of communication in the context of disasters and crises.

PRINCIPLES OF RISK COMMUNICATION AND DISASTER EVENTS

Risks are dangerous events that have an estimable probability of occurring and some potentially severe consequences. The probability estimates may or may not be accurate; therein is part of the challenge for their communication. Risks can be due to human or natural factors, and increasingly, the distinction between these is dissolving. Katrina was a natural disaster, but the scope of its consequences was largely based on lack of human infrastructure and response. A disaster can be defined as "an adverse impact that needs to be faced using special measures for planning, coordinating and utilizing appropriate resources" (Alexander, 2003, p. 118). Disasters are "sudden events of a catastrophic nature that affect a major portion of a human community or society and overwhelm the capacity of the community to quickly absorb and recover from the loss" (Rich & Winters, 2002, p. 326).

Disasters tend to create *crises*, which refer to the problems created when institutions are severely challenged in their response to a disaster. An earthquake that has no impact on people's lives is not a disaster. A disaster is something that evokes large-scale human threat response, and therefore calls forth issues of institutional response and responsibility (Kreps, 1985). When institutional response and responsibility are taxed by a disaster beyond an institution's readiness, it becomes a *crisis*. For example, an organizational "crisis should have 'some of all' of the following features: (1) severe disruption of operations; (2) negative public perception of the company; (3) financial strain; (4) unproductive of management time; and (5) loss of employee morale and support" (Shaluf, Ahmadun, & Mustapha, 2003a, p. 30).

A crisis may be related to intentional harm (e.g., a terrorist bombs a power grid) or to an "accident," which would be an event that is unusually "large-scale," "costly," "public," or some combination of these features (Shaluf et al., 2003, p. 305). Some crises are indirectly related to the disaster that triggers them. The *Exxon Valdez* was a disaster for the fishing industry of Prince William Sound, which created a crisis for the company and local residents. Katrina was a disaster that overwhelmed all institutional response, but it also created entirely unforeseen crises, such as crises of confidence and a public credibility problem for the President, the Department of Homeland Security, FEMA, and state and local governments. All disasters are local, and at the broader level, they tend to all share most characteristics (Bolin,

1988; Disaster Threat Reduction Agency, 2001; Paton & Johnson, 2001; Nigg & Perry, 1988; North, Price, & Smith, 1988; Taylor, 1987; Weinstein, 1987). Both natural disasters and terrorist attacks are usually sudden and occur with little warning (Christine, 1995). One of the most important similarities across disasters is that "communications links are almost always disabled and disrupted during the first hours of a major disaster" (Tampere Declaration on Disaster Communications, 1991, p. 7).

The premise that disasters are more alike than unique is reasonable given that "the manner in which individuals and society prepare for, respond to, and recover from natural or technological events is very similar" (Rich & Winters, 2002, p. 327). "An unstated but nevertheless central assumption of FEMA's standard operating procedures is that all disasters (man-made as well as natural) can be handled in exactly the same way" (Schneider, 1995, p. 76). Natural disasters and terrorism often have similar effects and require similar responses (Blondheim & Leibs, 2003). The importance of this premise is that it greatly facilitates preparation for and response to disasters. An "all hazards" approach means that full preparedness for a terrorist attack will enhance underlying capabilities for addressing natural disasters such as fires or earthquakes (Rudman, 2003).

Some important differences between natural disasters and terrorist attacks warrant consideration (Bolin, 1988). Tried and tested responses exist to most natural disasters deriving from human experiences over the centuries, but fewer obvious recommendations exist for responses to technological (e.g., gaseous chemical spills) or terrorist (e.g., hostage incident) events (Bolin, 1988; O'Brien, 2003). This is complicated by the fact that, unlike natural disasters, terrorists intentionally try to defeat prevention measures (Alexander, 2002).

The following are general principles that describe the nature of most disaster events. These common principles will often inform how communication will need to respond and compensate for various ramifications of the event.

- **All disasters are similar in important aspects.** As indicated above, the research is striking that disasters regardless of their origin, whether natural, technological or terrorist, share far more similarities than differences.
- **All disasters are "local" in character.** Despite their structural similarities, "Disasters and their subsequent responses are by their very nature unique social problems" (Drabek & McEntire, 2003, p. 99). Not surprisingly, therefore, "nearly all disaster-type incidents start out as local events reported only by the local media" (Hartsough & Mileti, 1985, p. 284). Moreover, local government takes the initial, and typically primary, responsibility for the management of disasters (Perry, 2003; Perry & Nigg, 1988). Given the enormous consequence of disasters to the locality where they occur, local media generally suspend normal programming and shift to crisis coverage during the emergency (Fischer, 2002). Research suggests that local media are more accurate and useful than network or national media in reporting on crises (Friedman, 1989). The local media "know" the area, the people involved, and how to best assist the local populace in responding to the disaster. In an analysis of disaster myths in the media following Hurricane Gilbert, Fischer (1998, p. 85) concluded: "the local print media was the most accurate, followed by the local television broadcast media and then the network news reporting which was judged to be the most likely to exaggerate," although "we found the television news, generally, to be relatively accurate." Local media are also in a unique situation to facilitate a local response to crises. "Local media will assist in disseminating needed information to the public to facilitate an effective response to the attack. National media will be less helpful in that their self-perceived role will be to describe the unfolding story that will often be largely fiction" (Fischer, 2000, p. 365). Thus, the initial response and the immediate media coverage are always predominantly local as a disaster unfolds.
- **Panic is *not* a common response to disasters.** Studies of numerous types of disasters suggest that maximum accurate information should be provided to the public because panic

is seldom the outcome of good information. Despite widespread stereotypes that people behave irrationally during disasters, the vast majority of research indicates that this is false (Alexander, 2002; Drabek, 1969; Drabek & McEntire, 2003; Fischer, 2002; O'Brien & Mileti, 1992; Omer & Alon, 1994; Perry & Nigg, 1988; Perry & Pugh, 1978; Schneider, 1995; Tierney, Lindell, & Perry, 2001). "Anecdotal evidence consistently supports the argument that the public can be trusted far more than decision makers think it can" (Fischer, 2000, p. 365).

- **Ineffective responses to disasters are costly.** Each decade millions of people die in disasters and tens of billions of dollars are lost. As humans become more interconnected, as world population increases, as humans live in more crowded conditions, and more infrastructure to support these populations is constructed, "fatalities and economic losses from disasters are rising" (Mitchell & Thomas, 2001, p. 77). Worldwide, "the number and impact of natural disasters are increasing at a dramatic rate.... Over three million people have been killed by disasters in the past two decades. At the same time media reports about disasters so word of any disaster seems more local than in the past. In constant dollars, the total economic cost of natural disasters has tripled in the last 30 years, from $40 billion to $120 billion in the 1980s" (Cate, 2004). In one disaster, "damages from the 1989 Loma Prieta earthquake in California are projected to total between $7 and $10 billion...about 13,000 people were rendered homeless" (Gillespie & Banerjee, 1993, pp. 237–253). Disaster losses are not merely tangible in nature. In a summary of over 160 samples of disaster victims totaling over 60,000 people studied, 11% experienced "minimal impairment, indicative of transient stress," 51% experienced "moderate impairment, indicative of prolonged stress," 21% experienced "severe impairment, indicative of significant psychopathology or distress," and 18% experienced "very severe impairment" (Norris et al., 2002, p. 218). Every community would benefit greatly from competent disaster preparation and crisis response.
- **Information is always incomplete in disaster situations.** Disruptions and overloading of traditional communication media during a disaster, the heightened state of arousal of the public, and the general confusion that surrounds initial media reporting of an unfolding event, all contribute to incomplete information about a disaster. Further, most disasters simply imply a variety of complex effects on an environment that is itself not well understood (Covello & Sandman, 2001).
- **Slowly unfolding disasters demand more media consumption and confirmation than sudden disasters.** When clear warnings are available as in hurricanes and floods, officials and the public can make more deliberate responses. Events such as earthquakes and terrorist bombing require immediate, ad hoc responses (Burkhart, 1991, pp. 34, 61, 96).
- **The more complex or technical the risk or disaster, the more media messages will be accepted by the public.** In the context of minimal information, people often cling to what little information is available, and therefore, the initial reports through the media become disproportionately salient in forming subsequent beliefs and perceptions (Burkhart, 1991, p. 81; Dougall, Hayward, & Baum, 2005, p. 37).

PRINCIPLES OF COMMUNICATION AFTER DISASTER EVENTS

Public Communication Is a Vital Tool in Responding to Any Disaster Event

Communication is the most important tool in gaining cooperation from the public and linking responders. Communication is more likely to save lives than any other community action. "Effective communication during a public health emergency can have profound effects ranging from increased compliance with recommended treatment to decreased development of long-term psychological sequelae" (Blanchard et al., 2005, p. 489).

An argument can clearly be made that planning and tangible infrastructure preparations have greater potential than communication for vouchsafing public health in the context of disasters. Had the warnings been heeded, and had the levies been better built and maintained, the argument goes, Katrina would have been an immensely less damaging disaster. Risk communication, however, has everything to do with establishing the public and policy agenda for precisely these types of planning and infrastructure preparations. One of the key reasons that such planning and preparations are not made is because they fall off the public's and government's radar. Furthermore, although better levies *might* have prevented the disaster (although there are theories that levies cause asymmetric subsidence that actually exacerbate long-term risks of flooding), better communication preparations, policies, and practices could have significantly diminished the most deleterious social impacts of the crisis that did occur. Nature and terrorism will find ways of surprising society's best anticipations, but communication is a dynamic process that can adapt to unexpected circumstances. Competently planned, guided, and trained communication will be more flexible in response to changing circumstances than any rigid fortification, piece of equipment, or shelter.

The role of communication in disasters typically falls into two camps: risk communication and crisis communication. Generally speaking, *risk communication* refers to messages that seek to anticipate disasters or threats that typically involve warning, avoidance, prevention, and cautionary advice. Typically, risk communication occurs prior to and anticipatory to a disaster. In contrast, disaster or *crisis communication* refers to the messages that occur during and immediately following a disaster that attempt to mitigate social harm and disruption. Though there are other ways types of disasters could be differentiated (e.g., Kreps, 1985; Shaluf et al., 2003b; Taylor, 1987), most disasters share enough in common to treat natural, technological, intentional and accidental disasters as a group.

Overlap also exists between risk communication and disaster communication. Specifically, with disasters that have some degree of lead-time, such as slow-onset fires, floods, hurricanes, or volcanic eruptions, risk communication warns citizens how to protect themselves (e.g., shelter in place, evacuate, prepare a survival kit, etc.). Importantly, in order to gain the compliance of a person or a particular public, it is essential that a message be perceived as relevant to some risk to the audience or some person(s) the audience cares about. Therefore, risk and crisis communication are integrally intertwined.

The following principles of communication represent general "best practice" lessons drawn from research across a broad range of crises, disasters, and terrorist events, but they are more grounded in and tethered to communication theory and research than more "how to" lists such as the "Seven Cardinal Rules of Risk Communication" (Covello & Sandman, 2001). Much of this discussion was adapted from a previous report summarizing over 220 scholarly and governmental sources (Foster, Andersen, McBride, & Spitzberg, 2004). The principles are organized by the relevant focal entity in the communication context. Specifically, the principles are organized around the traditional taxonomy: who (source), communicates what (message), to whom (receiver), where (context), through what means (media) and strategies (process).

The Source(s) of Risk and Disaster Messages

- **People are skeptical of threats, threat warnings, and recommendations.** People do not automatically believe threats or warnings; many ethnic minorities are especially skeptical of government sources and people in general may not take the advice of officials. One of the best-evidenced findings from the disaster literature is that people in general are skeptical of warnings and threat messages, regardless of source (Burkhart, 1991; Drabek, 1999; Mileti & Sorensen, 1988; Omer & Alon, 1994; Perry & Mushkatel, 1984). "The first principle in understanding disaster warning responses is to recognize explicitly that the initial response to any warning is denial" (Drabek, 1999, p. 515).

- **Warnings must come from high credibility sources and be repeated through many media.** Frequent warnings, in multiple media, with high credibility sources produce the most public compliance (Ice & Petersen, 2002; Mileti & Sorensen, 1987). A primary recommendation of the Homeland Security Council's (2005) report on Pandemic Influenza includes, "identifying credible spokespersons at levels of government to effectively coordinate and communicate helpful, informative messages in a timely manner" (p. 4). Police, firemen, university experts, physicians, well-known newspersons, and popular government officials should deliver warnings. For example, in the study of a smallpox outbreak scenario, credibility of official was critical to public compliance (Lasker, 2004). Research showed that 50–70% would trust a director of a local hospital, director of state or local police, and a director of the health department in the event of a local anthrax bioterrorism event (Pollard, 2003). Officials in the field are generally viewed as credible. "In the U.S., a face-to-face warning by a uniformed officer is probably the most credible warning mechanism for the majority of the population (Tierney et al., 2001, p. 85). The most credible initial information on flood evacuation was from public officials (Drabek, 1969). Officials were the most credible sources of warnings in a chemical emergency, while social networks were rated sharply lower than officials (Burkhart, 1991).
- **The public prefers its information directly from a known and trusted source.** People trust their own doctor. In studies of peoples' preferred sources of information in regard to anthrax specifically, Kittler, Hobbs, Volk, Kreps, and Bates (2004; see also Pollard, 2003) found that over 80% (by far the most) trust their physicians "a lot" or "completely" for information about anthrax, followed by health websites (30%), public radio (30%), newspaper (28%), online newspaper site (21%), television (19%), magazine (16%), and other people (10%). The Internet is underutilized, but when it is, 65% located their information by searching for the word 'anthrax' or 'bioterrorism' (Kittler et al., 2004; see also Hobbs et al., 2004; Pollard, 2003). Kahan et al. (2003) found in a survey that 30% of respondents "chose the hospital emergency department as their first choice for care or information if they were worried about an anthrax attack or the media communicated that an attack was in progress. The other two-thirds preferred their family doctor or the health authorities" (Kahan et al., 2003, p. 441). National surveys (Pollard, 2003) show that the officials "trusted most" in a local anthrax attack are local physicians (31–47%) and the local health department (36–48%), followed distantly by law enforcement agencies (12–14%), religious leaders (6–8%), and elected officials such as the mayor (5–13%). In the study of the smallpox outbreak scenario, Lasker (2004) found that:
  - "For free telephone support from a trained person in the smallpox situation, considerably more people [84%] would find it very helpful to talk with someone who they know wants what is best for them (like their health practitioner) than to talk with someone they don't know who works for their local government" [58%] (p. iv).
  - "The vast majority of the American people (87% of the population) say they would want to talk directly with someone who can give them information or advice to help them decide what to do in this [smallpox outbreak] situation" (p. 19).
  - "94% want to talk to someone who "knows a lot about smallpox," 88% want to talk with "someone who wants what is best for them," 64% want to talk to someone who "already knows their medical history," and 54% want "someone whom they know well" (p. 20).

A unified/centralized source of authoritative information is essential. Generally speaking, *the more agencies responsible for managing a crisis, the more likely there will be communication errors and problems* (Turner & Pidgeon, 1997, p. 87). It is vital that consistent with "incident command system" models of crisis management, a unified and centralized source of information is provided for inter-agency communication, communication with the public responders (Behm, 1991; Benson, 2004; Christine, 1995; Fischer, 1998; Nigg & Perry, 1988; Paton & Jackson, 2002; Perry, 2003; Rudman, 2003; Sood, Stockdale, & Rogers, 1987).

The Content and Design of Risk and Disaster Messages

- **Timely, accurate, specific, sufficient, consistent, and understandable information is essential for an effective public response.** Information needs to (a) occur in time for appropriate response, (b) provide information that reflects the actual state of affairs, (c) be in simple language and level of complexity for all levels of the population to understand and follow, (d) provide relevant details vital to effective response, (e) provide sufficient information to cover the most appropriate options of response, (f) emphasize information and recommendations consistent across sources and media, and (g) provide instructions that can be practically implemented under the circumstances (h) not include excessively horrifying details of the crisis (Behm, 1991; Homeland, Security Council. 2005, Ice & Petersen, 2002; Keinan, Sadeh, & Rosen, 2003; Mileti & Sorensen, 1987, 1988; Perry & Mushkatel, 1984; Rich & Winters, 2002).
- **Messages need to be simple to reach an entire population**: "High levels of illiteracy in the American public speak to the diminished ability to process complicated messages and the need to craft messages that are unambiguous, written in simple language, and take advantage of graphics and layout to facilitate comprehension" (Wray, Kreutler, Jacobsen, Clements, & Evans, 2004, p. 236).
- **Messages need to be personally relevant and provide actionable responses**: When a disaster strikes, people need to (1) receive the warning or message, (2) understand it, (3) believe it, (4) personalize it (i.e., see its relevance to them), (5) decide how to respond, and (6) take action (Defense Threat Reduction Agency, 2001; Miletti & Sorensen, 1987, 1988).
- **Messages designed to gain compliance should employ moderate levels of fear appeals**. Research on fear appeals suggests that while relatively strong fear appeals are most effective, such appeals are less likely to be processed than more moderate appeals (Witte & Allen, 2000). Lasker's (2004) scenario study of a smallpox outbreak indicated "cooperation is 91% higher than baseline (65%) among people who say they would be extremely or very worried about catching smallpox" (Lasker, 2004, p.17). Therefore, messages that can effectively instill a sense of personal risk should be far more successful than messages that fail to instill such a sense of personal risk. Not only do some people avoid horrifying or high fear messages, such messages can have adverse effect on their mental health (Keinan et al., 2003).
- **People seek confirmation of threat warnings and their response depends on the message confirmation**. People tend not to have a substantial amount of preexisting trust for the government or media, so they tend to rely instead on direct observation (which is often very dangerous in disaster contexts), or they seek confirmation from other people, or other media to confirm a threat (Burkhart, 1991; Wray et al., 2004, p. 238). Studies of earthquakes (Massey, 1995), tornados (McEntire, 2002), floods and chemical spills (Burkhart, 1991) all show people employing media or other people to confirm a warning or disaster information heard through another medium. Indeed, one of the more common sources of confirmation is a neighbor, either through directly observing their actions or discussing the situation with them (Drabek, 1969; Mileti & Sorensen, 1988).
- **Connecting family members is essential to functional public response**. During a crisis, the first instinct of most people is to unite with their families and secure the safety of their children. Numerous studies show that if people can communicate with their families and know they are safe, they are more likely to comply with disaster orders and recommendations (Mileti & Sorensen, 1988; Omer & Alon, 1994; Perry & Mushkatel, 1984). In the smallpox scenario study, "one-third of the people who would not cooperate fully in this [smallpox outbreak] situation would leave the shelter of their building in order to take care of their children; one-quarter would leave to take care of other family members" (Lasker, 2004, p. iii).
- **The more frequent the prior warnings, the less people attend to them**. Warnings of disaster are issued about once a day in the United States making them easy to ignore (Mileti & Sorensen, 1988). Warnings rapidly fade from consciousness, a process called habituation,

adaptation, or normalization and become relatively invisible in the already information-rich environment. Likewise the credibility of some media, especially newspapers, may diminish after false warnings (Major & Atwood, 1997; Mileti & Sorensen, 1988).

The Audience of Risk and Disaster Messages

- **All disasters increase uncertainty, public media consumption, and information-seeking.** The public already knows virtually nothing about disasters, actual personal risks of disasters, or what to do in response to disasters. Indeed, a study of the most widely publicized threat management system in the country found that "When respondents were asked, "Have you heard of the Homeland Security Advisory System?" just under half (49.5%) indicated they had heard of this system." Whites were more aware than blacks (Knight, 2005, p. 2). It follows therefore, that "only a tiny fraction of the American people know very much about the plans that are being developed in their communities" (Lasker, 2004, p. viii). Disasters exacerbate this uncertainty by interrupting people from normal routines and creating anxiety and ambiguity. Fast accurate information is essential in alleviating fear, uncertainty, and dysfunctional responses (Mileti & O'Brien, 1992; Perry & Lindell, 1989, p. 60).
- **People communicate at work and in social networks about disasters.** Mass media can expand their effectiveness though interpersonal communication by constructing warnings telling people to contact families, friends, and neighbors to pass on emergency information. Officials should recognize the danger of false rumors spread by word of mouth and mount aggressive multi-mediated efforts to debunk dysfunctional rumors. "In the absence of accurate and sufficient media information, more inaccurate rumor or intuition will dominate public response" (Fischer, 2000, p. 362). Gossip flourishes in the hothouse atmosphere of emergency shelters and along evacuation routes (Lewis, 2004). Authorities and the media need to be on guard against, and routinely refute, rumors during times of crisis (OSHA, 2003).
- **Parents communicate with their children about disasters:** "Two-thirds of parents also reported activities in their child's school in response to terrorism, such as conducting special classroom activities or assemblies (44%), providing counseling for students (44%), and providing materials or information for parents (44%) to help children cope" (Stein et al., 2004, p. 184). Children are often vital to disaster preparedness (Ronan, Johnston, Daly, & Fairley, 2001). Parents are vital in training children to have appropriate responses to a crisis, but the information can flow both ways. An "excellent method of disseminating information is through children at school" (Peuler, 1988, p. 255) who educate their families on preparedness. Furthermore, in preparation or in the aftermath of disasters, "many of the children will carry this information into the home" (Peuler, 1988, p. 256).
- **Socioeconomic status complicates disaster response.** Uneducated, illiterate, and poorer populations are less likely to receive messages from the government and the media, and are likely to be less trusting of these messages (Lasker, 2004). Even if these populations receive and believed such messages, they often lack resources (e.g., transportation) to assist in their compliance with recommendations.
- **Most people experience inaction and have an optimistic bias regarding disasters.** Phone surveys of corporate spokespersons displayed "a robust optimistic bias" in regard to their self-risk and their "awareness and preparedness for a bioterrorism attack at their corporation" (Salmon et al., 2003, p. 130). This occurs also among the general public (Covello & Sandman, 2001). People may not believe that a disaster will affect them for several reasons. (1) Because of the relative infrequency of disasters in a given locale, people find the prospect of such an event actually occurring as being incredible (Drabek, 1999, p. 516). (2) Because people look for signs of normalcy to rationalize away warnings (Omer & Alon, 1994). (3) People seem well equipped with a protective "It can't happen to me" syndrome (Mileti &

Sorensen, 1988). (4) Given the infrequency of disasters, in a real sense a careful cost/benefit analysis favors inaction (Mileti & Sorensen, 1987).

- **Most people assess personal risks in biased ways.** "There is only a low correlation between the level of physical risk in a situation and the amount of worry that it arouses" (Covello & Sandman, 2001). A variety of factors influence people's view of their personal risk. It stands to reason that people who perceive greater personal risk are generally more likely to respond to compliance-gaining messages. Some of the factors they ground in the research are as follow (Covello & Sandman, 2001):
  - The more involuntary, uncontrollable, and irreversible the risks, the more motivating relevant risk messages are: Involuntary exposure to risks, exposure to risks that could have been averted under appropriate circumstances, and risks that cannot be reversed are less acceptable, and more arousing.
  - The more salient, graphic, and specific the harms from risks are, the more motivating relevant risk messages are: Disasters with vague, diffuse, or intangible costs are less arousing than risks resulting in specific, visual, quantifiable harms to specific persons.
  - The larger the scope of harm, and the more horrific the harm, the more motivating risk messages are: Disasters with catastrophic potential, or that imply intense suffering, arouse greater response than disasters with more limited consequences.
  - The less familiar and well-understood a risk, the more motivating relevant risk messages are: Disasters resulting from complex ill-understood events (e.g., Chernobyl) are more arousing than familiar risks (e.g., smoking).
  - The more a risk threatens children, the more motivating risk messages are: The more a disaster targets children relative to adults, the more arousing the risks will be.
  - The more the source of a risk message is trusted, the more motivating relevant risk messages are: People tend to trust messages from their personal physician, but they are far less trusting of messages from the government, per se.
  - The more media attention a risk message receives, the more motivating relevant risk messages are: For example, due to the cultivation effect of media exposure, people tend to overestimate their personal risk of being a victim of a violent crime.
  - The more personally relevant a disaster or risk, the more motivating relevant risk messages are (e.g., living closer to the epicenter of anthrax release is likely to increase the salience of the risk than for those living at the periphery of exposure).
  - The more unfair, inequitable, immoral, and unethical a disaster, the more motivating relevant risk messages are: For example, a terrorist attack against innocent civilians is more arousing than against military personnel in a theatre of battle.

The Context of Risk and Disaster Messages

- **Family proximity during disaster complicates disaster response.** Unless all family members are accounted for *an evacuation will not take place* (Omer & Alon, 1994; Perry & Mushkatel, 1984). However, if there is communication among family members and they are assured of ongoing contact and reunification, people will comply with evacuation orders (Mileti & Sorensen, 1988; Omer & Alon, 1994).
- **Generally speaking, the more agencies responsible for managing a crisis, the more likely there will be communication errors and problems.** The more sources of communication in a disaster, the more likely the occurrence of error (Nacos, 2002; Turner & Pidgeon, 1997, p. 87; Turner & Gelles, 2003).

The Media Used to Deliver Risk and Disaster Messages (see Table 10.1)

- **Local media are vital in an emergency or disaster.** Local media are the most immediate, knowledgeable, and accurate during a disaster. "Media news reports are usually the only credible information source for the public during a disaster event" (Piotrowski & Armstrong, 1998 , p. 344). The information they provide is essential to the general populace, first responders, and government officials. Data from 6 national surveys "highlighted the importance of local television and radio and of cable and network news channels as information sources" on bioterrorism in fall of 2001 (Pollard, 2003, p. 93). People (31%) received most of their information about anthrax after the Washington incident from the "media" (Blanchard et al., 2005, p. 491; based on focus group interviews with people exposed to anthrax attack in Washington, DC).
- **Media are partially substitutable**. We live in a world in which people expose themselves to multiple media for news and entertainment. When there is no local television station, citizens tend to turn to other sources or media for their information (Burkhart, 1991, p. 62, 114). Often multiple media are sought out even when they are all available. During the September 11, 2001, terrorist attacks on New York and Washington, DC, most people reported watching television in groups and often making phone calls or sending email simultaneously (Carey, 2003). Therefore, the following principle adheres as well.
- **Multiple media provide the most effective crisis communication**. Communication to and from the public, to and from the media, to and from first responders, to and from disaster management centers, and to and from government agencies work best with consistent messages and a rich media mix.
- **Television is the most robust, multi-channeled communication medium during a crisis**. Television is the most widely used source during disasters and a redundant infrastructure that is difficult to disrupt. "Recent polling data indicated that the general public will turn to television and radio as primary sources of information in a terror attack" (Wray et al., 2004, p. 238). In the United States, television is the most commonly employed medium in today's society for receiving information including threat and disaster information. For the public at large, this is especially true during most disasters. "Under no other circumstances are the ratings for TV and radio stations as high as during crises" (Nacos, 2002, p. 175). After learning about the September 11 attacks, four out for five Americans turned to television as their main source of information (Carey, 2003), although the way people first found out about the attack varied by area of country. For example, in Albuquerque 32% of respondents first heard about the attacks on television (Rogers, 2003). In Los Angeles, 40% of respondents learned about them on television (Cohen, Ball-Rokeach, Jung, & Kim, 2003). Nevertheless, over 100 million people or 50% of all households watched CNN on September 11; its normal share is 10% (Rappoport & Alleman, 2003). This media fascination was sustained after the initial attack. People reported being mesmerized by the TV coverage and watched all day and into the night (Carey, 2003).
- **Radio is a vital primary and supplemental source of communication during disasters**. Radio is the surprising survivor of disaster response media. It is one of the older means of communicating with people during a disaster yet it is still one of the more prominent means through which at-risk populations receive vital information regarding the disaster. For example, in Los Angeles 19.5% of respondents heard about the events of September 11 on radio and 29.8% of respondents reported increased attention to radio following 9-11 (Cohen et al. 2003). In Albuquerque 27% of respondents heard of the 9-11 crisis on radio (Rogers, 2003). Overall, one in six people learned about the 9-11 attacks on radio (Carey, 2003; Noll, 2003). Listening to radio and National Public Radio (NPR) in general was much higher following

TABLE 10.1
Advantages and Disadvantages of Various Media in Crisis and Disaster Situations

Advantages:	*Disadvantages:*
Television	
Most prominent disaster information source (Hurricane Danny, San Diego fires) Immediacy, visual emphasis Less reliant on language Surprisingly resilient (9-11: 8 stations damaged but 90% had cable)	Sound byte compression simplifies complex disasters (e.g., Chernobyl) Vulnerable to infrastructure and power grid damage Disparities between local and national/international coverage Claims-makers have no control over gatekeepers and public exposure
Convergent Media: E-mail	
Sent instantaneously to large, pre-selected audience Rapidly adaptable to circumstance Resilient to infrastructure damage (9-11: mayor's chief of staff contacted office workers when phones didn't work)	Not widely diffused & adopted Not immediately available for many Typing and accessing may be untimely in disaster Dependent on literacy of audience
Convergent Media: Internet & WWW	
Potential for relatively instant exposure to large audience Potential for emergent therapeutic & response communities Involving, immediacy & visual interactive format Telecommuting & sheltering in place Extraordinarily resilient to infrastructure damage (e.g., 9-11) Blackberry's & VoIP show potential Potential for controlling rumor & misinformation	1% learned of 9-11 via Internet Internet still experiences congestion (9-11 video log-jam, FEMA site logged over 2 million hits on 9-11) Accessibility to terrorists (9-11 web sites had to be taken down) Potential for excessive or distorted information Current disaster sites lack interactivity & timeliness Dependent on literacy of audience Internet itself is a terrorist target
Conventional Radio	
A prominent source of disaster information Relatively high immediacy & high availability/access (e.g., Loma Prieta: rerouting traffic) Significant local presence & knowledge Promotes emergent therapeutic communities Resilient to power disruptions (radios survived 9-11 intact) Adaptable (12,000 shifted to all news during 9-11) Cal. Emergency Services Radio System, SECURE, RACES, Law Enf. Mutual Aid Radio System, HAM, ATS, etc.	Limited gate-keeping, permitting distorted information on air Local stations often controlled by headquarters out of region, diminishing sensitivity, expertise, and access from disaster location Still tends to take less prominent role relative to television
Two-Way Radio & Paging Systems	
Potential to reach large audience, especially responders Significant relative range HAM & CB radios (e.g., REACT, RACES) assist in diffusion (e.g., Beverly Hills supper club fire, Fort Worth tornado)	Not widely used or diffused Not widely interoperable (e.g., Mt. St. Helens, 9-11, S.D. fires) Limited range due to circumstance (e.g., 9-11,building interference) Management problems (i.e., who gets to talk to whom when)
Warning Systems & Sirens	
Historically proven very effective in many natural disasters (e.g., Ft. Worth tornado)	Do not provide specific information on type of hazard or response Limited to those with prior experience Even those with prior experience may have become habituated (jaded) Color-coded systems have proven widely misunderstood and useless for public response

TABLE 10.1
Continued

Advantages:	*Disadvantages:*
Mobile/Cellular Telephones	
Widely diffused & accessible in population Low-tech, highly operable Resilient to infrastructure damage (e.g., COWs during 9-11) Relatively immediate channel of communication	Limited footprints of coverage & signal Still vulnerable to infrastructure damage (e.g., 9-11: 15 sites lost) Vulnerable to congestion (9-11, TWA flight 800—Long Island) At present, no prioritizing or screening of traffic Limited security (i.e., 3rd parties can listen in)
Standard Telephone & Hotlines	
Widely diffused & accessible Low-tech, highly operable Resilient to some types of infrastructure damage (e.g., 911: phones operated despite 300,000 & 2 offices down) Hotlines easy to set up & program	Immobility a constraint during many disasters Limited exposure & audience (i.e., 1 person at a time) Susceptible to congestion (e.g., 911: 1/3rd experienced problems) Susceptible to infrastructure damage (e.g., lines being down) Hotlines often ill-managed, under-staffed, & insufficiently updated
Word-of-Mouth, Diffusion, & Social Networks	
Primary factor in determining public response (e.g., 70% Washington volcano, > half in hurricanes Danny, Alicia) Serves essential confirmation function Widely diffused (e.g., 911: average person told 4.8 others)	Varies in role by type of disaster, time of day, & immediacy of threat The more technical the threat, the less useful & accurate the source Subject to biases & misinformation (e.g., Niigata earthquake rumor)
Officers, Public Officials, Forums in the Field	
Sources in the field te nd to be viewed as highly credible Sources in the field tend to be effective in achieving public compliance to instructions (esp. commands)	Limited coverage (e.g., hurricanes Alicia & Danny, Mt. St. Helens) Time & resource expensive Slow, even impractical in certain situations Public forums difficult to manage agenda Dependent on matching language of information with community
Newspapers	
Medium of choice for detailed, complex, in-depth understanding of disasterRelatively static & slow (i.e., "yesterday's news") Relatively permanent medium (i.e., can be saved, transported)	Limited to literate public audience Still often not sufficiently in-depth (e.g., Chernobyl, TMI) Sometimes understaffed relative to disaster (e.g., *The Oklahoman*)
Flyers, Handouts, Inserts, Billboards, Etc.	
Relatively inexpensive Appropriate for short-term, one-message efforts (e.g., preparedness) Relatively permanent medium (i.e., can be saved, transported)	Limited to literate public audience Very limited exposure in information dense environment Untimely relative to disaster
Direct Observation	
Immediately intuitive, iconic, and understandable (e.g., seeing neighbors evacuate) Important factor in perceived readiness and efficacy	Promotes "disaster pornography" or voyeurism (e.g., flooding to see the flood) First-hand observers of disaster often have the worst vantage point for accurate comprehension (e.g., 911)

the 9-11 crisis (Carey, 2003). Radio was the leading medium of communication through which faculty learned about developments during the Kent State crisis (Tompkins & Anderson, 1971). A study of Washington state residents' perceptions of risk from volcano shows 91% reporting radio as a source of information (Perry, Lindell, & Greene, M. R., 1982). Radio flood warnings were sporadic, yet nearly half of residents reported their first information came from radio (Drabek, 1969). Between 17–25% of citizens heard their first warning from radio in hurricanes Alicia and Danny (Ledingham & Walters, 1989, p. 39). Local FM radio stations were ranked 3rd, AM stations ranked 7th, national radio stations 8th, weather-band radio 9th, marine-band radio 10th as sources of information on Hurricane Danny in one sample (Piotrowski & Armstong, 1998, p. 344). Because a large segment of the population may be en route, working at a desk, recreating, or engaged in some other activity during the immediate time frame of a disaster, radio represents an important source of real-time information during a disaster. Radio is relatively inexpensive, operates well "on the fly," and tends to represent considerable "local expertise" on issues that may be particularly relevant (e.g., specific locations of events). Furthermore, radio is often well suited for visually impaired populations and non-English speaking populations in markets that often have radio programs in their own language.

- **The Internet is becoming an increasingly important medium of contact**: "The Internet was underutilized during fall 2001, when it became important to convey information on the risks of anthrax" (Hobbs et al., 2004, p. 67). "While traditional media provided the primary source of information on anthrax and bioterrorism, 21% (95% CI, 15–27%) of respondents [N = 500 randomly selected primary care patients in Boston] reported searching the Internet for this information during late 2001. Respondents reported trusting information from physicians the most, and information from health websites slightly more than information from any traditional media source. Over half of those searching the Internet reported changing their behavior as a result of information found online" (Kittler et al., 2004, p. 1). However, the Internet can be vulnerable during a major disaster. In the 9-11 aftermath, "overload rapidly affected the celerity of net-based messaging" (Alexander, 2002, p. 236). Video streams on 9-11 put a huge burden on already overloaded web servers (Carey, 2003). Especially in New York City, congestion was substantial from 9-11 until the next day, slowing service significantly and rendering the Internet useless at times (Carey, 2003; Moss & Townsend, 2003; Rappoport & Alleman, 2003).
- **Disasters tend to reveal a reactive media cycle**. Disasters are extremely newsworthy (Sood et al., 1987). The ways in which media respond to disasters often display a period of "ramping up" to the disaster, a period of expanding the story, and then a period in which lessons learned in the aftermath are sought (Friedman, 1989, Herbert et al., 2003).
- **The media face constraints in disseminating disaster information**:
  - The media are themselves dependent on infrastructure to operate. A constraint in any given disaster is that communities lacking local media outlets and/or journalists will be dependent on media without much specific information regarding the locality of interest (Alexander, 2002; Toigo, 1989; Wrobel, 1990).
  - Media organizations also face time constraints. Specifically, media are disproportionately accessible and accessed depending on time of day or cycle of communication production and dissemination (Fischer, 1998).
  - Another constraint media face is language, specifically that not all relevant populations understand English (Rich & Winters, 2002; Schneider, 1995).
  - Finally, media tend to be selective and biased in the ways in which they present disaster relevant information. The "if it bleeds, it leads" tendency leads to a variety of gate-keeping biases in the pubic image of personal risk in a disaster situation (Covello & Sandman, 2001).
- **There are upper limits to the effect of media.** For example, "in Mount Vernon's [Washington] chemical emergency, almost nine out of ten of those warned by the media developed only

a slight sense of personal risk, and for Abilene's [Texas] floods the corresponding proportion was more than eight out of ten" (Burkhart, 1991, p. 85). In other words, people ignored the warnings of danger in the media, influenced more by their curiosity. Research to date in risk and disasters communication suggests that current models and knowledge can only go so far. "It is important to note that although much is known about factors affecting evacuation decisions at the household level, current explanatory models only account for 50 percent of variance in warning response at best" (Tierney, Lindell, & Perry, 2001, p. 92).

- **Exposure to media coverage of a disaster is associated with distress.** Several studies of terrorist attacks have shown a strong association between the degree of media exposure to the disaster and psychological distress (Dougall, Hayward, & Baum, 2005; Schlenger et al., 2002; Shuster et al., 2001). The causal direction is unclear; the most distressed individuals may have sought the most media. However, it is clear that viewing coverage of terrorism does not appear to lower distress and promote adjustment (Dougall, et al., 2005; Schlenger et al., 2002; Shuster et al., 2001).
- **Most media are still limited in their ability to reach non-English speaking populations:** After the Loma Prieta earthquake, many government assistance workers spoke only English, and they were unable to communicate with the Spanish-speaking segments of the affected population" (Schneider, 1995, p. 119).
- **There are significant disparities across certain populations' access to various media:** Transient populations tend to receive emergency information later than indigenous populations, and respond less effectively.
- **The media are a tool of terrorists as well as responders.** It is important to remember that because terrorists seek publicity, the media often play an unwitting accomplice. Further, the media sometimes report information that becomes tactically or strategically useful to terrorists.

The Process of Risk and Disaster Messages

- **Communication must be redundant across media and sources.** Messages should be repeated frequently through a variety of different media to reach either the public or first responders (Fischer, 1998; Mileti & Sorensen, 1988; Tierney et al., 2001). Likewise all communication technology should have redundant backup equipment and plans in place to make sure systems do not fail (Alexander, 2002; Kapsales, 2004; Mileti & Sorensen, 1987).
- **Communication must be two-way.** Any disaster communication plan must plan for two-way communication between the public and the media, the public and government officials, the public and their families, and the government and first responders. Across a variety of disasters many lives could be saved if two-way communication could have occurred. In his study of the general public in responding to two disaster scenarios, Lasker (2004) found that "one-third of the population has a strong personal interest in participating in planning" (p. viii).

Suggestions

- **Enlist help from physicians and the health care system:** Most disasters create crises for health care delivery. Consequently, virtually all disaster and crisis planning needs to include the health care delivery system a partner. Furthermore, because people trust their own physician, having prerecorded contingency messages recorded by physicians available on mass switchboard emergency numbers could significantly increase the credibility of messages.
- **Have a ready source for outsource phone banking of calls:** Having scalable automatic telephone messaging systems, and targeted emergency telephonic notification systems in place is a vital form of notification for response. The CDC found it was able to do this during the anthrax attacks (Robinson & Newstetter, 2003).

- **Polling feedback**: "Periodic surveys of public attitudes provide important, timely information for understanding audiences in communication planning" (Pollard, 2003, p. 93).
- **People support triage:** The public supports rational triage of service delivery in disaster and crisis contexts. For example, "almost everyone (94% of the population) supports providing the vaccine right away to people who are known to be exposed to the smallpox virus even if it means slowing down vaccinating people who have not yet been exposed" (Lasker, 2004, p. 23). Consequently, disaster plans need to incorporate, and administrators need to embrace, needs-based triage protocol contingencies.
- **People want a choice of responses:** When possible, the public needs to be given more than one option for responding to disaster contexts. For example, according to responses to a hypothetical smallpox outbreak, it was found that "the anxiety level of half of the American population (48%) would be reduced if the officials managing the smallpox outbreak gave them a choice of protective actions" (Lasker, 2004, p. 24).
- **People want planning:** "Three-fifths of the American population believe that the harm caused by a terrorist attack in their community could be reduced a great deal or a lot by preparing ahead of time to deal with the effects" (Lasker, 2004, p. viii). Indeed, in recent years planning has moved from a focus on deficit or loss to establishing community resilience networks designed to provide a strong local response to a crisis (MacDonald, 2005; Paton & Johnson, 2001).
- **Create a "buddy system" between PIOs and scientists:** The CDC moved to such a model during the anthrax attacks so as to help assure that neither the scientist nor the communicator would provide inconsistent messages or information (Robinson & Newstetter, 2004). Scientists are viewed with unique forms of credibility that can significantly complement governmental sources of information.
- **Be ready to engage in "telebriefings":** The CDC went to this approach during the anthrax attacks. It involved almost daily telephone-based news conferences, and transcripts from these were rapidly uploaded to a website for the media (Robinson & Newstetter, 2004).
- **Develop a central repository of information about the disaster to refer media inquiries to that is coordinated and ready via website.** The communication agents of the CDC noted how useful it would have been to have had a more coordinated and up-to-date source of general and background information, rather than answering the same questions over and over again with each new inquiry.
- **Have "technology go kits" for field communication teams:** This would consist of communication devices with ready directories and encryption (Robinson & Newstetter, 2004).
- **Develop a standardized form for distributing daily information to the media:** Everyone will want to know standard topics: how many are now ill, at what stage is their illness, what areas are now affected, what new resources or strategies are being employed, etc. Distribute (blast-fax, e-mail, etc.) daily or more frequently (Robinson & Newstetter, 2004).

CONCLUSION

By many measures, the world is becoming a more dangerous place. The fact that there are more people in more places, from more cultures, often in greater levels of density, means that when disasters occur, they have the potential to affect more people, and more organizations and institutions are responsible for managing such disasters. Consequently, the study and understanding of the processes involved in anticipating, preparing for, and responding to such disasters have emerged as vital professions and disciplines unto themselves. Comprehensive approaches to training and evaluating preparedness for communicating before, during, and after disasters are long overdue, and beginning to emerge (e.g., Brand, Kerby, Elledge, Johnson, & Magas, 2006; Homeland Security Council, 2005). The sooner a corpus of guiding principles regarding risk and crisis communication can be established and refined, the sooner societies can better manage the disasters that confront them.

BIBLIOGRAPHY

Alexander, D. (2002). *Principles of emergency planning and management.* Oxford: Oxford University Press.

Alexander, D. (2003). Towards the development of standards in emergency management training and education. *Disaster Prevention and Management, 12,* 113–123.

Beauchesne, A. M., Shanley, K., McIlroy, C., & Lee, E. (2002). *A governor's guide to emergency management (Vol. 2: Homeland security).* Washington, DC: National Governors Association.

Behm, A. J. (1991). Terrorism, violence against the public, and the media: The Australian approach. *Political Communication and Persuasion, 8,* 233–246.

Benson, B. A., (2004). *The incident command system's effect on public relations excellence.* Communications Thesis, San Diego University, California.

Blanchard, J. C., Haywood, Y., Stein, B. D., Tanielian, T. L., Stoto, M., & Lurie, N. (2005). In their own words: Lessons learned from those exposed to anthrax. *American Journal of Public Health, 95*(3), 489–495.

Blondheim, M., & Liebs, T. (2003). From disaster marathon to media event: Live television's performance on September 11, 2001 and September 11, 2002. In A. M. Noll (Ed.), *Crisis communications: Lessons from September 11* (pp. 185–198). Oxford: Rowman & Littlefield.

Bolin, R. (1988). Response to natural disasters. In M. Lystad (Ed.), *Mental health response to mass emergencies: Theory and practices* (pp. 22–51). New York: Brunner/Mazel.

Brand, M., Kerby, D., Elledge, B., Johnson, D., & Magas, O. (2006). A model for assessing public health emergency preparedness competencies and evaluating training based on the local preparedness plan. *Journal of Homeland Security and Emergency Management, 3* (article 3), 1–19. Retrieved April 1, 2008, from http://www.bepress.com/jhsem/vol3/iss2/3

Brookmeyer, R., Johnson, E., & Bollinger, R. (2004, Dec. 16). Public health vaccination policies for containing an anthrax outbreak. *Nature, 432* (7019), 901–904.

Burkhart, F. N. (1991). *Media, emergency warnings, and citizen response.* Boulder, CO: Westview Press.

Carey, J. (2003). The functions and uses of media during the September 11 Crisis and its aftermath. In A. M. Noll (Ed.), *Crisis communications: Lessons from September 11* (pp. 1–16). Oxford: Rowman & Littlefield.

Cate, F. H. (2004). *The media and disaster reduction: Roundtable on the media, scientific information and disasters at the United Nations World Conference on Natural Disaster Reduction.* Retrieved 8 June 2004, from http://www.annengberg.nwu.edu/pubs/disas /disas3.htm

Christine, B. (1995) Disaster management: lessons learned. *Risk Management, 42,* 19–26.

Cohen, E. L., Ball-Rokeach, S. J., Jung, J. Y., & Kim, Y. C. (2003). Civic actions after September 11: A communication infrastructure perspective. In A. M. Noll (Ed.), *Crisis communications: Lessons from September 11* (pp. 31–43). Oxford: Rowman & Littlefield.

Covello, V., & Sandman, P. M. (2001). Risk communication: Evolution and revolution. In A. Wolbarst (ed.), *Solutions to an environment in peril* (pp. 164–178). Baltimore, MD: Johns Hopkins Press. Retrieved from http://www.psandman.com/articles/covello.htm

Craft, D. L., Wein, L. M., & Wilkins, A. H. (2005). Analyzing bioterror response logistics: The case of anthrax. *Management Science, 51,* 679–694.

Defense Threat Reduction Agency, Federal Bureau of Investigation, & U.S. Joint Forces Command. (2001, March). *Human behavior and WMD crisis/Risk communication workshop.* Retrieved 10 June 2004, from http://www.dtra.mil/about/organization/finalreport.pdf

DeGrazia, A. (1951). *Public and republic.* New York, Knopf.

Dougall, A. L., Hayward, M. C., & Baum, A. (2005). Media exposure to bioterrorism: Stress and the anthrax attacks. *Psychiatry, 68,* 28–42.

Drabek, T. (1969). Social processes in disaster: Family evacuation. *Social Problems 16,* 336–349.

Drabek, T. E. (1999). Understanding disaster warning responses. *The Social Science Journal, 36,* 515–523.

Drabek, T. E., & McEntire, D. A. (2003). Emergent phenomena and the sociology of disaster: Lessons, trends and opportunities from the research literature. *Disaster Prevention and Management, 12,* 97–112.

Fischer, H. W. (1998). *Response to disaster: Fact versus fiction & its perpetuation, the sociology of disaster* (2nd ed.). New York: University Press of America.

Fischer, H. W. (2000). Mitigation and response planning in a bio-terrorist attack. *Disaster Prevention and Management, 9,* 360–367.

Fischer, H. W. (2002). Terrorism and 11 September 2001: Does the "behavioral response to disaster" model fit? *Disaster Prevention and Management, 11,* 123–127.

Folio, L. R., Lahti, R. L., Cockrum, D. S., Bills, S., & Younker, M. R. (2004). Initial experience with mass immunization as a bioterrorism countermeasure. *Journal of the American Osteopathic Association, 104,* 240–243.

Foster, J., Andersen, P. A., McBride, J., & Spitzberg, B. H. (2004, June). *Disaster/terrorism preparedness media and assessment plan* (pp. 1–119). Report to San Diego County Health and Human Services Department.

Fowler, R. A., Sanders, G. D., Bravata, D. M., Nouri, B., Gastwirth, J. M., Peterson, D., Broker, A. G., Garber, A. M., & Owens, D. K. (2005). Cost-effectiveness of defending against bioterrorism: A comparison of vaccination and antibiotic prophylaxis against anthrax. *Annals of Internal Medicine, 142*(8), 601–610.

Friedman, S. M. (1989). TMI: The media story that will not die. In L. M. Walters, L. Wilkens, & T. Walters (Eds.), *Bad tidings: Communication and catastrophe* (pp. 63–84). Hillsdale, NJ: Erlbaum.

Gillespie, D. F., & Banerjee, M. M. (1993). Prevention planning and disaster preparedness. *The Journal of Applied Social Sciences, 17,* 237–253.

Hagenbourger, M. (2003). The French Post Office and anthrax: Key lessons and new questions. *Journal of Contingencies & Crisis Management, 11,* 124–128.

Handmer, J. (2000). Are flood warnings futile? Risk communication in emergencies. *The Australasian Journal of Disaster and Trauma Studies, 2,* 1–12.

Hartsough, D. M., & Mileti, D. S. (1985). The media in disaster. In J. Laube & S. A. Murphy (Eds.), *Perspectives on disaster recovery* (pp. 282–294). Norwalk, CT: Appleton-Century-Crofts.

Herbert, W. R., Collins, C. A., & Rowland, W. B., Jr. (2003, December). *An assessment: Virginia's response to hurricane Isabel.* Arlington, VA: System Planning Corporation. Retrieved June 10, 2004, from http://pub.sysplan.com/Hurricane_Isabel_Assessment.pdf

Hobbs, J., Kittler, A., Fox, S., Middleton, B, & Bates, D. W. (2004). Communicating health information to an alarmed public facing a threat such as a bioterrorist attack. *Journal of Health Communication, 9,* 67–75.

Homeland Security Council. (2005, November). *National strategy for pandemic influenza.* Washington, DC: Homeland Security Council.

Ice, J. I., & Petersen, D. (2002). *Considerations in risk communication: A digest of risk communication as a risk management tool.* Washington, DC: National Risk Management Research Laboratory, Office of Research and Development.

Kahan, E., Fogelman, Y., Eliezer, K., & Shlomo, V. (2003). Patient and family physician preferences for care and communication in the eventuality of anthrax terrorism. *Family Practice, 20,* 441–442.

Kapsales, P. (2004). Wireless messaging for homeland security: Using narrowband PCs for improved communication during emergencies. *Journal of Homeland Security, 1,* 1–10.

Keinan, G. & Sadeh, A., & Rosen, S. (2003). Attitudes and reactions to media coverage of terrorist acts. *Journal of Community Psychology, 31,* 149–165.

Kerkvliet, G. J. (2004). What is the true number of victims of the postal anthrax attack of 2001? *Journal of the American Osteopathic Association, 104* (11), 452.

Kittler, A. F., Hobbs, J., Volk, L. A., Kreps, G. L., & Bates, D. W. (2004). The Internet as a vehicle to communicate health information during a public health emergency: A survey analysis involving the anthrax scare of 2001. *Journal of Medical Internet Research, 6*(1), 1–7. Retrieved from http://www.jmir.org/2004/1/e8/

Knight, A. J. (2005). Alert status red: Awareness, knowledge and reaction to the threat advisory system. *Journal of Homeland Security and Emergency Management, 2,* 1–10. Retrieved from http://www.bepress.com/jhsem/vol2/iss1/9

Kreps, G. A. (1985). Disaster and the social order. *Sociological Theory, 3,* 49–64.

Lasker, R. D. (2004). *Redefining readiness: Terrorism planning through the eyes of the public.* New York: New York Academy of Medicine.

Ledingham, J. A., & Walters, L. M. (1989). The sound and the fury: Mass media and hurricanes. In L. M. Walters, L. Wilkens, & T. Walters (Eds.), *Bad tidings: Communication and catastrophe* (pp. 35–45). Hillsdale, NJ: Erlbaum.

Lewis, H. (2004). Lessons learned from hurricane Floyd. *Bankrate.com.* Retrieved 8 June 2004, from http://www.bankrate.com/brm/news/special/floyd/19991119.asp

McDonald , M. (2005, November). *Stages in the evolution of disaster risk communication: how knowledge, science and interactive technologies are transforming communication in high risk, low trust environments.* Plenary presentation at the National Communication Association Convention, Boston, MA.

McEntire, D. A. (2002). Coordinating multi-organisational responses to disaster: Lessons from the March 28, 2000, Fort Worth Tornado. *Disaster Prevention and Management, 11,* 369–379.

Major, A. M., & Atwood, E. (1997) Changes in media credibility when a predicted disaster doesn't happen. *Journalism and Mass Communication Quarterly, 74,* 797–813.

Massey, K. B. (1995). Analyzing the uses and gratifications concept of audience activity with a qualitative approach: Media encounters during the 1989 Loma Prieta earthquake disaster. *Journal of Broadcasting & Electronic Media, 39,* 328–340.

Miletti, D. S., & O'Brien, P. W. (1992). Warning during disaster: Normalizing communicated risk. *Social Problems, 39,* 40–57.

Miletti, D. S., & Sorensen, J. H. (1987). Natural hazards and precautionary behavior. In N. D. Weinstein (Ed.), *Taking care: Understanding and encouraging self-protective behavior* (pp. 189–207). Cambridge: Cambridge University Press.

Miletti, D. S., & Sorensen, J. H. (1988). Planning and implementing warning systems. In M. Lystad (Ed.), *Mental health response to mass emergencies: Theory and practices* (pp. 321–345). New York: Brunner/ Mazel.

Mitchell, J. T., & Thomas, D. S. K. (2001). Trends in disaster losses. In S. L. Cutter (Ed.), *American hazardscapes: The regionalization of hazards and disasters* (pp. 77–114). Washington, DC: Joseph Henry Press.

Moss, M. L., & Townsend, A. (2003). Response, restoration, and recovery: September 11 and New York City's digital networks. In A. M. Noll (Ed.), *Crisis communications: Lessons from September 11* (pp. 55–68). Oxford: Rowman & Littlefield.

Nacos, B. L. (2002). *Mass-mediated terrorism: The central role of the media in terrorism and counterterrorism.* Lanham, MD: Rowman & Littlefield.

Nigg, J. M., & Perry, R. W. (1988). Emergency preparedness and response planning: An intergovernmental perspective. In M. Lystad (Ed.), *Mental health response to mass emergencies: Theory and practices* (pp. 346–370). New York: Brunner/Mazel.

Norris, F. H., Friedman, M. J., Watson, P. J., Byrne, C. M., Diaz, E., & Kaniasty, K., (2002). 60,000 disaster victims speak: Part I. An empirical review of the empirical literature. *Psychiatry, 65*, 207–239.

North, C. S., Price, P. C., & Smith, E. M. (1988). Response to technological accidents. In M. Lystad (Ed.), *Mental health response to mass emergencies: Theory and practices* (pp. 52–95). New York: Brunner/Mazel.

O'Brien, P. W. (2003). Risk communication and public warning response to the September 11th attack on the World Trade Center. In Natural Hazards Research and Applications Information Center, Public Entity Risk Institute, and Institute for Civil Infrastructure Systems (Eds.), *Beyond September 11th: An account of post-disaster research* (Special Publication No. 39, pp. 355–372). Boulder, CO: University of Colorado.

Occupational Safety and Health Administration. (2003). *Crisis communication plan.* 18–19. Washington DC: U.S. Department of Labor.

Omer, H., & Alon, N. (1994). The continuity principle: A unified approach to disaster and trauma. *American Journal of Community Psychology, 22*, 273–285.

Paton, D. (2003). Disaster preparedness: A social-cognitive perspective. *Disaster Prevention and Management, 12*, 210–216.

Paton, D., & Jackson, D (2002) Developing disaster management capability: An assessment centre approach. *Disaster Prevention and Management, 11,* 115–122

Paton, D., & Johnson, D. (2001). Disasters and communities: Vulnerability, resilience and preparedness. *Disaster Preparedness and Management, 10*, 270–277.

Payne, J. G., & Schulte, S. K. (2003). Mass media, public health, and achieving health literacy. *Journal of Health Communication, 8*, 124–125.

Perry, R. W. (2003). Municipal terrorism management in the United States. Disaster *Prevention and Management, 12*, 190–202.

Perry, R. W., & Pugh, M. D. (1978). *Collective behavior: Response to social stress.* St. Paul, MN: West Publishing.

Perry, R. W., & Lindell, M. K. (1989). Communicating threat information for volcano hazards. In L. M. Walters, L. Wilkens, & T. Walters (Eds.), *Bad tidings: Communication and catastrophe* (pp. 47–62). Hillsdale, NJ: Erlbaum.

Perry, R. W., & Mushkatel, A. H. (1984). *Disaster management: Warning response and community relocation.* Westport, CT: Quorum Books.

Peuler, J. N. (1988). Community outreach after emergencies. In M. Lystad (Ed.), *Mental health response to mass emergencies: Theory and practices* (pp. 239–261). New York: Brunner/Mazel.

Piotrowski, C., & Armstrong, T. R. (1998). Mass media preferences in disaster: A study of hurricane Danny. *Social Behavior and Personality, 26,* 341–346.

Pollard, W. E. (2003). Public perceptions of information sources concerning bioterrorism before and after anthrax attacks: An analysis of national survey data. *Journal of Health Communication, 8*, 93–103.

Pool, I. D. S. (1973). Public opinion. In I. D. S. Pool, W. Schramm, N. Maccoby, & E. B. Parker (Eds.), *Handbook of communication* (pp.779–835.) Chicago: Rand McNally.

Rappoport, P N., & Alleman, J. (2003).The internet and the demand for news: Macro- and microevidence. In A. M. Noll (Ed.), *Crisis communications: Lessons from September 11* (pp 149–166). Oxford: Rowman & Littlefield.

Rich, H. E., & Winters, L. I. (2002). Disasters. In C. F. Hohm & J. A. Glynn (Eds.), *California's social problems* (2nd ed.; pp. 325–352). Thousand Oaks, CA: Pine Forge Press.

Robinson, S. J., & Newstetter, W. C. (2003). Uncertain science and certain deadlines: CDC responses to the media during the anthrax attacks of 2001. *Journal of Health Communication, 8*(suppl. 1), 17–34.

Ronan, K. R., Johnston, D. M., Daly, M., & Fairley, R. (2001). School children's risk perceptions and preparedness: A hazards education survey. *The Australasian Journal of Disaster and Trauma Studies, 1,* 1–27.

Rogers, E. M. (2003). Diffusion of news of the September 11 terrorist attacks. In A. M. Noll (Ed.), *Crisis communications: Lessons from September 11* (pp. 1–16). Oxford: Rowman & Littlefield.

Rudman, W. (2003) *Emergency Responders: Drastically underfunded, dangerously underprepared.* Washington, DC: Council on Foreign Relations.
Salmon, C. T., Park, H. S., & Wrigley, B. J. (2003). Optimistic bias and perceptions of bioterrorism in Michigan corporate spokespersons, Fall 2001. *Journal of Health Communication, 8*(suppl. 1), 130–143.
Schlenger, W. E., Caddell, J. M., Ebert, L., Jordan, B. K., Rourke, K. M., Wilson, D., Thalji, L., Dennis, J. M., Fairbank, J. A., & Kulka, R. A. (2002). *Journal of the American Medical Association, 288*, 581–588.
Schneider, M. E. (1995). *Flirting with disaster: Public management in crisis situations.* Armonk, NY: M. E. Sharpe.
Shuster, M. A., Stein, B. D., Jaycox, L. H., Collins, R. L., Marshall, G. N., Elliott, M. N., Zhou, A. J., Kanouse, D. E., Morrison, J. L., & Berry, S.H. (2001). A national survey of stress reactions after the September 11, 2001, terrorist attacks. *New England Journal of Medicine, 345,* 1507–1512.
Shaluf, I. M., Ahmadun, F. R., & Mustapha, A. (2003a). A review of disaster and crisis. *Disaster Prevention and Management, 12,* 24–32.
Shaluf, I. M., Ahmadun, F. R., & Mustapha, A. (2003b). Technological disaster's criteria and models. *Disaster Prevention and Management, 12,* 305–311.
Sood, R., Stockdale, G., & Rogers, E. M. (1987). How the news media operate in natural disasters. *Journal of Communication, 37*, 26–41.
Stein, B. D., Jaycox, L. H., Elliott, M. N., Collins, R., Berry, S., Marshall, G. N., Klein, D. J., & Schuster, M. A. (2004). The emotional and behavioral impact of terrorism on children: Results from a national survey. *Applied Developmental Science, 8*, 184–194.
Tampere Declaration on Disaster Communications. (1991). *The Tampere declaration on disaster communications.* Retrieved 8 June 2004, from http://www.reliefweb.int/telecoms /tampere/tampdec.html
Taylor, A. J. (1987). A taxonomy of disasters and their victims. *Journal of Psychosomatic Research, 31*, 535–544.
Tierney, K. J., Lindell, M. K., & Perry, R. W. (2001). *Facing the unexpected: Disaster preparedness and response in the United States*. Washington, DC: Joseph Henry Press.
Toigo, J. W. (1989). *Disaster recovery planning: Managing risk and catastrophe in information systems.* Englewood Cliffs, NJ: Yourdon Press.
Tompkins, P. K., & Anderson, E. V. B. (1971) *Communication crises at Kent State*. New York: Gordon and Breach.
Turner, B. A., & Pidgeon, N. F. (1997). *Man-made disasters* (2nd ed.). Oxford: Butterworth-Heinemann.
Turner, J. T., & Gelles, M. G. (2003). *Threat assessment: A risk management approach.* New York: Haworth Press.
U.S. Postal Inspection Service. (2004). *FY 2004 Annual report of investigations of the United States Postal Inspection Service*. Washington DC: U. S. Postal Inspection Service.
Webb, G. F. (2003). A silent bomb: The risk of anthrax as a weapon of mass destruction. *Proceedings of the National Academy of Sciences, 100*(8), 4355–4356.
Wein, L. M., Craft, D. L., & Kaplan, E. H. (2003). Emergency response to an anthrax attack. *Proceedings of the National Academy of Sciences, 100*(7), 4346–4351.
Weinstein, N. D. (1987). Cross-hazard consistencies: Conclusion about self-protective behavior. In N. D. Weinstein (Ed.), *Taking care: Understanding and encouraging self-protective behavior* (pp. 325–335). Cambridge: Cambridge University Press.
Weiss, M. J. (1988). *The clustering of America*. New York Harper and Row.
Witte, K., & Allen, M. (2000). A meta-analysis of fear appeals: Implications for effective public health campaigns. *Health Education & Behavior, 27*, 591–615.
Wray, R. J., Kreutler, M. W., Jacobsen, H., Clements, B., & Evans, R. G. (2004). Theoretical perspectives on public communication preparedness for terrorist attacks. *Family Community Health, 27*, 232–241.
Wrobel, L. A. (1990). *Disaster recovery planning for telecommunications*. Boston: Artech House.

11

The Ecological Perspective and Other Ways to (Re)Consider Cultural Factors in Risk Communication

Linda Aldoory
University of Maryland

A traditional assumption in risk communication is that audiences will improve their decision making in response to risk if armed with more information that is accurate (Finucane, Slovic, Mertz, Flynn, & Satterfield, 2000; Lindell & Perry, 2004). However, as Finucane et al. (2000) found, "Extensive efforts to educate the public…have failed to move public opinion to coincide with the experts" (p. 160). When audiences do react to risk messages, organizations and governments often assume that the response will be either panic, about risks that have low probability, or denial, about risks prevalent in everyday life (Scherer & Juanillo, 2003). According to Scherer and Juanillo (2003), "Individuals may worry about the risks of West Nile Virus with family or friends as they continue to smoke, consume high-fat foods, or ignore their doctor's instructions" (p. 222).

The reality is that public responses to risk communication—and the relationships between risk communicators and audiences—are much more complicated than these traditional assumptions suggest (Lindell & Perry, 2004). Audiences react in a myriad of ways to risk communication about threats affecting them because culture mediates the impact of risk communication efforts and potential relationships between risk communicators and audiences (Airhihenbuwa, Makinway, & Obregon, 2000; Gandy, 2001; Hornik & Ramirez, 2006; Lundgren & McMakin, 2004). Over the past 20 years, dozens of books and articles have attested to the influence of culture on risk perceptions and risk situations (Edgar, Freimuth, & Hammond, 2003; Finucane, 2002; Guttman, 2003; Lundgren & McMakin, 2004; Mays & Cochran, 1988; Murray-Johnson, Witte, Liu, & Hubbell, 2001; Singer & Endreny, 1993; Wahlberg & Sjoberg, 2000; Witte & Berkowitz, 1998), and the influence of culture on the production and reception of communication (Korzenny & Ting-Toomey, 1992). A national symposium on risk communication concluded that one of the most important issues for future research was communicating with communities of different race, ethnic background, and income (Chess, Salomone, Hance, & Saville, 1995).Understanding the role of culture in risk communication has become critical with the increasingly multicultural population of the United States. The 2000 census showed a decline in the non-Hispanic white population, and the latest projections predict that by 2050, the non-Hispanic white population will be reduced to 50% (U.S. Bureau of the Census, 2004). This means that risk communicators will be more effective in building relationships and achieving their objectives if they understand the cultural factors that play a role in their communicating about risk.

In this chapter I explain some cultural factors by summarizing a literature review I conducted on culture and its relationship with risk communication in the United States.[1] First, however, I contextualize the review of literature by explaining the social constructionist perspective I take here, and by defining and delimiting the terms "risk communication" and "culture." I then describe some traditional ways that culture has been viewed and studied in risk communication and end with more recent views of how cultural factors may be incorporated into risk communication. One recent scholarly turn I emphasize here is towards an ecological perspective for risk communication that offers broader, contextual and social domains (Murray-Johnson & Witte, 2003). While a traditional focus for designing risk messages has been the individualized, cognitive level, an ecological perspective considers cultural, economic and political factors when designing messages (Airhihenbuwa, 1995; Airhihenbuwa, Makinwa, & Obregon, 2000; Airhihenbuwa & Obregon, 2000; Ford & Yep, 2003; Kar, Alcalay, 2001a; Witte, Meyer, Bidol, Casey, Kopfman, Maduschke, et al., 1996). While continuing to include the individual, an ecological approach de-emphasizes the importance of the individual and, therefore, diminishes the potential to blame the victim. This chapter details the ecological approach and offers examples of it in practice.

A SOCIAL CONSTRUCTIONIST PERSPECTIVE

This chapter is grounded in the social constructionist approach to communication. This perspective assumes that risk, the environment, and media are all socially constructed through interaction and discourse, and, therefore, dependent on interpretation by producers and audiences of risk communication (Beck, 2001; Finucane, 2002; Finucane & Holup, 2005; Mumby, 1997). Individuals bring their own preconceived ideas to interactions and meaning making (Beck, 2001; Mishler, 1981, 1984). According to Lundgren and McMakin (2004), the social constructionist approach to risk communication assumes that the scientific community, media personnel, and audiences all have "values, beliefs, and emotions that subtly affect how risks are assessed and communicated" (p. 21). They continued, "Understanding [the social] context and facilitating an exchange of information, attitudes, values, and perceptions in both directions ('expert' to 'stakeholder' and vice versa) can help build better risk decisions…" (p. 21).

A social constructionist approach assumes that culture has an influential role in constructing meaning, beliefs and actions. The selection and interpretation of risks and risk messages are influenced by the way in which different cultures operate (Anderson, 1997; Douglas & Wildavsky, 1982; Guttman, 2003). Cultural groups vary significantly from one another in terms of a multitude of factors. The apparent differences include language and communication behavior; historical and personal experiences; social and peer networks; and perceived stereotypes of other cultural groups. Research has also found that cultural groups differ by perceived life priorities; health related practices and beliefs; susceptibility to risks; mortality rates; media use; and leadership structures (Kar et al., 2001a).

The social constructionist perspective and the role of culture in this perspective can be found in several theoretical approaches to risk communication. For example, the social network contagion approach (Scherer & Cho, 2003) suggests that social networks of family, friends, neighbors and work colleagues affect how we view risk and react to risk communication. The stronger the social ties and the more frequent the interactions, the more likely the cohesiveness of the social group in their reaction to a risk message (Albrecht & Goldsmith, 2003; Scherer & Cho, 2003). These social groupings are often formed around cultural similarity or history. In another theory, the social amplification of risk (Kasperson & Kasperson, 2005; Kasperson, Renn, Slovic, Brown, Emel, Goble,et al., 1988; Pidgeon, Kasperson, & Slovic, 2003), psychological, social, and cultural meanings can amplify the threat that individuals perceive. This theory frames risk perceptions as social constructions (McComas, 2006). Finally, in the social trust approach to risk communication, research has shown that the higher the trust in organizational sources of information about risk, the lower the estimate of risk and the estimate of benefits (Cvetkovich & Lofstedt, 1999; Cvetkovich & Winter, 2001; Siegrist & Cvetkovich, 2000). Perceived trust is influenced by intercultural understandings. As Cvetkovich and Lofstedt asserted, "Judgments of risk are not limited to assessments of physical processes…[but] are also reflections of the understanding of social systems and the actors playing roles within them" (p. 3).

Anderson (1997) argued that perceptions of risk—public and organizational—are all equally biased, because they reflect different cultural meanings and systems (p. 109). Conflicting cultural constructions of meaning between communicators and audiences can cause misunderstandings or confusion (Sharf & Vanderford, 2003). This, in turn, can inhibit relationship building and maintenance that are important for effective community-based, risk communication efforts. Reducing the potential for misunderstandings or mistrust should be an important goal in risk communication.

DELIMITING RISK COMMUNICATION

In her review of risk communication research, McComas (2006) defined risk as the forces or circumstances that pose danger to people or to what they value; risk is typically measured as a likelihood or probability of loss occurring (p. 76). She used the National Research Council's definition for risk communication: the interactive process of exchange of information and opinions among individuals, groups, and institutions concerning a risk or potential risk to human health or the environment (NRC, 1989). While this definition includes an interactive component, it falls short of explaining the social constructions and interpretations of information and risk. Beck (2001) argued that communication is used to socially construct conceptions of "illness," "risk," and "disease" (p. 4). Through communication, she argued, we co-create information, "legitimate" treatment, identities, and what we define as "normal" in a turbulent and risky environment (p. 4).

In this chapter, risk communication is considered not only the content of risk messages, but also the production and reception of risk messages, disseminated via public relations programs and community campaigns. Public health risks are addressed in this chapter more than technological or environmental risks. Also, I limited the literature search to risk communication in the United States, for purposes of maintaining a defined focus and scope.

DEFINING CULTURE

While considered a significant area for study, the concept of culture is controversial (Anderson, 1997; Lindell & Perry, 2004). It has political meaning as well as social and theoretical meanings, and it has been overused and frequently ill-defined. Some authors chose not to define the term specifically (Korzenny & Schiff, 1992), while others offered limited perspectives on the concept. Culture has been studied as nationality (Chaffee, 1992; Finucane & Holup, 2005), as ethnicity (Kreuter, Lukwago, Bucholtz, Clark, & Sanders-Thompson, 2002; Lindell & Perry, 2004; Mays & Cochran, 1988), and as a way to assess groups of individuals, such as African Americans or women, who have been marginalized by dominant culture groups (Airhihenbuwa, 1995; Ford & Yep, 2003; Witte, 1992).

Given the social constructionist approach, I offer a definition of culture and what it encompasses for purposes of this chapter. In general, culture can be defined as a system of values and norms, ideology, subjective states, ritual and discourse that influences attitudes, perceptions, communication and actions, within a historical context (Airhihenbuwa, 1995; Anderson, 1997; Ford & Yep, 2003; Triandis, 1976). Triandis (1976) referred to "subjective" culture as the way humans who speak a mutually understandable dialect react subjectively to their social environment (p. 3). This subjective reaction includes "the way they attend to cues from the environment, the way they think about 'what goes with what,' and the way they feel about different aspects of the environment" (p. 3). Giroux (1992) asserted that culture and cultural norms are constantly changing. He explained that culture is "a mobile field of ideological and material relations that are unfinished, multilayered, and always open to interrogation" (p. 99). Moreover, Beck (2001) argued, "The advent of technology, the shrinking of global boundaries, and the splintering of previously taken-for-granted structures has contributed to confusing conglomerations of cultural influences" (p. 29). These conglomerations are illustrated in the current ways risk communication is constructed. As Beck (2001) explained, it is through communication that individuals co-create "ever-emergent constructions of what it is to be a legitimate member of [a] culture and what members of this culture should and can do at particular times and in particular ways" (p. 29). This can be applied to risk communication, where members of a culture use communication to co-create what they should and can do in times of risk and as receivers of risk messages.

TRADITIONAL TREATMENT OF CULTURE IN RISK COMMUNICATION

Traditionally, culture in risk communication has been considered a univariate concept that can be isolated for communication efforts. In other words, culture has equaled race alone, or sex alone, or language spoken. Some of the core cultural considerations in risk communication have included: ethnicity and race; language, sex and gender; and health outcomes and mortality rates (Beck, 2001). Researchers have shown how these factors influence perceived risk and can act as barriers to effective risk communication.

Ethnicity and Race

There is a large body of evidence supporting the fact that ethnicity and race can influence the production, meaning, and reception of risk communication (e.g., Beck, 2001; Braithwaite & Taylor, 2001; Gandy, 2001; Hornik & Ramirez, 2006; Kar et al., 2001a; Lassiter, 1995; Murray-Johnson et al., 2001; Pratt, Ha, Levine, & Pratt, 2003; Purnell & Paulanka, 1998; Robinson, 1998; Spector, 1996; Sylvester, 1998; Yancey, Kumanyika, Ponce, McCarthy, Fielding, Leslie, et al., 2004). The published literature in the United States has focused on people of color, but white Americans are just as influenced by their ethnicity and race as other ethnic groups are—the influence is less apparent due to their dominant cultural position in this country.

Much of the literature on ethnicity and race in risk communication has focused on African American and Latino communities. This research described characteristics or core values that authors stated might help communicators create more culturally sensitive messages (Yancey et al., 2004).[2]

Characteristics highlighted in the literature about African American cultural groups have included "an active folk medicine system" and a strong "sense of the present" (Sylvester, 1998, p. 16). The extended family and individual racial identity are other important influencers in some African American communities (Kreuter et al., 2002; Murray-Johnson et al., 2001; Scott, Gilliam, & Braxton, 2005). Jemmott, Jemmott III, and Hutchinson (2001) found that, in their study, urban, African American adolescent participants held a strong sense of identification with Africa. These researchers also found that perceptions about HIV risk were influenced by negative attitudes about homosexuality and a view that AIDS was a form of "racial warfare" against African American people (p. 328). Several researchers have documented similar perceptions of institutional racism by African American people; this distrust has constructed a culturally shared understanding of the U.S. public health system (Airhihenbuwa, 1995; Green, Maisiak, Wang, Britt, & Ebeling, 1997). Since the Tuskegee Syphilis Experiment by the U.S. Public Health Service (begun in 1932 and published in 1972), many African Americans, regardless of socioeconomic status, are legitimately suspicious of U.S. health care institutions and the risk messages that disseminate from these institutions (Harter, Stephens, & Japp, 2000). According to Harter et al. (2000), "If African Americans are suspicious of health care institutions, it may be because throughout history they have been exploited for medical experimentation and demonstration" (p. 20).

Icard, Bourjolly, and Siddiqui (2003) suggested that some African American men might prefer to hear about risk prevention from friends than from other sources. They also suggested that positive self-empowering messages might be more desirable to some low-income African Americans than those focusing on negative problems (p. 220). Pratt et al. (2003) recommended group approaches for communicating prevention messages over one-on-one approaches (p. 371). Scott et al. (2005) listed the following strategies to use in HIV risk prevention in African American communities: include information on African American culture and history; emphasize the role of the family; and use age-appropriate, ethnically familiar channels (p. 26).

Research with Latino communities has outlined different value systems that often guide perceptions and behavior (Kar & Alcalay, 2001b; Scott et al., 2005; Valdes & Seoane, 1995). For example, *familismo* is the belief that family needs and welfare take precedence over individual needs. *Familismo* might be illustrated when parents make sacrifices for the children, and in return, children are expected to show respect and gratitude and to assume responsibility for parents in their old age. A second value system is *machismo*, which frames men as providers, protectors, and representatives of the family to the outer world. It also refers to culturally acceptable masculinity that includes bravery, strength, and virility. Unfortunately, machismo may create problems: in some Latino communities, it is not appropriate for women to talk about sexual risk with partners, and heterosexual men have more sexual freedom that might translate into sexual partners outside of marital commitment or lack of condom use (Gomez & Marin, 1996; Scott et al., 2005). A third value system, *sympatia*, encourages people to be sociable, likable, and outgoing (Gomez & Marin; 1996; Triandis, Marin, Lisansky, & Betancourt, 1984). Being helpful and giving are also parts of *sympatia.* Scott et al. (2005) listed the following strategies to use in HIV risk prevention for some Latina communities: respect privacy; demand that bilingual/bicultural workers examine the value judgments they themselves hold; use role models from the Latino community; place machismo in a positive context; and develop resource materials that are more than just bilingual (p. 23).

Compared to Latino and African American cultures, much less has been documented on the broad grouping often labeled Asian Americans. Asian and Pacific Islander Americans comprise more than 40 different nationalities and over 100 languages and dialects, making it unrealistic to generalize any cultural norm or belief (Kar et al., 2001b). At an aggregate level, however, it has been shown that Asian Americans do well on most indicators of health and quality of life, which has encouraged a stereotypical image of them as a "model minority" (Kar et al., 2001b, p. 91). However, research has shown that many Asian Americans experience generational conflicts and, among the more recently immigrated, identity confusion (Wong, Lai, Nagasaway, & Lin, 1998), which increases emotional stress. Some Southeast Asian communities are motivated by the avoidance of shame and loss of face. Some may believe that it is impolite to confess to not understanding what another person is saying, so they do not ask for explanations. This affects relationships between risk communicators and these particular audiences. Among some Vietnamese American communities, risk behaviors are guided by modesty, discretion and privacy, community solidarity, and helpfulness (Kar et al., 2001b). Many families blend traditional or folk health practices with Western medicine, creating a type of pluralistic system of health care for themselves (Scott et al., 2005).

These examples of cultural characteristics not only influence the perceptions and reactions of audience members, but also of communicators. The ethnic and racial backgrounds of risk communicators help construct their meaning of risk. As Kar et al. (2001a) explained, "Prevailing stereotypes and myths about ethnic minorities often adversely affect communication and rapport between health professionals and minority groups" (p. 339).

Language

According to Ellis (1999), "Language is the most elemental quality of the discourse of ethnic identity and group formation" (p. 158). Van Dijk, Ting-Toomey, Smitherman, and Troutman (1997) stated that "group members culturally produce and reproduce their own identity—and hence their group—by using the group's own language variety and special discourse forms…" (p. 164). Language differences have often been studied on an interpersonal level in risk communication (Burger, McDermott, Chess, Bochenek, Perez-Lugo, & Pflugh, 2003), but they have also influenced media and campaign messages about risk.

After English, Spanish is the most commonly spoken language in the United States (U.S. Bureau of the Census, 2006). According to the U.S. Bureau of the Census (2006), about 17.5 million people speak Spanish at home. In response, Spanish-language media has rapidly expanded in the United States. Three Spanish television networks—Univision, Telemundo, and Galavision—transmit to 64 cities across the country via 95 stations, and Spanish-language radio is often on all day long (compared to drive time radio listening hours for Euro-Americans), particularly for Latinos age 25 to 64 (Kar & Alcalay, 2001c, p. 127).

Risk communicators have discovered the necessity to work with Spanish language media in disseminating risk messages. However, translating messages into other languages such as Spanish has had little success—the "special discourse forms" described by van Dijk et al. (1997) and culturally embedded signifiers cannot be easily translated. Beck (2001) explained that not only language, but also "linguistic and nonverbal patterns indicate and reify cultural preferences and orientations to the world" (p. 197). Therefore, there are ongoing misinterpretations and confusion among audience members when confronted with risk communication that may be written in their first language. Language barriers have been shown to be particularly prevalent with Asian and Pacific Islander American populations (Scott et al., 2005). Again, with over 100 dialects and languages, the ability to clearly communicate to a cultural grouping labeled Asian American is challenging if not impossible.

Sex and Gender

Several authors have considered sex and gender as cultural groupings that affect the production and reception of communication about risks (for greater detail, see Beck, 2001; Dosman, Adamowicz, & Hrudey, 2001; Gabbard-Alley, 1995; Gallant, Keita, & Royak-Schaler, 1997; Wood, 1994, 2005). This body of research has focused on the gendered and sociocultural differences between men and women and how these differences impact communication. Except for literature on AIDS/HIV risk, risk communication scholarship has virtually ignored lesbian, gay, bisexual, and transgendered (LGBT) cultures as distinct and relevant. In terms of AIDS/HIV, authors have focused on behavioral interventions for homosexual communities and resistance by U.S. heterosexual populations of messages due to strong anti-gay attitudes and norms (Johnson, Holtgrave, McClellan, Flanders, Hill, & Goodman, 2005; Kennamer & Honnold, 1995; Price & Hsu, 1992; Stipp & Kerr, 1989). For example, Kennamer and Honnold (1995) found that negative attitudes towards homosexuality and conservative AIDS policy attitudes helped predict low attention to news about AIDS. Similarly, Price and Hsu (1992) found that negative attitudes towards homosexuals and misinformation about AIDS transmission were strong predictors of support for stringent restrictions for persons with AIDS. More recently, Johnson et al. (2005) conducted a meta-analysis of behavioral interventions for prevention of HIV transmission among men who have sex with men; they found that overall the interventions helped reduce unprotected sex by 27% (p. 582). This study was not based in the communication field, and, unfortunately, limited research on LGBT communities has been conducted over the past 10 years in risk communication scholarship.

On the other hand, there have been several risk communication studies on male and female differences. In general, authors have argued that men and women are subtly guided by societal institutions, such as media and medicine, to enact ascribed gender roles. As Wood (2005) explained, individuals are bombarded with messages that present certain cultural prescriptions for gender. These prescriptions for certain gender roles are portrayed as natural and are pervasive and powerful in their ability to encourage role enactment by men and women. Such enactment then frames how men and women consider and approach each other and others of the same gender in the risk communication environment (Beck, 2001). Beck (2001) explained, "Perceptions about 'ideal' enactments of gendered roles may flavor the extent to which individuals opt to reveal such concerns (about risk) and seek help" (p. 205).

Research has shown that women rate a range of health risks higher than men due to sociocultural expectations and practices (Dosman et al., 2001; Knight & Warland, 2004). The number of children living at home has been found to affect risk perceptions of food safety, such that regardless of sex, the person primarily responsible for rearing the children considered food related risks higher (Davidson & Freundenburg, 1996; Dosman et al., 2001). In addition, gender expectations about work outside the household affects risk perceptions. Studies have shown that the more committed the individual is to employment outside the home and the more evenly distributed is household work, then the less likely were women to hold higher food related risk perceptions (Davidson & Freundenburg, 1996; Dosman et al., 2001; Lin, 1995). These studies support the notion that gender is socially constructed and gender role expectations guide risk perceptions. It also helps explain how gender is a cultural norm that has its own sets of beliefs, values, and expectations.

Health Outcomes and Mortality Rates

Differences in health outcomes and mortality rates have guided some risk communication efforts, and these differences are often a result of cultural differences. Research has indicated that different ethnic groups and genders have different rates of disease, morbidity, and mortality. Death rates from all causes were 30% higher among blacks than whites in 2002 (National Center for Health Statistics, 2005). On one level, there are genetic diseases that affect certain ethnic groups. Sickle cell anemia and lactose intolerance disproportionately affect African American populations; and Tay Sachs disease predominantly affects European American Jews (Beck, 2001).

On another level, sociocultural factors that affect certain groups create varying health outcomes. Dietary habits, socioeconomic status, and family and cultural traditions create differences in mortality rates between black women and white women for breast cancer, diabetes, and heart disease (Beck, 2001). With AIDS and HIV, gender, class and race combine to create significant differences in prevalence. Women of color in the United States, for example, account for about 25% of the female population in the United States, but they account for 83% of the AIDS cases reported among women in 2004 (CDC, 2005). African American diabetes and AIDS rates are double those for whites (Beck, 2001; Jemmott et al., 2001).

While Asian Americans have a high level of physical health and well being relative to other minority cultures in the United States, they experience serious mental distress due to intergenerational conflicts (Wong et al., 1998). One survey of Asian Indian, Japanese, and Korean college students reported that intergenerational and gender role conflicts were the most significant sources of psychological distress. These Asian cultural groups also reported higher percentages of depression than national populations (Kar, Campbell, Jimenez, & Gupta, 1995; Kar, Jimenez, Campbell, & Sze, 1998).

NEW AND ALTERNATIVE WAYS TO CONSIDER CULTURE IN RISK COMMUNICATION

Over the last decade, alternative views of culture have been considered for risk communication. Authors have combined or transformed the traditional ethnic, gender, and language boundaries—which are simplistic and incomplete pictures of culture—and have created more realistic perspectives about cultural factors that affect people's everyday lives and their production and reception of risk messages. As Freimuth and Quinn (2004) argued, "to consider culture requires significant exploration beyond the typical variables of race, ethnicity, and socioeconomic status" (p. 2054).

One reason for this evolution towards a more complex yet realistic understanding of culture is the acknowledgment of the great diversity among members of the same ethnic group or gender, which has complicated the practice of risk communication (Jemmott et al., 2001; Sylvester, 1998). People who speak the same language or share the same ethnicity may still be different from one another depending on socioeconomic status, religiosity, family structure, etc. (Kar et al., 2001b). Kreuter et al. (2002) stated, "Although it is true that certain cultural characteristics may cluster within a given racial or ethnic group, it is at least equally true that substantial differences exist between individuals and subgroups within these populations" (p. 134). With this in mind, the following are some of the cultural factors that have been included in recent risk communication research: socioeconomic status; religiosity; trust; intersectionality of identity; power; and an ecological perspective for risk communication.

Socioeconomic Status as a Culture

Health disparities between income groups have been well documented, and authors have continued to underscore the importance of communication programs targeting low income populations (Bradley, Given, & Roberts, 2004; Marshall, Smith, & McKeon, 1995). However, considering income differences in risk communication is more complex when socioeconomic status is viewed as culture. Socioeconomic status is not defined with just income level—although often income is the only criteria used to divide audiences for communication programs. Socioeconomic status is an index that includes income level, educational attainment, occupation, and often census tract, neighborhood or geographic location, and type of housing (Braveman, Egerter, Cubbin, & Marchi, 2004; Lawlor, Smith, & Ebrahim, 2004; Madison, Schottenfeld, James, Schwartz, & Gruber, 2004). There is evidence to suggest that socioeconomic status creates beliefs, norms, and values and guides food consumption, health and risk behaviors (Lawlor et al., 2004). These "criteria" construct cultural groupings of people that perceive and react to risk communication differently according to their socioeconomic status. One study, for example, showed that, among women 60 to 79 years old, indicators of socioeconomic deprivation in childhood were associated with a reduced likelihood to use hormone replacement therapy after menopause. These associations were independent of adult socioeconomic status, behavioral risk factors, and physiological risk factors (Lawlor et al., 2004, p. 2151). Lawlor et al. (2004) explained that childhood socioeconomic position (SEP) influenced future use of HRT by influencing

> …the individual's attitudes toward health, preventive treatment, and natural physiological processes such as menopause and aging gained from their parents' attitudes toward these; the ability to access health care; and discrimination based on patient characteristics…It is plausible that adult attitudes toward the use of HRT and access to HRT are formed by SEP in earlier life. (p. 2153)

This impact of childhood SEP found in this study supports the construction of socioeconomic status as a cultural factor that affects meaning making of risk communication. Socioeconomic status is considered more than just a lack of resources; it is embedded in socialization processes and family norms and beliefs to the extent that it supersedes other factors in guiding risk perceptions and health behaviors.

Icard et al. (2003) reminded communication practitioners—who might come from backgrounds with stable economic resources—to understand why certain risks might not be considered priorities among some low-SES communities, particularly when these risks are "compared to their day-to-day challenges" (p. 220). Campaigns targeting at-risk groups may be more successful "when linked to economic problems such as having money to pay for food, shelter, or clothing" (Icard et al., 2003, p. 220).

The Knowledge Gap Hypothesis. The knowledge gap hypothesis assumes that knowledge disseminated through media is gained at higher rates for individuals and communities of higher socioeconomic status than for those of low socioeconomic status (Tichenor, Donohue, & Olien, 1970; Viswanath, Kahn, Finnegan, Hertog, & Potter, 1993). The assumption is that people and organizations with more resources will gain knowledge faster than those who have fewer resources; therefore, there will be a widening of amount of knowledge after messages are disseminated to audiences. The significance of this theoretical perspective here is its understanding of socioeconomic status as a cultural factor that may impede risk communication objectives. Media have become so prevalent in our social constructions of meaning that it is not arguably a mere ownership and access issue. The difference in knowledge in today's global, mediated environment suggests differences in other characteristics that may be the result of differences in economic ability and access.

The knowledge gap affects not only individuals, but also organizations and communities. Kar et al. (2001c) offered an interesting case example of the California Smoking Control Programs for Targeted Populations. The program funded community programs that addressed smoking cessation and prevention among communities of color. In evaluating the funding awards made available to organizations, it was found that the organizations rich in resources were the ones that had the channels and means to find out about the funding opportunity and, therefore, were the ones that submitted proposals and received funding. Resource-poor, grassroots community organizations—who were serving and representing the targeted communities more directly and effectively—did not have access to the call for funding (p. 129).

Religiosity

Religiosity can be measured through church attendance, prayer, participation in religious ceremonies, and beliefs about God as a causal agent (Kreuter et al., 2002, p. 138). Religiosity is often associated with ethnic background and can profoundly influence health care beliefs and practices (Beck, 2001; Ellison & Levin, 1998). The religious beliefs of those producing and disseminating risk messages can also subtly and perhaps unconsciously be reflected in messages.

For some African American communities, religion has been cited as the "backbone" of the community (Jemmott et al., 2001, p. 329; Sylvester, 1998). In one national survey, 81% of low income African American women said it was important for them to go to church; 92% said they prayed at least once a week. In another study, African American participants were significantly more likely to believe that prayer can cure disease than were participants from other ethnic groups (Kreuter et al., 2002). Jemmott et al. (2001) found that African American participants responded to AIDS prevention efforts in light of their beliefs that illness was a form of punishment by God and that AIDS was a consequence of sinful behavior (p. 328). Several risk prevention programs have been coordinated with pastors of African American churches. However, one study found that the connection to church may be counterproductive for certain people whose "personal beliefs, lifestyle, or living conditions may be stigmatized or subject to moral judgments and scrutiny" (Icard et al., 2003, p. 220). Icard et al. (2003) included in these groups substance abusers, sex workers, and others at higher risk for certain health and environmental threats.

Less research has been published about other non-Christian faiths and their relationships to risk communication. AbuGharbieh (1998) described how some Muslims combined Western conventional medical treatments with their performance of daily prayers and listening or reading the Kuran. He explained, "The devout patient may request that his or her chair or bed be turned to face Mecca and that a basin of water be provided for ritual washing or ablution before praying" (p. 153). Other religious faith practices have not easily reconciled with the Westernized, Christian-based practices that are communicated as protection against risk. Some Native American and aboriginal populations, in particular, have traditional and spiritual practices (Beck, 2001; Cook, 2005; Kelm, 1998; Warry, 1998), which might conflict with recommended risk prevention practices.

Trust

Social trust is the willingness to rely on and find credible the actions and communications from institutions and management entities—this has been differentiated from interpersonal trust (McComas, 2006). Social trust is important to risk perceptions and communication (Finucane, 2002, p. 34), but "until quite recently, trust largely was unappreciated in risk management efforts" (McComas, 2006, p. 82). A lack of trust has been cited in several studies as a critical factor in the gap between expert and lay assessments of risk, which has posed a barrier to effective risk communication. In general, when trust has been lacking, greater risk has been perceived (Frewer, Scholderer, & Bredahl, 2003; Heath, Seshadri, & Lee, 1998; McComas & Trumbo, 2001; Siegrist & Cvetkovich, 2000; Siegrist, Cvetkovich, & Roth, 2000; Siegrist, Earle, & Gutscher, 2005; Trumbo & McComas, 2003). This association can be mitigated by level of personal knowledge about the communicated risk (Siegrist & Cvetkovich, 2000), such that individuals rely on social trust to make judgments about risks when personal knowledge is lacking. Also, trust has been found to be more easily lost than gained; and lost trust resulting from previous experience with an organization has continued to harm relations with an organization even if current information about the organization has been positive (Cvetkovich, Siegrist, Murray, & Tragesser, 2002).

Research has shown that trust and suspicion is greater among certain American cultures. Historical surveys that included African Americans as respondents showed that as an aggregate, these respondents had less trust in people compared to national totals measuring trust (Erskine, 1969). Again, historical medical practices by the U.S. government have afflicted African American communities to such an extent that some African Americans mistrust the medical community (Edgar et al., 2003; Johnson, 2004). Johnson (2004) reported that 74% of African Americans surveyed believed they were very or somewhat likely to be doctors' guinea pigs without consent (p. 1280). Jemmott et al. (2001) argued that, given this environment of historical racism, "There is little wonder that African Americans would be wary of health education programs, doubt medical research, distrust researchers who seek to recruit them for studies, and disbelieve government officials and health authorities who offer recommendations…" (p. 328). There has been similar concern by some African American communities that psychological testing has been used inappropriately to label African Americans as pathological or intellectually inferior (Jemmott et al., 2001, p. 328).

Intersectionality of Identity

A recent consideration in risk communication is that of the impact of intersectionality of identity: the multiplicative and intertwining effects of the multiple identities and cultures that influence an individual (Freimuth & Quinn, 2004; Fullilove, Fullilove III, Haynes, & Gross, 1990; Gomez & Marin, 1996). Gandy (2001) explained, "Our identity as a member of a group defined primarily by race or ethnicity is just one component of an extremely complex identity structure" (p. 600).

According to Russell (2001), it is imperative in risk communication to understand intersectionality and the relative influences of multiple reference groups on beliefs, values, norms, and behavior (p. 236). In her evaluation of a peer health education project for HIV risk reduction in California, Project ABLE, Russell (2001) explained the project's multiple understandings of culture in order to address homeless youth who derived from various ethnic backgrounds. On one level, there were certain norms and behaviors guiding homeless youth that created a sort of culture of homelessness. However, within that cultural context, the youth also brought their own ethnic, gender, and personal histories. The program, therefore, used dramatic theater to attract the attention of the age group, and used peers as actors to increase identification with audience members. The peer actors illustrated the multiple ethnic backgrounds of the audience members. The content of the story told through the theater incorporated events and situations that reflected the culture of youth homelessness. The evaluation of the program showed differential impact on knowledge, perceived risk, and intent to use condoms by interactions of age, gender and ethnicity. For example, audience members who were younger, Latino, and/or female seemed to have the most willingness to try condoms. There were greater increases in perceived risk among male, older, and/or Caucasian or African American (p. 241). The program and its evaluation illustrated how intersectionality created meaning for individuals in ways that were not reflected through individual identity assessment (i.e., age only, sex only).

The "White Male Effect." Recent research has revealed the existence of an interaction between gender and race in risk beliefs and attitudes, such that a person's gender or a person's ethnicity cannot be considered alone. In a national survey where respondents rated 25 risks related to the environment, health and their lifestyle, Flynn, Slovic, and Mertz (1994) found what they termed a "white male effect" on perceived risk (p. 1107). White men's mean ratings of risk were lower than those for white women, nonwhite women, and nonwhite men. Compared to all other gender/race groupings, white men with low perceived risk were generally better educated, had higher household incomes, were more likely to agree that it is acceptable to impose very small risks on individuals without consent, and disagreed that they have very little control over risks to their health. The white male effect also showed that the white men in this study had significantly higher trust in institutions and authorities making decisions about risks (p. 1006).

Support for the white male effect was found by other researchers (Finucane et al., 2000; Marshall, 2004; Palmer, 2003). Whereas Flynn et al. (1994) asked questions about risks posed to the American public, Finucane et al. (2000) included risks posed "to you and your family." Again, white males had significantly lower risk ratings. As with Flynn et al. (1994), Finucane et al. (2000) found the relationship remained strong even with other demographic variables controlled (i.e., income, education, political orientation, age, children living in household, and perceived control over health risks). Nonwhite women had the highest risk ratings. The white male effect showed up most significantly with the following risks: handguns, nuclear power plants, second-hand cigarette smoke, multiple sexual partners, and street drugs (Finucane et al., 2000, p. 164).[3] Similarly, Marshall (2004) found that white men had the lowest risk perceptions of cancer in communities with industrial plants while black women had the highest risk perceptions.

In Johnson's (2002) attempt to replicate these findings (with a semi-random sample of potential jurors in Philadelphia), white men were the most distinctive group on air pollution beliefs, and nonwhite women were the most significantly different from each other in air pollution beliefs (p. 735). This heterogeneity within nonwhite groups also showed up in Finucane et al.'s (2000) study, where African Americans, Asians, and Latino participants differed *among* each other in risk perceptions.

While findings were termed the "white male effect," they actually revealed much more about intersectionality and the role of culture for white females, black females, black males, and other intersected identities. In general, the findings support the claim that social constructions of norms, meanings, and practices about risk and communication differ by gendered-raced cultures. For example, socio-cultural expectations of white women as caregivers might lead these women to feel greater pressure to be sensitized to risk for the sake of children, parents and other loved ones. Previous research on religiosity and identification with Africa might guide black women's motivations when they are faced with risk messages. Much more research needs to be conducted within the area of intersectionality and risk communication. The research presented here singled out findings for white males, and many more identities need to be singled out in risk communication research.

Flynn et al. (1994) offered their rationale for the white male effect:

> Perhaps white males see less risk in the world because they create, manage, control, and benefit from so much of it. Perhaps women and nonwhite males see the world as more dangerous because in many ways they are more vulnerable, because they benefit less from many of its technologies and institutions, and because they have less power and control. (p. 1107)

Palmer (2003), who also found the white male effect in risk perceptions about a broader array of health and technical risks, concluded that the white male effect was important because "it helps to explain why experts, who primarily are white males in the USA, tend to view the risk of hazards differently from the lay public, especially when hazards whose effects are viewed as uncontrollable or catastrophic by the public are under consideration" (p. 72). Understanding the white male effect is critical to understanding relationships between risk communicators and their audiences. As Johnson (2002) clearly put it, "If women and nonwhites differ in risk beliefs from the white men who dominate risk research and policy making in the United States, risk policies and communications could be failures, counterproductive, or unethical" (p. 725).

Power

Some research has suggested that risk perceptions are related to individual levels of decision-making power. In other words, the perceived ability to influence decisions about the use of hazards in a community affects level of perceived risk as well as intent to take preventive actions (Finucane et al., 2000; Bord & O'Connor, 1997). Traditionally, risk communication has been produced by knowledgeable experts who may have control over community, economic, and health resources. If trust is lacking due to personal and historical experiences, then perceived power differentials between the source of risk messages and the audience members will discourage productive relationships and preventive outcomes.

Therefore, an important consideration for risk communicators is how to diminish the power imbalance between themselves and their sources and their audiences. Empowerment of communities and individuals has become a central organizing theme of health promotion strategies with marginalized populations (Ford & Yep, 2003, p. 250). According to Kar et al. (2001c), "empowerment is the act of increasing people's ability to cope constructively with their environments and control their own destinies" (p. 111). Empowerment should be both a process as well as an outcome of risk communication. Individuals and communities gain power through decision-making responsibility, accountability for others, increasing community capacity, and increasing social justice (Airhihenbuwa, 1995; Fawcett, Paine-Andrews, Francisco, Shultz, & Ricter, 1995; Ford & Yep, 2003).

Developing emancipatory projects is a "bottom up" approach for risk communication (Bell & Alcalay, 2001; Ford & Yep, 2003). Elements of this type of effort include: encouragement of grassroots organizing; use of established, community social networks; and creation of broad coalitions of organizations and groups. In addition, community health workers (CHWs) become integral in communicating risk. CHWs are residents within targeted communities who are knowledgeable about community needs, culture and language. They enact the role of "channel" through which risk is communicated to individuals. CHWs are typically similar in culture, language, and living arrangements as audience members, and they are trained in health services and intervention techniques. They are part of the decision-making team who designs risk messages and programs, and they are the ones to turn to for advice about how to empower audience members through the programs.

Ford and Yep (2003) provided a case study of an empowerment risk prevention program that was developed by the Casa en Casa project of La Clinica de la Raza (LCDLR) in East Oakland, California. The project began as a small medical clinic offering free health services to clients, who were mostly Mexican. Staff involvement in the community encouraged community involvement with the clinic's services, and a separate health education program evolved out of the collaboration. The staff used community organizing to create the Casa en Casa project where neighbors met weekly in each others homes to learn about health and to develop community actions. All the program information and communication provided by staff was connected culturally and linguistically to the community (Ford & Yep, 2003, p. 250).

This case showed how risk communicators hold a position of knowledge power and have resources to communicate risk. The relationship between risk communicators and audience members is inherently constructed with power differentials. Therefore, regardless of audience culture, communicators should consider their position as powerful and assess the opportunities for empowerment strategies for communities. If audiences and producers of risk messages were white/male/Euro-American and similar in culture, then the producers would not need to tap into "local knowledge" since they derive from similar cultural constructions. Both producer and audience would feel empowered through identification with the messages. However, in most risk communication programs, this homogenous audience is rarely a reality.

Ecological Perspective for Risk Communication

According to some authors, there has been a shift towards including broader, contextual and social domains in risk communication (Murray-Johnson & Witte, 2003). While a traditional focus for risk messages has been on an individual, cognitive level, a new focus is a wider, complex level that includes cultural, economic and political factors (Airhihenbuwa, 1995; Airhihenbuwa, Makinwa, & Obregon, 2000; Airhihenbuwa & Obregon, 2000; Ford & Yep, 2003; Kar et al., 2001a; Witte, Meyer, Bidol, Casey, Kopfman, Maduschke, et al., 1996). This move to focus on contexts offers advantages over individualistic models, which often ignore cultural influences (Ford & Yep, 2003). An ecological perspective is a more holistic and realistic portrayal of risk communication.

While continuing to include the individual, an ecological approach de-emphasizes the importance of the individual and, therefore, diminishes the potential to blame the victim. It also allows the use of alternative strategies for education and prevention because it includes so many other social, political, and economic factors (Ford & Yep, 2003; Kar et al., 2001c). One example of an ecologically based model is Airhihenbuwa's (1995) cultural empowerment model that argues for communication interventions constructed to reflect and incorporate cultural practices, norms and everyday realities of the audiences. While contextualizing risk within larger social and political levels, this model also "nurtures the individual and his or her family and community" (Airhihenbuwa & Obregon, 2000, p. 12).

There are a couple of studies with Latina and Asian women that also illustrated the ecological perspective for considering culture in risk communication (Bauer, Rodriguez, Quiroga, & Flores-Ortiz, 2000; Rodriguez, Quiroga, & Bauer, 1996; Zambrana, 1996). Research on domestic abuse identified a number of factors that prevented women from avoiding the risk of abuse even after they knew how to do so. Some of the Latina participants described feeling discriminated against by medical providers (Zambrana, 1996). Cultural factors for Asian women included feelings of shame and fear of ostracism from their communities (Bauer et al., 2000). Both Latina and Asian women expressed a need to maintain loyalty to family and to keep family together.

Kar et al. (2001b) proposed a type of ecological model that identifies three levels of cultural competency. The first level is cultural understanding, which they described as a working knowledge of the core beliefs, values, norms, and traditions unique to the target cultures. The second level is cultural acceptance, which includes sensitivity, respect, acceptance of differences, and recognition of the right of other cultures. The opposite of cultural acceptance is imposed or enforced assimilation. The third and highest level is reciprocal relationship. Here, communicators and audience members share friendships and trusting partnerships (p. 101).

Braithwaite and Taylor (2001) referred to the levels of cultural competence as surface structure versus deep structure of culture. Surface structure includes a consideration of different message elements, channels and sources, while deep structure reflects the social, psychological, environmental, and historical factors that affect susceptibility and response to risk. Risk communication may increase attention and receptivity by using surface structures, but it will affect salience, involvement, and intent to act by also including deep structures of culture (Braithwaite & Taylor, 2001).

There has been evidence to support the use of deep cultural structures. Research by Jemmott et al. (2001) showed that when HIV risk information and prevention techniques were designed to be culturally sensitive for African American youth, the race and gender of trainers and presenters of the techniques made no significant difference in intervention outcomes. The authors argued that had the intervention messages been culturally "inappropriate," differences in trainer behavior by race and gender might have emerged (p. 318). Similarly, Sylvester (1998) found in her study of African Americans that participants believed that it did not matter whether their physicians were black or white, "as long as their needs were being met" (p. 204). In other words, the participants in these two studies were more concerned with the risk messages that incorporated deep cultural structures than with the sources or channels that were enacted using surface structures of culture.

CONCLUSION

There will never be a realistic and parsimonious method for communicating risk to all cultural groupings and intersectionalities that construct reality for people in this country. Taking a pure, social constructionist view of risk communication prevents any communication effort from achieving its objectives. As Kar et al. (2001a) concluded, "there is no standard model of effective health promotion and disease prevention intervention, and even if there was one, it is not likely to be effective among all ethnic groups" (p. 339).

However, as the literature described here attests, there are ways to consider culture that will improve risk communication and build relationships between risk communicators and audiences. It is important to consider how the production and reception of risk communication is influenced by intersections of ethnicity, race, language, gender, health outcomes and mortality rates. There has been a shift towards more complex and deeper ways to consider culture: by considering socioeconomic status as a cultural structure rather than just a difference in income level; by addressing the role of religiosity, trust and the historical experiences that may have lowered levels of trust in some communities; by recognizing the implicit power relations embedded in producing and communicating risk; by assessing the intersectionality of identity on an individual level; and by taking an ecological perspective to address social, economic, political, and institutional effects on individual risk perceptions and actions.

Cultural barriers cause poor, intercultural communication between communicators who produce and disseminate risk messages and audiences who receive these messages (Lupton, 1994; Sylvester, 1998). Cultural barriers often result "when dominant and hegemonic cultural standards are applied to less privileged groups in a particular society (e.g., application and imposition of middle-class, male, European American beliefs and values about risk on poor, female, non-European American individuals)" (Ford & Yep, 2003, p. 248). One way dominant cultural standards are applied is through the traditional reliance on the biomedical model and individualistic models of health knowledge and behavior. According to Ford and Yep (2003), this "marginaliz[es] the role of culture in everyday communication practices" (p. 247). Jemmott et al. (2001) similarly concluded, "Culturally inappropriate program frameworks account for the failure of many social and behavioral programs formulated in a dominant group construct for later implementation in minority communities" (p. 336).

The underlying rationale for considering cultural factors in risk communication is that it will increase audience identification with risk messages, which will empower audience members and ultimately achieve organizational objectives. However, as Guttman (2003) reminds us, even with good intentions, there are ethical concerns when risk communication incorporates cultural symbols in messages. Guttman (2003) argued that communicators may be blamed for detaching themes and symbols from their original meaning and co-opting cultural meanings (p. 650). There are also ethical dilemmas in deciding whether certain cultural norms and values need to be challenged in order to achieve risk prevention and control. For example, encouraging individual empowerment among certain communities of women may go against cultural norms of traditional family and gender structures. With risk communication, the current challenge according to Guttman (2003) is to "develop sensitivity not only to which themes may be appropriate, but to the ethical issues their application may spawn" (p. 660).

In conclusion, audiences react in a myriad of ways to risk communication about threats affecting them because culture mediates the impact of risk communication efforts and potential relationships between risk communicators and audiences. Cultural sensitivity, understanding of deep cultural structures, and true cultural competence will increase audience identification with risk messages, empower communities, and achieve organizational objectives.

NOTES

1. The search for published research on culture and risk communication was by no means comprehensive. I first searched for literature in communication and mass media databases, but I found very little. I expanded the search to include social psychology, psychology, health and medicine, risk analysis, environmental studies, and general social science resources. I found a much larger body of knowledge to draw from after expanding the search in this manner.
2. There is a danger of essentializing cultural groups when writing about them in general terms. I am describing here the research that has illustrated how culture has been considered in risk communication; but in doing so, it may sustain or even encourage stereotyping and generalizing. In addition, as a white researcher, I am uncomfortable citing this literature about other cultural groups so simplistically and briefly. By purposively couching the descriptions with terms such as "some," "might," and "include," I hope to keep readers aware that there is no monolithic cultural characteristic or stereotype for the ethnic and racial groups discussed here.
3. There was an exception where Asian males gave lower risk ratings than white males on six items in Finucane et al.'s (2000) study: motor vehicles, tap water, cellular phones, imported foods, eating red meat, and hormones in meat. However, this exception does not negate the interaction of race and gender influencing risk perceptions. Palmer (2003) found supporting data in that Taiwanese-American males had lower risk ratings than white males in her study. To explain this, she noted that the Taiwanese-American males held similar endorsement of individualist attitudes, similar lack of endorsement of egalitarian attitudes, and higher hierarchist attitudes than white males (p. 80).

BIBLIOGRAPHY

AbuGharbieh, P. (1998). Arab Americans. In L. Purnell & B. Paulanka (Eds.), *Transcultural health care: A culturally competent approach* (pp. 137–162). Philadelphia: F. A. Davis.

Airhihenbuwa, C. O. (1995). *Health and culture: Beyond the western paradigm.* Thousand Oaks, CA: Sage.

Airhihenbuwa, C. O., Makinway, B., & Obregon, R. (2000). Towards a new communication framework for HIV/AIDS. *Journal of Health Communication, 5*(Suppl.), 101–111.

Airhihenbuwa, C. O., & Obregon, R. (2000). A critical assessment of theories/models used in health communication for HIV/AIDS. *Journal of Health Communication, 5*(Suppl.), 5–15.

Albrecht, T. L., & Goldsmith, D. J. (2003). Social support, social networks, and health. In T. L. Thompson, A. M. Dorsey, K. I. Miller, & R. Parrott (Eds.), *Handbook of health communication* (pp. 263–284). Mahwah, NJ: Erlbaum.

Anderson, A. (1997). *Media, culture and the environment.* New Brunswick, NJ: Rutgers University Press.

Bauer, H. M., Rodriguez, M. A., Quiroga, S. S., & Flores-Ortiz, Y. G. (2000). Barriers to health care for abused Latina and Asian immigrant women. *Journal of Health Care for the Poor and the Underserved, 11*, 33–44.

Beck, C. S. (2001). *Communicating for better health: A guide through the medical mazes.* Boston, MA: Allyn and Bacon.

Bell, R. A., & Alcalay, R. (2001). Health communication campaign design: Lessons from the California Wellness Guide Distribution Project. In S. B. Kar, R. Alcalay, with S. Alex (Eds.), *Health communication: A multicultural perspective* (pp. 281–307). Thousand Oaks, CA: Sage.

Bord, R. J., & O'Connor, R. E. (1997). The gender gap in environmental attitudes: The case of perceived vulnerability to risk. *Social Science Quarterly, 78,* 830–840.

Bradley, C. J., Given, C. W., & Roberts, C. (2004). Health care disparities and cervical cancer. *American Journal of Public Health, 94,* 2098–2103.

Braithwaite, R. L., & Taylor, S. E. (Eds.). (2001). *Health issues in the black community* (2nd ed.). San Francisco: Jossey-Bass.
Braveman, P. A., Egerter, S. A., Cubbin, C., & Marchi, K. S. (2004). An approach to studying social disparities in health and health care. *American Journal of Public Health, 94,* 2139–2148.
Burger, J., McDermott, M. H., Chess, C., Bochenek, E., Perez-Lugo, M., & Pflugh, K. K. (2003). Evaluating risk communication about fish consumption advisories: Efficacy of a brochure versus a classroom lesson in Spanish and English. *Risk Analysis, 23,* 791–803.
CDC. (2005). *HIV/AIDS surveillance report, 2004, Vol. 16.* Atlanta, GA: U.S. Department of Health and Human Services.
Chaffee, S. H. (1992). Search for change: Survey studies of international media effects. In F. Korzenny, S. Ting-Toomey, with E. Schiff (Eds.), *Mass media effects across cultures* (pp. 35–54). Newbury Park, CA: Sage.
Chess, C., Salomone, K. L., Hance, B. J., & Saville, A. (1995). Results of a National Symposium on Risk Communication: Next Steps for Government Agencies. *Risk Analysis, 15,* 115–125.
Cook, S. J. (2005). Use of traditional Mi'kmaq medicine among patients at a First Nations community health centre. *Canadian Journal of Rural Medicine, 10*(2), 95–99.
Cvetkovich, G., & Lofstedt, R. E. (Eds.). (1999). *Social trust and the management of risk.* London: Earthscan Publications.
Cvetkovich, G., Siegrist, M., Murray, R., & Tragesser, S. (2002). New information and social trust: Asymmetry and perseverance of attributions about hazard managers. *Risk Analysis, 22,* 359–367.
Cvetkovich, G., & Winter, P. L. (2001, December). *Social trust and the management of risks to threatened and endangered species.* Paper presented to the Society of Risk Analysis, Seattle, Washington.
Davidson, D. J., Freundenburg, W. R. (1996). Gender and environmental risk concerns: A review and analysis of available research. *Environment and Behaviour, 28,* 302–339.
Dosman, D. M., Adamowicz, W. L., & Hrudey, S. E. (2001). Socioeconomic determinants of health- and food safety-related risk perceptions. *Risk Analysis, 21,* 307–317.
Douglas, M., & Wildavsky, A. (1982). *Risk and culture: An essay on the selection of technical and environmental dangers.* Berkeley: University of California Press.
Edgar, T., Freimuth, V., & Hammond, S. L. (2003). Lessons learned from the field on prevention and health campaigns. In T. L. Thompson, A. M. Dorsey, K. I. Miller, & R. Parrott (Eds.), *Handbook of health communication* (pp. 625–636). Mahwah, NJ: Erlbaum.
Ellis, D. (1999). *Crafting society: Ethnicity, class, and communication theory.* Mahwah, NJ: Erlbaum.
Ellison, C. G., & Levin, J. S. (1998). The religion-health connection: Evidence, theory, and future directions. *Health Education and Behavior, 25,* 700–720.
Erskine, H. (1969). The polls: Negro philosophies of life. *Public Opinion Quarterly, 33,* 147–158.
Fawcett, S. B., Paine-Andrews, A., Francisco, V. T., Schultz, J. A., & Ricter, K. P. (1995). Using empowerment theory in collaborative partnerships for community health development. *American Journal of Community Psychology, 23,* 677–697.
Finucane, M. L. (2002). Mad cows, mad corn and mad communities: The role of socio-cultural factors in the perceived risk of genetically-modified food. *Proceedings of the Nutrition Society, 61,* 31–37.
Finucane, M. L., & Holup, J. L. (2005). Psychosocial and cultural factors affecting the perceived risk of genetically modified food: an overview of the literature. *Social Science & Medicine, 60,* 1603–1612.
Finucane, M. L., Slovic, P., Mertz, C. K., Flynn, J., & Satterfield, T. A. (2000). Gender, race, and perceived risk: The "white male" effect. *Health, Risk & Society, 2,* 159–172.
Flynn, J., Slovic, P., & Mertz, C. K. (1994). Gender, race, and perception of environmental health risks. *Risk Analysis, 14,* 1101–1108.
Ford, L. A., & Yep, G. A. (2003). Working along the margins: Developing community-based strategies for communicating about health with marginalized groups. In T. L. Thompson, A. M. Dorsey, K. I. Miller, & R. Parrott (Eds.), *Handbook of health communication* (pp. 241–261). Mahwah, NJ: Erlbaum.
Freimuth, V. S., & Quinn, S. C. (2004). The contributions of health communication to eliminating health disparities. *American Journal of Public Health, 94,* 2053–2055.
Frewer, L. J., Scholderer, J., & Bredahl, L. (2003). Communicating about the risks and benefits of genetically modified foods: The mediating role of trust. *Risk Analysis, 23,* 1117–1133.
Fullilove, M. T., Fullilove III, R. E., Haynes, K., & Gross, S. (1990). Black women and AIDS prevention: A view towards understanding the gender rules. *The Journal of Sex Research, 27,* 47–64.
Gabbard-Alley, A. S. (1995). Health communication and gender: A review and critique. *Health Communication, 7,* 35–54.
Gallant, S., Keita, G., & Royak-Schaler, R. (Eds.). (1997). *Health care for women: Psychological, social and behavioral influences.* Washington, DC: American Psychological Association.
Gandy, O. H. Jr. (2001). Racial identity, media use, and the social construction of risk among African Americans. *Journal of Black Studies, 31,* 600–618.

Giroux, H. A. (1992). *Border crossings: Cultural workers and the politics of education.* New York: Routledge.
Gomez, C. A., & Marin, B. V. (1996). Gender, culture, and power: Barriers to HIV-prevention strategies for women. *The Journal of Sex Research, 33*, 355–362.
Green, B. L., Maisiak, R., Wang, M. Q., Britt, M. F., & Ebeling, N. (1997). Participation in education, health promotion, and health research by African Americans: Effects of the Tuskegee Syphilis Experiment. *Journal of Health Education, 28,* 196–200.
Guttman, N. (2003). Ethics in health communication interventions. In T. L. Thompson, A. M. Dorsey, K. I. Miller, & R. Parrott (Eds.), *Handbook of health communication* (pp. 651–679). Mahwah, NJ: Erlbaum.
Harter, L. M., Stephens, R. J., & Japp, P. M. (2000). President Clinton's apology for the Tuskegee syphilis experiment: A narrative of remembrance, redefinition, and reconciliation. *The Howard Journal of Communications, 11*, 19–34.
Heath, R. L., Seshadri, S., & Lee, J. (1998). Risk communication: A two-community analysis of proximity, dread, trust, involvement, uncertainty, openness/accessibility, and knowledge on support/opposition toward chemical companies. *Journal of Public Relations Research, 10*, 35–56.
Hornik, R. C., & Ramirez, A. S. (2006). Racial/ethnic disparities and segmentation in communication campaigns. *American Behavioral Scientist, 49*, 868–884.
Icard, L. D., Bourjolly, J. N., & Siddiqui, N. (2003). Designing social marketing strategies to increase African Americans' access to health promotion programs. *Health and Social Work, 28*, 214–223.
Jemmott, L. S., Jemmott III, J. B., & Hutchinson, M. K. (2001). HIV/AIDS. In R. L. Braithwaite, & S. E. Taylor (Eds.), *Health issues in the black community* (2nd ed.; pp. 309–346). San Francisco: Jossey-Bass.
Johnson, B. B. (2002). Gender and race in beliefs about outdoor air pollution. *Risk Analysis, 22*, 725–738.
Johnson, B. B. (2004). Arguments for testing ethnic identity and acculturation as factors in risk judgments. *Risk Analysis, 24*, 1279–1287.
Johnson, W. D., Holtgrave, D. R., McClellan, W. M., Flanders, W. D., Hill, A. N., & Goodman, M. (2005). HIV intervention research for men who have sex with men: A 7-year update. *AIDS Education and Prevention, 17*, 568–589.
Kar, S. B., & Alcalay, R., with Alex, S. (2001a). *Health communication: A multicultural perspective.* Thousand Oaks, CA: Sage.
Kar, S. B., & Alcalay, R., with Alex, S. (2001b). A multicultural society: Facing a new culture. In S. B. Kar, R. Alcalay, with S. Alex (Eds.), *Health communication: A multicultural perspective* (pp. 79–107). Thousand Oaks, CA: Sage.
Kar, S. B., & Alcalay, R., with Alex, S. (2001c). Communicating with multicultural populations: A theoretical framework. In S. B. Kar, R. Alcalay, with S. Alex (Eds.), *Health communication: A multicultural perspective* (pp. 109–137). Thousand Oaks, CA: Sage.
Kar, S. B., Campbell, K., Jimenez, A., & Gupta, S. (1995). Invisible Americans: An exploration of Indo-American quality of life. *Amerasia Journal, 21*(3), 25–52.
Kar, S., Jimenez, A., Campbell, K., & Sze, F. (1998). Acculturation and quality of life: A comparative study of Japanese-American and Indo-Americans. *Amerasia Journal, 24*(1), 129–142.
Kasperson, J. X., & Kasperson, R. E. (2005). *The social contours of risk: Publics, risk communication and the social amplification of risk* (Vol. 1). London: Earthscan.
Kasperson, R. E., Renn, O., Slovic, P., Brown, H. S., Emel, J., Goble, J. X. et al. (1988). The social amplification of risk: A conceptual framework. *Risk Analysis, 8*, 177–187.
Kelm, M. (1998). *Colonizing bodies: Aboriginal health and healing in British Columbia, 1900–50.* Vancouver, BC: UBCPress.
Kennamer, J. D., & Honnold, J. A. (1995). Attitude toward homosexuality and attention to news about AIDS. *Journalism and Mass Communication Quarterly, 72,* 322–335.
Knight, A., & Warland, R. (2004). The relationship between sociodemographics and concern about food safety issues. *The Journal of Consumer Affairs, 38*, 107–120.
Korzenny, F., & Schiff, E. (1992). Media effects across cultures: Challenges and opportunities. In F. Korzenny, S. Ting-Toomey, with E. Schiff (Eds.), *Mass media effects across cultures* (pp. 1–8). Newbury Park, CA: Sage.
Korzenny, F., Ting-Toomey, S., with Schiff, E. (Eds.). (1992). *Mass media effects across cultures.* Newbury Park, CA: Sage.
Kreuter, M. W., Lukwago, S. N., Bucholtz, D. C., Clark, E. M., & Sanders-Thompson, V. (2002). Achieving cultural appropriateness in health promotion programs: Targeted and tailored approaches. *Health Education & Behavior, 30,* 133–146.
Lassiter, S. (1995). *Multicultural clients: A professional handbook for health care providers and social workers.* Westport, CT: Greenwood Press.

Lawlor, D. A., Smith, G. D., Ebrahim. S. (2004). Socioeconomic position and hormone replacement therapy use: Explaining the discrepancy in evidence from observational and randomized controlled trials. *American Journal of Public Health, 94,* 2149–2154.

Levy-Storms, L., Wallace, S. P., Goldfarb , F., & Burhansstipanov, L. (2001). The community as classroom: A health communication program among older Samoan and American Indian women. In S. B. Kar, R. Alcalay, with S. Alex (Eds.), *Health communication: A multicultural perspective* (pp. 251–280). Thousand Oaks, CA: Sage.

Lin, C.-T. J. (1995). Demographic and socioeconomic influences on the importance of food safety in food shopping. *Agricultural and Resource Economics Review, 24,* 190–198.

Lindell, M. K., & Perry, R. W. (2004). *Communicating environmental risk in multiethnic communities.* Thousand Oaks, CA: Sage.

Lundgren, R. E., & McMakin, A. H. (2004). *Risk communication: A handbook for communicating environmental, safety, and health risks* (3rd ed.). Columbus, OH: Battelle Press.

Lupton, D. (1994). Toward the development of critical health communication praxis. *Health Communication, 6,* 55–67.

Madison, T., Schottenfeld, D., James, E., Sherman, J. A., Schwartz, A. G., & Gruber, S. B. (2004). Endometrial cancer: Socioeconomic status and racial/ethnic differences in stage at diagnosis, treatment and survival. *American Journal of Public Health, 94,* 2104–2111.

Marshall, A. A., Smith, S. W., & McKeon, J. K. (1995). Persuading low-income women to engage in mammography screening: Source, message, and channel preferences. *Health Communication, 7,* 283–299.

Marshall, B. K. (2004). Gender, race, and perceived environmental risk: The "white male" effect in Cancer Alley, LA. *Sociological Spectrum, 24,* 453–478.

Mays, V. M., & Cochran, S. D. (1988). Issues in the perception of AIDS risk and risk reduction activities by black and Hispanic/Latina women. *American Psychologist, 43,* 949–957.

McComas, K. A. (2006). Defining moments in risk communication research: 1996–2005. *Journal of Health Communication, 11,* 75–91.

McComas, K. A., & Trumbo, C. W. (2001). Source credibility in environmental health-risk controversies: Application of Meyer's credibility index. *Risk Analysis, 21,* 467–480.

Mishler, E. G. (1981). The social construction of illness. In E. G. Mishler, L. R. Amarasingham, S. D. Osherson, S. T. Hauser, N. E. Waxler, & R. Liem (Eds.), *Social contexts of health, illness and patient care* (pp. 141–168). Cambridg: Cambridge University Press.

Mishler, E. G. (1984). *The discourse of medicine.* Norwood, NJ: Ablex.

Mumby, D. (1997). Modernism, postmodernism, and communication studies. *Communication Theory, 7,* 1–28.

Murray-Johnson, L., & Witte, K. (2003). Looking toward the future: Health message design strategies. In T. L. Thompson, A. M. Dorsey, K. I. Miller, & R. Parrott (Eds.), *Handbook of health communication* (pp. 473–495). Mahwah, NJ: Erlbaum.

Murray-Johnson, L, Witte, K., Liu, W. Y., & Hubbell, A. P. (2001). Addressing cultural orientations in fear appeals: Promoting AIDS-protective behaviors among Mexican immigrant and African American adolescents and American and Taiwanese college students. *Journal of Health Communication, 6,* 335–358.

National Center for Health Statistics. (2005, May). *Health, United States, 2004 with chartbook on trends in the health of Americans.* Retrieved from http://www.cdc.gov/nchs/data/hus/ hus04trend.pdf.

NRC. (1989). *Improving risk communication.* National Academy Press, Washington, DC.

Palmer, C. G. S. (2003). Risk perception: another look at the "white male" effect. *Health, Risk & Society, 5,* 71–83.

Pidgeon, N. F., Kasperson, R. E., & Slovic, P. (2003). *The social amplification of risk.* Cambridge: Cambridge University Press.

Pratt, C. A., Ha, L., Levine, S. R., & Pratt, C. B. (2003). Stroke knowledge and barriers to stroke prevention among African Americans: Implications for health communication. *Journal of Health Communication, 8,* 369–381.

Price, V., & Hsu, M. L. (1992). Public opinion about AIDS policies: The role of misinformation and attitudes toward homosexuals. *Public Opinion Quarterly, 56,* 29–52.

Purnell, L., & Paulanka, B. (Eds.). (1998). *Transcultural health care: A culturally competent approach.* Philadelphia: F. A. Davis.

Robinson, L. (1998). *"Race," communication and the caring professions.* Philadelphia: Open University Press.

Rodriguez, M., Quiroga, S., & Bauer, H. (1996). Breaking the silence: Battered women's perspectives on medical care. *Archives of Family Medicine, 5,* 153–158.

Russell, L. A. (2001). Health communication for HIV risk reduction among homeless youth. In S. B. Kar, R. Alcalay, with S. Alex (Eds.), *Health communication: A multicultural perspective* (pp. 235–249). Thousand Oaks, CA: Sage.

Scherer, C. W., & Cho, H. (2003). A social contagion theory of risk perception. *Risk Analysis, 23*, 261–267.
Scherer, C. W., & Juanillo Jr., N. K. (2003). The continuing challenge of community health risk management and communication. In T. L. Thompson, A. M. Dorsey, K. I. Miller, & R. Parrott (Eds.), *Handbook of health communication* (pp. 221–239). Mahwah, NJ: Erlbaum.
Scott, K. D., Gilliam, A., & Braxton, K. (2005). Culturally competent HIV prevention strategies for women of color in the United States. *Health Care for Women International, 26,* 17–45.
Sharf, B. F., & Vanderford, M. L. (2003). Illness narratives and the social construction of health. In T. L. Thompson, A. M. Dorsey, K. I. Miller, & R. Parrott (Eds.), *Handbook of health communication* (pp. 9–34). Mahwah, NJ: Erlbaum.
Siegrist, M., & Cvetkovich, G. T. (2000). Perception of hazards: The role of social trust and knowledge. *Risk Analysis, 20,* 713–720.
Siegrist, M., Cvetkovich, G. T., & Roth, C. (2000). Salient value similarity, social trust, and risk/benefit perception. *Risk Analysis, 20,* 353–362.
Siegrist, M., Earle, T. C., & Gutscher, H. (2005). Test of a trust and confidence model in the applied context of electromagnetic field (EMF) risks. *Risk Analysis, 23,* 705–716.
Singer, E., & Endreny. P. (1993). *Reporting on risk: How the mass media portray accidents, diseases, disasters, and other hazards.* New York: Russell Sage.
Spector, R. (1996). *Cultural diversity in health and illness* (4th ed.). Stamford, CT: Appleton & Lange.
Stipp, H., & Kerr, D. (1989). Determinants of Public Opinion about AIDS. *Public Opinion Quarterly, 53*, 98–106.
Sylvester, J. L. (1998). *Directing health messages toward African Americans: Attitudes toward health care and the mass media.* New York: Garland.
Tichenor, P. Donohue, G., & Olien, C. (1970). Mass media flow and differential growth in knowledge. *Public Opinion Quarterly, 34*, 159–170.
Triandis, H. C. (1976). *Variations in black and white perceptions of the social environment.* Urbana: University of Illinois Press.
Triandis, H. C., Marin, G., Lisansky, J., & Betancourt, H. (1984). Simpatia as a cultural script of Hispanic. *Journal of Personality & Social Psychology, 47*, 1363–1375.
Trumbo, C. W., & McComas, K. A. (2003). The function of credibility in information processing for risk perception. *Risk Analysis, 23,* 343–353.
U.S. Bureau of the Census. (2006). *Statistical abstract of the United States.* Washington, DC: U. S. Department of Commerce. Retrieved March 18, 2006, from http://www.census.gov/prod/2001pubs/statab/sec01.pdf.
U. S. Bureau of the Census. (2004). *Population projections.* Washington, DC: U. S. Department of Commerce. Retrieved March 18, 2006, from http://www.census.gov/population/www/projections/popproj.html.
Valdes, I., & Seoane, M. H. (1995). Hispanic buying power (marketing power). *American Demographics, 17*(10), S10.
Van Dijk, T., Ting-Toomey, S., Smitherman, G., & Troutman, D. (1997). Discourse, ethnicity, culture and racism. In T. A. van Dijk (Ed.), *Discourse as social interaction* (pp. 144–180). Thousand Oaks, CA: Sage.
Vaughan, E. (1995). The significance of socioeconomic and ethnic diversity for the risk communication process. *Risk Analysis, 15*, 169–180.
Viswanath, K., Kahn, E., Finnegan Jr., J. R., Hertog, J., & Potter, J. D. (1993). Motivation and the knowledge gap. *Communication Research, 20,* 546–563.
Wahlberg, A. A., & Sjoberg, L. (2000). Risk perception and the media. *Journal of Risk Research, 3*(1), 31–50.
Warry, W. (1998). *Unfinished dreams: Community healing and the reality of aboriginal self-government.* Buffalo, NY: University of Toronto Press Inc.
Witte, K. (1992). Preventing AIDS through persuasive communications. In F. Korzenny, S. Ting-Toomey, with E. Schiff (Eds.), *Mass media effects across cultures* (pp. 67–86). Newbury Park, CA: Sage.
Witte, K., & Berkowitz, J. H. (1998). Radon awareness and reduction campaigns for African Americans: A theoretically based evaluation. *Health Education & Behavior, 25*, 284–302.
Witte, K., Meyer, G., Bidol, H., Casey, M. K., Kopfman, J., Maduschke, K.. et al. (1996). Bringing order to chaos: communication and health. *Communication Studies, 47,* 229–242.
Wong, P., Lai, C. F., Nagasawa, R., & Lin, T. (1998). Asian Americans as a model minority: Self-perceptions and perceptions by other racial groups. *Sociological Perspectives, 41*(1), 95–121.
Wood, J. T. (1994). *Who cares? Women, care and culture.* Carbondale, IL: Southern Illinois University Press.
Wood, J. T. (2005). *Gendered lives: Communication, gender, and culture* (6th ed.). Belmont, CA: Wasdsworth Publishing.
Yancey, A. K., Kumanyika, S. K., Ponce, N. A., McCarthy, W. J., Fielding, J. E., Leslie, J. P. et al. (2004, January). Population-based interventions engaging communities of color in healthy eating and active living: A review. *Preventing Chronic Disease* [serial online]. Retrieved March 20, 2006, from http://www.cdc.gov/pcd/issues/2004/jan/03_0012.htm.

Zambrana, R. E. (1996). A research agenda on issues affecting poor and minority women: A model for understanding their health needs. In E. B. Ray (Ed.), *Communication and disenfranchisement: Social health issues and implications* (pp. 117–135). Mahwah, NJ: Erlbaum.

12

Science Literacy and Risk Analysis: Relationship to the Postmodernist Critique, Conservative Christian Activists, and Professional Obfuscators

Michael Ryan
University of Houston

Attention focused primarily on New Orleans when the Gulf Coast was pounded in August 2005 by Hurricane Katrina, one of the nation's worst natural disasters. This was inevitable because New Orleans was by far the largest city hit, because more deaths were recorded there, because the value of property destroyed set new records—and because the tragedy did not have to be as bad as it was.

Scientists had warned for years that New Orleans would be devastated by a hurricane striking near the city (Bourne, 2004). A direct hit by a Category 5 hurricane—which the U.S. Army Corps of Engineers predicted was a 1-in-500-years event—would be like filling a huge bowl with water, sewage, toxic chemicals, and bodies. The hurricane would drive water into Lake Pontchartrain, overwhelming the levees and pumps that keep water in the lake and out of the city, and flow over levees on the Mississippi River. Scientists warned that people and pets of New Orleans could be stranded for weeks waiting for flood waters to recede; that as much as 80 percent of the city could be destroyed; that the populace could face tuberculosis, dengue fever, malaria, cholera, and other diseases; and that rivers, lakes, bays, and land could be contaminated by toxic chemicals from nearby petrochemical plants.

They warned that levees and pumps needed to be upgraded and that the million acres of wetlands destroyed since the 1930s needed to be restored. Funds for projects that would minimize the damage were cut to the point that very little could be done to help minimize the tragedy if New Orleans were hit by a Category 4 or 5 hurricane. Louisiana's congressional delegation urged the government in early 2005 to fund safety improvements along the Gulf Coast, for instance, but President Bush proposed $10.4 million for southeast Louisiana's main hurricane protection project, a sixth of the amount local officials said they needed (Walsh, Alpert, & McQuaid, 2005). By this time, of course, it was too late.

Risk assessments often are ignored by politicians and activists who have other priorities (e.g., to lower taxes, fight wars, or fund projects that have greater priority for them). They can ignore them in part because of the uncertainty inherent in the scientific process. Because scientists produce knowledge about what was previously unknown, "uncertainty is a normal and necessary characteristic of scientific work" (Zehr, 1999, p. 3). Scientists, who engage uncertainty as they explore the unknown, identify problems to study by looking for questions raised in research by other scientists. They investigate such questions in their own research and that research points still other researchers to fruitful questions.

This characteristic of scientific inquiry reduces its power to educate as findings enter the public domain, for many Americans are not sufficiently literate about science to understand that uncertainty is a natural byproduct of the process. The difficulty is exacerbated by (a) those who exploit uncertainty as they attack science in general, and (b) opponents of a given study who exploit uncertainty simply to undermine that study's contribution to the public discourse (Rampton & Stauber, 2001).

Attacks against science by postmodernists, Conservative Christian activists, and professional obfuscators can pollute, polarize, and paralyze the public discussion of science to the point that policy makers, lawmakers, and others simply cannot use scientific research as a basis for action. The scientific enterprise that produces risk assessments and crisis plans has been marginalized by these critiques. This chapter describes each critique, shows how each can confuse and paralyze discussion, suggests that scientific literacy and journalism are affected by attacks against science, and poses some conclusions.

THE POSTMODERNIST CRITIQUE

The postmodernist critique blindsided the scientific community in the 1960s with all sorts of questions about the scientific enterprise, particularly about objectivity and the social role of science. Many scientists were baffled by the critique because they didn't know what postmodernism was and they tended to ignore it. It isn't easy to understand postmodernism for a number of reasons, including:

- "[C]larity is not conspicuous amongst its marked attributes. It not only generally fails to practise it, but also on occasion actually repudiates it" (Gellner, 1992, pp. 22–23).
- Postmodernist scholars draw from so many disciplines, theories, and approaches, it is impossible to define postmodernism as a coherent theory (Bloland, 2005). It is more aptly called a condition (Lyotard, 1984).
- Postmodernists typically do not claim objectivity, truth, moral superiority, or universality for their positions, primarily because they will not permit such claims by modernist scholars. "To be sure, certain arguments of the traditional kind are put forth (e.g., they follow certain conventions of rational argument, they make reference to an assumed reality, etc.), but this is not to impress them with the stamp of truth. It is only to engage in a cultural practice of sense making" (Gergen, 2001, p. 807).
- "[I]t is impossible to fully define the postmodern since the very attempt to do so confers upon it a status and identity which it must necessarily oppose" (Usher & Edwards, 1994, p. 7). The result, of course, is a critique that is extraordinarily difficult to pin down.[1]

Still, some aspects of the postmodernist critique are far from murky. Clearly, it is a reaction against the modern, which "refers to strongly held assumptions both in and out of academia regarding the core values of the Enlightenment: the centrality of reason, the belief in progress, the virtues of individualism, and faith in the scientific method" (Bloland, 2005, p. 122). It also challenges the function and adequacy of language as the channel through which scientists inform their colleagues and the public about their discoveries (Gergen, 2001).[2] Postmodernists argue that everything is relative, that reality has multiple meanings, that language reflects its culture and refuses to stand still, and that there are no objective facts.[3]

Postmodernists pose questions about the metanarratives that scientists use to legitimize their assumptions about the scientific enterprise. One of these is that science can help societies cope with risk. Ulrich Beck (1992) challenged that metanarrative when he said, "the sciences are *entirely incapable* of reacting adequately to civilizational risks, since they are prominently involved in the origin and growth of those very risks" (p. 59). Scientists—in part because they are so intertwined with political, judicial, and corporate interests—have done a poor job of protecting people from poisons in air, water, and food. "Science has *become the protector of a global contamination of people and nature*. In that respect, it is no exaggeration to say that in the way they deal with risks in many areas, the sciences *have squandered until further notice their historic reputation for rationality*" (p. 70).[4]

The following section focuses on one aspect of the postmodernist critique—the modernists' belief in an objectively knowable world—to illustrate the postmodernist approach.

Objectivity Is Not Possible

Individual knowledge has long been central to the modernist belief system, for within each individual lies "a bounded and sacred sanctuary of the mind, a domain governed by autonomous capacities for careful, conscious observation and rational deliberation" (Gergen, 2001, p. 804). Postmodernists observe that no mind is completely autonomous, however, because it is influenced by social, political, economic, and cultural attitudes, values, and assumptions. No scientist can construct a reasonably accurate representation of truth, or reality, because no researcher can transcend his or her own values, attitudes, and perceptions, which are influenced by class, race, gender, and other personal, professional, environmental, and psychological factors (e.g., Berger & Luckman, 1967).

Modernists also are bound by the language and approved codes they use to communicate their discoveries. For the postmodernist, private thought is simply a form of cultural participation. The question for them, according to Kenneth Gergen (2001), is:

> How could one deliberate privately on matters of justice, morality, or optimal strategies of action … except through the terms of public culture? (See also Sandel, 1982.) When this idea is applied to the domain of scientific knowledge, one sees that the individual scientist is deemed rational only if he or she adopts the codes of discourse common to his or her particular community of science. (p. 805)

Michel Foucault (1972) argued that knowledge flows from a structuring discourse. For example, "once one begins to describe or explain what exists, one inevitably proceeds from a forestructure of shared intelligibility" (Gergen, 2001, p. 806).[5] Sue Curry Jansen (1993) critiqued a male perspective as one structuring discourse: "[F]eminist epistemologies treat the forms of 'objectivity' science has valorized as contingent cultural artifacts: artifacts that were crafted by formalizing and codifying the subjective views of the men who participated in the founding conversations of modern science" (pp. 138–139).[6] An example of the kinds of case studies that some critics use to support their assertions is found in the work of Belgian philosopher Luce Irigaray (1985), whose ideas about the male perspective were summarized and interpreted by Katherine Hayles (1992):

> The privileging of solid over fluid mechanics, and indeed the inability of science to deal with turbulent flow at all, [Irigaray] attributes to the association of fluidity with femininity. Whereas men have sex organs that protrude and become rigid, women have openings that leak menstrual blood and vaginal fluids. Although men, too, flow on occasion—when semen is emitted, for example—this aspect of their sexuality is not emphasized. It is the rigidity of the male organ that counts, not its complicity in fluid flow. These idealizations are reinscribed in mathematics, which conceives of fluids as laminated planes and other modified solid forms. In the same way that women are erased within masculinist theories and language, existing only as not-men, so fluids have been erased from science, existing only as not-solids. From this perspective it is no wonder that science has not been able to arrive at a successful model for turbulence. The problem of turbulent flow cannot be solved because the conceptions of fluids (and of women) have been formulated so as necessarily to leave unarticulated remainders. (p. 17)[7]

This male perspective, Irigaray and others argue, has had a profound impact on scientific inquiry.

Structuring discourses—and, therefore, scientific truth assertions—can change because changing cultural and historical contexts ultimately render them vague and imprecise (e.g., Bloor, 1976; Latour, 1987; Latour & Woolgar, 1986). Sandra Harding (1997) argued that "distinctive 'standpoints on nature' are created by the fact that different cultures are exposed to different parts of nature and that cultures examine their parts of nature by way of culturally distinctive interests, discursive resources, and ways of organizing the production of empirical knowledge" (p. 199). Postmodernists deny the existence of "facts about the natural world that knowers in different times and places could recognize as more rational to hold on the grounds that they are based on better evidence, are better approximations of the truth, or have withstood serious attempts to refute them" (Nanda, 1998, p. 295).

Critics like Andrew Ross (1996) suggest that scientists should "talk about different ways of doing science, ways that downgrade methodology, experiment, and manufacturing in favor of local environments, cultural values, and principles of social justice. This is the way that leads from relativism to diversity" (p. 4). Helen Longino (1990) and Elisabeth Lloyd (1993) would simply redefine objectivity, claiming that it results from the interaction of different individuals and groups who hold different assumptions and have different stakes. In other words, some reality is knowable; it is what individuals in different times and places say it is.

One stream of literature argues that truth can be found only through a subjective approach that relies largely on personal experience. One of the personal approaches is standpoint epistemology, which requires "a reformulation of the term 'objectivity,' taking it away from any notion of eradicating bias toward a method of acknowledging and incorporating bias into the structure of the scientific method" (Durham, 1998, p. 127). This epistemology produces a "stronger" objectivity than does the scientific method, according to Sandra Harding (1993), a leading advocate of standpoint epistemology. Feminist epistemology, for example, is grounded in a woman's point of view (e.g., Clough, 1993; Hartsock, 1983).[8] One goal is "to define the nature of the truth claims that feminists advance and to provide a methodological grounding that will validate those claims" (Hekman, 1997, p. 341).[9]

A related approach is situated knowledge, or ethnoscience, which refers to "knowledges that are historically, culturally, and linguistically mediated, finite, and secured within, although not necessarily homologous with, a field of power relations" (Jansen, 1993, p. 139; see also Haraway, 1988). Proponents of situated knowledges often recommend that approach for non-Western cultures. The "universals" of objective scholarship, they assert, were "put in place by the violence and rapaciousness of colonialism and not by its superior claims to validity—non-Western cultures can never gain a true knowledge of the natural world as *they* experience it unless they develop their own 'alternative universals' grounded in indigenous categories, cultural idioms, and traditions" (Nanda, 1998, p. 287).

An example from India illustrates how situated knowledge can be privileged over objective knowledge. Anthropologist Frédérique Marglin (1990)—who used India's smallpox eradication program as an example "to challenge the entire project of modernization" (p. 102)—suggested that using a modern cowpox-based vaccine to eliminate smallpox was an affront to variolation, a local custom that "consisted in inoculating healthy persons by pricking the skin with a needle impregnated with human smallpox matter.... The technical operation was accompanied by worship of the goddess of smallpox" (p. 104). Although traditional variolation is approximately 10 times more likely to cause smallpox than the modern vaccine, Marglin, who used Derrida's (1976) deconstructive approach, said the modern vaccine represents an imposition of Western logocentric thought—which is characterized by binary oppositions (e.g., health is a binary opposite of illness)—over the non-logocentric, binary-denying view, which treats the goddess, Sitala Devi, as "*both* the presence and the absence of the disease" (p. 103).

Frédérique Marglin (1990) defended those who resisted the modern vaccine in the name of the goddess as fighting for a form of life that does not distinguish between natural and supernatural forces, and she condemns the vaccinators' logocentric language:

> Even when vaccination was presented to the people in a fashion that was not overtly repressive, the language of eradication violated the people's non-logocentric modes of thought. To speak of smallpox as an absolute evil that can and should be totally eradicated forever was an insult to Sitala, goddess of smallpox. Sitala is a concrete symbol or manifestation of a non-logocentric mode of thought and action. To dismiss belief in Sitala as simple superstition amounts to simple ignorance. (pp. 139–140)

Stephen Marglin (1990) suggested that the traditional non-logocentric views (as reflected in *techne*, or locally embedded, situated knowledge) should be privileged over logocentric views (as reflected in the value-free, impersonal *episteme* of science).

Many postmodernist theorists argue that scholarship must be marked by direct ideological intervention, which means in this context that scholars must use their research to redress grievances; to advance economic, cultural, political, or social goals; or to improve aspects of society. For some, ideological considerations must guide decisions about which questions they pose, how questions are framed, and what evidence they privilege. More fundamentally, an ideological approach "foregrounds its ideological perspective and analyzes texts or industry occurrences as evidence in support of that ideology" (Potter, Cooper, & Dupagne, 1993, p. 322). Proponents of ideological scholarship "want to subordinate science, but to a more severe agenda, whereby the scientific acceptability of a claim would be contingent on its perceived political expediency" (Koertge, 1996b, p. 271).

Summary

The postmodernist critique is reflected in higher education, professional and academic journals, and the popular media. "Newspapers and magazines, in chronicling abrupt changes in our lifestyles and life circumstances, report almost casually that we are already citizens in a postmodern world" (Bloland, 2005, p. 126). The critique has helped expose science's part in creating some of the very risks that many scientists are striving to resolve, the occasional insensitivity of science to culture and history, and the inadequacy of some scientific research. It has helped shine a light on "the way science and technology are situated in society, culture, and the economy" (Bloland, 2005, p. 130). It has helped scholars explore new ways to conduct research (Parsons, 1995), to produce better explanations of their efforts, to outline potentially transformative ideas, and to engage in an intercultural dialogue about knowledge and concepts of humanity (Gergen, 2001).

The critique also has helped polarize discussion and contributed to a general lowering of respect for the scientific enterprise. By arguing, for example, for epistemic charity (all ways of knowing are equal) critics send the message that all information is of equal value as individuals, groups, and societies make critical decisions. Epistemic charity can lead to reactionary modernity—which rejects scientific rationality and emphasizes technological advances—and a loss of faith in science (Nanda, 2003, pp. 125–159).[10] Arguments that science is a tool of Western oppression (F. Marglin, 1990) and that objective approaches cannot work also cast doubt on a scientific enterprise that relies heavily on an objective approach whose users must enjoy high credibility if their work is to be useful.

The critique, ironically, could lead to unnecessary suffering and disease in a traditional society in which traditional, non-logocentric approaches are privileged over scientific, logocentric approaches. Privileging traditional approaches seems to require (a) the rejection of the fundamental goal of modern health science—the elimination or mitigation of suffering and disease through scientific discovery—and (b) a denial that the research of scientists who pursue this goal has improved the quality of life for millions around the world. Further, rejection of the standard scientific models used to calculate risk could sidetrack or halt efforts to mitigate a risk's effects and even to stop its occurrence.

CONSERVATIVE CHRISTIAN ACTIVISTS

Conservative Christian activists have engaged for decades in a kind of war against modernity, and the science that reflects modernity. This is a coalition of activists from all Christian denominations—Greek Orthodox, Protestant, Roman Catholic—who think they are morally obliged to impose their views on everyone else. They believe that Jesus Christ was the son of God, that one can be "saved" only by accepting God's word as expressed in the Bible, and that they are part of a chosen elite that is obliged to interpret and to enforce God's word (Ryan & Switzer, in press).

They find the scientific enterprise lacking in many respects, but Conservative Christian activists reject the postmodernist view that reality—or truth—is relative and that it is found between the poles in a binary world (e.g., intelligent design versus evolutionary theory, right to choose versus right to life). For the postmodernist, no condition or situation is permanent and everything is relative because there are no universal truths. For the Conservative Christian activist, universal truth is embedded in the Bible, which contains metanarratives and authoritative discourses that apply to all peoples in all situations. The meanings Conservative Christian activists assign to words are unalterable and, for them, beyond any postmodernist or scientific challenge.

Conservative Christian activism appeared early in the 17th century in America, but it gained momentum in the 1800s, partly in response to Charles Darwin's *The Origin of Species by Means of Natural Selection* and, more generally, to the emerging scientific enterprise, which activists saw as undermining Christian values. They called themselves fundamentalists because their beliefs were "fundamental" to religious practice (Ammerman, 1991).[11]

Traditional views of science were being challenged at roughly the same time by scientific activists. The conflict over science, said Eva Marie Garroutte (2003), was a struggle pitting two approaches to the study of the natural world. "One, which we might call Baconianism, imagined a fundamentally *sacred science*, sustained by contributions from diverse practitioners. The other, which I will call positivism, assumed a strictly *secular science*, nurtured and presided over by a bounded set of professionals" (p. 197).

Advocates of secular science argued that they alone had the authority to make scientific claims. They excluded Baconian scholars, many of whom "had formerly justified their right to comment upon scientific activity by reference to the Christian scriptures," and they "undermined the ability of religious-friendly scientists to formulate meaningful claims about nature—indeed, about anything that had to do with reality" (Garroutte, 2003, p. 212). Secular scientists gained control of the intellectual scientific terrain and excluded religious interests from it. It was the prevailing model of universal, objective knowledge for decades and religious considerations were irrelevant.

The fundamentalists' offspring, who form the core of Conservative Christian activism today, did not concede the scientific terrain to the secular scientists for long. The future of the country and the "God-given mission" of these activists, as Linda Kintz (1998) put it, depend on "the reconstruction of U.S. culture so that it is in tune with the natural law of the Ten Commandments and Judeo-Christian values, as natural law and biblical law are conflated" (p. 7; see also Dinges & Hitchcock, 1991).

Conservative Christian activists were by the 1960s allying with secular groups holding similar views and they were using sophisticated technologies to get their messages to larger Christian and secular audiences. They were a formidable force in the 1970s, and their activism was endorsed by scholars like Robert Bellah (1967, 1973), who argued that an "American civil religion" would play a valuable role in national and international affairs. George Weigel (2004) suggested that the Catholic Church was "distinctively positioned to broker a new and wiser conversation throughout the world about the way in which moral truths impinge on the politics of nations" (p. 38).

Other scholars took a negative stance. Roderick Hart (1997), for example, noted that an American civil religion "is a type of ideological imperialism, a demand for a set of public symbols which will suffice for all Americans" (p. 106). Shadia Drury (2004) argued most forcefully against the kind of re-empowerment of the churches that religious activism required: "Any suggestion that the Churches should be re-endowed with political power has its source in historical amnesia. In my view, the political crimes committed in the name of Christianity were not historically contingent accidents; they were a logical consequence of Christian beliefs" (pp. xii–xiii). The negative critique had little impact, however, as religious activism was expanding rapidly and manifesting itself in a variety of fields—including science. This influence has continued and grown in the 21st century.

Activists—with the help of the conservative Bush administration, which often bends to their wishes—have enjoyed great success in the 21st century in attacking legitimate science from within the government (Kaplan, 2004). Scientists are so concerned, 20 Nobel Prize winners signed a letter expressing outrage about this politicizing of science:

> When scientific knowledge has been found to be in conflict with [the Bush administration's] political goals, the administration has often manipulated the process through which science enters into its decisions. This has been done by placing people who are professionally unqualified or who have clear conflicts of interest in official posts and on scientific advisory committees; by disbanding existing advisory committees; by censoring and suppressing reports by the government's own scientists; and by simply not seeking independent scientific advice.... Furthermore, in advocating policies that are not scientifically sound, the administration has sometimes misrepresented scientific knowledge and misled the public about the implications of its policies.... The distortion of scientific knowledge for partisan political ends must cease. ("Restoring Scientific," 2004)

The scientists' concern seems justified. "From global warming to lead poisoning, from AIDS research to pregnancy prevention, the Bush administration has chosen to sacrifice science whenever it conflicts with the needs of Bush's corporate patrons or his evangelical base" (Kaplan, 2004, p. 95).

This section does not attempt to summarize each battle in the Conservative Christian war against science. It focuses instead on the battle against evolution as one example of the Conservative Christian activists' strategy in the science war.

Evolution and Intelligent Design

Conservative Christian activists share a nostalgic, premodernist view of the world.[12] They yearn for a simpler past in which they were not isolated, alienated, and frustrated—or challenged by modernity's focus on rationality and objectivity. Their critique of science focuses primarily on those issues, ideas, and theories that most clearly challenge the world described in the Bible. Scientific evolution—which is questioned by very few scientists, even those who believe in a Christian God—is a lightening rod for this criticism, for many Conservative Christians fear that evolution undermines the biblical version of creation and challenges the uniqueness of human beings. "For two millennia," David Wilson (2002) noted, "Western civilization has imagined people as categorically different from and vastly superior to other animals. The list of supposedly unique human attributes has been almost endless, encompassing language, tool use, intelligence, morals and aesthetics" (p. 225). Charles Darwin challenged all of that.

Conservative Christian activists, who have fought evolution for nearly 100 years, have resorted to the two-pronged, somewhat contradictory strategy they have used in opposing other scientific inquiry: (a) They attack research they see as threatening, in part by framing it in political and legal terms, rather than in scientific terms, and (b) they use their own "science" to fight science. The strategy has worked in many instances, as when they managed to persuade some public schools to ban for decades the teaching of evolution and the adoption of textbooks mentioning evolution. This worked until the U.S. Supreme Court ruled in *Epperson v. Arkansas* (1968) that such bans were unconstitutional.

Following that defeat, Conservative Christian activists offered creation science as a "scientific" explanation for the world's creation. The battle was joined for 20 years and many Americans—including many in government, law, education, and the media—took the "scientific" arguments seriously. However, the U. S. Supreme Court, in *Edwards v. Aguillard* (1987), declared unconstitutional a Louisiana law that made creation science part of the science curriculum (Powell, 2004, p. A20).

Conservative Christian activists came back from the drawing board with "intelligent design," yet another "scientific" explanation for the universe, but without God at its center. Biochemist Michael Behe of Lehigh University, a high-profile proponent of intelligent design, argued that evolution cannot work when a system is irreducibly complex, meaning the system could not be formed by several successive, slight modifications. "Irreducible complexity is just a fancy phrase I use to mean a single system which is composed of several interacting parts, and where the removal of any one of the parts causes the system to cease functioning" (Behe, 1996).

Behe cited many systems as irreducibly complex, including the eye. If any part of the eye is nonfunctional, it cannot work. It strains credibility to suggest that each part of the eye evolved at the same speed. If this assumption is accurate, an irreducibly complex biological system constitutes evidence against Darwinian evolution. Behe's explanation for such a complex system is intelligent design, meaning that some biological systems were designed by an "intelligent agent," not necessarily God, and did not evolve over time. Intelligent design does not explain everything, and it "does not mean that any of the other factors [e.g., natural selection, population size, migration, and common descent] are not operative, common, or important" (Behe, 1996).

The new strategy has worked well, as Chris Mooney and Matthew Nisbet (2005) reported. Intelligent design received serious media attention, particularly in yet another high-profile trial. The trial began in October, 2005, in Dover, Pennsylvania, in a case in which the legality of teaching intelligent design in public schools was tested. The case, *Kitzmiller v. Dover Area School District*, was filed by the ACLU on behalf of concerned parents after the local school board voted 6-3 to endorse the following change to the biology curriculum: "Students will be made aware of gaps/problems in Darwin's Theory and of other theories of evolution including, but not limited to, intelligent design."

U. S. District Judge John E. Jones III dealt the intelligent design advocates a severe blow, however, when he ruled that Dover schools could not maintain the intelligent design policy or require teachers to disparage evolution or to refer to intelligent design. The Dover policy, Jones ruled, violated the Constitution's Establishment Clause. The judge left no doubt about his view of the Dover policy when he wrote:

> Those who disagree with our holding will likely mark it as the product of an activist judge. If so, they will have erred as this is manifestly not an activist Court. Rather, this case came to us as the result of the activism of an ill-informed faction on a school board, aided by a national public interest law firm eager to find a constitutional test case on ID, who in combination drove the Board to adopt an imprudent and ultimately unconstitutional policy. The breathtaking inanity of the Board's decision is evident when considered against the factual backdrop which has not been fully revealed through this trial. The students, parents, and teachers of the Dover Area School District deserved better than to be dragged into this legal maelstrom, with its resulting utter waste of monetary and personal resources. ("Memorandum Opinion," 2005, pp. 137–138)

Journalists covering the trial evidently did not recognize, as Judge Jones did, the "breathtaking inanity of the Board's decision," for most treated intelligent design as a serious alternative to evolution. Such trials often are covered by political reporters who focus on the false "controversy" between evolution and intelligent design and not by science writers who know the scientific case favors evolution overwhelmingly.

> [S]cience writers generally characterize evolution in terms that accurately reflect its firm acceptance in the scientific community. Political reporters, generalists, and TV news reporters and anchors, however, rarely provide their audiences with any real context about basic evolutionary science. Worse, they often provide a springboard for anti-evolutionist criticism of that science, allotting ample quotes and sound bites to Darwin's critics in a quest to achieve "balance." (Mooney & Nisbit, 2005, p. 32)

By treating intelligent design and evolution as scientific equals, the news media confer on intelligent design a credibility it does not deserve, for there is no evidence of an "intelligent agent's" hand in the shaping of the universe. "The pairing of competing claims plays directly into the hands of intelligent-design proponents who have cleverly argued that they're mounting a *scientific* attack on evolution rather than a religiously driven one, and who paint themselves as maverick outsiders warring against a dogmatic scientific establishment" (Mooney & Nisbit, 2005, p. 34).

Summary

Conservative Christian activists understand they must use science, and not religious teachings, as they try to influence public policy; U. S. courts have demonstrated repeatedly that religious teachings cannot be the basis for challenges to public policy. They attack scientific findings that contradict biblical teachings and they create research that supports their points of view. They have been quite successful in the 21st century, as their continuing struggle against evolution suggests.

Conservative Christian activists have created institutes like the Medical Institute for Sexual Health and the National Association for the Research and Therapy of Homosexuality to push their conservative scientific agenda and to attack legitimate science. The Institute for Youth Development has even started a "peer-reviewed" journal whose "referees" must pass a severe ideological test. The journal is a response to charges that activists' research is never peer-reviewed. Conservatives now argue that, because of this journal, their work is peer-reviewed and therefore is credible.

PROFESSIONAL OBFUSCATORS

James Tozzi, head of the Center for Regulatory Effectiveness, is one of thousands of professional obfuscators who has made a career of killing, delaying, or weakening regulations proposed by the Environmental Protection Agency, the Occupational Health and Safety Administration, and other government agencies. Paid by wealthy corporations "to delay or block efforts to protect public health and the environment," professional obfuscators were hard at work in the lead industry in the 1920s, the chemical industry in the 1950s, the asbestos industry in the 1960s, the plastics and oil industries in the 1970s, and the tobacco industry in the 1980s and 1990s ("The art," 2005, p. 30).

Tozzi's latest gambit is the Data Quality Act, which he conceived, Rep. Jo Ann Emerson (R-Mo.) introduced, and Congress passed in 2000 with little debate.[13] Section 515 of the act "directs the Office of Management and Budget (OMB) to issue government-wide guidelines that 'provide policy and procedural guidance to Federal agencies for ensuring and maximizing the quality, objectivity, utility, and integrity of information (including statistical information) disseminated by Federal agencies'" (U.S. Office of Management and Budget, 2002).

The act is supposed to ensure the government uses sound science in developing regulations, but "by demanding that the government use only data that have achieved a rare level of certainty, these critics maintain, the act dismisses scientific information that in the past would have triggered tighter regulation" (Weiss, 2004, p. A6). The act adds enormously to federal agencies' workloads by requiring them to respond to all complaints about the reports and studies they distribute.[14] The act has been used by a variety of corporations, industry groups, and liberal and conservative organizations. Syngenta Crop Protection is one corporation that has used the act to forestall regulation.

EPA scientists were most concerned when they discovered that atrazine, a leading weedkiller banned in 2005 by the European Union, "was disrupting hormones in wildlife—in some cases turning frogs into bizarre creatures bearing both male and female sex organs" (Weiss, 2004, p. A1). Several other studies documented the effects of atrazine on frogs and "some laboratory studies have linked atrazine to cancer in rats, and some epidemiological studies show a correlation between exposure and cancer in humans" (Lee, 2003, p. 20). At least one Syngenta-supported study found the link between atrazine and abnormalities in frogs while others did not. EPA scientists and other experts challenged the Syngenta studies because of their funding source, methodological problems, and lack of independent review.

Syngenta commissioned its own studies of atrazine's effects and hired James Tozzi to file a petition under the Data Quality Act charging the EPA "had not designated tests that would serve as the gold standard of proof of hormone disruption in frogs" (Weiss, 2004, p. A9). The EPA does have tests that measure some effects of chemicals on wildlife, but it does not have such tests for hormone disruption.

EPA scientists added in their final report a sentence that said hormone disruption "is not an acceptable reason to restrict a chemical's use—because the government had not settled on an officially accepted test for measuring such disruption" (Weiss, 2004, pp. A1, A6). Those words in effect cancelled all the scientific studies of the effects of atrazine. Jennifer Sass, a National Resources Defense Council scientist, said "the evidence of atrazine's effects was more than convincing by traditional standards. The act, she said, has 'hamstrung EPA's ability to express anything that it couldn't back up with a mountain of data. It basically blocked EPA scientists from expressing an expert opinion" (Weiss, 2004, p. A7).

This chapter does not attempt to list all the tools in the professional obfuscators' inventory or all the industries that use the technique. It focuses instead on one example: the tobacco industry's decades-long battle to avoid any kind of regulation.

Tobacco and Sound Science

The tobacco industry refined the art of obfuscation as it tried to deflect the regulation of its product, in part by discrediting scientific results documenting the harmful effects of cigarette smoke on smokers and non-smokers alike. An early tool was The Advancement of Sound Science Coalition (TASSC), a now-defunct front for its "sound science" campaign, which was intended to delay or to kill the Environmental Protection Agency's 1992 report documenting a link between secondhand smoke (environmental tobacco smoke) and cancer. The report "estimated that ETS causes approximately 3000 lung cancer deaths per year in nonsmokers" (Environmental Protection Agency, 1992). The Group A human carcinogen "had adverse effects on respiratory health, particularly in children" (Muggli, Hurt, & Repace, 2004, p. 175). APCO Associates, a subsidiary of the huge GCI/Grey advertising and public relations firm, coordinated the campaign.

Philip Morris wholeheartedly endorsed an attack against the EPA, as an internal memorandum authored by Philip Morris executive Victor Han suggests: "The credibility of EPA is defeatable, but not on the basis of ETS alone. It must be a part of a larger mosaic that concentrates all of the EPA's enemies against it at one time" (Han, 1993, p. 2). One of TASSC's jobs was "to make the case that efforts to regulate tobacco were based on the same 'junk science' as efforts to regulate Alar, food additives, automobile emissions, and other industrial products that had not yet achieved tobacco's pariah status" (Rampton & Stauber, 2001, p. 239). The goal of the "junk science" campaign was to highlight or create uncertainty about research that could be used as a basis for regulation. This and similar campaigns by other industries are designed to discredit or ridicule cutting edge science and researchers who threaten powerful interests regardless of the quality of the studies.

> Advocates for this perspective allege that many of the scientific studies (and even scientific methods) used in the regulatory and legal arenas are fundamentally flawed, contradictory, or incomplete, asserting it wrong or premature to regulate the exposure in question or to compensate the worker or community resident who may have been made sick by the exposure. (Michaels & Monforton, 2005, p. S40)

The tobacco industry was comfortable with this approach, as a statement by one industry executive suggests: "Doubt is our product since it is the best means of competing with the 'body of fact' that exists in the mind of the general public. It is also the means of establishing a controversy" ("Smoking and Health," 1969, p. 4).[15]

TASSC focused in the early 1990s on recruiting new members, raising funds from other sources so that Philip Morris could not be identified as the major funding source, developing a list of examples of unsound science, directing volunteers, and trying to identify and recruit contacts within the academic and scientific communities, according to a memorandum to Philip Morris executives from APCO's Margery Kraus. APCO also proposed updating all TASSC members each month, monitoring interest groups, arranging media tours, issuing news releases, serving as a clearinghouse of TASSC speakers, placing opinion pieces in trade publications, and "drafting 'boilerplate' speeches, press releases and op-eds to be utilized by TASSC field representatives" (Kraus, 1993, p. 5). TASSC focused primarily on media outside Washington, D.C., and New York City, where journalists might have asked pointed questions and opponents might have challenged them.

Garrey Carruthers, TASSC's public face, began a tour of the "secondary" markets in December 1993 with a list of "friendly" reporters supplied by Philip Morris and with news releases that described TASSC as a "grassroots-based, not-for-profit watchdog group of scientists and representatives from universities, independent organizations and industry, that advocates the use of sound science in the public policy arena. It is committed to monitoring all public policy related science to ensure that a sound science and valid peer-review process is used" (Advancement of Science, 1993, p. 3). Carruthers' fierce attack against science included arguments against the EPA, which, he charged, politicized science and made it conform to the political views of special interests.

Neal M. Cohen, an APCO vice president, described during a 1994 meeting of lobbyists in Longboat Key, Florida, some of the strategies his company used to establish front groups for TASSC. An overarching goal, according to Jane Fritsch (1996) of *The New York Times*, always was to keep clients' names hidden from the public, for revealing the names of unpopular or unsympathetic clients could jeopardize the grassroots campaigns so popular among lobbyists. "Typically, the client, often a large business, hires a Washington firm to organize a coalition of small businesses, nonprofit groups and individuals across the nation. The coalition draws public sympathy for the legislation sought by the original client, who recedes into the background" (p. A1).

Cohen described his grassroots campaign for tort reform in Mississippi to show the lobbyists how the model works.[16] Cohen attacked "greedy" trial lawyers; he paid a college teacher for a study showing that more money was going to the tort system than to education in Mississippi; and he recruited as many members as he could to agitate for tort reform. "Within four weeks, he said, the coalition had 1,200 members, including nonprofit agencies, schools, businesses and people who felt they had been victimized by frivolous suits" (Fritsch, 1996, p. A20). Corporate attorneys, tobacco interests, and insurance industry leaders—those who would benefit most from tort reform—were not encouraged to join. "In a tort reform battle, if State Farm…is the leader of the coalition, you're not going to pass the bill. It is not credible, O. K., because it's so self-serving," Cohen said (Fritsch, 1996, p. A20). The public did not know who was behind the campaign.

Management of TASSC was transferred soon after Fritsch's story appeared to the EOP Group, a lobby firm in Washington, D.C. TASSC named Steven Milloy its executive director to carry on the fight for "sound science" in public policy making. Milloy—an associate of James Tozzi at Multinational Business Services, which worked during the Reagan administration to gut environmental regulations—established the Regulatory Impact Analysis Project Inc., of which he was president, and created the Junk Science Home Page.

Milloy attacked environmentalists, food safety regulators, public health officials, the EPA, antinuclear and animal rights activists, and others, accusing them of, among other things, using faulty data and analyses to support special interests (Michaels & Monforton, 2005, p. S43). To Sheldon Rampton and John Stauber (2001), the Junk Science Home Page seemed designed to lower, not elevate, scientific discussion. "Using schoolyard taunts and accusations of 'mindless anti-chemical hysteria,' Milloy routinely attacked the world's most prestigious scientific journals, including *Science*, *Nature*, the *Lancet*, and the *Journal of the American Medical Association*" (p. 249). Milloy's attacks against critics of the tobacco industry were particularly harsh.

> He dismissed the EPA's 1993 [sic] report linking secondhand smoke to cancer as "a joke," and when the *British Medical Journal* published its own study with similar results in 1997, he scoffed that "it remains a joke today." After one researcher published a study linking secondhand smoke to cancer, Milloy wrote that she "must have pictures of journal editors in compromising positions with farm animals. How else can you explain her studies seeing the light of day?" (Rampton & Stauber, 2001, p. 250).

Steven Milloy, dismissed as a joke by some, is influential among conservatives. A scholar at the Cato Institute, he is an expert in politicizing scientific research and in mobilizing firestorms of criticism against the "junk science" that threatens the interests of his clients. His op-ed columns have appeared in many newspapers, including *The* (Phoenix) *Arizona Republic*, *The Washington Times*, *New York Post*, *Detroit Free Press*, *The* (San Francisco) *Examiner*, *Chicago Tribune*, and *The Philadelphia Inquirer*. Some newspapers, like the *Chicago Sun-Times*, run Milloy's articles without mentioning his ties to and background as an industry lobbyist. He built a case in one such article that genetically modified foods are no more dangerous than other foods (Milloy, 1999).

The Data Quality Act grew out of the tobacco industry's "sound science" project. Front groups like the Center for Regulatory Effectiveness, funded mainly by tobacco interests, carried the ball in this game. The tobacco industry's role in getting the Data Quality Act passed was revealed in documents made public as part of the multi-state tobacco settlement. Notes from a meeting in May 1996 showed that Philip Morris executives agreed that "the acquisition of data is a major goal," that a position paper about data sharing was desirable, and that Philip Morris executives should coordinate the strategy for ensuring data disclosure (Untitled Document, 1996, p. 1).

James Tozzi, a key player in that "strategy," contacted John Spotila of the Office of Management and Budget urging OMB to develop data quality guidelines. Tozzi noted that his Center for Regulatory Effectiveness had posted a model data quality document on the Internet for public comment. "CRE will then prepare a summary of the comments reviewed by CRE's 'interactive public docket,' make revisions to the Model NPRM guidelines based on the comments, and transmit a revised comment to OMB and other concerned parties" (Tozzi, 2000, p. 2). Philip Morris and CRE exchanged several memoranda in which Philip Morris helped "fine-tune" the language of the model data quality law. Philip Morris transmitted its recommendations in the summer of 2000 and declared, "We believe Data Quality forms the basis for high-quality research, collaboration, the exchange of information, and constructive dialogue" (Walk, 2000, p. 1). Congress passed the Data Quality Act soon after that.

The Environmental Protection Agency managed to release its 1992 report on December 11, 2002, after the 4th Circuit Court of Appeals in Richmond, Virginia, threw out the tobacco industry's suit against the EPA. The industry, however, had—in large part because of its "sound science" initiative—delayed the full report for a decade.

Meanwhile, the tobacco industry opened a second front in the battle for new smokers following the $369 billion multi-state agreement. It has applied the aggressive tactics it used for years in the United States to the Third World. Third World journalists, for example, get free trips like one to Miami during which the British American Tobacco company "paid for the visitors' air fare, hotel rooms and even dinners at expensive restaurants. At meetings like this, the reporters, from countries including Brazil, Argentina, Chile and Peru, heard company officials and paid speakers attack restrictions on smoking and cigarette advertising as scientifically unsound or artifacts of lawsuit-driven societies like the United States'" (Meier, 1998, p. A14). British American Tobacco has long passed to foreign journalists data that seem to minimize the health risks of smoking. "To head off indoor smoking restrictions, large cigarette producers have also begun public relations campaigns abroad that recycle the same theme" (Meier, 1998, p. A14).

Summary

Professional obfuscators are firmly entrenched in many American industries and advocacy groups. James Tozzi, Steven Milloy, and the tobacco industry are not the only ones who try to undermine the scientific enterprise to benefit themselves, their supporters, and their industries. A few of the other organizations that try to undermine sound science are the Washington Legal Foundation, which attacks "junk science" and government regulations in courts across America; the Hudson Institute, an anti-environmental think tank that argues, among other things, that organic foods are not as safe as those grown using pesticides; the Competitive Enterprise Institute, which is backed by major oil companies and argues that there is no evidence for global warming; the Heartland Institute, which parrots the junk science line on Alar, dioxin, biotechnology, broadband technology, and the tobacco industry's position on secondhand smoke; the American Policy Center, which regularly attacks the Environmental Protection Agency; and The National Anxiety Center, which tries to counter the fears fostered by "lying" consumer advocates and environmentalists.

Professional obfuscators, like Conservative Christian activists, typically use a two-pronged attack to achieve their goals: (a) attack the opposition's legitimate scientific research and (b) pass off their own poor science as good science. The attacks and the poor science regularly appear in the news media—as "legitimate" news stories, editorials, columns, and opinion pieces written by partisans who have monetary interests in the topics about which they write. The conflicts of interest of the contributors to America's news media often are not reported.

CONCLUSIONS

Science is not the only lens through which one may view the world, but it is an important one, for natural and social science research is a critical foundation for many debates about political, cultural, social, economic, and scientific issues and problems. Criticism is essential to the scientific process, for the history of science offers numerous examples of scientists who manipulate data for personal or professional advantage, lie about results, make honest errors, and politicize their findings. One example is the study by Andrew Wakefield that linked MMR (measles, mumps, and rubella) vaccinations to autism. Wakefield's six-year campaign proclaiming his finding as fact "led to a diminution of MMR vaccination in the United Kingdom, as well as continued distrust of advances related to therapeutic interventions in children" (Ratzan, 2004, p. 279). The U.S. Institute of Medicine later rejected the finding that MMR vaccination caused autism, and the health community eventually discovered that Wakefield was paid $102,690 by the U.K.'s Legal Aid Board to study vaccine-damaged children for potential legal action.

Such cases are unfortunate, but science has established safeguards against abuse. The peer review system ensures that research and grant proposals are vetted by a researcher's colleagues, and vast numbers of studies never are published or funded. Science's insistence on the replication of research helps ensure that abuses ultimately are exposed. The scientific method, which establishes the rules of the game, is intended to ensure that a scientist's work is transparent to other researchers and to the public, and that the scientist follows procedures that have been validated in thousands of studies. Scientists are expected to follow the rules—and to explain their procedures publicly when they do not. Transparency is crucial because all scientists make strategic decisions (e.g., what questions to ask, what subjects to study, which variables to measure), and they must explain those decisions.

Science is an easy target for individuals and groups seeking only to protect religious, ideological, or monetary interests because (a) the uncertainty built into the scientific process is easily and effectively exploited, and (b) many people are easily swayed or confused by partisan attacks because they are not sufficiently literate about science to judge its merits.[17] It is easy for a partisan inquisitor to raise enough questions to make virtually any research seem weak. "By magnifying and exploiting these uncertainties, polluters and manufacturers of dangerous products have been remarkably successful in delaying, often for decades, regulations and other measures designed to protect the health and safety of individuals and communities" (Michaels & Monforton, 2005, p. S40). Conservative Christian activists have enjoyed similar success in their attacks against science.

Professional obfuscators and Conservative Christian activists typically do not condemn the whole of the scientific enterprise and its methods, as do many postmodernist critics. They reserve their attacks for research that threatens their own or their organizations' interests. Professional obfuscators and Conservative Christian activists also use their own "scientific" research to counter legitimate studies that report unacceptable findings (i.e., those that do not support partisan positions). This partisan research typically is misleading at best because sympathetic scientists are expected to identify (with help from their partisan benefactors) potential findings that support partisan goals and then to supply "scientific" data that support these findings. Legitimate scientists, who begin with a hypothesis and then follow the scientific method as they collect evidence relating to that hypothesis, reject this approach. They do not cherry-pick evidence that supports their position and discard evidence that does not.

Postmodernist critics typically attack the entire scientific enterprise, often using single cases to show that "modern science is nothing more than a 'myth,' a 'narration' or a 'social construction' among many others" (Sokal & Bricmont, 1998, p. x). Single cases (e.g., one film) may in fact be aberrations, but one cannot know because postmodernist scholars cannot, and do not feel required to, demonstrate that an isolated case is representative of anything. Postmodernists reject the idea that a researcher can use an objective approach, arguing instead that it is impossible for a researcher to be objective, a proposition that is true, but irrelevant, for there is a difference between personal objectivity (which is impossible to achieve) and an objective approach (which can be used effectively).[18] They rarely provide systematic evidence to support their views, for they would then be using a modernist approach.

Much of the postmodernist critique has had a positive impact on science, but some has had a negative impact. Thomas Kuhn (2000) notes, for example, that:

> Talk of evidence, of the rationality of claims drawn from it, and of the truth or probability of those claims has been seen as simply the rhetoric behind which the victorious party cloaks its power. What passes for scientific knowledge becomes, then, simply the belief of the winners. I am among those who have found the claims of the strong program [the constructivist approach] absurd: an example of deconstruction gone mad. (p. 110)

Professional obfuscators, Conservative Christian activists, and postmodernist critics have had a broad impact in the United States and Europe, particularly in education, science, law and regulation, and mass communication. The focus in the following section is on science and mainstream media.

Science and Mainstream Media

Mass communication is a crucial site for discussion of problems and issues in science, and it is widely criticized when it fails to report science accurately and in context. Part of this failure is rooted in the U.S. educational system. Most journalists, including science writers, attend the same colleges, universities, and public schools that other Americans do. Like other Americans, they can be and are confused by curricula that have been molded by the attacks of postmodernists, Conservative Christian activists, and professional obfuscators.

Noretta Koertge (1998) argues, for example, that the postmodernist critique is firmly entrenched in higher education, and that its rejection of an objective approach and its emphasis on constructs like epistemic charity have made it increasingly difficult for students to understand fundamental scientific concepts. Furthermore, "Postmodernist perceptions of science are rapidly diffusing out from the graduate humanities seminar into the K–12 science classroom," and "we have reason to be concerned about their impact on education" (Koertge, 1998, p. 260). College students, and now public school students, learn, for example, that, "Since allegedly there can be no compelling evidential basis for scientific claims, the discerning citizen needs to ask not whether the claim is well supported but, rather, whose political interests are served by such a claim" (Koertge, 1998, p. 266).

The postmodernists' attempt to politicize science is bolstered by professional obfuscators and Conservative Christian activists who, in trying to protect their own interests, argue frequently that some scientific research is politically motivated and should be ignored. College and public school students who are taught that (a) science must be viewed as a political process, or (b) partisan "science" (e.g., intelligent design) is equal to legitimate science (e.g., evolution) are not well served. In fact, the best way to test a scientific claim is to *ignore* its political, religious, or social implications and to evaluate the *procedure* followed in the research that supports that claim.

The science curriculum that reflects partisan attacks and ideas leads to confusion, and that makes it extremely difficult for students to develop science literacy, which can be defined as "the evolving skills and competencies needed to find, comprehend, evaluate, and use [science and] health information and concepts to make educated choices, reduce health risks, and improve quality of life." Nor can they easily learn "to apply [science and] health concepts and information to novel situations" (Zarcadoolas, Pleasant, & Greer, 2003, p. 119).

This confusion inevitably follows students into their careers as science writers. The situation is worse for journalists who are not science specialists, but who cover politicized science. This lack of knowledge is evident in coverage of the fight over evolution, in which journalists confer unwarranted credibility on intelligent design and present evolution and intelligent design as if scientific evidence supported the two equally. It does not (Mooney & Nisbit, 2005).

The situation gets worse. Many of the human sources on whom journalists rely for information also are products of public institutions whose science curricula have been shaped by partisans. One example is the "scientific expert," who is so important to legal and regulatory systems. Anyone can be an expert witness if all ways of knowing have equal weight—if the views of partisans and the scientifically illiterate are assigned the same credibility as those of scientific experts. Many "experts," though sincere and passionate about their causes, simply do not know what they're talking about.

Journalists also must cope with experts who are recruited to mislead or to confuse. Partisans frequently lure these individuals to testify before regulators, courts, and legislatures with offers of money (often presented as "grants") or prestigious positions. They are selected because their views are consistent with those of the partisans who recruit them. Such "expert witnesses" are not always scientists, are not specialists in the industries under study, and are not disinterested observers.[19]

The Clearinghouse on Environmental Advocacy and Research analyzed in 1997 the backgrounds of many experts listed in the Directory of Environmental Scientists and Economists, published by the National Center for Public Policy Research, an industry front group. The directory purported to list experts in 27 scientific fields. The Clearinghouse discovered that fewer than half of the experts in the directory were scientists and that only 51 of 141 held Ph.D. degrees in any field (Rampton & Stauber, 2001, p. 256).

This is not to suggest that journalists should ignore non-scientists or that non-scientists have no role in determining acceptable levels of risk or what the future should look like. "The real battleground [in risk assessment and acceptance] is about the plausibility of diverse visions of utopia and dystopia and about who can claim the authority (in terms of both morality and expertise) to produce a credible version of the future" (Kitzinger & Williams, 2005, p. 739). The decision must not be left to scientists and their corporate and government sponsors alone (e.g., Beck, 1992). The argument here is that journalists must know enough about science to recognize and ignore "experts" who are uninformed or who simply want to confuse policy makers through sham science and empty attacks against legitimate science. Many do not know nearly enough.

It is important for journalists to be literate about science because so many Americans rely on them for science news. A 2002 Gallup poll that explored Americans' sources for health news showed that 64 percent get a "great deal" or a "moderate amount" from television, followed by newspapers, 52 percent; magazines, 51 percent; and the Internet, 37 percent. Sixty-four percent expressed a "great deal" or a "moderate amount" of trust and confidence in newspapers, followed by magazines and the Internet, 62 percent each, and television, 59 percent (Institute of Medicine, 2004, p. 121).[20]

These audiences may be ill-served by the media, for hundreds of examples of poor science coverage suggest that many journalists are illiterate or confused about science. A study of the embryo stem cell debate in the United Kingdom, for example, showed that journalists "presented the debate as a strict binary opposition with little room for ambivalence or 'cautious optimism....' The oppositional way in which the news media frame issues as two-sided controversies does not help to break through binary oppositions and may exclude people who fail to offer up 'black' or 'white' positions" (Kitzinger & Williams, 2005, p. 739). Journalists typically were unwilling to question such key terms as "hope" and "potential," and their lack of knowledge affected the types of questions they asked. Journalists failed for the most part to question potential health risks, women's views about being the sources of embryos, financial aspects of this research, and scientists' assertions.

Another example is coverage of the "deadly" broken heart syndrome. The media reported in mid-February, 2005, that "sudden stress—from, say, the shock of a surprise party or the death of a loved one—can cause a surge of adrenaline that can, essentially, poison the heart muscle and cause something that resembles a heart attack" (Skloot, 2005, p. 48). The media were crammed with frightening statements about the Johns Hopkins University study: "The syndrome is more common than doctors realize," "you can die of a broken heart," "there is no way to tell who is at risk," and "sudden stress breaks hearts." In fact, "There was no broken-heart study. There was a 'small observational case series,' which is basically a group of scientists saying, Here's something we noticed that warrants investigation" (Skloot, 2005, p. 50). Researchers studied only 19 of thousands of Baltimore patients who experienced sudden stress. Similar media "freak-outs" have occurred with West Nile virus, mad cow disease, hanta virus, and many other "deadly" health threats.

Jared Diamond (2005), who demonstrates forcefully that societies make decisions that can cause them to fail, notes that, "[H]uman societies and smaller groups may make disastrous decisions for a whole sequence of reasons: failure to anticipate a problem, failure to perceive it once it has arisen, failure to attempt to solve it after it has been perceived, and failure to succeed in attempts to solve it" (p. 438). Science is particularly useful as it helps societies anticipate and perceive problems, but only if the scientific enterprise is credible, and only if the public and its leaders are scientifically literate. Thoughtful critiques of individual research studies do not undermine science and are in fact useful. But the three groups analyzed here—postmodernists, Conservative Christian activists, and professional obfuscators—have fought a kind of guerrilla war against all studies, even good ones, that threaten partisan goals, and they have, together, challenged the entire scientific enterprise. The attacks, cumulatively, have undermined science's credibility and its efforts to educate the public about science issues—and this hinders society's efforts to anticipate and to avoid catastrophe.

NOTES

1. Gergen (2001) argued further that "one should not mistake the form of the constructionist arguments for their function. The attempt in these arguments is not to generate yet another first philosophy or foundation to replace all that has preceded—for example, to put logical empiricism to death. To construe the proposals in this way would be to give them a modernist reading" (p. 807).
2. For the postmodernist, "the truth of a story does not lie in *the facts*, but in the meaning. If people believe a story, if the story has a grip over them, whether events that it describes actually happened or not is irrelevant" (Gabriel, 1998, p. 85). For the modernist (journalists, scientists, and other chroniclers), accurate facts are critical. The former treats facts in a cavalier manner, while the latter "treats his/her material with the respect of an archaeologist, wishing to discover, preserve and display valuable objects, his/her own pride lying in his/her claim not to have tampered with the material" (p. 101). The distinction is important, but many critics reject it.
3. Modernists assume an objective reality that can be observed. Postmodernists argue that there is no evidence for that assumption (Gergen, 2001).
4. Beck (1992) argued that the only way to establish a level of safety is to use the real world as a laboratory: Establish the "acceptable level" of poisoning (e.g., .0001 parts per million is safe) and then measure the effects of the poisoning on real people. He was concerned that real people often are excluded from the process of establishing acceptable levels. They are not given the opportunity to consider "the not totally absurd premise of *not* poisoning *at all*" (p. 65).
5. For instance, "Western psychologists can unproblematically study the emotion of anger . . . because they have a long tradition of indexing people's actions in this way. However, they would be ill equipped to commence research on *Atman*, *liget*, or *fago* because these terms from other cultures are generally unintelligible to Western speakers" (Gergen, 2001, p. 806).
6. Postmodernist scholars often frame their critiques in ways that allow them to topple their strawpersons easily. Few social or natural scientists would argue with postmodernists that personal objectivity is impossible. They would, however, argue that it is possible and useful to follow an objective approach, which sets out standards that, when followed carefully, minimize many of the postmodernists' criticisms (Ryan, 2001). Recognition of this critical distinction would substantially weaken this aspect of the postmodernist critique of science.
7. For a scientist's critique of this view, please see Philip Sullivan (1998).
8. Critiques of feminist epistemology by Noretta Koertge (1996a) and Janet Richards (1996) reflected the views of many scientists toward their approach. Robin Usher and Richard Edwards (1994) noted that postmodernists and feminists agree about many issues, but that the alliance between them is uneasy, in part because (a) many feminists do not endorse a radical challenge to modernism, and (b) "feminism is itself located in the legacy of the Enlightenment tradition; the latter's emancipatory impulse nurtures the roots both of eighteenth- and nineteenth-century feminism and Marxism" (p. 20).
9. Science does not "validate" claims. Susan Haack (1996) argued that an inquiry that makes a case for a proposition identified in advance is a sham and a fake. "So they are motivated to avoid careful examination of any evidence that might impugn the proposition for which they are seeking to make a case, to play down or obfuscate the importance or relevance of such evidence, to contort themselves explaining it away" (p. 58).
10. Meera Nanda (2003) suggested in her analysis of India that the view that all ways of knowing are equal reflects the fascist claims of Hindu fundamentalists in India.
11. Their five *literal* truths were: The Bible was God's inerrant, infallible word; Jesus was born of a virgin; his death was the sacrifice made by Jesus for humanity's sins; Jesus rose physically from the dead and would eventually return; and God intervened in the world through what humans call miracles (such as the "virgin birth" and Jesus' resurrection). "Biblical law" *was* "natural law," in their view, and fundamentalism was a rational response to modernity (Ryan & Switzer, in press).
12. Premodern refers to a nostalgic view of and a searching for the past. Premodernists reject the isolation, alienation, and frustration that they say have resulted from the modern's emphasis on rationality and objectivity.

13. The Data Quality Act was preceded by the Data Access Amendment of 1999, which "provides affected parties with access to all of the raw data underlying published studies produced with federal support so that they can review and even reanalyze the data in the course of their scientific assessment" (Wagner, 2005, p. S100).
14. Professional obfuscators were fighting on the legal front even as they were attacking research that did not support their positions and offering their own bad science to counter good science. They won a victory of sorts in 1993 when the U.S. Supreme Court ruled in *Daubert v. Merrell Dow Pharmaceuticals Inc.* that federal judges must be "gatekeepers" of science; that is, judges were to decide what scientific testimony was relevant and reliable (Michaels & Monforton, 2005, p. S44). The problem was that few judges were knowledgeable about science and were not prepared to cope with the complexity and sheer bulk of scientific findings that litigants wanted to present in their courtrooms (Gatowski, et al., 2001). Federal judges have struggled with this responsibility for more than a decade.
15. The executive acknowledged the limits of the "doubt" campaign: "Doubt is also the limit of our 'product'. Unfortunately, we cannot take a position directly opposing the anti-cigarette forces and say that cigarettes are a contributor to good health. No information that we have supports such a claim" ("Smoking and Health," 1969, pp. 4–5).
16. The national and state campaign for tort reform was another part of the tobacco industry's attempt to protect its profits. Executives knew the industry could not afford to lose many judgments that they considered unreasonably large.
17. A study by the National Science Board (2004) suggested that many Americans and Europeans do not understand science fundamentals or how science works. The study showed "minimal gains over time in the public's knowledge of science and the scientific method and [suggested] that belief in astrology and other forms of pseudoscience is widespread and growing" (p. 7:5). Other researchers concluded that roughly 10 percent of U. S. adults "were well informed, or civic scientifically literate. This finding raises serious questions about the ability of citizens to comprehend the arguments in major scientific controversies..." (Miller, Pardo, & Niwa, 1997, p. 109).
18. Scientists and others who use an objective approach "report information that is complete, precise, balanced, and accurate; view powerful authorities and institutions with skepticism; consider new evidence and alternative interpretations; serve no religious, economic, social, or political agenda; attend to the views of the marginalized; try to be fair, disinterested, and impartial; recognize their own predispositions and not allow those predispositions to determine outcomes; use creativity in the search for facts and opinions that don't conform to the dominant narrative; and share all information freely.... Strategic decisions, critical analyses, and interpretations are based on professional norms, and not on personal values or emotion" (Ryan, 2001).
19. Holcomb Noble (1999) recounted the case of C. Edward Koop, the former U.S. Surgeon General, who urged Congress in 1999 to permit Schering-Plough Corporation to extend by five years its patent on the popular allergy drug Claritin. Schering-Plough stood to earn an additional $6 billion in sales by keeping the drug under its own patent. Koop did not think it necessary to tell Congress that the pharmaceutical giant had given his nonprofit Koop Foundation $1 million earlier that same year (p. A20).
20. Television, with its emphasis on conflict, gives considerable time to science's critics and typically leads viewers to think that partisan science and legitimate science are of equal value and should carry equal weight. Further, superficial television coverage has no time to fill the gaps in viewers' knowledge of science.

REFERENCES

The Advancement of Sound Science Coalition (1993, December 3). National watchdog organization launched to fight unsound science used for public policy comes to Texas, news release. Retrieved October 10, 2005, from http://www.tobaccodocuments.org/pm/2046988980-8982.html.

Ammerman, N. T. (1991). North American Protestant fundamentalism. In M. E. Marty & R. S. Appleby (Eds.), *Fundamentalisms observed* (pp. 1–65). Chicago: University of Chicago Press.

The art of obfuscation (2005, July 30). *St. Louis Post-Dispatch*, p. 30.

Beck, U. (1992). *Risk society: Towards a new modernity* (M. Ritter, Trans.). London: Sage.

Behe, M. J. (1996, August 10). Evidence for intelligent design from biochemistry. Speech delivered to the God and Culture Conference, Discovery Institute, Seattle, Washington. Speech retrieved October 2, 2005, from http://www.arn.org/docs/behe/mb_idfrombiochemistry.htm.

Bellah, R. N. (1973). American civil religion in the 1970's. *Anglican Theological Review*, *55*(1), 8–20.

Bellah, R. N. (1967). Civil religion in America. *Daedalus, 96*(1), 1–21.

Berger, P. & Luckman, T. (1967). *The social construction of reality: A treatise in the sociology of knowledge.* London: Routledge and Kegan Paul.

Bloland, H. G. (2005). Whatever happened to postmodernism in higher education? No requiem in the new millennium. *The Journal of Higher Education*, *76*(2), 121–150.

Bloor, D. (1976). *Knowledge and social imagery*. London: Routledge & Kegan Paul.

Bourne, J. K. Jr. (2004, October). Gone with the water. *National Geographic, 206*, 88–105.

Clough, P. T. (1993). On the brink of deconstructing sociology: Critical reading of Dorothy Smith's standpoint epistemology. *Sociological Quarterly*, *34*(1), 169–182.

Derrida, J. (1976). *Of Grammatology*. (G. C. Spivak, Trans.). Baltimore: Johns Hopkins University Press.

Diamond, J. (2005). *Collapse: How societies choose to fail or succeed.* New York: Viking.

Dinges, W. D., & Hitchcock, J. (1991). Roman Catholic traditionalism and activist conservatism in the United States. In M. E. Marty & R. S. Appleby (Eds.), *Fundamentalisms observed* (pp. 66–141). Chicago: University of Chicago Press.

Drury, S. B. (2004). *Terror and civilization: Christianity, politics, and the Western psyche*. New York: Palgrave Macmillan.

Durham, M.G. (1998). On the relevance of standpoint epistemology to the practice of journalism: The case for "strong objectivity." *Communication Theory*, *8*(2), 117–140.

Environmental Protection Agency (1992). *Respiratory health effects of passive smoking: Lung cancer and other disorders*. Washington, D.C.: Office of Research and Development, Office of Health and Environmental Assessment.

Foucault, M. (1972). *The archaeology of knowledge* (A. M. S. Smith, Trans.). New York: Harper & Row.

Fritsch, J. (1996, March 19). Sometimes, lobbyists strive to keep public in the dark. *The New York Times*, pp. A1, A20.

Fuller, C. L. (1994, March 17). February monthly report. Philip Morris memorandum to M. A. Miles from C. L. Fuller. Retrieved October 10, 2005, from http://www.tobaccodocuments.org/pm/2041424310-4316.html.

Gabriel, Y. (1998). Same old story or changing stories? Folkloric, modern and postmodern mutations. In D. Grant, T. Keenoy, & C. Oswick (Eds.), *Discourse and organization* (pp. 84–103). London: Sage.

Garroutte, E. M. (2003). The positivist attack on Baconian science and religious knowledge in the 1870s. In C. Smith (Ed.), *The secular revolution: Power, interests, and conflict in the secularization of American public life* (pp. 197–215). Berkeley: University of California Press.

Gatowski, S. I., Dobbin, S. A., Richardson, J. T., Ginsburg, G. P., Merlino, M. L., & Dahir, V. (2001). Asking the gatekeepers: A national survey of judges on judging expert evidence in a post-*Daubert* world. *Journal of Law and Human Behavior, 25*(5), 433–458.

Gellner, E. (1992). *Postmodernism, reason and religion*. London: Routledge.

Gergen, K. J. (2001). Psychological science in a postmodern context. *American Psychologist, 56*(10), 803–813.

Haack, S. (1996). Concern for truth: What it means, why it matters. In P. R. Gross, N. Levitt, & M. W. Lewis (Eds.), *The flight from science and reason* (pp. 57–63). New York: New York Academy of Sciences.

Han, V. (1993, February 22). Internal Philip Morris memorandum to E. Merlo. Document number 2023920035. Retrieved October 10, 2005, from http:/www.tobaccodocuments.org/pm/2023920035-0040.html.

Haraway, D. (1988). Situated knowledges: The science question in feminism and the privilege of partial perspective. *Feminist Studies*, *14*(3), 575–599.

Harding, S. (1993). Rethinking standpoint epistemology: What is "strong objectivity"? In L. Alcoff & E. Potter (Eds.), *Feminist epistemologies* (pp. 49–82). New York: Routledge.

Harding, S. (1997). Women's standpoints on nature: What makes them possible? In S. G. Kohlstedt & H. Longino (Eds.), *Women, gender, and science: New directions* (pp. 186–200). Chicago: Osiris, University of Chicago Press.

Hart, R. P. (1977). *The political pulpit*. West Lafayette, IN: Purdue University Press.

Hartsock, N. C. M. (1983). The feminist standpoint: Developing the ground for a specifically feminist historical materialism. In S. Harding & M. B. Hintikka (Eds.), *Discovering reality: Feminist perspectives on epistemology, metaphysics, methodology, and philosophy of science* (pp. 283–310). Dordrecht, Holland: D. Reidel.

Hayles, N. K. (1992). Gender encoding in fluid mechanics: Masculine channels and feminine flows. *Differences: A Journal of Feminist Cultural Studies, 4*(2), 16–44.

Hekman, S. (1997). Truth and method: Feminist standpoint theory revisited. *Signs: Journal of Women in Culture and Society*, *22*(2), 341–365.

Institute of Medicine (2004). *Health literacy: A prescription to end confusion*. Washington, DC: The National Academies Press.

Irigaray, L. (1985). *This sex which is not one*. (C. Porter & C. Burke, Trans.). Ithaca, NY: Cornell University Press, chapter 6.

Jansen, S. C. (1993). "The future is not what it used to be": Gender, history, and communication studies. *Communication Theory*, *3*(2), 136–148.

Kaplan, E. (2004). *With God on their side: How Christian fundamentalists trampled science, policy, and democracy in George W. Bush's White House*. New York: The New Press.
Kintz, L. (1998). Culture and the religious right. In L. Kintz & J. Lesage (Eds.), *Media, culture, and the religious right* (pp. 3–20). Minneapolis: University of Minnesota Press.
Kitzinger, J., & Williams, C. (2005). Forecasting science futures: Legitimising hope and calming fears in the embryo stem cell debate. *Social Science & Medicine, 61*(3), 731–740.
Koertge, N. (1996a). Feminist epistemology: Stalking an un-dead horse. In P. R. Gross, N. Levitt, & M. W. Lewis (Eds.), *The flight from science and reason* (pp. 413–419). New York: New York Academy of Sciences.
Koertge, N. (1998). Postmodernisms and the problem of scientific literacy. In N. Koertge (Ed.), *A house built on sand: Exposing postmodernist myths about science* (pp. 257–271). New York: Oxford University Press.
Koertge, N. (1996b). Wrestling with the social constructor. In P. R. Gross, N. Levitt, & M. W. Lewis (Eds.), *The flight from science and reason* (pp. 266–273). New York: New York Academy of Sciences.
Kraus, M. (1993, September 23). Memorandum to V. Han of Philip Morris. Retrieved October 10, 2005, from http://www/at tobaccodocuments.org/pm/2024233677-3682.html.
Kuhn, T. S. (2000). *The road since Structure*. Chicago: University of Chicago Press.
Latour, B. (1987). *Science in action: How to follow scientists and engineers through society*. Cambridge, MA: Harvard University Press.
Latour, B., & Woolgar, S. (1986). *Laboratory life: The construction of scientific facts*. Princeton, NJ: Princeton University Press.
Lee, J. (2003, June 18). Popular pesticide faulted for frogs' sexual abnormalities. *The New York Times*, p. A20.
Lloyd, E. A. (1993). Pre-theoretical assumptions in evolutionary explanations of female sexuality. *Philosophical Studies, 69*(2, 3), 139–153.
Longino, H. E. (1990). *Science as social knowledge: Values and objectivity in scientific inquiry*. Princeton, NJ: Princeton University Press.
Lyotard, J. F. (1984). *The postmodern condition: A report on knowledge*. (G. Bennington & B. Massumi, Trans.). Minneapolis: University of Minnesota Press.
Marglin, F. A. (1990). Smallpox in two systems of knowledge. In F. A. Marglin & S. A. Marglin (Eds.), *Dominating knowledge: Development, culture, and resistance* (pp. 102–144). Oxford, England: Clarendon.
Marglin, S. A. (1990). Losing touch: The cultural conditions of worker accommodation and resistance. In F. A. Marglin & S. A. Marglin (Eds.), *Dominating knowledge: Development, culture, and resistance* (pp. 217–282). Oxford, England: Clarendon.
Meier, B. (1998, January 18). Tobacco industry, conciliatory in U.S., goes on the attack in the Third World. *The New York Times*, p. A14.
Memorandum Opinion (2005, December 20). *Tammy Kitzmiller v. Dover Area School District*, U.S. District Court, Middle District of Pennsylvania. Retrieved February 6, 2006, from http://www.news.findlaw.com/hdocs/docs/educate/ktzmllrdvr122005opn.pdf.
Michaels, D., & Monforton, C. (2005). Manufacturing uncertainty: Contested science and the protection of the public's health and environment. *American Journal of Public Health, 95*(Suppl. 1), S39–S48.
Miller, J. D., Pardo, R., & Niwa, F. (1997). *Public perceptions of science and technology: A comparative study of the European Union, the United States, Japan, and Canada*. Bilbao, Spain: Fundacion BBV.
Milloy, S. (1999, October 6). Modified crops cause concern: European fears have little impact here. *Chicago Sun-Times*, p. 64.
Mooney, C., & Nisbit, M.C. (2005, September/October). Undoing Darwin: When the coverage of evolution shifts to the political and opinion pages, the scientific context falls away. *Columbia Journalism Review, 44*, 30–39.
Mooney, C. (2004, May). Paralysis by analysis: Jim Tozzi's regulation to end all regulation. *The Washington Monthly, 36*, 23–25.
Muggli, M. E., Hurt, R. D., & Repace, J. (2004). The tobacco industry's political efforts to derail the EPA report on ETS. *American Journal of Preventive Medicine, 26*(2), 167–177.
Nanda, M. (1998). The epistemic charity of the social constructivist critics of science and why the Third World should refuse the offer. In N. Koertge (Ed.), *A house built on sand: Exposing postmodernist myths about science* (pp. 286– 311). New York: Oxford University Press.
Nanda, M. (2003). *Prophets facing backward: Postmodern critiques of science and Hindu nationalism in India*. New Brunswick, NJ: Rutgers University Press.
National Science Board. (2004). Science and technology: Public attitudes and understanding. In *Science and engineering indicators 2004* (pp. 7:1–7:37). Arlington, VA: Author. Retrieved October 18, 2005, from http://www.nsf.gov/statistics/seind04/c7/c7h.htm.
Noble, H. B. (1999, September 5). Hailed as a surgeon general, Koop is faulted on web ethics. *The New York Times*, pp. A1, A20.

Parsons, C. (1995). The impact of postmodernism on research methodology: Implications for nursing. *Nursing Inquiry, 2*(1), 22– 28.

Potter, W. J., Cooper, R., & Dupagne, M. (1993). The three paradigms of mass media research in mainstream communication journals. *Communication Theory, 3*(4), 317–335.

Powell, M. (2004, December 26). Evolution shares a desk with "intelligent design." *The Washington Post*, pp. A1, A20, A21.

Rampton, S., & Stauber, J. (2001). *Trust us, we're experts*. New York: Jeremy P. Tarcher.

Ratzan, S. C. (2004). Truth and health consequences. *Journal of Health Communication*, *9*(4), 279–280.

Restoring scientific integrity in policymaking (2004, February 18). Union of Concerned Scientists. Letter to George W. Bush. Retrieved October 10, 2005, from http://www.ucsusa.org/global_environment/rsi/page.cfm?pageID=1320.

Richards, J. R. (1996). Why feminist epistemology isn't. In P. R. Gross, N. Levitt, & M. W. Lewis (Eds.), *The flight from science and reason* (pp. 385–412). New York: New York Academy of Sciences.

Ross, A. (1996). Introduction. *Social Text, 14*(1, 2), 1–13.

Ryan, M. (2001). Journalistic ethics, objectivity, existential journalism, standpoint epistemology, and public journalism. *Journal of Mass Media Ethics, 16*(1), 3–22.

Ryan, M., & Switzer, L. (in press). Mirror on a war agenda: Conservative Christian activists and media coverage of the invasion of Iraq. In D. O'Hair, R. Heath, K. J. Ayotte, & G. Ledlow (Eds.), *Terrorism: Communication and rhetorical perspectives*. Cresskill, NJ: Hampton.

Sandel, M. J. (1982). *Liberalism and the limits of justice*. Cambridge, England: Cambridge University Press.

Skloot, R. (2005, June). Hype that breaks your heart. *Popular Science*, *266*, 48, 50.

Sokal, A., & Bricmont, J. (1998). *Fashionable nonsense: Postmodern intellectuals' abuse of science*. New York: Picador USA.

Smoking and Health Proposal (1969). Internal Brown & Williamson memorandum, number 0000332506. Retrieved October 10, 2005, from http://www.tobaccodocuments.org/bw/332506.html.

Sullivan, P. A. (1998). An engineer dissects two case studies: Hayles on fluid mechanics, and MacKenzie on statistics. In N. Koertge (Ed.), *A house built on sand: Exposing postmodernist myths about science* (pp. 71–98). New York: Oxford University Press.

Tozzi, J. (2000, January 17). Memorandum to J. T. Spotila of the Office of Management and Budget. Retrieved October 10, 2005, from http://www.tobaccodocuments.org/pm/2072826846-6848.html.

Untitled Document (1996, May 14). Philip Morris. Retrieved October 10, 2005, from http://www.tobaccodocuments.org/pm/2064229275-9276.html..

Usher, R., & Edwards, R. (1994). *Postmodernism and education*. London: Routledge.

U. S. Office of Management and Budget (2002, January 3). *Guidelines for ensuring and maximizing the quality, objectivity, utility, and integrity of information disseminated by federal agencies*. Washington, DC: Author. Retrieved on October 12, 2005, from http:// www.whitehouse.gov/omb/fedreg/reproducible.html.

Wagner, W. (2005). The perils of relying on interested parties to evaluate scientific quality. *American Journal of Public Health, 95*(Suppl. 1), S99–S106.

Walk, R. A. (2000, June 26). Comments by Philip Morris USA worldwide scientific affairs on CRE proposed draft quality regulation. Retrieved October 10, 2005, from http://www.tobaccodocuments.org/pm/2078738342A-8343.html.

Walsh, B., Alpert, B., & McQuaid, J. (2005, August 31). Feds' disaster planning shifts away from preparedness. Newhouse News Service. Retrieved October 26, 2005, from http://www.nola.com/hurricane/t-p/katrina.ssf?/hurricane/katrina/stories/html/DISASTERPLAN31.html.

Weiss, R. (2004, August 16). A policy puts science on trial: "Data Quality" law is nemesis of regulation. *The Washington Post*, pp. A1, A6, A7.

Weigel, G. (2004, May). World order: What Catholics forgot. *First Things, 143,* 31–38.

Wilson, D. S. (2002). *Darwin's cathedral: Evolution, religion, and the nature of society*. Chicago: University of Chicago Press.

Zarcadoolas, C., Pleasant, A., & Greer, D. S. (2003). Elaborating a definition of health literacy: A commentary. *Journal of Health Communication*, *8*(Suppl. 1), 119–120.

Zehr, S. C. (1999). Scientists' representations of uncertainty. In S. M. Friedman, S. Dunwoody, & C. L. Rogers (Eds.), *Communicating uncertainty: Media coverage of new and controversial science* (pp. 3–21). Mahwah, NJ: Erlbaum.

13

Influence Theories: Rhetorical, Persuasion, and Informational

Jeffrey K. Springston
University of Georgia

Elizabeth Johnson Avery
University of Tennessee–Knoxville

Lynne M. Sallot
University of Georgia

> Security is mostly a superstition. It does not exist in nature, nor do the children of men as a whole experience it. Avoiding danger is no safer in the long run than outright exposure. Life is either a daring adventure or nothing.
>
> Helen Keller (1957, p. 28)

Indeed, life can be a dangerous proposition. As individuals we all face risks every day, as do the groups, organizations, and institutions we belong to and interact with. And on occasion those risks to individuals, groups, organizations, and institutions can develop into crises. Heath (2006) defined risk as "an occurrence that can have positive or negative consequences of varying magnitudes, the occurrence of which and the effects of which can be variously predicted, controlled, and harmful or beneficial. In this context, a crisis is a risk manifested" (p. 245).

According to Bostrom (2003), most risk communication practice and the majority of risk communication research studies have come out of two camps. The first are those that come from an *advocacy* position. Public health advocacy, often referred to as social marketing, is an example of an area where the grounds and motives of research, theory building, and interventions focus on advocating the reduction of risk. The second camp is what Bostrom termed *informed consent*. Here the focus is on providing valid and reliable information but not advocating for a specific position. Bostrom rightly pointed out that there are many connections in the theories that inform both camps. Much of the research on crisis communication has focused on best practices in negotiating the public relations implications of the crisis, usually from the organizational perspective.

One of the fundamental tenets of communication theory is the need to understand one's audience. Without insight into an audience's knowledge, attitudes, and beliefs, effective communication becomes much more difficult. This chapter explores some of the important rhetorical and social scientific theories and models available to facilitate understanding of the role of influence in risk and crisis environments. Some useful theories and models, such as the extended parallel process model (see chapter 14), the theory of image restoration (see chapter 5), and the mental models approach (see chapter 24), are covered elsewhere in this handbook. This chapter focuses on other important theories not covered in depth elsewhere.

RHETORIC AND INFLUENCE

Rhetoric *is* influence. Human action is contingent on knowing; we are finite and temporally constrained yet confronted with decisions that define the future. Often, available evidence to make the decisions is vague, leaving us to act in the face of uncertainty. Ultimately, humans make choices and are influenced; they are persuaded to act or not act, and they are persuaded how to act. Rhetoric occupies this sphere between reality and ideality, the disparity between what is reality and what we wish it to be. Rhetoric exists because humans are symbol-using creatures with the capacity to change.

Campbell and Burkholder (1997) acknowledged that one of the most plaguing aspects of rhetorical theory is the quest to understand the human capacity of, and vulnerability to, persuasion. They noted three explanations for human persuasibility, the first and most pervasive of which "locates the source of influence in argument and claims that humans are open to persuasion because they are beings capable of conceptualizing options and of exploring competing justifications as well as the implications and consequences of different courses of action" (p. 7). Thus, persuasive discourse presents options, the coherence and consistency of which are examined by humans who select a course of action based on a given rationale. The processes of choice and deliberation are central to all theories of influence; however, rhetorical theory departs from other theories of influence as it does not recognize verifiable answers to its central questions (Campbell & Burkholder, 1997).

Inasmuch rhetoric is influence, rhetorical theory gives us tools to understand this influence and, ultimately, persuasive communication. Yet, given the innate connection of rhetoric and persuasion, rhetoric is regarded with suspicion (Herrick, 2001) and sometimes as unethical (Heath, 2000); rhetoric has even been judged as "the harlot of the arts" (Burgess, 1973). Yet, rhetoric is quite salient to our understanding and analysis of risk and crisis and the discourse that surrounds such situations as we as practitioners, scholars, or members of a public make prescriptions for appropriate courses of action. The organization must persuade its stakeholders amidst crisis, be it to repair reputation and public confidence in its services, as was the case with Exxon and Tylenol, or to follow advisories for public safety, such as reporting suspicious white substances during the post 9/11 Anthrax alerts. Thus, placed in that very sphere in which rhetoric exists, that discrepancy between what is reality, which is so far from ideality in a crisis situation, crisis communication scholarship cannot neglect rhetorical theories of influence.

In crisis, the greatest disparity between reality and ideality exists, and those involved must make decisions under conditions of heightened uncertainty. Such imposes additional ethical considerations on the crisis communicator utilizing theories of influence; in the interest of quelling uncertainty she or he cannot mislead the public. Further, the organization must disclose all information that affects public safety whether or not that discourse is desirable for the reputation of the organization. Ethical responsibilities imposed on crisis and risk communicators are further discussed in chapter 17 of this handbook.

A review of scholarly literature reveals a burgeoning number of articles using rhetorical theory to analyze the crisis situation, such as apologia discourse (Marsh, 2006; Rowland & Jerome, 2004; Hearit & Brown, 2004), epideictic discourse (Huxman, 2004), constitutive approach studies (Stokes, 2005), and narrative theory (Heath, 2004; see also Palmlund, chapter 9 of this volume). To understand and utilize more contemporary rhetorical theory, however, the risk and crisis scholar must be well-versed in the earliest theorizing on rhetoric and the influence of Aristotle.

ARISTOTLE AND RHETORIC

Aristotle (trans. in 1991) gave us a vocabulary for talking about the available means of persuasion and defines rhetoric as "an ability, in each particular case, to see the available means of persuasion" (p. 36). In his classic book *On Rhetoric,* Aristotle identified three basic "pisteis," or means of persuasion—ethos, logos, and pathos. The first proof of persuasion, *ethos*, is based on the character and credibility of the speaker and is contingent on the evaluation of his or her reasoning and trustworthiness. *Logos* is the perceived truth or probability of arguments based on use of logical and rational evidence, and *Pathos* refers to the emotional appeals used by the speaker.

These three proofs emerge in three species, or genres, of rhetoric recognized by Aristotle—epideictic, forensic, and deliberative. A speaker, subject, and audience are present in each rhetorical situation; the audience participates in the capacity of judge or spectator depending on the nature of the discourse. A *deliberative* speech calls an audience to judge a future action and demonstrates the harm or benefit in engaging in that action. The audience evaluates past action based on available evidence in a *forensic* speech, which demonstrates the positive or negative aspects of what has been done or the truth or falsity of a claim. Finally, *epideictic* speeches, which are value-laden, do not invite the audience to make judgments but instead place praise or blame on someone or something while reminding the audience of the past and projecting the future.

Johnson and Sellnow (1995) employed Aristotle's conceptual framework of available means—and types—of persuasion to analyze Exxon President W. D. Stevens' speech following his company's 1989 oil spill crisis. Johnson and Sellnow (1995) argued crisis response is a two-step process, an assessment of the causes of the crisis—often using forensic discourse—followed by deliberative discourse, which utilizes coping mechanisms for the current crisis situation as well as avoidance measures for future crises. Throughout this process, epideictic rhetoric to improve the organization's reputation, a discourse of praise, is best when used throughout both steps, as character and policy of the organization are entwined in its defense (Johnson & Sellnow, 1995).

In their analysis of Stevens' speech, Johnson and Sellnow (1995) noted that "organizations that fail to enter the deliberative stage of their crisis response with an idea of what policies they desire to see adopted or rejected miss an opportunity to influence their future" (p. 59). Thus, crisis communication must not rely purely on forensic discourse. Although accountability and identification of responsibility are critical forensic elements of crisis rhetoric, a more involved and politicized society demands consistent effort on behalf of the organization or entity amidst crisis to strategically manage issues with an eye on the future (Johnson & Sellnow, 1995). Clearly, Aristotle's genres may lend crisis and risk communication scholarship a vital framework from which to analyze the crisis situation to learn from the past and inform the future.

In the two-step process in crisis response discourse posited by Johnson and Sellnow (1995), the first entails an assessment of causes leading to the crisis, or forensic discourse. NASA blamed the *Challenger* disaster on a failed O ring. Exxon blamed the oil spill on human error. Tylenol revealed that its product contamination was the result of human tampering. Post 9/11 an "us" v. "them" frame was quickly created by President Bush establishing Al Qaida as the enemy. Amidst every crisis, the public is oft reminded of the cause of the situation, typically through forensic elements in organizational discourse. For virtually all crisis types, it is generally in this first stage in the discourse, recognized by Johnson and Sellnow (1995), that the organization designates responsibility. It is in this stage of crisis rhetoric—designation of responsibility—that Kenneth Burke's dramatistic theory may be particularly useful to crisis and risk communication research.

"What is involved, when we say what people are doing and why they are doing it?" (Burke, 1945, p. xv). So opens Kenneth Burke's (1945) classic *A Grammar of Motives*, and the answer to that question is the focus of his book. Burke (1945) developed a vocabulary for analyzing a rhetorical act in order to understand its meaning. Burke's dramatistic approach assumes language does not simply represent reality; language *is* reality. Language is both to act and to convey information. Dramatism enables scholars to analyze the realities lived by different rhetors (Burgchardt, 2000);

thus, dramatistic analysis of crisis rhetoric may reveal the lived realities of rhetors amidst various crisis types and inform future responses.

As Burgchardt (2000) acknowledged, "the most concrete and describable feature of dramatism is the pentad" (p. 207). Burke's pentad has five constituent elements—act, scene, agent, agency, and purpose—that can be used to analyze the rhetorical situation as a mean of understanding human motivation. In Burke's conceptualization of the five elements, the *act* is what transpired, the *scene* is the setting of the act, the *agent* is the person or kind of person responsible for the act, the *agency* is the instrument used to perform the act, and the *purpose* is why that act was carried out. Although people may rarely agree on the purpose or other elements of the pentad with regard to a given act, inevitably discussion of motives, as Burke (1945) pointed out, will entail answers to "what was done (act), when or where it was done (scene), who did it (agent), how he did it (agency), and why (purpose)" (p. xv). For example, Burke's pentad may be used to analyze the classic crisis communication case study of the 1989 *Exxon Valdez* oil spill in Prince William Sound. The discourse surrounding the disaster revealed that an oil spill (act) occurred in Prince William Sound (scene) as a result of the captain and crew (agents) misguiding the ship (agency) into a reef clearly indicated on maps as a result of negligence (purpose).

Given that language is a selection and de-selection of the elements of a rhetor's reality, motivations of the speaker are revealed by analysis of the use and prioritization of the five pentadic elements, explaining why Burke called the system a "grammar of motives" (Campbell & Burkholder, 1997). Burke's pentad can be used to reveal the way an organization and its publics perceive and create a reality contingent on which elements or parts of the pentad are privileged in its crisis rhetoric. Exxon President Stevens' response to the disastrous oil spill opens with the issue of human error and establishes the ship's captain, Joseph Hazelwood, as the primary target of blame; Stevens insisted that "Hazelwood's appointment should not detract from Exxon's character, but, rather, should be viewed as unfortunate and inevitable consequence of delegating responsibility to employees" (Johnson & Sellnow, 1995, p. 57).

The rhetoric used to describe a crisis situation illustrates the organization's perspective on the situation and possible courses of future action (Ihlen, 2002), creating the reality surrounding the crisis. The initial reality created in Stevens' rhetoric was not one of corporate responsibility or rectification but instead one prioritizing the agent, who, in this case, was the cause of the disaster. The problem crafted was not one that regulations or restrictions on oil transportation could address; the *agent*, the captain representative of human error, was to blame. Dramatistic analysis of crisis communication may reveal the motivations of the communicator and the reality that he or she sought to create post-crisis; such provides a fascinating area of investigation into the implications of that reality in the court of public opinion. Organizational rhetoric may also be well-served by ratio analysis, the analysis of the prioritization of pentadic elements in its discourse (e.g., agent/act).

Each of the five elements of Burke's pentad can be linked in a ratio, or pairing, to every other element in the pentad, resulting in ten ratios (Campbell & Burkholder, 1997). A rhetorical critic may analyze the "scene/act" ratio to reveal how the scene may reveal the nature of the act; similarly, various ratios of elements may be highlighted indicative of the rhetor's strategy (Herrick, 2001). For example, Ling (1970) used a pentadic approach to analyze Senator Edward Kennedy's speech following the death of Mary Jo Kopechne and revealed Kennedy's emphasis on scene in order to shift responsibility for the accident away from him.

Burke's work emphasizes the role of symbolic action and is based on the understanding that language *is* action. Campbell and Huxman (2003) recognized the participatory and reciprocal nature of rhetorical action in their assertion, "just as the rhetor plays a role and takes on a persona, audiences are invited to play roles and take on one or more personas… advertising, for example, creates scenarios that are appealing and invite us to imagine ourselves playing roles in them" (p. 187). Burke's theory proffers great potential for crisis and risk communication scholarship. As action, language creates its audience; thus, theories such as Althusser's (trans. in 1971) notion of interpellation may also be used to study crisis and risk communication from a rhetorical perspective.

One function of language and its action is to render people subjects, perhaps through what French Marxist Philosopher Althusser termed *interpellation*. Interpellation is the process in which ideology creates its subjects; it is the textual operating mechanism through which audiences are positioned (O'Sullivan, Hartley, Saunders, Montgomery, & Fiske, 1994). A theory about the way communication works, interpellation is not purely an informational model with a transcendent subject waiting to receive a message. The audience is created in tandem with the message; the audience exists as the discourse invites it to play a particular role, to act in a way the speaker wants the audience to act. In crisis and risk communication, the communicator has a unique opportunity to invite an audience to play a role as a particular kind of shareholder. Instead of presupposing a fixed, determinable public, which in actuality may not exist, interpellation theory recognizes the autonomy and responsibility of the organization, which invites a constituted audience to play a particular role.

In his 1969 policy speech on Vietnam, President Nixon invited his audience to play the role of the "great, silent majority" that supports his policy of Vietnamization as opposed to dissenting. An audience may also be created inadvertently, underscoring the importance of ethical rhetoric. A record number of women candidates ran for political office and contributions for female candidates doubled following the 1991 Anita Hill-Clarence Thomas hearings. Although the economic power to affect political campaigns had always been present, that audience was mobilized by the hearings. As Campbell and Huxman (2003) acknowledged, "the so-called consciousness-raising groups in the women's liberation movement can be seen as transforming women into audiences—that is into people who believe that they can act effectively to become agents of change" (p. 188).

Rhetorical criticism may enhance existing crisis and risk communication theory and reveal audiences created through crisis response and communication of risk. It is important in crisis communication scholarship to consider what role we invite audiences to play lest they actually play that role. We must understand that we are calling a particular audience into being and that they are taking on the responsibilities we ask them to take on. In this vein or example, Foss and Griffin (1995) proposed a rhetorical perspective that invites the audience to consider a point of view different to the one they hold without proposing the position held by the audience is wrong, but a different one might be better. It is worth consideration.

Thus, rhetorical theory provides new ways to study the crisis or risk audience non-empirically, which can lend further insight into the practice and ethics of crisis communication. There is the possibility of a dynamic relationship between an organization and its stakeholders. Discourse can refigure that relationship by inviting its audience to play a more informed role or a more invested role.

The successful rhetorical act garners audience participation from the beginning to the end; the audience must internalize and consume discourse accurately. The audience must be able to realize the trustworthiness (*ethos*) and expertise (*logos*) of the source. The rhetorical act must be relevant to the audience with a clear purpose and give them means to achieve that goal (Campbell & Huxman, 2003). Finally, the audience must "come to believe that they can take action, here and now, that can reasonably to be expected to achieve the goal desired" (Campbell & Huxman, 2003, p. 188).

Undoubtedly, the crisis rhetor will face many obstacles in route to creating a participative audience. As fears of an avian influenza pandemic began to mount in the United State in 2004, crisis communicators were charged with creating a new audience equipped with all of the above criteria—purpose, efficacy, and trust. This audience must be informed, engaged, and ready-to-act. Analysis of the discursive elements in the rhetoric of major health institutions such as the Centers for Disease Control and Prevention and the National Institutes of Health may reveal *how* and *what kind* of audience is being created. Interpellation may be a useful theoretical approach in crisis communication literature as it exposes the possibilities of roles the audience can assume.

Like Althusser's (trans. in 1971) notion of interpellation, Charland's (1987) constitutive theory can inform our work in crisis and risk communication through its focus on how audiences are positioned and asked to participate in the construction of meaning. Rhetoric and public discourse have the capacity to create a sense of common identity. When the founders of the United States identified the nation as "we, the people," they constructed a national identity and what it means to be American (Beasley, 2004). In the same way, public relations and crisis communication enable organizations to constitute its publics. Yet, constitutive rhetoricians argue "what counts as good communication is often developed through what is accepted as good communication" (Stokes, 2005, p. 558). For example, Tylenol's good PR and transparent public discourse after its tampering crisis had the inadvertent consequence of pressuring other companies to be similarly open amidst crisis (Stokes, 2005).

Stokes (2005) called for a constitutive approach to the study of public relations using a case study of Metabolife International's response to a *20/20* television report on the danger of ephedra, a drug found in large amounts in the popular product. Stokes (2005) argued the study of public relations "needs to employ a constitutive lens that reveals how public relations discourse shapes, reflects, and is constrained by the larger public sphere...the types of public relations strategies used today have taken on a level of currency that extends beyond the instrumental understanding of how organizations emerge victorious in crisis, how they protect reputations, or how they increase profits" (p. 556).

Indeed, both public relations and crisis communication scholarship can identify and continue to analyze the influence of discourse on the audience and how that audience consumes and discusses the rhetorical situation. As Stokes (2005) asserted, audiences do not passively watch organizations handle a crisis situation; they identify norms and patterns present in communication. Thus, through a constitutive rhetorical lens, crisis and risk communication scholarship can analyze the crisis situation to explain why audiences expect certain things in a crisis situation as well as to prescribe the norms that can be appealed to through crisis. Thus, crisis communicators must be mindful of the implications of their communicative goal. As scholars, we must push beyond assessments of the success or failure of a crisis response to evaluations of the effect of that rhetoric on public discourse and consciousness.

Edwin Black's (1970) notion of the "second persona" provides another useful theoretical framework for studies of influence in crisis communication. Black makes the distinction between the rhetor as an actual person and the persona that he or she assumes during a communicative act. Given that the rhetor adopts this *first* persona, the rhetorical act invites the audience to assume the role of the *second* persona (Black, 1970; Campbell & Burkholder, 1997). Black (1970) asserted rhetorical criticism can be used to identify the second persona implied by discourse; such may reveal the ideological underpinnings of that discourse.

Personal identity is constructed by the knowledge and system of beliefs of the individual; thus, inviting the audience to play the role of second persona introduces significant ethical implications of the communicative act (Campbell & Burkholder, 1997). These ethical implications imposed on the rhetor may be particularly salient during a crisis situation. Black's (1970) second persona is an important theoretical lens for crisis and risk communication scholars to consider, as it may reveal the morality and ethics of crisis rhetoric. As we reveal the roles the crisis communicator implores the audience to assume amidst crisis, scholars will identify and advance a more nuanced set of ethical guidelines of and considerations for risk and crisis rhetoric. For example, is the rhetor inviting an audience to be one that is active or passive?

Certainly, rhetorical theories of influence provide an important framework for the future of crisis and risk communication scholarship. Scholars should increasingly look to the classic theory of Aristotle and Burke to inform their analysis of crisis discourse. Althusser's (trans. in 1971) notion of interpellation, Charland's (1987) constitutive rhetoric, and Black's (1970) second persona may reveal the audience that is created in crisis rhetoric and the role it is called to play. Crisis and risk communication scholarship, as it continues to develop its rhetorical perspective, may advance and more thoroughly understand the ethical challenges and responsibilities imposed on the rhetor amidst crisis. Crisis discourse calls a particular audience into being; through these rhetorical lenses, we can reveal what that being is from an audience perspective, moving beyond speaker-centered models.

In addition to revealing the success or failure of a crisis response, in using rhetorical theory we can reveal the enduring effects of the crisis situation. We can identify how it creates and shapes the audience and the norms established in the audience through certain communicative acts to inform future crisis communication. Certainly, as we have moved far beyond the assumption of a passive, inactive audience we must analyze what this very active audience does with and becomes through crisis and risk rhetoric. To be sure, rhetoric itself *is* influence, and influence is power. The rhetor *must* be mindful of the power he or she assumes in crisis and risk communication and the influence of that discourse.

Narrative theory offers another way of understanding and guiding the development of effective risk and crisis communication, in a way that can work in a complementary fashion with other rhetorical theories described. Fisher's (1987) narrative paradigm provides a model for developing and delivering messages (stories) that listeners find logical and compelling (Fisher, 1987). Fisher argued that humans are essentially storytellers and that the purpose of these stories is to provide "good reasons" to believe or act in certain ways. Two criteria can be used to assess the narrative effectiveness. The first is narrative probability, which is the gauge of whether a story is coherent and free of internal inconsistencies or contradictions. Second is narrative fidelity, which describes whether a story "rings true" with listeners' experiences in terms of the stories they know to be true in their lives. For stories to be effective, they must incorporate the perspectives of the listener.

In a given risk context such as in a health care setting, stories can be communicated in forms that recount, such as explaining one's health history, or in forms that account, such as scientific explanation and argument. Although patients and caregivers can use both forms, caregiver narratives most often account and patients most often recount. However, interventions that include both account and recount may be the most influential because such messages convey necessary health or other risk information in a way that acknowledges the context and values of the audience, in this case the patient. This type of approach may be particularly effective for women. A number of researchers have found that women tend to discuss their health in terms of contextual experiences, whereas men tend to report their symptoms (Meeuwesen, Schaap, & Van der Staak, 1991; Williams-Brown, Baldwin, & Bakos, 2002; Wodak, 1981).

Continuing with the health example, narratives are operationally defined as attempts at storytelling that portray the interrelationships among behavioral recommendations and physical symptoms, as well as the psychological, social, or cultural context of these behaviors and symptoms (Waitzkin, Britt, & Williams, 1994). Such narratives may include complete stories or brief fragments without a coherent beginning and end. Narrative is not an all-or-nothing proposition. The more a communicative act includes the elements of fidelity and probability the more it will fit Fisher's (1987) notion of a "good story."

SOCIAL SCIENTIFIC THEORY AND INFLUENCE

There are a number of models that integrate rhetorical and social scientific theories. In a framework reminiscent of transactional analysis, risk communication scholar Peter Sandman (2004) outlined a four-strategy approach open to risk communicators—follow-the-leader, echo, donkey, and seesaw. This framework builds on the components of a number of established rhetorical and social scientific theories, and it provides an interesting platform for examining influence in risk environments. The appropriateness and effectiveness of each strategy is predicated on differences in audience positions relative to any given issue.

Follow-the-leader is a strategy appropriate for audiences that have no awareness or opinion on a particular issue. That is not to say that people are a blank slate. Individuals will view any communication through their pre-existing perceptual filters. In other words, a story narrative must make sense to them. Sandman suggests that when someone has no prior knowledge or attitudes about a given issue, the best strategy is to tell them what to think. In a crisis situation, the audience is likely ready to attend to information and will gladly follow the lead.

In risk communication situations, however, the communicator must present his/her message in an interesting way to circumvent the potential of apathy. In the event the audience is likely to encounter an opposing position and the issue will become prominent, inoculation theory would suggest that it is wise to mention the opposing position and provide reasons why that opposing position should be disregarded (McGuire, 1961).

Echo, or communicating with individuals who already agree with you, is a useful approach for several reasons. Such interaction can remind them of details they may have forgotten and/or can prod them from inaction to action. For example, an audience might support the idea of recycling as a way of reducing impact on the environment, but they might not actually be doing it. Through the use of an echo strategy that incorporates behaviors that individuals can easily incorporate in their lives, it's possible to move people to action. Sandman (2004) argued that the key to this strategy is to make the message interesting by offering the audience new variations to the theme, and by inoculating the audience to potential naysayers.

Donkey refers to the suggested strategy when dealing with people who disagree with your position. The underlying logic of this strategy is that the communicator must start by validating that the opposing position has some merits. In this way the communicator pays tribute to those ascribing to the opposing position. Rather than just giving an audience reasons to support a position, the communicator attempts to offer them reasons that might work from the audience's perspective. At this point the communicator begins to lay a path from that position to the new one. For example, let's say that you are trying to convince a person with an indoor cat that he or she should administer heartworm protection, even though the pet never ventures outdoors. The message might go something like this: "I have an indoor cat too, and I used to think I didn't need to bother with heartworm protection. Then I found out that indoor pets are very vulnerable to mosquito-borne parasites. Even though my cat never goes outdoors, mosquitoes have a way of getting into the house by flying in as a door opens or closes, or by attaching onto clothing when I or my family enter from outside. Once in the house, the mosquito will zero in on any available food source, and that food source is often a pet."

The final strategy is seesaw, a strategy appropriate when an audience is ambivalent about an issue. Take the example of nuclear power for instance. Sandman (2004) argued that it is very possible to hold opposing views simultaneously. One might value the abundant, non-greenhouse producing supply of electricity that can be generated by nuclear power plants but also be troubled by the potential of a Cherynobyl-like catastrophe. Because of the uncertainty of both the risk of nuclear meltdown and of global warming, a person might have difficulty determining which side of the issue to adopt. Sandman (2004) outlined a fundamental paradox underlying the seesaw strategy. People tend to resolve their ambivalence by emphasizing the opposite side of the issue that others are advocating. This tendency reflects a boomerang effect, which is explained by reactance theory (see Brehm, 1966; Worchel & Brehm, 1970). In brief, the logic of reactance theory assumes that individuals can perceive incoming persuasive messages as a potential threat to their autonomy. By rejecting the message, individuals feel they are able to retain autonomy.

For example, if communication focuses on worst-case scenarios, an audience may focus on how unlikely they are; whereas, when communication focuses on how unlikely worst case scenarios are, the audience will focus on how terrible it would be. In the short run, a communicator might assume the position opposite of the one sought, all the while providing evidence to support the other position. Sandman (2004) rightly pointed out, however, that different audiences are likely to be listening at once. While donkey is the appropriate strategy with one audience, seesaw is the appropriate strategy with another. The long-term strategy is to slowly inch toward the center on the issue, meeting your audience in the middle. Sandman (2004) argued that, ultimately, seesaw is likely to win over more converts than donkey. As social judgment theory posits, it is much more difficult to influence individuals with positions that fall outside of their latitudes of acceptance (Sherif, Sherif, & Nebergall, 1965).

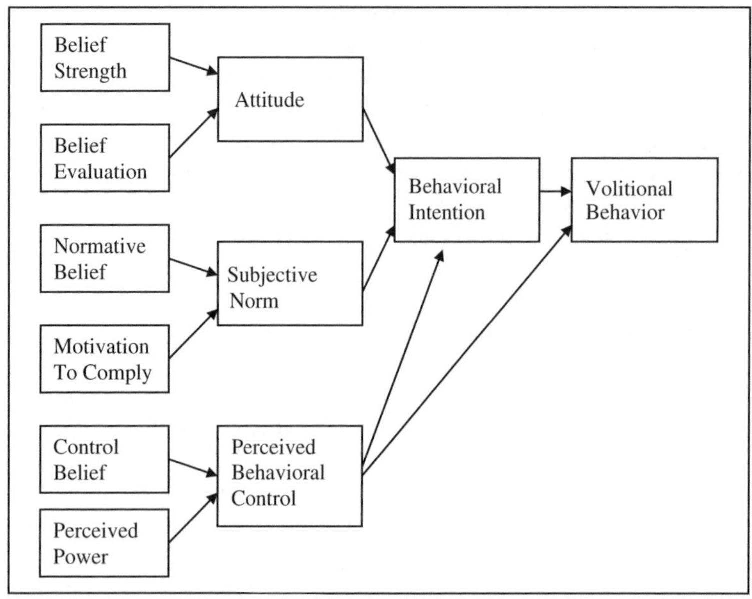

FIGURE 13.1 Theory of reasoned action model (Hale, Householder, and Greene, 2002).

Two prominent theories informing risk communication scholarship are Fishbein and Ajzen's (1980) *theory of reason action* and the related *theory of planned behavior* (Ajzen, 1988). Both theories have been fruitful in guiding insight into how people think and communicate about risks (e.g., Fishbein & Middlestadt, 1989; Montano & Taplin, 1991). In essence, the theory of reasoned action and the theory of planned behavior posit behavioral intention is the strongest predictor of volitional behavior (i.e., behavior that is not coerced). In a review of the theories, Hale, Householder and Greene (2002) developed a diagram outlining the components of both theories leading to volitional behavior, displayed in Figure 13.1.

An individual's *behavioral intention* is influenced by *attitudes* and *subjective norms*. Within the framework of the theory of reasoned action, an attitude refers to the positive or negative evaluation of performing a particular behavior. This positive or negative view is a function of one's *belief strength* and *belief evaluation*. Belief strength refers to the degree of confidence in that held belief. Belief evaluation refers to the degree to which an individual believes a behavior or condition is positive or negative.

A *subjective norm* is the function of *normative belief* and *motivation to comply* with the expected behavior. A normative belief refers to the extent to which an individual perceives that a given behavior or condition is expected and desirable in the eyes of others that are important to the individual. Motivation to comply with the expected behavior refers to how compelled the individual is to comply with the expectations of the various referents.

To draw an example of how the theory of reasoned action might unfold, let's assume that a person has concluded that it is both risky and undesirable to be overweight, and he has resolved to lose weight in order to become healthier. In this example, the *volitional behavior* is to follow one of the popular low-carbohydrate diets. While many weight loss strategies exist, our subject has read literature that has led him to *believe strongly* that an over-consumption of simple carbohydrates is one of the main reasons for weight gain, and that avoiding those foods is a positive thing (*belief evaluation*). He also perceives that his friends, family, and co-workers think negatively of his being overweight (*normative belief*), and he has a strong desire to satisfy these referents' desire for him to lose weight (*motivation to comply*). As a result, it is his *behavioral intention* to follow his diet carefully by eating fewer simple carbohydrates in order to lose weight.

While the theory of reasoned action has proved useful in explaining behavior, it is not without its critics. Hale, Householder, and Greene (2003) provide a thoughtful analysis of these criticisms. In essence, the theory of reasoned action is most criticized for its omissions, particularly for not considering non-volitional behaviors. As a result, Ajzen (1985) added the concept of *perceived behavioral control* to the theory of reasoned action to formulate the expanded *theory of planned behavior*. Perceived behavioral control is thought to predict both behavioral intentions and volitional behaviors. Perceived behavioral control is a product of *control belief*, which refers to the perceptions that adequate resources are available for the person to perform a behavior, and *perceived power*, the ability of the person to use those resources in a way that leads to successful behavior.

Returning to the earlier example, while it would be wonderful if one's behavioral intentions to eat healthier would automatically translate into successful behavior, judging from the high number of people that fail at their dieting goals, this is often not the case. In this example, the theory of planned behavior might be better at explaining the success or failure of our dieter, because the behavior is more goal-oriented. To succeed, our dieter will need to replace simple carbohydrates in his diet with healthier substitutes. Given that fresh fruits and vegetables tend to be more expensive than simple carbohydrates, our dieter must feel he has the financial ability to integrate this new food into his budget (control belief). Because of both selection options and costs, it is often more difficult to eat healthier food choices when eating out at restaurants. As a result, our dieter must feel that he has the ability to integrate home meal planning and preparation into his schedule, and he must also believe that he has the personal willpower to make healthy selections when eating out (perceived control).

The Elaboration Likelihood Model (ELM), proposed by Petty and Cacioppo (1981, 1986), is another important theory relevant to the study of risk communication. ELM integrates a variety of communication variables into a process-oriented framework. In a survey of the development of the ELM, Booth-Butterfield and Welbourne (2002) argued that the theory has provided coherence to an array of seemingly contradictory study findings examining individual variables including source, message, receiver, and context. ELM frames persuasion or influence into a dual-process model: central processing and peripheral processing.

Central processing is characterized as careful and thorough consideration of persuasive messages in a way that elaborates or exceeds what is specifically supplied in the message. When central processing, a person consciously evaluates the merits of an argument and considers how it could be incorporated in his or her life. It does not necessarily mean that persuasion has occurred, however (Petty & Wegener, 1999).

Attitude change can also occur through peripheral processing. This involves a much less involved, less thoughtful consideration of an argument. This would provide one explanation for the effectiveness of repetitious advertising. Choosing one brand of green beans over another is probably not something that many people devote much thought to, but because a person has seen a particular brand image repeatedly they may be influenced to pick it up off the shelf. The theory holds that central processing should result in more enduring attitude change, one that is more resistant to counterargument, and is more likely to promote actual behavior change.

Some scholars have conducted studies that link the use of narratives and the likelihood that people will centrally process risk messages. For example, Stephenson and Palmgreen (2001) conducted a study that revealed that the effectiveness of anti-marijuana public service ads was moderated by the amount of empathetic identification a viewer had to the characters portrayed in the ads.

Another dual process theoretical model that has been useful in studies of risk communication is the Heuristic-Systematic Model (HSM). Similar to ELM, HSM conceptualizes the risk information thought process as comprised of two levels. In a survey of HSM, Todorov, Chaiken, and Henderson (2003) pointed out that people rarely have the opportunity to process information in an ideal setting. There are often distractions, constraints, and pre-existing influences on processing both in the environment and within the individual. Because of these influences, unless a person has sufficient motivation and resources, it is assumed that many individuals process information in the easiest, most efficient way that they can. When a person perceives a particular issue to be important, he or she is more thoughtful about that issue. The person will be more systematic in his or her thinking on the issue and will consider the differences in how well-developed and reasoned different arguments are on the subject. Additionally, that person will be much less prone to attending to cues not central to the content of the argument, such as the length of messages or some physical attribute of the source of the information.

On the other hand, when a person sees an issue as less important, he or she is less motivated by the issue, and therefore he or she is likely to exhibit heuristic processing. A person engaged in heuristic processing will tend to be influenced by cues unrelated to message content such as a message source's level of physical attractiveness. Unlike systematic processing where a person carefully weighs different arguments, heuristic processing often relies on simple rules such as "those in authority can be trusted" or "the majority must be right" (Chen & Chaiken, 1999).

Building on HSM, Griffin, Neuwirth, and Dunwoody (1999) developed the *Risk Information Seeking and Processing model* (RISP). A key concept introduced in this model is information sufficiency. Information sufficiency in the RISP model refers to the size of the gap between the amount of information a person has about a given threat versus the amount the person feels he or she needs. The researchers argued that this variable affects whether the person uses a systematic or heuristic style of information processing, and also influences the style of information seeking. Griffin, Neuwirth, Dunwoody, and Geise (2004) conducted a study that tested elements of the RISP model using path analysis. An adaptation of the model is displayed in Figure 13.2.

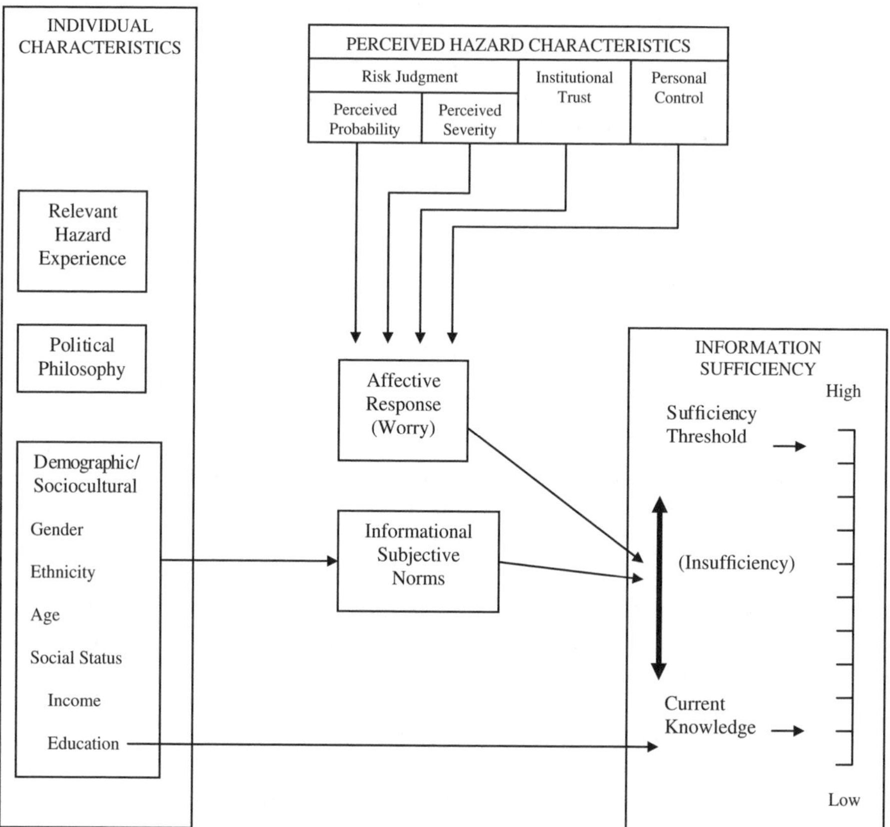

FIGURE 13.2 Risk information seeking and processing model (Griffin, Neuwirth, Dunwoody, and Giese, 2004).

According to the model, perceptions of information sufficiency are influenced by a number of factors. First, there are individual characteristics that come into play influencing how a risk or hazard is perceived. These characteristics have a bearing on how the individual perceives the characteristics of the risk or hazard, what informational subjective norms a person perceives, and how much knowledge a person has about a particular risk. Specific individual characteristics include prior experience with a particular risk, one's political philosophy, and one's demographic and sociocultural background.

Perceived hazard characteristics are comprised of three major elements: risk judgment, which is a function of perceived probability and perceived severity of the risk; personal control, and institutional trust. Two of the elements are analogous to variables articulated in the Extended Parallel Process Model (EPPM).[1] Risk severity is a central component in both models. Perceived probability is analogous to perceived susceptibility, and personal control is analogous to self-efficacy in the EPPM. Institutional trust is unique to the RISP model. It refers to the level of trust an individual has that an organization or agency will protect him or her from harm.

Griffin et al. (2004) argued that an individual's perceived hazard characteristics dictate the degree the person will worry (affective response) about the risk. Based on the work of scholars such as Batra and Stayman (1990) and Kuykendall and Keating (1990), Griffin et al. (2004) predicted that while positive emotions are likely to lead to heuristic information processing, negative affective states such as worry are more likely to lead to systematic processing. The authors point out that, unlike fear, which is an emotional response to an immediate threat, worry is linked to perceptions of future risk. The authors also argue that worry is probably much more common than fear.

In a study of the RISP model, Griffin et al. (2004) surveyed residents of two cities near the Great Lakes, specifically testing elements of the model relative to the potential contamination risks of the consumption of municipal drinking water and fish from the Great Lakes. Results supported the model. Individuals with higher levels of worry and those who perceived that important people in their lives would expect them to keep informed about the risks tended to perceive a higher gap between their current knowledge and the amount of knowledge that was sufficient to properly handle the risks.

A particular category of theories that has received much attention in health risk research is stage theory. A common assumption of stage theories is that individuals typically don't change risky behaviors in one step. Rather, they move along a continuum of cognitive and behavioral change. Weinstein, Rothman, and Sutton (1998) identified four key elements that provide the foundational logic of stage theories. First, the theories have a categorizing system that defines different stages of cognitive and behavioral change. The authors indicated that it is important to realize that these stages are theoretical constructs, and, as such, it is often difficult to identify the exact boundaries of each stage. Second, there is a coherent order to the stages that most people pass through. Third, there is an assumption that there will be common barriers in a particular stage that many individuals will face. Finally, individuals in a particular stage will likely face different common barriers than will individuals in a different stage. A major value of a stage theory approach is that it enhances the ability to tailor messages to a particular stage. There is a considerable amount of evidence that shows tailored messages are more influential than non-tailored messages (e.g., Campbell, Tessaro, DeVellis, Benedict, Kelsey, & Sanhueza, 2002; Kreuter, Farrell, Olevitch, & Brennan, 2000; Rimer, Halabi, Sugg-Skinner, Kaplan, Crawford, Samsa, Strigo, & Lipkus, 2001).

A risk behavior change theory very popular in health research is the transtheoretical model, often referred to as the stages of change theory (Prochaska & DiClemente, 1986). Originally developed for smoking cessation research, the transtheoretical model has been used in a variety of other health risk contexts, including cancer screening, alcohol and drug use (e.g., Champion, Maraj, Hui, Perkins, Tierney, Menton, & Skinner, 2003; Belding, Iguchi, & Lamb, 1997; Herzog, Abrams, Emmons, Linnan, & Shadel, 1999). As implied in the name, the model incorporates elements of a number of different theoretical constructs. According to Prochaska and colleagues (Prochaska & DiClemente, 1986; Prochaska, Redding, & Evers, 1997), risk behavior change can be viewed on a continuum wherein the individual moves from not considering an action or health behavior to maintaining adherence of the behavior (Prochaska et al., 1997). The model considers the history of the targeted behavior and intention regarding future behavior. A commonly used version of the model outlines five stages: precontemplation, contemplation, action, maintenance, and relapse.

The communication implications are different for each stage. To move a person from precontemplation to contemplation, communication must at least be compelling enough to catch the person's attention in order for him or her to begin contemplating a change. Once the person begins to contemplate changing his or her behavior, that person will need to perceive good reasons for moving to actual behavior change (action). They will also need to perceive that they are capable of enacting the change. Many situations require maintenance of a certain behavior (or in the case of issues like over-eating, smoking, or substance abuse, maintaining an avoidance of those behaviors). Getting a mammogram once or eating fruits and vegetables once in a while is not adequate to minimize a health risk. According to the transtheoretical model, individuals who have adopted healthy behavior changes often relapse to an earlier stage. Subsequent weight gain and relapse smoking are two prime examples of this behavior.

In a comprehensive review of research using the transtheoretical model, Spencer, Pagell, Hallion, and Adams (2002) found the model to be particularly useful for smoking cessation studies. The transtheoretical model is not without critics, however. Sutton (2001) conducted a meta-analysis of studies focusing on substance abuse that used the transtheoretical model as its guiding theory. Sutton (2001) found "meager and inconsistent" support for the model. While indicating that the notion of behavior change involving movement through sequential stages is an important idea, the researcher argued that the transtheoretical model is a "poor implementation of this idea" (2001, p. 183). He argued that there are serious problems with the existing measurement of stages and of the often arbitrary time periods used to define movement from one stage to the next.

A more recent iteration of stage change theory is the precaution adoption process model or PAPM (Weinstein & Sandman, 2002). While portions of the model are similar to the transtheoretical model, the contemplation stage is more discretely elaborated upon in the PAPM. Stage one describes individuals unaware of a particular risk issue, similar to the precontemplation stage in the transtheoretical model. Individuals in stage two of the PAPM are aware of an issue but not yet engaged in it and may never become engaged. Weinstein and Sandman (2002) argued that with the myriad of competing issues individuals face regularly, it is quite common that these individuals often don't consider doing anything about many of those issues. Stage three refers to those instances when an individual does consider whether or not he or she will act on an issue, similar to the contemplation stage of the transtheoretical model. However, between the contemplation and action stages, the PAPM identifies the conscious decision not to act (stage four). Stage five in the PAPM is a decision to act. Stage six is the point on which the individual takes action to avoid or minimize the risk, and stage seven is the maintenance of this behavior over time. As in the transtheoretical model, PAPM allows for individuals to relapse to an earlier stage.

The PAPM has been used to guide intervention studies on a number of topics. For example, Weinstein, Lyon, Sandman, and Cuite (1998) tested elements of the PAPM in a study that examined influencing homeowners to conduct home radon testing. The study focused particularly on two stage transitions, specifically the transition between being undecided to electing to doing a home radon test and the transition from deciding to test and actually ordering the testing kit. Results of the study supported the validity of the PAPM. Specifically, the results indicated that there were distinct differences in barriers between different stages. The results also confirmed that information about the risk had different effects on individuals, depending on their stage. Information emphasizing radon risk affected those undecided about testing more than it did among those already deciding to act. Conversely, information addressing the ease of testing was deemed more important to those that had already decided to act than for those still undecided. While this model needs to be further tested, the ability to identify distinct stages for tailoring risk messages appears promising.

CONCLUSION

This chapter reviewed a broad range of rhetorical, persuasion, and informational theories of influence, from the early work of Aristotle to more contemporary models such as PAPM. The breadth of literature that can inform scholarship in crisis and risk communication should be invigorating to scholars in this field. Charland's (1987) work on constitutive theory can inform our work by illuminating how audiences are positioned and asked to participate in the construction of meaning in risk and crisis situations. We can test the utility of Ajzen's (1985) Theory of Planned Behavior to make predictions about the behavioral response of that very audience following a crisis. Given that one of the most fundamental tenets of communication theory is the need to understand one's audience, scholars should be invigorated with all of the available tools that enable our getting closer to achieving this goal.

Rhetoric is influence, and influence is power. The rhetorical theories reviewed in this chapter can be used to reveal the ethical implications of risk and crisis discourse. As we engage theory such as Black's (1970) second persona, risk and crisis communication scholars can develop more thorough understandings of the audience that rhetoric creates, informing what are the *best* practices in negotiating the public relations implications of a crisis.

Yet, without insight into the knowledge, attitudes, and beliefs of the audience, rhetoric is less informed and, ultimately, less successful in reaching those target publics. Thus, HSM and EPPM enable our identifications of cognitive mechanisms that influence how publics may process a crisis situation. Stage theory forces crisis and risk scholars and practitioners to acknowledge and reconcile that change does not generally occur in one step and that the entire picture must be taken into account.

Taken together, the rhetorical and social scientific theories and models presented in this chapter that are available to facilitate the scholarly inquiry of influence in risk and crisis environments will yield the most well-rounded, comprehensive understanding of the situation, audience, and prescriptions for response. They must not be viewed as opposing forces but instead as complementary ontological and epistemological theoretical frameworks with great potential to inform scholarship in risk and crisis communications.

To be sure, life can indeed be a dangerous proposition. Our daily encounters with risk and, all too often, crises, underscore the importance of the role of influence in risk and crisis communication. As scholars, we must answer *how* publics are influenced amidst these periods of vulnerability and *why* this persuasion occurred. We must analyze *who* is the audience the rhetor creates and *what* they are called to do as well as identify *when* and *where* they are called to act. These questions can be best answered through a variety of theoretical approaches as we actively test, refine, extend, and develop theories and best practices in risk and crisis communication.

NOTE

1. For a full description of the Extended Parallel Process Model, see chapter 15, this volume.

BIBLIOGRAPHY

Ajzen, I. (1985). From intentions to actions: A theory of planned behavior. In J. Khul & J. Beckmann (Eds.), *Action control: from cognition to behavior* (p. 11–39). New York: Springer-Verlag.

Ajzen, I. (1988). *Attitudes, personality, and behavior*. Milton Keynes, UK: Open University Press.

Althusser, L. (1971). *Lenin and philosophy and other essays*. Trans. Ben Brewster. New York: Monthly Review.

Aristotle. (1991). *On rhetoric*. Trans. G. Kennedy. New York: Oxford.

Batra, R., & Stayman, D. M. (1990). The role of mood in advertising effectiveness. *Journal of Consumer Research, 17*, 203–214.

Beasley, V. B. (2004). *You the people: American national identity in presidential rhetoric.* College Station, TX: Texas A & M University Press.

Becker, M., & Maimon, L. (1975). Sociobehavioral determinants of compliance with health and medical care recommendations. *Medical Care, 13,* 10–24.

Belding, M. A., Iguchi, M. Y., & Lamb, R. J. (1997). Stages and processes of change as predictors of drug use among methadone maintenance patients. *Experimental and Clinical Psycholopharmacology, 5,* 65–73.

Black, E. (1970). The second persona. *Quarterly Journal of Speech, 56,* 109–119.

Booth-Butterfield, S., & Welbourne, J. (2002). The elaboration likelihood model: Its impact on persuasion theory and research. In J. P. Dillard & M. Pfau (Eds.) *The persuasion handbook: Developments in theory and practice* (pp. 155–173). Thousand Oaks, CA: Sage.

Bostrom, A. (2003). Future risk communication. *Futures, 35,* 553–573.

Brehm, J. W. (1966). *A theory of psychological reactance.* New York: Academic Press.

Burgchardt, C. R. (2000). *Readings in rhetorical criticism.* State College, PA: Strata.

Burgess, P. G. (1973). Crisis rhetoric coercion vs. force. *Quarterly Journal of Speech, 59,* 61–73.

Burke, K. (1945). *A grammar of motives.* Berkeley: University of California Press, 1969.

Campbell, M. K., Tessaro, I., DeVellis, B., Benedict, S., Kelsey, B. & Sanhueza, B. (2002). Effects of a yailored health promotion program for female blue-collar workers: Health works for women. *Preventive Medicine, 34*, 313–323.

Campbell, K.K., & Burkholder, T.R. (1997). *Critiques of contemporary rhetoric.* Belmont, CA: Wadsworth.

Campbell, K.K., & Huxman, S.S. (2003). *The rhetorical act: Thinking, speaking, and writing critically.* Belmont, CA: Wadworth.

Champion, V., Maraj, M., Hui, S., Perkins, A.J., Tierney, W.M., Menton, U., & Skinner, C.S. (2003). Comparison of tailored interventions to increase mammography screening in nonadherent older women. *Preventive Medicine, 36*(2) 50–158.

Charland, M. (1987). Constitutive rhetoric: The case of the *Peuple Quebecois. Quarterly Journal of Speech, 73,* 133–150.

Chen, S., & Chaiken, S. (1999). The heuristic-systematic model in its broader context. In S. Chaiken and Y. Trope (Eds.), *Dual-process theories in social psychology* (pp. 73–96). New York: Guilford.

Fishbein, M., & Ajzen, I. (1980). Predicting and understanding consumer behavior: Attitude-behavior correspondence. In I. Ajzen & M. Fishbein (Eds.), *Understanding attitudes and prediction social behavior* (pp. 148–172). Englewood Cliffs, NJ: Prentice Hall.

Fishbein, M., & Middlestadt, S. E. (1989). Using the theory of reasoned action as a framework for understanding and changing AIDS-related behaviors. In V. M. Mays, G. W. Albee, & S. F. Schneider (Eds.), *Primary prevention of AIDS: Psychological approaches* (pp. 93–110). Newbury Park, CA: Sage.

Fisher W. (1987). *Human communication as narration: Toward a philosophy of reason, value, and action.* Columbia: University of South Carolina Press.

Foss, S. J., & Griffin, C. L. (1995). Beyond persuasion: A proposal for an invitational rhetoric. *Communication Monographs, 62*, 2–18.

Griffin, R., Dunwoody, S., & Neuwirth., K. (1999). Proposed model of the relationship of risk information seeking and processing to the development of preventive behaviors. *Environmental Research, 80*, 230–45.

Griffin, R., Neuwirth, K., Dunwoody, S., & Geise, J. (2004). Information sufficiency and risk communication. *Media Psychology, 6*, 23–61.

Hale, J. L., Householder, B. J., & Greene, K. L. (2003). The theory of reasoned action. In J. P. Dillard & M. Pfau (Eds.), *The persuation handbook: Developments in theory and practice* (pp. 259–286). Thousand Oaks, CA: Sage.

Hearit, K. M., & Brown, J. (2004). Merrill Lynch: corporate apologia and business fraud. *Public Relations Review, 30,* 459–466.

Heath, R.L. (2000). A rhetorical perspective on the values of public relations: Crossroads and pathways toward concurrence. *Journal of Public Relations Research, 12,* 69–91.

Heath, R. L. (2004). Telling a story: A narrative approach to communication during a crisis. In D. P. Millar & R. L Heath (Eds.), *Responding to crisis: A rhetorical approach to crisis communication* (pp. 167–188). Mahwah, NJ: Erlbaum.

Heath, R.L. (2006). Best practices in crisis communication: Evolution of practice through research. *Journal of Applied Communication Research, 34*(3), 245–248.

Herrick, J.A. (2001). *The history and theory of rhetoric.* Needham Heights, MA: Allyn & Bacon.

Herzog, T. A., Abrams, D. B., Emmons, K. M., Linnan, L., & Shadel, W. G. (1999). Do processes of change predict smoking stage movemements? A prospective analysis of the transtheoretical model. *Health Psychology, 18*, 369–375.

Huxman, S. S. (2004). Exigencies, explanations, and executions: Toward a dynamic theory of the crisis communication genre. In D. P. Millar & R. L Heath (Eds.), *Responding to crisis: A rhetorical approach to crisis communication* (pp. 281–298). Mahwah, NJ: Erlbaum.

Ihlen, O. (2002). Rhetoric and resources: Notes for a new approach to public relations and issues management. *Journal of Public Affairs, 2*(4), 259–269.

Johnson, D., & Sellnow, T. (1995). Deliberative rhetoric as a step in organizational crisis management: Exxon as a case study. *Communication Reports, 8*(1), 54–60.

Keller, H. (1957). *The open door*. New York: Doubleday.

Kreuter, M., Farrell, D., Olevitch, L., & Brennan L. (2000). Tailoring health messages. *Customizing communication with computer technology*. London: Erlbaum.

Kuykendall, D., & Keating, J. P. (1990). Mood and persuasion: Evidence for the differential influence of positive and negative states. *Psychology & Marketing, 7*, 1–9.

Ling, D. A. (1970). A pentadic analysis of Senator Edward Kennedy's address to the people of Massachusetts. *Central States Speech Journal, 21*, 81–86.

Marsh, C. (2006). The syllogism of apologia: Rhetorical stasis theory and crisis communication. *Public Relations Review, 32*, 41–46.

McGuire, W. (1961). Resistance to persuasion conferred by active and passive prior refutation of the same and alternative counterarguments. *Journal of Abnormal and Social Psychology, 63*, 326–332.

Meeu wesen, L (1988). *Spreekuur of zwijguur. Somatische fixatie en sekse-asymmetrie tijdens het medisch consult* [Speaking or being silent. Somatic fixation and gender asymmetry during the medical interview]. Nijmegen, the Netherlands: University of Nijmegen.

Meeuwesen, L., Schaap, C., & Van der Staak, C. (1991). Verlal analysis of doctor-patient communication. *Social Science and Medicine, 32*, 1143–1150.

Montano, D. E., & Taplin, S. H. (1991). A test of an expanded theory of reasoned action to predict mammography participation. *Social Science and Medicine, 32*, 733–741.

O'Sullivan, T., Hartley, J., Saunders, D., Montgomery, M., & Fiske, J. (1994). *Key concepts in communication and cultural studies.* London: Routledge.

Petty, R. E., & Cacioppo, J. T. (1981). *Attitudes and persuasion: Classic and contemporary approaches.* Dubuque, IA: William C. Brown.

Petty, R. E., & Cacioppo, J. T. (1986). *Communication and persuasion: Central and peripheral routes to attitude change.* New York: Springer-Verlag.

Petty, R. E., & Wegener, D. (1999). The elaboration likelihood model: Current status and controversies. In S. Chaikeen & Y. Trope (Eds.), *Dual process theories in social psychology* (pp. 37–72). New York: Guildford.

Prochaska, J. O. & DiClemente, C. C. (1986). Toward a comprehensive model of change. In W. R. Miller & N. Heather (Eds.), *Treating addictive behaviors: Processes of change* (pp. 3–27). New York: Plenum.

Prochaska, J. O., Redding, C. A., & Evers, K. E. (1997). The transtheoretical model and stages of change. In K. Glanz, F. M. Lewis, & B. K. Rimer (Eds.), *Health_behavior and health education_*(p. 60–84)._San Francisco, CA: Jossey-Bass Publishers.

Rimer, B. K., Halabi, S., Sugg-Skinner, C., Kaplan, E. B., Crawford, Y., Samsa, G. P., Strigo, T. S., & Lipkus, I. M. (2001). The short-term impact of tailored mammography decision-making interventions. *Patient Educational Counselling. 43*(3), 269–285.

Rowland, R. C., & Jerome, A. M. (2004). On organizational apologia: A reconceptualization. *Communication Theory, 14*(3), 191–211.

Sandman, P. M. (2004, December 13). Games risk communicators play: Follow-the-leader, echo, donkey, and seesaw. Retrieved March 6, 2007, from http://www.Petersandman.com.

Sherif, C. A., Sherif, M., & Nebergall, R. E. (1965). *Attitude and attitude change: The social judgment-involvement approach.* Philadelphia: Saunders.

Spencer, L., Pagell, F., Hallion, M. E., & Adams, T. B. (2002). Applying the transtheoretical model to tobacco cessation and prevention: A review of the literature. *American Journal of Health Promotion, 7*(1), 7–71.

Stokes, A. Q. (2005). Metabolife's meaning: A call for the constitutive study of public relations. *Public Relations Review, 31*, 556–565.

Stephenson, M. T., & Palmgreen, P. (2001). Sensation seeking, perceived message sensation value, personal involvement, and processing of anti-marijuana PSAs. *Communication Monographs, 68*(1), 49–71.

Sutton, S. (2001). Back to the drawing board? A review of applications of the transtheoretical model to substance use. *Addiction, 96*, 175–186.

Todorov, A., Chaiken, S., and Henderson, M. D. (2003). The heuristic-systematic model of social information processing. In J. P. Dillard & M. Pfau (Eds.), *The persuasion handbook: Developments in theory and practice* (pp. 195–211). Thousand Oaks, CA: Sage.

Waitzkin, H., Britt, T., & Williams, C. (1994). Narratives of aging and social problems in medical encounters with older persons. *Journal of Health and Social Behavior,_35*(12), 322–348.

Weinstein, N. D., Lyon, J. E., Sandman, P. M., & Cuite, C. L. (1998). Experimental evidence for stages of precaution adoptions. *Health Psychology, 17*, 445–453.

Weinstein, N. D., Rothman, A., & Sutton, S. (1998). Stage theories of health behavior. *Health Psychology, 17*, 290–299.

Weinstein, N. D., & Sandman, P. M. (2002). The precaution adoption process model and its applications. In R. J. DiClemente, R. A. Crosby, & M. C. Kegler (Eds.), *Emerging theories in health promotion practice and research: Strategies for improving public health* (pp. 16–39). New York: Josey-Bass.

Williams-Brown, S., Baldwin, D. M. & Bakos, A. (2002, Winter). Storytelling as a method to teach African American women breast health information. *Journal of Cancer Education, 17*(4), 227–230.

Wodak, R. (1981). Women relate, men report: Sex differences in language behavior in a therapeutic group. *Journal of Pragmatics, 5*, 261–285.

Worchel, S., & Brehm, J. W. (1970). Effect of threats to attitudinal freedom as a function of agreement with the communicator. *Journal of Personality and Social Psychology, 14*, 18–22.

14

Raising the Alarm and Calming Fears: Perceived Threat and Efficacy During Risk and Crisis

Anthony J. Roberto
Arizona State University

Catherine E. Goodall
The Ohio State University

Kim Witte
Michigan State University

Tuesday, August 23rd, 5 p.m. EDT. Tropical depression twelve forms over the southeastern Bahamas.

Wednesday, August 24th, 11 a.m. EDT. Tropical depression twelve strengthens into tropical storm Katrina.

Thursday, August 25th, 5 p.m. EDT. Maximum sustained winds have increased to 75 MPH. Tropical Storm Katrina is upgraded to a Category 1 hurricane, the fourth hurricane of the 2005 season.

Thursday, August 25th, 7 p.m. EDT. Katrina makes landfall in Florida with 80 MPH winds.

Friday, August 26th, 11:30 a.m. EDT. Katrina is upgraded to a Category 2 hurricane, with maximum sustained winds near 100 MPH.

Saturday, August 27th, 5 a.m. EDT. Katrina is upgraded to a Category 3 storm with 115 MPH winds.

Sunday, August 28th, 1 a.m. CDT. Katrina is upgraded to a Category 4 storm with maximum sustained winds of 145 MPH.

Sunday, August 28th, 8 a.m. EDT. Katrina is upgraded to a Category 5 storm, the highest possible rating, with winds greater than 155 MPH.

Monday, August 29th, 6 a.m. EDT. Extremely dangerous Category 4 Hurricane Katrina, with maximum sustained winds of 145 MPH and higher gusts, makes initial landfall near southern Louisiana.[1,2]

According to the National Hurricane Center, Katrina was the costliest and one of the five deadliest hurricanes to ever strike the United States (Knabb, Rhome, & Brown, 2005). Many estimate that Katrina will be the biggest and costliest natural disaster in the country's history (Kofman, 2005;

Axtman, 2006). At the time this chapter was written, the official death toll across seven states stood at 1,310 (Roberts, 2006). Another 1,900 individuals are still missing, with many presumed dead (*Daily News*, 2006). Katrina displaced nearly 770,000 residents, and destroyed nearly 300,000 homes (Axtman, 2006). To date, it is estimated that Katrina caused nearly $60 billion in insured damages (Insurance Networking News, 2006), and government spending has topped $88 billion with another $20 billion requested (Department of Homeland Security, 2006).

Much of the damage and displacement caused by Katrina was clearly unavoidable. Katrina was an extremely powerful hurricane that made landfall at a particularly vulnerable location. However, it is also clear that a number of steps could have been taken to reduce the immense amount of chaos and suffering that occurred in the immediate aftermath of the storm. Individuals, as well as local, state, and federal government officials had several days to prepare: States of Emergency were declared in both Louisiana and Mississippi nearly 72 hours in advance, a State of Emergency was declared and voluntary evacuations were ordered for New Orleans nearly 48 hours in advance, and mandatory evacuations of New Orleans were issued nearly 24 hours before Katrina reached the city. Nonetheless, many individuals were unable or unwilling to take steps to prepare for or avoid the approaching hurricane, and substantial government relief for the effected areas did not arrive until three or more days after the storm had passed.

The main goal of this chapter is to highlight the important roles of perceived threat and efficacy when attempting to change people's behavior during risk and crisis. Toward this end, and using hurricane preparedness as its primary example, the balance of the chapter will focus on one useful tool for developing effective health-risk messages; the Extended Parallel Process Model (EPPM) (Witte, 1992; Witte, Meyer, & Martell, 2001). We will begin with an overview of the EPPM, including an example application and a brief review of the numerous risk-communication topics to which it has been applied. We will then discuss the concepts of *collective efficacy* and *societal level risk judgments*, and suggest a slight extension of the EPPM to include these two constructs.

THE EXTENDED PARALLEL PROCESS MODEL (EPPM)

A fear appeal is a persuasive message that attempts to scare people by describing the frightening things that may happen to them if they do not follow the persuader's recommendations. The EPPM (Witte, 1992) helps explain why some fear appeals succeed and others fail. Put simply, the EPPM is concerned with the effects of perceived treat and efficacy on behavior change (see Table 14.1). Perceived threat is composed of an individual's perceptions of both susceptibility and severity. *Perceived susceptibility* addresses the likelihood that the threat will occur, and *perceived severity* deals with the seriousness of the consequences of the threat. Perceived efficacy is comprised of an individual's perceptions of both response efficacy and self-efficacy. *Response efficacy* concerns the perceived safety and effectiveness of the recommended behavior, and *self-efficacy* deals with whether or not a person has the necessary skills and resources to engage in the recommended behavior.

TABLE 14.1
Components of Perceived Threat and Efficacy

Variable	*Key Question*
Perceived susceptibility	How likely is it that the threat will occur?
Perceived severity	How serious are the short- or long-term physical or mental consequences of the threat?
Respons e-efficacy	Is the recommended behavior safe and effective?
Self-efficacy	Do I have the necessary skills (e.g., knowledge, ability) and resources (e.g., time, money) to engage in the recommended behavior?

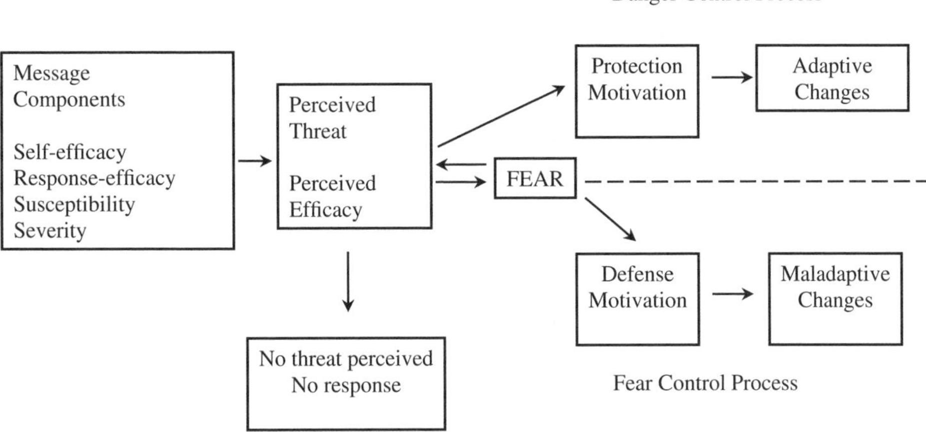

FIGURE 14.1 The extended parallel process model (Witte, 1992).

Three outcomes are possible depending on one's level of perceived threat and efficacy: (1) *no response* will occur when perceived threat is low; (2) a *fear control response* will occur when perceived threat is high and perceived efficacy is low; and (3) a *danger control* response will occur when both perceived threat and efficacy are high. This critical point, when perceived efficacy exceeds perceived threat, is an important concept in the development of effective risk communication messages. Figure 14.1 provides a visual representation of the EPPM.

Example Application of the EPPM

A glance at the disaster preparedness web sites created by the Department of Homeland Security and the American Red Cross illustrate how every region of the Unites States is prone to a myriad of potential manmade or natural disasters.[3] Examples of manmade disasters include chemical or biological threats, nuclear or radiation threats, or even a terrorist attack. Examples of natural disasters include extreme cold or heat, winter storms, thunder storms and tornados, floods or mudslides, earthquakes, hurricanes, and even a number of biological threats (e.g., pandemic flu). As such, federal, state, and local authorities strongly encourage citizens to take a number steps to prepare for, or minimize the potential impact of such risks. For example, these and other organizations recommend that households prepare personal evacuation and family communication plans, create a disaster supply kit, or simply to gather a three-day supply of food and water in the case of a known imminent threat (such as a hurricane).

When utilizing the EPPM to create risk communication messages, one must specify a goal (or recommended response) and also determine the threat (or what motivates the recommended response). To illustrate the three possible outcomes introduced at the end of the proceeding section, imagine you are developing a risk communication message for individuals living in the path of an approaching hurricane. For our example, the recommended response (or goal) is to get an individual to take steps to prepare for this hurricane (which is the threat). In this case, let us also assume that "taking steps to prepare" means (1) evacuating the area to decrease the likelihood of being stranded after the hurricane, or, (2) at a minimum, to gather a three day supply of food and water in case the individual stranded after the hurricane. The following sections illustrate the three different responses an individual might have depending on his or her levels of perceived threat and efficacy.

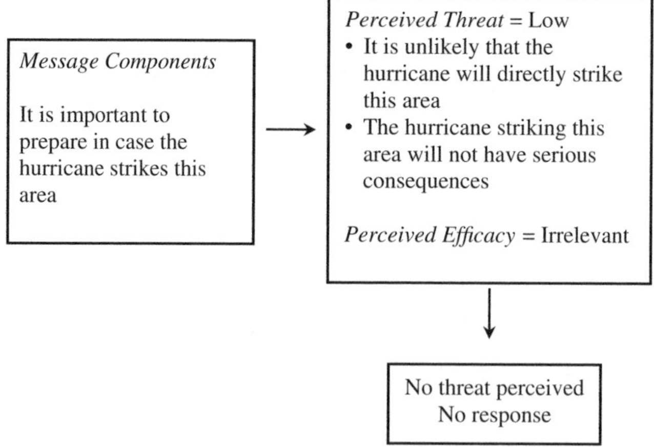

FIGURE 14.2 The extended parallel process model—low threat example.

Low-Threat Path

When perceived threat is low, there will be *no response* to the risk communication message (see Figure 14.2). That is, if an individual does not believe that he or she is susceptible to the threat (e.g., "It is unlikely that the hurricane will directly strike this area"), or if he or she does not believe the threat will have severe consequences (e.g., "The hurricane striking this area will not have serious consequences"), then the person will not be motivated to pay attention to the message and, therefore, will not respond. In this situation, the risk communication effort has failed to increase perceived threat. Importantly, both perceived susceptibility and perceived severity have to be high for one's appraisal of threat to be high.

This is undoubtedly why many people fail to prepare for or evacuate in the face of a potential risk or crisis situation. The path of a hurricane, for example, is not easily predicted, and residents may have taken steps to prepare in the past only to have the hurricane veer away at the last moment (thus the reason for the low susceptibility judgment). Or, any number of weaker hurricanes may have struck the area in the past and only caused minimal damage (thus the reason for the low severity judgment). In short, residents who live in an area for a long time may have seen many hurricanes in the past. Most bypassed the area or caused little damage, and they see no reason to expect the next one to be any different. Therefore, they do not take steps to prepare or evacuate.

High-Threat/Low-Efficacy Path

If perceived threat is high and perceived efficacy is low, the individual will engage in *fear control* (see Figure 14.3). That is, if the individual believes that he or she is susceptible to the threat of the hurricane (e.g., "The hurricane is likely to strike this area"), and if the individual believes that the threat of a hurricane is severe (e.g., "The hurricane striking this area will have serious consequences"), then the individual's level of perceived threat will be high. A high appraisal of the threat elicits fear, which motivates the individual to engage in the second appraisal of efficacy. If, during the appraisal of efficacy, the person does not believe the recommended response is effective (e.g., "Being prepared or evacuating will not help me"), or if the person does not believe that he or she has the ability to engage in the recommended response (e.g., "I do not have the time or means to prepare or evacuate"), then the person's level of perceived efficacy will be low. In this case, the risk communication message has not promoted high efficacy perceptions (i.e., although the person perceives a threat, the person does not perceive a viable option to reduce it). Consequently, the

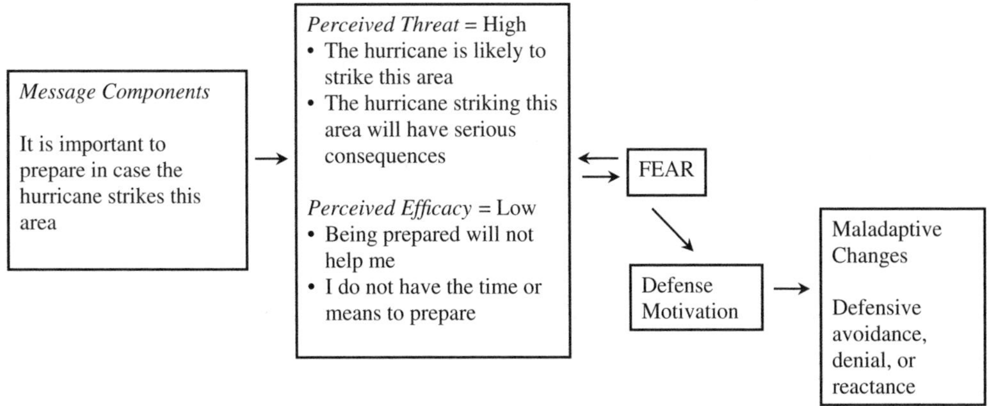

FIGURE 14.3 The extended parallel process model—high threat/low efficacy example.

risk communication messages are likely to fail, or worse, backfire (Stephenson & Witte, 2001). Notably, both response efficacy and self-efficacy must be high for one's appraisal of efficacy to be high.

Put somewhat differently, the high appraisal of threat leads to an uncomfortable state of fear, which motivates the individual to take action to remove the uneasy feeling. The adaptive way of dealing with this problem would be to follow the recommended action. However, because perceptions of efficacy are low, the only way the individual can deal with the problem is to try to control his or her fear rather than the actual danger. Three common strategies for controlling fear are *defensive avoidance* (e.g., ignoring the information), *denial* (e.g., refusing to believe that the risk is real), or *reactance* (e.g., rejecting the risk communication message as manipulative).

High-Threat/High-Efficacy Path

When perceptions of both threat and efficacy are high, the individual will engage in *danger control* (see Figure 14.4). In this situation, the risk communication message has accomplished all of its goals by convincing the person that both a personally relevant and serious threat exists, and by providing the person with means to reduce the threat that is both effective (i.e., high response-efficacy "My

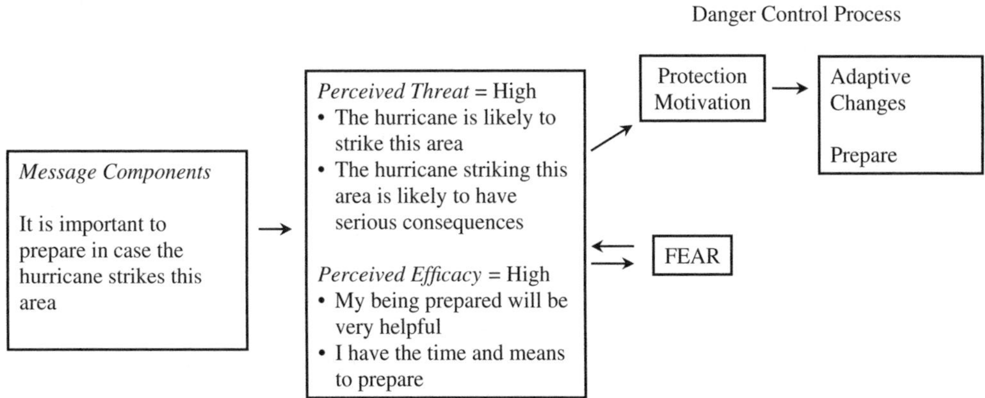

FIGURE 14.4 The extended parallel process model—high threat/high efficacy example.

being prepared or evacuating will be very helpful") and easily implemented (i.e., high self-efficacy "I have the time and means to prepare or evacuate"). It is only when *both* perceived threat and efficacy are high that a person will focus on potential solutions to the problem, which will likely lead to attitude or behavior change in the advocated direction.

Please keep in mind that this is just one application of the EPPM to a specific situation. But, the process would be essentially the same for any potential manmade or natural disasters. Further, the EPPM has regularly been used to guide health-risk messages designed to influence a wide variety of individual behaviors on a smaller scale (i.e., to get a gun owner to store his or her weapon locked and unloaded to prevent accidental firearm injury or death, to get sexually active college students to use condoms to prevent the spread of HIV/AIDS or other sexually transmitted diseases, etc.). But regardless of the topic or the scope of the risk, the fundamental idea of the EPPM always remains the same: for risk and crisis communication efforts to achieve their maximum effectiveness, *both* perceived threat and efficacy must be high.

A Brief History of the EPPM

The EPPM is an integration and extension of three previous theoretical perspectives on fear appeals: (a) the fear-as-acquired drive model, (b) the parallel process model, and (c) protection motivation theory (reviewed in Witte et al., 2001). The most notable difference between the EPPM and these other fear appeal theories is that previous theories focused largely on individuals who adopted the recommended response (i.e., "danger control") after being exposed to a fear appeal message, lumping everyone else into the no response category. In reality, however, the no response category is comprised of two groups: those who truly had no response to the campaign and those who engaged in fear control responses. The EPPM was the first fear appeal theory to specify how interactions between perceived threat and efficacy lead to danger control or fear control, and to explain when one process would be expected to dominate over the other.

Witte and Allen (2000) conducted a meta-analysis of 93 fear appeal studies. The data were largely consistent with propositions advanced by the EPPM. Specifically, strong fear appeals were found to produce higher levels of perceived severity and susceptibility, and to be more effective in changing attitudes, intentions, and behavior than weak fear appeals. Further, messages that were high in both threat and efficacy produced the greatest behavior change, and messages that were low in both threat and efficacy produced the least behavior change. However, the findings regarding other threat-efficacy combinations were not entirely consistent with EPPM predictions. Specifically, the EPPM predicts these other combinations should be similar in effectiveness to the low threat low efficacy condition when, in fact, they fell somewhere between these two other conditions. Finally, as predicted by the EPPM, messages high in threat and low in efficacy produced the greatest defensive responses. In sum, with only a few exceptions, the EPPM received a fair amount of support from the meta-analysis results.

Since the EPPM first was published in 1992, it has been used to guide dozens of studies focusing on numerous target populations and risk-communication topics around the world. Sample topics and target audiences include promoting gun safety for hunters and other gun owners (Meyer, Roberto, Atkin, 2003; Roberto, Meyer, Johnson, & Atkin, 2000; Roberto, Meyer, Johnson, Atkin, & Smith, 2002; Roberto, 2004); a computer-based pregnancy, sexually transmitted disease, and HIV prevention intervention for rural-Appalachian high school students (Roberto, Zimmerman, Carlyle, & Abner, 2007; Roberto, Zimmerman, Carlyle, Abner, Cupp, & Hansen, 2007); preventing hepatitis B in high-risk adolescents (Roberto, 2004; Slonim et al., 2005); promoting radon awareness and reduction among African-Americans (Witte, Berkowitz, Lillie, et al., 1998); preventing HIV and/or AIDS prevention among youth in juvenile detention centers (Witte & Morrison, 1995); preventing bulimia (Smalec & Klingle, 2000); preventing smoking in Canada (Thesenvitz, 2000); communicating occupational risks to workers (Tan-Wilhelm et al., 1999); and preventing genital warts (Witte,

Berkowitz, Cameron, & Lillie, 1998) and skin cancer (Stephenson & Witte, 1998). Most recently, the EPPM has been applied in several international family planning and HIV and/or AIDS prevention projects in Ethiopia (Belete, Girgre, & Witte, 2003; Witte, Girma, & Girgre, 2001, 2002–2003), Kenya (Witte, Cameron, Lapinski, & Nzyuko, 1998), Namibia (Smith, Witte, & Downs, 2006), Uganda (Mulogo et al., 2006), and India (Witte, Singhal, Muthuswamy, & Duff, 2003).

Until recently (see Witte, Ferrera, & Smith, 2005), research and interventions guided by the EPPM typically focused on and individual's perceptions of their own levels of threat and efficacy. For example, does the recipient of a health risk message recommending 20 minutes of cardiovascular activity four times a week to reduce the risk of heart disease believe she or he is susceptible to heart disease and that heart disease has severe consequences (i.e., does she or he perceive a threat)? And if so, does the message recipient believe the recommended response is effective, and that she or he has the ability to engage in the recommended response (i.e., does she or he have high efficacy)? If the answer is "yes" in all cases, then the individual is likely to engage in the recommended response to reduce the danger (i.e., danger control). Or, using the hurricane example presented earlier, how does the individual living in a potential strike zone of a powerful hurricane assess his or her personal threat and efficacy? If both are high, then the individual is likely to engage in the recommended response; otherwise, he or she will not.

Over the past decade, however, two lines of research suggest perceptions of threat and efficacy at the collective, or societal, level may also be important. The notion of "perceived collective efficacy" is an extension of social cognitive theory, and Bandura (1996, 1997) argued that the notion of self-efficacy is also applicable at the group level. The notion of "societal risk judgments" suggests that risks to others can also influence individual behaviors. The next sections of this chapter will define and briefly discuss perceived collective efficacy and societal risk judgments, with an emphasis on the potential use of these constructs in future risk and crisis communication efforts guided by the EPPM.

PERCEIVED COLLECTIVE EFFICACY

Bandura (1997) defined *perceived collective efficacy* as a group's shared belief in its combined ability to undertake courses of action to reach a goal. According to Bandura (1997, 1998), the primary difference between and self- and collective efficacy is that self-efficacy focuses on an individual's perceptions of his or her abilities to achieve designated levels of performance, whereas collective efficacy focuses on a group's ability. Bandura (1997) noted that "the strength of families, communities, organizations, social institutions, and even nations lies partly in people's sense of collective efficacy that they can solve the problems they face and improve their lives through unified effort" (p. 477). This would be particularly true during periods of large-scale risks and crises such as pandemic flu, terrorist attacks, or natural disasters. In each of these instances many challenges exist that would require collective effort to solve. In these and similar cases, it would be particularly difficult for people to exercise control of major aspects of their lives entirely on their own.

Research Regarding Perceived Collective Efficacy

The concept of collective efficacy has been applied to a number of contexts, including the performance of teams/groups (Diamond & Brannick, 2003; Karrasch, 2003), neighborhood violence and crime (Morenoff, Sampson, & Raudenbush, 2001; Sampson, Raudenbush, & Earls, 1997; Xu, Fiedler, & Flaming, 2005), family functioning (Caprara, Regalia, Scabini, Barbanelli, Pastorelli, & Bandura, 2004), and education (Bandura, 1993; Goddard, Hoy, & Woofolk Hoy, 2000). These studies suggest the important role of collective efficacy in influencing and improving a number of outcomes.

According to Bandura (1997), the degree to which collective efficacy predicts performance depends on how much of a collective effort is needed to achieve the goal. For example, highly interdependent groups (i.e., soccer teams, military) require a great deal of coordinated effort from all individuals in the group. If one group member decreases his or her level of performance, it affects the performance of the other group members. Conversely, some groups are not as interdependent (i.e., bowling teams). Although each individual score contributes to the final score, one member's level of performance is not as likely to directly affect the other members' performance (e.g., see Diamond & Brannick, 2003).

For example, Karrasch (2003) looked at the impact of collective efficacy on the Stabilization Force in Bosnia-Herzegovina. The military may be considered a highly interdependent group, as the members must work closely together in order to achieve goals. In the Karrasch (2003) study, members of the group reported a strong sense of collective efficacy. The researcher suggested that one of the reasons why the group's collective efficacy was so high was because they had achieved a number of successes in the past. This is in support of Bandura's (1977) proposition that initial success has a positive impact on an individual's efficacy beliefs. Because this research is in line with Bandura's theory of self-efficacy, it suggests that self-efficacy and collective efficacy are closely related. The results of this study seem to suggest that group success may depend partly on the group's level of perceived collective efficacy.

Other researchers have applied the concept of collective efficacy to the issue of crime. For example, Sampson et al. (1997) found that collective efficacy was negatively related to violence in a community. The researchers defined collective efficacy as the level of social cohesion among neighbors, and their willingness to take collective action for the common good. Results indicated that the higher the level of collective efficacy, the lower the level of violence in the community. Caprara et al. (2004) looked at the role of collective efficacy in the functioning of family systems. The researchers found evidence that a family's collective efficacy beliefs are important indicators of family functioning, which is demonstrated by family satisfaction, communication, parental monitoring and conflict management.

Research on collective efficacy has also looked at its role in promoting social change, particularly when such change comes as a result of exposure to entertainment-education programs. Papa et al. (2000) conducted a study in an Indian village looking at the effects of an entertainment-education radio soap opera on the villagers' sense of collective efficacy to address a variety of social issues facing the community. Results of in-depth interviews indicated that informal listening groups of the program had gradually become formalized into clubs with regular members. Members of the clubs would listen to the programs and then collectively discuss the content and come up with a course of action to address the issues emphasized in the program. The villagers appeared to have developed a sense of collective efficacy to address problems facing the community.

The important role of collective efficacy in each of these studies illustrates the potential usefulness of including this construct in the EPPM. It seems likely that in some situations, collective efficacy may be a better predictor than self-efficacy in producing desired outcomes (i.e., when people must work together to reach a goal), perhaps because some outcomes are better suited for collective, rather than individual action. Further, as noted by Witte et al. (2005), in some situation, high self-efficacy may not be sufficient. The importance of collective efficacy in the studies described above seems to illustrate this point.

The following section provides a discussion of the findings in the literature on collective efficacy in education. As noted by Bandura (1997), the academic system is well suited for studying the impact of perceived collective efficacy on group performance because each school district has multiple schools all pursuing the same goal. Additionally, teachers operate collectively in the interactive system rather than as detached individuals. According to Bandura (1994, 1997), when teachers collectively judge themselves as unable to help students achieve academic success, they communicate feelings of uselessness that can impact all individuals in the school. On the contrary, when they collectively judge themselves as able to impact the achievement of their students, they provide a positive atmosphere that is more conductive to academic development.

Bandura (1993) analyzed the impact of perceived collective efficacy in a study of 79 elementary schools in the same school district. To evaluate the role of collective efficacy in academic performance, path analyses were conducted to determine the causal order of the following variables: student and teacher characteristics (i.e., socioeconomic status and ethnic composition of student body, number of years teaching), collective efficacy, and prior level of academic achievement. Results showed that student body characteristics such as socioeconomic status, and ethnic composition had a small *direct* effect on school performance. However, the impact of these characteristics had a much stronger *indirect* impact on performance because they altered the teachers' collective efficacy to educate the students. The stronger the sense of collective efficacy among the teachers, the better their students performed academically.

Goddard et al. (2000) also looked at the relationship between collective teacher efficacy and student achievement. The researchers collected data from students and teachers in 47 elementary schools in a single school district. Results indicated that as expected, collective efficacy was a significant predictor of student achievement in both mathematics and reading. Additional results indicated that collective teacher efficacy and self-efficacy were moderately related, $r = .41$, $p <. 001$. The authors stated that this suggests that "collective teacher efficacy is an extension of individual teacher efficacy to the organizational level" (Goddard et al., 2000, p. 503). Bandura (1997) also noted the relationship between self- and collective efficacy, stating that "the sociocognitive determinants operate in much the same way at the collective level as they do at the individual level" (p. 482). The close relationship between self- and collective efficacy provides further evidence that collective efficacy can be easily and appropriately applied to the EPPM.

Witte et al. (2005) were among the first to suggest that the idea of perceived collective efficacy might be relevant to the EPPM. The researchers tested the usefulness of adding collective efficacy to the EPPM to predict willingness to help individuals affected by HIV in a community in Namibia. Collective efficacy was included in the study because the researchers thought that it may be even more influential than self-efficacy. The authors reasoned that even if an individual is high in self-efficacy, low collective efficacy may discourage community dialogue, collective action, and persistence of collective action in the face of barriers. The authors cite previous research suggesting that healthy behaviors are better determined by "collectively negotiated social identities" (Dutta-Bergman, 2003, p. 6) than individual choice.

Witte et al. (2005) operationalized collective efficacy as individuals' beliefs that members of their community would (a) be willing to help people affected by AIDS, (b) be able to work together to address the problem, and (c) be able to mobilize resources to help those affected by AIDS. Results indicate that individuals with a greater sense of collective efficacy had greater beliefs that members of their community would take in AIDS orphans. Results of this study seem to suggest the importance of including collective efficacy in EPPM studies, as this concept may help increase our understanding of the processing of fear appeal and health risk messages.

Estimating Perceived Collective Efficacy Regarding Disaster Preparedness

Bandura (1997; see also Figueroa, Kincaid, Rani, & Lewis, 2002) identified two possible methods to estimate perceived collective efficacy. The first method entails asking individuals to rate their personal capabilities (i.e., self-efficacy), and then aggregating the individual judgments of all group members. This would be similar to asking "how well prepared do you think you and your family are if a disaster were to happen in your area?" (Fox News/Opinion Dynamics Poll, 2005), and then estimating perceived collective efficacy of the group as a whole by averaging each member's self-perceptions. The second method of estimating perceived collective efficacy involves aggregating individual judgments of the group's capability as a whole. This would be similar to asking "How well prepared do you think your local authorities are if a disaster were to happen in your area?" (Fox News/Opinion Dynamics Poll, 2005), and then averaging these ratings into a single estimate of perceived collective efficacy. Similar questions could also be asked about other groups, including state and federal governments.

Bandura (1997) noted that opinion polls, while leaving much to be desired, are one way to estimate perceived collective efficacy. Thus, though no formal measures of perceived collective efficacy regarding disaster preparedness were found, numerous public opinion polls conducted after Hurricane Katrina provide rudimentary estimates of perceived collective efficacy using both of the methods outlined above. With this in mind, we sought to estimate the perceived collective efficacy of the American public in relation to disaster preparedness using recent public opinion poll data. So, how did perceived collective efficacy fare when using each of the two criteria identified above? Unfortunately, it appeared to be only modest at best.

For example, when asked "how well prepared do you think you and your family are if a disaster were to happen in your area?" (Fox News/Opinion Dynamics Poll, 2005), less than one-third (29%) of individuals reported being "very prepared," and over one-quarter (26%) felt "not very prepared" or "not at all prepared". These results are corroborated by another poll reported by Sacks and Flattery (2005), which found that nearly half of individuals (47%) did not feel prepared for a natural disaster or emergency weather event in their community. And, though the EPPM is primarily concerned with peoples' perceptions, a number of findings from a poll commissioned by the American Red Cross (2006) in May, 2006 are hard to ignore. Specifically, it was found that while many Americans believe they are at least somewhat prepared, most are not. For example, 69% have not established a meeting place to reunite with family members, 59% of pet owners have no plan to keep their pets safe, and 60% have no specific evacuation plan. These poll results suggest that the two primary reasons for failure to prepare are lack of time and knowledge (e.g., only 23% knew that a three-day supply of water equals three gallons of water per day per person). These are clearly important efficacy-related issues. These data are corroborated anecdotally by Governor Jeb Bush's suggestion that some residents failed to stock up adequately in advance of Hurricane Wilma, which caused significant disruptions in Southern Florida only six short weeks after Hurricane Katrina: "People had ample time to prepare, and it isn't that hard to get 72 hours' worth of food and water… just to do the simple things that we ask people to do" (CNN, 2005).

The preceding paragraph estimates perceived collective efficacy using the first method outlined by Bandura, which called for aggregating individuals' estimates of their personal capabilities. However, public opinion poll data also allows us to estimate perceived collective efficacy using the second method (i.e., by aggregating individual judgments of the group's capability as a whole). For example, when asked "How much confidence do you have in the ability of the U.S. government to respond to natural disasters," just over one-half of respondents (51%) reported "not very much" or "none at all" (CBS News Poll, 2006). These results were corroborated by a public opinion poll taken nearly six months later. When asked "How confident are you in the federal government's ability to handle a major disaster in the future," just over one-half (52%) of those polled responded "not too confident" or "not at all confident" (Associated Press/Ipsos Poll, 2006). Not surprisingly, a majority of respondents (56%) reported that the government's response to Hurricane Katrina made them *less* confident in its ability to respond to a terrorist attack or natural disaster (CBS News/New York Times Poll, 2005).

Estimates of collective efficacy at the state and local levels fared only somewhat better. For example, when asked "How well prepared do you think your state government is if a disaster were to happen in your state," only 18% of respondents reported "very prepared," while 29% reported "not very prepared" or "not at all prepared" (Fox News/Opinion Dynamics Poll, 2005). When asked this same question about local authorities, 22% of respondents reported "very prepared," while 30% reported "not very prepared" or "not at all prepared" (Fox News/Opinion Dynamics Poll, 2005).

Notably, public opinion data suggests that perceived collective efficacy toward other potential risks and crises appears to be even worse than it is for natural or weather-related disasters. For instance, only about one-third of households (35%) felt personally "prepared" or "very prepared" for a terror attack in their community; and less than one-half (42%) believed the government is capable of protecting their communities from a terrorist attack (Sacks & Flattery, 2005). Further, only about one-third of households (35%) were confident in the health care system's readiness to respond effectively to a deadly flu pandemic, or a biological, chemical, or radiological attack (Sacks & Flattery, 2005).

In sum, Bandura (1997) noted that "the major challenge to leadership is to forge a national sense of efficacy" (p. 521). This is in direct contrast to the current state of public opinion. Indeed, Bandura noted it is possible for individuals to experience a "crisis of efficacy" (p. 403), and Sacks and Flattery (2005) indicated that confidence in the government's ability to protect the American public has fallen to a new crisis level.

PERCEIVED SOCIETAL LEVEL RISK JUDGMENTS

Risk judgments have been conceptualized as the ways in which individuals characterize and evaluate hazards (Slovic, 1987). According to Dunwoody and Neuwirth (1991), risk perceptions contain cognitive and affective dimensions. The cognitive dimension refers to how individuals assess the likelihood of being affected by a risk (similar to perceived susceptibility) and the affective dimension refers to the concern or worry people experience as a result of that judgment (similar to perceived severity). Aside from these dimensions, others have proposed that risk judgments include a personal and societal component (Tyler & Cook, 1984). The emphasis of this section is on *perceived societal level risk judgments*, which refer to one's beliefs about the threat to the larger community.

Let us return once again to the hurricane example. Whereas personal risk perceptions refer to beliefs about how the risk will impact the individual, societal level risk judgments include beliefs and concerns about the impact the hurricane may have on others. Interestingly, Tyler and Cook (1984) proposed that personal and societal risk judgments are separate and that people may judge a risk to be present on one level, but not on the other. Further, these authors stated that even if individuals have high societal risk judgments, they may not necessarily draw implications for their personal risk from their societal risk judgments. More recent research, however, suggested that personal and societal risks are not completely distinct. For example, Snyder and Rouse (1995) reported a significant moderate positive relationship between personal and societal risk judgments ($r = .36$).

Research Regarding Societal Risk Judgments

Research looking at societal level judgments of risk, or risks to "others," suggests that individuals who do not feel personally at risk, but believe that others are at risk, can be motivated to engage in behaviors addressing the risk. A fairly good example of this is a study conducted by Morrison (2005). This study was guided by the EPPM and compared the effectiveness of direct and indirect fear appeals persuading men to encourage women to take self-defense classes to reduce the possibility of rape in the future. Because many women perceive that they are invulnerable to rape (i.e., they perceive low susceptibility), fear appeals targeting them directly may not be effective. As a result, Morrison developed an indirect fear appeal targeting men. The indirect fear appeal attempted to persuade men to talk to women (e.g., girlfriends, sisters, friends) about enrolling in a self-defense class. For the men in the sample, the threat was primarily to others, but the efficacy was personal. For the women, the threat and efficacy components were both personal. Results showed that men could be motivated by indirect fear appeal messages with a threat that did not necessarily affect them directly.

An even better example of the impact of societal judgments of risk on behavior was conducted by Lindsey (2005). The purpose of her study was to gain an understanding of the conditions in which individuals would be motivated to engage in behaviors that assist unknown others. The researcher used the EPPM as a guideline and developed messages designed to persuade healthy individuals to join the bone marrow donor registry. The risk component addressed the risk faced by adults and children with leukemia and lymphoma, and the efficacy component emphasized the role the healthy individuals can play by discussing a feasible and effective solution (to join the registry). Results indicated that a message addressing a threat to an unknown other could impact individuals' behavioral intentions and behaviors.

Research on the phenomenon of *sociotropic voting* also provides some insight into the impact of individuals' collective level judgments of issues. Studies have shown that individuals tend to make political judgments based on societal level, rather than personal level concerns. That is, people tend to vote for what they believe is good for the nation as a whole, rather than what is good for them personally. This is referred to as sociotropic voting (Funk, & Garcia-Monet, 1997; Mutz, 1992). Although the motivating factors that lead people to engage in sociotropic voting are not entirely clear, some evidence has supported the notion that people tend to make collective level considerations, rather than just focusing on their personal considerations (Funk, & Garcia-Monet, 1997). This phenomenon may provide some insight as to why individuals may be willing to take protective action to address a risk even if they perceive it is an issue on the societal level (or to others) rather than to themselves.

Most of the previous work guided by the EPPM tended to focus on messages addressing a personal level threat. However, as the examples discussed above suggest, there are circumstances in which it may be necessary and effective to develop risk and crisis communication messages targeting individuals who may not be personally at risk. These studies suggest that it is possible to motivate individuals to take action even if the threat is to others.

The inclusion of societal risk in the EPPM does not significantly change the original model. Societal risk can easily be incorporated in an EPPM study by changing the point of reference of the questions. For example, here are two typical perceived threat items (note: the respondent would be asked how strongly he or she agrees or disagrees with each statement): "I am at risk of being injured or killed by a hurricane" (personal susceptibility); and "Being injured or killed would have serious consequences" (personal severity). These items could easily be modified to measure perceived societal risk judgments: "A lot of people are at risk of being injured or killed by a hurricane" (societal susceptibility); and "Many people being injured or killed would have severe consequences" (societal severity). In order to determine whether personal or societal risk would be measured in the study and manipulated in the message, one would have to consider the target audience of the message (i.e., are they likely to be personally impacted by the risk, or is it more likely that others will be impacted?).

This can be illustrated using the hurricane example. Suppose a risk communication practitioner wants to develop a message advocating disaster preparedness to reduce the negative consequences of a hurricane. For residents living in coastal areas, the message would likely focus on the personal level risk of hurricanes. Such a message could emphasize the risk of a hurricane striking the individuals' neighborhood, and advocate developing a personal or family emergency kit and evacuation plan. However, for those residents in communities that are not likely to be directly affected by a hurricane, the preparedness message would emphasize the risk of a hurricane to individuals in neighboring counties (or even states). It could then emphasize that these individuals who are *not* personally at risk prepare their community to take in evacuees and prepare to assist those struck by the storm immediately after it hits.

Although the hurricane example illustrates this point, it may be useful to look at the issue of global warming, as it appears to be particularly well suited for messages addressing either personal or societal risk. For example, messages addressing global warming could emphasize the present risk to the individual (personal level risk). Additionally, these messages could emphasize the risk of global warming to future generations if we do not immediately take action to address the threat (societal level risk). Interestingly, the Ad Council (2006) has developed messages addressing the societal risk of global warming. These PSA ads provide good examples of messages addressing a societal level risk.

For example, one of the television PSAs features a man who appears to be in his 40s standing on the tracks of a railroad as a train approaches behind him (note: this ad can be viewed at http://

www.adcouncil.org/default.aspx?id=325). The man says: "Global warming: some say irreversible consequences are 30 years away. Thirty years? That won't affect me." Just as the train approaches the man, he steps off of the tracks. However, as he moves away to safety, the camera reveals that there is a young girl on the tracks where the man was originally standing. Because some individuals may not perceive that they are currently at risk to experience the consequences of global warming, the PSAs address the threat to future generations, emphasizing that our actions today impact the lives of others in the future.

Notably, Myers and Goodall (2006) looked at the impact of perceived threat and efficacy on individuals' attitudes and behavioral intentions regarding the issue of global warming. Unlike previous studies guided by the EPPM, however, these researchers looked at risk and efficacy at both the personal and societal levels. Results were consistent with the predictions of EPPM at both the personal and societal levels. At the *personal* level, those who perceived high risk and high efficacy were the most likely to hold favorable attitudes toward public policy addressing global warming, and intend to engage in behaviors that may reduce the progression of global warming. The same pattern was observed when threat and efficacy were measured at the *societal* level. In fact, when the personal and societal level variables were compared, societal level risk and efficacy actually explained *more* of the variance in both attitudes and behavioral intentions than personal risk and efficacy. These results illustrate that the predictions of the EPPM hold even when the primary variables of interest (perceived risk and efficacy) are measured on the societal levels, and that measuring these variables at the societal level might sometimes be an even stronger predictor of important outcome variables.

Estimating Perceived Societal Risk Judgments

Earlier, we used public opinion poll data to provide a rough estimate of perceived collective efficacy toward hurricane and disaster preparedness. We were also able to find a few public opinion polls that addressed individual or societal risk judgments regarding these and related issues. For example, 72% of U.S. adults surveyed in a recent Harris Poll say they think hurricanes are the most destructive natural or manmade disasters (PRNewswire, 2006). Notably, respondents rated hurricanes as most destructive whether or not they lived in an area that is directly affected by hurricanes; suggesting that both individual and societal judgments of severity are high in this instance. Further, results of the American Red Cross (2006) poll discussed earlier also indicate another key reason *why* many people do not prepare for such events: they do not think it is important. This is clearly related to the threat portion of the EPPM, as perceived threat motivates action (and it seems that people are currently not motivated to act). Unfortunately, whether this is due to low susceptibility, low severity, or both was not clear.

In this instance, public opinion poll data regarding terrorism provides even better example of perceived individual versus societal risk judgments. At the individual level, for example, when asked "How worried are you that you or someone in your family will become a victim of terrorism," 14% reported being very worried, and another 29% reported being somewhat worried (CNN/USA Today/Gallup, 2006). At the societal level, when asked "How worried are you that the United States will experience another major terrorist attack," 25% reported being very worried, and 23% reported being fairly worried (NBC News/Wall Street Journal, 2006). Thus, susceptibility judgments regarding the likelihood of a terrorist attack appear to be slightly higher at the societal level than they are at the individual level.

CONCLUSION

The primary goals of this chapter were to provide a brief overview and example of the EPPM, and to introduce the possibility of including perceived collective efficacy and perceived societal risk judgments into this model. Since the Extended Parallel Process Model was first introduced 15 years ago, it has become a popular tool for risk and crisis communication researchers and practitioners interested in the design, implementation, and evaluation of fear-arousing messages. The EPPM highlights the important roles of both perceived threat and efficacy during risk and crisis. Specifically, the model notes that perceived threat motivates action, and that perceived efficacy determines the nature of that action (i.e., whether a person will attempt to control the danger or control their fear). Thus, developing effective risk and crisis communication messages involves more than simply sounding the alarm that a personally relevant and serious threat exists. Such messages must also present a means of calming fears by providing a way to reduce the threat that is both effective and easy to perform.

NOTES

1. This timeline was adapted from National Weather Service National Hurricane Center Tropical Prediction Center "Hurricane Katrina Advisory Archive" (National Oceanic and Atmospheric Administration, n.d.).
2. In December 2005, the National Hurricane Center issued a report noting that Katrina was a Category 3 hurricane with 127 mph winds when it first made landfall in Louisiana, and a Category 1 or Category 2 hurricane when it reached New Orleans (Knabb, Rhome, & Brown, 2005).
3. Note, more detailed information and a wide variety of materials regarding disaster preparedness can be downloaded free of charge from the Department of Homeland Security web site at http://www.ready.gov/america/index.html, or at the American Red Cross web site at http://www.redcross.org/services/disaster/. Example materials include an Emergency Supply List, Family Communication Plan, and a *Ready Pets* brochure. Finally, numerous EPPM-related materials may be downloaded free of charge at http://anthony roberto/eppm.

REFERENCES

Ad Council (2006). *Global warming*. Retrieved July 29, 2006, from http://www.adcouncil.org/default.aspx?id=325.

American Red Cross (2006). *Survey reveals Americans not as prepared as they think*. Retrieved July 31, 2006, from http://www.redcross.org/pressrelease/0,1077,0_314_5398,00.html.

Associated Press/Ipsos Poll (February 13–16, 2006). Retrieved June 16, 2006, from http://www.pollingreport.com/disasters.htm.

Axtman, K. (2006, March 1). Life six months after Katrina [online]. *The Christian Science Monitor*. Retrieved March 22, 2006, from http://www.cbsnews.com/stories/2006/03/01/katrina/.

Bandura, A. (1977). Self-efficacy: Toward a unifying theory of behavior change. *Psychological Review, 84*, 191–215.

Bandura, A. (1993). Perceived self-efficacy in cognitive development and functioning. *Educational Psychologist, 28*, 117–148.

Bandura, A. (1994). Self-efficacy. In V. S. Ramachaudran (Ed.), *Encyclopedia of human behavior* (Vol. 4, pp. 71–81). New York: Academic Press.

Bandura, A. (1996). Personal and collective efficacy in human adaptation and change. In J. G. Adair, D. Belanger, & K. L, Dion (Eds.), *Advances in psychological science: Vol. 1. Personal, social and cultural aspects*. Hove, UK: Psychology Press.

Bandura, A. (1997). *Self-efficacy: The exercise of control*. New York: Freeman.

Bandura, A. (1998). Personal and collective efficacy in human adaptation and change. In J. G. Adair, D. Belanger, & K. L. Dion (Eds.), *Advances in psychological science: Vol. 1. Personal, social and cultural aspects* (pp. 51–71). Hove, UK: Psychology Press.

Belete, S., Girgre, A., Witte, K. (2003). *Summative evaluation of "Journey of Life": The Ethiopia reproductive health communication project*. Addis Ababa: JHU/CCP and Ethiopia National Office of Population.

Caprara, G. V., Regalia, C., Scabini, E., Barbaranelli, C., Pastorelli, C., & Bandura, A. (2004). Impact of adolescents' perceived self-regulatory efficacy on familial communication and antisocial conduct. *European Psychologist, 3*, 125–132.

CBS News Poll (February 22–26, 2006). Retrieved June 16, 2006, from http://www.pollingreport.com/disasters.htm.

CBS News/New York Times Poll (December 2–6, 2005). Retrieved June 16, 2006, from http://www.pollingreport.com/disasters.htm.

CNN (October 27, 2005). Gov. Bush: No gas shortage after Wilma. Retrieved June 27, 2006, from http://www.cnn.com/2005/WEATHER/10/27/wilma/index/html.

CNN/USA Today/Gallup (2006). Retrieved June 16, 2006, from http://www.pollingreport.com/disasters.htm.

Daily News (2006, March 7). *Katrina body hunt continues*. Retrieved March 14, 2006, from http://www.dailynews.co.za/index.php?fSectionId=501&fArticleId=3144380.

Department of Homeland Security (2006). *Hurricane Katrina: What the government is doing*. Retrieved March 22, 2006 from, http://www.dhs.gov/interweb/assetlibrary/katrina.htm.

Diamond, L. K., & Brannick, M. T. (2003, April). Performance and perceived team and player efficacy in bowling teams. Paper presented to the 18th Annual Conference of the Society for Industrial and Organizational Psychology, Orlando, FL.

Dunwoody, S., & Neuwirth, K. (1991). Coming to terms with the impact of communication on scientific and technological risk judgments. In L. Wilkins & P. Patterson (Eds.), *Risky business: Communicating issues of science, risk and public policy* (pp. 11–30). New York: Greenwood.

Dutta-Bergman, M. J. (2005). Theory and practice in health communication campaigns: A critical interrogation. *Health Communication, 18*, 103–122.

Figueroa, M. E., Kincaid, D. L., Rani, M., & Lewis, G. (2002). *Communication for social change: An integrated model for measuring the process and its outcomes*. New York: The Rockefeller Foundation.

Fox News/Opinion Dynamics Poll (September 27–28, 2005). Retrieved June 16, 2006, from http://www.pollingreport.com/disasters.htm.

Funk, C. L., & Garcia-Monet, P. A. (1997). The relationship between personal and national concerns in public perceptions about the economy. *Political Research Quarterly, 50*, 317–342.

Goddard, R. D. Hoy, W. K., & Woolfolk Hoy, A. (2000). Collective teacher efficacy: It's meaning, measure, and impact on student achievement. *American Educational Research Journal, 31*, 627–643.

Insurance Networking News (2006, March 21). *Insurers could be exposed to billions more in Katrina environmental damages*. Retrieved March 22, 2006, from http://www.insurancenetworking.com/protected/article.cfm?articleId=3934&pb=ros.

Karrasch, A. I. (2003). *Lessons learned of collective efficacy in multinational teams* (Army Project No. 2O262785A790). Alexandria, VA: U.S. Army Research Institute for the Behavioral and Social Sciences.

Knabb, R. D., Rhome, J. R., & Brown, D. P. (2005). *Tropical cyclone report: Hurricane Katrina 23–30 August 2005*. Retrieved March 14, 2006, from http://www.nhc.noaa.gov/pdf/TCR-AL122005_Katrina.pdf#search='Knabb%20Rhome%20katrina'.

Kofman, J. (2005, December 21). Katrina weaker than originally thought. *ABC News*. Retrieved March 14, 2006, from http://www.abcnews.go.com/US/HurricaneKatrina/story?id=1429373.

Lindsey, L. L. (2005). Anticipated guilt as behavioral motivation: An examination of appeals to help unknown others through bone marrow donation. *Human Communication Research, 31*, 453–481.

Meyer, G., Roberto, A. J., & Atkin, C. K. (2003). A radio-based approach to promoting gun safety: Process and outcome evaluation implications and insights. *Health Communication, 15*, 299–318.

Morenoff, J. D., Sampson, R. J., & Raudenbush, S. W. (2001). Neighborhood inequality, collective efficacy, and the spatial dynamics of urban violence (Report No. 00-451). Ann Arbor, MI: Population Studies Center at the Institute for Social Research.

Morrison, K. (2005). Motivating women and men to take protective action against rape: Examining direct and indirect persuasive fear appeals. *Health Communication, 18*, 237–256.

Mulogo, E. M., Witte, K., Bajunirwe, F., Nabukera, S. K., Muchunguzi, C., Batwala, V. K., et al. (2006). *Birth plans: Influence on decisions about seeking assisted deliveries among rural communities in Uganda*. Manuscript submitted for publication.

Mutz, D.C. (1992). Mass media and the depoliticization of personal experience. *American Journal of Political Science, 36*, 483–508.

Myers, T. A., & Goodall, C. E. (2006). *Individual and societal level perceptions of risk and efficacy: Addressing the issue of global warming*. Manuscript in preparation.

National Oceanic and Atmospheric Administration (n.d.). *Hurricane Katrina advisory archive*. Retrieved March 7, 2006, from http://www.nhc.noaa.gov/archive/2005/KATRINA.shtml.

NBC News/Wall Street Journal (2006). Retrieved June 16, 2006, from http://www.pollingreport.com/disasters.htm.

Papa, M. J., Singhal, A. Law, S., Pant, S., Sood, S., Rogers, E. M., et al. (2000). Entertainment-education and social change: An analysis of parasocial interaction, social learning, collective efficacy, and paradoxical communication. *Journal of Communication, 50*, 31–55.

PRNewswire (2006). *Hurricanes are the most destructive according to Harris Poll of U.S. adults*. Retrieved July 24, 2006, from http://www.prnewswire.com/cgi-bin/stories.pl?ACCT=109&STORY=/www/story/05-16-2006/0004363257&EDATE=.

Roberto, A. J. (2004). Putting communication theory into practice: The extended parallel process model. *Communication Teacher, 18*, 38–43.

Roberto, A. J., Meyer, G., Johnson, A. J., Atkin, C. K., & Smith, P. K. (2002). Promoting gun trigger-lock use: Insights and implications from a radio-based health communication intervention. *Journal of Applied Communication Research, 30*, 210–230.

Roberto, A. J., Meyer, G., Johnson, A. J., & Atkin, C. K. (2000). Using the extended parallel process model to prevent firearm injury and death: Field experiment results of a video-based intervention. *Journal of Communication, 50,* 157–175.

Roberto, A. J., Zimmerman, R. S., Carlyle, K. E., & Abner, E. L. (2007). A computer-based approach to preventing pregnancy, STD, and HIV in rural adolescents. *Journal of Health Communication, 12,* 53–76

Roberto, A. J., Zimmerman, R. S., Carlyle, K., Abner, E. L., Cupp, P. K., & Hansen, G.L. (2007). The effects of a computer-based pregnancy, STD, and HIV prevention intervention: A nine-school trial. *Health Communication, 21,* 115–124.

Roberts, M. (2006, February 11). Katrina death toll put at 1,310, with hundreds still missing. *The Boston Globe.* Retrieved March 14, 2006, from http://www.boston.com/news/nation/articles/2006/02/11/katrina_death_toll_put_at_1310_with_hundreds_missing/.

Sacks, R., & Flattery, J. (2005). *Crisis of confidence in government widens: Majority of public doubts government's abilities in face of hurricanes, pandemic flue, and threats of terrorism.* Retrieved June 16, 2006, from http://www.ncdp.mailman.columbia.edu/files/ Marist%20Survey%202005%20press%20release%20final.pdf#search='majority%20of%20public%20doubts%20government%27s'.

Sampson, R. J., Raudenbush, S. W., & Earls, F. (1997). Neighborhoods and violent crime: A multilevel study of collective efficacy. *Science, 277,* 918–924.

Slonim, A. B., Roberto A. J., Downing, C. R., Adams, I. F., Fasano, N. J., Davis-Satterla, L., et al. (2005). Adolescents' knowledge, beliefs, and behaviors regarding hepatitis B: Insights and implications for programs targeting hepatitis B and other vaccine- preventable diseases. *Journal of Adolescent Health, 36,* 178–186.

Slovic, P. (1987). Perception of risk. *Science, 236,* 280–285.

Smalec, J., & Klingle, R. S. (2000). Bulimia interventions via interpersonal influence: The role of threat and efficacy in persuading bulimics to seek help. *Journal of Behavioral Medicine, 23,* 37–57.

Smith, R., Witte, K., & Downs, E. (2006). *I want to be like you: Entertainment education, EPPM, and health education.* Manuscript submitted for publication.

Snyder, L. B., & Rouse, R. A. (1995). The media can have more than an impersonal impact: The case of AIDS risk perceptions and behavior. *Health Communication, 7,* 125–145.

Stephenson, M. T., & Witte, K. (1998). Fear, threat, and perceptions of efficacy from frightening skin cancer messages. *Public Health Reviews, 26,* 147–174.

Stephenson, M. T., & Witte, K. (2001). Creating fear in a risky world: Generating effective health risk messages. In R. E. Rice & C. K. Atkin (Eds.), *Public communication campaigns* (3rd ed., pp. 88–102). Thousand Oaks, CA: Sage.

Tan-Wilhelm, D., Witte, K., Liu, W. Y., Newman, L. S., Janssen, A., Ellison, C., et al. (1999). Impact of a worker notification program: Assessment of attitudinal and behavioral outcomes. *American Journal of Industrial Medicine, 36,* 1–9.

Thesenvitz, J. (2000). *Fear appeals for tobacco control.* Toronto, Canada: Council for a Tobacco-Free Ontario, the Program Training and Consultation Centre and the Health Communication Unit (University of Toronto).

Tyler, T. R., & Cook, F. L. (1984). The mass media and judgments of risk: Distinguishing the impact on personal and societal level risk judgments. *Journal of Personality and Social Psychology, 47,* 693–708.

Witte, K. (1992). Putting the fear back into fear appeals: The extended parallel process model. *Communication Monographs, 59,* 329–349.

Witte, K., Berkowitz, J., Cameron, K., & Lillie, J. (1998). Preventing the spread of genital warts: Using fear appeals to promote self-protective behaviors. *Health Education & Behavior, 25,* 571–585.

Witte, K., Berkowitz, J., Lillie, J., Cameron, K., Lapinski, M. K., & Liu, W. Y. (1998). Radon awareness and reduction campaigns for African-Americans: A theoretically-based formative and summative evaluation. *Health Education & Behavior, 25,* 284–303.

Witte, K., Cameron, K. A., Lapinski, M. K., & Nzyuko, S. (1998). Evaluating HIV/AIDS prevention programs according to theory: A field project along the Trans-Africa highway in Kenya. *Journal of Health Communication, 4,* 345–363.

Witte, K., & Allen, M. (2000). A meta-analysis of fear appeals: Implications for effective health campaigns. *Health Education & Behavior, 27,* 591–615.

Witte, K., & Ferrera, M, & Smith, R. (2005, May). *Social sides of health risks: Stigma and collective efficacy.* Paper presented to the Health Communication Division of the International Communication Association, New York, NY.

Witte, K., Girma, B., & Girgre, A. (2001). *Ethiopia reproductive health communication project: Family planning HIV/AIDS prevention formative and baseline study.* Addis Ababa: JHU/CCP and Ethiopia National Office of Population.

Witte, K., Girma, B., & Girgre, A. (2002–2003). Addressing the underlying mechanisms to HIV/AIDS preventive behaviors in Ethiopia. *International Quarterly of Community Health Education, 21,* 163–176.

Witte, K., Meyer, G., & Martell, D. (2001). *Effective health risk messages: A step-by-step guide*. Thousand Oaks, CA: Sage.
Witte, K., & Morrison, K. (2000). Examining the influence of trait anxiety/repression-sensitization on individuals' reactions to fear appeals. *Western Journal of Communication*, *64*, 1–27.
Witte, K., Singhal, A., Muthuswamy, N., & Duff, D. (2003). *Compilation of three quantitative reports assessing effects of* Taru [Report]. Athens: Ohio University.
Xu, Y., Fiedler, M. L., & Flaming, K. H. (2005). Discovering the impact of community policing: The broken windows thesis, collective efficacy, and citizens' judgment. *Journal of Research in Crime and Delinquency*, *42*, 147–186.

15

Post-Crisis Communication and Renewal: Understanding the Potential for Positive Outcomes in Crisis Communication

Robert R. Ulmer
University of Arkansas at Little Rock

Timothy L. Sellnow
University of Kentucky

Matthew W. Seeger
Wayne State University

Crisis communication is growing as a field of study due in part to the frequency and high profile nature of recent crises such as 9/11, Anthrax and bioterrorism in the mail, the Southeast Asian Tsunami, and Hurricanes Katrina and Rita. In each of these crises, communication's role is highlighted. Communication is particularly challenging during a crisis because an immediate response to the looming threat is necessary and because these situations are inherently uncertain. Much of the present literature suggests that managing image during a crisis is critical to an effective response (Allen & Caillouet, 1994; Benoit, 1995a; Coombs, 1999, 2007; Hearit, 1995; Rowland & Jerome, 2004). Although image is important and embedded within the threat, the uncertainty, and the chaos of crisis, so too is the opportunity for growth, renewal, and reconstitution (Seeger, Sellnow, & Ulmer, 2003; Seeger & Ulmer, 2002; Seeger, Ulmer, Novak, & Sellnow, 2005; Ulmer, Seeger, & Sellnow, 2007; Ulmer & Sellnow, 2002; Ulmer, Sellnow, & Seeger, 2007). We advocate that organizations must avoid the threat bias in crisis communication research and embrace the opportunities embedded in these events.

This chapter examines three dominant research lines that emphasize the importance of repairing an organization's image following a crisis. Next, we present the theoretical components of organizational renewal. After we articulate our vision for renewal, we examine two case studies. The first case study, Hurricane Katrina, illustrates how a discourse focused on image and blame emerged following that crisis and stifled renewal. The second case examines a more optimistic and renewing discourse following extensive flooding in North Dakota in 2006. The chapter concludes with implications for post-crisis communication. For our purposes, the crisis situation ends when immanent danger and crisis escalation diminish. At this time, during the post-crisis phase, the primary communication focus shifts from the short term efforts to diffuse harm to reflection and long-term corrective action.

TRADITIONS IN ORGANIZATIONAL CRISIS COMMUNICATION RESEARCH

For the past 20 years, communication researchers have developed theoretical approaches for responding to organizational crises. This research includes Corporate Apologia (Hearit, 2006), Image Restoration Theory (Benoit, 1995a), Situational Crisis Communication Theory (Coombs & Halladay, 2002), and Organizational Renewal (Ulmer, Sellnow, & Seeger, 2007). Corporate Apologia, Image Restoration Theory, and Situational Crisis Communication Theory identify strategies an organization can use to repair its image after a crisis. We briefly examine each of these research traditions.

Corporate Apologia

Research on corporate apologia was initially conceptualized as the speech of self defense (Ware & Linkugel, 1973). As Hearit (2001) pointed out, an apologia is not exactly an apology but rather "a response to criticism that seeks to present a compelling competing account of organizational accusations" (p. 502). In this case, a prerequisite for an apologia is some type of accusation or a *kategoria* (Ryan, 1982). Hearit and Courtright (2004) explained that apologetic crises "are the result of charges leveled by corporate actors (e.g., media or public interest groups) who contend that an organization is guilty of wrongdoing" (p. 210). In order to respond to these accusations, Ware and Linkugel originally developed four strategies for apologists: denial, bolstering, differentiation, and transcendence. Much of the initial research that analyzed post-crisis responses used these strategies as guides (Benoit & Lindsey, 1987; Sellnow & Ulmer, 1995). More recently, Hearit (2006) extended the work of Ware and Linkugel by offering "five distinct prototypical stances that company officials make use of to defend their actions: denial, counterattack, differentiation, apology, and legal" (p. 15). These strategies are used principally for an organization to account for its actions after a crisis.

Image Restoration Theory

Building upon the work of Ware and Linkugel (1973) and the account literature (Scott & Lyman, 1968), Benoit, developed a comprehensive theory of image restoration or image repair. Image refers to how the organization is perceived by its stakeholders and/or publics. Benoit (1997) mentioned that "the key to understanding image repair strategies is to consider the nature of attacks or complaints that prompt such responses" (p. 178). He explained that two components of the attack are essential. First, the organization must be "held responsible for an action" (Benoit, 1997, p. 178). Second, "that [action must be] considered offensive (Benoit, 1997, p. 178). Benoit (1995a) developed a list of 14 impression management strategies. The five major strategies include denial, evasion of responsibility, reducing the offensiveness of the event, corrective action, and mortification. Each strategy can be used individually or in combination (Sellnow & Ulmer, 1995; Sellnow, Ulmer, & Snider, 1998). Similar to corporate apologia, Benoit's image restoration strategies focus on how organizations respond to accusations or account for their actions after being accused of a transgression. An effective response is designed to repair the organization's damaged image.

Situational Crisis Communication Theory

Coombs developed a crisis theory by linking attribution theory and crisis response strategies (Coombs, 2007; Coombs & Halladay, 2002). His theory "evaluates the reputational threat posed by the crisis situation and then recommends crisis response strategies based upon the reputational threat level" (p. 138). The crisis response strategies in Situational Crisis Communication Theory are a synthesis of work on corporate apologia, impression management strategies, and image restoration theory. He developed the list by selecting "those [strategies] that appeared on two or more lists developed by crisis experts" (p. 139). He provided four major postures, including denial, diminishment, rebuilding, and bolstering. In all, he delineated 10 crisis response strategies. His approach evaluates the threat to the organization's reputation based upon "crisis type, crisis history, and prior reputation" (Coombs, 2007, p. 141).

The first variable that can have an impact on an organization's image is crisis type. Coombs (2007) argued there are three general crisis types: "victim crisis cluster, accidental crisis cluster, and preventable crisis cluster" (p. 142). The victim cluster involves crises such as natural disasters, rumors, workplace violence, and malevolence. Accidental crises involve challenges, technical error accidents, and technical error product harm. Preventable crises include human error, accidents, human error product harm, and organizational misdeeds.

The second and third variables that can impact the organization's image are the crisis history and the organization's prior reputation. Crisis history and prior reputation are important because organizations that have recurring crises or poor reputations are not likely to have their messages accepted by stakeholders. Coombs' theory suggests that stakeholders "assign responsibility for negative unexpected events" (p. 138). Depending upon the crisis type, crisis history, and prior reputation, Coombs' provides crisis response strategies to address the attributions of responsibility toward the organization.

SUMMARY OF THE ROLE OF IMAGE IN CRISIS COMMUNICATION RESEARCH

The major research traditions in evaluating post-crisis communication clearly denote the importance of threat to the image of an organization following a crisis. Both Corporate Apologia and Image Restoration Theory focus on the role of accusations and responses in crisis communication. In this case, their focus is on how an organization's image is damaged or threatened and repaired through communication. Coombs (2007) takes a somewhat broader approach by moving beyond accusations and responses to include a range of crises such as natural disasters. He also examined crisis longitudinally by including issues such as crisis history and the organization's prior history. Clearly, though, Coombs is interested in the role of image and how to repair the organization's threatened image following a crisis. A discussion of how the discourse of renewal breaks from these past research traditions follows.

DISCOURSE OF RENEWAL

Although much of the research on crisis communication focuses on managing threat to the image of the organization, we argue there is also potential for an optimistic discourse that provides a vision for the organization as it moves beyond a crisis. Image can and does play a role in organizational crises. However, we argue that crises also carry the potential for opportunity. We see four theoretical objectives central to the discourse of renewal: organizational learning, ethical communication, a prospective rather than retrospective vision, and sound organizational rhetoric (see Table 15.1). We discuss each of these objectives below.

Organizational Learning

Much research suggests that learning is a critical approach to effectively managing a crisis (Elliott, Smith, & McGuinness, 2000; Kovoor-Misra & Nathan, 2000; Mittelstaedt, 2005; Nathan, 2000a,

TABLE 15.1
Theoretical Elements Related to the Discourse of Renewal

1. Organizational Learning
2. Ethical Communication
3. Prospective rather than Retrospective Vision Following the Crisis
4. Effective Organizational Rhetoric

2000b; Roux-Doufort, 2000; Seeger, Sellnow, & Ulmer, 1998; Simon & Pauchant, 2000; Ulmer, Sellnow, & Seeger, 2007). Crisis creates an opportunity for an organization to confront its problems or deficiencies. Sitkin (1996) argued that failure is an *essential* part of the learning process for organizations. Mittelstaedt (2005) suggested that "learning to identify mistakes in an analytic and timely fashion is often the difference between success and failure" (p. 287).

Simon and Pauchant (2000) delineated three types of learning critical to learning from and overcoming a crisis. Behavioral learning is the lowest form of learning because changes are not internalized by members of the organization but rather are "maintained by external control, through rules, regulations or technological systems" (p. 7). Paradigmatic learning involves "both changes due to an external agency and changes enacted by the organization itself" (p. 7). Systemic learning involves an organization learning in advance of a crisis and preventing it. Organizations seeking renewal are more likely to employ paradigmatic or systemic learning rather than having a regulatory agency enforce behavioral learning on them. Behavioral learning suggests that the organization is experiencing impediments to learning and as a result needs external verification that learning is taking place.

Elliott, Smith, and McGuinness (2000) delineated several barriers to organizational learning. They explain that the key barriers include

> rigidity of core beliefs, values and assumptions, ineffective communication and information difficulties, failure to recognize similar or identical situations that happen elsewhere, maladaption, threat minimization and environmental shifts, cognitive narrowing and event fixation, centrality of expertise, denial and disregard of outsiders, lack of corporate responsibility, and focus upon "single loop" or single cause, learning. (p. 18)

We believe that organizations that emerge from crisis successfully and capitalize on the opportunities of crisis will avoid these barriers and emphasize the importance of what they can learn from the event. It is also important that the organization illustrate to stakeholders how its learning will help ensure that the organization will not experience a similar crisis in the future. Schwan's Sales Enterprises provides an excellent example of an organization that avoided the barriers to learning and exhibited paradigmatic learning.

In 1994, Schwan's Sales Enterprises experienced a large salmonella outbreak linked to their trademark vanilla ice cream (Sellnow et al., 1998). Rather than focusing on blame and responsibility for the event, Alfred Schwan, the owner, focused on taking care of his customers and learning from the event. Following the salmonella outbreak, the company built a new facility to pasteurize all of its products before shipping and contracted for a dedicated fleet of sealed tanker trucks to transport its products (Ulmer et al., 2007). Although these changes were costly, they illustrated to customers and the industry that Schwan's had learned from its crisis. In addition, Schwan's learning allowed the company to renew and grow as a result of the crisis.

Ethical Communication

A second key factor in creating a renewing response is communicating ethically before, during, and after the crisis. Organizations that have not prepared adequately for crisis or are unethical in their business practices are going to have to account for those actions in the wake of the crisis. In fact, unethical actions are often the cause of a crisis. One of the key factors in crisis is that it reveals the ethical values of the organization. If an organization is unethical before the crisis, those values are likely to be identified during the crisis. Crises provide the opportunity to identify failures that have built up over time and have been ignored or gone undetected. Organizations that institute strong positive value positions with key organizational stakeholders such as openness, honesty, responsibility, accountability, and trustworthiness before a crisis happens are best able to create renewal following the crisis.

Stakeholder Relationships. Included in ethical communication are the relationships organizations have with their stakeholders. There are few opportunities for the public and stakeholders to view these organizational values prior to crisis. If organizations are going to benefit from a reservoir of goodwill following a crisis, they must invest in true equal partnerships with their stakeholders prior to the crisis. Organizations that want to benefit from renewal focus on developing clear understandings and amicable relationships with their stakeholders. When strong relationships are developed before a crisis an organization is able to depend upon a reservoir of good will from its stakeholders that can help it overcome the negative effects of the crisis.

For instance, Ulmer (2001), in his examination of a plant fire, argued that the strong relationships Malden Mills CEO Aaron Feuerstein had with his stakeholders based upon openness, honesty, trust, reciprocity, and loyalty enabled the organization to recover from the crisis. The opportunities created by these stakeholders were best illustrated by the stakeholders' support of Feuerstein following the crisis. The community in which the company operated provided over $300,000 in donations and wrote letters of support for Aaron Feuerstein's employees. The media supported Malden Mills by serving as a conduit of information to reduce crisis-induced uncertainty. Finally, vendors supported the company by trusting that Malden Mills would be able to meet their orders after the fire.

Provisional Rather than Strategic Communication. Renewal and ethics also focus more on provisional or instinctive responses to crisis rather than on strategic communication. Strategic communication can be seen as unethical when it is designed to protect the image of the organization by employing "spin" to deflect blame from the organization. Because renewal is a leader-based form of communication, renewal is often based upon the leaders' established ethical character. These leaders often respond in provisional or instinctive ways deriving from long established patterns of doing business. Typical of the discourse of renewal is an immediate and instinctive response based upon the positive values and virtues of a leader rather than a strategic response that emphasizes escaping issues of responsibility or blame.

Seeger and Ulmer (2001) examined two plant fires and found that the leaders' virtues and character were central to their instinctual crisis responses. For instance, prior to their crises both leaders had long established patterns of corporate and social responsibility and philanthropy. In addition, both leaders had established strong positive connections with their employees based upon openness, trust, honesty, and reciprocity. At the time of their crises, both CEOs responded immediately by explaining that they would rebuild their plants and would pay workers until the plants were rebuilt. Both CEOs made these statements while their plants were still burning, which suggests that the decisions were made less on cost benefit analysis and more on the leaders' instinct, character, and personal values. In both cases, issues of culpability and wrong-doing were largely absent. With a lack of focus on legal liability or image damage, time was freed up for rebuilding their organizations.

Significant Choice. Nilsen (1974) is credited with developing the concepts of significant choice in communication research. He explained that much of human dignity resides in the capacity to make rational decisions. We advocate the ethic of significant choice as a criterion for ethical crisis communication. In this case, we advocate always communicating the essential information about what is best for the stakeholders while never manipulating information. We use the notion of significant choice as criteria for evaluating the ethicality of post-crisis messages. Nilsen argued for clear and unbiased communication in order for citizens to make rational choices and decisions. In terms of crisis communication, providing unclear or biased information to stakeholders can distort their decision-making process and as a result deny them the opportunity to make a rational decision. Nilsen argued for five standards to be met when engaging stakeholders in significant choice:

1. Stakeholders are free from physical or mental coercion
2. The choice is made based on all the information that is available
3. All reasonable alternatives are included in the discussion
4. Both short-term and long-term consequences are disclosed and discussed
5. Both senders and receivers of messages are open about the personal motives they have that may influence their decision making

These five criteria provide an initial framework for better understanding how to avoid bias in crisis communication.

Prospective vs. Retrospective Vision

A third feature of a renewing response is communication focused on the future rather than the past. Organizations that have created renewing responses to crisis typically are more prospective than retrospective in their crisis communication. These organizations focus on the future, organizational learning, optimism, their core values, and rebuilding rather than on issues of blame or fault. Issues of blame and fault are important but seem to be less so than moving the organization and its stakeholders forward and building a vision for the future.

Optimism. The discourse of renewal is inherently an optimistic form of communication and focuses on the ability of the organization to reconstitute itself by capitalizing on the opportunities embedded in the crisis. For instance, Meyers and Holusha (1986) explained that "[c]rises present opportunities as well as challenges, opportunities that are not available at any other time" (p. 45). In their research, they described seven opportunities associated with crisis: heroes are born, change is accelerated, latent problems are faced, people are changed, new strategies evolve, early warning systems develop, and new competitive edges appear (Meyers & Holusha, 1986, p. 46). In fact, a number of scholars have suggested more recently that crisis has the potential to create opportunities (Hurst, 1995; Mitroff, 2005; Nathan, 2000b; Witt & Morgan, 2002). With this in mind, similar to Fink (1986), we argue that crisis is a turning point for an organization. The discourse of renewal takes into account the potential opportunities associated with crisis and focuses on the organization's fresh sense of purpose and direction after it emerges from a crisis.

Ulmer and Sellnow (2002) examined the national discourse following the 2001 terrorist attacks and found that a renewing effect took place. They based their analysis of this renewal primarily on commitment to stakeholders and values. One of the key areas of renewal focused on stakeholder commitment, particularly to New York City police officers and fire fighters. There were surprisingly few complaints about the service these public servants provided throughout the terrorist attacks. Instead, public spokespersons and the nation responded with sympathy for first responders who died on 9/11 and contributed millions of dollars to the families affected by the terrorist attacks.

In addition, the United States experienced renewal based on core values. Following the terrorist attacks, there was a renewal of patriotism, optimism, and a sense of cooperation. The President, Congress, and other federal officials pledged to renew and engage in the lifestyles they led before the terrorist attacks, and companies lowered fares and fees in order to get citizens back into their previous lifestyles. There was a sense that the world had changed but also a message that people had a renewed belief in the core values of the United States.

Effective Organizational Rhetoric. The discourse of renewal is grounded in a larger framework of effective organizational rhetoric (Ulmer, Seeger et al., 2007). Cheney and Lair (2005) explained: "Organizational *rhetoric* involves drawing attention to issues and concerns in contemporary organizational life with a focus on issues of persuasion and identification" (p.75).

We see the discourse of renewal as a leader-based form of communication. Because we see the discourse of renewal as a leader-based form of communication we argue that leaders structure a particular reality for organizational stakeholders and publics. Managing a crisis most often involves communicating with stakeholders in order to construct and maintain perceptions of reality (Gandy, 1992). Establishing renewal involves leaders motivating stakeholders to stay with the organization through the crisis, as well as rebuilding the organization better than it was before. We advocate that organizational leaders who hope to inspire others to imitate and embrace their view of crisis as an opportunity must establish themselves as models of optimism and commitment (Ulmer, Seeger, et al., 2007; Ulmer, Sellnow, et al., 2007). Perelman and Olbrechts-Tyteca (1969) characterize arguments based upon models as follows: "In the realm of conduct, particular behavior may serve, not only to establish or illustrate a general rule, but also to incite to an action inspired by it" (p. 362). Conversely anti-model arguments involve behaviors that the rhetor believes should be avoided.

Cantor Fitzgerald CEO Howard Lutnick's response to the September 11, 2001, terrorist attack's devastating impact on his bond trading firm is an example of a leader exemplifying how to become a model of optimism and moving forward following a crisis. Cantor Fitzgerald, the largest and most productive bond-trading firm in the world, occupied floors 101–105 of the World Trade Center Tower 1. When one of the terrorist planes hit Tower 1 just below floor 101, most of the Cantor Fitzgerald employees were trapped and 658 employees died. In response to the crisis, Lutnick vowed to rebuild the bond trading firm and support the families who lost loved ones in the terrorist attacks. Lutnick explained, "There is only one reason to be in business—it is because we have to make our company be able to take care of our 700 families…700 families… That is my American dream now" (Russakoff & Eunjung Cha, 2001, p. A24). Seeger, Ulmer, Novak, & Sellnow (2005) found that initially framing the event in terms of this new vision had a clear impact on creating renewal following the crisis. Howard Lutnick's vision was to focus on helping his primary stakeholders—the families of those who lost members in the tragedy. When Cantor Fitzgerald reopened on the Monday following the attacks, it experienced one of the busiest days ever as money, hedge funds, and mutual funds managers tried to help it by sending it business. This response was certainly tied to Howard Lutnick's vision and the context of the 9/11 attacks. Eventually, Cantor Fitzgerald was able to rebuild its organization and support the families who lost loved ones.

SUMMARY OF THE DISCOURSE OF RENEWAL

The discourse of renewal provides a different perspective to crisis communication than is presently examined in the research on Corporate Apologia, Image Restoration Theory, or Situational Communication Theory. Rather than protecting or repairing the image of the organization following a crisis, the discourse of renewal emphasizes learning from the crisis, ethical communication, communication that is prospective in nature, and effective organizational rhetoric. The discourse of renewal focuses on an optimistic, future-oriented vision of moving beyond the crisis rather than determining legal liability or responsibility for the crisis. In many examples of renewal, issues of blame, culpability, or image never arise as dominant narratives following the crisis. What makes these responses so effective is they mobilize the support of stakeholders and give these groups a vision to follow in order to overcome the crisis. Crises that emphasize threat to the image of the organization typically lack these qualities and often have the potential to extend the lifecycle of the crisis. What follows are two cases. One, Hurricane Katrina, focuses on threat and does not generate a renewing response. The other, the 2006 North Dakota Flood, illustrates how a renewing response can be generated following a natural disaster. These cases serve as examples of the potential obstacles to achieving renewal, along with the benefits of a renewing crisis response.

HURRICANE KATRINA

According to the National Oceanic and Atmospheric Administration, hurricane Katrina was among the strongest hurricanes to ever strike the United States. The category 5 storm spawned more then 30 tornadoes and flooded an estimated 80% of New Orleans up to the level of 20 feet. Over 1,500 causalities in five states are attributable to the storm (National Hurricane Center, 2005, p. 1). The official death toll in Louisiana was 1,464. The White House estimated that Katrina may eventually cost $100 billion ("The Federal Response," 2006). A study by the Rand Corporation estimated that New Orleans' population will not return to 50% of its pre-hurricane levels until sometime in 2008. Over 250,000 people have been displaced since the disaster (Rand, 2006). Katrina reverberated through the social, economic, and political fabric of the country. What has been widely described as a failed response has been associated with a significant drop in President Bush's approval ratings. Moreover, the response has been seen as evidence that the federal government's efforts to create a robust and coordinated disaster response capability after the 9/11 tragedy have failed. Major areas of New Orleans remain uninhabited and some areas still await clean-up. While the levee system has been repaired, comprehensive emergency response plans are not complete some 20 months after the disaster, and many experts still consider the city very vulnerable.

The communication failures in the Katrina response were widespread and vivid. Most of the responses by individuals and organizations were based upon shifting responsibility, assigning blame, framing divisiveness among stakeholders, and failed attempts at image restoration. An initial communication failure was in the warning and evacuation system. While hurricanes warnings are often inadequate because they fail to create sufficient concern or address individual circumstances (see Norris, Riad, & Waugh, 2001; Mileti & Sorenson, 1990), the Katrina warning failed in light of the overwhelming scope and scale of the disaster, along with basic problems in evacuation and logistics. A study of early Katrina evacuees found that 73% heard of the mandatory evacuation. Some 55% of those who did not evacuate explained that they did not have access to a car. Other reasons included "I waited too long" (42%), "I was physically unable to leave" (22%), "I needed to take care of some one who was physically unable to leave" (23%) (Spence, Lachlan, & Burke, 2008). Simply stated, a significant proportion of the residents of New Orleans did not have the resources to evacuate or were unable to evacuate due to other obligations. The evacuation order was also perceived as coming too late. Post-event communication was equally flawed. The communication of FEMA Director Michael Brown and other senior officials seemed out of touch with the realities on the ground. Significant public conflicts developed between Mayor Ray Nagan, Louisiana Governor Blanco, and the Bush Administration. Issues of race, class, and poverty came to the forefront and became a significant component of the post-crisis communication.

Lack of Organizational Learning

Significant efforts have been made to critique the Katrina response and learn the important lessons from this disaster. For example, according to the White House document, *The Federal Response to Hurricane Katrina: Lessons Learned,* (2006) Hurricane Katrina reveals 17 critical challenges (see Table 15.2).

The United States Government Accountability Office also undertook a major study of the Katrina response. The GAO identified four lessons it concluded were critical.

1. Clearly defining and communicant leadership roles, responsibilities, and lines of authority for catastrophic response in advance of such events
2. Clarifying the procedures for activating the National Response Plan and applying them to emerging catastrophic response in advance of such events
3. Conducting strong advance planning and robust training and exercise programs
4. Strengthening response and recovery capabilities for a catastrophic disasters. (GAO, 2006)

TABLE 15.2
Seventeen Lessons from Hurricane Katrina

1. National Preparedness
2. Integrated Use of Military Capabilities
3. Communications
4. Logistics and Evacuations
5. Search and Rescue
6. Public Safety and Security
7. Public Health and Medical Support
8. Human Services
9. Mass Care and Housing
10. Public Communications
11. Critical Infrastructure and Impact Assessment
12. Environmental Hazards and Debris Removal
13. Foreign Assistance
14. Non-Governmental Aid
15. Training, Exercises, and Lessons Learned
16. Homeland Security Professional Development and Education
17. Citizen and Community Preparedness

While many of the deficiencies described by the GAO and the White House are technological and logistic, many are also a function of inadequate communication. Moreover, it is not clear that these deficiencies have been addressed in a systematic way.

Most experts suggest that New Orleans is still vulnerable to hurricanes, despite the fact that the levees have been repaired. FEMA has yet to create a comprehensive emergency management plan for New Orleans and has even missed its own deadlines for doing so. While it is impossible to assess at this point how fully the lessons of Katrina have been learned, the initial analysis suggests that the learning is incomplete. New post-Katrina understandings of the risk concern the vulnerability of coastal regions, issues of building codes, and a heightened appreciation of the need for preparation and evacuation during the threat of hurricanes. Interestingly, an additional understanding concerns the inability of the public to count on government agencies during disasters.

Unethical Communication

Disasters and crises often reveal fundamental ethical challenges (Seeger et al., 2003). Fundamental issues in ethical standards and values were evident in the Hurricane Katrina response. Katrina demonstrated basic and long-stranding inequities in terms of class and race. Issues of appropriate treatment of medical patients arose during the evacuations. Inadequate information and access to information compromised the ability of individuals to make significant decisions related to their safety and security.

Among the most visible and dramatic ethical issues to emerge from Katrina concerned inequities surrounding race and class. While research has indicated that the poor and minorities are usually more vulnerable in a crisis, the inequities were dramatically highlighted in this episode. The poor lived in more vulnerable, often lower-lying neighborhoods, and their houses were often older and more susceptible to damage. Those who did not have cars or who could not afford gasoline were stranded in New Orleans. The Center on Budget and Policy Priorities estimates that in 2000, 65% of the New Orleans' poor residents did not have cars or trucks. Many evacuated to the Superdome. As a shelter of last resort, the Superdome became a dramatic, over-crowded illustration of the heightened vulnerabilities of the poor and the minority populations of New Orleans. Quinn (2006) notes, "The hurricane was only the disaster agent; what created the disaster was the underlying vulnerability of the affected communities." (p. 204). The poverty rates in Mississippi and Louisiana in 2004 were both close to 20%, and New Orleans had a poverty rate of 28%, according to US Census Data. Nowhere were the issues of racism illustrated more dramatically than in the case of the Gretna bridge blockade. During the Gretna bridge blockade, minority evacuees from New Orleans were turned back by armed police as they sought refuge in the suburb of Gretna (CNN.com, 2005).

Other dramatic ethical lapses involved vulnerable patients stranded by the rising waters. Many patients were immobile and could not be evacuated and mortalities at medical facilities where very high. Some media reports indicated that patients were abandoned by their caregivers. Johnson (2007) reports a number of cases were hospital evacuation plans were inadequate and where staff was overwhelmed. When phone lines were cut, some administrators were forced to use canoes to coordinate with other facilities. Some administrators noted that critically patients died because of systematic failures in evacuation. In still other cases, medical staff was charged with murder after they were reported to have injected patients with a lethal cocktail so medical staff could evacuate (Konigsmark & Johnson, 2006). Clearly the ethical duty to care for those most vulnerable, the poor and the sick, was not met in the case of Hurricane Katrina.

A final ethical issues concerned access to information. Hurricane predications are an inexact science and warnings often come with little lead time. Once it was clear that the city could not be completely evacuated because time was short and transportation inadequate, residents were directed to the Superdome. This facility was soon overrun with over 40,000 evacuees and inadequate food and waters. In addition, little official information was reaching the superdome or stranded residents. Many reported feeling abandoned and cut off from information, including information about friends and family and about what was being done to help them.

Retrospective Vision

These debates about blame and competing image restoration strategies have carried over as a kind of barrier or bias that precludes the emergence of a more optimistic prospective discourse. In the case of Katrina, debates regarding the relative role of the federal government, the State of Louisiana, and the role of the city of New Orleans continue. These debates have also become personalized in the form of prominent personalities. While there is general agreement about the inadequacy of the response to Katrina, surprisingly little consensus about the lessons of Katrina have emerged or about how to go forward. The Katrina discourse has remained largely retrospective, with the primary focus on failures and blame. In fact, the post-crisis discourse is most consistent with traditional images restoration strategies, including blame-shifting, evading responsibility through good intentions, reducing offensiveness by attacking accusers, as well as some level of mortification through corrective action. Although efforts have been made by politicians—including Mayor Nagin, Governor Blanco, and President Bush—to discuss a way forward, no leader has emerged with a compelling and unifying vision of a rebuilt Gulf Coast. Rather than a unifying prospective discourse, Katrina has reignited long-standing race, class, political, and regionalism tensions. Coombs (2007) describes this as a crisis Velcro effect, where a crisis can collect previous issues and controversies in ways that significantly complicate the current crisis.

Significant disagreements have developed over which neighborhoods should be rebuilt; what role should local, state, and federal government play; who should pay; how should future risk be accommodated; and who should have a voice in the rebuilding. While some discussions have focused on the "opportunities" embedded in the crisis, these are largely isolated to specific issues such as heath care, education, or housing (Zwillich, 2005). An overarching prospective and consensual vision of a rebuilt Gulf Coast has not emerged.

Ineffective Rhetoric

As described earlier, the rhetoric associated with Katrina can best be characterized as a larger campaign of image restoration where various actors employ strategies of denial and blame shifting, evasions or responsibility, and mortification to bolster their image. These strategies have been widely employed by FEMA, the Bush Administration, the city of New Orleans, and the State of Louisiana as they have argued among themselves about who is most at fault. Long regional, political, and historical tensions have exacerbated the level of conflict. Most dramatic are the references to the region's history of racism. Hip Hop artist Kanye West's early accusation that President Bush "does not care about black people" brought issues of race into the forefront. The prominence of race as a theme in post-Katrina rhetoric was reified by media reports describing "refugees" and almost exclusively showing African Americans. Others focused on basic questions of competence in the government's response to the disaster. Two significant addresses characterize the Katrina rhetoric: President Bush's September 15 address from New Orleans' historic Jackson Square and Mayor Ray Nagin's January 16, 2006, speech on the future of New Orleans.

Bush's speech was described as an effort to show his concern and demonstrate that he was engaged and in touch with the facts on the ground. He acknowledged that New Orleans was devastated, without water and electricity, and grieving for the dead and displaced. Bush sought to recast questions of inadequate rescue and the associated "sorrow and outrage" toward questions of "recovery and rebuilding" ("President Discusses Hurricane," 2005). To support this effort, President Bush offered three commitments. The first was to meet the immediate needs of the evacuees. This included an allocation of $60 billion for immediate relief. Second was "to help the citizens of the Gulf Coast to overcome this disaster, put their lives back together, and rebuild their communities" ("President," 2005). This included a focus on both immediate and long-term housing. Finally, President Bush acknowledged the region's "deep and persistent poverty" and "history of racial discrimination which had cut off generations from opportunity" ("President," 2005). He promised to listen to good ideas and look for ways to create economic opportunity. The facts on the ground continued to belie the President's remarks and commitments. Most stark was the fact that generators had been brought in to light up Jackson Square and power the television cameras for the speech. When Bush left, the generators were removed and the city was again dark

Mayor Ray Nagin made many controversial remarks about the response to Katrina but arguably his most controversial were delivered on January 16, 2006. Speaking on the occasion of Martin Luther King Day, Nagin imagined a conversation with the late Dr. King where he related the details of the hurricane and its aftermath:

> I said, "What is it going to take for us to move on and live your dream and make it a reality?" He said, "I don't think that we need to pay attention any more as much about other folks and racists on the other side." He said, "The thing we need to focus on as a community—black folks I'm talking about—is ourselves." ("Transcript," January 17, 2006)

Like Bush's speech, Nagin's remarks were designed to be about the future and rebuilding and to offer a message of responsibility and self-reliance for the African American community. He spoke of long-standing problems in the community and about the cause of the disaster. In so doing, however, he created more controversy and divisiveness.

Nagin argued that Katrina was an act of God undertaken because New Orleans did not take care of its people. "We are not taking care of our children. We are not taking care of our women. Moreover, "surely he [God] is not approving of us being in Iraq under false pretenses" ("Transcript," January 17, 2006).

Later in his brief remarks, Nagin offered a vision of rebuilding, but one that many saw as divisive.

> We ask black people… It's time for us to come together. It's time for us to rebuild a New Orleans, the one that should be a chocolate New Orleans. And I don't care what people are saying in Uptown or wherever they are. This city will be chocolate at the end of the day. ("Transcript," January 17, 2006)

Nagin's "chocolate city" remark was widely criticized and eventually he would apologize. The vision of a rebuilt New Orleans that emerged from this controversy served to reify the divisions of race and class that historically characterized the region.

While renewal is grounded in cooperation and the emergence of a new post-crisis consensus, the responses of both Bush and Nagin were characterized by further disagreement and heightening of pre-existing tensions and divisions. In the former case, the failures of Bush's "commitments" were evident as soon as the generators were tuned off. These failures enhanced the perception that the promises were hollow and that New Orleans was indeed abandoned. Ray Nagin's portrayal of a rebuilt New Orleans was seen as playing into old racial divisions. Critics suggested that there was no room in the rebuilt chocolate city for people of other races and backgrounds. These speeches, by two of the leaders with primary responsibility for renewal, failed to generate consensus; rather, both speeches exacerbated the lack of consensus about moving forward from one of the nation's worse natural disasters. Little space was left in the public discourse for a prospective vision of a rebuilt and renewed region.

An additional factor precluding the emergence of a renewing discourse was the ongoing possibility of additional harm. Although the Army Corps of Engineers had promised to rebuild the levee system before the onset of the 2007 hurricane season, the system was damaged and degraded, offering even less protection than it did before Katrina. Accusations were made by independent experts that shortcuts were being taken and that substandard materials were being used (Warrick, 2006). The larger issue of damaged wetlands and coastline degraded by decades of human activity remained essentially unaddressed. Initial plans for restoring the protective buffer of wetlands and costal islands were downsized due to costs ("Grabbing our last chance," 2007). Without the immediate protection of the levees and assurances that longer-terms issues of enhanced vulnerability to hurricanes would be addressed, the threat remained and opportunities for renewal of New Orleans and much of the Gulf Coast have been suppressed.

THE CASE OF THE RED RIVER VALLEY FLOOD

The winter of 1996–1997 brought more snow than had ever been recorded to the Red River Valley, the area along the border between Northern Minnesota and North Dakota. Not surprisingly, the spring of 1997 ushered in the most extensive and expensive flood the region had seen in more than 100 years. Ultimately, the flood displaced more than 50,000 residents, some permanently, and accumulated a total of $5 billion in damages. When the waters receded, communities in the region responded with a spirit of renewal. Dikes replaced homes in low-lying areas. Flood walls were built to protect buildings and, wherever possible, diversions were constructed to divert water away from populated areas. Despite the turmoil experienced by residents in 1997, most cities maintained their population levels and proclaimed they were now much safer from Red River's flooding than at any other time in history. This spirit of renewal was severely put to the test in the spring of 2006, when the valley again experienced a major flood.

Aside from high water levels, the 2006 flood had very little in common with the tribulations of 1997. Rather than record snowfall, the winter of 2006 brought only an average level of snow. The problems of 2006 actually began in the fall when heavy rains saturated the soil just before the winter freeze occurred (Olson, 2006e). Thus, the winter's snow fell upon a sheet of ice over soil that was already heavy with moisture. The mild winter produced another complication. As an administrator for the region's watershed district explained, "Snow didn't blow around very much and consequently it didn't pile up in the windbreaks and ditches, where it takes longer for snow to melt" (Olson, 2006e, p. A11). These conditions were compounded by the simultaneous effects of a rapid warm-up and heavy rain. Snow that had lingered for months was literally gone overnight as temperatures remained high as rain fell persistently. Within days, the flood warning levels moved from low to extreme. The mayor of Fargo, North Dakota, the largest city in the region, summarized the situation by saying, "No one has seen a flood like this where it came so quickly… I was concerned we wouldn't get in all done in time" (Wagner, 2006a). Despite the swiftly rising waters, the residents were able to minimize the damage, largely because of the renewal efforts in their communities. Organizational learning, ethical communication, a prospective focus, and effective rhetoric from leaders in the region resulted in a concerted effort that spared the region from the devastation it had encountered less than a decade earlier. As this case illustrates, the Red River Valley's renewal efforts enabled them to endure a second major flood with only a fraction of the losses they experienced in 1997.

Organizational Learning

A daily newspaper in the region, *The Forum*, published an editorial bluntly summarizing the value of organizational learning for the region: "If anything good came out of the 1997 experience, it's the comprehensive flood emergency plans that today are routine elements in city management" ("If it floods," 2006, p. A9). Similarly, while touring the flooded region Minnesota's governor proclaimed, "Many communities are benefiting from flood mitigation work that's been done in the past" (Frank, 2006, p. A14). Much of the work referenced by *The Forum* and the Minnesota governor was inspired by the flood of 1997. There are many examples of organizational learning based on the 1997 flood. Two of most compelling examples involve the prediction of flood levels and new dike construction.

In 1997, the National Weather Service was severely criticized by community leaders and residents for failing to provide accurate predictions of the Red River's crests. In 1997, the agency relied upon outdated gauges posted along the river. On occasion, the gauges were frozen or damaged by floating debris. Consequently, the agency gave contradicting reports that over-reassured some residents while frightening others into building sandbag dikes that were higher than necessary. The agency also failed to communicate the level of uncertainty or potential error in its estimates. Thus, some communities assumed the flood would not exceed the projected crests (Sellnow, Seeger, & Ulmer, 2002). The National Weather Service's performance in 2006 was much improved.

A spokesperson for the National Weather Service gave the agency the grade of A–/B+ for its predictive role in the 2006 flood. He admitted that, in the past, the agency had "gotten our Cs before and we've gotten our Ds" (Olson, 2006f, p. A1). Adaptations in measuring techniques based on the failures of 1997 enabled the agency to maintain consistently accurate projections despite one of the fastest occurring floods ever seen by the agency. The information provided by the National Weather Service enabled city officials in the region to focus their efforts and to complete their flood protection procedures in record time. The agency could not have experienced this degree of success had it not adapted and innovated based on the 1997 flood.

Based on what was learned in 1997, new dike systems costing hundreds of millions of dollars were erected throughout the region. The new dike systems served two valuable purposes during the 2006 flood. First, new dikes meant that far fewer sandbag dikes had to be constructed. Permanent dikes had replaced vulnerable areas where, prior to 1997, residents routinely sandbagged each spring. The swiftly rising waters of 2006 would not have afforded residents the time necessary to construct these temporary dikes. The flood coordinator of one city in the region explained the value of his city's new dike system: "It sure simplified what we had to do here" (Olson, 2006d, p. A3). Another example involved a Fargo high school that had flooded badly during the 1997 flood. After 1997, the high school erected a flood wall designed to protect the campus from the Red River. When the water started to rise in 2006, the high school simply closed the floodwall gates. An administrator at the high school said simply: "If the city floods, we're probably going to be the safest of anybody, even though we're closest to the river" (Olson, 2006a, p. A10).

A second advantage produced by the new dike system was related to their location. The new dikes were built on land where vulnerable houses once stood. Hundreds of houses were purchased and destroyed after 1997 because they were considered indefensible in the case of a severe flood. The 1997 flood revealed the vulnerability of houses that had been in place for decades. Had these houses not been removed and their residents relocated, they surely would have been consumed by the 2006 flood. Because residents and city officials did not have to devote time to protecting these low-lying and susceptible homes, they could focus their efforts on responding quickly to other more pressing needs.

The organizational learning that took place in response to the 1997 flood gave the region the confidence and reassurance necessary to wage a successful battle against the 2006 flood. One resident, a veteran of the severe flooding of 1997, echoed the sentiment of many residents in her comparison of 2006 and 1997: "Thank God we're prepared for it. Thank God it won't be that bad again" (Schmidt, 2006, p. A12).

Ethical Communication

During any natural disaster, the open flow of communication is essential. Those in harm's way need information on how and when to prepare for the impending crisis. Poor communication can lead to unnecessary harm or even death. For renewal to take place in a flood situation, organizational leaders must offer ethical communication. By ethical, we mean that residents are deserving of open, honest, and truthful communication. In 1997, community leaders set a very high standard for ethical communication. For example, an AM radio station with the broadcasting power to cover the entire region broadcast flood information, commercial free, around the clock. For its dedication, the radio station earned a Peabody award for meritorious service. Similarly, one of the region's daily newspapers continued to publish even after its building was destroyed by the flood. The newspaper printed its copies in another city and trucked them back to the flood-ravaged area, where they were distributed free. The paper served as a means for residents to get information related to flood recovery and to find the whereabouts of family, friends, and colleagues. The newspaper won a Pulitzer Prize for community service due to its dedication to the community (Sellnow & Seeger, 2001).

In 2006, residents again relied on their community leaders to use the available means of communication to inform residents and to coordinate flood fighting efforts. The Fargo mayor earned tremendous credibility with his open and honest communication in 1996. Still mayor in 2006, he capitalized on this credibility when he described the urgency of the situation to residents. The mayor used the newspaper and radio to express the city's "desperate need" for volunteers (Rogers, 2006, p. A8). In response to this request, 2,000 residents volunteered to fill and stack sandbags (Wagner, 2006b). As the 2006 flood fight continued, the number of volunteers expanded. Among the volunteers were high school and university students and faculty who were released from classes to help with sandbagging. One city official said of the young volunteers: "For the kids out of school they don't stop…it just renews your faith in youth" (Nowatzki, 2006a, p. A14). Volunteers came from throughout the community, and some cities from more than 200 miles outside the region sent bus loads of volunteers to help with the battle against the flood.

In contrast to the open and honest communication pertaining to the region's vulnerability and need for volunteers, the communication related to the cause of the flood was far less ethical. The fall rain and fast melt were the primary causes of the 2006 flood. Yet, subtle changes in the environment throughout the region may have contributed to the flood's severity. For example, North Dakota residents living near the Canadian border insisted that flooding in 2006 was far worse than necessary because of a raised road running 26 miles along border. The residents argued that the road was actually a dike that kept the water from flowing northward. Canadian officials refused to open the road, claiming that road was not a dike. An attorney for the North Dakota residents argued that "for the past 60 years, the Canadians have built an earthen structure, we call it a dike, and it has effectively interrupted and blocked the natural flow of water into Canada" (Wagner, 2006d, A1). Other residents complained that expansive ring dikes around new housing developments were impeding the flow of water, causing water to rise and pool in areas where only minimal flooding had occurred in the past. The coordinator for the Red River Joint Water Resource District explained that ambiguity and complexity are inherent in the politics of water, "because what you do in the business always affects someone else" (Nowatzki, 2006b, A8).

The lessons of ethical communication learned during the 1997 flood paid dividends during the 2006 flood. Officials were open and honest about their fears and the need for assistance. Their ethical communication resulted in a mammoth response to their call for volunteers. Conversely, the lack of open and honest communication in the debates concerning the "politics of water" remains a frustration in the region (Nowatzki, 2006b, p. A8). This frustration also has the potential to delay or diminish the region's ability to fully experience renewal in response to the 2006 flood.

Prospective Outlook

For an organization or community to realize its potential to renew, a prospective outlook is essential. During a crisis, messages focusing on survival and recovery foster the energy and commitment needed to visualize and enact a positive outcome. During the 2006 flood, residents and community leaders established a prospective focus by emphasizing progress and by maintaining a healthy sense of humor.

The emphasis on progress was based on a comparison of the 1997 flood with 2006 conditions. Community leaders emphasized the progress that had been made since 1997 and pledged to continue the ongoing effort to fortify the region against catastrophic flooding. In Fargo, the city engineer lauded the effectiveness of the dike system constructed at a cost of $70 million. Concurrently, he discussed options for further improving the defensibility of the southern part of the city. As the flood waters began to recede, he and other city leaders were already discussing possible options for improvement and their costs (Nowatzki, 2006b).

Many area residents were quick to make light of inconveniences caused by the 2006 flood. Standing on a sandbag dike protecting his house from the rising river, one resident joked, "[My] wife says, 'Let's put a swimming pool back there,' so I delivered" (Wagner, 2006a, p. A10). Another resident whose backyard was engulfed by encroaching flood water said, "There's a nice cove in the backyard, out of the wind" (Domaskin, 2006, p. A1). A rural resident whose home served as a "fortress" in the midst of the surrounding water said her "family feels like they're in an episode of Gilligan's Island" (Finneman, 2006, p. A1). The sense of humor displayed by residents reflected a form of optimism. This optimism was based on a sincere belief that they would endure the flood and that life would soon return to normal.

The prospective focus enabled residents of the region to focus on withstanding the flood and emerging from it better prepared to deal with future flooding. One resident, whose home could only be reached by boat, summarized the region's prospective focus by saying, "Sooner or later with God's help and smart minds, it will end" (Finneman, 2006, A1).

Effective Rhetoric

The community and state leaders in the Red River Valley displayed model behavior by rhetorically emphasizing a balance between reassurance and alarm. As the flood waters began rising swiftly, Fargo's mayor told the community, "We don't view this as a crisis. We view this as an inconvenience" (Olson, 2006b, p. A14). The coordinator of a town 70 miles upriver assured residents that their community was prepared, but he admitted his uncertainty by saying, "The wildcat in all of this is the rain" (Olson, 2006b, p. A14). Similarly, when was asked how their flood preparation was progressing, the chairman of a township near Fargo said, "Amazingly, frighteningly well … nothing pulls people together like this" (Wagner, 2006c, p. A13). This rhetoric of cautious confidence persevered throughout the 2006 flood, even as conditions worsened.

The rain that community leaders feared arrived as communities scrambled to complete their flood preparation. The Fargo mayor reflected on the consequences of the hard rainfall by saying that the valley was not in a crisis situation, but "it's certainly more serious than it was yesterday" (Olson, 2006c, p. A1). As the rain fell, swelling tributaries began consuming portions of county roads. An area sheriff admitted that the situation was worsening and offered a warning that balanced precaution with confidence: "Stick to the major roads. If you do encounter water on the roadway, it's not a good idea to drive through it because you don't know what's underneath the water" (Finneman, 2006, p. A20). Sadly, one day later a 57-year-old woman failed to heed this advice and was found face-down in a flooded ditch after she abandoned her car when it became stuck on a flooded road (Gilbertson, 2006, p. A14). This was the only death attributed to the 2006 flood.

With flood waters rising precipitously, Fargo's mayor urged residents to complete their flood preparations quickly. The mayor explained the situation to a reporter, "We don't want them to get complacent thinking the crest might be less than (37 feet). We urge them to get [sand]bags and be ready to place those bags based on previous experience" (Rogers, 2006, p. A8). As the city awaited the river's crest two days later, Fargo's mayor said: "We're kind of in wait and watch mode now... We think we've done everything we need to do" (Nowatzki, 2006a, p. A1).

As the fortified region awaited the river's descent, North Dakota and Minnesota governors toured the region, offering optimistic messages. North Dakota's governor acknowledged the seriousness of the flood: "It's really the Red Lake right now. I mean, it's just really spread out" (Nowatzki, 2006a, p. A14). Minnesota's governor offered an acknowledgement of the flood's severity along with encouragement: "This is a significant concern and challenge, but in most areas it is under control and is going to be OK" (Frank, 2006, A14). Both governors also pledged to provide financial assistance for the flood recovery and further flood mitigation efforts. North Dakota's governor vowed to continue the state's support in the lawsuit involving the road in Canada that was functioning as a problematic dike. He also offered the state's assistance in paying for a portion of the cleanup, recovery, and ongoing flood prevention and planning. Minnesota's governor summarized his position by saying, "Clearly a great deal of work has been done over the years but more needs to be done... We're certainly going to make another step in that direction, a big step with the bonding bill and probably cleanup costs as well" (Frank, 2006, p. A14).

The rhetoric provided by key leaders associated with the 2006 Red River flood was consistent, optimistic, and reassuring. When residents faced the uncertainly about the height of the Red's crest, they received messages emphasizing the ongoing preparation as well as messages encouraging residents in vulnerable areas to work quickly to compete their flood management efforts. Once the flood began, the residents received advice for maintaining their safety and, again, reassurance that the community leaders were doing everything possible to protect them. Finally, when the flood waters began to recede, the states' governors acknowledged the damage and pledged assistance. These messages formed an ideal rhetorical response to the crisis.

The 1997 flood threatened to destroy entire cities in the Red River Valley. The region prevailed despite what was then the most costly flood in the history of the United States. Nine years later, the river threatened to equal the 1997 crests. The region's renewal efforts fostered by the 1997 flood resulted in an improved flood resistance program that minimized damage in 2006. Cities were able to prepare more quickly and more effectively in 2006 due to improved protective measures and the relocation of highly vulnerable homes. The renewal effort between 1997 and 2006 enabled the communities to learn from their previous mistakes and oversights. Residents acquired resilience from their 1997 experiences that enabled them to maintain a prospective outlook of optimism and endurance. Moreover, the community leaders in the region used their experience and credibility to communicate ethically and to offer a rhetoric that balanced caution and confidence. Thus, the Red River Valley provides a representative case of how effective renewal can be in meeting the challenge of persistent risk or crisis conditions.

SUMMARY AND CONCLUSIONS REGARDING RENEWAL

Organizations that are willing to view from a balanced perspective including both threat and opportunity have a much greater potential for experiencing renewal. Despite this potential, we observe a persistent bias toward viewing crises solely from the perspective of threat. In this section we offer conclusions and recommendations for eliminating the threat bias and for recognizing and overcoming key impediments to renewal.

The Threat Bias in Crisis Communication Research

Research in crisis communication often defines crisis events "as unexpected, non-routine events or series of events that create high levels of uncertainty and threaten or are perceived to threaten an organization's high priority goals" (Ulmer, Sellnow, et al., 2007, p. 7). Much of the research in crisis communication accentuates the perceived threat associated with crisis, and this threat is typically emphasized as potential harm to an organization's image. We argue, however, that crises hold unrealized potential if viewed only from the perspective of threat. We believe crises have the capacity to both threaten an organization's fundamental goals and viability and hold forth the promise for growth, renewal, change, and opportunity. We suggest that future research must mindfully define and examine crisis events from this inclusive perspective. Nathan (2000a) concurs, he explains that:

> [I]n crisis the threat dimensions are usually seen most quickly and are then acted upon, while the potential for opportunity lies dormant. When a crisis is anticipated or when it occurs, the manager should be able to see both threat *and* opportunity features before deciding how to proceed. (p. 4)

It stands to reason that "our crisis definitions, perceptions and subsequent actions are inextricably linked" (Nathan, 2000b, p. 12). Focusing solely on the role of threat in crisis "promotes threat response that may, in turn, magnify and even intensify the state of [the] crisis" (Nathan, 2000b, p. 12). Much of the research on crisis communication focuses on obvious failures as a result in part because organizations focus excessively on the perceived threat associated with the event (Benoit, 1995b; Seeger & Ulmer, 2003; Shrivastava, 1987; Small, 1991; Ulmer & Sellnow, 1997; Williams & Treadaway, 1992). These failures are littered with denials, scapegoating, obscuring responsibility, and general unethical and ineffective communication. We argue that full consideration of both the potential threat and opportunity associated with crisis is a more appropriate and effective way to think about and communicate about crises. Clearly, we do not advocate a single-minded focus on opportunity without an understanding of the seriousness of crisis events. Rather, we argue for mindfully reconsidering our definitions of crisis to include the perceived threat as well as the potential for opportunity emerging from the crisis.

Impediments and Limitations to Creating Renewal Following a Crisis

We see four potential limitations or impediments to creating renewal following a crisis: resistance to learning based upon the organization's culture, mindlessness, whether a company is privately or publicly owned, and crisis type (Seeger & Ulmer, 2002; Ulmer et al., 2007).

Organizational learning and change is a key aspect of generating a renewing response to a crisis. Stakeholders must believe that the organization is going to change and that a similar crisis is not likely to happen in the future. Organizations that create barriers to learning or fail to learn from a crisis will experience resistance from stakeholders and impediments to moving beyond the crisis. If organizations are going to overcome these limitations, they must be open to change and generate a culture that focuses on organizational learning.

Langer (1989) characterizes mindlessness as individuals or organizations responding in routine, habitual ways to situations and acting from a single perspective. In crisis situations, we advocate organizations thinking paradoxically about both the threat and opportunities associated with crisis. However, we further advocate a more mindful approach to managing crises that emphasizes awareness that both threat and opportunity are inherent to crisis and to respond automatically to the threat and leave the opportunity dormant is ineffective. Nevertheless, mindless organizations are likely to experience severe impediments to creating a renewing response to a crisis.

Presently, the empirical evidence that supports creating a renewing response comes primarily from private rather than public companies. One reason for this dominance may be that there is more entrepreneurial spirit and greater autonomy in private rather than in public companies. In addition, a greater willingness to spend money on rebuilding and moving beyond the crisis in appears evident in private compared to public companies. Private owners appear more likely to create a renewing response, to buy into change, and to learn as a result of a crisis.

Finally, there appear to be conditions that are most conducive to renewal. For instance, disasters and floods create such devastation that space is created for renewal to occur. Fires that typically destroy old buildings often free up the space for new, state of the art structures, and technologically superior workspaces. However, we have documented a wide variety of cases that have illustrated the characteristics of renewal outside the parameters of natural disasters and plant fires. For example, organizations that have not typically been praised or appreciated by the general public, such as Cantor Fitzgerald, have responded to crises in such a socially responsible manner that they have created an opportunity for renewing their public image. In crisis situations, mindful organizations are capable of recognizing opportunities to take corrective action, to serve those in need, and to set new standards of service, responsibility, and compassion. When organizations are willing to respond in this manner, they create opportunities for learning, admirable and ethical behavior, rhetorical sensitivity, and a prospective outlook.

Crises, by their nature, are a threat to the survival of organizations. Certainly, no organization should hope for a crisis simply to experience the opportunities described here. Rather, crises are an inherent and inevitable element of the organizational experience. Those organizations that see crises solely as threats to their public image are likely to respond in a defensive and potentially manipulative manner. This defensive posture, at best, offers one benefit—survival. We contend that a combined emphasis on the threat and opportunity of crises fosters the simultaneous benefits of survival and growth. This growth manifests itself in the organization's willingness to respond with rhetorical sensitivity, make ethical decisions, learn from the crisis, and focus on the future. As we have argued throughout this chapter, these elements exemplify a balanced approach to crisis. Applying these elements can produce an opportunity for renewal that far exceeds basic survival.

BIBLIOGRAPHY

Allen, W. M., & Caillouet, R. H. (1994). Legitimation endeavors: Impression management strategies used by an organization in crisis. *Communication Monographs, 61*, 44–62.

Benoit, W. L. (1995a). *Accounts, excuses and apologies*. Albany: State University of New York Press.

Benoit, W. L. (1995b). Sears' repair of its auto service image: Image restoration discourse in the corporate sector. *Communication Studies, 46*, 89–105.

Benoit, W. L. (1997). Image repair discourse and crisis communication. *Public Relations Review, 23*, 177–186.

Benoit, W. L., & Lindsey, J. J. (1987). Argument strategies: Antidote to Tylenol's poisoned image. *Journal of the American Forensic Association, 23*, 136–146.

Cheney, G., & Lair, D. J. (2005). Theorizing about rhetoric and organizations: Classical, interpretive, and critical aspects. In S. May & D. K. Mumby (Eds.), *Engaging organizational theory and research: Multiple perspectives* (pp. 55–84). Thousand Oaks, CA: Sage.

Coombs, W. T. (1999). *Ongoing crisis communication: Planning, managing, and responding*. Thousand Oaks, CA: Sage.

Coombs, W. T. (2007). *Ongoing crisis communication: Planning, managing, and responding*. Thousand Oaks, CA: Sage.

Coombs, W. T., & Halladay, S. J. (2002). Helping crisis managers protect reputational assets: Initial tests of the situational crisis communication theory. *Management Communication Quarterly, 16*, 165–186.

Elliott, D., Smith, D., & McGuinness, M. (2000). Exploring the failure to learn: Crises and the barriers to learning. *Review of Business, 21*, 17–24.

Domaskin, A. (2006, April 6). Boating only way to travel in subdivision. *The Forum*, pp. A1, A14.

Fink, S. (1986). *Crisis management: Planning for the inevitable*. New York: AMACOM.

Finneman, T. (2006, April 1). Cities, counties brace as floodwaters rise. *The Forum*, pp. A1, A20.

Frank, T. (2006, April 5). Experience helps Minn. Residents prepare for rise. *The Forum*, pp. A1, A14.

Gandy, O. H. (1992). Public relations and public policy: The structuration of dominance in the information age. In E. L. Toth & R. L. Heath (Eds.), *Rhetorical and critical approaches to public relations* (pp. 131–164). Hillsdale, NJ: Erlbaum.

Gilbertson, B. (2006, April 2). Region fights flooding. *The Forum*, pp. A13–A14.

"Grabbing our last chance" (March 6, 2007). *The Times Picayune*. Retrieved June 16, 2007, from http://www.nola.com/timespic/stories/index.ssf?/base/news-3/1173165389150860.xml&coll=1.

Hearit, K. M. (1995). "Mistakes were made": Organizations, apologia and crises of social legitimacy. *Communication Studies, 46*, 1–17.

Hearit, K. M. (2001). Corporate apologia: When an organization speaks in defense of itself. In R. L. Heath (Ed.), *Handbook of public relations* (pp. 595–605). Thousand Oaks, CA: Sage.

Hearit, K. M. (2006). *Crisis management by apology: Corporate response to allegations of wrongdoing*. Mahwah, NJ: Erlbaum.

Hearit, K. M., & Courtright, J. L. (2004). A symbolic approach to crisis management: Sears' defense of its auto repair policies. In D. P. Millar & R. L. Heath (Eds.), *Responding to crisis: A rhetorical approach to crisis communication* (pp. 201–212). Mahwah, NJ: Erlbaum.

"Hurricane Katrina: GAO's Preliminary Observations Regarding Preparedness, response and recovery" (2006). Government Accountability Office, Washington, DC. GAO-06-442T

Hurst, D. K. (1995). *Crisis and renewal: Meeting the challenge of organizational change*. Boston, MA: Harvard Business School Press.

If it floods, the valley is prepared. (2006, March 23). *The Forum*, pp. A9.

Johnson, C.W. (2007). "Emergency Planning After Hurricane Katrina: Using Task Analysis with Observational Studies to Simulate Hospital Evacuations. Retrieved May 1, 2007, from http://www.dcs.gla.ac.uk/johnson.edu.

Konigsmark, A. & Johnson, K. (2006). Katrina hospital deaths lead to 3 arrests. *USA Today*. Retrieved June 29, 2007, from http://www.usatoday.com/news/.nation/2006-07-18-katrina-deaths_X.htm.

Kovoor-Misra, S., & Nathan, M. (2000). Timing is everything: The optimal time to learn from crises. *Review of Business, 21*, 31–36.

Langer, E. J. (1989). *Mindfulness*. Cambridge, MA: Perseus Books.

Meyers, G. C., & Holusha, J. (1986). *When it hits the fan: Managing the nine crises of business*. Boston: Haughton Mifflin.

Mileti, D. S., & Sorenson, S. (1990). Communication of emergency public warnings: A social science perspective and the state of the srt assessment. Oak Ridge, TN: ORNL-6609. Oak Ridge National laboratory, Department of Energy.

Mitroff, I. I. (2005). *Why some companies emerge stronger and better from a crisis: 7 essential lessons for surviving disaster*. New York: AMACOM.

Mittelstaedt, R. E. (2005). *Will your next mistake be fatal? Avoiding the chain of mistakes that can destroy*. Upper Saddle River, NJ: Wharton.

Nathan, M. (2000a). From the editor: Crisis learning—Lessons from Sisyphus and others. *Review of Business, 21*, 3–5.

Nathan, M. (2000b). The paradoxical nature of crisis. *Review of Business, 21*, 12–16.

National Hurricane Center (2005). Hurricane History. Retrieved April 11, 2007, from http://www.nhc.noaa.gov/HAW2/english/history.shtml.

Nilsen, T. R. (1974). *Ethics of speech communication* (2nd ed.). Indianapolis, IN: Bobbs-Merrill.

Norris F., Riad J., & Waugh W., Jr. (2001). The psychology of evacuation and the design of policy. In A. Farazmand (Ed.), *Handbook of crisis and emergency management* (pp. 309–325). New York; Marcel Dekker.

Nowatzki, M. (2006a, April 5). Fargo left to 'wait and watch' after days of work. *The Forum*, pp. A1, A14.

Nowatzki, M. (2006b, April 9). Ring dikes popular in Canada, but not with southern neighbor. *The Forum*, pp. A1, A8.

Olson, D. (2006a, March 20). A new season arrives. *The Forum*, pp. A1, A10.

Olson, D. (2006b, March 31). Warmth moves up crest prediction. *The Forum*, pp. A1, A14.

Olson, D. (2006c, April 1). Temporary dikes go up on 2nd St. *The Forum*, pp. A1, A20.

Olson, D. (2006d, April 5). Major damage not expected as floodwaters inundate area. *The Forum*, pp. A1, A3.

Olson, D. (2006e, April 6). What caused the flood? Well, a lot of things, really. *The Forum*, pp. A1, A11.

Olson, D. (2006f, April 12). Riding a crest. *The Forum*, p. A1.

Perelman, C., & Olbrechts-Tyteca, L. (1969). *The new rhetoric: A treatise on argumentation*. Notre Dame, IN: University of Notre Dame Press.

"President discusses hurricane relief in address to the nation." (September 15, 2005). Retrieved May 12, 2007, from http://www.whitehouse.gov/news/releases/2005/09/20050915-8.html.

Quinn, S. C. (2006). Hurricane Katrina: A social and public health Disaster. *American Journal of Public Health*, 96, 2. Retrieved May 12, 2007, from http://www.ajph.org/cgi/content/short/AJPH.2005.080119v1

"Racism, resources blamed for bridge incident." (Sept 13, 2005). CNN.com. Retrieved June 29, 2007, from http://www.cnn.com/2oo5/US/)(/13/katrina.bridge/index.html.

Rogers, M. (2006, April 3). Mayor warns against complacency. *The Forum*, pp. A1, A8.

Roux-Doufort, C. (2000). Why organizations don't learn from crises: The perverse power of normalization. *Review of Business, 21*(21), 25–30.
Rowland, R. C., & Jerome, A. M. (2004). On organizational apologia: A reconceptualization. *Communication Theory, 14*, 191–211.
Russakoff, D., & Eunjung Cha, A. (2001, September 14, 2001). Sketches of the missing: Hard-workign early risers. *The Washington Post,* p. 24.
Ryan, H. R. (1982). Kategoria and apologia: On their rhetorical criticism as a speech set. *Quarterly Journal of Speech, 68*, 254–261.
Schmidt, H. (2006, April 5). Forks, EGF ready for Red. *The Forum*, p. A12.
Scott, M. H., & Lyman, S. M. (1968). Accounts. *American Sociological Review, 33*, 46–62.
Seeger, M. W., Sellnow, T. L., & Ulmer, R. R. (1998). Communication, organization and crisis. In M. E. Roloff (Ed.), *Communication Yearbook* (Vol. 21, pp. 231–275). Thousand Oaks, CA: Sage.
Seeger, M. W., Sellnow, T. L., & Ulmer, R. R. (2003). *Communication and Organizational Crisis*. Westport, CT: Praeger.
Seeger, M. W., & Ulmer, R. R. (2001). Virtuous responses to organizational crisis: Aaron Feuerstein and Milt Cole. *Journal of Business Ethics, 31*, 369–376.
Seeger, M. W., & Ulmer, R. R. (2002). A post-crisis discourse of renewal: The cases of Malden Mills and Cole Hardwoods. *Journal of Applied Communication Research, 30*, 126–142.
Seeger, M. W., & Ulmer, R. R. (2003). Explaining Enron: Communication and responsible leadership. *Management Communication Quarterly, 17*, 58–84.
Seeger, M. W., Ulmer, R. R., Novak, J. M., & Sellnow, T. L. (2005). Post-crisis discourse and organizational change, failure and renewal. *Journal of Organizational Change Management, 18*, 78–95.
Sellnow, T., & Seeger, M. (2001). Exploring the boundaries of crisis communication: The case of the 1997 Red Rive Valley Flood. *Communication Studies, 52(2),* 153–167.
Sellnow, T. L., Seeger, M. W., & Ulmer, R. R. (2002). Chaos theory, informational needs, and natural disasters. *Journal of Applied Communication Research, 30*, 269–292.
Sellnow, T. L., & Ulmer, R. R. (1995). Ambiguous argument as advocacy in organizational crisis communication. *Argumentation and Advocacy, 31*, 138–150.
Sellnow, T. L., Ulmer, R. R., & Snider, M. (1998). The compatibility of corrective action in organizational crisis communication. *Communication Quarterly, 46*, 60–74.
Sherman, A. & Shapiro, I. (2005). "Essential facts about the victims of Hurricane Katrina." Center for Budget Policy and Priorities." Center on Budget and Policy Priorities. Retrieved May 12, 2007, from www.cbpp.org/9-19-05pov.htm.
Shrivastava, P. (1987). *Bhopal: Anatomy of a crisis*. Cambridge, MA: Ballinger Publishing Company.
Simon, L., & Pauchant, T. C. (2000). Developing the three levels of learning in crisis management: A case study of the Hagersville tire fire. *Review of Business, 21*, 6–11.
Sitkin, S. B. (1996). Learning through failure: The strategy of small losses. In M. D. Cohen & L. S. Sproull (Eds.), *Organizational learning* (pp. 541–578). Thousand Oaks, CA: Sage.
Small, W. (1991). Exxon Valdez: How to spend billions and still get a black eye. *Public Relations Review, 17*, 9–26.
Spence, P. R., Lachlan, K. A., & Burke, J. (2008). Crisis preparation, media use, and information seeking: Patterns across Katrina evacuees and lessons learned for crisis communication. *Journal of Emergency Management.*
"Transcript of Nagin's speech" Times-Picayune, Tuesday, January 17, 2006. Retrieved April 12, 2007, from: http://www.nola.com/news/t-p/frontpage/index.ssf?/news/t-p/stories/011706_nagin_transcript.html.
"The Federal Response to Hurricane Katrina: Lessons Learned" (2006). Retrieved April 10, 2007, from http://www.whitehouse.gov/reports/katrina-lessons-learned/.
Ulmer, R. R. (2001). Effective crisis management through established stakeholder relationships: Malden Mills as a case study. *Management Communication Quarterly, 14*, 590–615.
Ulmer, R. R., Seeger, M. W., & Sellnow, T. L. (2007). Post crisis communication and renewal: Expanding the parameters of post-crisis discourse. *Public Relations Review*, 130–134.
Ulmer, R. R., & Sellnow, T. L. (1997). Strategic ambiguity and the ethic of significant choice in the tobacco industry's crisis communication. *Communication Studies, 48*, 215–233.
Ulmer, R. R., & Sellnow, T. L. (2002). Crisis management and the discourse of renewal: Understanding the potential for positive outcomes of crisis. *Public Relations Review, 28*, 361–365.
Ulmer, R. R., Sellnow, T. L., & Seeger, M. W. (2007). *Effective crisis communication: Moving from crisis to opportunity*. Thousand Oaks, CA: Sage.
Wagner, S. (2006a, April 6). River levels start the fall in F-M area; fight ongoing. *The Forum*, pp. A1, A10.
Wagner, S. (2006b, April 7). Good news trumps bad. *The Forum*, pp. A1, A11.
Wagner, S. (2006c, April 8). Floodwaters continue to recede. *The Forum*, pp. A12, A13.

Wagner, S. (2006d, April 20). A bitter road. *The Forum*, pp. A1, A14.

Ware, B. L., & Linkugel, W. A. (1973). They spoke in defense of themselves: On the generic criticism of apologia. *Quarterly Journal of Speech, 59*, 273–283.

Warrick, J. (March 6, 2006). "Levee fixes falling short, experts warn. Washington Post.com. Retrieved June 17, 2007, from http://www.washingtonpost.com/wp-dyn/content/article/2006/03/05/AR2006030500976.html.

Williams, D. E., & Treadaway, G. (1992). Exxon and the Valdez accident: A failure in crisis communication. *Communication Studies, 43*, 56–64.

Witt, J. L., & Morgan, G. (2002). *Stronger in broken places: Nine lessons for turning crisis into triumph*. New York: Times Books.

Zwillich, T (2005) "Rebuilding New Orleans." *The Lancet, 366*, 9493, 1256–1256.

16

Risk Communication by Organizations: The Back Story

Caron Chess and Branden Johnson
Rutgers University

To study risk communication as an interactive process, research should encompass key participants in the interaction. However, risk communication research has attended to public perception to a greater extent than organizational behavior—even though organizations vitally shape the communication process and messages. While senior managers in corporations or government agencies make decisions about the form and content of risk communication, rarely are their actions studied. Instead, risk communication research has focused on those outside the organization, who are often considered merely receivers of these messages.

In this chapter, we "study up" to provide insight into how organizational dynamics have shaped risk communication in the United States. Risk communication was born of Bhopal, matured with implementation of the federal Right to Know law, and entered a mid-life crisis post-September 11. We begin with an adaptation of an article from *Risk Analysis* (Chess, 2001) that describes the organizational genesis of corporate risk communication. After Bhopal, chemical companies voluntarily undertook risk communication to bolster their credibility. Nonetheless, concerns about chemical safety and corporate integrity provided the impetus for Congress to pass a federal Right to Know law to force chemical companies to release information about toxic chemicals.

We then update this history by looking at risk communication in the post-September 11 world. We provide two examples that illustrate the trade offs between information access and security. Since the attack on the World Trade Center on September 11, 2001, chemical companies have successfully argued that information on worst case scenarios, the potential results of catastrophic accidents, should not be available to the public. Although never comfortable with releasing information about where plumes of toxic chemicals might waft, the companies' arguments were far more persuasive after September 11.

We also explore how government agencies handled one of their major risk communication challenges: risk communication about anthrax.[1] The interactions among organizations on the federal level, particularly the Centers for Disease Control (CDC) and the Federal Bureau of Investigation (FBI), restricted the information available to the country. However, we demonstrate that in some instances long-standing relationships on the local level reduced interorganizational communication problems that plagued federal agencies. The result was greater transparency among local organizations and with those they served.

TABLE 16.1
Stages of Risk Communication

All we have to do is get the numbers right.
All we have to do is tell them the numbers.
All we have to do is explain what we mean by the numbers.
All we have to do is show them that they've accepted similar risks in the past.
All we have to do is show them it's a good deal for them.
All we have to do is treat them nice.
All we have to do is make them partners.
All of the above.

(Adapted from Fischhoff, 1995)

ORGANIZATIONAL THEORY AND THE HISTORY OF RISK COMMUNICATION

Fischhoff (1995) suggested that risk communication has moved through seven stages of different "focal communication strategies which practitioners hope will do the trick" (p. 137). His stages (see Table 16.1) range from content-oriented risk communication intended to persuade to process-oriented risk communication involving partnerships. Thus, Fischhoff posited both a change in content and a change in process. In doing so, he suggested that the morphing of risk communication is not simple, but begins with getting the data right.

Fischhoff's intention was to speed learning about risk communication: "Every year (or perhaps every day), some new industry or institution discovers that it, too, has a risk problem. It can, if it wishes, repeat the learning process that its predecessors have undergone. Or, it can attempt to short-circuit that process and start with its product, namely the best available approaches to risk communication" (1995, p. 137).

Fischhoff acknowledged that organizational learning was more complex than any evolutionary description, no matter how apt. He also noted that his evolutionary account was speculative because no one has systematically documented the history of risk communication.

Risk communication evolved for the most part without the benefit of an organizational framework. Instead, risk communication research began with theoretical frameworks provided by psychologists such as Fischhoff. However, the broader risk field is based on a variety of disciplinary frameworks, including the sociology of risk (e.g., Krimsky & Golding, 1992). According to some sociologists of risk (e.g., Clarke, 1992; Freudenburg,1993; Rosa, 1997), the story of risk is the story of organizations.

We argue that the impetus for and effectiveness of risk communication are also tied to organizational variables. The organizational aspects of the risk communication story are complex and would benefit from multiple tellings from a variety of viewpoints, among them organizational learning, culture, and leadership. However, one chapter cannot provide a definitive version of the organizational story behind the history of risk communication. Instead, we hope to provide a perspective that considers the interactions between organizations and their organizational environments as a factor in risk communication.

BACKGROUND: ORGANIZATIONAL THEORY AND RISK COMMUNICATION

> To understand the behavior of an organization you must understand the context of that behavior—that is the ecology of the organization. (Pfeffer & Salancik, 1978, p. 1)

The following organizational perspective on risk communication is based on the dominant theoretical paradigm currently subscribed to by organizational theorists. This open systems paradigm (derived from systems theory) suggests that an organization's external environment is the major influence on the organization and its ability to succeed. This paradigm contrasts with two other organizational paradigms that previously dominated organizational theory and continue to influence corporate and governmental practice. The first, the rational paradigm, assumes an organization is a closed mechanical system and focuses on increasing organizational efficiency (Scott, 1992). The second, the natural systems paradigm, emphasizes that dynamics of groups and styles of leadership are fundamental to organizational success (Scott, 1992).

In contrast, the open systems approach discussed in this chapter tends to emphasize the ways an organization's external environment can constrain such dynamics. While CEOs have been described as having power over the closed system of an organization (e.g., Weber, 1968), senior managers have far less discretion than previously thought, according to open systems theory. For example, actions of CEOs are subject to scrutiny by financial institutions that look for short term gain (Mintz & Schwartz, 1985). The power of financial institutions is so great that they can topple regimes of CEOs whose strategies are incompatible with those of banks and institutional shareholders, such as large pension investors.

The open systems paradigm has also been adopted by other fields. For example, a normative theory of public relations suggests that an organization's form of public relations is influenced by the organization's external environment (e.g., Grunig.1992). The history of the greening of industry has also been discussed in terms of pressure from the external environment (e.g., Schot & Fischer, 1993).

However, defining where an organization ends and its environment begins is fraught with problems. One approach is to define organizational boundaries by the extent of organizational discretion. When an organization's discretion is less than the discretion of another organization to control an activity, the activity is outside the organization's boundary (Pfeffer & Salancik,1978). Boundaries are conceived of as dynamic, defined by relationships that often change over time

The definition of the organizational environment has evolved with the maturation of organizational theory. The *task environment* is the part of the environment that is relevant to production activities and considers organizations largely in terms of the work they do (Scott, 1992). This definition looks at exchanges between the environment and the focal organization (the organization under study) largely in terms of resources (Thompson, 1967). Thus, customers, suppliers, and competitors constitute the task environment (Dill, 1958).

The more recent conception of an institutional environment is far broader, including rules, norms, roles and expectations, which can affect organizations independent of resources (Scott, 1987). In contrast to the concept of a task environment, "the new formulation stresses the role played by cultural elements—symbols, cognitive systems, normative beliefs—and the sources of such elements" (Scott, 1987, p. 498). *Institutional environments* can reward organizations not only for output quality, quantity, or efficiency, as do task environments, but also for developing appropriate structures or procedures. For example, schools are evaluated on obedience to institutional rules about student attendance, certification of teachers, and accreditation (Meyer & Rowan, 1980, 1991). Managers need not consciously decide to adapt the organization to norms. Organizations assimilate societal norms, rules and expectations, "creating the lenses through which actors see the world and the very categories of structure, action, or thought" (Dimaggio & Powell, 1991, p. 13). The norms and values can be so taken for granted that organizations do not even realize they are acceding to them: "...every outcome is not the result of a decision process" (Scott, 1987, p. 505). For example, senior managers have symbolic trappings of power in this society. It is a given that these managers have perks that the rest of us do not. While the perks may vary by organization, the notion that hierarchy has its privileges is a given. This does not suggest that givens cannot be challenged. In fact, this theory of institutionalism seeks to unmask these assumptions to show their influence (Dimaggio & Powell, 1991).

Most theorists see organizational environments as socially constructed, not merely a collection of attributes that can be measured: "Organizational environments are not given realities; they are created through a process of attention and interpretation" (Pfeffer & Salancik, 1978). In other words, organizations' perceptions of their reality are shaped by what companies and corporations choose to notice in their external environments and how they understand events. (One perplexing question is: who or what perceives the environment? Is perception of the environment the summation of perceptions of individuals in the organization, perceptions of powerful leaders, units within organizations, and/or organizations as a whole? Reviews of some of these questions, which are beyond the scope of this chapter, are found in Downey and Slocum (1975) and Downey, Hellriegel, & Slocum (1975).

THE RISK COMMUNICATION GROWTH SPURT: THE POST-BHOPAL ENVIRONMENT

The relationship between chemical manufacturers and their external environments provides a basis for interpreting the post-Bhopal history of risk communication. In March, 1985, three months after Americans watched on the evening news men, women, and children dying as a result of the accident at the Union Carbide plant, the company's Chief Operating Officer, Warren Anderson, spoke to Congress about the company's Institute, West Virginia plant, which used the same chemical responsible for the tragedy in India. He reassured senators that the plant had been examined with a "fine tooth comb" (Shabecoff, 1985, p. A1). The release of methyl isocyanate that caused the deaths in Bhopal was "inconceivable" in the United States. Fifty percent of the American people believed him, according to a Harris poll.

On the morning of Sunday, August 11, less than five months after Anderson's assurances, a cream-colored cloud of gas ended golf at the country club near Union Carbide's Institute plant. (Franklin, 1985). Eyes of residents near the plant also started stinging and the air reeked. More than 130 people in Institute, West Virginia, were treated for eye, throat, or lung irritation caused by release of aldicarb oxime from Union Carbide's plant (Diamond, 1985). The havoc in Bhopal followed by the leak in Institute (even though a less toxic chemical) caused a crisis of public confidence that sent an alarm through the chemical industry (Lueck, 1985). After the West Virginia incident, another Harris poll showed that 91% of Americans felt that government "should crack down a lot harder on chemical companies such as Union Carbide than they have." While the industry braced itself for tougher regulation (Lueck, 1985, p. A1), it also sought to rescue its credibility by demonstrating competence and caring. After Bhopal, the Chemical Manufacturers Association (CMA) initiated the Community Awareness and Emergency Response Program, which encouraged CMA member corporations to work voluntarily with communities to improve emergency response and community awareness of hazardous chemicals.

However, the Institute release also gave more credence to the claims of environmentalists and union leaders that chemical companies could not be trusted. Despite the deaths in India, Union Carbide had not developed adequate systems to warn Institute residents. Senator Frank Lautenberg of New Jersey saw the release as evidence of the need for federal legislation: "Here we had a company that could not operate in a safe fashion even with a public microscope" (Diamond, 1985, p. 1).

Because a company under international pressure failed to act responsibly, the assumption was that others under less pressure would need to be watched closely. Congress responded to unions' and environmentalists' demands for a federal law to force corporations to disclose information about the toxics they handle and to give community residents the right to know about the environmental releases. On October 17, 1986, after much opposition from the chemical industry, the Emergency Planning and Community Right to Know Act was finally passed (Hadden, 1989). Subsequent to these events, the Chemical Manufacturers Association (now named the American Chemistry Council) developed its Responsible Care program which has spawned a variety of codes of conduct and guidance about how to communicate with communities about risk.

AN ORGANIZATIONAL INTERPRETATION OF EVENTS

Risk communication in its various forms can be seen as a strategy to adapt to the increasingly hostile environment in which chemical manufacturers found themselves. Particularly after Bhopal, manufacturers felt pressure from risk stakeholders[2] who questioned the legitimacy of chemical manufacturers. Major accidents "acted as a catalyst for intensified public hostility and distrust inspired new regulations and new business action" (e.g., Schot & Fischer 1993). Reduced legitimacy had the potential to reduce access to resources (e.g., Pfeffer & Salancik, 1978), such as land for expansion and permitting needed for increased production. Turbulence, resulting from reduced legitimacy in the external environment, made the future, and successful strategies to deal with contingencies, difficult to predict.

Essentially, as a result of organizational threat, risk communication became a corporate survival mechanism. The threat was not only tied to access to resources but more fundamentally to corporations' legitimacy and the uncertainty of the external environment: "History shows us that no industry has survived a permanent conflict with society. Dialogue, adjustment, and cooperation are therefore not a luxury but a necessity" (Loudon, 1987, p. 8).

Legitimacy and the External Environment

The restructuring of relationships with communities, manifest in the rise of risk stakeholders, came about because chemical manufacturers had lost legitimacy and with it power to control formerly proprietary information. Legitimacy is difficult to specify and may be more apparent by its absence than presence (Pfeffer & Salancik, 1978).

One interpretation views legitimacy as the amount of "cultural support for an organization—the extent to which the array of established social accounts provide explanations for its existence" (Scott, 1987, p. 201). Seen from this perspective, "A completely legitimate organization would be one about which no question could be raised" (Scott, 1987, p. 201).

Legitimacy can also be framed in terms of the "congruence between social values associated with or implied by their activities and norms of acceptable behavior in the larger social system in which they are a part. In so far as the two value systems are congruent, we can speak of organizational legitimacy. When an actual or potential disparity exists between the two value systems, there will exist a threat to organizational legitimacy (Dowling & Pfeffer, 1975, p. 122).

The long-standing technical expertise of chemical manufacturers had previously granted legitimacy to exclude those with less expertise. Power over risk confers expertise, and expertise confers power, according to risk assessor Chauncey Starr (1969): "Society has generally clothed many of its controlling groups in an almost impenetrable mantle of authority of undisputed wisdom." (p. 86). Thus, prior to enactment of the federal Right to Know legislation corporations' power was based, in part, on exclusive information about chemical releases and that expertise helped to maintain corporations' authority. Without that exclusive authority, industry representatives were concerned that the information from Right to Know would spark irrationality about risk.

Corporations saw risk communication as a possible palliative for "chemophobia." In the face of decreasing legitimacy, the pressure to communicate became greater. As one corporate leader suggested at the first national conference on risk communication: "For too long, industry in general has viewed risk communication as unnecessary. We have reasoned that our scientists indicate the risk to the public is insignificant, and that is all that matters. Why should we bother talking about something that is no concern to someone else?" (Blair, 1986, p. 37).

Another industry leader exhorted companies to accept "the public challenge" because "The reaction may well be staggering. If we don't voluntarily change in our approach to public concerns, the public will force us to do it" (Corbett, 1988, p. 18). These reactions to threats to legitimacy have also been recognized by some who study the "greening" of industry and see the transition towards sustainability as "foremost a result of firms seeking normative conformity and external legitimation" (Schot & Fischer, 1993, p. 15).

Environmental Uncertainty

Because the organizational environment changes, and organizational knowledge about the environment is imperfect, corporate forecasts of the future may be no more accurate than the monthly horoscopes sold in drugstores. While organizations may intend to make rational choices, they often need to act on incomplete information (March & Olsen, 1975). As other prominent organizational theorists have pointed out: "Problems arise not merely because the organizations are dependent on their environment but because this environment is not dependable. When environments change, organizations face the prospect either of not surviving or of changing their activities in response to these environmental factors" (Pfeffer & Salancik, 1978, p. 3).

Uncertainty in the organizational environment can be defined in a variety of ways, but most definitions include an element of unpredictability, whether of the environment itself, the effect of the environment on the organization, or the effect of an organization's response to the environment (Spicer, 1997). Thus, change in the environment does not necessarily lead to uncertainty because the implications of changes may be fairly predictable: "Uncertainty refers to events that the organization cannot forecast. It is not mere change or the rate of change, but the unpredictable change in variables that affects organizational decision making" (Lorenzi, Sims, & Slocum, 1981, p. 27).

Organizations seek to reduce or avoid uncertainty in the environment (Pfeffer & Salancik, 1978). As Simmons and Wynne (1993) have suggested: "The reduction or domestication of uncertainty is a central concern of all social actors, who function best when everyday life can be more or less predictable... When institutions come into question, or are no longer acceptable, uncertainty is increased" (p. 202). Environmental stability allows organizations to see the horizon, but turbulence obscures the view. An organization's ability to survive is defined by its ability to conduct activities that reduce such turbulence and allow the corporation to predict the future accurately. As a result, some corporations have preferred to anticipate stringent environmental regulations and plan for them rather than to be caught unaware.

The aftermath of Bhopal and the subsequent enactment of the federal Right to Know law was a particularly turbulent time for chemical manufacturers. Their previous ability to withhold information buffered them from outside scrutiny and concerns of risk stakeholders that might arise as a result. The loss of that control meant less stability in the interactions between corporations and risk stakeholders. For example, the director of EPA's Office of Toxic Substances predicted a revolution in the way society viewed toxics (Shabecoff, 1988). With toxic release inventory (TRI) information citizens would be able to develop a chemical portrait of the plants in their neighborhood, monitor threats to their health, provide relevant information to their doctors, and develop meaningful emergency response plans (Hadden, 1989).

Corporations were particularly concerned about further erosion of trust caused by risk stakeholders having access to large amounts of data without information about exposure or health effects (Hadden, 1989). From the manufacturers' perspective, the volume of emissions might have appeared large but the impact on health was minimal due to limited exposure and dilution of toxics in the ambient air. Risk communication was a key to survival: "We said 'look out guys. We are going to end up in worse shape then the atomic industry if we don't do something,'" said the then chair of the Chemical Manufacturers Association (Holusha, 1991, p. F10). One "something" was risk communication. Thus, risk communication in its various guises served as a corporate strategy to reduce environmental turbulence.

Previous to Bhopal and the passage of the federal Right to Know law, for the most part, the chemical industry's relationships to risk stakeholders were not part of an explicit social contract. However, Right to Know made some of these previously ambiguous, unimportant relationships both salient and unpredictable.

In short, loss of legitimacy, increase in environmental uncertainty, and threat to resources were intertwined. Following Bhopal and the enactment of Right to Know legislation, the loss of legitimacy led to destabilization of the authority of the chemical industry and to increased environmental uncertainty for companies that previously had not had to deal with risk stakeholders. With this loss of legitimacy and increased environmental uncertainty, some corporations feared for their survival. Risk communication was a tool to increase legitimacy, thereby decreasing uncertainty and potential impact on resources.

THE ENVIRONMENT AND THE ORGANIZATION: MUTUAL CAUSALITY

Risk communication is not merely a response to the external environment; it also creates that environment. As described, the loss of legitimacy following the Bhopal and Institute releases encouraged industry adaptations. But an organization's actions can *influence* socially constructed notions of legitimacy as well as *be influenced by* societal expectations. For example, Union Carbide's accident in India and its subsequent release in West Virginia changed the perception of the legitimacy of the chemical manufacturing industry. Union Carbide also played a major role in changing the regulatory environment; Congress resisted advocates' pressure for a federal Right to Know law after Bhopal but caved to increased public pressure after the release in Institute. The threat was so great that corporate leaders acknowledged it publicly. "We are going to get a lot more scrutiny from the public and the Congress, and it may be warranted," said one vice-president for safety, health, and environment (Lueck, 1985, p. A1). This threat of new laws also made the regulatory environment less predictable. Thus, industry both created and responded to the environment; organizations are not passive receivers of pressure from their environment, they are also powerful creators of the conditions under which they function.

Union Carbide created an environment in which corporations needed to deal with stakeholders about risk issues. But the organizational environment did not constrain organizational actions so greatly that risk communication was the *only* response available to manufacturers. For example, some companies chose to speak about their TRIs only if asked by the press (Chess, Tamuz, & Greenburg, 1995). In other words, only if the environment changed further due to media attention would a company release TRI data. On the other hand, some companies chose to respond to their environment with proactive risk communication activities. For example, the Bristol site of Rohm and Haas framed the TRI figures so the numbers could be more easily assimilated by risk stakeholders and more readily understood in a favorable light. The site public affairs manager contacted reporters before they called him, and he prepared press kits specifically for releasing TRI data (Chess et al., 1995). In addition, some companies moved from merely disseminating messages to becoming more collaborative as seen in the rise of community advisory panels.

Thus, decline in public confidence that affected manufacturers did not *determine* what form of risk communication a company chose as a strategy for coping with the changing external environment. The environment does not dictate that a company will choose to persuade rather than collaborate (or, even more complex, toy with collaboration as a means of persuasion). We do not argue that the organizational environment is the sole influence on corporate use of risk communication. We do contend, however, that the chemical industry's perception of a decrease in legitimacy, increase in environmental uncertainty, and potential loss of resources prompted various risk communication practices. Without such conditions, risk communication would not have been so prominent in chemical manufacturers' vocabulary.

CORPORATE AND GOVERNMENT RISK COMMUNICATION POST-SEPTEMBER 11

Risk communication has changed profoundly since the attacks on the World Trade Center and the Pentagon. Government agencies and corporations now deal with huge uncertainties about how to prevent, mitigate, and respond to terrorism. These pressures in this external environment are different than those after the Bhopal tragedy. While Bhopal led to calls for greater transparency and accountability, terrorism led to calls for greater security.

After Bhopal, risk communication was seen as a means to reduce risks posed by corporations to the surrounding community. After 9/11, risk communication was seen as a practice that might increase risks of terrorism. As discussed in the following section, concerns about security risks led to minimizing the communication about them. We provide two examples of how organizational interactions affected risk communication. The first deals with implementation of regulations governing disclosure of information about the potential impact of chemical facilities' accidental releases of toxics. The second describes the role of organizations in communicating about anthrax in 2001.

Risk Management Plans

The fate of Risk Management Plans (RMPs) is emblematic of corporate (and associated government) risk communication in the post-September 11 world. While Right to Know required companies to file information about the toxics they used and released, RMPs asked them to go several steps further. To reduce the likelihood and consequences of a catastrophic accident Section 112 (r) of the Clean Air Act of 1990 required certain facilities to file by 1999 a Risk Management Plan with the USEPA. The most controversial aspects of these plans were "worst case scenarios." These scenarios required "offsite consequence analyses" (OCAs) that indicated how far certain chemicals with catastrophic potential would travel under specified conditions and the potential impact to nearby populations. RMPs were to be made public.

Industry largely complied, but the disclosure of RMPs was controversial even before 9/11. Among the criticisms was that worst-case scenarios required by federal regulations for firms' accident planning and communication were unrealistic and would unnecessarily alarm citizens. Companies complained that communication of such plans to industry neighbors was of limited value (Erekson & Johnson, 1999, and NICS, 2000, both cited in Beierle, 2004, p. 340; Chemical Emergency Preparedness and Prevention Office, 2000; Johnson & Chess, 2003). Some firms argued that they did not need more regulation: prevention of worst case scenarios was in their corporate self-interest because their own staff and businesses would be harmed far sooner than anyone in the community. Industry also noted their close cooperation with emergency response officials in frequent training and exercises.

The loudest and most compelling argument dealt with the potential use of the information by terrorists. Companies argued that RMP descriptions of the potential chemical plumes provided a tool for terrorists. As a result of concerns specifically about abuse of this information by terrorists and other criminals, USEPA chose not to post the OCAs on the Internet, as had originally been planned. Concerns of the CIA and other security organizations that USEPA would be forced to release the data anyway, due to Freedom of Information Act (FOIA) rules, led to the Chemical Safety Information, Site Security and Fuels Regulatory Relief Act of 1999 (Chemical Emergency Preparedness and Prevention Office, 2000), which exempted OCAs from FOIA.

Putting aside security concerns, this restriction of information was unlikely to win companies points with communities surrounding their plants. Some research suggests strong public interest in such information even among those who believed industry provided net benefits to their community (Johnson & Chess, 2003). While there was much skepticism among industry neighbors about business' trustworthiness and competence, this research suggested that a bit more imagination and perseverance by industry might pay off in improved relations with its neighbors (Johnson & Chess, 2003).

How did 9/11 affect this dynamic on management and communication of catastrophic chemical risks? There was an initial rush of activity by USEPA to use its powers to tighten security, by Congress to request reports and funding, and by the Bush administration to limit FOIA applications to its proposed national security department. Meanwhile environmentalists argued that the likelihood of further terrorist attacks would not be affected by cutting public access to accident scenario information (Johnson & Chess, 2003). Rather than force more public accountability on potentially catastrophic risks, the upshot of the events of September 11 seems to have been a reification of positions, with industry resisting and environmentalists urging fuller public disclosure. Government agencies and legislators have taken positions that support their ideological positions or organizational interests.

Environmentalists lost this round. "Under the original rule, facilities were required to include a brief description of this [OCA] analysis in the executive summary of their RMPs" (Chemical Emergency Preparedness and Prevention Office, 2004). The nongovernmental organization OMB Watch had been posting these executive summaries on its Right to Know web site. However, by 2004, USEPA's Chemical Emergency Preparedness and Prevention Office noted "EPA and federal law enforcement agencies have become concerned that OCA descriptions in executive summaries may pose a security risk, so EPA has revised the rule to remove this requirement" (Chemical Emergency Preparedness and Prevention Office, 2004). USEPA has still not re-posted any RMP information on its website, despite this removal of "dangerous" information.[3]

The remaining Internet information, the executive summaries posted by OMB Watch on its RT-KNet web site (http://www.rtknet.org/rmp/), leave something to be desired for the inquiring neighbor. For example, a 2006 query for one of the zip codes targeted by Johnson and Chess (2003) found only two facilities listed. One had deregistered itself from the RMP database in 2002 on grounds that it no longer met the reporting criteria (presumably this meant also that it no longer posed a significant offsite risk), but the available information did identify the worst-case scenario and chemical very briefly. The other facility's summary only provided a table of contents but no details. Neither identified the size or distance of affected offsite populations.

Thus, the only way that citizens can read worst-case and other OCA analyses is in 56 federal reading rooms around the country. People may read and take notes on OCA information, but not remove, photocopy or otherwise mechanically reproduce it. One may access OCA information for up to 10 facilities per calendar month, without restriction on these facilities' location, by showing photo identification issued by a federal, state, or local government agency (such as a driver's license or passport) and signing a certification on a sign-in sheet.

One also may access OCA information for all facilities that are located in or potentially affect the jurisdiction of the Local Emergency Planning Committee where the inquirer lives or works. Those who want this information must document their residence or work address and provide their name and signature. Reading rooms may offer access by appointment only, "so that paper copies [for specific requested facilities] can be printed and delivered from elsewhere," or by walk-in (but with an advance call recommended to "confirm its availability and learn of any site-specific requirements, and it gives the Reading Room a chance to prepare for your visit" http://epa.gov/emergencies/content/rmp/readingroom.htm, accessed 30 May 2008).

Most states have only one such reading room, and not always located where one might expect. New York's sole room is in Buffalo; California has two, situated in San Francisco and Sacramento, so residents of southern California have a long way to travel. Evidence suggests that few people have sought information in these reading rooms (National Institute for Chemical Studies, 2001, cited in Beierle, 2004, p. 339).

We noted earlier the critical roles that perceptions of greater environmental uncertainty, and of threats to legitimacy or resources, can play in organizational risk communication strategies. Clearly, the events of 9/11 drastically increased uncertainty from a source (terrorists) hitherto little considered in facility operations. But threats to legitimacy and resources also changed. Resolution of current battles over legitimacy and resources could define the risk communication environment for decades. Therefore, we discuss the debates within the policy community over the appropriate boundary for organizational discretion. The outcome of the competition of ideas within the policy community will ultimately not only affect management of risks but also communication about them.

Changes in the government's organizational infrastructure for overseeing chemical security reflect perceptions of agencies' legitimacy. Once changes are made an agency may have its authority constrained or amplified. This shift may raise further questions about both legitimacy and resources. The interactions among the Bush administration, the new Department of Homeland Security (DHS), EPA and the chemical industry illustrate the potential complexity of these dynamics. Shortly after 9/11, President Bush stripped USEPA of responsibility for chemical plant security and awarded such responsibility to the DHS. For several years DHS, in effect, relegated that responsibility informally to the firms themselves; for example, the American Chemistry Council worked through its Responsible Care program to add a Responsible Care Security Code, adopted June 2002, in partnership with DHS, USEPA, FBI, and Defense Department, among others (Heath, McKinney, & Palenchar, 2005, p. 136) to earlier provisions on reducing environmental emissions and catastrophic releases. This non-regulatory approach reflected the legitimacy of corporate America and, in turn, further legitimized corporate efforts to oversee security.

In 2003, a push was made for legislation that would have essentially codified the industry's voluntary standards (Lipton, 2005), although even that was apparently too strong for the chair of the House Energy and Commerce Committee. He argued that there was no point given the low probability of any specific facility being attacked and the inability of security short of "Fort Knox" levels from preventing a determined attack from succeeding (Cohen, 2005). However, there were questions about how effective a voluntary approach was; for example, only 7% of facilities that USEPA had identified as risky belonged to Responsible Care. After reporters found little evidence of plant security at several facilities, the *New York Times* urged tighter plant security and the use of safer chemicals. The editorial also pushed for reducing onsite amounts of dangerous chemicals, moving dangerous facilities out of densely populated areas where feasible, and government overseeing chemical safety (Inside the Kill Zone, 2005). The U.S. Department of Homeland Security, however, insisted that it used "a risk-based method" for identifying high-consequence sites superior to "an outdated [USEPA] model" that exaggerates consequences, and had inspected "all of the highest consequence chemical facilities in the New Jersey area and nationwide." DHS believed facility operators had made substantial improvements in law enforcement coordination, access control, detection technologies and response preparedness (Stephan, 2005, p. A20).

By 2005, DHS argued that it needed greater statutory authority, given that "the entirely voluntary efforts of those companies alone will not sufficiently address security for the entire sector" (Lipton, 2005, p. A20). Twenty percent or more of the highest-risk plants were not covered by the voluntary efforts (Risk Policy Report, 2005a). At the same hearing at which Robert Stephan, the assistant secretary of DHS' Office of Infrastructure Protection, made those statements, Steven P. Bandy testified on behalf of the National Petrochemical and Refiners Association and the American Petroleum Institute that "Industry does not need to be prodded by government mandates to take aggressive and effective steps to secure its facilities.... Chemical security legislation would be counterproductive" (Lipton, 2005, p. A20). Here we see DHS raising questions about the legitimacy of corporate self-enforcement efforts, and corporations parrying DHS' challenge.

This shift in perspective by DHS on the need for chemical security legislation and a flurry of bills introduced in the U.S. Congress beginning in 2005 appeared to dampen industry resistance to any legislation at all. While opposition to any legislation was presumably a lost cause, the battle escalated over its content, in particular over appropriate boundaries for where the limits of corporate and government discretion should lie. In April 2006, in advance of markup of a U.S. Senate bill, lawmakers were "still divided on whether to force companies to reduce the hazards their products pose, whether EPA should have any role in the issue, and whether federal legislation should preempt state plans" (Risk Policy Report, 2006b). We discuss in detail below only the first of these elements, concerning hazard reduction.

The hazard reduction element in potential legislation has been labeled by its proponents as "inherently safer technologies" (IST), and concerns the reduction of quantities of hazardous chemicals onsite (e.g., by replacing the chemical with a "safer" chemical, or by making more efficient use of the chemical so less is needed). It covers chemicals used as feedstock for product manufacturing, as well as the products themselves. A New Jersey state official had predicted less than two months after 9/11 that terrorism potential "will push companies toward eliminating the use of the hazardous chemicals in the first place" (Cooper, 2001, AO-1).

This prediction turned out to be flawed. Industry has argued that IST "could transfer risk to other points in the supply chain,... result in government micromanagement of industry processes, duplicate requirements and could lead to manufacturing to be shipped overseas. "No federal program mandating [IST] will change how these processes are run in any significant way," Matthew Barmasse said on behalf of the Synthetic Organic Chemical Manufacturers Association (Risk Policy Report, 2005d, pp. 6–7). Industry officials raised other concerns, including that inherent safety "may be a back-door way to eliminate use of toxic chemicals that are necessary for their production processes... subject facilities to vague requirements, lead to a host of lawsuits against companies and not necessarily make plants safer" (Risk Policy Report, 2005c, p. 6). Michael Chertoff, the DHS Secretary, said requiring the industry to use safer chemicals would be "mission creep"—even though that would be precisely the kind of precautionary step that should be a core part of his department's mission (*New York Times*, 2006c, p. 3). What we see here are several new arguments about threats to resources, with issues of legitimacy more in the background ("government micromanagement," no significant process change due to federal mandates, "back-door" elimination of toxics).

By contrast, environmentalists, labor groups and other supporters of inherent safety argued "that reducing the source of threats is a critical way to complement physical security measures," and "employing physical security is not enough to protect communities in the event of a terrorist attack or accidental release." As Carol Andress of Environmental Defense put it, source reduction "cuts the need for security measures and minimizes the likelihood of a major chemical accident" (Risk Policy Report, 2005c, pp. 1, 6). The legitimacy issues did not change for IST supporters; they merely added security to their communications in favor of IST.

By way of analogy, we can summarize this tale by saying that chemical companies and the US Department of Homeland Security focused upon the arsonist's match as a target for preventing the "fire" of chemical catastrophe, while environmentalists and other advocates of "inherently safer" approaches focused upon the potential fuel. Change in type or quantity of fuel could reduce the consequences of a conflagration, whether caused by a successful arsonist or by some other source of heat. To put it another way, the firms and USDHS focus on cause, arguing that to allow USEPA a larger role would entail "mission creep," with intrusion of environmental goals and specialists into a realm solely concerned with national security. Critics focused on consequences, arguing that any chemical agent that could result in possibly hundreds or thousands (or, in the most extreme scenarios, one million) of casualties should be removed or reduced, regardless of the instigating cause of a catastrophe.

We see here the competition of various narratives that frame both the development of policy (including inaction as one option) and "the lives of people who live in communities near manufacturing" (Heath et al., 2005). These narratives are, in essence, competing stories about organizational legitimacy. Organizations with large stocks of chemicals onsite—for use in processing (e.g., chlorine to kill microorganisms in drinking water) or manufacturing, or as products of manufacturing—have engaged in a continuing battle with organizations concerned about the risks entailed in these chemical stocks. Heath et al. (2005) have rightly said that facilities “are often caught between a rock and a hard spot in their responsibility” to both “take actions to prevent and minimize the threat to their facilities and to communicate with various members of the public in a responsible manner” (p. 134).

Questions can be raised, however, about how stark the choices actually are. For example, the drinking water treatment sector has reduced the degree to which toxic chlorine is used or stored as a treatment technology (Beierle, 2004), and other facilities also have reduced inventories in order to avoid becoming subject to the RMP rules (Beierle, 2004). Orum (2006) reported 284 of the 14,000 facilities originally covered by RMP have taken themselves off the list of those required to report by “switching to less acutely hazardous processes or chemicals or moving to safer locations” (p. 3). Thus, at least some facilities can adopt seemingly safer technology, whatever the rhetoric from “their” side. Similarly, while tradeoffs between the benefits and costs of risk disclosure can be challenging, creative tactics may avoid or reduce the tension, as in Beierle’s (2004, p. 339) suggestion that listing of high-risk facilities or their parent firms would be one way to disclose OCA information useful to communities that could not also be useful to terrorists. In another example, an activist suggested that if a voluntary approach were used, companies should be required to report to the public, DHS, and the Securities and Exchange Commission “the choices they are making” (Risk Policy Report, 2006a, p. 1).

The issue of terrorism since 9/11 has expanded the scope of the debate somewhat but, by and large, has not altered the thrust of these contending groups’ arguments. Legitimacy has become even more important in this debate, since in the battle over proposed federal legislation on chemical facility security DHS alternates as an ally and a foe of business regarding IST and the roles of federal or state environmental regulators. Perceived legitimacy and resource threats in an environment of uncertainty both fuel and provide rhetorical content for the contending arguments within the policy community.

Regardless, risk communication about potential chemical catastrophes has been powerfully affected by events in the external environment. Just as Bhopal was a catalyst for legislation promoting disclosure of information, the attacks on 9/11 provided legitimacy for corporate arguments about the need to restrict information. Just as Union Carbide accidents in India and West Virginia undermined the credibility of industry arguments against disclosure, terrorism undermined environmentalists’ arguments for release of information.

Risk communication is no longer seen as key to corporate survival. Instead the strength of corporations’ containment of information has been defined by much of government and industry as central to the country’s survival. Arguably, community interests in chemical companies have become less important than the interests of national security. While the federal Right to Know law made the relationship between industry and communities salient, terrorism made that relationship seem far less important than preventing attacks on facilities. Terrorism and the fear of future attacks on the United States have created sufficient turmoil in the organizational environment that once again the history of risk communication has been profoundly changed.

RISK COMMUNICATION ABOUT ANTHRAX

The anthrax attacks of 2001 were the CDC’s Bhopal. While far fewer people were injured or died, the anthrax attacks have fundamentally altered how this federal agency, the county’s premier medical investigative unit, views communication (Sellnow, Seeger, & Ulmer, 2005). The agency was put in the position of having to investigate under tremendous time pressure and international attention the first terrorist release of a bioengineered weapon in the United States. To do so, it needed to collaborate with two organizations with vastly different missions and cultures: the FBI and the United States Postal Service (USPS). The friction that resulted helped to shape the risk communication process.

During September and October of 2001, at least four letters containing anthrax spores were mailed to media figures and politicians in the United States, resulting in 22 cases of anthrax, 5 of them fatal, including the deaths of two postal workers (GAO, 2004). More than 10,000 people were advised to take antibiotics to prevent disease (Gerberding , Hughes, & Koplan, 2002) and the Hart Senate Office Building and 23 postal facilities were found to be contaminated (Government Accounting Office, 2004).

The CDC, which is responsible for surveillance of disease, provided advice to the USPS and local and state agencies who handle public health emergencies. The CDC pulled together the agency's largest epidemiological effort (Altman, 2001a) to investigate cases in Florida, New York, New Jersey, and Washington, DC. The agency also faced unprecedented pressure to communicate about what it found.

The CDC was faced with the "perfect storm" of uncertainty: scientific uncertainty (e.g., Can anthrax spores be released from a sealed envelope?); medical uncertainty (e.g., What quantity of spores will cause illness?); and institutional uncertainty of all kinds: unpredictability of the organizational environment, the effect of the environment on the organization, or the effect of an organization's response to the environment (Spicer, 1997).

Bioterrorism was both a public health and security issue that involved all levels of government as well as private organizations, such as hospitals. As we describe, often there was considerable ambiguity about which organization had the authority to investigate, manage, or communicate aspects of the risk. In other words, as with RMPs, the issues of legitimacy and resources were very much in play.

The CDC and the FBI both investigated the first case of anthrax in Florida, a tabloid photo editor who died on October 5. The interactions within and among federal agencies dealing with anthrax contamination were so poor and so public that the failings, and the resulting risk communication problems, were reported in the *New York Times* on several occasions (Altman, 2001a; 2001b.) In short, the war on terror was fought among organizations as well as against terrorists.

Not surprisingly, from the outset the first case of anthrax was as much a political story as a medical one, with Tommy Thompson, then head of the Department of Health and Human Services, calling it an "isolated case." The implication of the press conference was that the victim, Bob Stevens, described as an outdoorsman, may have contracted anthrax from natural sources on a visit to North Carolina. When it became clear that Stevens' disease and subsequent death had nothing to do with his trip, the story was immediately portrayed as a follow up to 9/11, and another battle in the U.S. war on terrorism, rather than discussed largely as a public health issue (Maxwell, 2003).

As described in the following sequence of events, the interagency competition for legitimacy dramatically affected risk management and risk communication. In one instance, the FBI worked with the Army to test the anthrax-contaminated letter sent to Senator Tom Daschle, but did not permit the CDC to examine it. Instead the CDC was informed via conference calls that the letter was well-sealed (Siegel, 2002). "Army scientists, who are not accustomed to making public health proclamations, wrongly reassured the CDC without sufficiently testing the spread potential of this dangerous anthrax," according to one analysis (Siegel, 2002, p. 16). The CDC's acceptance of second-hand information may have contributed to the CDC giving false reassurances to the USPS and its workers, said Siegel (2002).

The conflict between the CDC and FBI had serious consequences but mundane causes: the agencies had different missions, goals, cultures, and structures (Waugh & Sylves, 2002). The FBI and other law enforcement agencies solve and prosecute crimes. As a result, the FBI safeguards information to preserve evidence and maintain the integrity of the investigation (Butler et al., 2002; Siegel, 2002). Success and secrecy are synonymous in the FBI. Intimidation is an important weapon in the law enforcement arsenal. It was inevitable the FBI could take out the CDC in the first round of the turf war.

Risk Communication at the Local Level

Dealing with anthrax was a local issue as well as a national one. While the FBI was the lead enforcement agency and CDC the most prominent public health agency, they were by no means the only agencies fighting the war on terror. State, county, and local agencies had the responsibility for critical emergency response and public health roles. Not surprisingly, interagency communication also affected risk communication and risk management on the local level.

For example, New Jersey was the site of contamination of a huge postal processing and distribution facility in Hamilton, which processes about two million pieces of mail a day. All told, at least four letters containing anthrax were processed in the facility, which on October 18, 2001, was the first postal facility in the country to close. Ultimately, two workers in the state were diagnosed with inhalation anthrax and another four workers were either confirmed or suspected of having cutaneous anthrax as a result of the attacks in the fall of 2001. While state and federal attention focused on Hamilton, seen as the state's ground zero for anthrax, citizens around the state were deciding how to handle their mail. Frightened residents turned to a variety of sources for information, including local and county health and enforcement agencies.

For example, many towns in New Jersey experienced white powder scares, none of which turned out to be anthrax. Nonetheless, offices of local government officials were flooded with calls. What organization should handle the phone calls? How should the calls be triaged? Where should they be referred? What calls merit field investigation? These basic questions did not have obvious answers. They could be seen as health issues, law enforcement issues, or both. As with the battle at the federal level, these questions were fundamentally ones of organizational legitimacy. The question was which organizations had the expertise, authority, or resources to respond to each of these issues.

A team of Rutgers researchers (Caron Chess, Lee Clarke, and Karen O'Neill) undertook a study of how communication about anthrax varied by location in New Jersey, a home-rule state where municipalities have power to take very different approaches to issues. The Rutgers team conducted four geographically based case studies in the state including those with (a) multiple cases of anthrax (Hamilton township); (b) false reports of two suspect cases (Monmouth county); (c) a case initially labeled as suspect (the town of Bellmawr); and (d) no anthrax detected (the town of Morristown). The interview protocol included a range of issues about risk communication, including the sources of information used by interviewees as well as the information they provided to others. The team also asked how decisions regarding risk communication were made within and among organizations.

The experience in one town with a major postal facility, which routinely handled mail from the Hamilton facility, illustrates some of the differences between the federal and local interactions. This case study of Eatontown, which is about an hour's drive away from Hamilton, was based on more than 20 interviews by the lead author as well as review of newspaper articles, government documents, and electronic communication.

In this locality, public health did not need to fight for legitimacy. The local public health officer was respected by law enforcement and emergency response officials. A coordinator for the Office of Emergency Management related that "I talk to [the health officer] quite often… I listen to what he says because he knows what he is doing." This reliance on the health officer's expertise continued as officials prepared for the possibility of future bioterror events: "He has sent us information as to what to watch for. With the smallpox thing, he's got a store on that if we ever had to do a mass vaccination and stuff like that. He has given me some ideas already" (Personal communication, Chess et al., 2004).

Police departments were concerned about protecting their own personnel and recognized that they lacked expertise to do so. Police called the local health department to coordinate response to anthrax-related calls. According to a local health officer, "The police are very good with the typical law enforcement, but when you get to bugs, they get kind of worried about that... they don't have a lot of dealings with it so there's a lot of apprehension and they look for a lot of direction and hopefully proper information" (Personal communication, Chess et al., 2004).

However, other problems with interorganizational communication were responsible in large measure for a false media report of two workers from the Eatontown facility having anthrax (Chess et al, 2004). Although CDC and the N.J. Department of Health and Senior Services (NJDHSS) cautioned that nasal swabs were not useful for diagnosis of individual cases, one hospital in the area responded to postal workers' requests for "testing" with nasal swabs. On October 29, that hospital informed the local health officer that two workers, including one with respiratory symptoms, had nasal swabs that were positive for *Bacillus*. Such preliminary screening indicates the presence of *Bacillus* bacteria—but not necessarily *Bacillus anthracis*. A number of different respiratory illnesses can produce a positive swab. Thus, these results and the clinical symptoms (without the substantiation of abnormal X-rays or other supporting evidence) did not meet federal or state criteria for suspected or potential cases of anthrax.

That evening a meeting for postal workers was held at the Monmouth facility. Unfortunately, the NJDHSS official who was supposed to speak was called to a meeting with Congressional representatives, The mayor asked the local health officer to fill in and address the anxious workers who had heard about their ill colleagues.

The local health official described the situation: "I just happened to be there at the invitation of the mayor ... and the next thing I knew I felt like I was the private, and all of a sudden they say, 'Well, you're now the general, you're the health expert.'... I mean, I know a lot, but I am not the be-all, end-all, one-stop shopping for anthrax." Instead of a representative from NJDHSS addressing workers' concerns and heading off rumors, the local public health officer spoke of two "suspect cases" of workers having anthrax: "I very definitely said it was a suspect case, not definitive cases.... The terminology was wrong.... I thought 'suspect' meant not proven—maybe, maybe not—but a lot of people took it to mean it was more likely to be a case." The story was carried in the local paper and then picked up by CNN, according to those we interviewed (Chess et al., 2004).

This story of how Eatontown made it to CNN also had a largely organizational plot line. While county and state officials fault the local health official for this miscommunication, in truth the problems are greater than one flawed individual. There was tremendous uncertainty about organizational responsibility for managing and communicating the risk. The hospital either did not know of the CDC and NJDHSS guidance about swabbing or failed to comply. (We do not know which because this local hospital refused numerous requests for interviews.) The NJDHSS' limited risk communication resources meant that the local health officer was unexpectedly the source of information. Finally, in a home rule state such as New Jersey, county and state officials often have tense relationships with local officials who have tremendous authority. Given the above, it is not surprising that we heard different versions of the protocols for officials on the local, county and state level to keep each other informed of information such as the hospital's diagnosis the two workers

When many organizations are involved in solving major problems under time constraints with limited science and unclear institutional authority, communication problems were bound to occur. However, to the credit of New Jersey officials, regardless of the communication problems, there was not a single death in the state.

CONCLUSION

As this chapter describes, close reading of risk communication efforts reveal organizational narratives. We argue that much risk communication is influenced by organizational realities and vice versa. While the evolution of risk communication is no doubt affected by myriad factors, from communication technology to sophistication of various publics, communication is fundamentally an organizational process. This process is likely to be influenced by organizational environments, including dramatic events such as Bhopal, the attacks of September 11, 2001, and the release of the anthrax bacillus.

Far more research on the links between organizational issues and risk communication is needed. But organizations can make such research difficult. The Rutgers team was turned down for a number of interviews when studying anthrax. Few current USPS officials were willing to speak with the researchers. Interviewees at all levels of government expressed concerns about being truthful about the interactions within their organization or the links with other agencies. One federal official told the lead author that any study of his organization would be so sensitive that it could not be published. A local official feared that honesty about her relationships with other agencies would derail current programs.

Organizational researchers have often confronted similar access issues. Risk communication researchers may also need to deal with this fact of life. It helps to look at successful case studies, which people are more eager to discuss than organizational failures. (However, when discussing what they perceive as successes, they will talk about failures, e.g., Chess et al., 1995). Those who work for an organization may also have an easier time with access although organizational buy-in may be problematic. In addition, consultants who are assisting organizations with their risk communication activities might pair with researchers who could design studies to look at the back stories.

Yet, when conducting such studies, the difficulties posed by organizational access are more than balanced by the existing, rich scholarship in organizational research. Risk communication researchers interested in organizational issues can jump start their research by working with researchers from related fields. For example, the research team for this study of anthrax communication included two sociologists, Lee Clarke and Karen M. O'Neill, who provided expertise on a range of issues from organizational legitimacy to emergent networks. Academics outside the risk communication field have spent years studying topics that are extremely relevant to risk communication such as internal organizational communication, organizational culture, and organizational learning. The application of such theory to risk communication also provides an opportunity for the field to gain greater theoretical traction. Because organizational aspects of risk communication have been little-studied, the opportunities are great. Following are a very few that are relevant to the topics discussed in this chapter.

Research is needed about organizations that have not been touched directly by risk communication crises. What motivates their risk communication? To what extent do they learn from organizations that have undergone crises?

Longitudinal studies could track risk communication efforts in the same organization over time. How do changes in the organizational environment affect risk communication and vice versa? Once crises are resolved does the organization go back to business as usual? Do perceptions of external stakeholders vary over time? What about the links between risk communication and risk management?

The anthrax research discussed in this chapter confirms the findings of disaster researchers about networks that emerge during and after such crises. However, risk communication is rarely a major focus of such research or practice. It should be.

To improve risk communication research and practice, we need to increase our attention to those organizations that communicate. Otherwise, we will continue to know far more about public response to risk communication than the communication process itself. Interactive communication necessarily involves understanding the actors, and organizations usually have lead roles.

ACKNOWLEDGMENTS

The original article in *Risk Analysis* (Chess, 2001) from which this chapter was adapted was supported by the New Jersey Institute of Technology's Hazardous Substances Management Research Center and an EPA STAR fellowship. Thanks to Ginger Gibson, Susan Santos, and two anonymous reviewers for providing comments on an early draft of the post-Bhopal section of the chapter. Erin Beare provided invaluable, patient assistance on that section. The research on anthrax was supported by the National Science Foundation SGER-03-041 and the United States Department of Homeland Security through the National Consortium for the Study of Terrorism and Responses to Terrorism (START), grant number N00140510629. The research on chemical security post 9-11 was supported by the New Jersey Department of Environmental Protection. However, any opinions, findings, and conclusions or recommendations are ours and do not necessarily reflect views of NJIT, USEPA, NSF, USDHS, NJDEP, or Rutgers University.

NOTES

1. As Clarke et al, (2006) pointed out, technically *B. anthracis* is the bacterium that creates the disease called *anthrax.* So, it wasn't really an "anthrax" attack but a *B. anthracis* attack. For simplicity, we refer to the "anthrax attack."
2. Organizational stakeholders have been defined variously. This chapter defines stakeholders in the manner of Clarkson (1995): "persons or groups that have, or claim, ownership rights or interests in a corporations and its activities past, present or future. ...stakeholders with similar interests claims or rights can be classified as belonging to the same group..." (p. 106). Stakeholders traditionally have been considered customers, suppliers, and shareholders. The extent to which other interests have been seen as important varies. When we use the term risk stakeholders, we will be referring to stakeholders concerned with company activities that may affect their risks, broadly construed. In this chapter, the definition of risk conforms to the National Research Council's 1996 definition of the term—what poses danger to people or "to what they value." This conception of risk includes but is not limited to a loss of quality of life, human health, or the natural environment (Stern & Fineberg, 1996).
3. USEPA did not release required 2004 corporate updates of RMPs as requested in an OMB Watch FOIA request, until the group filed a lawsuit (Risk Policy Report, 2 August 2005b).

BIBLIOGRAPHY

Altman, L. K. (2001a, October 16). The doctor's world; CDC Team tackles Anthrax. *New York Times,* F1.

Altman, L. K. (2001b, November 13). When everything changed at the C.D.C. *New York Times,* F1.

Beierle, T.C. (2004). The benefits and costs of disclosing information about risks: What do we know about right-to-know? *Risk Analysis, 24,* 335–346.

Blair, E. (1986). Panel on risk communication. In T. Davies, V. Covello & F. W. Allen (Eds.), *Proceedings of the National Conference on Risk Communication.* Washington: Conservation Foundation.

Butler, J. C., Cohen, M. L., Friedman, C. R., Scripp, R. M., & Watz, C. G. (2002). Collaboration between public health and law enforcement: New paradigms and partnerships for bioterrorism planning and response. *Emerging Infectious Diseases, 8*(10), 1152–1156.

Chemical Emergency Preparedness and Prevention Office. (2000). *Assessment of the incentives created by public disclosure of off-site consequence analysis information for reduction in the risk of accidental releases.* Retrieved April 17, 2006, from http://yosemite.epa.gov/oswer/ceppoweb.nsf/vwresourcesbyfilename/incenass.pdf/$file/incenass.pdf.

Chemical Emergency Preparedness and Prevention Office. (2004). *Changes to the chemical accident prevention rule (risk management program) in 2004* (EPA Publication No. 550-F-04-002). Washington, D.C.: U.S. Environmental Protection Agency, Office of Solid Waste and Emergency Response.

Chess, C. (2001). Organizational theory and the stages of risk communication. *Risk Analysis, 21*(1), 179–188.

Chess, C., Calia, J., & O'Neill, K. (2004). Communication triage: An Anthrax case study. *Biosecurity and Bioterrorism: Biodefense Strategy, Practice, and Science, 2*(2), 106–111.

Chess, C., Tamuz, M., & Greenberg, M. (1995). Organizational learning about environmental risk communication: The case of Rohm and Haas' Bristol plant. *Society and Natural Resources, 8,* 57–66.

Clarke, L. (1992). Context dependency and risk decision making. In J. F. Short & L. Clarke (Eds.), *Organizations, uncertainties, and risks* (pp. 27–38). Boulder, CO: Westview.

Clarke, L., Chess, C., Holmes, R., & O'Neill, K (2006). Risk communication lessons from the US anthrax attacks. *Journal of Contingencies and Crisis Management,14*(3), 160–169.
Clarkson, M. B. (1995). A stakeholder framework for analyzing and evaluating corporate social performance. *Academy of Management Review*, *20*(1), 92–117.
Cohen, A. (2005, May 24). A lawmaker works, oddly enough, to keep his voters' backyards dangerous. [Editorial]. *New York Times*, A28.
Cooper, C. J. (2001, November 5). Chemical industry assessing terror risks. *The Bergen Record,* AO-1, AO-11/c.
Corbett, H. J. (1988). Chemicals and the public. Meeting of British Institute of Engineers and American Institute of Chemical Engineers. c1, c2.
Diamond, S. (1985, August 18). Credibility a casualty in West Virginia. *New York Times*, V1, V3.
Dill, W. R. (1958). Environment as influence on managerial autonomy. *Administrative Science Quarterly*, pp. 409–443.
Dimaggio, P. J., & Powell, W. W. (Eds.). (1991). Introduction. *The new institutionalism in organizational analysis* (pp. 1–40). Chicago: University of Chicago.
Dowling, J., & Pfeffer, J. (1975). Organizational legitimacy: Social values and organizational behavior. *Pacific Sociological Review*, *18*(1), 122–134.
Downey, K. H., & Slocum, J. W. (1975). Uncertainty: Measures, research, and sources of variation. *Academy of Management*, *18*(3), 562–576.
Downey, H. K., Hellriegel, D. H., & Slocum, J. W. Jr. (1975). Environmental uncertainty: The construct and its application. *Administrative Science Quarterly*, *20*, 613–629.
Erekson, O. H., & Johnson, P. C. (1999). Community-industry dialogue in risk management: Responsible care and worst case scenarios in the valley of the shadow, case study number 10. In O. L. Loucks, O. H. Erekson, J. W. Bol, R. F. Gorman, P. C. Johnson, & T. C. Krehbiel (Eds.), *Sustainability perspectives for resources and business* (pp. 337–353). Washington, D.C.: Lewis Publishers.
Fischhoff, B. (1995) Risk perception and communication unplugged: Twenty years of process, *Risk Analysis, 15*(2), 137–145
Franklin, B. A. (1985, August 12). Toxic cloud leaks at Carbide plant in West Virginia. *New York Times*, A1, A12.
Freudenburg, W. (1993). Risk and recreancy: Weber, the divisions of labor and the rationality of risk perceptions. *Social Forces*, *4*(71), 909–932.
Gerberding, J. L., Hughes, J. M., & Koplan, J. P. (2002). Bioterrorism preparedness and response: Clinicians and public health agencies as essential partners. *Journal of American Medical Association, 287*(7), 898–899.
Gladwin, T.N. (1993). The meaning of greening: A plea for organizational theory. In K. Fischer & J. Schot (Eds.), *Environmental strategies for industry: International perspectives on research needs and policy implications* (pp. 37–62). Washington, D.C.: Island Press.
Government Accountability Office (2004). *Better Guidance is needed to ensure an appropriate response to anthrax contamination.* (No. Report No.: GAO-04-239.). Washington, D.C.
Grunig, L. A. (1992). How public relations/communications departments should adapt to the structure and environment of an organization ... and what they actually do. In J.E. Grunig (Ed.), *Excellence in public relations and communication management* (pp 467–482). Hillsdale, NJ: Erlbaum.
Hadden, S. (1989). *A citizen's right to know: Risk communication and public policy*. Boulder, CO: Westview.
Heath, R.L., McKinney, D.B., & Palenchar, M.J. (2005). Community right-to-know vs. terrorists' exploitation of public information. In H. D. O'Hair, R. L. Heath, & G. R. Ledlow (Eds.), *Communication and media* (pp. 125–166). Westport, CT: Praeger.
Heck, K. (2005). *New Jersey becomes first state to require chemical plant security measures to protect against terrorist attack.* Retrieved July 12 2006, from http://www.nj.gov/cgi-bin/governor/njnewsline/view_article.pl?id=2815.
Holusha, J. (1991, October 13). The nation's polluters: Who emits what and where? *New York Times*, F10.
Inside the kill zone [editorial]. (2005, May 22). *New York Times*, WK11.
Johnson, B.B., & Chess, C. (2003). Communicating worst-case scenarios: Neighbors' views of industrial accident management. *Risk Analysis, 23,* 829–840.
Krimsky, S., & Golding, D. (Eds.) (1992). *Social theories of risk.* Westport, CT: Praeger.
Lipton, E. (2005, June 15). Administration to seek antiterror rules for chemical plants. *New York Times,* A20.
Lorenzi, P., Sims, H. P., & Slocum, J. W. (1981). Perceived environmental uncertainty: An individual or environmental attribute. *Journal of Management*, *7*(2), 27–41.
Loudon, A.A. (1987). *The chemical industry and the environment.* Paper presented at the European Conference of Industrial and Environmental Management, Interlaken, Austria.
Lueck, T. J. (1985, August 15). Chemical industry braces for tougher regulation. *New York Times*, A1.
March, J. G., & Olsen, J. P. (1975). The uncertainty of the past: Organizational learning under ambiguity. *European Journal of Political Research, 3,* 147–171.

Maxwell, T. A. (2003). The public need to know: Emergencies, government organizations, and public information policies. *Government Information Quarterly, 20,* 233–258.

Meyer, J. W., & Rowan, B. (1980). The structure of educational organizations. In M. W. Meyer (Ed.), *Environments and organizations* (pp. 78–109). San Francisco: Jossey-Bass.

Meyer, J. W., & Scott, R. W. (1983). Centralization and legitimacy problems of local government. In J. W. Meyer & W. Richard (Eds.), *Organizational environments: Ritual and rationality* (pp. 199–216). Newbury Park, CA: Sage.

Meyer, J. W., & Rowan, B. (1991). Institutionalized organizations: Formal structure as myth and ceremony. In W. W. Powell & P.J. Dimaggio (Eds.), *The new institutionalism in organizational analysis* (pp. 41–62). Chicago: University of Chicago.

Mintz, B., & Schwartz, M. (1985). *The power structure of American business.* Chicago: University of Chicago.

National Institute for Chemical Studies (NICS). (2001*). Local emergency planning committees and risk management plans: Encouraging hazard reduction.* Retrieved July 12 2006, from, http://www.nicsinfo.org/LEPCStudyFinalReport.pdf.

Secretary of homeland insecurity [editorial]. (2006, March 24). *New York Times,* WK11.

Nussbaum, A. (2006, March 22). A way around N.J.'s tough chemical security rules? *The Bergen Record,* p. A1.

Orum, P. (2006). *Preventing toxic terrorism: How some chemical facilities are removing danger to American communities.* Retrieved May 10, 2006, from http://www.nytimes.com/packages/pdf/national/20060425c hemicalplantreport.pdf.

Perrow, C. (1984). *Normal accidents: Living with high-risk technologies.* New York: Basic.

Pfeffer, J., & Salancik, G. R. (1978). *The external control of organizations: A resource dependence perspective.* New York: Harper and Row.

Risk Policy Report. (2005a, June 21). EPA, DHS argue for limit on facilities subject to security risk rules. *Inside EPA's Risk Policy Report, 12,* 1, 8–9.

Risk Policy Report. (2005b, August 2). EPA releases long-awaited facility risk data after group sues. *Inside EPA's Risk Policy Report, 12,* 2–3.

Risk Policy Report. (2005c, July 19). Key senator eyes options for 'safer' chemical rules in security bill. *Inside EPA's Risk Policy Report, 12,* 1, 7.

Risk Policy Report. (2005d, December 13). Senator eyes possible changes to chemical bill to win over Democrats. *Inside EPA's Risk Policy Report, 12,* 6–7.

Risk Policy Report. (2006a, May 2). Analyst says chemical plants should report efforts to boost safety. *Inside EPA's Risk Policy Report, 13,* 1, 2, 6.

Risk Policy Report. (2006b, April 11). Competing chemical security bills show panel split ahead of markup. *Inside EPA's Risk Policy Report, 13,* 10–11.

Risk Policy Report. (2006cMarch 7). EPA's chemical security role looms as key issue ahead of Senate debate. *Inside EPA's Risk Policy Report, 13,* 3–4.

Rosa, E. A. (1997, March). *Sociological approaches to risk: Friend or foe to the rational actor paradigm.* Paper presented at the Risk Assessment and Policy Association International Meeting, Alexandria, Va.

Schot, J. & Fischer, K. (1993). Introduction: the greening of the industrial firm. In K. Fischer & Schot (Eds.), *Environmental strategies for industry: International perspectives on research needs and policy implications.* (pp. 3–36). Washington, D.C.: Island Press.

Scott, W. R. (1987). The adolescence of institutional theory. *Administrative Science Quarterly, 32,* 493–511.

Scott, W. R. (1992). *Organizations: Rational, natural, and open systems.* Englewood Cliffs, NJ: Prentice Hall.

Sellnow, T. L., Seeger, M. W., & Ulmer, R. R. (2005). Constructing the "New Normal" through the post-crisis discourse. In D. H. O'Hair, R. L. Heath & G. R. Ledlow (Eds.), *Community preparedness and response to terrorism* (pp. 167–189). Westport, CT: Praeger.

Shabecoff, P. (1985, March 27). Industry chiefs back U.S. curbs on polluted air. *New York Times,* A1, A23.

Shabecoff, P. (1988, February 14). Industry to give vast new data on toxic perils. *New York Times,* A1.

Siegel, M. (2002). The anthrax fumble. *Nation, 274*(10), 14–16.

Simmons, P., & Wynne, B. (1993). Responsible care: trust, credibility, and environmental management. In K. Fischer & J. Schot (Eds.), *Environmental strategies for industry: international perspectives on research needs and policy implications* (pp. 201–226). Washington, D.C.: Island Press.

Spicer, C. (1997). *Organizational public relations: A political perspective.* Mahwah, NJ: Erlbaum.

Starr, C. (1969). Social benefit versus technological risk: What is our society willing to pay for safety? *Science, 165,* 1232–1238.

Stephan, B. (2005, May 17). Chemical plant security. [Editorial]. *New York Times,* A20.

Stern, P., & Fineberg, H.V. (1996). *Understanding risk: Informing decisions in a democratic society.* Washington, D.C.: National Academy Press.

Thompson, J. D. (1967). *Organizations in action: Social science bases of organizational theory.* New York: McGraw-Hill.

Waugh, W. L., & Sylves, R. T. (2002). Organizing the war on terrorism. *Public Administration Review*, *62*, 81–89.

Weber, M. (1968). *Economy and society: An interpretive sociology* (G. Rosh & C. Wittich, Trans.). New York: Bedminster Press.

17

Ethical Responsibility and Guidelines for Managing Issues of Risk and Risk Communication

Shannon A. Bowen
Syracuse University

INTRODUCTION

This chapter takes an issues management perspective on risk management to explore the ethical responsibilities imposed by the impact of risk on organizations, publics, and on society. A perspective combining the disciplines of risk and crisis management, issues management, public relations, moral philosophy, and applied ethics is used to frame the discussion of ethical risk management and communication. Progress and growth in public relations scholarship over the past few decades has created a theoretically-based framework for understanding the consequences and ties between an organization and publics, as well the relationship variables that contextualize communication in this milieu. Social responsibility, corporate accountability, and ethics also play a major role in this discussion. Relationships between organizations and publics often flourish or founder due to the way in which risk is managed. As seminal work by Ulrich Beck (1992, 1995, 1998) and Mary Douglas (1992; Douglas & Wildavsky, 1982) discussed, risk management occurs at the societal level and has sociopolitical consequences for not only for the risk-bearers in that society, but also for businesses, governments, and culture in general. Society counts on a flow of honest and reliable communication in order to enable decisions about risk, and the interplay of these multitudes of moral duties creates ethical responsibilities to multiple publics. This complex interplay is examined in light of those moral duties with an eye toward creating normative—yet practical—recommendations for ethical risk management.

Risk is a term fraught with controversy in its own definition, and impassive arguments over the nature of "the relative riskiness" (p. 39) of many topics (Fischhoff, Watson, & Hope, 1990). Some scholars see risk as a probability-based discipline, lending itself to an analytical decision-making framework (Fischhoff et al., 1990) while others view the very development of society itself as the management of risk and uncertainty (Luhmann, 1993). This chapter combines the thought in each of those perspectives, first looking at the societal-level consequences of risk on publics and its ethical implications. The chapter then moves to a moral philosophy analysis of the ethical implications stemming from risk, and offers guidelines for risk management from Kantian deontological ethics.

SOCIAL SYSTEMS THEORY, ISSUES, AND RISK

Following the tradition of the critical theorists of the Frankfurt School, Beck (1992) created the notion of the "risk society" in which man-made risks are both products and attempts at control of their byproducts, and become inescapable problems and issues for the whole society. This society, for the purposes of this chapter, is best framed through systems theory, in which organizations interact with publics through communication, both proactively and in response to their environment. Luhmann's (1984) theory of social systems provides a foundation for issues management in that it helps an organization adapt to a changing environment and to change pressures from publics. In fact, Luhmann (1984) argued that social systems and communication were inextricably linked: "Thus we give a double answer to the question of what comprises a social system: communications and their attributions as actions. Neither aspect is capable of evolving without the other" (p. 174). The strength of Luhmann's argument indicates the need for a societal level focus of the communication function of issues management. Systems theory conceives of society as a system, made up of smaller systems, of which organizations are one. The interplay of communication between these different systems allows a conceptualization of risk management as a crucial part of the moving equilibrium between the systems constituting society.

Communication plays a large role in the interaction between a system and its environment (Lauzen & Dozier, 1994; Stoffels, 1994): systems theory has contributed to our understanding of how public relations and issues management are involved in that interaction (Plowman, 2005). Katz and Kahn (1966) also drew parallels of organizations as social systems with a complex interplay of variables affecting how the organization attempts to accomplish its goals and interact effectively with other systems, such as publics in its environment. The risk management function, through the use of communication, allows the organization to interact with its environment in a way that allows a balanced amount of risk to be born by publics who are aware and informed about that risk. This state of balance between organizational interests and the interests of publics is known as a moving equilibrium in which the system inherently seeks balance, but recognizes that a continual state of flux is both normal and desirable (Plowman, 2005).

Communication is vital for allowing understanding among risk-bearing publics, appropriate and timely responses, and adapting to heightened levels of risk or new risks. For instance, a failure to conduct ethical communication was found to be responsible for the continued spread of the Severe Acute Respiratory (SARS) virus throughout China and resulted in increased deaths (Bowen & Heath, 2007). The ethical implications of communicating about risk, as seen in that example, are not to be undervalued as they might result in drastic shifts in consequences on large numbers of people.

Predicting ethical consequences is never an accurate science, and when managing risk a plethora of many unknown factors can impact the system. Funtowitz and Ravetz (1983) argued, "'Systems uncertainty' contains the elements of inexactness, uncertainty, and ignorance encountered in the scientific and technical studies; whereas 'decision stakes' involves the costs and benefits to all the interested parties, of all the various available policy options, including delays in decision of some definite or indefinite duration" (p. 227). Systems theory provides an adequate rubric within which to frame this complex web of decisions, providing that information is collected through the use of public relations boundary spanning capabilities to lessen inherent uncertainty. Even when uncertainty is reduced, the most sophisticated and rigorous methods of moral analysis still prove difficult.

BOUNDARY SPANNING AND ENVIRONMENTAL SCANNING

The dominant coalition, separated from the environment by the hierarchy of the organizational structure, needs a link to the environment to provide information on strategic publics and stakeholders.

The communication function is a natural fit in this "boundary-crossing" (Luhmann, 1984, p. 205) or boundary-spanning role (Spicer, 1997). Researchers (L. A. Grunig, Grunig, & Dozier, 2002) found that in order for the communication function to contribute its maximum to organizational effectiveness, the top issues manager should be a part of the decision-making core, or dominant coalition. One method of gaining membership in the dominant coalition is to become the conduit of information on the external environment for the dominant coalition. That information is gained through the boundary-spanning role in which the issues manager interacts with publics in the environment, seeking to learn and understand their points of view, values, and priorities. Membership in this group allows one to hold both the power (Mintzberg, 1983) and influence (Berger & Reber, 2006) to engage in active analysis of ethical risk communication.

Environmental scanning is the process of seeking information from outside the organization from publics, stakeholders, and even competitors, to aid in the identification of issues (Stoffels, 1994). Environmental scanning enables communicators to identify issues for discussion and resolution at a nascent stage before they evolve into intractable positions (Lauzen, 1995). As Miller (1999) noted, environmental scanning is not strategic unless the information is used in the strategic planning of issues management. Another feature of its strategic nature is the decision of what material is relevant and important from among all the information acquired in environmental scanning. Luhmann (1984) described this process:

> Communication must be viewed not as a two-part, but as a three-part selection process. It is not just a matter of sending and receiving with selective attention on both sides; instead, the selectivity of the information itself is an aspect of the communication process, because selective attention is actualized only in reference to the very selectivity of information. Selectivity as such attracts further communication: it recruits communications that direct themselves to aspects that selectivity has excluded. (p. 140)

We can see that the very selection of information in the environmental scanning process is part of communication as well as part of risk management. Making meaning of risks and defining the extent of the threat is part of the ethical responsibility of the issues management function.

Lauzen (1995) found that environmental scanning provided opportunities for communicators to build relationships with valuable external information sources. Dozier, Grunig, and Grunig (1995) concluded his discussion of dominant coalition membership through boundary spanning and environmental scanning by stating that "Scanning. . .provides senior managers in excellent organizations with the ticket they need to make an impact at the decision-making table" (p. 206). Both boundary spanning and environmental scanning provide outlets for publics to petition organizations for a redress of grievance, explanations of behavior, or alterations in policy. These venues for beginning and engaging in discussions allow a continual flow of communication between different groups in society for the resolution of problematic issues. Such a conduit of information flow as input is important for the functioning of society because of the power differential between organizations and publics involved in such debates.

This argument is consistent with Habermas' (1984, 1996) conception of the public sphere in which public discussion and debate takes place, meaning that issues management serves a social role in enabling discourse in the public sphere. Further, discussion between organizations and publics about what constitutes acceptable levels of risk performs a valuable function in deciding how business will operate and can be supported by the community. How, where, and by whom risk is borne are considerations relevant not only in specific cases but also in defining the larger role of governmental regulation and business self-regulation.

Risk and crisis are not issues to be determined and studied solely from the biased perspective of an organization, often a corporate or for-profit entity. Political economy theory argues that the organizations with the most funding and access to media are the ones who control dominant message themes (Adorno, 1991; Bagdikian, 1985; Murdock, 1996; Olasky, 1989). However, activist research shows that even a small public can have an impact on the policy of an enormous and well-funded organization (L. A. Grunig, 1992; Murphy & Dee, 1996; Olson, 1982). Issues management functions as a forum for conducting these debates through which problematic issues can be addressed often regardless of funding or power differentials. This role is an ethical one for managing risk because it allows open access to dialogue about risk for many parties to the debate. Risk management provides a means of access to organizations and input at the policy level for publics.

A CLOSER LOOK AT AN ISSUE

There are many definitions of an issue in the literature. Crable and Vibbert (1985) wrote: "An issue is created when one or more human agents attached significance to a situation or a perceived problem" (p. 5). This definition is valuable because it separates issues management from crisis management by noting that some issues are situations whereas others may be perceived as problems. Not all issues are problems; they may be matters of importance, concern, or even benefit to the organization. The Crable and Vibbert (1985) definition allows for that contingency through its inclusion of a significant situation.

Chase, author of the seminal book *Issue Management: Origins of the Future* (1984), defined an issue as "an unsettled matter which is ready for decision" (p. 38). He contrasted his simple definition of an issue against "trends" by noting that trends are more subtle and often precede issues. In a more recent discussion, Chase and Crane (1996) stated, "an issue exists when there is a gap between corporate action and stakeholder expectation," and he views issues management as the process of bridging that gap (p. 130).

In Renfro's (1993) definition of an issue, he pointed out that a broad area of concern can give rise to several issues. Heath (1997), building on his 1986 definition with Nelson (1986), defined an issue as a "contestable question of fact, value, or policy that affects how stakeholders grant or withhold support and seek changes through public policy" (p. 44). J. E. Grunig and Repper (1992) emphasized how issues are perceived by publics in their definition: "Publics make issues out of problems that have not been resolved" (p. 146). For example, rising costs of prescription medications is an issue that resonates with aged publics who are often dependent on medications yet living on fixed incomes. This issue is one which generated public concern and debate in many arenas, such as public policy organizations, government, the pharmaceutical industry, the health care sector, and the aging lobby.

Two elements should be added to the understanding of an issue to make it comprehensive: frames of reference and diversity. A person's frame of reference is a set of learned beliefs and values that frames all subsequent learning and attitude formation on an individual level (Bettinghaus & Cody, 1987). Frames of reference can vary across cultures and societies, and the frame of reference a person brings to an issue influences how that issue is perceived. The second factor in defining an issue is diversity; Wilson (1990) criticized previous attempts to define issues management as ethnocentric. Given the nature of the global economy and the demands for organizations to deal with multinational publics (Wakefield, 1996), it is reasonable to expect issues management to grapple with questions of diversity and tolerance. Kruckeberg (1995–96) wrote, "Virtually everyone is being forced into new relationships within social systems that are becoming both increasingly diverse and divisive" (p. 37). Such divisive topics carry an inherent element of risk in the very nature of their resolution. Incorporating cultural, racial, gender, orientation, religious, or other types of diversity, as well as the frames of reference unique to these perspectives, will be of importance to risk management as it takes on an enhanced significance and responsibility stemming from its social role in facilitating discussion and resolution of social issues.

DEFINING ISSUES MANAGEMENT IN RELATION TO RISK

Issues management, risk, and crisis, intersect at the juncture of communicating in the public interest. Issues management seeks to ethically and responsibly communicate about issues, risks, and concerns of publics through a framework of socially responsible management. Issues management seeks to anticipate and strategically, and ideally ethically, communicate about issues. Gaunt and Ollenburger (1995) wrote, "Issues management is the organized activity of identifying emerging trends, concerns, or issues likely to affect an organization in the next few years and developing a wider and more positive range of organizational responses toward that future" (p. 201). A definition that accentuated the social role of issues management was offered by Murphy (1996): "Issues management attempts to discern trends in public opinion so that an organization can respond to them before they amplify into serious conflict which breaches the social fabric and eludes control" (p. 103). A similar definition of issues management emphasizing the management role was given by Wilson (1990), who wrote, "Issues management can be best understood as an action oriented management function which seeks to identify potential or emerging issues. . .then mobilizes and coordinates organizational resources to strategically influence development of those issues" (p. 41). Heath (1997) added that issues management "helps organizations grow and survive: by reconciling their interests with those of the publics in their environments who have the ability to influence public policy" (p. 3).

Where do risks and issues intersect, then? Issues management coordinates communication about issues of interest in the organization with the stakeholders and publics in its environment enabling the organization to continue its business with minimal interference. These issues do not *necessarily* involve risk, but in light of the heightened levels of physical insecurity, financial instability, and health and safety risks brought on by modern society, almost all issues can be said to involve some element of risk. Many scholars (Chun, 2005; Koehn, 2005; Sauser, 2005; Stormer, 2003; Zwetsloot, 2003) also noted increasing demands for accountability, transparency, and responsibility in the years following high-level corporate scandals such as Enron (Bowen & Heath, 2005; Sims & Brinkman, 2003), public health crises such as the aforementioned SARS example, or the security threats posed by terrorism (Hoffman, 2002). In this light, issues management is defined as the organizational conscience or ethical decision-making counsel. Issues management is the function of strategically aligning the corporation with the environment, allowing continued survival and development of a long-term relationship with members of that environment, so this logic holds that issues management should include the consideration of how ethical implications and values of publics affect that mission.

Defining issues management as the "corporate conscience" has much support in recent scholarly literature and empirical inquiry (Bowen, 2004; Dando & Swift, 2003; Huang, 2004). Many organizations have hired ethics experts in response to increased pressure for accountability from publics (Grojean, Resick, Dickson, & Smith, 2004), but whether business follows theory in implementing this practice on a large and permanent scale remains to be seen. One method of maintaining social responsibility and ethical rectitude is to use the issues management function in a manner of encouraging dialogue with publics. Responsibility and responsiveness follow knowledge and discussion of issues of importance to publics—including risks to these publics. A normative social role is maintained by facilitation of information and debate surrounding problematic issues.

ORIGINS AND DEVELOPMENT OF ISSUES MANAGEMENT

Ewing (1997) deemed W. Howard Chase the "father of issues management" and credited Chase with the term "issues management" used in the inaugural edition of his 1976 newsletter, *Corporate Public Issues and Their Management*, although the activities of issues management had been carried out regularly by senior-level public relations counselors since at least the 1940s (Heath & Bowen,

2002). Chase used the term "issues management" to describe an activity taking place in forward-thinking corporations and businesses (Hainsworth, 1990). In the social turbulence of the late 1960s and early 1970s, many executives were struggling to maintain control of the environment, to predict changes, and to regain stability (Ansoff, 1980). The function of issues management grew out of management's reaction to a tempestuous environment brought on by social changes and demands for businesses to justify their existence.

Heath and Cousino (1990) argued that issues management was a result of the pressures of activism and increasing demands for corporate social responsibility from both inside and outside the industry. L. A. Grunig (1992) defined an activist public as "a group of two or more individuals who organize in order to influence another public or publics through action that may include education, compromise, persuasion, pressure tactics, or force" (p. 504). J. E. Grunig and Repper (1992) traced the development of issues management to a fundamental belief by Chase and other early proponents that an organization would be at the mercy of activist groups without issues management. The history of issues management and activism are inextricably linked. However, issues management has grown to include many areas of concern in addition to activism, such as contributions to overall organizational effectiveness, strategic planning, optimization of organizational communication, end-user satisfaction of an organization's goods or services, and ethical decision making (Buchholz, Evans, & Wagley, 1994; J. Coates, V. Coates, Jarratt, & Heinz, 1986). The extension of issues management to a societal level function is, therefore, a natural one. Issues management serves not only to help an organization resolve issues with publics, but also to facilitate the resolutions of problems within society through the dialogical flow of communication. This function is an important contribution to society because the continued cohesion of a society is dependent on the collective resolution of issues and the management of risk.

EMPLOYING STRATEGIC ISSUES MANAGEMENT AND RISK MANAGEMENT

Organizations will consistently have consequences, intentional or not, on the stakeholders and publics around them (Dozier & Ehling, 1992; Dozier, L. A. Grunig, & J. E. Grunig, 1995; J. E. Grunig & Hunt, 1984; L. A. Grunig, J. E. Grunig, & Ehling, 1992; Heath, 1998; Heath, Seshadri, & Lee, 1998). Hung (1999) argued, "Strategically implement[ed] issues management will help an organization understand what kind of consequences it has and the impacts of these consequences" (p. 5). The understanding and planning for consequences afforded by issues management helps the organization maintain good relationships with publics. The important role of communication in this capacity is heightened when an element of risk is involved, because risk-bearing publics normally require more communication that non-risk-bearing publics. Ongoing, frequent communication is an essential component of risk communication in order to minimize uncertainty (Palenchar & Heath, 2006). The communication among issues, risk, and crisis management takes place in a larger social context that affects our understanding of these matters, and results in a societal level impact. See Figure 17.1 for a representation.

Relationships, Dialogue, and Collaborative Problem Solving

Relationships based on two-way communication are the foundation of issues, risk, and crisis communication. A leader in public relations scholarship, J. E. Grunig (2000) wrote, "Recently, my research has moved toward the development and maintenance of relationships as the central goal of public relations" (p. 33). Vercic, L. A. Grunig, and J. E. Grunig (1996) argued, "Building good relationships with strategic publics maximizes the autonomy of organizations to pursue their goals" (p. 37). Of course, effective risk and issues management contributes to these goals. In the societal level function of managing risks and issues, these functions can be said to maintain relationships between many groups in society: publics, governments, industries, organizations,

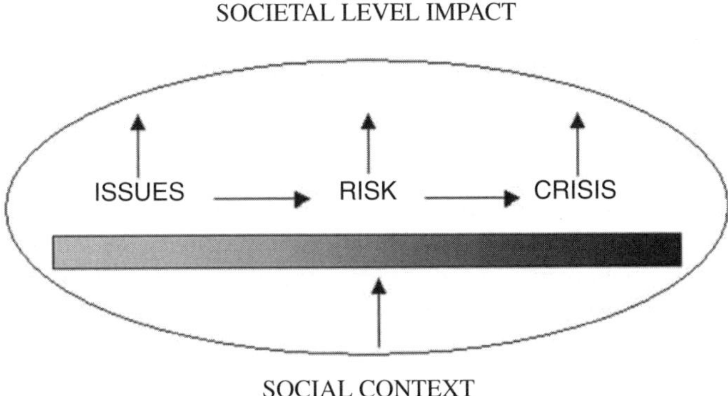

FIGURE 17.1 Continuum of issues, risk, and crisis.

and communities. With regard to managing risk, the maintenance of relationships has been argued by researchers (Palenchar & Heath, 2002) to substantially increase comfort with risk-bearing publics.

Other researchers in issues, risk, and crisis management have also conducted research on the importance of relationship building (Broom, Casey, & Ritchey, 1997; Heath, 1998; Ledingham, Bruning, & Wilson, 1999; Lerbinger, 1997, 2006; Spicer, 1997). Researchers (Huang, 1997, 2001; Kent & Taylor, 2002; Ledingham & Bruning, 2000; Ledingham, 2006; Taylor & Doerfel, 2005) who specialize in the relationship management approach to public relations typically report four variables that quantify the relationship: control-mutuality, satisfaction, trust, and commitment (J. E. Grunig & Huang, 2000). These relationship indicators generally illustrate the theoretical components of successful organization-public relationships, and allow communicators to have benchmark and evaluative measures to build or maintain relationships in practice. All of the relationship indicators have a vital role in risk management, but perhaps none is more important than trust. Ethics and careful attention to the ethical management of risk communication can both support the trust variable. Researchers (Bowen, 2006; Bowen et al., 2006) argued that ethics enhances trust in organization-public relationships by reinforcing credibility, expectations of consistency, and encouraging dialogue.

The emphasis of relationship building is dialogue—a view that coincides with the concepts inherent in symmetrical theory. The symmetrical model of communication is one that naturally seeks to maintain and enhance relationships with publics. The recent emphasis on relationship building in public relations research is an understanding promulgated by J. E. Grunig's symmetrical (dialogical) theory. The growth of relationships with strategic publics is an area of equal importance to issues management, because issues are normally defined and acted on by publics in the organization's environment. Dialogue is a central part of problem resolution, making issues management invaluable to the discussion of social problems. Issues management allows organizations to interact effectively with their environments (Lauzen & Dozier, 1992) making it a central component of the discussion and resolution of social ills. For instance, it is hard to imagine effectively addressing risk in the post-9/11 age without the issues management function (Bowen, 2005; Hoffman, 2002). Security issues are a new but important component of risk in modern life, constituting an area in which society must use issues management to engage in dialogue about what security means, what civil liberties can or should be abridged in the interest of security, and acceptable versus unacceptable risk (Beck, 1995, 1998; Douglas & Wildavsky, 1982). Further, the risk-bearing publics in terms of terrorist activities have been dramatically expanded by large-scale and far-reaching terrorist acts

(Clair, MacLean, & Greenberg, 2002; Hoffman, 2002). The ramifications of risk management at the societal level even on the single issue of terrorism are enormous. One can see from this example that the importance of communication is often magnified when the issues involves a substantial element of risk.

Another approach to issues management centered on the development of relationships is the rhetorical or rhetorical enactment approach (Heath, 1998). This theory conceptualized public relations along a continuum with sophistry, self-interest, and persuasion at one end of the spectrum and dialogue, the contest of ideas, and collaborative decision making at the other end (Heath, 1998). Heath's view of public relations through rhetorical enactment theory emphasized "mutually beneficial relationship development and maintenance between organizations and their stakeholders/stakeseekers" (p. 16). Public relations researchers (Huang, 1997, 2001; Plowman, 1998, 1999) have incorporated much knowledge from the areas of interpersonal communication, negotiation, and conflict resolution. Moreover, the field continues to strengthen its understandings of the symmetrical precepts of dialogue and relationship maintenance (Huang, 1997, 2001; Ledingham & Bruning, 2000) as central concerns in issue resolution and risk management. Integrative problem-solving strategies (Lewicki, Litterer, Saunders, & Minton, 1993) which attempt to collaboratively manage issues of risk, have led to a large role for organizations as social actors and socially responsible agents.

Issues managers can use the theories of relationship, symmetry, dialogue, and collaborative problem solving to advise an organization not only on the ethically responsible way to mange risk, but also to have an impact on the outcomes of risk at the level of affecting their communities and, ultimately, an impact at the social level. Integrating these theoretical approaches and combining that management perspective with an ethical analysis provides a tool that can help to effectively manage risk and communicate about risk in the most effective manner possible.

Organizational Approaches to Problem Solving and Social Implications

Management theorist Ackoff (1974) defined four attitudes organizations might take toward problems, issues, or crises. The organization could be inactive, in that it does nothing or "stonewalls;" reactive, being the response of an ill-prepared organization to crisis; hyperactive, an overly aggressive stance defining all issues as crises; and preactive, in which an organization predicts problems that may arise and prepares a concerted response. These four approaches are similar to those described by other scholars, such as Buchholz, Evans, and Wagley (1989), who found reactive, accommodative, proactive, and interactive approaches to issues. To these classic attitudes, Roth, Ryder, and Voehl (1996) added the interactive approach, which viewed "problems as having a positive as well as negative side" and as an "ongoing part of any healthy operation rather than a nuisance at best. It defines problem solving as a pastime critical to positive organizational and individual development" (p. 16). Perhaps an ethically and socially responsible approach to managing risk aligns best with their definition because those considerations could add a positive element to even the most grave issues. As illustrated in chaos theory literature, issues and risk communication have an intrinsic nature of unpredictability. However, planning for potentialities can help the organization react in well-conceived ways even when a particular situation eludes prediction or control.

Is interactivity a socially valuable principle in and of itself, or is it simply the approach that best contributes to organizational effectiveness? The interactive view of issues management described by Roth, Ryder, and Voehl (1996) is similar to J. E. Grunig and Hunt's (1984) two-way symmetrical model of public relations in which collaborative problem solving is valued as a social good. Both the dialogical perspective and the two-way symmetrical model depend on a two-way flow of information, and both have realized that the deliberate resolution of problems is crucial to continued organization existence. In the societal level of analysis applied in this chapter, these integrative approaches are also crucial in resolving problems concerning segments of society. Issues management consists largely of resolving issues that have (or are about to) become problems and could move on to become crises. The interactive and two-way symmetrical approaches to issues have their bases in the contributions of scholarship on negotiation, conflict resolution, organizational behavior, and organizational effectiveness. These constructs allow issues management to be used to effectively engage in problem solving at a level that has implications for the society itself. Even when issues are not in and of themselves an overt concern for large portions of society, the facilitation of dialogue and the resolution of smaller issues function as a social binder of relationships and interests. Issues management is literally a facilitator of social problem solving and figuratively the oil greasing the wheels of communication flow between different segments of society, organizations, and publics.

Crisis management (Coombs, 1998) can also be viewed as part of issues management. Crises can result from issues that have not been satisfactorily resolved, or from accidents, explosions, natural disasters, or other unpredictable events such as terrorist activities. For instance, few could have predicted the devastation and social turmoil that Hurricane Katrina inflicted on the U.S. gulf coast in 2005, much less the significant issues emerging with the Federal Emergency Management Agency (FEMA) and many other government entities. A risk management perspective would anticipate these risks, and incorporate an ethical and socially responsible element into crisis plans. Much of the turmoil in a case such as Hurricane Katrina could have been prevented with socially responsive ethical analysis. For instance, such analyses could have avoided the allegations against government agencies of institutionalized racism or discrimination against those of lower socioeconomic status.

Risk Communication and Complexity Theory

Topics of risk communication and the emergence of crisis situations are still arenas in which social problems can be discussed and resolved. However, the level of complexity and unpredictability of these problems makes managing the many issues surrounding an issue of inherent risk or a crisis challenging. The application of complexity and chaos theory can shed light on the uncertainties and social implications of communicating in a dynamic and ever-changing context.

Chaos theory emerged from an amalgamation of physics and mathematics, systems theory, and topology, and has grown into a theory of complex adaptive systems. This school of thought asserted that systems do not operate in a predictable cause-and-effect manner, but are in unpredictable and interlocking systems of complexity and change. In this view, systems operate on a non-linear basis in which outcomes evolve exponentially and have little resemblance to inputs. Feedback will create "noise" in the system that could cause destabilization and new patterns. Sudden bifurcation of the system due to these new patterns can be expected but outcomes remain unpredictable. According to Murphy (2007), actors and decision makers in a complex system do not generally follow fixed rules, but:

> The 'rules' for interaction are dynamically developed by the agents themselves in the course of their interaction. Furthermore, the agents' actions are nonlinear, and thus the results of individual interactions are unpredictable: Small causes can have a profound impact on the system and large causes may have minimal effect. (p. 121)

Complexity and chaos scholars also hold that self reorganization and renewal are inherent in the chaotic system and do not require external intervention to generate new forms and inner guidelines (Murphy, 1996).

Risk management and communication about risk are clearly areas with a large theoretical overlap in complex adaptive systems. The uncertainty involved in risk implies that risk communication can hardly be "strategically managed." Intrinsic in the nature of risk itself is an element of chaos, and this feature is what makes the "management" of risk an ever-elusive endeavor. Perhaps a more responsible approach is to ethically interact with risk, increasing the importance of a stringent ethical analysis in any risk communication. The application of complexity and chaos theory is important to understanding the societal level function of risk management because it explains how many social issues arise unexpectedly and hold extremely complex causal chains. As a result, issues involving social implications, an element of risk, or crisis are notoriously unpredictable and volatile. In the words of Beck (1998), "The basic question is: how can we make decisions about a risk we know nothing about?" (p. 12).

Both complex adaptive systems and chaos theory are particularly applicable to risk management because each can explicate the volatile and unmanageable nature of risk. As Murphy (1996) explained, "In public relations, few phenomena appear more unstable than public opinion, and it is here that chaos theory has most relevance" (p. 102). Murphy's (1996) application of chaos theory to issues management is seminal in that it provided a conceptual framework for managing risk, and understanding of how issues can develop in unforeseen ways. Many permutations of the complex system are completely unpredictable, even when using the best predictive research methods and scenario building strategies (Sung, 2007). Murphy's (2007) conceptualization is also instrumental in that it allows us to see risk-bearing publics and interest groups themselves as chaotic social systems (Murphy & Dee, 1996). Chaos can be a good approach to use in assessing the potential implications of risk and crisis situations. Murphy (1996) stated, "This vulnerability of chaotic systems to small changes explains why organizations can be caught off guard by initially small-scale events that undergo catastrophic social amplification" (p. 105). This dynamic was lamented by strategy scholar Mintzberg (1983) when he stated that it had become commonplace to see the most powerful of corporations capitulate to the smallest of activist groups.

Under the application of complexity and chaos theory, the degree of control the organization might have when dealing with certain risks would be negligible, especially once a risk becomes a topic of public policy debate. Gonzales-Herrero and Pratt (1995) advised managers to "assess the degree of control an organization has" (p. 28) in such circumstances, noting that often that control is very limited. However, rather than attempting to control change, communicators can use symmetrical communication to open a dialogue that facilitates change in both the organization and the publics, risk bearers, or social interest group (Murphy, 1996). Murphy (1996) concluded, "Chaos theory balances out overly rational management approaches and provides useful reminders that context-sensitivity, patience, and careful timing may effect change where wholesale proactivity cannot" (p. 111). Murphy's concepts are based on the idea of socially responsible risk and issues management, providing further support for the application of ethical analyses in risk management. Despite the growth of scholarship in this area (Coombs, 1999; Millar & Heath, 2004), communicating about risky issues has not been thoroughly researched through the theoretical frame of complexity or chaos theory. However, it is clear that complexity and chaos theory explain our limited predictive ability regarding the outcomes and potential impacts of risk. For this reason, an analysis of risk must include a rational approach and the ethical consideration of our obligation to protect publics, minimize risk, and communicate ethically about those elements of our risk management. Conducting a rigorous and rational ethical analysis is one of the only lines of defense against the inherently chaotic and complex nature of risk.

ETHICAL IMPLICATIONS OF RISK COMMUNICATION

Many situations necessitate the bearing, understanding, and management of risk. These imperatives require communication between the risk creator and the risk bearer, but there are larger ethical decisions looming behind any issue of risk. For instance, taking any medication also brings a risk of side effects, and that risk must be communicated about on multiple fronts, understood, and weighed by those who consider using the medication. In order to communicate about risk in an ethically responsible manner, one should consider the many duties and obligations accepted by the organization who engages in risk generating activities. The very nature of risk itself implies a moral responsibility to consider the consequences of these actions and potential actions on many varied publics. Therefore, issues of risk are inherently matters of ethics—both consequence and duty are implied.

For guidance on how to resolve the ethical dilemmas common in risk communication, moral philosophy will be examined from both consequence and duty-based perspectives. The moral utility perspective of John Stuart Mill will be discussed as a framework for the ethical analysis of risk due to its heavy reliance on consequentialist argumentation. Then, the moral philosophy and the rigorous ethics of German philosopher Immanuel Kant (1724–1804) will be applied in the context of risk communication. Ethical guidelines will be reviewed and applied to risk communication, including the standards of a morally good will, objective rational analysis, maintaining dignity and respect, and honesty and disclosure.

A CONSEQUENTIALIST MORAL ANALYSIS OF RISKY CONSEQUENCES

Why should one consider risk as a matter of ethics at all? If such examination is based on probabilities, hard science, and chemistry, then why complicate the issue with moral philosophy? One must consider moral philosophy because risk involves a human decision-making process of determining what is a risk, defining related concepts, weighing and judgments about fact, and decisions about worthwhile risk for a greater good in the form of some probable outcome. This area is the realm of consequentialist philosophy, in determining the moral utility of decisions and defining what will be judged as the good outcome that should be maximized. Furthermore, scholars in public relations (J. E. Grunig & L. A. Grunig, 1996) have asserted that a consequentialist moral perspective is most suited for analyzing ethical decisions in communication because the organization and publics are inextricably linked by the consequences each has upon the other. The consequences publics and organizations have on each other are what bind them together and turn publics into more closely-tied strategic publics "that many theorists have called stakeholders" (J. E. Grunig, 1992, p. 12). Whether termed publics or stakeholders, there are many ethical implications in the decisions they make, how they interact with others based on those decisions, and the potential and real consequences of these actions. This consequence-based view holds true equally for both organizations and publics (or stakeholders).

Those consequences were examined in moral philosophy most stringently (De George, 2006) by John Stuart Mill (1861/1957). Mill, taking up the utilitarian mantle of Bentham's limited philosophy, sought to apply a consequence-based analysis to moral decisions. Utilitarianism is an analysis method in which consequences, or predicted, potential consequences are weighed and analyzed in terms of creating a greater moral good for a greater number of people. Moral good can be defined in different ways according to which type of utilitarianism is being applied. In act utilitarianism, one seeks to maximize the good and minimize the harm in a situation-specific decision, in all of its detail. In rule utilitarianism, one seeks to maximize the good and minimize the harm based upon similar situations in the past and underlying principles of right or wrong. In either approach, the principle of utility is applied, in which a "maximum utility" decision is the ethically correct choice—that is, the decision which maximizes whatever is defined as good while minimizing whatever is defined as bad. "The greater good for the greater number" is a simple synopsis of utilitarianism's consequentialist decision-making imperative, although it loses some of the fine distinctions found in rule versus act approaches.

Applying a utilitarian framework for analysis of risk is reasonably, even deceptively, simple – the greater good for the greater number principle is often used in decisions regarding whether a benefit is "worth" the risk. In applying a utilitarian analysis, the decision maker must make sure that all possibilities have been considered and predicted as accurately as possible. As we know, chaos theory explains why this is a difficult task. Further, utilitarianism is limited by several other flaws (Gorovitz, 1971; Posner, 2002) which should be borne in mind any time a utilitarian analysis is employed. Utilitarian philosophy has the disadvantage of having to accurately predict numerous potential outcomes before any decision can be made. Once a utilitarian calculus is employed, the option favoring the majority is always chosen, creating a potentially dangerous reinforcement of the status quo. Finally, utilitarian approaches, particularly act utilitarianism judging only a single situation, ignore moral principle in favor of outcomes. As numerous critics have discussed, utilitarian judgment looks only at the potential utility of outcomes rather than the 'rightness' or 'wrongness' implied in moral principle. Christians (2007) explained the problem with using only utility and not moral principle: "Theft, suicide, euthanasia, deceit are not wrong in themselves, but only if their consequences are less productive than their alternatives" (p. 115). Using only outcomes as a decision-making basis or putting the ends before the means is problematic if the risk manager does not hold the most pure of motives. Despite its inherent weaknesses, some (Elliott, 2007) asserted that a utilitarian approach is a viable framework for the analysis of ethical dilemmas because of its alliance with the democratic ideal of maximizing individual self-interest, ultimately leading to collective good for all.

Despite the appealing simplicity of acting on behalf of the greatest good for the greatest number, this author must caution against applying an exclusively utilitarian moral framework within the context of risk management. The notions of inherent ambiguity and high uncertainty involved in risk lead to the conclusion that reliably predicting the potential outcomes of decisions with unknown or vague factors of risk would render the utilitarian paradigm of ethical judgment by outcome useless. As discussed in the above section on chaos theory, many unpredictable outcomes are seen and even exponentiate with issues of high uncertainty. The many vagaries that comprise the very nature of risk are at odds with reasonably employing any standard of the utilitarian calculus "the greatest good for the greatest number" since one has no way of reliably estimating these numbers.

Rosa (2003), writing on the metatheoretical foundations of risk considered unpredictable possibilities essential, and argued: "Risk is a situation or an event where something of human value (including humans themselves) is at stake and where the outcome is uncertain" (p. 56). Thus, risk itself is too unpredictable to employ a utilitarian paradigm because it uses potential consequences to determine the ethical action. These consequences are often simply unknown and cannot be anticipated in matters of risk. If outcomes were no longer ambiguous, unpredictable, or uncertain, then the problem would likely not qualify as risk management but would be handled by the more certain parameters of research and scenario-building involved in issues management. In order to ethically manage risk, we need a philosophical framework less reliant on uncertain outcomes and based on a less mutable determinant of what is ethical. The primary alterative to utilitarianism is the non-consequentialist paradigm of deontology.

DEONTOLOGY: KANT'S DUTY-BASED PERSPECTIVE OF MORAL PHILOSOPHY

Non-consequentialist philosophy does not ignore the consequences of decisions, but those consequences are not the standard by which the rightness or wrongness of a decision is judged. Noting that a more stable delimiter of what is ethical was needed than that offered by the consequentialist philosophers, Kant set out to create a universal measure of morality (Sullivan, 1989). Paton (1967) asserted: "Kant contrived to say something new about morality. This remarkable achievement has compelled every subsequent writer on moral philosophy to examine his views" (p. 15). All philosophers must include Kant in their philosophizing and argue for or against his work because his impact is so great that his theory cannot be ignored (Sullivan, 1989). Basing an ethical judgment on Kant's non-consequentialist, duty-based paradigm of deontology offers a solid and rigorous foundation in moral analysis and some degree of consistency for risk management.

Rational and objective analysis is the cornerstone of Kant's moral philosophy (Paton, 1967;

Sullivan, 1989). Using our reason to differentiate "between objective and subjective judgments" (Bennett, 1966, p. 133), bases decisions on more rigorous footing than that of intuition, expeditiousness, or other factors which could potentially impinge on a moral analysis. Using reason alone is the way in which Kant's paradigm levels the playing field, dispersing power differentials and more subjective concerns which could bias a moral analysis. More is explained on enacting this cornerstone of Kantian analysis below, but this requirement seeks to minimize uncertainty and bias, and encourage reasoned objectivity for the decision maker.

A deontological analysis is particularly suited to risk communication because it seeks to minimize uncertainty through its reliance on universal principles that apply across various situations. Minimizing uncertainty is a common goal with risk management, even if the approaches used toward attaining that goal are radically different in nature. Deontology uses a perspective of a universal condition for a decision, and only if it can meet the three general tests of universalizability is the action then deemed ethical. This decision-making test is called the categorical imperative, specifying a universal standard of ethics. It holds that ethical decisions should apply in all similar situations regardless of context of individual perspectives of decision makers. Analysis of risk using reason alone and meeting the tests of the categorical imperative in terms of duty, maintaining respect for those involved, and a morally good will can ensure that a decision meets this universal ethical principle. Each of these imperatives is discussed below in terms of risk communication and ethical responsibility to risk bearers.

Good Will and Risk Responsibility

Philosophers (Kant, 1785/1993; Rawls, 1971) argued that the greatest moral standard is to hold good will toward others. A morally pure or good will means that not only is no harm intended, but also, the moral good will upholds the highest requirement of moral behavior possible. The good will trumps the utilitarian measure of creating the greatest happiness for the greatest number because it does not fail under rigorous scrutiny. Only the moral good will is incorruptible in the most stringent sense when put through rigorous philosophical analyses. Other conditions that seem to hold inherent good and value on first glance, such as courage, can become corrupted when taken to extremes—such as courage becoming foolhardiness. Kant (1785/1993; 1793/1974) argued that of all human values, only a morally good will was absolutely unassailable.

For risk communication, a morally good will is the factor of importance that should be tested above all other decision-making considerations. Taken from the organizational perspective, an organization must hold a morally good will at the center of its decision making with issues of risk having an impact on publics. This willingness to maintain a morally good will is essential when dealing with matters of risk, acceptable and unacceptable potential harm, and informed choice among publics. A good will in risk communication can be evidenced by providing the necessary and complete information with which publics can make an informed decision, free of coercion or subjective bias of their own. In this manner, moral responsibility for risk bearing is then shared by an organization and an engaged public who make informed choices with regard to acceptable versus unacceptable levels of risk.

Risk bearing entails a higher level of ethical responsibility than non-risk related issues due to the gravity of potential outcomes. The serious nature involved in taking risk or bearing risk in association with doing business implies a moral obligation of good will in that the attempt to do no harm is maintained. Harm is a real possibility in situations of risk communication. The moral imperative of maintaining a good will implies that the organization goes a step further in its deliberations of causal moral responsibility than "doing no harm." The level of moral responsibility associated with a good will implies that decisions made with only good intention toward publics will be deemed ethical. Actions undertaken from the perspective of "doing no harm" are on dangerous moral footing because of the uncertainty inherent in risk and also because they do not reach the ethical standard of Kant's categorical imperative commanding good intention. For example, an organization could decide that quietly dumping a nontoxic substance in a river near a community would do no harm. However; the issue is to also behave with a morally good will—so such dumping would be ruled unethical because it does not contribute to a purely moral ethic of good will—in this example, the betterment of the community through good-intentioned stewardship. According to Kantian philosophy, the morally good will would hold that no dumping of this sort should take place because a good will would mean that all dumping should be in accordance with agreed-upon standards, even if it is more expensive to the organization.

Morally, the right thing to do is to proceed in all decisions with the utmost integrity, maintaining a good will even toward those publics perceived to be of little consequence, those bearing an "insignificant" amount or risk, or those hostile toward the organization, such as environmental activist groups. Although this standard might prove difficult when the organization is faced with obstructionist activist groups who do not want to resolve issues (L. A. Grunig, 1992; Heath & Douglas, 1991; Murphy & Dee, 1992), or in cases of clear wrongdoing on behalf of some party (Sims & Brinkman, 2003), considering the pure good will stands the organization in better position for explaining the rigor of its procedures, and also provides a defensible policy if challenged. In many cases, policy decisions regarding risk or crisis are examined in excruciating detail by the news media, and using the measure of a morally good will provides the organization with a sound basis from which to justify and, if necessary, defend. Communicating matters of risk is the ethical responsibility of the organization, and as such the test of the morally good will offers a rigorous test of motives.

Objective Application of Moral Standards Related to Risk

One dictum of ethical decision making based on Kantian philosophy that is often misunderstood is the requirement to make decisions from the basis of objective reason alone. This philosophical requirement asks the decision maker to rule out personal inclinations, subjective or self-interested desires, and so forth, and make ethical judgments from the basis of a rational analysis. Critics often misunderstand this requirement because they believe that the requirement is for an automaton-type of objectivity that is simply not possible within the human condition. Kant did not require a mathematical precision, but asked all moral decision makers to attempt to rule out personal influence and concerns to the greatest extent possible. Therefore, understood within the constructivist context of a socially-created reality, as Kant's original writings on this topic convey (Kant, 1785/1964; Paton, 1967), it is possible to be rational and objective when making moral judgments. Although it is true that being bound to the use of values-laden language limits our application of perfect rationality, the effort of making an objective analysis of a situation using our reason alone is often enough to make the decision detached from our own desires (Bennett, 1966), morally worthy in terms of the categorical imperative, and rationally defensible.

Ethical decisions can be said to be objective to the greatest extent possible when using a Kantian paradigm. Kant (1963/1930) explained the connection between morality and objective, rational analysis:

> Moral goodness is, therefore, objective in character because it does not depend on any harmony with our inclinations, but on itself as such. Every subjective law is derived from the character of this or that subject and is valid only in respect of that subject, but moral laws ought to be of general validity and ought to apply to all free actions irrespective of the diversity of subjects. (p. 24)

Ruling out prudential self-interest, subjective desires, and other influences that cloud objectivity can be a challenging task. But, it is an essential component of conducting a thorough risk analysis and arriving and a well-reasoned and sound organizational policy. Risk managers can then communicate with confidence knowing that a rigorous and thoroughly considered rationale buttresses their communications with publics.

In order to analyze ethical dilemmas involving an element of risk, it is necessary to delineate stakeholders and publics who could be affected by the issue. Those groups, as well as the perspective of the organization, should be considered in decision making. Management traditionally considers the needs of the organization first and foremost in these situations. However, to do that would violate the ethical norm of rationality imposed by a Kantian philosophical analysis because it would be privileging the organization above all other parties in the decision. Such privilege violates objective rationality, in which all parties must be considered from a reasoned—as opposed to selfish—perspective. Each perspective is to be weighed upon its merits in a rational analysis, not upon the source. In an objective analysis of facts and perspectives, a logical and morally defensible organizational approach to managing and communicating about risk is the goal. This goal is arduous but attainable, and provides a sound rationale for management action and risk communication.

MAINTAINING DIGNITY AND RESPECT FOR RISK BEARERS

Another tenet of Kantian moral philosophy requires the decision maker to consider whether possible decision alternatives maintain the dignity and respect of those involved in and affected by the ethical issue. In order for the morally good will to be maintained, a respectful attitude of others and the self must be maintained in the decision-making process. Decisions that take advantage of certain groups or blatantly devalue or disregard the interests of some would fail this ethical test. According to Sullivan (1989), a renowned Kantian scholar, Kant believed that rationality and dignity were inextricably linked, because all rational moral beings are worthy of equal status under the moral law of ethics. This moral equality warrants equal consideration of the ideas, values, and perspectives of others in a rational decision-making process.

Maintaining the dignity and respect the organization has for risk bearing publics includes incorporating their perspectives and values into decision making that could potentially affect these groups, as well as encouraging the freedom of informed choice about the risks one finds acceptable. Heightened importance and scrutiny are often placed on communication involving risk by involved publics. Their desire for honest, timely, complete, clear and factual information is increased with the level of personal risk they believe to exist (J. E. Grunig & Repper, 1992). Oftentimes, these publics merely want to be heard on an issue and have some reassurance that the organization has considered their positions on the risk (Bowen, 2000). Even if their view is not represented in the ultimate decision, knowing it was contemplated by management is normally enough to allow the dignity and respect of these publics to be maintained (Bowen, 2002). Research supports this ethical theory: If risk-bearers are aware that their position has been considered by the organization, they are likely to be more supportive of that organization, even when resulting decisions do not directly further their interests (Heath et al., 1998).

Access to the organization and its decision-making process is another aspect of maintaining dignity and respect for publics and stakeholders. Opening channels of communication so that publics and stakeholders have access to the decision-making process in the organization is a vital component of maintaining relationships with both publics and risk bearers (Heath et al., 1998; Palenchar & Heath, 2002). When publics have access to the decision-making process of the organization, they can contribute ideas and input which is often valuable in creating long-term solutions. Organizations that do not provide access of this kind to publics often find that they are faced with opposition because these publics feel ignored. Not only is it ethical to provide access to publics because it mitigates power differentials, it is also one method of building support and maintaining relationships with those who must bear the risk associated with the organization.

Maintaining an open dialogue with publics (Pearson, 1989) and risk bearers is ethical in that it affords them the dignity and respect of the organization. An additional benefit of this approach is that it is integrative. Collaborative decision making can occur when publics are afforded a role in the strategic decision-making process regarding risks, encouraging a sound and balanced decision. Decisions integrating the views and interests of publics outside the organization, in addition to the view of management, will often result in better decisions over the long term. Decisions tend to be more inclusive and enduring when they are crafted with many perspectives in mind. When publics are encouraged to participate in this manner, they develop a sense of ownership of the decision and a collaborative working relationship with management (Hung, 2007). These factors might not insulate the organization from criticism, but should help to engender more positive relationships on the whole. Research (L. A. Grunig, 1992; Heath & Douglas, 1991; Lerbinger, 2006; Lewicki et al., 1993) consistently finds that publics are more likely to support an organization and its policies when they have some role, even a small one, in its policy deliberations.

ACTING ON A DUTY OF HONESTY AND DISCLOSURE

Moral philosophy obligates people to act from a basis of honesty in their actions and communication. Honesty is obligated for all people by arguing that the rational will applies equally to all people and therefore holds a uniform obligation for all to behave honestly. Truth telling can be universalized, because all would want to be dealt with honestly themselves. Deceit cannot be universalized because the very fabric of society would be eroded if an assumption of honesty were not possible. The deontological imperative of honesty comes from a duty to uphold the moral law that is implied by the rational will, as a higher-order cognitive function of human reason. In Kantian philosophy, the ability to use rationality concurrently implies a duty to uphold moral principle. The duty applies as consistently to individuals as it does to organizations and their publics.

Issues of risk often involve decisions on the importance of information, prioritizing topics, disclosure, and the nature of how communication takes place. Palenchar and Heath (2006) explained, "Strategic and ethical risk communication entails science and information within dialogic advocacy, the framing and interpretation of facts, values, and policies" (p. 133). As Palenchar and Heath (2006) pointed out, the framing of facts should be enacted within an ethical context but it also requires ethical sensitivity to the decision making involved in determining what facts are important, which issues are relevant, and how they should be resolved. Part of that process includes engaging in dialogue with publics, but that dialogue must be based on honest and full disclosure on behalf of both the organization and publics.

The moral imperative of honesty is imposed equally on both organizations and the risk bearers or publics with whom they interact. This universal imperative means that organizations and publics must maintain a relationship based on forthright communication of facts, honest interpretation of those facts, and full disclosure of information. One must respect the power that comes with framing (Entman, 1993; Goffman, 1974) definitional and factual issues surrounding risk, and the moral duty to wield that power ethically. What is considered full disclosure, when to disclose, and similar concerns are difficult determinations, but must be considered and reasoned through a moral paradigm in the interest of maintaining relationships based on dignity and respect.

Full disclosure of honest and accurate information can help build relationships and understanding in the risk communication context even when the information itself involves conflict or is not of a positive nature. When communicating about risks with risk-bearing publics, research shows that higher levels of information actually lower fear and dread among community publics (Heath et al., 1998). Further, research has found a positive correlation between conflict resolution skill and increased levels of moral reasoning (W. Heydenberk, R. Heydenberk, & Bailey 2003). These findings illustrate that honest and candid communication adds value to the relationships an organization holds with publics in numerous ways, from reducing fear of risks to applying sophisticated ethical analyses to questions and issues of risk.

SUMMARY AND CONCLUSIONS

This chapter reviewed arguments explaining the moral implications of risk communication and offered guidelines for engaging in ethical risk management. Bodies of research from systems theory, issues management, and public relations theory indicate that risk communication has an impact at the societal level, and some scholars (Beck, 1992; Douglas, 1992; Luhmann, 1993) have argued that society enables humans to collectively manage risk. Societal-level consequences point to a large-scale moral responsibility and duty inherent in risk communication. The extent to which operational consequences involve an element of risk determines how much ethical analysis is required in risk management and communication.

This chapter is but one step in the direction of creating a comprehensive ethical paradigm for conducting risk communication in a socially responsible manner, with a responsibility not only to an employer, but to a larger ideal of a universal social good. Risk management is needed to assess, evaluate, and plan for risky consequences, as well as to communicate about them with publics who bear the risks associated with a particular issue. Future research in the areas of applied ethics, character and virtue ethics, and paradigms of communitarian justice also need to be explored with regard to risk communication.

There is little doubt that risk management and the communication surrounding risk plays a valuable role in society. Risk management helps to inform and educate about risk, to create an acceptable level of risk tolerance for those who bear the risk. It also serves a positive social role by building understanding of risk and knowledge of response strategies for crises. Finally, risk management helps to resolve social problems by engaging in a public dialogue about levels of risk, helping to determine what type and amount of risk is and is not acceptable to publics.

As industrialization grows and industry expands to previously underdeveloped countries, the demand for greater and more responsible risk communication will also grow. The role of dialogue about risk and issues impacting society cannot be underestimated in its importance. Indeed, much of this communication shapes society itself, and in doing so carries a great burden of ethical and social responsibility. Engaging in ethically thoughtful and socially aware risk communication is a primary responsibility for communication professionals, who should strive to implement risk management with moral courage and integrity. The result of pursuing ethical goals is that the information and dialogue created by risk management is a morally-responsible social good, existing to the benefit not only of risk-bearers, but also for the betterment of society itself.

BIBLIOGRAPHY

Ackoff, R. L. (1974). *Redesigning the future*. New York: Wiley.

Adorno, T. W. (Ed.). (1991). *The culture industry: Selected essays on mass culture*. London: Routledge.

Ansoff, H. I. (1980). Strategic issue management. *Strategic Management Journal, 1*, 131–148.

Bagdikian, B. (1985). The US media: Supermarket or assembly line? *Journal of Communication, 35*(5), 97–109.

Beck, U. (1992). *Risk society: Towards a new modernity* (M. Ritter, Trans.). London: Sage.

Beck, U. (1995). *Ecological politics in an age of risk* (A. Weisz, Trans.). Cambridge: Polity Press.

Beck, U. (1998). Politics of risk society. In J. Franklin (Ed.), *The politics of risk society* (pp. 9–22). Cambridge: Polity Press.

Bennett, J. (1966). *Kant's analytic*. Cambridge: Cambridge University Press.

Berger, B. K., & Reber, B. H. (2006). *Gaining influence in public relations: The role of resistance in practice*. Mahwah, NJ: Erlbaum.

Bettinghaus, E. P., & Cody, M. J. (1987). *Persuasive communication*. New York: Holt, Rinehart, and Winston.

Bowen, S. A. (2000). *A theory of ethical issues management: Contributions of Kantian deontology to public relations' ethics and decision making*. Unpublished doctoral dissertation, University of Maryland, College Park, MD.

Bowen, S. A. (2002). Elite executives in issues management: The role of ethical paradigms in decision making. *Journal of Public Affairs, 2*(4), 270–283.

Bowen, S. A. (2004). Organizational factors encouraging ethical decision making: An exploration into the case of an exemplar. *Journal of Business Ethics, 52*(4), 311–324.

Bowen, S. A. (2005). Communication ethics in the wake of terrorism. In H. D. O'Hair, R. L. Heath & G. Ledlow (Eds.), *Communication, communities, and terrorism* (pp. 114–151). Westport, CT: Praeger.

Bowen, S. A. (2006). Autonomy in communication: Inclusion in strategic management and ethical decision-making, a comparative case analysis. *Journal of Communication Management, 10*(4), 330–352.

Bowen, S. A., & Heath, R. L. (2005). Issues management, systems, and rhetoric: Exploring the distinction between ethical and legal guidelines at Enron. *Journal of Public Affairs, 5*, 84–98.

Bowen, S. A., & Heath, R. L. (2007). Narratives of the SARS epidemic and ethical implications for public health crises. *International Journal of Strategic Communication, 1*(2), 73–91.

Bowen, S. A., Heath, R. L., Lee, J., Painter, G., Agraz, F. J., McKie, D., et al. (2006). *The business of truth: A guide to ethical communication.* San Francisco, CA: International Association of Business Communicators.

Broom, G. M., Casey, S., & Ritchey, J. (1997). Toward a concept and theory of organization-public relationships. *Journal of Public Relations Research, 9*(2), 83–98.

Buchholz, R. A., Evans, W. D., & Wagley, R. A. (1989). *Management response to public issues.* Englewood Cliffs, NJ: Prentice-Hall.

Buchholz, R. A., Evans, W. D., & Wagley, R. A. (1994). *Management responses to public issues: Concepts and cases in strategy formulation* (3rd ed.). Upper Saddle River, NJ: Prentice Hall.

Chase, W. H. (1984). *Issue management: Origins of the future.* Stamford, CT: Issue Action Publications.

Chase, W. H., & Crane, T. (1996). Issue management: Dissolving the archaic division between line and staff. In L. B. Dennis (Ed.), *Practical public affairs in an era of change.* Lanham, MD: University Press of America.

Christians, C. G. (2007). Utilitarianism in media ethics and its discontents. *Journal of Mass Media Ethics, 22*(2&3), 113–131.

Chun, R. (2005). Ethical character and virtue in organizations: An empirical assessment and strategic implications. *Journal of Business Ethics, 57*(3), 269–284.

Clair, J. A., MacLean, T. L., & Greenberg, D. M. (2002). Teaching through traumatic events: Uncovering the choices of management educators as they responded to September 11th. *Academy of Management Learning and Education, 1*(1), 38–54.

Coates, J. F., Coates, V. T., Jarratt, J., & Heinz, L. (1986). *Issues management: How you can plan, organize and manage for the future.* Mt. Airy, MD: Lomond.

Coombs, W. T. (1998). An analytic framework for crisis situations: Better responses from a better understanding of the situation. *Journal of Public Relations Research, 10*(3), 177–191.

Coombs, W. T. (1999). *Ongoing crisis communication: Planning, managing, and responding* Thousand Oaks, CA: Sage.

Crable, R. E., & Vibbert, S. L. (1985). Managing issues and influencing public policy. *Public Relations Review, 11*(2), 3–16.

Dando, N., & Swift, T. (2003). Transparency and assurance: Minding the credibility gap. *Journal of Business Ethics, 44*(3), 195–200.

De George, R. T. (2006). *Business ethics* (6th ed.). Upper Saddle River, NJ: Pearson Prentice Hall.

Douglas, M. (1992). *Risk and blame: Essays in cultural theory.* New York: Routledge.

Douglas, M., & Wildavsky, A. (1982). *Risk and culture: An essay on the selection of technical and environmental dangers.* Los Angeles: University of California Press.

Dozier, D. M., & Ehling, W. P. (1992). Evaluation of public relations programs: What the literature tells us about their effects. In J. E. Grunig (Ed.), *Excellence in public relations and communication management* (pp. 159–184). Hillsdale, NJ: Erlbaum.

Dozier, D. M., Grunig, L. A., & Grunig, J. E. (1995). *Manager's guide to excellence in public relations and communication management.* Mahwah, NJ: Erlbaum.

Elliott, D. (2007). Getting Mill right. *Journal of Mass Media Ethics, 22*(2&3), 100–112.

Entman, R. (1993). Framing: Toward clarification of a fractured paradigm. *Journal of Communication, 43*, 51–58.

Ewing, R. P. (1997). Issues management: Managing trends through the issues life cycle. In C. L. Caywood (Ed.), *The handbook of strategic public relations & integrated communications* (pp. 173–188). New York: McGraw-Hill.

Fischhoff, B., Watson, S. R., & Hope, C. (1990). Defining risk. In T. S. Glickman & M. Gough (Eds.), *Readings in risk* (pp. 30–42). Washington, DC: Center for Risk Management.

Funtowitz, S. O., & Ravetz, J. R. (1983). Three types of risk assessment: A methodological analysis. In C. Whipple & V. T. Covello (Eds.), *Risk analysis in the private sector* (pp. 217–231). New York: Plenum Press.

Gaunt, P., & Ollenburger, J. (1995). Issues management revisited: A tool that deserves another look. *Public Relations Review, 21*(3), 199–210.

Goffman, E. (1974). *Frame analysis: An essay on the organization of experience*. Cambridge, MA: Harvard University Press.

Gonzales-Herrero, A., & Pratt, C. B. (1995). How to manage a crisis before—or whenever—it hits. *Public Relations Quarterly*(Spring), 25–34.

Gorovitz, S. (Ed.). (1971). *Utilitarianism, with critical essays*. Indianapolis, IN: Bobbs-Merrill.

Grojean, M. W., Resick, C. J., Dickson, M. W., & Smith, D. B. (2004). Leaders, values, and organizational climate: Examining leadership strategies for establishing an organizational climate regarding ethics. *Journal of Business Ethics, 55*(3), 223–241.

Grunig, J. E. (1992). Communication, public relations, and effective organizations: An overview of the book. In J. E. Grunig (Ed.), *Excellence in public relations and communication management* (pp. 1–30). Hillsdale, NJ: Erlbaum.

Grunig, J. E. (2000). Collectivism, collaboration, and societal corporatism as core professional values in public relations. *Journal of Public Relations Research, 12*(1), 23–48.

Grunig, J. E., & Grunig, L. A. (1996, May). *Implications of symmetry for a theory of ethics and social responsibility in public relations*. Paper presented at the meeting of the International Communication Association, Chicago.

Grunig, J. E., & Huang, Y. H. (2000). From organizational effectiveness to relationship indicators: Antecedents of relationships, public relations strategies, and relationship outcomes. In J. Ledingham & S. Bruning (Eds.), *Public relations as relationship management: A relational approach to the study and practice of public relations* (pp. 23–53). Mahwah, NJ: Erlbaum.

Grunig, J. E., & Hunt, T. (1984). *Managing public relations*. New York: Holt, Rinehart and Winston.

Grunig, J. E., & Repper, F. C. (1992). Strategic management, publics, and issues. In J. E. Grunig (Ed.), *Excellence in public relations and communication management* (pp. 117–157). Hillsdale, NJ: Erlbaum.

Grunig, L. A. (1992). Activism: How it limits the effectiveness of organizations and how excellent public relations departments respond. In J. E. Grunig (Ed.), *Excellence in public relations and communication management* (pp. 503–530). Hillsdale, NJ: Erlbaum.

Grunig, L. A., Grunig, J. E., & Dozier, D. M. (2002). *Excellent public relations and effective organizations: A study of communication management in three countries*. Mahwah, NJ: Erlbaum.

Grunig, L. A., Grunig, J. E., & Ehling, W. P. (1992). What is an effective organization? In J. E. Grunig (Ed.), *Excellence in public relations and communication management* (pp. 65–90). Hillsdale, NJ: Erlbaum.

Habermas, J. (1984). *The theory of communicative action: Reason and the rationalization of society* (T. McCarthy, Trans. Vol. 1). Boston: Beacon Press.

Habermas, J. (1996). The public sphere. In P. Marris & S. Thornham (Eds.), *Media studies: A reader* (pp. 55–59). Edinburgh: Edinburgh University Press.

Hainsworth, B. E. (1990). Issue management: An overview. *Public Relations Review, 16*(1), 3–7.

Heath, R. L. (1997). *Strategic issues management: Organizations and public policy challenges*. Thousand Oaks, CA: Sage.

Heath, R. L. (1998, November). *Rhetorical enactment theory: Another piece in the paradigm shift*. Paper presented at the meeting of the National Communication Association, New York.

Heath, R. L., & Bowen, S. A. (2002). The public relations philosophy of John W. Hill: Bricks in the foundation of issues management. *Journal of Public Affairs, 2*(4), 230–246.

Heath, R. L., & Cousino, K. R. (1990). Issues management: End of first decade progress report. *Public Relations Review, 16*(1), 6–18.

Heath, R. L., & Douglas, W. (1991). Effects of involvement on reactions to sources of messages and to message clusters. In J. E. Grunig & L. A. Grunig (Eds.), *Public relations research annual* (Vol. 3, pp. 179–194). Hillsdale, NJ: Erlbaum.

Heath, R. L., & Nelson, R. A. (1986). *Issues management: Corporate public policymaking in an information society*. Beverly Hills, CA: Sage.

Heath, R. L., Seshadri, S., & Lee, J. (1998). Risk communication: A two-community analysis of proximity, dread, trust, involvement, uncertainty, openness/accessibility, and knowledge on support/opposition toward chemical companies. *Journal of Public Relations Research, 10*(1), 35–56.

Heydenberk, W. R., Heydenberk, R. A., & Bailey, S. P. (2003). Conflict resolution and moral reasoning. *conflict Resolution Quarterly, 21*(1), 27–45.

Hoffman, B. (2002). Rethinking terrorism and counterterrorism since 9/11. *Studies in Conflict and Terrorism, 25*, 303–316.

Huang, Y. H. (1997). *Public relations strategies, relational outcomes, and conflict management strategies.* Unpublished doctoral dissertation, University of Maryland, College Park.

Huang, Y. H. (2001). Values of public relations: Effects on organization-public relationships mediating conflict resolution. *Journal of Public Relations Research, 13*(4), 265–302.

Huang, Y. H. (2004). Is symmetrical communication ethical and effective? *Journal of Business Ethics, 53*(4), 333–352.

Hung, C.-J. F. (2007). Toward the theory of relationship management in public relations: How to cultivate quality relationships? In E. L. Toth (Ed.), *The future of excellence in public relations and communication management: Challenges for the next generation* (pp. 443–476). Mahwah, NJ: Erlbaum.

Hung, C. J. (1999, June). *Public relations and issues management: How they contribute to organizational effectiveness.* Paper presented at the meeting of the Public Relations Society of America Educators Academy, College Park, MD.

Kant, I. (1785/1964). *Groundwork of the metaphysic of morals* (H. J. Paton, Trans.). New York: Harper & Row. (Original publication 1785)

Kant, I. (1785/1993). Metaphysical foundations of morals (C. J. Friedrich, Trans.). In C. J. Friedrich (Ed.), *The philosophy of Kant: Immanuel Kant's moral and political writings* (pp. 154–229). New York: The Modern Library. (Original publication 1785)

Kant, I. (1793/1974). *On the old saw: That may be right in theory but it won't work in practice* (E. B. Ashton, Trans.). Philadelphia: University of Pennsylvania Press. (Original publication 1793)

Kant, I. (1930/1963). *Lectures on ethics* (L. Infield, Trans.). Indianapolis, IN: Hackett Publishing. (Original publication 1930)

Katz, D., & Kahn, R. L. (1966). *The social psychology of organizations* (2nd ed.). New York: Wiley.

Kent, M. L., & Taylor, M. (2002). Toward a dialogic theory of public relations. *Public Relations Review, 28*(1), 21–37.

Koehn, D. (2005). Integrity as a business asset. *Journal of Business Ethics, 58*(1), 125–136.

Kruckeberg, D. (1995–96). The challenge for public relations in the era of globalization. *Public Relations Quarterly*, 36–39.

Lauzen, M. M. (1997). Understanding the relations between public relations and issues management. *Journal of Public Relations Research, 9*(1), 65–82.

Lauzen, M. M., & Dozier, D. M. (1992). The missing link: The public relations manager role as mediator of organizational environments and power consequences for the function. *Journal of Public Relations Research, 4*(4), 205–220.

Lauzen, M. M., & Dozier, D. M. (1994). Issues management mediation of linkages between environmental complexity and management of the public relations function. *Journal of Public Relations Research, 6*(3), 163–184.

Ledingham, J., & Bruning, S. (Eds.). (2000). *Public relations as relationship management: A relational approach to the study and practice of public relations.* Mahwah, NJ: Erlbaum.

Ledingham, J. A. (2006). Relationship management: A general theory of public relations. In C. Botan & V. Hazleton (Eds.), *Public relations theory II* (pp. 465–483). Mahwah, NJ: Erlbaum

Ledingham, J. A., Bruning, S. D., & Wilson, L. J. (1999). Time as an indicator of the perceptions and behavior of members of a key public: Monitoring and predicting organization-public relationships. *Journal of Public Relations Research, 11*(2), 167–183.

Lerbinger, O. (1997). *Crisis manager: Facing risk and responsibility.* Mahwah, NJ: Erlbaum.

Lerbinger, O. (2006). *Corporate public affairs: Interacting with interest groups, media, and government.* Mahwah, NJ: Erlbaum.

Lewicki, R. J., Litterer, J. A., Saunders, D. M., & Minton, J. W. (1993). *Negotiation: Readings, exercises, and cases* (2nd ed.). Boston, MA: Irwin.

Luhmann, N. (1984). *Social systems* (J. Bednarz & D. Baecker, Trans.). Stanford, CA: Stanford University Press.

Luhmann, N. (1993). *Risk: A sociological theory* (R. Barrett, Trans.). New York: Aldine De Gruyter.

Mill, J. S. (1861/1957). *Utilitarianism.* New York: The Liberal Arts Press.

Miller, K. (1999). Issues management: The link between organization reality and public perception. *Public Relations Quarterly*(Summer).

Millar, D. P. & Heath, R.. L. (Eds.). (2004). *Responding to crisis: A rhetorical approach to crisis communication.* Mahwah, NJ: Erlbaum.

Mintzberg, H. (1983). *Power in and around organizations.* Englewood Cliffs, NJ: Prentice-Hall.

Murdock, G. (1996). Concentration and ownership in the era of privatization. In P. Marris & S. Thornham (Eds.), *Media studies: A reader* (pp. 91–101). Edinburgh: Edinburgh University Press.

Murphy, P. (1996). Chaos theory as a model for managing issues and crises. *Public Relations Review, 22*(2), 95–114.

Murphy, P. (2007). Coping with an uncertain world: The relationship between excellence and complexity theories. In E. L. Toth (Ed.), *The future of excellence in public relations and communication management: Challenges for the next generation* (pp. 119–134). Mahwah, NJ: Erlbaum.

Murphy, P., & Dee, J. (1992). DuPont and Greenpeace: The dynamics of conflict between corporations and activist groups. *Journal of Public Relations Research, 4*(1), 3–20.

Murphy, P., & Dee, J. (1996). Reconciling the preferences of environmental activists and corporate policy makers. *Journal of Public Relations Research, 8*(1), 1–33.

Olasky, M. N. (1989). The aborted debate within public relations: An approach thorough Kuhn's paradigm. In J. E. Grunig & L. A. Grunig (Eds.), *Public relations research annual* (Vol. 1, pp. 87–96). Hillsdale, NJ: Erlbaum.

Olson, M. (1982). *The logic of collective action: Public goods and the theory of groups*. Cambridge, MA: Harvard University Press.

Palenchar, M., & Heath, R. L. (2002). Another part of the risk communication model: Analysis of communication processes and message content. *Journal of Public Relations Research, 14*(2), 127–158.

Palenchar, M., & Heath, R. L. (2006). Responsible advocacy through strategic risk communication. In K. Fitzpatrick & C. Bronstein (Eds.), *Ethics in public relations: Responsible advocacy* (pp. 131–153). Thousand Oaks, CA: Sage.

Paton, H. J. (1967). *The categorical imperative: A study in Kant's moral philosophy*. New York: Harper & Row.

Pearson, R. (1989). Beyond ethical relativism in public relations: Coorientation, rules, and the idea of communication symmetry. In J. E. Grunig & L. A. Grunig (Eds.), *Public relations research annual* (Vol. 1, pp. 67–86). Hillsdale, NJ: Erlbaum.

Plowman, K. D. (1998). Power in conflict for public relations. *Journal of Public Relations Research, 10*(4), 237–261.

Plowman, K. D. (1999, June). *Strategic management, conflict, and public relations.* Paper presented at the meeting of the Public Relations Society of America Educators Academy, College Park, MD.

Plowman, K. D. (2005). Systems theory. In R. L. Heath (Ed.), *Encyclopedia of Public Relations* (Vol. 2, pp. 839–842). Thousand Oaks, CA: Sage.

Posner, R. S. (2002). Some problems of utilitarianism. In L. P. Hartman (Ed.), *Perspectives in business ethics* (2nd ed., pp. 37–42). Boston: McGraw-Hill.

Rawls, J. (1971). *A theory of justice*. Cambridge, MA: Harvard University Press.

Renfro, W. L. (1993). *Issues management in strategic planning*. Westport, CT: Quorum Books.

Rosa, E. A. (2003). The logical structure of the social amplification of risk framework (SARF): Metatheoretical foundations and policy implications. In N. Pidgeon, R. E. Kasperson & P. Slovic (Eds.), *The social amplification of risk* (pp. 47–79). Cambridge: Cambridge University Press.

Roth, W., Ryder, J., & Voehl, F. (1996). *Problem solving for results*. Delray Beach, FL: St. Lucie Press.

Sauser, W. I., Jr. (2005). Business ethics: Answering the call. *Journal of Business Ethics, 58*(4), 345–357.

Sims, R. R., & Brinkman, J. (2003). Enron ethics (or, culture matters more than codes). *Journal of Business Ethics, 45*(3), 243–256.

Spicer, C. (1997). *Organizational public relations: A political perspective*. Mahwah, NJ: Erlbaum.

Stoffels, J. D. (1994). *Strategic issues management: A comprehensive guide to environmental scanning*. Milwaukee, WI: Pergamon.

Stormer, F. (2003). Making the shift: Moving from "ethics pays" to an inter-systems model of business. *Journal of Business Ethics, 44*, 279–289.

Sullivan, R. J. (1989). *Immanuel Kant's moral theory*. Cambridge: Cambridge University Press.

Sung, M. J. (2007). Toward a model of scenario building from a public relations perspective. In E. L. Toth (Ed.), *The future of excellence in public relations and communication management: Challenges for the next generation* (pp. 177–198). Mahwah, NJ: Erlbaum.

Taylor, M., & Doerfel, M. L. (2005). Another dimension to explicating relationships : Network theory and method to measure inter-organizational linkages. Public Relations Review, *31*(1), 121–129.

Vercic, D., Grunig, L. A., & Grunig, J. E. (1996). Global and specific principles of public relations: Evidence from Slovenia. In H. M. Culbertson & N. Chen (Eds.), *International public relations: A comparative analysis* (pp. 31–65). Mahwah, NJ: Erlbaum.

Wakefield, R. I. (1996). Interdisciplinary theoretical foundations for international public relations. In H. M. Culbertson & N. Chen (Eds.), *International public relations: A comparative analysis* (pp. 17–30). Mahwah, NJ: Erlbaum.

Wilson, L. J. (1990). Corporate issues management: An international view. *Public Relations Review, 16*(1), 40–51.

Zwetsloot, G. I. (2003). From management systems to corporate social responsibility. *Journal of Business Ethics, 44*(201–207).

18

Linking Public Participation and Decision Making through Risk Communication

Katherine A. McComas
Cornell University

Joseph Arvai
Michigan State University and Decision Research

John C. Besley
University of South Carolina

INTRODUCTION

Although risk communication often occurs on a one-on-one basis, such as when a patient consults with his or her family physician about a particular medical condition, it also takes place in the public sphere, such as when people gather together for collective deliberation about a public or environmental health risk. Although both contexts require careful consideration of how communication shapes attitudes and behaviors, risk communication that occurs in the public sphere requires additional thought into how social dynamics and the processes themselves can send competing or conflicting messages. An added consideration involves the role of the individual in the decision-making process. Whereas a patient has, for the most part, the ultimate say in the course of action vis-à-vis the physician's diagnosis, any one individual has relatively less of a voice in decisions regarding the management of public or environmental health risks having societal as well as personal consequences.

In light of the growing emphasis on involving the public in collective deliberation about risk assessment and risk management, the last three decades have been witness to considerable advancement in systematic research on public participation. The results of this research has included influential books (e.g., Beierle & Cayford, 2002; Renn, Webler, & Wiedemann, 1995), National Research Council (NRC) reports (1989, 1996, 2005), and hundreds of peer-reviewed journal articles spanning multiple disciplines and offering conceptual and empirical insight into theory and practice of public participation. This chapter offers a synthesis of a portion of this existing research in an effort to create a foundation upon which to move theoretical and practical discussions forward. It begins with a brief overview of public participation, leading into a discussion of the most common rationales or justifications for involving citizens in risk assessment and risk management. The chapter then summarizes research examining key issues to consider in the design and implementation of public participation, which includes a review of related developments in the decision sciences and the use of decision aids to improve the quality of deliberative risk judgments. The chapter concludes with a discussion of current limitations in knowledge and understanding and promising avenues for future research.

DEFINING PUBLIC PARTICIPATION

Just as definitions of risk communication vary widely, so do the meanings of public participation. At one extreme, public participation can be equated with holding a single public hearing during an environmental permitting process. At the other extreme, it can entail a series of iterative, intense, and deliberative meetings that involve both expert and public participants, as is the case in many watershed planning initiatives. And just as the extent of public participation varies, so does its intent. Some public participation efforts are oriented primarily toward informing people about decisions already made while others are actively used to elicit participants' values, objectives, and concerns as a means of improving the overall quality of risk management decisions.

In this chapter, we limit our discussion of public participation to intentional efforts on behalf of organizations or institutions to involve citizens in the process of risk assessment and management. In this sense, we find affinity with Renn, Webler, and Wiedemann's (1995) definition of public participation as "forums for exchange that are organized for the purpose of facilitating communication between government, citizens, stakeholders and interest groups, and businesses regarding a specific decision or problem" (p. 2). Our focus is primarily on public participation sponsored by government agencies at the federal, state, and local level. Left out of this discussion are other forms of grassroots citizen action, such as boycotts, marches, or protests, which are important types of political engagement but beyond the scope of this chapter.

Some discussion may also be warranted regarding our use of the term *public* participation, as opposed to *stakeholder* participation or *citizen* participation. Arguably, the term "public" suggests the widest spectrum of possible participants, whereas "stakeholder" suggests a much more targeted or invested individual or group. Likewise, the term "citizen" implies that all of the participants are either legal residents or members of a clearly defined community. We make no such distinction and use the term "public participation" to include each of the above potential participants in the risk assessment or risk management process. Because these processes are grounded in the of the context of risk, a participatory process fundamentally entails risk communication, understood here as the iterative exchange of information among individuals, groups, and institutions regarding the assessment, characterization, and management of risk (NRC, 1989).

Focusing on the process itself, some researchers and practitioners have preferred the term *engagement* to *participation*. In particular, Rowe and Frewer (2005) proposed using "public engagement" as an overarching concept to encompass public communication, public consultation, and public participation. They differentiated among the three sub-concepts according to information flow, with public communication referring to the transmission of information from authorities to participants, consultation referring to transmission from participants to the authorities, and participation reflecting a two-way exchange of information. While agreeing with the need to differentiate among levels of engagement or participation, we prefer to orient our analysis according to the degree of public deliberation (see Table 18.1).

An approach that has seen growing attention in the research literature, public *deliberation,* suggests an intentional, careful weighing of facts and arguments prior to making decisions or informed judgments. Many consider deliberation to represent an important element of public participation in political activities (Burkhalter, Gastil, & Kelshaw, 2002; Fishkin, 1997; Fishkin & Laslett, 2003; Gastil & Dillard, 1999) although some have suggested its role has been undervalued in characterizing risk (NRC, 1996). In describing the value of deliberation in risk characterization, for example, the NRC (1996) argued that although deliberation may not—and in some cases,

TABLE 18.1
Selection of Studies Examining Common Public Participation Processes According to Degree of Public Deliberation

	Participation Process	*Description*	*Citations*
Less Public Deliberation/ Discussion-oriented	Survey	Random sample or targeted population used to assess the attitudes and desires of residences; survey delivery may include background information.	(Ballard & Kuhn, 1996; Burger, 2004; Charnley & Engelbert, 2005; Heath & Palenchar, 2000; Jardine, 2003; Maharik & Fischhoff, 1993; McComas & Scherer, 1999; Milbrath, 1981; Pellizzoni & Ungaro, 2000; Pidgeon et al., 2005; Smith & Tyler, 1997)
	Focus groups or other controlled discussion group	Participants recruited by sponsors; discussion occurs behind closed doors and may only be available to decision makers.	(Charnley & Engelbert, 2005; Dietrich & Schibeci, 2003; Dürrenberger, Kastenholz, & Behringer, 1999; Jardine, 2003; Pellizzoni & Ungaro, 2000; Rowe, Horlick-Jones, Walls, & Pidgeon, 2005; Smith & McDonough, 2001)
	Written comments on draft material/ Interactive web site	Open call for comments on an issue of concern and/or proposed policies or actions. Can be provided in hard copy or through an electronic forum. Potential for multiple iterations.	(Lidskog & Soneryd, 2000; O'Riordan, 1976; Pidgeon et al., 2005; Roth, Dunsby, & Bero, 2003; Rowe et al., 2005; Schotland & Bero, 2002; Witt, Andrews, & Kacmar, 2000)
	Availability session/ Open house	Individual representatives from sponsors or other experts answer one-on-one questions.	(McComas, 2003b)
	"Traditional" Public meeting/ Public hearing	Open access to all citizens but agenda set by officials. Likely includes presentation followed by opportunity for questions or comments.	(Gundry & Heberlein, 1984; Hamilton, 2003; Kuhn & Ballard, 1998; Lidskog & Soneryd, 2000; McComas, 2001, 2003a; McComas & Scherer, 1998; O'Riordan, 1976)
	Advisory board/ Stakeholder groups	Select group of citizens/ stakeholders with potential for substantial within-group deliberation, but primarily within elite groups. Discussion may be open or closed.	(Aronoff & Gunter, 1994; Branch & Bradbury, 2006; Burroughs, 1999; Kinney & Leschine, 2002; McDaniels et al., 1999; Murdock, Wiessner, & Sexton, 2005; O'Riordan, 1976; Rothstein, 2004; Santos & Chess, 2003; Wolfe & Bjornstad, 2003)
	Discussion events/ community dinner/ Workshops/Priority setting	Public events designed to facilitate and encourage discussion, more than might be true than with a traditional public meeting.	(Abelson et al., 2003; Halvorsen, 2001, 2003; Renn et al., 1995)
More Public Deliberation/ Discussion-Oriented	Decision-aiding initiatives/ Deliberative forum/ Deliberative workshops	Public events that typically involve expert and non-expert participants. Deliberations are often structured to incorporate principles from the decision sciences (such as eliciting participants' objectives, developing management options, and addressing tradeoffs).	(Abelson et al., 2003; Arvai & Mascarenhas, 2001; Einsiedel, 2002; Einsiedel & Eastlick, 2000; Einsiedel, Jelsoe, & Breck, 2001; Goven, 2003; J. Gregory & Miller, 1998; Joss & Durant, 1995a, 1995b; Maguire & Servheen, 1992; Mayer, Jolanda, & Geurts, 1995; Renn, Webler, & Johnson, 1991; Rowe, Marsh, & Frewer, 2004)

should not—lead to consensus, it "brings into consideration knowledge and judgments coming from various perspectives so that participants develop understandings that are informed by other views" (p. 74). The NRC noted that deliberation "captures in part the meaning of democracy… and contributes to making decisions more rational and legitimate" (p. 74). In turn, it proposed an iterative and cyclical analytic-deliberative model of characterizing risk, discussed in greater detail below, which places equal value on the fact-finding and the deliberative side of risk assessment and risk management.

Examining the extent to which a public participation process emphasizes public deliberation offers one lens through which to view previous research. Table 18.1 provides a summary of key studies in public participation classified according to the extent to which their design facilitates public deliberation. On one end of the spectrum are surveys, which can provide a useful "snapshot" of representative opinions yet do not—in themselves—entail public deliberation. On the other end are decision-aiding initiatives or deliberative forums, which are expressly designed to stimulate public discussion or deliberation. It is important to recognize that different decisions may require different degrees of deliberation (NRC, 1996); at times, it may be more appropriate to use one process over another. Depending on the objectives, different processes may also complement one another, such as when availability sessions or open houses are combined with traditional public meetings or when surveys or polls are used as a component of public deliberations (Fishkin & Luskin, 1999; NRC, 1996).

JUSTIFICATIONS FOR PUBLIC PARTICIPATION

Developing a richer appreciation of the various approaches to and ideas about public participation requires exposure to the tensions that have doggedly pursued its development and implementation. For risk management, perhaps the greatest source of tension stems from the question of how much control over risk management decisions should agencies or authorities cede to members of the public. Few will argue against at least some level of participation by concerned publics. But, there are those who are in favor of strict, consensus-based approaches such as alternative dispute resolution that argue for near-complete control of the process to be in the hands of the participants, effectively granting each of them a veto over potential decisions (Bleiker & Bleiker, 1995; Carnes, Schweitzer, & Peelle, 1996). Others, by contrast, recognize that most decisions will rest in the hands of risk managers and argue for a more measured approach where input from various stakeholders—expert and non-expert alike—is elicited through deliberation and decision-aiding procedures that aim to highlight areas of agreement and disagreement as it relates to people's support for competing risk management options (Arvai & Mascarenhas, 2001; J. Gregory & Miller, 1998; R. Gregory, McDaniels, & Fields, 2001).

For risk assessment and risk management, an additional source of tension concerns questions about the value that ought to be placed on different types of knowledge. Specifically, to what extent should risk assessments and risk management decisions rely primarily on scientific or technical inputs versus also incorporating lay or non-expert opinions or, in the extreme, traditional (i.e., aboriginal) knowledge (Wynne, 1992a, 1992b)? In response, much of the recent and influential work in the context of participatory risk assessment and management processes calls for extensive consultation with members of diverse publics beginning at the early stages of project development. Leading endorsements of these processes in the United States have come from the NRC (1996) and the Presidential Commission on Risk (1998). Internationally, strong endorsements have come from the Canadian Standards Association (1997) and the UK Parliamentary Office of Science and Technology (2001). However, there are still significant concerns that the democratization of the risk assessment and management processes will lead to the inclusion of superficial scientific and technical assessments. The EPA's Science Advisory Board (2001), for example, has recently warned that processes that invest heavily in public participation frequently do not do an adequate job of addressing and dealing with relevant science.

Underlying many of these questions about the degree and content of public participation is a third tension: its overall purpose. Arguments in support of public participation are generally characterized as being instrumental, normative, or substantive (Fiorino, 1990; NRC, 1996). Instrumental arguments contend that having citizens participate during decision making helps to legitimate the outcomes of these processes, leading to a higher degree of public acceptance of the resulting decisions. Normative arguments emphasize the democratic underpinnings of public participation, namely that government should obtain the consent of the governed and citizens have the right to participate meaningfully in policy decisions that ultimately affect them. Finally, substantive arguments contend that the wisdom relevant to the decision may not be limited to scientific or technical experts and that participation from diverse groups of citizens may, in fact, improve decision making.

Although some public participation efforts can satisfy instrumental, normative, and substantive criteria, it is often the case that a given participatory approach places greater emphasis on one criteria over others. Beierle and Cayford (2002), for example, recounted how traditional approaches to public participation reflected managerial models, which give decision-making power to authorities that were expected to make choices in the public's behalf. These approaches tended to emphasize instrumental uses of public participation, such as government accountability. The legislation that followed, spurred on by grassroots movements, carried a much more pluralistic appeal and is credited with a variety of reforms, among them sunshine laws, freedom of information laws, workplace health and safety reforms, and consumer rights legislation (Beierle & Cayford, 2002; Lynn, 1990). Rather than viewing expert officials as objective decision makers, pluralism considered managers or expert officials as arbitrators among different interests in the public. Pluralist approaches, by contrast, tended to serve normative purposes and largely under-appreciated substantive goals. For risk assessment and risk management, pluralistic approaches still prioritized scientific, technical, and managerial authority over public input. The most recent approach, referred to as popular or participatory democracy, stresses the substantive benefits of public participation, such as the creation of social capital, political efficacy, and community capacity (Beierle & Cayford, 2002).

The evolution of thinking among risk professionals and researchers about the role of public participation in risk assessment and management has largely mirrored the development of approaches to risk communication. As chronicled in Fischhoff (1995) and Leiss (1996), early approaches to risk communication emphasized the superiority of scientific assessments or expert knowledge. Thus, rather than seeking information from citizens, risk communication more often entailed one-way transfers of information from scientists or technical experts to citizens or non-experts. The next phase of risk communication evidenced a greater awareness that citizens were not always willing to accept what the experts were saying, thus ushering in a period where persuasive approaches were more common. In the 1990s, a parallel body of research developed around issues of trust and credibility, concepts central to persuasion yet found largely neglected in risk communication (Slovic 1993). The current phase of risk communication is said to include a growing recognition that risk is, in part, a social construct and that trust plays a major role in people's orientation toward risks (Cvetkovich, 2000; Leiss, 1995; Lofstedt, 2005; Slovic, 1993).

Striking a similar chord, Lynn (1990) has described early approaches to public participation in risk assessment and risk management as "a right-to-hear-what-has-already-been-decided approach" (p. 96). In this manner, early attempts at participation seemed more geared to having the public "buy into" decisions that were already made, while also allowing agencies to claim that they had satisfied their civic mandate (Heberlein, 1976; Lynn, 1990). The second phase of risk communication is reflected by public participation efforts often referred to as "decide-announce-defend" methods. While still maintaining the superiority of technical assessments over non-expert knowledge, these approaches manifested an awareness that citizens were often unwilling to accept what the experts were saying, and so considerable attention was given to persuading citizens that the experts had made the "right" choice. The current phase, which recognizes the social dynamics of public participation, is reflected in the awareness that certain efforts to involve the public may have unintended consequences, including exacerbating rather than reducing conflict about the environment. Slovic (1993), for example, has suggested that:

> Conflicts and controversies surrounding risk management are not due to public irrationality or ignorance but, instead, can be seen as expected side effects of…psychological tendencies interacting with our remarkable form of participatory democratic government, and amplified by certain powerful technological and social changes in our society. (p. 679)

As Slovic (1993) continued, these tendencies include people's inclination for noticing—and in many instances, giving greater weight to—so-called "trust-destroying" events (such as overly technocratic communication with the public, failed safety inspections, accidents, cover-ups, etc.) as compared to the reciprocal "trust-building" events (such as operational transparency, successful inspections, the creation of local advisory boards, flawless safety records, etc.). Although many still practice more traditional (read: antiquated) versions of public participation, others have demonstrated a greater awareness of the need to view citizens as more than audience members but as stakeholders (Dandoy, 1990).

The current orientation toward risk communication and public participation is perhaps best documented by the NRC (1996), which laid out compelling justifications for incorporating greater stakeholder involvement during the process of risk characterization. To do so, the NRC criticized the traditional separation of risk assessment from risk management, which it argued has hindered effective risk characterization. To elaborate, risk assessment refers to the process whereby scientists seek to understand and characterize risk and has typically been conducted without the inclusion of citizen or public input, such as the consideration of risk perceptions. As such, it has traditionally been presumed to be value-free or, by some measure, more "objective." Risk management, in comparison, encompasses the regulatory activities of evaluating options and alternatives in relation to risk assessments. Although the distinction between risk assessment and risk management has proved useful at times, such as when scientists seek to avoid political pressure, the NRC argued that a strict separation has limited deliberation and suggested that effective risk characterization must integrate scientific analysis with deliberation, both at the scientific and public level.

IMPROVING THE QUALITY OF PARTICIPATORY RISK MANAGEMENT APPROACHES

As risk management debates increasingly examine ways to incorporate the values of concerned citizens into policy decisions, the following section addresses methods designed to enable members of the lay public (e.g., residents of potentially affected communities and regions) as well as broader interest groups to participate effectively alongside technical experts and government representatives. In particular, we focus on a series of relevant findings from research in the decision sciences that support the development and use of decision aiding tools during participatory risk assessment and management processes.

As the previous discussion implies, effective public participation during risk assessment and management requires, at minimum, a requisite level of competence on the part of both the public participants and the facilitators or analysts who elicit, summarize, and transmit information to decision makers. However, effective public participation also requires the collection and transmission of accurate technical information to which people can respond; this information typically comes in the form of scientific and technical inputs used to answer participants' questions—or to spark thoughtful discussion—about a given risk in question. In response to the need for accurate technical inputs, a significant amount of effort has been devoted to developing improved analytic tools for risk assessment.

Regrettably, a similar level effort has not been undertaken with respect to improving methods for public participation in risk management. Despite recent advances in our understanding of individual and group judgmental processes (Koehler & Harvey, 2004; NRC, 2005), there continues to be little agreement about what constitutes a successful or high quality participatory risk management process. From our perspective, as researchers who also work as analysts and facilitators with both expert and public groups, one important reason for this lack of agreement is the general absence of understanding among risk managers about what constitutes high-quality information *from* (vs. *to*) stakeholders and then how this information can be used in the risk management process. This situation is a sharp contrast to that for technical or expert input: Although differences across disciplines and methods exist, there is significant agreement among experts regarding what constitutes careful scientific identification of the anticipated impacts of a risk and how this information should be analyzed and presented.

In response to the deficiency, recent studies and practical applications of "decision aiding" approaches have shown promise in terms of enhancing the quality of public input and resulting decisions. These approaches, which have their basis in behavioral decision research (e.g., see Kahneman, Slovic, & Tversky, 1982; Kahneman & Tversky, 2000; Plous, 1993; Simon, 1956; e.g., see Slovic, Lichtenstein, & Fischhoff, 1977; Tversky & Kahneman, 1981) and on recent research focusing on the constructive nature of preferences (Payne, Bettman, & Johnson, 1993; Slovic, 1995).

Public participation efforts that ask people to think about and respond to risks—or to articulate their values or choices—provide cues to people that, in turn, help them to form their preferences across options (Arvai & Mascarenhas, 2001). As a result, public participation and risk communication cannot be viewed simply as a kind of "cognitive archaeologist" that provides information and relies upon deliberation to uncover attitudes and preferences about risks that, in some basic form, preexist in the minds of those involved. Instead, the participatory risk communication efforts are better viewed as "judgmental architects" where the information that people receive—along with how the process is structured—influences the way in which peoples' decisions, and therefore their behavioral responses, are constructed.

Of course, this constructive view of preferences is problematic because it means that risk communication—and by extension, public participation—can be manipulated to inform desired preferences and motivate specific behaviors. Just like the practitioner of contingent valuation who, with the right instrument, can obtain a desired willingness-to-pay judgment for almost any non-market good, a skillful facilitator can structure deliberations such that they lead to predetermined outcomes (e.g., see Fisher, Ury, & Patton, 1991).

On the other hand, a participatory risk communication approach can also be viewed as a kind of tutorial that builds understanding of a risk management problem and works to overcome common problems as it informs a choice (or set of choices). For example, risk communication can be designed to help participants recognize and address common problems that people often face when presented with complex choices in unfamiliar contexts. Some of these problems include difficulties associated with identifying and clarifying the full range of objectives or concerns that can be influenced by a decision. Others relate the tendency to neglect important value tradeoffs when these objectives and alternatives inevitably conflict (J. Gregory & Miller, 1998). Similarly, risk communication efforts can be designed to help people overcome their tendency to place a greater weight during decision making on their affective (i.e., instinctive emotional) responses as compared to the need for more effortful analyses driven by deliberation and reasoning when faced with many salient risk problems (Arvai & Mascarenhas, 2001; Wilson & Arvai, 2006) .

Each of these issues—as well as a host of others—can be addressed through the inclusion in risk communication and public participation processes of decision structuring tools that help people to more fully define their decision and risk-specific objectives, identify or understand the available risk management options that are sensitive to these objectives and then address the often difficult tradeoffs that choosing among options entails (Clemen, 1996; Hammond, Keeney, & Raiffa, 1999; Kleindorfer, Kunreuther, & Shoemaker, 1993). These decision structuring tools are based on insights from a number of sources, including the work of Keeney (1992) on value-focused thinking, and the structured analytical basis provided by multiattribute utility theory (Keeney & Raiffa, 1993) and behavioral decision analysis (von Winterfeldt & Edwards, 1986).

The starting point for a public participation process is to determine whose values or concerns matter in the decision: which individuals or groups legitimately are in and which are out? Being clear about the objectives of the consultation will help to determine whose values are essential. In most small-group or survey efforts, for example, it will be important to include both local residents and technical experts (who might be from industry, government agencies, or the academic community) and to include representatives of the range of different viewpoints (Edwards & von Winterfeldt, 1987). The scale of the initiative also matters. For a small, local project selecting participants may not be too difficult but for a larger, more complex undertaking some limits will need to be placed on the set of participating stakeholders. Ultimate decisions about who to include is linked to the evaluation techniques that will be employed: the selection of a small group of representative citizens who might meet in person once or twice a month over a one-year period implies a different participant base than does a survey that can be sent out over the Internet.

Beyond identifying the participants in such a process, four additional and interrelated tasks stand out as essential. These four are addressed briefly below. In each case, a key element of a structured approach is the use of specific analytical tools to encourage and deepen deliberation. The ultimate objective is to provide information that will be most helpful to the decision makers in the context of the specific risk-management problem under consideration.

Defining the Decision Problem

Any approach that seeks public input to improve the quality of risk management decisions should first highlight the importance of thinking carefully about the problem at the forefront of the consultation. This aspect of the process entails working with participants first to assess the trigger for their initial decision problem and then to evaluate the constraints—real or imagined—that may guide how it is ultimately addressed (Hammond et al., 1999).

Many public decisions are triggered by the need to respond to a specific option; for example, should the local planning commission allow a nationally recognized big box retailer to locate one of its stores to a remediated brownfield? People invited to respond to this questions will, undoubtedly, come armed with answers: "*Of course it should be allowed!*" Or, "*No; we should build a community-focused neighborhood with coffee shops, independently owned stores, and a library instead.*" Having worked as consultants and analysts on similar problems, we know that—despite the trigger presented by the choice to build a department store—a more fundamental problem often drives these decisions. In the case of the previous example, it can be stated this way: *what do we do with our remediated brownfield?*

As this example highlights, decision makers and stakeholders must be prepared, often at the urging of facilitators, to think more broadly about the decision problem. The overall goal of taking time to carefully define a decision problem is to help participants—and decision makers—distinguish between what Dawes (1988) labels "decision thinking" and "automatic thinking." Decision thinking involves defining a problem in a way that opens it to a more thoughtful consideration of objectives and later, the creation of alternative courses of action from which to choose. Automatic thinking, in contrast, occurs in situations where there has been an incomplete assessment of the decision problem as a result of, for example, an over-reliance on readily available management alternatives.

Clarifying Participants' Objectives

Structured decision processes also ask participants to express all those things that matter to them, including both content and process considerations, in the context of the risk management initiative that is the focus of their involvement. Identifying and defining the values, objectives, and concerns that arise in the context of a novel problem is frequently difficult work and requires both introspection and deliberation on the part of participants. A variety of techniques are used to assist stakeholders to think through and express their values, using iterative processes to refine their definitions. For example, one of the key distinctions made during value elicitations is between the means and ends objectives identified by stakeholders. Although this distinction is straightforward conceptually—ends are valued in and of themselves, whereas means are valued insofar as they contribute to the availability or amount of some other objective—it is often less clear in practice and can lead to informative discussions among participants about the relationships among possible actions and their principal concerns (R. Gregory, 2000).

Beyond simply listening to the views of participants, the focus on identifying and clarifying objectives as part of a decision-aiding consultation also requires the facilitator also be a skilled communicator and analyst. For example, the analyst may help stakeholders to move from vague, qualitative expressions of uncertainty (using words such as "unlikely" or "reasonably probable" to describe impacts) to quantitative expressions (using percentages, probabilities, or frequencies). To accomplish this, a short primer on decision making under uncertainty or an introduction to probability is often required. As another example, a facilitator may spend a significant amount of time working with participants to develop effective measures of for each objective. In doing so, the approach works to minimize disagreements between participants because all parties come to understand what is meant by a specific objective or desired management endpoint. For example, the objective of "improving environmental health" often means very different things to different people. To some, it may mean the restoration of scenic vistas or the return of threatened species; to others, it might represent a much more specific endpoint such as an increase in the overall productivity (typically measured in grams of carbon per meter squared) of a system such as an estuary or grassland. Clarifying, in specific terms, what is meant by these objectives ensures that the input provided by participants—e.g., as it relates to the creation or evaluation of risk management options—is consistent insofar as it is provided in a common language (J. Gregory & Miller, 1998).

Creating Management Alternatives

Helping participants to distinguish between *means* and *ends* objectives also allows for greater creativity in identifying alternatives for evaluation in decision making. For example, a common approach to managing fisheries is to restrict commercial and recreational angling. Whereas various fishing restrictions are *means* objectives, the *ends* objective is to rehabilitate the populations of certain species. Focusing on this *ends* objective helps to avoid anchoring on a single course of action by opening the door to other alternatives besides just fishing restrictions (e.g., habitat rehabilitation, manual restocking techniques, restricting development around spawning channels, etc.). Differentiating *means* and *ends* is a straightforward process that involves first asking people as part of a consultation to think of all the things they would like to see achieved with a decision followed by the following simple question: why is that important? If the answer is that something is important for its own sake, then it is an *ends* objective. If not (i.e., if something is important because it leads to something else, which is also important), then it is a *means* objective (R. Gregory & Keeney, 2002).

When structuring consultations about options, it is critically important to couch the discussion in terms of the earlier work on means and ends objectives. The reasoning behind doing so is straightforward: Because stakeholders' objectives are the basis for considering any decision, the first step in any decision process is for the stakeholders to carefully consider their values by clearly defining what it is they want to achieve in the decision context. This values-focus is in contrast to an emphasis on alternatives (Keeney, 1992), which is based on analyzing the most readily available or obvious management options and then selecting the "best" one from a set of implied, and often poorly defined, criteria.

Selecting Alternatives and Addressing Tradeoffs

For most decisions, a given alternative will not satisfy all of the participants' stated objectives equally well. To facilitate meaningful comparisons across the available options, each alternative needs to be the focus of a detailed analysis to assess the degree to which it meets the objectives identified during the stakeholder elicitations. This analysis is conducted by carefully analyzing the predicted consequences of each alternative against the participants' stated objectives.

Once the predicted outcomes of the alternatives have been established, participants in risk consultations should be invited to help evaluate the tradeoffs that choosing one over another entails. Recent research (Arvai & Mascarenhas, 2001) emphasized the need for clear tradeoffs in the context of balancing such policy-relevant attributes as economic, environmental, and ethical or moral concerns, in part because devoting more resources to any one policy initiative means devoting less to others. If stakeholders refuse to consider such tradeoffs, then technical experts will likely make these tradeoffs themselves and develop policies without the benefit of insight about the views of stakeholders.

Yet in spite of their importance, the avoidance of tradeoffs by stakeholders—and by extension, those who convene public participation processes—is a common feature of many risk management decisions. When tradeoffs are avoided, people often end up selecting alternatives that only partially address their objectives because they fail to evaluate alternatives across conflicting dimensions of value (Bohnenblust & Slovic, 1998). Similarly, when people fail to address tradeoffs, they may reject otherwise strong alternatives because they do not agree with a single dimension. In sum, making the need to address tradeoffs an explicit component of a structured and participatory risk management process helps stakeholders to overcome the well-documented natural tendency to emphasize single objectives when addressing difficult choices (March, 1978).

Being explicit about the need to consider tradeoffs sets these structured decision approaches apart from other participatory strategies such as alternative dispute resolution or other negotiation-based approaches. The goal is not to broker an agreement so as to resolve conflicts among all of the stakeholders; in sharp contrast, a structured decision approach acknowledges the possibility that a single alternative may not fully satisfy all of the stakeholders. Rather than working to resolve disputes, a structured decision approach works to provide insight, or "decision aiding," for public participation so as to capture important stakeholder objectives for the creation and selection of management alternatives. Providing insight to decision makers about the values, beliefs, perspectives and preferred tradeoffs of stakeholder groups is far more in keeping with normal governance structures, in which legitimate agencies make decisions that work exclusively to achieve socially desirable ends.

In our experience, engaging participants in this four step process is more difficult than typically thought. Much more than "careful listening" is required, in part because the participants themselves are often unsure of how they feel about the problem or its proposed solutions. They may have little understanding of choices or tradeoffs that they have not been asked to think about before in any detail. Not all practitioners would agree with this assessment. Some believe that the required input from participants can be obtained in a straightforward manner so long as the measurement process conforms to rules set by established or contingent markets. Others—often trained exclusively as facilitators or mediators—believe that their own ability to listen and to bond with participants will lead to decision-focused input.

In our view, however, neither of these will lead to meaningful public participation because the reasoned opinions of many, especially in the context of novel or unfamiliar problems, do not exist prior to their elicitation (as we note above). In other words, input from participants is context-specific and is constructed over the course of the elicitation. This perspective of constructed preferences (Payne, Bettman, & Johnson, 1992; Slovic, 1995), which is supported by a rich body of research by psychologists and decision scientists (Arvai & Mascarenhas, 2001; R. Gregory & Slovic, 1997) speaks directly to the need for matching the information and guidance that participants receive with the requirements of the decision at hand.

EVALUATING PUBLIC PARTICIPATION

Accompanying greater pressure to involve stakeholders in risk assessment and risk management has been greater attention to understanding what methods are most effective and why (Berry, Portney, Bablitch, & Mahoney, 1997; Chess & Purcell, 1999; Fiorino, 1990; Tuler & Webler, 1999; Webler & Tuler, 2006; Webler, Tuler, & Krueger, 2001). The diversity of goals and objectives of public participation programs, their organizers, and their participants has made it challenging to establish criteria for evaluation (Chess & Purcell, 1999; Webler, 1999). Some have also suggested that researchers who study public participation have also hindered efforts by failing to adequately define the meaning of key variables (Rowe & Frewer, 2005).

As one means of organizing these ideas, Chess and Purcell (1999) suggested distinguishing evaluations in terms of process-oriented and outcome-oriented criteria. Process-oriented criteria weigh a program's success against the execution of the particular technique. Measures of effectiveness include attendance, fairness of the process, variety of viewpoints, one-on-one communication, clear presentations, and so on. Outcome-oriented criteria, in comparison, gauge success against the results of the participation effort. These include whether participants' comments were considered useful, whether they influenced the decision, whether participants were satisfied with the process, or whether relationships between the agencies and participants improved.

We suggest an alternative framework for examining criteria for effectiveness grounded in the social psychological theories of organizational justice (Greenberg, 1993). This research has focused on matters of fairness and what individuals perceive as fair. In their historical overview of organizational justice, Colquitt, Greenberg, and Zapata-Phelan (2005) described four "waves" of research focusing on justice: distributive, procedural, interactional, and integrative. Distributive justice focuses on the perceived fairness of outcomes or, in relation to workplace environments, allocation of rewards. In allocation decisions, standards for fairness can appeal to concerns of equity (rewards equal contributions), equality (everyone gets equal shares), or need (those with greater need receive greater shares) (Ambrose & Arnaud, 2005).

Procedural justice argues that people care about more than the fairness of outcomes; in other words, the means by which ends are realized. Thus, the fairness of decision-making or participatory procedures plays a large role in these evaluations. Judgments of procedural fairness typically include a consideration of participant control or "voice", meaning the degree to which participants believe they can influence the process. In pioneering work on procedural justice, Thibaut and Walker (1975) argued that people favored having more control over the process because it allowed them to exert indirect control over decisions. In turn, research has shown that these fairness judgments influence satisfaction with the decision-making procedures (Thibaut & Walker, 1975) the authorities wielding the procedures (Colquitt, 2001; Lauber & Knuth, 1997; Thibaut & Walker, 1975), and willingness to accept the outcomes (Arvai & Mascarenhas, 2001; Tyler, 1994; Weiner, Alexander, & Shortell, 2002). When participants do not view the procedures as just, consequences may include a reduced commitment to decisions or policies (Colquitt, Conlon, Wesson, Porter, & Ng, 2001; Fuller & Hester, 2001; McFarlin & Sweeney, 1992) and a decrease in the extent to which people voluntarily comply with them (Colquitt et al., 2001; Tyler, Degoey, & Smith, 1996).

Although the instrumental aspect of procedural control is an important part of fairness evaluations, subsequent research suggested that control was not the only factor that influenced participant judgments of procedural justice. Treatment by authorities mattered as well (Tyler & Folger, 1980). In this regard, Lind and Tyler (1988) proposed an alternative model that emphasized relational aspects of procedural justice. Specifically, the relational model posits that, when forming relational judgments, individuals pay attention to the trustworthiness and neutrality the authorities in charge of the process, as well as the degree to which they are treated with respect (Tyler, 1989, 1994, 2000; Tyler et al., 1996; Tyler & Lind, 1992). Other notable research that broadened research on procedural justice included work by Leventhal and colleagues (Leventhal, 1980) suggesting six criteria for just decision making in organizational contexts: (a) consistent application, (b) unbiased judgments, (c) use of accurate information, (d) a desire to redress flawed decisions, (e) ethicality, and (f) representativeness.

Departing slightly from these ideas, some have suggested that the perceived fairness in interpersonal treatments should be viewed as a distinct dimension of justice rather than a component of procedural justice. Specifically, Bies and Moag (1986) and Greenberg (1993) endorse an interactional viewpoint whereby justice is comprised of interpersonal and informational justice dimensions, with interpersonal justice focusing on respect and appropriateness of treatment and informational justice relating to the adequacy of explanations, transparency of the process, or sharing of information. Since being proposed, the appeal of interactional justice has been growing among organizational justice researchers (Bies, 2005; Colquitt, 2001), who have largely confirmed an important role for interactional treatment in justice evaluations, if not effectively eliminating doubts over the concept's unidimensionality.

Table 18.2 categorizes some of the key articles in public participation that have suggested criteria for evaluation that mirror organizational justice dimensions. As the table illustrates, the criteria for assessing the effectiveness of public participation have generally focused on procedural justice. In addition, most have emphasized control or voice aspects of procedural justice. For example, representation of affected parties is often suggested as a criteria for effectiveness (Checkoway, 1981; Fiorino, 1990; Heberlein, 1976; Rowe & Frewer, 2000), as is sharing of decision-making authority (Fiorino, 1990; Irvan & Stansbury, 2004; Rowe & Frewer, 2000). Interpersonal or relational elements of procedural justice are present (Beierle & Cayford, 2002; Irvan & Stansbury, 2004; Rowe & Frewer, 2000; Webler & Tuler, 2000), as are criteria that speak more to informational aspects of justice (Beierle & Cayford, 2002; Checkoway, 1981; Fiorino, 1990; Heberlein, 1976; Irvan & Stansbury, 2004; Rowe & Frewer, 2000; Webler & Tuler, 2000; Webler et al., 2001).

Research examining public participation in risk assessment and risk management, as well as natural resource management, has offered evidence that procedural justice matters (P. D. Smith & McDonough, 2001). For example, research has shown that the perceived fairness of discussion procedures can influence the audience's satisfaction with the process (Lauber & Knuth, 1999; McComas, 2003a; Webler & Tuler, 2000) and acceptance of the decisions (Arvai, 2003). Sharing control over the decision-making procedures is also important to perceptions of fairness (Heath, Bradshaw, & Lee, 2002). Others have emphasized the importance of fairness of deliberative procedures among efforts seeking to maintain or rebuild trust in risk management institutions (Lofstedt, 2005). On the other hand, some have argued that normative dimensions of fairness are not as important to building trust in risk managers as perceived shared values (Earle, 2004). Still, our hope is that by highlighting this existing body of research on justice, scholars can use this research to engage more systematically in the process of evaluating methods of public participation.

MOTIVATING CITIZENS TO PARTICIPATE

When examining any public participation process, issues of representativeness are likely to arise. Representativeness can be defined as the extent to which participants in a given public participation

TABLE 18.2
Summary of Key Articles' Criteria for Evaluating Public Participation Using a Justice Framework

Citation	*Procedural Justice —Voice/Control*	*Procedural Justice — Relational/ Interpersonal*	*Informational Justice*	*Other*
Heberlein (1976)	- involvement of citizens to avoid obstructionism ("cooptation function") - incorporation of citizen views and priorities, noting concern for representativeness of participants ("interactive function")		- information about the nature of a project ("informational function")	
Checkoway (1981)	- suitability of engagement timing - representativeness of participants - influence on agency decisions		- technical information made understandable to non-specialists	
Fiorino (1990)	- possibility of participation by amateurs (non-experts) - sharing of authority - adequate deliberation and discussion		- relative equality in access to information	
Webler & Tuler (2000)	- non-officials able to influence agenda and discourse rules - non-officials able to influence moderator selection - all interested parties able to take part in discussion	- promotion of discussion about the sincerity and authenticity of truth claims	- access to commonly agreed-on standards and definitions - means of submitting disputed truth claims to outside experts - means of assessing and recognizing normative truth claims	
Rowe & Frewer (2000)	- representativeness of participants - early involvement of non-officials - non-officials able to influence final decision	- independence/ unbiased management of engagement - transparency of decision process to facilitate trust	- non-officials have access to resources (i.e., to hire independent expertise) - clarity of decision-making process	- cost-effectiveness - nature of task clearly defined

(*continued*)

TABLE 18.2
Continued

Citation	*Procedural Justice —Voice/Control*	*Procedural Justice — Relational/ Interpersonal*	*Informational Justice*	*Other*
Webler, Tuler, & Krueger (2001)	- non-officials can gain access to the process - non-officials have some power to influence process and outcomes - structure of engagement promotes constructive interactions		- non-officials have access to information - adequate analysis of options presented	- creation of social conditions for future community processes
Beierle & Cayford (2002)	- the incorporation of public values into decisions - helping to improve the substantive quality of decisions	- building trust in institutions - resolving conflict among competing interests	- educating and informing the public	
Irvan & Stansbury (2004)	- non-officials have some control over policy process	- engagement structured to build trust/relationships		- development of citizens' education and skills - avoidance of litigation - strategic alliances - legitimacy
Branch & Bradbury (2006)	- power shared among participants-mechanisms in place to ensure accountability and provide avenues for recourse - decision making process is fair and open and decision makers identified and accessible	- relationships convey mutual respect and recognition - behaviors demonstrate consideration of others' values	- information disclosed in timely manner	

process share similar characteristics (e.g., demographics, attitudes, values, opinions) as people who did not participate yet who still arguably have some interest in the outcomes (e.g., live in an affected area, are a member of a particular interest group). Representativeness is worth considering for several reasons. From a normative sense, having a representative sample of participants ensures that people have a voice in their own governance, which is considered vital to the functioning of a healthy democracy (Fiorino, 1990). From an instrumental sense, representation is considered an important criteria for procedural fairness (Leventhal, 1980; Renn, Webler, & Kastenholz, 1996; Renn et al., 1995). Accordingly, having an unrepresentative audience can be grounds for dismissing any decisions or recommendations as being unfair. Finally, from a substantive sense, representativeness can ensure that important target audiences (or their surrogates) are present to share insights and help inform the assessment and management of risk. Thus, to inform efforts to increase the representativeness of participants, a growing number of studies have examined what factors influence participation.

In the sections that follow, we organize this literature into research examining rational incentives, socio-economic status, and relational factors. Rather than suggesting that one category of incentives is more important than the others, we believe that a more accurate picture would consider the complexity surrounding any decisions to participate.

Rational Incentives

By rational, we mean that people participate for very practical or logical reasons. For example, they participate to provide input to public officials or to support other community members' ability to voice concerns (Checkoway, 1981). People who feel more involved with the issue or more at risk are also be more likely to participate in risk management debates (Gundry & Heberlein, 1984; McComas, 2003b; McComas & Scherer, 1998). Wanting to hear what the authorities have to say is another very reasonable reason to participate; so, too, is wanting to hear what other citizens have to say (McComas, 2003a, 2003c).

The desire to influence decisions is another rational reason to attend (Adams, 2004). So, too, is deciding not to attend depending because of the timing of the opportunity to participate. For example, if the opportunity to participate comes too early in the decision-making process, the decision context may not be salient enough to motivate people to attend (Renz, 1992). On the other hand, if the opportunity to participate comes late in the decision-making process, people may not attend because they believe that the decisions have already been made and, therefore, their input will not matter.

Socio-Economic Incentives

Research suggests that an individual's social and economic circumstances, as well as the context of the risk, may influence their attendance. As a means of predicting civic participation in political activities, resource-oriented scholars, such as Verba and his collaborators, have highlighted the individual-level factors that underlie public participation. In general, this research has found that people most likely to participate are those who have the greatest capacity to participate, due to levels of education and relevant political experience, and those who believe that they can make a difference (Almond & Verba, 1989; Rosenstone & Hansen, 1993; Verba, Schlozman, & Brady, 1995). A related body of communication research looks at the role of media use, interpersonal discussion, and knowledge in fostering public engagement (McLeod et al., 1999; Norris, 2000; Shah, 1998; Shah, McLeod, & Yoon, 2001; Sotirovic & McLeod, 2001), suggesting that people who pay more attention to political news and engage more often in political discussion are more likely to participate.

Relational Incentives

A third cluster of incentives centers around citizens' experiences with participation or with authorities in charge of the process. We characterize these as relational incentives and believe that they can provide an important link between predictors of participation and participation's outcomes (Besley & McComas, 2005). As discussed earlier, research on the relational aspects of procedural justice has demonstrated the importance of authorities' treatment of participants in the development of perceptions of fairness. In turn, these perceptions of fairness can influence outcomes, such as satisfaction with the process and willingness to engage in future activities (Tyler, 1989, 1994, 2000; Tyler & Lind, 1992).

Along these lines, recent research has found that perceived treatment at public meetings held about local health risks was related to participants' willingness to attend future public meetings

(McComas, Trumbo, & Besley, 2007). Research also found that the perceived fairness of authorities also influenced decisions to attend local public meetings about area health risks (McComas, Besley, & Trumbo, 2006).

FUTURE DIRECTIONS

The key contributions of public participation in risk assessment and management go well beyond just involving a broad cross-section of people in the process. While one of the clear benefits of the participatory approaches discussed in this chapter rests in their ability to engage concerned parties in a process that leads to decisions that are likely to affect them, public participation efforts can also be designed such that they help to structure and clarify the important elements of a complex decision. In doing so, new and often complex risk problems—and the range of possible solutions to them—can become more easily understood by the full range of participants. On the one hand, it becomes easier for non-expert participants—often the public—to understand the expected environmental, health-related, economic, or social impacts of a problem because the technical information that is brought to bear on it is tied to their own expressed values, objectives, and concerns. On the other hand, it also becomes easier for experts and agency decision makers to understand the linkages back to what people care about and thus to anticipate variations in the support for, or opposition to, various risk management options. This higher level of understanding among all of the participants in these processes, we believe, leads to the more thoughtful selection of risk assessment endpoints or management options. But despite some early successes that have combined the principles of public participation, risk communication, and decision aiding (e.g., see Arvai & Mascarenhas, 2001; Failing, Horn, & Higgins, 2004; J. Gregory & Miller, 1998; Keeney & McDaniels, 1992; Maguire & Servheen, 1992; McDaniels, Gregory, & Fields, 1999) many questions—and thus, opportunities for future research—remain.

For example, while we and many others advocate public participation in most risk assessment and management contexts, at what point is it appropriate to terminate these processes? The default assumption among many researchers and practitioners is that these processes will end when decisions are made. However, many decision-making processes that have relied upon public participation have not even come close to reaching a decision despite many years—or in some cases, decades—of work. A short list of such contexts includes decisions about the adoption of genetically modified organisms in agriculture, the long-term storage of nuclear waste, and the management of endangered species. At what point can a decision maker defensibly terminate public participation and make a decision based on the weight of available evidence?

Other open questions relate to the media through which public participation in risk assessment and management may take place. Broadband access to the Internet has opened doors to a degree of global communication that we could have scarcely imagined 10 short years ago. We now possess the capability to engage in a cross-national deliberation about global risks complete with real-time audio, video, and data transfer. For example, climate scientists in India have the ability to hold data-intensive meeting with policy makers from Canada and the United States with concerned citizens in all three—and very likely more—of these countries given the opportunity to evaluate and respond to the unfolding deliberation; all of this can happen without a single participant leaving their home. These capabilities have been at our fingertips for the last several years, and yet there has been virtually no research aimed at the suitability, effectiveness, or defensibility of these processes.

In many ways, the science of public participation is trying to catch up to the practice. In our experience, people who conduct participatory processes are hungry for research-based evidence to justify their approaches or support their inclinations to try something new. Recently, the National Research Council established a panel on Public Participation in Environmental Assessment and Decision Making to review empirical research in the field and to develop propositions to guide federal agencies in public participation. Although the final report is not yet assembled, the work underscores the importance of continued research in public participation.

BIBLIOGRAPHY

Abelson, J., Eyles, J., McLeod, C. B., Collins, P., McMullan, C., & Forest, P. G. (2003). Does deliberation make a difference? Results from a citizens panel study of health goals priority setting. *Health Policy, 66*(1), 95–106.

Adams, B. (2004). Public meetings and the democratic process. *Public Administration Review, 64*(1), 43–54.

Almond, G. A., & Verba, S. (1989). *The civic culture: Political attitudes and democracy in five nations* (New ed.). Newbury Park, CA: Sage Publications.

Ambrose, M. L., & Arnaud, A. (2005). Are procedural justice and distributive justice conceptually distinct? In J. Greenberg & J. A. Colquitt (Eds.), *Handbook of organizational justice* (pp. 59–84). Mahwah, NJ: Erlbaum.

Aronoff, M., & Gunter, V. (1994). A pound of cure — Facilitating participatory processes in technological hazard disputes. *Society & Natural Resources, 7*(3), 235–252.

Arvai, J. L. (2003). Using risk communication to disclose the outcome of a participatory decision-making process: Effects on the perceived acceptability of risk-policy decision. *Risk Analysis, 23*(2), 281–289.

Arvai, J. L., & Mascarenhas, M. J. (2001). Print media framing of the environmental movement in a Canadian forestry debate. *Environmental Management, 27*(5), 705–714.

Ballard, K. R., & Kuhn, R. G. (1996). Developing and testing a facility location model for Canadian nuclear fuel waste. *Risk Analysis, 16*(6), 821–832.

Beierle, T. C., & Cayford, J. (2002). *Democracy in practice: Public participation in environmental decisions*. Washington DC: Resources for the Future.

Berry, J. M., Portney, K. E., Bablitch, M. B., & Mahoney, R. (1997). Public involvement in administration: The structural determinants of effective citizen participation. *Journal of Voluntary Action Research, 13*, 7–23.

Besley, J. C., & McComas, K. A. (2005). Framing justice: Using the concept of procedural justice to advance political communication research *Communication Theory, 15*, 414–436.

Bies, R. J. (2005). Are procedural justice and interactional justice conceptually distinct? In J. Greenberg & J. A. Colquitt (Eds.), *Handbook of Organizational Justice* (pp. 85–112). Mahwah, NJ: Erlbaum.

Bies, R. J., & Moag, J. F. (1986). Interactional justice: Communication criteria of fairness. In R. J. Lewicki, B. H. Sheppard & M. H. Bazerman (Eds.), *Research on negotiaions in organizations* (Vol. 1, pp. 43–55). Greenwich, CT: JAI Press.

Bleiker, A., & Bleiker, H. (1995). *Public participation handbook for officials and other professionals serving the public*. Monterey, CA: Institute for Participatory Management and Planning.

Bohnenblust, H., & Slovic, P. (1998). Integrating technical analysis and public values in risk-based decision making. *Reliability Engineering and System Safety, 59*(1), 151–159.

Branch, K. M., & Bradbury, J. A. (2006). Comparison of DOE and Army Advisory Boards: Application of a conceptual framework for evaluating public participation in environmental risk decision Making. *Policy Studies Journal, 34*, 723–754.

Burger, J. (2004). Fish consumption advisories: knowledge, compliance and why people fish in an urban estuary. *Journal of Risk Research, 7*(5), 463–479.

Burkhalter, S., Gastil, J., & Kelshaw, T. (2002). A conceptual definition and theoretical model of public deliberation in small face-to-face groups. *Communication Theory, 12*(4), 398–422.

Burroughs, R. (1999). When stakeholders choose: Process, knowledge, and motivation in water quality decisions. *Society & Natural Resources, 12*(8), 797–809.

Canadian Standards Association. (1997). *Risk management guidelines for decision makers*. Ottawa, Ontario: Canadian Standards Association.

Carnes, S. A., Schweitzer, M., & Peelle, E. B. (1996). *Performance measures for evaluating public participation activities in DOE's Office of Environmental Management* (No. ORNL-6905). Oak Ridge, TN: Oak Ridge National Laboratory.

Charnley, S., & Engelbert, B. (2005). Evaluating public participation in environmental decision-making: EPA's superfund community involvement program. *Journal of Environmental Management, 77*(3), 165–182.

Checkoway, B. (1981). The politics of public hearings. *The Journal of Applied Behavioral Science, 17*(4), 566–582.

Chess, C., & Purcell, K. (1999). Public participation and the environment: Do we know what works? *Environmental Science & Technology, 33*, 2685–2692.

Clemen, R. T. (1996). *Making hard decisions: An introduction to decision analysis*. Boston, MA.: PWS-Kent Publishing Co.

Colquitt, J. A. (2001). On the dimensionality of organizational justice: A construct validation of a measure. *Journal of Applied Psychology, 86*(3), 386–400.

Colquitt, J. A., Conlon, D. E., Wesson, M. J., Porter, C., & Ng, K. Y. (2001). Justice at the millennium: A meta-analytic review of 25 years of organizational justice research. *Journal of Applied Psychology, 86*(3), 425–445.

Colquitt, J. A., Greenberg, J., & Zapata-Phelan, C. P. (2005). What is organizational justice? A historical overview. In J. Greenberg & J. A. Colquitt (Eds.), *Handbook of organizational justice* (pp. 3–56). Mahwah, NJ: Erlbaum.

Cvetkovich, G. (Ed.). (2000). *Social trust and the management of risk.* London: Earthscan Publications

Dandoy, S. (1990). Risk communication and public confidence in health departments. *American Journal of Public Health, 80*, 1299–1300.

Dawes, R. (1988). *Rational choice in an uncertain world.* New York: Harcourt, Brace, and Jovanovich.

Dietrich, H., & Schibeci, R. (2003). Beyond public perceptions of gene technology: community participation in public policy in Australia. *Public Understanding Of Science, 12*(4), 381–401.

Dürrenberger, G., Kastenholz, H., & Behringer, J. (1999). Integrated assessment focus groups: bridging the gap between science and policy? *Science and Public Policy, 26*(5), 341–349.

Earle, T. C. (2004). Thinking aloud about trust: A protocol analysis of trust in risk management. *Risk Analysis, 24*(1), 169–183.

Edwards, W. & von Winterfeldt, D. (1987). Public values in risk debates. *Risk Analysis, 7*, 141–158.

Einsiedel, E. F. (2002). Assessing a controversial medical technology: Canadian public consultations on xenotransplantation. *Public Understanding of Science, 11*(4), 315–331.

Einsiedel, E. F., & Eastlick, D. L. (2000). Consensus conferences as deliberative democracy — A communications perspective. *Science Communication, 21*(4), 323–343.

Einsiedel, E. F., Jelsoe, E., & Breck, T. (2001). Publics at the technology table: The consensus conference in Denmark, Canada, and Australia. *Public Understanding Of Science, 10*(1), 83–98.

Environmental Protection Agency Science Advisory Board. (2001). *Improved Science-Based Environmental Stakeholder Processes* (No. EPA-SAB-EC-COM-01-006). Washington, DC: Environmental Protection Agency.

Failing, L., Horn, G., & Higgins, P. (2004). Using expert judgment and stakeholder values to evaluate adaptive management options. *Ecology and Society, 9*, 13–32.

Fiorino, D. J. (1990). Citizen participation and environmental risk: A survey of institutional mechanisms. *Science, Technology & Human Values, 15*(2), 226–243.

Fischhoff, B. (1995). Risk perception and communication unplugged: Twenty years of process. *Risk Analysis, 15*, 137–145.

Fisher, R., Ury, W., & Patton, B. (1991). *Getting to yes: Negootiating agreement without giving in.* New York: Penguin Books.

Fishkin, J. S. (1997). *The voice of the people: Public opinion and democracy* (2nd ed.). New Haven, CT: Yale University Press.

Fishkin, J. S., & Laslett, P. (2003). *Debating deliberative democracy*. Malden, MA: Blackwell.

Fishkin, J. S., & Luskin, R. C. (1999). Bringing deliberation to the democratic dialogue. In M. McCombs & A. Reynolds (Eds.), *The poll with the human face: The national issues convention experiment in political communication* (pp. 3–38). Mahwah, NJ: Erlbaum.

Fuller, J. B., & Hester, K. (2001). A closer look at the relationship between justice perceptions and union participation. *Journal of Applied Psychology, 86*, 1096–1105.

Gastil, J., & Dillard, J. P. (1999). Increasing political sophistication through public deliberation. *Political Communication, 16*(1), 3–23.

Goven, J. (2003). Deploying the consensus conference in New Zealand: Democracy and de-problematization. *Public Understanding of Science, 12*(4), 423–440.

Greenberg, J. (1993). The social side of fairness: Interpersonal and informational classes of organizational justice. In R. Cropanzano (Ed.), *Justice in the workplace: Approaching fairness in human resource management* (pp. 79–103). Hillsdale, NJ: Erlbaum.

Gregory, J., & Miller, S. (1998). *Science in public*. Cambridge, MA: Perseus Publishing.

Gregory, R. (2000). Using stakeholder values to make smarter environmental decisions. *Environment, 42*(5), 34–44.

Gregory, R., & Keeney, R. L. (2002). Making smarter environmental management decisions. *Journal of the American Water Resources Association, 38*, 1601–1612.

Gregory, R., McDaniels, T., & Fields, D. (2001). Decision aiding, not dispute resolution: Creating insights through structured environmental decisions. *Journal of Policy Analysis and Management, 20*(3), 415–432.

Gregory, R., & Slovic, P. (1997). A constructive approach to environmental valuation. *Ecological Economics, 21*, 175–181.

Gundry, K. G., & Heberlein, T. A. (1984). Do public meetings represent the public? *Journal of the American Planning Association, Spring*, 175–182.

Halvorsen, K. E. (2001). Assessing public participation techniques for comfort, convenience, satisfaction, and deliberation. *Environmental Management, 28*(2), 179–186.

Halvorsen, K. E. (2003). Assessing the effects of public participation. *Public Administration Review, 63*(5), 535–543.
Hamilton, J. D. (2003). Exploring technical and cultural appeals in strategic risk communication: The Fernald radium case. *Risk Analysis, 23*(2), 291–302.
Hammond, J., Keeney, R. L., & Raiffa, H. (1999). *Smart choices: A practical guide to making better decisions.* Cambridge, MA: Harvard Business School Press.
Heath, R. L., Bradshaw, J., & Lee, J. (2002). Community relationship building: Local leadership in the risk communication infrastructure. *Journal of Public Relations Research, 14*(4), 317.
Heath, R. L., & Palenchar, M. (2000). Community relations and risk communication: A longitudinal study of the impact of emergency response messages. *Journal of Public Relations Research, 12*(2), 131–161.
Heberlein, T. A. (1976). Some observations on alternative mechanisms for public involvement: The hearing, the public opinion poll, the workshop and the quasi-experiment. *Natural Resources Journal, 16*, 197–212.
Irvan, R. A., & Stansbury, J. (2004). Citizen participation in decision making: Is it worth the effort? *Public Administration Review, 64*(1), 55–65.
Jardine, C. G. (2003). Development of a public participation and communication protocol for establishing fish consumption advisories. *Risk Analysis, 23*(3), 461–471.
Joss, S., & Durant, J. (1995a). The UK National Consensus Conference on Plant Biotechnology. *Public Understanding of Science, 4*, 195–204.
Joss, S., & Durant, J. (Eds.). (1995b). *Public participation in science: The role of consensus conferences in Europe*. London, UK: British Science Museum & European Commission Directorate General XII.
Kahneman, D., Slovic, P., & Tversky, A. (1982). *Judgment under uncertainty: Heuristics and biases.* Cambridge, UK.: Cambridge University Press.
Kahneman, D., & Tversky, A. (2000). *Choices, values, and frames*. Cambridge, UK: Cambridge University Press.
Keeney, R., & McDaniels, T. (1992). Value-focused thinking about strategic decisions at B.C. Hydro. *Interfaces, 22*, 94–109.
Keeney, R. L. (1992). *Value-focused thinking. A path to creative decision making.* Cambridge, MA: Harvard University Press.
Keeney, R. L., & Raiffa, H. (1993). *Decisions with multiple objectives: Preferences and value tradeoffs*. Cambridge, UK: Cambridge University Press.
Kinney, A. G., & Leschine, T. M. (2002). A procedural evaluation of an analytic-deliberative process: The Columbia River Comprehensive Impact Assessment. *Risk Analysis, 22*(1), 83–100.
Kleindorfer, P. R., Kunreuther, H. C., & Shoemaker, P. J. H. (1993). *Decision sciences: An integrative perspective*. New York: Cambridge University Press.
Koehler, D., & Harvey, N. (2004). *Blackwell handbook of hudgment and decision-making*. London: Blackwell Publishing.
Kuhn, R. G., & Ballard, K. R. (1998). Canadian innovations in siting hazardous waste management facilities. *Environmental Management, 22*(4), 533–545.
Lauber, T. B., & Knuth, B. A. (1997). Fairness in moose management decision-making: The citizens' perspective. *Wildlife Society Bulletin, 25*(4), 776–787.
Lauber, T. B., & Knuth, B. A. (1999). Measuring fairness in citizen participation: A case study of moose management. *Society & Natural Resources, 12*(1), 19–37.
Leiss, W. (1995). Down and dirty: The use and abuse of public trust in risk communication. *Risk Analysis, 15*(6), 685–692.
Leiss, W. (1996). Three phases in the evolution of risk communication practice. *Annals AAPSS, 545*, 85–94.
Leventhal, G. S. (1980). What should be done with equity theory? New approaches to the study of fairness in social relationships. In K. Gergen, M. Greenberg & R. Wilis (Eds.), *Social exchange: Advances in theory and research.* New York: Plenum Press.
Lidskog, R., & Soneryd, L. (2000). Transport infrastructure investment and environmental impact assessment in Sweden: Public involvement or exclusion? *Environment and Planning A, 32*(8), 1465–1479.
Lind, E. A., & Tyler, T. R. (1988). *The social psychology of procedural justice*. New York: Plenum Press.
Lofstedt, R. E. (2005). *Risk management in post-trust societies*. London: Palgrave Macmillan.
Lynn, F. M. (1990). Public participation in risk management decisions: The right to define, the right to know, and the right to act. *Risk: Health, Safety & Environment, 1*, 95–102.
Maguire, L. A., & Servheen, C. (1992). Integrating biological and sociological concerns in endangered species management: Augmentation of grizzly bear populations. *Conservation Biology, 6*, 426–434.
Maharik, M., & Fischhoff, B. (1993). Risk knowledge and risk attitudes regarding nuclear energy sources in space. *Risk Analysis, 13*, 345–353.
March, J. (1978). Bounded rationality, ambiguity, and the rationality of choice. *Bell Journal of Economics, 9*, 587–608.

Mayer, I., Jolanda, d. V., & Geurts, J. (1995). An evaluation of he effects of participation in a consensus conference. In S. Joss & J. Durant (Eds.), *Public participation in science: The role of consensus conferences in Europe* (pp. 109–124). London: British Science Museum & European Commission Directorate General XII.
McComas, K., Besley, J., & Trumbo, C. (2006). Why citizens do and don't attend public meetings about local cancer clusters. *Policy Studies Journal, 34*(4), 671–698.
McComas, K., Trumbo, C., and Besley, J. (2007). Public meetings about suspected cancer clusters: The impact of voice, interactional justice, and risk perception on attendees' attitudes in six communities. *Journal of Health Communication, 12,* 527–549.
McComas, K. A. (2001). Public meetings about local waste management problems: Comparing participants to non participants. *Environmental Management, 27*(1), 135–147.
McComas, K. A. (2003a). Citizen satisfaction with public meetings used for risk communication. *Journal Of Applied Communication Research, 31*(2), 164–184.
McComas, K. A. (2003b). Public meetings and risk amplification: A longitudinal study. *Risk Analysis, 23*(6), 1257–1270.
McComas, K. A. (2003c). Trivial pursuits: Participant views of public meetings. *Journal of Public Relations Research, 15,* 91–115.
McComas, K. A., & Scherer, C. W. (1998). Reassessing public meetings as participation in risk management decisions. *Risk; Health, safety, and Environment, 9,* 347–360.
McComas, K. A., & Scherer, C. W. (1999). Providing balanced risk information in surveys used as citizen participation mechanisms. *Society & Natural Resources, 12*(2), 107–119.
McDaniels, T., Gregory, R., & Fields, D. (1999). Democratizing risk management: Successful public involvement in local water management decisions. *Risk Analysis, 19,* 497–510.
McFarlin, D. B., & Sweeney, P. D. (1992). Distributive and procedural justice as predictors of satisfaction with personal and organizational outcomes. *The Academy of Management Journal, 35,* 626–637.
McLeod, J. M., Scheufele, D. A., Moy, P., Horowitz, E. M., Holbert, R. L., Zhang, W. W., et al. (1999). Understanding deliberation — The effects of discussion networks on participation in a public forum. *Communication Research, 26*(6), 743–774.
Milbrath, L. W. (1981). Citizen surveys as citizen participation mechanisms. *Journal of Applied Behavioral Science, 17,* 478–496.
Murdock, B. S., Wiessner, C., & Sexton, K. (2005). Stakeholder participation in voluntary environmental agreements: Analysis of 10 Project XL case studies. *Science Technology & Human Values, 30*(2), 223–250.
National Research Council. (1989). *Improving risk communication.* Washington, DC: National Academy Press.
National Research Council. (1996). *Understanding risk: Informing decisions in a democratic society.* Washington, DC: National Academy Press.
National Research Council. (2005). *Decision making for the environment: Social and behavioral science research priorities.* Washington, DC: The National Academies Press
Norris, P. (2000). *A virtuous circle: Political communications in postindustrial societies.* Cambridge, UK: Cambridge University Press.
O'Riordan, J. (1976). The public involvement program in the Okanagan Basin study. *Natural Resources, 76,* 177–196.
Payne, J. W., Bettman, J. R., & Johnson, E. J. (1992). Behavioral decision research: A constructive processing perspective. *Annual Review of Psychology, 43,* 87–132.
Payne, J. W., Bettman, J. R., & Johnson, E. J. (1993). *The adaptive decision maker.* Cambridge, MA: Cambridge University Press.
Pellizzoni, L., & Ungaro, D. (2000). Technological risk, participation and deliberation. Some results from three Italian case studies. *Journal of Hazardous Materials, 78*(1–3), 261–280.
Pidgeon, N. F., Poortinga, W., Rowe, G., Jones, T. H., Walls, J., & O'Riordan, T. (2005). Using surveys in public participation processes for risk decision making: The case of the 2003 British GM nation? Public debate. *Risk Analysis, 25*(2), 467–479.
Plous, S. (1993). *The psychology of judgment and decision making.* New York: McGraw-Hill, Inc.
Presidential Commission on Risk. (1998). *Risk management.* Washington, DC: The White House.
Renn, O., Webler, T., & Johnson, B. B. (1991). Public participation in hazard management: The use of citizen panels in the U.S. *Risk: Health, Safety & Environment, 2*(197–226).
Renn, O., Webler, T., & Kastenholz, H. (1996). Procedural and substantive fairness in landfill siting: A Swiss case study. *Risk: Health, Safety & Environment, 7,* 145–168.
Renn, O., Webler, T., & Wiedemann, P. (1995). A need for discourse on citizen participation. In O. Renn, T. Webler & P. Wiedemann (Eds.), *Fairness and competence in citizen participation: Evaluating models for environmental discourse* (Vol. 10, pp. 1–15). Dordrecht: Kluwer.
Renn, O., Webler, T., & Wiedemann, P. M. (1995). *Fairness and competence in citizen participation: Evaluating models for environmental discourse.* Dordrecht: Kluwer.

Renz, M. A. (1992). Communicating about environmental risk: An examination of a Minnesota County's communication on incineration. *Journal of Applied Communication Research*(February), 1–18.
Rosenstone, S. J., & Hansen, J. M. (1993). *Mobilization, participation, and democracy in America*. New York: Macmillan.
Roth, A. L., Dunsby, J., & Bero, L. A. (2003). Framing processes in public commentary on US federal tobacco control regulation. *Social Studies of Science, 33*(1), 7–44.
Rothstein, H. F. (2004). Precautionary bans or sacrificial lambs? Participative risk regulation and the reform of the UK food safety regime. *Public Administration, 82*(4), 857–881.
Rowe, G., & Frewer, L. J. (2000). Public participation methods: A framework for evaluation. *Science, Technology & Human Values, 25*(1), 3–29.
Rowe, G., & Frewer, L. J. (2005). A typology of public engagement mechanisms. *Science Technology & Human Values, 30*(2), 251–290.
Rowe, G., Horlick-Jones, T., Walls, J., & Pidgeon, N. (2005). Difficulties in evaluating public engagement initiatives: Reflections on an evaluation of the UK GM Nation? Public debate about transgenic crops. *14*(4), 331–352.
Rowe, G., Marsh, R., & Frewer, L. J. (2004). Evaluation of a deliberative conference. *Science Technology & Human Values, 29*(1), 88–121.
Santos, S. L., & Chess, C. (2003). Evaluating citizen advisory boards: The importance of theory and participant-based criteria and practical implications. *Risk Analysis, 23*(2), 269–279.
Schotland, M. S., & Bero, L. A. (2002). Evaluating public commentary and scientific evidence submitted in the development of a risk assessment. *Risk Analysis, 22*(1), 131–140.
Shah, D. V. (1998). Civic engagement, interpersonal trust, and television use: An individual-level assessment of social capital. *Political Psychology, 19*(3), 469–496.
Shah, D. V., McLeod, J. M., & Yoon, S. H. (2001). Communication, context, and community — An exploration of print, broadcast, and Internet influences. *Communication Research, 28*(4), 464–506.
Simon, H. (1956). Rational choice and the structure of the environment. *Psychological Review, 63*, 129–138.
Slovic, P. (1993). Perceived risk, trust, and democracy. *Risk Analysis, 13*(6), 675–682.
Slovic, P. (1995). The construction of preference. *American Psychologist, 50*, 364–371.
Slovic, P., Lichtenstein, S., & Fischhoff, B. (1977). Behavioral decision theory. *Annual Review of Psychology, 28*, 1–39.
Smith, H. J., & Tyler, T. R. (1997). Choising the right pond: How group membership shapes self-esteem and group-oriented behavior. *Journal of Experimental Social Psychology, 33*, 146–170.
Smith, P. D., & McDonough, M. H. (2001). Beyond public participation: Fairness in natural resource decision making. *Society & Natural Resources, 14*(3), 239–249.
Sotirovic, M., & McLeod, J. M. (2001). Values, communication behavior, and political participation. *Political Communication, 18*(3), 273–300.
Thibaut, J. W., & Walker, L. (1975). *Procedural justice: A psychological analysis*. Mahwah, NJ: Erlbaum.
Tuler, S., & Webler, T. (1999). Voices from the forest: What participants expect of a public participation process. *Society & Natural Resources, 12*(5), 437–453.
Tversky, A., & Kahneman, D. (1981). The framing of decisions and the psychology of choice. *Science, 211*, 453–458.
Tyler, T. R. (1989). The Psychology of Procedural Justice — A Test of the Group-Value Model. *Journal of Personality and Social Psychology, 57*(5), 830–838.
Tyler, T. R. (1994). Psychological models of the justice motive: Antecedents of distributive and procedural justice. *Journal of Personality and Social Psychology, 67*, 850–863.
Tyler, T. R. (2000). Social justice: Outcome and procedure. *International Journal of Psychology, 35*(2), 117–125.
Tyler, T. R., Degoey, P., & Smith, H. J. (1996). Understanding why the justice of group procedures matters: A test of the psychological dynamics of the group-value model. *Journal of Personality and Social Psychology, 70*(5), 913–930.
Tyler, T. R., & Folger, R. (1980). Distributional and procedural aspects of satisfaction with citizen-police encounters. *Basic and Applied Social Psychology, 4*, 281–292.
Tyler, T. R., & Lind, E. A. (1992). A Relational Model of Authority in Groups. *Advances in Experimental Social Psychology, 25*, 115–191.
United Kingdom Parliamentary Office of Science and Technology. (2001). *Open channels: Public dialogues on science and technology*. London: House of Commons.
Verba, S., Schlozman, K. L., & Brady, H. E. (1995). *Voice and equality: Civic voluntarism in American politics*. Cambridge, MA: Harvard University Press.
von Winterfeldt, D., & Edwards, W. (1986). *Decision analysis and behavioral research*. Cambridge, UK: Cambridge University Press.

Webler, T., & Tuler, S. (2000). Fairness and competence in citizen participation: Theoretical reflections from a case study. *Administration & Society, 32*, 566–595.

Webler, T., & Tuler, S. (2006). Four perspectives on public participation process in environmental assessment and decision making: Combined results from 10 case studies. *Policy Studies Journal, 34*, 699–722.

Webler, T., Tuler, S., & Krueger, R. (2001). What is a good public participation process? Five perspectives from the public. *Environmental Management, 27*(3), 435–450.

Weiner, B. J., Alexander, J. A., & Shortell, S. M. (2002). Management and governance processes in community health coalitions: A procedural justice perspective. *Health Education & Behavior, 29*, 737–754.

Wilson, R. S., & Arvai, J. L. (2006). When less is more: How affect influences preferences when comparing low and high-risk options. *Journal of Risk Research, 9*(2), 165–178.

Witt, L. A., Andrews, M. C., & Kacmar, K. M. (2000). The role of participation in decision-making in the organizational politics-job satisfaction relationship. *Human Relations, 53*(3), 341–358.

Wolfe, A. K., & Bjornstad, D. J. (2003). Making decisions about hazardous waste remediation when even considering a remediation technology is controversial. *Environmental Science & Technology, 37*(8), 1485–1492.

Wynne, B. (1992a). Misunderstood misunderstandings. *Public Understanding of Science, 2*, 112–133.

Wynne, B. (1992b). Sheep farming after Chernobyl: A case study in communication scientific information. In B. Lewenstein (Ed.), *When Science Meets the Public* (pp. 43–67). Washington, DC: American Association for the Advancement of Science.

19

Warming Warnings: Global Challenges of Risk and Crisis Communication

David McKie
University of Waikato

Christopher Galloway
Swinburne University of Technology

This chapter takes the issue of global warming as an exemplary warning in relation to 21st century global risk. It focuses on the central role of communication in shaping social perceptions of risk in general, and on one potential catastrophe with global impact in particular. It explores the limits of rationality within an ecology of risk communication by looking back—to an earlier 20th century risk perceived as global—and considers how global warming has more recently passed a critical point in public consciousness. It focuses on how different discipline weightings can align advances in knowledge with contemporary contexts; on encouraging environmentally responsible business actions without relying too heavily on a legalistic approach; on how new communication infrastructures are evolving; and on how to engage emotions in catalyzing the international collaboration needed to tackle global challenges.

INTRODUCTION: INTERWEAVING DISCIPLINES AND LIMITING LAW

Global warming is simultaneously raising planetary temperatures and interest in interdisciplinary interfaces between catastrophe, communication, and risk. This is not new insofar as risk studies already has a history of crossing conventional knowledge boundaries and synthesizing inputs from a range of diverse fields. Increasingly, however, such crossovers intensify as society "is enlarging the number and complexity of activities that are known to carry the risk of degrading the quality of human life and its natural environment" (White, 2000, p. xv). These comments preface Slovic's (2000a) edited collection on *The Perception of Risk*, which covers an extensive socio-environmental-economic context.

The diversity of disciplinary intersections carries over into extreme risk considerations. Posner's (2004) *Catastrophe: Risk and Response*, for example, situates certain feasible events, "such as a major asteroid collision, global bioterrorism, abrupt global warming" (p. v) as having "unimaginably terrible consequences up to and including the extinction of the human race, possibly within the near future" (p. v). While Althaus (2005) positions individual discourses as "having a particular knowledge approach with which they confront the unknown" (p. 567), an interdisciplinary cluster is inevitable in relation to large-scale risk. For Posner (2004), for example, while there is a vast body of popular and scientific writing dealing with "possible megacatastrophes" (p. v), "law and the social sciences, with the partial exception of economics ... have paid little attention to such possibilities" (p. v). To address catastrophic risk, Posner's proposed prototype reaches beyond the usual input subjects for risk, and beyond his own home discipline of law, to update research into a more effective disciplinary mix (especially in combining natural sciences with social sciences). His prototype for augmented knowledge points less in the direction of expanding, and establishing, a static body of knowledge, and more toward forming an interpretative community able to adapt to and synthesize appropriate interdisciplinary inputs that draw from often distinct research traditions in humanities, science, and social science.

Interpretative syntheses are vital and demand historically-informed communities pulling different disciplines together. Posner (2004) further noted how catastrophic risks are evident and expanding and, along with "the mathematical methods sometimes used in the analysis of extreme events" (p. v), "the social sciences, in particular economics, statistics, cognitive psychology, and law, have an essential role to play in the design of policies and institutions for combating them" (p. v). Despite his attempts at bridging the natural sciences-social sciences gap, however, Posner's (2004) named disciplines excluded politics and communication, which can offer a check on, and supplement to, contemporary tendencies to depend on legally-oriented risk prevention.

These tendencies are observable in the attention devoted to the precautionary principle. This principle "has emerged over recent decades as a widely and increasingly accepted general principle of environmental policy, law, and management" (Cooney, 2004, p. xii) that, as an approach to uncertainty, "provides for action to avoid serious or irreversible environmental harm in advance of scientific certainty of such harm" (p. xii). In this way, the principle usefully suggests legal safeguards for the prevention of harm. Supporters see it as a moral standard, a "decision-making and action tool with ethical power and scientific rigor" (Tickner, Raffensperger, & Myers, 1999, p. 1), which becomes almost transcendent as "a principle of justice, that no-one should have to live with fear of harm to their health and environment" (p. 16). On the positive side, despite 20% of Americans believing that no preventative steps—at least none with an economic cost—should be taken against global warming prior to scientific proof, Jurisprudence Professor Cass Sunstein (2005) made a strong case that: "Modest steps can certainly be justified" (p. 25) and "Insofar as the Precautionary Principle counteracts the tendency to demand certainty, it should be approved" (p. 25).

Less usefully, as Sunstein (2005) went on to report, there is no canonical definition of the principle and the twenty or more on offer are often incompatible with each other. As a result, while the precautionary principle provides a popular front for action against the global warming "denial industry," and suggests how to underpin legal safeguards for the prevention of harm, its growing "shibboleth status" (Berry, cited in Marchant & Mossman, 2005, p. xi) gives cause for concern. Legalized caution can, for example, come with other costs and can increase other risks by eliminating "technologies and strategies that make human lives easier, more convenient, healthier, and longer" (Sunstein, 2005, p. 25). In fact, retrospective application of the principle might have inhibited life-enhancing innovations that range from antibiotics and aircraft through measles vaccines and open-heart surgery, to X-rays (Starr, 2006).

HISTORICIZING FEARS: CONTEXT MATTERS AND OLDER FUTURE THREATS

Nor is it just scientific advances that might be threatened. Writing for the World Conservation Union, Cooney (2004) saw that the "core of the [precautionary] principle can be understood as *countering the presumption in favor of development*" (p. 5) [italics in original] and tilting "the balance in decision-making toward 'prudent foresight' ... a broad notion susceptible of supporting a very wide range of operational measures" (p. 5). With the move outside of law, the principle's lofty goals do not exempt it from controversy and it becomes subject to political struggles. These struggles are also struggles for communicative advantage that involves context not as a passive surrounding, but as co-creator of meaning.

In arguing that the shift in prioritizing global warming as high risk comes from the interaction between communication messages and their context as well as scientific findings, we focus on the need for self-reflection on the risk communication process and an awareness of how it changes over time. At present, key contexts have been characterized by what both Glassner's (1999) and Furedi's (2002) book titles call the *Culture of Fear*, in which people, individually and collectively, seek to practice the *The Risk Management of Everything* (Power, 2004). Sunstein (2005) pushes the characterization toward a planetary dimension with what his book calls *Laws of Fear: Beyond the Precautionary Principle*.

By inevitably, and irrevocably, globalizing the context, climate change calls into question the capacity of even developed conceptions of risk communication as "a community infrastructure, transactional communication process among individuals and organizations regarding the character, cause, degree, significance, uncertainty, control and overall perception of a risk" (Palenchar, 2005, p. 752). The definition provides impressive coverage of local and national instances. However, further fundamental questions, with massive practical implications, arise in a global context: What does community infrastructure mean in global terms? What is involved in transactional communication processes that transcend national boundaries? What consideration should be given to non-humans (such as endangered species)? What individuals and organizations are key players in overall perceptions of which risks? More than linear extensions of existing risks, these questions have significant communication and historical dimensions.

While Posner, himself a judge as well as a legal scholar, and other law-oriented theorists, may omit communication as a component in current interdisciplinary risk considerations, our emphasis finds some endorsement in the sociologically-oriented work of Ulrich Beck. Beck, who has historically contextualized recent fear and risk, gained global prominence with his early description, published in German in 1986—and later in English as *Risk Society: Towards a New Modernity* (Beck, 1992)—of modern society as a risk society only a few months prior to the Chernobyl disaster. Chernobyl offered an almost immediate confirmation of his thesis with regard to society's production of technologies beyond its control, and Beck is credited with creating the sociological terms *Risikogesellschaft* (risk society) and *Zweite Moderne* (second modernity) as the later reflexive period of modernity.

RISK SIGNS OF THE TIMES (1): BEYOND MODERNITY AND NUCLEAR FEAR

In his later *World Risk Society* (1999), Beck characterized the first period of modernity as "based on nation-state societies … essentially understood in a territorial sense" (1999, pp. 1–2), which exhibited "collective patterns of life, progress and controllability, full employment and exploitation of nature" (p. 2), has "now been undermined by interlinked processes" (p. 2), including the process of globalization and the extension of "global risks (as ecological crisis and the crash of global financial markets)" (p. 2). Globalization comes with an increase in interlinked risks as well as in interlinked markets and contributes to the growing trend to move responsibility for environmental and social matters away from government and toward corporations (see Makower "and Business for Social Responsibility," 1994; McKie & Munshi, 2007).

Beck's stress, on global risks beyond national territories, finds strident confirmation in Rees' (2003) book title, *Our Final Hour: A Scientist's Warning: How Terror, Error, and Environmental Disaster Threaten Humankind's Future in this Century—on Earth and Beyond*, and opening sentence: "THE TWENTIETH CENTURY BROUGHT US THE BOMB, and the nuclear threat will never leave us" [capitals in original] (p. 1). For Beck (1999), this second period of modernity is marked by the need for society to respond reflexively to such challenges, as "unforeseen consequences of the victory of the first, simple, linear, industrial modernization based on the national state" (1999, p. 2). The rest of this chapter accepts that 21st century society is indeed a high risk society, with global and reflexive dimensions. It is further guided by the communication core of an earlier Beck (1992) insight: "Troubled times and generations can be succeeded by others for which fear, tamed by interpretations, is a basic element of thought and expression" (p. 75).

As part of the movement to adapt atomic power for peaceful purposes, Chernobyl postdates the closest prototype of 21st century global fear and risk: the spread of atomic anxiety across the planet after 1945: "During the Cold War years, the main threat looming over us was an all-out thermonuclear exchange, triggered by an escalating superpower confrontation" (Rees, 2003, p. 2). That earlier phase of global anxiety illuminates Beck's (1992) observation because fear, during the decades after the World War 2, was far from being "tamed by interpretations" (p. 75). Indeed, recent research reveals Pentagon interpretations of the USSR as having as many as a thousand ICBMs with massive destructive capacity, when, in fact, only "four Soviet missiles were operational" (Ghamani-Tabrizi, 2005, p. 2).

This salutary reminder of the influence of geo-political paranoia on risk interpretation finds 21st century parallels in exaggerated claims for Iraq holding weapons of mass destruction. Such tracking, of the spread of anxiety, also remains a useful method of reflecting on the mutation of popular and institutional risk assessments and their communication depth and range. Other facets of Ghamari-Tabrizi's (2005) research can also be usefully adapted to contemporary concerns. One is her discussion of the post-World War 2 shift in power away from military experience to techno-scientific research and simulation. Another, which perceptively captures the importance of inter-disciplinarity, is her insight into simulation's imbrication in disciplinary disputes because, once they had "distinguished their approach from the uniformed military, the simulationists wrangled over competing techniques ... economists squabbled with the systems analysts; others rebuked them both for methodology folly; and the physicists snubbed everyone" (Ghamari-Tabrizi, 2005, p. 126).

RISK SIGNS OF THE TIMES (2): FROM KAHN'S COLD WAR TO GORE'S WARMING WARNING

The first of these facets, the shift away from prior experience, matters because it formed the mold for subsequent risk assessment team approaches. Among its drivers were the success of operations research during World War 2 and the breakthroughs of non-military interdisciplinary teams as diverse as the Manhattan Project (see Bennis & Biederman, 1997) and the Enigma codebreakers (see Johansson, 2004). The main proponents of the move were engineers, mathematicians, and scientists, and, in the United States, those working with the Rand Institute. They argued that, in the face of a third world war, which would be a nuclear war, the locus of expertise had moved from military veterans, whose experience was now outmoded, to civilian experts skilled in the "new technologies of simulation" (Ghamari-Tabrizi, 2005, p. 124), and able to imagine fighting a third world war "as a science fiction, a hypothetical physical, military, and social construct ... accessible only through experiments, models, and simulations" (p. 124).

The immediate post-war battle between military experience and simulation expertise was won by the latter group. That victory left marks that are still discursively and practically legible in the dominance of an interpretative style that features figures, graphs, and mathematically- and scientifically-oriented research, the core of "technical" expert-driven approaches to risk communication.

Another of Ghamari-Tabrizi's (2005) facets, the heaping together of future simulation methodologies "not as a science but as a style, a mood, and an aesthetic" (p. 126), can also be adapted to engage more reflectively with public fears of climate change risk. The post-World War 2 simulation philosophy became a significant part of risk texts through media channels and prominent public figures. Herman Kahn—through his 1961 book *On Thermonuclear War*; his impact on government policy makers, Pentagon committees, national and international lecture audiences; and fictionalizations of him in such films as *Dr Strangelove*—emerged as the talisman figure for nuclear fear. Al Gore, from his transition from the man who was once the next president of the United States, through lecture circuits, book fairs, government consultancies, to a successful Oscar-winning documentary star in *An Inconvenient Truth*, has become the equivalent figurehead for global warming.

The environment has had *Economist, National Geographic* and multiple *Time* magazine covers since 1997, but the May 2006 "Green Issue" of *Vanity Fair* featured a cover with Julia Roberts surrounded by Al Gore, George Clooney, and Robert F. Kennedy—all suitably somber faced—alongside the headline: "A THREAT GRAVER THAN TERRORISM: GLOBAL WARMING" [capitals in original] and the question: "How much of New York, Washington, and other American cities will be underwater?" Observing the phenomenon of the mediatization of global warming, *The Australian Financial Review Magazine* noted that while it "remains to be seen if the media's Damascene conversion will have any real impact.... The wise money would be on the smart eco-investors and entrepreneurs ... who see big greenbacks" (Huck, 2006, p. 18). Within a year, *The Atlantic* drafted a tighter assessment of possible winners and losers because climate change "could also be a windfall for some people, businesses, and nations" (Easterbrook, 2007, p. 52).

These typical media summations of the importance of the bottom line parallel recent larger political policy initiatives along financial lines, most prominently, the British government-commissioned *The Economics of Climate Change: The Stern Review* (Stern, 2007). In updating the contemporary aesthetic from Kahn, we can see the shift of Gore and global warming into the mainstream through newer media as well as magazines. Certainly, there is mounting evidence that a critical mass has been reached in two areas of the contemporary Zeitgeist: the overtaking of terrorism by climate change as the current global threat; and the reforging of relations between the economic and the environmental.

CRITICAL POINTS: SUSTAINABLE BUSINESS, SELF-INTEREST, AND RATIONAL LIMITS

Currently, a less precautionary-inclined market environmentalism can be seen not as part of the problem of sustainable global growth but rather as part of the solution. Hart's (2005) *Capitalism at the Crossroads: The Unlimited Business Opportunities in Solving the World's Most Difficult Problems*, for instance, argues that "the corporate sector could become the catalyst for a truly sustainable form of global development" (p. xli). And, with this business and economic co-option of global warming as an issue, it seems to have reached one of Breakwell and Barnett's (2001) "critical points" (p. 9): "when the orientation, tempo or strength of the social image of a hazard changes significantly" and, they further note, how "Self interest, moral outrage and the arousal of fear are identified as principles that are instrumental in leading to an event achieving critical point status" (p. 9).

Yet, there is something surprising in global warming reaching "critical point status" because it has to transcend present day time and space self interests in favor of future generations and distant populations. Even while pointing out how the financial justification for the UN climate negotiation process and the Kyoto protocol stems from a market failure to reduce greenhouse gas emissions, economists conclude that the financial rationale for change is unconvincing:

> If we leave it to the decision-making processes of individual consumers, businesses and/or countries, then we get too much pollution because the private costs of polluting activities are typically much lower than the social costs. To drive a car, for example, we pay for the petrol and the car but not for the damages that arise in faraway countries and to future generations because of the car's carbon dioxide emissions. Worse, most people and organizations, even at the country level, are too small for their individual action to make a difference. If one country alone reduced pollution, it would incur all

> the costs of that effort without any benefits as long as the other countries continue to pollute. Thus, it is rational for countries and individuals alike to keep on polluting even if they are concerned about the effects. (Martin, 2006, p. 2)

That has already emerged in relation to economic resource allocation. If less research had been concentrated on disproving, or doubting, global warming, much more in grants and research and development could have been invested in generating adaptations and implementing responses. In risk communication terms, the choice is not only how to weight the differing inputs but also to pay attention to, and to draw attention to, how self interest, whether corporate, personal, or national, can distort media representation. This can happen through disproportionately large or small public exposure being obtained by different bodies such as activists, corporations, and (dis)interested scientists.

This messy and politically contested public arena needs to be borne in mind. It undermines the illusion of rational control saturating much risk communication and the tendency to gravitate around an outmoded sender-receiver message theory even among sophisticated mental model researchers. Granger Morgan, Fischhoff, Bostrom, and Atman (2002), for instance, typify a common approach to risk, and its communication, as a rationally-knowable, and essentially one-way process through trying to solve the communication problems faced by risk specialists and ensuring "that, if they choose to, laypeople can understand how the risks they face are created and controlled, how well science understands those risks, and how great they seem to be" (p. 14).

Often risk communicators attempt to downplay emotion and assign it a small or even misleading role in the process. Granger Morgan et al. (2002), for example, agree that, in some situations, people have the right to become "emotionally involved" (p. 8) and suggest such "emotions need not mean that risk communication is hopeless" (p. 8), but they can at best "provide motivation for acquiring competence" (p. 8). Others, with some ethical justification, consciously deploy fear as a communications tool since the "promotion of fear and the propagandist manipulation of information is often justified on the grounds that it is a small price to pay to get a good message across to the public" (Furedi, 2002, p. 25).

SPREADING RISK: MEDIA AND DISCOURSE ECOLOGY

In the not so distant past, nuclear age strategists were able to formulate "a doctrine of deterrence by 'mutually assured destruction' (with the singularly appropriately acronym MAD)" (Rees, 2003, p. 2), but today it is conceivable that "ordinary citizens could command the destructive capacity that in the twentieth century was the frightening prerogative of the handful of individuals who held the reins of power in states with nuclear weapons" (p. 2). Global warming exacerbation, and reduction, is similarly out of the control of any small nuclear club. It involves everyone from small Pacific islands, whose total landmass may vanish beneath the ocean, to powerful nations signing, or not signing, protocols such as Kyoto.

In essence, large scale and fluid processes, beyond the rational control of individual agents—whether corporations, governments, or citizen movements—are refocusing approaches, in different time scales, to both nuclear and global warming risks. The refocus is occurring in a context of a changing media sphere. Debates on the fundamentals of the environment and economics—independently and in concert—and their interrelationship with global risk have moved well beyond the academy, expert discourses, and small membership fora. Nevertheless, although the results are hidden in open sight (and multiple web sites), the wider ecology of global warning communications remains an understudied factor.

A sense of this interactive evolution can be tracked through just one example. In Poole's (2006) popular book *Unspeak*™—a term defined on the front cover's mock dictionary entry as "1. n. mode of speech that persuades by stealth. *E.G., climate change, war on terror*" [italics in original] —he notes attempts to present a more semantically comforting communication environment by redefining labels through the example of pollster Frank Luntz' leaked memo of advice to the US Republicans: "The terminology in the upcoming environmental debate needs refinement.... *It's time for us to start talking about 'climate change' instead of global warming*" (Luntz, cited, Poole, 2006, p. 42) because "*Climate change' is less frightening than 'global warming*" [italics and underlining in original] (p. 42), after all, as "one focus group participant noted, climate change 'sounds like you're going from Pittsburgh to Fort Lauderdale.' While global warming has catastrophic connotations attached to it, climate change suggests a more controllable and less emotional challenge" (p. 42).

Emotionally-informed economic considerations carry over into the internationally expanding ecology of contemporary global risk communications. This expanding ecology encompasses the technical dissemination of large-scale, people-friendly access to information through the internet. In that arena, diverse fora appeal to the cognitive and scientific as well as the emotional and provide continuity with their simulationist predecessors. In addition, on a site such as YouTube, conflicting viewpoints collide in close proximity because a common feature of cyberspace is how enemies often become close neighbors by occupying adjacent territories as part of the same onscreen list of search results.

In 2006, for example, the list produced by a YouTube search for global warming displayed the promotional video for *An Inconvenient Truth*, Al Gore's slide show on the risk of Global Warming filmed with added animation and illustrative footage, immediately alongside its satiric send-up, *Al Gore's Penguin Army*, which presents Gore as a bore who blames global warming for almost everything (including a picture of an anorexic-looking Lindsay Lohan). When we viewed it, that spoof was closely followed by a further offering headed "The same liars who conned and used kids about smoking made 'Al Gore's Penguin Army'" (http://www.youtube.com/watch?v=e6SSKWpBJHY). That offering in turn went on to cite a *Wall Street Journal* investigation that the *Al Gore's Penguin Army* posting was not an ordinary amateur, as claimed on its YouTube listing, but "actually came from a slick Republican public relations firm called DCI, which just happens to have oil giant Exxon as a client" (http://www.youtube.com/watch?v=fzHN73nQAzk). The circle was temporarily completed when, as part of a posting in the same search list, the Republican pollster Frank Luntz, who featured in Poole's (2006) analysis, is interviewed in a video on *The Bush Administration's Approach to Global Warming* (http://www.youtube.com/watch?v=CKJ2fu_Gluo&mode=related&search). This video is critical of that administration and features Luntz himself on screen claiming that the advice he provided the Bush administration in 2000 was valid then but was no longer defensible.

In effect the emerging communication infrastructure is enabling an informed, albeit intermittently, and politically open, albeit unstructured, debate. This takes place in mediated forms that invite involvement in interpretation and an evolving community, whose members participate in posting, often relatively inexpensive, visual or verbal contributions. Millions of people also distribute personal blogs and broadcasts into the interactive maelstrom known as the blogosphere. The internet also provides easy access to credible economic (the *Stern Review* is downloadable at http://www.hm-treasury.gov.uk/index.cfm) and scientific sources. At the time of writing, for example, Wikipedia's excellent entry on global warming (http://en.wikipedia.org/wiki/Global_warming) offers a sober introduction to the science for non-scientists with links to further information; and, the BBC web site (http://news.bbc.co.uk/2/hi/science/nature/6322083.stm), provides scientifically-informed graphics on climate change designed to be easily comprehensible to publics who only need access to the internet and English. Such web fora, blogs, and other forms effectively extend Palenchar's (2005) community infrastructure toward global participation. The interactive fora also admit emotion—evident in the language and images of many posts—to environmental discussions and economic discussions alike.

MORE FEAR MATTERS: LIMITING RATIONALITY AND DEPLOYING EMOTIONS

Emotions in general, and fear in particular, are important drivers—of individual, national, and international processes—that influence message design, delivery, and reception. What de Becker's (1998) book cover claims in relation to individuals: "True fear is a gift. Unwarranted fear is a curse," applies equally to risk at a social level. People can be afraid with little logical cause. People may also be without fear, when there are rational reasons for them to be frightened enough to take drastic action and to change long established behaviors. Let us stress that this is not an argument, especially in relation to global warning, to exclude rational considerations because beliefs are also "correlated with behavior in the expected way" (Cutler & Glaeser, 2005, p. 10) so that people "who think that smoking or drinking poses a greater risk are unsurprisingly less likely to smoke or drink" (p. 10).

Part of the communication difficulty is that, in risky situations, apathy is the most common reaction because "low-probability, high magnitude risks are hard to think about" (Sandman, 2002). Risk communication can help address the gap that may exist "between expert pronouncements about risks and what the public chooses to dread" (Ungar, 1992, p. 485). In fact, dramatic environmental events may need to occur before publics pay concerted attention (Jagtenberg & McKie, 1997). Meantime, in the absence of disaster or near-disaster, a risk response strategy based on "rational concern" (Fischhoff, Gonzalez, Small, & Lerner, 2003 , p. 97) is more desirable than either panic or fearlessness. However, it must also take account of the limits or rationality and cannot exclude consideration of emotions, which should also be updated with recent findings—accessibly summarized in Gazzaniga, Ivry, and Mangun's (2002) summary of cognitive neuroscience as "a hybrid of disciplines" (p. 7), with "roots in neurology, neuroscience, and cognitive science" (p. 7).

Changing public attitudes to global warming offer an illustrative example. Over the last twenty-five years, an international scientific consensus on the dangers of global warming has emerged with evidence from substantial reports by the U.S. National Academy of Sciences (National Research Council, 1983, 2001), and globally-focused international groups and fora such as the World Climate Program (1985) and the Intergovernmental Panel on Climate Change, 1990, 1995, 2001). They concur in concluding that it poses a clear, and if not present, at least near-future, danger.

Leading scientists mount attacks on the activities of the "contrarian" movement, which denies that there is convincing evidence of global warming, and which they perceive as an alliance of corporate-funded public relations practitioners and scientists. In 2005, Lord May (2005) of Oxford, then President of the Royal Society, and former chief scientific adviser to the British Government, warned against the entry of what he calls a US oil industry funded "climate change denial lobby" (see also Demeritt, 2001) and divided the opposition into two parts: those recognizing the risk of global warming included the majority of informed scientists and those questioning its existence "a small band of sceptics, including lobbyists funded by the US oil industry, a sci-fi writer (in the shape of Michael Crichton) and the *Daily Mail* who deny the scientists are right."

Since, as Ungar (1992) observed, "risk analysis reveals that fear of a phenomenon increases with the number of people exposed and is particularly great when the impact is global" (p. 491), it is unsurprising that the anti-environmentalist movement mobilized globally through transnational operations and international fiction bestsellers. Both critics, and their opponents, often hinge their arguments around emotions, usually fear. The environmentalists, since the frightening implication of imminent mortality in Rachel Carson's (1962) *Silent Spring*, have gathered momentum through Merchant's (1980) *The Death of Nature* to terminal confirmation such as *The End of Nature* (McKibben, 1990). On the anti-environmental side, Bailey's (2002) *Global Warming and Other Eco-Myths: How the Environmental Movement Uses False Science to Scare Us to Death* aligns with Crichton's (2004) novel *State of Fear*, which attributes our present fear not to global warming but to exaggerated and violent environmentalist distortion of its minimal risk.

After all, democratic governments nations seek to be accountable to the public through periodic elections and "require officials to pay close attention to the popular will" (Sunstein, 2005, p. 1) so that responsiveness "to public fear is, in this sense, both inevitable and desirable" (p. 1). Anxieties can be further compounded by the media playing an important role in prioritizing legislation in reaction to perceived problems, often by the use of compelling media imagery, which creates an emotional response. Moreover, because media interventions are often critical, and tied to the commercial demands of a short news cycle that pushes for just-occurring events with pictures, media play an important role in constructing—and, often, amplifying—certain easily-visible, risk-related concerns (e.g., oil spills) and in minimizing less dramatic and slow moving ones (e.g., the loss of the ozone layer). Ultimately, these distortions have to be addressed by risk communicators around such core concerns as building trust, especially public trust, and credibility, especially public credibility, as attributes of communicative relationships. Slovic's (2000b) research found that "much to the distress of agency [US Environmental Protection Agency] technical experts who argue that other hazards deserve higher priority" (p. 390), the major part of the EPA's budget went "to hazardous waste primarily because the public believes that the cleanup of Superfund sites is the most serious environmental problem for the country" (p. 390).

ASYMMETRY RULES: NEW WARMING AND THE WEALTH OF SOME NATIONS?

A further problem is what risk experts call "the asymmetry principle" (Slovic, 2000b, p. 410), so that when "it comes to winning trust, the playing field is not level ... [but] tilted toward distrust" (p. 410). So agents that consciously attempt to publicize scientific disagreements at the expense of scientific consensus further load the weighting against trust. While this stands as a useful warning, it is not to claim that such attempts are always wrong, or that science is not also socially constructed or free of subjectivity—see, for example, Slovic's (2000b) evidence on the different constructions of risk by men and women in the revealingly titled chapter, "Trust, Emotion, Sex, Politics, and Science."

Asymmetry is not just restricted to trust. Rational self-interest may hinder the need for transnational solutions to climate change. In fact, the possible return of Beck's early-modern nation-state territoriality might weigh the balance further in favor of the already wealthy. On the basis of its recent findings, the 2007 Intergovernmental Panel on Climate Change (IPCC) Report can confidently claim an increase in human-induced global warming: "Much more evidence has accumulated over the past five years to indicate that changes in many physical and biological systems are linked to anthropogenic warming" (http://www.ipcc.ch/).

However, with an increase in availability of information "across the regions of the world concerning the nature of future impacts, including for some places not covered in previous assessments," the IPCC evidence extends the scope from what global warming will do to the environment, to what it might do for the international distribution of power and wealth. In Easterbrook's (2007) hypothetical example of "a primary impact of an artificially warmed world" (p. 57) making "land in Canada, Greenland, Russia, Scandinavia, and the United States more valuable" (p. 58), then the impact will have large economic and political ramifications for "the 21st-century global situation" (p. 58), so that: "if northern societies find that climate change makes them more wealthy, the quest for world equity could be dealt a huge setback" (p. 58). Commenting on the IPCC Report summary that billions of people faced shortages of essentials, including food and water, the chairman concluded "It's the poorest of the poor in the world, and this includes poor people even in prosperous societies, who are going to be the worst hit" (http://news.bbc.co.uk/2/hi/science/nature/6532323.stm).

On top of exacerbating equity issues, which are likely to be a matter of life and death to millions, self-interested responses could also put planetary survival at stake longer term. Accordingly, attempts to create Palenchar's (2005) "climate of participatory and effective discourse to reduce friction and increase harmony and mutuality" (p. 753) will require risk communication to move beyond Beck's (1999) "first, simple, linear, industrial modernization based on the national state" (p. 2). New fora, and new transnational institutions not tied to existing territorial blocs or regions, will be better placed to set a less interested planetary agenda for engaging with the expansion of megacatastrophic risks. Ironically, while the UN climate change process, especially through the IPCC, has not impacted positively on the actual climate, it has probably made the single largest institutional contribution to the public climate of acceptance of global warming as a real, major, present, and future danger requiring urgent action. Perhaps the IPCC's key contribution to date has been to establish, and to model, an informed interpretative community where many different countries contribute scientists and knowledge and coordinate actions to identify detailed dimensions of the problem in the face of denial.

Now that the warming warning has reached a critical point in much of civil society internationally, it is time the scientists were enabled to focus more on solutions, and risk communicators to deploy their resources to prepare publics for the sacrifices and lifestyle changes that preventative measures will require. In shifting from the drive for communicative advantage, they would do well to parallel, and learn from already existing examples: the Global Environment Facility, which is an independent organization that gives grants for projects that benefit the global environment and sustainability; the Forest Stewardship Council, which issues a consumer label to wood products constructed from sustainably-managed forests; and the IPCC itself (see Simmons & Jonge Oudraat, 2001). In the absence of emergent, globally-concerned, and environmentally-aware risk communication fora, and institutions, appropriate adaptive action is unlikely to win enough public support in time. Since fear of global warming is no longer "tamed by interpretations" (Beck, 1992, p. 75), which had called its very existence into doubt, it can now be channeled to set agendas for urgent action.

BIBLIOGRAPHY

Althaus, C. E. (2005). A disciplinary perspective on the epistemological status of risk. *Risk Analysis*, *25*(3), 567–588.

Bailey, R. (Ed.). (2002). *Global warming and other eco-myths: How the environmental movement uses false science to scare us to death.* Roseville, CA: Prima Publishing.

Beck, U. (1992). *World risk society.* Cambridge: Polity Press.

Beck, U. (1999). *Risk society: Towards a new modernity.* London: Sage.

Becker, G. de (1998). *Gift of fear and other survival signals that protect us from violence*. New York: Dell.

Bennis, W., & Biederman, P. W. (1997). *Organizing genius: The secrets of creative collaboration.* London: Nicholas Brealey.

Marchant, G. E., & Mossman, K. L. (2005). *Arbitrary and capricious: The precautionary principle in the European courts.* London: International Policy Press.

Breakwell, G. M., & Barnett, J., with Lofstedt, R., Kemp, R., & Glaser, C. (2001). *The impact of social amplification of risk on risk communication.* London: HM Stationery Office.

Cooney, R. (2004). *The precautionary principle in biodiversity conservation and natural resource management: An issues paper for policy-makers, researchers and practitioners.* Cambridge: International Union for Conservation of Nature and Natural Resources. Retrived 28 March, 2006, from http://www.pprinciple.net/publications/PrecautionaryPrincipleissuespaper.pdf

Carson, R. (1962). *Silent spring*. Boston: Houghton Mifflin.

Crichton, M. (2004). *State of fear.* New York: HarperCollins.

Cutler, D., & Glaeser, E. (2005). *What explains differences in smoking, drinking and other health-related behaviours.* Harvard Institute of Economic Research, *2060.* Retrieved 23 March, 2006, from http://post.economics.harvard.edu/hier/2005papers/2005list.html.

Demeritt, D. (2001). The construction of global warming and the politics of science. *Annals of the Association of American Geographers, 9*(2), 307–337.

Easterbrook, G. (2007). Global warning: Who loses and who wins? *The Atlantic*, April, 52–64.

Furedi, F. (2002). *Culture of fear*. London: Continuum.

Gazzaniga, M., Ivry, R., & Mangun, G. (2002). *Cognitive science* (2nd. ed.). New York: W. W. Norton.

Ghamari-Tabrizi, S. (2005). *The worlds of Herman Kahn: The intuitive science of thermonuclear war.* Cambridge, MA: Harvard University Press.

Glassner, B. (1999). *The culture of fear: Why Americans are afraid of the wrong things.* New York: Basic Books.

Granger Morgan, M., Fischhoff, B., Bostrom, A., & Atman, C. J. (2002). *Risk communication: A mental models approach.* Cambridge: Cambridge University Press.

Hart, S. (2005). *Capitalism at the crossroads: The unlimited business opportunities in solving the world's most difficult problems.* Upper Saddle River, NJ: Wharton School Publishing.

Huck, P. (2006). Facing up to climate change. *The Australian Financial Review Magazine*, April 52–64.

Intergovernmental Panel on Climate Change. (1990). *Policymakers' summary: Working group III.* Geneva, Switzerland: IPCC.

Intergovernmental Panel on Climate Change. (1995). *IPCC second assessment report: Climate change 1995.* Geneva, Switzerland: IPCC.

Intergovernmental Panel on Climate Change. (2001). *IPCC third assessment report: Contributions of IPCC working groups.* Geneva, Switzerland: IPCC.

Jagtenberg, T., & McKie, D. (1997). *Eco-impacts and the greening of postmodernity: New maps for communication studies, cultural studies and sociology.* Thousand Oaks, CA: Sage.

Johansson, F. (2004). *The Medici effect: Breakthrough insights at the intersection of ideas, concepts and cultures.* Boston, MA: Harvard Business School.

Kahn, H. (1961). *On thermonuclear war.* Princeton, NJ: Princeton University Press.

Martin, R. (2006). *Climate change: Economic sense and non-sense of carbon mitigation policies.* London: London School of Economics CEP Policy Analysis Paper (downloadable at http://cep.lse.ac.uk/about/news/2007.asp)

May, B. (2005, January). Under-informed, over here. Retrieved 6 April, 2006, from http://www.guardian.co.uk/life/lastword/story/0,,1398885,00.html

McKibben, B. (1990). *The end of nature.* London: Viking.

McKie, D., & Munshi, D. (2007). *Reconfiguring public relations: Ecology, equity, and enterprise.* London: Routledge.

Makower, J., and Business for Social Responsibility. (1994). *Beyond the bottom line: Putting social responsibility to work for your business and the world.* New York: Simon & Schuster.

Merchant, C. (1980). *The death of nature: Women, ecology and the scientific revolution.* San Francisco: Harper and Row.

National Research Council. (1983). *Changing climate.* Washington, DC: National Academy Press.

National Research Council. (2001). *Climate change science.* Washington, DC: National Academy Press.

Palenchar, M. J. (2005). Risk communication. In R. Heath (Ed.), *Encyclopedia of public relations, Vol 2* (pp. 752–755). Thousand Oaks, CA: Sage.

Penman, R. (2000). *Reconstructing communicating: Looking to a future.* Mahwah, NJ: Erlbaum.

Poole, S. (2006). *Unspeak™: How words become weapons, how weapons become a message, and how that message becomes reality.* New York: Grove Press.

Posner, R. A. (2004). *Catastrophe: Risk and response.* New York: Oxford University Press.

Power, M. (2004). *The risk management of everything: Rethinking the politics of uncertainty.* London: Demos.

Rees, M. (2003). *Our final century: Will the human race survive the twenty-first century.* London: William Heinemann.

Sandman, P. M. (2002). Beyond panic prevention: Addressing emotion in emergency communication. Retrieved 1 May, 2006, from http://www.psandman.com/articles/beyond.pdf

Simmons, P. J., & Jonge Oudraat, C. de, (2001). *Managing global issues: Lessons learned.* Washington, DC: Carnegie Endowment for International Peace.

Slovic, P. (Ed.). (2000a). *The perception of risk.* London: Earthscan.

Slovic, P. (2000b). *Trust, emotion, sex, politics and science.* In P. Slovic, P. (Ed.), *The perception of risk* (pp. 390–412). London: Earthscan.

Starr, S. (2006). Science, risk, and the price of precaution. Retrieved 30 September, 2006, from http://www.spiked-online/Articles/00000006DD7A.htm

Stauber, J, & Rampton, S. (1995). *Toxic sludge is good for you! Lies, damn lies and the public relations industry.* Monroe, ME: Common Courage Press.

Stern, N. (2007). *The economics of climate change: The Stern Review.* Cambridge: Cambridge University Press.

Sunstein, C. R. (2005). *Laws of fear: Beyond the precautionary principle.* Cambridge: Cambridge University Press.

Tait, J., & Bruce, A. (2004). Global change and transboundary risks. In T. McDaniels & M. J. Small (Eds .), *Risk analysis and society: An interdisciplinary characterization of the field* (pp. 367–419). Cambridge: Cambridge University Press, in association with the Society for Risk Analysis.

Tickner, J., & Raffensperger, C., Myers, N. (1999). *The precautionary principle in action: A handbook.* Windsor, ND: Science and Environmental Health Network. Retrieved 21 February, 2006, from http://www.biotech-info.net/handbook.pdf

Ungar, S. (1992). The rise and (relative) decline of global warming as a socia l problem. *The Sociological Quarterly, 33*(4), 483–501.

White, G. (2000). Decision processes: Rationality and adjustment. In P. Slovic, P. (Ed.), *The perception of risk* (p. xv). London: Earthscan.

World Climate Program. (1985) *Report of the international conference on the assessment of the role of carbon dioxide and of other greenhouse gases in climate variations.* Geneva, Switzerland: World Meteorological Association.

20

Risk, Crisis, and Mediated Communication

Kurt Neuwirth
University of Cincinnati

In a world of greater interdependency, globalization and change, the important role of mediated channels to understanding risk and crisis communication processes increasingly is apparent to scholars and concerned citizens alike. Indeed, it is difficult to imagine mediated portrayals of major events or public debates that do not touch upon some aspect of risk. This chapter seeks to 1) sketch several major approaches to mediated communication, 2) underscore their relevance to risk and crisis communication and accentuate possible unifying factors, 3) explore the potential impact of new media, and 4) emphasize areas of potential research.

There are, in addition, several background assumptions informing the discussion below worth noting in detail. First, while some scholars and many practitioners often conceptualize the media's role as a simple transmission mechanism useful for PR and propaganda purposes, this discussion presumes that communication is constitutive (Giddens, 1984), with mediated communication seen as a transaction involving a confluence of participants (sources, channel operators, and receivers) who actively construct social meanings. Second, consistent with the above, is the notion that risk itself is socially constructed (Nelkin, 1989; Stallings, 1990). Third, the discussion assumes that a) crisis communication is a special case of risk communication, b) risk communication is subsumed by public opinion, which incorporates both risk and benefit and incorporates considerations based on objective "real world" conditions and subjective social and cultural factors, c) that public opinion can only be understood by incorporating both macro and micro levels of analysis (Mcleod, Pan, & Rucinski, 1995), and d) the media provide the essential link between individuals and groups and organizations dedicated to political action (Price & Roberts, 1987).

The theoretical perspectives discussed below differ somewhat in the particular micro and macro-level effects they seek to explain, time span referenced, extent of audience activity assumed, degree of social consensus and social conflict associated with a risk, theoretical focus on privileging the sender, receiver, or both, and relative support of or critical stance toward the status quo. However, these theories, except where otherwise noted, share several important features as well, including: spanning more than one level of analysis, an implied or explicit social constructionist stance, and incorporation of interpersonal communication as an integral part of the theory.[1]

INFORMATION DIFFUSION

The direction and flow of information—often known as *diffusion* (Rogers, 1995; Rogers & Kincaid, 1981)—is a topic of longstanding concern among communication scholars. And of all theories of mediated communication, diffusion is most widely known and cited by scholars in allied fields. Briefly, diffusion is a process by which ideas, relevant information, technical practices and commercial products spread throughout a social system. Although time-scales may vary from hours to decades–depending upon what is spreading, be it news about *e-coli* in spinach to the adoption of kindergarten in school curricula—the normal pattern of dispersal resembles an S-shaped curve characterized by a slow start, rapid acceleration, and finally a lengthy deceleration. Researchers use deviations from this "null" pattern as diagnostic tools make inferences about underlying social processes. For example, whereas patterns of incomplete diffusion are suggestive of source constraints (e.g., too low a budget) or receiver-based constraints based on social, cultural and economic factors (Chaffee, 1975), an above "normal" rate of diffusion suggests sources and mediated channels are stimulating information dispersal. Diffusion studies tend to cluster in the areas of innovations and news, and each is taken up in detail below.

Diffusion of Innovations

Diffusion of innovations—new products and social practices, public health measures and medical advances—is characterized by a low level of controversy and high level of consensus regarding the appropriateness of the innovation. The working assumption, not without considerable empirical support, is that the media are most influential in creating initial awareness of an innovation, but that interpersonal influence processes (change agents) are deemed more important in determining actual adoption of an innovation. Researchers have undertaken literally thousands of diffusion studies and many key diffusion concepts have been incorporated into the broader literature on communication campaigns.

It is important to note that the diffusion approach, given its early and widespread influence, has been criticized on several grounds, including a sender-based definition of communication success, a view of the audience as passive, and the assumption of a linear communication flow (Buran & Davis, 2006).

News Diffusion

Studies of news diffusion examine the spread of awareness of "critical events" through a population. As with studies of innovations, news diffusion studies also are characterized by a high degree of consensus regarding an event's importance. What appears to distinguish news diffusion studies is that the events in question involve severe consequences for the social system being studied. With few exceptions, crises are the very template researchers use in their study of *news* diffusion. Wars, assassination attempts, major disasters such as shuttle failures and hurricanes, and attacks on the homeland are all examples of what are known as *critical events* (Chaffee, 1975).

The study of critical events reveals not only how well or poorly authorities discharge their responsibilities, but can also demonstrate how patterns of media coverage serve to condition the public's response. Typically, media performance during a crisis or critical event shifts considerably from what is considered "normal" operation. Mediated channels switch from regular scheduled programming to continuous broadcast coupled with a suspension of commercial content. The increased coverage stimulates rapid information flow throughout the population. Public concern and emotional reactions increase and this provokes greater rates of interpersonal relay. Regardless whether the initial source was mediated or interpersonal communication, people tend to consult mediated channels for confirmation and further information seeking as the crisis unfolds. However, short of a crisis, one also might inquire about public matters that become the subject of debate, and to that end, take up the topic of agenda-setting.

AGENDA-SETTING AND FRAMING

Agenda-Setting

The journalistic practice of reducing the quantity of information received to fit available space and time is known as gatekeeping (Shoemaker & Reese, 1991) and gives rise to agenda-setting—the idea that news story placement conveys to readers and viewers cues about an issue's relative importance or salience. This agenda-setting effect is 1) non-directional insofar as these cues encourage receivers not what to think, but what to think about (McCombs & Shaw, 1972; McCombs, 1982; McCombs, 2005), 2) may be or may not be intentional on the media's part, and 3) spans the micro and macro levels of analysis. The agenda-setting literature itself is robust, with hundreds of published studies appearing under that rubric since its inception, and the term itself is one of the few to migrate from a specialized academic lexicon to common usage in contemporary political discourse (see Dearing & Rogers, 1996; Kosicki, 1993, for reviews).

At the individual level the media are thought to influence *intrapersonal* (one's own salience judgments) agendas, *perceived community* (what others in the community consider important) agendas, and *interpersonal* (actual discussion of issues) agendas (Mcleod, Becker & Byrnes, 1974). As a general proposition, agenda-setting studies, particularly those exploring perceived community agendas, have received broad, although not perfect, support. In response, researchers have offered at least two contingent conditions considered particularly conducive to strong agenda-setting effects; both of which are linked to audience experience and circumstances. First, issues should be assessed in relation to a person's level of experience with the topic. Issues are considered *obtrusive* (Zucker, 1978) when audience experience is high (e.g., gasoline prices) and *unobtrusive* when respondents' experience is low (e.g., environmental regulations), with the media showing greater influence for unobtrusive issues. Second, a person's *need for orientation* (Weaver, 1977) stems from higher levels of 1) *uncertainty* about, and 2) *interest* in an issue (e.g., an unknown substance found in local water supplies is making people sick), and it is these two factors combined that enhance an agenda-setting effect. Of course, external events that are highly uncertain and are of major consequence, are likely to increase a person's need for orientation, and thus judgments about issue importance are likely to be maximized during times of great moment and crisis.

In addition, judgments about an issue's relative salience or importance involve cognitive estimates of risk and emotional reactions such as fear and worry evoked by the hazard or problem at hand (Dunwoody & Neuwirth, 1991). The exact functional relationship of these elements to salience estimates is, at present,unknown, but elements of mediated content (e.g., portrayal of severe, unndesirable consequences) have been shown to give rise to both risk and worry estimates (Dunwoody et al., 1992), a finding consistent with a multidimensional view of risk (Slovic, 1992) entailing the knowability of and dread about a risk.

The macro-level view of agenda-setting entails the study of three distinct yet interdependent agendas: media (issues stressed by the media), public (problems the public believes are important), and policy (topics considered important by executive and legislative incumbents, as well as those seeking to influence government actions). Although these elements are interrelated, researchers typically have studied only one of these relationships (e.g., media and presidential agendas) at a time and, given the intellectual interests of media scholars, it is not surprising that most research activity has examined how the media influence the public's agenda.

The findings suggest several noteworthy points. First, a minimal amount of media coverage (Newman, 1990) is necessary for an issue to achieve prominence as an important problem. Second, although there is an upper limit to the number of issues considered as important, and even though issues must "compete" for a place on the public agenda or risk being displaced, the number of issues on an agenda can vary (Hertog, Finnegan, & Kahn, 1994). Third, the various media demonstrate high levels of agreement concerning issue importance (Atwater, Fico, & Pizante, 1987). Fourth, print media, in particular the wire services and the prestige press such as the *New York Times* tend to influence electronic media agendas (Atwater et al., 1987). Finally, smaller community size appears to mitigate local media influence on community agendas due to greater rates of interpersonal discussion (Atwater, Salwen, & Anderson, 1985). Indeed, reverse causal direction is more likely in smaller communities, that is, the public agenda in smaller communities is more likely to influence the local media's agenda (Schweitzer & Smith, 1991) rather than the reverse.

Given the robustness of research findings in this area, it is not surprising that research focusing on risk and environmental issues also demonstrates that variations in the frequency of media coverage are associated with increases and decreases in public concern (Trumbo, 1995, Mazur, 2006). Perhaps more interesting is research showing a *lack* of convergence when comparing real-world indicators of hazards and problems with media coverage (Funkhauser, 1973; Ader, 1995). This null relationship between real-world and media generated agendas, coupled with a more direct correspondence of media and audience agendas, has several implications for risk and crisis scholars. First, if any further evidence were needed, this overall pattern is consistent with the view that risk, through the media or otherwise, is socially constructed (Nelkin, 1989). Second, these findings also suggest that peoples' reactions to risk and crisis information is "rational" in that it is responsive to the information presented in the media. Third, the broader question of the media's provision of content at variance with real-world "facts" remains unresolved, particularly for scholars and policymakers seeing a close alignment of these agendas as desirable. Some scholars have argued that such "bias" is a direct result of the media's use of sensationalism in the pursuit of larger audiences, profits, and industry consolidation (McChesney, 2004) and/or ideological tilt (Lewis, 2001). Regardless whether one accepts these arguments and gives credence to the causal mechanisms that they imply, the issue of an "agenda gap" between real-world indicators and media portrayals of hazards, as well as large differences between expert and lay estimates of risk remains, and achieving possible remedies to these gaps remains both vital and open.

Media Framing

More recently, researchers (see McCombs, 2005) have distinguished two levels of agenda-setting. First-order agenda-setting, as outlined above, involves media-suggested importance assigned to issues (so-called objects), whereas second-order agenda-setting entails the media suggesting to the public the dimensions or attributes by which *each* issue should be evaluated. Although at least one study (Kim, Scheufele, & Shanahan, 2002) has been conducted, at this juncture, no research examining mediated portrayals of risk and crisis events and second-order (attribute) agenda setting have been conducted. McCombs (2005) also has advanced the view that second-order agenda setting is equivalent to what other scholars have termed *framing* (Gamson, 1992: Reese et al., 2001).

Although many risk communication researchers likely are familiar with Kanheman and Tversky's (1974) notion of framing a message in terms of loss and gain, or of framing as a general strategy of message production (Entman, 1993), it is important to note that other scholars (e.g., Scheufele, 1999; Pan & Kosicki, 1993) argue that framing 1) is more than a simple message design strategy, but rather is a social process that crosses levels of analysis and, 2) is distinct from second-order agenda-setting since framing involves priming of an entire perspective or framework rather than elements within an issue.

The relationship between agenda-setting and framing is most well-developed by Nisbet and colleagues (Nisbet, Brossard, & Kroepsch, 2003; Nisbet & Huge, 2006), who have argued that issues develop in alternating cycles of media coverage. Lower levels of media attention to an issue are associated with the use of technical and administrative framing, with participation limited to a relatively narrow set of directly interested stakeholders. A precipitating event frequently shifts media attention, provoking 1) increased rates of media coverage, 2) shifts in media content to the overt use of dramatic frames emphasizing wider social conflict and ethical concerns surrounding the issue, and 3) participation in discourse by a broadened set of actors, often including the general public.

It is important to note that, although the debate about how frames function at the individual level is ongoing, and its ultimate resolution will be of great importance to scholars. However findings concerning macro processes entailing issue cycles and the ways in which the public becomes engaged by an issue, although somewhat tentative, show the greatest potential for guiding future research.

KNOWLEDGE GAP

As people become aware of an issue, it also seems reasonable to examine how much they might be learning, a topic which has emerged under the rubric of knowledge gap. Research into the role played by the media in communities has given rise to the Knowledge Gap hypothesis (Ettema & Kline, 1977; Tichenor, Donohue, & Olien, 1980; Gaziano, 1983), a systems based approach that refers to patterned differences of information levels between different strata or groups in communities of different sizes, themselves considered subsystems within state, regional or national systems. The theory posits that under normal or "consensus" conditions, the "information rich"—elites with high educational attainment and/or wealth—are more knowledgeable about an issue than are those of lower socioeconomic status (SES). The passage of time exacerbates the situation, as high SES groups acquire knowledge at a more rapid rate than do lower SES persons who have not have attended quality schools or whose access to mediated channels is limited. As a general proposition, then, knowledge gaps are thought to increase over time, and as McQuail (2005, p. 492) noted, basic social inequalities likely are the source of many gaps, which, realistically, the media cannot be expected to change.

However, research does suggest that two factors influence media so as to narrow knowledge gaps, the first centering on coverage of social conflict by the media and the second, more distal, involves elements of community structure as they influence media coverage. The former case is straightforward; media coverage of conflict in a community increases learning through greater rates of media exposure, attention to media fare, and processing of information.

The latter argument is more complex, and centers on community size and the media's "embeddedness" in a community. Larger, more pluralistic communities are characterized by greater diversity, a larger number of interest and occupational groups, and politics is characterized by competition and coalition politics.

Greater community complexity means that interpersonal channels are not adequate carriers of knowledge, and citizens are dependent on the media for knowledge of public affairs. And owners, editors, and reporters attain status and influence in the community by covering conflict and strife. Conversely, smaller, more homogeneous communities tend to operate more on the basis of a "consensus" model where local community elites, including those in the media, operate out of a sense of community boosterism involving conflict minimization and suppression, with press coverage completely absent or limited to providing minimal information about growing conflicts. Consequently, persons in these smaller communities often are forced to access information from larger regional media, which cover the conflict in greater detail.

The original knowledge gap research was conducted in Minnesota covering controversies such as environmental pollution and placement of high voltage lines and has been replicated in other locations (Dunwoody & Rossow, 1989; Griffin & Dunwoody, 1997), applied to opinions and opinion holding (Olien, Donohue, & Tichenor, 1995), and extended into ancillary areas such as health and politics (see Visvanath & Finnegan, 1996; Gaziano & Gaziano, 1996 for extended reviews).

Channel differences between print and TV have been found, with print exposure appearing to favor highly educated groups whereas exposure to television news, because of its widespread use and acceptance by lower SES groups, would appear to narrow existing gaps (Robinson, 1972; Shingi & Mody, 1976). More recent research suggests countervailing trends may be operating, dependent upon conflict levels. Knowledge gaps do narrow for contested national issues such as presidential elections (Holbrook, 2002), yet research examining Internet use (Bonfadelli, 2002) suggests that patterns of exposure under normal conditions tend to widen existing gaps between those who are more or less affluent. Whether the Internet might function as a source of outside information when more traditional mediated channels may be attempting to "put a lid" on local controversies is an open question.

The broader implication for risk and crisis communication is that the knowledge gap literature challenges the commonly held view that social conflict is something that is negative and to be avoided; widely publicizing a conflict can have the salutary effect—one consistent with the democratic ideal of an informed citizenry—of increasing knowledge levels for everyone in a community or larger social system.

Media Dependency

Beyond basic knowledge, the extent to which the well-being of a social system and its citizens hinges upon media performance is a theme that has come to be termed media dependency. Media Dependency Theory (Ball-Rokeach & DeFleur, 1976; Ball-Rokeach, 1985) is a systems-based framework integrating macro and micro levels of analysis that provides an account of variations in societal structure, media functioning, and audience response, particularly in times of social change and crisis. For individuals, dependency is considered the degree to which a person *relies* on the media (or a particular medium) to meet his/her goals. Dependency, at least in part, is the degree to which a particular channel or group of channels satisfies the central needs of individuals, with variations in channel content and individual needs (e.g., surveillance, acting effectively, entertainment) combining to produce effects. As a general proposition, greater reliance on any one channel or the media as a whole implies greater media influence.

At the societal level, media institutions shape their content streams to serve receiver needs and maintain their competitiveness. And as an urbanized and post-industrial society becomes more complex and interpersonal social networks become less influential, greater numbers of people come to rely increasingly on the media for the completion of essential tasks. Under such circumstances, the media's role becomes increasingly central as society and its citizens become almost completely dependent upon media systems for effective and efficient operation.

A second source of dependency stems from changing conditions inherent in processes of structural change occurring in a society. Structural stability is not a constant, but varies with changing circumstances, particularly in times of exacerbated conflict, social change, and crisis. Typically, such circumstances mean that people will experience a greater need for information and interpretation of events, and their use of and dependency upon the media will increase. The clear implication is that media influence is most likely to be strongest during times of crisis, and more limited during normal and routine circumstances. The greatest challenge for researchers utilizing this theoretical framework has been to find relatively rare instances in which the theory can be tested. In one study (Ball-Rokeach, 1998), change in media coverage of Vietnam War news produced generalized scepticism about the war, provoking greater dependency on the media for information about the war, and greater interpersonal discussion of the war. More recent work (Matei & Ball-Rokeach, 2003; Ball-Rokeach, Kim, & Matei, 2001) suggests that community storytelling, reinforced by media infrastructure, provides essential links to the broader society and inculcate a sense of community belonging. Although not addressed, the more recent findings strongly suggest that storytelling and narrative in communities likely influence collective responses to risk and crises. The direct application of Media Dependency Theory to risk and crisis communication would appear to be a good fit, particularly in the case of crisis communication. Yet to date, many communication researchers, and the wider risk research community, have not taken advantage of this opportunity.

SPIRAL OF SILENCE

Although it is well-established that the media can and do influence estimates of risk, what individuals do with these estimates, in particular interpersonal relay of information and opinion, has been found to be influenced by media-generated impressions of the social environment. That impressions can serve to facilitate discussion and debate is a widely-held assumption consonant with normative democratic theory. Yet it is also possible to suppose that some aspects of media coverage may serve to inhibit free-wheeling public debate, and it is toward the possibility of opinion suppression that the Spiral of Silence is directed.

Originally developed in an effort to account for macro-level fluctuations in polling data of German elections the Spiral of Silence (Noelle-Neumann, 1984; Noelle-Neumann,1991; Noelle-Neumann & Petersen, 2004) theory posits that the media, through mechanisms such as agenda-setting, framing and selective provision of content (opinion columns, editorials, letters to the editor, visual characterization of crowd at a demonstration, and the like), creates a "climate of opinion"—a potentially inaccurate if not false impression—from which individuals estimate the prevalence of viewpoints surrounding controversial, value-laden issues. Individuals, motivated by an aversion for becoming socially isolated, are less inclined to give their actual views on an issue when they perceive that their opinion is contradicted by that of the majority.

The accumulation of research through the 1990s lead to the prevailing view that the silencing effect attributable to perceptions of majority opinion was small in magnitude (Glynn, Hayes, & Shanahan, 1997). More recently, however, this area has seen a resurgence in activity as researchers shifted the focus of their efforts to an examination of the role fear of isolation (Scheufele, Shanahan, & Lee, 2001), factors inhibiting and enhancing opinion expression (Neuwirth & Frederick, 2004), and assessing conformity-based avoidance of opinion expression (Neuwirth, Frederick, & Mayo, in press).

The relevance to risk and crisis communication is straightforward: Pressures toward conformity—with attendant amplification and attenuation of perceived risks across time promulgated by the media—are most likely to occur during major crises and during highly contentious debates about policy alternatives. For those viewing mediated channels as simple transmission mechanisms, this may not seem problematic, and indeed may represent welcome opportunities for partisan advantage. However, for those regarding mediated communication from a transactional or critical perspective, the potential for premature closure or outright truncation of robust debate based on the Enlightenment ideal unbridled discourse likely will be viewed with some trepidation. To date, several studies have utilized the Spiral of Silence framework to study relevant topics such as genetically modified foods (Scheufele, Shanahan, & Lee, 2001) and biotechnology (Priest, 2006), and there is every indication that this area will provide opportunities for future research and insights, particularly when circumstances surrounding an issue are emotionally (e.g., Sandman, 1993) and morally charged.

CULTIVATION

So far the discussion has centered on theoretical approaches to news and public affairs content considered important to public debate and discourse. Yet it is apparent to even the casual observer that mediated content, especially TV and cable, is dominated by entertainment fare. The bulk of research examining entertainment content has examined shorter-term, individual-level effects.

Traditionally, approaches to entertainment have focused on factors leading to individuals' program choice and enjoyment (Rosengren, 1985; Ruggiero, 2000), factors associated with emotional reaction (pleasure) to typical narrative structure (Bryant & Zillmann, 1991), and imitation (Bandura, 1986). Relevant here too is the idea that a single exposure (e.g., exposure to the film *Jaws* and fear of sharks) can have a long-lasting, memorable influence—the so-called drench effect (Greenberg, 1988; Bahk, 2001).

Somewhat in contrast is the Cultivation approach promulgated by Gerbner and colleagues (Signorelli & Morgan, 1990; Gerbner, Gross, Morgan, Signorelli, & Shanahan, 2002), who approach the media's—particularly television's—longer-term, cumulative influence on the distribution and concentration of fundamental beliefs about social reality from a critical perspective. Cultivation assumes that television itself is ubiquitous and that its entertainment content (including cable fare) is highly constrained by the requirement that dramatic content (high status, beautiful people in exotic locations facing danger and negotiating risky situations) appeal to a mass audience in a commercial context. When compared to actual statistics, content analysis of typical programming reveals that these portrayals present a distorted picture of the social world: over-representation of males, high status professions, crime, disease, and natural and human-generated hazards. These TV-generated biases about elements of the world carry though to peoples' beliefs, as evidenced by numerous studies (mostly correlational) showing a positive correlation between hours spent watching television and beliefs consonant with a "TV worldview." Moreover, television content also is thought to lower the expectation about others' good behavior and is characterized by an outlook named a "Mean World syndrome."

Researchers (Hawkins & Pingree, 1990) have distinguished between first-order beliefs—cognitions about the frequency that an event will occur (e.g., likelihood of becoming involved in a plane crash), from second-order beliefs—broader ideas about the general nature of the world, and work continues as researchers attempt to refine the cognitive processes operating at the individual level (Tapper, 1995, Shrum, 1995; Bilandic, 2006).

In addition, two other Cultivation processes are worth noting. The first, named *resonance*, is an individual level effect occurring when fictional content coincides with a person's actual experience or real world events (e.g., terrorist threat of a nuclear attack, as portrayed in the movie *True Lies*, before and after the events of 9-11-2001). The second, termed *mainstreaming*, is a societal-level effect in which viewers, particularly those most exposed to television, become homogenized in their beliefs about the world.

As alluded to above, the relationship of communication about a crisis–from a news and entertainment content perspective, is most closely related to a drench effect (Greenberg, 1988), which posits that a single exposure to a sufficiently memorable stimulus forever alters knowledge and attitudes about a particular object or situation (e.g., sharks and exposure to the film *Jaws*). However, it is Cultivation's emphasis on the longer-term, cumulative effects of media influence that researchers may find particularly useful in that we can see a more direct link between mediated exposure and beliefs about and emotional reactions to hazards. For example, exposure to entertainment fare and first-order beliefs about the frequency of objectively rare events is likely to shape the background and contextual cognitions and emotional states that persons implicitly incorporate when confronting a hazard. And resonance can be seen as amplifying perceptions of risk. This point is particularly relevant, given that some researchers long have lamented the empirical finding of a gap between lay and expert risk estimates. Indeed scholars might do well to consider the possibility that entertainment, not news content as so often is supposed, may be the broadest and most extensive source of risk and hazard information available to the general population.

A possible link between Mean World—beliefs entailing a form of general social distrust studied by Cultivation scholars—and research suggesting that social trust (Slovic, 1993; Earle & Cvetkovich,1995) functions as key mediating variable in risk communication, is a connection that often is unappreciated by researchers. Yet second-order beliefs—general beliefs and attitudes about the world and how it functions (termed *Mean World*)—have been indexed by statements invoking an expectation of the worst in others. Conceptually, Mean World seems to be broader in scope than current ideas about social trust, which appear reference the adequate performance of those charged with managing hazards. The extent to which Mean World distrust overlaps empirically with research examining social trust is an open question, but one well worth exploring. In addition, researchers working within the Cultivation framework may indeed find that social trust (of institutional and incumbent role performance) is predominantly influenced by mediated entertainment content.

THE STORY SO FAR

If one were to put the theories and approaches of mediated communication about risk and crisis into a broader story-line, the narrative might unfold something like this: Many of the general notions that people develop about risk, hazards and whether authorities charged with their management can be trusted come not only from news accounts, but from the entertainment programs they see (Cultivation). By dint of seeing similar programs, many people develop general and fairly uniform worldviews that they apply to hazards (mainstreaming). When news about real-world hazards corresponds closely to dramatic narratives people have seen, the effect is amplified (resonance), whereas when news runs counter to popular understandings, influence may be lessened. But the news media are influential as well, particularly when it comes to more immediate responses to risk and crises; throughout, the factors that seem to matter most are the degree of social conflict involved, and how severe the problem is. When conflict is low and there is consensus on how to manage risk, then hazards often are handled by regulatory agencies. An example would be routine garbage disposal. Media coverage is fairly low, restricted to reporting on official actions; there is no conflict frame for journalists to utilize as an organizing principle for their stories. Should the consequences become greater and social consensus hold, one finds that the media play a larger role, as socially approved messages are sent to citizens who are most affected by the hazard in question (diffusion of innovations). An instance can be seen in a campaign directed at early breast cancer detection via self-examination techniques. As the magnitude of the hazard becomes severe, socially agreed upon messages are sent urgently and frequently via news channels (news diffusion) to inform the public of some kind of imminent danger. News about contaminated spinach causing severe illness or death or a terrorist attack exemplify this kind of situation.

As consensus breaks down and social conflict increases and/or because the outcomes are more consequential, other processes—and applicable theories—come to the fore. A minimal amount of social conflict serves as a "threshold" for the media to cover stories about risk and hazard (Framing). At first only an interested few—often the highly educated or well-off—are likely to pay much attention to and form opinions about an issue (knowledge-gap). But as people become increasingly aware of an issue's importance (agenda-setting), they start to pay closer attention, and earlier differences in knowledge and opinion holding lessen or disappear entirely. In such a situation, all citizens in a community can work towards attaining agreement on how to proceed using the same set of agreed-upon "facts."

But sometimes resolution of an issue does not come easily (e.g., abortion, or radioactive waste depository). The community, state, or nation becomes polarized and competing groups and partisans start to apply moral criteria (right and wrong) to opponents and become coercive in their tactics. The media present cues about majority sentiment and how "dangerous" expressing an opinion might be. People become fearful of expressing their opinion (spiral of silence) and fall silent, thereby diminishing the overall quality of discourse.

Crisis can be found at the extreme range of consequence, conflict or both. And it is during a crisis that media's influence is most important (dependency theory). Under such severe conditions, both society and individuals find themselves at the apex of their dependency on mediated communication. Individuals rely on the media for essential information and guidance. And the media are essential for authorities in their coordination efforts as they mobilize society's resources to respond to an emergency. During a crisis, there appears to be a greater emphasis on maintaining a social consensus in support of authorities.

The media, too, are more likely to be supportive of the authority's efforts and to mute possible criticisms, and this tendency appears to be reflected in public sentiment (spiral of silence) as well.

NEW TECHNOLOGY AND FUTURE RESEARCH

The introduction of newer mediated technologies carries with it a series of implications for risk and crisis communication and theories about media. Recent trends include increased availability of information via the Internet, greater connectivity and a rise in mobility due to portable devices (Kurzweil, 2005), all of which combine to challenge established ways of delivering mediated content. Although the final outcomes cannot be known at present—indeed several countervailing tendencies appear to operate simultaneously—the significance of certain developments, representing an admixture of system—and individual-level changes for both theory and practice, slowly are becoming apparent. Some of these developments directly influence risk and crisis communication, whereas others serve as more general background influences. And, it's important to underscore that many of the points about new media sketched below are conjectural, if not contradictory. Ultimately, though, they can and should be the object of productive empirical examination.

Perhaps foremost among these changes are issues surrounding access to and the quality of information about hazards. One might suppose that Title III SARA information posted on the Web would be of great interest to organizations (including the press) and individuals concerned about the level of chemical discharges in a community. Indeed, this development portends the potential for higher levels of information diffusion and narrowing of knowledge-gaps. However, national security concerns stemming from the "war on terror" have eliminated the public availability of information deemed useful to terrorists. In addition, political considerations directed at lessening regulatory "burdens" have reduced the frequency in which discharge reports are filed, thus causing any data base to be less current. Thus, governmental control and regulation of the information store associated with SARA suggests that knowledge levels about chemical discharges in a local community are likely to decline due to self-imposed source constraints, and decision-making about chemical discharges is likely to be restricted to a limited number of elite actors. The upshot is that a media system can only be as good—understood as the provision of adequate and necessary information for effective participation—as the basic information that is available. A related concern focuses on media ownership (McChesney, 2004), namely, that a pattern of increased concentration has lead to the production of content designed to maximize profit at the expense of adequately representing the full range of public interest and opinion on matters of common concern, thereby shrinking the public sphere and possibilities of participation. A convergence of content, as implied by ownership concentration, also suggests that agenda-setting and cultivation effects will be more uniform than in the past.

While the above is derived from normative democratic expectations, a further implication of the media's concentration of ownership can be drawn when considering entertainment programming. As media concentration increases, one would expect that standardization and uniformity of content also will increase, and one can easily suppose that the use of plot devices employing a plethora of hazards and risks (as outlined above) will continue unabated. This portends that Cultivation effects also will, if not increase, certainly endure.

However, the existence of the Internet itself provides hints of several countervailing processes, particularly as many of the older media are eclipsed as the new medium assumes a predominant role in peoples' lives. First, greater choice exercised by Internet users suggests a developing trend toward greater audience fragmentation. Such a development is likely to mean that it will be less likely that people will share common informational and cultural experiences, thus making social coordination more difficult. And as a result, people may find that fewer matters will be seen as common concerns and problems and so a fairly high threshold will be needed for all issues to be considered as part of an agenda.

Greater use of mobile devices and increased Internet connectivity likely will mean faster rates of diffusion for those issues that are considered important. And the increased use of technology also intimates that social system dependency, and individual level reliance on mediated channels will increase over time.

Greater interconnectivity has produced (e.g., Ned Lamont campaign) and will continue to generate new forms of social organization that can easily connect people based on interest and experience with groups confronting risks and crises situations. And recently the Internet has given rise to some of the most popular sites (e.g., YouTube, Myspace, and the like) ever seen, where content—from simple blogs to videos—is created and shared by and among users. This last form is of great interest, since it represents a potential challenge the authority of established media organizations. Traditionally, journalists have vetted information by fact checking procedures designed to weed out rumor and speculation. People creating a blog or a vlog are under no such restrictions. Under ordinary circumstances, established facts have time emerge from a background welter of gossip and conjecture. However, in crisis situations, where facts are scarce but ambiguity and uncertainty are at their highest levels, one might suspect that rumors will be greatly amplified and viral-diffuse throughout the "blogosphere."

The Internet also is likely to influence the Spiral of Silence. Certainly Internet access makes it easier to find information bolstering ones's arguments and enhances ones ability to garner social support for one's position. On the other hand, the organizing potential of the Internet may make it easier to rally people against someone or some position, thus increasing the coercive potential of the social environment.

A commensurate shift to greater access and user control of information means that theoretical inquiry about patterns of information search and seeking behaviors (Griffin, Dunwoody, & Neuwirth, 1999; Trumbo, 1998) will become an increasingly important topic of study. Research also is likely to focus on the extent to which mediated channels themselves facilitate information seeking and processing—a form of information subsidy designed to direct a user's attention (Gandy, 1993).

There are two further points to be made in summary. First, research on the media and some aspect of risk or crisis communication usually is conducted from the perspective of a single theory or approach. At present, no one has attempted to examine risk and crisis communication using several theories, if not simultaneously, then in conjunction with one another. Yet this is certainly possible. Missing ingredients appear include: work on theoretical integration, imagination, and, of course, resources. All of which raises the question: If one were to study risk and crisis communication using several theories of media, how much influence might we find? The answer, one suspects, is: a lot.

Finally, the discussion above should make it clear that most, if not all risk communication has some public opinion and policy component and involves discourse directed at the social construction of risk and social efforts in response to risk. Considering risk and crisis communication as part of larger public opinion processes allows scholars 1) to go beyond an overly simplified accounts of the media as simple conduits that facilitate the transmission of facts concerning objective elements of mortality and morbidity, 2) to consider a range of theories that implicate political, social, and cultural values that people commonly consider when forming opinions about the risks and crises they face, and the actions they consider, and ultimately take.

NOTE

1. There are, of course, aspects of mediated communication not covered in this chapter but are treated elsewhere in this volume, or otherwise lie outside of the purview of this book. These include: Message effects (see chapter 8, this volume), and journalistic practices related to the production of risk information (see Friedman, Dunwoody, & Rogers, 1999).

BIBLIOGRAPHY

Ader, C. A. (1995). A longitudinal study of agenda setting for the issue of environmental pollution. *Journalism and Mass Communication Quarterly, 72*(2), 300–311.

Atwater, T., Fico, F., & Pizante, G. (1987). Reporting on the state legislature: A case study of inter-media agenda-setting. *Newspaper Research Journal, 8*(2), 53–61.

Atwater, T., Salwen, M. B., & Anderson. (1985). Media agenda-setting with environmental issues. *Journalism Quarterly, 62,* 393–397.

Atwater, T., Salwen, M. B., & Anderson, R. B. (1985). Interpersonal discussion as a potential barrier to agenda setting. *Newspaper Research Journal, 6*(4), 37–43.

Bahk, C. M. (2001). Drench effects of media portrayal of fatal virus disease on health locus of control beliefs. *Health Communication, 13*(2), 187–204.

Ball-Rokeach, S. J. (1985). The origins of individual media system dependency: A sociological framework. *Communication Research, 12,* 485–510.

Ball-Rokeach, S. J. (1998). A theory of media power and a theory of media use: Different stories, questions, and ways of thinking. *Mass Communications & Society,* 1(1-2), 5–40.

Ball-Rokeach, S. J., Kim, Y., & Matei. (2001). Storytelling neighborhood: Paths to belonging in diverse urban environments. *Communication Research, 28,* 392–428.

Ball-Rokeach, S. L., & DeFleur, M. L. (1976). A dependency model of mass media effects. *Communication Research, 3,* 3–21.

Bandura, A. (1986). *Social foundations of thought and action: A social cognitive theory.* Englewood Cliffs, NJ: Prentice-Hall.

Bilandzic, H. (2006). The perception of distance in the cultivation process: A theoretical consideration of the relationship between television content, processing experience, and perceived distance. *Communication Theory, 16*(3), 333–355.

Bonfadelli, H. (2002). The internet and knowledge gaps: A theoretical and empirical investigation. *European Journal of Communication, 17,* 65–85.

Bryant, J., & Zillman Dolf (Eds). (1991). *Responding to the screen: Reception and reaction processes.* Mahwah, NJ: Erlbaum.

Buran, S. J., & Davis, D. K. (2006). *Mass communication theory: Foundations, ferment, and future.* Belmont, CA: Thompson Higher Education.

Chaffee, S. H. (1975). The diffusion of political information. In S. H. Chaffee (Ed.), *Political communication: Issues and strategies for research* (pp. 85–128). Beverly Hills, CA: Sage.

Dearing, J. W., & Rogers, E. M. (1996). *Agenda Setting.* Beverly Hills, CA: Sage.

Dunwoody, S., & Neuwirth, K. (1991). Coming to terms with the impact of communication on scientific and technological risk judgments. In L. Wilkins & P. Patterson (Eds.), *Risky business: Communicating issues of science, risk, and public policy* (pp. 11–30). New York: Greenwood Press.

Dunwoody, S., & Rossow, M. (19??). Community pluralism and newspaper coverage of a high-level nuclear waste siting issue. In L. A. Grunug (Ed.), *Environmental activism revisited. Monographs in Environmnetal Education and Environmental Studies, 5,* 5–21.

Dunwoody, S., Neuwirth, K., Griffin, R. J., & Long, M. (1992). The impact of risk message content and construction on comments about risks embedded in "Letters to friends." *Journal of Language and Social Psychology, 11,* 9–33.

Earle, T. C., & Cvetkovich, G. T. (1995). *Social trust: Toward a cosmopolitan society.* Westport, CT: Praeger Publishers.

Entman, R. M. (1993). Framing: Toward a clarification of a fractured paradigm. *Journal of Communication, 43*(4), 51–58.

Ettema, J. S., & Kline, F. G. (1977). Deficits, differences, and ceilings: Contingent conditions for understanding the knowledge gap. *Communication Research, 4*(2), 179–202.

Friedman, S. M., Dunwoody, S., & Rogers, C. L. (Eds.). (1999). *Communicating Undertainty: Media coverage of new and controversial science.* Mahway, NJ: Erlbaum.

Funkhauser, G. R. (1973, The issues of the sixties: An exploratory study of the dynamics of public opinion). *Public Opinion Quarterly, 37*(1), 62–75.

Gamson, W. A. (1989). News as framing. *American Behavioral Scientist, 33,* 157–161.

Gamson, W. A. (1992). *Talking politics.* Cambridge: Cambridge University Press.

Gandy, J., Oscar. (1993). *The panoptic: A political economy of personal information.* Boulder, CO: Westview Press.

Gaziano, C., & Gaziano, E. (1996). Theories and methods in knowledge gap research since 1970. In M. B. Salwen & D. W. stacks (Eds.), *An integrated approach to communication theory and research* (pp. 127–144). Mahway, NJ: Erlbaum.

Gaziano, C. (1983). The knowledge gap: An analytical review of media effects. *Communication Research, 10*(4), 447–486.

Gerbner, G., Gross, L., Morgan, M., Signorelli, N., & Shanahan, J. (2002). Growing up with television: Cultivation Processes. In J. Bryant & D. Zillmann (Eds.), *Media Effects: Advances in theory and research* (pp. 43–68). Hillsdale, NJ: Erlbaum.

Giddens, A. (1984). *The constitution of society: Outline of the theory of structuration.* Berkeley: University of California Press.

Glynn, C. J., Hayes, A. F., & Shanahan, J. (1997). Perceived support for one's opinions and willingness to speak out: A meta-analysis of survey studies on the "spiral of silence." *Public Opinion Quarterly, 61,* 452–463.

Greenberg, B. S. (1988). Some uncommon television images and the drench hypothesis. In S. Oskamp (Ed.), *Applied Social Psychology Annual, Vol. 8* (pp. 88–102). Beverly Hills: Sage.

Griffin, R. J., & Dunwoody, S. (1997). Community structure and science framing of news about local environmental risks. *Science Communication, 18*(4), 362–384.

Griffin, R. J., Dunwoody, S., & Neuwirth, K. (1999). A proposed model of the relationship of risk information seeking and processing to the development of preventive behaviors. *Environmental Research, 80*(2), S230–245.

Hawkins, R. P., & Pingree, S. (1990). Divergent psychological process in constructing social reality from mass media content. In N. Signorielli & M. Morgan (Eds.), *Cultivation analysis: New directions in media effects research* (pp. 35–50). Newbury Park, CA: Sage.

Hertog, J., Finnegan, J., & Kahn, E. (1994). Media coverage of AIDS, cancer, and sexually transmitted diseases: A test of the public arenas model. *Journalism Quarterly, 71*(2), 291–304.

Holbrook, T. M. (2002). Presidential campaigns and the knowledge gap. *Political Communication, 19,* 437–465.

Kahneman, D., & Tversky, A. (1974). Judgment under uncertainty: Heuristics and biases. *Science, 185,* 1124–1131.

Kosicki, G. M. (1993). Problems and opportunities in agenda-setting research. *Journal of Communication, 43,* 100–127.

Kim, S-H, Scheufele, D. A., & Shanahan, J. (2002). Think about it this way: Attribute agenda-setting function of the press and the public's evaluation of a local issue. *Journalism & Mass Communication Quarterly, 79*(1), 7–25.

Lewis, J. (2001). *Constructing public opinion: How political elites do what they like and why we seem to along with it.* New York: Columbia University Press.

Matei, S., & Ball-Rokeach, S. (2003). Th internet in the communication infrastructure of urban residential communities: Macro- or Mesoliknage? *Journal of Communication, 53,* 642–658.

Mazur, A. (2006). Risk perception and news coverage across nations. *Risk Management, 8,* 1–26.

McChesney, R. W. (2004). *The problem of the media: U. S. communication politics in the 21st century.* New York: Monthly Review Press.

McCombs, M. (2005). A look at agenda-setting: Past, present and future. *Journalism Studies, 6*(4), 543–557.

McCombs, M. E. (1982). The agenda-setting approach. In D. D. Nimmo & K. R. Sanders (Eds.), *Handbook of political communication* (pp. 121–140). Beverly Hills, CA: Sage.

McCombs, M. E., & Shaw, D. L. (1972). The agenda-setting function of the mass media. *Public Opinion Quarterly, 36,* 176–187.

McLeod, J. M. B., Lee B., & Byrnes, J. E. (1974). Another look at the agenda-setting function of the press. *Communication Research, 1,* 131–166.

McLeod, J., & Pan, Z., Rucinski. (1995). Levels of analysis in public opinion research. In T. L. Glasser & C. T. Salmon (Eds.), *Public opinion and the communication of consent* (pp. 55–85). New York: Guilford.

McQuail, D. (2005). *McQail's mass communication theory.* Thousand Oaks, CA: Sage.

Nelkin, D. (1989). Communication technological risk: The social construction of risk perception. *Annual Review of Public Health, 10,* 95–113.

Neuwirth, K., Frederick, E., & Mayo, C. (In press). The spiral of silence and fear of isolation. *Journal of Communication.*

Neuwirth, K., & Frederick, E. (2004). Peer and social influence on opinion expression: Combining the theories of planned behavior and the spiral of silence. *Communication Research, 31*(6), 669–703.

Newman, W. R. (1990). The threshold of public attention. *Public Opinion Quarterly, 54,* 159–176.

Nisbet, M. C., Brossard, D., & Kroepsch, A. (2003). Framing science: The stem cell controversy in an age of press/politics. *The Harvard International Journal of Press/Politics, 8*(2), 36–70.

Nisbet, M. C., & Huge, M. (2006). Attention cycles and frames in the plant biotechnology debate. *The Harvard International Journal of Press/Politics, 11*(2), 3–40.

Noelle-Neumann, E. (1984). *The spiral of silence: Our social skin.* Chicago, IL: University of Chicago Press.

Noelle-Neumann, E. (1991). The theory of public opinion: The concept of the spiral of silence. In J. A. Anderson (Ed.), *Communication Yearbook 14* (pp. 256–287). Newbury Park, CA: Sage.

Noelle-Neumann, E., & Petersen. (2004). The spiral of silence and the social nature of man. In L. L. Kaid (Ed.), *Handbook of political communication research* (pp. 339–356). Mahwah, NJ: Erlbaum.

Olien, C. N., Donohue, G. A., & Tichenor, P. J. (1995). Conflict, consensus and public opinion. In T. L. Glasser & Salmon Charles T. (Eds.), *Public opinion and the communication of consent* (pp. 301–322). New York: Guilford.

Pan, Z., & Kosicki, G. M. (1993). Framing analysis: An approach to news discourse. *Political Communication, 10,* 55–75.

Price, V., & Roberts, D. F. (1987). Public opinion processes. In C. Berger & S. H. Chaffee (Eds.), *Handbook of communication science* (pp. 781–816). Newbury Park, CA: Sage.

Priest, S. H. (2006). Public discourse and scientific controversy: A spiral of silence analysis of biotechnology opinion in the United States. *Science Communication, 28*(2), 1–21.

Reese, S. D., Gandy, J., Oscar H., & Grant, A. E. (Eds.). (2001). *Framing public life: Perspectives on media and our understanding of the social world.* Mahwah, NJ: Erlbaum.

Robinson, J. P. (1972). Perceived media bias in the 1968 election: Can the media affect behavior after all? *Journalism Quarterly, 49,* 239–246.

Rogers, E. M. (1995). *Diffusion of Innovations, 4th ed.* New York: The Free Press.

Rogers, E. M., & Kincaid, D. L. (1981). *Communication networks : Toward a new paradigm for research.* New York: The Free Press.

Rosengren, K. E. (1985). *Media gratifications research: Current perspectives.* Beverly Hills, CA: Sage.

Ruggiero, T. E. (2000). Uses and gratifications theory in the 21st century. *Mass Communication & Society, 3*(1), 3–37.

Sandman, P. (1993). *Responding to community outrage: Stragegies for effective risk communication.* Fairfax, VA: American Industrial Hygiene Association.

Scheufele, D. (1999). Framing as a theory of media effects. *Journal of Communication, 49*(1), 103–122.

Scheufele, D. A., Shanahan, J., & Lee, E. (2001). Real Talk: Manipulating the dependent variable in spiral of silence research. *Communication Research, 28*(3), 304–324.

Schweitzer, J. C., & Smith, B. L. (1991). Community pressures on agenda-setting: How West Texas newspapers covered the nuclear waste-dump site selection process. *Newspaper Research Journal, 12*(3), 46–62.

Shanahan, J., Morgan, M., & Stengjerre, M. (1997). Green or Brown? Television's cultivation of environmental concern. *Journal of Broadcasting & Electronic Media, 41,* 305–323.

Shingi, P. M., & Moody, B. (1976). The communication effects gap: A field experiment on television and agricultural ignorance in India. *Communication Research, 3*(2), 171–190.

Shoemaker, P. J., & Reese, S. D. (1991). *Mediating the message: Theories of influences on mass media content.* New York: Longman.

Shrum, L. (1995). Assessing the social influence of television: A social cognition perspective on cultivation effects. *Communication Research, 22,* 402–429.

Signorelli, N., & Morgan, M. (Eds.). (1990). *Cultivation analysis: New directions in media effects research.* Newbury Park, CA: Sage.

Slovic, P. (1992). Perception of risk: Reflections on the psychometric paradigm. In S. Krimsky & D. Golding (Eds.), *Social theories of risk* (pp. 117–152). New York: Praeger Publishers.

Slovic, P. (1993). Perceived risk, trust, and democracy. *Risk Analysis, 13*(6), 675–682.

Stallings, R. A. (1990). Media discourse and the social construction of risks. *Social Problems, 37*(1), 80–95.

Tapper, J. (1995). The ecology of cultivation: A conceptual model for cultivation research. *Communication Theory, 5*(1), 36–57.

Tichenor, P. J., Donohue, G. C., & Olien, C. N. (1980). *Community conflict and the press.* Beverly Hills, CA: Sage.

Trumbo, C. (1995). Longitudinal modeling of public issues: An application of the agenda-setting process to the issue of global warming. *Journalism and Mass Communication Monographs, No. 152.*

Trumbo, C. (1998). Communication channels and risk information: A cost-utility model. *Science Communication, 20*(2), 190–203.

Visvanath, K., & Finnegan, J. R. (1996). The knowledge gap hypothesis 25 years later. In B. R. Burleson (Ed.), *Communication Yearbook 19* (pp. 187–227). Thousand Oaks, CA: Sage.

Weaver, D. H. (1977). Political issues and voter need for orientation. In D. L. Shaw & M. E. McCombs (Eds.), *The emergence of American political issues: The agenda-setting function of the press* (pp. 107–119). St. Paul, MN: West Publishing.

Zucker, H. G. (1978). The variable nature of news media influence. In Brendt D. Ruben (Ed.), *Communication Yearbook 2* (pp. 235–246). New Brunswick, NJ: Transaction Books.

21

Crises and Risk in Cyberspace

Kirk Hallahan
Colorado State University

Since the mid-1990s, the Internet and related technologies have become integral parts of the way people and organizations communicate. Not surprisingly, these have become commonplace tools in crises and risk communication.

Today, Internet technologies include Web 1.0 tools such as e-*mail, Web sites, chats* and *discussion boards* (also known as *newsgroups*). More recent innovations include Web 2.0 technologies such as *blogs* (Web logs), *wiki's* that permit the collaborative creation of content, audio *podcasts* and video *vodcasts*, and *social networking media*. The latter allow users to maintain friendships (e.g., MySpace.com and Facebook), share music and video files, recommend and rate news (e.g., Digg.com), and post and stream videos (e.g., YouTube). Merging into the mix is cellular telephony. Cell technology uses over-the-air digital transmissions instead of networked coaxial cable connections and relies on hand-held phones or personal digital assistants (PDAs). Nonetheless, the converging systems now allow the exchange of the same varieties of content.

Technology is not an altogether new trend in crisis or risk communication. In the 1970s and 1980s, telephony, private telegraph systems, telecopiers and facsimile machines, computerized data bases, audio and video conferences, and satellite news distribution were all recognized as potentially valuable tools in crisis and issues management (Calloway, 1991; Calloway & Keen, 1996; Heath, 1997; Ramsey, 1993). However, electronic communications are more important today than ever before based on high levels of adoption of and dependence upon personalized telecommunications devices by individuals. More than two-thirds of people in leading industrialized countries have Internet access in some form, while three-quarters of them use cell phones (Horrigan, 2007).

Crisis management and risk management operate in a new communication technology age (Heath & Millar, 2004, pp. 2–3) where new technologies have changed how organizations communicate with stakeholders and how people communicate with one another (Massey, 2004, pp. 245–246). Moore (2004) summed up the recent changes as a "seismic but dangerously neglected shift in the world of crisis" where "Constant enhancement in the ability of IT [information technologies] to merge rapid information exchange, opinion formation, and decisive stakeholder action will force crisis-hit companies to rethink crisis response strategies" (p. 29).

Information technologies found in and outside of cyberspace are *organizing resources* that can be deployed by organizations to manage crises and risk (Calloway & Keen; 1996; Calloway, 1991). Coombs (2007) noted the Internet can be a tool for environmental scanning and issue monitoring, for employee communications, for access to third-parties by organizations and media, and for assessing impact. Yet, the importance of cyber media has not yet been recognized universally. For example, although communication with traditional media was identified as one of 10 best practices in crisis communications, *direct* communications with affected publics via the Internet or cellular communications was not addressed (Seeger, 2006).

New media technologies provide organizations with new options for dealing with crises, but also can be the sources of new varieties of organizational crises to which they must respond. At the same time, new media are used by people and organizations confronted with risks but also pose new risks for them. This review surveys current trends and the evolving research related to crises and risk as they relate to Internet- and cellular-based communications.

CRISIS RESPONSES

Early Online Crises

In 1994, widespread public use of the Internet began following the advent of the first easy-to-use graphical Web browser. By 1996 organizations had begun employing the then-available Internet technologies to deal with crises. Early notable examples include Odwalla's contaminated product recall in 1996 (Coombs, 2007, p. 100; Lerbinger, 1997, p. 218; Thomsen & Rawson, 1998) and the Red River Valley flood in North Dakota in 1997 (Harris, 1997; Seeger, Sellnow & Unger, 2003, pp. 72–93, 154–177). Other disasters ensued, including the September 11 attacks in 2001, the Indonesian tsunami in 2004, Hurricane Katrina in 2005, and the shootings at Virginia Tech in 2007.

Several authors cited crisis communication as an important application in early books dealing with online public relations (Haig, 2000; Holtz, 1999, 2002; Levine, 2002; Middleberg, 2001; Phillips, 2000; Sherwin & Avila, 1997). The role of online media in crises also began to receive attention in other reviews within public relations (Baines, Egan & Jefkins, 2004; Bertolucci, 1999; Campbell, 2002; Doucette, 1998; Hallahan, 2001, 2004a; James, 2000; Guth & Marsh, 2005; Regester & Larkin, 2005; Shankman, 2000) and within the crisis management literature (Berkeley & Woolard, 2001; Boyd, 2000; Bucher, 2002; Caponigro, 2000; Sweetman, 2000; Mak, Malloard, Bui & Au, 1999; National Research Council, 1998; Neil, 2000; Seymour & Moore, 2000).

In large measure the importance of new technologies in crisis response reflects the integration of interactive media into the mix of media used by organizations generally and public relations in particular. The past two decades saw the rise of virtual managements and teams that rely on computer networks to function. The result has been more structurally flattened (vs. hierarchical) post-modern organizations that are highly decentralized, interactive, collaborative and transparent (Boje, Gephart & Thatchenkery, 1996; Boone, 2001; Clegg, 1990). Virtually every managerial function has been computerized in some way, including conflict resolution (Ford, 2004).

Within public relations, interactive or digital media have become an integral part of the mix of media used in public relations (Hallahan, 2001) and have transformed the practice (Key, 2005; Pavlik, 2007; Ziegler, 2006). Although many organizations adopted Internet technologies cautiously (Hill & White, 2000; Johnson, 1997; White & Raman, 1999), practitioners soon embraced and promoted the Internet (Gregory, 2004; Institute of Public Relations, 2000; Mickey, 1998). Practitioners previously had recognized the value of computers and data bases (Petrison & Wang, 1993; Ramsey, 1993; Thomsen, 1995) and quickly adopted the Net as a research tool (Gaddis, 2001; Lordan, 2001). In addition to its value for exchanging ideas among practitioners (Neff, 1998; Thomsen, 1996), the Web provided a basis for empowerment of public relations professionals (Porter & Sallott, 2003, 2005; Sallot, Porter & Acosta-Alzuru, 2004) Practitioners recognized the value of the new technologies as tools for advocacy, demonstrating social responsibility, building relationships and reputation management (Brier, DeWitte & van den Bergh, 2006; Capriotti & Moreno, 2007; Eccles, Newquist & Schatz, 2007; Esrock & Leichty, 1998, 1999, 2000; Galloway, 2005; Jo & Kim, 2003; Kang & Norton, 2004; Kanson & Nelson, 2006; Kent & Taylor, 1998; Kent, Taylor & White, 2003; Park & Lee, 2007; Reber, Gower & Robinson, 2005; Springston, 2001).

The importance of new technologies in crisis responses also reflects how technology changed journalism, including crisis coverage (Pavlik, 2003). News organizations quickly adopted computer-assisted reporting, e-mail contacts with sources, e-mail interviews, online newsrooms, Web conferences, RSS feedbacks from blogs and other sources, and cellular technologies as basic methods of newsgathering (Alfonso & Miguel, 2006; Callison, 2003; Duke, 2002; Hachigian & Hallahan, 2003; Hallahan, 1994; Porter, Sallot, Cameron & Shamp, 2001; Sallot & Johnson, 2006; Shin & Cameron, 2003; Woodall, 2006).

New Media in Crises Responses

Around the time the new millennium began, most organizations had addressed online communications in their general crisis planning (Few companies 2001; Hanna, 2005; Internet disaster recovery, 1997). Later research indicated a growing number of tools had been deployed in crisis responses by corporations (Perry, Taylor & Doerfel, 2003; Taylor & Perry, 2005). One recent study found that the Internet was employed in at least half of 175 surveyed crises and suggested that a series of best practices was emerging (Taylor & Kent, 2007). A separate study found that technology was incorporated in crisis preparedness planning: Practitioners are paying particular attention to e-mail and test messaging as a communication tools, and large organizations monitor the Internet at levels equal to broadcast media (Cloudman & Hallahan, 2006).

New media have proven valuable in both the anticipation of and response to crisis. For example, businesses have launched online campaigns to seek a favorable judgment in litigation or passage of legislation that would allow them to maintain business practices essential to their operations (Bounds, 2007; MP3.com launches, 2000). Online communications have been used in product recalls by companies, including Ford and Bridgestone, to avert potential crises (Copeland, 2000; Gibson, 2000a, b; Tillet, 2000). *Southern Living* even used the Web to withdraw the entire run of its April 2004 issue because of a problematic recipe that could explode "like napalm" (McKay & Mollenkamp, 2004). Financial institutions similarly used the Web to educate bank customers and others about potential problems with Y2K problem as the year 2000 approached (DiNardo, 2002).

During the response phase of crises, standard planning practices today call for organizations to use e-mail, Web sites, discussion boards, and short-message services (Instant Messaging) to inform stakeholders and media about crises—what happened, instructions for actions, and reassurances about effort to solve problems. For example, Yum Brands effectively posted its own video—not merely a press statement—to apologize to the public after a widely circulated Web video depicted rats scurrying around one of its franchised restaurants undergoing renovations in New York City (Macarthur, 2007). Organizations have recognized the value of telephony and text messaging for groups where numbers are readily available, such as student and employee groups affected by the shootings at Virginia Tech (Irvine, 2006; Swartz & Hopkins, 2007; Yuan, Dade & Prada, 2007).

Organizations now understand that crises dramatically increase traffic to Web sites. For example, Hurricane Katrina generated 1.7 million search engine searches and 9 million visits to Weather Bug and the Weather Channel, while the Red Cross.org Web site saw a 32-fold increase in daily visitors during the crisis (Francisco, 2005). Web sites, e-mails and text messages are particularly valuable to present and maintain accurate perceptions of the organization; present timely, accurate, up-to-date information; facilitate the work of media; manage negative publicity; and direct the activities of staffs and others affected by a triggering event (Bagg & Pyle, 2001).

As a result both content and technological Webmasters and e-mail/text messaging specialists have become essential members of crisis response teams (Alvey, 2005) and organizations must consider alternative methods of communication when e-mail is not available (Krupa, 2002). Prudent organizations are ready to expand computing capacity through access to additional servers and/or alternative hot sites operated by third-party service bureaus that now specialize in emergency recovery services (Bird, 1997; Callan, 2002; Fried, 1995; Mason, 1991; Robinson, 2003; Wallace & Webber, 2004).

Best practices suggest that organizations create *in advance* templates (also known as *ghost* or *dark sites*) to replace a site's home page whenever a major crisis occurs. Alternatively, organizations can establish microsites for managing crises and their aftermath. These are special-purpose sites with unique names and/or Web addresses (URLs) and can include victim assistance information (Middleburg, 2001). These complement phone banks of trained staff who answer telephone calls coming to previously designated phone numbers. Importantly, many organizations—or the survivors or families of victims—create special Web sites to commemorate a tragic event—a virtual forum for the survivors and others to express grief.

E-mail, intranets and extranets, and cellular telephones have proven to be valuable channels to collect intelligence from employers, customers and other interested parties during crises (Krupa, 2002). Electronic communications are particularly valuable for people in remote locations not affected by utility outages. Public discussion boards, for example, allow people to post questions or provide answers about missing people or property, or to make appeals for assistance. Social networking sites such as MySpace or Facebook can serve as similar function for registered members, such as the students at Virginia Tech (Kantor, 2007; Shneiderman & Preece, 2007). Following the 9/11 attacks, organizations used the public Internet (in lieu of their out-of-commission private intranets) to locate and organize employees and to resume operations (Kiger, 2001). Internet communications also complemented traditional media in communicating crisis news and updates to employees (Downing, 2004; Glass, 2002; Greer & Moreland, 2003; Wolfington & Wyatt, 2004, pp. 388–394).

The Internet has proven to be a powerful tool to organize disaster relief efforts. One of the earliest such applications was the Red Cross's intranet, ARC Online, which fed updates on Hurricane Fran from its central office to affiliates across the country in 1996 (Deck, 1996). Relief agencies used the Internet to coordinate relief activities in the wake of the Indonesian tsunami and Hurricane Katrina (Coren, 2005; Still, 2005). Meanwhile, information technology has been recognized for its role in the management of emergency medicine (Matthew, 2005). Relief agencies such as the Red Cross and Salvation Army routinely use Web sites and make solicitations to prospective contributors via e-mail following major disasters. One of the easiest forms of collecting contributions is to set up arrangements with cellular firms so cell phone users can call a designated number and have their cellular account charged a specified amount, which is automatically forwarded to the designated charity (Buckman & Pringle, 2005).

Government and relief agencies are also seeking to understand how to utilize new communications technologies in disasters. During Hurricane Katrina, for example, the Federal Emergency Management Agency (FEMA) used a Web site to coordinate the donation of goods from the public. Sponsored research and other initiatives are under way related to geo-collaborative crisis management (MacEachern, Fuhrmann, McNeese, Cai & Sharma, 2005), improved inter-agency cooperation (Horan, Marich & Schooley, 2006; Batteau, Brandenburg & Seeger, 2006) and the enhancement of humanitarian relief networks (Genova, 2006; Stephenson, 2005).

CRISES CREATED IN CYBERSPACE

While organizations use online communications to *respond* to natural disasters and human-generated crises created offline, new media can *create* crises for organizations in their own right (Fearn-Banks, 2007). Not surprisingly, the Institute for Crisis Management has added computer manufacturers to its list of the most crisis-prone industries (Woyke, 2007).

Internet-caused crises are a special case of *technology-based crises*, which are typically rooted in the system's complexity and the inter-connectedness of components in the system (Perrow, 1984, pp. 348–349). Such *cybercrises* involve triggering events that occur in cyberspace, create significant uncertainty, disrupt organizational operations, and might mar the organization's relationships or reputation—either online or offline.

Online crises fall into three broad areas: 1) outages and unplanned disruptions in service, 2) harmful comments, hoaxes or rumors, and 3) outright attacks by detractors.

Outages and Unplanned Disruptions in Service

With the increased interdependence of users and organizations on information technologies, a particular problem involves system failures that interrupt business or other interactions. Organizations are under continuing pressure to maintain the *uptime* or reliability of systems. Thus crisis management has become a priority for organizations (E-Business emergencies, 1999; Internetweek, 1999). Notable lapses in performance during the past decade included frequent disconnections of customers by Internet service providers (ISPs) during periods of heavy demand (Anthes & Wagner, 1996). Major e-businesses also suffered from user demand that exceeded system capacities—Charles Schwab in 1997, H&R Block in 2000, and TurboTax in 2007, to name a few (Dalton, 1999; Sullivan, 2000; Tax traffic swamps, 2000). In April 2007, owners of BlackBerry PDAs found themselves out of service due to a wayward system software upgrade. The result was a service crisis bungled by the company (Bulik, 2007; Meyerson, 2007).

Disasters that disrupt local electrical service have an obvious impact on the ability of organizations to maintain online systems in affected areas. Surprisingly, a National Academy of Science study showed that damage to the Internet was limited following the 9/11 attacks (Internet damage, 2002). Yet an electrical blackout in New York City only two years later illustrated dependability concerns (Harmon, 2003).

Systems are also subject to deliberate attempts to interrupt continuity—a vulnerability attenuated by the increased dependence by organizations upon just-in-time supplies delivery systems. Computer system operators must now be vigilant against computer hackers who try to break into systems for financial or political gain, as well as distributors of software program viruses and e-mail worms whose motivation might be the mere notoriety when such outages are reported in the press (Hallahan, 2004b). Although software viruses and e-mail worms are hardly new, the varieties of malicious software (*malware*) used to commit computer crimes are growing (Brandt, 2006; Richmond, 2006a) despite efforts to thwart criminals (Acohido, 2006; Acohido & Swartz, 2006a, b; Ante & Grow, 2006; Grow, 2005; Hamm, 2006).

The most extreme form of disruption involves *cyberterrorism*, which involves the creation of weapons (malicious software and electromagnetic weapons) intended to disrupt the physical world, often for political purposes (Barnes, 2003, pp. 260–261; Embar-Seedon, 2002; Keegan, 2002; Matusitz, 2005; Stanton, 2002). Despite a lack of any evidence, press reports about the bombing of the Murrah Federal Office Building in Oklahoma City in 1995 claimed the bombers used the Internet to communicate their plans. Following the event, discussion boards (personal Web sites were in their infancy) were rife with militant rantings (Barnes, 2003, p. 261).

Federal officials acknowledged the United States' cybervulnerabilities as early as 1997 when a commission called for the creation of a National Infrastructure Protection Center (U.S. Department of Justice, 1998; Sauter & Carafano, 2005). A small-scale preview of the potential danger occurred in the Big Hack Attack of 2001, where Chinese and American hackers commandeered sites in each others' countries following the collision of an American spy plane and a Chinese jet. The incident resulted in the shuttering of sites in both countries by hackers but mostly involved minor *cybergraffiti* (Smith, 2001). Today, *Internet jihad* refers to the use of online technologies by political extremists in the Middle East (A world wide web of terror, 2007).

Following 9/11, the United States saw renewed warnings about cyberterrorism (Schwartz, 2001), and many organizations stepped up their vigilance (McMahon, 2000; Murray, 2004; Quinley & Schmidt, 2002; Thomas & Loaders, 2000). The 9/11 attacks led the U.S. government to remove already widely available public information from government agency Web sites (Fox, Rainie & Madden, 2002; Lehmert, 2002; Reporters Committee, 2003). The military also beefed up its Internet arsenal (Michaels, 2007) while testing a variety of systems in the Iraq War (Balfour & Ante, 2003; Crock, Magnusson, Walczak & Balfour, 2003).

Harmful Comments, Hoaxes and Cyber-Rumors

Although preceded by a very similar event more than year before (Roper, 1995), the first major cybercrisis is generally acknowledged to be the user revolt in 1994, when giant computer chip manufacturer Intel ignored comments in a computer discussion group that its new Pentium chip contained a flaw that resulted in errors when making advanced mathematical calculations. Intel did not act until the controversy made its way into the trade and business press, and IBM—its largest customer—announced it would suspend use of Intel chips as components in its personal computers (Marlow, 1999, pp. 169–174; Burgelman & Grove, 1996; Emery, 1996; Hallahan, 2008, pp. 62–63; Hearit, 1999).

As the Intel case showed, the Internet is a powerful communications channel that can create awareness among albeit small and fragmented audiences. However, Internet communications also can set the public agenda in cyberspace and beyond (Dzwo, 1998; Dzwo, Roberts, Baker & Sutherland, 1999; Roberts, Wanta & Dzwo, 2002). Internet communities can moderate public opinion and thus can be contingent factors for how an organization might respond to a crisis (Cho & Cameron, 2006; Kim & Shin, 2005).

Advocates of Internet communication argue that the Internet is today's equivalent of Jürgen Habermas' public sphere (Couldry & Curran, 2003; Gimmler, 2001; Habermas, 1962/1989; Motion, 2001; O'Donnell, 2001). Benefits cited include the facilitation of community (Badaracco, 1998; Rheingold, 1993), dialog between organizations and their constituents (Ainsworth, Hardy & Harley, 2005; Heath, 1998; Kent & Taylor, 1998), and the promotion of social corporate responsibility (Coombs, 1998). However, critics point out the Internet is not truly egalitarian but, instead is an oligarchy of public opinion (Schild & Oren, 2005).

Due to easy access and the Internet's power to dissemination information quickly and broadly, organizations can be thrown into disarray from comments online in the same way organizations can be hurt by negative publicity in traditional media. Only its ability to quickly reach highly segmented audiences directly makes the Internet more powerful than traditional media. Examples abound of how e-mails have disclosed information unflattering or incriminating information about government officials and organizational executives (Abrahamowitz, 2007; Hagan, 2007; Rundle, 2007), both intentionally and unintentionally. Many of these comments were made by users who mistakenly believed their writings were private. E-mail forwarding can spread negative information in the same fashion that viral marketers use the Internet to create "buzz" about new products and services (Warren & Jugenson, 2007).

Bulletin boards and chats continue to draw diatribes. In one example in 2007, U.S. retailer Home Depot saw 4,000 angry posts from customers following negative remarks by the moderator in an MSN comment room. Another 10,000 disgruntled customers e-mailed the company (Conlin, 2007). Although bulletin boards and chat rooms are intended to encourage and facilitate the free exchange ideas, online anonymity or pseudonymity often emboldens users to be nasty and to make comments they would not in face-to-face exchanges (Fost, 2007; Noveck, 2007; Simpson, 2005). Reader vitriol in 2006 led the *Washington Post* to discontinue accepting comments from readers on its ombudman's blog (Seelye, 2006a). Because many chats are no longer monitored, the chances are greater than with traditional media that inflammatory or crisis- triggering comments will go unchecked.

Blogs have become fixtures in cyberspace that allow individuals to express personal and organizational opinions (Flynn, 2006; Holtz & Demopoulos, 2006; Kline & Burnstein, 2005; MacDougall, 2005; Reese, Rutiglianao, Kideuk & Jaekwan, 2007). Blogs can be used to promote the blogger's self-interest—such as Paris Hilton's blog where the overly publicized actress appealed for public forgiveness and leniency following a drunk drinking conviction in 2007 (Mutter, 2007). However, many bloggers serve as astute and thoughtful observers and commentators on the public scene—and serve as third-party social influencers on various topics in the same way that the press was believed to accord explicit or implicit third-party endorsements (Gillin, 2007; Lenhart & Fox, 2006). Soldiers have even used blogs to share their experience in war (Burden, 2006). Although millions of blogs have been established, only about 20% of them are really active, i.e., updated at least quarterly (Green, 2007). Blogs are easily monitored by both organizations (Green, 2007; Nail, 2006a) and by news media (Dylko & Kosicki, 2006) through RSS (real simple syndication) software. Blogs have also have become the source of revelations about missteps by government officials and media. For example, the Clinton-Lewinsky scandal made headlines in 1998 only after blogger Matt Drudge revealed *Newsweek* had "spiked" (withheld) the story. Similarly, Dan Rather resigned as news anchor after bloggers revealed CBS's faulty sourcing in its coverage of President Bush's military record (Nail, 2006a).

Hoaxes are also an unintended consequence of the free exchange of ideas in cyberspace. One small California company, for example, averted a crisis only because of its quick response following distribution of a fake news release announcing the company's CEO had resigned, that the company was under investigation by the Securities and Exchange Commission, and that its earnings would be restated (Battey, 2000). Hoaxes also can involve *spoof sites* intended to parody or lampoon well-know people or organizations (Ossinger, 2006). Similarly, with the advent of collaborative media such as Wikipedia (Tapscott & Williams, 2006), so-called "dirty tricks" can be performed without any extensive knowledge of how the system works. Examples include the hoax played by a Tennessee businessman to alter John Seigenthaler Sr.'s biography in Wikipedia to falsely report that the former journalist and government official was involved in the assassination of John F. Kennedy and Seigenthaler's former boss, Robert F. Kennedy (Goodin, 2005; Seigenthaler, 2005; Seelye, 2005). Other notable incidents involved their staffers altering biographical and other information on U.S. Senators (Wikinews investigates, 2006).

Rumors involve (often untrue) information passed on from user to user without verification of facts and without a verifiable source—and are particularly difficult to trace online (Kibby, 2005). One study suggests that at more than two-thirds of publicly held companies have been targets of rumors in Web-based chats or bulletin boards and that half of these companies have received queries about information or rumors appearing in chat or message board threads (Ryan, 2004). Among major brands that have been the targets of crisis-triggering rumors during the past decade are Procter and Gamble, Tommy Hilfinger, Kentucky Fried Chicken, Nieman Marcus, Microsoft and Costa Rican bananas (Fearn-Banks, 2007, pp. 95–99).

Attacks. Rumors can be shared unwittingly by users who believe the information to be true, but many rumors and uncorroborated information is circulated by people who purposely want to point out misbehaviors or to defame others. Attack Web sites were created as early as 1996 when critics of Ford Motor Company created a Web site called FlamingFords.com and activists created an anti-McDonald's Web site called Mcspotlight.org (Middleberg, 1996). Similar feuds continue today targeting large companies such as Coca-Cola (Coombs, 2007, p. 31) and Wal-Mart (Fearn-Banks, 2007, p. 7; Kabel, 2006).

Although trademark laws in many countries dissuade detractors from using organization's names in site addresses, attack Web sites proliferate. Many of these homesite derivatives add the suffix "-sucks.com" to their names (Farrell, 2000). Other *rogue sites* carefully select Web site names or addresses that sound deceptively similar to the names or Web addresses of targeted organizations (Fearn-Banks, 2002, 2007; Hallahan, 2004b; Holtz, 2002, pp. 291–305; Philips, 2001). A goal is to distract gullible users searching for legitimate sites on search engines (Pelline, 1997). Attack, spoof and rogue sites have augmented with through the creation of heavily trafficked public *complaint* or *gripe sites* where individuals can vent against specific companies (Appleman, 2001). Complaints illustrated with videos also appear on YouTube (Hart, 2006).

Attack and rogue sites, as well as *cybersmears* (Cásarez, 2002; Crawford, 1999) and hate e-mail (Barnes, 2003, pp. 262; Levin, 2002), underscore the important role that new media have assumed in politics, the discussion of public issues and the exercise of power in modern societies. One study found that almost two-thirds of online community members involved in social issues through the Internet say those issues were new to them when they began participating on the Internet. More than 40% of online community members reported they participate more in social activism since they started participating in online communities (USC Annenberg Digital Future Project, 2007).

Politics has been transformed by the Internet (Chadwick, 2006; Klotz, 2001) with the advent of candidate and issue Web sites and e-mail (Valla, 2007), streaming video and Webcasts (Fine. 2006), sponsored and independent blogs (Craig, 2007; MacDougall, 2005; Schatz, 2007) and social networking sites where voters can exchange ideas with candidates and others (Vargas, 2007a; Seelye, 2007). As result, new specialists have emerged: online political operatives (OPOs) and online political advertising consultants (Vargas, 2007b, c).

Not surprisingly, social activists such as MoveOn.Org have gained notoriety for their use of new media, while groups such as NetAction.Org specialize in training activists on Internet strategies and tactics in the tradition of radical community organizer Saul Alinksy. Cyberactivists use distributed networks (Arquilla & Ronfeldt, 1998) to advance their cause, enlist followers, and affect legislation and the public affairs agenda (Kolko, 2003; Lerbinger, 2006; Nelson, 2006). They also strive to effect organizational and social change more generally (Brabbs, 2000; Coombs & Holladay, 2007, pp. 70–73; Cyberadvocacy, 2000; Ford & Gill, 2001; Gillespie, 2000; Harkinson, 2001; Hick & McNutt, 2002; Hill & Hughes, 1998; Holtz, 2002; Kim & Shin, 2004; Meisner, 2000; Now, a gadfly, 2000; Rauch, 2006; Thomas, 2003; Turnbull, 2001; Youngblood, 2006). Online movements are especially evident at the global level (Bennett, 2003; Dartnell, 2006; Hick, Halpin & Hoskins, 2000; Rogers, 2003; Warkentin, 2001) and include use of new media by marginalized groups (Mitra, 2004; O'Donnell, 2001) as well as groups characterized as outright anarchists (Atton, 2002; Whitsel, 2000).

How should organizations respond (Shortman, 2003)? The rise of cyberactivism has led to the development of models for classifying cyber attacks (Ye, Newman & Farley, 2005/2006) and assessing and prioritizing online threats from an issues management perspective (Coombs, 2002). While some argue that it is possible for organization to control or create a symbolic "space" in which to address cybercritics (Courtright, 2007; Kent & Taylor, 1998; Smudde, 2005), others argue all online crises are political and thus an "enemy" is involved inevitably (Chrysler CEO rips, 2002; Dezenhall & Webber, 2007). The result is a combative mentality punctuated with metaphors such as firefighting (O'Keefe, 1997, pp. 341–369), cyberwarfare (Aftab, 2005) and nail 'em! (Dezenhall 2003, pp. 156–168).

The trend has also focused attention on the online techniques used by activists groups to maximize their advantage and their use of new media. Researchers have examined the use of *message framing* by activists (e.g., Collins, Zoch & Walsh, 2005), *dialogic communications* (Taylor, Kent & White, 2001) and *hate language* (Barnes, 2003, p. 262; Levin, 2002). As an example, see Allen et al. (chapter 22, this volume).

RISK RESPONSES

The rise of cyberactivism underscores the reality that these new media provide a readily accessible channel for people to respond to risks, which are defined here as perceived hazards or threats to a person's physical, psychological, social, political or economic well-being. With increasing frequency, the public turns to the Internet or cell phones to learn details of crisis-and risk-related events. Members of the general public with little or no prior involvement with responsible organizations attempt to find out what happened, how organizations are responding, and how the consequences might affect their lives. More involved publics—people with whom the organization has established relationships, goodwill and trust—might use new media to reconcile new information with their extant knowledge.

Beyond crises, users also rely on new media to cope with routine problems in their lives. The Internet and cell phones thus operate as *risk management tools* that are readily available and convenient. Various private, not-for-profit and governmental agencies also use the Internet and related media in *risk education* programs. A good example is the Ready.Gov Web site, where the federal government promotes personal emergency preparedness to adults and kids (Coombs & Holladay, 2007, pp. 96–97). Campaign designers increasingly integrate new media into public information programs and have developed an emerging body of knowledge about successful strategies and tactics (Bortree, 2007; Lieberman, 2001).

In managing personal risks generally, people engage in both *information-seeking* and *information sharing. Situational theory*, which has been widely studied in public relations, posits that people will engage in active information seeking (vs. passive information processing) when confronted with a problem—particularly when problem recognition and cognitive involvement are high and constraint recognition is low (Grunig, 1997). Publics are formed around issues as people share ideas, opinions and emotions with others. New media facilitate this process by making it easy to find information and by linking together people separated by geographic distance. Other theorists rely upon *structuration theory* to suggest that very process of collaborating online can create publics or social organizations. Electronic environments allow people to communicate freely in an unregulated, uncensored, public environment (Cozier & Witmer, 2001). The result has been referred to as *communities* (Feenberg & Barney, 2004; Hallahan, 2004c; Rheingold, 1993), *networks* (Castells, 2000) and, most recently, *social networking..*

Information-Seeking

When confronted with uncertainty, people either avoid *or* seek information (Case, Andrews, Johnson & Allard, 2005; Palenchar & Heath, 2007, p. 125; Seeger, Vennette, Ulmer & Sellnow, 2002). One obvious source of information is the traditional media, which have been augmented with Web sites mobile phone services operated by newspapers, magazines and broadcasters as well the growing array of other online news aggregators such as Yahoo! News, Digg, Reddit and Slashdot and specialized news sources. For example, Al Jazeera, the independent Arab television network based in Qatar, operates an English language Web site as a way to present an alternative Arab perspective to English speakers worldwide (Auter, 2006).

The late 1990s saw heavy public reliance on the Web for news about the death of Princess Diana in 1997 (Sorkin, 1997, Tedesco, 1997), the Clinton-Lewinsky scandal (Rosen, 1998/1999; White House crisis, 1998), and the Kosovo war (Guensburg, 1999; Malushi, 1999).

The 9/11 attacks in 2001 were seminal events that demonstrated the power of the Web to supply news to people facing risk (Blair, 2002; Martin & Phelan, 2003; Palser, 2002; Rappoport & Alleman, 2003: Seeger, Vennette, Ulmer & Sellnow, 2002; Vengerfeldt, 2003). Although not the initial source of information (Kanilian & Gale, 2003) and despite delays by newspapers in covering the event on their Web sites (Randle, Deveport & Bossen, 2003; Salaverria, 2005), nearly one-third of Americans went online to search for information (Rainie, 2001). Many users found the Internet a superior source compared to traditional media (Jones & Rainie, 2002; Kellner, 2004; Spence et al., 2006). Topics searched online closely paralleled topics covered in traditional media (Aikat, 2005; Frith & Aikat, 2003). Internet use led to a greater connectedness and a broader range of civic activities following 9/11 (Kim, Jung, Cohen & Ball-Rokeach, 2004), and people who participated in online discussions also were more likely to participate in similar community activities offline (Dutta-Berman, 2006).

Web search engines are used by roughly one-fifth of Americans on a typical day and allow users to readily locate virtually any topic available in text, image, audio or visual formats (Fallows, 2005; Rainie, 2005). When searching for health information online, most users begin with search engines; 80% of Americans have used search engines to search on at least 1 of 17 health topics (Fox, 2006). At the same time, 36% of online adults consult Wikipedia (Rainie & Tancer, 2007) for various topics.

Today, 1 out of 6 Americans accesses news online. But among "high powered" Internet users (defined as active users with broadband connections) more than 70% go online for news in a typical day (Horrigan, 2006). Alternatively, users can go directly to organizations that are covered in the media. Today, organizations use direct communication to bypass media (Hallahan, 1994) and can incorporate a variety of tools—blogs, transcripts, e-mail messages and links to search engines—to counterbalance negative publicity received in the mainstream press (Seelye, 2006).

Emerging evidence suggests that online news complements rather than displaces traditional news consumption (Dutta-Bergman, 2004). Users are more likely to follow their own interests (Tewksbury, 2003) and employ selective exposure when seeking utilitarian information (Knobloch,-Westerwick, Carpenter, Blumhoff & Nickell, 2005) or topics involving political opinion (Best, Chmielewski & Krueger, 2005). Researchers have conducted analyses of how online (versus traditional) media cover such highly visible risks as severe acute respiratory syndrome (SARS—Lee, 2005a, b; Tian & Stewart, 2005), genetic cloning (Hyde, 2006), and the Iraq War (Dimitrova, Kaid, Williams & Trammell, 2005; Schwalbe, 2006).

Online news is considered rich in *mobilizing information*, i.e., supplying information that aids people to act on attitudes they already hold. However, evidence suggests the amount of mobilizing information is no higher in online versus traditional news (Hoffman, 2006). Other research suggests the availability of mobilizing information does not lead to risk avoidance (Samarajiva, 2004).

Information Sharing

Responses to major disasters covered in the news illustrate the interactive nature of new media, which enables users to both receive and *create* content shared with others. Indeed, the web has become a *coping mechanism* (Associated Press, 2007a).

The 2004 Indonesia tsunami prompted numerous tourists and residents to post messages on both text and video blogs (vlogs)—and was considered a breakthrough event for consumer-generated content and for *citizen journalism* on the Web—a trend that had begun the previous year in the wake of Hurricane Fran on east coast of the United States (Palser, 2004). (Subsequently, many mainstream media adopted crowdsourcing to encourage audiences to submit images and information via the Internet and cell phones.) As had been evidenced in earlier disasters, people displaced by the tsunami and Hurricane Katrina in 2005 used the Internet to search for survivors and regain or maintain contacts with friends and family (Dewan, 2005; Hafner, 2005; Moore, 2005; Regaldo & Mintz, 2005; Schwartz, 2004, 2005). The process was facilitated by the quick establishment of cybercafes in the devastated areas (Internet café, 2005; Katrina public web, 2005). Public access terminals were augmented with the Web-based tracing services operated by entities such as the Red Cross to help locate missing persons. Research documents how online communities can emerge following news or a disaster such as the Gujarat earthquake in India (Kodrich & Laituri, 2005) and Hurricane Katrina (Procopio & Procopio, 2007).

Online information sharing is popular because many people are interested in establishing a personal presence or identity on the Web (Hunt, 1996; Killoran, 1999) and are not reticent to share personal information or assist others. To illustrate, user Juan Mann posted a clip on YouTube offering "Free Hugs" to strangers. Meanwhile, user Ryan Fitzgerald offered to talk to anyone who called him on his cell phone—an offer to which 5,000 people responded (Associated Press, 2007b).

Discussion boards, chats and blogs that enable readers to add comments are devoted to a myriad of special topics—including how people can avoid or solve problems with products or services. Other personal problems about which people freely share information range from dating and sexual relationships to parenting, grieving and debt management (Leland, 2007).

Health and nutrition are areas where new media have been particularly important in helping people manage risk. Telemedicine encompasses a wide range of activities from emergency triage to long-distance diagnosis by physicians and transmission of medical images and data (Turner, 2003). Among its most important applications, however, are disease prevention, public health education, and relationship building between medical providers and patients and at-risk populations (Springston & Lariscey, 2003, p. 551). People increasingly engage in self-diagnosis and obtain information before and after consulting physicians from medical Web sites such as the pioneering Medscape.com (Tanne, 1999) and WebMD (Stoltz, 2006), as well as Web sites operated by nonprofit and governmental agencies, medical providers and insurers interested in promoting wellness (Weintraub, 2006).

Online patient groups have become important components in health care by serving as channels for social support and research (Landro, 2007). Discussion boards and chats operate as online health communities devoted to a broad range of topics (Maloney-Krichman & Preece, 2001). Recent research about online health groups has focused on information sharing about topics such as bovine spongiform encephalopathy or "mad cow disease" (Richardson, 2001), sleeping disorders (Weisgerber, 2004), syphilis and HIV (Anderton & Valdiserri, 2005; McFarlane, Bull & Reitmeijer, 2002; Shernoff, 2006), vegan diets (Sneijder & Te Molder, 2005), and alcoholism (VanLear, Sheedhand, Withers & Walker, 2005). For a general discussion about the analysis of computer-mediated discourse, see Herring (2001).

Consumer preferences for *user-generated content* (also known as *consumer-generated media*) explain the vital role of interactive Web 2.0. More than one-quarter of online consumers now submit a rating or review or a product or service or contribute to a discussion board (Haven, 2007), and one-half of users are either creators or readers or such comments (Parr, 2007). User-generated content drives many of the fastest growing Web sites such as MySpace, Facebook and You Tube (Burns, 2006; *Never Ending Friending*, 2006)—a trend expected to continue on the Web (In-Stat, 2006) and to expand to mobile phones (Stone & Richtel, 2007). This same trend is expected to continue in the arena of user-generated news with sites such as Digg.com and Reddit.com (comScore Media Matrix, 2006).

Research consistently suggests that consumers prefer obtaining information from peers online (Altus, 2007; Leggatt, 2007). In the case of online news, for example, users employ the same criteria to assess online and traditional news stories (Sundar, 1999). However, experimental research showed the same stories were more liked and perceived to be of higher quality when attributed to other users compared to stories attributed to news editors, computers or the user himself/herself (Sundar & Ness, 2001). Beyond user satisfaction, research suggests that collaboration enhances article quality in Wikipedia (Wilkinson & Huberman, 2007).

RISKS CREATED IN CYBERSPACE

Both individuals and organizations now find themselves coping with a variety of new risks that did not exist prior to the advent of cyber-communications. Although many of these risks do not involve triggering events associated with a crisis, they can create levels of uncertainty and disruption in the lives of people and entities.

Risks for Individuals

People express concerns about various aspects of using the Internet. This has been demonstrated in a personality trait labeled *Internet anxiety*, a special case of fears or concerns about a person's ability to successfully use computers (Joiner et al., 2005; Joiner, Brosnan, Duffield, Gavin & Maras, 2007; White & Scheb, 2000; Zhang & Zhang, 2002). More specifically, however, six key risks exist for individuals in cyberspace.

Disclosure risk involves the embarrassing revelation—whether accidental or intentional—of mailings, postings or other information that reveal indiscretions, unethical behaviors or character shortcomings (O'Hara, 2006). The misstep might have occurred years ago, but survives in electronic files only to be released due to a lack of system security (Barr, 2006; Pegoraro, 2007; Zambroski, 2006) or due to the deliberate actions of others (Greenhouse & Barbaro, 2006). Former U.S. Representative Mark Foley and BP chief executive John Browne are two examples of prominent people ousted from positions of power because of sexual scandals (Jesdanun, 2006; Kidman, 2007). For ordinary individuals, current and prospective employers enjoy easy access to a wealth of information through organizational intranets and e-mails, personal Web pages, chats, bulletin boards and blogs. Information has been used by employers to terminate present or avoid hiring potential employees (Dell & Cullen, 2006; Lambert et al., 2005; Nashaskima, 2007; Stone, 2006). These reference checks are facilitated by search engines, for-profit services (Hart, 2007), and Web sites where people can complain about the misbehavior of others (Alvarez, 2006; Saranow, 2007).

Deception risk involves not knowing the sources of information or being able to easily verify information. Deception can be as simple of misunderstanding content, but often involves information that is deliberately incomplete or fragmentary. Today's users must become cyber-literate to assess the veracity of online content. Deception also includes the use of devices that distract attention—including pop-ups and spam (Palmer, 2006). Purposeful deception takes various forms (Hallahan, 2006). Examples include digital manipulation of images (Hafner, 2004), and schemes to gain more prominent listings on search engines (a technique euphemistically referred to as search engine optimization). Other recent examples include anonymous self-serving attacks on competitors (Kesmodel & Wilkie, 2007; White, Lubline & Kesmodel, 2007), fake blogs or *flogs* (Barabaro, 2006; Siebert, 2006), *astroturfing* or the use of fake grassroots campaigns and front organizations (Ahrens, 2007; Greenberg, 2007), fake ads for fictional characters on MySpace.com (Holmes, 2006), and anonymous video postings (Regalado & Searcey, 2006).

Crime risk involves deception aimed at extracting economic, political or other losses from users, particularly vulnerable groups such as seniors and youth (Dibble, 1998). One private study suggests that 86% of targeted cyberattacks are aimed at consumers (Richmond, 2006). According to the FBI, auction fraud was the most commonly reported online offense, followed by non-delivered merchandise/payments (Federal Bureau of Investigation, 2007). Other swindles include *e-mail scams* such as the infamous Nigerian mail scam (Fearn-Banks, 2007, pp. 5–6) and fake online appeals that have become commonplace after major disasters (Gray, 2005; Krebs & Mayer, 2005).

Although the problem is actually more pervasive offline than online, *identity theft* is a growing concern (Bryan-Low, 2005; Cullen, 2007; Ellis, 2006; Mattioli, 2006; Nierengarten, 2006; Swartz, 2005; Vaca, 2003; Vasccellaro, 2006b). Among techniques commonly used to obtain valuable details about individuals are *phishing*—sending e-mails from fictitious but familiar- or official-sounding e-mail addresses that instruct people to buy online or disclosure personal information (Shin, 2007). A variation of this scam is *vishing*, which requires online users to leave a voice mail message on the telephone (LaValle, 2006). Other techniques involve spyware or adware (including "empty spam" messages) where thieves embed software in users' computers without the users' knowledge to capture keystrokes or passwords (Elgin, 2006; Hallahan, 2004b; Krebs, 2006; Zeller, 2006).

Other examples include outright deception, such as the major electronic retailer found to operate an intranet that mimicked sites of major competitors to show customers competitive prices—only the prices shown were deliberately inaccurate and equal to higher than the store's prices (Gombossy, 2007). Separately, government officials are concerned about consumer protection issues more generally and trafficking in illegal commodities. A particular problem involves the purchase of unauthorized pharmaceuticals and the safety of Internet pharmacies (Fox, 2004; U.S. General Accounting Office, 2004). Securities regulators are concerned about trading losses by "day trading" among investors and stock manipulation in penny stocks and other equities (Nakashima, 2007b).

Research in marketing has focused on the question of risk-taking and trust in e-commerce. With the expanded use of secure transaction and online payment systems (Grow, 2006), researchers have explored on issues such as development of trustworthy systems (Schaffer, 2004; Whitworth and De Moor, 2003), warranties (Lwin & Williams, 2006) and social aspects of online shopping (Blake, Valdiserri, Neuendorf, & Powers, 2006). In particular, e-marketers have strived to develop a conceptual understanding as well as scales to measure online trust (Camp, 2001; Eggert, 2006; Fogg, 2003; Forsythe, Liu, Shannon & Gardner, 2006; Garbarino & Strahilevitz, 2004; Lacohee, Phippen & Furnell, 2006; Littler & Melanthiou, 2006).

Privacy risk is the largest single concern among online users (Hallahan, 2006; Holtzman, 2006). About two-thirds of Americans say they don't trust Web sites even if the site has a posted privacy policy (Junnarkar, 2002). In the late 1990s, problems with disclosure of personal information led to major problems for computer giants such as AOL and DoubleClick (Crisis Rx, 2000; This just in, 1997) and resulted in the establishment of guidelines by the Direct Marketing Association and other trade groups (Hallahan, 2006). Although privacy disclosures are valuable, research has raised questions about their effectiveness because such notices are often ignored by users (Milne & Culnan, 2004). Many leading American technology companies favor passage of a stronger privacy laws at the federal level to avoid an emerging crazy-quilt of discrepant state rules (Hart, 2006).

New forms of privacy invasion continuously emerge. One example is the easy accessibility of satellite imagery, such as Google's Street View, that depicts the details of neighbors, streets, and public buildings—down to people's backyards (Helft, 2007). The privacy problem has been confounded in the United States by the Bush administration's position that it was authorized to engage in surveillance of suspected terrorists without warrants or other oversight under the 2006 renewal of the USA Patriot Act adopted following the 9/11 attacks (Eggen, 2007; Risen & Lichtblau, 2005). Meanwhile, government Web sites are tracking visits to U.S. government sites in violation of the 2003 government directive (McCullagh, 2006) and engage in data mining activities without oversight (Lichtblau, 2005; Nakishima, 2007c).

Addiction risk involves an array of allegedly compulsive or anti-social behaviors involving Internet use—including excessive time spent online overall, game playing, viewing pornography, pathological behaviors in chatrooms, and gambling (Grohol, 2005). *Internet addiction disorder* was labeled by Dr. Ivan Goldberg as a spoof in 1995, but received serious attention in response to growing concerns about the impact of the new medium as it was quickly adopted. More than 20 research articles and several books were published in the late 1990s. (For a review of the current state of research, see Yellowlees & Marks, 2007.)

Alternative explanations for addiction can be found in communications research suggesting that users merely attempt to manage impressions online (O'Sullivan, 2000), or lose their anchor to reality as they become engrossed in the flow of the online activity (Webster, Trevino & Ryan, 1993) and to abandon or lose their sense of personal identity (Simpson, 2005; Walther, 1996; Walther & Tidwell, 1992). Such behaviors might be explained by the more limited nonverbal and social cues associated with online communications (Barnes, 2003).

At least three research centers operate in the United States and China to study or treat the malady, and but researchers are sharply divided on the question. Dr. Kimberly Young of the Center for Internet Addition (www.netaddiction.co) has pushed for inclusion of IAD in the 2012 revision of the American Psychiatric Association's *Diagnostic and Statistical Manual of Mental Disorders.* However, in separate actions in 2007, the American Society of Addiction Medicine opposed calling overuse of Internet and video games a true addiction and the American Medical Association called for further research on video game overuse (Internet addiction disorder, 2007; Video games no addiction for now, 2007).

Exploitation risk involves users being taken advantage of, including the prospect if incurring physical harm. Critics argue that the rise of new technologies, particularly the easy access to pornography, has perpetuated a culture created by the mass media that promotes abuse, exploitation and violence against women and children, both online and offline (Gillespie, 2000). In addition to perpetuating a culture where women are objectified and marginalized, teenage and adult women can be tracked online by *cyberstalkers* who engage in harassing and sometimes aggressive behavior (Jenkins, 2007; Hallahan, 2004b). Importantly, women have used also deployed the Internet as an advocacy tool to overcome such abuses (Passariello, Johnson & Vranica, 2007).

Children are vulnerable to cyberbullying by peers (Willard, 2007), deception by commercial concerns related to products sold online, and sexual exploitation. Children are especially at risk because they are frequently incapable of making judgments about the appropriateness of age-related content, the veracity of information, or the identity and truthfulness of sources (Holloway & Valentine, 2003; Shade, 2002). Easily lured into exhilarating Web sites and chatrooms filled with pornographic content (Zimmer & Hunter, 2003), one in five children report having received unwanted sexual solicitations online. The exploitation problem has been exacerbated with the emergence of social networking sites, where 55% of online uses have created online profiles (Lenhart & Madden, 2007; Zeller, 2005). Teens generally are not shy about disclosing the most intimate personal insights about themselves (Nussbaum, 2007), and both Facebook and MySpace have been forced to restrict disclosures of about online activity and personal identifying information (PII) by members (Hansell, 2006; Nogouchi, 2006). Fortunately, higher levels of risk perception among teens appear to lead to less willingness to provide information (Yuom, 2005). Laws have been passed by virtually every major western industrial nation outlawing the trafficking or possession of child pornography in efforts to eliminate child abuse by pornographers. Several online public information campaigns against sexual abuse and pedophilia have been launched by advocacy groups (Arnolado, 2001; Coombs & Holladay, 2007, pp. 94–95).

Exclusion risk involves risks related to having no or only limited access to Internet or cellular communications and thus not being able to fully participate in society. The problem of the "digital divide" between information-haves and have-nots places individuals at risk of not having access to information that might be required as a matter of right or might be required, for example, in order to vote or conduct business with government (Couldry, 2004; Dance, 2003; Hindman, 2000; James, 2003; Kuttan, 2003). The potential societal risks are unintended *knowledge gaps* among people in society (see Neuwirth, chapter 20, this volume)—a social threat that has led some critics to call for universal access for all Americans.

The digital divide in the United States and globally is largely an artifact of socio-economic factors. Yet others would contend it is also a matter of personal choice. One recent study proposed and found significant support among experts for a scenario in which, by 2020, people left behind by accelerating information and technologies might form a new cultural group of technological "refuseniks" who self-segregate and commit acts of terror or violence in protest against technology (Anderson & Rainie, 2006, pp. 59–66). Thus, the elimination of disparities is an important social concern for both disenfranchised individuals as well as society as a whole.

Risks for Organizations

Organizations engaged in e-commerce and other types of exchanges such as fund-raising confront unique problems stemming from their limited knowledge of the people with whom they are dealing in cyberspace (Halpern & Mehrotra, 2000). While fraud is the most egregious concern, other examples abound. Individual investors can now lend money to others via sites such as Prosper.com (Kim, 2007). Businesses also can lose control of information about products—witness the leaks related to content of the final Harry Potter novel prior to its official release in 2007 (Trachtenberg & DeAvila, 2007).

Janal (1998) was the first book author to focus attention on the *reputation-related* risks to organizations in the new world of online communications. Hallahan (2004b) later focused on the need to protect an organization's *digital assets* and argued that organizations confront risks from five principal sources: *attackers, hackers, lurkers, rogues* and *thieves.* He also outlined the ethical and legal problems confronting organizations (Hallahan, 2006).

Importantly, many risks for organizations have the potential to escalate into full-blow crises but never do so. An error by an employee in the Alaska Department of Revenue, for example, led to the deletion of all computerized records related to the $38 billion Alaska Permanent Fund. However, officials were able to reconstruct the files from 300 cardboard boxes of paper records, and public concern was minimized (Oops!, 2007).

Cyber-risk containment for organizations requires a combination of *engineering*, *enforcement*, *education* and *encouragement.*

Engineering. One study in 2001 by Jupiter Media Matrix found that 70% of companies surveyed described their level of cyber-risk as "low" or "medium" (Stateman, 2001). Since then organizations have invested heavily in enhanced computer security systems in the aftermath of 9/11 (Held, 2002; Kliem, 2003; Sager, 2001; Schwartz, 2002). Nonetheless, a Conference Board report five years later found that the United States was poorly prepared for a major disruption of the Internet (Vara, 2006a). Particularly vulnerable are the most popular Web sites (Larkin, 2007; Goo, 2007), colleges (Markelein, 2006) and the federal government (GAO says, 2004; Gross, 2007; U.S. General Accounting Office, 2005). The nation's goal is to avoid the nationwide cyber attack that crippled governmental, financial, media and corporate Web sites in Estonia in Spring 2007 (Rhoads, 2007).

Enforcement. *Enforcement* includes the establishment and pursuit of consistent organizational policies regarding communications technology practices (Flynn, 2001). Managers need to establish routine Web site and related audits to determine both the extent of holdings and potential risk vulnerabilities (Hallahan, 2004b). This requires melding physical security and information security functions—a task sometimes difficult (Vara, 2006b). Organizations must be vigilant in pressing criminal and civil charges against perpetrators of crime who pose risks (Goldfarb, 2006). Plagiarism appears to be increasing (Goldsborough, 2004), along with *brandjacking*. The latter involves fraud, counterfeiting and other abuses against businesses such as cybersquatting (Klapper, 2006), false association, pay-to-click (PTC) fraud, domain kiting or tasting, objectionable content, unauthorized sales channels, and phishing (MarkMonitor, 2007). Legal remedies are often difficult because of jurisdictional differences across cyberspace (Bryan-Low, 2007; Hallahan, 2004b, 2006).

Education. *Education* requires enlightening users of an organization's systems about potential risks. Responsibility begins with organizational directors who must be increasingly involved in policy pertaining to risk-related issues (Hicks, 2001; Vispoli, 2006). Employees and others must be instructed about potential risks and scams, such as *cyber-blackmail* (Argenti & Forman, 2003; Warner, 2003). Security experts note that employees create significant risks for organizations through misdeeds or misjudgments. Many staffers are unwittingly duped by hackers who use *social engineering* to gain the confidence of staff while extracting seemingly innocuous information or cooperation (Brandt, 2006; Totty, 2006). Particular problems for business involve the unintended disclosure of proprietary information or trade secrets to lurking competitors engaged in legal competitive intelligence or illegal industrial espionage. Publicly traded firms also must be watchful to avoid the premature release of material information that might influence investors' purchase or sale of equities without providing for prompt and full disclosure to all investors as required under federal securities laws (Hallahan, 2006). All types of organizations must be concerned about the violation of various privacy laws pertaining to employees, customers, students, and patients and cretitors. Many educational and membership organizations face a particular challenge in enlisting cooperation from users over whom those organizations exercise little control (Marklein, 2006).

Encouragement. *Encouragement* includes enhancing the self-efficacy of organizations and users to show they can make a difference in containing cyber-risks. Among the most important efforts in this arena are efforts for large complex organizations to develop crisis plans that encourage risk containment (Andrijcic & Horowitz, 2006; Vijayan, 2004). Various major corporate insurance underwriters have developed actuarial models of cyber-risks and encourage best practices as part of offering *cyberliability insurance* (Boyle, 2000; Lindhe, 2000; Mukopadhyray, Saha, Chakrabarti, Mahanti, & Podder, 2005). Beyond education about risk avoidance, an organization's users must understand the *importance* of risk reduction. Organizations can facilitate this process by developing usable systems (Hallahan, 2001b; Kesmodel, 2006) that foster self-efficacy among users. Risk reduction can be further encouraged through public policies that encourage investment and incentives so organizations manage and discourage cyber-risks (Gross, 2007; Krebs 2007a, b).

CONCLUDING OBSERVATIONS

This review suggests that people's uses of new communications technologies have undergone significant changes over past decade. No one quite knows for certain how the Internet will evolve, despite the best prognostications by experts (see Anderson & Rainie, 2005). New applications, new technologies and new concerns will undoubtedly emerge.

Not surprisingly, the study of crises and risks in the context of cyberspace is an emerging field that blends research on crises and risk with the emerging field of *informatics* (how people use computers) and *captology* (the use of computers as persuasive technologies; Fogg, 2003). In keeping with Coombs' (1996) observation about the state of crisis communications in general, more conceptual and empirically-based investigation is required.

Despite these changing circumstances, it is clear that new technologies have much to offer organizations and individuals as resources in dealing with crises and risks. This is particularly true for mobile communications devices, which are just now beginning to be exploited as organizational communication tools. This is also especially true for younger generations who have grown up as *digital natives* (vs. their elders, *digital immigrants*) and are fully comfortable with Internet and cellular technologies (Prensky, 1991). Generational differences are especially noteworthy in crisis and risk communication: A 2006 study showed that 20% of Americans overall relied on the Internet as their primary source of news and information about science. But, for adults ages 18–30, who also had broadband access at home, that figure was 44%—more than double (Horrigan, 2006).

Although lingering generational differences can be expected to conflate in coming years as the population ages, inconsistent patterns of use pose important implications for new technologies and for the communicators that reply upon them. Research suggests that while dependence on new media has increased, and considerable variation remains in the adoption and commitment to new media across user groups (Horrigan, 2007). For this reason, new media are not panaceas to all crisis and communications challenges—and cannot be examined out of context of a more integrated approach that also incorporates traditional media (see Neuwirth, chapter 20, this volume).

Experts agree that crisis and risk communicators must use *both* traditional and cyber media in order to be effective in creating the most effective messages and targeting and reaching key audiences most efficiently (Coombs, 2007, pp. 102, 171–172; Hallahan, 1994; Looker, Rockland & Taylor, 2007). Although using new technology is fashionable and organizations confront rising expectations about their technological prowess (Kazoleas & Teigan, 2006), evidence from a study of 2,847 global companies suggests that organizations are guarded in their investment in Web 2.0 technologies (McKinsey, 2007; see also Business crawls, 2007). Indeed for some entities, it might be appropriate to forego social pressures (Flanagin, 2000, White, Lublin & Kesmodel, 2007) to engage in the wholesale adoption of new technologies and to deploy these new tools selectively.

This discussion has focused on the implications of communications for crises and risk that might exist in the real world. Yet, as online experiences become a part of our everyday experiences, it is not inconceivable to expect the emergence of *virtual crisis and risk specialists* whose roles will be to cope with incidents that take place entirely within the realm of cyberspace.

Consider the emergence of Second Life—the fantasy Web world where users create and act out life through avatars, or customized cartoon-like characters. More than 80 major brands have created (and paid for) a virtual presence in Second Life in order to reach the site's more than 13 million visitors. Yet, the netizens of Second Life have crashed planes into the Nissan building, murdered customers going into the American Apparel retail store, plastered the NBC Universal logo on a S&M sex parlor, and vandalized the headquarters of thenU.S. presidential candidate John Edwards. Such misdeeds are called "griefing" in Second Life parlance (Fass, 2007; Semuels, 2007). Nevertheless these incidents represent potential crises and risks that might need to be addressed by future virtual crisis and risk managers who undoubtedly will soon inhabit this virtual world.

REFERENCES

A world wide web of terror (2007, July 12). *The Economist.* Retrieved July 21, 2007, from http://www.economist.com/world/displaystory.cfm?story_id=9472498.

Abramowitz, M. (2007, April 13). Rove e-mail sought by congress may be missing. *Washington Post*, p. A1.

Acohido, B. (2006, August 3). Cybercrooks constantly find new ways into PCs. *USA Today.* Retrieved August 15, 2007, from http://www.usatoday.com.

Acohido, B. & Swartz, J. (2006, April 23). Malicious-software spreaders get sneakier, more prevalent. *USA Today.* Retrieved April 24, 2006, from http://www.usatoday.com.

Acohido, B. & Swartz, J. (2006, October 11). Cybercrime flourishes in online hacker forums. *USA Today.* Retrieved October 13, 2006, from http://www.usatoday.com.

Aftab. P. (2005, Summer). The PR professional's role in handling cyberwarfare. *Strategist, 11*(3), 28–30.

Ahrens, F. (2007, February 12). Crackdown on fake blogs, Astroturf. Post I.T. Retrieved February 13, 2007, from http://www.washingtonpost.com.

Aikat, D. (2005, May). The blending of traditional media and Internet: Patterns of media agenda setting and web search trends before and after the September 11 attacks. Paper presented to International Communication Association, New York.

Ainsworth, S., Hardy, C. & Harley, B. (2005). Online consultation: E-democracy and E-resistance in the case of the Development Gateway. *Management Communication Quarterly, 19*, 120–145.

Alfonso, G. H. & Miguel, R. (2006). Trends in online media relations: Web-based corporate press rooms in leading international companies. *Public Relations Review, 32*, 262–275.

Altus, C. (2007, March 20). Survey finds boomers serve as sources for others. *PR Week.* Retrieved March 22, 2007, from http://www.prweek.com.

Alvarez, L. (2006, February 16). (Name here) is a liar and cheat. *New York Times*. Retrieved February 20, 2006, from http://www.nytimes.com.

Alvey, R. J. (2005, December). Creating an effective crisis communication team. Managing media work at Hurricane Katrina field hospital. *Public Relations Tactics, 17*(12), 12.

Andrijcic, E. & Horowitz, B. (2006). A macro-economic framework for evaluation of cyber security risks related to protection of intellectual property. *Risk Analysis: An International Journal, 26*(4), 907–923.

Anderson, J. Q. & Rainie, L. (2006, September 26). The future of the Internet II. Washington, DC: Pew Internet & American Life Project. Retrieved September 30, 2006, from http://www.pewinternet.com.

Anderton, J. P. & Valdiserri, R. O. (2005). Combating syphilis and HIV among users of Internet chatrooms. *Journal of Health Communication, 10*, 665–671.

Ante, S. E. & Grow, B. (2006, May 29). Meet the hackers. *Business Week*, pp. 58–63.

Anthes, G. H. & Wagner, M. (1996, July 1). Internet outages spark disaster fears. *Computerworld, 30*(27), 14.

Appleman, H. (2001, March 4). I scream, you scream: Consumers vent over the net. *New York Times.* Retrieved March 4, 2001, from http://www.nytimes.com.

Argenti, P. & Forman, J. (2002). *The power of corporate communication.* New York: McGraw-Hill.

Arguilla, J. & Ronfeldt, D. (1998). Preparing for information-age conflict. *Information, Communication & Society, 1*(1), 1–22.

Arnaldo, C. A. (2001). *Child abuse on the Internet: Ending the silence*. New York: Berghahn Books.

Associated Press (2007a, April 17). Web becomes a coping mechanism. Retrieved April 20, 2007, from http://msnbc.com/id/18158063/.

Associated Press (2007b, April 23). Man gets 5,000 calls for YouTube posting. Retrieved April 23, 2007, from http://www.usatoday.com.

Atton, C. (2002). *Alternative media.* London: Sage.

Auter, P. J. (2006). Developing and maintain the Al Jazeera websites. In M. G. Parkinson & D. Ekachai (Eds.), *International and intercultural public relations. A campaign case approach* (pp. 239–253). Boston: Allyn & Bacon.

Badaracco, C. H. (1998). The transparent corporation and organized community, *Public Relations Review, 23*(3), 265–272.

Bagg, F. & Millar, D. P (2001, June). *New technologies in successful crisis management. Summary of Professional Development Seminar.* New York: Public Relations Society of America.

Baines, P., Egan, J. & Jefkins, F. (2004). *Public relations. Contemporary issues and techniques.* New York: Elsevier Butterworth Heinemann.

Balfour, F. & Ante, S. E. (2003, March 31). The wired war has arrived. *Business Week*, p. 36–39.

Barbaro, M. (2006, March 7). Wal-Mart enlists bloggers in P.R. campaign. *New York Times.* Retrieved March 9, 2006, from http://www.nytimes.com.

Barkow, T. (2004, Fall). Blogging for business. *Strategist, 10*(4), 40–42.

Barnes, S. B. (2003). *Computer-mediated communication. Human-to-human communication across the internet.* Boston: Allyn & Bacon.

Barr, S. (2006, August 17). Re: What you say in work e-mails. *Washington Post*, p. D04

Batteau, A. W., Brandenburg, D. & Seeger, M. (2006). Project highlights: Multiple agency and jurisdiction organized responses (M.A.J.O.R.) disaster management research. Proceedings of the 2006 International Conference on Digital Government Research, San Diego, CA (pp. 126–127). ACM International Conference Proceeding Series, vol. 151.

Battey, J. (2000, November 20). Saving a shattered image. *InfoWorld, 22*(47), 47–49.

Bennett, W. L. (2003). New media power: The Internet and global activism. In N. Couldry & J. Curran (Eds.), *Contesting media power: Alternative media in a networked world* (pp. 17–38). Lanham, MD: Rowman & Littlefield.

Berkeley, S. & Woolard, T. (2001). Corporate reputation and the Internet. In R. Hillary (Ed.), *The CBI environmental management handbook* (pp. 97–103). Sterling, VA: Earthscan.

Best, S. J., Chmielewski, B. & Krueger, B. S. (2005, Fall). Selective exposure to online foreign news during the conflict with Iraq. *Harvard International Journal of Press/Politics, 10*(4), 52–70.

Bertolucci, J. (1997, February 10). Crisis managing on the Web. *Denver Post*, p. 12C.

Bird, J. (1997, August). Apocalypse when? *Management Today, 86*(8), 56–58.

Blair, T. (2002, April 2). Internet performs global role, supplementing TV. *Online Journalism Review.* Retrieved January 29, 2007, from http://www.ojr/org.

Blake, B. F., Valdiserri, J., Neuendorf, K. & Powers, J. (2006, August). Social desirability effects in the reporting of online shopping and Internet usage. Paper presented to Association for Education in Journalism and Mass Communication, San Francisco.

Boje, D. M., Gephart, Jr., R P. & Thatchenkery, T. J. (Eds.) (1996). *Postmodern management and organization theory.* Thousand Oaks, CA: Sag.

Bortree, D. (2007). Building relationships with child publics: Study of the content of nutrition web sites for children. Unpublished paper, University of Florida, Gainesville.

Bounds G. (2007, May, 22). A growing dispute: Fertilizer start-up uses web as defense. *Wall Street Journal,* pp. B1, B10.

Boyle, C. E. (2000, October 2). Cyberliability: Identifying the risks in cyberspace can be tricky. *Insurance Journal.* Retrieved July 1, 2007, from http://www.insurancejournal.com/magazines/west/2000/10/02/fetures/22552.htm.

Brabbs, C. (2000, September 21). Web fuels consumer activism. *Marketing*, p. 23.

Brandt, A. (2006, August). The 10 biggest security risks you don't know about. *PC World*, pp. 76–88.

Briers, B., De White, S. & van den Bergh, J. (2006, June). E-Zines silence the brand detractors. *Journal of Advertising Research, 46*(2), 199–208.

Bryan-Low, C. (2005, July 13). As identity theft moves online, crime rings mimic big business. *Wall Street Journal*, pp A1, A6.

Bryan-Low, C. (2007, January 17). How legal codes can hinder hacker cases. *Wall Street Journal*, p. A8.

Bucher, H. (2002). Crisis communication and the Internet: Risk and trust in a global media. Retrieved June 25, 2007, from http://www.firstmonday.org/issues/issue7_4/bucher/.

Buckman, R. & Pringle, D. (2005, January 3). Cellphones help with disaster relief. *Wall Street Journal,* p. B5.

Buktaman, S. (1993). *Terminal identity*. Durham, NC: Duke University Press.

Bulik, B. S. (2007, April 23). BlackBerry bungles blackout. *Advertising Age.* Retrieved April 23, 2007, from http://adage.com/print?article_id=116217.

Burden, M. C. (2006). *The blog of war: Front-line dispatches from soldiers in Iraq and Afghanistan.* New York: Simon & Schuster Paperbacks.

Burgelman, R. A. & Grove, A. S. (1996, Winter). Strategic dissonance. *California Management Review, 38*(2), 8–28. "Inside Intel" retrieved July 1, 2007, from http://gsb.stanford.edu/community/bmag/sbsm0696/bellweather2.htm.

Burns, E. (2006, August 14). Report: CGM sites dominate fastest-growing web brands. Retrieved August 25, 2006, from http://www.clickz.com/3623137/print.

Business crawls into Web 2.0 (2007, May 1). Retrieved May 2, 2007, from http://www.emarketer.com/Articles/Print.aspx?100486.

Callan, J. (2002). *How to keep operating in a crisis. Managing a business in a major catastrophe*. Burlington, VT: Bower.

Callison, C. (2003). Media relations and the Internet: How Fortune 500 company web sites assist journalists in gathering news, *Public Relations Review, 29*(1), 29–42.

Calloway, L. J. (1991). Survival of the fastest: Information technology and corporate crises, *Public Relations Review, 17*(1), 85–92.

Calloway, L. J. & Keen, P. G. W. (1996). Organizing for crisis response. *Journal of Information Technology, 11*, 13–26.

Camp, L. J. (2001). *Trust and risk in Internet commerce*. Cambridge, MA: MIT Press.

Campbell, S. B. (2002). Internet public relations: A tool for crisis management. In E. Gilboa (Ed.), *Media and conflict. Framing issues. Making policy. Shaping opinions*. Ardsley, NY: Transnational Publishers.

Caponigro, J. R. (2000). *The crisis counselor. A step-by-step guide to managing a business crisis*. New York: Contemporary Books.

Capriotti, P. & Moreno, A. (2007). Corporate citizenship and public relations. The importance and interactivity of social responsibility issues on corporate websites. *Public Relations Review, 33*, 84–91.

Cásarez, N. B. (2002, Summer). Dealing with cybersmears: How to protect your organization from online defamation. *Public Relations Quarterly, 47*(2), 40–45.

Case, D. O., Andrews, J. E., Johnson, J. D. & Allard, S. L. (2005). Avoiding versus seeking: The relationship of information seeking to avoidance, blunting, coping, dissonance and related concepts. *Journal of the Medical Library Association, 93*(3), 353–362.

Castells, M. (2000). *The rise of the network society* (2nd ed.). Malden, MA: Blackwell.

Chadwick, A. (2006). *Internet politics: States, citizens and new communications technologies*. New York: Oxford University Press.

Cho, S. & Cameron, C. T. (2006). Public nudity on cell phones: Managing conflict in crisis situations. *Public Relations Review, 32*(2), 199–201.

Chrysler CEO rips advocacy groups (2002, May 10). *O'Dwyer's PR Daily*. Retrieved May 10, 2002, from http://www.odwyerpr.com.

Clegg, S. (Ed.) (1990). *Modern organizations: Organization studies in the postmodern world*. London: Sage.

Cloudman, R. & Hallahan, K. (2006). Crisis communications preparedness among U.S. organizations: Activities and assessments by public relations practitioners. *Public Relations Review, 32*(4), 367–376.

Collins, E. L, Zoch, L.M. & Walsh, D.C. (2005, August). Closing the deal: The use of Snow & Benford's core framing functions on activist web sites. Paper presented to Association for Education in Journalism and Mass Communication, San Antonio, TX.

Companies underestimate online financial risks (2001, December). *PR Tactics, 8*(12), p. 3.

comScore Media Matrix (2006, August 16). The score: User-generated news grows. Retrieved July 11, 2007, from http://www.imediaconnection.com.

Conlin, M. (2007, April 16). Web attack. *Business Week*, pp. 54, 56.

Coombs, W. T. (1998). The internet as potential equalizer: New leverage for confronting social irresponsibility. *Public Relations Review, 24*(3), 289–303.

Coombs, W. T. (2002). Assessing online issue threats: Issue contagions and their effect on issue prioritization. *Journal of Public Affairs, 2*, 215–229.

Coombs, W. T. (2006). Crisis management. A communicative approach. In C. H. Botan & V. Hazelton (Eds.), *Public relations theory II* (pp. 171–197). Mahwah, NJ: Erlbaum.

Coombs, W. T. (2007). *Ongoing crisis communications* (2nd ed.). Thousand Oaks, CA: Sage.

Coombs, W. T. & Holladay, Sherry, J. (2007). *It's not just PR. Public relations in society*. Madden, MA: Blackwell.

Copeland, L. (2004, August 21). Web plays key role in drive toward tire recall. *Computerworld, 38*(34), p. 6.

Coren, M. (2005, January 5). Internet aids tsunami relief. CNN. Retrieved January 7, 2005, from http://www.cnn.com/2005/TECH/01/05/tech.tsunami/index.html.

Couldry, N. (2004). The digital divide. In D. Gauntlett & R. Horsley (Eds.), *Web studies* (pp. 185–194. New York: Oxford University Press.

Couldry, N. & Curran, J. (Eds.) (2003). *Contesting media power: Alternative media in a networked world*. Lanham, MD: University Press.

Courtright, J. L. (2007). Internet activism and institutional image management. In J. L. Courtright and P. M. Smudde (Eds.), *Power and public relations* (pp. 131–178). Cresskill, NJ: Hampton Press.

Cozier, Z. R. & Witmer, D. F. (2001). The development of a structuration analysis of new publics in an electronic environment. In R. L. Heath (Ed.), *Handbook of public relations* (pp. 615–624). Thousand Oaks, CA: Sage.

Craig, T. (2007, January 26). Video blogging spurs new brand of politics. *Washington Post,* p. B06.

Crawford, A.P. (1999). When those nasty rumors start breeding on the web, you've got to act fast. *Public Relations Quarterly, 44*(4), 43–45.

Crisis Rx for DoubleClick (2000, February 28). *Advertising Age, 71*(9), 58.

Crock, S., Magnusson, P. Walczak, L. & Balfour, F. (2003, April 7). The doctrine of digital war. *Business Week*, pp. 30–32.

Cullen, T. (2007, July 18). Using your credit report to protect against identity theft. *Wall Street Journal*, p. D5.

Cyberadvocacy (2000, October/December). *Futurist, 34*(5), 67.

Dalton, G. (1999, September 6). Coping with e-business emergency. *Informationweek,* no. 751, 42–53.

Dance, F. E. X. (2003). The digital divide. In L. Strate, R. L. Jacobson & S. B. Gibson (Eds.), *Communication and cyberspace: Social interaction in an electronic environment* (pp. 171–182). Creskill, NJ: Hampton Press.

Dartnell, M. (2006). *Insurgency online: Web activism and global conflict.* Toronto: University of Toronto Press.

Deck, S. (1996, September 9). 'net aids Red Cross. *Computerworld, 30*(37), 12.

Dell, K. & Cullen, L. T. (2006, September 11). Snooping bosses. *TIME*, pp. 62–64.

Dewan, S. (2005, September 3). The desperate cry out for loved ones still lost. *New York Times*. Retrieved September 7, 2005, from http://www.nytimes.com.

Dezenhall, E. (2003). *Nail 'em. Confronting high-profile attacks on celebrities and businesses*. Amherst, NY: Prometheus Books.

Dezenhall, E. & Webber, J. (2006). *Damage control: Why everything you know about crisis management is wrong*. New York: Penguin.

Dibble, J. (1998). My *Tinylife: Crime and passion in a virtual world.* New York: Henry Holt and Company.

Dimitrova, D. V., Kaid, L. L., Williams, A. P. & Trammell, K. D. (2005). War on the web: The immediate news framing of Gulf War II. *Harvard International Journal of Press/Politics. 10*(1), 22–24.

DiNardo, A. M. (2002). The Internet as a crisis management tool: A critique of banking sites during Y2K, *Public Relations Review 28*(4), 367–378.

Doucette, N. (1998, December). Disaster planning: Considering the contingencies. *Rough Notes, 14*(12), 38–40.

Downing, J. R. (2004). American Airlines' use of mediated employee channels after the 9/11 attacks. *Public Relations Review, 30*, 37–48.

Duke, S. (2002). Wired science: Use of World Wide Web and e-mail in science public relations, *Public Relations Review 28*(3), 311–324.

Dutta-Bergman, M. J. (2004). Complementarity in consumption of news types across traditional and new media. *Journal of Broadcasting and Electronic Media, 48***.** 41–60.

Dutta-Bergman, M. J. (2006). Community participation and Internet use after September 11: Complementarity in channel consumption. *Journal of Computer-Mediated Communication, 1*, 469–484.

Dylko, I. B. & Kosicki, G. M. (2006, August). Sociology of news and new media: How the blogsphere transforms our understanding of journalism and changes news. Paper presented to Association for Education in Journalism and Mass Communication, San Francisco.

Dzwo, T. (1998, August). Crises on the cyberspace: Applying agenda-setting theory to on-line crisis management. Paper presented to Association for Education in Journalism and Mass Communication, Baltimore, MD. Retrieved June 25, 2007, from http://list.msu.edu/cgi-bin/wa?A2=ind9811D&L=aejmc&P=R1069 7.

Dzwo, T., Roberts, M. S., Baker, G. F., & Sutherland, J. C. (1999, May). Corporate crises in cyberspace: The role of on-line communication in shaping the public agenda. Paper presented to International Communication Association, San Francisco.

E-Business emergencies (1999, September 6). *InformationWeek*, no. 751, p. 42.

Eccles, R. G., Newquist, S. C. & Schatz, R. (2007, February). Reputation and its risks. *Harvard Business Review, 85*(2), 104–114.

Eggen, D. (2007). Court will oversee wiretap program. *Washington Post*, p. A01.

Eggert, A. (2006). Intangibility and perceived risk in online environment. *Journal of Marketing Management, 22*(5/6), 553–572.

Elgin, B. (2006, July 17). The plot to hijack your computer. *Business Week*, pp. 41–48.

Ellis, J.E. (2006, July 24). Spyware, Inc. *Business Week*, pp. 82–83.
Embar-Seedon, A. (2002). Cyberterrorism. Are we under siege? *American Behavioral Scientist, 45*(6), 1033–1043.
Esrock, S. L. & Leichty, G. B. (2000). Organization of corporate web pages: Publics and functions, *Public Relations Review, 26*(3), 327–344.
Esrock, S. L. & Leichty, G. B. (1999). Corporate world wide web pages: Serving the news media and other publics, *Journalism & Mass Communication Quarterly, 76*(3), 456–467.
Esrock, S. L. & Leichty, G. B. (1998). Social responsibility and corporate web pages: Self-presentation or agenda-setting, *Public Relations Review, 24*(3), 305–320.
Fallows, D. (2005, January 23). Search engine users: Internet searchers are confident, satisfied and trusting – but they also are unaware and naïve. Washington, DC: Pew Internet and American Life Project. Retrieved June 25, 2007. from http://www.pewinternet.org.
Farrell, G. (2000, April 7). From sour grapes to online white. *USA Today*, pp. 1B–2B.
Fass, A. (2007, July 2). Sex. pranks and reality. *Forbes, 180*(1). Retrieved July 7, 2007, from http://members.forbes.com/forbes/2007/0702/048_print.html.
Fearn-Banks, K. (2002). *Crisis communications. A casebook approach* (2nd ed.), Mahwah, NJ: Erlbaum.
Fearn-Banks, K. (2007). *Crisis communications. A casebook approach* (3rd ed.), Mahwah, NJ: Erlbaum.
Federal Bureau of Investigation (2007). Internet fraud [Web site]. Retrieved June 25, 2007, from http://www.fbi/gov?majcases/fraud/internetschemes.htm.
Feenberg, A. & Barney, D. (2004). *Community in the digital age. Philosophy and practice.* Lanham, MD: Rowman & Littlefield.
Few companies have web crisis policies (2001, July 9). *Investor Relations Business*, pp. 1, 18.
Fine, J. (2006, July 3). Screamfests are so old media. *Business Week*, p. 26.
Flanagin, A.J. (2000). Social pressures on organizational website adoption. *Human Communication Research, 26*(4), 618–646.
Flynn, N. (2001). *The e-policy handbook.* New York: AMACOM.
Flynn, N. (2005). *Blog rules! A business guide to managing policy, public relations and legal issues.* New York: AMACOM.
Fogg, B. J. (2003). *Persuasive technology: Using computers to change what we think and do.* Boston: Morgan Kaufmann.
Ford, J. (2004, Summer). Integrating the Internet into conflict management systems. *The Journal of Quality & Participation, 27*(2), 28–30.
Ford, T. V. & Gill, G. (2001). Radical Internet use. In T. V. Ford & G. G (Eds.), *Radical media. Rebellious communication and social movements* (pp. 201–234). Thousand Oaks, CA: Sage.
Forsythe, S., Liu, C. Shannon, D. & Gardner, L.C. (2006). Development of a scale to measure the perceived benefits and risks of online shopping. *Journal of Interactive Marketing, 20*(2), 55–75.
Fost, D. (2007, March 29). Bad behavior in the blogosphere. *San Francisco Chronicle*. Retrieved March 30, 2007, from http://www/SFgate.com.
Fox, S., Rainie, L. & Madden, M. (2002, September 5). One year later: September 11 and the Internet. Washington, DC: Pew Internet & American Life Project. Retrieved September 10, 2002, from http://www.pewinternet.org/report_display.asp?r=69.
Fox, S. (2004, October 10). Prescription drugs online. Washington, DC: Pew Internet & American Life Project. Retrieved July 1, 2007, from http://www.pewinternet.org/PPF/r/139/report_display.asp.
Fox, S. (2006, October 29). Online health search 2006. Washington, DC: Pew Internet & American Life Project. Retrieved June 25, 2007, from http://www.pewinternet.org.
Francisco, B. (2005, September 2). Web provides critical during Katrina. *Market Watch.* Retrieved September 2, 2005, from http://www.marketwatch.com/news/.
Fried, L. (1995). *Managing information technology in turbulent times*. New York: Wiley.
Frith, C. R. & Aikat, D. (2003, July). The interplay of old and new media: How the traditional news media affected Web searches before and after September 11, 2001. Paper presented to the Association for Education in Journalism and Mass Communication, Kansas City.
Gaddis, S. (2001). On-line research techniques for the public relations practitioner. In. R. L. Heath (Ed.), *Handbook of public relations* (pp. 591–602). Thousand Oaks, CA: Sage.
Galloway, C. (2005). Cyber PR and the "dynamic touch," *Public Relations Review, 31*(4), 572–577.
Garbarino, E. & Strahilevitz, M. (2004). Gender differences in the perceived risk of buying online and the effects of receiving a site recommendation. *Journal of Business Research, 57*, 768–775.
Genova, G. L. (2006). Crisis communication practices of an international relief agency. *Business Communication Quarterly, 69*(3), 329–337.
Gibson, D. C. (2000, Summer). The cyber-revolution in product recall public relations. *Public Relations Quarterly, 45*(2), 24–26.

Gibson, D. C. (2000, Winter). Firestone's failed recalls, 1978 and 2000: A public relations explanation. *Public Relations Quarterly, 45*(4), 10–13.

Gillespie, T. (2000). Virtual violence? Pornography and violence against women on the Internet. In J. Radford, M. Friedberg & L. Harne (Eds.), *Women, violence and strategies for action: Feminist research, policy and practice* (pp. 40–56). Philadelphia, PA: Open University Press.

Gillin, P. (2007). *The new influencers*. Sanger, CA: Quill Driver Books.

Gimmler, A. (2001). Deliberate democracy, the public sphere and the internet. *Philosophy & Social Criticism, 27*(4), 21–39.

Glass, A. J. (2002). The war on terrorism goes online: Media and government response to the first post-Internet crisis. Working Paper 2002-3. Boston: Joan Shorenstein Center on the Press, Politics and Public Policy.

Goldsborough, R. (2004, November). Stop, thief! Preventing web plagiarists from stealing your content. *Public Relations Tactics 11*(11), 19.

Goldfarb, Z. A. (2006, July 18). To agency insiders, cyber theft and slow response are no surprise. *Washington Post*, p. A17.

Gombossy, G. (2007, March 2). Best Buy confirms it has secret website. *Hartford Courant*. Retrieved March 7, 2007, from http://www.courant.com.

Goo, S. K. (2007, January 30). Google moves to disarm search "bombs." *Washington Post*, p. D03.

Goodin, Dan (2005, December 5). Wikipedia writers told to register. Associated Press.

Gray, T. (2005, January 6). FBI warns of tsunami charity scams. Retrieved January 12, 2007, from http://www.internetnews.com/xSP/article.php/3455501.

Green, H. (2007, May 7). The big shots of blogdom. *Business Week*, p. 66.

Greenberg, K. (2007, April 30). When Google works too well. MediaPost Publications. Retrieved April 30, 2007, from http://www.mediapost.com.

Greenhouse, S. & Barbaro, M. (2006, February 17). On private web site, Wal-Mart chief talks tough. *New York Times*. Retrieved March 20, 2006, from http://www.nytimes.com.

Greer, C. F. & Moreland, K. D. (2003). United Airlines' and American Airlines' online crisis communication following the September 11 terrorist attacks. *Public Relations Review, 29,* 427–441.

Gregory, A. (2004). Scope and structure of public relations: A technology driven view, *Public Relations Review, 30*(3), 245–254.

Grohol, J. M. (2005). Internet addiction guide. Retrieved June 25, 2007, from http://www.psychcentral.com/netaddition/.

Gross, G. (2007, April 11). Cybersecurity group calls for new gov't approaches. *PC World*. Retrieved March 16, 2007, from http://www.washingtonpost.com.

Grow, B. (2005, May 30). Hacker hunters. An elite force takes on the dark side of computing. *Business Week*, pp. 74–82.

Grow, B. (2006, January 9). Gold rush. *Business Week*, pp. 69–73.

Grunig, J. E. (1997). A situational theory of publics: conceptual history, recent challenges and new research. In D. Moss, T. MacManus & D. Verčič (Eds.) Public *relations research: An international perspective* (pp. 3–48). London: International Thomson Business Press.

Guensburg, C. (1999, May). Online access to the war zone. *American Journalism Review, 21*(4), 12–13.

Guth, D. W. & Marsh, C. (2007). *Public relations: A values-driven approach* (3rd ed.). Boston: Allyn & Bacon.

Guth, D. W. & Marsh, C. (2005). *Adventures in public relations: Case studies and critical thinking*. Boston: Allyn & Bacon.

Habermas, J. (1962/1989). *The structural transformation of the public sphere. An inquiry into a category of bourgeois society* (T. Burger with F. Lawrence, trans.). Cambridge, MA: MIT Press.

Hachigian, D. & Hallahan, K. (2003). Perceptions of public relations web sites by computer industry journalists, *Public Relations Review, 29*(2), 43–62.

Hafner, K. (2004, March 11). The camera never lies, but the software can. *New York Times*. Retrieved June 25, 2007, from http://www.nytimes.com

Hafner, K. (2005, September 5). For victims, news about home can come from strangers online. *New York Times*. Retrieved September 7, 2005, from http://www.nytimes.com.

Hagan, N. (2007, June 11). Libby's supporter's who wrote to judge learn that letters take on new life on the web. *New York Times*. Retrieved June 11, 2007, from http://www.nytimes.com.

Haig, M. (2002). *E-PR: The essential guide to public relations on the Internet*. London: Kogan Page.

Hallahan, K. (1994, Summer). Public relations and circumvention of the press. *Public Relations Quarterly, 39*(2), 17–19.

Hallahan, K. (2001a). Strategic media planning. Toward an integrated public relations media model. In R. L. Heath (Ed.), *Handbook of public relations* (pp. 461–470). Thousand Oaks, CA: Sage.

Hallahan, K. (2001b). Improving public relations web sites through usability research, *Public Relations Review, 27*(2), 223–240.

Hallahan, K. (2004a). Online public relations. In H. Bidgoli (Ed.), *The Internet encyclopedia* (vol. 2, pp. 769–783). Hoboken, NJ: Wiley.
Hallahan, K. (2004b). Protecting an organization's digital public relations assets. *Public Relations Review, 30*, 255–268.
Hallahan, K. (2004c). 'Community' as the framework for public relations theory and research. *Communication Yearbook, 28*, 233–279.
Hallahan, K. (2006). Responsible online communication. In K. Fitzpatrick & C. Bronstein (Eds.), *Ethics in public relations. Responsible advocacy* (pp. 107–130.
Hallahan, K. (2008). Organizational-public relations in cyberspace. In T. Hansen-Horn & B. Neff (Eds.), *Public relations theory: From theory to practice* (pp. 43–70). Boston: Allyn & Bacon, 2005.
Halpern, M. & Mehrotra, A.K. (2000, February). The tangled web of e-commerce: Identifying the legal risks of online marketing. *The Computer Lawyer, 17*(2), 8–14.
Hamm, S. (2006, August 21/28). Heading off the hackers. *Business Week*, p. 36.
Hanna, G. (2005, January). How to take a computer disaster in stride. *Strategic Finance, 86*(7), 49–52.
Hansell, S. (2006, June 21). MySpace to add restrictions to protect younger teenagers. *New York Times*. Retrieved June 24, 2006, from http://www.nytimes.com.
Harkinson, J. (2000, July-August). On line and active. *E 12-14*, no. 4, 12–14.
Harmon, A. (2003, August 18). The bits are willing, but the batteries are weak. *New York Times*. Retrieved August 18, 2003, from http://www.nytimes.com.
Harris, M. (1997, April 12). Flood provides the World Wide Web a chance to display its usefulness. *Grand Forks Herald*, p. 1. Retrieved 1997 from http://www.gfherald.com/life/local/412marciacol.htm.
Harshman, E. M., Gilsinan, J. F., Fisher, J. E., & Yeager, F. C. (2005). Professional ethics in a virtual world: The impact of the Internet on traditional notions of professionalism. *Journal of Business Ethics, 58*, 227–236.
Hart, K. (2006, July 6). Angry customers use web to shame firms. *Washington Post*, p. D1.
Hart, K. (2007, January 27). Tracking who's saying what about whom. *Washington Post*, p. D01.
Haven, B. (2007, January 25). Leveraging user-generated content. Retrieved July 12, 2007, from http://www.forrester.com.
Hearit, K. M. (1999). Newsgroups, activist publics and corporate apologia: The case of Intel and its Pentium chip. *Public Relations Review, 25*(3), 291–308.
Heath, R. L. (1997). *Strategic issues management*. Thousand Oaks, CA: Sage.
Heath, R. L. (1998). New communication technologies: An issues management point of view. *Public Relations Review, 24*(3), 274–288.
Heath, R. L. & Millar, D. P. (2004). A rhetorical approach to crisis communication: Management, communication processes and strategic responses. In D P. Millar, & R. L. Heath (Eds.), *Responding to crisis. A rhetorical approach to crisis communication* (pp. 1–17). Mahwah, NJ: Erlbaum.
Held, G. (2002). Security and the Internet. In S. Purba (Ed.), *New directions in Internet management* (pp. 537–546). Boca Raton, FL: Auerbach Publications.
Helft, M. (2007, May 31). Google photos stir a debate over privacy. *New York Times*. Retrieved June 1, 2007, from http://www.nytimes.com.
Herring, S. C. (2001). Computer-mediated discourse. In D. Sciffrin, D. Tannen & H. E. Hamilton (Eds.), *The handbook of discourse analysis* (pp. 612–634). Malden, MA: Blackwell.
Hick, S., Halpin, E. F. & Hoskins, E. (Eds.) (2000). *Human rights and the Internet*. New York: St. Martin's Press.
Hick, S. & McNutt, J. (Eds.) (2002). *Advocacy, activism and the Internet. Community organization and social policy.* Chicago: Lyceum Books
Hicks, W. M. (2001, September). Cyber-risk meets corporate governance. *Directorship, 27*(8), 1–4.
Hill, K. A. & Hughes, J. E. (1998). *Cyberpolitics: Citizen activism in the age of the Internet*. Lanham, MD: Rowman & Littlefield.
Hill, L. N. & White, C. (2000). Public relations practitioners' perceptions of the World Wide Web as a communications tool, *Public Relations Review, 26*(1), 31–52.
Hindman, D. B. (2000). The rural-urban digital divide. *Journalism & Mass Communication Quarterly, 77*, 549–560.
Hoffman, L. H. (2006). Is Internet content different after all? A content of mobilizing information in online and print newspapers. *Journalism & Mass Communication Quarterly, 83*(1), 58–76.
Holloway, S. J. & Valentine, G. (2003). *Cyberkids. Children in the information age*. New York: Routledge-Falmer.
Holmes, E. (2006, August 7). On MySpace, millions of users make "friends" with ads. *Wall Street Journal*, pp. B1, B3.
Holtz, S. (1999). *Public relations on the net. Winning strategies to inform and influence the media, the investment community, the government, the public and more*. New York: AMACOM.

Holtz, S. (2002). *Public relations on the net. Winning strategies to inform and influence the media, the investment community, the government, the public and more* (2nd ed.). New York: AMACOM.
Holtz, S. (2007, April). Keynote remarks at New Communications Forum. Retrieved April 9, 2007, from http://www.newcommreview.com?p=689.
Holtz, S. & Demopoulos, T. (2006). *Blogging for business: everything you need to know and why you should care*. Chicago, IL: Kaplan Publishing.
Holtzman, D. H. (2006). *Privacy lost. How technology is endangering your privacy*. San Francisco: Jossey-Bass.
Horan, T. A., Marich, M. & Schooley, B. (2006). Time-critical information services: analysis and workshop findings on technology, organizational, and policy dimensions to emergency response and related e-governmental services. Proceedings of the 2006 International Conference on Digital Government Research, San Diego, CA (pp. 115–123). ACM International Conference Proceeding Series, vol. 151.
Horrigan, J. B. (2006, November 20). The internet as a resource of news and information about science. Washington, DC: Pew Internet & American Life Project. Retrieved November 25, 2006, from http://www.pewinternet.org.
Horrigan, J. B. (2007, May 6). A typology of information and communication technology users. Washington, DC: Pew Internet & American Life Project. Retrieved May 8, 2007, from http://www.pewinternet.org.
Hunt, K. (1996). Establishing a presence on the World Wide Web. A rhetorical approach. *Technical Communication, 43*(4), 376–387.
Hyde, J. (2006). News coverage of genetic cloning: When science journalism becomes future-oriented speculation. *Journal of Communication Inquiry, 30*(43), 229–250.
Irvine, M. (2006, July 18). E-mail has become the new snail mail as younger set sets goes with text message. *USA Today*. Retrieved July 20, 2006, from http://www.usatoday.com/tech/news/2006-07-18-snail-e-mail_x.htm.
Institute of Public Relations (2000). *The death of spin. Summary report of Public Relations Consultants Association Internet Commission*. London: IPR.
Internet addiction disorder (2007, July 17). Retrieved July 25, 2005, from http://en.wikipedia.com/wiki/Internet_Addiction#_note-0.
Internet café heals tsunami-hit area (2005, January 19). Retrieved January 25, 2005, from http://sify.com/news/internet/fullstory.php?id=136561607.
Internet damage from 9/11 said minor. (2002, November 20). Associated Press. Retrieved November 21, 2002, from www.nytimes.com.
Internet disaster recovery (1997, March). *Managing Office Technology, 42*(3), 14.
In-Stat (2006). User generated content—More than just Watching the You Tube and Hangin in MySpace. Abstract of report by analyst Michael Inouye. Retrieved July 12, 2007, from http://www.instat.com/abstract.asp?id=212&SKU=IN0602976CM
James, D. (2000, November 6). When your company goes code blue: How crisis management has planned. *Marketing News, 34*(23), 1, 15.
James, J. (2003). *Bridging the global digital divide*. Cheltenham, UK: Edward Elgar.
Janal, D. S. (1998). *Risky business. Protect your business from being stalked, connected or blackmailed on the Web*. New York: Wiley.
Jesdanum, A. (2006, October 5). Instant-messaging conversations can easily linger for years as evidenced in Foley case. Associated Press. Retrieved October 6, 2007, from http://www.usatoday.com.
Jenkins, C. L. (2007, April 14). Stalkers go high tech to intimidate victims. *Washington Post*, p. A01.
Jo, S. & Kim, Y. (2003). The effect of web characteristics on relationship building. *Journal of Public Relations Research, 15*(3), 199–224.
Johnson, M.A. (1997). Public relations and technology: Practitioner perspectives. *Journal of Public Relations Research, 3*, 213–236.
Joiner, R., Gavin, J., Duffield, J., Brosnan, M., Crook, C., Durndell, A. L., Maras, P., Miller, J., Scott, A.J. & Lovatt (2005). Gender, Internet identification and Internet anxiety: Correlates of Internet use. *CyberPsychology & Behavior, 8*(4), 371–378.
Joiner, R., Brosnan, M., Duffield, J., Gavin, J. & Maras, P. (2007). *Computers in Human Behavior, 23*(3), 1408–1420.
Jones, S. & Rainie, L. (2002). Internet use and the terror attacks. In B. S. Greenberg (Ed.), *Communication and terrorism* (pp. 27–38). Cresskill, NJ: Hampton Press.
Junnarkar, S. (2002, January 2). Report: half of net users mistrust sites. CNet. Retrieved June 24, 2007, from http://news.com
Kabel, M. (2006, July 18). Gloves come off as Wal-Mart critics slam each other on Web. Associated Press. Retrieved July 20, 2006, from http://www.usatody.com.
Kang, S. & Norton, H.E. (2004). Nonprofit organization's use of the World Wide Web: Are they sufficiently fulfilling organizational goals? *Public Relations Review, 30*(3), 279–284.

Kanilian, S. & Gale, K.L. (2003, Winter). With 3 hours, 97 percent learn about 9/11 attacks. *Newspaper Research Journal, 24*(2), 78–91.

Kanso, A. M. & Nelson, R.A. (2006). Corporate reputation under attack: A case study of Nike's public relations campaign to blunt negative perceptions of its labor practices. In M. G. Parkinson & D. Ekachai, D. (Eds.*), International and intercultural public relations. A campaign case approach* (pp. 99–116). Boston: Allyn & Bacon.

Kantor, A. (2007, April 27). Virginia Tech tragedy highlights differences between old, new media. *USA Today*, pp. A1. Retrieved April 28, 2007, from http://www.usatoday.com.

Katrina public web kiosk project wants volunteers (2005, September 5). Retrieved September 9, 2005, from http://www.desktoplinux.co/news/NS4984662030.html.

Kazoleas, D. & Teigen, L. G. (2006). The technology-image expectancy gap: A new theory of public relations. In C. H. Botan and V. Hazleton (Eds.), *Public relations theory II* (pp. 415–433). Mahwah, NJ: Erlbaum.

Keegan, C. (2002, November). Cyber-terrorism risk. *Financial Executive*, *20*(11), 35–37. Retrieved December 3, 2006, from http://www.fei.com.

Kellner, D. (2004). 9/11, spectacles of terror and media manipulation. *Critical Discourse Studies, 1*(1), 41–64.

Kent, M. L. & Taylor, M. (1998). Building dialogic relationships through the World Wide Web, *Public Relations Review, 24*(3), 321–334.

Kent, M. L., Taylor, M. & White, W. J. (2003). The relationship between Web site design and organizational responsiveness to stakeholders, *Public Relations Review, 29*(2), 63–78.

Kesmodel, D. (2006, May 31). Codes on sites "captcha" anger of web users. *Wall Street Journal*, pp. B1–B2.

Kesmodel, D. & Wilke, J. R. (2007, July 12). Whole Foods is hot, Wild Oats a dud—so said "Rahodeb." *Wall Street Journal*, p. A1, 10.

Key, R.J. (2005, November). How the PR profession can flourish in this new digital age. *Public Relations Tactics, 12*(11), 18.

Kibby, M.D. (2005). Email forwardables: folklore in the age of the internet. *New Media & Society, 7*(6), 770–790.

Kidman, A. (2007, May 2). The resignation of BP's CEO .... Retrieved May 3, 2007, from http://www.itwire.com.

Kiger, P. (2001, November). Lessons from a crisis: How communication kept a company together. *Workforce, 80*(11), 28–36.

Killoran, J. B. (1999). Under construction: A "PR" department for private citizens. *Business Communication Quarterly, 62*(2), 101–104.

Kim, J.J. (2007, July 18). Options grow for investors to lend online. *Wall Street Journal*, pp. D1, D10.

Kim, J. R. & Shin, H. (2005). How an issue in cyberspace shifts to the real world: Three-stage cyber-issue diffusion (CID) model. Paper presented to International Communication Association, Seoul, Korea.

Kim, Y., Jung, J., Cohen, E. L. & Ball-Rokeach, S. J. (2004). Internet connectedness before and after September 11, 2001. *New Media & Society, 6*(5), 611–631.

Klapper, B. S. (2006, January 25). U.N. reports rise in cybersquatting. *Seattle Post-Intelligencer*. Retrieved January 26, 2006, from http://seattlepi.nwsource.com/business/1700AP_UN_Cybersquatting.html.

Kliem, R. L. (2002). Managing risk in an intranet environment. In S. Purba (Ed.), *New directions in Internet management* (pp. 345–351). Boca Raton, FL: Auerbach Publications.

Kline, D. & Burnstein, D. (2005*). Blog! How the newest media revolution is changing politics, business and culture.* New York: CDS Books.

Klotz, R. (2001). Internet politics: A survey of practices. In R. P. Hart & D. R. Shaw (Eds.), *Communication in U.S. elections. New agendas* (pp. 185–202). Lanham, MD: Rowman & Littlefield.

Kodrich, K. & Laituri, M. (2005). The formation of a disaster community in cyberspace. The role of online news media after the 2001 Gujarat earthquake. *Convergence: The Journal of Research Into New Media Technologies, 11*(3), 40–56.

Kolko, B. E. (Ed.) (2003). *Virtual publics: Policy and community in the electronic age*. New York: Columbia University Press.

Knobloch-Westerwick, S., Carpentier, F. D., Blumhoff, A., & Nickel, N. (2005). Selective exposure effects for positive and negative news: Testing the robustness of the information utility model. *Journalism & Mass Communication Quarterly, 82*(1), 181–195.

Krebs, B. (2006, February 19). Invasion of the computer snatchers. *Washington Post*, p. W10.

Krebs, B. (2007a, April 12). Federal government sees modest computer security gains. *Washington Post*. Retrieved April 16, 2007, from http://www.washingtonpost.com.

Krebs, B. (2007b, April 26). Nation's cyber plan outdated, lawmakers told. *Washington Post*. Retrieved April 26, 2007, from http://www.washingtonpost.com.

Krebs, B. & Mayer, C. E. (2005, September 1). Scammers hit web in Katrina's wake. *Washington Post,* p. D12.

Krupa, T. (2002, November). Surviving without e-mail: Effective communicating and managing information during technology crisis. Proceedings of the 30th annual ACM SIGUCCS Conference on User Services (pp. 186–190). New York: Association for Computing Machinery Special Interest Group of University and College Computing Services. Providence RI.

Kutan, A. & Peters, L. (2003). *From digital divide to digital opportunity*. Lanham, MD: Scarecrow Press.

Lacohee, H, Phippen, A. D. & Furnell, S. M. (2006). Risk and restitution and how users establish online trust. *Computer & Security, 25*(7), 486–493.

Lambert, P., Herbst, D., Achilles, J., Richardson, S., Steele, D., & Egan, N. (2005, August 8). Blogged out of their jobs. *People*, pp. 107–108.

Landro, L. (2007, June 12). The growing clout of online patient groups. *Wall Street Journal,* p. D1.

Larkin, E. (2007, April 19). Popular web sites highly vulnerable to attack. *PC World*. Retrieved January 20, 2007, from http://www.washingtonpost.com.

LaValle, A. (2006, July 17). Email scammers try new bait in "vishing" for fresh victims. *Wall Street Journal,* pp. B1, B6.

Lee, A. Y. L. (2005a, May). Internet press freedom and online crisis reporting. The role of news sites in SARS epidemic. Paper presented to International Communication Association, New York.

Lee, A. Y. L. (2005b). Between global and local: The glocalization of online news coverage on the trans-regional crisis of SARS. *Asian Journal of Communication, 15*(3), 255–273.

Leggatt, H. (2007, April 30). Online travel consumers prefer use-generated content. Retrieved June 25, 2007, from http://www.bizreport.com/2007/04/online_travel_consumers_prefer_usergenerated__content__html.

Lehmert, A. (2002, September). Bringing back the web. *Quill, 90*(7), 17–19.

Leland, J. (2007, February 18). Debtors search for discipline via blogs. *New York Times*. Retrieved February 18, 2007, from http://www.nytimes.com.

Lenhart, A. & Fox, S. (2006). Bloggers. A portrait of the internet's new story tellers. Washington, DC: Pew Internet & American Life Project. Retrieved July 20, 2006, from http://www.pewinternet.org/PPF/r/186/report_display.asp.

Lenhart, A. & Madden, M. (2007, April 18). Teens, privacy and online social networks: How teens manage their online identities and personal information in the age of MySpace. Retireved July 27, 2007, from http://www.pewinternet.org/report_display.asp?r=211.

Lerbinger, O. (1997). *The crisis manager. Facing risk and responsibility*. Mahwah, NJ.

Lerbinger, O. (2006). *Corporate public affairs. Interacting with interest groups, media and government.* Mahwah, NJ: Erlbaum.

Levin, B. (2002). Cyberhate. A legal and historical analysis of extremists' use of computer networks in America. *American Behavioral Scientist, 45*(6), 958–988.

Levine, M. (2002). *Guerilla PR wired: Waging a successful publicity campaign online, offline, and everywhere in between.* Chicago: McGraw-Hill.

Lichtblau, E. (2005, December 20). FBI watched activist groups, new files show. *New York Times*. Retrieved December 21, 2005, from http://www.nytimes.com.

Lieberman, D. A. (2001). Using interactive media in communication campaigns for children and adolescents. In R. E. Rice & C. K. Atkin (Eds.), *Public communication campaigns* (3rd ed.) (pp. 373–388). Thousand Oaks, CA: Sage.

Lindhe, L. (2000, May 3). Taking cover. *Computerworld.* Retrieved July 1, 2007, from http://www.computerworld.com.

Littler, D. & Melanthiou, D. (2006). Consumer perceptions of risk and uncertainty and the implications for behaviour toward innovative retail services; The case of Internet banking. *Journal of Retailing & Consumer Services, 13*(6), 431–443.

Looker, A., Rockland, D. & Taylor, E. (2007, June). Media myths and realities: A study of 2006 media usage in America. *Public Relations Tactics, 14*(6), 10, 21.

Lordan, E.J. (2001). Cyberspin: The use of new technologies in public relations. In R. L. Heath (Ed.), *Handbook of public relations* (pp. 583–590). Thousand Oaks, CA: Sage.

Lwin, M. O. & Williams, J. D. (2006). Promises, promises: How consumers respond to warranties in Internet retailing. *Journal of Consumer Affairs, 40*(2), 226–260.

Macarthur, K. (2007, March 1). Yum releases its own (rat-free) video. President Emil Brolick apologizes. *Advertising Age.* Retrieved March 2, 2007, from http://adage.com/print?article_id=115258.

MacDougall, R. (2005). Identity, electronic ethos and blogs. *American Behavioral Scientist, 49*(4), 575–599.

MacEachren, A.M., Fuhrmann, McNesse, M., Cai, G., & Sharma, R. (2005). Project highlight: Geo-Collaborative crisis management. [Summary of GEO Vista project at Pennsylvania State University] Retrieved May 15, 2007, from http://www.geovista.psu.edu/publications/2005/dgo2005-projecthighlight-gccm.pdf

Mak, Y, Mallard, A. P. Bui, T. & Au, G. (1999). Building online crisis management support using workflow systems. *Decision Support Systems, 25,* 209–224.

Maloney-Krichmar, D. & Preece, J. (2001). A multilevel analysis of sociability, usability and community dynamics in an online health community. *ACM Transactions on Computer-Human Interaction, 12*(2), 201–232.

Malushi, S. (1999, May 8). Kosova voices, e-mail messages: Where journalists and others can go for the latest information. *Editor & Publisher, 132*(19), 62.

Marklein, M. B. (2006, August 2). The new learning curve: Technological security. *USA Today.* Retrieved August 15, 2006, from http://www.usatoday.com.

MarkMonitor (2007). MarkMonitor releases first quarterly brandjacking index [news release]. Retrieved May 3, 2007, from http://www.markmonitors.com/news/press-070430.html.

Marlow, E. (1999). *Electronic public relations.* Belmont, CA: Wadsworth.

Martin, P. & Phelan, S. (2003). History and September 11: A comparison of online and network TV discourses. In A. M. Noll (Ed.), *Crisis communications. Lessons from September 11* (pp. 167–184). Lanham, MD: Rowman & Littlefield.

Massey, J.E. (2004). Managing organizational images: Crisis response and legitimacy restoration. In D. P. Millar, & R. L. Heath (Eds.), *Responding to crisis. A rhetorical approach to crisis communication* (pp. 233–246). Mahwah, NJ: Erlbaum.

Mason, J. (1990, April 23). Disaster protection: Hot sites turn up the heat on America. *Computerworld, 24*(17), 88–89.

Matthew, D. (2005). Information technology and public health management of disasters—a model for South Asian countries. *Prehospital and Disaster Medicine, 20*(1), 54–60.

Mattioli, D. (2006, October 17). Who's reading online resumes? Identity crooks. *Wall Street Journal,* p. B5.

Matusitz, J. (2005). Cyberterrorism: How can American foreign policy be strengthened in the information age? *American Foreign Policy Interests, 27,* 137–147.

McCullagh, D. (2006, January 5). Government web sites follow visitors' movement. CNet. Retrieved January 5, 2006, from http://www.news.com.

McFarlane, M., Bull, S. S. & Reitmeijer, C. (2002). Young adults on the Internet: Risk behaviors for sexually transmitted diseases and HIV. *Journal of Adolescent Health Care, 31*(1), 11–16.

McKay, B. & Mollenkamp, C. (2004, March 31). Classic recipe burns editors at magazine. *Wall Street Journal,* p. B1.

McKinsey & Co. (2007, March 22). How businesses are using Web 2.0: A McKinsey global survey. *The McKinsey Quarterly.* Retrieved June 1, 2007, from http://www.mckinseyquarterly.com.

McKeown, C. A. & Plowman, K. D. (1999). Reaching publics on the web during the 1996 presidential campaign. *Journal of Public Relations Research, 11*(4), 321–347.

McMahon, D. (2000). *Cyber threat: Internet security for home and business.* Toronto: Warwick.

Meisner, M. (2000, Fall). e-activism. Environmental activists are using the Internet to organize, spoof and subvert. *Alternatives Journal, 26*(4), 34–38.

Meyerson, B. (2007, April 20). System update led to BlackBerry outage. Associated Press. Retrieved April 20, 2007, from http://www.washingtonpost.com.

Michaels, J. (2007, March 8). Military beefs up Internet arsenal. *USA Today*, p. A1.

Mickey, T. J. (1998). Selling the internet: A cultural studies approach to public relations, *Public Relations Review, 24*(3), 335–350.

Middleberg, D. (1996, November). How to avoid a cybercrisis. *Public Relations Tactics, 3*(11), 1, 15

Middleberg, D. (2001). *Winning PR in the wired world. Powerful communications strategies for the noisy digital space.* New York: McGraw-Hill.

Milne, G. R. & Culnan, M. J. (2004). Strategies for reducing online privacy risks: Why consumers read (or don't read) online privacy notices. *Journal of Interactive Marketing, 18*(3), 15–29.

Mitra, A. (2004). Voices of the marginalized on the Internet: Examples from a website for women of South Asia. *Journal of Communication, 54*(3), 492–510.

Moore, M. (2005, January 2). Internet brings disaster home. *Rocky Mountain News*, pp. 44A, 45B.

Moore, S. (2004, January-February). Disaster's future: The prospects for corporate crisis management and communication. *Business Horizons, 47*(1), 39–36.

Motion, J. (2001). Electronic relationships: Interactivity, Internet branding and the public sphere. *Journal of Communication Management, 5*(3), 217–230.

MP3.com launches e-mail campaign. (2000, September 29). Associated Press. Retrieved September 30, 2000, from http://www.nytimes.com.

Mukhopadyay, A., Saha, D., Chakrabarti, B. B., Mahanti, A. & Podder, A. (2005). Insurance for cyber-risk: A utility model. *Decision, 32*(1), 153–169.

Murray, B. H. (2004). *Defending the brand: Aggressive strategies for protecting your brand in the online arena.* New York: American Management Association.

Mutter, Z. (2007, May 9). Paris Hilton blogs for forgiveness. *PC World.* Retrieved May 10, 2007, from http://www.washingtonpost.com.

Nakashima, E. (2007a, March 7). Harsh words die hard on the web. *Washington Post,* p. A1.

Nakashima, E. (2007b, January 26). Hack, pump and dump. *Washington Post.* Retrieved January 26, 2007, from http://www.washingtonpost.com.

Naskahima, E. (2007, March 21). Senate bill would mandate disclosure of data mining. *Washington Post,* p. D03.

Nail, J. (2006a, March). Mining the blogosphere for consumer insight. What can a company find? *Public Relations Tactics, 13*(3), 24.

Nail, J. (2006b, December). Don't try to beat the blogs: Integrating new media tactics, influence into traditional reporting. *Public Relations Tactics, 13*(12), 20.

National Research Council (1998). *Information technology research for crisis management.* [Summary of workshop sponsored by the Committee on Computing and Communications Research to Enable Better Use of Information Technology in Government] Washington, DC: National Academy Press.

Neff, B. D. (1998). Harmonizing global relations: A speech act theory analysis of PR Forum, *Public Relations Review, 24*(3), 351–376.

Nelson, R. A. (1996). Activist groups and new technologies. Influencing the public affairs agenda. In L.B. Dennis (Ed.), *Practical public affairs in an era of change* (pp. 413–422). Lanham, MD: University Press of America

Neil, B. (2000, January/February). Crisis management and the Internet. *Ivey Business Journal, 64*(3), 13–17.

.NetAction.Org (2007). The virtual activist 2.0. A training course. Retrieved June 25, 2007, from http://www.netaction.org/training/

Never ending friending (20067, April 12). Research commissioned by Fox Interactive and Isobar & Carat and conducted by TNS, TRU & Marketing Evolution. Retrieved April 12, 2007, from http: http://blogs.forrester.com/Never_Ending_Frieding_April_2007.pdf.

Newman, G. R. & Clarke, R. C. (2003). *Superhighway robbery: Preventing e-commerce crime.* Cullompton, Devon, UK: Willan.

Nierengarten, N. (2006, Winter). A plan for wealth managers to reduce the risk of cyber threats. *Journal of Wealth Management, 9*(3), 24–30.

Noack, D. (1997, May 10). Online coverage of the floods, Editor *& Publisher, 130*(19), 26–27.

Now, a gadfly can bite 24 hours a day (2000, January 24). *Business Week*, no. 3665, p. 150.

Nogouchi, Y. (2006, September 8). Saying it "messed up," Facebook modifies controversial feature. *Washington Post*, p. D01.

Noveck, J. (2007, March 22). Online anonymity lets users get nasty. Associated Press. Retrieved March 22, 2007, from http://www.usatoday.com.

Now, a gadfly can bite 24 hours a day (2000, January 24). *Business Week*, no.3665, p. 150.

Nussbaum, E. (2007, February 12). Say everything. *New York.* Retrieved June 25, 2007, from http://nymag.com/news/features/27341/.

O'Donnell, S. (2001). Analyzing the Internet and the public sphere: The case of Womenslink. *Javnost—The Public, 8*(1), 39–58.

O'Hara, T. (2006, October 2). Hard-learned lesson: Don't try to censor a blogger. *Washington Post*, p. D01.

O'Keefe, S. (1997). *Publicity on the Internet. Creating successful publicity campaigns on the Internet and commercial online services.* New York: Wiley.

O'Sullivan, P. B. (2000). What you don't know won't hurt me: Impression management functions of communication channels in relationships. *Human Communication Research, 26*(3), 403–431.

Oops! Computer tech wipes out info on $38B fund (2007, March 19). Associated Press. Retrieved March 20, 2007, from http://www.usatoday.com.

Ossinger, J. L. (2006, February 13). The problem with parody. *Wall Street Journal,* p. R 7.

Pegoraro, R. (2007, April 14). Delete doesn't mean disappear. *Washington Post*, D01.

Palenchar, M. J. & Heath, R. L. (2007). Strategic risk communication: Adding value to society. *Public Relations Review, 33*, 120–129.

Palmer, D. E. (2006). Pop-ups, cookies, and spam: Toward a deeper analysis of the ethical significance of Internet marketing practices. *Journal of Business Ethics, 58*, 271–280.

Palser, B. (2002, November). Not so bad: the performance of online news sites on September 11 was better than most reviews suggest. *American Journalism Review, 24*(9), 26–27.

Palser, B. (2004, February March). The difference a year makes. *American Journalism Review, 26*(1), 58.

Parr, B. (2007, May 7). User-generated content. Jupiter Research. Retrieved July 12, 2007, from http://www.jupiterresearch.com.

Park, N. & Lee, K. M. (2007). Effects of online news forum on corporate reputation. *Public Relations Review, 33*(3), 346–348.

Passariello, C., Johnson, K. & Vranica, S. (2007, March 22). A new force in advertising—Protest by e-mail. *Wall Street Journal*, p. B1.

Pavlik, J. (2003). New technology and news flows: Journalism and crisis coverage. In K. Kawanto (Ed.), *Digital journalism. Emerging media and the changing horizons of journalism* (pp. 75–89. Lanham, MD: Rowman & Littlefield.

Pavlik, J. (2007). Mapping the consequences of technology on public relations. Gainesville, FL: Institute for Public Relations.

Pelline, J. (1997, September 5). Whitehouse.com goes to porn. CNet. Retrieved July 1, 2007, from http://news.com.com/2100-1023-202985.html.

Perrow, C. (1984). *Normal accidents: Living with high risk technologies*. New York: Basic Books.

Perry, D.C., Taylor, M. & Doerfel, M.L. (2003). Internet-communication in crisis management. *Management Communication Quarterly, 17*(2), 206–232.

Petrison, L. A. & Wang, P. (1993). From relationships to relationship marketing: Applying database technology to public relations. *Public Relations Review, 19*(3), 235–246.

Pew Internet & American Life Project (2007, January 7). Social networking websites and teens. An overview. Retrieved January 9, 2007, from http://www.pewinternet.org.

Phillips, D. (2001). *Online public relations*. London: Kogan Page.

Preece, J. (2001). *Online communities. Designing usability, supporting sociability*. New York: Wiley.

Prensky, M. (2001). Digital natives, digital immigrants. *On the Horizon, 9*(5), 1–6.

Porter, L.,V. & Sallot, L.,M. (2003). The internet and public relations: Investigating practitioners' roles and the world wide web. *Journalism & Mass Communication Quarterly, 80*(3), 603–622.

Porter, L. V. & Sallot, L. M. (2005). Web power: A survey of practitioners' world wide web use and their perceptions of its effects on their decision-making power, *Public Relations Review, 31*(1), 111–120.

Porter, L. V., Sallot, L. M., Cameron, G. T., & Shamp, S. (2001). New technologies and public relations: Exploring practitioners' use of online resources to earn a seat at the management table. *Journalism & Mass Communication Quarterly, 78*(1), 172–190.

Postmes, T., Spears, R. & Lea, M. (1998). Breaching or building social boundaries? SIDE-effects of computer-mediated communication. *Communication Research, 25*(6), 689–715.

Procopio, C. H. & Procopio, S. T. (2007). Do you know what it means to miss New Orleans? Internet communication, geographic community, and social capital in crisis. *Journal of Applied Communication Research, 35*(1), 67–87.

Quinley K. M. & Schmidt, D. L. (2002). *Business risk: how to assess, mitigate, and respond to terrorist threats*. Cincinnati, OH: National Underwriter Co.

Rainie, L. (2001, September 15). How Americans used the Internet after the terror attack. Washington, DC: Pew Internet & American Life Project. Retrieved June 25, 2007, from http://www.pewinternet.org/reports/toc.asp?Report=45.

Rainie, L., Fox, S. & Madden, M. (2002). One year later: September 11 and the Internet. Washington, DC: Pew Internet & American Life Project. Retrieved November 6, 2002, from http://www.pewinternet.org/reports/toc.asp?Report=69.

Rainie, L. (2005, November 20). Search engine use shoots up in the past year. Washington, DC: Pew Internet & American Life Project. Retrieved June 25, 2007, from http://www.pewinternet.org.

Rainie, L. & Tancer, B. (2007, April). 36% of online American adults consult Wikipedia. Washington, DC: Pew Internet & American Life Project. Retrieved June 25, 2007, from http://www.pewinternet.org.

Ramsey, S. A. (1993). Issues management and the use of technologies in public relations, *Public Relations Review, 19*(3), 261–276.

Randle, Q., Davenport, L. D. & Bossen, H. (2003, Winter). Newspapers slow to use Web sites for 9/11 coverage. *Newspaper Research Journal, 24*(1), 58–71.

Rappoport, P. N. & Alleman, J. (2003). Internet and the demand for news: Macro- and microevidence. In A. M. Noll (Ed.), *Crisis communications. Lessons from September 11* (pp. 149–166). Lanham, MD: Rowman & Littlefield.

Rauch, J. (2006, August). Activists as interpretive communities. Rituals of consumption and interaction in an alternative media audience. Paper presented to Association for Education in Journalism and Mass Communication, San Francisco.

Reese, S. D., Rutigliano, L., Kideuk, H. & Jaekwan, J. (2007). Mapping the blogosphere: Professional and citizen-based media in the goal news arena. *Journalism, 8*(3), 235–261.

Reber, B. R., Gower, K. & Robinson, J. A. (2005). The Internet and litigation public relations, *Journal of Public Relations Research, 18*(1), 23–44.

Regalado, A. & Mintz, J. (2005, January 3). Video blogs break out with tsunami scenes. *Wall Street Journal*, p. B1.

Regalado, A. & Searcey, D. (2006, August 3). Where did that video spoofing Gore's film come from? *Wall Street Journal*, p. B1.

Regester, M. & Larkin, J. (2005). *Risk issues and crisis management. A casebook of best practice* (3rd ed.). London: Kogan Page.

Reporters Committee on Freedom of the Press (2003, Spring). Ramifications of 9-11 Web takedowns still unclear. *News Media & Law*, *27*(2), 5. Retrieved June 15, 2003, from http://www.rcfp.org/elecaccess/elec_access_911takedown.htm.

Rheingold, H. (1993). *The virtual community: Homesteading on the electronic frontier*. Reading, MA: Addison-Wesley.

Rhoades, C. (2007, May 18). Cyber attack vexes Estonia, poses debate. *Wall Street Journal*, p. A6.

Richardson, K. (2001). Risk news in the world of internet newsgroups. *Journal of Sociolinguistics, 5*(1), 50–72.

Richmond R. (2006a, September 25). Hackers' use of web applications in attacks rises. *Wall Street Journal*, p. B5.

Richmond, R. (2006b, February 13). Anatomy of a threat. *Wall Street Journal*, p. R5.

Risen, J. & Lichtblau, E. (2005, December 16). Bush lets U.S. spy on callers without courts. *New York Times*. Retrieved December 19, 2005, from http://www.nytimes.com.

Roberts, M., Wanta, W. & Dzwo, T. (2002). Agenda setting and issue salience online. *Communication Research, 29*(4), 452–465.

Robinson, M.K. (2003). *Disaster recovery planning for nonprofits*. Dallas, TX: Hamilton Books.

Rogers, J. (2003). *Spatializing international politics: Analyzing activism on the Internet*. New York: Routledge.

Roper, H. (1995). Letters from cyberhell. *Inc., 17*(13), 67–70.

Rosen, R. (1998/1999, December/January). Crisis in context. *Communication World, 16*(1), 34–35.

Rundle, R. L. (2007, April 24). Critical case: How an email rant jolted a big HMO. *Wall Street Journal*, pp. A1, A16.

Ryan, S. (2004, November). Protecting your business from Internet rumors. *Public Relations Tactics, 11*(11), 19.

Sager, I. (2001, October 22). Preparing for a cyber-assault. *Business Week*, p. 50.

Sallot, L. M. & Johnson, E. A. (2006). To contact … or not? Investigating journalists' assessments of public relations subsidies and contact preferences. *Public Relations Review, 32*(1), 83–86.

Sallot, L. M., Porter, L. V. & Acosta-Alzuru, C. (2004). Practitioners' web use and perceptions of their own roles and power: A qualitative study, *Public Relations Review, 30*(3), 269–278.

Salaverría, R. (2005). An immature medium. *Gazette: International Journal for Communication Studies, 67*(1), 69–86.

Samarajiva, R. (2005). Mobilizing information and communications technologies for effective disaster warning: Lessons from the 2004 tsunami. *New Media & Society, 7*(6), 731–747.

Saranow, J. (2007, January 12). The snoop next door. *Wall Street Journal*, pp. W1, 12.

Sauter, M. A. & Carafano, J. J. (2005). *Homeland security. A complete guide to understanding preventing and surviving terrorism.* New York: McGraw-Hill.

Schaffer, S. (2004). *The role of trust on the Internet. The development of an online trust creation model for etravel agents*. Munster: Lit.

Schatz, A. (2007, February 14). Candidates find a new stump in the blogosphere. *Wall Street Journal,* p. B1.

Schwalbe, C. B. (2006, November). Remembering our shared past: Visually framing the Iraq war in the U.S. news websites. *Journal of Computer-Mediated Communication, 12*(1), 264–289.

Schneiderman, B. & Preece, J. (2007, February 16). 911.gov. *Science, 351*, 944.

Schild, S. & Oren, K. (2005, Spring). The party line online: An oligarchy of opinion on a public affairs listserve. *Journalism & Communication Monographs, 7*(1), 5–47.

Schwartz, J. (2001, November 23). Cyberspace seen as potential battleground. *New York Times,* p. B5.

Schwartz, J. (2002, September 9). Year after 9/11, cyberspace door is still ajar. *New York Times*. Retrieved September 9, 2002, from http://www.nytimes.com.

Schwartz, J. (2004, December 28). Blogs provide raw details from scene of disaster. *New York Times*. Retrieved January 3, 2005, from http://www.nytimes.com.

Schwartz, J. (2005, January 3). Myths run wild in blog tsunami debate. *New York Times*. Retrieved January 3, 2005, from http://www.nytimes.com.

Seeger, M. W. (2006). Best practices in crisis communication: An expert panel process. *Journal of Applied Communication Research, 34*(3), 232–244.

Seeger, M. W., Sellnow, T. L. & Ulmer, R. R. (2006). *Communication and organizational crisis*. Westport, CT: Praeger.

Seeger, M. W., Vennette, S., Ulmer, R. R. & Sellnow, T. L. (2002). Media use, information seeking, and reported needs in post crisis contexts. In B. S. Greenberg (Ed.), Communication *and terrorism: Public and media responses to 9/11* (pp. 53–63). Cresskill, NJ: Hampton Press.

Seelye, K. Q . (2005, December 4). Snared in the Web of a Wikipedia liar. *New York Times*. Retrieved December 9, 2005, from http://www.nytimes.com

Seelye, K. Q. (2006, January 20). Paper closes reader comments on blog, citing vitriol. *New York Times*. Retrieved January 20, 2006, from www.nytimes.com.

Seelye, K. O. (2006, January 2). Answering back to the news media, using the Internet. *New York Times*. Retrieved January 5, 2006, from http://www.nytimes.com.

Seelye, K. O. (2007, July 23). Debates to connect candidates and voters online. *New York Times*. Retrieved July 24, 2007, from http://www.nytimes.com.

Seigenthaler, J. (2005, November 29). A false Wikipedia "biography." *USA Today*. Retrieved June 25, 2007, from http://www.usatoday.com.

Semuels, A. (2007, February 22). Virtual losses its virtues. Los *Angeles Times*, p.A1. Retrieved May 25, 2007, from http://www.latimes.com/entertainment/.

Seymour, M. & Moore, S. (2002). *Effective crisis management. Worldwide principles and practice.* London: Casell

Shade, L. R. (2002). Protecting the kids? Debates over Internet content. In S. D. Ferguson & L. R. Shade (Eds.), *Civic discourse and cultural politics in Canada. A cacophony of voices* (pp. 76–87). Westport, CT: Ablex Publishing.

Shankman, P. (2000, October 2). PR Insight: Crisis management, Internet style. Retrieved November 14, 2000, from http://www.internetprguide.com/pr_insight/article/0,,10123_473731.00.html.

Shernoff, M. (2006). *Without condoms. Unprotected sex, gay men & barebacking.* New York: Routledge.

Sherwin, G. R. & Avila, E. N. (1997). *Connecting online: creating a successful image on the Internet.* Grants Pass, OR: Oasis Press.

Shin, A. (2007, February 10). Taking the bait on a phish scam. *Washington Post*, p. D01.

Shin, J. & Cameron, G.T. (2003). The potential of online media: A coorientational analysis of conflict between PR practitioners and journalists in South Korea. *Journalism & Mass Communication Quarterly, 80*(3), 583–602.

Shortman, M. (2003, March 17). When should you respond to online attacks? *PR Week*, p. 18.

Siebert, T. (2006, October 20). Edelman reveals two more Wal-Mart flogs. MediaPost Publications. Retrieved October 20, 2006, from http://publications.mediapost.com.

Simpson, B. (2005). Identify manipulation in cyberspace as a leisure option: Play and the exploration of self. *Information & Communications Technology Law, 14*(2), 115–131.

Smith, C. S. (2001, May 13). The first world hacker war. *New York Times*. Retrieved May 13, 2001, from http://www.nytimes.com.

Smudde, P. M. (2005, Fall). Blogging, ethics and public relations: A proactive and dialogic approach. *Public Relations Quarterly, 50*(3), 34–38.

Sneijder, P. & Te Molder, H. F. M. (2005). Moral logic and logical morality: Attributions of responsibility and blame in online discourse on veganism. *Discourse & Society, 16*(5), 675–696.

Sorkin, A. (1997, September 8). Diana's death expands web's news role. *New York Times*. Retrieved July 8, 2007, from http://query.nytimes.com.

Spence, P.R., Westerman, D., Skalski, Seeger, M. Sellnow, T.L. & Ulmer, R.R. (2006). Gender and age effects on information-seeking after 9/11. *Communication Research Reports, 23*(3), 217–223.

Springston, J. (2001). Public relations and new media technology: The impact of the Internet, In R. L. Heath (Ed.), *Handbook of public relations* (pp. 603–614). Thousand Oaks, CA: Sage.

Springston, J. & Lariscey, R. A. W. (2003). Health as profit: Public relations in health communication. In T. L. Thompson (Ed.), *Handbook of health communication* (pp. 537–556). Mahwah, NJ: Erlbaum.

Stanton, J. J. (2002). Terror in cyberspace. Terrorists will exploit and widen the gap between governing structures and the public. *American Behavioral Scientist, 45*(6), 1017–1032.

Stateman, A. (2001, December). Companies underestimate online financial risks. *Public Relations Tactics, 8*(12), 3.

Stephenson, M., Jr. (2005). Making humanitarian relief networks more effective: operational coordination, trust and sense making. *Disasters, 29*(4), 337–350.

Sweetman, B. (2000, May). Managing a crisis. *Airport Transport World, 37*(5), 71–74.

Still, T. (2005, January 12). Outpouring of tsunami relief displays power of Internet. Wisconsin Technology Network. Retrieved June 25, 2007, from http://wistechnology.com/printarticle.php?id=1482.

Stoltz, C. (2006, August 1). A 10-year check up. *Washington Post*, p. HE01.

Stone, B. (2006, August 21/28). Web of risks. *Newsweek*, pp. 76–77.

Stone, B. & Richtel, M. (2007). Social networking leaves confines of the computer. *New York Times*. Retrieved May 1, 2007, from http://www.nytimes.com.

Sullivan, T. (2004, December 4). Bracing for disaster. *InfoWorld*, p. S35.

Sundar, S. S. (1999). Exploring receivers' criteria for perception of print and online news. *Journalism & Mass Communication Quarterly, 76*(2), 373–386.

Sundar, S. S. & Nass, C. (2001). Conceptualizing sources in online news. *Journal of Communication, 51*(1), 52–72.

Swartz, J. (2007, February 9). Tech experts plot to catch identity thieves. *USA Today*. Retrieved February 9, 2007, from http://www.usatoday.com.

Swartz, J. & Hopkins, J. (2007, April 18). Could cell text alert have helped at Va. Tech? *USA Today*, p. 3B.

Tanne, J.H. (1999, July-August). Speed the science. *Columbia Journalism Review, 38*(2), 16.

Tapscott, D. & Williams, A. D. (2006). *Wikinomics. How mass collaboration changes everything.* New York: Portfolio Penguin Group.

Tax traffic swamps H&R Block tax site (2000, February 3). *New York Times*. Retrieved February 3, 2000, from http://www.nytimes.com.

Taylor, M. & Kent, M. L. (2007). Taxonomy of mediated crisis responses. *Public Relations Review, 33*(1), 140–146.

Taylor, M. & Perry, D. C. (2005). Diffusion of traditional and new media tactics in crisis communication, *Public Relations Review, 31*(2), 209–218.

Taylor, M., Kent, M. L. & White, W. J. (2001). How activist organizations are using the internet to build relationships. *Public Relations Review, 27*, 263–284.

Tedesco, R. (1997, September 8). Websites enhance TV cover of princess's death. *Broadcasting & Cable, 127*(37), 61.

Tewksbury, D. (2003). What do Americans really want to know? Tracking the behavior of news readers on the Internet. *Journal of Communication, 53*(4), 694–710.

This just in.... (1997, August/September). *Communication World, 14*(8), 62.

Thomas, C. (2003). Cyberactivism and corporations. New strategies for new media. In S. John & S. Thomson (Eds.), *New activism and the corporate response* (pp. 115–135). New York: Macmillan Palgrave.

Thomas, D. & Loader, B. C . (Eds.) (2000). *Cybercrime: Law enforcement, security and surveillance in the information age.* London: Routledge.

Thomsen, S. R. (1995). Using online data bases in corporate issues management. *Public Relations Review, 21*(2), 103–122.

Thomsen, S. R. (1996) @Work in Cyberspace: Exploring practitioner use of the PR Forum, *Public Relations Review*, *22*(2), 115–132.

Thomsen, S. R. & Rawson, B. (1998, Fall). Purifying a tainted corporate image: Odwalla's response to an E.coli poisoning. *Public Relations Quarterly,* 35–46.

Tian, Y., & Stewart, C. (2005). Framing the SARS crisis: A computer-assisted text analysis of CNN and BBC online news reports of SARS. *Asian Journal of Communication, 15*(3), 289–301.

Tillet, L.S. (2000, August 28). Tire recall stresses Ford's Internet site. *Internetweek*, p. 9

Totty, M. (2006, February 13). The dangers within. *Wall Street Journal*, pp. R1, 4.

Trachtenberg, J.A. & De Avila, J. (2007, July 19). Mischief unmanaged. *Wall Street Journal*, p. B1.

Turnbull, N. (2001). Issues and crisis management in a convergent environment. *Journal of Public Affairs, 1*(1), 85–92.

Turner, J. W. (2003). Telemedicine: Expanding health care into virtual environments. In T.L. Thompson (Ed.), *Handbook of health communication* (pp. 515–535). Mahwah, NJ: Erlbaum.

U.S. Department of Justice (1999). Critical infrastructure protection [web site]. Retrieved June 25, 2007, from http://www.usdoj.gov/criminal/cybercrime/critinfr.htm#Vc

U.S. GAO says control systems at risk of cyber attacks (2004, May). *Control Engineering, 51*(5), 11–12.

U.S. General Accounting Office (2005, May 13). Information security: Emerging cybersecurity issues threaten federal information. Report GAO 05-231. Retrieved from http://www.gao.gov./cig-bin/getreprt?GAO-05-231.

U.S. General Accounting Office (2004, June). Internet pharmacies. Some pose safety risks for consumers. Report GAO-04-820. Washington, DC: GAO. Retrieved June 30, 2004, from http://www.gao.gov/cig-bin/getrpt?GAO-04-820.

USC Center for the Digital Future (2000). Online world as important to Internet users as real world. Los Angeles, CA: University of Southern California Annenberg School for Communication. Retrieved January 5, 2007, from http://www.digitalcenter.org/pdf/2007-Digital-Future-Report-Press-Release-112906.pdf.

Vaca, J.R. (2003). *Identity theft.* Upper Saddle River, NJ: Prentice-Hall.

Valla, M. (2007, May 2). In French election, web plays big role. *Wall Street Journal*, p. B7.

VanLear, C.A., Sheehan, M., Withers, L.A. & Walker, R.A. (2005). AA Online: The enactment of supportive computer mediated communication. *Western Journal of Communication, 69*(1), 5–26.

Vara, V. (2006a, June 23). In event of big Web disruption, U.S. is ill-prepared, study says. *Wall Street Journal*, p. B2.

Vara, V. (2006b, October 23). Intruder alerts. *Wall Street Journal*, p. R10.

Vargas, J. A. (2007a, February 17). Young voters find voice on Facebook. *Washington Post*, p. A01.

Vargas, J. A. (2007b, March 17). Online firms boot up for political campaigns. *Washington Post*, p. D01.

Vargas, J. A. (2007c, May 4). Meet the OPOs. *Washington Post*, p. A01.

Vascellaro, J. E. (2006a, August 2). "Empty spam" feasts in in-boxes. *Wall Street Journal*, p. D3.

Vascellaro, J. E. (2006b, August 3) New ways to prove you are who you say you are online. *Wall Street Journal*, pp. D1, D4.

Vengerfeldt, P. (2003). Internet as a news medium for the crisis news of terrorist attacks in the United States. In A. M. Noll (Ed.), *Crisis communications. Lessons from September 11* (pp. 133–148). Lanham, MD: Rowman & Littlefield.

Vijayan, V. (2004, March 22). Big four accounting firms join in cyber-risk effort. *Computerworld, 38*(12). Retrieved May 25, 2007 from http://www.computerworld.com.

Violence against women and Department of Justice reauthorization act (2006). 42 USC 13701.

Vispoli, T. (2006, October). Cyber risks: Beware the new pirates. *Directorship*, 24-25. Retrieved June 1, 2007 from http://www.directorship.com

Wall, D. S. (Ed.) (2001). *Crime and the Internet*. London: Routledge.

Wallace, M. & Webber, L. (2004). *The disaster recovery handbook*. New York: AMACOM,

Walther, J.B. (1996) Computer-mediated communication: Impersonal, interpersonal and hypersonal interaction. *Communication Research, 23*(1), 3–43.

Walther, J. B. & Tidwell, L. (1992). When is mediated communication not interpersonal? In K. M. Galvin & P. Cooper (Eds.), *Making connections: Readings in relational communication* (pp. 300–307). Los Angeles: Roxbury.

Warkentin, C. (2001). *Reshaping world politics: NGOs, the Internet, and global civil society*. Lanham, MD: Rowman & Littlefield.

Warner, B. (2003, December 29). Cyber blackmail wave targets office workers. Reuters News Service. Retrieved July 1, 2007, from http://www.organissimo/org/forum/index.php?showtopic=6324.

Warren, J. & Jurgensen, J. (2007, February 10–11). The wizards of buzz. *Wall Street Journal*, pp. P1, P4.

Web becomes a coping mechanism (2007, April 17). MSNBC. Retrieved April 19, 2007, from http://www.msnbc.com.

Webster, J., Trevino, L. K. & Ryan, L. (1993). The dimensionality and correlates of flow in human-computer interactions. *Computers in Human Behavior, 9*, 411–426.

Weintraub, A. (2006, February 20). How good is your online nurse? *Business Week*, pp. 88–89.

Weinberger, C. (2004). Turning to the Internet for help on sensitive medical problems. *Information, Communication & Society, 7*(4), 554–574.

White, C. & Raman, N. (1999). The World Wide Web as a public relations medium: The use of research, planning and evaluation in web site development, *Public Relations Research, 25*(4), 405–420.

White, C. & Scheb II, J. M. (2000). Impact of media messages about the Internet: Internet anxiety as a factor in the adoption process in the USA. *New Media & Society, 2*(2), 181–194.

White, E., Lublin, J. S. & Kesmodel, D. (2007, July 13). Executives get the blogging bug. *Wall Street Journa*l, pp. B1–B2.

White House crisis draws to the "net" (1998, February 2). *Broadcasting & Cable, 128*(5), 80.

Whitsel, B. C. (2000). Catastrophic new age groups and public order. *Studies in Conflict and Terrorism, 23*(1), 31–36.

Whitworth, B. & De Moor, A. (2003). Legitimate by design: Towards trusted socio-technical systems. *Behaviour & Information Technology, 22*(1), 31–51.

Wikinews investigates Wikipedia usage by U.S. Senate staff members (2006, February 7). Retrieved February 9, 2006, from http://en.wikinews.org.

Wilkinson, D. M. & Huberman, B. A. (2007, February 26). Assessing the value of cooperation in Wikipedia. Palo Alto, CA: HP Labs. Retrieved March 1, 2007, from http://www.firstmonday.org/issues/issue12_4/wilkinson/.

Willard, N. (2007). *Cyberbullying and cyber threats: Responding to the challenge of online social aggression, threats and distress.* Champaign, IL: U.S. Research Press.

Wolfington, L. & Wyatt, L.M. (2004). Health care's response to 9-11 and Anthrax attacks in the nation's capital. In J.A. Hendrix, *Public relations cases* (6th ed.) (pp. 388–394). Belmont, CA: Thomson Wadsworth.

Woodall, I. (2006, July). Journalists relay what is expected from an online newsroom. Meaningful trends revealed in 2006 survey. *Public Relations Tactics, 13*(7), 18.

Woyke, E. (2007, July 30). Getting on the glitch list. *Business Week*, p. 10.

Ye, N., Newman, C. & Farley, T. (2005/2006). A system-fault-risk framework for cyber attack classification. *Information Knowledge Systems Management, 5,* 135–151.

Youngblood, N. E. (2006). The international campaign to ban landmines and the 1997 ban bus campaign. In M. G. Parkinson & D. Ekachai, D. (Eds.), *International and intercultural public relations. A campaign case approach* (pp. 133–145). Boston: Allyn & Bacon.

Younglees, P. M. & Marks, S. (2005). Problematic Internet use or Internet addiction? *Computer in Human Behavior, 23*(3), 1447–1453.

Yuan, L., Dade, C. & Prada, P. (2007, April 18). Texting when there's trouble. *Wall Street Journal,* p. B1, 10.

Yuon, S. (2005). Teenagers' perceptions of online privacy and coping behaviors: A risk-benefit appraisal approach. *Journal of Broadcasting and Electronic Media, 49*(1), 86–100.
Zambroski, R. (2006, May-June). Think before you send. *Communication World, 23*(3), 38–40.
Zeigler, T. (2006, December). Eight ways for organizations to employ new media. *Public Relations Tactics, 13*(12), 20.
Zeller, Jr., T. (2005, November 3). The lives of teenagers now: Open blogs, not locked diaries. *New York Times.* Retrieved November 7, 2005, from http://www.nytimes.com.
Zeller, Jr., T. (2006, February 26). Cyber thieves quietly copy your passwords as you type/. *New York Times.* Retrieved March 3, 2006, from http://www.nytimes.com.
Zhang, Y. & Zhang, Y. (2002). Comparison of Internet attitudes between industrial employees and college students. *CyberPsychology & Behavior, 5*(2), 142–149.
Zimmer, E. A. & Hunter, C. D. (2003). Risk and the Internet: Perception and reality. In L. Strate, R. Jacobson & S. B. Gibson (Eds.), *Communication and cyberspace. Social interaction in an electronic environment* (2nd ed.), (pp. 183–202). Buffalo: State University of New York.

22

Virtual Risk: The Role of New Media in Violent and Nonviolent Ideological Groups

Matthew T. Allen, Amanda D. Angie, Josh L. Davis, Cristina L. Byrne, H. Dan O'Hair, Shane Connelly, and Michael D. Mumford

University of Oklahoma

In January 2007, Senator Hillary Clinton of New York declared her candidacy for the 2008 presidential elections by posting a video on her web site declaring "I'm in." She followed this with a series of "web chats" with voters on current issues and concerns (CNN, 2007). Senator Clinton's use of the Internet as her initial medium for communicating with voters is emblematic of the importance new media plays in today's society. According to the World Bank, in the United States in 2004, roughly 63 percent of the population could be considered "Internet users" (Internet World Stats, 2007). Of that group, 88 percent say the Internet plays a role in their daily routines (Pew Internet and American Life Project, 2004). Over one billion people worldwide are online (Internet World Stats, 2007), and the material they are being exposed to is not always prosocial. For example, according to the an intelligence report by the Southern Poverty Law Center (SPLC), there were 524 U.S. hate web sites online in 2005, up 12 percent from the previous year (Potok, 2006).

The Internet then has become the engine that drives many sources of new media, such as online videos, blogs, streaming radio, instant messaging, and so forth. What is notable about these new media sources is the lack of regulation relative to traditional sources, such as television, radio, and newspapers. Any person with access to the Internet can create a web site to deliver their message to a target group, gather material from a variety of sources, and interact with other like-minded individuals in synchronous or asynchronous formats. Given the broad audience and relative ease of dissemination, these new media sources are fertile ground for the proliferation of ideological groups and their messages.

Ideological groups can be defined as those with strongly held values that form a mental model for how they interpret events in the world (Mumford, Bedell-Avers, Hunter, Espejo, Eubanks, & Connelly, in press). This definition covers a broad range of viewpoints and therefore includes a number of forms of ideological groups. Some ideological groups, such as the Republican and Democratic parties, hold ideological views that are consistent with those of many in the populace in which they operate. Other groups, such as the Libertarian Party, can be considered more on the fringe of their sphere of influence. In fact, many political, civic (e.g., the American Civil Liberties

Union [ACLU]), and religious (e.g., the Catholic Church) groups can be considered ideological in nature. At the most extreme, ideological groups can have antisocial or even violent worldviews. For example, the Army of God is a fundamentalist Christian group whose members have been linked to a number of threats and attacks on abortion clinics (FBI, 2003).

The purpose of this chapter will be to further explore the role that media, and new media in particular, plays in the communication of violent and nonviolent ideological groups. The unregulated and decentralized nature of new media translates into new avenues for growth and communication for ideologues. For good or for ill, new media sources have provided a new outlet for ideological groups to take hold. While most ideological groups have benign or even prosocial messages, others promote violence, hatred, racism, and other antisocial beliefs and behaviors. From the perspective of risk and crisis communication, ideological groups take on special meaning. Ideological beliefs can exacerbate preexisting perceptions of risk and crisis in the environment, thus increasing the likelihood that these groups will react violently. In turn, these violent ideological groups and their members pose a risk in the form of potential *crisis conditions* for specific subgroups (e.g., African Americans with the Ku Klux Klan) or, in extreme cases, to a society's structure itself (e.g., the United States with terrorist groups). For this reason, understanding the role of media in these groups is critical to study of risk and crisis communication.

The above discussion brings forth a number of observations regarding the relationship between media and ideological groups. First, it is clear that ideological groups want to use media sources to influence non-ideologues in a way that is consistent with the group's goals. This can come in a variety of forms. One reason for the use of new media is to "get the word out" about their cause. For example, ideological groups, especially those that have become associated with negative press, may want to dispel any misconceptions about their beliefs and values. Another reason may be to draw together like-minded individuals who share the same ideals for potential recruitment. In the case of nonviolent groups, it may simply be a matter of getting people actively involved in something they are passionate about. In the case of violent ideological groups, it may be to draw in people who are disenchanted and therefore vulnerable to the violent ideology being offered (e.g., Blazak, 2001; Moghaddam, 2005).

A second observation is to recognize that new media is dynamic, and therefore people not affiliated with a particular group may actively seek to disrupt the influence processes used by the ideological groups above. These nonmembers can use new media sources via the World Wide Web (WWW) to produce countermessages to the ones that the ideological group is presenting. For example, on the popular video web site YouTube.com, online members can post comments about the videos on the web site. These comments are available for public viewing and videos that convey an ideological message can be disputed using this commenting feature. However, there are special considerations in communicating with violent ideological groups because people heavily invested in extremist ideologies tend to perceive more threat from outside sources of influence (Post, Ruby, & Shaw, 2002). For this reason, it is difficult to change the mind of group members who are heavily invested in the ideology.

The process of influencing members of ideological groups and vice versa has in the past been an extremely difficult exercise, particularly for those groups on the fringe of accepted societal norms. The difficulty lies in the nature of ideological groups and the limitations of traditional media. Violent ideologues are often not open about their viewpoints, making it difficult to know who to talk to in the first place. Likewise, it is difficult for ideological groups to influence others because traditional media sources are either expensive, highly regulated, or both. Other methods of influence, such as pamphlets or newsletters are difficult to disseminate to wide audiences. With these traditional influence avenues cut off, violent ideological groups are more likely to act on their violent beliefs. However, new media sources have made both the process of communicating with ideologues and the process of ideological groups communicating with non-ideologues much easier. It has removed many of these barriers by making violent ideologues "anonymously open" and by allowing groups to disseminate their beliefs in online formats. However, it has also opened doors for researchers to examine this interplay between non-ideologues, nonviolent ideologues, and violent ideologues.

New media provides a unique opportunity for researchers to examine this complex interaction between ideologues and those that oppose them in an open-source setting. However, with a few notable exceptions, researchers have rarely taken advantage of this opportunity. The remainder of this chapter will outline some literature and propositions to guide future crisis communication research in this area. This will be accomplished by first relaying relevant literature in psychology and communication related to ideological groups and new media. Next, based on these corpora, a number of propositions will be advanced. Third, these propositions will be illustrated with one violent and one nonviolent ideological group. Finally, implications and future directions for how these propositions can be applied for both researchers and practitioners will be offered.

IDEOLOGICAL GROUPS

Ideological groups are a unique type of social group comprised of a collection of individuals that hold shared viewpoints related to their goals and interests in relation to other groups (Van Dijk, 2006). In contrast to other types of social groups, which may hold only shared general beliefs such as knowledge, norms, and values, ideological groups satisfy a number of social criteria (e.g., permanence, continuity, and so forth) for its members that are used to coordinate their actions in accordance with their beliefs. Underlying these notions is the idea of an ideology, which involves the specification of goals and values that are determined by a fixed set of beliefs about goal attainment (Mumford et al., in press). This specification involves using mental models to structure one's understanding of and reactions to different events. Collections of individuals who have adopted a particular framework (i.e., mental model) for understanding and acting in different situations belong to an ideological group (Friedland, 2001). These individually held models may be ideologically biased based on the underlying, socially shared attitudes of the group members (Van Dijk, 2006). This, in turn, can give rise to the representation and expression of events and actors (e.g., news reports, opinion articles, etc.) as more or less negative or positive depending on the nature of the mental model.

Ideological Group Structure and Characteristics

The structure inherent in ideological groups can be attractive to individuals for a number of different reasons. First, ideological groups help manage environmental uncertainty and any perceived external threats (Jost & Hunyady, 2005). For this reason, individuals who possess heightened needs for uncertainty avoidance, order, structure, closure, intolerance for ambiguity or perceptions of a dangerous world tend to favor ideological group membership. Ideological groups also effectively address perceptions of environmental threat (Ezekiel, 2002). For example, one of the main foci of Neo-Nazi and Klan groups is their fear of the destruction of the white race by Jews and other ethnic minorities. These groups provide their members with the comfort that they are effecting change through their actions (i.e., saving the white race from annihilation). Additionally, these feelings of uncertainty are reduced through the groups' representation of the future and the confidence that its goals will be accomplished (Hoffman, 1999). This provides a clear, normative prescription of behaviors in which the group and its members should be engaged. Specifically, the goals of the group become the goals of the individual members themselves and guide their actions.

Second, ideological groups provide a sense of identity, meaning, and reality for their members (Watts, 2001). In particular, groups promote the development of a social identity by providing a feeling of belongingness and a way of locating oneself in relation to other people in order to define their personal selves (e.g., personal traits that differentiate self from all others) and collective selves (e.g., group membership that differentiates "us" from "them") (Hogg, 2003; Van Dijk, 2006). Therefore, ideological groups can satisfy these two opposing needs (i.e., the need for differentiation and the need for assimilation) by providing a sense of family or community, using organized symbolic and cultural events so members can feel as if they are part of something bigger, reward conformity through valued social and personal means, and alleviate identity issues in threatened individuals (Combs, 2003; Hewstone, Rubin, & Willis, 2002; Watts, 2001). Ideological groups also draw in and shape individuals' beliefs and provide a sense of meaning through their representation of the "truth" about the salient issues.

Third, ideological groups help foster a more positive self-concept through the enhancement of self-esteem (Aberson, Healy, & Romero, 2000). In relation to social identity, individuals seek to maintain a positive identity through association with positively valued groups and through comparisons with other groups (Tajfel, 1982). In other words, individuals attempt to enhance differences between groups in ways that favor the ingroup in accordance with their beliefs. This tendency toward positive evaluation of one's own group and negative evaluation of outgroups is termed intergroup bias and has been linked to the self-enhancement and the self-esteem of individual group members (Aberson et al., 2000; Hewstone et al., 2002). In particular, self-enhancement through positive social identity seems to play a key role in intergroup bias and social identity development (Hogg, 2003). More specifically, an individual's tendency to exhibit intergroup bias is influenced by the congruence between their self-concept and the intergroup bias strategies of the group, such as the goals the group sets forth (Aberson et al., 2000). This can lead to a stronger identification with the ingroup and more differentiation from the outgroup.

Fourth, ideological groups provide a structure through which individuals can make sense of and understand the world around them (Murray & Cowden, 1999). As discussed above, ideological groups provide a sense of identity and thus standards or guidelines for the type of behavior in which members can engage. In this sense, these groups also promote limited (i.e., heuristically based) information processing regarding outgroup perceptions and instill a sense of moral and legal justification for the group's actions (Bandura, 2004; Combs, 2003; Murray & Cowden, 1999). Because ideology is used as the driving force within the group, individuals will be less likely to attend to external information in the environment. This can lead to a perpetuation of blame on certain outgroups (i.e., scapegoating) for hardships or negative outcomes that the ingroup is suffering (Watts, 2001). In addition, this also produces the means through which ideological groups provide a sense of justification for their beliefs and actions. The conduct of the group is made personally and socially acceptable by portraying it as serving socially worthy and moral purposes (Bandura, 2004). The cognitive redefinition of right and wrong can sanctify even destructive acts if necessary.

Ideological Group Emergence Factors

While the foregoing suggests a number of characteristics of ideologues, generally, these observations provide little specific information about the nature of violent ideological groups. In the present analysis, violent ideological groups are defined as groups of individuals united by a specific set of values that either openly condone violence or its members have been linked to multiple acts of violence. These groups also tend to be identified by their alignment with an extremist ideology that is used to justify the aggressive acts they pursue. Nonviolent ideological groups, by contrast, are united behind a strong belief and work toward mutual goals, but do so in less aggressive ways. While the formation of ideological groups arises through the adoption of a mental model (Friedland, 2001), there is also reason to believe that certain environmental conditions give rise to the promotion of violent ideological groups (Mumford et al., in press).

In particular, the emergence of violent ideological groups is linked with certain external and internal conditions such as group rivalry, social conflict, social disruption, feelings of victimization, and moral superiority. These social and environmental conditions are intertwined with the notion of perceived threat or the sensitivity of the ingroup to criticism from some outgroup or to inequality that exists externally (Cameron, Duck, Terry, & Lalonde, 2005). More specifically, group rivalry tends to arise when social identity is threatened by comparison of the ingroup to a highly similar outgroup or if an ingroup's superiority is challenged on a particularly salient dimension. This can result from opponents threatening a group's identity or forcing it to act decisively to prove its worth (Post et al., 2002). In addition, social conflict is comprised of the presence of multiple ideological groups, fragmentation in society, fear of social loss, threats to tradition, and economic displacement (Mumford et al., in press). This can be the result of disputes over resources, political power, or even ethnic and religious differences (Post et al., 2002).

Moreover, social disruption consists of a loss of social pattern, fragmentation of society, and middle-class marginalization (Mumford et al., in press). This can be a result of open discrimination by a dominant outgroup, historical conflicts and divisions among groups, or persecution of a subordinate group (Post et al., 2002). Lastly, perceptions of victimization and a strong sense of moral superiority by the group can arise from feelings of injustice, corruption, and limitations in opportunity and may provide the justification necessary for the use of force (Mumford et al., in press). Each of these factors on its own or in concert can lead to members' further psychological entrenchment in the group's ideology and thus the potential for resorting to violent means for resolving conflict.

Violent Ideological Group Characteristics

In light of the conditions for the emergence of these violent ideological groups, there is also reason to believe that these types of groups possess unique characteristics that distinguish them from nonviolent ideological groups. In addition, these characteristics may also contribute to the susceptibility of these groups to violence (Mumford et al., in press). First, violent ideological groups can be distinguished by the characteristics of their leaders. Specifically, violent ideologues tend to be more narcissistic, paranoid, sociopathic, and extreme in their ideological views than nonviolent group leaders (Mumford et al., in press; Post et al., 2002). Second, these groups tend to encourage their members to surrender their individual identity for that of a more group-oriented identity. It may push members to "become a part of the greater good" either by adopting the group's identity or through individual sacrifice for the group (e.g., becoming a martyr) (Burdman, 2003). Third, violent ideological groups engage in socialization practices that emphasize obedience to authority, loyalty to the group, and a reshaping of previously held beliefs to fall in line with those of the group (Burdman, 2003; Post et al., 2002; Mumford et al., in press).

Additionally, these groups promote oppositional bonding or negative outgroup comparisons with other groups (i.e., intergroup bias) (Hewstone et al., 2002). A fifth violent tendency is for ideological groups to exhibit a sense of ideological righteousness which entails group feelings of superiority, strong group values, feelings of victimization, group sacrifice, and symbolic commitment (Mumford et al., in press). In addition, these groups attempt to instill in their followers a new mental model through ideological indoctrination which includes sense breaking (breaking down currently held mental models), sacrifice for the organization, sensemaking (building new mental models in line with the group), and training in ideology (Mumford et al., in press). Lastly, violent ideological groups have often been distinguished from other nonviolent groups by their practice of dehumanization or identifying outgroup members as subhuman through the removal of all positive characteristics while reassigning negative ones (Kent, 2005; Stahelski, 2005).

Violent Ideological Member Characteristics

In correspondence with the characteristics discussed above that are unique to violent ideological groups, individuals who become interested in and seek membership with these groups tend to exhibit a fairly consistent pattern of characteristics as well. Of course, there are specific types of people who are attracted to some groups and not others; however, certain social and psychological factors tend to play a large role in an individual's intentions to identify with or join violent ideological groups. Some social factors include age, education, gender, socio-economic status, and family structure. Typically, membership will consist of young males (ages ranging from 16 to 30 with the majority in their lower 20s) from lower socio-economic levels, with mid- to lower education levels (high school degree or lower), and single parent or dysfunctional households (Ezekiel, 2002; Watts, 2001).

In addition, some psychological factors characterizing group members include malleable identities and thrill-seeking tendencies, beliefs, perceptions of reality, temporal orientation, and search for meaning. Younger individuals tend to have a more pliable collective identity, lending them to the structure and opportunities provided by these groups (Taylor & Louis, 2004). Also, their tendencies toward thrill-seeking or other opportunistic motives may enhance the attraction of violent ideological groups to these potential members (Watts, 2001). Individuals with a more future-orientated view look for ways of defining themselves, promoting a positive identity, and achieving goals including engaging in meaningful and satisfying behavior. They will tend to gravitate more toward others who share similar worldviews or interpret their environment in the same way. In particular, they need a direction to their lives and crave a sense of meaning or purpose (Taylor & Louis, 2004). Overall, then, individuals matching these characteristics are at greater risk of messages intended to sway their ideological perceptions.

Each of the characteristics discussed above point to the multitude of influences that act upon individuals and the formation of ideological groups. When examining the group characteristics and membership of these groups, the implications for behavior become apparent. In particular, certain circumstances may interact with group characteristics that can lead to conditions that increase the risk of antisocial and even violent behavior. In addition, these characteristics may also have implications for the ways in which violent and nonviolent ideological groups communicate with their followers and with the population at large. Specifically, these groups may use different types of media for different purposes such as attracting new membership or disseminating information about their cause. In the following section, we will review the extant literature regarding old and new media and make predictions for the ways in which violent and nonviolent ideological groups will use each.

NEW MEDIA

Technological advancements are continuously developing and enhancing the ways in which individuals and groups communicate with each other through media. These new forms of media are appropriately referred to as new media. Currently new media is primarily in a digital format, which permits high levels of flexibility in form and functionality, and is often marked with a degree of interactivity for its audience. Some examples of today's new media include the Internet, email, podcasts, and mobile phones (including text messaging). New media has recently gained considerable attention in the literature, and it is suggested by this chapter that properties of these new media formats may be particularly important with respect to how ideological groups communicate.

New media is defined by the period of time in which it exists. As new technologies develop, new media becomes "old media". Furthermore, as a particular form of new media becomes utilized more, it can to some extent take on the role of old media (Flanagin & Metzger, 2001). For example, the increased reliance on email as a communication channel has led it to take on a similar role to that of the telephone. In a similar fashion, the increased use of the Internet has led to web sites taking on a role similar to that of the TV, as a source of both information and entertainment (Flanagin & Metzger, 2001). Table 22.1 presents some examples of new and old media formats.

While differences exist between media formats, it should be noted that the general purposes for communication remain the same. This assumption has led researchers to hold the position that people generally do not behave differently when using new media and the Internet in particular, than

TABLE 22.1
Examples of Old Media and New Media

Media	*Categories*	*Examples*
Old Media	*Print*	letters, books, newspapers, magazines
	Images	photographs, film, television
	Sound	phonograph, telephone, radio
New Media	*Print*	The Internet, email, palm pilots, text messaging
	Images	DVDs, satellite television, the internet, cellular telephones, web cams, digital video recorders
	Sound	Ipods, MP3s, mobile telephones, the internet, web radio, digital cable music

Note. "New Media" section of table adapted from Marshall (2004).

in other domains (e.g., Matei, 2005). In other words, media simply provides the means or resources to more easily do the things that people already do, or in some circumstances do the things that they already wanted to do (Calhoun, 1998). This assertion provides an important function in permitting us to hypothesize about the psychological and social nature of the relationship between individuals or groups and the media with which they choose to interact.

To examine this potential relationship between media use and ideological groups, it is necessary to explore the connection between the motives of media use, and the attributes of ideological groups. The Uses and Gratification approach has been used to unearth a variety of motivations and reactions related to different media types. The motivation for media use typically concerns the attainment of various interactive and informational needs, depending on the availability, and the instrumentality of the media to meet these needs (e.g., Rubin, 1993, 1994). More specifically, Uses and Gratification research has determined that media use is often utilized for diversion or escape, to meet social needs, to meet personal identity needs (such as reinforcing attitudes, beliefs and values), or to learn about one's community, events and affairs (Ruggiero, 2000). More recently this approach has been extended to include new media (e.g., Newhagen & Rafaeli, 1996; Papacharissi & Rubin, 2000; Ruggiero, 2000). For example, Papacharissi and Rubin (2000) discovered that individuals who were less satisfied with life, and who felt less socially valued were more likely to use the Internet to facilitate interpersonal communication. These motivations and characteristics are some examples of the psychological needs that resonate with characteristics of ideological groups or the group members. In general we can conclude from this research that a variety of psychological needs, in conjunction with social and situational characteristics can interact with the media characteristics to determine media choice and use. While the Uses and Gratification research has indicated a general relationship between psychological needs and media use, the number of contingencies involved in this approach combined with the unique nature of ideological groups prevents any useful generalizations from being made. We hope to contribute to this area by exploring the possible role that ideology and identity formation play in media selection and use.

While the focus of this chapter concerns new media, this does not preclude the examination of ideological groups' use of old media. In fact, a cursory examination into the literature yields some useful findings. Ideological groups have in the past utilized old media formats to communicate their beliefs and values both among group members and the general public. This type of ideologically-oriented media has been termed "alternative media" and is defined as media produced by non-commercial sources that attempt to transform existing social roles and routines by critiquing and challenging power structures (Downing, 2003). For example, the Communist party produced a local newspaper which was commonly referred to as "The Wall." This publication eventually garnered Communist governmental support, and subsequently editorial control in many communist countries (Downing, 2003).

Alternative media has also taken on more extremist forms known as radicalized alternative media. This media type is often associated with social and political movements, where it is frequently focused on challenging the structures of power and mainstream-media uses (Downing, 2003). Currently, the rise in use of new media has expanded the occurrence of radicalized media, with one such example being the web site Indymedia.org (Garcelon, 2006). Indymedia.org is a group of open domain web sites whose purpose is to be an alternative to the corporate mass media in the United States. It has since attracted a large presence of anarchic radicals who post content from a large number of countries.

Blogs are an additional form of new media that combine news and information with self-expression (Kaye, 2005). In these venues, a blogger reports a variety of news, opinions, and links to information. While often utilized as an alternative source of information, blogs do not undergo formal editorial reviews. Blog readers also may interact with the blogger and other blog readers through participation in online discussion boards. As noted previously, mainstream political movements have become actively involved in presenting their ideological viewpoints or policies on the Internet using media such as blogs. As an example, Iranian President Mahmoud Ahmadinejad currently maintains a blog that is presented in a number of different languages (http://www.ahmadinejad.ir). In line with this phenomenon, in the United States it was estimated in 2003 that more than 17,000 political web sites were maintained by bloggers and were visited by at least 25 million Americans, with the top 100 political blogs attracting 100,000 Americans a day (Jost, Glaser, Kruglanski & Sulloway, 2003).

In addition to political groups, religious groups have also recently become involved in new media (Sturgill, 2004). Fundamentalist Evangelistic Christians have frequently utilized the media as a source to spread their teachings, from radio to television, and now the Internet. The Internet Evangelism Coalition (http://ied.gospelcom.net) even provides several resources that demonstrate how to utilize podcasts, blogs, chat rooms, and other tactics to spread evangelism. With six national TV networks and 2,000 radio stations, the large presence of conservative evangelical Christians in today's media is evident. The Christian Broadcasting Network characterizes the general trend of these evangelical faith-based media networks covering a mix of religion, news, politics and family-oriented shows. This convergence of media sources is a salient example of how ideological groups use new media to spread their ideology. This phenomenon is perhaps best summarized by Frank Wright, the current president of the National Religious Broadcasters, who once said, "We don't just tell them what the news is, we tell them what it means…" (Blake, 2005, p. 35). When presenting risk information then, it seems that these more specialized media types facilitate and perhaps even enhance the capability of ideological groups to selectively present information within the group. Furthermore, ideological groups may also be able to utilize these media types to communicate risks with the general public, as a way of gaining wider acceptance or even attracting members.

Virtual Communities

The advantages of new media, and in particular of the Internet, for ideological groups can be seen from the discussion above. It provides groups and their members with relative anonymity if needed, and easily accessible meeting grounds for those that have similar interests, values, and beliefs. One particularly salient advantage for these groups is the formation of virtual communities. A virtual community is an online group of people that through interaction create a sense of belonging, feelings of membership, influence, fulfillment of needs, and a shared emotional connection, where participants regularly engage in communication processes (Jones, 1997). These characteristics can create a sense of perceived similarity, homogeneity, and group cohesion, which can create a psychological attachment to the virtual community and ultimately to the group as a whole. Some virtual communities also afford the opportunity for individuals, who may have either naïve associations with a group's ideology or are simply curious about the group, to access their propaganda and gain exposure.

These virtual communities offer a unique structure for social interaction. For example, these interactions can be conducted anonymously (Bargh & McKenna, 2004). These anonymous communications inherently reduce the risks associated with self-disclosure, which in time can lead to a sense of intimacy. In this case, the anonymity of the virtual community may in fact perpetuate the members' identification with the ideological group. For example, consider the individual who holds extremist views yet his current environment does not permit him to routinely socialize with other like minded individuals, or to openly voice his beliefs for fear of being publicly stigmatized. The Internet provides the means for both, thus permitting the individual to routinely socialize with other like minded individuals, and act on their extremist views. As an example, consider the example of the reclusive social deviant who secretly affiliates with a militant wing of the Black Panthers, a fact unknown to even close family members. These virtual communities have the ability to provide structure and support to their violent extremist views.

Concerning the production and consumption of media messages by ideological groups, the idea of the "reach" of the media may be an instrumental part of determining the utility and use of a particular media format. The concept of reach can be defined as the scope or size of the audience a media source is intended to be consumed by. A low reach channel is media that has little or no apparent outside audience (Gunther & Liebhart, 2006). In comparison, a high reach channel would have a wide audience, such as that of a national newspaper or national news broadcast. These low reach channels are viewed in a self affirming way and in reference to ones' own opinion. This leads one to perceive confirming views as acceptable, and to dismiss disconfirming views. On the other hand, when individuals have strong convictions regarding a topic (i.e., views held by ideologues), they tend to perceive widely disseminated information on that topic as negatively biased, regardless of the true nature of the information (Vallone, Ross, & Lepper, 1985). Based on its perceived reach, different media are often viewed as more or less credible (Metzger, Flanagin, Eyal, Lemus, & McCann, 2003), especially in terms of partisan issues which are often the topic of ideological group discussions. Therefore, it seems as though the reach of the media may influence ideological group perceptions of its credibility as well as what media outlets they choose to disseminate their information.

As this section notes, the various properties of new media will permit a number of flexible, decentralized, and convenient media channels and formats. Over time, it seems plausible that due to the low cost and ease of producing new media this trend will lead to a number of media sources created by both organizations and users. Therefore, as Chaffee and Metzger (2001) indicate, the study of media communication may no longer be about what the media is doing to people, but what the people are doing with the media.

Media Credibility

Perhaps one of the more important consequences of new media is the fact that the responsibility of verification of the content falls on the consumer. In old media, such as newspapers, books, magazines, and television, all forms received some level of factual verification. For new media, those sources on the Internet, this may not be the case (Gilser, 1997; Scheuermann & Langford, 1997). This poses a risk when ideological groups are communicating with the general public, or among its own members. A number of studies have examined issues involving credibility assessments of media, and more specifically the Internet. In a recent review of credibility assessment, Metzger and colleagues (2003) identified three facets, namely credibility regarding the source, the message, or the medium. For web site credibility or source credibility, it was demonstrated that perceptions of site trustworthiness, expertise, attractiveness, and dynamism were all found to be important contributions in credibility assessments (Flanagin & Metzger, 2001). In regard to web site message credibility, it was found that online message credibility is influenced by perceived authority, and is further increased with connection to other authorities (Rieh & Belkin, 1998). This finding is relevant to ideological groups as these groups can often be highly authoritarian (Post et al., 2001). Furthermore, individuals attracted to these groups are susceptible to this type of influence (Henry, Sidanius, Levin, & Pratto, 2002). In regard to medium credibility, it was shown that credibility is often measured much along the same lines as traditional media with believability being the most often cited characteristic, and accuracy, trustworthiness, bias, and information completeness included as well. Overall, then, credibility assessment may vary by what is determined salient at the time by the user (Metzger et al., 2003).

The idea that the effect of the media rests predominately on what people do with it is a critical component to the study of ideological groups. The new media format may provide individuals the pathway to orient themselves toward specialized worldviews of their own choosing (Chaffee & Metzger, 2001). With the ability to select and filter media content and integrate it into their preexisting ideas, new media will allow users to surround themselves with like-minded ideological media and potentially further enhance their views through socialization online Internet with other like-minded individuals (Chaffee & Metzger, 2001). These ideologues, through new media, have the ability to make their beliefs and values easily accessible and perhaps influence individuals who are more susceptible to their messages. Examples of this, ranging from terrorist groups to pornography, are abundant on the Internet where social constraints are reduced and content is both user generated and unregulated. Fortunately, the use of new media by these groups can be seen as an opportunity to study the functioning and influential characteristics of ideological groups. In the following section, we present several suggestions for avenues of risk communication research by offering various propositions on how violent and nonviolent ideological groups communicate using new media.

PROPOSITIONS

In the above sections, we have established some of the social and psychological characteristics of both violent and nonviolent ideological groups as well as attempted to describe the state of the new media literature in a broad sense. The ideological literature is much better-formed at this point than the literature regarding new media, which is not surprising considering the recent development and constant transformation of new media. The goal of this section is to synthesize these two seemingly disparate literatures into a set of researchable propositions that are relevant to risk and crisis communication. In keeping with this, the propositions are framed as comparisons between violent and nonviolent ideological groups. By developing propositions framed in this way, two objectives are accomplished. First, interested researchers can test these propositions through systematic research on the web. Second, research in this vein informs risk communication scholars as to the forms of media where potentially dangerous ideologues may be found.

Prior to describing the propositions, a few caveats should be noted up front. First, the propositions should be treated as general guidelines and not rules applicable to all groups of that particular type. For example, the following propositions would not apply to cults or militia groups that oppose the use of new technology. Second, the role of culture is extremely important to the development of an individual's identity (Cross & Gore, 2003). While some cultural considerations are mentioned, the distinct role of culture is generally not described in any detail in the subsequent sections. Therefore, it should be recognized that the following has a more Western orientation. These points should be borne in mind in the following analysis.

The propositions are broken into three sections that are organized roughly in terms of the unit of analysis. The first section deals with new and traditional media, and its uses for violent and nonviolent ideological organizations. We also explore the purpose this new media serves for the organizations. Second, we will describe a number of propositions related to virtual community formation, size, and structure. Finally, propositions regarding the online behavior of the ideological group members themselves, rather than the groups as a whole, will be offered. These sections are described in more detail below.

Media Use

In the 1928 presidential election, Al Smith, a democratic governor from New York, became the first Catholic to represent a major party in a presidential election. In reaction to his nomination, the Ku Klux Klan (KKK) launched a media campaign that involved pamphlets and newspapers, one with a cartoon of Smith kneeling next to the pope and kissing his ring (Slayton, 2001). The ideas expressed by this known violent ideological group were granted an audience by more mainstream or traditional media, which would seem almost inconceivable in the United States today. However, this observation does not indicate that there is an absence of ideological messages in traditional media. For example, the National Youth Anti-Drug Media Campaign, a project established by the United States Congress to discourage youths from taking drugs, has a number of advertisements on the Internet, television, radio, and in print (see www.mediacampaign.org for more details). The broader point is that ideology per se does not preclude the use of traditional media; rather it is the content of the ideological message that matters most.

The reasons for this are relatively obvious. First, while the first amendment does protect the opinions of citizens, messages that incite others to violence are of questionable legality (see, for example, the Supreme Court decision regarding "fighting words," *Chaplinsky v. New Hampshire*). Second, private broadcasters, publishers, and so forth of traditional media would not stay in business long if they catered to the more extreme views of violent ideological groups. Most violent ideological groups, almost by definition, hold viewpoints that may be considered "extreme" by members of the society in which they operate. In fact, groups that are at-risk for violence tend to have more extreme and polarizing attitudes within their group (Pynchon & Borum, 1999), and toward out-group members (Bandura, 2004; Mumford et al., in press). This is especially true with groups that categorize all non-members as "enemies" (Moghaddam, 2005; Post, 2005; Post et al., 2002). There are of course exceptions, such as the violent ideological group Hamas, which in January 2006 was elected as the majority party of the Palestinian Authority (PA). However, these exceptions are rare. Nonviolent ideological groups on the other hand, when resources allow, will want to use any media source that can reach the largest audience possible to deliver its message. This analysis leads to our first proposition:

> *Proposition 1*: Nonviolent ideological groups will find traditional media sources more attractive than violent ideological groups.

As stated earlier, describing new media is difficult because it is constantly changing and incorporating more forms of multimedia (Marshall, 2004). For example, comparing the richness of online forms of media and television can be difficult because online media can come in the form of text, streaming audio, audiovisual, interactive games, and so on. It is precisely this flexibility that makes new media so attractive to all groups, whether ideological or non-ideological, violent or nonviolent. However, there are also a number of specific reasons ideological groups may want to use new media. First, ideological groups can produce high quality media at a relatively low cost. Second, using new media, online ideological messages can be tailored to specific audiences. By targeting ideological messages, new media can be used to bring together like-minded individuals for recruitment and fundraising (Damphousse & Smith, 2002; Lee & Leets, 2002). For example, Blazak (2001) explains how white hate groups such as White Aryan Resistance (WAR) target alienated youths for potential membership in their groups.

A third reason, which almost seems inconsistent with the second, is that new media can be used to deliver ideological messages to a wider audience. Recall that ideological groups have a particular worldview that they are trying to enact (Mumford et al., in press), and thus are naturally going to want to "get the message out" about their ideological views, whether it is to market their group (Levin, 2002), legitimize their movement (Corman & Schiefelbein, 2006), or clarify misconceptions about their beliefs. For example, on the Animal Liberation Front (ALF) web site, their "Frequently

Asked Questions" (FAQ) section elaborates on the distinction between the Animal Rights, Animal Welfare, and Animal Liberation movements, and why their movement is not one of "political correctness" or a type of religion (see www.animalliberationfront.com).

One implication of the first proposition is that violent ideological groups will be particulaly drawn to new media. In addition to the reasons suggested above, violent groups may have more malevolent reasons for being drawn to new media. Research has shown that new media can also be used for cyberterrorism (Stanton, 2002), intimidation (Corman & Schiefelbein, 2006), written attacks (Damphousse & Smith, 2002), and for tactical reasons (Levin, 2002). For example, Stanton (2002) describes a scenario where intelligent programs, or *bots*, are used by terrorist groups to interact with users and spread propaganda online. Likewise, Levin (2002) describes how techniques such as "steganography" can be used by violent ideologues to embed secret documents and messages within e-mails. For reasons such as these, new media will appeal to ideological groups generally, but particularly to violent ideological groups. This leads to our second proposition:

Proposition 2: Both violent and nonviolent ideological groups will use new media.

The discussion regarding the use of media by violent ideological groups begs the question of how new media is used differentially between violent and nonviolent ideological groups. In general, new media can be used for a diversity of reasons, such as shopping online, information seeking, finding companionship, and so forth, satisfying a number of individual needs (Ang, 1995; Flanagin & Metzger, 2001; Matusitz & O'Hair, in press). However, ideological groups will want to center users' activities on their particular ideological viewpoint. For example, white hate groups can propagate their ideology through the sale of culturally relevant music using companies such as Resistance Records (Damphousse & Smith, 2002). New media is also frequently used in concert with traditional media. For example, one study demonstrated that web searching increases after key events such as the September 11, 2001, terrorist attacks, suggesting that people often get news from traditional media, but turn to new media for additional details (Aikat, 2005; O'Hair & Heath, 2005). Consistent with this research, Dennis and Ash (2001) suggest that new media can be used to replace or work alongside traditional media. The avenue that is chosen may depend, at least in part, on the ideological orientation of the group or web site. Specifically, the extent to which the group distrusts traditional media may depend on whether the group is violent or nonviolent.

Research with violent ideologues suggests that they have an alternative view of reality than the mainstream masses. It has long been recognized that human beings have basic needs and these needs can be frustrated by social and economic hardships and turbulence in the environment (Maslow, 1943). For this reason, *perceived* deprivation is a key initial step for becoming a violent ideologue (Etzioni-Halevy, 1975; Moghaddam, 2005; Staub, 1996; 2003). The word "perceived" is of key importance because people can live with a lifetime of economic hardship and not turn to violence, while others can come from affluence and become ideological extremists. Osama bin Laden is a notable example of the latter case because of his educated background and economic advantage (Taylor & Louis, 2004). This perceived deprivation can come from a variety of sources, such as a history of devaluation of the group one belongs to (Staub, 1996, 2003), a lack of potential for upward mobility, and perceptions of procedural injustice (Moghaddam, 2005). New media from violent ideological groups can step in and fill this void in an individual's needs by providing a worldview that gives them someone to blame for their plight.

One implication of this discussion is that these feelings of deprivation and needs fulfillment can lead to collective identities in violent ideological groups that are marked by extreme viewpoints (Post, 2005; Taylor & Louis, 2004). To engender these viewpoints in other ideological group members, violent ideological groups will first want to strip away old identities and worldviews, and then reformulate them (Kent, 2005). New media can be an excellent medium for breaking free from traditional norms (Wheeler, 2003) and, therefore, a medium where this process can take place. Nonviolent ideological groups on the other hand do not share the ideological extremism and righteousness that define violent ideological groups (Mumford et al., in press). This suggests nonviolent ideological groups will not engage in as much of the "sense-breaking" as their violent counterparts. If we operate under the assumption that traditional media often represents a more "mainstream" worldview, we are led to the following proposition:

> *Proposition 3*: Nonviolent ideological groups are more likely to use new media to complement traditional media while violent ideological groups are more likely to prioritize new media over traditional media sources.

A second implication of the above discussion is that violent ideological groups will want to focus their recruitment on those that feel they are deprived, and thus more susceptible to violent ideologies. Research has shown that this is exactly how violent ideological groups operate (Blazak, 2001; Post et al., 2002). Blazak (2001), in particular, has shown that white hate groups such as the KKK and WAR specifically target frustrated, alienated, and angry youths for recruitment to their groups. They will even go to schools and neighborhoods where a factory has been shut down to talk to youths whose parents have been laid off. This is a time when they are particularly susceptible to ideological messages. Online, white hate groups recruit using a number of tools, such as persuasive storytelling (Lee & Leets, 2002), appeals to white masculinity, appeals to patriotism and Christianity, vivid imagery, and targeted messages for white women and children (Bostdorff, 2004). These groups may also recruit members of other groups who share ideologies with similar characteristics, blending distinct characteristics of the two groups, but keeping the same violent ideas (Watts, 2001). It comes as no surprise then that groups with more intensive and selective recruitment are more at risk for violence (Post et al., 2002). Nonviolent ideological groups however, do not have any reason to recruit from this pool of people as they are trying to get the message of their ideology out to the greatest number of people. This leads to the following:

> *Proposition 4*: Nonviolent ideological groups will target the general population in which the group operates, while violent ideological groups will target frustrated individuals with more malleable identities.

Underlying this discussion is the notion that people can use new media to interact with others. This has long been recognized by communications scholars (Morris & Ogan, 1996), but there has been little examination of the role of virtual communities and ideological groups. This is our next topic of discussion.

Ideological Groups and Virtual Communities

Research suggests that people have a natural need to feel like they are part of a group (Buss, 2000). Social identity theory in particular proposes that the groups we belong to, whether they are ideological or not, play a substantial role in our personal identity (Tajfel, 1982). The strength of this tendency is demonstrated in a number of studies using the "minimal group differences" paradigm (Tajfel, Billig, Bundy, & Flament, 1971). These studies demonstrate that we make negative attributions about outgroup members and positive attributions of ingroup members, even when the actual group differences are trivial (Hogg, 2003; Tajfel et al., 1971). One can imagine then the strength of this intergroup bias tendency when the group differences are highly meaningful or salient, as is the case with ideological groups (Hewstone et al., 2002). Because our self-esteem is strongly linked to what others think of us (Leary, Tambor, Terdal, & Downs, 1995), our collective identity may be the most important part of our self-concept because it gives us a basis for comparing ourselves to others (Taylor & Louis, 2004).

This natural need for affiliation may help explain why virtual communities have formed on the Internet for all types of groups, whether ideological or non-ideological, violent or nonviolent (Ridings & Gefen, 2004). The open format of the Internet can draw members from all over the world for even the most obscure interests. One would surmise then that both violent and nonviolent ideological groups have a long history of virtual communities on the web. For example, Levin (2002) traced the first use of new media for extremist activity to 1983, when the Liberty Bell Net bulletin board system was established to post racist material. Groups in general frequently form out of a collective discontent where no group at present meets individual needs (Bargh & McKenna, 2004; Worchel, Coutant-Sassic, & Grossman, 1991). Ideological groups of course are no different, and can reduce uncertainty and draw others in due to their articulation of a meaningful worldview (Blau, 1964), regardless of the extremity of the ideology. This leads to our next proposition:

Proposition 5: Nonviolent and violent ideological groups will both form virtual communities online.

This proposition only deals with the existence of virtual communities, and not their purpose. What goes on in a virtual community? The communications literature seems to coalesce around two main themes: 1) information exchange, and 2) social relationship building (Ridings & Gefen, 2004). Given the purpose that all ideological groups share, a commitment to a common worldview, it seems logical that they would want to promote information exchange in their own virtual communities to spread their ideological ideals. It is especially important for ideological groups to have information online given that the Internet is the media source most conducive to structuring the knowledge of readers, compared to television and print newspapers (Eveland, Seo, & Marton, 2002). Information exchange includes a number of online behaviors, such as announcements (both information and personal), queries (both to the group and to specific individuals), group projects, and responses to queries (Burnett & Buerkle, 2004). This suggests that certain media types may be more conducive to information exchange.

Group members engage in information exchange activities for a number of reasons, such as altruism, reciprocity, and group status (Lampel & Bhalla, 2007). Status may be particularly important in the context of violent ideological groups because group membership is such an important part of collective identity (Bargh & McKenna, 2004; Post et al., 2002). In nonviolent ideological groups, status may also be important (especially for those that want to be seen as an "expert" in the ideology), as well as an altruistic motive for furthering the group's cause. There are also a number of advantages to exchanging information via the web for group members and web surfers as well. First, given the amount of misinformation on the Internet (Lewis, 2006), the ideological groups, by virtue of their belief, may be seen as the only credible source for ideologically-loaded information. Second, the Internet can be used to get much more in-depth coverage of a topic of interest (e.g., Aikat, 2005; McKeown & Plowman, 1999). Regardless of the reasons, from the perspective of either the group or the user, it seems that information exchange is vital to the virtual communities of both violent and nonviolent ideological groups, leading to the following proposition:

Proposition 6: Nonviolent and violent ideological groups will both emphasize information exchange in their virtual communities.

However, there may be differences between violent and nonviolent ideological groups in their emphasis on relationship building within their virtual communities. As described earlier, violent ideological groups seek out individuals who are deprived, frustrated, and impressionable. These individuals have a sense of "anomie," or normlessness, that a violent ideological group can exploit (Blazak, 2001). One way groups do this is by establishing strong social networks that these individuals can join (Turpin-Petrosino, 2002). Once involved in these social networks (whether online or not), violent ideological groups can take hold of potential recruits through a number of influence tactics. For example, virtual communities can be used to provide "social proof" that others believe as they do and that their violent ideology is normal (Blazak, 2001; Damphousse &

Smith, 2002; Post, Sprinzak, & Denny, 2003). Groups can also capitalize on affiliation motives by ingratiating themselves to potential recruits, making it difficult to disagree with them in the future (Blazak, 2001; Cialdini & Goldstein, 2004). These social networks then can be used as a gateway for violent groups to indoctrinate individuals into an ideology that solves all of their problems. They provide them with an ideology that scapegoats outgroup members, creates a positive vision of the future, and creates a fictional world where the offending outgroup does not exist (Staub, 1996; 1999).

For nonviolent ideological groups, there is no evidence that similar processes are involved. While nonviolent ideological groups are concerned with social disruption, they also have higher levels of social concern (Mumford et al., in press). This implies that, while nonviolent ideological groups would like for the world to change, they do not share the desperation that violent ideological groups do for recruiting members, indoctrinating them, and forcing them to stay involved in the group. They seem to prefer using more mainstream means for convincing the population at large. This analysis leads to our next proposition:

Proposition 7: Violent ideological groups, more than nonviolent ideological groups, will emphasize virtual communities for social interactions and relationship building.

If our previous analysis is correct, then the emphasis on community building has implications for other aspects of the web sites of violent and nonviolent ideological groups. Web sites are often described in terms of interactivity. One of the central dimensions of interactivity is interaction efficacy, which can be described as the extent to which people feel comfortable talking to others online and how real-time the communication is (Sohn & Lee, 2005). This is sometimes also called synchronicity (e.g., Morris & Ogan, 1996; Porter, 2004). Certain forms of web communication are more conducive for information exchange, while others are more conducive for social interaction (Maclaran & Catterall, 2002). For example, message boards are more conducive for information exchange (a more asynchronous form of communication), while chat rooms are more conducive for social interaction (a more synchronous form of communication). If we presume that violent ideological groups are more likely to emphasize community building than nonviolent groups, then we may also presume that these groups will also seek more interaction efficacy in their web sites. Higher interaction efficacy facilitates community building through participation in more "real" dialogue than in more asynchronous forms of communication. This will also allow group members to form more personal relationships with potential recruits. This leads to the following proposition:

Proposition 8: Violent ideological groups will seek more interaction efficacy in their web sites (i.e., more synchronous forms of communication) than nonviolent ideological groups.

Another way to describe virtual communities is how loose or tight they are (Maclaran & Catterall, 2002). Tight communities are characterized by heavy-handed control of the web community's content, whereas loose communities are characterized by less control. Research has suggested that, over time, groups will often move toward more conformity norms to reduce uncertainty within the groups (Hogg, 2003). In violent ideological groups however, this tendency may be exacerbated by the extremity of the ideology and threat perceived from the outside world (Post et al., 2002; Pynchon & Borum, 1999). A number of factors may contribute to this tendency. First, violent ideological groups are often characterized by categorical "us versus them" thinking (Moghaddam, 2005). Categorical ideologies leave little margin for disagreement among members, thus contributing to the conformity of the group. Second, violent ideological groups are more likely to arise in cultures that are monolithic and authority oriented (Staub, 1996; 1999). As Burdman (2003) demonstrated in her study of Palestinian children, authoritarian societies can increase the ease with which violent acts are carried out. In this particular case, it was accomplished by indoctrinating children into a culture of violence through textbooks, radio, and television. Third, the types of individuals that are drawn to violent ideological groups are less likely to challenge authority. For example, Henry and colleagues found that high right wing authoritarianism (partially characterized by respect for authority) were more likely to support violence in American and Arab samples (Henry et al., 2002).

There are a number of clear and dangerous implications to this conformity. For one, this conformity over time can lead the members of violent ideological groups to subordinate their personal identity to the collective identity of the group (Moghaddam, 2005; Post, 2005; Post et al., 2003). When this happens, individual members can displace or diffuse their responsibility for harmful or violent consequences (Bandura, 2004). A second implication is that group decision-making is more likely to be characterized by groupthink (Post et al., 2002; Pynchon & Borum, 1999). Groupthink is the tendency for a group to seek concurrence in making decisions, even when the decision may overall be harmful to the group (Janis, 1972). When this occurs, people will be more likely to go along with an action that leads to violent outcomes, even when it may hurt the group in the long run. The emphasis that ideological groups place on authority and conformity leads to our next proposition:

Proposition 9: Violent ideological groups will have tighter (i.e., more regulated, more constrained, and more homogeneous) virtual communities than nonviolent ideological groups.

Implicit in the previous discussion is that violent ideological groups must take severe steps toward gaining conformity in their organization. As groups move more toward violence, they become more polarized through demonizing and dehumanizing members of the outgroup (Kent, 2005; Moghaddam, 2005; Post et al., 2002). The result of this is the loss of members who are more moderate than their counterparts in their views (Post et al., 2002). Groups may also lose members whose involvement can be partially attributed to their youth, and therefore they do not become fully indoctrinated into the ideology and eventually leave (Blazak, 2001). Also, it may be easier to control communication leaks or indiscretions in smaller groups. Additionally, violent groups are also unlikely to positively reinforce new members who have questions about the group. Therefore, ideologues who might be interested in getting involved are more likely to not participate again when given negative feedback (Bargh & McKenna, 2004). This leads to our next proposition:

Proposition 10: Nonviolent ideological group communities will be larger than violent ideological group communities.

Readers will notice that this proposition seems somewhat inconsistent with the proposition above that states violent ideological communities will emphasize social interactions and relationship building. This represents a quandary that these groups face. On the one hand, they want to recruit people to their cause to form a collective and carry out violent activities. On the other, they do not want any sign of dissent within the organization, leaving their options limited. This is what attracts these groups to people with less crystallized identities. These individuals can be "molded" in the image of their archetype of what an "ideal member" should look and act like. They can then indoctrinate these people to keep them involved in group activities and solidify their ideology through tight community structures and a rigid application of doctrine rules.

This leads to another observation regarding the nature of violent ideologues—once someone is fully indoctrinated into a violent ideology, it is very difficult to change that person's world view (Moghaddam, 2005; Staub, 1996). One reason is that, once a person has become fully indoctrinated, they begin to circumvent the cognitive, emotional, and cultural norms that prevent doing harm to others. For example, Bandura (2004) describes how violent ideologues disengage themselves from violent acts by giving them a more sanitized label. Thus, civilian deaths become "collateral damage" and people become "infidels." When this occurs, group members become desensitized to the violence and no longer see it as amoral. Violent ideological group members may also bypass inhibitory mechanisms by exaggerating the differences between them and the outgroup, redefining morality, attributing blame to the outgroup for violence against them, and so forth (Bandura, 2004; Moghaddam, 2005; Stillwell & Baumeister, 1997).

A second reason it is difficult to change people once they have become fully indoctrinated is the need for psychological coherence and self-consistency (Swann, Rentfrow, & Guinn, 2003). People yearn for a self-concept that they can understand and that is consistent with previous actions. To remain consistent then, once a violent ideologue has become fully indoctrinated, it is less likely they will break from it and sacrifice this consistency. Much like the above propositions, there is little reason to believe that nonviolent ideological groups share this extreme indoctrination because "moral disengagement" is unnecessary for members of these groups. For this reason, the following proposition is offered for indoctrinated members of ideological groups:

> *Proposition 11*: Violent ideologues will remain part of a virtual community for a longer duration than nonviolent ideologues.

Member Behaviors

The previous section dealt with the formation and characteristics of ideological communities online. This section will deal with the behaviors of those members in relation to media. Specifically, we are concerned with the types of media that violent and nonviolent ideological group members will view as credible and the scope of their media reach. As mentioned, researchers who study credibility distinguish between source, message, and media credibility (Metzger et al., 2003). Researchers can run into difficulty in pinpointing the specific aspect that the perceiver views as credible. For example, people can attribute credibility to the author of the information, the media type, the people's actions that are being reported, and so forth (Schweiger, 2000). Despite this difficulty, the consistent finding that people who are highly involved in a topic view only consonant messages as credible, is particularly germane to this analysis (Flanagin & Metzger, 2001). When one views this research through the lens of ideological groups generally, and violent ones specifically, these findings are not surprising.

The central reason to believe these findings may be particularly strong for violent ideological group members is that these groups perceive more threat in their environment than nonviolent ideological groups (Post et al., 2002). As discussed at length above, violent ideological groups socialize their members into the view that anybody who is not part of the ingroup is an enemy (Bandura, 2004; Jost & Hunyady, 2005; Moghaddam, 2005; Post, 2005). The consequence of this categorical thinking is that violent groups often see threat as proximate and plausible (Blazak, 2001; Post et al., 2002), leading them to distrust all messages that come from outside the group. For example, Charles Manson used what was to him an imminent threat of a race war to encourage members of his violent ideological group to commit murder (Bugliosi & Gentry, 2001). This analysis leads to our next proposition:

> *Proposition 12*: Nonviolent ideologues will view both traditional and new media as credible, while violent ideologues will only view ideologically-related new media sources as credible.

It stands to reason then that if violent ideologues view outside sources as noncredible, that they will also seek sources that are consistent with their own ideology. Research has shown that groups tend to prefer to discuss material that they all know and believe rather than information that is novel (Kerr & Tindale, 2004; Tindale & Kameda, 2000). The implication is that ideological group members may only seek information that confirms their ideology and ignore information that disconfirms it. For nonviolent ideological groups, they may find confirming information in a variety of media sources, both traditional and new. On the other hand, violent ideological groups may only be able to find confirming information in new media sources that share the same ideology as they do. This may help to explain why violent groups often develop new cultural artifacts such as music and language that celebrate their ideology (Blazak, 2001; Damphousse & Smith, 2002; Vigil, 2003). In lower reach channels and lower reach web sites, violent ideologues are less likely to find challenges to their beliefs and threats to their ideology (Lord, Ross, & Lepper, 1979). This leads to the following proposition:

Proposition 13: Violent ideologues will prefer lower reach channels (i.e., channels that reinforce their beliefs and values) than nonviolent ideologues.

At the beginning of this section, we suggested that these propositions will provide a testable set of hypotheses for future researchers. In the next section, we will take a cursory look at the fidelity of these propositions by examining them in the context of two ideological groups' web sites, one violent and one nonviolent.

ILLUSTRATION

To explore the differences between violent and nonviolent ideological groups' use of new media, two prototypical web sites were examined for the elements previously discussed and outlined in the propositions. Table 22.2 presents a comparison between the web sites of two ideological groups: a) Greenpeace (www.greenpeace.org), a nonviolent environmentalist group, and b) Aryan Nations (www.aryan-nations.org), a violent white hate group. The table includes information collected from the two web sites that was readily available in order to demonstrate the application of these propositions for these two ideological groups.

The first grouping of propositions explores how ideological groups use new vs. traditional/old media. On their web site, Greenpeace provides links to recent television interviews, as well as newspaper articles about the organization, its relevant issues of activism, and its current missions. The web site has a section titled "In the News", which contains links to relevant articles or video clips of Greenpeace missions or issues making national news headlines. For example, on the issue of oceans and whaling, a viewer could click on links to news articles located on the BBC or Boston Globe web sites about this topic. This suggests that this organization is embracing and using traditional media alongside new media. However, Aryan Nations provides no links or connections with any type of traditional media. Some of the sections on their web site include merchandise, literature (e.g., racist manifestos), activist tips, and leaflets to distribute, but no mention or direct attention is paid to national level news stories.

While the purpose and structure is somewhat varied, both web sites make extensive use of new media including discussion boards, photographs, video, and virtual communities. For example, the Greenpeace web site provides information and communication that is targeted towards the general public (e.g., international web sites and a discussion of a variety of issues that impact different groups of people), while the Aryan Nations web site is primarily devoted to providing information targeted towards ingroup members and their specific interests (e.g., little variety in areas of concern or causes, and not inclusive of any other viewpoints).

The second set of propositions discusses the nature of online ideological communities. It should be noted that both web sites had strong elements of virtual communities, but they varied in both purpose and structure. While both web sites provided extensive information to viewers on their issues and beliefs, the Aryan Nations web site had a strong focus on building relationships among members. For example, members had the ability to contact other members via a private instant and e-mail messaging system. Information regarding face-to-face gatherings in local areas was also

TABLE 22.2
Comparison of Two Ideological Websites

	Nonviolent Ideological Group Greenpeace	*Violent Ideological Group Aryan-Nations*
Proposition 1: Nonviolent ideological groups will use traditional media sources while violent ideological groups will not	Organization members participate in interviews with traditional media sources, as well as post traditional news coverage related to the group on the web site	No connection with traditional media
Proposition 2: Both violent and nonviolent ideological groups will use new media	Extensive use of web site, virtual communities, photos, and videos	Extensive use of web site, virtual communities, photos, and videos
Proposition 3: Nonviolent ideological groups are more likely to use new media to work alongside or bend traditional media while violent ideological groups are more likely to use new media to replace traditional media sources	Website has a link devoted to regularly updated press releases, as well as a Greenpeace "In the News" section	No connection with traditional media
Proposition 4: Nonviolent ideological groups will target the general population in which the group operates, while violent ideological groups target frustrated individuals with low identity	Website provides open access to both the community and information to the general public	Information and community focus on recruiting members, especially individuals that feel betrayed by US government and hate minorities
Proposition 5: Nonviolent and violent ideological groups will both form virtual communities online	Discussion boards, blogs, and e-mailing capabilities to friends, Congress, etc.	Discussion boards, web site founder blog, and live chats
Proposition 6: Nonviolent and violent ideological groups will both emphasize information exchange in their virtual communities	Extensive amount of information provided on each of the organization's causes, including news reports, articles, etc.	Extensive amount of information provided on the groups principles, beliefs, and activism in the form of manifestos, articles, videos, humor, etc.
Proposition 7: Violent ideological virtual communities, more than nonviolent ideological communities, will emphasize social interactions and relationship building	Communities not focused on building personal relationships but working together for a common goal	Communities focus on bonding between group members with chat discussions, private messaging systems, as well as information about face to face events and meetings
Proposition 8: Violent ideological groups will seek more interaction efficacy in their web sites (i.e., more synchronous forms of communication) than nonviolent ideological groups	No live chat, but a live web cam and a possible private messaging system but it was not functional at the time	Live chat rooms on various topics of discussion, as well as a private IM and e-mail system
Proposition 9: Violent ideological groups will have tighter virtual communities than nonviolent ideological groups	Open access to community for members and visitors to view and participate	Must be a registered member to view and participate in community
Proposition 10: Nonviolent ideological group communities will be larger than violent ideological group communities	World wide communities with discussion boards, and blogs in several different languages	2,420 members for online discussion boards, live chats, and private messaging systems
Proposition 11: Violent ideologues will remain part of a virtual community for a longer duration than nonviolent ideologues	No information	Three years duration for the earliest member, but system was redesigned 3 years ago
Proposition 12: Nonviolent ideologues will view both traditional and new sources of media as credible, while violent ideologues will only view ideologically-related new media sources as credible	Reports news stories from traditional media which can be discussed in communities	Does not acknowledge traditional media or derides it (e.g., refers to it as Jew Media)
Proposition 13: Violent ideologues will prefer lower reach channels than nonviolent ideologues	Relied mainly on high reach channels for sources of information, like CNN.com, or other large online news organizations	Extensively use low reach channels like group newsletters or sources from similar web sites

available, and members were encouraged to participate in discussion boards with other members from their own state. In a similar vein, the Aryan Nations web site provided live chat rooms which were not available on the Greenpeace web site, suggesting that violent ideological groups make use of more synchronous forms of media.

Another notable difference was the ease with which a viewer could access the community and participate. The Greenpeace web site provided open access to the discussion boards for viewing messages, while the Aryan Nations web site required registration and approval to become a participating member. Another difference in the tightness of these communities was the extent of moderation on the discussion boards. It was unclear whether or not Greenpeace had any moderators for the discussion, but Aryan Nations was in the process of recruiting new moderators for their forums. Also, some of the posts on the Aryan Nations discussion boards were from established members asking for different posters to be banned from the forum for not adhering to the ideology. For example, a member was deleted because others believed him to be a black individual ("Member deletion, [name omitted] has been removed from the registry. It would appear he didn't agree with our ideology!"). In contrast, there were several derogatory posts that remained online in the Greenpeace forums. Information regarding the size of the community and duration of membership was unavailable for Greenpeace, but Aryan Nations discussion forum had approximately 2,400 virtual community members, with the most senior member being active for three years. However, the length of membership duration information may not be completely accurate due to the recent discussion board redesign that reset member profiles.

The third set of propositions dealt with the online behavior of individual group members. The first issue of concern is media credibility. It appears from the available discussions on these forums that members of Aryan Nations do not trust traditional media. The members ridiculed traditional media by claiming that it was under the control of Jewish individuals and thus, inaccurate and slanted. For example, one member stated, "If only we in Amerika [sic] could pry ourselves away from the jew-tube and all the lies it feeds us! I wish my countrymen would seriously question the information they recieve [sic] from the liberal media and instead believe the evidence of thier [sic] own eyes!" On the other hand, the participants on the Greenpeace forums freely used traditional media sources and seemingly trusted them for accuracy. Along similar lines, individuals in the Aryan Nations forum relied heavily on low reach channels for the information that they posted in their discussions. For example, members would post articles from newsletters written by white supremacist leaders, or other similar hate group publications instead of national, widely recognized news sources (e.g., CNN). It should be noted, however, that the members of this forum did not always exclude high reach channels, but favored lower reach sources of information. From the information that was available on the web sites about these groups and their members, it appears that the propositions put forth in this discussion are generally indicative of the distinctions that can be made between violent and nonviolent ideological groups.

CONCLUSION

If nothing else, the above discussion should leave one with the impression that new media will play an important role in the study of risk and crisis communication generally, and violent ideological groups specifically. With an audience of over one billion worldwide, violent ideological groups can exponentially expand their influence using new media driven by a global Internet. However, the vast and open medium of online communication also poses a number of problems for ideological groups. For example, with so much information, how does an ideological group draw an audience to the content it wants to espouse? How do these groups get people from a passive interest in the ideology to an active involvement? These and a number of other questions have yet to be answered. However, the foregoing observations do have a number of practical and theoretical implications for scholars studying risk and crisis communication.

As discussed earlier, the propositions are designed to provide a framework for a testable set of hypotheses regarding new media in relation to violent and nonviolent ideological groups. Risk and crisis communication scholars should be particularly interested in the avenues for research that these propositions afford. One avenue may be to examine the content and structure of the communication strategies that violent and nonviolent ideological groups use and respond to within different strands of new media. For example, if one wanted to convince a nonviolent ideologue of a particular viewpoint, what communication strategies would be more effective in a chat room (a synchronous format) versus a message board (an asynchronous format)? How would this change for violent ideological group members? What are some key moderating factors? Does the topic of conversation matter? Also, what types of media are better for reaching different audiences? How often are online video games played by youths susceptible to predatory violence? These and other questions can be answered through deeper examination of the propositions above. The broader implication here is that new media provides an excellent source by which to answer these questions, and researchers should be prepared to take advantage.

In a more applied sense, risk and crisis communication researchers may also be interested in methods for disrupting the recruitment and indoctrination of potential violent ideologues. For example, as mentioned at the beginning of this chapter, the number of online hate group sources has been increasing over the last five years (Potok, 2006), suggesting a need for countermessages to combat this online culture of violence. However, the implication of the above discussion is that these groups and their members are insulated and tend to operate within a constrained, ideologically-bound culture. This makes the production of effective countermessages difficult, because individuals considering a violent ideology need to be engaged within online communities and through sources that are culturally and ideologically relevant to them. Through an in-depth examination of the rationale surrounding the propositions above, one can begin to make strategic communication metrics similar to that shown in Table 22.3. As opposed to the general hypotheses presented above, Table 22.3 introduces specific sources for influencing violent and nonviolent ideologues and non-ideologues.

Two limitations to this table are 1) it is only a small sampling of the universe of factors that may influence violent and nonviolent ideologues and 2) it has, as of now, little to no basis in empirical research. To get to the point where a full matrix along these lines is useful, many of the basic issues presented in the above propositions must be resolved. For example, if one were to set out a goal for dissuading less crystallized individuals from participating in online hate communities, one would need to consider what is known about the psychological characteristics of these violent ideologues

TABLE22. 3
Influence Mechanisms for Violent Ideological Groups

Media Source	*Audience Reach*	*Ideological Relevance*
1. Open source communities (e.g., MySpace)	Low	Yes
2. Online video game	High	Yes
3. Blogs	Low	No
4. Message Boards	Moderate	No
5. Chat Rooms	Low	Yes
6. Open source information (e.g., Wikipedia)	Low	No
7. Streaming Music	High	Yes
8. Traditional TV	High	No

to determine the specific media that would be most effective. As suggested above, these individuals are frustrated, view mainstream media as less credible, and are more likely to prefer lower reach channels. If these propositions are found to be correct, we can use this information to evaluate certain media on different outcomes. Some outcomes include, for example, the number of people that are reached with the media source within the group of interest, whether the media source is ideologically relevant, the flexibility with which a countermessage can be produced, and so forth. In this instance, traditional television may be a good source in that it may reach the population of interest, but may have little effect because it is not considered ideologically relevant. Chat rooms by contrast may reach a fewer number of people, but are more ideologically relevant.

From a broader perspective, we notice that the issues examined in this modest chapter reflect two broader trends apparently occurring in the world today. The first trend is toward the "clash of ideas" and the role that ideology plays in our daily lives. The proliferation and violence of extremist Islamic viewpoints, the strength of the hard line right-wing in the U.S. government, and the extermination of entire groups of people due to differing belief systems all point to a growing recognition of the role that ideology plays in the world. A second trend is toward the proliferation of technology generally, and the Internet specifically, as a vehicle for new media. These two trends can simultaneously lead to a rapidly changing and potentially dangerous world. Terrorist groups can spread their ideology and plan attacks through new media. Hate groups can scoop up the young and disenfranchised and recruit to their ranks. Anti-government militias can use new media as a tactical battleground to inflict damage on society. Given the potential and already realized risks associated with these trends, it is incumbent upon risk and crisis communication scholars to better understand these phenomena and how they interact. Only through this understanding can we prevent risk from becoming crisis, and crisis from becoming tragedy.

BIBLIOGRAPHY

Aberson, C. L., Healy, M., & Romero, V. (2000). Ingroup bias and self-esteem: A meta-analysis. *Personality & Social Psychology Review, 4*(2), 157–173.

Aikat, D. (2005, May). *The blending of traditional media and the internet: Patterns of media agenda setting and web search trends before and after the September 11 attacks.* Paper presented at the 55th Annual Meeting of the International Communication Association, New York, NY.

Ang, I. (1995). *The nature of the audience* (2nd ed.). Thousand Oaks, CA: Sage.

Bandura, A. (2004). The role of selective moral disengagement in terrorism and counterterrorism. In F. M. Moghaddam & A. J. Marsella (Eds.), *Understanding terrorism: Psychosocial roots, consequences, and interventions* (pp. 121–150). Washington, DC: APA.

Bargh, J. A., & McKenna, K. (2004). The internet and social life. *Annual Review of Psychology, 55*, 573–590.

Blake, M. (2005). Stations of the cross: How evangelical Christians are creating an alternative universe of faith-based news. *Columbia Journalism Review, 44*(1), 32–39.

Blau, P. M. (1964). *Exchange and power in social life*. New York: Wiley.

Blazak, R. (2001). White boys to terrorist men: Target recruitment of Nazi skinheads. *American Behavioral Scientist, 44*(6), 982–1000.

Bostdorff, D. M. (2004). The internet rhetoric of the Ku Klux Klan: A case study in web site community building run amok. *Communication Studies, 55*(2), 340–361.

Bugliosi, V. & Gentry, C. (2001). *Helter Skelter: The true story of the Manson murders*. London: W. W. Norton & Company.

Burdman, D. (2003). Education, indoctrination, and incitement: Palestinian children on their ways to martyrdom. *Terrorism and Political Violence, 15*, 96–123.

Burnett, G., & Buerkle, H. (2004). Information exchange in virtual communities: A comparative study. *Journal of Computer-Mediated Communication, 9*(2), 1–22.

Buss, D. M. (2000). The evolution of happiness. *American Psychologist, 55*(1), 15–23.

Calhoun, C. (1998). Community without propinquity revisited: Communications technology and the transformation of the urban public sphere. *Sociological Inquiry, 68*(3), 373–397.

Cameron, J. E., Duck, J. M., Terry, D. J., & Lalonde, R. N. (2005). Perceptions of self and group in the context of a threatened national identity: A field study. *Group Processes & Intergroup Relations, 8*(1), 73–88.

Chaffee, S. H., & Metzger, M. J. (2001). The end of mass communication? *Mass Communication & Society, 4*(4), 365–379.

Cialdini, R. B., & Goldstein, N. J. (2004). Social influence: Compliance and conformity. *Annual Review of Psychology, 55*, 591–621.

Combs, C. C. (2003). *Terrorism in the 21st century* (3rd ed.). Upper Saddle River, NJ: Pearson.

Corman, S. R., & Schiefelbein, J. S. (2006). *Communication and media strategy in the jihadi war of ideas* (Arizona State University, Consortium for Strategic Communication Report No. 0601). Retrieved April 14, 2007, from http://www.asu.edu/clas/communication /about/csc/.

CNN (2007). *Hillary Clinton launches White House bid: 'I'm in'*. Retrieved March 2, 2007, from http://www.cnn.com/2007/POLITICS/01/20/clinton.announcement/index.html.

Cross, S. E., & Gore, J. S. (2003). Cultural models of the self. In M. R. Leary & J. P. Tangney (Eds.), *Handbook of self and identity* (pp. 536–564). New York: Guilford Press.

Damphousse, K. R., & Smith, B. L. (2002). The internet: A terrorist medium for the 21st century. In: H. W. Kushner (Ed.), *Essential readings on political terrorism: Analyses of problems and prospects for the 21st century.* Lincoln: University of Nebraska Press.

Dennis, E. E., & Ash, J. (2001). Toward a taxonomy of new media - Management views of an evolving industry. *JMM: The International Journal on Media Management, 3*(1), 26–32.

Downing, J. D. H. (2003). Audiences and readers of alternatives media: The absent lure of the virtually unknown. *Media, Culture & Society, 25*(5), 625–645.

Etzioni-Halevy, E. (1975). Patterns of conflict generation and conflict 'absorption:' The cases of Israeli labor and ethnic conflicts. *Journal of Conflict Resolution, 19*(2), 286–309.

Eveland, W. P. J., Seo, M., & Marton, K. (2002). Learning from the news in campaign 2000: An experimental comparison of TV news, newspapers, and online news. *Media Psychology, 4*(4), 353–378.

Ezekiel, R. S. (2002). An ethnographer looks at Neo-Nazi and Klan groups: The racist mind revisited. *American Behavioral Scientist, 46*(1), 51.

FBI (2003). *Counterterrorism facts and figures 2003.* Retrieved March 2, 2007. from http://www. fbi.gov/libref/factsfigure/counterterrorism.htm.

Flanagin, A. J., & Metzger, M. J. (2001). Internet use in the contemporary media environment. *Human Communication Research, 27*(1), 153–181.

Friedland, R. (2001). Religious nationalism and the problem of collective representation. *Annual Review of Sociology, 27*(1), 125–153.

Garcelon, M. (2006). The 'Indymedia' experiment. *Convergence: The Journal of Research into New Media Technologies, 12*(1), 55–82.

Gilser, P. (1997). *Digital literacy*. New York: Wiley.

Gunther, A.C., & Liebhart, J. L. (2006). Broad reach or biased source? Decomposing the hostile media effect. *Journal of Communication*, 56, 449–466.

Henry, P.J., Sidanius, J., Levin, S., & Pratto, F. (2002). Social dominance orientation, authoritarianism, and support for intergroup violence between the Middle East and America. *Political Psychology, 26*(4), 569–583.

Hewstone, M., Rubin, M., & Willis, H. (2002). Intergroup bias. *Annual Review of Psychology, 53*(1), 575–604.

Hoffman, B. (1999). The mind of the terrorist: Perspectives from social psychology. *Psychiatric Annals, 29*(6), 337–340.

Hogg, M. A. (2003). Social identity. In M. Leary & J. Tangney (Eds.), *Handbook of self and identity* (pp. 462–479). London: Guilford Press.

Internet World Stats (2007). *Internet usage statistics: The big picture*. Statistics retrieved March 26, 2007, from http://www.internetworldstats.com/stats.htm.

Janis, I. L. (1972). *Victims of groupthink: A psychological study of foreign-policy decisions and fiascoes.* Oxford, England: Houghton Mifflin.

Jones, S. G. (1997). *Virtual culture: Identity and communication in cybersociety*. Thousand Oaks, CA: Sage.

Jost, J. T., Glaser, J., Kruglanski, A. W., & Sulloway, F. J. (2003). Political conservatism as motivated social cognition. *Psychological Bulletin, 129*(3), 339–375.

Jost, J. T., & Hunyady, O. (2005). Antecedents and consequences of system-justifying ideologies. *Current Directions in Psychological Science, 14*(5), 260–265.

Kaye, B. K. (2005). It's a blog, blog, blog world: Users and uses of weblogs. *Atlantic Journal of Communication, 13*(2), 73–95.

Kent, S. A. (2005). Education and reeducation in ideological organizations and their implications for children. *Cultic Studies Review, 4*(2), 119–145.

Kerr, N. L., & Tindale, R. S. (2004). Group performance and decision making. *Annual Review of Psychology, 55*, 623–655.

Lampel, J., & Bhalla, A. (2007). The role of status seeking in online communities: Giving the gift of experience. *Journal of Computer-Mediated Communication, 12*(2), 434–455.

Leary, M. R., Tambor, E. S., Terdal, S. K., & Downs, D. L. (1995). Self-esteem as an interpersonal monitor: The sociometer hypothesis. *Journal of Personality and Social Psychology, 68*(3), 518–530.

Lee, E., & Leets, L. (2002). Persuasive storytelling by hate groups online: Examining its effects on adolescents. *American Behavioral Scientist, 45*(6), 927–957.

Levin, B. (2002). Cyberhate: A legal and historical analysis of extremists' use of computer networks in America. *American Behavioral Scientist, 45*(6), 958–988.

Lewis, T. (2006). Seeking health information on the internet: Lifestyle choice or bad attack of cyberchondria? *Media, Culture, & Society, 28*(4), 521–539.

Lord, C. G., Ross, L., & Lepper, M. R. (1979). Biased assimilation and attitude polarization: The effects of prior theories on subsequently considered evidence. *Journal of Personality and Social Psychology, 37*(11), 2098–2109.

Maclaran, P., & Catterall, M. (2002). Researching the social web: Marketing information from virtual communities. *Marketing Intelligence & Planning, 20*(6), 319–326.

Marshall, P. D. (2004). *New media cultures*. New York: Oxford University Press.

Maslow, A. H. (1943). A theory of human motivation. *Psychological Review, 50*, 370–396.

Matei, S. A. (2005). From counterculture to cyberculture: Virtual community discourse and the dilemma of modernity. *Journal of Computer-Mediated Communication, 10*(3).

Matusitz, J., & O'Hair, D. (in press). The role of the internet in terrorism. In D. O'Hair, R. Heath, K. Ayotte, & J. Ledlow (Eds.), *Terrorism: Communication and rhetorical perspectives*. Cresskill, NJ: Hampton Press.

McKeown, C. A., & Plowman, K. D. (1999). Reaching publics on the web during the 1996 presidential campaign. *Journal of Public Relations Research, 11*(4), 321–347.

Metzger, M. J., Flanagin, A. J., Eyal, K., Lemus, D. R., & McCann, R. M. (2003). Credibility for the 21st century: Integrating perspectives on source, message, and media credibility in the contemporary media environment. *Communication Yearbook, 27*, 293–335.

Moghaddam, F. M. (2005). The staircase to terrorism: A psychological exploration. *American Psychologist, 60*(2), 161–169.

Morris, M., & Ogan, C. (1996). The Internet as mass medium. *Journal of Communication, 46*(1), 39–51.

Mumford, M. D., Bedell-Avers, K. E., Hunter, S. T., Espejo, J., Eubanks, D., & Connelly, M. S. (in press). Violence in ideological and non-ideological groups: A quantitative analysis of qualitative data. *Journal of Applied Social Psychology*.

Murray, S. K., & Cowden, J. A. (1999). The role of `enemy images' and ideology in elite belief systems. *International Studies Quarterly, 43*(3), 455–481.

Newhagen, J. E., & Rafaeli, S. (1996). Why communication researchers should study the internet: A dialogue. *Journal of Communication, 46*, 4–13.

O'Hair, D., & Heath, R. (2005). Conceptualizing communication and terrorism. In D. O'Hair, R. Heath, & J. Ledlow (Eds.), *Community preparedness, deterrence, and response to terrorism: Communication and terrorism* (pp. 1–12). Westport, CT: Praeger.

Papacharissi, Z., & Rubin, A. M. (2000). Predictors of internet use. *Journal of Broadcasting & Electronic Media, 44*(2), 175–197.

Pew Internet and American Life Project (2004). Abstract of research report retrieved March 26, 2007, from http://www.pewinternet.org/PPF/r/88/press_release.asp.

Porter, C. E. (2004). A typology of virtual communities: A multi-disciplinary foundation for future research. *Journal of Computer-Mediate Communication, 10*(1).

Post, J. M. (2005). When hatred is bred in the bone: Psycho-cultural foundations of contemporary terrorism. *Political Psychology, 26*, 615–636.

Post, J. M., Ruby, K. G., & Shaw, E. D. (2002). The radical group in context: 1. An integrated framework for the analysis of group risk for terrorism. *Studies in Conflict & Terrorism, 25*(2), 73–100.

Post, J. M., Sprinzak, E., & Denny, L. M. (2003). The terrorists in their own words: Interviews with 35 incarcerated Middle Eastern terrorists. *Terrorism and Political Violence, 15*(1), 171–184.

Potok, M. (2006). *The year in hate: 2005*. Article retrieved April 18, 2007, from http://www. splcenter.org/intel/intelreport/article.jsp?aid=627.

Pynchon, M. R., & Borum, R. (1999). Assessing threats of targeted group violence: Contributions from social psychology. *Behavioral Sciences & the Law, 17*(3), 339–355.

Rieh, S.Y., & Belkin, N.J. (1998). Understanding judgment of information quality and cognitive authority in the WWW. *Journal of the American Society for Information Sciences, 35*, 279–289.

Ridings, C. M., & Gefen, D. (2004). Virtual community attraction: Why people hang out online. *Journal of Computer-Mediated Communication, 10*(1).

Rubin, A. M. (1993). Audience activity and media use. *Communication Monographs, 60*, 98–103.

Rubin (1994). Media uses and effects: A uses-and-gratifications perspective. In J. Bryant & D. Zillmann (Eds.), *Media effects: Advances in theory and research* (pp. 417–436). Hillsdale, NJ: Erlbaum.

Ruggiero, T. E. (2000). Uses and gratifications theory in the 21st century. *Mass Communication & Society, 3*(1), 3–37.

Scheuermann, L. E., & Langford, H. P. (1997). Perceptions of internet abuse, liability, and fair use. *Perceptual and Motor Skills, 85*(3), 847–850.

Schweiger, W. (2000). Media credibility – Experience or image?: A survey on the credibility of the World Wide Web in Germany in comparison to other media. *European Journal of Communication, 15*(1), 37–59.

Slayton, R. A. (2001). *Empire statesman: The rise and redemption of Al Smith.* New York: Free Press.

Sohn, D., & Lee, B.K. (2005). Dimensions of interactivity: Differential effects of social and psychological factors. *Journal of Computer-Mediated Communication, 10*(3).

Stahelski, A. (2005). Terrorists are made, not born: Creating terrorists using social psychological conditioning. *Cultic Studies Review, 4*(1), 30–40.

Stanton, J. J. (2002). Terrorism in cyberspace: Terrorists will exploit and widen the gap between governing structures and the public. *American Behavioral Scientist, 45*(6), 1017–1032.

Staub, E. (1996). Cultural-societal roots of violence: The examples of genocidal violence and of contemporary youth violence in the United States. *American Psychologist, 51*, 117–132.

Staub, E. (1999). The origins and prevention of genocide, mass killing, and other collective violence. *Peace and Conflict: Journal of Peace Psychology, 5*(4), 303–336.

Staub, E. (2003). Notes on cultures of violence, cultures of caring and peace, and the fulfillment of basic human needs. *Political Psychology, 24*(1), 1–21.

Stillwell, A. M., & Baumeister, R. F. (1997). The construction of victim and perpetrator memories: Accuracy and distortion in role-based accounts. *Personality and Social Psychology Bulletin, 23*(11), 1157–1172.

Sturgill, A. (2004). Scope and purposes of church web sites. *Journal of Media & Religion, 3*(3), 165–176.

Swann Jr., W. B., Rentfrow, P. J., & Guinn, J. S. (2003). Self-verification: The search for coherence. In M. R. Leary & J. P. Tangney (Eds.), *Handbook of self and identity* (pp. 367–383). New York: Guilford Press.

Tajfel, H. (1982). Social psychology of intergroup relations. *Annual Review of Psychology, 33*, 1–39.

Tajfel, H., Billig, M. G., Bundy, R. P., & Flament, C. (1971). Social categorization and intergroup behaviour. *European Journal of Social Psychology, 1*(2), 149–178.

Taylor, D. M., & Louis, W. (2004). Terrorism and the quest for identity. In F. Moghaddam & A. Marsella (Eds.), *Understanding terrorism: Psychosocial roots, consequences, and interventions* (pp. 169–185). Washington, D.C.: APA.

Tindale, R. S., & Kameda, T. (2000). "Social sharedness" as a unifying theme for information processing in groups. *Group Processes & Intergroup Relations, 3*(2), 123–140.

Turpin-Petrosino, C. (2002). Hateful sirens . . . who hears their song?: An examination of student attitudes toward hate groups and affiliation potential. *Journal of Social Issues, 58*(2), 281–301.

Vallone, R. P., Ross, L., & Lepper, M.R. (1985). The hostile media phenomenon: Biased perception and perceptions of media bias in coverage of the Beirut Massacre. *Journal of Personality and Social Psychology, 49*(3), 577–585.

Van Dijk, T. A. (2006). Ideology and discourse analysis. *Journal of Political Ideologies, 11*(2), 115–140.

Vigil, J. D. (2003). Urban violence and street gangs. *Annual Review of Anthropology, 32*, 225–242.

Watts, M. W. (2001). Aggressive youth cultures and hate crime: Skinheads and xenophobic youth in Germany. *American Behavioral Scientist, 45*(4), 600–615.

Wheeler, D. L. (2003). The internet and youth subculture in Kuwait. *Journal of Computer-Mediated Communication, 8 (2)*, 1–18.

Worchel, S., Coutant-Sassic, D., & Grossman, M. (1991). A developmental approach to group dynamics: A model and illustrative research. In S. Worchel, W. Wood, & J. A. Simpson (Eds.), *Group process and productivity* (pp. 181–202). Newbury Park, CA: Sage.

23

Community Building through Risk Communication Infrastructures

Robert L. Heath
University of Houston

Michael J. Palenchar
University of Tennessee

H. Dan O'Hair
University of Oklahoma

From the early moments after the release of MIC in Bhopal, India, practitioners and theorists worked feverishly for a model to use to describe how communication could best be brought to serve the interest of people at risk for various similar disasters. This discussion was not really new. Throughout history, in various ways by many inventive means, human society has been deeply engaged in discussions that can understand, mitigate, and manage risks, however individually or collectively. Despite this legacy, in the days after a crisis results from the manifestation of a risk, members of society are likely to turn to one or more individuals for answers to why the risk occurred and to whether those who were affected deserved to so suffer. Something of that kind of reasoning buzzed through media coverage in early 2006 after the 12 miners died and one lived at the Sago Mine in West Virginia.

As voices have called for risk democracy answers, experts and lay people tend to think in terms of the one individual as well as the many participating parts of networks that need to come together to address and mitigate risks. Soon after Bhopal, critics asked who best could explain risks in a convincing way. At the same time, experts were advising members of society to create and sustain well-crafted infrastructures to identify risks, create emergency plans, and formulate messages and advice on actions that increase the public safety. Thus, the concept of the local emergency planning committee was created.

By federal mandate, state level LEPC (local emergency planning committee) preparation was set into motion. Below the state system, was a complementary complex of such committees. A single committee might serve many counties, whereas many committees might serve one county, such as large metropolitan areas (e.g., Houston, Texas). Part of the logic in the design was that there needed to be sufficient span of control based on a mix of number of people in a community who could be affected by a risk, especially an industrial disaster, and the magnitude individually or collectively of such a potential disaster. The committees were mandated to consist of company managements, city/government officials, corporate first responders, government responders, citizens, and members of the media. This logic worked, in large part, to the degree that individual members were willing and able to coordinate and motivate the other members to respond.

Thus was created one of the most comprehensive infrastructures to address risks that has ever occurred in the United States. For various reasons, this was a brilliant concept and design. For as many reasons, LEPC's were doomed from the start. One weak link was citizen input tended to be weak. Another weakness was the unwillingness of media reporters to serve as advisors for how LEPCs should communicate and what would constitute news. Many reporters did not want to wear a planning hat and a reporting hat. For many, this was a dramatic conflict of interest. Reporters are trained (although celebrity reporters often forget that training) to report the news not to make it. So, the role of communication expert often fell to independent contractors (public relations/risk communication counselors and practitioners), company public affairs experts/community relations experts, or governmental public affairs experts.

All of the risk communication efforts, both collective and individual, throughout history have often been easier to imagine and create than to implement successfully. The key to success and failure simply is the "human factor." We are constantly reminded of observations as challenging as the one Susan Hadden (1989) used to open her article on institutional barriers: "Risk communication is fraught with difficulty" (p. 301). She believed that most risk communication only occurred under legal requirement and was intended to help laypeople make better choices based on the rationale "that the expert's risk assessment formed the best basis for making some decision involving risks" (p. 301). To this end, statutes often have required that information be provided even though they might define how the information should best be used by any community. Thus, the standard of community right to know may in actuality be limited to community right to some data dump. Scientists may disagree regarding what data are relevant and how they should be interpreted. We need not point to instances where scientific reports in any one year contradict those from a pervious time which had become standard wisdom. Those which seem so revolutionary today stand a good chance of being refined or contradicted. It may also assume that the typical format of risk communication is an expert source seeking to persuade various targets regarding preferred risk choices. For these reasons, risk communication tends not to exhibit the characteristics of dialogue.

To explain community infrastructures and advise on ways to make them more serviceable to society, this chapter undertakes several topics. Throughout, the theme is central to that of risk democracy, within association with various experts, individual voices of risk bearers must be brought together to create systems and shared perspectives that appropriately assess, mitigate, and respond to risks that may be unevenly borne throughout any community or larger society. The logics explored in this chapter parallel the analysis by Scherer and Cho (2003) who have reasoned that an individual cognitive approach to risk perception ignores myriad social influences. Preferring to feature network contagion theory, they found "that social linkages in communities may play an important role in focusing risk perceptions" (p. 261). Opinions are formed, held, shared, and reinforced by social units, what can be called community units of like-minded people. Decades of interpersonal communication research have also confirmed this "birds of a feather flock together" view of knowledge, attitudes, and behaviors. Themes of this sort are traditionally expanded by general systems theory and principles of propinquity.

MANY AND VARIED INFRASTRUCTURES

We begin this section with perhaps the most obvious statement in this volume: There would be no discipline called risk communication if all of the people of any relevant society perceived the same risks, perceived them in the same way, and reacted to them as of one mind. Instead, we are confronted at the basis of analysis with the reality that differences of many kinds and for many reasons account for the discipline and all of what makes it interesting. In one of her many provocative criticisms, Hadden (1989) observed that statutes (as put into play by government administrators) most often address the "availability of information, as opposed to its utility, relevance, or ease of understanding" (p. 303). One of the obvious differences exists between government experts/regulators, scientists, and lay publics of every flavor. Thomas, Swaton, Fishbein, and Otway (1980) found that policymakers' attitudes tend to be more favorable toward risk conditions than are members of the lay public. In the controversy over nuclear regulation, policymakers do not have an accurate perception of the feelings and beliefs of those publics. It's likely that conversations, however quiet or contentious, are likely to result in misunderstanding and biases that frustrate every attempt to develop shared understanding and interpretations of risks and risk management policy. Hadden (1989) reported that 60% of the local emergency planning chairman in Texas "thought that citizens would not understand information made available under Title III" of SARA (p. 305). Other findings suggest how fractured an infrastructure can be. "While the elected officials (of these LEPCs) were most likely to believe that citizens can understand information about hazardous substances, they were least likely to agree that it is important for citizens to know about hazardous substances" (p. 305).

Is it a mystery why different disciplines as well as various publics perceive risks, their benefits/costs, abatement, and mitigation differently. Gardner and Gould (1989) opened their article with the telling sentence: "Scientists, engineers, and government regulators have had increasing difficulty in understanding public reactions to technological development, especially in the last 10–15 years" (p. 225). They follow that observation with an attribution of cause for this frustration with the general public: "Many technical experts believe that this opposition results from an overestimation by the public of the risks of technology caused by a lack of technical education, misinformation appearing in the media, or even irrationality" (p. 225). In addition to this tentative possibility for misunderstand and loss of trust for scientific conclusions and recommendations, another problem is the likelihood that technically trained individuals and lay publics simply speak "different languages." Some of the reasons for these interpretive differences result from reward/cost estimations that may be subjective/objective, "the degree of apparent disagreement in the scientific community concerning the risks, the degree to which benefits are equitably distributed among those at risk, and the degree to which the technology can kill many people at once in a catastrophic accident" (p. 226). In this way, Gardner and Gould postulated that "the general public appears to use a broader and more complex definition of 'risk' and 'acceptability' than does the technical community" (p. 226). To examine this infrastructural barrier to community decision making, Heath and Palenchar (2003) conducted a study and found that the public follows the predictions of expressed-preference conclusions in their risk perceptions. The public tends to define risk, acceptability, and benefits idiosyncratically, in a complete, multidimensional matter. "Their definitions differ significantly from those used by professional risk-managers and other technical experts in quantitative assessments of risk and acceptability" which are sensitive to sociodemographics (p. 225).

Dueling scientists complicate the interpretation and understanding of various risks that are needed for the development of relevant risk policy. Parkin and Balbux (2000) probed the clarity and consensus among scientific disciplines regarding the Safe Drinking Water Act and the Food Quality and Protection Act. A key concept in the controversy is "susceptibility." The researchers concluded: "The present analysis of definitions from the fields of ecology, biology, engineering, medicine, epidemiology, and toxicology revealed different emphases that relate to the underlying perspectives and methods of each field" (p. 603). After considering differences and similarities among definitions falling along disciplinary lines, they noted the need for one definition to reduce controversy (although achieving one definition would be controversial) and irregularity in policy making and implementation. To Parkin and Balbus, the need for one definition "is increasingly urgent" but not 'readily met.' A new working consensus on the definition of susceptibility will require development over time with input from many perspectives" (p. 609).

Lack of knowledge on the part of lay publics is one problem. Dueling science is another since it leads to conflicting opinions, frustration regarding what knowledge is worth knowing, and which authorities are best to believe. Infrastructures are fractured by such perplexities. Siegrist and Cvetkovich (2000) explored some of these matters as they examined the role of social trust, knowledge, and benefits. They found that when lay publics have knowledge about a risk and its benefits/harms, the role of the expert is diminished. In the absence of such knowledge, trust for experts predicts whether people will believe the benefits of the risk are worth the potential harms. Such publics exhibit a negative relationship between risks and benefits. Social complexity is such that lay people look for experts whom they can trust in the absence of knowledge—and when such knowledge seems to lead to conflicting conclusions. People seem willing to trust their own knowledge, but in its absence turn to respected authorities. It is likely that their knowledge originates with trusted sources. One of the logics of risk communication is that risks can be seen as more tolerable if they are accompanied by benefits. Nevertheless, social trust is a factor in the perception of the risk/benefit ratio. Such findings may suggest that trust is idiosyncratic and related to the amount of knowledge people have. Trust, however, is a key factor (Kasperson, Kasperson, Pidgeon, & Slovic, 2003; White & Eiser, 2005).

At least in the case of biotechnology, knowledge of the technology, its risks, and benefits may not be as strong a predictor of acceptance/rejection as is trust. For this reason, assessment of the challenges of risk communication success or failure need to address the "trust gap" as a primary factor (Priest, Bonfadelli, & Rusanen, 2003). It is likely, for that reason, that independent of knowledge, efforts to impose controls over sources of risks and of risk impacts are likely to reflect doubts regarding the trustworthiness of the source more than knowledge of the risk per se (O'Hair, 2004).

How much the regulatory environment has changed in many countries, and other locale, the truth is that the amount of legislation and regulation regarding risk perception, management, and communication has dramatically increased. Renfro (1982) and Heath (1997) listed dozens of federal agencies that have been created in the United States since the Dangerous Cargo Act in 1877. Such regulatory agencies touch most if not all aspects of the public's lives. Nuclear materials and processes, tobacco, noise, alcohol, chemicals, dust, toxics, abrasives, modes of transportation, and such have been put under the watchful eye of regulators. Even Mother Nature is under surveillance. Most recently efforts have increased, for instance, to foretell and monitor the emergence and progress of a tsunami. Since the attack on the World Trade Center, the Department of Homeland Security has been added to this long list. Recent mine crises in West Virginia and Utah will bring substantial attention to the risks of miners, as well as to the regulators. That sort of watch also continues in China where mining deaths are more routine than many observers around the world think acceptable.

Contributing a Scandinavian perspective, Sjoberg (2000) chronicled the growing list of organizations of this kind in Sweden. The conclusion: "…a study of private bills submitted to the Swedish Parliament showed that the share of risk-related bills had tripled during the last 30 years from 11 to 29%" (p. 1). Such regulation necessarily brings into dialogue the competing relationship between economic benefits and safety related subjective assessments. Starr (1969) is often credited as bringing the cat of economic benefits into the pigeons of various cultural and social concerns for safety and health, environmental quality, the fairness of the level of risk people are expected to bear, and whether there is equal distribution of risk across a population (Heath, 1997).

In any discussion of risk, scientists and the lay public both seek some insight into the paradoxes of real risk and perceived risk. The two types often are not the same, not viewed in the same way by either scientists or the unscientific community. Such paradoxes, concurrences, and divisions result from the fact that beliefs and values correlate as predictors of risk perception (Sjoberg, 2000). As well, a key dimension in the infrastructural approach to risk is comparative risks. This factor raises the question of whether people believe they are more or less at risk than are other members (however similar or dissimilar) in a society. One of the battles in the tobacco risk war centers on whether people are more or less likely to start and continue smoking based on how they perceive their risk in comparison to that of other members of society (Slovic, 2001).

Sjoberg (2000) reasoned that denial is one reason why people think others are more at risk than they are. We can also imagine some degree of altruistic interest in the welfare of others may be at work. People may have relatively accurate or inaccurate data (and interpretation) to draw on to attribute degree of risk to self, but may worry that others are more at risk than they are. This may be one of the reasons why women tend to report higher risk aversion than men (Slovic, 1992). For reasons that seem relatively obvious, the forces of social amplification of risk (Kasperson, 1992; Kasperson, et al., 2003) would seem sensitive to the perception on the part of individuals, NGOs, and reporters that at least some part of the population has a high enough sensitivity to any risk that reporting is likely to attract viewers, listeners, and readers. People may receive and be concerned by mediated messages regarding risks because of how that information may be relevant to friends, families, and others socially close to each of us (i.e., peer networks).

As much as denial and altruistic sensitivity to others' well-being can account for varying perceptions of risk, another key factor is the differences between one's own perception of ability to control a risk relevant to one's own interest as opposed to the perception of how capable others are to control risks relevant to their behavior. Parents, for instance, generically worry that their children are likely to encounter (and even willfully bring onto themselves) risks greater than their ability to control. Whereas various populations, because for various psychometric reasons, may believe they are able to exert sufficient control and even more control than others can over a risk, it is likely that if they worry about other's deficiency in this regard they will support increased control (either by the source of the risk or by government). That logic, for instance, has been central to the anti-tobacco campaigns, even including reducing youth access to cigarettes. The logic is that children/young teens cannot control their urge to engage in such risky behavior and therefore they must be protected by eliminating cigarette vending machines, restricting sales to minors, and even keeping cigarettes beyond easy access by locking them into storage areas in places where they are sold to persons above a certain age. That same logic applies to access to alcohol.

Sjoberg (2000) compared risk assessment models used by various researchers to explain risk perception and aversion. This review has included specifically the economic model, psychometric model, and cultural model. Out of the review come insights useful for understanding risk perception, mitigation, and communication infrastructures. One of the universal logics is that knowledge (K), attitude (A), and behavior (B) logics tend to predict how people perceive and respond to risks. One of the corrections Sjoberg offered is that attitude (A) on the part of lay publics may precede rather than follow knowledge (B as in belief). Whereas scientists might, but also might not, approach risk evaluation by focusing on knowledge that drives belief (KBA) and then progresses to attitude, lay publics may reverse this equation (AKB). Whereas Sjoberg's studies have centered on nuclear energy, other studies giving similar insights to the KAB logic have addressed perception of unprotected sex and pregnancy (Valente, Paredes, & Poppe, 1998). Looking at the underlying logic beneath this line of analysis, Sjoberg (2000) reasoned: "Risk perception is hard to understand" (p. 9). Considering perception of nuclear energy, Sjoberg shared these insights:

> The fact that attitude plays such a prominent role in the models is interesting. It suggests that risk perception is to a large extent a question of ideology in a very specific sense, not in the general sense, that is posited by Cultural Theory. People who, for some reason, are strongly in favor of nuclear power tend to see it is risk free, and vice versa. (p. 9)

For this reason, when we find that experts see risks as smaller than do specific publics, we must be concerned that the logic is that attitude drives such perceptions in such a way that data are found to confirm the attitude. For this reason, we may find that presentations of fact do not change attitudes.

In fact, what is seen as a fact and how it is seen as compelling of belief may result from the attitude the person holds. As any infrastructure may want to feature fact in the discussion, giving scientific finding primacy in such discussions, it might be better to locate, examine, and attend to the potency of attitudes as primary rather than secondary variables in risk perception and management.

One of the dominant models of risk perception and management features the logic that once scientists have reasonably raised doubts about the safety of some public health matter or concluded that some technology is reasonably safe, the sheer reporting of such conclusions should resolve public doubts and concerns. The outcome would be public opinion that squared with scientific opinion. Any difference, such logics reason, could only result if some force, such as an industry or some activist communication efforts, should confuse and confound the reporting and interpretation of such information. Many cases can be examined to worry this theme, but one that is highly relevant and substantially studied is the effects of tobacco products on health and the public reactions.

As long ago as 1944, Gallup Poll data reported that 36% of the public believed smoking was very harmful, and 42% believed it was somewhat harmful. Starting in 1953, several prominent scientists offered what they thought were compelling data about the health hazards of using tobacco products. At the time, society in general treated smoking as a social attribute. Nevertheless, in January 1954, 70.47% of the public believed cigarette smoking is harmful (no = 23.52%). Even though smoking was steeped in social attractiveness, many people, according to Gallup Poll data, could articulate harms associated with smoking in early 1954. These included shortens breath (7.98%), harmful to nose and throat sinuses (13.98%), harmful to general well-being (4.53%), harmful to heart (2.32%), causes cancer, throat cancer (1.40%), and causes tuberculosis (8.87%). Many other irritants were mentioned as harms of smoking. In the same series of questions, Gallup asked whether the respondents had "heard or read anything recently that cigarette smoking may be a cause of cancer of the lung." Yes was the answer of 82.52%; no = 17.48%). And, then the telling question: "What is your own opinion—do you think cigarette smoking is one of the causes of lung cancer, or not?" Yes answered 41.01% versus no (30.63%), no opinion (27.76%), qualified yes (0.40%), and qualified no (0.2.20%). Later in that year 59.77% believed that smoking is harmful, whereas 34.42% believed the opposite. Two years later, Gallup found that 77.52% reported they had read or heard "about the recent report of the American Cancer Society reporting the results of a study on the effects of cigarette smoking" versus 22.48% who said no. In the face of the report, people had many reasons to not stop smoking, including the belief that the report was not proven (6.25%), a lack of will power (10.66%), and desire to not stop because smoking was enjoyable (11.97%) (Gallup Brain, accessed February 12, 2006). In the ensuing years, non-profits (such as American Cancer Association and American Heart Association), various medical researchers, public health officials, and undoubtedly friends and family members debated the health consequences of using tobacco products. In 1964, the Surgeon General concluded the practice was harmful, recommending regulation including the use of health warnings.

RISK PERCEPTION AND MANAGEMENT AS COLLECTIVE PROCESSES

In the 1950s and 1960s in the United States, one of the most popular television programs was *Dragnet* which starred Jack Webb as Sgt. Joe Friday. This intrepid detective often told those he was questioning that all he wanted was the facts, nothing but the facts. This advice is often the centerpiece and the logistic downfall of risk perception, analysis, management, and communication. Even when there are facts, the key players may disagree as to their relevance, completeness, and accuracy. They may be subject to various interpretations. As Hadden (1989) observed, "Multiple overlapping jurisdictions, difficulties in collecting and disseminating the information that is the essence of RC (risk communication), liability, and many other social/institutional barriers inhibit the proper conduct of RC" (p. 306). Often risk efforts do not succeed because of "a failure to determine in advance exactly what information is appropriate to the decisions envisioned or what people want to know. Many of the laws collect too much information, imposing inappropriate costs on the regulated industry and hampering efforts to disseminate it; others disseminate too much, or the wrong kind, imposing unnecessary costs on risk bearers" (p. 306).

Even the passing media scanner will encounter periodic claims regarding medical science which at least modify, if not contradict, studies that had become "conventional wisdom." Part of the confusion, ambiguity, and contradiction results from differences in data gathering and interpretation by various scientific and other groups relevant to various risks. Two relevant news stories appeared side by side in the February 16, 2006, *Wall Street Journal*. One, authored by Zhang and Gray (2006) opened with this paragraph:

> The Food and Drug administration yesterday issued guidelines to tell food companies when they should—and shouldn't—use the term "whole grain" on packages. But the nonbinding advice may not offer much relief, at least in the short term, to consumers pondering an array of confusing claims on food labels. (p. D1)

In a companion story on health advice, Forelle and Westphal (2006) asked whether calcium really does help women prevent bone loss and fractures. The story included the following lines:

> The study may cause some women and doctors to rethink the wisdom of routine use of the supplements. But the findings were peppered with caveats that suggest the study wouldn't be the final word on the subject, and the study's authors said there is still reason to believe that supplementing diet with calcium is beneficial for some women. (p. D1)

After discussion of the results compared to other assumptions and previous results, the authors of this news story observed: "Past WHI (Women's Health Initiative) results have also been confusing, and subject to later attacks" (p. D1). And so goes the march of public health research, media risk communication, and personal decision making about personal health risks and their mitigation.

No risk infrastructure is better than its ability to perceive and interpret any specific risk. The entire process begins with perception. Since our earliest moments of childhood, others were teaching us to look out for risks. Such risk perception will depend on various levels of scientific education, training and ability—largely vested in key individuals throughout society. As such, someone who would be trained to observe chemical toxicity might merely be a member of a lay public regarding risks related to fraudulent financial instruments and planning. The heuristics and biases of a society may best be accounted for by sociological theory. Specific and collective sensitivities may be explained by cultural theory. Distribution of risk and commitment to mitigation may combine science, society, and culture.

Disciplines do not agree and often assume substantially different interpretive approaches to risks. Althaus (2005) offered a provocative comparative analysis of the disciplines approach to risks by starting with "economic conceptualizations that distinguish risk from uncertainty and argue that risk is an ordered application of knowledge to the unknown" (p. 567). As such this review considered "each of the disciplines as having a particular knowledge approach with which they confront the unknown so as to order its randomness and convert it into a risk proposition" (p. 567). Rather than suggesting that one discipline's approach is superior to others, she reasoned that the various disciplines should work in concert to bring to bear on risk perception and interpretation the best each has to offer. This is an epistemological view of risk perception than "places the personal decision maker at the center of attention, forcing analysis to concentrate on the nature of uncertainty and the available knowledge that is brought to bear on this uncertainty" (p. 567). Accordingly, each discipline is an epistemological system that focuses on risk matters with a unique set of bifocals and varying interpretive screens.

This epistemological approach, outlined by Althaus (2005), recognizes five dimensions of risk, each of which may vary because of heuristics and assumptions of each discipline. These dimensions are subjective risk ("the mental state of an individual who experiences uncertainty or doubt or worry as to the outcome of a given event"), objective risk (weighting losses and gains), real risk ("the combination of probability and negative consequence that exists in the real world"), observed risk (the measurement of such risk), and perceived risk ("the rough estimate of real risk made by an untrained member of the general public") (p. 568). Extending this logic to each of several disciplines, she reasoned that logic and mathematics see "risk as a calculable phenomenon" which is similar to science and medicine ("risk as an objective reality") (p. 569). Among the social sciences, anthropology views risk as a cultural phenomenon, sociology (societal phenomenon), economics ("a decisional phenomenon, a means of securing wealth or avoiding loss"), law ("risk as a fault of conduct and a judicable phenomenon"), psychology ("behavioral and cognitive phenomenon"), linguistics (as a concept), history (as a story), arts (emotional phenomenon), religion (act of faith), and philosophy (a problematic phenomenon) (p. 569). Such review "demonstrates that each discipline brings its own knowledge form to its understanding of risk" (p. 580).

One factor in the epistemology of risk is the preference of experts to categorize risks, rank them, and pose exposure/impact models to help assess any risk alone and by categories. This logic also stems from preferences for the logic that experts perform assessment and the risk communication task is to foster understanding and agreement on the part of risk bearers so their logic becomes similar, identical, or at least comfortable with that of experts. Such analysis is solid in conception but problematic in implementation. Agencies often lack the resources and resolve to make such comparisons and rankings. Lay publics may not understand and agree with expert assessment. Experts may disagree among themselves. In this collision of politics and society, such models and heuristics may, at least for the moment, work best as logics for discussion where expert and public input can support democratic risk-management decision-making (Morgan, Florig, DeKay, & Fischbeck, 2000).

Participation

Without seeming facile, a long-standing finding of group dynamics is that people are more satisfied with decisions if they (or if they know others) engage in collective decision making. Under such conditions, people not only approve of the process as such but also the product if they believe their input was carefully and reasonably considered. By a similar logic, Arvai (2003) explored publics' satisfaction of knowing that risks had been openly and thoughtfully considered. Empirical findings suggest that people under conditions of knowledge of group discussion approve of the process, as democratic, even if they are less than fully supportive of the outcome of such discussion. Risk communicators, therefore, should be cautious in predicting that participation (or knowledge of participation) will not necessarily lead to concurrence with the decisions made but risk bearers are nevertheless pleased to know that participatory processes are working.

A strong body of research demonstrates that community organizations (businesses, non-profits, religious, schools, etc.) can play a pivotal role in communication campaigns (Stephens, Rimal, & Flora, 2004). Results from the Stanford Five City Project revealed that organizations outside of the media have the potential of reaching about half of a community's households (Flora, Jatilus, Jackson, & Fortmann, 1993). Community organizations also serve an audience segmentation function primarily because of the communication infrastructure in place (bulletin boards, listservs, newsletters, etc.). One advantage of community organizations is that membership is voluntary and messages originating from them are usually viewed with greater levels of trust. A key strategy for communication campaign managers is to enlist the support of key organizational leaders who would then serve as opinion leaders and promote the messages of the campaign (Stephens et al., 2004). There is little doubt that enlisting the support of community organizations can increase the reach of communication campaigns.

Community involvement is not a new phenomenon; recently a National Research Council committee (Stoto, Abel, & Dievler, 1997) recommended that deliberative and participative community processes should be engaged to inform public policy choices. The committee argued that these processes lead to a more informed public and more support for decisions. *Project Impact*, established in 1997 by FEMA, was meant to actively engage communities in the process of disaster resistance. Research from *Project Impact* discovered that communities were better able to secure resources from support organizations and were better positioned to understand their community's relative risks and better equipped for managing those risks. In essence, these communities became more resilient as a result (Rodriquez, 2004). Several subsequent studies have verified the positive effect of community involvement during risk policy decision making in a variety of contexts (McDaniels, Gregory, & Fields, 1999; Gregory, Arvai, & McDaniels, 2001; Arvai, Gregory, & McDaniels, 2001). Even community members who do not directly participate in the planning and deliberating process have more positive views of the policy decision based on their perception that the process was fair and inclusive of community members' viewpoints (Arvai, 2003). In sum, public meetings that genuinely involve citizens in dialogue and stress the importance of interactive exchange have greater chances of success. These types of communication processes not only increase perceptions of participation, but build relationships important in the trust credibility areas (McComas, 2003).

Another challenge of community involvement and local participation is *awareness*. Heath, Bradshaw, and Lee (2002) conducted a study examining the impact of local risk communication infrastructures (local emergency planning committees and citizens advisory committees) on risk communication activities in communities. The study found that community members were relatively unaware of these organizations and did not perceive them as options for expressing viewpoints. Citizen-research participants revealed that when healthy local communication infrastructures were in place stronger communities resulted and were positioned better for responding to risks and crises.

Discussion coupled with monitoring of the fit between perceptions of risk by management and employees also seems to predict the likelihood of successful risk management within an organization. Such efforts not only result in better design of risk messages relevant to each workplace but also serve as a means by which employees gain more knowledge of hazards in the workplace. This process increases the likelihood that the organization will be more effective in risk management and improves chances that employees will engage in self-protection (Cox et al., 2003).

Given the difficulties of predicting the success of risk communication, those who are responsible for such discussions need to realize that a top-down linear model is less likely to work than one where process, message, and decision output is seen as a community effort than by experts alone. To that end, Chess (2001) advised that organizations responsible for risk management are wise to constantly monitor not only agreement/disagreement and understanding but also evaluative parameters for success that are sensitive to the values and interests of the risk bearers. "Without such self-reflection, corporate risk communication efforts may not adapt sufficiently quickly to changes in their organizational environment" (p. 187).

Organizing Risk Management

It does not take long to create a substantial list of agencies, even only at the U.S. federal government level, to show how many expert bodies exist to obtain, interpret, communicate, and manage risks. Here are a few: Federal Drug Administration, Environmental Protection Agency, Occupational Safety and Health Administration (OSHA), which has a Health Communication Standard, and the National Transportation and Safety Board. The storms of the summer of 2005 gave front page and top of the hour news visibility to the Army Corps of Engineers, Federal Emergency Management Administration (FEMA), and Department of Homeland Security. The Sago and Utah mine deaths in 2006 and 2007 gave the federal Mine Safety and Health Administration its latest 15 minutes of glory. The International Atomic Energy Agency was thrust into the spotlight over the challenges posed by leaders in Iran over nuclear policies and sanctions, both economic and military.

A complete list of all of the federal, state, and local committees, agencies, and departments would make a lengthy table. Suffice it to say that virtually every aspect of people's lives have some relevant agency review. Much of this review features data collection, review, policy compliance, policy formation, and penalty. Sometime the entity creating the risk is a business or another government agency. Perhaps, as in the case of faulty personal health practices, the culprit in this risk drama is categories of individuals, one or two individuals at a time. They might be younger people engaging in a list of potentially harmful behaviors. They might be male or female, old or young.

As long as the list is for government agencies, we can imagine that it is replicated in many iterations by departments or at least specialties within businesses. Human resources, for instance, might be primarily responsible for OSHA compliance. Health, Safety, and Environmental Responsibility departments abound in industrial organizations, in individual companies and trade associations.

Add to these lists myriad non-profit activist groups, NGOs, or special interest organizations. For decades, as problems became apparent one or more organizations, by narrow or broad category, formed to advocate the interests of members and those individuals or aspects of nature for whom the members had an altruistic interest.

Two of the authors of this chapter have conducted extensive research in communities that live and work in the shadows of one of the largest petrochemical complexes in the world, essentially running from the Mississippi River to Port Lavaca, Texas. A glimpse of this segment of the United States (and one not indifferent to the rest of the world since many of the companies are multinationals) suggests the complexity of such an infrastructure. Let's probe that infrastructure.

The U.S. government has several primary agencies assigned to provide routine oversight, dialogue, and policy development/implementation: For instance, Environmental Protection Agency, Occupational Safety and Health Administration, National Transportation and Safety Board, Chemical Emergency Preparedness and Prevention Office, and Department of Highway Safety. Each has regulatory power. Typically, states where these sorts of facilities operate have agencies that parallel (and perhaps conflict with) OSHA and EPA. One of these in Texas is the Texas Commission on Environmental Quality. Another is the State of Texas Department of Human Resources. One recently added player on this field is the Department of Homeland Security and its state counterparts.

Several federal and state agencies have investigative power in the event of a reportable incident, such as an explosion that injures or kills employees. Three of these at the federal level are the Federal Bureau of Investigation, the National Transportation and Safety Board, and the National Chemical Safety Board. In addition to these federal agencies, comparable state agencies have investigative power.

Cities and counties have regulatory agencies or departments who are responsible for emergency response, planning, and policy development. One of the relevant regulatory agencies in the matrix explained here is Harris County Pollution Control. This is one of the departments in the County's Environmental Public Health Division. Of related interest is the Houston – Galveston Area Council, a "think tank" and planning body that is charged with research and policy recommendation. Given the size of the Houston Ship Channel, it not only falls within the jurisdiction of Harris County but also Chambers, Brazoria, and Galveston counties. Other counties would have jurisdiction over other parts of this immensely complex array of industrial facilities. The Port Authority is a local agency that coordinates with other local and state agencies as well as the U. S. Coast Guard. These persons link with local policy and fire officials, and some emergency management experts at the city and county levels. Some facilities are both in cities and counties while others operate in unincorporated areas. Boundaries of plants as well as the impact of environmental releases cross over county and city boundaries.

As far as elected officials are concerned, there are U.S. Senators as well as members of the House of Representatives. Similar state offices exist. There are elected heads of each county in Texas, county judges. Each county has other elected officials, such as county commissioners. As well, each city has a mayor and members of city council.

LEPCs

Among the key elements in these infrastructures are the local emergency planning committees. Mandated by the EPA in the 1980s, these committees were organized under the auspices of each state and in Texas through county LEPC's. In this case there was limited business for them to do, a county was either unlikely to add more with specific jurisdictions and even perhaps combine with other adjacent counties. According to federal mandate, these committees conduct research, provide technical environmental impact data, and manage community relations. Given that these committees are largely composed of technically trained individuals, they are often not skilled in communication techniques and even prefer a linear reporting style that does not easily accommodate to the communication needs of area residents. Studies conducted soon after their creation often faulted the communication ability of such committees while giving them high marks for strategic planning. Anecdotal study suggests that how well any LEPC communicates depends on the skills of the community relations experts for one or more local companies or of a communication expert working for the city or county. Even elected officials serve these communication purposes, as do the occasional fire chief, police chief, or city emergency manager.

One additional element of the infrastructure, community action panels (or committees: CACs or CAPs) were created, often by interested community relations personnel and/or public spirited managers of petrochemical facilities. One can also imagine that internally corporate councils advised against these panels because both the LEPCs and the CACs/CAPs have as one of their operating missions to serve as a public forum for plant managers to report that an incident occurred, the impact of the incident, and the lessen learned. In the event the incident resulted in death or injury, even property damage outside a plant, corporate council must shudder in its boots at such candid public admission. Whereas LEPC membership is biased toward technical expertise, the CACs truly are more dependent on and structured for dialogue between managers, technical experts, and concerned citizens.

Both the LEPCs and CACs/CAPs are hosted by industry, usually in cooperation with local city and/or county government. Meetings may occur at plant facilities, but they are more likely to occur in government or other public buildings. Both kinds of organizations operate under open meeting guidelines, but in the case that discussions might center on issues of community security that could be compromised by those intent on harm, as in the case of terrorists, discussions of technical and strategic nature, can be conducted in executive session.

The value of such organizations, especially each one's idiosyncratic operations vis-à-vis its local jurisdiction, will be debated and responsible changes are likely. However, research suggests that communities where the LEPC/CAC is well known to operate, where it is visibly supported by companies, and known to operate in conjunction with local government result in greater expressions of support than occurs in neighborhoods without such infrastructures (Heath, Bradshaw, & Lee, 2002).

In the case of the Houston Ship Channel area, at least two additional organizational types need mention. One is the trade association, East Harris County Manufacturers Association (EHCMA), in this case. Although its size varies by voluntary membership and company ownership, EHCMAs size tends to be slightly more than 100 companies. Most are engaged in manufacturing and refining, but some generate electricity and operate material handling facilities. At the local level, this organization also has state and national counterparts such as the American Chemistry Council (formerly Chemical Manufacturers Association) and the Vinyl Institute, as well as the Texas Chemical Council.

The other kind of governmental institution is any local school district or school facility. Because of the possibility or eventuality of a toxic release into the community, emergency planning protocols are worked out between the industry and the local school district or relevant school. Children need to be kept safe, primarily through emergency response and shelter in place protocols. Schools are also an excellent venue for discussion of topics on personal and public safety (Ronan & Johnston, 2005). Science classes are often supported by local industry as a venue for students to learn about the chemicals and industry operating nearby.

So far, the organizational infrastructure described as an illustration has centered on government and industry. Additional pieces include media (print and electronic, including the Internet). Industry, for instance, as well as local government steadily builds more of its discourse into the Internet. Activists, a topic to be more developed during the rest of this illustration, also utilize this communication tool. Industry puts out emergency management information, as well as crisis response statements, many of which end up on the Internet or originate there.

Activitists

In this description of infrastructures, citizens range from unattached critics to well coordinated activists. The range of criticism emanates from the telephone and in person complaints by local residents focusing on issues such as odors and flares (two recurrent themes as predictable as the rise and setting of the sun). Some area residents create activist groups of their own. As one would predict, the Houston Ship Channel is rife with such groups. One such activist group using the acronym, GHASP (Galveston Houston-Association for Smog Prevention) gathers information, conducts modest amounts of research, and reports its findings. The Web is a powerful tool for such organizations that otherwise would be substantially disadvantaged by the deep pockets of corporate communication departments against which activists battles. Once often narrowly circulated, reports by groups such as this, can reach any interested reader with a search engine and a few seconds to spend. However strong or weak the information of the group, its voice can be heard locally in meetings, through standard media, and via the Internet. Dozens of similar local activist groups emerge in infrastructures such as these.

National and international activist groups lend their credibility, voice, and communication channels to the risk communication debates. For instance, due to its size and prominence, the Houston Ship Channel is periodically visited by local, state, and national representatives of these groups, such as the Sierra Club, Environmental Defense Fund, Audubon Society, National Wildlife Federation, and Greenpeace, to name only a few.

Local scientists and attorneys with environmental safety interests also play a role in such infrastructure. Research organizations, university researchers, public relations agencies, and other components make up vital parts of such infrastructures. So do all of the traditional and grassroots media, local, state, federal, and international.

In conclusion, these sections have laid theory but more importantly given details about one of the largest and most complex risk communication and emergency response infrastructures in the world to illustrate how complex and tangled the dialogue might be. In fact, the illustration only focused on the elements of process; the actual dynamics of discourse, the crafting of sense making and shared meaning, would require a separate illustration. Such illustration would not only focus attention on a specific topic, at a particular time, but demonstrate how the mix of science, corporate policy, public policy, myth, self-interest, outrage, and unvoiced concern can be fruitful, as well as frustratingly dysfunctional. One caveat in closing: As much as industry can be assumed to frustrate the dialogue at the process and content levels, years of experience suggest that industry members also know the virtues of continual conversation and scrupulous attention to community spirited interpretations and responsiveness.

INFRASTRUCTURE AS ZONES OF MEANING

Anyone who has studied or responded as a professional to crisis or risk situations understands that society—however broadly or narrowly defined—consists of multiple publics or opinion pockets. On a given matter, at the top of the discussion, are people highly involved cognitively whereas others may be oblivious of the crisis or risk. Beyond awareness, we have substantial differences of knowledge, attitude or evaluation, motivation, and policy preferences. For this reason, we can imagine that communities consist of zones of meaning. That meaning may evidence an array of differences in the degree to which people are interested, aware, knowledgeable, willing and able to voice support or opposition, and tolerant or intolerant of the crisis or risk.

One of the vital discoveries in the early years of risk studies was the presence and power of various interpretative and response heuristics. Based on his research and that of others, Covello (1992) featured a list of heuristics: Catastrophic potential, familiarity, understanding, uncertainty, controllability, voluntariness of exposure, effects on children, effects manifestation, effects on future generations, victim identity, dread, trust in institutions, media attention, accident history, equity, benefits, reversibility, personal stake, and origin. The value of such lists is the ability to gain insights into predictable patterns that focus key publics' attention and predict their responses, interpretations, and reactions to crises and risks. Such factors are weighted, situational, and multi-dimensional. They are useful for planning, prevention, and the rubrics of dialogue. They can help participants in a risk situation predict and interpret who will be outraged and why that reaction is likely to occur.

One of the primary interpretive heuristics is the degree to which people in a specific risk situation are tolerance or intolerant of the specific risk. Assuming they know about it and care, the degree of tolerance is likely to be function of knowledge of the risk (and attendant information such as its source), who benefits versus who bears the risk, how much control is exerted by the source of risk and other players in the infrastructure, the degree to which people are cognitively involved by their self-interest with the risk, and the degree to which experts and lay people can be variously certain in their understanding of the risk (Nathan, Heath, & Douglas, 1992).

Slovic (1992) following similar logics reported that not only do men and women exhibit various degrees of risk tolerance on an array of risks, women are almost universally less tolerant of such risks, especially those which are associated with technologies or chemicals. Such differences, although in a similar pattern across many risks, also evidence national biases, at least in samples drawn from Canada and Sweden. One of the dimensions that corresponds to tolerance in systematic ways is the perception of the benefits of the risk. These two dimensions (tolerance and benefit) seem more to depend on specific risks that exhibit a pattern with a high correlation across all risks. Perceptions of such risks are influenced by the degree to which subjects believe them to be well known, the source of dread, foreseeable and likely to produce severe and uncontrollable damage. Such perceptions appear to be sensitive to high/low peer influence and admiration as well as being perceived to be socially approved.

Investigations of this kind led Slovic to advocate a psychometric paradigm. That view is reasonable, but only completely useful when connected to the dynamics of infrastructures, suggested by sociometrics. Combining psychometrics and sociometics gives the ingredients of infrastructures where risks are discussed, shared, and individuals become variously supportive or intolerant of them. Such patterns not only are relevant to community reactions to weather risks, but also those relevant to industrial and governmental agency policies and activities. So is the case for individual reactions to such risks an smoking initiation, abuse of alcohol and drugs (legal and illegal), and sexual activity. When we consider how people learn about and evaluate risks leading them to support or oppose the risks as well as organizations associated with them, we need not dig far into the data to realize that "it takes a village" to help people understand, accommodate to, and even oppose such risks and their source—even when those sources are the people in the community itself.

For these reasons, we are further convinced that risk discussions and crisis response occur in infrastructures of society where experts interact with non-experts, and individuals have idiosyncratic information needs and evaluative/response heuristics. We can well imagine that how attentive people are to mass-mediated messages as well as the content of interpersonal conversation and public meetings is likely to reflect the nature and quality of the infrastructure as well as the preferences of the individuals involved. To this end, we postulate that how well a crisis is predicted and responded to as well as how productive risk communication is depends less on the communication ability of any one source but rather on the quality of the infrastructure where the dialogue occurs.

Although many residents might live and work in the shadow of a major refining and chemical manufacturing complex, the citizens are quite unlikely to have a singular and easily defined set of opinions on the industry, the risk of living and working near it, and the ways in which the risk is best managed. People who, for instance, believe they are at risk exhibit higher levels of cognitive involvement (concern), lower trust in government as potential source of control over the source of the risk, more knowledge of shelter in place as an emergency response concept, a greater willingness to receive more information about shelter in place by that name as well attend a meeting to learn more about how do shelter in place. Women are more likely to hold these views than are men. Drawing on this finding, a community relations expert who hosts or attends a public meeting on shelter in place protocols is more likely to encounter women who are at least minimally knowledgeable and highly motivated to learn more. They may also be less willing to easily trust the company as a single source of advice, but may also worry that government conspires with industry against the "public interest" (Heath & Abel, 1996a).

Emergency response campaigns occur across the nation as corporate and government officials seek to inform key publics of what to do in the face of an emergency. These events would include severe weather and chemical releases, for instance. Persons who report lower levels of knowledge of such emergency response options tend to also be less well connected in the community, less knowledgeable of the source of such information (such as a relevant manufacturing company), and less knowledgeable that emergency response protocols exist. So, reaching this individual would be dramatically more difficult than communicating with those who were more aware of the protocols and interested in learning more. Even so, the kinds of communication and relationship building efforts would likely to be different. One target would require awareness, which is not easy to overcome when they are either disinterested or focused on other matters to the exclusion of safety. Those who are more aware and more involved may be willing to hear more information, but they may distrust the motives and even recommendations (Heath & Abel, 1996b).

In such communities, people may trust some government officials and not others. Or, they might trust school officials, who are often part of the emergency response network because of the need to prepare students for a crisis event as well as to prepare the parents to respond properly. School officials may be more trusted than elected officials, but not specialists such as fire and police personnel. In the communities at risk then, who the spokespersons are and who they should be are worth considering (O'Hair, 2004). The key to understanding such matters sensitive to infrastructures is that one size does not fit all, each as the spokesperson or the members of the audience. In such situations, how long people have lived in a community is also likely to influence the credibility they hold for the elected and appointed officials (Heath & Abel, 1996a).

Investigating the impact of knowledge about radon on citizens' reaction, Sandman, Weinstein, and Klotz (1987) discovered that knowledge did not influence homeowners' degree of distress about indoor radon and willingness to take action to mitigate risk. The researchers found that information was reaching the public, but did not affect residents' decisions to monitor for radon gas, intention to take remedial action, degree of distress about the gas, and evaluation of the seriousness of one's own radon level. While 64.5% answered factual questions correctly, just 16% had monitored or planned to monitor for radon. Only 18% of those with high radon levels had taken remedial action by modifying their homes. To show how radon can ignite concern, researchers told of angry protests over the disposal of industrial radon waste. They reasoned that the difference in response resulted because laypeople tend to base risk estimates on subjective factors like fairness, naturalness and familiarity of the risk. In contrast, experts base risk estimates on mortality rates and other objective data across an entire community. The researchers termed risk estimates based on objective data a "hazard" and estimates based on subjective data an "outrage." They said risk communicators need ways to teach the public to attend to serious hazards and to avoid being outraged by modest risks.

Because of the inherent and apparent incentives for people in a community of risk to be attentive to information flow and systematically evaluative in their approach to the risks in the community, research often finds this paradigm lacks empirical support. People who live in a community where substantial risks occur—whether from exposure to sudden release, fire or explosion, or to long-term exposure—are often quite uninformed.

Environmental Protection Agency protocol as well as the motivation behind community activism assumes that once people are aware of problems they will seek more information, develop and apply evaluative heuristics, and take action as well as call for corporate and/or governmental action. That model of behavior may fit the activist individuals in the community, those who are active or likely to become active but the pattern is not found to exist universally in a community of risk. Most people in such communities evidence much more ignorance of the conditions and organizations involved than they reveal being knowledgeable and appropriately evaluative. One extensive study found great gaps in knowledge of companies, potentially harmful chemicals, and government actions on such matters as well as the benefits (jobs, taxes, and community income) from living and working near such facilities. In fact, predicting whether people (and if so which ones) will support or oppose the industry is confronted with understanding and using idiosyncratic information and opinion patterns. Worth noting is the fact that the track record of the industry working with local government is highly predictive of support whereas the opposite can lead to opposition for both the industry and government in such matters (Heath & Abel, 1996b).

CONCLUDING REMARKS

Increasing community involvement and participation in risk management spawns positive civic and social effects often referred to as resilience. Resilient communities have the capacity to recognize conditions, mobilize resources, and self-organize in response to a crisis. It is through resilient acts that communities and their members construct strategies that manage risks. Building resilient, socially networked communities where stores of communication capital reside offer greater comfort and security than disconnected communities (O'Hair, Heath, & Becker, 2005). The obstacles in building community infrastructures are not impossible but challenging. What this chapter demonstrates is that multiple players operating from diverse motives and conceptions of science present a system of collaboration that requires proactive involvement by those who can perspective-take from a multi-facet lens—one that captures viewpoints that are often occluded if not hidden from normal view.

BIBLIOGRAPHY

Althaus, C. E. (2005). A disciplinary perspective on the epistemological status of risk, *Risk Analysis, 25*, 567–588.

Arvai, J. L. (2003). Using risk communication to disclose the outcome of a participatory decision-making process: Effects on the perceived acceptability of risk-policy decisions. *Risk Analysis*, *23*, 281–289.

Arvai, J., Gregory, R., & McDaniels, T. (2001). Testing a structured decision approach: Value focused thinking for deliberative risk communication. *Risk Analysis: An International Journal, 6*, 1065–1076.

Chess, C. (2001). Organizational theory and the stages of risk communication. *Risk Analysis, 21*, 179–188.

Covello, V. T. (1992). Risk communication: An emerging area of health communication research. In S. A. Deetz, (Ed.), *Communication yearbook 15* (pp. 359–373). Thousand Oaks, CA: Sage.

Cox, P., Niewohner, J., Pidgeon, N., Gerrard, S., Fischhoff, B., & Riley, D. (2003). The use of mental models in chemical risk protection: Developing a generic workplace methodology. *Risk Analysis*, *23*, 311–324.

Flora, J., Jatilus, D., Jackson, C., & Fortmann, S. (1993). The Stanford Five-City Heart Disease Prevention Project. In T. E. Backer & E. Rogers (Eds.), *Organizational aspects of health campaign: What works?* (pp. 101–128). Thousand Oaks: Sage.

Forelle, C., & Westphal, S. P. (2006, February 16). Does calcium really help women prevent bone loss, fractures? *Wall Street Journal*, pp. D1, D8.

Gallup Brain (accessed February 12, 2006). The Gallup Organization online service, http://www.brain.gallup.com.

Gardner, G. T., & Gould, L. C. (1989). Public perceptions of the risks and benefits of technology, *Risk Analysis, 9*, 225–242.

Gregory, R., Arvai, J., & McDaniels, T. (2001). Value focused thinking for environmental risk consultations. *Environmental Risk: Perceptions, Evaluation, and Management, 9*, 249–273.

Hadden, S. G. (1989). Institutional barriers to risk communication. *Risk Analysis*, 9(3), 301–308.

Heath, R. L. (1997). *Strategic issues management*. Thousand Oaks, CA: Sage.

Heath, R. L., & Abel, D. D. (1996a). Proactive response to citizen risk concerns: Increasing citizens' knowledge of emergency response practices. *Journal of Public Relations Research, 8*, 151–171.

Heath, R. L., & Abel, D. D. (1996b). Types of knowledge as predictors of company support: The role of information in risk communication. *Journal of Public Relations Research, 8*, 35–55.

Heath, R. L., Bradshaw, J., & Lee, J. (2002). Community Relationship Building: Local Leadership in the Risk Communication Infrastructure, *Journal of Public Relations Research, 14*, 317–353.

Kasperson, R. E. (1992). The social amplification of risk: Progress in developing an integrative framework. In S. Krimsky & D. Golding. (Eds.), *Social theories of risk* (pp. 153–178). Westport, CT: Praeger.

Kasperson, J. X., Kasperson, R. E., Pidgeon, N., & Slovic, P. (2003). The social amplification of risk: Assessing fifteen years of research and theory. In N. Pidgeon, R. E. Kasperson, & P. Slovic (Eds.), *The social amplification of risk* (pp. 13–46). Cambridge: Cambridge University Press.

McComas, K. A. (2003). Citizen satisfaction with public meetings used for risk communication. *Journal of Applied Communication Research, 31*(2), 164–184.

McDaniels, T., Gregory, R., & Fields, D. (1999). Democratizing risk management: Successful public involvement in local water management decision. *Risk Analysis, 19*, 491–504.

Morgan, M. G., Florig, H. K., DeKay, M. L. , & Fischbeck, P. (2000). Categorizing risks for risk ranking. *Risk Analysis, 20*, 49–58.

Nathan, K., Heath, R. L., & Douglas, W. (1992). Tolerance for potential environmental health risks: The influence of knowledge, benefits, control, involvement and uncertainty. *Journal of Public Relations Research, 4*, 235–258.

O'Hair, D. (2004). Measuring risk/crisis communication: Taking strategic assessment and program evaluation to the next level. *Risk and crisis communication: Building trust and explaining complexities when emergencies arise* (pp. 5–10). Washington, DC: Consortium of Social Science Associations.

O'Hair, H. D., Heath, R., & Becker, J. (2005). Toward a paradigm of managing communication and terrorism and communication. In H. D. O'Hair, R. L. Health, & G. R. Ledlow (Eds.), *Community preparedness and response to terrorism: Communication and the media* (pp. 307–327). Westport, CT: Praeger.

O'Hair, H. D. & Heath, R. L. (in press). Conceptualizing communication and terrorism. In H. D. O'Hair, R. L. Heath, & G. R. Ledlow (Eds.), *Community preparedness and response to terrorism: Communication and the media* (pp. 1–12). Westport, CT: Praeger.

O'Hair, H. D., Matusitz, J., & Eckstein, J. (in press). The role of communication in terrorism. In H. D. O'Hair, R. Heath, K. Ayotte, & G. R. Ledlow (Eds.), *Terrorism: Communication and Rhetorical perspectives.* Cresskill, NJ: Hampton Press.

Parkin, R. T., & Balbux, J. M. (2000). Variations in concepts of "susceptibility" in risk assessment. *Risk Analysis, 20*, 20, 603–611.

Priest, S. H., Bonfadelli, H., & Rusanen, M. (2003). The "trust gap" hypothesis: Predicting support for biotechnology across national cultures as a function of trust in actors. *Risk Analysis, 23*, 751–766.

Rodriquez, H. (2004). The role of science, technology and media in the communication of risk warnings. *Risk and crisis communication: Building trust and explaining complexities when emergencies arise.* Washington, DC: Consortium of Social Science Associations.

Renfro, W. L. (1982). Managing the issues of the 1980s. *The Futurist, 16*, 61–66.

Ronan, K. R., & Johnston, D. M. (2005). *Promoting community resilience in disasters: The role for schools youth, and families.* New York: Springer.

Sandman, P. M., Weinstein, N. D., & Klotz, M. L (1987). Public response to the risk from geological radon. *Journal of Communication, 37*(3), 93–107.

Scherer, C. W., & Cho, H. (2003). A social network contagion theory of risk perception. *Risk Analysis, 23*, 261–267.

Siegrist, M., & Cvetkovich, G. (2000). Perception of hazards: The role of social trust and knowledge. *Risk Analysis, 20*, 713–719.

Sjoberg, L. (2000). Factors in risk perception. *Risk Analysis, 20*, 1–11.

Slovic, P. (1992). Perception of risk: Reflections on the psychometric paradigm. In S. Krimsky & D. Golding, D. (Eds,), *Social theories of risk* (pp. 117–152). Westport, CT: Praeger.

Slovic P. (2001). (Ed.). *Smoking: Risk, perception, & policy*. Thousand Oaks, CA: Sage.

Starr, C. (1969). Social benefit versus technological risk. *Science, 165*, 1232–1238.

Stephens, K., Rimal, R., & Flora, J. (2004). Expanding the reach of health campaigns: Community organizations as meta-channels for the dissemination of health information. *Journal of Health Communication, 9*, 97–111.

Stoto, M., Abel, C., & Dievler, A. (1997). *Healthy communities: New partnerships for the future of public health.* Washington, DC: National Academies Press.

Thomas, K., Swaton, E., Fishbein, M., & Otway, H. J. (1980). Nuclear energy: The accuracy of policy makers' perceptions of public beliefs. *Behavioral Science, 25*, 332–344.

Valente, T. W., Paredes, P., & Poppe, P. R. (1998). Matching the message to the process: The relative ordering of knowledge, attitudes, and practices in behavior change research. *Human Communication Research, 24*, 366–385.

White, M. P., & Eiser, J. R. (2005). Information specificity and hazard risk potential as moderators of trust asymmetry. *Risk Analysis, 25*, 1187–1198.

Zhang, J., & Gray, S. (2006, February 16). The whole truth about whole grain: FDA guidelines on use of term on food labels; bread makers vs. cereal makers. *Wall Street Journal*, pp. D1, D8.

III

CONTEXTS OF CRISIS AND RISK COMMUNICATION

Section Three examines risk and crisis challenges in several typical and often daunting contexts. Following the themes developed in the first and second sections, this section brings principles discussed above to bear on questions relevant to various health and safety contexts. However, theoretical and research based these disciplines are, they also have their practical or applied side. They are only as good as their ability to put matters right. The overarching theme of this section is the challenges that occur for effective and ethical communication regarding risks and crises relevant to various contexts, each of which has its own demands, limits, and success. Central to the applications featured in this section runs a consistent theme: Facts count, but are interpreted through cultural frames which are sensitive to self and political interests which may in various ways distort the more simplistic role of information in these matters. Sense making and interpretation are not trivial, but the essence of risk and crisis communication—a model that diminishes the information sharing or exchange model to the point of being trivial. Getting the facts right is important, but only a starting point.

Chapter 24 focuses on one of the many challenges faced by the Centers for Disease Control (CDC) in the United States. The specific challenge addressed by Seeger, Reynolds and Sellnow is pandemic influenza. The chapter's centerpiece is the CERC model which grows out of the CDC's mission to provide information which key publics can use to make the best possible decisions under trying circumstances. The model begins with the initiation of a pre-crisis plan, continues through the start of the crisis event, and fosters maintenance and resolution. As is typical for such plans, it allows for an evaluation stage in which assessment occurs to determine whether refinements are needed and which ones if so.

Applying the logic of the Mental Models Approach to risk communication, chapter 25 addresses the challenges of effective communication and cancer prevention and treatment. At both points in a person's life, fear and the complexity of cancer are likely to impede individuals' understanding. Downs, Brune de Bruin, Fischhoff, Hesse, and Maibach reason that campaigns can wage war on myths and misunderstanding by bringing the understanding of the lay public closer to the science based knowledge of experts. This logic is the essence of the Mental Models Approach which bases the success of communication on how large or narrow the understanding gap is between experts and targets of such campaigns. Messages need to be carefully designed and targets need time and support to understand and appreciate the science set before them.

However peaceful and idyllic one might think educational settings used to be, the reality is that they have long been dangerous. In medieval times, for instance, academics lived in walled cloisters. Academic garb worn today, especially the material hanging from the sleeves, was used to carry stones and other means for resisting attacks. And, of course, academic decisions could be seen as heresy. Nevertheless, academic settings, as discussed in Chapter 26 are in various ways repositories of risk and in need of crisis prevention and response plans. One of the basic rhetorical options of such plans is the need for restoration. No matter how horrific the violence on campus, all members of the campus community need eventually to be healed and able to return to business as normal. Atkinson, Vaughn, and VanCamp explore the risk potential based on past events and current conditions. A risk of violence is likely. Restoration is a key strategic response in the arsenal of the crisis responders. It requires actions, as well as words.

One strategy that can lead to restoration is apologia, a more complex concept than is inferred by those who define the strategy as apology. In chapter 27, Hearit and Robeson address the recurring question raised by those facing a crisis event: What shall we say and how should we say "it" to best restore ourselves and our organization? First, we acknowledge that even the best response never returns the status quo. So, we are forced to ask what statements, then, move us forward. First, we must acknowledge that crisis response can never be only communicative. Various restorative actions are required. In doing so, inevitably some clash of interests occurs. The authors observe that when the crisis draws attention to organizational missteps, and the motives behind them, in ways that questions the legitimacy of the organization's ability and willingness to properly exert control apologia opens the door for statements and actions that can lead to restoration. But time will test the efficacy of the response.

As noted in the discussions on the precautionary principle, one of the most contentious areas of risk communication centers on the challenges of new technologies. People and other organisms, so critics worry, are often the guinea pigs used to test the health and safety risks of such technologies. In chapter 28, Leitch and Motion examine this issue which they claim has become more controversial than nuclear physics. From a discourse perspective, heavily sensitive to cultural interpretations of risk, the authors examine the dialectic of privatization of benefit and socialization of risk, a counterpart to the dialectic of harm and benefit as a conceptual heuristic for understanding the benefits and negative consequences of risk.

A recurring theme in the discussion of risk and crisis is the rhetorical or dialectical tension between presentation of facts, interpretation of facts, and decision making that results from the mutually beneficial balancing of interests. Cultural interpretations contend against what others pose as sound science. As discussed in chapter 6, the precautionary principle was proposed and has been debated as a decision heuristic to be used when sound science is incapable to resolving the uncertainties relevant to a risk decision. In chapter 29, Prouthou and Heath use the principle as a means for examining the dialogue between activists and regulators on the matter of genetically modified organisms. As much as those engaged in the contest of new and emerging technologies have fostered or acquiesced to dialogue as the basis for risk decisions, as discussed in chapter 28, the challenge is to employ a heuristic such as the precautionary principle without bringing so much caution into the discussion that no decision becomes the decision. The context for this dialogue is the World Trade Organization and the European Union, among the several interlocking decision-making bodies charged with advancing and maintaining public health and safety in matters of commercial scientific innovation.

The ability to understand and adapt to the environment is a timeless aspect of risk communication, perhaps its root cause. The march of human society has been inseparable from the impact people have on the environment and the impact the environment has on people. In chapter 30, Peterson and Thompson examine this theme to better understand how lay people learn about environmental risks, how the media influence their understanding and perceptions, and how public opinion and public policy are formed. As others in this volume have, these authors center their attention on the battle between what is offered as sound science and the resistance from cultural interpretations of science based interpretations of risk. The centerpiece of this discussion is the relevance and rhetorical twisting of the concept of uncertainty, the universal principle of risk, whether in a casino or from exposure to toxic substances, for instance. However, sound scientific risk interpretations and recommendations are, the authors caution, we cannot ignore the political implications that pit interests against one another in ways that may distort a more reasoned discourse.

Since the terrorist attacks on the World Trade Center and the Pentagon in 2001, academic and political interest in terrorism has become an almost all-consuming issue, despite some simple comparatives. In the United States, approximately 40,000 people die each year in automobile accidents, and about 18,000 die from complications related to influenza. But the loss of 3,000 people in the 2001 attack has led to war, destruction, international tensions, and challenges to national image, character, and Constitutional protections. In chapter 31, Ayotte, O'Hair, and Bernard demonstrate how what is thought (or thought not) to be a risk or crisis is a matter of interpretation, subject to rhetorical framing. Framing is a central theme of other chapters, and here is brought to bear on the tensions that result when some event (probable or actual) requires or allows interpretation that is contestable—and political. Getting and sharing information on matters as problematic and contestable as terrorism can be a misleading paradigm of crisis and risk communication. Distortion and dysfunction is not possible, but probable and perhaps dysfunctional to more systematic and collective (collaborative) decision making. In such matters, facts count, but in action, the question is this: as interpreted by what decision heuristic and how much. In the name of protecting a population or responding to individuals, nations, or assemblages, merely calling them terrorists has become politically sufficient to define the rhetorical problem and frame its response.

Chapter 32 continues the analysis of terrorism as a context for risk and crisis communication. Bruce, Shamas, and O'Hair observe how new communication technologies become not only a tool but a means for the social amplification of risk and crisis in the context of terrorism. Via communication terrorism becomes a reality created, perceived, and understood. The Internet gives terrorists and people who discuss terrorism an access to listeners, readers, and viewers not typically allowed by the traditional media. This, of course, includes the use of the Internet to show beheadings by groups dubed terrorists by their opponents. These same groups, as discussed in chapter 31, either vilify or claim as heroes the persons perpetrating such acts. The Internet allows alternative channels for such discourse and does so in a way that avoids the interpretive clout of traditional media. In these and other ways, new communication technologies have become the driving force behind terrorism, by whatever name, in the 21st century.

Although the nature of travel has changed over the decades, it has always been associated with various risks, that once manifested, become a crisis for some organization and various individuals and groups. Nevertheless, travel is essential to commerce and personal lifestyles. In chapter 33, Sallot, Springston, and Avery note that travel truly is big business, and even an essential part of regions' and nations' economies. In travel, not only is risk associated with the mode of travel, but also the circumstances of the travel, such as war, violent weather, or communicable disease. With these matters as their foundation, the authors examine performance of various organizations regarding their crisis and risk management and communication. The assessment is that academic research could provide better management and communication responses, as well as trained individuals to work on behalf of organizations fostering travel and the travelers who put themselves at risk.

24

Crisis and Emergency Risk Communication in Health Contexts: Applying the CDC Model to Pandemic Influenza

Matthew W. Seeger
Wayne State University

Barbara Reynolds
Centers For Disease Control and Prevention

Timothy L. Sellnow
University of Kentucky

The Centers for Disease Control and Prevention (CDC) has been at the epicenter of health communication efforts. Not only is the CDC a primary practitioner of health communication in the form of heath promotion, it has also used risk communication strategies to address emerging threats such as the anthrax attacks, the threat from smallpox, Sudden Acute Respiratory Syndrome (SARS), and the risk associated with pandemic influenza. Recently, however, the CDC has begun to integrate strategies for crisis communication as the agency has adopted responsibilities most often associated with first responder groups.

Crisis communication and risk communication have developed as essentially independent bodies of scholarship and practice. Crisis communication has focused primarily on issues of image restoration and strategic responses to crises after an event occurs, often from the standpoint of an organization or agency (Benoit, 1995; Coombs, 1995). Risk communication has roots primarily in persuasion and the perception of risk. This includes methods for educating the public about risk and constructing strategic messages to modify risky behavior (Covello, 1992; Witte, 1992, 1995). Risk communication has been driven largely by environmental safety, by larger issues of public health, and to a lesser degree by corporate interests such as the chemical and food industries (Plough & Krimsky, 1987).

As the public health community in particular has faced the broadened mission of responding to large-scale crises and disasters, the agency has embraced new communication strategies and tactics. The CDC has developed an integrated approach to communication known as Crisis and Emergency Risk Communication, or CERC (Reynolds, Galdo, & Sokler, 2002). Reynolds and

Seeger (2005) have described the CERC approach as a systemic form of interaction that requires ongoing communication processes throughout the various stages or phases of a crisis. Moreover, this merged approach can also be understood as a meta-strategy of crisis preparation and response that informs other strategies and tactics of communication about risks and crises (Seeger & Reynolds, 2008).

Following the 2001 anthrax episode, the CDC was moved to the forefront as an essential resource for health-related risk and crisis communication. In response to this charge, the CDC has worked to enhance its capacity for delivering accurate, audience-centered messages to the public. In addition the CDC has developed complex global relationship in hopes of managing crises such as pandemic influenza. As part of this preparation, the CDC has developed and applied the Crisis and Emergency Risk Communication (CERC) Model. This chapter applies the CERC model to the CDC's ongoing efforts to develop a management plan for an inevitable pandemic influenza. The application confirms that effective planning is essential to managing global crises. This planning must be done in a manner that builds relationships, maintains flexibility, avoids risk inflation, and devotes time to all stages in the CERC mode.

In this chapter, we explore the development of risk communication as a form of health communication and describe those factors that led the CDC to adopt the CERC approach. Specifically, we identify CDC's response to the anthrax episode as a primary factor that precipitated the emergence of CERC as a framework. We also explore how the CDC's CERC framework has been used to inform communication efforts associated with avian influenza (H5N1) and the threat of pandemic influenza. Pandemic influenza is arguably the most significant public heath threat to emerge in the last several decades. We also seek to demonstrate, through this case, how an integrated crisis and risk communication approach can function to inform the early states of a crisis. Our purpose is to illustrate how an integrated communication approach is used in responding to a global threat to pubic health. Finally, we offer suggestions for how the CERC model might inform future efforts to communicate about public health issues.

RISK COMMUNICATION IN HEALTH CONTEXTS

Before the events of September 11, 2001, or the episode of anthrax-contaminated letters, the CDC had developed a very robust capacity for risk communication. Employing health educators and message designers, the CDC had a multi-faceted strategy for informing and persuading the public regarding health issues. One approach was grounded primarily in uncertainty management models. In this approach, relevant health information is delivered to the public in an accessible, targeted, and timely manner. Health educators present information to groups who are at particular risks. Brochures, video-presentations, and web-based messages are carefully crafted and tested to meet audience needs, comprehension levels, and language preferences. Information about specific diseases, treatment options, risk factors, and related issues has been disseminated in these ways by the CDC.

Another set of risk communication approaches are targeted more broadly as persuasive messages using large-scale advertising campaigns. These campaigns employ a variety of strategies such as fear appeals and related strategies to persuade publics to change behaviors. Anti-smoking campaigns, safe sex, drug abuse, and a variety of life-style issues have been addressed in these ways. These messages are often distributed through more general media channels, such a television commercials and magazine advertisements. They have become an ubiquitous feature of public communication channels.

In both cases, the CDC uses carefully scripted and tested messages. Emphasis is placed on insuring that health information reflects sound science. The CDC carefully vets health messages with appropriate subject-matter experts to ensure consensus about the accuracy of the message. Messages are framed, targeted, and adapted to reach specific audiences, usually those most at risk for the health issues being addressed. Messages are often crafted as part of larger campaigns, using multiple channels and continuing over extended periods of time.

Crisis and Emergency Risk Communication

A third model, known as CERC, was originally developed by the CDC following the anthrax attacks and the events of 9/11. Based on these experiences, management at the CDC concluded that traditional strategies of risk communication alone were insufficient for responding to cases of large-scale public crisis. Using existing models, the CDC struggled to rapidly mount an effective response to an emerging, poorly understood, and dynamic threat. Both resources and expertise were inadequate and, in some cases, the basic strategies for communication were ineffective (Cole, 2003).

The events of 9/11, for example, created a broad set of communication needs that had to be executed within the confines of high uncertainty, severe threat, and restricted response time. Moreover, the scope and nature of the event was such that a coordinated federal response was required. Although the CDC's responsibilities, in the case of 9/11, were limited primarily to questions of the environmental health risks associated with debris, dust, ash, and assorted compounds, the scope of the disasters taxed available resources. The CDC's primary role involved testing and monitoring air and issuing warnings and guidelines to both first responders and community members. Mental health information was also distributed. These responsibilities were relatively familiar and well understood, as was the role of supporting agency. The CDC had often played a tertiary, supporting role in responding to the public health dimensions of disasters, usually natural disasters.

The subsequent anthrax episode, however, placed the CDC in a much more central role and required substantial communication resources and crisis communication expertise that extended beyond the agency's experience or capability. Moreover, the CDC encountered a number of challenges in communicating effectively during the anthrax episode (Robinson & Newstetter, 2003; Vanderford, 2003). These failures prompted the agency to develop new approaches, strategies, and models.

THE ANTHRAX ATTACKS

The anthrax attacks, involving letters tainted with highly refined anthrax spores, began within one month of the 9/11 attacks. As a consequence, these acts of bio-terrorism were understandably interpreted, at least initially, as a second wave of attacks from the same terrorist source. During a period of roughly two weeks, several letters containing anthrax were mailed to media organizations and federal officials. These included *The Sun,* a Boca Raton newspaper, and *The New York Post.* A letter was also mailed to Tom Brokaw, the anchor of NBC nightly news. Senators Tom Daschle of South Dakota and Patrick Leahy of Vermont also received contaminated letters resulting in 12 Senate offices being closed (Anthrax Case Timeline, 2003).

Given the biological nature of the event, the CDC took a lead role in the federal response. The CDC issued a number of statements through various spokespersons. While these statements were designed to clarify the public's understanding of the risk and reduce anxiety, they likely had the opposite affect. First, the CDC had inadequate information about the attacks (Robinson & Newstetter, 2003). Inhalation anthrax had been eradicated from this country in the early 1900s. Moreover, the anthrax spores in at least some of the letters behaved in unexpected ways due to the degree of refinement and so called "weaponization." The spores were highly aerosolized and were able to pass through small gaps in envelopes. Only military organizations had any significant experience with anthrax in this form. To further compound the inherent uncertainty, no one could predict the ways in which cross contamination would occur because letters were processed through automated mail sorting machines. Second, efforts to reassure the public resulted in additional concern as the CDC's predications proved inaccurate. On at least two separate occasions, the CDC's reassuring statements were followed by additional infections and deaths. The CDC's communication capacity was overwhelmed (Vanderford, 2003). Moreover, several of the strategies employed were particularly ineffective in communicating with the postal workers, who had been exposed to anthrax (Quinn, Thomas, & McAllister, 2005).

By the time the crisis ended, a total 22 cases of inhalation anthrax and 8 cases of cutaneous (skin) anthrax were associated with the contaminated letters (Anthrax Case Timeline, 2003). In addition, five people died, including two postal workers and a retired widow, Ottie Lundgren. Novak and Barett (2008) observed that "by the time the crisis ended, the public and other stakeholders viewed the CDC as a slow and rigid organization with ineffective communication and serious credibility problems; the CDC became an organizational casualty of the anthrax-related crisis." Clearly, new approaches to communication were required.

As noted earlier, the development of CERC was a direct consequence of the failure of the CDC to communicate effectively during the anthrax episode. Observers have suggested that the CDC lacked capacity to meet the volume of requests for information. Messages were inconsistent and some reports suggest that far too many spokespersons were speaking for the CDC (Novak & Barrett, 2008). Problems also arose regarding the speed of communication and, in some cases. the accuracy of information provided (Cole, 2003).

THE CERC MODEL

The CDC suggests that the CERC model is designed:

> to provide information that allows an individual, stakeholder, or entire community to make the best possible decisions during a crisis emergency about their well-being and communicate those decisions, within nearly impossible time constraints, and ultimately to accept the imperfect nature of choices as the situation evolves. (Reynolds, Galdo, & Sokler, 2002, p. ii)

Taken as a whole, the CERC model is an integrative framework that seeks to merge strategies of risk and crisis communication (Reynolds, Galdo, & Sokler, 2002). The framework specifies a broad set of communication activities that vary as the crisis evolves through various stages or phases. The CERC model describes five general stages of a crisis: pre-crisis, initial event, maintenance, resolution, and evaluation. In each stage, a set of recommended communication activities is described. According to the CDC, specific and distinct communication activities should occur in each stage (see Table 24.1). During pre-crisis, for example, public health communicators should undertake the kinds of activities most often described as risk communication. These activities include educating the public about risks and appropriate responses to specific adverse events, and seeking to change behaviors so that risks are reduced. In the crisis stage, a variety of communication activities such as information about the nature of the threat, responses by officials, and recommendations for self-efficacy or individual response may be required. As the crisis moves into the resolution stage, health communicators face a different set of exigencies. At this point, the public seeks more detailed insight into the nature of the event. During the resolution stage, questions of cause, blame, and responsibility typically emerge. These questions, then, require officials to respond with a broad-based, honest, and open discussion of these issues. Finally, the evaluation stage is an opportunity to create and communicate the lessons from the crisis. Evaluation creates the opportunity for health communicators to prepare for the next infectious disease or food borne illness outbreak.

Subsequent investigations have refined the CERC model (Reynolds & Seeger, 2003) and have begun testing its efficacy (Ballard-Reisch et al., 2008). Ballard-Reisch et al. emphasized the developmental features of a crisis and noted that failures to communicate effectively in one stage may influence the development of subsequent stages. "If done well, stage 1 initiatives lay the foundation

TABLE 24.1
Crisis and Emergency Risk Communication Model

I. **Pre –Crisis (Risk Messages; Warnings; Preparations)**
Communication and education campaigns targeted to both the public and the response community to facilitate:
- Monitoring and recognition of emerging risks
- General public understanding of risk
- Public preparation for the possibility of an adverse event
- Changes in behavior to reduce the likelihood of harm (self-efficacy)
- Specific warnings messages regarding some eminent threat, such as evacuation notices, take shelter warnings, product recalls, etc.
- Alliances and cooperation with agencies, organizations, and groups
- Development of consensual recommendations by experts and first responders
- Message development and testing for subsequent stages

II. **Initial Event (Uncertainty Reduction; Self-Efficacy; Reassurance)**
Rapid communication to the general public and to affected groups seeking to establish:
- Empathy, reassurance, and reduction in the public's emotional turmoil
- Designated crisis/agency spokespersons and formal channels and methods of communication
- General and broad-based understanding of the crisis circumstances, nature of the threat, consequences, and anticipated outcomes based on available information
- Reduction of crisis related uncertainty
- Specific understanding of emergency management and medical community responses
- Understanding of self-efficacy and personal response activities (how/where to get more information; check on neighbors; avoid contaminated water, etc.)

III. **Maintenance (Ongoing Uncertainty Reduction; Self-Efficacy; Reassurance)** Communication to the general public and to affected groups seeking to facilitate:
- More accurate public understandings of ongoing risks
- Understanding of background factors and issues
- Broad based support and cooperation with response and recovery efforts
- Feedback from affected publics and correction of any misunderstandings/rumors
- Ongoing explanation and reiteration of self-efficacy and personal response activities (how/where to get more information) begun in Stage II.
- Informed decision-making by the public based on understanding of risks/benefits

IV. **Resolution (Updates Regarding Resolution; Discussions about Cause and New Risks/New Understandings of Risk)** Public communication and campaigns directed toward the general public and affected groups seeking to:
- Inform and persuade about ongoing clean-up, remediation, recovery, and rebuilding efforts
- Facilitate broad-based, honest, and open discussion and resolution of issues regarding cause, blame, responsibility, and adequacy of response.
- Improve/create public understanding of new risks and new understandings of risk as well as new risk avoidance behaviors and response procedures
- Promote the activities and capabilities of agencies and organizations to reinforce positive corporate identity and image

V. **Evaluation (Discussions of Adequacy of Response; Consensus about Lessons and New Understandings of Risks)** Communication directed toward agencies and the response community to:
- Evaluate and assess responses, including communication effectiveness
- Document, formalize, and communicate lessons learned
- Determine specific actions to improve crisis communication and crisis response capability
- Create linkages to pre-crisis activities (Stage I)

Reynolds, B., & Seeger, M. W. (2005). Crisis and Emergency Risk Communication as an integrative model. *Journal of Health Communication Research, 10*(1), 43–55.

for all other stages in the CERC model" (2008). CERC became an important framework when the agency was called on to respond to what was arguably the worst natural disaster to affect the United States in the last century, Hurricane Katrina.

Vanderford, Nastoff, Telfer, and Bonzo (2007) undertook an extensive analysis of the CDC's communication in response to Katrina. The CDC's responsibilities during natural disasters such as hurricanes focus on public health. The CDC distributes health information before and after these events in hopes of reducing or mitigating harm. The agency had used the CERC framework to developed extensive communication resources and capabilities before the onset of the 2005 hurricane season. Following the CERC model, the agency had anticipated many of the communication exigencies associated with Katrina. In addition, Vanderford (2007) and her colleagues point out that the CDC had learned important lessons from previous hurricane responses. The agency had established partnerships with local agencies and organizations, including Lowes, Inc., home improvement stores, to distribute messages and resources. Multiple health protection messages and guidance concerning preparedness, carbon monoxide poisoning, chain-saw safety, and boiling water were developed. These messages were distributed in advance and were pre-positioned for post-event delivery.

In addition to partnerships with various local groups and agencies, the CDC had engaged in significant message testing and adaptation. This process included public service announcements and messages distributed through local media. The crisis itself created additional exigencies requiring further adaptation and localization of messages. Moreover, the prolonged nature of Hurricane Katrina extended the CDC's communication requirements. Vanderford (2007) and her colleagues note "communication tasks emerged and evolved as the incident focus changed" (pp. 23–24). This evolution required new messages, sources, and channels. In fact, the agency remained in the disaster zone and provided support at evacuation centers to inform and persuade affected publics about ongoing clean-up, remediation, and recovery efforts.

Finally, the CDC has conducted extensive evaluations of its response to Katrina. Vanderford (2007) and her colleagues note three areas where important lessons were learned. First, the agency learned that rapid dissemination of messages was critical and that, in many instances, the conditions on the ground severely impeded rapid response. Second, messages had to be adapted for diverse location, audiences, and circumstances. Finally, as the CERC model suggests, various messages and message strategies were required at different phases in the crisis.

In the following section, we describe the ways in which CERC has informed pandemic preparedness efforts. This discussion draws from a variety of planning documents and training materials developed by the CDC and partner public health agencies to address the threat of pandemic influenza. While pandemic influenza, as of this writing, is still in the pre-crisis stage, it has precipitated a great deal of pre-crisis communication and planning at a variety of levels.

AVIAN INFLUENZA (H5N1) AND PANDEMIC INFLUENZA

While Katrina was one of the United States' most devastating natural disasters, it is dwarfed by the potential devastation of pandemic influenza. Most observers use the 1918 pandemic influenza as a reference for clarifying the threat. This event, which also involved a bird virus, claimed as many as 25 million lives world wide and 700,000 in the United States in 1918 and 1919. The outbreak occurred in three waves, affecting a disproportionate number of young and healthy individuals. An estimated 28% of the U.S. population was infected (Crosby, 2003). Other much smaller instances of pandemic influenza occurred in 1957 and in 1968. Projections from the CDC place the possible casualty rate from a modern pandemic flu at between 200,000 and 2 million.

Not surprisingly, the threat posed by pandemic influenza had generated a great deal of effort by federal agencies, including a variety of communication initiatives. Moreover, avian influenza (H5N1) and the possibility of emergent pandemic influenza illustrate one of the fundamental challenges of the CERC framework. More specifically, public health officials must warn people of the risk and prepare them psychologically for the possibility of an avian outbreak and for the more remote possibility of a human pandemic. Officials must also encourage the public to take appropriate precautions. This warning must be modulated so as not to create social disruption and a sense of futility or despair: public health officials must raise awareness and concern without inducing irrational behavior. This is a daunting challenge due to the need for public health officials to prepare the public for the possibility of severe social disruption, mass causalities, and inadequate medical resources. This line of communication must also clearly distinguish avian influenza (H5N1) and virulent and non-virulent forms from pandemic influenza, while clarifying the potential of one to precipitate the other. The communication activities associated with these challenges are clearly specified by the CERC process as part of the pre-crisis stage. Beyond public preparation, CERC also suggests that coordination among responders as well as how the development of resources and response capability should occur.

The CDC, the Department of Health and Human Services (DHHS), the World Health Organization (WHO), and other public health groups are active in developing crisis communication plans, coordinating response capabilities, and in communicating pre-event guidance and preparation messages to the public. In fact, HHS officials have described communication as a sort of societal medication, or "social Tamiflu," which can help manage the sociological aspects of a pandemic in ways that could actually contain and reduce harm. In this manner, effective communication is generally seen as a central component of any response (Reissman, Watson, Klomp, Tanielian, & Prior, 2006; Osterholm, 2005). For example, one of the strategies most often proposed for managing and containing a widespread infectious disease outbreak is social distancing. Social distancing is a broad class of strategies ranging from reduction of social interaction, to isolation and voluntary home quarantine of patients and their contacts, and travel restrictions (Glass, Glass, Beyeler, & Min, 2006). Businesses, for example, are being encouraged to plan for telecommuting as a strategy for maintaining social distance among employees (Gill, 2006; U.S. Department of Labor, 2007). School closing will likely be used as a way to reduce exposure and transmission of the virus. Social distancing requires a great deal of pre-event planning, education, justification, and persuasion. Effective communication, therefore, is necessary for the use of social distancing as an intervention strategy for pandemic influenza.

DHHS has also announced a number of additional initiatives for state and federal agencies. These include the stockpiling of appropriate medication, such as the anti-viral agent Tamiflu (oseltamivir phosphate) and continued research and development of new vaccines and new vaccine technologies. The web site Pandemicflu.gov has been used as a central location for educational materials, press releases, planning documents and guidances. Public health agencies and independent spokespersons have issued statements that are largely consistent with one another and with the larger agency message. The CDC, for example, has hosted a number of state and regional summits, which include public health officials, business leaders, community leaders, and members of the preparedness community (Centers for Disease Control and Prevention, 2007). These meetings have been designed to promote partnerships and cooperation within communities and across agencies. In its messages, the CDC has sought to carefully differentiate avian influenza (H5N1) from the possible mutation that might occur, leading to pandemic. These messages are also consistent with the messages offered by WHO. Before his death in May 2006, then WHO Director General Lee Jong-wook spoke to a major summit of African public health officials on March 6, 2006. In this address, the director sought to differentiate avian influenza from pandemic flu and offered specific recommendations for preparation and response.

> Countries on this continent must be equipped to take many important actions. **One:** they must be able to find, confirm and quickly report H5N1 in birds—whether wild or domestic. They must then take immediate action to stop the bird outbreaks. In Africa in particular, immediate "on-the-spot" cash compensation to backyard poultry owners is necessary, or they will have no incentive to cull. **Two:** countries must be equipped to find, confirm and treat people who may be ill with this bird virus. **Three:** countries must be able to collect, examine and share virus samples from these people, in order to determine whether the virus is changing in any way. Every country must have an avian influenza and human pandemic influenza preparedness plan. (Jong-wook, 2006)

In addition to his efforts to distinguish avian influenza from pandemic, Jong-wook also offered a clear preparedness message consistent with the recommendations of the CERC model.

One of the deficiencies in the pandemic influenza plan concerns what kinds of preparedness activities should be undertaken. In hurricane episodes, for example, pre-crisis preparedness would include stockpiling food and water, preparing for evaluations, boarding up houses, and closely monitoring weather reports. In the case of avian flu and the possibility pandemic influenza, appropriate preparedness advice is much less self- evident and, as described below, much more difficult to effectively communicate.

Although specific recommendations have been distributed to public health and preparedness agencies both domestically and locally, more limited information has also been disseminated about personal preparedness. As noted above, this may be in part due to the difficulties in offering specific advice about a highly equivocal situation. In one example of this difficulty, the DHHS issued an individual preparedness checklist that included recommendations for stockpiling food (HSS, 2006). In response to a question, DHHS Secretary Mike Leavitt recommended buying extra cans of tuna and powdered milk. The recommendation resulted in the same level of media ridicule as did Secretary of Homeland Security, Tom Ridge's earlier remarks about duct tape and plastic sheeting as an effective defense against bio terrorism. In subsequent comments, Leavitt was able to clarify and contextualize his remarks.

By far, the most important Stage 1 communication about pandemic influenza has been the release of the official *National Strategy for Pandemic Influenza: Implementation Plan*. This 386-page document outlines plans for response; clarifies authority relationships, including command, control, and coordination protocols; and identifies available resources. The document also outlines an approach to communication, which is largely consistent with the CERC model:

> The need for timely, accurate, credible, and consistent information that is tailored to specific audiences cannot be overstated. This requires coordinated messaging by spokespersons across government, at the local, State, tribal, and Federal levels, and by our international partners. It also requires the designation and training of a cadre of spokespersons within relevant organizations, the ability to provide guidance in the setting of incomplete information, and the acknowledgement that this guidance may change as more information becomes available. Such a capability should be developed before a pandemic, as should the key messages that we know we will have to communicate upon the emergence of a pandemic virus. (National Strategy for Pandemic Influenza: Implementation Plan, 2006, p. 20)

As noted earlier, DHHS and the CDC have initiated a number of training activities for state, local, and federal officials who might be expected to communicate about pandemic influenza. Moreover, these activities have brought together representatives across agencies, including U.S. Fish and Wildlife, U.S. Department of Agriculture, Department of Homeland Security, CDC, and DHHS. Also included are state-level counterparts to these agencies as well as governors' press secretaries and representatives from tribal nations. The goals of this training are to build awareness of the threats, create capacity, and to foster coordination and cooperation. In addition, a variety of communication resources have been made available on the official pandemic web site(Pandemicflu.gov.) These resources include media guides from DHHS and WHO, as well as training materials, background information, and fact sheets from the CDC.

Even more recently, the CDC issued its Interim Pre-pandemic Planning Guidance: Community Strategy for Pandemic Influenza Mitigation in the United States (2007). This document focuses on the use of "layered, non-pharmaceutical interventions" as ways to contain and control an outbreak. The guidance plan outlines four primary interventions:

> 1) Isolation and treatment (as appropriate) with influenza antiviral medications of all persons with confirmed or probable pandemic influenza; 2) Voluntary home quarantine of members of households

> with confirmed or probably case(s) and consideration of combining this intervention with others (sic); 3) Dismissal of students (including public and private schools as well as colleges and universities and school based activities ... 4) Use of social distancing measures to reduce contact between adults in the community and workplace, including, for example, cancellations of large public gatherings (sic). (Centers for Disease Control and Prevention, 2007, p. 4)

These four interventions represent the primary social dimensions to an integrated pandemic influenza response. They are grounded in a traditional infections disease methodology of containing and limiting an outbreak. The National Strategy for Pandemic Influenza: Implementation Plan, for example, includes the strategy of using ring vaccinations and distribution of Tamifue as a containment and control strategy. The Guidance for Community Strategies builds upon these pharmaceutical approaches with various behavioral changes.

The Guidance outlines a wide variety of assumptions about effective response and recommends specific strategies. This includes a specific view of the role of communication as central to success:

> [G]enerating appropriate risk communication content/materials and an effective means for delivery, soliciting active community support and involvement in strategic planning decisions, and assisting individuals and families in addressing their own preparedness needs are critical factors in achieving success. (Centers for Disease Control and Prevention, 2007, p. 14)

As described by the CERC model, pre-event communication supports the development of plans at various levels by providing information about preparedness. The Guidance also describes "coordinated" and "consistent" communication as necessary to building and maintaining public trust and as strategy for containing anxiety and fear (Centers for Disease Control and Prevention, 2007, p. 48).

The Guidance also fulfills another important CERC function by specifying the various audiences to whom pandemic influenza messages should be targeted. This includes businesses and other employers, childcare programs, elementary and secondary schools, colleges and universities, faith-based and community organizations, and individuals and families. The Guidance outlines specific preparedness suggestions for each of these groups, including recommendations for communicating with their constituencies. Schools, colleges, and universities are encouraged to "provide faculty, staff and students with information about the importance of hand hygiene ... and about covering coughs..." (p. 96). In addition, the Guidance makes recommendations about communicating about college and university preparedness plans to with faculty, staff, and students.

The various planning documents and training initiatives have been robust, and communication strategies have been central to these efforts. These initiatives have been structured as general outlines of strategies as opposed to specific tactics or messages. This approach allows agencies and organizations at other levels to implement the recommendations by adapting them to local circumstances and audiences. These initiatives are also general in a manner that reflects the larger uncertainty associated with the pandemic influenza threat.

Pandemic Through the Lens of CERC

As discussed earlier, CERC is an integrated, developmental approach to communication. It is based on the assumption that effective pre-event communication and planning will improve the response and mitigate the harm in subsequent stages. While the threat of an influenza pandemic, as of this writing, can still be placed in late Stage 1 Pre-Crisis, notable resources and activities have been invested in communication and planning. Moreover, significant outbreaks of H5N1 continue to occur throughout Asia, Africa, and Europe, and 166 human deaths have been reported by WHO. From the perspective of the CERC model, the Stage 1 response to the threat of pandemic influenza has been vigorous, although challenges continue to emerge. The CERC model describes communication activities as largely educational and preparatory, with significant emphasis placed on developing cooperative relationships, alliances, and consensual recommendations by the medical community. Public messages should seek to create a realistic understanding of the threat, and establish specific actions that may be taken should the threat emerge. In addition, Stage 1 actions should focus on establishing and communicating the specific policies, procedures, and plans that would be executed in subsequent stages.

As described earlier, the complexities of creating a broad-based public understanding of pandemic influenza and avian influenza (H5N1) have challenged the CDC, DHHS, WHO, and many state and local heath departments. It is not clear that these agencies have been successful in distinguishing between the two in ways that allow the public to develop an accurate or realistic understanding of the risk. Some critics have also charged that the risk level is actually being inflated (Normile, 2005). Moreover, Stage 1 communication has the potential to desensitize the public to the issue and create the perception of futility and inevitability particularly if the communication is not grounded in sound science that presents the threat in a realistic manner. The post-anthrax and post-SARS environment within which messages about pandemic influence are being communicated encourages frequent communication and direct public warnings (Wilkins, 2005). In addition, it is not entirely clear as to how the public should prepare. Advice such as that offered by Secretary Levitt has the potential to confuse the public and trivialize preparedness. CDC's web-based guidance for individuals and families describes food stockpiling, maintaining an adequate supply of prescription drugs, and staying informed (U.S. Department of Labor, 2007). Other actions, such as those proposed by the Interim Pre-Pandemic Planning Guidance, are community- or organizationally-based.

One striking feature of Stage 1 communication has been the high level of coordination across agency and across international, national, state, and local levels. Perhaps as a consequence of the coordination failures with the anthrax event, subsequent efforts have emphasized building cooperative relationships among agencies. Moreover, there is also a broad recognition that pandemic influenza will require a multi-agency approach and that the treat is global. Modern transportation systems will likely spread any outbreak very rapidly. This coordination is largely a function of multi-agency training and the general guidance documents issued by WHO and the CDC.

An additional feature of Stage 1 communication about pandemic flu has been the remarkable consistency of message. This consistency of message is likely a consequence of the coordination efforts described above. With few exceptions, the various government agencies and public health groups have offered very similar advice and suggestions. This consistency includes both domestic and international groups. The level of concern expressed has also been generally consistent. In part, this may be due to the 1918 pandemic as a common reference. This form of consistent Stage 1 communication has served to reduce the overall ambiguity with what is inevitably a highly uncertain issue.

The ongoing challenge with communication regarding pandemic influenza is how to communicate appropriate concern and a realistic understanding of the risk at this early stage without promoting unnecessary fear or inappropriate responses. Alternatively, public health agencies risk creating complacency or reducing their own credibility if their predictions are found to be inaccurate. The consensus of the scientific and public health communities is that pandemic influenza is a certainty. Significant uncertainty exists about timing and severity. Effective communication in these circumstances is challenging.

DISCUSSION

This analysis of the communication and preparedness for pandemic influenza using the elements specified by CERC validates some aspects of the model and illustrates the challenges in planning for a major crisis. Initially, the CERC model and this assessment of it provide a clear endorsement for crisis planning in general. The message development, message testing, alliances, and resource coordination that have already taken place in response to H5N1 would not exist without thoughtful planning. Any agency can greatly increase its chances of responding effectively to a crisis situation by engaging in the type of assessment and planning emphasized in the CERC model.

Another area of success for the CERC model is its comprehensive view of risk and crisis. A primary goal in establishing the CERC model was to create a planning mechanism that encompassed both risk and crisis communication. The model provided a seamless transition from risk communication to crisis communication in response to Hurricane Katrina. Similarly, the CERC model informs CDC officials as they develop risk messages in the United States and participate in crisis management as human cases of H5N1 occur throughout Asia, Africa, and Europe.

The monitoring and preparation aspects of the CERC model are also validated by this analysis. The CDC is currently engaged in an unprecedented degree of world-wide monitoring for H5N1. Preparation continues to expand as more information and resources become available. The need for alliances and cooperation are also illustrated in the H5N1 case study. The CERC model effectively establishes such collaboration as essential for successfully transitioning from risk communication to crisis communication. In addition, the ongoing message development and message testing continue to enhance the CDC's ability to respond appropriately as the H5N1 situation evolves.

The CERC model is also successful in addressing the complexity of audiences in risk and crisis situations. Empathy, an appropriate spokesperson, uncertainty reduction, and self-efficacy are essential aspects of risk and crisis communication that are often overlooked. The H5N1 case reflects a clear and effective dedication to these aspects by the CDC, DHHS, and WHO. Those who apply the CERC model in other crisis situations will certainly benefit from the model's emphasis on audience adaptation.

The CERC model's focus on interagency coordination is another key strength. When planning for and responding to a crisis as vast and complex as a pandemic influenza, no nation can or should operate independently. By collaborating with WHO, CDC has developed unprecedented relationships with health officials in countries already coping with H5N1. Monitoring and resource coordination are also occurring at a global level. This strength of the CERC model, however, also reveals an inherent weakness. The collaboration advocated by the CERC model is, by its nature, precarious. Any nation or region could severely impede effective risk and crisis communication by violating the trust of other nations. For example, China's unwillingness to cooperate with WHO in the early stages of the SARS crisis illustrates the potential danger of disunity. The CERC model appropriately emphasizes the need for interagency and international collaboration, but establishing and maintaining this collaboration is a difficult and tenuous process.

A concern for the CERC model and for crisis management plans in general is that considerably more attention is paid to the initial steps than to the later stages. The preparation and coordination phases can and should be enacted and assessed with regularity. The later stages, however, cannot be fully examined without the onset of a crisis event. Two observations are important in addressing this potential weakness. First, when crises do occur, the CERC model allows for learning from the crisis event. This learning can be done by the agency facing the crisis or the learning process can be accomplished vicariously through observation. Second, the later stages of the CERC model can be applied and evaluated through simulations and tabletop exercises. For example, the CDC has engaged in table exercises as it prepares for a potential pandemic influenza. These activities allow agencies to test their readiness in all aspects and at all stages of a crisis situation.

Another area of concern raised in this analysis is the potential for perceived risk inflation through overly zealous communication. The CERC model advocates considerable preparation and thoughtful communication at all stages. The CDC cautions, however, against too much communication at the early pre-event stages (Reynolds, Deitch, & Schieber, 2006). There is always the temptation to initiate a general campaign at these stages rather than target only those who are actively seeking information or provide more general infection control advice. In some recent cases, public health agencies have been overly zealous in their pandemic communication. These tendencies are exacerbated by media organizations willing to sensationalize issues to build ratings (Lewis, 2008). Such general campaigns and media sensationalizing has the potential to desensitize the public or foster a cynical reaction from some portions of the public. Moreover, at this stage such communication may be an inefficient use of communication resources. Thus, constant monitoring of audience needs and interests and ongoing message testing are paramount. Messages must be carefully modulated and the CERC model should not be misinterpreted as a license to signal general public alarms at the early pre-crisis stages. Risk and crisis communicators must also be mindful of the potential for such communication to foster feelings of helplessness and responses that increase the potential for the "worried well" to burden the medical system.

As the CERC model is applied and refined in the future, practitioners must also remain cognizant of the unpredictability of crisis situations. Although the CERC model may provide essential advice, no model can fully comprehend the complexity of a crisis situation. Those applying the CERC model must be mindful of the unique and unanticipated aspects of every risk and crisis situation. Agility in managing the unanticipated aspects of a crisis is essential. The National Center for Food Protection and Defense makes this point clear in their recommendations for best practices in risk and crisis communication. They advise risk and crisis communicators to "continuously evaluate and update their crisis plans" (Seeger, 2006, p. 236). This is important advice when applying the CERC model.

The 2001 anthrax episode forever changed the role of the CDC. From that point forward, the CDC has been recognized as a primary source of public communication in health-related risk and crisis situations. The CERC model is a product of the CDC's increased communication vigilance. The comprehensive nature of the model allows for a sophisticated and audience-sensitive approach for managing risk and crisis situations. As such, the CERC model offers a cutting edge approach to managing risk and crisis communication.

CONCLUSION

The threat posed by pandemic influenza is profound and warrants a substantive level of preparation and planning. In fact, the CDC describes pandemic influenza as a certainty. The only significant questions concern the timing, scope of harm, and the nature and effectiveness of the response. A critical component of any effective response will involve strategic communication. Application of the CERC model developed by the CDC significantly improves the likelihood that many of these communication activities will help contain and limit the harm. Any communication strategy, however, must be sufficiently dynamic and equivocal to match the inherent complexity and uncertainty that accompanies the threat

REFERENCES

Anthrax Case Timeline (2003). *Journal of Health Communication, 8*(supplement), 1–2.

Ballard-Reisch, D., Clements-Nolle, K., Jenkins, T., Sacks, T., Pruitt, K., & Leathers, K. (2008). Applying the Crisis and Emergency Risk Communication (CERC) Integrative Model to Bioterrorism Preparedness: A Nevada Case Study. In M. Seeger, T. Sellnow, & R. R. Ulmer (Eds.), *Crisis communication and the public health* (pp. 203–220). Cresskill, NJ: Hampton.

Benoit, W. L. (1995). *Accounts, excuses, and apologies.* Albany: State University of New York Press.

Centers for Disease Control and Prevention (2007). Interim pre-pandemic planning guidance: Community strategy for pandemic influenza mitigation in the United States. Retrieved February 3, 2007, from http://pandemicflu.gov/plan/community/mitigation.html.

Cole, L. A. (2003). *The anthrax letters.* Washington, DC: Joseph Henry Press.

Coombs, W. T. (1995). The development of guidelines for the selection of the "appropriate" crisis response strategies. *Management Communication Quarterly, 4,* 447–476.

Covello, V. T. (1992). Risk communication: An emerging area of health communication research. In S. A. Deetz (Ed.), *Communication Yearbook 15* (pp. 359–373). Newbury Park, CA: Sage.

Crosby, A. W. (2003). *America's forgotten pandemic: The influenza of 1918.* New York: Cambridge University Press.

Glass R. J., Glass, L. M., Beyeler W. E., & Min H. J. (2006). Targeted social distancing design for pandemic influenza. *Emerging Infectious Disease, 12.* Retrieved December 15, 2006, from http://www.cdc.gov/ncidod/EID/vol12no11/06-0255.htm.

Gill, T. (2006). Countering the economic effects of bird flu through telework. *Journal of Business Continuity and Emergency Planning, 1,* 27–36.

Health and Human Services (2006). Individual and Family Preparedness Checklist. Retrieved January 15, 2007, from http://www.pandemicflu.gov/planguide/checklist.html.

Interim Pre-pandemic Planning Guidance: Community Strategy for Pandemic Influenza Mitigation in the United States. (2007). Retrieved February 7, 2007, from http://www,pandemicflu.gov/plan/community_mitigation.pdf

Jong-wook, L. (2006, March). WHO Statement to press conference, 9 March, 2006. Retrieved March 11, 2006, from http://www.who.int/dg/lee/speeches/2006/mbagathi_hospital/en/index.html.

Lewis, M.. (2008). Breaking news: and a public health crisis. In M. Seeger, T. Sellnow, & R. R. Ulmer (Eds.), *Crisis communication and the public health* (pp. 257–272). Cresskill, NJ: Hampton.

National strategy for pandemic influenza: Implementation plan, (2006). Retrieved February 17, 2006 from http://www.whitehouse.gov/homeland/pandemic-influenza.html.

Normile, D. (2005). Avian influenza: Pandemic skeptics warn against crying wolf. *Science, 18,* 1112–1113. Retrieved December 15, 2006, from http://www.sciencemag.org/cgi/content/summary/310/5751/1112.

Novak, J.M., & Barrett. M. S. (2008). Tracking the Anthrax story: Spokespersons and effective risk/crisis communication. In M. Seeger, T., Sellnow, & R. R. Ulmer (Eds.),*Crisis communication and the public health* (pp. 43–58). Cresskill, NJ: Hampton.

Osterholm, M. (2005). Preparing for the next pandemic. *New England Journal of Medicine. 352,* 1839–1842.

Plough, A., & Krimsky, S. (1987). The emergence of risk communication studies: Social and political context. *Science, Technology, and Human Values,* 12, 4–10.

Plough, A., & Krimsky, S. (1990). The emergence of risk communication studies: Social and political Context. In T. S. Glickman & M. Gough (Eds.), *Readings in risk* (pp. 223–231). Washington, DC: Resources for the Future.

Quinn, S. Q., Thomas, T., & McAllister, C. (2005). Postal workers' perspectives on communication during the anthrax attack. *Biosecurity and Bioterrorism: Biodefense Strategy, Practice, and Science, 3,* 207–215.

Reissman D. B., Watson, P. J., Klomp, R. W., Tanielian, T. L., & Prior, S. D. (2006). Pandemic influenza preparedness: Adaptive responses to an evolving challenge. *Journal of Homeland Security and Emergency Management, 3,* 2. Retrieved December 15, 2006, from http://www.bepress.com/jhsem/vol3/iss2/13.

Reynolds, B., Galdo, J. H., & Sokler, L. (2002). *Crisis and emergency risk communication.* Atlanta, GA: Centers for Disease Control and Prevention.

Reynolds, B, Deitch, S., & Schieber, R. (2006). *Crisis and emergency risk communication: Pandemic influenza.* Atlanta, GA: Centers for Disease Control and Prevention.

Reynolds, B., & Seeger, M. W. (2005). Crisis and emergency risk communication as an integrative model. *Journal of Health Communication Research, 10*(1) 43–55.

Robinson, S. J., & Newstetter, W. C. (2003). Uncertain science and certain deadlines: CDC responses to the media during the anthrax attacks of 2001. *Journal of Health Communication, 8,* 17–35.

Seeger, M. W. (2006). Best practices in crisis and emergency risk communication. *Journal of Applied Communication Research, 34,* 232–244.

Seeger, M. W., & Reynolds, B. (2008). Crisis communication and the public health: Integrative approaches and new imperatives. In M. Seeger, T. Sellnow, & R. R. Ulmer (Eds.), *Crisis communication and the public health* (pp. 3–23). Cresskill, NJ: Hampton.

Wilkins, L. (2005). Plagues, pestilence and pathogens: The ethical implications of news reporting of a world health crisis. *Asian Journal of Communication. 15,* 247–254.

Witte, K. (1992). Preventing AIDS through persuasive communications: A framework for constructing effective, culturally specific, preventative health messages. *International and Intercultural Health Communication Annual, 16,* 67–86.

Witte, K. (1995). Generating effective risk messages: How scary should risk communication be? In B. B. Burleson (Ed.), *Communication Yearbook, 19* (pp. 229–254). Thousand Oaks. CA: Sage.

U.S. Department of Labor (2007). Guidance on preparing workplaces for an influenza pandemic. OSHA 3327-02N 2007. Retrieved January 15, 2007, from http://www.osha.gov/Publications/influenza_pandemic.html#maintain_operations.

Vanderford, M. (2003). Communication lessons learned in the Emergency Operations Center during CDC's anthrax response: A commentary. *Journal of Health Communication*, *8*, 11–12.

Vanderford, M., Nastoff, T., Telfer, J. L., & Bonzo, S. E. (2007). Emergency communication challenges in response to Hurricane Katrina: Lessons for the Centers for Disease Control and Prevention. *Journal of Applied Communication Research*, *35*, 9–25.

25

How People Think about Cancer: A Mental Models Approach

Julie S. Downs, Wändi Bruine de Bruin, and Baruch Fischhoff
Carnegie Mellon University

Bradford Hesse
National Cancer Institute's Health Communication and Informatics Research Branch

Ed Maibach
George Mason University

BACKGROUND

Fear and Complexity of Cancer May Impede Understanding

People fear cancer: the diagnosis, the treatments, and the prognosis (Freimuth, Stein, & Kean, 1989). That is true not only for adults, but also for children, who worry about getting cancer themselves (Chin, Schonfeld, O'Hare, Mayne, Salovey, Showalter, & Cicchetti, 1998). Perceived seriousness is one of the major organizing factors by which people differentiate diseases (Turk, Rudy, & Salovey, 1985), making cancer particularly salient. One possible source of the intense reaction to cancer risks is how easily worst-case cancer scenarios come to mind (Tversky & Kahneman, 1973). Another is the tendency of mass media to infuse cancer with fear, in part by portraying cancer as inevitable and fatal (Clarke & Everest, 2006). Exceptionally bad experiences with cancer are more salient than cases treated early and effectively—many of which never come to others' attention at all. As a result, people may overestimate cancer's uncontrollability and the negative consequences that will follow a diagnosis (Silverman, Woloshin, Schwartz, Byram, Welch, & Fischhoff, 2001). Such fear can be a barrier to screening (Subramanian, Klosterman, Amonkar, & Hunt, 2004) and contribute to choosing extreme treatments such as radical mastectomy among women who are candidates for breast-conserving surgery (Nold, Beamer, Helmer, & McBoyle, 2000) and prophylactic mastectomy among women with a family history of breast cancer, which they regret later (Montgomery, Tran, Heelan, van Zee, Massie, Payne, & Borgen, 1999; Peters, McCaul, Stefanek, & Nelson, 2006).

Another potential barrier to informed decisions about cancer is the sheer number and complexity of the decisions that might need to be made (Fischhoff, 2005; McCaul, Peters, Nelson, & Stefanek, 2005). There are many cancers, each posing choices regarding prevention, screening, and treatment—often requiring mastery of unfamiliar and uncertain domains. In response to this complexity, health care educators and providers have labored to bring the facts of cancer to people, for example using decision aids aimed at patients facing cancer-related decisions (O'Connor, Fiset, DeGrasse, Graham, Evans, Stacey, Laupacis, & Tugwell, 1999). Where such interventions have been evaluated, the results have been mixed. Although patients rate complex decision aids as more helpful than simpler ones, their actual knowledge of cancer is similar with both (O'Connor, Stacey, Rovner, Holmes-Rovner, Tetroe, Llewellyn-Thomas, Entwistle, Rostom, Fiset, Barry, & Jones, 2001).

Many agencies try to raise awareness of cancer, with actions like community events and public service announcements. Unfortunately, that well-meaning strategy may undermine the decision making of individuals who lack an overall understanding of cancer risks. For example, they may disproportionately increase cancer's perceived risks, without creating a balanced appreciation of the control options. Of course, awareness can have benefits as well: increasing citizens' demands for cancer research, eliciting compassion for survivors and those who have lost loved ones, and promoting timely screening. Communication strategies must weigh these benefits against the risks of creating an unrealistic fear of cancer. They can only do that with a comprehensive view of the decisions that people face, accompanied by an empirically grounded understanding of the beliefs and values brought to them. Without such perspective, communications risk rousing fearful emotions, without providing the factual knowledge needed to stabilize them.

Understanding New Information

People try to make sense of the world around them by integrating new information with existing beliefs. If those old beliefs are erroneous or confused, new information may be hard to process (Karasz, McKee, & Roybal, 2003). Successful integration requires creating coherent *mental models*, allowing people to make sense of what they hear and make consistent inferences regarding the situations that they face. Affording people such mental models requires understanding the beliefs that they already hold in their intuitive formulations. Cancer communications structured around such existing sets of beliefs will be capable of building on correct beliefs and fixing incorrect ones. A scientific examination of lay beliefs should focus on the topics identified by cancer science as most relevant to achieving the goals that matter most to people. The *mental models* approach seeks these ends by integrating decision theory and behavioral research (Morgan, Fischhoff, Bostrom, & Atman, 2001).

In past work, we have focused on the facts most relevant to specific cancer-related decisions, including ones involving prosthetic breast implants (Byram, Fischhoff, Embrey, & Bruine de Bruin, 2001), exposure to carcinogenic household chemicals (Riley, Fischhoff, Small, & Fischbeck, 2001), and the capabilities of mammography (Silverman et al., 2001). Each application typically focused on one or two aspects of the complex processes by which a particular cancer risk is created and controlled. However, each such choice is also embedded in people's general beliefs about the processes creating and controlling cancer risks. For example, people care about risk factors because they worry about what might happen if they got cancer. Those in treatment often wonder how they got their cancer. And so on. Narrowly targeted communications may not provide needed context, leaving people with disparate beliefs, loosely organized around whatever overall mental model of cancer they happen to have. The resulting communications can be inefficient, by starting from scratch each time, and ineffective, by creating a fragmented and confusing overall picture, making people feel overwhelmed by a problem that they can't get their minds around. More comprehensive, basic education about cancer can provide broader understanding, which serves as a basis for future, more specific messages (Schonfeld, Bases, Quackenbush, Mayne, Morra, & Cicchetti, 2001).

Consequences of Broad Misconceptions

Without basic understanding of a domain, people have difficulty using whatever knowledge they do have. For example, experiences with minor diseases are sometimes inappropriately generalized to major diseases, resulting in misleading mental models (Lau & Hartman, 1983). In the context of cancer, that might account for the tendencies to blame general targets, such as stress and diet, and adopt unsuitable treatments, such as antibiotics or insulin (Payne, 1990). During the 1990s, most women followed the debate about routine mammography screening for women aged 40–49, but many believed that the only drawback to such screening was the cost to insurers, failing to recognize the increased risk of false positives (Woloshin, Schwartz, Byram, Sox, Fischhoff, & Welch, 2000). That misunderstanding is consistent with a mental model in which all tumors grow rapidly (Carlsson & Strang, 1997).

These facts are not hard to explain. However, they do need to be conveyed in a way that contributes to a coherent, accurate mental model. Thus one might build on the standard approach of developing communications focused on changing specific behaviors (e.g., Hornik, 2002) by embedding them in a broader context. Here, we provide such complementary research, by seeking to identify a common conceptualization that will help people to interpret decision-specific communications and to make appropriate inferences in situations where relevant, authoritative communications are absent.

National Cancer Institute's Challenge Goal

In 2003, the National Cancer Institute (NCI) described its Challenge to the Nation: "to eliminate the suffering and death due to cancer" (von Eschenbach, 2005). More specifically, the Institute committed itself to reducing the burden of cancer, casting it as no longer mysterious and frightening, but as a challenge that was being overcome through progress in research and practice. Implicitly, the Institute asked the public to stop hoping for the elusive "cure" for cancer and, instead, to fight cancer at each stage of the process: preventing it, delaying its onset, slowing its progress, or living a healthy, productive life with it (see Culliton, 2006, for a similar perspective).

This reformulation requires a major shift in public understanding of cancer—one that is unlikely to be achieved with piecemeal communications about specific cancer risks, screening techniques, and treatments. Pursued in isolation, these messages may undermine the desired transformation, by reinforcing the existing mental models that they evoke. The Institute's strategic formulation is, necessarily, quite abstract. An intermediate conceptualization is needed to create the bridge between the general framework and more specific content that can guide inferences and decisions, in a way that is faithful to both the scientific evidence regarding cancer and people's intuitive ways of thinking. Given the heterogeneity of the processes that need to be understood, we propose that such a model should be metaphoric, providing a general script for organizing narratives about cancer.

A useful metaphor would convey understanding about how cancer acts in the body and can be treated. It would be neither the cancer metaphor denounced by Susan Sontag (1978) as blaming victims and mystifying disease, nor the "military metaphor" of the War on Cancer (Penson, Schapira, Daniels, Chabner, & Lynch Jr., 2004), which undermines the idea of living with a chronic disease caused by a body at war against itself (Skott, 2002). Like other heuristic devices, metaphors cannot provide complete accounts. At best, they can guide generally accurate inferences. As a result, a metaphor that works for the public might sometimes offend experts, who can readily identify its limitations. Those experts would have to be convinced that: (a) a deliberately selected metaphor leads to better inferences and choices than the intuitively selected metaphors it replaces, and (b) a metaphor's limitations are understood well enough to avoid mistaken inferences (e.g., by explicitly contradicting them).

APPROACH

The Interviews

The research reported here implements the initial steps of a mental models approach, describing lay beliefs in their intuitive formulations, focused on cancer-related issues identified by NCI domain specialists. These issues cover the full range of cancer concerns, including risk factors, disease progression, symptom identification, test choice and interpretation, treatment risks and benefits, recovery, and risk of death. We use the mental models approach to interviewing, in which open-ended questions focus interviewees with increasing specificity on the target issues. Participants are encouraged to express their full range of beliefs and concerns in their own words. The beliefs and language revealed in these interviews show conceptions and misconceptions that people bring to their cancer-related choices and to their interpretation of cancer risk communication.

With given research resources, such intensive interviews can reach a relatively limited sample. However, they provide the foundation for developing structured knowledge tests that could be administered to larger samples, capable of estimating the population prevalence of beliefs (e.g., Bruine de Bruin, Downs, & Fischhoff, 2007; Palmgren, Morgan, Bruine de Bruin, & Keith, 2004) and interventions targeting specific knowledge gaps and misconceptions (e.g., Downs, Murray, Bruine de Bruin, Penrose, Palmgren, & Fischhoff, 2004). The interviews identify not only the content of such tests and interventions, but also the language that they should use.

The Metaphors

One goal of this research was to identify metaphors that could bridge NCI's strategic concept with specific inferences. To that end, we identified eight candidate metaphors, then examined how people apply each to six key cancer topics: risk factors, disease progression, symptoms, testing, treatment, and outcomes (recovery, recurrence, death).

Based on existing research and consultation with NCI experts, we anticipated finding that many people think of cancer as a kind of invasion by contaminants. Individuals relying on this metaphor may feel the need to remove every single cancerous cell—or else risk death. A contamination metaphor could also prime (useful or exaggerated) thoughts about exposure to hazardous chemicals. It would not prompt thinking about genetic predisposition. Thus, a contamination metaphor could be both useful (e.g., by reducing needless exposures) and damaging (e.g., by encouraging needless anxiety or medical treatment). Another possible metaphor views cancer as a natural process that might be delayed long enough to avoid cancer altogether. That metaphor might help people treat cancer as "just" a part of life, something to live with, rather than have it as an overhanging fear. However, it could also encourage fatalism, leading them to ignore preventive measures. Because the natural process concept is so central to the Institute's thinking, we tested several metaphors representing it, in order to examine their intuitive appeal and associated inferences. We also chose metaphors suggesting less natural processes.

METHODS

Participants

We completed telephone interviews with 30 individuals drawn randomly (by a market research firm) from a national sample, ages 18 to older than 75. Overall, 33% were white, 23% African American, 20% Asian, and 23% Hispanic. Approximately one-third of the sample reported having been diagnosed with cancer, all of whom had relatively mild and easily treated cases (i.e., without chemotherapy or radiation treatments), and were in complete remission. We also interviewed 10 community leaders who serve as cancer outreach communicators in diverse communities across the country. Of those, five were white, one African American, two Asian, and two Hispanic. Consent forms were approved by Carnegie Mellon's Institutional Review Board, and sent by mail or email, with any remaining questions answered over the phone. Differences between the responses of outreach communicators and other participants were minimal; as a result, we pooled responses from all 40 participants (except where noted).

Materials

We included a few key questions from a related national survey with a rigorously developed item pool, in order to compare our participants' cancer knowledge with those of a nationally representative sample. The Health Information National Trends Survey (HINTS) was developed by the Health Communication and Informatics Research Branch of the Division of Cancer Control and Population Sciences as one product of the National Cancer Institute's Extraordinary Opportunity in Cancer Communications (Nelson, Kreps, Hesse, Croyle, Willis, Arora, Rimer, Viswanath, Weinstein, & Alden, 2004). HINTS has a nationally representative, Random Digit Dial (RDD) sample of adults 18 years and older. Like our study, it is administered in one-on-one interviews, eliciting open-ended responses that are then coded. We selected three of its key questions about cancer knowledge to include in our own interviews for comparison.

Our interview protocol began by asking participants to describe their understanding of cancer, focusing, in turn, on six domains determined through our consultation with cancer experts: Risk Factors (causing and preventing cancer), Symptoms (cues that might signal cancer), Testing (routine and diagnostic), Disease Progression, Treatments, and Outcomes (recovery, recurrence and death). Embedded in these general questions were three specific ones from HINTS. They tested knowledge about (a) general risk factors: "Can you think of anything people can do to reduce their chances of getting cancer?"; (b) specific risk factors: "Are there any changes people could make in their eating habits to reduce their chances of getting cancer?"; and (c) screening and testing: "What kinds of tests should people get to find out whether they have cancer?"

The interview protocol described eight metaphors, drawn from the research literature and expert input: (a) heart disease; (b) an infection caused by a parasite, such as a tapeworm or a tick; (c) allergies, such as to dust or peanuts; (d) auto-immune diseases, "where the body attacks its own cells," such as multiple sclerosis or diabetes; (e) the health problems that people get as their body ages, such as osteoporosis or dementia; (f) contamination with something toxic, such as lead poisoning or pesticides in food; (g) infections caused by a virus, such as measles or HIV; and (h) an accident waiting to happen, "such as running with scissors or driving a car that is in very poor condition."

Procedure

Interviewees were asked to start by describing their beliefs regarding each of the six domains (e.g., "Can you think of anything people can do to reduce their chances of getting cancer?" "Can you tell me what you know about how cancer is treated?"). They were asked to expand on each belief that they provided (e.g., how a behavior reduced or increased risk, how a treatment worked). Prompts continued until interviewees reported having nothing more to add. For each domain, interviewees were asked to think of another disease that was like cancer in that respect, then to describe similarities and differences. They were then asked which of the diseases that they had mentioned was most similar to cancer, and why. They were invited to share any personal experience with cancer, if they felt comfortable doing so.

Finally, interviewees considered three of the eight metaphors for cancer, drawn according to a partial Latin-square design. For each, they were asked what conclusions they would draw after learning that a new disease "was kind of like" it (e.g., kind of like being contaminated with something toxic) and how the metaphor did and did not fit cancer. They rated how well each metaphor fit cancer on a 1–5 scale, from "very different" to "very similar."

Qualitative Content Coding

Interviews were transcribed verbatim and each sentence coded into the protocol's topics. A set of codes was created for each, starting with those used by HINTS, then supplemented with new concepts mentioned in the interviews. Any statement that reflected an incorrect assertion or a misunderstanding of a concept was coded as such.

RESULTS

Overall Picture: Fragmentary Mental Models

Risk Factors. When asked what people could do to reduce their chances of getting cancer, 63% of interviewees mentioned "not smoking" (Table 25.1). Most (78%) mentioned improving nutrition (e.g., "eat better"), although they often could not elaborate how or why such a change would be helpful, beyond just listing a couple of basic rules (e.g., eat more vegetables or less red meat; Table 25.2). When asked for a specific dietary change that should reduce cancer risk, 30% could not name even one.

Only 30% mentioned environmental causes as contributing to cancer risk. A mere 13% mentioned exposure to sun (despite the extensive publicity on those risks). Some of those who men-

TABLE 25.1
Responses to "Can You Think of Anything People Can Do to Reduce Their Chances of Getting Cancer?"

Risk factors and strategies	*Interview responses*	*Population (HINTS)*
Don't smoke/Quit smoking	63%	59%
Eat better/Better nutrition	78%	51%
Exercise/Exercise more	48%	25%
Get a check up/Go to the doctor	33%	16%
Don't drink alcohol/Drink less alcohol	18%	11%
Stay out of the sun/Wear sunscreen	13%	9%
Environmental, Chemicals, Pollution, 2nd hand smoke, Pesticides, Wear protective gear	23%	8%
Healthy lifestyle, Positive attitude, Good state of mind, Safe sex, Meditation, Yoga, Moderation, Do not have multiple partners	33%	6%
Get screened for cancer/Get tested	25%	5%
Education, Well informed, Awareness, Books, Research	8%	4%
Reduce stress, Rest, Get enough sleep	8%	3%
Self exams, Body change awareness	15%	2%
Don't do drugs	3%	2%
Knowledge of family history, Good genes, Genetic testing	30%	1%
Limit exposure to carcinogens, Reduce toxins, Avoid causes of cancer	8%	1%
Reduce weight, Maintain healthy weight	3%	1%
Religion, Prayer	0%	0%
Mean number of ways mentioned	*4.03*	*2.31*

TABLE 25.2
Responses to "What Specific Changes Should People Make in Their Eating Habits to Reduce Their Chances of Getting Cancer?"

Proposed changes in eating habits	*Interview responses*	*Population (HINTS)*
Eat more vegetables	50%	51%
Eat less fat	20%	35%
Eat more fruits	35%	34%
Eat more fiber	8%	18%
Eat less red meat	10%	15%
Eat less fast food	5%	11%
Eat a balanced diet/All food groups/Follow food pyramid	10%	9%
Eat less/Healthy/Watch weight/Lose weight	28%	8%
Less processing/chemicals/ preservatives/additives	18%	8%
Take vitamin & mineral supplements/herbal supplements/specific vitamin - food recommendations	8%	6%
Stop drinking alcohol/Reduce alcohol	20%	4%
Less sugar/sweets/sodas	5%	4%
Eat organic/natural/homegrown foods	10%	4%
Drink more water	5%	3%
Watch/lower cholesterol	0%	3%
Research foods/Read labels	0%	1%
Eat less salt/sodium	0%	1%
Mean number of changes mentioned	*2.32*	*2.40*

tioned environmental causes expressed a lack of control (e.g., "Don't breathe the air, I guess." "I don't know what you can do about that, other than, short of moving away."). A few mentioned stress as a cause of cancer or avoiding stress as a way to prevent it.

Although some major cancer risk factors were mentioned by many participants, few could explain how those factors contributed to cancer. Indeed, most did not even try, merely saying that they did not know, as illustrated in these quotations:

- I know that diet affects many other illnesses, diabetes and heart and so forth, but I don't know about cancer. (Hispanic male, age 65–74, no cancer history)
- I don't know much about skin cancer, but I went to tanning beds a lot, and I have lots of moles now, and everyone is telling me that I should go and get them checked because, you know, they say that tanning beds cause cancer. (Hispanic female, age 25–34, history of cervical cancer)

These results indicate a tenuous grasp of cancer risk factors. Even when interviewees knew about a risk factor, they could rarely say very much about its mechanism of action. Without such knowledge, it can be difficult to select and implement effective risk-reduction behaviors, respond to changing circumstances, overcome obstacles, or follow debates about conflicting evidence. For example, without knowing what constitutes a "better" diet, people may waste their energies on fads, possibly even increasing their cancer risk. Conversely, not knowing how a recommended behavior reduces cancer risk may make it easier to make excuses for stopping it.

Symptoms. Interviewees offered various symptoms. About half (45%) said, at some point during the interview, that it is possible to have cancer without knowing it, often sharing stories about people who were surprised to discover that they had cancer. About a third (35%) said that people can have cancer without any symptoms at all. Symptoms ranged from very specific, the most common being lumps in the breast, to very general, such as ill health. Typically, symptoms were seen as a prompt for additional evaluation, rather than as proof of cancer.

- The easiest thing is to just go and get tested for your symptom, what the symptom is, and then you can find out why it's there. (Asian female, age 25–34, no cancer history)
- They wouldn't think they had cancer until they saw something, or felt something … unless they saw a growth or something like that. (Asian male, age 25–34, no cancer history)

Most interviewees said that they would not get cancer tests after every suspicious cough or headache, but could not specify their decisions further. Without a better mental model of symptoms, there seem to be substantial risks of both excessive testing and missing opportunities.

Testing and Screening. On average, interviewees mentioned 2.6 different tests for cancer, with mammography being the most common (Table 25.3). In one of the few differences from lay interviewees, our cancer outreach specialists made fewer statements about the general need for testing or screening, $t(36) = 3.62$, $p < .001$, and more about specific screening recommendations, such as testing people at high risk, $t(38) = 2.13$, $p < .05$, teaching people more about cancer, $t(25) = 2.12$, $p < .05$, and distinguishing among disease processes, $t(25) = 2.12$, $p < .05$. Interviewees generally described testing in terms of following up observed symptoms or engaging in routine screening practices, especially for those at higher risk.

- I have heard of people who have had a sore throat or a problem, thinking it was just a virus that they had or a cold and seek medical advice and find out that, sure enough, they got cancer of the throat or the esophagus or whatever. (Hispanic male, age 65–74, no cancer history)

TABLE 25.3
Responses to "What Kinds of Tests Should People Get to Find Out Whether They Have Cancer?"

Tests	*Interview responses*	*Population (HINTS)*
Mammogram	50%	65%
Pap test	23%	40%
Colonoscopy/Sigmoidoscopy	15%	38%
PSA test	15%	33%
Clinical breast exam	20%	13%
Stool blood test / Fecal occult blood test	8%	12%
Blood test	40%	9%
X-ray	35%	6%
MRI/CT scan	32%	6%
Breast self-exam	18%	6%
Digital rectal exam	3%	3%
Mean number of tests mentioned	*2.58*	*2.76*

- Until my doctor found it out, and in my case I have this prostate thing, it was my doctor who found it out and said, hey, you have something of a cancer in your prostate. (Asian male, over 75, history of prostate cancer)

Such descriptions reflect an image of cancer "lurking" in the body, surreptitiously polluting it and needing to be found before it is too late. Although this metaphor could prompt people to get screened regularly, its vagueness could contribute to problems like the common belief that any physician, performing any kind of examination, could discover a lurking cancer. Few saw drawbacks to testing, apart from possibly receiving the unpleasant news that one has cancer. Only 15% mentioned the risk of false positives. Although many listed cancer-specific tests, some believed that there was one test (usually a blood test) that could screen for all cancers. If people exaggerate the comprehensiveness of screening, they may exaggerate the extent to which no news is good news, leading them to neglect additional screening and protective behaviors.[1]

Disease Progression. Few interviewees had any confidence in their understanding of how cancer develops. Many answered simply, "I don't know," to basic questions about how cancer starts (35%) or progresses (21%). Those who did answer typically had little to say about how cancers begin, using rudimentary language about "bad" cells. Most described cancer as growing, spreading, or multiplying, with general phrases like "it just continues to grow." Few gave enough biological detail to indicate any real understanding. About a third (35%) mentioned treatments, saying that cancer will grow if nothing is done about it. Those who mentioned risk factors typically cited the same ones for cancer's initiation and progression, with the most common being smoking and exposure to the sun. African Americans talked more than others about how cancer can progress before it is noticed, $F(3,35) = 3.33$, $p < .01$, and about their need for more information, $F(3,35) = 4.77$, $p < .01$. Only Asian interviewees talked about the importance of a positive attitude or religion in preventing cancer, $F(3,35) = 3.01$, $p < .05$. Very few mentioned the possibility of cancers growing at different rates.

- I have to suppose that it's like an infection that just starts in one spot and continues to spread into other parts of the body or into the rest of the organ it started in, for instances, the lung or colon or whatever. (Hispanic male, age 65–74, no cancer history)
- I think in youngsters [there is] much quicker expanding or spread, well adults it may spread in other areas; it may spread in others; maybe if they have it in the lungs, they may have it in their brain or their back or their neck. (Asian female, over 75, no cancer history)
- So I can't really say how it really gets start[ed] because it is just a puzzle of questions that's in the body when the chemicals and your body cells are malfunctioning, and nobody really knows what type of exposure these people have had during their life that have cause this or rather has gone down from generations to generations. (African American female, age 55–64, no cancer history)

Treatments. Most interviewees listed at least two ways to treat cancer, with the most common being surgery (73%), radiation (73%), and chemotherapy (68%). All mentioned at least one method, except one individual who talked about the importance of maintaining a positive attitude and "accepting death" as a possible outcome. Interviewees tended to prefer surgery because it offered a chance of removing all of the "cancer cells," while recognizing that cancer can come back if "there was something left" or "it had spread to different parts of the body." They saw less value in chemotherapy and radiation, because they did not seem to offer hope of complete eradication (e.g., "[These treatments] more or less prolong suffering and the pain, and [a patient] must see the doctor more often, go to chemotherapy."). Most people believed that cancer could be cured (79%).

Those who believed in a cure also talked more about factors affecting treatment effectiveness, $t(36) = 2.74$, $p < .01$, and about the importance of detecting cancers, $t(36) = 2.07$, $p < .05$. Those who did not think that cancer could be cured did not appear to value strategies for slowing or containing it, $t(29) = 2.11$, $p < .05$.

- I don't have any idea how [medications] know where to go, but once you get it in your blood stream, it goes throughout your whole body, then attacking the cancerous growth. (White male, age 65–74, history of prostate cancer)
- I guess the surgery, like, kind of picks it out and the medication goes through your body, blood and fluids, to keep it out. (African American female, age 35–44, no cancer history)
- Surgery I think is better, if a person can stand the surgery, because that's once and for all thing. (Asian male, over 70, history of prostate cancer)

Outcomes. Most interviewees (78%) understood that "remission" meant (just) containing growth, which some explicitly described as different from being cured (e.g., "When I am not in remission anymore, I don't have cancer anymore."). They believed that people could do very little to prevent a re-occurrence, other than perhaps "just follow what the doctor says." White and African American interviewees were less likely to have misconceptions about remission (7% and 13%, respectively), compared to Hispanic (25%) and Asian (56%) interviewees, $\chi^2(3) = 8.28$, $p < .05$. A common mistake was confusing remission and recurrence. Most (72%) mentioned the possibility that cancer can recur, often believing that it happened when the cancer hadn't been treated properly and could come back elsewhere in the body. Nearly all mentioned that cancer was fatal, typically in general terms.

- I think remission means that it was there, but then it stopped for a while, and then it came back. (Hispanic female, age 25–34, no cancer history)
- It feels like there's a way to cure cancer there, but if it's inherent in the person on some level—I don't know, genetically or something like that—and it feels like, without some sort of gene therapy, then that form of, that cancer is incurable. (White male, age 25–34, no cancer history)
- So why did it come back, if they had surgery or radiation, and it was supposed to be gone. (African American female, age 55–64, no cancer history)

The older the interviewees were, the more likely they were to know that cancer can return after it has gone into remission ($r = .41$) and the more often they talked about the possibility of having cancer without knowing ($r = .39$). They were more likely to cite the importance of scientific or other credible evidence ($= .50$) and less likely to hold misconceptions about remission ($r = -.52$). They talked more about cancer being pervasive ($r = .48$) and having unknown risks ($r = .34$).

Experience with Cancer

Comparing the cancer outreach workers, cancer survivors, close family members of individuals with cancer, and interviewees with no close experience revealed surprisingly little effect of experience on general understanding. The less experience interviewees had had with cancer (either personally or through people very close to them), the more often they mentioned factors affecting the cancer process (such as differences between people or types of cancer, $r = -.55$) and the more often they mentioned that risks were not known ($r = -.31$). This may suggest that such variability is appreciated in the abstract, but becomes less relevant once there are particular examples focusing one's thoughts.

Outreach workers did not appear to have greater cancer knowledge than the lay interviewees, as measured by either the HINTS knowledge scores or the misconceptions revealed in the rest of the interview. Interviewees who had had cancer also had beliefs similar to others, except that (a) they gave fewer caveats in their description of the cancer process, mentioning less often that the process depends on various factors, $t(36) = 2.64$, $p < .05$; (b) they mentioned fewer HINTS factors that could reduce cancer risk, $t(38) = 2.05$, $p < .05$; and (c) they more frequently discussed asymptomatic aspects of cancer, $t(38) = 2.20$, $p < .05$.

Appeal of Metaphors

When asked to name conditions similar to cancer, interviewees most frequently mentioned infectious diseases (68%, including HIV, Hepatitis, TB and the common cold), followed by heart disease (45%), and autoimmune diseases (43%). Only one interviewee indicated contamination (citing asbestos). About one-fifth could not pick any metaphor as most similar, unable to compare cancer to any other diseases. When asked how their volunteered metaphors applied to each of the six different aspects of cancer that we asked about, the ones seen as having the most similar risk factors were heart disease and autoimmune disease. For disease progression, symptoms, treatment, and outcomes, infectious disease was seen as the most similar metaphor. For testing, heart disease was most similar. Across all aspects of cancer, however, the percentage of interviewees who could not name any metaphor remained relatively large.

After the interview section on different domains of cancer, where interviewees could generate their own metaphors, we asked them to discuss how well cancer fit three focal metaphors in terms of the six domains. Table 25.4 shows these metaphors in order acsending of judged similarity to cancer. The second and third columns describe ways in which cancer seemed similar and different.

(a) An accident waiting to happen, "such as running with scissors or driving a car that is in very poor condition," was judged to be similar to cancer mostly in terms of being preventable. Interviewees believed that the metaphor did not explain genetic factors of cancer as well.

TABLE 25.4
Explanations of metaphors

Metaphor	*Mean Rating*	*Cancer is similar*	*Cancer is different*
Accidents	2.80 (1.36)	Prevention is possible	Cancer has genetic factors
Contamination	2.73 (1.39)	Environmental exposure, abnormal cell growth	Cancer also has internal causes
Autoimmune Disease	2.69 (1.30)	Recurrence, no symptoms	Easier to treat, more localized, more suffering
Heart Disease	2.66 (1.18)	Behavioral, environmental and genetic risk factors, progressive disease	More difficult to prevent or treat
Infectious Disease	2.59 (1.29)	Reccurrence	Disease process
Parasitic Infection	2.20 (1.21)	Environmental exposure, disease process	More difficult to treat
Body Aging	1.96 (1.34)	Weaker body and more diseases with age	Affects all ages
Allergies	1.37 (.81)	Environmental exposure	More serious, more difficult to treat

Rating scale: 1 (very different from cancer) to 5 (very similar to cancer)

- If you know that a disease is in your family and you don't do anything about it, then it is an accident waiting to happen. (Hispanic female, age 45–54, history of skin cancer)
- If you are educated, you can almost keep, maybe, maybe you can keep it from happening by education and, and food and diet and, and how you live and how you, you know, how you take care of yourself. [But if] somewhere in that family somebody had cancer [in] their genetics, it's there, that certain disease. (African American female, over 75, no cancer history)
- Other than lung cancer I think the rest of the cancers are just there and it just happens. (60-year old white male with history of prostate cancer)

(b) Contamination with something toxic, "such as lead poisoning or pesticides in food," rarely arose spontaneously, but was strongly endorsed when interviewees were asked explicitly about its degree of similarity. One recurrent analogy was exposure to toxic substances in the environment, which then caused abnormal cell growth, which should be completely removed from the body and which will return with continued exposure. For example:

- A foreign object, a foreign substance in the body that shouldn't be there. (Hispanic female, age 25–34, history of cervical cancer)
- It could be something in the air. They could have been in Vietnam and got agent orange. You know, that caused the cancer. (African American male, age 55–64, history of prostate cancer)
- [It's similar] because you are still trying to go in there … to get rid of the bad cells vs. the good cells or the bad whatever is in you, trying to take over. (White female, age 35–44, no cancer history)
- [It's different] because it's an exogenous cause as opposed to cancer being an endogenous cause. (White female, age 45–54, no cancer history)

(c) Auto-immune diseases, "where the body attacks its own cells," such as multiple sclerosis or diabetes, were judged to be similar to cancer in that they could recur after they had been treated. Although cancer was seen as a more serious disease, some interviewees believed that it was more localized, hence easier to treat.

- It might be curable, but yet it could come back. And there might be ways to live [with] it, but you know, still keep it under control. (White female, age 35–44, no cancer history)
- You don't actually know it's in there, because a lot of people walk around with cancer everyday and don't even know it.… [It's also similar] in the way it is treated, the therapy, because you don't know if it has been eliminated completely from the body. (Hispanic female, age 45–54, history of skin cancer)
- To me, they might be a little similar because they both take medicine that controls it, but then there's that time that the medicine doesn't work anymore so it kind of takes over on its own. (Hispanic female, age 25–34, no cancer history)

(d) Heart disease arose spontaneously with some frequency but was not rated as particularly similar to cancer. Typical references invoked similarities to cancer in terms of both having behavioral, genetic, and environmental risk factors, as well as being hidden problems that grow progressively worse. Cancer, however, was seen as less sudden, more difficult to prevent, and more difficult to treat.

- They both feel like the kind of disease where if you have a [family] history of it then you're more at risk and you should think about this. And there are behavioral, I think, things that you can do like you can smoke or you can become obese. (White male, age 25–34, no cancer history)
- If you don't take care of it, it will progress to death, you have to do something. [And] if you are prone to heart disease, just like you are prone to certain cancers there's always a chance of reoccurrence. (Hispanic female, age 35–44, no cancer history)

(e) An infection caused by a virus, such as measles or HIV, was seen as similar in that it can be treated, but come back again. HIV was singled out for similarity because of its perceived lethality. Interviewees stressed, however, that the disease processes are different.
- With cancer, if treated properly and caught in time and everything, it, you could be in remission, so that means it will go away. Same with the virus, if treated properly it will go away. You will be cured. (African American female, age 35–44, no cancer history)
- There is somebody that has it that passes it on to you, in one form or another, either air-borne, fluid borne, and it's given to you or passed on from person to person vs. cancer, cancer is not passed on that way. (Hispanic female, age 35–44, no cancer history)

(f) Parasitic infections, such as those caused by a tapeworm or a tick, were seen as similar in terms of the role of environmental exposure, and the possibility of spreading through the body and growing through cell division. The most important differences were cancer being more difficult to treat and having no cure.
- They both function the same way I guess. The cell division or whatever multiplication process they have or whatever, whatever mechanism it is that causes them to grow. They both spread. The cancer would spread. The parasite infection would spread. (White male, age 65–74, history of prostate cancer)
- You might be able to be cured for a while, but eventually you're not going to cure that all together. I think that with the parasitic infection, you'll, you'll be able to cure it. (African American female, over 75, no cancer history)

(g) The health problems that arise as people's bodies age, such as osteoporosis or dementia, were seen as similar in that they occurred systemically, with the body's defense system becoming less able to protect it. The most commonly noted difference referred to cancer affecting people of all ages.
- You know, when the cell divides, and with the wear and tear of the environment and what you do to your own body could make these changes occur. (African American female, age 35–44, no cancer history)
- Cancer doesn't come with old age, cancer is something that develops in your body. (African American male, age 55–64, no cancer history)

(h) Allergies, such as to dust or peanuts, were seen as least similar to cancer, although some participants mentioned environmental exposure as being similar.
- Allergies in my understanding are very, very treatable. Whereas even with all the advances made by, in the area of the study of cancer, they can't get them all. They can't cure them all. (White male, age 65–74, history of prostate cancer)
- I guess it could be similar because it's environmental. (White male, age 55–64, no cancer history)

The ailments invoked by each metaphor were seen as different from cancer in their severity, often emphatically so. Even participants with personal cancer experiences, which in this sample had been mild cases in remission, felt that cancer was extremely severe and deadly.

HINTS Questions

Our sample was designed for diversity (of experience and background), rather than representativeness. Nonetheless, their knowledge of cancer is broadly similar to that found when the HINTS question were administered to a representative U.S. adult population (Nelson et al., 2004). Table 25.1 shows mentions of the risk factors listed in the coding scheme. Our participants mentioned slightly more factors overall, possibly reflecting differences in population, interview, or application of the coding scheme. One striking difference is our interviewees' lower emphasis on smoking. One possible methodological reason is that this was the first question asked in our survey, whereas it was the second question in the HINTS interview, directly following a question mentioning smoking as a cause of death.

This similarity extends to beliefs regarding changes in eating habits that might reduce cancer risk (Table 25.2). Our participants mentioned about the same number of factors as HINTS interviewees, with similar relative frequency. HINTS posed this question only to those who mentioned diet as a way to reduce cancer (in response to the first question), whereas we posed it to all participants. In part because most of our participants mentioned diet as a way to reduce cancer, following the HINTS protocol would have made little difference in the results.

Participants in our interviews and HINTS produced somewhat different descriptions of tests for cancer (Table 25.3). Here, the HINTS protocol may have made a difference, as the question was posed only to the 5% of participants who mentioned getting screened or tested for cancer as something that people could do to reduce their risk. The seemingly greater knowledge of HINTS interviewees about tests might reflect this restriction to those mentioning testing in the first place. More of our participants (20% vs. 5%) mentioned screening. However, they are too small a group (8) to compare. One suggestive result is that those who did not volunteer screening were more likely, when asked, to talk merely about generic tests (e.g., blood tests, x-rays, MRIs, CT scans).

DISCUSSION

Most interviewees knew very little about cancer. On the surface, some seemed relatively well informed, talking about risk factors, eating habits, and treatments, using words like "remission." However, further probing showed that many knew the terms, but not the underlying concepts. Their mental models were typically incomplete, inconsistent, and error-laden. They were particularly confused about risk factors (e.g., what constitutes a "better" diet), testing and screening (e.g., assuming that non-specific blood tests performed by any physician would be able to discover a lurking cancer), disease progression (e.g., being unclear about how cancer starts), and treatment (e.g., emphasizing the need to remove all cancer cells).

Without such critical details, people cannot act on their beliefs, communicate effectively with physicians and family, or make sense of their circumstances. They need accurate mental models in order to make effective decisions regarding eating habits, screening, treatment, and other cancer-related choices. Both the lack of such mental models and the awareness of that absence contribute confusion to the fear raised by cancer.

Problematic Metaphors

The worst news in these interviews was that a metaphor with great intuitive appeal was also quite inappropriate, in terms of fitting the facts of cancer and facilitating emotional equanimity regarding the threats. Interviewees strongly endorsed the contamination metaphor when described to them in the final section of the interviews. Unfortunately, this metaphor implies the need to remove cancer risk entirely. It raises impossible demands (and sometimes expectations) for screening and treatment procedures. Commercial "full-body" screening centers exploit this misconception by promising detection without warning against false alarms. Focusing on contamination suggests few prevention measures, except for avoiding any exposure to perceived carcinogens. It leaves a stain on those who have, or think they have, any semblance of cancer. Moreover, the details of the interviews suggested that other metaphors may be acceptable to people. Not only is contamination emotionally unsatisfying, but people also realize that decontamination is not a realistic aspiration. Such lack of hope may underlie much of the fear of cancer, partially contributing to failures to screen and devastation following diagnosis.

The metaphoric image of cancer growing and spreading that emerged from people's descriptions of disease progression might provide the foundation for a more complete mental model, incorporating ways in which that growth can be slowed, stopped, or reversed. However, very few interviewees currently saw any chance of influencing disease progression, "once cancer has started." Indeed, their default belief appears to be that cancers grow quite quickly. That fear was expressed by people who had never been diagnosed with cancer, as well as women who had had cervical cancer and men who had had prostate cancer. The cancer survivors almost uniformly saw themselves as lucky to have caught it early. The sole exception was a man who believed that his prostate cancer had been slow growing.

Thus, it may be feasible to refine the widely shared growth metaphor by adding the idea of differential growth rates. That would accommodate the realities of tragically fast cancers, inherently slow-growing cancers, and treatments slowing growth rates. Conveying the specific implications of differential growth rates would have to confront the well-documented difficulty that people have in estimating how risks accumulate through repeated exposure (e.g., Shaklee & Fischhoff, 1990). That difficulty leads them to underestimate both the cumulative effects of exponential growth and the impacts of changes in growth rates (Fischhoff, Bostrom, & Quadrel, 2002).

Interviewees' focus on eradication when describing treatments seems to reflect a mixture of belief (that eradication is essential for effective treatment) and desire (for a way to put cancer out of mind). As a result, it may be a potent obstacle to improving their understanding of cancer. People need an alternative organizing metaphor that not only leads to accurate inferences, but also provides emotional relief. Some grounds for crafting more nuanced messages can be found in the detailed text of the interviews. For example, many people describe eradication as more hope than reality, suggesting that they might embrace a growth model if it were expressed in a way that conveyed a realistic feeling of hope. That expression would have to address the common belief that when cancers are not removed entirely, re-growth will be very fast and uncontrollable. That belief was found even among people who had received seemingly successful cancer treatments, reinforcing the overwhelming role of fear.

One metaphor that was introduced to take advantage of the idea that cancer might grow slowly and be confined to later life was that of the body aging. Interviewees were particularly resistant to this idea, as were the domain experts, although for somewhat different reasons. Experts felt that such a metaphor confused natural growth and aging of cells with the unnatural, uncontrolled growth of cancer cells. Interviewees were more disturbed by the fact that cancer does not only affect the elderly but can happen even to children. Thus, any potential this metaphor might have had to convey particular ideas of slowing but not curing cancer is undone by its inherent differences and the overwhelming reluctance to consider it. Two other metaphors that were included to explore the sense of the body reacting to processes inside it, allergies and parasitic infections, were also met with a lack of enthusiasm. The ease of treating both of these ailments set them apart from cancer, and few similarities were seen to redeem them.

Useful Metaphors

As seen in the contrast between Table 25.4's rating and the frequency with which metaphors were produced spontaneously, many participants could see the relevance of many metaphors, once they were presented. Particularly promising alternatives include (a) heart disease, (b) "an accident waiting to happen," (c) auto-immune disease, and (d) infectious disease. Among these, heart and infectious disease were most often evoked without prompting.

Interviewees intuitively saw how heart disease had risk factors similar to those of cancer and could have equally sudden onset. As an organizing metaphor, heart disease has the further benefit that some behavioral, life-style changes may protect against both heart disease and cancer (although some drugs may decrease one risk at the price of increasing the other). Unfortunately, interviewees could not easily apply the heart disease metaphor to other aspects of cancer. A communication program built on this metaphor would have to find intuitively compelling ways to address the presence of affected areas throughout one's body, increasing growth and susceptibility with age, and the likelihood of re-growth and re-occurrence of disease after treatment. Conceptualizing heart disease as arteriosclerosis might provide some of these goals, at least for those familiar with it.

Another intuitively appealing metaphor, "an accident waiting to happen," may have more general promise. It suggests that many factors must come together for cancer to arise. Conversely, there may be many different things that one can do to reduce that risk. Although these steps cannot eliminate all risk, they might reduce it to an emotionally manageable level, while giving the feeling that one has acted prudently. In order to use the accident metaphor effectively as a guide to cancer-related decision making, people need authoritative information about what the risk and protective factors are, presented in an intuitively appealing way. Feelings of empowerment will be undermined if they have to sort through conflicting claims or, worse, discover that they have unwittingly invested in strategies lacking scientific support or having trivial impact. (Witness the recent controversies over pain-killing drugs and hormone replacement therapy.) A communication challenge inherent in the accident metaphor is avoiding producing a disorganized list of seemingly unrelated facts. Some internal organization is needed if communications are to transform existing mental models into frameworks for broader understanding.

Autoimmune disease has promise in promoting understanding of cancer, especially in its tendency to recur and occasional lack of symptoms while damage may be done to the body undetected. The need to follow through in treatments over the course of time may be reinforced by analogy to chronic, autoimmune conditions. Infectious disease, including the flu, HIV, TB and others, can be useful especially in their variability. Interviewees focused on the lethality of HIV in making a case for its similarity, an association that perhaps could be exploited by comparing less lethal cancers to more mild diseases. While the prognosis for lung cancer may call to mind HIV, cervical cancer may have a better comparison in a highly treatable infection that requires quick treatment.

Using Metaphors to Facilitate Education

These preliminary data provide a well-grounded starting point to explore further metaphors that are promising in terms of their ability to capture difficult concepts and provide a framework for education about cancer. The metaphors will need to be fleshed out into a broader explanatory capacity to determine whether they are not just compelling but can also facilitate understanding. Such a study would compare the best metaphors, along with a control group receiving a similarly intense exposure to conventional information, in their ability to improve understanding and to lead to correct inferences about new information. A good metaphor will not only make specific content easier to understand, but will provide a basis to make sense of new information in a way that is correct and useful. An in-depth study could identify possible applications of metaphors to education, and a randomized controlled trial could then pit metaphors against each other (and against a similar amount of general cancer information without any organizing metaphor) to determine viable strategies for educating the public about broad cancer processes and prevention. Finally, metaphors that appear particularly useful in helping people to understand cancer can be paired with more specific messages tied to relevant behaviors, in order to determine whether they enhance the effectiveness of directed communication and lead to more, better, or longer-lasting behavior changes.

NOTE

1. An analogous misconception is found with tests for sexually transmitted infections: many people believe that any blood sample will automatically be tested for HIV and that a pap smear detects sexually transmitted diseases other than HPV, the virus that causes genital warts (Bruine de Bruin, Downs, Fischhoff, & Palmgren, 2007).

BIBLIOGRAPHY

Bruine de Bruin, W., Downs, J.S., & Fischhoff, B. (2007). Adolescents' thinking about the risks and benefits of sexual behavior. In: Lovett, M. & Shah, P. (Eds.) *Thinking with Data*. Mahwah, NJ: Erlbaum.

Bruine de Bruin, W., Downs, J. S., Fischhoff, B., & Palmgren, C. (2008). Development and evaluation of an HIV/AIDS knowledge measure for adolescents focusing on gaps and misconceptions. *Journal of HIV/AIDS Prevention in Children and Youth, 8*, 35–57.

Byram, S., Fischhoff, B., Embrey, M., Bruine de Bruin, W., & Thorne (2001). Mental models of women with breast implants: Local complications. *Behavioral Medicine*, *27*, 4–14.

Carlsson, M. E., & Strang, P. M. (1997). Facts, misconceptions, and myths about cancer. What do patients with gynecological cancer and the female public at large know? *Gynecologic Oncology*, *65*, 46–53.

Culliton, B. J. (2006). Extracting knowledge from science: A conversation with Elias Zerhouni. *Health Affairs (Millwood), 25,* w94–103.

Chin, D. G., Schonfeld, D. J., O'Hare, L. L., Mayne, S. T., Salovey, P., Showalter, D. R., & Cicchetti, D. V.(1998). Elementary school-aged children's developmental understanding of the causes of cancer. *Developmental and Behavioral Pediatrics*, *19*, 397–403.

Clarke, J. N., & Everest, M. M. (2006). Cancer in the mass print media: Fear, uncertainty and the medical model. *Social Science & Medicine*, *62*, 2591–2600.

Downs, J.S., Murray, P.J., Bruine de Bruin, W., White, J.P., Palmgren, C., & Fischhoff, B. (2004). Interactive video behavioral intervention to reduce adolescent females' STD risk: A randomized controlled trial. *Social Science & Medicine*, *59*, 1561–1572.

Fischhoff, B. (2005). Decision research strategies. *Health Psychology*, *21*, S1–S8.

Fischhoff, B. (1999). Why (cancer) risk communication can be hard. *Journal of the National Cancer Institute Monographs*, *25*, 7–13.

Fischhoff, B., Bostrom, A., & Quadrel, M. J. (2002). Risk perception and communication. In R. Detels, J. McEwen, R. Beaglehole & H. Tanaka (Eds.), *Oxford textbook of public health*. (pp. 1105–1123). London: Oxford University Press.

Fischhoff, B., Downs, J., & Bruine de Bruin, W. (1998). Adolescent vulnerability: A framework for behavioral interventions. *Applied and Preventive Psychology*, *7*, 77–94.

Freimuth, V. S., Stein, J. A., & Kean, T. J. (1989). *Searching for health information: The Cancer Information Service model*. Philadelphia: University of Pennsylvania Press.

Hornik, R. C. (2002). *Public health communication: evidence for behavior change*. Mahwah, NJ: Erlbaum.

Karasz, A., McKee, M. D., & Roybal K. (2003). Women's experiences of abnormal cervical cytology: Illness representations, care processes, and outcomes. *Annals of Family Medicine*, *1*, 196–202.

Lau, R. R., & Hartman, K. A. (1983). Common sense representations of common illness. *Health Psychology*, *2*, 167–185.

McCaul, K. D., Peters, E., Nelson, W., & Stefanek, M. (2005). Linking decision-making research and cancer prevention and control: Important themes. *Health Psychology, 24*, S106–S110.

Morgan, M.G., Fischhoff, B., Bostrom, A., & Atman, C. (2001). *Risk communication: The mental models approach*. New York: Cambridge University Press.

Montgomery, L. L. Tran, K. N., Heelan, M. C., van Zee, K. J., Massie, M. J., Payne, D. K., & Borgen, P. I. (1999). Issues of regret in women with contralateral prophylactic mastectomies. *Annals of Surgical Oncology*, *6*, 546–552.

Nelson, D. E., Kreps, G. L., Hesse, B. W., Croyle, R. T., Willis, G., Arora, N. K. Rimer, B. K., Viswanath, K. V., Weinstein, N., & Alden, S. (2004). The Health Information National Trends Survey (HINTS): Development, design, and dissemination. *Journal of Health Communication, 9,* 443–460.

Nold, R. J., Beamer, R. L., Helmer, S. D., & McBoyle, M. F. (2000). Factors influencing a woman's choice to undergo breast-conserving surgery versus modified radical mastectomy. *American Journal of Surgery, 180*, 413–418.

O'Connor, A. M., Fiset, V., DeGrasse, C., Graham, I. D., Evans, W., Stacey, D., Laupacis, A., & Tugwell, P. (1999). Decision aids for patients considering options affecting cancer outcomes: Evidence of efficacy and policy implications. *Journal of the National Cancer Institute. Monographs, 25*, 67–80.

O'Connor, A. M., Stacey, D., Rovner, D., Holmes-Rovner, M., Tetroe, J., Llewellyn-Thomas, H., Entwistle, V., Rostom, A., Fiset, V., Barry, M., & Jones, J. (2001). Decision aids for people facing health treatment or screening decisions. *Cochrane Database of Systematic Reviews (Online), 3*, CD001431, retrieved April 1, 2008, from http://www.cochrane.org/reviews/en.ab001431.html

Palmgren, C., Morgan, M.G., Bruine de Bruin, W., & Keith, D. (2004). Initial public perceptions of deep geological and oceanic disposal of carbon dioxide. *Environmental Science & Technology, 38*, 6441–6450.

Payne, S. (1990). Lay representations of breast cancer. *Psychology and Health*, *5*, 1–11.

Penson, R. T., Schapira, L., Daniels, K. J., Chabner, B. A., & Lynch, T. J. Jr. (2004). Cancer as metaphor. *The Oncologist, 9*, 708–716.

Peters, E., McCaul, K. D., Stefanek, M., & Nelson, W. (2006). A heuristics approach to understanding cancer risk perception: contributions from judgment and decision-making research. *Annals of Behavioral Medicine, 31*, 45–52.

Riley, D. M., Fischhoff, B., Small, M., & Fischbeck, P. (2001). Evaluating the effectiveness of risk-reduction strategies for consumer chemical products. *Risk Analysis, 21*, 357–369.

Schonfeld, D. J., Bases, H., Quackenbush, M., Mayne, S., Morra, M., & Cicchetti, D. (2001). Pilot-testing a cancer education curriculum for grades K-6. *Journal of School Health, 71*, 61–65.

Shaklee, H., & Fischhoff, B. (1990). The psychology of contraceptive surprises: Judging the cumulative risk of contraceptive failure. *Journal of Applied Psychology, 20*, 385–403.

Silverman, E., Woloshin, S., Schwartz, L. M., Byram, S. J., Welch, H. G., & Fischhoff, B. (2001). Women's views of breast cancer risk and screening mammography: A qualitative interview study. *Medical Decision Making, 21*, 231–240.

Skott, C. (2002). Expressive metaphors in cancer narratives. *Cancer Nursing, 25*, 230–235.

Slovic, P., Fischhoff, B., & Lichtenstein, S. (1980). Facts and fears: Understanding perceived risk. In R. C. Schwing & W. A. Albers, Jr. (Eds.). *Societal Risk Assessment: How Safe is Safe Enough?* (pp. 181–214). New York: Plenum.

Sontag, S. (1978). *Illness as Metaphor*. New York: Strauss and Giroux.

Subramanian, S., Klosterman, M., Amonkar, M. M., & Hunt, T. L. (2004). Adherence with colorectal cancer screening guidelines: a review. *Preventive Medicine, 38*, 536–550.

Taylor, S. E., Lichtman, R. R., & Wood, J. V. (1984). Attributions, beliefs about control, and adjustment to breast cancer. *Journal of Personality and Social Psychology, 46*, 489–502.

Turk, D. C., Rudy, T. E., & Salovey, P. (1985). Implicit models of illness. *Journal of Behavioral Medicine, 9*, 1986.

Tversky, A., & Kahneman, D. (1973). Availability: A heuristic for judging frequency and probability. *Cognitive Psychology, 5*, 207–232.

Von Eschenbach, A. C. (2005). The national cancer program. In V. T. DeVita, S. Hellman & S. Rosenberg (Eds.), *Cancer: Principles and practice of oncology* (7th ed., pp. 2788–2793). Philadelphia: Lippincott Williams & Wilkins.

Woloshin, S., Schwartz, L. M., Byram S. J., Sox, H. C., Fischhoff B., & Welch, H. G. (2000). Women's understanding of the mammography screening debate. *Archives of Internal Medicine. 160*, 1434–1440.

26

Killing and Other Campus Violence: Restorative Enrichment of Risk and Crisis Communication

Cindi Atkinson and Courtney Vaughn

University of Oklahoma

Jami VanCamp

Oklahoma City University

Due to the number of school shootings (one of the ultimate campus crises) in recent years, many citizens view future occurrences as likely and have put pressure on school districts to minimize this risk but also to deal with such crises should they erupt. To understand the social psychology of violence, researchers and practitioners must appreciate the concept of alienation (Seeman & Anderson, 1983). During the latter part of the 20th century, American scholars took the Germans' lead and identified alienation as a key cause of violence. The school killer, for example, is so desensitized and disconnected from others that he can feel no one else's pain (Blauner, 1964; Fromm, 1994; Lipset & Schneider, 1983; Seeman & Anderson, 1983). Friedland (2001), a communication researcher theorizing restorative justice suggests that educators could more successfully minimize alienation by promoting democracy through various proactive measures (Ahmed, Harris, & J. Braithwaite, 2001, & V. Braithwaite, 1989; Chavis, 1998; Karp, 2001; Karp & Breslin, 1995; Morrison, 2001; Sullivan & Tifft, 2005; Wachtel, 2000).

Restorative justice is a response to crime focused on repairing victims' losses and encouraging offenders to take responsibility for their actions. It also helps schools build bridges between federal and state authorities and school communities when making decisions regarding risk and crisis communication (defined in chapter 1 of this volume), and, in turn, prevents or minimizes further infractions (e.g., Sampson, 1995; Strang & J. Braithwaite, 2001; Sergiovanni, 1994, Sullivan & Tifft, 2005). The role of restoration does not negate the largely retributive justice system and school discipline plans that are intended to deter violent crises by severely punishing the offender while largely excluding victims from the process. Rather, restorative justice can be woven into current risk and crisis theory and practice to help minimize the peril of shootings, nevertheless increasing the ability to deal with such crises when they come about.

To curtail school violence and communicate to the public the serious retribution that could follow, federal officials launched the war on drugs in the 1980s, based on the principal of zero tolerance. In 1985, *New Jersey vs. T.L.O.* approved warrantless school locker searches and the immediate suspension of students in possession of drugs. Five years later, the Gun Free School Zones Act made it a federal offense to possess a firearm on or near school property, however it was later declared unconstitutional. So, in 1994, the Gun-Free Schools Act corrected earlier constitutional issues while retaining the spirit and consequences of the parent law. It mandated that any state receiving federal funds must expel a student who breaks this law. The required expulsion period is a year, but some case-by-case time considerations could take place. Although the zero tolerance laws were one part of a larger package of federal school violence prevention initiatives, they were judicially enforced in 1995 when the Supreme Court upheld student expulsions (Blair, 1999; *Gross vs. Lopez*, 1995; Ogle & Eckman, 2002; Peterson & Skiba, 1999; Schiffbauer, 2000; Skiba, 2004).

Inspired by national edicts, school disciplinary rules were fortified to lessen the risk of killing on campus and other more minor offenses. Official school decision makers formalized and, in many cases, made these policies quite rigorous. In 1998, the National Center for Education Statistics reported that most schools required visitors to sign in at the office, prohibited students from leaving the campus, and maintained zero-tolerance policies toward serious student offenses (Brady, 2004; Cook, 2001 ; Schiffbauer, 2000). Some supporters of zero tolerance defended the above measures but stated they were not always the sole source of school discipline (Blair, 1999). Moreover, Anderson (1999) spotlights the inequities involved in resorting to unilateral retributive punishment. For example, poor and non-White students who live in neighborhoods where violence is visible and more pronounced than in wealthier parts of town are suspended from school with greater regularity, even though middle-class White students commit campus murders at much higher rates.

School district risk policies also focused on safety, which became a major factor in designing and protecting school buildings (e.g., Taylor & Graves, 1998). During the late 1990s, school facility studies noted that 74% of all buildings needed to be repaired or rebuilt immediately, and another 12% were not suitable for learning activities (Schiffbauer, 2000). School administrators examined every aspect of their institutions from the arrangement of classrooms, hallways, and common areas to the legal issues involved in creating student handbooks and implementing violence-prevention programs. The ideal school building should have few exterior access points, no dark or isolated hallways, and sunlight pouring into each classroom (Kaufman, Chen, Choy, Ruddy, Miller, Fleury, Chandler, Rand, Klaus, & Planty, 2000; Schiffbauer, 2000). Further, the ideal school representative considered and addressed the following questions when evaluating school safety measures:

- How close is the office area to the main access door?
- Are hallways safe?
- What communication system is in place?
- What traffic patterns are feasible?
- What lighting is in place?
- Is the crisis-management plan up-to-date?
- Do in-service programs enhance staff members' coping skills?
- Do school policies emphasize safety?
- Does the school curriculum address school safety issues?
- Does the school meet necessary legal requirements?
- Is the community part of the school safety plan? (Schiffbauer, 2000, p. 73)

Although school safety and discipline policies were intended to deter infractions by threatening extreme punishment and protecting schools, all too frequently strong crisis communication efforts failed. During the mid to late 1990s, parts of the country witnessed a rash of deadly school shootings. Those at Columbine High School in Littleton, Colorado, were perhaps the most publicized, however, crime scenes and chaos devastated residents of Pearl, Mississippi; West Paducah, Kentucky; Jonesboro, Arkansas; Edinboro, Pennsylvania; and Springfield, Oregon, to name only a few. Many Americans were shocked to find that so-called stable spots throughout the United States were subject to the same kind of disruption that larger urban areas had experienced for years (Chavez, 2006; Dwyer & Newman, 2004; Osher & Warger, 1998).

A second wave occurred in 2006, when a principal became the sole victim of a 15-year-old shooter in Baraboo, Wisconsin. The next incident took place in Nickel Mines, Pennsylvania, which is a peaceful Amish community where people's lives are based around the soil, hard work, and faith. Charles Carl Roberts, a 32-year-old man, was bent on killing young schoolgirls. The Pennsylvania attack bore striking similarities to a deadly shooting in Bailey, Colorado, only the week before. Despite these murders, some researchers continued to assert that American schools are safer for children than the larger society (Boyd, 2003; Burns & Crawford, 1999). Regardless, it was clear that retributive laws and school practices were not deterring all school violence. In addition, particularly when the offender took his own life, his family was left alongside those of the victims to pick up the pieces of their lives and deal with the emotions and questions without resorting to violence themselves. In short, communities were left torn apart. (See Figure 26.1 and the corresponding web site for details on particular school shootings.)

Myriad campus crises made good copy for the media but did little to help school communities humanely and stealthfully handle a crisis when risk measures failed (Mitchell, 2006). A major network reporter explains, "If it bleeds it leads" (Dwyer, 1999, p. 2). Along with the resulting public awareness and very real devastation for communities struck by violence, Americans are always hungry for unfiltered coverage from real people's perspectives. And they got it—due to heightened technology such as 24-hour news stations, pagers, cellular telephones, text messaging, and Amber

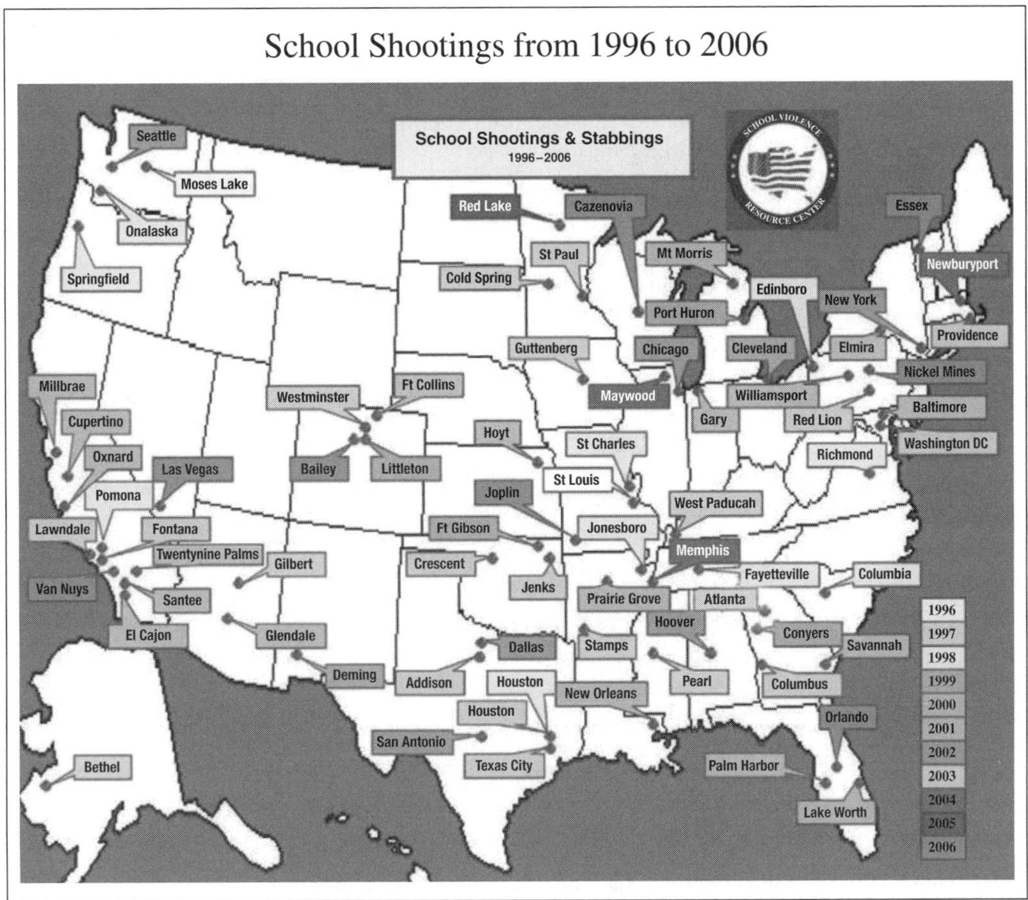

FIGURE 26.1 School Shootings from 1996 to 2006. *Source:* School Violence Resource Center. www.svrc.net/ShootingsMap.htm (retrieved November 18, 2006).

Alerts. The first 24 hours after the shooting at Columbine, Colorado's Jefferson County Public Schools logged 1,500 telephone calls from the media. Even though the district, which operated 145 schools, had its own telecommunication system, the lines were so jammed that cellular telephones were useless for large blocks of time. A temporary cellular tower was built in the media city and landlines eventually were installed at the area's crisis communication headquarters, which was temporarily set up in the library (Cook, 2001; Goodman & Goodman, 2004).

Researchers and practitioners alike learned that to maintain their credibility, schools with good crisis communication must form working relationships with national and international media such as the Associated Press. Then, schools can take the first line of defense in the event of violence on campus (Cook, 2001). Ironically, when school districts maintain the upper hand, the media is the most important means of communicating expeditiously with school patrons, including parents, students, staff, and faculty.

The Plano School District, located 25 miles north of Dallas, Texas, learned the importance of preparation the hard way. Also during the 1990s, the district, which had 59 schools and 47,300 students, was faced with a hostage situation at a daycare center that stood next to a school where a suicide had taken place on campus and several recent Plano High School graduates had overdosed on heroin. "As much media training as you may have had, unless you've had a lot of experience dealing with the media, you're not prepared," claimed Plano school district official Carole Greisdorf. "You're never quite prepared for what may come at you. You can never cover every eventuality, but you do as much as you can and you never stop looking at what could happen" (cited in Cook, 2001, p. 19) One crisis communication researcher made a simple but profound suggestion for a school or any other institution that fails to protect its own. "Time and time again, it seems that organizations that own up to their mistakes fare well in the court of public opinion, if not the legal courts as well. Sometimes, the best crisis strategy is to simply apologize" and strive to make things right (Wilson, 2002, p.159). Wilson is suggesting that such heartfelt commitments can create authentic bonds between schools and their communities (Sturges, 1994).

Reiterating and augmenting the research and practice concerning formal public disclosures through the ever-present media, school crisis communication advocates direct administrators to:

- Be prepared to act rather than react. Have a plan in place and review it each year.
- Determine who is responsible for calling whom and under what circumstances.
- Identify a spokesperson.
- Establish district and school chains of command.
- Prepare a list of emergency telephone numbers.
- Have a fact sheet with information about the district ready to distribute to media.
- Establish a hotline for information and rumor control.
- Identify a location for a crisis communication center.
- Plan for backup communication equipment in case phones and address systems fail.
- Prepare a statement that secretaries and receptionists can read to callers in the first 30 minutes of a crisis.
- Have the appropriate person handle the situation.
- Understand the circumstances and define the problem.
- Consider options.
- Act decisively to ensure safety of students, staff, and property.
- Communicate with staff.
- Update students periodically in classrooms.
- Avoid large group meetings.
- Send a letter home to parents at the end of the day explaining the situation.
- Update your telephone hotline message to include important information.
- Post important information related to the incident on district/school web sites.

- Get information to the community through key communicators such as parents. (Cook, 2001, p. 19)

Investigating systemic ways effectively to implement these suggestions, Cornell and Sheras (1998) conducted a study, which focuses on five school crises involving an alcohol-related fatality, self-injurious behavior, staff homicides, racial and ethical conflict, and community violence. The study does not include natural disasters, where there is less responsibility for anticipation and prevention. While Cornell and Sheras (1998) agree that planning is important to successful crisis responses in the event that risk prevention is unsuccessful, they believe implementation is just as important. They contend that qualities of leadership, teamwork, and responsibility are essential ingredients of successful crisis communication. They demonstrate the value of these qualities through analysis of these five case examples (Cornell & Sheras, 1998;also see Sturges, 1994).

Initially attending to victims' needs through critical-incident debriefing sessions with victims is also encouraged, but rarely are victims given the opportunity to work with perpetrators' families or in the communities. Nevertheless, in victim-centered therapy open flow of information is crucial. Obsessing about the future is a persistent source of anxiety for survivors, in particular what might be the prosecutorial outcomes of an offender's trial should he still be alive, or where his family members are living and what community they are a part of (Asmussen & Creswell, 1995). The National Organization for Victim Assistance (NOVA) has a model for the process where "each student and teacher in a classroom sits in a circle and a facilitator begins by asking sensory perception questions, thus guiding students to a discussion of emotions, prediction of the future and identification of coping skills." Art, writing, and music also provide emotionally constructive outlets (Waddell, & Thomas, 1999, p. 8).

Long-term victim issues involve retriggering incidents. Schools must follow up by disseminating information about post-traumatic stress disorder and provide or recommend other counselors who offer continuing individual counseling for the people most closely victimized. Anniversary dates for violent incidents can easily foment dreadful memories. Often, students display numerous fear-related behaviors; eating disorders and fragmented attention spans are only two. Holding memorial services in a relatively short period of time and reviewing the agenda for potentially disruptive content can help (Asmussen & Creswell, 1995; Hiley-Young & Gerrity, 1994; Poland, 1999; Poland & Pitcher, 1992; Pynoos & Nader, 1998; Waddell & Thomas, 1999).

Despite these efforts with students, the school community is often frustrated when offenders take their own lives, because it destroys their need for retribution. When left to their own devices, having no access to what could be school-initiated restorative practices, community members often strike out at the culprit's family and friends. This aggravates the risk of further violence by perpetuating the alienation that promotes campus rampages in the first place (Huggins, 2002; Newman, 2004). Delving deeper into community characteristics that schools must tap into to prevent renewed attacks, Newman (2004) examines the school shootings at Heath High School near Paducah, Kentucky, and Westside Middle School near Jonesboro, Arkansas. Lack of communication among local residents and between parents and children regarding youngsters that are clearly alienated and bent on taking out their frustrations on the school, a focal point for most small towns, lays the groundwork for otherwise preventable surprise attacks (Newman, 2004).

Although not a K–12 campus killing, the Virginia Tech massacre that erupted in April of 2007 exemplifies the failure of campus officials to communicate reputability to the public. To save face, Virginia Governor Timothy Kaine would later delegate an independent review of the university's lack of risk and crisis management, because numerous students and faculty had observed Cho Seung-Hui's, the shooter's, erratic and troubling behavior. Yet, little if anything was done to investigate the possibility that he might become violent. Moreover, the shootings occurred in two waves, and the university was not shut down after the first, when Cho shot and killed two students in a dormitory. That same day Cho shot 60 students, staff, and faculty in a science and engineering building, killing 30 of them. He then turned his weapon on himself. Panic spurred rumors that there was a second shooter. The entire affair went on record as the deadliest school killing field in United States history (ABC News, April 8, 2007; Beachy, 2007; *New York Times*, 2007; Shapira & Ruane, 2007).

Cho's family, unassuming dry cleaners, was harassed by the media and threatened by numerous community citizens. This lead to speculation that his parents might commit suicide. They did go into hiding, perhaps because FBI Assistant Director in Washington D.C., Joe Persichini did not place them in protective custody. However, Persichini stated that his organization and Fairfax, Virginia, county police would react to any hate crime that might crop up. That would be cold comfort to the Chos, if they were already dead. However, five days after the shooting, representing the family, Sun-Kyung, Cho's sister and Princeton graduate, wrote to the public that her family shared the darkness that enveloped the families of her brother's 32 victims. She penned, "We feel hopeless, helpless, and lost. This is someone I grew up with and loved. Now I feel like I don't know this person.... He has made the world weep. We are living a nightmare" (Breed & Beard, 2007, n.p.). Even so, other Korean students still feared retaliation just because of their ethnicity (ABC News, Feb. 10, 2007; CNN.com, 2007; *New York Times*, 2007; Shapira & Jackman, 2007). To the authors' knowledge, the university has not initiated any survivor community discussions that include the Chos nor encourage them to share their feelings of deep regret and anger, which might squire all involved toward some type of healing or restorative condition, fortifying rather than disintegrating their communities.

As indicated in the Virginia Tech disaster, much of the research and practice in risk and crisis school communication, especially in public relations, does not democratically involve the school community in dealing with the worst of campus crises. However, some sources do investigate violence on campus and offer detailed ways in which they can motivate school officials to get help for individuals who are traumatized. For example, schools could also organize and monitor other discussion groups that might identify potential perpetrators before they offend, and through shared decision making in conjunction with offender accountability (related to current retribution-centered justice and discipline) avoid another rash of school killings (Millar & Heath, 2004; e.g., Katz, Noddings, Kenneth, & Strike, 1999).

HISTORICAL BACKGROUND

Restorative and Retributive Justice

To deepen the understanding of the restorative and retributive dialectic in Western culture, we must first review the edicts of Hebrew tribal justice. Ideally, it focused on achieving shalom (restitution or recompense, not retribution) that embodied individual and collective voices to provide wholeness and harmony in relationships. It was considered the ideal state in which humans were created to live (Galaway & Hudson, 1996; Johnstone, 2002; Trebilcock, 2000; Yoder, 1987). Along with restitution came the notion of vindication for the victim and the law itself. Justice, when viewed through this lens, focuses on making things right through a process of settlement. In other words, crime creates a social imbalance and must be corrected by finding solutions among all of those who are involved (Van Ness & Strong, 1997; Yoder; 1987; Zehr, 1990).

Tribal control of justice eroded, shifting from city-state to some type of larger centralized control, until restoration and retribution could be detected in medieval European justice. Largely, it focused on community negotiation and, in rare occasions, the courts. Crime was viewed primarily in an interpersonal context. Most offenses represented an injustice toward or a conflict between people. Such wrongs created obligations and liabilities that had to be made right in some way. Victim and offender, as well as kin and community, played vital roles in this process. Feuds or revenge retaliations were ways of resolving such situations. However, more common ways included restitution and reconciliation, mediated by official representatives (Cragg, 1992; Zehr, 1990)·. Occurring simultaneously with restorative medieval practices was an undercurrent from retributive ancient Roman law that eventually blanketed restorative intentions. Retribution emerged "within the context of an overall struggle for power" and control (Zehr, 1987, p. 110). The development of canon law (a codified body of general decrees) in the early Catholic Church paralleled the Roman cultural and governmental civil code. Congregational self-rule evolved into ecclesiastical law and often embraced severely punitive measures (Hamilton, 2002). A primary concern of the papacy during the medieval years was to consolidate its authority as competing centers emerged in the early Christian churches. But, gradually, secular authorities formed to consolidate their supremacy and find ways to subordinate other power centers, including the church (Zehr, 1990). A declaration of royal authority, torture, and public executions were utilized as a tool for determining truth and exacting punishment (Foucault, 1977).

Beccaria's (1764) *On Crime and Punishment* is often cited as the foundation of modern penal law. His position was that people decide or choose their behavior on the basis of expectations about pain and pleasure. Kant (1797, 2000) used a debt metaphor to discuss the notion of just deserts. Citizens in a society enjoy the benefits of a rule of law. According to the principle of fair play, the loyal citizen must do his part in this system of reciprocal restraint. An individual who seeks the benefits of living under the rule of law without being willing to make the necessary sacrifices is dangerous (Murphy, 1992). In time, citizens tired of viewing nightmarish persecution and death, so, fueled by modernization, prisons developed as less visible means of dealing with mental illness and crime. Sentences could be calibrated and administered in private (Foucault, 1977). With monarchies in the throws of revolution, Paine's (1794) *Age of Reason* critiqued Christianity and theocracy and suggested that rational law (easily co-opted by the new governments) was even above the government.

The 19th century witnessed a complete metamorphosis of the approach to crime and justice. Berman (1993) terms this transitional time a legal revolution, where courts moved from reactive, accusatorial, umpiring roles to a more inquisitional form that claimed ownership of certain types of crimes. When these changes occurred, the nature of the outcomes also changed, including fines paid to the state, not restitution to victims. It was a matter of interpretation whether the law, as Paine suggested, was a hallowed thing that loomed above government or visa versa.

The following century's definition of punishment itself came to be governed by a few basic conceptual distinctions clarified by Hart (1959) in England and Rawls (1955, 1957) in the United States. Zalta (2005) delineates these analytical distinctions. Defining the concept of punishment and the institutions that inflict it must be kept distinct from justifying punishment. The practice of punishment must be defined as either backward-looking or forward-looking negotiation. The former was considered deontological, where no single idea captures all of the features in virtue, though the latter was preferable. Punishment served a utilitarian purpose but was only administered when an alleged offender was "proven" guilty (Sarker, 1998). Because crime gives the offender unfair advantage over the victim, forward-looking retribution advocates that the only way to even the score is to have the offender punished in the amount required to equalize the disruption (Maiese, 2004; Murphy, 1992; Zehr, 1990).

A major international exception to this modern trend was the Truth and Reconciliation Commission, chaired by Bishop Desmond Tutu and formed near the end of South African apartheid in 1993. It functioned in a restorative fashion: sought out the truth, required full disclosure by the perpetrator in face-to-face encounters with the victims, and granted amnesty from crimes committed. This act initiated communication between the country's citizens and their communities and the oppressive officials that had abused them. Because, it was argued, judges and lawyers, representatives of institutions far above schools and other local communities, meted out retributive justice alone, thwarting comprehensive post-crisis communication.

On the contrary, the Truth and Reconciliation Commission's mode of communication resembled a needs-based restorative philosophy that recognizes the value of every life and seeks to insure that the system does not deny any person the opportunity to exercise choice in meaningful ways. When an offense occurs or a conflict arises, one of the primary questions is to again use the concept of what can be done to make things right for all involved. Needs-based justice is concerned with communication between all of the social-structural conditions that exist within a community—families, schools, places of work, and worship. They, in turn, conduct empowering discussions with higher legal authorities (Sullivan & Tifft, 2005; Truth and Reconciliation Commission web site, 2003).

RESTORATIVE PRACTICES

Implications for Risk and Crisis Communication in Schools

Ted Wachtel, president of the International Institute for Restorative Practices (IIRP), based in Bethlehem, Pennsylvania, is often credited with bringing restorative justice to schools. During the mid-1990s, Wachtel developed SaferSanerSchools (Chmelynski, 2005). One of its intentions is to decrease the risk of school violence and help educators communicate to the public, especially, but not solely, when violent and other infractions are committed. Hopefully, the cycle of inadequate risk communication and poorly dealt with crises can diminish the risk of new violent outbursts. This metamorphosis leads to a fundamental change in the nature of a school climate, explains IRRP Director of Training Bob Costello. "It is the relationships, not specific strategies, which bring about meaningful change" (cited in Chmelynski, 2005, n.p.). The SaferSanerSchools program, currently in 30 to 40 schools nationwide, helps students understand the causes of their behavior while still understanding it as inappropriate (for some examples, see Table 26.1). In addition, there are several similar school-based programs, such as Tribes; Discipline Without Stress, Punishments, or Rewards; Positive Discipline; and The Responsive Classroom that incorporate many of the tenets of restorative practices while providing elaborate procedures for classroom or school-wide implementation.

Wachtel blames rising truancy and dropout rates, increasing disciplinary problems, violence, and mass murder largely on an absence of connectedness (alienation) in modern society. These are exactly some of the points Friedland (2001) and others make when arguing that risk and crisis communication theory and practice should explore how to create democratic reciprocal communication among and between rule makers (federal and state), schools and communities (V. Braithwaite, 2001; Morrison, 2001; Sullivan & Tifft, 2005; Wachtel, 2000). Speaking specifically about the disconnect within the educational community, Wachtel explains, "Schools have become larger, more impersonal institutions, and educators feel less connected to the families whose children they teach. Restorative practices [do things with people] rather than to them or for them, providing both high control and high support at the same time" (Carey, 1997; cited in Chmelynski, 2005, p. 18; Johnstone, 2002; Sullivan & Tifft, 2005). When this is done the risk of school killing, the ultimate offense, may be minimized.

Ed Baumgartner, principal of Palisades Middle School in Kintnersville, Pennsylvania, offered one example, claiming that participating in restorative justice programs encourages students' willingness to help address communicative behavior in other students. The school started using restorative practices in the fall of 2000. Baumgartner states, "There's also been a significant increase in students reporting other students for behavior problems, students self-reporting, and parents reporting their children" (cited in Chmelynski, 2005, n.p.). Moreover, in September 2006, a potential school crisis was averted in Green Bay, Wisconsin when a student notified authorities of a threat (Phelps, 2006). Parents and administrators at Green Bay East High School recognize the importance of students' willingness to communicate with authorities. McBride (2006) reported,

TABLE 26.1
Restorative Schools

State	*School*
CA	Center for Peacemaking & Conflict Studies, Fresno Pacific Univ.
CA, CT, GA, MA, VT	Educators for Social Responsibility, ESR serves over 375 schools in the United States
CO	Boulder High School, CO School Mediation Program
IA	Iowa Peace Institute
IL	Chicago Area Project in Chicago Public Schools
IN	Indiana's Safe & Responsive School's Project
MI	Safe Successful Schools, LLC
MN	PEASE Academy
NC	New Garden Friends School
NJ	Haddonfield School District
NY	Albany City School District, Safe Harbor
NY, NJ, PA	Safer Saner Schools
OK	John Wesley Charter School
PA	Buxmont Academy, Centennial School District, Green St. Friends School, Hatboro-Horsham School District, Haverford Township School District, Mastery Charter High School, Philadelphia City School District, Springfield Township School District, Souderton Area School District, Upper Darby School District, & Upper Merion Area School District
TN	SHHS Alternative Learning Center
VT	Hartland School District, Windsor School District
WI	Restorative Justice Experiment in Detroit, Janesville, Kenosha, Milwaukee, Racine, & Waukensha
WI	Madison Metro School District, Verona Area School District

Sources: SaferSanerSchools. Http://www.restorativepractices.org/Pages/safersanerschools.html; International Institute for Restorative Practices, http://www.iirp.org/.
Other web sites include: http://www.ojp.usdoj.gov/ovc/; http://www.iapeace.org/rj%20schools%20article.htm; http://www.schoolmediationcenter.org/; http://www.casel.org/home/index.php; http://restorativejusticeproject.org/; http://www.bcrjp.org/school_init.html; http://www.esrnational.org/home.htm; and http://www.chicagoareaproject.org/ (retrieved February, 10, 2007).

> Since the alleged threats were reported to authorities, school and community officials continually have praised the relationships that led a fellow East student to tell an associate principal about the purported plot. Those kinds of relationships are just as important as external measures, said board member and East parent Katie Maloney. 'The issue is not, what can we do to the structure, to try and keep vile things from happening,' she said. 'It's what we can do [to] teach people to work from within.' (n.p.)

When offenses do occur, as earlier noted, an important part of restoration is to hold offenders accountable to victims, legal authorities, and the school community for the harm they have caused. But unlike zero tolerance and authoritarian punishment, a proposed deterrence to potential violent offenders, restorative practices involve face-to-face encounters and encompass several informal procedures, such as peer mediation (when involved parties work to resolve the crisis through group discussion of all involved) (Cohen, 1995). Terry O'Connell, a community policing sergeant in Wagga Wagga, New South Wales, Australia (O'Connell, Wachtel, & Wachtel; 1999) created a circle group script to give novices guidance for the important points that should be covered. The questions and especially the participants could be altered to fit various minor or major crises, such school killings.

Circle groups usually involve the offender (or representatives if the offender is deceased) and the victim (or representatives); supporters for each party can also include various community members (Colorado School Mediation Project, 2000). Considerable counseling and preparation may take place to ready each participant to listen to the other. Willingness is a key to any successful resolution. The degree to which all are involved in meaningful emotional exchange and shared decision-making is the degree to which any form of social communication and discipline can be termed fully restorative (McCold & Wachtel, 2002, 2003). In fact, victims and other school community members are often allowed to negotiate the terms of such accountability with legal officials (J. Braithwaite, 2001; Trebilcock, 2000). Also, before the conference, several forms are signed including a justice referral and restorative justice conference agreement; and restorative justice pre-conference for person harmed, restorative justice pre-conference for student who caused harm, restorative justice pre-conference supporter or witness, and restorative justice conference forms (http://isd742.org/rj/tools.html). Figure 26.2 provides a sample script for a circle encounter.

Especially in New Zealand and Canada, but also in the United States, legal authorities are working with schools and other community organizations to create holistic and restorative juvenile justice practices, which, it is held, can minimize the risk of future offenses that may escalate into murders like the campus killings discussed earlier in this chapter. In effect they are risk measures. In 1993, the Balanced and Restorative Justice (BARJ) Project grew from the Office of Juvenile Justice and Delinquency Prevention's (OJJDP) grant to Florida Atlantic University (FAU). The next year, FAU developed a partnership arrangement with the Center for Restorative Justice & Peacemaking (Mediation) at the University of Minnesota. Usually these programs are for first-time offenders of lesser property crimes, including shoplifting and vandalism, while a committee interviews prospective participants and his or her families to familiarize itself with each juvenile's case. The project goal is to train and consult with committed juvenile justice officials and community members to create a balanced system that incorporates three key components: community safety, offender accountability to individuals and the community, and competency development for offenders. Reiterating the already discussed restorative intentions, the objective is to make things as "right" as they can be in the aftermath of an offense through involving victims' perspectives and the juvenile offender's meaningful atonement (see Figure 26.3.) BARJ proponents maintain that this can be achieved when juvenile justice professionals reconceptualize crime and penitence as a community problem and convince all stakeholders that together they can create solutions (Bilchik, 1998; Goodwin, 2001; Umbreit, 1999).

Beginning contextually within one community setting, in 1993 BARJ selected the Department of Juvenile Justice in Palm Beach County, Florida, to pilot its program. Palm Beach County was a jurisdiction with a diverse population that had been increasing exponentially since 1980. By 1993, the area employed a new county manager who was knowledgeable about and dedicated to restorative justice. He assiduously worked with judges, public defenders, the state attorney, law enforcement, staff from juvenile residential facilities, and case managers, augmented by community activists, business leaders, and victim-services providers. Meetings with many of these stakeholders produced dedicated well-educated representatives of restorative practices willing to become part of the three-pronged BARJ canon. Although at this writing much is left to be done, some successes have addressed each of the three major premises. (For a thorough discussion of the Florida and other state efforts, see Bilchik, 1998.)

A department of juvenile justice delinquency counselor was headquartered at Palm Beach County's Glades Glen Apartment complex. Adjudicated youngsters reported each day, and after school five days a week obtained tutoring and engaged in appropriate recreational activities. The project supervisor made arrangements with the Red Cross to train certain offenders to operate a day-care within the facility. Other participants spoke on crime prevention and the consequences of crime to the elementary and middle schools. Juvenile justice case managers and other staff worked with local schools during lunch periods and spent time in those institutions at least once a week. They

At the actual encounter, all parties sit in a circle located in a neutral place. Seating plans are predetermined. The mediator introduces him or herself and then explains the disaster or more minor offense that took place. Then s/he individually asks all involved some questions, insisting that each party should have an uninterrupted turn to participate. Of course the script would have to be modified when the offender has committed suicide, as is often the case in school shootings, family members could replace him. In our view, key school community or neighborhood members should also be included and asked similar questions like the ones presented below. This exercise may have to be repeated time and time again with considerable modifications due to the extreme emotions erupting from campus slaughters.

Speaking to the offender, the mediator asks, "What happened on November 3rd," for example?
"What were you thinking about at the time?"
"What have you thought about since this incident?"
"Who do you think has been affected by your actions?"
"How have you been affected?"

Then, the victim or (if deceased) his or her family is addressed.
"What was your reaction at the time of the incident?"
"How do you feel about what happened?"
"What has been the hardest thing for you?"
"How did your family and friends react when they heard about the incident?"

The victim's friends or supporters are addressed.
"How did you feel when this happened"?
"What has been the hardest thing for you?"
"What do you think are the main issues?"

The principal and/or teachers could also be included.
"As principal what was your reaction at the time of the incident?"
"How do you feel about what happened?"
"What has been the hardest thing for you?"

The offender or his or her representatives are asked to respond.
"How do you feel about what happened?
"What has been the hardest thing for you?"
"What do you think are the main issues?"
"What has been the hardest thing for you?"

The offender or representatives are given another opportunity to speak.
"Is there anything you want to say at this time?"

Victims then could add to the discussion by asking,
"What would you like from today's conference?"

Then, the mediator offers the offender or another of his or her representatives a chance to be heard.
"How do you feel about that?"

Teachers and the principal are then queried.
"What would you like from today's conference, and how could they be used to prevent further violence?"

The offender or representatives are asked to respond to the above remarks, after which time the mediator asks,
"Is there anything else anyone here would like to see come from today's conference?"

The mediator concludes by saying,
"Before I formally close this conference, I would like to provide everyone with a final opportunity to speak. Is there anything anyone wants to say?"

Finally s/he says,
"Thank you for your contributions in dealing with this difficult matter. [Possibly], Congratulations on the way you have worked through the issues. Please help yourselves to some refreshments while I prepare the agreement for your signatures."

FIGURE 26.2 Adapted from a sample script. *Source:* http://www.realjustice.org/Pages/script.html (retrieved August 4, 2007).

Clients/Customers	Goals	Values
Victims	Accountability	When an individual commits an offense the offender incurs a responsibility to individual victims and the community.
Youth	Competency Development	Offenders who enter the juvenile justice system should leave more competent than they were when they entered
Community	Community Safety	Juvenile justice has a responsibility to protect the public from juveniles in the system

FIGURE 26.3 Balanced and Restorative Justice. *Source:* http://ojjdp.ncjrs.org/pubs/implementing/balanced.html (retrieved December 12, 2007).

also provided seminars to teachers, parents, and administrators to better prepare them to identify the risk of violence through early warning programs and to learn how to manage a crisis should it arise (Bilchik, 1998).

To provide offenders with meaningful competencies, the program eschewed mindless traditional types of community service such as writing repetitive essays, digging holes, and picking up trash. The juvenile justice system expanded its infrastructure to support youth development projects that developed marketable skills. For example, the U.S. Department of the Interior U.S. Fish and Wildlife Service trained offenders for public service-oriented employment, the proceeds from which are used for financial remuneration to victims (Bilchik, 1998).

Restoration is never achieved without offender accountability, only a part of which is financial. Palm Beach County case managers and counselors in two Florida residential juvenile offender facilities offered awareness programs based on National Organization for Victim Assistance protocols. Texas's Giddings State School and Ohio's Buckeye Training Program provide curricula for youthful offenders that highlight the human devastation of their offences. Part of this includes a victim-dialogue to put a human face on the harm an offender has caused. Because this sometimes involved direct contact, offenders and victims were prepared through counseling and interviewing to deal with such encounters without being further hardened into self-justification or re-victimized, respectively. For any number of reasons, early on in Palm Beach, victim participation was limited, so individual staff members, who were also crime victims, were some of the first to participate. Progress is apparent, but much time is needed to change what we have already explained is a highly entrenched retributive system that teaches victims to feel helpless through alienation and shuttles offenders into the penitentiary's great abyss (Bilchik, 1998).

BARJ has also consulted with the Community Intensive Supervision Project (CISP), a part of Pittsburgh Pennsylvania's Allegheny County Juvenile Court Services. By 1996, there were five neighborhoods sites that provided an alternative to institutionalization for youthful offenders. The Allegheny County youngsters were primarily African American, as was the staff, many of which hailed from the same area. To reassure the hosting areas of their residents' safety, the program was rigorous and strenuously supervised; school attendance was mandatory as was daily attendance at a CISP center. Electronic monitoring, drug and alcohol testing, meaningful offender community service, and family counseling were also required (Bilchik, 1998).

CISP worked to avoid "fixing" offenders to reintegrating them back into the community. One means was through a drug and alcohol treatment program that, particularly in classic Twelve Step literature, offered offenders the opportunity to self-reflect and atone to victims and their communities. The results were working with disabled residents, painting low-income homes and cleaning graffiti from building walls; keeping vacant lots clean and, in some cases, planting community gardens; shoveling snow in parking lots and driveways of local businesses; doing yard work for elderly citizens; taking part in voter registration drives; preparing bulk mailings for various community organizations; and helping to make a community Christmas party come alive (Bilchik, 1998).

A CISP site, the Garfield Center, developed an excellent relationship with the Bloomfield-Garfield Corporation (BGC), a neighborhood-based community development group that viewed offenders as potential "extended staff," paying them to do any number of projects such as the all popular community garden and to learn trades through affiliated constructions companies. The Garfield Center's supervisor served on BGC's board of directors. In so doing the Center developed mutually beneficial relationships with other community organizations. Slowly, formerly skeptical residents began to trust the program, but it remains to be seen whether the community is united enough to sustain the evolving restorative juvenile process (Bilchik, 1998).

No matter how restorative a school or community's justice system might be, as is all too apparent, the most heinous of all violent school crises, murder, can still become a reality. However, some citizens and educators are dedicated enough to maintain a restorative attitude in the midst of such a crisis, almost automatically initiating victim-offender conferencing that can help all affected parties regain some sense of efficacy and hope which may, in turn, lead to future crisis prevention (Palk, Hayes, & Prenzler, 1998). One such instance was the earlier mentioned murder of several Amish school children. The perpetrator's wife told investigators that the husband she knew could not have done such a horrible thing. Flimsy as it may seem, the only explanation was that Roberts was haunted by a 20-year-old trauma of losing an infant daughter, taking out his rage on his student victims. Despite Roberts' ruthless acts, the Amish created a fund for the victims' families, *including the Roberts*. When a reporter asked one victim's grandfather how he made sense of this senseless act, he said that it was by forgiving the perpetrator (Kaufman & Gately, 2006 ; Raffaele, 2007; Simmons, 2007).

Consider another example of voluntary restorative practices as told from a victim's perspective: Bud Welch's educator daughter, Julie, was killed in the 1995 Oklahoma City bombing of the Murrah Federal Building. Welch fell into a chasm of depression and heavy drinking, harboring deadly vengeance against Timothy McVeigh and Terry Nichols, the crime's perpetrators. Welch (2002) explained, "Perhaps you recall TV images of Nichols being rushed from an automobile to a building with bulletproof vests on. The reason that the police did that is because people like me would have killed him" (p. 277). But something changed. In a search for healing and escape from his pain Welch paid a visit to McVeigh's father Bill and sister Jennifer, who like Julie, was a teacher aware of the potential for retributive actions toward her because of her brother's deadly deeds. Welch continued, "After our hour-and-a-half-long visit, I got up from the kitchen table and Jennifer came from the other end of the table, and gave me a hug, and we sobbed, and I was able to hold her face in my hands…and tell her, 'Honey, the three of us are in this for the rest of our lives'" (p. 280).

CONCLUSION

Not every constructed or voluntary restorative practice will completely eliminate the risk of major events, such as school shootings, from reoccurring. But even when offenders take their own lives or are jailed through established procedures and the primary victims are deceased, there are still many offenders' and victims' friends and family members, in addition to community representatives left to make sense of the debacle. In other words, the crisis is left unmanaged. In the case of school-based violence, sufferers should be attended to, and the school should take the lead in doing so. Participating in restorative communicative practices does have the potential to prevent further fragmentation of the community, which can only lead to more and more alienation among its members, and the potential for retaliatory violence. Discussion groups might include high-powered business owners or political leaders and any number of citizens whose lives, homes, or business are affected by school rampages (Newman, 2004). School personnel should familiarize themselves about restorative justice and its practices. Armed with such expertise, educators could more successfully encourage the school community to participate. It is worth a try to add restoration to current risk and crisis communications theory and practice by embedding it into school safety policy and making it part of the emergency crisis plan.

BIBLIOGRAPHY

ABC News (2007, February 10). Looking for blame and souvenirs from the 'obliterated' Cho family: Unabomber's brother David Kaczynski draws on his own nightmare to help family of Virginia Tech shooter. Retrieved August 10, 2007, from http://abcnews.go.com/US/VATech/story?id=3078950&page=1.

ABC News (2007, April 18). The facts of the Virginia massacre: The dead, The injured and the investigation so far. Retrieved August 10, 2007, from http://abcnews.go.com/US/story?id=3053832&page=1.

Ahmed, E., Harris, N., Braithwaite, J. & Braithwaite, V. (2001). *Shame management through reintegration*. Cambridge, UK: Cambridge University Press.

ajamom. (2007, April 23). Tough one. *Demons Register*. Retrieved August 10, 2007, from http://forums.dm-moms.com/viewtopic.php?t=21.

Anderson, E. (1999). *Code of the street; Decency, violence and the moral life of the inner-city*. New York: Norton.

Asmussen, K. J., & Creswell, J. W. (1995). Campus response to a student gunman, *Journal of Higher Education, 66*, 575–591.

Beachy, L. (2007, April 17). AC: The Peoples Media Company Breaking News Part II: Two shootings at Virginia Tech updated information and eyewitness accounts of the worst college campus tragedy in U.S. History. Retrieved August 10, 2007, from http://www.associatedcontent.com/article/217339/breaking_news_part_ii_two_shootings.html.

Beccaria, M. Trans. Ingraham, E. D. (1764, 1778, 1819). *An essay on crimes and punishment*. Philadelphia: Philip H. Nicklin.

Berman, H. J. (1993). *Faith and order: Reconciliation of law and religion*. Cambridge, MA: Scholars Press.

Bilchik, S. (1998). Guide for implementing the balanced and restorative justice model. Washing D.C.: US Department of Justice Office. Retrieved December 10, 2007, from http://www.ncjrs.gov/pdffiles/167887.

Blair, F. (1999). Does zero tolerance work? *Principal, 79*, 36–37.

Blauner, R. (1964). Alienation and freedom, the factory worker and his industry. Chicago: University of Chicago Press.

Brady, P. (2004). Just deserts: Can a retributivist theory of punishment be justified? *Irish Student Law Review*.12. Retrieved December 8, 2006, from http://www.islr.ie/Reviews/2004/retributivism.php.

Braithwaite, J. (1989). *Crime, shame and reintegration*. Cambridge: Cambridge University Press.

Braithwaite, J. (2001). Youth development circles. *Oxford Review of Education*. 27(2), 239–252.

Braithwaite, V. (2001). Values and restorative justice in schools. In H. Strang & J. Braithwaite (Eds.). *Restorative justice: Philosophy in practice* (PDF version). Burlington, VT: Ashgate. Retrieved November 7, 2006, from http://crj.anu.edu.au/menus/submenus/school_publications.php.

Breed, A. G., & Beard A. (2007). Student wrote about death and spoke in whispers, But no one imagined what Cho Seung Hui would do. Associated Press Archive (April 21). Retrieved August 10, 2007, from http://www.ap.org>www.ap.org.

Carey, M. (1997). Taking down the walls: Measures to integrate the objectives of the justice system with the community's. *Community Corrections Report*. Retrieved April 6, 2005, from http://www.ojp.usdoj.gov/nij/rest-just/ch6/takingdown.html.

Chavez, N. (2006). Experts weigh in on series of school shootings. Retrived October 3, 2006, from http://www.news10.net/storyfull2.aspx? Storied=20414.

Chavis, D. (1998). Building community capacity to prevent violence through coalitions and partnerships. In D. R. Karp. (Ed.) *Community justice: An emerging field*. Lanham (pp. 81–94). Lanham, MD: Rowman and Littlefield.

Chmelynski, C. (2005). Restorative justice for discipline with respect. *Education Digest: Essential Readings Condensed for Quick* Review, *71*(1), 17–20.

Chmelynski, C. (2005). Schools find 'restorative justice' more effective than expulsion. School Board News. Retrieved November 2006, from http://nsba.org/site/doc_sbn_issue.asp?TRACKID=&VID=55&CID=682&DID=35966.

CNN.com. (2007, April 21). Massacre at Virginia Tech: Virginia Tech killer's family: We are 'living a nightmare. Retrieved August 10, 2007, from http://www.cnn.com/2007/US/04/20/cho.family.statement/index.html.

Cohen, R. (1995). *Students resolving conflict: Peer mediation in schools*. Glenview, IL: GoodYear Books.

Colorado School Mediation Project. (2000). Restorative justice for schools: A guide to understanding the principles and practices of school-based restorative justice. Boulder, CO. Retrieved October 10, 2006, from http://www.csmp.org.

Cornell, D. G., & Sheras, P. L. (1998). Common errors in school crisis response: Learning from our mistakes. *Psychology in the* Schools, *35*(3), 297–307.

Cragg, W. (1992). *The practice of punishment: Towards a theory of restorative justice*. New York: Routledge.

Dwyer, K. (1999). Children killing children: Strategies to prevent youth violence. *Communique* (Spring), 1–9.

Dwyer, K., Osher, D., & Warger, C. (1998). *Early warning, timely response: A guide to safe schools*. Washington, DC: U.S. Department of Education.

Foucault, M., Trans. Sheridan, A. (1977). *Discipline and punish: The birth of the prison*. New York: Pantheon Books.

Friedland, L. A. (2001). Communication, community, and democracy: Toward a theory of the communicatively integrated community. *Communication Research*, *28*(4), 358–391.

Fromm, E. (1947). *Man for himself: An inquiry into the psychology of ethics*. New York: Holt.

Galaway, B., & Hudson, J. (Eds.). (1996). *Restorative justice: International perspectives*. Monsey, NY: Criminal Justice Press.

Goodwin, T. (2001). The role of restorative in teen courts: A preliminary look. Retrieved July 27, 2007, from http://www.hopehealing.org.

Hart, H. L. A. (1959). Definition and theory in jurisprudence, *Law Quarterly Review*, 51, 1935–1375.

Hess, H. (2002). *The early development of canon law and the council of Serdica*. Oxford: Oxford University Press.

Hiley-Young, B., & Gerrity, E. T. (1994). Critical incident stress debriefing (CICD): Values and limitations in disaster response. *NCP Clinical Quarterly, 4*, 1–4.

Huggins, D. (2002). Educational support services: From old paradigms to boundary spanning. *Learning Matters*, *7*(1), 3–7.

Johnstone, G. (2002). *Restorative justice*. Portland, OR: Willan Publishing.

Kant, I. (1797/2000). *The metaphysics of morals*. Cambridge: Cambridge University Press.

Karp, B. (2001). Restorative justice in school communities. *Youth and Society*, *33*(2), 249–272.

Karp, B. & Breslin, B. (1995). Institutions as the infrastructure of democracy. In A. Etzioni (Ed.), *New communitarian thinking* (pp. 170–180). Charlottesville: University of Virginia Press.

Katz, M. S., Noddings, N., Kenneth A., & Strike, K. A. (Eds.). (1999). *Justice and caring*. New York: Teachers College Press.

Kaufman, P., Chen, X., Choy, S. P., Ruddy, S. A., Miller, A. K., Fleury, J. K., Chandler, K. A., Rand, M. R., Klaus, P., & Planty, M. G. (2000). *Indicators of school crime and safety*. Washington, DC: U.S. Departments of Education and Justice.

Kocieniewski, D., & Gately, A. (2006). Milk truck driver in Pennsylvania killed four young girls and wounded seven others before killing himself. (Oct. 3). Posted by: Amish America. (Feb. 19, 2007). Retrieved July 31, 2007, from http://www.amishamerica.typepad.com/amish_america/2007/02/miracle_girls.html.

Lipset, S. M., & Schneider, W. (1983). The confidence gap: Business, labor and government in the public mind. New York: The Free Press.

Maiese, M. (2004). What retributive justice is. Retrieved November 2006, from http://www.beyondintractability.org/essay/retributive_justice.

McBride, K. (Posted 2006, September). Workshop to examine school safety. Crisis preparedness in focus after alleged East High threat. *Green Bay Press Gazette*. Retrieved December 9, 2007, from http://www.greenbaypressgazette.com/apps/pbcs.dll/article?AID=/99999999/.

McCold, P., & Wachtel, T. (2002). Restorative justice theory validation. In E. Weitekamp & H-J Kerner. (Eds.). *Restorative justice: theoretical foundation* (pp.110–142). Devon, UK: Willan Publishing.

McCold, P., & Wachtel, T. (2003). In pursuit of paradigm: A theory of restorative justice. Paper presented at the XIII World Congress of Criminology, August 10–15. Rio de Janeiro. Retrieved November 6, 2006, from http://www.realjustice.org/library/paradigm.html.

Mitchell, B. (2006). Testing school security: Anatomy of two decisions. *Poynter On-line. www.poynter.org*. Retrieved November 10, 2006, from http://www.poynter.org/content/content_view.asp?id=113126 - 37k – (Oct 31).

Morrison, B. (2001). Restorative justice and school violence: Building theory and practice. Center for Restorative Justice. Paper presented at the International Conference on Violence in Schools and Public Policies, Palais de l'UNESCO. Paris. (March 5–7).

Murphy, J. G. (1992). *Retribution reconsidered: More essays in the philosophy of law*. Dordrecht: Kluwer. Retrived July 31, 2007, from http://www.beyondintractability.org/essay/retributive_justice/.

New Jersey v. T.L. O. (1985). 94 N. J., at 343, 463 A. 2d, at 934, 940. (January 15).

New York Times (2007). Virginia Tech shooting leaves 33 dead Retrived August 10, 2007, from http://www.nytimes.com/2007/04/16/us/16cnd-shooting. html?ex=1186027200&en=24b3ba3bef0f0fb0&ei=5070.

Newman, K. (2004). *Rampage: The social roots of school shootings*. Boulder, CO: Perseus Books.

O'Connell, T., Wachtel, B., & Wachtel, T. (1999). *Conferencing handbook: The new real justice training manual*. Pipersville, PA: The Piper's Press.

Ogle, J. P. & Eckman, M. (2002). Dress-related responses to the Columbine shootings: Other-imposed and self-designed. *Family and Consumer Sciences Research Journal*, *31*(2), 155–194.

Paine, T. (1794). *The age of reason*. Luxembourg, 8th Pluviose (January 27). Retrieved July 15, 2006, from http://www.ushistory.org/Paine/reason/index.htm.

Palk, G., Hayes, H., & Prenzler. T. (1998). Restorative justice and community conferencing: Summary of findings form a pilot study. *Current Issues in Criminal Justice*, *10*(2),138–155.

Peterson, R., & Skiba, R. (1999). The dark side of zero tolerance: Can punishment lead to safe schools? *Phi Delta Kappan*, *80*, 372-376, 381-382.

Phelps, N. (2006). 'I decided it was my duty to inform the authorities,' East student says, Green Bay Gazette. (Sept. 21). Retrieved November 1, 2006, from http://www.greenbaypressgazette.com/apps/pbcs.dll/article?AID=/99999999/GPG0101/609210543/0/theme.

Poland, S., & Pitcher, G. (1992). *Crisis intervention in the schools*. New York: Guilford.

Poland, S. (1999). *School violence: Lessons learned.* Longmont, CO: Sopris West.

Pynoos, R. S., & Nader, K. (1998). Psychological first aid and treatment approach to children exposed to community violence: Research implications. *Journal of Traumatic Stress*, *1*(4), 445–473.

Raffaele, M. (2007, October 12). *Demolition crew razes Pa. Amish schoolhouse where 5 girls were killed*. Associated Press.

Rawls, J. (1955). Two concepts of rules. *Philosophical Review*, *64*(1), 3–32.

Rawls, J. (1957). Justice as fairness. *Journal of Philosophy*, *54*(22), 653–662.

Sampson, R. J. (1995). The community. In J. Q. Wilson & J. Petersilia (Eds.), *Crime* (pp. 193–216). San Francisco: Institute for Contemporary Studies.

Schiffbauer, P. (2000). A checklist for safe schools. *Educational Leadership, 57*(6), 72–75.

Seeman, M., & Anderson C. S. (1983). Alienation and alcohol: The roll of work, Mastery, and community in drinking behavior. *American Sociological Review*, *48*(1), 60–77.

Sergiovanni, T. J. (1994). *Building community in schools*. San Francisco: Jossey Bass.

Shapira, I., & Jadkman, (2007). T. Gunman kills 32 at Virginia Tech in deadliest shooting in U.S. History. *Washington Post* (April 17), p. A01. Retrived August 10, 2007, from http://www.washingtonpost.com/wpdyn//,content/article/2007/04/16/AR2007041600533.html.

Shapira, I., & Ruane, M. E. (2007, April 18). Student wrote about death and spoke in whispers, But no one imagined what Cho-Seung Hui would do. *Washington Post*, p. A01. Retrived August 10, 2007, from http://www.washingtonpost.com/wp-dyn/content/ article/2007/04/17/AR2007041700563_pf.html.

Simmons, M. (2007, Jan. 31). Letting go after shooting, Amish school embodies effort to heal. *New York Times*, Final section A, p. 12.

Skiba, R. (2004). Zero tolerance: The assumptions and the facts. *Education Policy Briefs*, 2(4), 1–8.

Strang, H., & Braithwaite, J. (2001). *Restorative justice and civil society*. Cambridge: Cambridge University Press.

Sturges, D. C. (1994). Communicating through crisis. A strategy for organizational survival. *Management Communication Quarterly*, 7(3), 297–316.

Sullivan, D., & Tifft, L. (2005). *Restorative justice: Healing the foundations of our everyday lives and contemporary issues in organized crime*. Monsey, NY: Willow Tree Press.

Taylor, C. M., & Graves, L. C. (1998). Trainees endorse crisis response, recovering training. *School Safety*, (Fall), 20–30.

Trebilcock, R. (2000). From silos to circles: Reclaiming restorative practices. Correctional Services Canada, Ottawa, on assignment with Real Justice. Retrieved July 31, 2007, from http://www.iirp.org/library/t2000/t2000_rtrebilcock.html.

Truth and Reconciliation Commission Website, (2003). Retrieved August 9, 2007, from http://www.doj.gov.za/trc/.

Umbreit, M. S. (1999). Avoiding the marginalization and "McDonaldization" of victim offender mediation: A case study in moving toward the mainstream. In G. Bazemore & L. Walgrave. (Eds.). *Restorative juvenile justice* (pp. 213–234). Monsey, NY: Criminal Justice Press.

United States v. Lopez. (1995). (93-1260), 514 U.S. 549.

Van Ness, D., & Strong, K. H. (1997). *Restoring justice*. Cincinnati, OH: Anderson.

Wachtel, T. (2000). Safer saner schools: Restoring community in a disconnected world. Retrieved November 2006, from http://www.restorativepractices.org/Pages/safersanerschools.html.

Waddell, D., & Thomas, A. (1999). Helping children cope. *Communique*, (Spring), 12–14.

Welch, B. (2002). Speaking out against the execution of Timothy McVeigh. In D. R. Dow & M. Dow (Eds.), *Machinery of death: The reality of America's death penalty regime* (pp. 275–282). New York: Routledge.

Wilson, S. (2002). *Real people, real crisis: An inside look at corporate crisis communications*. Winchester, VA: Oakhill Press.

Yoder, P. B. (1987). *Shalom: The Bible's word for salvation, justice and peace*. Newton, KS: Faith and Life Press.

Zalta, E. N. (Ed.). (2005). Punishment. *The Stanford encyclopedia of philosophy*. Stanford: The Metaphysics Research Lab Center For The Study of Language and Information. Retrieved September 5, 2006, from http://plato.stanford.edu/entries/punishment.

Zehr, H. (1990). *Changing lenses: A new focus for crime and justice*. Scottdale, PA: Herald Press.

27

Denial, Differentiation, and Apology: On the Use of Apologia in Crisis Management

Keith Michael Hearit
Western Michigan University

Kasie Mitchell Roberson
Miami University

The terrorist attacks of September 11, 2001, dramatically changed the operating landscape for the entire airline industry. As a result of planes being used as terrorist weapons, as well as the shock to the United States economy, previously profitable carriers were forced to alter their business model. One such carrier that faced dramatic losses was American Airlines. In order to stave off a Chapter 11 bankruptcy filing, in April 2003 the airline asked for and was granted $1.8 billion in wage concessions from its 110,000 employees in its mechanics' and flight attendants' unions (Wong, 2003a). The American Airlines executive team, then, in an act of wrong-headed management, subsequently announced that it was giving retention bonuses to its six most senior executives as well as offering $41 million in pensions to another 45 senior executives (Wong, 2003a, 2003b). When the news of the decision broke, the outcry of the unions was significant and thrust the company into a public relations maelstrom. Union leader John Ward said: "It's the equivalent of an obscene gesture from management" (Horowitz, Athitakis, Lasswell, & Thomas, 2004, n.p.). Chief Executive Officer Donald Carty quickly recognized the misstep, cancelled the retention agreements, and apologized for the company's decision.

> I have apologized to our union leaders for this and for the concern it has caused our employees. Those executives who have made the personal commitment to remain with American during the financial crisis, myself included, are not here solely for monetary reasons and we have all agreed to give up these retention payments in order to give our employees confidence in management's on-going commitment to shared sacrifice. (ARM Corporation, 2003, p. 1)

Observers praised Carty's quick response and forthrightness in response to the misstep.

In effect, Carty responded to the public relations crisis with what communication scholars have characterized as an apologia, or a "speech of self-defense" (Ware & Linkugel, 1973, p. 273). This compulsion to "clear one's name" is a familiar motive both to human and organizational actors, and as such, the use of an apologia to respond to a crisis is well-established by communication scholars as a necessary vehicle by which to extract social actors from intractable situations (Burke, 1984; Fisher, 1970; Hearit, 2006). To take such an approach to crisis situations does not mean that crisis management is solely communicative; indeed, good management decisions must be made to extricate a company from a crisis. Rather, the point is that regardless of the nature of a crisis there is a communicative dimension, one in which social actors must use apologetic discourse to respond to rhetorical exigencies and audience expectations.

As such, this chapter will seek to review the extant research literature on the relationship of apologia to crisis management; arguing that corporations respond to difficult contexts by balancing compelling and competing interests as they apply an "appropriate" response which is sensitive to the strategic, legal, and contextual dynamics that inhere to the particular context. To support this claim, the chapter first surveys a number of definitional issues as to what constitutes an apologia as well as the contexts that typically result in apologetic communication; second, it addresses the variety of contemporary approaches to the study of apologia and crisis management; third, it reflects on the constraining effect of liability on corporate speech; and finally, it draws some conclusions as to the use of corporate apologia in public relations crises.

DEFINITIONAL ISSUES

Allegations

As alluded to earlier, an apologia is discourse used in the defense of a reputation. When first studied, scholars primarily viewed it solely as a defense of an individual's character. In the seminal piece on apologia, for instance, Ware and Linkugel (1973) wrote that: "an attack on a person's character ... does seem to demand a direct response" (p. 274). Likewise, Harrell, Ware, and Linkugel (1975) argued that apologia concerned itself with the defense of an individual's "morality, motive, and reputation" (p. 246). However, scholars soon began to recognize that the situations in which social actors delivered apologiae were not just in the defense of character, but also included the defense of policies (Gold, 1978). Drawing from a political context, Gold (1978) asserted that it often is difficult to separate a defense of policies from a politician's public character. Similarly, Ryan (1982) argued that since allegations of wrongdoing are not limited to attacks on character, apologiae should not be limited to the defense of character—but to the defense of character *and* policy. The argument as to whether apologia is about the defense of character or policies is of direct relevance when apologia is applied to the organizational context—in that it is difficult, if not impossible, to separate an organization's actions from its organizational identity; the two are self-reflexive. In effect, a corporate apologia is a "response to a social legitimization crisis" (Hearit, 1995, p. 3).

Legitimacy is the "... right or title to exercise authority" (Francesconi, 1982, p. 49). For an organization to be perceived as legitimate, it must be seen as behaving in an appropriate manner by balancing utility and social responsibility concerns (Dowling & Pfeffer, 1975; Epstein & Votaw, 1978). Specifically, its "... acts must demonstrate responsibility, create trust, and be legal" (Hearit, 1995, p. 3). Legitimacy is critical because organizations are dependent on the support of key publics and the approval of political institutions to ensure their survival (Roper, 2005).

Organizations respond with apologiae when they find their legitimacy is threatened in times of crisis (Boyd, 2000; Brummer, 1991; Coombs, 1992; Deephouse, 1996; Holmstrom, 2005; Metzler, 2001; Seeger, 1986). The defense of actions or statements that have impugned an organization's legitimacy must be addressed quickly if an organization is to survive. Only when they acquiesce to public pressure and political consensus is their legitimacy restored. Failure to do so is likely to result in a negative regulatory result (Roper, 2005).

If an organization is found to have broken the law, there may be fines or sanctions to be faced, but earning back the public's trust may be much more difficult. It goes without saying that a key actor in the circulation of allegations against organizations is the media. One of the most significant aspects of the media is its ability to set the agenda with regards to which stories citizens pay attention. As such, journalists exercise a great deal of influence in communicating what is important as well as what topics are up for debate and those which are settled (Jamieson & Waldman, 2003). In so doing, the media decides what stories are worth covering and how to interpret the stories that are covered. Concomitantly, one of the most important features the media possess is the ability to frame issues. Graber (2002) states,

> The media set the public agenda when news stories rivet attention on a problem and make it seem important to many people. The media build the public agenda when they create the political context that shapes public opinions. (p. 175)

Therefore, the media has the power to transform an issue over time by framing it in a new light.

Because of the media's power to influence and shape public opinion, the role of the media in apologia is pervasive. The media have an interest in keeping the crisis interesting, and often do so by describing it as a morality tale of good versus evil (Campbell, 1991). When a crisis occurs, the media present it to the public, often reporting third-party criticism of how the crisis is being handled, and provide those directly involved in the response to the crisis an opportunity to discuss the situation. This gives individuals and organizations the opportunity to engage in apologia.

However, because of short news segments, when organizations do respond, most find that only a small portion of their defense is broadcast. This means that many organizations typically divide their response into short, but complete segments that clearly articulate their defense. This "sound bite defense," characterized by: (1) being 15–30 seconds in length, (2) a plausible counter-accounting for the "facts," and (3) the ability to stand-alone and not be taken out of context, is vital for an organization to ensure its defense is not misconstrued by media.

Contexts

A wide-variety of different approaches exist to explain the different crisis contexts that organizations face (Coombs, 1995, 1999; Hearit, 1999; Marcus & Goodman, 1991; Seeger, Sellnow & Ulmer, 1998, 2003). In an exhaustive review of the contexts that organizations often confront, for instance, Seeger et al. (2003) propose the following types of crises: crises in public perception; natural disasters, product or service crises (including product recalls, food-borne illness, and media-induced crises); terrorist attacks; economic crises; human resource crises; industrial crises; oil and chemical spills; and transportation disasters.

Yet it should be noted that not all crises described by Seeger et al. (2003) result in apologiae delivered by organizational and governmental officials. To draw from a scientific metaphor, crisis is the *genus*, while apologia is the *species*. The sine qua non of what makes a crisis context an apologetic one is the fact that there is a critical ring to an accusation. For instance, in a food borne illness crisis, there is an urgent need for a quick response, though little information is known; yet that fact alone does not necessarily make it an apologetic crisis. It is only when and if criticism is spouted for the slowness of a government's response that the need for an apologia becomes evident. To this end, we propose that there are four primary types of apologetic crises: scandals and illegalities, accidents, product safety incidents, and crises of social irresponsibility.

Scandals and Illegalities. The first context, scandals and illegalities, refers to those incidents in which there is a violation of a social code, whether it be a key executive whose private indiscretion has become public or, alternatively, engaged in some form of dishonest behavior that has exposed the organization to significant legal attention. The recent case of Enron, which used a form of off-the-books accounting to inflate its profits and defraud investors is an example of this type of wrongdoing. For organizations, the fortunate feature of this type of wrongdoing is that the guilt usually is centered in the actions of a small cadre of individuals and, as such, often can be dealt with cleanly and directly.

Accidents. In the second crisis context, accidents, due to the intersection of complex technology with human actors, there is an unexpected outcome in which lives are lost or the environment is despoiled (Hearit, 2001). Such was the case with the infamous *Exxon Valdez* oil spill. While the moniker of an "accident" does suggest that the outcome was accidental and unintended, post-accident investigations often reveal that the root causes were much more systemic and, as such, was an "accident waiting to happen" (Perrow, 1984; Seeger, 1986).

Product Safety Incidents. Unlike accidents, which happen dramatically, product safety incidents, conversely usually unfold over time, and only gain rhetorical currency as alert media or watch-dog groups string together seemingly unrelated incidents to find a common cause or theme. In this context, usually some latent design flaw becomes evident, resulting in death or injury to innocents, such as was the case in 2000–2001 with the Firestone Wilderness AT and ATX tires made at the company's Decatur, Illinois, plant (Hearit, 2006). With the proliferation of class action lawsuits, a whole cottage industry of lawyers and "safety-advocates" has arisen to find such incidents and sue on behalf of a damaged class (Hearit, 2006). For the organizations named in the class action lawsuits, the need to defend their reputation is self-evident.

Social Irresponsibility. Finally, in a social irresponsibility context, individual and corporate actors have been shown to violate a public social code. In this "other" category, corporate actors are seen to act in ways that violate publicly held social values, speak in politically incorrect ways, or have otherwise behaved in such a way as to give fuel to special interest or advocacy groups looking to "make an issue" with regards to their enemies. One example of this context is the comments in 2006 by Frederick Rouzaud, president and CEO of Champagne Louis Roederer, the maker of Cristal. Rouzaud admitted a certain discomfort with regards to the exclusive champagne's association with hip-hop culture, but noted: "We can't forbid people from buying it" (Century, 2006, p. 8). Critics, including the rapper Jay-Z, immediately charged that the company was racist and urged boycotts of the product (Franklin, 2006).

Having now reviewed the four primary types of apologetic crisis contexts, the following section hones in on the central part of apologetic address. That is, we shift here from context to a discussion of content strategies.

APPROACHES TO THE STUDY OF APOLOGIA

There are a variety of approaches that have been taken that have attempted to account for the central part of what constitutes apologetic address. Rooted in a generic approach to the study of apologia generally and the identification of what constitutes the substance of apologia specifically, these approaches have attempted to isolate how best to define the constitutive components of apologetic address. As such, the majority of scholarly effort since the publication of Ware and Linkugel's (1973) seminal study of apologia has focused on identification of the strategies used by apologists to extricate themselves from difficult situations (Benoit, 1995; Campbell & Jamieson, 1978; Coombs, 1995, 1999; Hearit, 1995). While extended reviews of all the permutations of this form of discourse exist, this analysis focuses only on those strategies that account for primary strategies used by organizations (Benoit, 1995).

Shifting Attention away from Accusations	Addressing Accusations
Counterattack/Shifting the Blame	Denial
Differentiation	Mortification
Transcendence	Corrective Action
Bolstering	Compensation
Victimage	
Minimization/Misrepresentation	

FIGURE 27.1 Apologetic Strategies.

Strategies

Organizations caught in a wrong tend to take one of two approaches in their attempts to respond to allegations: one which seeks to shift attention away from accusations and another which seeks to confront allegations (Roberson, 2005) (see Figure 27.1). These strategies, which attempt to divert attention, include: counterattack, shifting the blame, differentiation, transcendence, bolstering, victimage, minimization and misrepresentation. Conversely, strategies that serve to directly address accusations are: denial, corrective action, mortification, and compensation.

Shifting Attention Away from Accusations. In apologetic situations, organizations seek to restore their damaged credibility. One way to accomplish this is through shifting attention away from the charges made. If negative attention is shifted to another source, as often occurs when shifting the blame, organizations believe that their damaged image is repaired, because there is another to blame for the crisis. One variant of shifting blame is counterattack. Counterattack is a defensive strategy organizations use to redirect negative attention from themselves by pointing out others' faults (Ryan, 1988). This strategy is useful to shift negative attention in another direction, a tack often taken when there is more than one party involved in a crisis. This type of approach generates considerable media attention because the conflict adds additional drama to the existing crisis. Such was the case in 2000–2001 with the aforementioned Firestone case; when chief executive John Lampe sought to lessen blame on Firestone, he shifted some of the blame to the Ford Motor Company and its Explorer sport utility vehicle. By Spring 2001, there were approximately 174 deaths linked to the crashes—for which Firestone had received much of the blame (Tharp, 2001). Finally, on May 21, 2001 Bridgestone/Firestone severed its 100 year relationship with Ford Motor Company and argued that the accidents and deaths that occurred were the result of problems with the Ford Explorer (Tharp, 2001). Firestone CEO John Lampe stated: "The question must be asked, why does this [174 deaths] seem to be happening only on Ford Explorer and not on other vehicles?" (Tharp, 2001, p. 33). In so doing, Lampe shifted the blame from Firestone onto the Ford Corporation.

Differentiation is a second defensive strategy that organizations and their leadership use to separate themselves from attacks (Ware & Linkugel, 1973). Differentiation illustrates the particularities of a situation and frames the nature of an action as justified or acceptable. President George W. Bush used differentiation in his defense of the federal government's slow response to Hurricane Katrina. On September 15, 2005, he delivered a live nationwide address from Jackson Square in New Orleans. In this address, Bush used differentiation to defend the pace of the response, arguing that the disaster was unique. Bush stated: "The storm involved a massive flood, a major supply and security operation, and an evacuation order affecting more than a million people. It was not a normal hurricane—and the normal disaster relief system was not equal to it" (Bush, 2005a, p. 5). Bush used differentiation to justify the federal government's actions and to persuade the audience that because of the uniqueness of the situation the slow response could not have been avoided.

Transcendence shifts negative attention from specific charges by arguing that an organization's overall actions are honorable when considered within a broader context (Ware & Linkugel, 1973). In so doing, it often contains an appeal to higher values (Hearit, 1997; Wilson, 1976). This strategy has been used by politicians to respond to criticism that their energy policies are flawed (Dionisopoulos, 1986). President George W. Bush, for instance, in 2005 argued that his administration was doing all it could to bring down the price of gasoline for American consumers. He claimed: "... [E]very time we use home-grown biodiesel, we support American farmers, not foreign oil producers (Bush, 2005b, p. 5). In other words, Bush used transcedence to show that every time an American consumer fills up at the pump with biodiesel, he or she is working to promote America's energy independence. Note that with transcendence the attention shifts from Bush's flawed energy policies to consumers' role in America's energy independence.

Another defensive strategy used by organizations caught in a barrage of criticism is bolstering. With bolstering, organizations discount a charge by directing attention towards a favorable impression they had prior to the accusation (Gold, 1978; Ware & Linkugel, 1973). Here organizations try to get their audience to identify with their positive past reputation in the hope that it will overshadow the current situation they find themselves in. When using bolstering, individuals and organizations do not directly address charges; instead they shift attention away from the charges and onto a more favorable image of themselves. This defensive strategy also can be used to identify with a common past history that signals that there is hope for the future. Such was the approach taken by the Toshiba Corporation in 1987 in response to disclosures that the company had sold top secret milling equipment to the then Soviet Union—equipment which would enable them to produce dramatically quieter submarines which would be difficult to track. Toshiba apologized for the actions of its subsidiary, the Toshiba Machine Company, and instead emphasized the corporation's long history in the United States and the many jobs it has created for Americans (Hearit, 1994). President and CEO Joichi Aoi wrote:

> At a time when many of the U.S.-based corporations competing with Toshiba are moving production facilities and jobs abroad, Toshiba's American companies are steadily expanding the extent to which their products are manufactured in the United States. Today, Toshiba employs thousands of Americans in 21 states from New York to Texas to California. (Aoi, 1987, p. 18)

The implication of the bolstering strategy, of course, is that to punish the company too severely would cost some Americans their jobs.

A fifth strategy used by organizations is victimage. Victimage is a defensive strategy that enables organizations to portray themselves not only as innocent of wrongdoing—but victims of unwanted and unnecessary attention, often from an over-zealous prosecutor or media (Benoit, 1988; Katula, 1975). This strategy shifts attention away from the charges and is used to gain sympathy from the audience as well as to demonstrate that the individual or organization is a victim in the situation, just like everyone else. Martha Stewart, CEO of Martha Stewart Omnimedia used victimage as a defense strategy after she was charged with using insider information to sell her ImClone shares in 2001, estimated to be worth $45,000. Throughout her trial and after her sentencing, she proclaimed her innocence and claimed that she was the victim of an eager prosecution who was targeting her because of her celebrity status in an effort to show that the government was taking a strong stance against corporate scandals. Throughout the ordeal, Stewart described herself as "choked and almost suffocated to death" (Hays, 2004, p. A1). She portrayed herself as a victim in order to gain sympathy from the public and to maintain her innocence. The public's acceptance of Stewart as victim remains divided, thus showing the strategies are somewhat limited by public perception.

A final strategy used to shift attention away from accusations is minimization. Minimization is a defensive strategy that tries to portray the negative act as less serious than initially perceived (Benoit, 1995). In conjunction with this strategy, organizations may try to argue that the situation has been misrepresented by their competition or the media. As such, misrepresentation is a justification strategy used to distance individuals or organizations from the crisis (Coombs, 1995). Minimization and misrepresentation can be important in shifting attention away from the crisis or, at the very least, away from the individuals or organizations and on to others involved. It also can be used as a strategy to try to move past a crisis. This was the initial stance taken by the Intel Corporation after allegations surfaced in 1994 that there were flaws in its Pentium II chip; these flaws resulted in errors when mathematical calculations were performed on the Pentium chip (Hearit, 1999). Intel used minimization to argue that the defects in the chip were not serious and that most consumers would likely never face an error caused by the defects. The company argued: "an average spreadsheet user could encounter this subtle flaw of reduced precision once in every 27,000 years of use" (Grove et al., 1994, p. 7). The effort largely was successful until IBM produced independent data which suggested that the flaw would show itself every 24 days (Hearit, 1999).

Addressing Accusations. Another way organizations defend themselves when they face a crisis is to directly address the accusations made against them. This may be a wise course when a crisis is too severe to ignore or when evidence requires a response. In these situations, to shift attention away from the charges typically is seen as evasive. Instead, despite the legal consequences, organizations choose to directly address the charges. In doing so, they engage in strategies of denial, mortification, corrective action, or compensation.

Denial is an apologetic strategy organizations use to refute attacks; it is a rejection of the charges at hand (Ware & Linkugel, 1973). This often is the best strategy for organizations to use when they are innocent of charges. However, to use denial as a delay tactic is a dangerous strategy, for if any truth to the charges made is shown to exist, this would complicate further the task of repairing a reputation. Enron used this defensive strategy after the company faced a fraud indictment in 2003 which stemmed from an investigation in which prosecutors charged the company was "illegally pumping up the company's stock price by lying about the existence of certain Internet technology" (Eichenwald & Markoff, 2003, p. 1). Enron executives defended the company; they argued that Enron Broadband Services (E.B.S.) did possess the technical abilities as claimed. Larry Ciscon, a former vice-president for the company denied the charges; he stated:

> I do not think the technical capabilities were overstated.... And comparing E.B.S. to the other software companies I've seen in my 15 years in the software industry, I did not see anything outside of the standard product-development process. (Eichenwald & Markoff, 2003, p. 1)

This use of denial was problematic because evidence revealed Enron executives relied on half-truths to defend themselves, which seriously diminished whatever credibility the failing company possessed.

Mortification is a defensive strategy often used when organizations say they regret making a particular statement or engaging in a particular act (Benoit, 1995). In essence, this strategy is what most people (incorrectly) think of when they hear the world apologia—an apology. Yet, a mortification strategy only occurs when a company accepts responsibility and asks for forgiveness. This strategy is not implemented often because when a company admits fault it makes itself susceptible to lawsuits. A recent example of corporate officials using mortification occurred when mining rescuers apologized for an erroneous report that led family and friends of 13 trapped Sago Miners in West Virginia in January 2006 to believe that 12 of the 13 miners had survived. The miscommunication that led to the false report and not telling the families in a timely manner drew great criticism from the families themselves, as well as the media and the general public (Bishop & Alpert, 2006). Testifying publicly about the mining rescue mission, one of the rescuers Ronald Hixson, used a strategy of mortification: "We apologize for any of the problems or the heartache that the miscommunication caused. That was not meant to be" (Roddy & Twedt, 2006, p. A1). Such a response functioned to silence much of the hue and outcry.

Another strategy that directly addresses accusations is corrective action. Corrective action often is coupled with an apology, and shows key publics what actions are being taken to rectify the situation; that is, it articulates what is needed to remedy the situation and prevent it from occurring again (Benoit, 1995; Coombs, 1999; Hearit, 1995). If implemented correctly, the use of corrective action is highly persuasive, in that it reassures key publics, as well as draws upon a cultural faith in the redemptive power of technology which asserts that technology can be harnessed to solve some of the very problems it has created (Hearit, 2001; Sellnow, Ulmer & Snider, 1998). Such was the strategy used by the American Red Cross in the face of criticism for its administration of the Liberty Fund, which was initiated to take care of the families of the victims of the terrorist attacks of September 11, 2001. In late October 2001, the Red Cross admitted that it planned for some of the nearly $550 million to go to other relief efforts and other needs within the organization, including telecommunications upgrades (Ibarguen, 2001). Facing a public outcry and a Congressional investigation, the Red Cross soon changed course, replaced CEO Dr. Bernadine Healy, and announced that all money raised for the Liberty Fund would go to the victims of September 11. Chairman of the American Red Cross David McLaughlin used corrective action when he announced the change; he said: ... "[T]oday we are making a course correction for the Red Cross Liberty Fund.... A hundred percent of that fund and our efforts will be devoted to support those who are affected by the terrible tragedies that occurred on September 11 ..." (McLaughlin, 2001, p.1). Through the use of corrective action, the Red Cross was able to rectify the situation, appease its critics and effectively repair its reputation.

A final strategy that addresses accusations is compensation. Compensation offers to reimburse victims for injuries and losses that occurred as a result of the crisis (Benoit, 1995). While this strategy often is successful in forestalling lawsuits, it also shows that organizations responsible for a crisis are taking responsibility for their actions. When organizations use compensation, it typically is not discussed in detail to the public. Often, the compensation paid to victims remains undisclosed because a company and its victims do not want the information to be made public. This occurred in the aforementioned case in which Firestone tires were alleged to explode on Ford Explorers. Both companies frequently offered compensation to the victims or their families before they went to trial. By offering compensation to the victims, the companies were able to avoid an astronomical jury-ordered settlement and the negative press that would accompany it.

A strategic approach has constituted the bulk of academic research on the topic of apologia (Benoit, 1995; Coombs, 1995). As a result, a great deal is known as to the communicative options available to corporate officials as they face a crisis. While a number of criticisms have been leveled against a strategy-based approach to the study of apologia (i.e., it is a rediscovery Aristotle's *topoi*; it is more taxonomic than theoretical; or it lacks a critical edge), the knowledge of apologia is greatly informed by the thoroughness of those who have published in this area (see Benoit, 2000; Burns & Bruner, 2000; Conley, 1986; Simons, 2000). Subsequently, the next two approaches really are variations on the strategic approach, and have attempted to use this research in order to determine how these strategies cluster together in apologetic response.

A Reconceptualization of Apologia

Taking the oeuvre of Benoit (1995) and others (Coombs, 1995, 1999; Seeger, Sellnow & Ulmer, 2003) whose work constitutes the bulk of the strategy-based approach to apologia into account, Rowland and Jerome (2004) have argued that in spite of a flurry of academic inquiry, there has been no consensus on what specific apologetic strategies are necessary to use within an apologetic address. In fact, they argued that over the years this lack of consensus brings into question apologia's generic status, stating: "... one could argue that the failure to find a predictable set of characteristics across the range of organizational apologia studies has the effect of undercutting any claim of generic status or generalizability across a range of cases" (p. 193).

At root, Rowland and Jerome (2004) argue that scholars must take a step back in order to try to find some consistency within the characteristics that define organizational apologia in a broader effort to discover a "... theory-based explanation for why organizational advocates choose (or should choose) particular strategies in particular situations" (p. 193). To address this problem, they argue that what has been overlooked in apologetic literature is that organizational apologia often entails two conflicting purposes: image repair and image maintenance (Rowland & Jerome, 2004). Image repair is concerned with "presenting justification of action or denial of guilt in the particular case" whereas image maintenance has to do with the "maintenance of an overall positive image" (Rowland & Jerome, 2004, p. 195). Through their discussion of image repair and image maintenance, they offered an alternative approach to understanding the use of crisis-response strategies in apologia when they suggested that:

> ... it would be more sensible to attempt to identify the invariant characteristics found in all organizational apologia serving an image maintenance function and then seek the equivalent of argumentative subfields to explain variation of image repair strategies across apologia. (Rowland & Jerome, 2004, p. 199)

They further offered four strategies (of which at least one must be used) organizations use to maintain their reputation; they include: demonstrating concern for victims, bolstering organizational values, denying intent to do harm, and preventing recurrence by pursuing the root cause (Rowland & Jerome, 2004).

While Rowland and Jerome (2004) offered specific strategies that can be used in image maintenance, they contended that it is more difficult to determine which image repair strategies to use in a crisis because the response often is heavily influenced by the context of the situation (Dionisopoulos & Vibbert, 1988; Hearit, 1995). Rowland and Jerome (2004) further argued that by first understanding image maintenance, which has generalizable characteristics, then subgenres of apologia may be identified. Once these subgenres are identified, they argued that then "an appropriate typology of [image-repair] strategies" may be identified (Rowland & Jerome, 2004, p. 204). They go on to identify the following five key variables that they suggest "constrain the options of the individual or organization presenting the apologia" and would help to identify specific subgenres of apologia and subsequently appropriate image-repair strategies used in apologia; these include: "... perceived guilt, magnitude of harm (including the nature of the victim), data indicating the actual responsibility for the harm, the presence or absence of involved third parties, and whether the actions fit traditional moral standards in the culture" (Rowland & Jerome, 2004, p. 205).

Overall, Rowland and Jerome's (2004) reconceptualization of organizational apologia offers valuable insight into understanding the complexity of organizational crisis discourse and takes a step back from the discussion of what apologetic strategies are used and reveals conflicting purposes that organizations often face (image repair and image maintenance). Similarly, Hearit (2001, 2006) has offered an approach that attempts to use the research that constitutes the strategic approach as a starting place in identifying the "predictable set of characteristics across the range of organizational apologia studies" which Rowland and Jerome (2004, p. 193) argued are necessary to support a generic claim.

Prototypical Stances

Apologia is a situationally-driven genre; that is, the substance of apologetic address is driven largely by the nature of the allegations at hand. That being said, research into apologia shows that the apologetic discourse that faces these diverse contexts does tend to cluster into a limited number of prototypical forms (Hearit, 2001, 2006). This does not mean to say that there is no variation between or within these apologetic stances; simply that the oft-cataloged apologetic strategies tend to cluster into a relatively limited list of specific incarnations. These forms constitute a continuum that ranges from a denial stance that disavows any wrongdoing to an apology posture that fully acknowledges wrongdoing. While these stances have a distinctive posture, they tend to utilize a multiplicity of strategies in the defense of their position (e.g., a denial stance may use strategies of denial, defeasibility, bolstering and shifting the blame).

We Didn't Do It. It seems that the initial impulse of most apologists, when allegations surface, is to deny that they have done anything wrong; that is, they respond with a denial stance (Fitzpatrick, 1995). Here an organization may claim that it did not commit the act in question, had no knowledge of it, nor did it participate in similar acts. Such a stance only is effective to the degree that the apologist can convince auditors that the allegations are mere opinions that do not hold much weight or credibility. In the aforementioned Intel case, the company denied that the problem was a significant one and that the lion's share of its consumers had nothing to worry about. CEO Andrew Grove continued to deny that there was a problem: "I don't think it is part of our open and honest culture to make a commitment that we don't believe in [to replace the chips—no questions asked], and that we could not deliver. I think that would be an irresponsible thing to do" (Clark, 1994, p. A3). For many auditors, the forcefulness of the denial often acts as a signal as to how readily it should be believed.

Counter Attack. A second stance taken by apologists is a variant of a denial strategy. In this context, apologists continue to deny having committed any wrongdoing. Yet recognizing that it is rhetorically necessary for guilt to be addressed and allocated, they instead point the finger at another. The use of counter-attack is a highly-aggressive form of apologetic response, one in which the apologist tries to one-up the accuser, and assume his or her role as interrogator (Hearit, 1996; Ulmer, 1999). The target of a counter-attack may be an organization's competition, but it also may be the media in general—with charges directed against individual reporters. Here organizations claim that said journalists have carried out "sloppy reporting," or have not acted in the public interest but instead have published sensational reporting in an effort to garner ratings. Such was the approach taken in 1992 by General Motors to a story produced by *Dateline NBC* that accused GM of having produced C/K pick-ups that would explode in side-impact collisions (Hearit, 1996). GM argued that the trucks were safe, and that *Dateline NBC* had used incendiary devices to make the trucks explode on camera—a counter-charge eventually shown to be correct. It should be noted that such a fact-based counter-charge is rare; in most cases a counter-attack is seen as a futile, last-ditch effort by a guilty company to spread the blame.

It's Not Really Our Fault. A third stance taken by apologists is to acknowledge some wrongdoing, but to feature a differentiation stance. Here a company claims that while said act may have occurred, it really has limited culpability for the act. In such a context, a company is likely to locate the guilt for the act not in the company *qua* company but instead in the actions of a small cadre of its employees. In other words, an organization subtly or explicitly suggests that the offensive act was caused by a drunken captain, a disgruntled employee, a corrupt CEO, or a group of cowboy employees who acted without organizational sanction. The most rhetorically expedient factor of this approach is that said employees can be fired—and all organizational guilt can be removed from the company by separating from the employee(s). This was the stance taken by the Merrill Lynch brokerage firm in 2002. New York Attorney General Elliot Spitzer accused the firm of having "pumped-up" the value of telecom stocks with poor earnings prospects to investors—many of them retirees, in order to gain or retain lucrative investment banking fees from those same telecom companies. When the telecom boom went bust, these individual investors lost substantial sums. In solving the problem of its guilt, Merrill Lynch fired noted telecom analyst Henry Blodget and paid a $100 million fine, yet did not acknowledge any wrongdoing (Hearit & Brown, 2004).

We Promise Not to Do It Again. By far, the most accommodative prototypical approach is one of apology. In this stance, organizations are conciliatory—and try to reach an accommodation with outraged consumers by offering a mortification stance. Here a company, in effect, agrees with its critics that its actions were wrong, and also engages in a corrective action strategy whereby it promises not to engage in such behavior again. This stance is rhetorically efficacious because it communicates to consumers that the problem that precipitated the wrongdoing has been identified and fixed, so that the problem will not recur in the future. Such was the stance taken by the Christian & Missionary Alliance in the late 1990s to revelations that the church had covered-up instances of abuse in missionary schools in Africa from 1950–1971 (Courtright & Hearit, 2002). The church engaged in a full apology, worked to bring reconciliation, and put in place policy changes and controls to ensure that such acts never could occur again.

Talk to Our Lawyers. The final prototypical approach to dealing with the problem of wrongdoing is to take an "uncommunicative" stance. In such an instance, a company accused of wrongdoing takes a "no comment" approach whereby it refuses to participate in the media drama that surrounds allegations of wrongdoing. Instead, an organization recognizes that the only drama that matters is the one held in the courtroom and, as such, communicates solely and primarily through its lawyers. As such, any public statements that are offered tend to incorporate some form of "no comment" which often cites company policy in the area of privacy as justification. In the rare cases that public statements are made, the focus does tend to be on denial strategies (regardless of guilt) and shifting the blame (Benoit, 1995; Fitzpatrick & Rubin, 1995). The justification for a legal approach, it goes without saying, is concern for the legal and liability implications that accompany wrongdoing. In defense of the Dalkon Shield, an intrauterine device (IUD) designed to prevent pregnancy that instead ended up causing injury to a large number of women during the 1970s, the A. H. Robins company featured a legal approach that only took into account social concerns when it was required to do so (Mintz, 1985). While there is much to criticize from a public relations perspective, Fitzpatrick and Rubin (1995) report that a legal approach is one of the most widely-used stances by companies that are caught in a public relations crisis.

While the use of prototypical approach to the study of apologia offers a useful vehicle by which to understand the approach used by apologists to extricate themselves from crises, attempts to move beyond generic concerns constitute a final approach to the study of crisis management, one that seeks to explain the ritualistic dimensions that inhere in apologetic discourse.

Ritualistic Approach

Noting the degree to which apologetic responses primarily are a response to the problem of "guilt" (Burke, 1984) and, as such, tend to follow a readily recognized script for the purgation of that guilt, an alternative approach to the study of apologia features the role of ritual. This approach takes the strategies of denial, mortification, and scapegoating as a starting place, but observes that the application of these strategies tends to result in rhetoric that fails rather than succeeds. Indeed, the primary justification for delivering an apologia tends to be the fact that it stops the steady drumbeat ofnegative media stories. Rather, the use of such strategies tends to complete the cycle of accusation, guilt, confession and restoration. Because of this, apologia can be conceptualized as a secular remediation ritual, one in which organizations follow an identifiable script whereby they enter into the public "dock" and draw upon familiar conventions of guilt and restoration. By doing so, they perform a social action by completing the drama, thus depriving journalists of an ongoing story (Miller, 1984).

An emphasis on the role of ritual is rooted in the belief that an apologist not only has to "explain" his or her actions but has to demonstrate "proper regard for the *process* of correction" (Goffman, 1971, p. 100). This provides auditors a vehicle by which to measure the degree to which an apologist "really means it;" as evidenced by the carefulness that they give to following the particulars of the ritual. Ritual, according to Rothenbuhler (1998), "is the voluntary performance of appropriately patterned behavior to symbolically effect or participate in the serious life" (p. 27). A conceptualization of apologia as a public ritual recognizes that an apologia cogently accomplishes a task—the exculpation of guilt through speech (Austin, 1979; Tavuchis, 1991). The use of speech recognizes the degree to which an apologia is a performance—an "aesthetically marked and heightened mode of communication, framed in a special way and put on display for an audience" (Bauman, 1989, p. 262). This public performance, which hardly ever reveals any new information, is then judged by critics as to its quality—to which the apologist is seen to accept guilt (Rosenfield, 1968).

Yet not only must an apologia be well-performed, there are other characteristics that aid in the conceptualization of apologia as ritual. These characteristics include the fact that apologiae are sacred; they are socially structured in that they draw from the language and conventions of a given culture, and they are non-instrumental (Rothenbuhler, 1998). That is, they economically and convincingly accomplish a complex outcome—absolution. Additionally, an apologia must be seen to be voluntary to be perceived as effective—not an act performed under compulsion but rather one in which the apologist enters into voluntarily. A final factor in the conceptualization of apologia as ritual acknowledges that apologiae are not private exchanges but that in contemporary Western culture they are very much packaged as drama and then mediated for public consumption—often to the point of public spectacle. By doing so, one of their most critical factors is that they place the nature of the wrongdoing and the acknowledgement of that wrongdoing on the public record—for all to see and hear. As such their outcome is not to seek forgiveness but rather to demonstrate a sense of proportional humiliation (Courtright & Hearit, 2002; Tavuchis, 1991). Because of this fact, the emphasis on apologia is not on achieving forgiveness but rather on the *meaning* an apologia creates; their public performance demonstrates, on the part of the apologist—and vicariously by all who audit its mediated version—a re-adherence to those social values that were endangered by the initial wrongdoing. Socially, then, the entire community can proceed forward, recognizing that those social values, once again, have been shown to be imperative (Hearit, 1995).

Conceptualizing apologia as ritual requires a reconstitution of what it means to have a "successful" apologia. Hearit (2006), for instance, argues that "successful apologiae" are characterized by six features. First, they are able to locate a plausible place for guilt to go; guilt cannot simply be denied, it has to be expatiated. Second, they are well-performed; critics have to be able to "look the offender in the eye" and determine if the apologist really meant it. Third, they must be seen to be voluntary—and not done under compulsion, lest they be seen as performing an act and not really meaning it. Fourth, they must "complete the story" by meeting expectations that the guilt that brought about the need for an apologia has been absolved satisfactorily. Fifth, they must demonstrate adherence to the values they are charged with violating—reaffirming belief in the current social system. And finally, they must be seen to be ethical, lest it leave those who expected a full explanation unsatisfied—and fail to complete the ritualistic script that ends with absolution and resolution.

While the scholarship that makes up the study of apologia has done a thorough job in explicating the motives, contexts, and strategies that constitute apologetic discourse, there is indeed one glaring weakness in our understanding of apologia, and that is the role and effect that the problem of legal liability has on the rhetorical choices of corporate apologists. Indeed, as recently as 2001, Hearit wrote:

> While a few scholars have offered conclusions that corporations carefully craft their messages to avoid lawsuits (Fitzpatrick, 1995; Hearit, 1995a; Kaufmann et al., 1994; Tyler, 1997), little work has been done to arrive at a complete understanding of what probably is the core determinant that apologists consider when formulating their response to criticism. (p. 510)

This next section will attempt to lay out the influence that fears of legal liability have on corporate speech. To do so, it will first discuss the competing choices that corporate officers face, discuss those situations in which a corporation may safely apologize as well as those when it is advised against, and finally, offer a potential third way to deal with the problem of liability.

THE EFFECTS OF ETHICS & LIABILITY ON CORPORATE SPEECH

Of course, all of the research on what individuals and organizations "say" in a crisis management situation has to be tempered by the very real role of legal liability and its chilling effect, particularly on corporate speech. In a nutshell, corporations accused of wrongdoing face a set of competing challenges (Tyler, 1997). On one hand, company officials feel compelled to meet the needs of consumers who desire an accommodating statement that displays responsibility and displays concern for victims (that may even include an apology), thus demonstrating their ethical and social responsibility (Botan, 1997; Van Es & Meijlink, 2000; Kernisky, 1997). Conversely, members of the business community often expect the opposite response, one which features a strategy of denial—for an accommodating response often will result in lawsuits due to the assumption of responsibility (Marcus & Goodman, 1991). It should be noted that the fiduciary responsibility to stockholders is the only responsibility ensconced in law (Epstein, 1972).

Once such way in which corporations have attempted to meet the problem is to issue a statement of regret, in which they offer carefully-crafted statements that show concern but are worded so as to be ambiguous as to whether they accept responsibility (Hearit, 1994). Recently, a consensus has begun to emerge among scholars that it is too simple to say an organization can or cannot apologize and instead recognizes that while there are situations in which an organization cannot apologize there surely are situations in which an organization can apologize—or, at minimum, offer accommodating statements (Cohen, 1999; 2002; Hearit, 2006; Patel & Reinsch, 2003).

Situations in Which It Is Safe to Apologize

There are a number of circumstances in which organizations can—and should—safely apologize; in these, not only is it ethically right to apologize, it also makes strategic sense. One such situation is when the offense is in the realm of defamation. Simply put, it follows that if the offense is one of "speech" that then the primary way to rectify the situation is through "speech" as well (Wagatsuma & Rosett, 1986).

A second context in which an apology is both strategically wise as well as ethically necessary are those crises that are described best as "media flaps." Media flaps are crisis contexts in which an offense has occurred, though it is one in which the harm is social and not corporal, and as such, no real "victims" exist.

Similarly, scholars suggest additional contexts in which it is safe to apologize are those in which the costs of the wrongdoing are well known and, because of this, damages can be calculated easily (Cohen, 1999; Wagatsuma & Rosett, 1986). This occurs in situations in which there are injuries that result in missed work but no substantial pain and suffering (that could lead to substantial punitive damage awards). In this way, an organization is likely to know, or at least have a good idea up front, as to what an accommodative statement is likely to "cost" the company financially, as it measures the expense of compensation with the goodwill it is likely to gain for "doing the right thing."

An additional context in which it is safe to apologize is when the apology is part of a larger settlement (Cohen, 1999). While the original idea of an apology is that it is voluntary (Hearit, 2006), and as such, stops the rancor and makes legal sanction unnecessary, it nevertheless may be the case that an apology is delivered as part of a larger legal settlement.

Finally, organizations are wise to apologize in those situations in which their guilt can be established without an apology (Cohen, 1999; Hearit, 2006). In such a context, an organization is likely to be sued successfully anyways; it makes sense to offer an apology and generate the social goodwill that accompanies an apology. To do so is likely to limit larger punitive damages.

Situations in Which to Avoid Apologies

While there are situations in which an organization can safely apologize, scholars are just as adamant that there are situations in which organizations are wise not to apologize—or at minimum to wait (Kauffman, Kesner, & Hazen, 1994; Cohen, 1999). One such context occurs when the facts of the case are not yet fully known nor is the extent of the wrongdoing abundantly clear. In this case, an organization might offer an accommodating statement without knowing the extent to which it is setting itself up for long-term obligations. Similarly, while the calculus to determine the earnings potential of a successful executive is relatively straightforward (a factor of age, income, and time), it is much more difficult to put a price on the life of a child or harm to the environment.

A second situation in which an organization should be hesitant to apologize is when the damages would put the company out of business (Hearit, 2006). Ethical theorists agree that in such a situation an organization, in order to protect its employees sustenance, can avoid offering an apology, in that it is a well-accepted ethical standard that one may not be required to perform an action of which one is incapable (Hearit, 2006). Similarly, those contexts in which there is a group of victims who would likely lead to a class action lawsuit, offers a situation in which it would be wise for an organization to communicate carefully.

Private/Public Apology. In those contexts in which it is difficult to decide, the earlier aforementioned statement of regret does offer some sense of direction for apologists. Cohen (1999, 2002), for instance, does advocate that the idea of a "safe apology" is legally accurate. In so doing, he argues that sentiment can be divided from responsibility. Here a company can apologize (i.e., "We're sorry") without assuming responsibility (e.g., "We did it").

Hearit (2006) conversely has advocated for the presence of a third way for organizations to act both strategically and ethically. Specifically, he has argued that in an apologetic crisis management context organizations are wise to demonstrate public concern for those who are harmed, are obligated to offer public corrective action, and then are wise to make an apology—in private. In so doing, they can repair relationships with those who are injured or harmed without putting their company in a position that exposes them to larger liability issues (Fitzpatrick, 1995; Hearit, 1995; Kaufmann et al., 1994; Tyler, 1997).

CONCLUSION: A RHETORIC OF FAILURE

This chapter has reviewed the research on the topic of apologia as it relates to crisis management. In particular, it has argued that the use of apologia is a helpful vehicle by which to understand the "motives" of corporate speech in those particular crisis management contexts that are the result, not of some external forces, but rather due to their own organizational missteps or wrongdoing. As such, it has attempted to isolate the key definitional issues, described the most likely contexts of wrongdoing that are likely to result in apologiae, surveyed the different approaches to the study of corporate apologia, as well as articulated the critical nature of the role of liability on corporate speech.

It should be noted that apologia often are seen as a vehicle by which organizations are able to deliver a speech or publish an advertisement in which they "successfully" extricate themselves from the negative social sanction that occurs because of their alleged wrongdoing. Such an assumption illustrates a fundamental misunderstanding of how apologia works. Indeed, evidence suggests that the use of an apologia is largely an ineffectual instrument by which to transform peoples' understandings of a company's motives; instead, apologia may be characterized more by their failures than their successes. Indeed, in the opening narrative of this chapter, the American Airlines executive, Don Carty, after delivering a speech that was roundly lauded for his forthrightness and willingness to confront the situation, nevertheless, was forced to resign days later for his handling of the incident (Wong, 2003c). As such, Hearit (2006), borrowing from Payne (1989a, 1989b), described apologia as a "rhetoric of failure," in that the outcomes an apologia brings about are rarely transformative and seldom favorable.

Having said that they are ineffective at solving an organization's public relations problem, apologiae do have one singular virtue: According to Hearit (2006):

> At root, their primary virtue is that they complete the typical wrongdoing, guilt, and restoration drama; by doing so, they deny media a continual story. As such, apologia constitute a ritualistic form of communication, one in which an organization enters into a public confessional, taps into well-established themes of guilt and restoration, and in so doing, completes the story and gets the individual or organization off the front page. (pp. 17–18)

In the end, from a public relations manager's perspective, completion of the story in the media spotlight is, indeed, in an organization's best interest.

BIBLIOGRAPHY

Aoi, J. (1987, June 15). Toshiba Corporation extends its deepest regrets to the American people. *U.S. News & World Report,* p. 18.

ARM Corporation. (2003, April 18). American Airlines management voluntarily cancels retention agreements. Retrieved September 22, 2003, from http://www.amrcorp.com/news/april03/18_retention.htm.

Austin, J. L. (1979). A plea for excuses. In J. O. Urmson & G. J. Warnock (Eds.), *Philosophical Papers* (pp. 123–152). Oxford: Clarendon Press.

Bauman, R. (1989). Performance. In E. Barnouw (Ed.), *International encyclopedia of communications* (Vol. 3, pp. 262–266). New York: Oxford University Press.

Benoit, W. L. (1995). *Account, excuses, and apologies: A theory of image restoration strategies.* Albany: State University of New York Press.

Benoit, W. L. (1988). Senator Edward M. Kennedy and the Chappaquiddick tragedy. In H. R. Ryan (Ed.), *Oratorical encounters* (pp. 187–199). New York: Greenwood Press.

Benoit, W. L. (2000). Another visit to the theory of image restoration strategies. *Communication Quarterly, 48,* 40–43.

Benoit, W. L., and Brinson, S. L. (1994). AT&T: Apologies are not enough. *Communication Quarterly, 42,* 75 – 88.

Bishop, I., & Alpert, L. I. (2006, January 5). Anatomy of a cruel mistake: Bosses knew miners were dead – but waited three hours to tell loved ones. *The New York Post.* Retrieved May 15, 2006, from http://www.lexis-nexis.com.

Botan, C. (1997). Ethics in strategic communication campaigns: The case for a new approach to public relations. *Journal of Business Communication, 34,* 188–202.

Boyd, J. (2000). Actional legitimation: No crisis necessary. *Journal of Public Relations Research, 12,* 341–353.

Brummer, J. J. (1991). *Corporate responsibility and legitimacy: An interdisciplinary analysis.* New York: Greenwood Press.

Burke, K. (1984). *Permanence and change: An anatomy of purpose* (3rd ed.). Berkeley: University of California Press.

Burns, J. P., & Bruner, M. S. (2000). Revisiting the theory of image restoration strategies. *Communication Quarterly, 48,* 27–39.

Bush, G. W. (2005a, September 15). President addresses hurricane relief in address to the nation. Retrieved May 19, 2006, from http://www.whitehouse.gov.

Bush, G. W. (2005b, May 16). President discusses biodiesel and alternative fuel sources. Retrieved May 19, 2006, from http://www.whitehouse.gov.

Campbell, K. K., & Jamieson, K. H. (Eds.) (1978). *Form and genre: Shaping rhetorical action.* Falls Church, VA: Speech Communication Association.

Campbell, R. (1991). *60 Minutes and the news.* Urbana: University of Illinois Press.

Century, D. (2006, July 2). Jay-Z puts a cap on Cristal. *New York Times*, pp. 9-1, 9-8.

Clark, D. (1994, December 14). Intel balks at replacing Pentium chip without asking owners any questions. *The Wall Street Journal*, p. A3.

Cohen, J. R. (1999, May). Advising clients to apologize. *Southern California Law Review, 72,* 1009–1069.

Cohen, J. R. (2002, Spring). Legislating apology: The pros and cons. *University of Cincinnati Law Review, 70,* 819–872.

Conley, T. (1986). The Linnaean blues: Thoughts on the genre approach. In H. W. Simons & A. A. Aghazarian (Eds.), *Form, genre, and the study of political discourse* (pp. 59–78). Columbia: University of South Carolina Press.
Coombs, W. T. (1992). The failure of the task force on food assistance; A case study of the role of legitimacy in issue management. *Journal of Public Relations Research, 4*(2), 101–122.
Coombs, W. T. (1995). Choosing the right words: The development of guidelines for the selection of the "appropriate" response strategies. *Management Communication Quarterly, 8,* 447– 475.
Coombs, W. T. (1999). *Ongoing crisis communication: Planning, managing, and responding.* Thousand Oaks, CA: Sage.
Courtright, J. L., & Hearit, K. M. (2002). The good organization speaking well: A paradigm case for religious institutional crisis management. *Public Relations Review, 28,* 347–360.
Deephouse, D. L. (1996). Does isomorphism legitimate? *Academy of Management Journal, 39* (4), 1024–1039.
Dionisopoulos, G. N. (1986). Corporate advocacy advertising as political communication. In L. L. Kaid, D. Nimmo, and K. R. Sanders (Eds.), *New perspectives on political advertising* (pp. 82–106). Carbondale: Southern Illinois University Press.
Dionisopoulos, G. N., & Vibbert, S. L. (1988). CBS vs. Mobil: Charges of creative book-keeping in 1979. In H. R. Ryan (Ed.), *Oratorical encounters* (pp. 241–251). New York: Greenwood Press.
Dowling, J., & Pfeffer, J. (1975). Organizational legitimacy: Social values and organizational behavior. *Pacific Sociological Review, 18,* 122–136.
Eichenwald, K., & Markoff, J. (2003, June 8). Deception or just disarray, at Enron? *The New York Times.* Retrieved May 15, 2006, from http://www.lexis-nexis.com.
Epstein, E. M. (1972). The historical enigma of corporate legitimacy. *California Law Review, 60,* 1701–1717.
Epstein, E., & Votaw, D. (Eds.), (1978). *Rationality, legitimacy, responsibility: Search for new directions.* Santa Monica, CA: Goodyear Publishing Company.
Fisher, W. R. (1970). A motive view of communication. *The Quarterly Journal of Speech, 56,* 131–139.
Fitzpatrick, K. R. (1995). Ten guidelines for reducing legal risks in crisis management. *Public Relations Quarterly, 40,* 33–38.
Fitzpatrick, K. R. & Rubin, M. S. (1995). Public relations vs. legal strategies in organizational crisis decisions. *Public Relations Review, 21,* 21–33.
Franklin, M. (2006, July 4). Some brands welcome rappers' attention; others shy away from hip-hop association. *Kalamazoo Gazette,* p. C4.
Francesconi, R. A. (1982). James Hunt, the Wilmington 10, and institutional Legitimacy. *Quarterly Journal of Speech, 68,* 47–59.
Goffman, E. (1971). *Relations in public.* New York: Basic.
Gold, E. R. (1978). Political apologia: The ritual of self-defense. *Communication Monographs, 45,* 303–316.
Graber, D.A. (2000). *Media power in politics.* (4th ed.). Washington, D.C.: Congressional Quarterly, Inc.
Graber, D.A. (2002). *Mass media and American politics.* (6th ed.). Washington, D.C.: Congressional Quarterly, Inc.
Grove, A. S., Barrett, C. R., & Moore, G. E. (1994, December 21). To owners of Pentium™ processor-based computers and the pc community. *The Wall Street Journal*, p. A7.
Harrell, J., Ware, B. L., & Linkugel, W. A. (1975). Failure of apology in American politics: Nixon on Watergate. *Speech Monographs, 42,* 245–261.
Hays, C. L. (2004, June 17). 5 months in jail, and Stewart vows, 'I'll be back'. *New York Times.* Retrieved May 15, 2006, from http://www.lexis-nexis.com.
Hearit, K. M. (1994). Apologies and public relations crises at Chrysler, Toshiba, and Volvo. *Public Relations Review, 20,* 113–125.
Hearit, K. M. (1995). "Mistakes were made": Organizations, apologia, and crises of social legitimacy. *Communication Studies, 46,* 1–17.
Hearit, K. M. (1996). The use of counter-attack in public relations crises: The case of General Motors vs. NBC. *Public Relations Review, 22,* 233–248.
Hearit, K. M. (1997). On the use of transcendence as an apologia strategy: The case of Johnson controls and its fetal protection policy. *Communication Studies, 46,* 1–17.
Hearit, K. M. (1999). Newsgroups, activist publics, and corporate *apologia*: The case of Intel and its Pentium Chip. *Public Relations Review, 25,* 291–308.
Hearit, K. M. (2001). Corporate *apologia*: When an organization speaks in defense of itself. In R. L. Heath & G. M. Vasquez (Eds.), *Handbook of public relations* (pp. 595–605). Thousand Oaks, CA: Sage.
Hearit, K. M., & Brown, J. (2004). Merrill Lynch: Corporate apologia and fraud. *Public Relations Review, 30*(4), 459–466.
Hearit, K. M. (2006). *Crisis management by apology: Corporate response to allegations of wrongdoing.* Mahwah, NJ: Erlbaum.

Holmstrom, S. (2005). Reframing public relations: The evolution of a reflective paradigm for organizational legitimation. *Pubic Relations Review, 31*(4), 497–504.

Horowitz, A., Athitakis, M., Lasswell, M., & Thomas O. (January 1, 2004). 101 Dumbest Moments in Business. Retrieved June 16, 2006, from http://money.cnn.com/magazines/business2/business2_archive/2004/01/01/359611/index.htm.

Ibarguen, D. (2001, October 29). Some money raised for Red Cross' Liberty Fund to go to long-term plans. *The Associated Press State & Local Wire.* Retrieved May 15, 2006, from http://www.lexis-nexis.com.

Jamieson, K. H., & Waldman P. (2003). *Politicians, journalists, and the stories that shape the political world.* New York: Oxford University Press.

Katula, R. A. (1975). The apology of Richard M. Nixon. *Communication Quarterly, 23,* 1–5.

Kauffman, J. B., Kesner, I. F., & Hazen, R. L. (1994, July-August). The myth of full disclosure: A look at organizational communication during crisis. *Business Horizon's, 37,* 29–39.

Kernisky, D. A. (1997). Proactive crisis management and ethical discourse: Dow Chemical's issues management bulletins 1979–1990. *Journal of Business Ethics, 16(8),* 843–853.

Marcus, A. A., & Goodman, R. S. (1991). Victims and shareholders: The dilemmas of presenting corporate policy during a crisis. *Academy of Management Journal, 34,* 281–305.

McLaughlin, D. (2001, November 14). American Red Cross news conference: Major changes in Liberty Fund. Retrieved May 15, 2006, from http://www.redcross.org.

Metzler, M. (2001). The centrality of organizational legitimacy to public relations practice. In R. L. Heath (Ed.), *Handbook of public relations* (pp. 321–334). Thousand Oaks, CA: Sage.

Miller, C. R. (1984). Genre as social action. *Quarterly Journal of Speech, 70,* 151–167.

Mintz, M. (1985). *At any cost: Corporate greed, women, and the Dalkon Shield.* New York: Pantheon.

Patel, A., & Reinsch, L. (2003). Companies can apologize: Corporate apologies and legal liability. *Business Communication Quarterly, 66,* 17–26.

Payne, A. D. (1989a). *Coping with failure: The therapeutic uses of rhetoric.* Columbia: University of South Carolina Press.

Payne, A. D. (1989b). The Wizard of Oz: Therapeutic rhetoric in a contemporary media ritual. *Quarterly Journal of Speech, 75,* 25–39.

Perrow, C. (1984). *Normal accidents.* New York: Basic.

Roberson, K. M. (2005). *Political campaign trail apologia: A case study of the 2004 presidential campaign.* Unpublished doctoral dissertation, Purdue University, West Lafayette.

Roddy, D. B., & Twedt, S. (2006, May 4). Relatives sorry for 'heartache': Relatives of the Sago mine victims hear apologies for the confusion that had them believing their loved ones survived the January disaster. *Pittsburgh Post-Gazette.* Retrieved May 15, 2006, from http://www.lexis-nexis.com.

Roper, J. (2005). Symmetrical communication: Excellent public relations or a strategy for hegemony? *Journal of Public Relations Review, 17(1),* 69–86.

Rosenfield, L. W. (1968). A case study in speech criticism: The Nixon-Truman analog. *Speech Monographs, 35,* 435–450.

Rothenbuhler, E. W. (1998). *Ritual communication: From everyday conversation to mediated ceremony.* Thousand Oaks, CA: Sage.

Rowland, R. C., & Jerome, A. M. (2004). On organizational apologia: A reconceptualization. *Communication Theory, 14*(3), 191– 211.

Ryan, H. R. (1988). Senator Richard M. Nixon's apology for the fund. In H. R. Ryan (Ed.), *Oratorical encounters* (pp. 99–120). New York: Greenwood Press.

Ryan, H. R. (1982). Kategoria and apologia: On their rhetorical criticism as a speech set. *Quarterly Journal of Speech, 68,* 254–261.

Seeger, M. W. (1986). The Challenger tragedy and search for legitimacy. *Central States Speech Journal, 37,* 147–157.

Seeger, M. W., Sellnow, T. L., & Ulmer, R. R. (1998). Communication, organization, and crisis. In B. R. Burleson (Ed.), *Communication yearbook, 21* (pp. 231–275). Thousand Oaks, CA: Sage.

Seeger, M. W., Sellnow, T. L., & Ulmer, R. R. (2003). *Communication and organizational crisis.* Westport, CT: Praeger.

Sellnow, T. L., Ulmer, R. R., & Snider, M. (1998). The compatibility of corrective action in organizational crisis communication. *Communication Quarterly, 46*(1), 60–74.

Simons, H. W. (2000). A dilemma-centered analysis of Clinton's August 17th apologia: Implications for rhetorical theory and method. *The Quarterly Journal of Speech, 86,* 438–453.

Tavuchis, N. (1991). *Mea culpa: A sociology of apology and reconciliation.* Stanford, CA: Stanford University Press.

Tharp, P. (2001, May 22). Detroit's car clash: Firestone blasts Ford, ends century-old partnership. *The New York Post.* Retrieved May 15, 2006, from http://www.lexis-nexis.com.

Tyler, L. (1997). Liability means never being able to say you're sorry: Corporate guilt, legal constraints, and defensiveness in corporate communication. *Management Communication Quarterly, 11,* 51–73.
Ulmer, R. R. (1999). Responsible speech in crisis communication: The case of General Motors v. Dateline NBC. *Free Speech Yearbook, 37,* 155–168.
van Es, R., & and Meijlink, T. L. (2000). The dialogic turn of public relations ethics. *Journal of Business Ethics, 27,* 69–77.
Wagatsuma, H., & Rosett, A. (1986). The implications of apology: Law and culture in Japan and the United States. *Law & Society Review, 20 (4),* 461–497.
Ware, B. L., & Linkugel, W. A. (1973). They spoke in defense of themselves: On the generic criticism of apologia. *Quarterly Journal of Speech, 59*, 273–283.
Wilson, G. L. (1976). A strategy of explanation: Richard M. Nixon's August 8, 1974, resignation address. *Communication Quarterly, 24,* 14–20.
Wong, E. (2003a, April 18). American's executive packages draw fire. *New York Times,* p. C2.
Wong, E. (2003b, April 22). Furious, American's unions talk of new votes. *New York Times,* p. C1.
Wong, E. (2003c, April 25). Under fire for perks, chief quits American Airlines. *New York Times,* p. C1.

28

Risk Communication and Biotechnology: A Discourse Perspective

Shirley Leitch and Judy Motion

University of Wollongong

INTRODUCTION

During the closing years of the twentieth century, biotechnology overtook nuclear physics as the most controversial public issue in relation to scientific endeavour. The growing ability to manipulate genes, the basic building blocks of all life forms, gave rise to a range of environmental, economic, political, ethical, cultural, and spiritual concerns. Scientists and governments found themselves ill-prepared to deal with the complex issues associated with these concerns. Opposition to the technologies of genetic modification (GM) coalesced into an international social movement which saw citizens staging varying forms of protest action ranging from civil disobedience to attacks on laboratories and threats against the lives of scientists (Pringle, 2003). In India, peasant farmers marched against the Monsanto "terminator gene" which threatened the traditional practice of seed-saving from harvest to harvest. In the UK, activists dressed as mutant vegetables and danced on supermarket roofs to draw attention to the GM foods sold inside and all around the world thousands of people rallied in their capital cities and signed petitions calling for a halt to the release of GM organisms into the environment. The dominant message from those opposed to GM was that the risks of these new technologies were unknown and potentially too great to allow scientists and the biotechnology industry to proceed.

Governments and industry turned to communication professionals for assistance in dealing with public concern about modern biotechnology. For the most part, the form of assistance sought was the staging of public information and dialogue campaigns. These campaigns embodied, what Palenchar and Heath (2002) have termed the "atheoretical approach" whereby the problem is defined as public ignorance for which the obvious solution is the provision of information and advice by experts. This deficit model of communication assumes that publics will become more accepting of complex issues such as biotechnology once they come to know more about them (Irwin & Wynne, 1996). The deficit model is not supported by communication theory or research, or by the experiences of those who have launched campaigns based on deficit model thinking (Hansen, Holm, Frewer, Robinson, & Sandoe, 2003). For example, in June 2003, the UK Government sponsored a nationwide series of public discussion fora entitled *GM Nation?* The official report produced after the fora were completed concluded that "The more people engaged in GM issues, the harder their attitudes and more intense their concerns" (Dept. of Trade and Industry, 2003). Providing additional information about GM did not lead UK publics to become more receptive to the potential benefits of the technologies. Rather, increasing information appeared to increase public unease about rather than acceptance of GM (Leitch & Davenport, 2007/2008). In this chapter, we offer an alternative approach to risk communication and biotechnology, drawing upon discourse and social theory. First, however, we outline our understanding of the key terms of *risk* and *discourse*.

RISK AND DISCOURSE

The need for risk communication only arises when there is a perception of risk. The perception of risk is the perception of potential danger or a hazard of some kind. However, risk is also often closely associated with notions of statistical probability (Lupton, 1999). We talk of spreading risk with our investments by, for example, putting some of our money in the bank, which will give us an almost guaranteed return but at a low rate, while putting other money into speculative ventures like gold mining, that may pay off spectacularly or not at all. We also speak of reducing risks by, for example, careful preparation and testing of safety equipment associated with risky activities like scuba diving or whitewater rafting. Risk is not, therefore, necessarily to be avoided and in some cases, such as whitewater rafting, is actually the point of the activity. Risk may represent danger but it can also be the reason a particular activity is beneficial or fun. Heath (1997) argued:

> Risk is a dialectic of benefit and harm. We engage in games of chance such as buying a lottery ticket while being cognizant that we will likely lose our dollar.... We believe that seeing friends, relatives, business associates and recreational sites offsets the risks of traveling by air, car, bus, foot, water, or rail. Farmers engage in work involving dangerous equipment, hazardous chemicals and powerful animals—all in the name of income and personal freedom. (p. 325)

The challenge for communicators, then, is to negotiate the dialectic of benefit and harm that arises from risk.

The kinds of risks described above by Heath (1997) are those into which individuals enter either knowingly or with at least some degree of choice. There are, however, many risks over which individuals may perceive that they have little or no control. Biotechnology and the potential risks associated with GM constitute one set of risks that potentially fall into this category. We now turn to the work of Ulrich Beck who offered insights into these kinds of risks.

Beck (1986/1992) used the term "risk society" to describe what he saw as the dawning of a new historical epoch that was defined by the relationship between individuals and *risk* (Jones, 2002). Whereas industrial society had been concerned with the distribution of *goods*, risk society was concerned with the distribution of "*bads*"(Lash & Wynne, 1992, p. 3). That is, whereas power relations within industrial society had been marked out by the unequal access to the objects produced by society, power relations within risk society were marked out by the degree of unwanted exposure to the dangerous or lethal by-products of production. Beck's analysis, like all analyses that suggest distinctive historical periods, has been critiqued on the basis that the unequal distribution of *bads* was and remains a feature of industrial societies (Lash & Wynne, 1992, p. 3). It has also been critiqued from the perspective that the *bads* of some current risks are not unequally distributed. Nuclear annihilation of the planet would, for example, eventually destroy rich and poor, developed nations and less developed nations, presidents and peasants, regardless of race, creed or access to resources (Lash & Wynne, 1992).

While Beck (1986/1992) may have overstated his argument in terms of historical disjuncture, we would contend that his emphasis on the emergence of risk as an increasingly important feature of contemporary society that is unequally distributed is valid. Support for Beck's (1986/1992) central thesis has come from a number of empirical studies of risk perception by publics. For example, Finucane, Slovic, Mertz, Flynn, and Satterfeld, (2000) found that race and gender were strong determinants of risk perception. They contended that sociopolitical factors had a significant impact on how vulnerable publics felt in relation to particular risks, with white males reporting the lowest levels of risk vulnerability. In a follow-up study conducted on perceptions of risk in relation to blood transfusions, Finucane, Slovic, and Mertz (2000) found that,

> The people who tend to perceive the greatest personal and public risk from blood transfusions are female, nonwhite and less educated, and they have not previously received a transfusion. (p. 1017)

The life experiences of the less-fortunate in society have taught them not to trust that *society*, or *science* or some other abstract construct will ensure that risks will be mitigated and that they will not suffer as a result of the actions of others. That is, those who have the least reason to trust, trust least.

Beck (1986/1992) argued that the belief in and support for science and technology to drive continuous progress waned in the twentieth century. One of the reasons for this was the risks that were embedded in the technologies. For example, the car gave freedom of movement to millions of people but it also killed hundreds of thousands, polluted the environment and made cities less pleasant to live in. A further reason, according to Beck (1986/1992), was the fact that technological decisions that have the potential to fundamentally change our lives are made before they enter the realm of democratic politics. The logics which lead to the development of technologies are primarily economic and scientific. Public debate and government regulation follow on behind, often driven by the actions of environmental organizations and other activist groups. Some degree of protection from the risks of scientific progress has had to be fought for in the political realm and has often only been gained after much damage has already been done to people or the environment. The fundamentally undemocratic character of science and technology may then be one reason for the growing distrust of scientists and suspicion of the risks embedded in each new technology.

Beck (1986/1992) also offered insights into the reasons why increasing public knowledge about technology does not increase public trust in or support for those technologies. He argued that "the sources of danger are no longer ignorance but *knowledge*; not a deficit but a perfect mastery over nature" (Beck, 1986/1992, p. 183, emphasis in original). That is, the risks we experience are not due to our ignorance, they are created by our expertise. Increasing public understanding of science and technology thus increases public awareness of the risks that we are manufacturing for ourselves. Modernity, Beck (1986/1992) contended, "has become the threat *and* the promise of emancipation from the threat that it creates itself" (p. 183, emphasis in original). That is, science creates risk and then promises to provide the solution to that risk at some future time. Following the logic of this argument, the primary outcome of some kinds of public information campaigns may therefore be to increase public anxiety about and awareness of risks over which they have little or no control. Risk communication, therefore, becomes a highly problematic arena of activity.

In this chapter we offer a discourse perspective on risk communication and therefore need to outline what we mean by *discourse* before proceeding further. There are multiple definitions of discourse but for our purposes here we draw on the constitutive perspective offered by Fairclough (1992) who stated that:

> Discourse contributes to the constitution of all those dimensions of social structure that directly or indirectly shape and constrain it: its own norms and conventions, as well as the relations, identities and institutions which lie behind them. Discourse is a practice not just of representing the world, but of signifying the world, constituting and constructing the world in meaning. (p. 64)

In accordance with this view of discourse, our concern is not just with the portrayal of concepts and objects but also with the way in which that portrayal simultaneously constructs the concepts and objects that it describes (Foucault, 1975/1995). Thus, the constitutive view of discourse has two dimensions. The first is that the world—including the relations between people, the identities of individuals and organizations, and the social structures we populate—is reproduced through discourse. Reproduction is the conservative face of discourse which leads to continuities of the status quo at all levels of society. The second dimension is that these same identities, relations and structures may also be transformed through discourse. Transformation is the creative face of discourse which leads to the possibility of change (Fairclough, 1992). A discourse approach to risk communication therefore encompasses both the reproductive and transformational dimensions of discourse.

The reproductive and transformational dimensions of discourse operate from the micro-level to the macro-level and may involve discursive struggle between discourse actors. A micro-level discursive struggle may involve a professor and a graduate student contesting the meaning of results in a laboratory. A macro-level discursive struggle may involve citizens and governments contesting control within a nation. It is the macro-level with which we concerned in this chapter: the discursive struggle between a variety of discourse actors in a variety of discourse contexts over the way in which the risks of GM biotechnology would be regulated and managed for society as a whole (Jones, 2002). The discourse actors in the case we discuss, included Government and its agencies, citizens, activist groups, lobby groups, research organizations and biotechnology companies. The discursive struggle over GM has been global in character and while we draw on a case study of just one nation—New Zealand—in our discussion, the events took place against this global backdrop.

THE DISCURSIVE STRUGGLE OVER GM IN NEW ZEALAND

The New Zealand case was chosen for analysis for two major reasons. The first was that the potential risks of GM came to public prominence in New Zealand before GM organisms were released into the environment. The primary GM crops such as cotton, wheat and soya developed by companies such as Monsanto were not common crops in New Zealand. While millions of acres of farmland were devoted to GM crops in other parts of the world, none have at the time of writing ever been grown in New Zealand outside of small, contained field trials in science facilities. The opportunity for public debate over the risks of GM prior to public exposure to these risks was therefore possible. Such was not the case in the United States which had led the development of GM crops and whose farmers were early adopters of the technology.

The second reason for selecting the New Zealand case was that much of the public debate occurred through the vehicle of a government appointed royal commission of inquiry into GM. Much of the discursive struggle between the various actors was played out through the processes of the Royal Commission on Genetic Modification (RCGM) and was recorded in the RCGM's publications and on its website. Moreover the *Report of the RCGM* (RCGM, 2001a) provided the framework for the regulation of the risks of GM and thus set the framework for permissible action by research organizations and biotechnology companies. Indeed, the *Report of the RCGM* may be seen as an exercise in risk communication in its own right because it directly addressed the risk-related concerns of submitters in its recommendations and also sought to allay concerns if the weight of evidence made this possible. The *Report of the RCGM* was widely circulated in hard copy, could be downloaded from a public website and was widely quoted in the news media. The New Zealand experience of GM thus constituted an accessible case study of the discursive struggle centered on the dialectic of benefit and harm in relation to the perceived risks of GM that occurred within one nation (Davenport & Leitch, 2005).

Due to the campaigns undertaken by activist organizations such as Greenpeace, the GM issue gained prominence in New Zealand in the late 1990s. The Green Party, which positions itself as the parliamentary voice of the New Zealand environmental movement, also became actively involved in voicing strong opposition to GM technology. Immediately prior to the 1999 general election, the Green Party presented a petition to the national Parliament calling for the staging of a royal commission on GM and a moratorium on field trials or field release of GM organisms. These demands were subsequently adopted as campaign promises by the Labour Party who went on to win that election.

The establishment of the RCGM was formally announced on 17 April 2000 along with a voluntary moratorium which allowed laboratory-based research to continue but prevented the release of GM organisms into the environment, at least until after the RCGM's findings were known. The Government directed the RCGM to receive representations upon, inquire into, investigate and report upon:

(1) the strategic options available to New Zealand to address, now and in the future, genetic modification, genetically modified organisms and products; and
(2) any changes considered desirable given the current legislative, regulatory, policy, or institutional arrangements for addressing, in New Zealand, genetic modification, genetically modified organisms, and products. (RCGM, 2001a, p. 6)

The RCGM was, then, asked to provide macro-level advice to the Government as to the strategy that the nation should adopt in relation to GM as well as advice about the supporting policy and administrative infrastructure that needed to be put in place to support this strategy. In carrying out their work, the RCGM was also "directed ... to adopt procedures that would encourage people to express their views on the subject matter and to consult with the public in a way that allowed people to express their views clearly" (RCGM, 2001a, p. 7). The RCGM was not, then, a forum reserved for scientific and policy elites. Rather it was open to all citizens and the RCGM was directed to ensure that citizens were able to participate in meaningful ways. For this reason, the processes associated with the RCGM became the primary space for the discursive struggle over GM in New Zealand.

CONSTRUCTION OF RISK THROUGH DISCOURSE

The concept of *risk* functioned, in Williams (1976) terms, as a keyword within the discourses associated with the RCGM. Keywords, as defined by Williams, were words that "at some time, in the course of some argument, virtually forced itself on my attention, because the problems of its meanings seemed to me inextricably bound up with the problems it was being used to discuss" (Williams, 1976, p. 15). Keywords are, therefore, words that are highly salient for an issue but which do not have a settled or agreed meaning according to their usage by the major discourse actors in relation to that issue. Disagreement over the meanings attached to keywords may arise out of conflicting interests or ideological positions. An analysis of keywords is then an analysis of the points of conflict and power relations within a particular discourse. As Slovic (1999) contended:

> Whoever controls the definition of risk controls the rational solution to the problem at hand. If risk is defined one way, then one option will rise to the top as the most cost-effective or the safest or the best. If it is defined another way, perhaps incorporating qualitative characteristics and other contextual factors, one will likely get a different ordering of action solutions. Defining risk is thus an exercise in power. (p. 68)

We will now examine the multiple ways in which the keyword *risk* was deployed and understood by discourse actors during the discursive struggle over the future of GM technologies in New Zealand. These actors were, we would contend, all engaged in risk communication as they sought to gain ascendancy within the GM debate for their particular definitions and interpretations of the risks posed by GM technologies.

Submissions to the RCGM can be divided into those who were opposed to GM and those who were in support of GM but there were numerous subtleties and nuances within the two camps and the ways in which they conceptualised risk. The *Report of the RCGM* summarized the concerns of those opposed to GM as follows:

> During the course of our consultation, many concerns were expressed about the risks of gene technology. Some people were so opposed to the technology for cultural, ethical and spiritual reasons they

> did not wish it to be used in any circumstances. The main issue discussed, however, was whether genetic modification could be used safely in the wider environment or whether such use should be confined to the laboratory, either for research or for some health purposes. Many people said the risks of genetic modification could be contained within the laboratory where, within reason, its safe use could be assured. But they submitted the technology was inherently unsafe outside the laboratory and there was an unacceptably high level of risk associated with its use, even under field trial conditions. The belief that risks were unacceptably high reflected submitters' underlying concerns that negative impacts of uncontained genetic modification may be irreversible and rapidly get beyond control. (RCGM, 2001a, pp. 42–44)

The major issue for opponents, then, was the potential for harm associated with the release of GM organisms into the environment. However, there was a substantial minority of dissenters whose conceptions of risk were not rooted in concerns that might be addressed scientifically. These concerns were presented within a variety of discourse contexts, the major ones being: spiritual/cultural, economic, environmental, socio-economic and medical. The submissions of GM advocates covered a more limited range of discourse contexts, primarily economic, scientific and medical. We now briefly outline the various conceptions and perceptions of risks within their discourse contexts.

The spiritual/cultural discourse was primarily concerned with the risks associated with mixing the DNA of different species. Maori, who are the indigenous people of New Zealand, were predominant in this category of anti-GM submitters. According to the *Report of the RCGM*:

> Maori differed from Pakeha [European New Zealanders] submitters in the use of the concept of mauri to explain why transgenics involving living creatures was wrong. Mauri is the life energy or the soul and is shared by all living things. Even inanimate objects like cliffs, stones and especially water have their own mauri. Many submitters took the view that mixing this mauri by creating transgenic animals was wrong. (RCGM, 2001a, p. 35)

GM practices that mixed the mauri of different species were seen by these Maori submitters as belonging in the realm of the gods. Rather than outline specific risks, they retold Maori legends in which human arrogance had led people to stray into the realm of the gods where they generally perished or were severely punished. This spiritual discourse was incommensurable with the economic and scientific discourse of pro-GM submitters.

The Maori spiritual/cultural discourse also raised concerns that the mixing of the DNA of different species could lead to the risk of incest or cannibalism. One Maori submitter stated:

> Your elders should teach you about your genealogy, who your relations are. But listen to this scenario. Hohepa took Merania the cow as a wife. Moo! They begat Doughboy, Salt, and Lambchop. Now, Lambchop married Puha [an edible plant] and they begat Boilup [stew]. (RCGM, 2001a, p. 37)

The passing down of genealogy is a central element of Maori culture in which the rights and status of individuals is derived from their lineage. This submitter was clearly concerned that if human DNA sourced from Maori was mixed with the DNA of other species then genealogy would become highly problematic, particularly if it meant that one was related to one's dinner. This concern was echoed by another submitter who stated:

> What happens in terms of crossing a human gene with a tomato? And we as people inadvertently eat the tomato. Is that comparable to cannibalism? (RCGM, 2001a, p. 34)

This risk of committing a serious spiritual transgression was not one that could be countered by scientific evidence or argument. Spiritual transgressions were the preserve of Tohunga, Maori spiritual advisers or priests, who also dealt with illness because spiritual and physical health were considered by Maori to be closely interconnected. Thus, scientifically-based evidence that eating a tomato containing a human gene was safe was not sufficient to counter the belief that such an act would constitute a serious spiritual transgression which would have serious consequences, possibly illness or death for the transgressor. In practical terms, these submitters wanted complete traceability of genetic material and a tight labelling regime so that they could avoid contact with GM organisms. However, even these measures would not address their central concern, which was that the creation of transgenic organisms was simply wrong.

One of the points of contention between opponents and supporters of GM was the extent to which GM differed from the manipulation of genetic characteristics of organisms by traditional means. Those who opposed GM saw it as a new category of technologies that brought with them new and much greater risks. For example a submission from an organic sector group argued that:

> The levels of uncertainty that are socially, administratively and politically appropriate are not a scientific matter. They are societal—we can accept those levels of uncertainty and risk whose consequences we can manage... In the case of released GMOs, the uncertainty that we as a society can tolerate cannot include uncertainty about our own survival, and the survival of the natural environment. (RCGM, 2001b, Submission IP61 from the Bio Dynamic Farming and Gardening Association)

For this group, the key point was that because the risks of GM included potentially catastrophic consequences for everyone, GM was a legitimate matter for societal concern and, therefore, the future directions of GM research should be decided by society rather than left to scientists.

In contrast, supporters of GM attempted to portray GM as part of a continuum of biotechnology that was the backbone of the economy:

> Hundreds of millions of dollars are already directly invested in New Zealand in the science and development of genetic modification of existing production animal species and plants.... Indirectly and directly, the majority of our total economy is dependent on the knowledge that the biological sciences have already given us.... New Zealand is unlikely to ever be anything other than a nation developing products from the growing of plants and animals for the majority of its wealth, therefore our future wealth, political and economic security, depend on our ability to continue to develop products to meet the needs of a global marketplace. (RCGM, 2001b, Submission IP24 from the Life Sciences Network)

Again, this disagreement over the way in which GM should be categorised—as a new set of technologies or as an addition to an existing set of technologies—was not one that could be solved by scientific argument. Rather it was rooted in an historical discourse of either continuity or disjuncture and risk was either reduced or amplified accordingly.

In contrast the potential risks in relation to human health, other than those that had spiritual origins, were addressed by scientific arguments and statistical calculations. The health related submissions to the RCGM, which raised a large number of potential risks of GM, were therefore generally framed within a scientific discourse. One risk related to the use of vector sequences such as viruses and bacteria to aid the incorporation of new genes into an organism's genome. New diseases might be generated through the recombination of such vector sequences with DNA from known pathogens. As one scientist explained in his submission to the RCGM, "Genes, like viruses, can infect the body, which should warn of the potential risks of transgenic organisms serving as a reservoir for new diseases and as a medium for the evolution of new pathogens because of their altered physiology and biochemistry" (RCGM, 2001a, p. 46). This risk had been realized in a case in which a new mouse pox virus had been created by accident by scientists who had been attempting to make a vaccine for fertility control and were using mice in their experiments. The *Report of the RCGM* noted that in this case the risk was contained within a laboratory environment and had been dealt with successfully. A second perceived risk was the unintentional activation or suppression of genes by gene promoter sequences which are used to 'switch on' the transgene in the new GM organism. Such an event could lead to the creation of new diseases. However, there were no known cases in which this risk had eventuated.

Selection marker genes enable a transgenic organism to be identified. A third health-related risk arose from the concern that antibiotic resistant genes were being used as markers. The use of these genes as markers had the potential to increase the spread of antibiotic resistance and thus hasten the demise of antibiotics as useful drugs. The *Report of the RCGM* noted that the weight of scientific evidence was that this risk was not significant when compared with that posed by the continuing use and overuse of antibiotics in the treatment of human and animal ailments.

A fourth health risk related to concerns about what happened to GM DNA if it was eaten. DNA was known to cross the gut barrier into the blood stream and into organs. It had also been shown to transfer to fetuses via the placenta. While there was no known evidence that DNA in GM food had adverse effects on human or animal health, there was also no conclusive evidence that it would not do so in the future. The opening statement of the RCGM's chapter on 'Food' was that:

> From the submissions received and the statements made at the public hearings it was clear genetically modified food was one of the issues that dominated discussion. This was no surprise. Food is a matter of personal importance to individual New Zealanders. As food production for domestic consumption and for export contributes significantly to the economy, it is also of national importance. (RCGM, 2001a, p. 180)

The potential risks of GM food to human health were, then, a central concern for many New Zealanders. However, from the outset, the *Report of the RCGM* positioned concerns relating to the unknown food-related harms of GM as secondary to the equally unknown but estimated economic benefits offered by such food. Economic concerns were considered to be paramount. For example, the *Report of the RCGM* stated:

> For reasons we will set out, the Commission does not accept that it is a viable option to ban the production, importation or sale of genetically modified food in New Zealand. It considers, however, to ensure the health and safety of the public, the food industry must be subject to rigorous standards enforced and monitored by competent and careful regulatory bodies. (RCGM, 2001a, p. 182)

The solution offered to the unknown risks of GM food was, then, a regime of standards and labeling to ensure compliance with established international practices and provide consumer information. New Zealanders were to be offered the choice of whether or not to expose themselves to this set of risks in place of guarantees that the food was safe to eat.

The viability of a labeling regime, however, rested on the possibility of clearly delineating GM from non-GM organisms. Some submitters argued that this would not be possible if field-release of GM organisms occurred because of the risk of cross-pollination and out-crossing. On this issue the *Report of the RCGM* noted that:

> Environmentalists and Maori expressed concern at the potential for indigenous plants to be cross-pollinated by exotic, genetically modified plants of the same genus. Maori were particularly concerned that plants that had traditionally provided food resources would be altered by cross-pollination, affecting their value as a resource and causing spiritual pollution. (RCGM, 2001a, p. 57)

The potential risk to indigenous plants was, then, framed within both spiritual and environmental discourses and the concept of risk was understood differently depending upon which discourse was invoked. For example, the Green Party framed their submission in relation to this risk in environmental terms which meant that the primary concern was the potential to cause indigenous species to diminish in numbers or become extinct:

> Purdue University researchers found last year that a 0.1 percent intrusion of transgenic fish into a wild stock could bring that population to extinction within 40 generations where the gene reduces the offspring's ability to survive. They dubbed this theory the 'Trojan gene hypothesis' on the grounds that the gene gets into the population looking like something good but ends up destroying the population. (RCGM, 2001a, p. 53)

The reason for focusing on transgenic fish was that such fish were already being farmed in New Zealand by a company called *King Salmon*, who had made news media headlines when 'mutant' fish were found amongst their stock (Weaver & Motion, 2002).

Transgenic fish were, however, cited as just one example of the potential risk that GM organisms posed for the environment. Dr David Suzuki, a Canadian ecologist, wrote in his submission that:

> The difference with this technology is that once the genie is out of the bottle, it will be very difficult or impossible to stuff it back. If we stop using DDT and CFCs, nature may be able to undo most of the damage—even nuclear waste decays over time. But GM plants are living organisms. Once these new life forms have become established in our surroundings, they can replicate, change and spread, so there may be no turning back. (RCGM, 2001a, p. 55)

The environmental discourse conceptualized the environment as a delicate and complex system. The introduction of GM organisms into the environment was portrayed as a highly risky venture that could have potentially catastrophic consequences. A submission from the Royal Forest and Bird Protection Society stated:

> Our natural ecosystems in New Zealand are unique, and their isolation, until recently, has made them vulnerable and valuable beyond measure. Indigenous forest—indigenous flora and fauna and fish belong here in their own right.... The forest is one of our living ecosystems which has successfully adapted and developed to a complex self-maintained diverse community, which has sustained its integrity over eons. Yes, there has been genetic change as adaptation applies, but this has not been engineered by humans in haste. (RCGM, 2001a, p. 60)

This submission was typical of the environmental discourse which emphasized the special character of New Zealand as an isolated island nation that was one of the last habitable places on the planet to be inhabited by humans. This special character was presented as a reason for New Zealand to be particularly risk-averse on issues such as GM. That science could not guarantee the safety of GM organisms, was presented within the environmental discourse as a good reason not to allow field release.

There was also an economic dimension to the environmental discourse on the risks of GM. The Royal Forest and Bird Protection Society, for example, argued that:

> Our "clean and green" environment is a major selling point in itself and will reap increasing rewards in the 21st century. New Zealand primary producers target customers who enjoy high-quality products that come from a healthy and unpolluted environment. This is also the foundation of our tourism industry. However, our increasingly demanding international clients expect the green image to be backed up by reality. (RCGM, 2001a, p. 95)

Both primary producers such as farmers and tourism operators were said to be at risk from the introduction of GM organisms into New Zealand. This position was lent legitimacy by the fact that the Government's multi-million dollar international campaign to increase New Zealand's tourist numbers centered on the slogan "100% Pure" and portrayed the nation as an untouched Garden of Eden. Organic farmers, distributors and retailers were also likely to position risk within an economic discourse. Organic certification agency, BIO-GRO, for example, argued that "New Zealand would gain a very strong economic advantage from being able to brand all its food as genetic modification free" (RCGM, 2001a, p. 94). Thus, discourse actors who invoked economic risks did so primarily in relation to the potential effects on their own livelihoods which they then extrapolated to "the economy" or "New Zealand" as a whole.

The economic discourse was predominately a dialectic about the winners and losers from GM technologies. Inevitably, once the issue of economic or other loss is raised, legal issues also come to the fore. For this reason, there was also a legal discourse within the proceedings of the RCGM. This discourse centred on the issue of liability—who should pay if any of the risks raised in relation to GM were realised? Expertise in this area was assigned to the legal profession and the RCGM's chapter on 'Liability Issues' comprises a review of the existing New Zealand and international legal statutes, precedents, policies and regulatory agencies. The RCGM (2001a) concluded that:

> As technology advanced with ever-increasing pace throughout the 20th century, the common law... showed that it was well able to mould new remedies for novel situations. Parliamentary intervention has rarely been needed in this area. From a legal liability perspective we have not been persuaded that there is anything so radically different in genetic modification as to require new or special remedies. (p. 328)

The debate within the historical discourse as to whether GM represented continuity or disjuncture was discussed above. Clearly, the RCGM was persuaded more by the continuity perspective in relation to the possible legal liabilities of GM.

Biotechnology has been a central driver of the New Zealand economy and so it was not surprising that many of the submissions were either situated within a socio-economic discourse or made some reference to this discourse. Central to these concerns was the view that almost all of the benefits of GM technologies would accrue to major corporations such as Monsanto while the risks would be widespread and would disproportionately accrue to the poor. This "privatization of benefit and socialization of risk" argument echoed Beck's (1986/1992) thesis which was discussed above. Friends of the Earth explored these types of risk equity issues in their submission:

> GM food may appear to advantage poorer families by being cheaper and more affordable than more expensive, organic non-GM alternatives, but the resulting widespread intake of GM food would have the especially large potential to adversely affect human and other species. Children of poorer families would have no choice but to eat GM foods and could therefore be disadvantaged in terms of health, immunity, food diversity and other potential harms unknown to us at this point in time. In effect, any advantages of GM products in the short term are insignificant compared with the potential disadvantages to humans and other species in the longer term.... (RCGM, 2001a, p. 100)

Similar sentiments were expressed by a speaker at one of the RCGM's public meetings who was quoted in the *Report of the RCGM*:

> With problems worsening in South Auckland and other low income areas around the country, I find it an utter disgrace that GM food sits on our supermarket shelves waiting for these unsuspecting buyers. For the kiddies in these areas brought up on soft drink, highly refined foods and takeaways [fast foods], all of which now contain GM ingredients, the future currently looks extremely bleak. (RCGM, 2001a, p. 101)

Labeling of GM food was not, therefore, seen as necessarily providing choice for citizens if they lacked the educational or financial resources to make such choices.

In addition to concern for the disproportionate accrual of risk to the least advantaged citizens, the socio-economic discourse also focused on what was seen as the capture of any potential benefits of GM technologies by major corporations and elite individuals. For example, one submitter who was a genetics consultant appearing for the Pesticide Action Network New Zealand stated:

> As regards the much discussed cauliflower mosaic virus 35S (CaMV) promoter patented by Monsanto—I believe that the patent for the worldwide use of the enhancer gene that goes with it is or was owned (at least in part) by Lord Sainsbury, who also happens to be or have been the UK Minister of Science, and has sat on committees promoting GM foods ... Lord Sainsbury has decided me against GM for the immediate future. (RCGM, 2001a, p. 47)

This submission was typical of those that expressed lack of trust in the development of GM technologies on the basis that they would be owned by people or organizations that were not themselves trusted or respected by the submitters.

The socio-economic discourse also extended to the risk of placing trust in science to solve problems that science itself had created. As one submitter stated, "People don't trust genetic engineering.... They also don't trust genetic engineers. Some groups described how scientists have let us down too many times" (RCGM, 2001a, p. 64). This lack of trust was linked to the fear that scientists had compromised their integrity by accepting private sector funding from organizations that had an interest in achieving particular outcomes from the science. For example, Dr Morgan Williams, New Zealand's Parliamentary Commissioner for the Environment, in discussing work on the control of the pest species, possums, through the use of genetic modification technology, told the RCGM:

> What we've found, and it came out through this possum GE study, was that [the] New Zealand community's asking, how independent is our science voice today? Who actually owns that voice? ... and there's a widespread perception that the soul of science is, or has been, bought, and ... the objectivity, rightly or wrongly that was bestowed upon science in previous decades, is not seeking to be as strong as it was. (RCGM, 2001a, p. 64)

Trust is a central factor within risk communication (Hansen et al., 2003) and as these examples illustrate, trust in major institutions including major corporations and governments is low with some publics.

PRO- GM DISCOURSES

We now discuss submissions to the RCGM that were positive towards GM. These submissions were primarily situated within economic, medical or scientific discourses which generally framed *risk* in relation to GM in positive terms. That is, the risks presented were those of rejecting the potential benefits of GM research. The Dairy Board expressed this view of GM risk in its submission:

> The major social and economic risk to New Zealand (and to the New Zealand dairy industry in particular) is that the New Zealand dairy industry will be prevented from developing and using genetic modification, while its competitors are not. The New Zealand dairy industry is uniquely placed to benefit from research and development into, and possible commercial use of, genetic modification technologies. These are essential tools to the New Zealand dairy industry in maintaining its competitive position. If the New Zealand dairy industry is prevented from using these tools, they will be locked up by the very type of multinational corporation seen as posing a threat. The threat to New Zealand from such corporations will be increased, not decreased, by a ban on genetic modification use. (RCGM, 2001a, pp. 85–86)

Similar submissions were received from other industry associations who saw a risk to their competitiveness if they were prevented from accessing the same GM technologies that might become available to their competitors in other nations. This economic risk was then extrapolated out to become a social risk if negative economic outcomes led to a decline in living standards.

Research organizations also expressed strong support for allowing GM research to continue based on their opinion of the risks associated with not proceeding. The Association of Crown Research Institutes said in its submission that:

> The economic risks in avoiding genetic modification were significant as the technology offered significant strategic opportunities for New Zealand. The benefits from niche genetic modification products flowed on to all New Zealanders. (RCGM, 2001a, p. 86)

Again, the economic benefits of GM research were generalized to "all New Zealanders" in contrast to negative views expressed above where economic benefits were seen to accrue more selectively to a small number of individuals and organizations.

Advocates of GM also presented GM technologies as capable of reducing a variety of health risks posed by technologies currently in use. For example, the RCGM (2001a) was advised that, "Genetic modification makes it possible to eliminate the risks of contamination by infectious pathogens through avoiding raw material from human and animal sources" (p. 241). The Ministry of Health advised the RCGM that GM insulin was a "purer product with less risk of infection" than non-GM insulin (RCGM, 2001a, p. 242). Similarly, Dr Sean Devine asserted that human health "would be a 'winner' because drugs sourced from genetically modified organisms had a lower risk of HIV infection than those derived from human blood or blood products" (RCGM, 2001a, p. 242).

Pro-GM submissions emphasized that there were risks associated with any medical technology, such as undesirable side-effects of drug therapies. Thus GM technologies were, as noted above, part of a continuum of scientific development within medicine rather than some new class of technology which had to be considered differently. Interestingly, the submission from the Green Party made a similar point, stating that testing processes for medicines "does lower the risk from genetically modified medicines to the point where they are probably not dissimilar to the risks from other synthetic medicines, and that is why we are not opposed to the development of genetically engineered medicines in the laboratory" (RCGM, 2001a, p. 246). Thus, the Green Party made a clear distinction between the potential for harm posed by the field release of GM organisms and GM organisms in the food chain, to which it was opposed, and the potential for benefit of the development of medicines and therapies in contained laboratory conditions using GM technologies, which it supported.

DISCUSSION: RISK IN MULTIPLE DISCOURSE CONTEXTS

In this section, we analyze the transformational and reproductive strategies deployed by discourse actors as they sought to position GM either positively or negatively within the dialectic of benefit or harm. This dialectic was played out within the spiritual/cultural, economic, environmental, socio-economic and medical discourse contexts outlined in the previous section. The arguments made by discourse actors were sometimes competing but at other times were simply incommensurable because they arose from alternative world views. For example, within the spiritual/cultural discourse of some Maori groups, the risks were of divine retribution following transgressions of spiritual laws that forbade, for example, the mixing of the life forces of different species. Expertise in relation to such risks did not rest with scientists and could not be calculated in terms of statistical probability of occurrence. If the spiritual risk was accepted as valid, then the best course was to avoid the risk altogether by restricting the permissible uses of GM technologies particularly if they involved human DNA. However, there was no scientific means of determining the validity of such spiritual claims, which were a matter of faith.

The historical discourse ran through many submissions, as discourse actors offered competing accounts of GM technologies. Those who were opposed to GM, portrayed the technologies as constituting a radical change in science, one that involved a disjuncture with existing practices and presented a whole new category of potential risks. The necessary response to these risks was extreme caution and the creation of new sets of procedures, regulations and controls. The representation of GM as a radical and unknown scientific practice was, then, part of a reproductive discourse strategy designed to protect the status quo. In contrast, supporters of GM portrayed GM as a continuation of modern biotechnology which had underpinned New Zealand's economic progress from the beginning of its history as a nation. The necessary response to GM was to incorporate it within existing processes and to treat it no differently than any other kind of technological development. Here the representation of GM as a normal scientific practice was part of a transformational discourse strategy designed to change the status quo and enable the use of GM.

The environmental discourse was dominated by those opposed to GM who warned of a wide range of potential risks posed by GM technologies. These risks ranged from the genetic pollution of indigenous plant species due to unwanted cross pollination from GM species, through to species extinction and possible irreversible damage to eco-systems. These risks were open to scientific debate and evidence and the RCGM drew on this debate and evidence during its proceedings. Scientific opinion was, however, clearly divided in relation to many of the environmental risks. As Lofstedt (2004) has argued, while division amongst scientists is normal, when it is aired publicly in forums such as the RCGM, it fosters public distrust of science. That is, divisions are not seen as evidence of robust ongoing debate between scientists but as evidence that some scientists are telling the truth and others are not. In such a climate of distrust, publics are then able to pick the scientific argument that matches their pre-existing opinion or supports their interests. Global warming provides a telling case study of the consequences of selectively using science for political purposes. In the absence of scientific consensus, the general trend has been to adopt what is known as the precautionary principle and such was the case with the RCGM (Maguire, 2003; Maguire & Hardy, 2006).

The precautionary principle was laid out in the 1992 Rio Declaration on Environment and Development:

> In order to protect the environment, the precautionary approach shall be widely applied by States according to their capabilities. Where there are threats of serious or irreversible damage, lack of scientific certainty shall not be used as a reason for postponing cost-effective measures to prevent environmental degradation. (UNCED, 1992 cited in Maguire & Hardy, 2006, p. 7)

The major outcome of the application of the precautionary principle to the introduction of new technologies has been to allow regulators to place restrictions around such technologies even if there is no conclusive proof that they will do harm. Rather, the burden of proof has been shifted onto those who propose to deploy technologies to prove that they are safe and that their benefits outweigh any potential they may have to cause harm. In the face of uncertainty over the possible effects of GM on the environment, application of the precautionary principle would, and in this case did, lead the RCGM to recommend tight restrictions on the field release of such organisms.

There was also significant uncertainty over the degree and nature of risk within the medical discourse. In this context the debate was between those who placed emphasis on the potential of GM technologies to produce safer medicines and therapies that would replace riskier existing technologies and those who emphasised the risk inherent in the GM technologies themselves. As with the environmental discourse, the dialectic of benefit and harm was played out between competing scientific arguments. However, the medical discourse differed from the environmental discourse in one significant way; the GM technologies in question were laboratory-based rather than intended for field release. For this reason, the weight of submissions, including those from anti-GM groups such as the Green Party, was in favour of allowing scientists to continue GM medical research. Another difference, perhaps, was that GM medicines and therapies were intended for those who were unwell, who presumably would have some choice over whether or not to accept the prescribed cure. GM organisms released into the environment or the food chain would potentially impact on everyone and the degree to which individuals would be able to exercise choice in relation to their exposure to the risks potentially posed by these organisms was contentious.

The dialectic within the economic discourse was between those who saw the major risk as resulting from the rejection of GM technologies and those who saw the major risk as resulting from the acceptance of GM. In all cases the arguments were based on the self-interest of the particular submitters, which was an interesting difference between the economic discourse and the medical, political and spiritual/cultural discourses where the interests of everyone or of the planet more generally were positioned as paramount. The organic sector was concerned about the risk to their status as organic producers if GM crops became widespread. Eco-tourism operators were concerned about the potential risk to the "100% Pure" image of clean, green and GM-free New Zealand, which underpinned their industry. Some primary sector organizations, particularly from the dairy industry, saw the risk of being "left behind" other nations if GM technologies were banned. Other primary sector organizations, such as Zespri, saw the risk that GM posed for their brand identity in nations whose consumers had rejected GM produce, particularly those in Europe. Science organizations saw risks to the whole science sector if a ban were put in place, in that such a ban might lead science programmes and leading scientists to move offshore. In this discourse context, the validity of one risk did not negate the validity of another risk. That is, it was possible that the field release of GM organisms might advantage one sector economically and disadvantage another. The task of the RCGM, then, was to determine potential winners and losers rather than to weigh up the evidence in relation to competing risk claims.

The RCGM's task within the legal discourse was somewhat different: it was to determine what legal recourse the losers from GM would have to seek compensation should any of the myriad of risks raised in submissions come to fruition. Thus, the RCGM had to consider what legal processes and frameworks were required to deal with the submitters' worst case scenarios rather than to consider the likelihood that these scenarios would eventuate. The expert opinions that guided the RCGM in this area were those of the legal profession who were only concerned with access to legal redress. Risks within the legal discourse were simply outcomes that could render some parties liable to be sued and other parties liable for compensation according to established law and precedent.

The final discourse considered in this chapter was the socio-economic discourse. Within this discourse context, the emphasis was on the distribution of harm and benefits rather than on the nature of the risks themselves. Political actors agued that if GM foods did turn out to be less nutritious or more likely to trigger allergies or disease then it would be the least advantaged in society who would inevitably end up consuming these foods if they were allowed on the market. Moreover, the benefits in terms of profits would accrue to the major corporations who dominated the biotechnology sector globally. The issue, then, was why all people should bear the risks of GM, particularly those less advantaged, while the primary benefits of these technologies would be captured by the fortunate few.

CONCLUSION

The discourse on GM centred on what Heath (1997, p. 325) termed a "dialectic of benefit and harm" arising from risk perceptions and evaluations. These perceptions and evaluations arose from a range of world views which meant that they were sometimes incommensurable. The responsibilities of the RCGM were to, first, provide a forum that could accommodate all of these world views and, second, make recommendations to Government that were both evidence-based and politically acceptable. The necessity of establishing the RCGM as a public forum arose, we would contend, because of the undemocratic nature of much of the decision-making that occurs in relation to science and technology (Beck, 1986/1992). Most decisions are made by individual scientists, research groups and companies, within the context of established regulatory environments, and never enter the public sphere. Challenges to this mode of decision making can arise when developments come to the attention of publics for whom they pose potential risks. GM was such a development, which not only came to public attention but led to widespread public protest as well as activism by environmental groups. Faced with such a contentious issue, Government was compelled to create the RCGM as a means of both dealing with the issue and calming the political unrest that it had invoked. The establishment of the RCGM, then, was part of a process of risk communication by the Government. It involved both the gathering of material that could be used to assess the various risk claims as well as the provision of a communication forum within which these claims could be publicly made and debated.

The second responsibility of the RCGM, to make recommendations to Government that were evidence-based and politically acceptable, involved navigating within a range of discourse contexts including spiritual/cultural, economic, environmental, socio-economic and medical. Discourse actors who emphasised the potential of GM to cause harm deployed a reproductive discourse strategy in that they presented GM as posing various types of threats to the status quo. In their submissions they emphasised the radical nature of GM technologies and the potentially catastrophic consequences of unleashing such technologies. They sought the application of the precautionary principle which put the onus on scientists to demonstrate the absence of harm before they could proceed. In contrast, GM proponents used a transformational discourse strategy which, perhaps ironically, sought to position GM technology as part of the continuum of biotechnology that had underpinned the New Zealand economy for hundreds of years.

In fulfilling their second responsibility, the RCGM had to provide a means of reconciling what were in some instances, irreconcilable claims and counterclaims. We would argue that their report represented a superb piece of risk communication in that it acknowledged and gave voice to all claims and, in the end, found solutions that enabled most discourse actors to claim at least some degree of victory (Davenport and Leitch, 2005). The RCGM concluded that New Zealand should "keep its options open" on the grounds that it would be "unwise to turn our back on the potential advantages on offer, but that we should proceed carefully, minimising and managing risks" (RCGM, 2001a, p. 2). The *Report of the RCGM* thus placed emphasis on both "preserving opportunities" (RCGM, 2001a, pp. 174, 330) and "proceed[ing] with caution" (RCGM, 2001a) which amounted to a reconciliation of the dialectic of benefit and harm that had pervaded RCGM submissions. That GM had all but disappeared as an issue in New Zealand by the time of the 2005 general election provided the strongest evidence of the success of the RCGM process as an effective mode of risk communication for dealing with highly contentious and politicized issues.

REFERENCES

Beck, U. (1986/1992). *Risk Society* (M. Ritter, Trans.). London: Sage.

Davenport, S., & Leitch, S. (2005). Agoras, ancient and modern, and a framework for science-society debate. *Science and Public Policy*, 32(2), 137–153.

Department of Trade and Industry. (2003). *GM Nation? The Findings of the Public Debate.* London: DTI.

Fairclough, N. (1992). *Discourse and Social Change*. Cambridge: Polity.

Finucane, M. L., Slovic, P., Mertz, C .K., Flynn, J., & Satterfeld, T. A. (2000). Gender, race, and perceived risk: The "white male" effect. *Health Risk and Society*, *2*(2), 159–172.

Finucane, M. L., Slovic, P., & Mertz, C. K. (2000). Public perception of the risk of blood transfusion. *Transfusion*, *40*(8), 1017–1022.

Foucault, M. (1975/1995). *Discipline and Punish: The Birth of the Prison* (A. Sheridan, Trans.). New York: Vintage Books.

Hansen, J., Holm, L., Frewer, L., Robinson, P., & Sandoe, P. (2003). Beyond the knowledge deficit: Recent research into lay and expert attitudes to food risks. *Appetite*, *41*, 111–121.

Heath, R. L. (1997). *Strategic Issues Management: Organizations and Public Policy Challenges*. Thousand Oaks, CA: Sage.

Irwin, A., & Wynne, B. (1996). *Understanding Science?: The Public Reconstruction of Science and Technology*. Cambridge: Cambridge University Press.

Jones, R. (2002). Challenges to the notion of publics in public relations: Implications of the risk society for the discipline. *Public Relations Review*, *28*(1), 49–62.

Lash, S., & Wynne, B (1992). Introduction. In U. Beck (1986/1992). *Risk Society* (M.Ritter, Trans.), (pp.1–8). London: Sage.

Leitch, S., & Davenport, S. (2007/2008). Corporate brands and social brands:

Co-branding GM-Free and UK supermarkets. *International Studies in Management and Organization, 37*(4), 46–64.

Lofstedt, R. (2004). Risk Communication in the Twenty-First Century. *International Public Management Journal*, *7*(3), 335–346.

Lupton, D. (Ed.). (1999). *Risk and Sociocultural Theory: New Directions and Perspectives.* New York: Cambridge University Press.

Maguire, S. (2003). The co-evolution of technology and discourse: A study of substitution processes for the insecticide DDT. *Organization Studies*, *25*(1), 113–134.

Maguire, S., & Hardy, C. (2006). The emergence of new global institutions: A discursive perspective. *Organization Studies*, *27*(1), 7–29.

Palenchar, M. J., & Heath, R. L. (2002). Another part of the risk communication model: Analysis of communication processes and message content. *Journal of Public Relations Research, 14*(2), 127–158.

Pringle, P. 2003. *Food Inc. Mendel to Monsanto – The Promises and Perils of the Biotech Harvest.* New York: Simon & Schuster.

RCGM (Royal Commission on Genetic Modification). (2001a). *Report of the Royal Commission on Genetic Modification: Report and recommendations.* (Vol.1). Wellington, New Zealand: Royal Commission on Genetic Modification.

RCGM (Royal Commission on Genetic Modification). (2001b). *Submissions to the Royal Commission on Genetic Modification.* Retrieved 10 August 2006 from www.mfe.govt.nz/publications/organisms/royal-commission-gm/

Slovic, P. (1999). Trust, emotion, sex, politics, and science: Surveying the risk assessment battlefield. *Risk Analysis*, *19*(4), 689–701.

Weaver, C. K., & Motion, J. (2002). Sabotage and subterfuge: Public relations, democracy and genetic engineering in New Zealand. *Media, Culture & Society, 24*(3), 325–343.

Williams, R. (1976). *Keywords*. London: Fontana.

29

Precautionary Principle and Biotechnology: Regulators Are from Mars and Activists Are from Venus

Stephanie Proutheau
CELSA, Paris IV – Sorbonne University

Robert L. Heath
University of Houston

Risk communication theory and best practices have opened many windows of opportunity for environmental communication scholarship. As an intellectual and pragmatic challenge, the environment poses the most daunting challenge to humans. The risks suffered from technologies raise concerns about the ethical responsibilities of those who write about the environment. Is it an ethical issue, a matter of crisis management (Cox, 2007)? Without reservation, scholars believe it is normative. A central theme in environmental research is the management of the unknown, matters of uncertainty (Heath, Palenchar, Proutheau, & Hocke, 2007). To this end, it has been concluded,

> Environmental communication, like risk communication, integrates a focus on the probative force of various facts in the context of symbolic processes that result from the dynamics of a functional or dysfunctional communication infrastructure. (Heath et al., 2007, pp. 45–46)

The centerpiece in this potential dysfunction is the lack of a coherent decision heuristic that can be used to balance the advantages sought against the potential harms of industrialization, growth, technology, and policy. Centering attention on the need for a shared sense of reality, scholars and other experts have advanced an analytic stream centering on the relatively recent policy innovation known as the precautionary principle, the discussion of which has produced a vast literature and strident debate (Maguire & Ellis, chapter 6, this volume).

In the development of environmental policy and business planning, few of these challenges have more importance to human's quality of life than does the science and public policy as well as business plans relevant to agricultural biotechnology. It opens the window to visions of an enhanced quality of life for various key publics, but it also is one of those technologies where humans necessarily are their own experimental guinea pigs. On how to navigate these waters, the World Trade Organization (WTO) has unexpectedly moved to center stage over the past ten years. As the adjudicating authority in the trade conflict opposing the United States (joined by sixteen other complainants) to the European Union over the legitimate framework to regulate the international movements and utilizations of genetically modified organisms (GMOs) (Reports of the Dispute Panel, 2006), the WTO was overtaken by the multilateral making of technology choices; already one of the prevailing sound voices in such decision processes on the international scene, it has also been expected to become a forum for debate and dialogue. Because sound and precautionary standards have both been called in by the WTO stakeholders and stakeseekers as competing treatment of scientific uncertainty in framing GMOs' hazards and benefits, a key stake in the biotech case lies with the elucidating ambiguities in risk regulatory language so antagonisms can be mitigated and compatibilities fostered. The authors advance here along the lines of the rhetorical approach to issues management in order to understand the constraints and opportunities of the new discourse of precaution (Andrée, 2005) in multilateral risk decision making processes. As a centerpiece in that discussion, academics and policy makers strive to create participatory risk management and communication rationales so enlightened technology choices can be made by the whole of society, new and emerging technologies developed and applied through legitimate and effective planning, and potential crises avoided or mitigated.

At the most fundamental level, risks are defined as probabilistic occurrences that can have positive or negative outcomes of various magnitudes. In varying ways, science—including probabilistic reasoning, societal and cultural institutions, and individual predilections—becomes part of the challenge to those who seek to advance the human condition through sound science and those who work to assure that the risk creators do not unfairly burden others in the name of this advancement.

Risks do not come with a specified set of instructions on how to interpret, evaluate, minimize, and communicate about them. Thus, we are interested in the ways in which communication occurs, preferring to focus on the quality of infrastructures in which risks are made known, analyzed, judged, and managed. In such debates, the sound rationale for policy science necessarily plays a major role, instantiated in risk literature as the Mental Model Approach (MMA) (Morgan, Fischhoff, Bostrom, & Atman, 2002). Set against this preference for getting the facts through sound science and setting them into dialogue is the challenge of wrestling with the cultural institutions which tend to either support the sound assessment methods and conclusions, oppose them by preferring other interpretative heuristics, or remaining neutral for lack of ability to participate or indifference to the process and its products. Thus, in the risk decision equation, we ask, whose science is put into place, how good is that science, and whose lives and interests are benefited or harmed by the process and the outcomes?

The relationship between science and society becomes visible in the unfolding of policy-making processes within public institutions concerned with issues of science and thereby raises the question of the role of science in legitimating preferences for a specific social order.

> Although one should be very careful about making metaphorical allusions to science as the religion of modernity, our scientific contemporaries often appear to occupy a privileged position in relation to institutions of governance and commerce analogous to that enjoyed by the priesthood in earlier areas. Governments and managements both rely on scientists and technologists as the interpreters of the world, operating through an increasing array of scientific assessment processes as diverse as environmental protection, public health and economic policy.... Science is not simply one activity or aspect of society; it has become the primary culture of legitimation for modern society. (Rayner, 2004, p. 352)

The increased internationalization and public participation (sometimes undesired and unexpected) in risk policy over the past decades have opened the window to the emergence of several diverging science-for-policy rationales that compete against the single, unambiguous science and among themselves for social influence; this state of affairs therefore brings in uncertainty in the scientific voice but also risk decision making.

In the context of the debate over the safety of GMOs, the precautionary principle has been advanced as a potential solution by some, but its practical application is, on the other hand, argued by others to be an impediment to traditional risk decision processes. This chapter reviews the precautionary principle and the efficacy of its role as a particular framing of scientific uncertainty and the quality of its participation to the debate over the advances, advantages, and liabilities of the genetic engineering of crops and foods and corresponding international trade obligations. This discussion has two primary objectives: to isolate the factors that advance and frustrate the decision making process and offer suggestions as to how it can be enhanced.

THE EUROPEAN UNION: DEBATING THE LIMITS OF PRECAUTION

In the midst of the debates over degrees of risk, scientific uncertainty and risk management policy options, the precautionary principle has enlivened and frustrated the dialogue. This concept was introduced into the policy arena via a multitude of environmental protection conferences and conventions (see Maguire & Ellis, chapter 6, this volume) to foster restraint against environmental degradation; by inserting a principle and a procedure into risk policy debates, its aims at maximizing the visibility of the intolerance some advocates have for certain risks. Thus, it was intended to focus the controversy, but in fact became itself a centerpiece for controversy, especially as it has been interjected into discussions of the tolerability of risks attached to biotechnological applications in agriculture and food production.

The logic of this principle is that if the consequences of an action are not well known and the subject of substantial controversy regarding the potentiality of irreversible consequences, then actions and decisions should err on the side of caution. As such this principle marks a difference with the prevention of known risks and can be invoked to slow or even deny approval for new and emerging technologies characterized by risks which are not yet well known and the manifestation of which are uncertain but can in fact result in impacts of great magnitude (Maguire & Ellis, chapter 6, this volume).

This principle has often been captured in various cultural truisms. "Look before you leap." "Two wrongs do not make a right." "Better safe than sorry." "An ounce of prevention is worth a pound of cure." Colloquialisms such as these can be challenged by other familiar sayings. "The early bird gets the worm" suggests that the bird willing to judge the risks of daylight or spring time is more likely to get the reward than will the more cautious one. We might add this one, "nothing ventured, nothing gained."

These ordinary expressions suggest not only the boundaries but the essence of contention regarding this concept. If we are too cautious, goes the argument regarding certain modern agricultural technologies that could increase crop production, people will die of famine while we are worrying about the consequences of new crop technologies. The likelihood of death by famine, so the sound advocates would say, is starkly demonstrable, whereas the uncertainty about the long-term effects on human and ecological health of the new technology is merely or essentially only potential and perhaps a quite manageable risk. From the sound point of view, the precautionary advocacy may be nothing more than politically motivated caution by worriers to throw a cold blanket over the fire of innovation.

Introduced to improve the quality of deliberations and outcomes of risk decision processes regarding situations characterized by scientific uncertainty, the precautionary principle may in fact raise the level of uncertainty, according to the sound viewpoint. Some scientific premises can only be tested through implementation. If they are kept from being tested, the degree to which they increase or decrease risk may not be known. Critics of the principle, who often focus on its aggressive version (Maguire & Ellis, chapter 6, this volume), suggest that outcome is contradictory to the desires of the advocates of the principle. If, for instance, science knows the hazards of lead pipes, should the precautionary principle reduce the implementation of an alternative, such as vinyl pipe, until the health hazard of that technology is determined? If public health specialists know that X percent of the population will die or suffer severe consequences from smallpox inoculation, what then would be the advisability of inoculating health care workers on the assumption that one or the many potential means of bioterrorism is smallpox?

In regard to the European ban, the US's main objection rests with the EU not justifying its decision to impose stricter levels of protection against importations of GM products on the basis of demonstrated risks characterized by sound risk assessment. On the other hand, the EU has argued that there are components of scientific uncertainty pertaining to the applications of recombinant DNA technology and to the consequences of the consumption and open field cultivations of bioengineered organisms, foods and crops that does not rule out potential hazards for human and environmental health and thereby legitimize the application of precautionary measures to delay their commercialization while adequate EU-level regulations are developed and implemented. The EU, besides constituting a key Biosafety Protocole (BSP) signatory, had also officially endorsed the precautionary principle as soon as 2000 (Commission of European Communities, 2000). Therefore, the biotech trade dispute is not treated as one over the soundness of science but as one of cultural preference over the treatment of scientific uncertainty for risk assessment and management purposes; against this background the European policy action constitutes, in the mind of the US trade representatives, an overly precautionary framing of scientific uncertainty.

The public controversy over the determination of the safety of agricultural biotechnology pits issues and protocols of sound science against cultural interpretations of risk. Over the years, this latter perspective has become empowered by the precautionary principle. First a moral principle, it was later introduced in public policy making as it was forcefully championed via numerous international conventions on environmental protection. One of its most high-profile embodiments constitute the signature of the BSP in 2000, which is since then brought against the sound standards of the Codex Alimentarius for the determination of the appropriate level of scientific uncertainty within the WTO; international trade rules require that scientific uncertainty be characterized by sound risk assessment procedures in the context of procedures authorizing stricter levels of protection by individual country members against importations of GMOs. The current controversy is one of many battles this relatively new state of affairs promises. However, much the controversy seems to be a simple matter of getting and reporting risks, within parameters of acceptability, it poses something larger. It centers attention on how, within risk controversies, various advocates formulate preferred perspectives, central to which is their specific treatment of scientific uncertainty. As the stakeholders of sound science privilege their risk regime and attendant treatment of scientific uncertainty, they shun the pressure to acknowledge and respond to absolute scientific certainty implicit in the precautionary advocacy. The controversy over GMOs is presently treated as a clash between the sound and precautionary framings of scientific uncertainty in multilateral regulatory setting; the battle takes place where science must simultaneously serve as inquiry and advocacy.

Traditional risk analysis relies on evidence produced by sound science to determine potential harms; as such, the sound perspective embraces scientific uncertainty as an inherent component of advancing knowledge and relies on the ongoing process of scientific inquiry to identify or rule out hazards (DeGregori, 2004, pp. 124–126). On the other hand, the precautionary definition of scientific uncertainty involves the principle of not bowing to ignorance; it emphasizes the possibility that a piece of knowledge is still lacking in the state of the scientific knowledge as it defines a the likelihood of a manifestation and its impact at some point in time (Harremoës, Gee, Macgarvin, Stirling, Keys, Wynne, & Guedes Vaz, 2002). In regard to assessing biotechnological risks, sound stakeholders rely on the principle of substantial equivalence whereby a GMO is considered equivalent to its non-modified counterpart, until proven different (Kuiper, Kleter, Noteborn, & Kok, 2001). On the other hand, the precautionary reasoning operates inversely: it assumes a fundamental difference between modified and non-modified organisms and seeks to obtain scientific certainty to prove their equivalence. At the moment, in absence of what it considers to be compelling scientific evidences to prove the sound risk assessment results with absolute certainty, the overly precautionary advocacy features the consumption of GMOs and the cultivation of GM crops and plants as hazardous for human and environmental health. The lay out of these framings of scientific uncertainty reveal parts of the rhetorical process whereby the precautionary and sound perspectives on the GMO risk have grown incompatible.

"One of the characteristics of [risk] controversies is that hitherto accepted social definitions lose their validity. Shifts occur in what is considered the problem, as well as in what are defined as solutions" (Nowotny, cited by Schwartz & Thompson, 1990, p. 36). The assumptions and definitions on which risk managing organizations build their regulatory efforts are vetted by public discourse (Heath, 1997). As they enact new definitions or re-enact old ones, organizations create interpretive frames that compete, conflict or are compatible with those of their stakeholders (Heath, 1993). Critical to the present inquiry into the nature of risk controversies is the understanding that "the rhetorical paradigm adds value to organizations by increasing their sensitivity to how stakeholders create interpretative frames to impose limits on their … activities" (p. 142).

Rhetorical perspectives are useful, perhaps invaluable, in matters of understanding risk communication issues. As important as the process of risk communication is, perhaps even more important is the social crafting of meaning and the ways in which it is shared sense making or deeply conflicting perspectives. Burke (1966) also proposed that meaning is created because we see our physical realm *in the light of words*. Once identifiable groups have enacted narratives or adopted terministic screens, their discourses become treatable as zones of meaning (Heath, 1993, 1997), the identification and understanding of which is imperative for risk communicators (Heath & Abel, 1996; Heath & Palenchar, 2000; Palenchar & Heath, 2002). In risk controversies,

> science typically lies at the center of the debate, where those who advocate some line of action are likely to claim a scientific justification for their position, while those opposing the action will either invoke scientific uncertainty or competing scientific results to support their opposition. (Sarewitz, 2004, p. 386)

Around the biotech case, narratives of sound and precautionary science are enacted by opponent governments and organizations which wrangle to legitimize their rationale for the treatment of scientific uncertainty not only for the case at hand, but also for matters of science-for-policy in general. The present argument therefore advances the examination of the relationship between the content and the dynamics of these zones as a predictor of the quality of the risk policy decision-making process.

THE RHETORICAL MANAGEMENT OF RISK DECISIONS: DEFINING PRECAUTIONARY THRESHOLDS

The WTO biotech case is illustrative of policy issues demanding that sound and precautionary rationales coexist in risk decision makings for appropriate resolution. The integration in 1998 of precautionary measures as exemptions to free trade obligations within the WTO framework echoed with the shift in the framing of precaution established by the United Nations' Cartagena Protocole on Biosafety (BSP) signed in 2000. The ambiguities maintained about the status of these precautionary dispositions in international trade law provide sufficient leeway to countries signatories to both the WTO agreements and the BSP to broaden the interpretation of the WTO precautionary measures until they are made equivalent to the BSP precautionary principle; this interpretation is then brought against the sound policy rationale on which traditionally rests the enforcement of international trade rules. As a consequence of this regulatory configuration, two conditions of applicability for these precautionary measures exist and ought to be harmonized for the WTO to guarantee the legitimacy and durability of its activities and their outcomes: the status of the precautionary framing of scientific uncertainty introduced to the WTO can either be the one of a simple rule operating under sound procedures (traditionally the operating risk rationale at the WTO), or of a principle of international law superseding to the risk policy recommendations put forth by the sound rationale (operating rationale for the BSP signatories).

Such considerations on the case's regulatory dimensions are mobilized here for they can be used to define the communication situation as to productively guide risk communicators' research for the symbolic and discursive processes causing policy gridlocks. First, the differential between the formulations of precaution as a simple rule or as a principle of international law exemplifies the communication reality of harmonizing a modest version of precaution (see Maguire & Ellis, chapter 6, this volume) with the sound version, the proponents of which focus on the environmentalist lineage of the precautionary principle to warn against the consequences of more radicalized environmentalist claims bleeding into modest precaution, the role of which thereby reduced to serving as the Trojan Horse of environmentalist exigencies into sound public policy.

Also, because both interpretive frames of scientific uncertainty are endorsed by distinct international organizations, along with their own affiliated institutions and national governments, they as such constitute specific international risk regimes (Gerlach & Rayner, 1988) that can be apprehended by risk communicators as zones of meaning (Heath, 1993, 1997) competing for hegemony on the international scene. International risk regimes result from alliances between organizations endorsing the same risk culture (Douglas, 1992; Schwarz & Thompson, 1990). A key assumption underpinning cultural theory accounts for the function of risk beliefs across societies and is found to assist risk communicators in circumscribing the themes that are not spontaneously considered as integrative dimensions of risk advocacies. Indeed, cultural theory postulates that power institutions, guarantors of a given social order, are legitimated through the mobilization of corresponding myths of nature and conversely challenged or held accountable via the mobilization of myths of nature attendant to competing cultures. Cultural theory therefore holds nature as a potent source of social legitimation and, as a corollary, advances that risk controversies primarily function to cope with cultural boundary crises between social institutions (see Tansey & Rayner, chapter 3, this volume). Relevant to our discussion is therefore the possible reading of the biotech case controversy as the analogous echo to the wrangle between the WTO and other institutions within the UN on non-technological, social, issues. Indeed, the WTO, on one hand, and the UN social and environmental agendas, on the other, traditionally advocate for diverging international development rationales and priorities. Furthermore, the WTO, its regulatory content and procedural design, and, above all, the free trade movement as its foundational mission and vision for international development, are increasingly under attack by the international opinion, which on the other hand regularly gathers in the context of international conferences held in the UN round table tradition in order to develop and update world development orientations. International trade rules, although decided among governments democratically elected in their countries (although not all member countries are democracies), have been increasingly perceived by member states citizens as anti-democratic, especially when they are perceived to threaten meaningful cultural foundations with which already existing national regulations conflict. "The resulting demonstrations in Paris, Geneva, London and Seattle since 1998 have elicited little response from the governments. Such reluctance to confront the NGOs can only encourage them and weaken international agencies" (Robertson, 2001a, p. 2). However, "All the recent turmoil surrounding the WTO contrasts sharply with the staid image of multilateral diplomacy in general and a history of trade negotiations played out in relative obscurity" (Jones, 2004, p. 4).

These considerations hold valuable insights to determine the location of the threshold at which the precautionary principles is deemed applicable by its proponents: For risk communicators working to foster auspicious discursive, dramatic and thematic conditions for the accession of a new encompassing risk regime at the WTO, the reading of the role of risk controversies proposed by cultural theory forces investigations for key compatibilities between the two competing zones of precautionary meaning along the lines of a double questioning: one concerned with themes and plots pertaining to the physical dimensions (public health and environmental) of GMO risk narratives as well as an analogous questioning of the extent to which trade liberalization and sustainable development perspectives on international development can be made compatible, at least to a functional extent. Both zones of precautionary meaning therefore endorse narratives and themes of both the social and the physical dimensions of the GMO risk; assessing their contents and their progressions in order to spot antagonism by analogy and opportunities for compatibilities on both levels provides a communication model to risk communicators working in the context of risk policy gridlocks involving the framing of components of scientific uncertainty, such as the one over the safety of GMOs and corresponding international trade obligations. The present discussion attempts to formulate a compelling incentive for the strategic integration of risk bearers' (Palmlund, 1992) logics at early stages of the policy decision-making process. By proposing a rhetorical rationale for the management of risk dialogues about scientific uncertainty in pluralistic policy settings, the present study provides risk communicators with insights on the strategic investigation of key compatibilities between sound and overly precautionary zones of meaning, so society can keep functioning.

At the moment, the sedimentation of the contemporary environmentalist framing of scientific uncertainty into the precautionary principle has chipped away at the fundamental assumptions of sound science-for-policy. Given the rhetorical advantage of the precautionary advocacy in regard to agricultural biotechnology, the EU and other BSP signatories turn the tables, demanding that science prove safety beyond the shadow of a doubt. That is an extraordinary standard, one characterized as overly precautionary by sound advocates, given the nature of risk and the scientific inquiry.

In regard to their respective treatments of scientific uncertainty, the zones of precautionary meaning competing in the biotech case are found to be incompatible due to the emergence of what the authors call a zone of overly precautionary threshold, embracing a treatment of scientific uncertainty that is found, due to crucial aspects of its current version, disabling for the collaborative making of risk management decisions.

Risk narratives are susceptible to a dual impulse to scapegoating: One is inherent to the narrative logic, proposed Kenneth Burke (1964, 1973, esp., pp. 191–220), and the other results from risk beliefs being functional to maintaining a preferred social order against outside encroachment, advanced Mary Douglas (1992). Building on these insights, this chapter proposes that, in order for them to culminate into an overly precautionary risk diagnosis, narratives of organic (bodily and environmental) pollution must progress analogically to the narratives of social pollution, whereby the scripts of the social and the organic systems' dynamics and perturbations merge in language. The authors therefore argue that the management of both sound and overly precautionary zones of meaning necessitates the awareness of the symbolisms embedded in the treatment of organic and social themes in risk narratives, in order to identify and monitor the emergence of thematic, dramatic, and idiomatic correspondences that lay the script of overly precautionary narratives. Detailed attention to the political underpinnings of regulatory developments at the WTO guides the analysis along these lines.

THE WTO: ENLARGING MISSION AND ADJUSTING VISION?

The apparition of issues of risk at the WTO results from the regulatory developments of the corpus of trade rules; when country members implement importation and exportation policy choices that are inconsistent with their free trade obligations, the WTO requires justification on the basis of demonstrated risks, characterized by sound science, in order to authorize these policies. When a country erects trade barrier on the basis of scientific uncertainty, interpretative conflicts tend to emerge. It is in the context of trade dispute settlement procedures between WTO member countries, among which some are signatories to both the WTO and the BSP, that the challenge of managing the precautionary principle arose and has become an ongoing point of contention; risk claims can be advanced by WTO member countries to benefit from temporary exemptions to free trade obligations such as restoring trade barriers. Because these protective measures are not only authorized when risks are demonstrated but also when relevant scientific evidence is deemed insufficient, allowing member countries to invoke precautionary measures within the WTO framework becomes highly hazardous for it can pave the way to disguised protectionist importation policies, free trade proponents argue (Crawford-Brown, Pauwelyn, & Smith, 2004). Indeed, the WTO routinely operates under the sound science-for-policy rationale for the creation and enforcement of its trade rules; as such the sound rationale comes as a guarantor of the free trade movement: This is a start in defining the WTO's specific risk regime.

Further defining the mission of the WTO begins with an investigation of the genesis of the United Nations. The latter created the former as part of its mission to bring peace and to prevent war. To that end, the UN and eventually the WTO have sought to accomplish the vision of eliminating the reasons for war. Many of these deal with economic interests and public health issues. As the League of Nations, created in the aftermath of World War I, failed to prevent the breakout of World War II, the victorious allied powers replaced it with the UN in 1945. The UN's mission was unequivocally set toward prohibiting war by strictly regulating risks and manifestations of military conflicts. In order to successfully manage issues of peace, justice, and international assistance, the UN was flanked with a multitude of counterpart agencies with specific focuses on themes that have become central to international cooperation, among which today are education, intellectual property rights, refugee populations, atomic energy, trade and development, environmental protection, agriculture and public health. It is along these lines that the Convention on Biological Diversity, to which the BSP is appended, was held and came to erect regulatory obligations in regard to the environmental impact of human activities.

On the ground of an economic logic for international development, the UN Monetary and Financial Conference held in 1944 concluded with member states signing the Bretton Woods agreements which created the institutions dedicated to the management of monetary, economic and financial post-war reconstruction: The first chapter to the present World Bank Group, the International Monetary Fund, and the International Trade Association. The latter failed as the US Congress refused to endorse it. However, negotiations on issues of trade continued and eventually the parties were able to reach minimal agreement on the GATT 44 (General Agreement of Tariffs and Trade), three years later.

As the new world economic order was emerging under the influence of these international organizations, different perspectives on opportunities and priorities for international development also began to take shape. One is embodied in the GATT 44 and further amendments, and rests on the vision that one priority for international integration lies with fostering deregulation to alleviate distortion in international trade. Then and now, the heart of the agreement is the mission to promote free and fair international trade through the multilateral commitment to developing, implementing and observing facilitating trade rules, which are formulated under the premise that deregulation will facilitate the economic development of member countries. A large segment of international trade rules is concerned with regulating importation policies so they will be least trade-restrictive or eliminated because deemed unfair or unjustified (Howse, 2000). Obligations to fair trade are specified in two key regulatory provisions: Article I of the GATT stipulates the non-discriminatory treatment of importations from different exporter countries—this is the clause of the Most Favored Nation—and article III binds member countries to non-discriminatory treatment between importations from foreign sources and domestic production—this is the National Treatment provision. The principle of non-discrimination thus specified not only defines obligations but also the limits within which exemptions to free trade can be assessed and granted or denied. While international trade intensified over the years, with accelerating pace and growing volumes of exchanges, new trade issues developed notably due to new kinds of products and services traded transnationally; obligations to non-discriminatory trade needed to be adapted to these new situations and negotiations started to define these amendments.

Amendments to Trade Rules and Issues of Risk

When the GATT was amended during the 1994 annual Ministerial Conference, known as the Uruguay Round, the WTO was created and took on many of the GATT rules in addition to new amendments. Among these amendments were two partially new agreements on technical (non-tariff) barriers to trade: The TBT agreement (regulating all Trade Barriers to Trade and including the pre-existing Most Favored Nation and National Treatment rules) and, most importantly for the focus of the present discussion, the SPS agreement (regulating the use by countries of Sanitary and Phytosanitary "quarantine" measures).

The negotiations toward this agreement first started in 1986; after eight years of difficult negotiations, many ambiguities were purposefully maintained in the SPS and TBT agreements in order to reach the necessary level of consensus among member countries for them to sign and ratify the agreements. On the other hand, it is because these ambiguities were left unresolved that the interpretations of the new agreements have grown more complex and contentious and have led to the development of a new "in house" dispute settlement capacity (Jackson, 2000). Policy makers considered the dispute settlement process as "one of the more farsighted innovations" (Robertson, 2001a, p. 1), "the jewel in the WTO institutional structure" (Jackson, 2000, p. 272), but it was designed to cope with a side effect of the necessity to manage the difficult harmonization process between member countries' national regulations and the dispositions of the new SPS and TBT agreements, that is on-economic risks. This reality therefore required improvements in the WTO risk assessment capacity, but what this new responsibility would entail for the WTO was at first not fully conceivable.

Precautionary Measures Incorporated to International Trade Rules: Interpretation and Power

Before the Uruguay Round, quarantine measures to protect human, animal or plant life and health were allowed under GATT article XX(b). "The complicated effects on trade, however, required more precise rules" (Sampson, 2001, p. 23) and that is why the SPS agreement was negotiated, and the GATT article XX(b) was further specified under the SPS article 5.7. This article not only implicitly confirms the relevance of the GATT XX(b) rule, it explicitly introduces the precautionary principle within the WTO, the proponents of which try to increase its weight and broaden its interpretation, notably through high-profile dispute settlements such as the biotech case. On the other hand, some of the WTO members intended the precautionary measure to be brought into play exclusively within the sound risk assessment guidelines.

Understandably, the SPS agreement became soon after its ratification the focal point in the wrangling between the precautionary and the sound advocates (Cottier, 2001, p. 47). Within the first four years, it had been tested in three major cases before dispute panels: The hormone-treated beef case opposing the US and Canada to the importation ban by the EU, the Australian ban on the importation of fresh chilled and frozen salmon brought before the WTO by Canada, and the complaint by the US against the measures affecting agricultural products put in place by Japan.

> These disputes were complex legal undertakings. The panels and the Appellate Body were confronted with adjudicating politically sensitive and legally difficult matters under the new agreement, and required to assess extensive scientific evidence for the first time in the history of GATT/WTO. (Cottier, 2001, p. 42)

Given the salience of issues of public health and environmental protection on the international scene, a critical deficit in the WTO regulatory development was missing attention to issues of risk. One of the ways of addressing them was to define and instantiate the precautionary disposition contained in the SPS agreement. Such ambiguities do not constitute an issue until specific guidelines and its underlying assumption is needed to police the importation policies of dissident member countries. This is the exact rationale for the present reading of the controversy over the application of the precautionary principle to agricultural biotechnology: The growth of regulatory language has currently reached a stalemate whereby clarification is needed. However, the mechanism for that clarification is not readily functional since it does not include ways to bring into the final discussion the logics of risk bearers. Thus, the continual stumbling block of risk democracy brings to a focal point the matter of deciding between the privileges of sound science and the legitimate concerns of parties whose interests may not be served or well managed without serious dialogue.

Controversial Grounds

Therefore, there is an attendant challenge to the development of new rules that the WTO must tackle: "The strengthening of trade rules through the adoption of more extensive and complicated agreements increased the scope for disputes among members and placed unexpected pressures on the new dispute settlement understanding" (Roberston, 2001a, p. 1).

One of the unforeseen consequences of the comprehensive WTO agreements has been risk controversies. Indeed, the new dispute settlement procedures introduced unforeseen issues, including the concept of "risk" which had to be assessed in dispute hearings. A complaint by a plaintiff member country of unfair or unjustified trade protection arising from quarantine or technical measures taken by another member country requires an assessment of the consequences of changing them to meet international standards, which could include an analysis of risk of disease or damage.

> The WTO is not equipped to assess scientific risk or to establish international standards, and now disputes include arguments about social, environmental and cultural risks too. This has placed severe pressure on dispute panels and the Appellate Body, and has exacerbated differences among members over interpretations of the WTO agreements. (Roberston, 2001a, p. 27)

The WTO's preferred treatment of risk has come to the center of the international stage through these high profile dispute cases. Conversely, it is essential to understand that the choice of a risk assessment framework has tremendous repercussions on the enforcement of international economic rules (Crawford-Brown et al., 2004; Goldstein & Carruth, 2004):

> The prevention of unwarranted discriminatory barriers to trade is the *raison d'être* for WTO rules and disciplines. The present challenge facing WTO members is implementing its component agreements to provide flexibility for domestic policies without creating disguised barriers to trade. Balancing these conflicting interests can lead to controversy and disputes in international trade. Moreover, public perceptions of risk and their management differ between WTO member countries. (Sampson, 2001, p. 15)

Various players undoubtedly participated to the debate over the legitimacy of international trade rules to override national regulations, but none had predicted the magnitude with the challenge of scientific assumptions on which international trade policy is decided would impact WTO's authority.

International Standards of Risk Assessment in Antagonism?

Formal deliberations on economic issues at the WTO have been relying on sound science: SPS measures as exceptions to non-discriminatory standards are allowed (SPS article 5.7), but must be backed by science (SPS article 2.2), "If not, they are presumed to be trade protectionist" (Crawford-Brown et al., 2004, p. 462). More generally, under the TBT and SPS agreements, there is explicit "hope in science as the decisive factor" (p. 462). Within the rhetoric of sound science, then, the agreements would rest on the assumption that risk assessment required little more than knowing the facts, getting them straight, and calculating probabilities.

"The SPS agreement encourages the adoption of international standards, guidelines and recommendations" (Wilson & Gascoine, 2001, p. 161) thereby instituting "reliance upon internationally agreed science … as the foundation for any decision making" (Holland & Kellow, 2001, p. 241). Correspondingly, the WTO member states are bound to sound risk assessment standards established by the Codex Alimentarius Commission that was created in 1962 by a joint FAO/WHO (Food and Agriculture Organization and World Health Organization) initiative and which determines the safety of food product on the basis of assessment involving toxicological studies of pesticide residues, microbiological contaminants, chemical additives and veterinary biologics among others. "These international standards are not binding except under the provisions of the SPS Agreement" (Wilson & Gascoine, 2001, p. 161), and this has created commitment problems for countries who are signatories to both the WTO and the BSP agreements; indeed, the Codex risk assessment framework does include precautionary dispositions, but does not allow member countries to invoke them; only the Counsel retains this power and its application remains subjected to evidences resulting from sound science and this is under the same assumption that the precautionary measure of the SPS agreement was first introduced within the WTO.

Competing Standards as a Threat to the Free Trade Movement

The WTO's mission is to avoid unjustified impediments to international trade; however, the creation of the Committee on Trade and Development in 1994 as well as the ratification of environmental agreements within other intergovernmental bodies—such as the BSP in 2000 under the UN—come against some of the fundamental antidiscriminatory trade rules and can trigger paradoxes in the overall international system. "This confrontation is one of the most dangerous because it could end up restoring trade protection and reducing environmental protection" (Robertson, 2001a, p. 5). However, it is important to note here that this paradox has always existed since the GATT came into effect: Articles XX(b) and (a) already respectively allowed exceptions for the protection of environmental and human health, and to the protection of public morals (Howse, 2000).

More than a real exacerbation, it can be argued that it is now the growing perception of this ambiguity as a paradox that renders this state of affairs threatening to the WTO as its opponents try to establish an alternative system that would create a situation whereby two entirely autonomous paradigms co-exist within the international legal body; this regulatory manifestation signals the urgency of rendering compatible, at least to some functional extent, the different risk policy making cultures. The paradox, however, needs not to be one. As such, the perspectives initially embody the two trends that have rapidly emerged in the involvement of the international public opinion in the debate surrounding international policy decisions. Indeed, parallel to this increased involvement in public issues of science, the international civil society has been successfully instigating an appeal to the international community to start committing to environmental protection. This way, social realities on biotechnology on one hand and on biodiversity on the other have progressed along analogous plots, the content meaning of which have fostered antagonisms:

> The debates provide two different views on popular representations of science and technology. Biodiversity conservation is represented as a common goal of humankind, whereas modern biotechnology divides people into various camps of supporters and opponents. Modern biotechnology is often covered in terms of sudden techno-scientific breakthroughs, biodiversity loss is discussed in the context of earlier environmental problems. Furthermore, modern biotechnology is represented as the discovery of genes and the development of genetically modified organisms, whereas biodiversity conservation aims to calculate the loss of specifies and ecosystems and to suggest ways in which the environment could be conserved. The debates provide mirror images of public representations of science: that of conquering new areas in nature (modern biotechnology) in contrast of that of protecting and conserving (wild) nature (biodiversity conservation). (Hellsten, 2002, p. 5)

THE PRECAUTIONARY PRINCIPLE AND INTERNATIONAL LAW: THE PRECAUTIONARY AGENDA AT THE WTO

The BSP is claimed by its proponents to be an acknowledgement by signatory countries that the transnational movements of biotechnology products need special attention and regulation. The foundational standard of this corpus of treaties is the precautionary principle. Although the BSP is not acknowledged by the WTO as embodying risk assessment standards, precautionary member states mobilize the BSP's precautionary principle to interpret the precautionary measures of the SPS agreement and thereby justify trade barriers against GMOs that would otherwise not be justified by the outcome of sound risk assessment.

Countries that are signatories to both the GATT 1994 and the BSP attempt to create and benefit from the assessment of the legality of their trade policy as subjected to two different applicability conditions. Another problematic aspect under these auspices is the fact that the relationship between the rules of the BSP and the WTO trade rules are defined in the Protocol but remain largely unclear; it is simultaneously stated that member countries' obligations under other existing international agreements should not be altered by the Protocol, but that this declaration should not subordinate the Protocol to other international agreements (Anderson & Nielson, 2000, p. 8). As an issue of international law, the regulatory debate does not pertain to the legitimacy of the precautionary principle per se since it is already included in sound standards of risk assessment; rather, it is its degree of autonomy and applicability within regulatory frameworks that is in question. The framing of precaution by the precautionary principle reflects an official enactment at the international level, by key nations, of a new discourse of precaution (Andrée, 2005). Because one discourse on precaution already undergirds sound narratives of scientific uncertainty, this new definition of precaution is perceived by sound stakeholders as an overly precautionary account.

Part of the precautionary advocates' agenda at the Uruguay Round was to establish a specific set of rules within the WTO in reference to the GMO issue, but they were instead left dispersed across several agreements. Although several aspects relevant to the GMO debate were discussed within the Committee on Trade and Development, the establishment of a new agreement specific to GMOs under the WTO could undermine the system.

The article 5.7 of the SPS agreement authorizes trade exemptions in the form provisional measures while a full risk assessment is being conducted. Accordingly, the EU maintained a moratorium on GMOs while creating more adequate risk assessment capacities and management regulations. However, the new European Food Law created to manage issues relating to the importations and utilizations of GMO rests on references to the precautionary principle and the BSP, notably to the institute the mandatory labeling of GM products to ensure traceability in the food production chain. Introducing such dispositions within the WTO framework would undermine the trade system by delaying the development of systematic approval procedures for GM foods for several years (Robertson, 2001b).

In September 2006, the panel of experts found the European moratorium illegal; the delay allowed to the EU to harmonize GMO-related importation policies with the panel's recommendations is set to expire in November 2007. At this point in time, the audit of the adequacy between the new EU-level dispositions and international trade rules will reveal major inconsistencies and can motivate new trade conflicts and dispute settlement procedures. If the applicability of precautionary measures is not further defined in regard to the BSP precautionary principle, new conflicts could result in severe repercussions on the integrity of the trade system, or deteriorate into trade wars. Given the growing rhetorical advantage of the precautionary framing of scientific uncertainty within and outside of the WTO, negotiations of an agreement on the labeling and traceability rules, as requested by the EU, in order to bind WTO member states with the dispositions embodied in the European Food Law is looming. However, the weight of this interpretation will depend on which advocate will retain the rhetorical advantage; "The SPS agreement will be a major target for governments and NGOs seeking to establish new trade rules to cover biotechnology in the upcoming WTO rounds" (Robertson, 2001b, p. 217).

The precautionary principle was already used in formal deliberation on past cases. The asbestos case made precedent as the WTO Appellate Body allowed the use of the principle by the EU and thereby ruling in favor of the applicability of the principle as a basis for erecting trade barriers. However, precaution was earlier deemed by the same body ruling on the beef hormone case "not acceptable as an alternative basis for actions that are supposed to be based on scientific risk assessment" (Goldstein & Carruth 2004, p. 493). Since scientific risk assessment lies at the core of the international trade system, the attempt to promulgate the use of the precautionary principle in trade disputes is perceived as initiating a radically different, conflicting trend by displacing the burden of proof from the members who infringe trade rules to a burden of proof of absolute innocuity of science. Thus, the application of the principle within the WTO risk assessment is perceived by experts as instituting a shift from scientific expert judgment to risk perception and constitutes what some say is the basis for fostering discriminating trade barriers.

Therefore, the WTO—if it is to acknowledge and integrate the claims of its critics in order to alleviate the increasing pressure that they exert on the integrity of the international trade system—must also work to redefine the role of sound scientific expertise in risk policy making; this starts with accounting for the adequacy of its discourse with the nature of moral public debates. Considering that expert discourse on GMOs was found to have contributed to estrangement of the lay audience (Gaskell & Bauer, 2001), we can conceive of the overly precautionary narrative as a rhetorical retaliation without thereby justifying the radicalization of its design.

One cannot, however, grasp the full symbolic terrain on which such retaliation takes place until one also considers it as a challenge against not only sound discourse but against *WTO*'s sound discourse; it is indeed the whole risk regime, within which the sound framing of scientific uncertainty is functional to maintaining the free trade mission and vision as a priority of international development, to which the overly precautionary voice answers by mobilizing the overly precautionary framing. In this way, it lends support to the challenging of the free trade development rationale with the vision of sustainable development and its preferred representation of the good international solidarity.

From these considerations, it can be conjectured that the WTO's ability to reconcile the sound and overly precautionary decision rationales will partly depend upon its ability to enact narratives of international development that endorse plots, idioms and themes that overarch between sound and overly precautionary narratives. Nonetheless, cultural pluralism guarantees ongoing mutations in societies and serves as a resource for the making of enlightened risk decisions. This way, considering consensus as dysfunctional, the successful hybridization between trade liberalization and sustainable development narratives into an overarching narrative is not anticipated to yield a stable construction. Rather such hybrid narratives are expected to be goaded with local symbolic adaptations that constitute enabling symbolic resources for the strategic management of discursive ambiguities, notably in the language of precaution. Risk communicators' contribution to fostering the reasonable adaptation of the sound decision rationale to overly precautionary pressures is decisive because the emergence of policy innovations also largely depends upon the transformative capacities of language as symbolic action.

CONCLUSION

For the purpose of proposing a reading of the symbolic and discursive processes underlying policy gridlocks in context of scientific uncertainty, the present discussion has centered on how the progress of the precautionary rationale to redefine the risk analysis rationale within the WTO has paralleled the shift in the framing of precaution institutionalized by the BSP. Because the corpus of trade rules contains *de facto* both the sound and the precautionary rationales for the management of risks, how then can it now reconcile controversies? A key controversy illustrating and testing this theme centers on the risk attached to the regulation of the transboundary movement of GMOs in regard to the safety of genetic engineering applications to agriculture and food production. On the one hand, one interest stands on the principles of sound science which argues that within "reason" enough is known to predict risks and ascertain that they are ethically and legally acceptable. Such reasoning occurs despite the inability to predict outcomes of this kind with certainty. By definition, after all, uncertainty characterizes risks: The probability of an occurrence and the estimation of the magnitude of positive or negative impact in the event of the occurrence. In fact, sound science can even estimate who the risk bearers are.

The advocates of the precautionary principle reason that in the absence of sufficient predictability in risk characterization, occurrence and magnitude, precaution is needed. This is not an idle intellectual debate but is brought in the arena by powerful foes. Each has constituent stakeholders and stakeseekers, a classic case of issues management. In that context, the precautionary principle is confounded by the entanglements of language, logics, and interests that support the conflict. Whether it leads to resolution through consensus or defeat of one interest is a matter of contest. In the end, it is possible that the decision-making rationale in the context of scientific uncertainty will either become clearer or be found to be hopelessly devoid of principle and merely a matter of power resource management.

BIBLIOGRAPHY

Anderson, K. & Nielsen, C. P. (2000). *GMOs, food safety and the environment: What role for Trade Policy and the WTO?* Policy Discussion Paper No. 0034. Adelaide, Australia: Center for International Economic Studies.

Andrée, P. (2005). The Cartagena Protocol on Biosafety and shifts in the discourse of precaution. *Global Environmental Politics*, *5*(4), 25–46.

Burke, K. (1964). "Act" as many-in-one. *Location*, *1*, 94–98.

Burke, K. (1973). *The philosophy of literary form* (3rd ed.). Berkeley: University of California Press.

Cottier, T. (2001). Risk management experience in WTO dispute settlement. In D. Robertson & A. Kellow (Eds.), *Globalization and the environment: Risk assessment and the WTO* (pp. 41–63). Northampton, MA: Edward Elgar.

Cox, R. (2007). Nature's "crisis disciplines": Does environmental communication have an ethical duty? *Environmental Communication: A Journal of Nature and Culture*, *1*, 5–20.

Crawford-Brown, D., Pauwelyn, J., & Smith, K. (2004). Environmental risk, precaution, and scientific rationality in the context of WTO/NAFTA trade rules. *Risk Analysis*, *24*(2), 461–469.

Commission of European Communities. (2000). Communication from the commission on the Precautionary Principle. Brussels: COM 1. Retrieved March 22, 2005, from http://ec. europa.eu/dgs/health_consumer/library/pub/pub07_en.pdf.

DeGregori, T. R. (2004). *Origins of the organic agriculture debate*. Ames, IA: Blackwell.

Douglas, M. (1992). *Risk and blame*. London: Routledge.

Gaskell, G. & Bauer, M. W. (2001). Biotechnology in the years of controversy: A social scientific perspective. In G. Gaskell & M. W. Bauer (Eds.), *Biotechnology 1996–2000: The years of the controversy* (pp. 3–11). London: Science Museum Publications.

Gerlach, L. P. & Rayner, S. (1988). Culture and the common management of global risks, *Practicing Anthropology*, 10(3-4), 15–18.

Goldstein, B. & Carruth, R. S. (2004). The precautionary principle and/or risk assessment in the World Trade Organization decision: A possible role for risk perception. *Risk Analysis*, *24*(2), 491–499.

Harremoës, P., Gee, D. Macgarvin, M., Stirling, A., Keys, J., Wynne, B., & Guedes Vaz, S. *The precautionary principle in the 20th century: late lessons from early warnings* (pp. 184–217). London: Earthscan Publications Ltd.

Heath, R. L. (1993). A rhetorical approach to zones of meaning and organizational prerogatives. *Public Relations Review*, *19*(2), 141–155.

Heath, R. L. (1997). *Strategic issues management: Organizations and public policy challenges*. Thousand Oaks, CA: Sage.

Heath, R. L. & Abel, D. D. (1996). Types of knowledge as predictors of company support: The role of information in risk communication. *Journal of Public Relations Research*, *8*, 35–55.

Heath, R. L. & Palenchar, M. (2000). Community relations and risk communication: A longitudinal study of the impact of emergency response messages. *Journal of Public Relations Research*, *12*(2), 131–161.

Heath, R. L., Palenchar, M. J., Proutheau, S., & Hocke, T. M. (2007). Nature, crisis, risk, science, and society: What is out ethical responsibility? *Environmental Communication*, *1*, 34–48.

Hellsten, I. (2002). *The politics of metaphor: biotechnology and biodiversity in the media*. Tampere, Finland: Tampere University Press.

Holland, I. & Kellow, A. (2001). Trade and risk management: exploring the issues. In D. Robertson & A. Kellow (Eds.), *Globalization and the environment: Risk assessment and the WTO* (pp. 229–248). Northampton, MA: Edward Elgar.

Howse, R. (2000). Democracy, science and free trade: risk regulation on trial at the world trade organization. *Michigan Law Review, 98*, 2329–2357.

Jackson, J. J. (2000). Dispute settlement and a new round. In J. J. Schot (Ed.), *The WTO after Seattle* (pp. 269–282). Washington, DC: Institute for International Economics.

Jones, K. (2004). *Who's afraid of the WTO?* New York: Oxford University Press.

Kuiper, H. A., Kleter, G. A., Noteborn, H. P. J. M., & Kok, E. J. (2001). Assessment of the food safety issues related to genetically modified foods. *The Plant Journal, 27*(6), 503–528.

Morgan, M. G., Fischhoff, B., Bostrom, A., & Atman, C. J. (2002). *Risk communication: A mental models approach.* Cambridge: Cambridge University Press.

Palenchar, M. & Heath, R. L. (2002). Another part of the risk communication model: Analysis of communication processes and message content. *Journal of Public Relations Research, 14*(2), 127–158.

Palmlund, I. (1992). Social drama and risk evaluation. In S. Krimsky & D. Golding (Eds.), *Social theories of risk*_(pp. 197–212). Westport, CT: Praeger.

Rayner, S. (2004, December). The novelty trap. *Industry & Higher Education*, 348–355.

Reports of the Dispute Panel. (2006). European Communities - Measures affecting the approval and marketing of biotech products. *World Trade Organization / Dispute Settlements 291, 292, 293.* Adopted September 29, 2006.

Robertson, D. (2001a). Accounting for risk in trade agreements. In D. Robertson & A. Kellow (Eds.), *Globalization and the environment: Risk assessment and the WTO* (pp. 1–11). Northampton, MA: Edward Elgar.

Robertson, D. (2001b). GM foods and global trade. In D. Robertson & A. Kellow (Eds), *Globalization and the environment: Risk assessment and the WTO* (pp. 207–226). Northampton, MA: Edward Elgar.

Sampson, G. P. (2001). Risk and the WTO. In D. Robertson & A. Kellow (Eds.), *Globalization and the environment: Risk assessment and the WTO* (pp. 15–26). Northampton, MA: Edward Elgar.

Sarewitz, D. (2004). How science makes environmental controversies worse. *Environmental Science and Policy, 7*, 385–403.

Schwartz, M. & Thompson, M. (1990). *Divided we stand.* Philadelphia: University of Pennsylvania Press.

Wilson, D. & Gascoine, D. (2001). National risk management and the SPS agreement. In D. Robertson & A. Kellow (Eds.), *Globalization and the environment: Risk assessment and the WTO* (pp. 155–168). Northampton, MA: Edward Elgar.

30

Environmental Risk Communication: Responding to Challenges of Complexity and Uncertainty

Tarla Rai Peterson
Texas A&M University

Jessica Leigh Thompson
Colorado State University

The months of January and August, 2006, were the warmest on record for the continental U.S. July broke more than 2,300 daily records and more than 50 all-time high temperature records (NOAA. 2006). High temperatures from July 27 through August 5 "caused 40 heat stroke deaths," and an 8% increase in deaths by natural causes in New York City (New York City 2006). Western Europe suffered similarly, with Paris also reporting an 8% increase in deaths from natural causes during the heat wave (Cadot, Rodwin, & Spira, 2007). A summer heat wave in 1995 killed over 750 people in Chicago, and another in 2003 killed tens of thousands of people in Europe. Physicians warn that these and other, more subtle responses to climate change pose severe danger to human health and safety (Epstein, 2005).

Global climate change did not become a major risk communication issue until 1988, the hottest year on record up to that point (Christianson, 1999). On June 23, 1988, James Hansen, a leading climate modeler and director of the NASA Goddard Institute of Space Studies testified to the U.S. Senate Energy and Natural Resources Committee that "the greenhouse effect has been detected and it is changing our climate now" (Christianson, 1999, p. 196). Although scientists had been reporting this information for decades, the American public had not worried. Hansen's testimony, delivered during a record-breaking heat wave, immediately became front-page news across the United States and much of the international community. Nearly 10 years later, the International Panel on Climate Change (IPCC) published a report detailing current and expected risks posed by climate change (IPCC, 2007). Since the summer of 1989, numerous public opinion polls have found that Americans believe global climate change poses a threat, although the level of concern varies (Leiserowitz 2005). Leiserowitz noted that Gallup found that 63% of Americans were worried about global warming in 1989, 50% in 1997, 72% in 2000, and 58% in 2002. A Time/CNN poll conducted in 2002 found that 76% of Americans thought global warming was a "serious" problem, and most viewed it as a threat to themselves and future generations (Leiserowitz, 2005). Survey research suggests that most Americans are generally willing to pay for policy to mitigate climate change. At the same time, they show little willingness to voluntarily restrain behavior that contributes to climate change, and when presented with specific policies to mitigate climate change, they rarely support those that would mandate such restraint (Jamieson 2006). This paradoxical response is not unique to Americans. For example, in 2005, significant majorities of British voters described climate change as a threat (87% of Conservative voters, 92% of Labour voters, 95% of Liberal Democrat voters). A full 86% of those questioned believed the risk was sufficiently severe that the government should take action, although 61% opposed an environmental tax on air travel (Glover, Vidal, & Clark, 2005).

The chapters in this volume form part of a large body of research that has attempted to explain this paradoxical response by learning how people seek information about risk, how the mass media influence perceptions of risk, and how specific risks fit into the larger risk picture. Two of the most influential strands of environmental risk communication research have grown from the psychometric work associated with Paul Slovic and colleagues (Slovic, Fischhoff, & Lichtenstein, 1980, 1985; Slovic 1987, 1997), and the cultural theory school of anthropologist Mary Douglas and her associates (Douglas, 1966, 1982, 1994, 1999; Douglas & Wildavsky 1982). The first camp, rooted in psychological research, has focused on identifying and measuring subjective attributions of environmental risk based on aggregated individual responses, while the latter group has sought to understand environmental risk perception and risk-related behavior in terms of world view and culture. For example, Slovic defined risk perception "as the judgments people make when they are asked to characterize and evaluate hazardous activities and technologies" (Slovic, 1987, p. 280), whereas Douglas (1999) argued that risk beliefs are part of social and political culture.

Although these two approaches are not mutually exclusive, they suggest different strategies for effective risk communication. In this chapter we first review literature emanating from both of these approaches to risk, focusing on how they relate to risk communication about the environment. Because mass media are so important in late industrial society, we then examine what impact mass media channels have on awareness and understanding of environmental risks. We conclude with a discussion of the similarities and differences between communication about environmental risk as a potential hazard to human health and as a potential hazard to the biosphere. Because global warming/climate change epitomizes environmental risk so fully, we focus on this topic.

PSYCHOLOGICAL RESEARCH ON PERCEPTIONS OF ENVIRONMENTAL RISK

Psychological influences on perception of environmental risks have been studied extensively by many researchers since the mid-1980s. Slovic, Fischhoff, and Lichtenstein (1985) argued that the two most important elements to shape risk perceptions are "dread" risk and "unknown" risk. Especially in environmental communication these two categories of risk perception are not mutually exclusive, but may emphasize different elements of the risk. Dread risk includes characteristics such as "dread, perceived lack of control, catastrophic potential, fatalities, and the distribution of risks and benefits," (Slovic et al., 1985, p. 93). Unknown risk includes such characteristics as "the extent to which it is observable, known, new and delayed in its manifestation of harm," (Slovic et al., 1985, p. 93).

The media have communicated climate science both as a dread risk and an unknown risk. Ungar (1992) explained that scientists' claims about global warming failed to garner much attention until the extreme drought and heat of the summer of 1988, which Ungar suggested created a massive social scare. According to Ungar, the combination of dramatic events with catastrophic consequences including fatalities and uncertainty elevated global warming in the public's mind to a more serious social problem than historically conceptualized. McComas and Shanahan (1999) also concluded that media narratives on climate change tend to be driven by dramatic story constructions. Using Slovic's et al.'s (1985) categories of risk perception, we can see how a dramatic event, including the droughts and deaths of the summer of 1988, led to global warming being communicated as a "dread" risk, because It was something people could not control.

Similarly, global warming fits within Slovic et al.'s (1985) conceptualization of risk as an "unknown." In a survey of adults in metropolitan areas Stamm, Clark, and Eblancas (2000) found that people were aware in a general sense of global warming, but had limited understanding of its particular causes and possible consequences. Among the 512 respondents, the researchers identified widespread misconceptions and uncertainty. It is possible that messages framing global warming as "uncertain" also presented the audience with the idea that global warming is an unknown risk. Messages of uncertainty and unknown risks make it difficult to advocate behaviors that may positively change the rate of global warming. Gelbspan (1998), in his Pulitzer Prize-winning book, *The Heat Is On*, argued that, despite strong scientific consensus about the likely negative impacts of global warming, political commitment to the portrayal of doubt and uncertainty about both its existence and impacts have undermined public understanding of the issue and provided a rationale against adopting strong measures to reduce greenhouse gas emissions. Oreskes (2004) noted that the former U.S. Environmental Protection Agency (EPA) administrator, Christine Whitman advocated that the risks of climate change were unknown and uncertain as a means of protecting corporations whose revenues might be adversely affected by controls on carbon dioxide emissions. Whitman's statements responded directly to recommendations laid out in a memo prepared by Frank Luntz for the Republican Party. Luntz (1993) urged Republicans to maintain control over the global warming argument by emphasizing scientific uncertainty: "voters believe that there is no consensus about global warming within the scientific community. Should the public come to believe that the scientific issues are settled their views about global warming will change accordingly. Therefore, you need to continue to make the lack of scientific certainty a primary issue in the debate" (p. 137). Political messages such as Whitman's have been designed to emphasize uncertainty and unknown aspects of global warming, thus encouraging the public to believe that the scientific community had not reached consensus on global warming. Ironically, the strength of scientific consensus that global warming poses a serious risk to human health and wellbeing may have led to this political backlash.

Slovic (1987) also studied risk perceptions using cognitive maps of risk attitudes and perceptions and found that experts and laypersons often disagree about the meaning of risk. Again, using the example of global warming, large differences have been reported between the general public's awareness of global warming and scientific consensus on the topic. A 2001 National Science Foundation survey found that 77% of adults believed that global warming was real (Public belief in global warming 2002), compared to a survey of 928 peer-reviewed research articles, in which all scientists not only recognized the reality of global warming, but also offered its existence as justification for targeting funds toward additional research focused on potential strategies for mitigation (Oreskes, 2004). Despite the relatively strong consensus among scientists, many studies demonstrate that the vast temporal and spatial scales of global warming may contribute to public misunderstanding of the risks associated with climate change. Ethnographic studies (e.g., Henry, 2000; Kempton, 1991; Kempton, 1997) and research using mental modeling tactics similar to Slovic's (1987) cognitive maps (e.g., Bostrom, Morgan, Fischhoff, & Read, 1994) indicates that people are particularly confused about the precise nature, causes and consequences of global warming.

Fischer, Morgan, Fischhoff, Nair, and Lave (1991) attempted to discover what types of risk members of the public are most concerned about by asking research participants to make a list of risks that most concerned them. Most people cited threats to life and limb, accidents, disease, and crime, and some also mentioned economic risks, personal concerns, and eternal damnation. Only 10% of the risks cited stemmed directly from environmental or natural hazards. Using Slovic's definition of risk perception to interpret Fischer et al.'s results could lead to the conclusion that people do not typically identify or evaluate environmental hazards as risks.

The complexity of environmental risk may contribute to this situation. Stamm, Clark, and Eblancas (2000) claimed that most people do not think about environmental hazards accurately or completely, and this cognitive gap is likely to influence both their willingness and ability to participate in solving environmental problems (see also Grabe, Lang, Zhou, & Bolls, 2000). Morgan, Fischhoff, Bostrom, and Atman (2002) amplify Stamm et al.'s claim by arguing that people are too busy with jobs, families, friends, and other demands of daily living to deal with environmental risks. Rather, when people have to deal with risk, their attention is most often directed toward more mundane, day-to-day hazards they associate with individual choices (Morgan et al., 2002; Fischer et al., 1991). When perceiving health risks, for example, Klaidman (1991) "found that 54 percent of respondents believed that a serious illness couldn't happen to them." At the same time most people also believed that "everything causes cancer" and therefore "there is no way to avoid cancer" (1991, p. 5). This research suggests that perceived control exerts an important influence on individual decisions about risk. People tend to focus on risks they believe they can directly control (e.g., through diet, exercise, or driving habits), rather than those they can only influence indirectly (e.g., enacting clean water legislation, establishing criteria for siting hazardous facilities, or developing an international carbon credit system).

The choice to focus attention on a type of risk should not be confused with how tolerable people find that risk. In fact, to minimize cognitive dissonance people may choose to focus attention on the more tolerable risks over which they believe they can exert some control, rather than less tolerable risks over which they believe they have no control. Slovic and Fischhoff (1982) addressed how individuals are able to tolerate certain risks, yet find other risks unacceptable. They found that easily tolerated risks include those people can choose to avoid (e.g., chainsaws, skiing), risks they are familiar with (e.g., smoking), and risks that have been around for a long time (e.g., fireworks). Individuals have more difficulty tolerating risks that are involuntary (e.g., exposure to nuclear waste), have delayed effects (e.g., pesticides), and have unknown effects (e.g., genetic engineering).

Recent research has built upon these early studies of the psychological factors of risk perception by investigating the role of affect and emotion in risk perception and behavior. Specifically, Finucane, Alhakami, Slovic, and Johnson (2000) and Slovic, Finucane, Peters, and MacGregor (2002) explored the use of affective image analysis as a tool to study the relationship between affect, cognitive imagery and perceived risk. Slovic (1997) had previously conceptualized affect as "an orienting mechanism that directs fundamental psychological processes such as attention, memory and information processing," (p. 292). For Slovic, affect is not synonymous with mood or emotion, but is a specific, experienced state about the positive or negative aspects of any stimulus, which could include risk communication messages. And affective images are "broadly construed to include sights, sounds, smells, ideas and words to which positive and negative affect or feeling states have become attached through learning and experience" (Slovic, MacGregor, & Peters, 1998, p. 3). Leiserowitz (2005) used Slovic's definitions and conceptualizations to analyze a national survey on public perceptions of risk associated with climate change. Some of Leiserowitz's questions included: "What is the first thought or image that comes to your mind when you think of global warming?" (p. 1437) and "Which of the following are you most concerned about? The impacts of global warming on… (1) you and your family; (2) your local community; (3) the U.S. as a whole; (4) people all over the world; (5) non-human nature; or (6) not at all concerned." (p. 1437). Sixty eight percent of his 551 respondents were most concerned about the impacts on people around the world and nonhuman nature. Only 13% were most concerned about the impacts on themselves, their family or their local community. Most importantly, Leiserowitz (2005) found that Americans did not associate the impacts of global warming with risks to human health. Although climate change already has negatively impacted human health and is expected to cause additional harm (Epstein 2005), Leiserowitz's respondents made "no associations to temperature-related morbidity and mortality, health effects of extreme weather events (e.g., tornadoes, hurricanes or precipitation extremes), air-pollution health effects, water and food borne disease, or vector and rodent borne disease, all of which are potential health consequences of global climate change" (p. 1438). Leiserowitz (2005) concluded that the lack of personal concern explains American's failure to attend to climate change. Although the effects of climate change are not readily avoidable through individual choices such as diet, people may assume they can avoid the effects, simply because they have not heard about them. So long as people perceive climate change as impacting beings (whether human or not) other than themselves, there is no reason for it to become a high-priority issue.

Taken together, these studies have significant implications for environmental risk communication. They suggest that when an individual does not have direct, voluntary control over a risk, that risk becomes less tolerable. Tolerability, however, does not necessarily translate into attention or action. Individuals often focus on hazards they believe they can protect themselves from, rather than wasting their efforts attending to risks over which they believe they have no control. From one perspective, global warming should be a relatively intolerable risk because consequences are likely to impact all segments of the global population in various ways. The intolerability of this risk does not, however, translate into attention or action, because individuals may feel they do not have direct control over reducing the rate of global climate change. In the case of climate change, as with many environmental hazards, lack of awareness may trump any concerns about acceptability and tolerability. If people are not aware that an environmental hazard has the potential to harm them directly, they are unlikely to waste time worrying over it.

SOCIAL INFLUENCES ON PERCEPTION OF ENVIRONMENTAL RISKS

Although important, psychological explanations of environmental risk perception provide only part of the picture. Human beings are social animals, and our attitudes, understandings, and behaviors are influenced by our culture. Current research in the area of social influences on risk perception is rooted in cultural and anthropological studies of risk. Luhmann (1993) argued that risk is strongly influenced by sociological factors. "Cultural anthropologists, social anthropologists, and political scientists point out that the evaluation of risk and the willingness to accept risk are not only psychological problems, but above all social problems," (p. 3). Rosa, Mazur, and Dietz (1987) used a sociological perspective to analyze how people understood risks about the nuclear waste repository in Hanford, Washington. Their informants perceived the risks associated with nuclear waste through perceptual lenses shaped by social and cultural meanings that have been transmitted via primary influences such as family, friends, and fellow workers. They also found that secondary influences such as public figures and the mass media affected risk perceptions (Rosa et al., 1987). As Luhmann (1993) argued, people behave as they believe their primary reference groups expect them to behave, as they conform to their social surroundings.

Douglas and Wildavsky (1982) specifically examined how culture impacts perceptions of environmental risk. Their research was grounded in Douglas's (1966, 1982, 1994, 1999) anthropological perspective. Douglas forged a theoretical synthesis of Western philosophy and social scientific theory that provides an explanatory framework for how people organize their world, including what they believe to be dangerous. Wildavsky (1979) used this perspective to guide his examination of risk perception as a political, rather than an individual process, writing that "what to favor and what to fear are cultural constructs that enable us to walk right past snarling monsters and run away from little-bitsy things. If we want to know why we are fearful about what and whether we should be, this is equivalent to asking the cultural question, 'how should we live'?" (p. 36).

Thus, social factors play a prominent role in a person's awareness of environmental risks. Horlick-Jones, Sime, and Pidgeon (2003) recognize that environmental risk communication has evolved to incorporate the social dynamic of risk perception and policy development, specifically by inviting the lay public to be partners through decision making processes. This line of research comes out of an approach called the social amplification of risk framework (SARF) (e.g., Kasperson, Renn, Slovic, Brown, Emel, Goble, Kasperson, & Ratick, 1988; Kasperson 1992; Pidgeon, 1999; Pidgeon, Kasperson, & Slovic, 2003; Renn 1992). Empirical studies that described the various dynamic social processes underlying risk perception and response emerged from early SARF research. Pidgeon et al. (2003) explained that the theoretical starting point for SARF was inspired by Luhmann's (1979, 1993) social theory. Basically, Kasperson et al. (1988) launched from the assumption that risk events that might include actual or hypothesized accidents and incidents (or even new reports on existing risks), will be largely irrelevant or localized in their impact unless human beings observe and communicate them to others (Pidgeon et al., 2003). Ultimately, scholars advocating the SARF approach argued that the experience of risk is not so much an experience of physical harm, as it is an outgrowth of systemic social processes by which groups and individuals learn to create interpretations of risk. These interpretations provide rules people use to select, order and explain signals emanating from the physical world (Renn, Burns, Kasperson, Kasperson, & Slovic, 1992; Pidgeon et al., 2003).

Beck's influential *Risk Society* (1992) extended the cultural perspective specifically into contemporary environmental risks. Beck posits that one characteristic of "reflexive modern" society is a growing awareness of the unintended consequences of our technological development. These unintended consequences are the pervasive risks associated with technologies originally developed to protect human society from nature. Although Beck does not self-consciously focus on communication, he portrays politics in the risk society as revolving around presenting, justifying and arguing about ubiquitous self-induced risk, more than around revolution or counter-revolution. At the same time, they establish the inescapability of these risks, these rhetorically based practices may point out how risks are unevenly distributed throughout society. Beck's discussion of acceptable levels of risk is particularly relevant to communication. He noted that the establishment of "acceptable levels" indicates that the agency responsible for setting the levels has mitigated the risk to provide greater safety and security. Beck pointed out, however, that the existence of these acceptable levels justifies the claim that organizations must establish mechanisms that are guaranteed to pollute and create greater danger. Thus, the phrase, "acceptable levels" constrains creative thinking that might encourage people to envision alternate methods to achieve our socioeconomic goals.

Although most risk communication research is grounded in some variant on positivist social science, a small number of researchers have explored risk communication from a critical or rhetorical perspective (Farrell & Goodnight, 1998; Grabill & Simmons, 1998; Hamilton, 2003; Katz & Miller, 1996; Peterson, 2003; Sattell, 2006; Sauer, 2002). This research on environmental risk is unified by a humanistic curiosity about the epistemology of risk, and an insistence that risk assessment and risk communication are two sides of the same endeavor. They explore questions such as how individual beliefs about appropriate power relationships in society may contribute to increased risk associated with some social control frameworks over others (Peterson, 2003); how risk communicators might employ a rhetorical framework to discover what arguments might be most effective when explaining environmental risks (Sauer, 2002); and how collective memory of specific controversies may set the stage for risk perception, thus animating future argumentation pertaining to environmental risk (Sawtell, 2006). Dessai, Adger, Hulme, Turnpenny, Köhler, and Warren (2004) argued that, although climate scientists and others with related formal expertise may develop technically appropriate responses to climate change, these responses (whether adaptation or mitigation focused) remain unsustainable unless they integrate experiences and perceptions drawn from informal knowledge into technical responses. Concepts and strategies drawn from a critical or rhetorical perspective may enable the appreciation for both formal and informal expertise that is required to achieve a robust policy response to global warming.

Related to social interpretation of risks, it has also been argued that people underrate their own vulnerability to harm, but judge others as being at a greater risk. Weinstein (1989) first proposed the "optimistic bias" theory, stating that individuals do not believe they are susceptible to health or environmental risks, while rating society as a whole to be vulnerable to the same risk. Optimistic bias inhibits a person's ability to understand or seek information about potential risks to his or her health. Klein and Helweg-Larsen (2002) conducted a meta-analysis of 27 studies investigating the relationship between optimistic bias and perceived control and concluded that greater perceived control was significantly related to greater optimistic bias. Leiserowitz's (2005) survey results, indicating that 68% of respondents were most concerned about climate change as it impacted people around the world and nonhuman nature, while only 13% believed that global warming would impact them or their family directly, illustrate this bias.

Coleman (1993) tested optimistic bias theory when she studied the relative influences of mass media, interpersonal channels, and self-efficacy on risk judgments. She asked participants to assess their probability of encountering various health risks, the amount of exposure they have to mass media channels of risk information, and how often they talked about these risks with other people. The participants who saw certain risks to be more of a societal problem had engaged in more interpersonal discussion of those issues, while people who focused on their individual vulnerability or the potential risk to themselves were most influenced by the mass media.

Research has demonstrated that interpersonal communication directly contributes to the amount of information people have regarding potential health risks (Coleman, 1993; Robinson & Levy, 1986; Dunwoody & Neuwirth, 1991). The influence of that information, however, depends on how trustworthy the receiver perceives the source to be. Worsley (1989) found that information from credible, interpersonal sources is more likely than information gained from mass media to influence behavioral change regarding risk perceptions. Thus, interpersonal communication influences the judgments people make by extending the influence of mediated reports. For example, Robinson and Levy (1986) argued that not only does news reporting communicate risk information to mass media audiences, but also to acquaintances with whom audience members discuss what they have seen, heard or read. This research should not, however, be interpreted as demonstrating that either face-to-face communication or mediated communication is more central to environmental risk communication. As Singer and Endreny (1993) point out, despite the evidence that people are motivated to change their behavior based on interpersonal conversations, it is important to recognize that the interpersonal sources most likely obtained their information from the mass media (Singer & Endreny, 1993).

MEDIA AS A CHANNEL FOR COMMUNICATING ENVIRONMENTAL RISK

While it is not possible to delineate a clean boundary between psychological factors and cultural dynamics of risk communication, it is frequently argued that the media serve as the public's primary introduction to risk (Luhmann, 2000). Environmental and science-related risks are especially more likely to be discovered through a mediated channel than from any other source. Nelkin (1995) and later Wilson (1995) concluded that the general public gets most of its knowledge about science from the mass media. Most people, therefore, obtain their information about environmental risk through this channel. Research has shown that media attention to risk can influence people's understanding of risky behavior or potential health risks. For example, in 1988 the U.S. government launched a media campaign about AIDS. From that point on, media coverage increased 10-fold and public awareness has increased significantly. A 1991 survey in the Los Angeles Times reported that only 15–20% of the population personally knew anyone who was ill with AIDS. More than 99% had heard or read through the mass media about Magic Johnson's decision to quit professional basketball because he had tested positive for the AIDS virus, however (Janny, 1991). There has also been a substantial increase in condom sales in the U.S. since 1989 (Singer, Rogers, & Glassman, 1991), indicating that media attention to risks can influence public understanding of issues, as well as public behavior related to those issues. Numerous studies have demonstrated strong correlations between media coverage, public awareness, and political agendas regarding risks (Walgrave & Van Aeist, 2006). This should not be taken as a simple claim that media set the political agenda, however, for considerable debate remains regarding "under what specific circumstances the mass media are able to boost political attention for issues" (Walgrave & Van Aiest, 2006, p. 89). Donohue, Tichenor, and Olien (1995) argued that the rather than setting the political agenda, the media maintain the status quo, while Kepplinger and Daschmann (1997) reasoned that daily news establishes the context within which future information is judged.

Research also has shown that media preoccupation with some types of risk has led the public to overestimate the likelihood of some incidents, while underestimating the likelihood of other. For example, because the media over-represent severe, intentional, and gruesome incidents, the public overestimates their frequency. Westfeldt and Wicker (1998) observed that, "In 1997, even as the prison population was going up and the crime rate was falling, the public rated 'crime / gangs / justice system' as 'the most important problem facing the country today' and 'by a large margin'" (p. 2). As they chronicled the preoccupation with crime by local newspapers and TV broadcasters, they also observed that national media followed the same pattern. Even though the Center for Media and Public Affairs "reported in April 1998 that the national murder rate had fallen by 20% since 1990, … the number of murder stories on network newscasts rose in the same years by approximately 600%" (Westfeldt & Wicker, 1998, p. 2).

A similar effect has been identified in mass media reporting of global warming. Many scholars have investigated how mass media report the scientific findings related to global warming, greenhouse gases and climate change (Bell, 1994a, b; Boykoff & Boykoff, 2004; Dunwoody & Peters, 1992; Nissani, 1999) and many have explored factors that lead to inaccurate, insufficient or otherwise confusing coverage of global warming (Corbett & Durfee, 2004; Cottle, 2000; Wilson, 2000). Scholars have identified failures on behalf of scientists in transmitting their high-level expertise to journalists (McComas & Shanahan, 1999; Ungar, 1992, 2000; Zehr, 2000) and others have investigated the transmission failures between the media and the public (Bell, 1994b; Stamm, et al., 2000; Wilson, 1995, 2000; Ungar, 1992, 2000). Boykoff and Boykoff (2004) explained that when it comes to journalistic coverage of global warming, balanced reporting has led to informational bias. For example, a traditional journalist is trained to incorporate both sides of an issue to balance the story. Such inclusion actually makes the audience member less certain about global warming than a news story that provides more details on the history and context of global warming (Corbett & Durfee, 2004). Therefore, traditional global warming coverage has historically confused audiences about the degree and magnitude of environmental risk associated with changing global climates.

For environmental health risks generally, several studies have linked media coverage to changes in public opinion about the health and safety of environmental risks, such as air pollution, toxic waste, and nuclear energy production. Wallis (2007) argued that one reason the British public were unaware of the strong relationship between air quality and human health was that media representations minimized the links. He suggested better understanding could be achieved by increasing public access to the inputs for "Headline Indicators," a program carried over all national network sites through the United Kingdom. Galvez, Peters, Grager, and Forman (2007) analyzed communication about environmental risk to children following the World Trade Center attack on September 11, 2001. They found that parents generally obtained information about environmental risks posed to their children from mass media, both traditional and Internet. They argued that the official response made good use of risk communication principles (Covello, 1993) to reduce anxiety by providing specific suggestions (such as closing windows and replacing air filters) that gave the public a sense of individual control. Although considerable uncertainty regarding environmental risks to children younger than 18 years exists, communication messages did not emphasize the uncertainty. Further, the information was broadly available, because it was distributed through both traditional (print and electronic) media and the Internet. They also found that the media were helpful in providing historical context for specific air quality information, which alleviated additional concern (Galvez, Peters, Grager & Forman, 2007).

Many researchers have concluded that economic drivers for the news industry determine that coverage is generally event-driven. Since the accident at Three Mile Island, for example, media coverage of nuclear energy has focused overwhelmingly on public safety, and most of it has negatively framed the industry. Although the nuclear industry argues that civil uses of nuclear power are drastically different from military use of nuclear weapons, the production processes and waste products are similar. Following from this similarity, the general tenor of news coverage since Three Mile Island has suggested that nuclear power automatically poses a serious threat or health risk.

Media also focus on stories emphasizing human interests and short-term economic impacts (Klaidman, 1991; Murray, Schwartz, & Lichter, 2001; Singer & Endreny, 1993; Stamm, Clark, & Eblancas, 2000). They tend to cover bizarre and mysterious health hazards before they address more mundane or long-term risks to humans (Klaidman, 1991; Murray et al., 2001; Singer & Endreny,

1993). Although incorporating wild-caught fish into the diet frequently poses an immediate and localized health risk, for example, the media rarely devote attention to this chronic issue. Despite the fact that both state and national agencies update safety advisories regularly, there are few stories focusing on the risks associated with the mundane practice of eating wild-caught fish (Burger & Gochfeld, 2006). Again, due to the nature of the news industry, journalists do not have the time or energy to investigate all of the world's problems and propose solutions.

Many researchers indicate that the news media play a special role in developing the public's perceptions of risk because media link technical assessments of experts with the psychological assessments of laypersons (Gregory, 1989; Gregory & Mendelsohn, 1993; Murray et al., 2001; Singer & Endreny, 1993). Gregory argued that the media facilitate two-way communication about risks from technical experts to the public and from the public to scientists and government or industry decision-makers. "Media play a role in interpreting scientific findings for the public, providing key information, selective summaries and overall assessments of the quality and relevance of the study" (Gregory, pp. 2–3). In Gregory's analysis, the media weigh heavily in influencing public perceptions of risk. Murray et al. conjectured that "by now it is almost commonplace that many Americans are overly afraid of risks," and their fears are often magnified by "alarmist reporting" (p. 115). Although the specific influence and salience of mass media remains uncertain, research clearly indicates that media influence perceptions of environmental risk in numerous ways.

Through the multiple channels available, "most of the information we have about risks comes to us by way of the mass media" (Singer & Endreny, 1993, p. 2). Risk information does not, for the most part, come as explicit reporting about risk, but instead comes in the guise of news and feature stories about accidents, illnesses, natural disasters, and scientific breakthroughs. For certain classes of hazards, especially those that are serious and rare, the mass media are the most likely source of information for most people (Singer & Endreny, 1987). Even if a person lives through the hottest summer on record, record drought or severe forest fires, as experienced in 1988 and 2002, it is the media that connects such events to scientific evidence for the public. Bell (1994a) found that the media were the sole source of information on global warming for New Zealanders, and Wilson (1995) reported that the media, especially television media, were the primary information source in the United States.

Griffin, Dunwoody, and Neuwirth (1999) found that although the mass media were relatively popular sources of information about lead in tap water, those influences did not necessarily translate into public recognition of specific health risks posed by their environment, nor do they lead people to take preventive actions. It appears then that people tend to pick their risks and act accordingly. Klaidman (1991) argued that people prefer to decide for themselves, "usually in seat-of-the-pants fashion," whether the payoff in pleasure or profit is worth the risk (Klaidman, 1991, p. 4). Klaidman claimed that people generally make their decisions based on information that is incomplete, confused, misleading, or wrong, and when accurate and substantially complete information is available to them from the news media and other sources, they still may make irrational choices in behavior toward the risk. This suggests that even when the press pays a great deal of attention to environmental risks, it does not guarantee that readers and viewers will choose to be concerned about them. Even when consumers of news are reasonably well informed and concerned about environmental risks, this does not guarantee that individuals will change their behavior. People often hold preferences that are not easily swayed by awareness that their chosen activities are risky. Conversely, they may be outraged by the trivial risks that are imposed on them (Klaidman, 1991).

Many researchers of environmental risk focus on how the mass media influence risk judgments at the societal level (Culbertson & Stempel, 1985; Pilisuk & Acredolo, 1988). Some researchers have gone further to claim the mass media influence risk perceptions at the personal level (Dunwoody & Neuwirth, 1991; Culbertson & Stempel, 1985). However, Dunwoody and Neuwirth (1991) maintained that the mass media only make risk issues salient initially, and that interpersonal channels are used to make informed judgments at a later time. Although they found that informed judgments are made after interpersonal interactions, the media frames used to introduce the issues initially may influence the interpersonal interaction, and eventually the risk judgments made. Although content is not irrelevant, many of the variances in media's impact on individual's risk perceptions could be due to the different reporting styles and frames used to construct stories. Kosicki and McLeod (1990) found that media images were critical to audience reception, Hornig (1992) found strong interactions between framing of risk and audience factors, and Wakefield and Elliot (2003) found that media's perceived trustworthiness influenced whether people judged news about environmental risk to be credible.

Most research about media influence on risk perceptions has focused on attitudes and opinions formed after exposure to a specific media source. One current challenge is to discover how risk perception operates as a dependent variable. The assumption that risk is something "out there" to be measured fuels a tendency to view the concept as unidimensional, the ubiquitous risk estimate. Such estimates are often defined as "quantitative measures of hazard consequences that can be expressed as conditional probabilities of experiencing harm" (Hohenemser, Kates, & Slovic, 1983, p. 379). If such a measure captures the likelihood of harm, researchers argue, then reasonable public perceptions of the risk in question should coincide with the estimate, meaning that a person's estimate of the risk is as close as researchers can come to measuring a person's risk perception. Risk perception, according to this approach, is defined as "a measure of the closeness of fit between the risk estimate and individual personal evaluations of the hazards" (Dunwoody & Neuwirth, 1991, p. 13).

In an attempt to operationalize and measure perception of risks portrayed in the media, Griffin, Dunwoody, Dybro, and Zabala (1994) created an "index of perception of personal risk." Their index was constructed by combining respondent answers to two items. The first item was cognitive, and the second affective: "the respondent's risk estimate of the likelihood that he or she would become ill from tap water lead in the future on a scale from zero (= no chance) to 100 (= certainty), and the extent to which the respondent worries about becoming ill from tap water lead in the future on a scale of zero to 100" (Griffin et al., 1994, p. 16). The researchers standardized the two items to form a single measure of risk perception. Coleman (1993) tapped the cognitive dimension of risk perception by asking respondents to rate their likelihood of coming into harm, or being at risk using a six-point Likert scale.

The development and refinement of metrics such as these are critical to understanding how environmental risk is communicated generally, and how the media contribute to public understanding of environmental risk specifically. It is clear that mass media coverage plays an important role in informing audiences about potential environmental risks. It could also be argued that communicating about environmental risks, especially those associated with global warming, requires extensive scientific and technical knowledge, high level cognitive skills, and a sophisticated understanding of psycho-social dynamics. As Morgan, Fischhoff, Bostrom, and Atman (2002) reasoned, "people need a diverse set of cognitive, social and emotional skills to deal with information about risks" (p. 2).

Individuals encounter enormous amounts of risk information on a daily basis, and regardless of whether the information came from the mass media or their mothers, they must make decisions on what to worry about. Because of life's daily demands, people are too busy to deal with environmental problems they feel are beyond their control. Risk perception regarding environmental hazards appears to be influenced by the fact that humans prefer to focus on risks they believe are straightforward, as well as those that can be controlled at the individual level. At the same time, people have less tolerance for risks they perceive to be beyond their control. Individuals tend to assume that "others" are more at risk than they are, and these beliefs are reinforced through social interactions. A person's cognitive constructs, cultural norms, and interpersonal interactions all influence their perceptions about health and environmental risks. Once a risk appears on an individual's radar screen, do they seek more information about the causes and effects? If so, from whom or what sources do they most rely on for accurate information about health and environmental risks?

SEEKING INFORMATION ABOUT ENVIRONMENTAL RISK

People are motivated to gather information about a risk when they feel they need the information to cope with daily challenges. Ungar (2000) argued that it is a daunting task for members of the public to go beyond simple recognition of an issue and grasp some of its scientific underpinnings, because the sources and channels for doing so are quite limited. "Except *The New York Times*, few of the other mass media provide sufficiently accurate, detailed, sophisticated, or concerted coverage to take someone much beyond simple awareness of the issue" (Ungar, 2000, p. 297). Ungar argued that for people willing to take the initiative, there are books, films, and Internet sites that afford a "social scientific" perspective on the issues. However, most people rely on experts to evaluate risks, threats, and environmental problems for them (Ungar, 2000). Ungar discussed the knowledge-ignorance paradox, which simply means that as more specialized information emerges, there is a simultaneous growth in ignorance, and people have to be motivated to seek information to counter the ignorance. According to Ungar, there are many motivations for knowledge or seeking information about risks: personal motivations, pragmatic uses, good citizenship, knowledge (for knowledge's sake), and the social utility of knowledge for conversations. Whatever the motivation, however, there are limits on the amount and intensity of information seeking people will undertake.

Griffin, Dunwoody, and Neuwirth (1999) articulated a model to predict the extent to which a person will seek information about risks. Their study focused on human characteristics that might predispose someone to seek and process information about risks in different ways. Specifically, they identified seven factors that influence the extent to which people will seek out risk information and the extent to which they will spend time and effort analyzing the risk information critically. First, they found that people's gender, ethnicity, age, socioeconomic status, and political philosophy influenced their decision to seek more information about a risk. Second, they argued that people's believed control over susceptibility or harm, their trust in risk management, and perceived threats to personal values influenced whether or not they engaged in information-seeking behaviors. Griffin et al. also found that "affective responses to the risk," (such as worry, anger, and uncertainty manifested in fear and anxiety) influenced a person's formation of risk judgments. The researchers found that worry motivates information seeking and processing more than cognitive components of risk perception. Anger was related to an individual's attempt to reassert control over the risk, and uncertainty was perceived as a loss in control. Likewise, the amount of information people feel they need in order to cope with the risk influenced whether or not they seek more information. They found that beliefs about the usefulness of information from various channels directly influenced a person's information-seeking behavior.

Ungar (2000) described how metaphors can provide valuable assistance when attempting to either highlight or downplay environmental risks. The widely recognized "ozone hole" and "greenhouse effect" illustrate his point. Whereas people understand that a "hole is an aberration in a protective shield," the effect of a greenhouse "seems like something natural and benign" (p. 299). As Corbett and Durfee (2004) argued, the metaphor of a hole in the ozone layer has been an effective linguistic strategy for motivating both individual and corporate action (such as the Montreal Protocol), whereas the metaphor of a greenhouse effect has not proven effective in motivating similar action on global warming. On the other hand, Farrell and Goodnight (1998) demonstrated how the metaphors used in an attempt to downplay the accident at Three Mile Island backfired on the industry.

Pidgeon, Kasperson, and Slovic (2003) suggested that the world is witnessing rapid changes, wherein risk communication is highly dependent upon a huge expansion of traditional media, electronic communication and cultural fragmentation. According to Pidgeon et al. (2005) these changes have produced a politicization of risk issues in the public sphere. Risks associated with global warming have been especially politicized in recent years (Gelbspan, 2005; Michaels, 2004; Tolan & Berzon, 2005).

CONCLUSIONS

We close with a description of an extended memorandum Frank Luntz prepared for the Republican Party in 1993 (Luntz, 1993). Nowhere is the importance of communication within the politicized realm of environmental risk more evident than in this document, which has been spun into successful political campaigns, serious speeches downplaying environmental risks, and websites poking fun at those who abide by its tenets (see for example, Luntzspeak, at http://www.luntzspeak.com/). The use of technically sound communication principles in the memo is explicit. Luntz advised politicians to "think of environmental (and other) issues in terms of 'story.' A compelling story, even if factually inaccurate, can be more emotionally compelling than a dry recitation of the truth" (p. 132). In keeping with his advice to focus on a good story, rather than "truth," he provided a set of "communication recommendations [for] global warming," beginning with:

> 1. The scientific debate remains open. Voters believe that there is no consensus about global warming within the scientific community. Should the public come to believe that the scientific issues are settled their views about global warming will change accordingly. Therefore, you need to continue to make the lack of scientific certainty a primary issue in the debate. (p. 137)

Just to make sure readers get his point about how important language is, Luntz provided examples of "words that work," such as

> Scientists can extrapolate all kinds of things from today's data, but that doesn't tell us anything about tomorrow's world. You can't look back a million years and say that proves that we're heating the globe now hotter than it's ever been. After all, just 20 years ago scientists were worried about a new Ice Age. (Luntz, 1993, p. 138)

He added variety while being consistent by including boxes titled, "Language that works." In these, he showed his readers how to appeal to public fears:

> Unnecessary environmental regulations hurt moms and dads, grandmas and grandpas. They hurt senior citizens on fixed incomes. They take an enormous swipe at miners, loggers, truckers, farmers—anyone who has any work in energy intensive professions. Then mean less income for families struggling to survive and educate their children. (p. 139)

Finally, he opined, "It's time to start talking about 'climate change' instead of 'global warming'. "Climate change is less frightening than global warming. Climate change sounds like you're going from Pittsburgh to Fort Lauderdale. Global warming has catastrophic connotations attached to it (p. 142)." In case anyone is not persuaded, he closed with the claim, "the words on these pages are tested - they work!" (Luntz, 1993, p. 142).

We hope this brief review of the Luntz memo foregrounds the potential power of environmental risk communication. Leiserowitz (2005) and Lorenzoni, Pidgeon, & O'Connor (2005) noted that the development and implementation of appropriate climate change policy requires integration of both experts' and non-experts' perceptions and definitions of what they understand to be dangerous climate change. Although some environmental risks may be less uncertain and less complex than risks associated with global warming, the same principles apply. To the degree risk communicators are aware of the complex social practices that go into the social construction of environmental risk, they will be better able to respond and then foreground their craft as a powerful means for framing ethical audience involvement in the always uncertain and complex decisions about environmental risk.

BIBLIOGRAPHY

Beck, U. (1992). *Risk society: Towards a new modernity*. Newbury Park, CA: Sage.
Bell, A. (1994a). Media (mis)communication on the science of climate change. *Public Understanding of Science, 3*, 259–275.

Bell, A. (1994b). Climate of opinion: Public and media discourse on the global environment. *Discourse and Society*, *5*(1), 33–64.

Bostrom, A., Morgan, M. G., Fischhoff, B., & Read, D. (1994). What do people know about global climate change? *Risk Analysis*, *14*, 959–970.

Boykoff, M.T. & Boykoff, J.M. (2004). Balance as bias: Global warming and the US prestige press. *Global Environmental Change*, *14*, 125–136.

Burger, J. and Gochfeld, M. (2006). A framework and information needs for the management of the risks from consumption of self-caught fish. *Environmental Research, 101,* 275–285.

Cadot, E., Rodwin, V. G., & Spira, A. (2007). In the heat of the summer: Lessons from the heat waves of Paris. *Journal of Urban Health*, *84*(4), 466–468.

Christianson, G. E. (1999). *Greenhouse: The 200-year story of global warming*. New York: Walker and Company.

Coleman, C.L. (1993). The influence of mass media and interpersonal communication on societal and personal risk judgments. *Communication Research*, *20*(4), 611–628.

Corbett, J. B., & Durfee, J. L. (2004). Testing public (un)certainty of science: Media representations of global warming. *Science Communication*, *26*(2), 129–151.

Cottle, S. (2000). TV news, lay voices and the visualization of environmental risks. In S. Allan, B. Adam & C. Carter (Eds.). *Environmental Risks and the Media* (pp. 29–44). London: Routledge.

Covello, V. (1993). Risk communication, trust, and credibility. Journal of Occupational Medicine, 35, 18–19.

Culbertson, H. M., & Stempel, G. H., (1985). "Media malaise": Explaining personal optimism and societal pessimism about health care. *Journal of Communication*, *35*, 180–190.

Dessai, S., Adger, W. N., Hulme, M., Turnpenny, J., Köhler, J., & Warren, R. (2004). Defining and experiencing dangerous climate change. *Climatic Change, 64*(1–2), 15.

Donohue, G. A., Tichenor, P. J., & Olien, C. N. (1995). A guard dog perspective on the role of media. *Journal of Communication, 45*(2), 115–132.

Douglas, M. (1966). *Purity and danger: An analysis of the concepts of pollution and taboo*. London: Routledge & Kegan Paul.

Douglas, M. (1982). *Essays in the sociology of perception*. London: Routledge and Kegan Paul.

Douglas, M. (1994). *Risk and blame: Essays in cultural theory*. London: Routledge.

Douglas, M. (1999). Environments at risk. In M. Douglas (Ed.), *Implicit meanings: Selected essays in anthropology* (2nd ed., pp. 204 – 217). London: Routledge.

Douglas, M., & Wildavsky, A. (1982). *Risk and cultur: An essay on the selection of technological and environmental dangers.* Berkeley: University of California Press.

Dunwoody, S., & Neuwirth, K. (1991). Coming to terms with the impact of communication on scientific and technological risk judgments. In L. Wilkins & P. Patterson (Eds.), *Risky business: Communicating issues of science, risk and public policy* (11–30). Westport, CT: Greenwood Press.

Dunwoody, S., & Peters, H. P. (1992). Mass media coverage of technological and environmental risks. *Public Understanding of Science*, *1*(2), 199–230.

Epstein, Paul R. (2005). Climate change and human health. *New England Journal of Medicine*, *353*(14), 1433–1436.

Farrell, T. B., & Goodnight, G. T. (1998). Accidental rhetoric: The root metaphors of Three Mile Island. In C. Waddell (Ed.), *Landmark essays on rhetoric and the environment* (pp. 75–105). Mahwah, NJ: Erlbaum.

Finucane, M. L., Alhakami, A., Slovic, P., & Johnson, S. M. (2000). The affect heuristic in judgments of risks and benefits. *Journal of Behavioral Decision Making*, *13*, 1–17.

Fischer, G. W., Morgan, M.G ., Fischhoff, B., Nair, I., & Lave, L. B. (1991). What risks are people concerned about? *Risk Analysis, 11*, 303–314.

Galvez, M. P., Peters, R., Grager, N., & Forman, J. (2007). Effective risk communication In children's environmental health: Lessons learned from 9/11. *Pediatric Clinics of North America, 54,* 33–46.

Gelbspan, R. (1998). *The heat is on: The climate crisis, the cover-up the prescription*. New York: Perseus.

Gelbspan, R. (2005). Disinformation, financial pressures, and misplaced balance. *Nieman Reports, 59*(4), 77–79.

Glover, J. Vidal, J., & Clark, A. (June 21, 2005). Blair told: Act now on climate. Guardian Unlimited. Retrieved October 30, 2007, from http://politics.guardian.co.uk/polls/story/0,11030,1511097,00.html#article.

Grabe, M.E., Lang, A., Zhou, S., & Bolls, P.D. (2000). Cognitive access to negatively arousing news: An experimental investigation of the knowledge gap. *Communication Research, 27*, 3–26.

Grabill, J. T., & Simmons, W. M. (1998). Toward a critical rhetoric of risk communication: Producing citizens and the role of risk communicators. Technical Communication Quarterly, 7, 415–441.

Gregory, R. (1989). Improving risk communications: Questions of content and intent. In W. Leiss (Ed.), *Prospects and problems in risk communication* (pp. 98–132). Waterloo, Ontario: University of Waterloo Press.

Gregory, R., & Mendelsohn, R. (1993). Perceived risk, dread, and benefits. *Risk Analysis, 13*, 259–264.

Griffin, R. J., & Dunwoody, S. (1994). *Community structure and press coverage of health risks from environmental contamination.* Report prepared for the U.S. Environmental Protection Agency, Office of Policy, Planning and Evaluation, Risk Communication Project.

Griffin, R. J., Dunwoody, S., Dybro, T., & Zabala, F. (1994). *The relationship of communication to risk perceptions and preventative behavior related to lead in drinking water.* Presented to the Science Communication Interest Group, Association for Education in Journalism and Mass Communication, at the 1994 Annual Convention, Atlanta, GA.

Griffin, R. J., Dunwoody, S., & Neuwirth, K. (1999). Proposed model of the relationship of risk information seeking and processing to the development of preventive behaviors. *Environmental Research* Section A 80, S230–S245.

Hamilton, J. D. (2003). Exploring technical and cultural appeals in strategic risk communication: The Fernald radium case. *Risk Analysis, 23*, 291–302.

Henry, A.D. (2000). Public perceptions of global warming. *Human Ecology Review*, *7*(1), 25–30.

Hohenemser, C., Kates, R.W., & Slovic, P. (1983). The nature of technological hazard. Science, 220, 376–384.

Horlick-Jones, T., Sime, J. & Pidgeon, N. (2003). The social dynamics of environmental risk perception: Implications for risk communication research and practice" In N. Pidgeon, R. E. Kasperson & P. Slovic (Eds.). *The social amplification of risk* (pp. 262–285). Cambridge, UK: Cambridge University Press.

Hornig, S. (1992). Framing risk: Audience and reader factors. *Journalism Quarterly, 69*(3), 679–690.

IPCC. (2007). Summary for policymakers. In . M. L. Parry, O. F. Canziani, J. P. Palutikof, P. J. van der Linden, & C. E. Hanson (Eds.), *Climate change 2007: Impacts, adaptation and vulnerability. Contribution of Working Group II to the Fourth Assessment Report of the Intergovernmental Panel on Climate Change* (pp. 7–22). Cambridge, UK: Cambridge University Press.

Jamieson, D. (2006). An American paradox. *Climatic Change, 77*, 97–102.

Janny, S. (1991, November 28). Johnson case raises AIDS concerns if not caution. *Los Angeles Times*. Retrieved January 10, 2003, from http://pqasb.pqarchiver.com/latimes/2099010.html.

Kasperson, R. E. (1992). The social amplfication of risk: Progress in developing an integrative framework. In S. Krimsky & D. Golding (Eds.), *Social theories of risk* (pp. 153–178 London: Praeger.

Kasperson, R. E., Renn, O., Slovic, P., Brown, H. S., Emel, J., Goble, R., Kasperson, J. X., & Ratick, S. (1988). The social amplification of risk conceptual framework. *Risk Analysis, 8*, 177–187.

Katz, S., & Miller, C., (1996). The low-level radioactive waste siting controversy in North Carolina: Toward a rhetorical model of risk communication. In C. Herndl & S. Brown (Eds.), *Green culture: Environmental rhetoric in contemporary America* (pp. 111–140). Madison: University of Wisconsin Press,.

Kempton, W. (1991). Lay perspectives on global climate change. *Global Environmental Change, 1,* 183–208.

Kempton, W. (1997). How the public views climate change. *Environment, 39*(9), 12–21.

Kepplinger, H., & Daschmann, G. (1997). Today's news – tomorrow's context: A dynamic model of news processing. *Journal of Broadcasting & Electronic Media, 41*, 548–565.

Klaidman, S. (1991). *Health in the headlines: The stories behind the stories.* New York: Oxford University Press.

Klein, C. T. F., & Helweg-Larsen, M. (2002). Perceived control and the optimistic bias: A meta-analytic review. *Psychology and Health, 17*(4), 437–446.

Kosicki, G. M., & McLeod, J. M. (1990). Learning from political news: Effects of media images and information-processing strategies. In S. Kraus (Ed.), *Mass communication and political information processing* (pp. 69–83). Hillsdale, NJ: Erlbaum.

Leiserowitz, A. A. (2005). American risk perceptions: Is climate change dangerous? *Risk Analysis 25*(6), 1433–1442.

Lorenzoni, I., Pidgeon, N. F., & O'Connor, R. E. (2005). Dangerous climate change: The role for risk research. *Risk Analysis 25*(6), 1387–1398.

Luhmann, N. (1979). *Trust and power*. New York: Wiley Press.

Luhmann, N. (1993). *Risk: A sociological theory*. (R. Barrett, Trans.). Hawthorne, NY: Aldine de Gruyter.

Luhmann, N. (2000). *The reality of mass media*. (K. Cross, Trans.). Stanford, CA: Stanford University Press.

Luntz, F. (1993). The Environment. A cleaner, safer, healthier America. The Luntz Research Companies — Straight Talk. Retrieved October 30, 2007, from http://www.luntzspeak.com/memo.html.

McComas, K. (2006). Defining moments in risk communication research: 1996–2005. *Journal of Health Communication, 11*, 75–91.

McComas, K., & Shanahan J. (1999). Telling stories about global climate change. *Communication Research, 26*(1), 30–57.

Michaels, P. J., (2004). *Meltdown: The predictable distortion of global warming by scientists, politicians, and the media.* Washington, D.C.: Cato Institute.

Morgan, M. G., Fischhoff, B., Bostrom, A., & Atman, C. J. (2002). *Risk communication: A mental models approach.* New York: Cambridge University Press.

Murray, D., Schwartz, J., & Lichter, S. R. (2001). It ain't necessarily so: How media make and unmake the scientific picture of reality. Lanham, MD: Rowman & Littlefield.

Nelkin, D. (1995). *Selling science: How the press covers science and technology*. New York: Freeman.

New York City Department of Health and Mental Hygiene. (2006, Nocember). Deaths associated with heat waves in 2006. NYC Vital Signs. Special Report. Retrieved September 1, 2007, from http://www.nyc.gov/html/doh/downloads/pdf/survey/survey-2006heatdeaths.pdf.

Nissani, M. (1999). Media coverage of the greenhouse effect. Population and Environment: A *Journal of Interdisciplinary Studies, 21*(1), 27–43.

NOAA. (2006, September). U.S. has second warmest summer on Record: Nation experienced warmest January – August period on record. NOAA Satellite and Information Service. Retrieved October 1, 2007, from http://www.noaanews.noaa.gov/stories2006/s2700.htm.

Oreskes, N. (2004). Beyond the ivory tower: The scientific consensus on climate change. *Science, 306*, 1686.

Peterson, T. R. (2003). Social control frames: Opportunities or constraints? *Environmental Practice, 5*, 232–238.

Pidgeon, N. F. (1999). Social amplification of risk: models, mechanisms and tools for policy. *Risk, Decision and Policy,* 4(2), 145–159.

Pidgeon, N. F., Kasperson, R. E., & Slovic, P. (2003). *The social amplification of risk.* Cambridge, UK: Cambridge University Press.

Pidgeon, N. F., Poortinga, W., Rowe, G., Horlick-Jones, T, Walls, J., & O'Riordan, T. (2005). Using surveys in public participation processes for risk decision making: The case of the 2003 British GM nation public debate. *Risk Analysis, 25*(2), 467–479.

Pilisuk, M., & Acredolo, C. (1988). Fear of technological hazards: One concern or many? *Social Behavior, 3,* 17–24.

Public belief in global warming. (2002). Table 7-28 in Chapter 7. In Science and Engineering Indicators 2002. Arlington, VA: National Science Foundation. http://www.nsf.gov/sbe/srs/seind02/c/cs2.htm#gallup.

Renn, O. (1992). Risk communication: Toward a rational discourse with the public. *Journal of Hazardous Materials, 29,* 465–519.

Renn, O., Burns, W. J., Kasperson, J. X., Kasperson, R. E., & Slovic, P. (1992). The social amplification of risk: Theoretical foundations and empirical applications. *Journal of Social Issues, 48*, 137–160.

Robinson, J. P., & Levy, M. R. (1986). Interpersonal communication and news comprehension: *The Public Opinion Quarterly, 50*(2), 160–175.

Rosa, E., Mazur, A., & Dietz, T. (1987). *Sociological analysis of risk impacts associated with the string of a high level of nuclear waste repository: The case of Hanford. Proceedings of the workshop on Assessing Social and Economic Effects of Perceived Risk.* Seattle: Battelle Human Affairs Research Centers.

Sauer, B. J. (2002). *The rhetoric of risk: Technical documentation in hazardous environments*. Mahwah, NJ: Erlbaum.

Sawtell, S. S. (2006). The rhetoric of risk: Institutional controversies over agricultural biotechnology. Ph.D. dissertation, Northwestern University, Evanston, Illinois. Retrieved November 2, 2007, from ProQuest Digital Dissertations database. (Publication No. AAT 3212804).

Singer, E. T., & Endreny, P. M. (1987). Reporting hazards: Their benefits and costs. *Journal of Communication, 37*(3), 10–26.

Singer, E. T., & Endreny, P. M. (1993*). Reporting risk: How the mass media portray accidents, diseases, disasters and other hazards.* New York: Russell Sage Foundation.

Singer, E. T., Rogers, F., & Glassman, M.B. (1991). Public opinion about AIDS before and after the U.S. government information campaign of 1988. *Public Opinion Quarterly, 55*, 161–179.

Slovic, P. (1987). Perceptions of risk. *Science, 236*, 280–285.

Slovic, P. (1997). Trust, emotion, sex, politics and science: Surveying the risk-assessment battlefield. In M. Bazerman, D. Messick, A. Tenbrunsel, & K. Wade-Benzoni (Eds.), *Environment, ethics and behavior* (pp. 277–313). San Francisco: New Lexington Press.

Slovic, P., Finucane, M., Peters, E., & MacGregor, D. G. (2002). The affect heuristic. In T. Gilovich, D. Griffin, & D. Kahneman (Eds.), *Heuristics and biases: The psychology of intuitive judgment* (pp. 329–342). Cambridge, UK: Cambridge University Press.

Slovic, P., & Fischhoff, B. (1982). Determinants of perceived and acceptable risk. In L. C. Gould & C. A. Walker (Eds.), *Too hot to handle: The management of nuclear wastes* (pp. 112–150). New Haven, CT: Yale University Press.

Slovic, P., Fischhoff, B., & Lichtenstein, S. (1980). Facts and fears: Understanding perceived risk. In R. C. Schwing & W.A . Albers (Eds.), *Societal risk assessment: How safe is safe enough* (pp. 181–214). New York: Plenum Press.

Slovic, P., Fischhoff, B., & Lichtenstein, S. (1985). Characterizing perceived risk. In R. W. Kates, C. Hohenesmer, & J. Kasperson (Eds.), *Perilous progress: Technology as hazard* (pp. 91–123). Boulder, CO: Westview.

Slovic, P., MacGregor, D. G., & Peters, E. (1998). Imagery, affect, and decision-making. Eugene: Decision Research.

Stamm, K. R., Clark, F., & Eblancas, P. R. (2000). Mass communication and public understanding of environmental problems: The case of global warming. *Public Understanding of Science, 9,* 219–237.

Tolan, S., & Berzon, A. (2005). Global warming: What's known vs. what's told. *Nieman Reports, 59,* 91–94.

Ungar, S. (1992). The rise and relative decline of global warming as a social problem. *The Sociological Quarterly, 33*(4), 483–501.

Ungar, S. (2000). Knowledge, ignorance and the popular culture: Climate change versus the ozone hole. *Public Understanding of Science, 9,* 297–312.

Wakefield, S. E. L., & Elliot, S. J. (2003) Constructing the news: The role of local newspapers in environmental risk communication. *The Professional Geographer, 55,* 216–226.

Wallis, M. K. (2007). Clean air strategies: An environmental nongovernmental organization perspective on the science-policy interface. *Journal of Toxicology and Environmental Health, Part A, 70,* 369–376.

Weinstein, N. (1989). Optimistic biases about personal risks. *Science, 246,* 1232–1233.

Westfeldt, W., & Wicker, T. (1998). Indictment: The news media and the criminal justice system. Nashville, TN: First Amendment Center.

Wildavsky, A. B. (1979). *Speaking truth to power: The art and craft of policy analysis.* Boston: Little, Brown.

Wilkins, L., & Patterson, P. (1987). Risk analysis and the construction of news. *Journal of Communication, 37,* 80–92.

Wilson, K. M. (1995). Mass media as sources of global warming knowledge. Mass *Communication Review, 22*(1), 75–89.

Wilson, K. M. (2000). Drought, debate and uncertainty: Measuring reporters' knowledge and ignorance about climate change. *Public Understanding of Science, 9*(1), 1–13.

Worsley, A. (1989). Perceived reliability of sources of health information. *Health Education Research, 4,* 367–376.

Zehr, S. C. (2000). Public representations of scientific uncertainty about global climate change. *Public Understanding of Science,* 9, 85–103.

31

Knowing Terror: On the Epistemology and Rhetoric of Risk

Kevin J. Ayotte
California State University, Fresno

Daniel Rex Bernard and H. Dan O'Hair
University of Oklahoma

Studies of risk and crisis communication differ in a multitude of ways, such as in the objects of danger to which they turn their attention, the types of audiences they analyze and, of course, in the theoretical and methodological frameworks that drive their analyses. Barbara Reynolds' (2002) introductory training manual, *Crisis and Emergency Risk Communication*, developed by the Centers for Disease Control and Prevention, distinguishes among crisis communication, risk communication, and crisis and emergency risk communication according to several factors such as time pressure (ranging from anticipatory to urgent) and general purpose of the respective messages (pp. 5–6). Perhaps the most obvious distinction between risk and crisis communication derives from their relative relationship to the dangerous event. Risk communication tends to consider the probability of a dangerous phenomenon (e.g., disease, environmental harm, etc.) occurring and the magnitude of such an event in terms of its impact on something a community values. Crisis communication addresses a dangerous event in progress or after it has occurred, usually to manage institutional relations with the community and/or mitigate the harmful effects of the hazard (Reynolds & Seeger, 2005, pp. 46–47), what Heath and O'Hair refer to as "risk manifested" (chapter 1, this volume). Crisis and risk communication might thus be said to differ in terms of the ontological status of the hazardous event at issue, in terms of whether the danger is merely probabilistic or has actually come into Being.

In their common concern for the nature of, and prospective reactions to, a hazardous event, however, crisis and risk communication might both be said to represent histories, histories of the present or future occurrence of hazardous events. Rather than a study of institutional or public communication about a particular event or category of hazard, this chapter explores technical and public discourses about risk as discourses about what we might call a risky history of the world. Public communication about risks often defers to the premise of an objective world of dangers, generally with little self-reflexive examination of our perceptions of the risk. The epistemological premise of the ability to read accurately and transparently that true nature of worldly risks is generally simply assumed in both lay and expert risk communication. Thus, we have then-Secretary of Defense Donald Rumsfeld articulating the nature of security risks following the events of September 11, 2001, where he makes uncharacteristically explicit the epistemology of much risk communication (including, but not limited to, the risks surrounding terrorism and other dangers to security). In response to concerns about the treatment of prisoners by the Afghan Northern Alliance during the "war on terrorism," Rumsfeld asserted, "I guess we have to take the world like we find it. And the way we find it is that a group of people killed thousands of Americans on September 11" (Rumsfeld, 2001). Similarly, and despite their theoretical and methodological differences, technical studies of risk and crisis communication tend to contrast descriptions of an "accurate" or "correct" understanding of the nature of a hazard to a public "misunderstanding" or "irrational" fear of it. Both types of risk communication, public uses and technical studies of it, thus similarly operate as a discursive history of a hazard. The sense of history emphasized here regards the epistemological function of it noted by Michel Foucault, where historical description works discursively "to circumscribe the 'locus' of an event, the limits to its fluidity and the conditions of its emergence" by "seeking out the regularity of phenomena and the probable limits of their occurrence" (Foucault, 1971/1972, p. 230). In their efforts to define and put into language the nature of a particular risk and the likelihood of its emergence from probability into the Being of a hazardous event, risk communication scholars take on the epistemological role that Foucault associates with the practice of historical commentary, which is "to say *finally*, what has silently been articulated *deep down*" (p. 221; italics in original) by the objective reality of our risky world. Foucault summarizes this epistemology of history as one that takes the "possibility of speaking of experience" as a necessary complement to the ability "to designate and name it,...to know it in the form of truth" (p. 228).

To explore risk and crisis communication generally, and risk and crisis communication about terrorism in particular, as histories of threatening events, this chapter employs a methodology that Foucault has termed "genealogical," to the extent that it explores the conditions of emergence of certain discourses of risk and the field of knowledge they construct. The method herein is also "critical" in the sense that it examines how mechanisms of power, in this case rhetorical features of risk discourse, work to produce particular knowledge formations surrounding the threat of biological terrorism (Foucault, 1971/1972, pp. 231–232). Recognizing that knowledge in various disciplines "cannot be distinguished from the ways it is expressed" (Preda, 2005, p. 31), this chapter will draw from diverse theories of rhetoric beyond Foucault to consider how what is taken to be knowledge of terrorism risks is constructed in significant part by the rhetoric through which those risks are described. In short, we argue that the objectivist epistemology driving much of the extant risk and crisis communication scholarship, as well as the rhetorical practices employed by much public and expert communication about terrorism, themselves play a substantial role in producing the meaning of risk ultimately communicated to various audiences. In offering an epistemological critique of a wide array of existing risk and crisis scholarship, we do not suggest that those studies are invalid or lack utility in helping to explicate the best approach to communicating risk. Nor, in highlighting aspects of risk and crisis communication research that themselves rhetorically demonstrate certain epistemological commitments, do we seek to impute ideological or political motives to any of the authors cited as examples. Rather, we conclude that the absence of attention to the rhetorical implications of risk and crisis discourse results in a potentially more limited understanding of public knowledge about, and reactions to, risk and crisis communication than could be gleaned from analyses that also take into account the rhetorical production of that knowledge. Despite calls for an integrated community informatics system that accounts for multiple and diverse stakeholders, the rhetorical processes described here go beyond simple information management.

The first section of this chapter surveys a wide swath of recent risk and crisis communication scholarship in order to trace what might be termed broadly a "modernist" epistemology underlying present ways of thinking and communicating about risk. This section therefore serves as a genealogy of contemporary epistemologies of risk. Taking the discourse about biological terrorism as a rhetorical archive especially relevant to American concerns about risks in the world today, the second section of the chapter explores the ways in which modernist epistemologies of risk manifest in risk and crisis communication about bioterrorism, in academic studies of that communication, as well as in their resulting recommendations for risk and crisis communication policy. The third section of the chapter presents a rethinking of the rhetorical implications of risk and crisis communication, including but not limited to that addressed to the threat of biological terrorism, in the light of questions raised here and elsewhere about the manner in which humans communicate knowledge about the world. The purpose of this rethinking is to highlight both the analytical and practical consequences of the epistemological assumptions that inform risk and crisis communication. It is to those epistemological frameworks in risk and crisis communication that we turn first.

MODERNIST EPISTEMOLOGIES OF RISK

The emergence of modernism as an intellectual paradigm is most often traced to the Enlightenment in 18th-century Europe, with the ascendance during that period of a faith in human reason's ability to perceive objectively and measure accurately an external world supposedly organized according to scientific laws. It was modernist thinking that codified the scientific method and more significantly the prevalence of positivism that finds its legacy in many contemporary studies of communication, including risk and crisis communication. As Deborah Lupton (1999) observed, this "modernist concept of risk" relies upon the premise that phenomena are, at bottom, "knowable" to the extent that the magnitude of their dangers and the probabilities of their occurrence are objective, measurable, and communicable via human discourse (pp. 6–7). While much communication research, particularly that associated with social scientific methods, does not explicitly dwell on its modernist foundations, these theoretical assumptions underlie virtually all empirical studies. In relying upon empiricist procedures of observation to gather data about the phenomenal world, statistical analyses of the probabilistic likelihood that phenomena will happen with a given regularity, and the general notion that language and other communication media are capable of adequately transmitting the resulting knowledge (either to other researchers or to the public), most risk and crisis communication research falls squarely into the modernist paradigm with its positivist epistemological orientation (Grabill & Simmons, 1998, p. 417). As we will see later, even many studies of risk and crisis communication that operate from an interpretivist or rhetorical methodology fit within the aforementioned modernist premises (see Heath & O'Hair, chapter 1, this volume).

Beyond methodology, Jeffrey Grabill and Michele Simmons (1998), identified two broad categories of risk communication scholarship differentiated by their respective attitudes toward public participation in the evaluation of dangers: the "technocratic approach," in which communication about risk is a "one-way flow of technical information from 'experts' to the public" (p. 421); and a loosely related group of "negotiated approaches," where public participation allows two-way communication about risk with the assumption that all parties can be made to argue rationally about the nature of risks and appropriate responses to them (pp. 422–423). Several examples of each approach are discussed below in order to demonstrate that, despite the differences in method, theory, object of analysis, and orientation to the public (technocratic or negotiated), all share common epistemological assumptions about the nature of our risky world and humans' ability to acquire knowledge of it.

Variations on a Technocratic Theme

Although research on risk communication sometimes declines to foreground its epistemological premises, assumptions about the nature of the world and our knowledge of it are nonetheless embedded in all such work. Lupton (1999) describes the ontological and epistemological bases of the positivist model of risk research, where "[r]isks...are pre-existing in nature and in principle are able to be identified through scientific measurement and calculation and controlled using this knowledge" (p. 18). In addition to enabling the description and specification of hazards, the positivist premise of a world of dangerous phenomena ascertainable with objective accuracy also provides the foundation for the technocratic approach to risk communication. Within the technocratic framework, cognitive science and psychometrics are mobilized to contrast "'objective facts' of risk" to the "subjective understanding of lay people" in that public knowledge of dangers can be more or less "accurate" (Lupton, 1999, p. 19). Thus, technocratic risk communication scholarship often characterizes the failure of risk communication efforts as a lack of audience understanding or a rejection of messages from experts, despite the objective truth of that expert knowledge (Grabill & Simmons, 1998, p. 416). In this way, much of the risk communication literature, as Vincent Covello (1992) noted, focuses on the goal of "communicating risk information effectively" (p. 360) given a variety of "characteristics and limitations of the public in evaluating and interpreting risk information" (p. 366).

The contrast between a "truthful" expert assessment of hazards and the public's supposed misunderstanding of these objective truths about risk hearkens back to Paul Slovic's (1987) archetypal research claiming to show that people's "difficulties in understanding probabilistic processes... causes...risks to be misjudged" (p. 281). Because the public is not significantly trained to interpret scientific data or understand the relative meaning of myriad statistical measures, the primary problem faced in risk communication is the public's inability to understand the "true" nature of assorted risks. Lay people misjudge the comparable value of large numbers, have difficulty comparing hazards of differing magnitude and probability, and too often let emotion prevail over reason in their evaluation of risks. One example of this noted by Slovic is that the most significant factor in "lay people's risk perceptions" are "dread risks," those dangers that are "uncontrollable," "fatal" or "catastrophic," and to which exposure is involuntary or "inequitable" (p. 283). Dread risks tend to encompass hazardous phenomena of enormous magnitude, events such as terrorism, nuclear war, and certain diseases, and Slovic's point is that the public tends to fear these hazards to a degree disproportionate with their probability of occurrence and thus their risk in relation to more mundane threats; even if the extent of their magnitude is potentially tremendous, the infinitesimally low likelihood that an individual will experience one of these dreaded harms, in comparison to risks that are statistically much more common (e.g., automobile accidents, food poisoning, heart disease from poor diet), leads many risk communication researchers to conclude that the problem is one of public cognitive shortcomings.

Katherine Rowan (1991), for example, identified a series of "obstacles" to effective risk communication and has promoted various problem-solving strategies for overcoming these difficulties. One possible explanation for the public's failure to correctly apprehend the nature of a given threat and act according to official risk management procedures is a "lack of clarity...about what action to take" that can be solved "by mass warnings suggesting specific behaviors" (p. 323). The metaphor of clarity is significant here, as it belies an epistemological commitment in the study's operative vision of communication. Here, communication is implicitly posited within a relatively simply "channel" or "conduit" model, where the act of transmitting information is a process that, done correctly, can serve as a kind of transparent window between sender and receiver. The communication of information about risks may be obscured by confusing technical jargon, contradictory instructions, or vague language, but the possibility is held out for a pure exchange of knowledge about hazard if the warnings would include greater specificity about what to do in the event of a crisis. While Rowan did not directly address the epistemology driving the determination of what information about hazards and ameliorative behaviors the messages should contain, the epistemic framework can be inferred not only from the absence of such a discussion (presuming in Lupton's terms an "objective fact of risk") but also the implicit conduit model of communication. To the extent that the communication of risk information to the public need only be "clarified," the experts assessing risks are presumed to have unmediated access to the reality of hazardous phenomena despite their need to describe that reality through linguistic and rhetorical devices.

A different problem identified by some risk communication scholars, the public's disinclination to trust the messages provided by government or industry experts about hazards, displays a similarly modernist epistemological orientation. For example, Katherine McComas (2003) juxtaposed public "skepticism" of government-supplied information to the "credibility" of expert sources of information on risks (p. 169). In doing so, McComas implied that skepticism, specifically a lack of belief or credence in the information handed over, is the problem, without questioning the adequacy of the initial determination of the nature of the risk itself. While the choice to focus on public attitudes rather than the evaluation of risk assessment cannot be considered a fault in the study, the consequences of this supposition regarding the experts' unmediated access to the reality of hazardous phenomena may nonetheless be significant. Rather than encouraging the participation of public audiences in critically evaluating the meaning of the danger facing them and the propriety of proposed responses to it, the effort simply to fix public skepticism suggests that the nature of the risk is not in question, and perhaps even more disconcerting, not to be questioned. Issues involving environmental risks have repeatedly demonstrated the lack of public focus on information pertaining to hazardous materials (Peterson & Franks, 2006).

Concerns about media misrepresentation of hazards are especially illustrative of this technocratic approach to risk communication. While there are many critically-oriented studies of media coverage of innumerable events where the goal of the research is to emancipate the public from institutional (i.e., expert) ideologies, a great deal of the risk communication scholarship in this area instead views the media as an obstacle to the communication of true information from government and industry experts to the general public about hazards. Two examples of the technocratic orientation to media criticism illustrate this point.

In examining journalism covering risks to public health and safety, Jim Willis and Albert Adelowo Okunade (1997) promised to assess the quality of the news media's representation of "the true nature of risks" (p. 3). The goal of this study is, in part, to help journalists "get closer to the truth of these health dangers" (p. ix). The ontological assumption about the nature of a risky world identified earlier by Lupton (1999), specifically that there is an objectively "true nature" to any given hazard, as common to positivist risk communication inquiry is clear. The magnitude of the harm possible from the hazard is apparently pre-given, as if one did not have to ascertain the impact of that harm in relation to an assortment of human values (e.g., life, property, rights, wealth), the relative weight of which are unavoidably subjective in their different significances to different peoples across regions, classes, and individual worldviews. The probability of the occurrence of these dangers is also presumably part of the "true nature of risks," where the likelihood that a certain dangerous event will happen can be determined statistically based on a history of similar events and an examination of current factors that might impinge on the possibility of the hazard's manifestation. Questions about the prospect of such objective knowledge of the truth of risks will be considered in the third section of this chapter, but for now it is sufficient to note that the epistemological assumptions of Willis and Okunade's argument conform to the positivist framework of risk communication discussed above. Willis and Okunade's book also displays an understanding of communication according to the conduit model covered earlier, in that they emphasize the problem of "noise" in the communication channel (p. 23), as if fully transparent communication of risk "truths" were possible but for flaws in the presentation of the message. Rather than considering the possibility that "noise" is endemic to human communication, in the way that Kenneth Burke (1969) described language use as always both a "selection" and "deflection of reality" (p. 59), Willis and Okunade imagined a perfectability to the communicative enterprise that relies again on a positivist and thoroughly arhetorical perspective on communication.

A second example of technocratic media criticism, the claim by Murray, Schwartz, and Lichter (2001) to provide a "demystification" (p. 2) of the media's representation of reality, operates from within an explicitly positivist framework despite the seemingly more interpretivist leanings of their goal of educating consumers in critical media literacy. They noted, for instance, that the mediated representation of reality includes multiple layers of interpretation and message transmission (p. 8), which would seem to demonstrate a sensitivity to the ways in which communication about an event unavoidably inflects the resulting message with the subjective elements of language choice, rhetorical style, emphasis on some features rather than others, and so forth. Yet the self-description of the authors asserted an objectivist confidence that their position as researchers "endow[s] us with a certain virtue, that of interested and observant outsiders, able to perceive and question the practices and assumptions of both science and journalism from an objective position that is sometimes referred to as the 'immaculate perception'" (p. 11). More disturbing than the dubious divinity of the study's insights is the notion that, even while questioning the pretensions of both scientists and the media, the researchers are themselves able to escape unproblematically the constraints of interpretation and communication to which the hapless scientists and journalists are bound. Again, the implications of this general faith in objectivity will be explored in depth later, but for now a couple points regarding the limitations of the epistemological orientation adopted by this particular study may suffice.

One conclusion reached by Murray et al. (2001) is that "media exaggeration of risk ultimately stems from activist exaggeration of risk" (p. 118). The description of media accounts of hazards as "exaggerated" reflects an epistemological assumption similar to that relied upon by Willis and Okunade (1997), specifically that there is an objectively true nature of the risk's magnitude and probability that are in some way distorted via "exaggeration." This language of "exaggeration" is particularly common in critiques of the news media and demonstrates the belief on the part of many researchers that an unmediated access to the reality of risk is not only possible but in fact has already been attained by them. The difficulty in positing a world knowable as essence is amply demonstrated by the complication wrought through the very language Murray et al. (2001) relied upon when describing the constructedness of media representations of crime via a simple distinction between the commission of crime and reports of crime (pp. 133–137). The sharp distinction between reality and its representation betrays the positivist epistemological conceit that assumes the pre-given nature of the material reality labeled by the authors as the occurrence of crime; for the authors, the material occurrence of crime precedes its discursive reporting. Yet, the nature of the phenomena *as crime* is a legal evaluation of representations of material reality (i.e., judgment by a jury that a reported phenomenal act constitutes a violation of the law); thus, the crime (in the sense of the *criminality* of the act, the act *as crime*) can never occur before the speech act that reports it to law enforcement authorities. While the reliance of the criminal justice system upon the speech acts of juries (and sometimes judges) for the determination of crimes makes this a particularly convenient example, it illustrates well that the descriptive practices of human communication may in fact shape the meaning of supposedly pre-discursive risky phenomena.

Other communication scholars have identified limitations of the positivist, technocratic approach to the study of risk and crisis communication. Sellnow, Seeger, and Ulmer (2002) noted in particular the difficulty of attempting to measure the probability of hazards, the occurrence of which does not correspond to the regularity of natural phenomena such as the rising of tides or chemical reactions. In their words, there is a "tension between the fundamental absence of predictability in complex, non-linear systems and the continued tendency of crisis managers, even in the face of chaos, to assume that traditional methods for prediction are adequate" (p. 287). Events such as a pandemic outbreak of avian flu, the detonation by Al Qaeda of a dirty bomb, or another release of anthrax-laced letters in U.S. mail represent exactly the kind of events in the non-linear system of our social world that comprise the hazards at the heart of contemporary risk communication, and yet positivist models in risk communication studies presume the occurrence of these types of hazards can be predicted with the same sort of precision claimed in the natural sciences. The result may be an inability on the part of risk communicators to address adequately what Sellnow et al. referred to as "cosmology episodes," where an audience's meaningful reality is disrupted by a crisis that precipitates "a collapse of sensemaking" because of an organization's inability to interpret adequately a unique situation according to the model of past events (p. 271). The same difficulty they note for crisis communication occurs with predictions regarding as-yet unrealized risks, such as nuclear terrorism, since there is no past analogue that could be used to measure with objective certainty the magnitude or probability of such a hazard. As a potential solution, Sellnow et al. (2002) concluded that "probabilistic statements, reflecting more realistically the lack of precise predictability in many crisis situations" while also "allowing stakeholders to make their own qualitative assessments" may be more useful in assisting citizens "to respond more effectively to the crisis" (p. 288). While this proposal seems to offer a useful alternative to the uncritical application of positivist methods to many risk phenomena, a rigorous genealogy of our knowledge of risk might still wonder about the epistemology presumed in "sensemaking" before the "collapse" precipitated by a crisis. In a fashion similar to the way that the language of "exaggeration" implies an objectively correct perception before hyperbole, so too does the notion of a "collapse" of interpretation imply some sort of pre-interpretive knowledge that was epistemically more pristine before the fall. The need for attention to the always already interpreted status of risks will be explored at length later in this chapter, but Sellnow et al.'s advocacy of risk communication that is inclusive of all stakeholders echoes another concern that has been raised regarding the technocratic impulse of much risk scholarship.

Rowan (1991) noted that the technical model of risk communication has been criticized for the elitism of its expertist orientation (p. 303). In framing risk communication as a dyadic relationship between a group of experts in possession of accurate knowledge about hazards and a lay public that is the passive recipient of such knowledge, failures of risk communication too easily become characterized as failures of the public audience to accept or understand the information proffered by the experts. As Barbara Reynolds and Matthew Seeger (2005) put it, "ineffective communication, poor trust, low credibility, or a case of misunderstanding" (p. 47) are often code for the public's refusal to adopt the technical view of a risk. Rather than allowing space for public input in the evaluation and comparison of risks in terms of individual and community values, the technocratic style of risk communication frequently sets itself in the paternalistic role of deciding what is best for us because we cannot be trusted to come to the "correct" conclusions ourselves. These concerns about the elitism of certain visions of risk communication have led some researchers to advocate a more democratic approach to the analysis of, and communication about, risk.

Democracy and the Public Negotiation of Risk

In contrast to the "mass-mediated hypodermic communication" evident in the technocratic approach to risk communication, some scholars have pursued the creation of opportunities for community-based decision making founded on dialogue about public hazards, a practice labeled by Gay and Heath (1995) as "risk democracy" (p. 212). As described above, such dialogue geared toward the negotiation of a consensus among experts and public stakeholders regarding risks has not been the goal of all risk communication. Recognizing the elitist implications of presuming that understandings of risk promulgated by government or industry officials need simply to be grafted onto a passive public audience, the expectation is that dialogue about risk would entail a dialectical determination of hazards and appropriate responses through the mutual participation of experts and the lay public. This pursuit of a theory and practice of risk communication that makes deliberative space for, in fact demands, the engagement of the public on such decisions would go a long way toward enabling more robust public debate about a host of issues from environmental pollution to foreign policy in the "war on terrorism." In fact, the present authors' rhetorical criticism of the epistemology of terrorism risk discourse must presume itself a part of the dialogue in such a "risk democracy" if this chapter hopes to inform the ongoing discourse about terrorist violence. Several other chapters in this volume join the call for engaged dialogue within the broader risk community.

It is also the present chapter's commitment to epistemological inquiry that leads us to perceive a still distinctly modernist tenor to the ontological and epistemological foundation on which Gay and Heath's (1995) risk democracy is built. Gay and Heath identified the problem of ineffective risk communication as one of epistemological inadequacy, labeled "misperceptions of risk," where the public's "cognitive limitations" leave "lay persons...at a disadvantage" vis-à-vis "experts" because of the public's "difficulty judging probabilities, making predictions,...coping with uncertainty" and "evaluating expertise" (p. 216). To the extent that limitations on the part of official "experts" are ruled out of possibility by the very terms of the problem, one modernist premise here is that the nature of the risk (the true perception of it rather than the "misperception") is pre-given in the phenomenal world. The goal is not so much to encourage a critical appraisal of the nature of the risk itself but rather to encourage public relations officials to talk *with* the public instead of *at* them. This element of public participation should not be minimized, as it is undoubtedly a prerequisite to the sort of specifically rhetorical public engagement we advocate here. It is important to note, however, the potential problems attendant to assuming *prima facie* that experts have no "cognitive limitations" (in this study of terrorism discourse, perhaps "rhetorical limitations") and are somehow outside the workings of language and rhetoric that ineluctably shape the meaning of the risky world around us. In characterizing the problem of undemocratic risk discourse as one of a cognitively unskilled public unable to comprehend the correct perception of risk, Gay and Heath may encourage risk communicators to presume uncritically that the public simply needs to be trained to understand what the experts were saying all along. As Grabill and Simmons (1998) worry, the promotion of public participation in decision making generally "asserts that the solution lies in educating the public and bringing public perception into conformity with scientific rationality." Risk communication thus maintains both its modernist and positivist impulses as simply "the transfer of information" (p. 418) between parties that happen to be more or less communicatively and cognitively savvy. The goal of risk democracy, then, is undeniably vital, but the question remains whether we can have an adequate dialogue about risk unless we also consider the ways in which "risks [are] constructed as social facts" (Lupton, 1999, p. 18) by the rhetoric through which they are described.

Grabill and Simmons (1998) have observed that many studies of risk communication are "arhetorical" (p. 416), but especially noteworthy is the way in which some positivist scholarship actively attempts to distance the communication practices it advocates from anything like the persuasion sought by rhetorical discourse. One researcher implies that risk communication does not always involve persuasion with the admonition that, "[o]ut of respect for the democratic process and individual rights of choice, risk communicators may not want to engage in persuasion constantly" (Rowan, 1991, p. 324). Reynolds and Seeger (2005) displayed a similar perspective, arguing that "[c]risis messages often are focused more directly on informing than persuading" (p. 48). The assumption in both of these cases is that individuals have at their disposal a mode of communicating about risk that does not involve trying to persuade public audiences that a world of risks *is* a certain way. The communicative option of informing implicitly acts as a conduit conveying meaning from sender to receiver, presuming not only an arhetorical presentation of the message by risk communicators but also an objective and self-evident nature of the hazard translated as pure information. While we will consider at greater length the implications of failing to account for the rhetorical work done by all risk discourse, we turn first to a couple of the existing studies of the rhetoric of risk.

Rhetorics of Risk: An Alternative to Modernist Epistemology?

One of the archetypal studies of risk rhetoric is an article by Farrell and Goodnight (1981) examining the technical and public rhetorics surrounding the 1979 accident at the Three Mile Island nuclear power plant. In that piece, the authors conclude that the "loss of public [rhetorical] competence combines with an anomaly of the natural world to thwart effective discourse" (p. 272). This article made substantial contributions to theories of the public and technical spheres in rhetorical studies, but the quote excerpted above illustrates an epistemological commitment in that study directly relevant to the analysis at hand. In emphasizing the source of the problem in the risk communication at Three Mile Island as one of inadequate communication competence, on the part of nuclear safety experts for their reliance on technical reasoning and on the part of the public for their inability to comprehend that reasoning, Farrell and Goodnight operated as if the meaning of the "anomaly" (the accident at the nuclear plant) as a particularly risky event is objective and not itself a rhetorical construct. Thus, they identified the "causes of" the rhetorical crisis surrounding the Three Mile Island nuclear power plant accident in the "systemic failures" of a "flawed discourse" that failed to help the various audiences for the disaster understand "all that was going on" (p. 273). In so doing, Farrell and Goodnight displayed an epistemological allegiance to the world as potentially fully present via adequate rhetorical discourse capable of communicating true knowledge in the production of public understanding of a hazard. Thus, while acknowledging the inevitable rhetoricity of risk communication, recognizing that it will always involve persuasion, Farrell and Goodnight's epistemology implies that the rhetorical presentation of risk information simply needs to be corrected as "effective discourse" so that it adequately conveys "all that was going on" *as it really was*. While this approach to the rhetoric of risk can provide useful insights about the ways in which certain rhetorical styles can affect an audience's reception of a message, Farrell and Goodnight's view of rhetoric as a mode of presentation does not help us to answer Lupton's (1999) question about how risks come to be considered social knowledge. Echoing Foucault's line of thinking, Preda (2005) argues that rhetoric cannot be thought of merely as the "form of the knowledge content," but rather must be understood as "a social practice producing knowledge" (p. 6).

Grabill and Simmons (1998) claimed to provide this sort of an epistemological genealogy of the idea of risk through a "'critical rhetoric' of risk communication" tracing the "epistemology within communicative processes" in order to undo "the separation of risk assessment from risk communication" (pp. 416–417). Paralleling in many ways Gay and Heath's (1995) articulation of "risk democracy," Grabill and Simmons called for risk communication consistent with "*participatory* democracy." In it, they imagine a process "that involves the public in fundamental ways at the earliest stages of the decision making process." Their description of this involvement, however, is confined to the public's "participation in producing the policy itself" (p. 429; italics in original), rather than from the initial identification, description, and evaluation of the hazard. It is in this vein that Grabill and Simmons emphasized the need for "usability testing" of risk communication on the grounds that citizens are "users" who "have important knowledge often excluded from decision making" (p. 432). Despite their notion of a "critical rhetoric" of risk, even this critical epistemology construes knowledge of hazards as objectively pre-given in the minds of public citizens rather than constructed and reconstructed by the rhetoric through which threats are discussed. Rather than pursuing a true genealogy of how risks come historically to acquire the status of public knowledge, Grabill and Simmons suggested that, with "the inclusion of user/citizen knowledge, such [risk decision] processes might also be [made] more 'intelligent' by including multiple perspectives" (p. 437). To a large degree, their proposal applies a view of rhetoric as epistemic, capable of producing objective knowledge, articulated by Cherwitz and Hikins (1983) in the notion that a "thorough understanding of a particular social phenomena can occur only when *all* relevant perspectives have been discovered, evaluated, and juxtaposed" (p. 266; italics in original). The specific difficulties with perspectivist rhetorical epistemology have been discussed at length elsewhere (Whitson & Poulakos, 1993), but the one of central concern here is the epistemological faith in the possibility of achieving an understanding simultaneously so "thorough" and uninflected by rhetoric that it could be considered "knowledge" in any objective sense. Despite its critical intent, the rhetorical perspective outlined by Grabill and Simmons reflects much of the same modernist epistemology we have traced in other strands of risk communication scholarship (e.g., community risk profiling, stakeholder analyses, systemic informatics, etc.).

What we see in common across these varying theoretical and methodological approaches to the study of risk is the similar treatment of the history of risky events along the lines of what Foucault referred to as commentary. All of these modernist versions of risk communication represent "attempt[s] to stabilize" meaning "for the record," despite the fact that the total informational picture about any hazardous phenomena is always "in flux" (Sauer, 2003, p. 67). What is needed is not necessarily a rejection of modernist analyses of risk communication, but rather a relentlessly critical genealogy of those constant fluctuations in the meaning of a given risk so that we can include in any study attention to the construction of what comes to be considered the facts of a risky world. This genealogy of the epistemology of risk will employ methods of rhetorical criticism, but with an eye to explaining how particular risks come to be persuasive *as* facts of the world rather than only why a particular rhetorical framing of pre-given facts does or does not move public audiences. As Beverly Sauer (2003) put it, "when individuals represent knowledge in new rhetorical forms, they see the world differently through the lens of new representations; they produce new knowledge and new understanding in the transformation" (p. 83). The next section of this chapter takes as an artifact the case of risk communication about biological terrorism, thought broadly as a component of the larger discourse of risks of terrorism in general, for the type of epistemological genealogy described above.

KNOWING BIOTERRORISM

Having traced, in the first section of this chapter, the modernist epistemology predominant in risk communication scholarship, this next section traces similarly modernist epistemological assumptions across what might be called a discourse of bioterrorism. Rather than taking a single or small group of discrete texts as the object of rhetorical criticism, this sense of "discourse" connotes an array of communicative artifacts that together can be said to comprise the discontinuous set of language practices that is our risk communication about biological terrorism. Foucault (1971/1972) himself noted the "heterogeneous ensembles of enunciations" (p. 234), which others would term "intertextuality," that comprise most, perhaps all, discourses. While it would be convenient for communication scholars if audiences relied upon only one measurable source of information about terrorism, it would be naïve for us to imagine that this is the case (O'Hair, Heath, Ayotte, & Ledlow, 2008; O'Hair & Heath, 2005). At the cognitive level, the post-structuralist concept of intertextuality seems to be an almost self-evident necessity when one tries to imagine a hermetically-sealed understanding of the post-September 11 reference to "nuclear terrorism" without the complication of memories of photographs of a nuclear mushroom cloud, perhaps the Hollywood film *The Sum of All Fears*, and, of course, the backdrop of 9/11. At the pragmatic level, it seems equally obvious that in addition to whatever official (governmental, industrial, etc.) messages are disseminated, there will inevitably be an assortment of competing messages from news and entertainment media, including potentially conflicting messages from other official sources (Miller, Matusitz, O'Hair, & Eckstein, 2008). The Centers for Disease Control and Prevention (CDC) acknowledge exactly this need for awareness of the breadth of risk communication in their introductory training text, *Crisis and Emergency Risk Communication* (CERC) (Reynolds, 2002). The CERC text notes that various experts, officials, and commentators will contribute to the public discourse about a crisis, although the extent of the discussion consists of warning that this added discourse may "sometimes contradict or misinterpret your messages" (p. 65).

In recognition of the intertextuality of bioterrorism discourse, we include in the analysis below several different textual artifacts. The CDC's *Crisis and Emergency Risk Communication* training manual (Reynolds, 2002) brings together the work of several risk communication scholars with an organization in clear proximity to U.S. federal government risk communication about bioterrorism. The Federal Emergency Management Agency (FEMA) developed a civilian training program, *Community Emergency Response Team* (CERT) (Human Technology Inc., 2003), that attempts to educate lay citizens in basic disaster response assistance ranging from first aid to light search-and-rescue; the participant training manual for CERT is incorporated in the present analysis as an application of risk communication. The CDC also initiated a risk communication program dubbed the "Pre-Event Message Development Project," which coordinates researchers at the University of Alabama-Birmingham, the University of California-Los Angeles, the University of Oklahoma, and Saint Louis University in developing "an armory of 'pre-event' message content for a range of terrorism agents and scenarios" (Vanderford, 2004, p. 193). We include a series of articles from the journal *Biosecurity and Bioterrorism: Biodefense Strategy, Practice, and Science*, which report on the CDC's "Pre-Event" study. Rounding out the texts for analysis are several examples of bioterrorism discourse found in the major national news media, including statements by U.S. government officials during and shortly after the bioterrorist dissemination of anthrax in U.S. mail during October and November 2001. Given both the intertextual nature of bioterrorism discourse and the focus in this chapter primarily upon theoretical questions, we do not claim that this is an exhaustive list of the messages comprising this discourse nor a comprehensive rhetorical criticism of any one of them. Instead, our selection of artifacts for analysis is meant to highlight a representative sample of especially prominent components of the discourse surrounding bioterrorism that are sufficient to illustrate key epistemological and rhetorical patterns.

To begin, across much of the talk and writing about the threat of bioterrorism there is a relatively consistent epistemological framework, one that presumes basic positivist tenets from the ontology of risk to empiricist methods for measuring it, and ultimately, then, the process of communicating about that risk. The purpose of tracing the predominance of positivist theory and methodology in discourse about bioterrorism risks is not simply to illustrate the epistemological critique offered in the first section of the chapter. In identifying the reliance of bioterror discourse on a host of claims to the objective "truth" of bioterrorist hazards, we seek to demonstrate the utility of this Foucauldian attention to the "internal rules" of what can be read as an historical discourse. As Foucault (1971/1972) intimated, we will find that the internal epistemological rules informing the risk communication about bioterrorism seek "mastery of another dimension of discourse: that of events and chance" (p. 220) in the present and future threat of terrorism. As suggested at the beginning of the chapter, we will see that the discourse about bioterrorism very often seeks to present a history of bioterror risks in the form of the "truth" about the risk.

It should be noted from the outset that the majority of risk communication about bioterrorism is founded on assumptions about the material "facts" of this hazard that together can be said to constitute the ontology of biological danger. In short, ontologically the danger of bioterrorism is presumed to be a pre-discursive phenomenon, the properties of which are objectively determinable. We should emphasize that this ontology is very much *assumed* in most of this discourse, discernable largely from the ways in which explicitly epistemological claims of knowledge regarding bioterror risks take as unproblematic the hazardous object of inquiry. It is in fact the ubiquitous hallmark of bioterrorism risk communication that the problems to be overcome are ineffective communication and imperfect knowledge of the risk, both of which necessarily imply the possibility of communicating transparently the objective truth about bioterrorist threats.

Crisis and Emergency Risk Communication (Reynolds, 2002) opens with the announcement that a key concern for risk and crisis communication is that the information provided by the media and other sources "may not be accurate" (p. 8). In this view, the nature of a given crisis can in fact be defined and described in objective terms, such that it makes sense to specify that the role of the crisis communication official "is to learn the facts about what happened…and to verify the true magnitude of the event" (p. 64; see also pp. 8, 81). Similarly, the *CERT Participant Manual* (Human Technology Inc., 2003) acknowledges that "[b]ystanders may be confused by the event. They may tend to exaggerate potential numbers or may not even remember the event accurately" (pp. 5–21). Wray, Kreuter, Jacobsen, Clements, and Evans (2004), while acknowledging the diversity of communication theories that can be brought to bear in analyzing the event of the 2001 anthrax attacks, highlighted the need for officials "to accurately convey risk level to appropriate audiences" (p. 235). All of these texts display the positivist impulse discussed in the first section that underlies the fundamentally epistemological contrast between a distorted or "exaggerated" representation and a risky reality that can be known in "true" and "accurate" terms.

A series of articles in the journal *Biosecurity and Bioterrorism* reporting on the initial findings from focus group research in the "Pre-Event Message Development Project" operates with identical epistemological premises. Writing about the need for truth in the context of a hypothetical terrorist event involving VX nerve gas, Henderson, Henderson, Raskob, and Boatright (2004) contrasted the need for "valid information on self-protection" to "barriers to communication" (p. 228). Wray and Jupka (2004) concluded that crisis communication in the event of a bioterrorist attack with plague must "describe general means of prevention of transmission," "provide a clear description of symptoms," identify when and how to seek medical care for diagnosis and treatment, and alert the public to "effective information sources" (p. 209). Becker's (2004) recommendations for effective risk communication about radiological terrorism focus on the inclusion of key health information content and the clarity of its presentation (p. 204). All share the ontological premise of an objective nature to the respective bioterror hazards, insofar as none of the articles interrogate the definition of bioterrorism threats, and all presume that the essence of these threats is both accessible to human knowing and can be transparently ("clear[ly]," "effective[ly]," without "barriers") communicated via language. None consider the rhetorical effects of what is assumed to be arhetorical scientific risk discourse dispensing the "true" nature of bioterrorism risks.

In only two of the articles about the "Pre-Event Message Development Project" do the authors explicitly reflect on the epistemological implications of their subject position as researchers; both articulate epistemologies eschewing any notion of subjective interpretation and proclaiming a scientifically disinterested "view from nowhere." Henderson et al. (2004) described the epistemological orientation of their study as adopting an "*emic* perspective," which "purposely takes the professional expert *away* from his or her perspective in order to avoid projection of potentially incorrect assumptions" by instead assessing threat awareness "in people's own words." Such an epistemology allegedly allows for "a panoramic window into the perceptions and behaviors of the public" (p. 225; italics in original). Hale, Dulek, and Hale (2005) asserted that their "qualitative research approach immersed the researchers in the data and encouraged their objectivity" (p. 116). The validity of such epistemologies within social scientific research is beyond the scope of this chapter, but this notion that phenomenal reality, of risks or people's perceptions of them, is immediately present to human knowledge has been the subject of extended critique from rhetorical and linguistic perspectives (Derrida, 1967/1973; Nietzsche 1873/1979; Whitson & Poulakos, 1993). The relevant point of these critiques for the purpose of the argument at hand is merely to establish a theoretical warrant for considering the ways in which the inevitably rhetorical elements of risk communication inflect what comes to be considered knowledge of bioterrorism. Before we examine some of the rhetoric at work in bioterrorism discourse, we first need to establish the absence, or inadequacy, of rhetorical perspectives in risk communication about bioterrorism. While self-reflexive attention to the rhetoric present in all risk communication is relatively infrequent in the literature, the explicit reliance on Aristotle in the *CERC* text (Reynolds, 2002) sets the stage for our later reflection upon the rhetorical implications of fear in risk communication.

The CDC's *CERC* manual (Reynolds, 2002) included a laudable effort to consider rhetoric in its training procedures, listing its indebtedness to Aristotle's *Rhetoric* among the bibliographic resources used in creating the text (pp. 29, 42). Ironically, despite Aristotle's admonitions regarding the importance of aesthetic form and linguistic style, in many ways he might be considered a rhetorical positivist. For Aristotle (trans. 1991), knowledge of objective "facts" was not only possible but the preferred grounds for rhetorical deliberation; the rhetorical techniques of metaphor and other tropes followed from the need to compensate for the epistemological "corruption" of some audiences (1404a). It is to a large degree this sense of rhetoric as a tool of "effective communication" capable of solving public "misunderstanding" that the *CERC* manual then relies upon for the extent of its rhetorical sensibility. While not explicitly labeled as a rhetorical concern, in setting out instructions on "how to communicate effectively in a crisis," the *CERC* manual recommends attention to the arrangement of main points by suggesting that speakers "put the good news in subordinate clauses" (Reynolds, 2002, p. 23) in order to reassure audiences after first demonstrating that a threat is being taken seriously. The text provides various tips for arranging presentations of emergency information during a crisis (pp. 48–53) as well as specific form guidelines for relating facts to the audience: make the message simple and accessible to non-experts, avoid jargon, etc. (p. 41). Without diminishing the value of Aristotelian insight to the persuasive power of rhetorical form, it is noteworthy that, in thinking of rhetoric as only a ripple in the communication conduit rather than a mechanism for constructing the social facts of risk, the *CERC* manual perpetuates the limitations of modernist rhetorical epistemology discussed earlier in this chapter. Especially illustrative of the need for greater rhetorical analysis in risk communication is the way in which the various texts comprising bioterrorism risk communication do or do not address the effect fear will have on public understandings of the nature of the risk posed by biological terrorism (McComas, 2006).

The *CERC* manual (Reynolds, 2002) observes that a terrorist event using weapons of mass destruction (WMD) will be especially fear-inspiring because of the general public aversion to chemicals and disease (p. 182), yet here and in the CDC's "Pre-Event Message Development Project," fear is considered only as an obstacle to effective communication. Fear becomes part of the "noise" obscuring the communication of the true facts about a given risk, rather than a component of the very meaning of the hazard. Henderson et al.'s (2004) study therefore attempts to "most closely simulate a real attack situation, where information is scarce at first and then accrues over time" (p. 226), but does so by simply "rolling out" increasingly more information about a VX gas attack, without, of course, the fear effects that would accompany a real event. Thus, the absence of risk information, or the presence of inaccurate risk information, is portrayed as the primary source of fear, as if the emotional fearsomeness can somehow be excised from the official, "accurate" information about bioterrorism. Wray and Jupka (2004) described how, in their study, a "hypothetical [plague bioterrorism] scenario elicited a rising level of fear over the course of the scenario, but this concern was tempered in many with added information" (pp. 212–213). While the authors acknowledge that a real bioterrorist attack would "cause even higher levels of panic" than were generated by the hypothetical scenario, they conclude based on focus group results that "the release of information can allay such fears" (p. 214). In a similar vein, Glik, Harrison, Davoudi, and Riopelle (2004) concluded their article on public risk perceptions of terrorism using botulinum toxin with a quotation from a focus group participant summarizing the expected effectiveness of accessible accurate information about the threat: "'if someone would have had the information when we were panicking, everybody wouldn't have panicked'" (p. 223). The audience's access to the "reality" of the risk supposedly increases with either the quantity or quality of arhetorical bioterror "information."

Even if we accept this narrow role of fear in bioterrorism discourse as simply an obstacle that competes with a hypothetically dispassionate account of "true knowledge" of the risk from government and industry officials, the public's reliance on the mass media for such information creates the prospect that official "truths" will be drowned amid a sea of sensationalist media appeals to the fear associated with bioterrorism. Research has recognized for some time that the news media are the public's primary source of information about terrorism in general (Dobkin, 1992; O'Hair & Heath, 2005; Vincent, 1992), and several of the studies linked to the "Pre-Event Message Development Project" acknowledge this same dominant role for the news media in providing public information about potential bioterrorism risks (Becker, 2004; Henderson et al., 2004; Wray & Jupka, 2004). At the same time, it has become a truism in risk communication research that media coverage of risks emphasizes dangers that are unusual, dramatic, and the exposure to which is involuntary, because these qualities are considered newsworthy, making informational messages about these hazards extremely visible in public discourse (O'Hair, 2005; Rowan, 1991). The media thus play up "drama, conflict, expert disagreements, and uncertainties" (Covello, 1992, p. 364) by devoting attention to "sensational material" and "potentially catastrophic effects" above more common, yet mundane, risks that actually harm more people (p. 365). If the news coverage of bioterrorism before and after the 2001 anthrax attacks in U.S. mail is any indication, media descriptions of the fear-inducing characteristics of biological terrorism may quickly overwhelm even official risk communication efforts. ABC news anchor Peter Jennings reported on September 18, 2001, that "[t]he secretary of defense [Rumsfeld] said this week…that a germ warfare attack anywhere could bring about loss of lives not in the thousands but in the millions" (Jennings, 2001). *Time* cited a report by the Congressional Office of Technology Assessment that "showed that a broad dispersal of anthrax spores over a major city could cause 3 million casualties. Another report estimated that a smallpox release could kill 40 million" (Gibbs, 2001, p. 54). Another *Time* article, like many media accounts, provided a hypothetical scenario to help the public organize their fears into a comprehensible and terrifying image: "a single suicidal terrorist spraying a few drops of smallpox virus—or a liquid solution of Ebola or even plague—in a crowded mall or into the ventilation system of a large building could cause untold harm" (Golden, 2001, p. 45). The hope for risk communication about bioterrorism sanitized of appeals to fear seems fruitless in the face of a media industry that has every incentive to fan the flames of terror in order to reap the profits of viewership. As will be argued in the next section, however, by far the most significant aspect of the fear surrounding the threat of bioterrorism is the rhetorical role such fear plays in constructing, rather than obscuring, the very reality of the hazard itself.

RISK *AS* RHETORIC: FEAR AND THE REALITY OF BIOTERRORISM

The modernist epistemology of risk communication, rhetorical or social scientific in method, displays a bifurcation of logic and emotion with the idea that logical inquiry is capable of discerning an objective knowledge regarding hazards that is then sometimes obscured by emotional appeals and other barriers to the "effective" and transparent communication of an unveiled reality of risk. Thus, Singer and Endreny (1993) lamented that news media coverage of hazards provides "often inadequate and sometimes inaccurate" information about reducing risks, with the result that "emotion, not reason" (p. 41) guides public reaction to threats. This sharp delineation between emotion and logic echoes the almost identical distinction posited by Aristotle between *pathos* and *logos* as different types of rhetorical appeals. As noted above, Aristotle's ideal schema of deliberation consisted purely of objective facts and so would have been evaluated on the basis of *logos* alone. And while contemporary social scientists might find themselves reluctant to admit a reliance upon rhetoric in their analyses of risk, Aristotle's sense that *logos* belonged to the realm of rhetoric rather than scientific reasoning lay in his stipulation that science dealt with absolute certainties while rhetoric's purview was probability. Since risk analysis and communication, however, are intimately intertwined with evaluations of probability, we might profitably consider some of the rhetorical implications of a commitment to the "reason" of risk probabilities before turning to the exploration of *pathos* in greater depth.

As Rowan (1991) has observed, the "technical" model of risk communication generally defines risk "as a multiplicative function of the severity of some hazard and its likelihood of occurrence (Risk = Severity × Likelihood)" (pp. 302–303). At first glance, the reductive simplicity of the risk equation makes some mathematical sense; zero likelihood of even an infinite impact would appropriately be assigned a nil risk value, and a true certainty about sufficiently unpleasant consequences would constitute a significant risk. Sauer (2003), for example, notes the reliance on "crude mathematical formulas" (p. 86) by miners who define risk as the magnitude of a hazard multiplied by the probability it will occur. The *CERT Participant Manual* (Human Technology Inc., 2003), under the topic of "Light Search and Rescue Operations," instructs students to "consider probabilities" in assessing a disaster situation by "considering what *will probably happen* and what *could happen*" (pp. 5–14, italics in original). These sorts of efforts illustrate Sauer's (2003) point that, whereas much of rhetorical theory, from classical to postmodern, has at its core a recognition of the intrinsic uncertainty that accompanies discursive representations of the phenomenal world, risk analysis often attempts to circumscribe that uncertainty by quantifying it (pp. 99–101). In Singer and Endreny's (1993) view, the news media may thus present a phenomenon that is a "probabilistic process" with a "spurious element of precision" (p. 14) in ways that amplify the perceived magnitude of a problem. Some risk communication scholars actually encourage the presentation of worst-case scenarios to the public. Renz (1992) recommended mobilizing the public to participate in decision making about risks by characterizing hazards "in worst case terms" through "high estimates when no close calculations have been done" (p. 16). Heath, Seshadri, and Lee (1998) recommended identifying worst-case scenarios in order "[t]o gain [public] trust" (p. 43) by demonstrating that officials are not hiding bad news. In any case, all of the instances above essentially result in the ultimate elision of any emphasis on the probabilistic nature of the risk by the logic of the risk equation itself; in worst-case interpretations, the risk equation becomes an enthymeme where the probability variable serves as an unstated premise. The "reality" of the risk may thus seem to derive from the implied certainty of occurrence conveyed by the worst-case scenario and rhetorically call into Being the meaning of the threat as immediately present (rather than as-yet only probabilistic) to audiences.

The risk equation is sometimes negotiated the other way as well, where probabilistic uncertainties are in fact explicitly acknowledged by risk communicators. The CDC's *CERC* text (Reynolds, 2002), for instance, emphasizes that effective communication requires officials to "[a]cknowledge uncertainty" (p. 23) to avoid artificially high expectations from public audiences. Doing so, however, does not necessarily guarantee the pristinely objective knowledge of a risk cognizant of its merely probable nature. As Singer and Endreny (1993) observed, news coverage of risks focuses almost exclusively on the magnitude of a hazard but far less on its probability of occurrence (p. 89). A particularly illustrative incident can be seen in a CNN broadcast on the threat of bioterrorism immediately before the rash of anthrax mailings. Joe Waeckerle of the American College of Emergency Physicians was explaining the low probability of a successful bioterrorist attack due to the multitude of technical and logistical obstacles when he was asked by CNN anchor Jonathan Karl to confirm that although the probability of occurrence was low, the consequences could be devastating should a biological attack occur. Waeckerle, relating the potential impact of attack by biological weapons, admitted that "there are studies that have demonstrated that it's equal to the consequences of a nuclear bomb" (Karl, Robertson, Garrett, Kelley, & Sesno, 2001). The problem arises with very small probabilities of infinitely large impact, as is the case with bioterrorism threats. In such cases, the evaluation of probability often effectively vanishes as the description of bioterrorism hazards seemingly infinite in magnitude makes even low risks rhetorically irrelevant when the mathematics of a low risk multiplied by its infinite magnitude still equals infinity. But the rhetoricity of this logic, namely the fundamentally rhetorical character of evaluations of probability, is obscured because the contingent element of probability is treated as a necessary (and already fulfilled) condition in the amplification of worst-case scenarios.

One of the weaknesses of the positivism underlying Aristotle's faith in an objective world of facts divorced from the rhetorical style with which they are described is his conclusion that the appeal to *logos* via reasoning through probabilities is entirely distinct from the rhetorical work done by appeals to the *pathos* of fear. We should consider instead the prospect that the fear associated with bioterrorism may operate in a mutually reinforcing fashion with logical appeals to probabilistic risk analysis, where fear functions to magnify the values associated with variables in the logical reasoning. Even without exaggeration on the part of the news media or foreign policy officials, the emotive, fearsome magnitude of the impact of biological weapons may come to define the threat itself, such that the emotional dread and horror associated with WMD overwhelm traditional evaluations of probability in public risk perceptions (Stern, 1999). Henderson et al. (2004) acknowledged that the public fears chemical terrorism regardless of objective measures of an agent's biochemistry, but this point is articulated only in the author's admonition to judge the impact of an attack on more than "mortality potential alone" (p. 225). A rethinking of Aristotle's definition of fear from beyond the modernist framework, taking the nature of the feared hazard not as pre-given but in fact as constructed in part by the rhetorical operation of fear, demonstrates the insights that might be gleaned from a rigorous rhetorical criticism of risk communication.

The desire for security is by definition not motivated simply by a recognition of one's vulnerability to harm but by the anticipation that one will in fact be harmed. This anticipation of harm is echoed in Aristotle's (trans. 1991) definition of fear as "a sort of pain or agitation derived from the imagination [*phantasia*] of a future destructive or painful evil" (1382a). His choice of the word "*phantasia*," an "appearance" that is "visualized" (Kennedy, in Aristotle, trans. 1991, p. 139, n. 43), is significant in the light of his subsequent claim that "even the signs of such things are causes of fear; for that which causes fear seems near at hand. (This is danger: an approach of something that causes fear)" (Aristotle, trans. 1991, 1382a) To the extent that the fearsomeness of their description is constitutive of the perceived "approach" that transforms material capability into "danger," representations of weapons of mass destruction as dangerous phenomena must be read rhetorically:

> If we accept the claim that the emotion of fear makes its cause "seem near at hand," descriptions of the material condition of "danger" transform *phantasia* into a rhetorical phantasmagoria. This is not to suggest that the destructive potential of a particular threat does not exist, but rather that rhetorical appeals to fear operate emotively like an optical illusion where the potential for destruction appears to rush toward the audience, growing disproportionately in magnitude instead of size. The "reality" identified by any (presumably frightening) analysis of "danger" in the form of international security threats, then, is always and already "approaching" the audience of such discourse. (Ayotte, 2002, p. 49; see also Derrida, 1982, pp. 315–316)

When the amplification of the fearsomeness of WMD deployment comes to represent the essence of the threat for the purposes of public deliberation, we may find that it is the rhetorical construction of the magnitude of destruction that frames the "reality" of the threat as immediate presence known by the audience. From a rhetorical perspective, we might therefore understand better why dangers "are judged as more frequent or likely if they are easy to imagine or recall" (Snyder & Blood, 1992, p. 39; see also Heath, Seshadri, & Lee, 1998, p. 39); the imagination of especially feared dangers works rhetorically to make the reality of the hazard seem immediately present to the audience of risk discourse. As Burgess (1973) concluded, the compelling power of crisis rhetoric comes from its transformation of probability into perceived certainty, where "certainty is present to the victim as an experience of imminence; and the experience of imminence of dangerous consequences *presents* those consequences in their fullness if not in detail" (p. 69; italics in original).

The impetus for this chapter's critique of the modernist epistemology of risk communication is that the unavoidably rhetorical aspects of risk discourse demonstrate the validity of Foucault's (1971/1972) warning that "we should not imagine that the world presents us with a legible face," and instead we "must conceive discourse as a violence we do to things" (p. 229). The positivist commitment to a risky world knowable as "accurate" "truth" fails to account for the way in which the intrinsically fearsome qualities of risks like bioterrorism will always and already shade any discursive efforts to communicate a supposedly objective nature of the hazard. While positivist approaches to risk communication may provide immensely important insights regarding public understandings of danger and appropriate policy responses, the analysis herein illustrates the necessity of incorporating a critically rhetorical sensibility as well that goes beyond existing modernist interpretations of Aristotelian rhetorical theory.

Implications

The primary purpose of this chapter has been to trace the epistemological implications of risk communication that fails to attend to the rhetorical elements of bioterrorist threats, and so it will be the task of future scholarship to further explore the political and pragmatic implications that follow from particular understandings of bioterrorism risks. As a beginning, however, we must note that the material consequences of ignoring the rhetorical nature of risk communication in the analysis of bioterrorism discourse are varied, diffuse, and significant. Perhaps one of the most obvious concerns is that, to the extent that any of the modernist risk communication studies examined throughout this chapter are correct in identifying problems with the public understanding of risk, failure to attend to one of the key factors, rhetoric, contributing to that understanding will leave analyses of risk inadequate to the task of improving public response to dangers like bioterrorism. A related concern is that the rhetoric of risk will be accepted uncritically as the objective reality of a dangerous world and so incite risk management policies and practices that are either inappropriate to addressing the hazard or significantly disadvantageous in some way (Willis & Okunade, 1997). While serious speculation regarding the rhetorical causes of the 2003 U.S. invasion of Iraq is beyond the scope of this chapter, the rampant amplification that marked official discourse about the ultimately non-existent Iraqi WMD threat can only be described as a profound failure of risk communication. The effects may also be tactical rather than strategic, confounding disaster management efforts, as Reynolds (2002) observes, when people distant from the danger respond with panic to risk discourse that they have more time to process than the victims immediately affected by a hazard (p. 25). Such was the case with an accident in Goiania, Brazil, in 1987 when a small amount of cesium 137 was discovered in an abandoned medical clinic and contaminated unknowing residents. Public fear following reporting of the event led people far away in other regions of the country to react as if they were in immediate proximity to the event, wasting scarce public health resources in the process (Becker, 2004). The immediacy and perceived narrowing of proximity of risks has demonstrated magnified effects in other contexts as well (O'Hair, 2004).

Absent an epistemology of risk that is both sensitive to and critical of the rhetoric framing biological threats in the contemporary world, we may find that counter-terrorism and bioterror mitigation policy are too often exercises in ideology as much as the protection of human life. Although diseases like anthrax, smallpox, and plague dominate worries about bioterror agents, avian flu, SARS, and mad cow disease capture news media headlines, and dramatic and gory "emerging viruses" like Ebola are highly publicized, the risk of contracting any of these diseases remains significantly lower than that for other infectious agents. The ideological work performed by risk communication about biological hazards leads Jessica Stern (2002/03) to note that unusual diseases like Ebola inspire lots of attention in popular culture, while real killers like malaria are generally absent from the public's consciousness (p. 105). Marshaled by a sense of urgency, exotic diseases terrify, in part, because they come from physical locations and boundaries of science that appear unfamiliar; yet, a risk epistemology that imagines that publicized representations of disease threats are socially and rhetorically neutral may fail to account for the extent to which classist and ethnocentric ideologies creep into public understandings of disease. Despite the fact that some diseases have afflicted particular populations for years, concern about a disease is often only heightened when it affects the affluent. Thus, diseases that afflict the affluent are labeled as "emerging" infectious diseases, while diseases that predominately afflict the poor are considered "tropical" diseases (Farmer, 1999). Objectivist epistemologies that imagine bioterrorism threats and disease risks as transparently existing in the world, available to unadulterated empirical perception and explanation, may fail to attend to economic, social, and political involvement in the definition and management of threats and diseases alike. Research funding into disease prevention and cures then mirrors the ideologically-inf(l)ected knowledge of these diseases provided by risk communicators.

While there can be little doubt of the need for significant funding for the prevention and mitigation of bioterrorism, a comparison of the money spent on bioterror defense to the dollars devoted to "tropical" diseases such as malaria reveals the truly disturbing material consequences that follow from an un-reflexive approach to bioterror risk communication. American casualties from bioterrorism consist entirely of those exposed to anthrax in the U.S. mail in October and November 2001, which ultimately resulted in 22 infections, 11 of which were the inhalation version of the disease. Five of the victims of inhalation anthrax died (CDC, 2007). Driven not only by those casualties but also the possible carnage of a perfectly dispersed anthrax attack over a major city or a contagious agent like smallpox released by terrorists, the U.S. budget for bio-defense spending in 2007 was brought $5.24 billion, which total U.S. spending on bio-defense since 2001 to $32 billion (Lam, Franco, & Schuler, 2006, p. 114). In contrast, over 350 million people are infected with malaria each year, the vast majority in sub-Saharan Africa, resulting in more than one million annual deaths (World Health Organization, 2005). U.S. funding to combat malaria in Africa through the "President's Malaria Initiative" was $30 million in 2006 (USAID, 2006). Millions die each year from preventable and treatable "tropical" diseases such as malaria, yet the specter of bioterrorism risks remains far more publicly compelling and firmly ensconced as the "truth" about serious disease risks currently facing humanity. Even allowing for the worst-case scenarios of bioterrorism involving contagious and highly lethal pathogens, the size of the disparity between bioterror and malaria efforts in the light of their respective death tolls suggests a strongly ideological influence in the American attitude toward catastrophic disease risks. The exact nature of that ideology is beyond the scope of this chapter—some might say ethnocentrism is to blame, others classism—but in any case our understanding of the urgency of this threat (and the funding priorities that follow) is guided by something other than merely the concern for human life. Rather than an objective empirical phenomenon awaiting measurement by positivist risk analysis, bioterrorism as a meaningful concept turns out to be always and already constructed by the rhetorical practices through which it is described and that knowledge disseminated. Nonetheless, very real material impacts follow from the varying knowledge of disease threats made available to us by risk communication about bioterrorism.

Obviously a public health threat very different from bioterrorism, the early history of HIV/AIDS offers a useful illustration of the ideological entailments of an un-reflexive epistemology of risk in seemingly scientific (i.e., positivist) discourse. Such discourse produced "truths," or "hard facts" about the virus, disease, and the implications of the virus in our society and the world. HIV/AIDS, stigmatized early on as a "gay" disease by the authority of science and technology, made future efforts to re-conceptualize the disease difficult. While there are several accounts of HIV/AIDS throughout the scientific community, few have studied the way that scientific knowledge about HIV/AIDS has been constructed through controversy and claims-making (Epstein, 1996). Scientific accounts of HIV/AIDS have historically begun with the *a priori* assumption that the scientific field generates knowledge about HIV/AIDS. For example, while empirical studies helped to spotlight the appearance of HIV/AIDS, the studies also spotlighted the gay community as a link to HIV/AIDS. The early construction and conception of HIV/AIDS as a "gay disease" within society is evident in the July 3, 1981, *New York Times* article that "broke the story" on HIV; the title of the article read, "Rare Cancer Seen in 41 Homosexuals" (MacKinnon, 1992). Of course, this single article was not solely responsible for the conceptualization of HIV/AIDS as a "gay disease." However, this article does serve as an exemplar of how objectivist epistemology communicated a type of "truth," one that linguistically forged the link between homosexuals and HIV/AIDS. Science and society embraced the representation of a "gay cancer," which later became known as gay-related immunodeficiency (GRID), despite the fact that intravenous drug users, hemophiliacs, and Haitian immigrants in the United States were also known to be infected with the virus (MacKinnon, 1992). On this rhetorical foundation, an active campaign to link homosexual males with the virus emerged.

The social demonization of HIV/AIDS as a "gay disease" allowed for the emergence of supposed moral implications to the virus. Grmek (1990) suggested that the "diabolical virus" has its origins in Africa (p. xi). Since the disease was first reported in Ugandan smugglers in Kasensero, in the Rakai district, the disease was thought to be divine retribution for sins committed, such as robbery and smuggling (Grmek, 1990). The belief that the HIV/AIDS virus is a divine plague resonated with similar historic claims made about syphilis, the bubonic plague, and leprosy. "Plague," as the principal metaphor by which the AIDS epidemic is understood, is significant because mass incidences of illness are understood as inflicted, not just endured (Sontag, 1989). In other words, if illness is seen as punishment by God for an "evil" or "immoral" lifestyle, then those who have the disease are being punished by illness for lack of morality. The meaning of the threat of HIV/AIDS quickly became inseparable from moral ideology.

The definite biography of HIV/AIDS, or bioterrorism, or any other disease risk, cannot be written until contemporary scientific research intersects with epistemological and rhetorical criticisms, thus preparing us to analyze disease in relation to questions of language, representation, interpretation, narrative, ideology, social, and intellectual differences (Treichler, 1999). Paul Farmer (1999) noted that a critical epistemology of emerging infectious diseases is still in the early stages of development. He continued, stating,

> [a] subtle and flexible understanding of emerging infections would be grounded in critical and reflexive study of how our knowledge develops. Units of analysis and key terms would be scrutinized and regularly redefined. These processes would include regular rethinking.... [T]hey would allow reflection on the limits of human knowledge. (p. 39)

Epistemological discussions about HIV/AIDS are grounded in empirical modalities of explanation, prediction, and control because HIV/AIDS is inherently connected to scientific and medical vernaculars of disease. However, we cannot overlook the usefulness of other theoretical and epistemological perspectives in building a body of knowledge that centers on saving lives. While there is no one theory best designed to discuss bioterrorism or disease risk, we must be critical of the theories used to discuss such risks as each theoretical perspective produces material consequences. A failure to recognize how the rhetoric of risk constructs our ideas of bioterrorism threats and disease risks severely limits our ability to engage contemporary discussions involving the communication of such risks. Thus, it is of particular interest to examine how the vehicle of rhetorical amplification educes unwarranted fears of "exotic" or "tropical" diseases while simultaneously diminishing the fear of preventable/treatable diseases and ignoring the material consequence of this under-(re)presentation. If risk communication about disease, whether or not derived from bioterrorism, is to address the needs of public health, applied communication scholars must be willing to reflect critically on the implications of the epistemological frameworks that we adopt in our analysis.

CONCLUSION

The epistemological and rhetorical criticisms advanced in this chapter beg the question of what sort of alternative practices can be incorporated into risk communication studies in order to both encourage and enable greater sensitivity to and respect for the rhetorical force of the language we rely upon to communicate the nature of our risky world. Part of the alternative is theoretical, specifically a commitment to thinking about risk communication outside of the modernist epistemological framework so commonly relied upon in methods ranging from the positivist to the rhetorical. While such theoretical movement might be sufficient for academic research, the government and industry officials involved in defining and communicating various risks to public audiences, along with members of the public themselves, must possess the rhetorical skills necessary to function as critical consumers and responsible producers of risk discourse. As Sauer (2003) argued, the rhetorical illiteracy of audiences is an additional complication of the inevitable epistemological inadequacy in available discourse about risks (p. 98). Consequently, "[d]ecision makers...need rhetorical knowledge to understand how audiences construct and negotiate meaning" (p. 16). Part of the solution of better risk communication would be to involve critically trained rhetoricians in the crafting of technical documentation about and communication of risk (Sauer, 2003). In this way, risk discourse itself could be made more accessible to the public and other stakeholders, not in the sense of epistemological transparency, but through self-conscious awareness of the inevitably rhetorical characteristics of that communication about risk.

For the general public, rhetorical literacy will only be possible with training in understanding the meanings of a range of discursive media beyond written text so that individuals can interpret and navigate the complexly intertextual rhetoric in a given risk or crisis environment (Sauer, 2003). Whether the medium of risk discourse is national television news, *Time* magazine, an Internet blog, or a conversation with a neighbor, members of the public must be educated and empowered not only about specific risks but also about how to evaluate critically the very nature of those risks *as* rhetoric through and through.

BIBLIOGRPAHY

Aristotle. (1991). *On rhetoric: A theory of civic discourse* (G. A. Kennedy, Trans.). New York: Oxford University Press.

Ayotte, K. J. (2002). The art of war: Aristotle on rhetoric and fear. In K. Boudouris and T. Poulakos (Eds.), *Studies in Greek philosophy: No. 40. The philosophy of communication: Vol. 2* (pp. 45–57). Athens: Ionia Publications.

Becker, S. M. (2004). Emergency communication and information issues in terrorist events involving radioactive materials. *Biosecurity and Bioterrorism: Biodefense Strategy, Practice, and Science, 2*(3), 195–207.

Burgess, P. G. (1973). Crisis rhetoric: Coercion vs. force. *Quarterly Journal of Speech, 59*(1), 61–73.

Burke, K. (1969). *A grammar of motives*. Berkeley: University of California Press.

Centers for Disease Control and Prevention. (2007, February). Anthrax. In *Epidemiology and prevention of vaccine-preventable diseases* (10th ed.). Waldorf, MD: Public Health Foundation. Retrieved March 7, 2007, from http://www.cdc.gov/nip/publications/pink/anthrax.pdf

Cherwitz, R. A., & Hikins J. W. (1983). Rhetorical perspectivism. *Quarterly Journal of Speech, 69(3),* 249–266.

Covello, V. T. (1992). Risk communication: An emerging area of health communication research. In S. A. Deetz (Ed.), *Communication Yearbook 15* (pp. 359–373). Newbury Park, CA: Sage.

Derrida, J. (1973). *Speech and phenomena and other essays on Husserl's theory of signs* (D. B. Allison, Trans.). Evanston, IL: Northwestern University Press. (Original work published 1967)

Derrida, J. (1982). Sending: On representation (P. Caws & M. A. Caws, Trans.). *Social Research, 49,* 294–326.

Dobkin, B. A. (1992). *Tales of terror: Television news and the construction of the terrorist threat*. New York: Praeger.

Epstein, S. (1996). *Impure science: AIDS, activism, and the politics of knowledge*. Berkeley: University of California Press.

Farmer, P. (1999). *Infections and inequalities: The modern plagues*. Berkeley: University of California Press.

Farrell, T. B., & Goodnight, G. T. (1981). Accidental rhetoric: The root metaphors of Three Mile Island. *Communication Monographs, 48(4),* 271–300.

Foucault, M. (1972). The discourse on language (R. Swyer, Trans.). In *The archaeology of knowledge and the discourse on language* (A. M. Sheridan Smith, Trans.) (pp. 215–227). New York: Pantheon Books. (Original work published 1971)

Gay, C. D., & Heath, R. L. (1995). Working with technical experts in the risk management infrastructure. *Public Relations Review, 21*(3), 211–224.

Gibbs, N. (2001, October 29). Homeland insecurity. *Time, 158,* 40–54.

Glik, D., Harrison, K., Davoudi, M., & Riopelle, D. (2004). Public perceptions and risk communication for botulism. *Biosecurity and Bioterrorism: Biodefense Strategy, Practice, and Science, 2(3),* 216–223.

Golden, F. (2001, November 5). What's next? *Time, 158,* 44–45.

Grabill, J. T., & Simmons, W. M. (1998). Toward a critical rhetoric of risk communication: Producing citizens and the role of technical communicators. *Technical Communication Quarterly, 7*(4), 415–441.

Grmek, M. D. (1990). *History of AIDS: Emergence and origin of a modern pandemic* (R. C. Maulitz & J. Duffin, Trans.). Princeton, NJ: Princeton University Press. (Original work published 1989)

Hale, J. E., Dulek, R. E., & Hale, D. P. (2005). Crisis response communication challenges: Building theory from qualitative data. *Journal of Business Communication, 42*(2), 112–134.

Heath, R. L., Seshadri, S., & Lee, J. (1998). Risk communication: A two-community analysis of proximity, dread, trust, involvement, uncertainty, openness/accessibility, and knowledge on support/opposition toward chemical companies. *Journal of Public Relations Research, 10(*1), 35–56.

Henderson, J. N., Henderson, L. C., Raskob, G. E., & Boatright, D. T. (2004). Chemical (VX) terrorist threat: Public knowledge, attitudes, and responses. *Biosecurity and Bioterrorism: Biodefense Strategy, Practice, and Science, 2*(3), 224–228.

Human Technology Inc. (2003, June). *Community emergency response team: Participant manual*. Washington, D.C.: U.S. Government. Retrieved January 14, 2007, from http://www.citizencorps.gov/cert/training_mat.shtm#CERTSM

Jennings, P. (2001, September 18). America fights back. *ABC News Special*. Retrieved January 15, 2007, from http://www.lexis-nexis.com

Karl, J., Robertson, N., Garrett, M., Kelley, D., & Sesno, F. (2001, September 29). America's new war: How far should government go to keep people safe? *CNN*. Retrieved January 15, 2007, from http://www.lexis-nexis.com

Lam, C., Franco, C., & Schuler, A. (2006). Billions for biodefense: Federal agency biodefense funding, FY2006–FY2007. *Biosecurity and Bioterrorism: Biodefense Strategy, Practice, and Science, 4*(2), 113–127.

Lupton, D. (1999). *Risk*. London: Routledge.

MacKinnon, K. (1992). *The politics of popular representation: Reagan, Thatcher, AIDS, and the movies*. London: Associated University Presses.
McComas, K. A. (2006). Defining moments in risk communication research: 1996–2005. *Journal of Health Communication, 11*, 75–91.
McComas, K. A. (2003). Citizen satisfaction with public meetings used for risk communication. *Journal of Applied Communication Research, 31*(2), 164–184.
Miller, C., Matusitz, J., O'Hair, H. D., & Eckstein, J. (2008). The role of communication and the media in terrorism. In H. D. O'Hair, R. L. Heath, K. J. Ayotte, & G. R. Ledlow (Eds.), *Terrorism: Communication and rhetorical perspectives.* Cresskill, NJ: Hampton Press.
Murray, D., Schwartz, J., & Lichter, S. R. (2001). *It ain't necessarily so: How media make and unmake the scientific picture of reality*. Lanham, MD: Rowman & Littlefield.
Nietzsche, F. (1979). On truth and lies in a nonmoral sense. In *Philosophy and truth: Selections from Nietzsche's notebooks of the early 1870's* (D. Breazeale, Ed. and Trans.) (pp. 79–97). Atlantic Highlands, NJ: Humanities Press International. (Original work published 1873)
O'Hair, D. (2005). Research statement before US Congress. *The role of social science research in disaster preparedness and response.* Hearing before the Subcommittee on Research. Committee on Science. House of Representatives. Washington, DC: Government Printing Office.
O'Hair, D. (2004). Measuring risk/crisis communication: Taking strategic assessment and program evaluation to the next level. *Risk and crisis communication: Building trust and explaining complexities when emergencies arise* (pp. 5–10). Washington, DC: Consortium of Social Science Associations.
O'Hair, H. D., Heath, R. L., Ayotte, K. J., & Ledlow, G. R. (2008). The communication and rhetoric of terrorism. In H. D. O'Hair, R. L. Heath, K. J. Ayotte, & G. R. Ledlow (Eds.), *Terrorism: Communication and rhetorical perspectives.* Cresskill, NJ: Hampton Press.
O'Hair, D., & Heath, R. (2005). Conceptualizing communication and terrorism. In D. O'Hair, R. Heath, & J. Ledlow (Eds.), *Community preparedness, deterrence, and response to terrorism: Communication and terrorism* (pp. 1–12). Westport, CT: Praeger.
Peterson, T. R., & Franks, R. R. (2006). Environmental conflict communication. In J. Oetzel & S. Ting-Toomey (Eds.), *The Sage handbook of conflict communication* (pp. 419–450). Thousand Oaks, CA: Sage.
Preda, A. (2005). *AIDS, rhetoric, and medical knowledge*. Cambridge: Cambridge University Press.
Renz, M. A. (1992). Communicating about environmental risk: An examination of a Minnesota county's communication on incineration. *Journal of Applied Communication Research, 20*(1), 1–18.
Reynolds, B. (2002, October). *Crisis and emergency risk communication* (V. F. Freimuth, A. Eberl-Lefko, L. Weinberg, E. Williams, C. R. Wood, & A. Zawislanski, Eds.). Atlanta, GA: Centers for Disease Control and Prevention. Retrieved July 26, 2006, from http://www.orau.gov/cdcynergy/erc/CERC%20Course%20 Materials/CERC_Book.pdf
Reynolds, B., & Seeger, M. W. (2005). Crisis and emergency risk communication as an integrative model. *Journal of Health Communication, 10,* 43–55.
Rowan, K. E. (1991). Goals, obstacles, and strategies in risk communication: A problem-solving approach to improving communication about risks. *Journal of Applied Communication Research, 19*(4), 300–329.
Rumsfeld, D. (2001, November 30). Secretary Rumsfeld interview with CNN Novak and Hunt. Retrieved January 14, 2007, from http://www.defenselink.mil/transcripts/2001/t11302001_t1130cnn.html
Sauer, B. (2003). *The rhetoric of risk: Technical documentation in hazardous environments.* Mahwah, NJ: Erlbaum.
Sellnow, T. L., Seeger, M. W., & Ulmer, R. R. (2002). Chaos theory, informational needs, and natural disasters. *Journal of Applied Communication Research, 30*(4), 269–292.
Singer, E., & Endreny, P. M. (1993). *Reporting on risk: How the mass media portray accidents, diseases, disasters, and other hazards*. New York: Russell Sage Foundation.
Slovic, P. (1987, April 17). Perceptions of risk. *Science, 236,* 280–285.
Snyder, L. B., & Blood, D. J. (1992). Caution: Alcohol advertising and the Surgeon General's alcohol warnings may have adverse effects on young adults. *Journal of Applied Communication Research, 20*(1), 37–53.
Sontag, S. (1989). *AIDS and its metaphors*. New York: Farrar, Straus and Giroux.
Stern, J. (1999). *The ultimate terrorists*. Cambridge, MA: Harvard University Press.
Stern, J. (2002/2003). Dreaded risks and the control of biological weapons. *International Security, 27(3),* 89–123.
Treichler, P. A. (1999). *How to have theory in an epidemic: Cultural chronicles of AIDS*. Durham, NC: Duke University Press.
United States Agency for International Development. (2006, June 8). The president's malaria initiative (PMI) (Fact Sheet). Washington, DC: USAID. Retrieved March 5, 2007, from http://www.usaid.gov/press/factsheets/2006/fs060608.html
Vanderford, M. L. (2004). Breaking new ground in WMD risk communication: The pre-event message development project. *Biosecurity and Bioterrorism: Biodefense Strategy, Practice, and Science,* 2(3), 193–194.

Vincent, R. C. (1992). CNN: Elites talking to elites. In H. Mowlana, G. Gerbner, & H. I. Schiller (Eds.), *Triumph of the image: The media's war in the Persian Gulf* (pp. 181–201). Boulder, CO: Westview Press.

Whitson, S., & Poulakos, J. (1993). Nietzsche and the aesthetics of rhetoric. *Quarterly Journal of Speech, 79*(2), 131–145.

Willis, J., & Okunade, A. A. (1997). *Reporting on risks: The practice and ethics of health and safety communication*. Westport, CT: Praeger.

World Health Organization. (2005). World malaria report 2005. Geneva: WHO. Retrieved March 5, 2007, from http://www.rollbackmalaria.org/wmr2005/pdf/WMReport_lr.pdf

Wray, R., & Jupka, K. (2004). What does the public want to know in the event of a terrorist attack using plague? *Biosecurity and Bioterrorism: Biodefense Strategy, Practice, and Science, 2*(3), 208–215.

Wray, R. J., Kreuter, M. W., Jacobsen, H., Clements, B., & Evans, R. G. (2004). Theoretical perspectives on public communication preparedness for terrorist attacks. *Family & Community Health, 27*(3), 232–241.

32

Magnifying Risk and Crisis: The Influence of Communication Technology on Contemporary Global Terrorism

Michael D. Bruce and H. Dan O'Hair
University of Oklahoma

In the 1990s, as the Cold War came to an end, many Westerners hailed what they saw as a new era of peace and prosperity being ushered in across the globe. After the fall of the Berlin Wall, during what Ikenberry (2004) referred to as the "American unipolar age," (p. 1), the United States appeared to stand as the world's only remaining "superpower." Subsequently, with the demise of the Soviet Union, mainstream Westerners, their perspectives shaped by decades of anti-Soviet popular and political rhetoric, suddenly deemed the world to be much less "scary." Concurrent discussions and/or ratification of various weapons treaties—i.e., the Nuclear Nonproliferation, Comprehensive Test Ban, and Chemical Weapons Convention treaties—underscored the sense among politicians, foreign policy analysts and the general public that the security threat posed by other states was on the decline (Matthews, 1997). Van Belle's (2000) study of foreign policy and international affairs provided academic support for the perception of the reduced threat, stating that the institutionalization of press freedoms, a more characteristic component of U.S. unipolar hegemony than the Cold War political cultures of either the Soviet Union or the United States, "shapes some aspects of foreign policy decisions in a consistent and empirically identifiable manner, most notably by limiting international conflict" (p. 9).

Thus the prevalent notion of "reduced security threat" was not only accompanied by, but actually correlated to a simultaneous "opening" of media systems and means of information access. In addition to Cold War thawing and a subsequent increase in press freedoms, the 1990s were marked by a celebration of the coming "information age." Satellite television, mobile telephones, 24-hour news channels and, most importantly, the Internet were widely endorsed for their potential to bring about widespread social, cultural and political change. "Convergence," the coming together of media technologies (satellite, fiber-optic, computer, telephony) that allow near real-time, asynchronous sorting and retrieval of audio, video, communication, and data, came to be a media industry buzzword. Recognizing that new decentralized technologies would allow anyone with access to such technologies to produce and distribute mediated communication, many proponents lauded digital technologies for their potential to free communication from government and corporate "gatekeepers" and thus to increase "democratization" around the globe. Such optimism, as described by Kalathil (2002), anticipated a process of "technologically enhanced Pax Americana, in which borders disintegrate and democratic values spread rapidly throughout a networked world" (p. 347).

Communication and media scholars also recognized the potential impact of new information technologies on global societies. However, their assessments of the widespread distribution of information and communication technologies were not so sanguine. In fact, Postman (1992) bemoaned the cultural hegemony of "technophiles," or those "who see only what new technologies can do and are incapable of imagining what they will undo" (p. 5). Even McLuhan (1962), known for having depicted a technologically-enabled "global village" characterized by a mutual sense of human responsibility, was highly ambivalent in his assessment of communication technologies: he also prophesied a global village of new conditions and thus "turmoil and chaos" which could invite "a mandate for war."[1]

As Innis pointed out in *Empire & Communications* (1972) and *The Bias of Communication* (1951), throughout history new communication technologies have undermined old bases of social power—for better or worse, depending on your position and/or perspective. Postman (1992) elaborates on Innis to state, "Every technology is both a burden and a blessing; not either-or, but this-and-that" (pp. 4–5). As Bauman (1999) reminded us of media in general, they do not cause culture, they are the tools of culture, and their implications rest in the way they are used. Mishra further pointed out that, "for each 'technology', there is an 'anti-technology'" produced, "making it a double edge weapon" (Mishra, 2003, p. 1). Thus all technologies, including media technologies, must be recognized as both emerging from and operating within an already-existent sphere of contested human processes and relations.

Hence, as explored in this chapter, rather than a "unipolar" age of ameliorated differences brought on by institutionalized press freedoms and Internet-leveled hierarchies and barriers, the 21st century heralded a more fragmented set of conflicts and actors than previously known in modern history. With the September 11, 2001, attacks on the World Trade Center in New York City and the Pentagon in Washington D.C., "superpower" metaphors were quickly replaced by an awareness of non-centralized, non-state actors with long-lists of grievances, particularly against the United States. That realization led to an immediate acknowledgement among scholars, analysts and pundits that new communication technologies—the nascent "golden child" of Western development, tied-aid and policy initiatives—had played a key role in increasing the risk of violence and terrorism against both state and civilian targets.

This chapter, therefore, examines how the communicative networks of the "information age" facilitate contemporary global terrorism, a risk system made up of decentralized actors ideologically and/or tactically webbed through new information technologies. After describing some potential actors and grievances associated with decentralized terrorist organizations, the chapter considers the role of mass communication in public opinion formation, the rising influence of non-state actors, the increasingly sophisticated media strategies employed by those with Middle Eastern interests, and the U.S. government's attempts to use media to counter the influence of terrorist organizations.

TERRORISM AND COMMUNICATION

Although, in retrospect, it was the coupled enthusiasm for U.S. superpower status and new communication technologies which led analysts and "experts" to underestimate the risk of violence and terrorism posed by technologically-enabled networks of non-state actors. Those same analysts and intelligence now concur that a unifying characteristic of the new breed of decentralized terrorist organizations of the 21st century is their sophisticated and pervasive use of information and communication technologies.

While most Westerners fixate on fundamentalist/Islamisist terrorism, or terrorism based on an underlying Islamic religious cause, Islamic identity itself is never a single-factor impetus for committing terrorist acts, nor, by a long shot, are all terrorists Muslim. Rather, recent history demonstrates how tactics and grievances are being shared among a broad set of dispersed groups with varying demographic profiles and divergent interests. For instance, the Movement for the Emancipation of the Niger Delta (MEND), operating in the Niger delta since 2006, provides an example of an emergent terrorist group sharing grievances with other resource- and geography-oriented groups; operating against multiple targets, including Western oil companies and the state of Nigeria; and being situated within multiple networks of alliances (Junger, 2007). This demonstrates how contemporary global terrorism comprises a dispersed set of risks of deliberate damage to life and property, and is being perpetrated by a variety of actors against a variety of targets.

If, as some scholars and analysts assert, terrorism is ultimately an act of symbolic communication (O'Hair, Heath, & Ludlow, 2005; Tuman, 2003), then it follows that emergent forms of terrorism reflect changing communicative modes. Whether face-to-face or facilitated by technology, communication is more than just the passing of words and information; it is the shared process through which individuals and groups construct and frame, or come to understand, their subjective world (Carey, 1988). In other words, it is via communication that "reality" is created, perceived and understood. Terrorism is an effort to produce certain realities, aims to impact symbolic construction by "deliberately exacting pain, suffering, and death on civilians for the purpose of accomplishing specific goals without regard for human rights and creating a climate of fear through violent means" (O'Hair et al., 2005, p. 12). Thus, as an attempt to construct social meaning—to achieve goals, to demonstrate power, to provoke fear—terrorism is primarily a communicative act.

As advancing communication technologies enable a broader construction of mutual realities, "terrorism" as a communicative process reflects these widening circles of shared meaning. However, as theoretically explained later in this chapter, mediated realities are both broad yet fragmented. While shared macro-media systems such as global television networks and satellite news create a broadly-shared symbolic framework, this macro-"reality" is nevertheless differentiated at the level of lived historical experience, as people actively decode media content according to their position in a variety of lived social realities and networks (Hall, 1980; Terranova, 2004). Similarly, on the ground experiences and networks strongly motivate the use of information and communication technologies (ICTs), such as the Internet and telephone, through which actors reciprocally contribute to the construction of broader social spheres. Contemporary global terrorism thus must be situated both in terms of the macro-symbolic framework within which it resonates and the "nuancing" channels which facilitate it, e.g., it must be situated in terms of the "global-local" nexus so salient within contemporary cultural theory.

Although fragmented and dispersed, those "local" grievances and social factors which most frequently generate a disposition toward or commitment to carrying out violent terrorist acts can be very generally summarized as: 1) occupation (Pape, 2003), which elicits resource, geography, representation, and/or identity based responses; 2) the emergence of an anti-state mode of fundamentalist Islam (Kramer, 2004, 2006), coupled with a "democracy deficit" in the originating nations of some terrorist actors (Gambill, 2003; Hass, 2004); and, 3) specific "single-issue" grievances among some non-government organizations, such as environmentalism, animal rights, and abortion (Smith 1998). Contemporary global terrorists use ICTs to project these particular grievances through the prism of global media culture, where it symbolically resonates as "terrorism"—a violent communication of power that attempts to produce fear for the purpose of achieving subjective goals.

Both Beck (1992) and Giddens (1999) remind us that risk is differentiated from hazard in the fact that risk incorporates an element of human assessment of probability. As Lerbinger (1997) defines risk, it is "the probability that death, injury, illness, property damage, and other undesirable consequences will stem from a hazard" (p. 267). Thus the presence of risk depends on the "likelihood" that a crisis will happen—with "likelihood" being based in human perception. Subsequently, risk must be situated within the various social, institutional and rhetorical dimensions affecting human perception.

"Terrorism," the risk of suffering deliberate damage, derives the bulk of its symbolic power through the mere presence of threat. Thus terrorism constitutes a risk system based on human perception. It therefore is also comprised of social, institutional, and rhetorical dimensions. As Beck

(1992) points out, in an age of global industrialization, these dimensions of risk are no longer local. In this way contemporary global terrorism—with its myriad of actors, grievances, methods and targets—demonstrates technological delocalization and dispersal of risk as a system.

PUBLIC OPINION

For much of this decade, the image of the United States has suffered in international public opinion. This negative image, often perpetuated by the media, is most prevalent in the Middle East. The University of Maryland/Zogby International 2006 Annual Arab Public Opinion Survey revealed that 72% of respondents considered the United States as "one of two countries that pose the biggest threat to them" (Zogby, 2007). In addition, findings from the The Pew Global Attitudes Project (Pew Research Center, 2006) revealed that less than 30% of respondents from predominantly Muslim countries had a favorable opinion of the United States. In the past when the U.S. government (as an official entity) has suffered from a negative image in other parts of the world, the image of the average American has remained positive. However, current trends in public opinion reveal that this "dual pattern" of opinion concerning the U.S. government and American citizens is disappearing (Nisbet, Nisbet, Scheufele, & Shanahan, 2004). In a study of young people from 12 different countries, DeFleur and DeFleur (2003) found "negative views of both the U.S. government and of ordinary Americans" (p. 19). Young people's responses were measured on a 12-item attitude scale, with questions ranging from American's generosity to sexuality. In particular, the responses of Middle Eastern teens revealed a generally negative attitude towards Americans on all 12 items in the scale. The negative opinion of Americans also carried over to other regions that were surveyed. Only teens from two of the twelve surveyed countries (Italy and Argentina) had a favorable opinion of Americans. A Pew Research Center (2006) survey found that positive opinions of the United States among most Europeans (excluding Great Britain) were less than 40%. A BBC poll found that of those polled in more than 25 countries, most had an unfavorable rating of the U.S. involvement in Iraq and the U.S. presence in the Middle East (Sullivan, 2007).

In his book, *Public Opinion*, Walter Lippman (1956) wrote of pictures in our heads and the world outside. His thesis was that man does not act on "certain knowledge, but on pictures made by himself or given to him" (p. 25), often by the media. Van Ginneken (2003) argued that it is the rise of mass media, particularly the penny press at the end of the 19th century, that established the concept of a mass (public) opinion. He added that people in "pre-modern, traditional, agrarian society were held together by permanent bonds between families, villages, and regions; between trades, classes and institutions" (p. 74). Thus, relational bonds served as the replacements for the first hand knowledge needed in opinion formation. With the increasing prevalence and influence of transnational media, the traditionally strong bonds of opinion formation and decision making—between family, tribes, and religion—can be increasingly co-opted by media or virtual bonds (Lippman, 1956; Moy & Pfau, 2000; Stivers, 1994; Van Ginneken, 2003). Research on media use during stressful events and isolation has found the media can serve "linking" and "social utility" functions that facilitate these virtual bonds (Dominick, 1996; Perez-Lugo, 2004).

Mass communication scholars use macro-level theories to examine the shaping of public opinion by the media. These theories: cultivation, agenda setting, framing, and priming examine how media use reconstructs decision-making and behavioral responses. Each of these theories attempts to explain how the media shape public opinion and personal conceptions of reality. These theories suggest that media alter opinion formation and decision making by making certain information more easily accessible, through the "frequency," "recency," and "distinctiveness" of media portrayals (Schrum, 2001, p. 98; see also Nisbet, et al., 2004; Sheafer, 2007). Iyengar (1990) referred to this process as the "accessibility bias." Thus, the amount of coverage and the frequency of attention given to a particular item can influence the process of opinion formation and decision making.

Numerous studies based on these theoretical constructs have been conducted on audiences in

North America, Europe and Asia to examine the media's influence. The general consensus is that the media does play a role in influencing public opinion and in altering individual's conceptions of reality. However, fewer theoretical studies have examined the influence of the new media in the Middle East. DeFleur and DeFleur (2003) argue that the negative attitudes of teens in their study were significantly influenced by repeated negative images of Americans in the entertainment media. Ayish (2002) studied how three Arab broadcasters, using three different patterns of political communication framed local, regional and international news, revealing an obsession with political news and a pan-Arab worldview. Nisbet, et al. (2004) examined the effect of TV news viewing on anti-American attitudes among Muslims. Their findings suggest that "TV news viewing is an important influence on anti-American attitudes" (p. 31).

Sageman (2004a, 2004b) argued that terrorism can't be understood through individual characteristics, rather it is based on group dynamics. While the numbers of individuals actively involved in jihad are reported to be relatively small, their support structure is said to be based on a large community of sympathizers and supporters. For example, a former head of the British MI5 intelligence service has estimated the number of sympathizers in Britain to be in excess of 100,000 (Waiting on al-Qaeda's, 2007). Thus, the media's influence in shaping public opinion and linking like-minded individuals are key aspects of community building.

"Community" constitutes an elemental first step in the construction of new media-based terrorist groups. Tönnies (2001) specifically conceived "community" as connoting something much more intimate than the res publica; he saw community as a "shared" symbolic space between individuals and the contested symbolic space of the social. While "all communities are imagined, given that their very production and reproduction always presumes the employment of a range of symbolic devices" (p. 149), until recently, large "imagined" communities revolved around the concept of "nation-ness" (Anderson, 1991; Slevin, 2002), or the "Westphalian system" of states (Mathews, 1997).

However, new communication technologies have facilitated "communities" of people with shared interests beyond national borders or shared national identities. Communication scholars often label these communities "virtual communities," focusing on computer-mediated communication (CMC) as the enabling technology. These formed communities can revolve around such diverse interests as Star Trek, sexual orientation, medical conditions, environmentalism, religion, or geo-political orientation. Frequently, individuals seek to co-produce virtual communities based on shared interests due to 1) their minority status within other broader communities; 2) the geographic dispersal of people with similar interests; or 3) the intensity of their feelings for the interest in which they seek a like-minded community (McQuail, 2000).

As ICTs enable the formation of "community" through processes of shared symbolic communication, community-formation simultaneously allows diverse grievances to come to resonate within a shared cultural milieu. New communication technologies allow humans to organize in new ways and "in situations where collective action was not possible before" (Rheingold 2002; p. xviii). With collective action, a community begins to function like a social movement, demonstrating political motivation to accomplish goals in response to a cause or set of grievances, and linking "for joint action without building a formal institutional presence" (Mathews, 1997, p. 52). Various labels allude to the novelty of symbolically-formed and technologically-enhanced social movements—"geopolitical tsunami" (Bollier, 2004); "power shift" (Mathews, 1997); "smart mobs" (Rheingold, 2002); and the "second superpower" (Moore, 2003) all reflect the empowering yet subversive potentials of political action based in ICTs.

RISE OF NON-STATE ACTORS

Multiple scholars (Hoffman, 2006; Smith, 1998; van Ginneken, 2003) recognize Greenpeace as an early organization/social movement that gained international attention for its grievances through strategic media use. Although Greenpeace did not undertake the more radical and violent actions of some later movements, such as Animal Liberation Front (ALF) and Earth First!, Greenpeace was one of the first environmental groups to employ "direct action" (Smith, 1998), or physical response packaged for the media, in its demands for environmental social justice.

Greenpeace, as a non-governmental organization (NGO), represents how media use can transform organizations from a structured hierarchy into a network based social movement. NGOs are typically organizations with a singular focus, cause or issue, which work locally to gain greater international relevance as they harness the power of the media. As the Aspen Group (Bollier, 2004) explained, NGOs operate in two roles: 1) that of partners with governments, or "useful proxies for helping them;" and 2) as independent players (p. 29). As independent players, NGOs can be perceived as "activist" or "extremist," and thus many activist NGOs promote "direct action" in pursuit of their goals (Smith, 1998). Some extremist NGOs promoting violence, threats, and/or destruction of property, are classified as single issue terrorists by the FBI.

Greenpeace gained notoriety during the 1980s for its actions protesting seal hunting, whaling, nuclear weapons testing and other activities (Smith, 1998; Van Ginnekin, 2003). As a pacifist movement, Greenpeace avoided the promotion of violence, but encouraged "peaceful interference" into activities it saw as objectionable. When French commandos sunk Greenpeace's ship, the Rainbow Warrior, in 1985, the organization seized the opportunity to raise media and public attention for its campaign against nuclear weapons testing. On the tenth anniversary of the incident, Greenpeace again staged protests in restricted waters near French nuclear weapons tests. French officials stormed the ship using tear gas. As television cameras recorded the events, the images were beamed worldwide via satellite news channels. By harnessing the power of satellite television, Greenpeace evolved into one of the largest and most successful global NGOs, gaining millions of members, acquiring multi-million dollar budgets, and ultimately obtaining policy changes, bans, and treaties that promoted its environmental agenda (Van Ginnekin, 2003).

While Greenpeace demonstrates the transformation of an NGO to the status of an international organization of political and cultural significance through strategic media use, the demonstrations accompanying the 1999 meetings of the World Trade Organization (WTO) in Seattle illustrate how ICTs enable a variety of actors to coalesce into a diffuse social movement. Moore (2003) explains that the Internet allows NGOs to "execute a kind of near-instantaneous, mass improvisation of activist initiatives" (p. 2). In what has been dubbed the "Battle of Seattle," protestors disrupted the WTO meetings by using cell-phones, "dynamically updated websites" and "swarming tactics" (Rheingold, 2002). Kidd (2002) described the WTO demonstrations as the "high-water mark of NGO advocacy networks" (p. 6). The protests of the WTO's neo-liberal globalist policies were orchestrated by more than a half-dozen NGOs and involved tens of thousands of demonstrators representing a variety of interests (Downing, 2001; Kidd, 2002).

In much the same way that international NGOs evolved as sources of soft power in the global community, al Qaeda and other like-minded movements have extended their influence and power through media use. A brief examination of al Qaeda's history illustrates the evolution of its communication strategies and the resulting structural changes from a structured hierarchical organization into a globally networked social movement.

Although the origins of al Qaeda's activities can be traced back to the waning moments of the Soviet-Afghan war, most Westerners outside the intelligence community were fairly unfamiliar with the terrorist organization until the late 1990s. Since September 11, 2001, however, Osama bin Laden and his jihadi terrorist organization al Qaeda have provided the face for contemporary global terrorism. Security apparati and the Western media have continually worked to link foiled terrorist plots and accomplished attacks back to al Qaeda, no matter how tenuous the connection. This reveals widespread confusion regarding both the organization and its influence. Al Qaeda provides an example of the impact of communication technologies on contemporary global terrorism, as patterns of communication transformed al Qaeda from an organization into a franchise, before fragmenting it into a highly dispersed social movement.

Al Qaeda is frequently referred to as a hierarchical organization controlling all Islamic terrorism through the activation of "sleeper cells." Conversely, some analysts suggest that al Qaeda is just a "brand name" for any anti-American terrorism (Kepel, 2002). What is clear is that there was a rapid increase in terrorism following the dispersal of Afghan freedom fighters back to their homelands in 1992 (Kepel, 2002). Al Qaeda is generally credited with having unified these "freedom fighters" and other disparate terrorist groups under a single ideological goal.

The source of unifying ideology for the original leaders of al Qaeda is found in fundamentalist Salafism. Derived from the Arabic word salaf, or "ancient ones," Salafists seek the restoration of "authentic Islam" (Sageman, 2004a, 2004b). Not all salafists promote the use of violence as a means to this end. However, some fundamentalist components of the movement have called for the use of struggle or jihad to create a utopian Islamic society. The original goal of these jihadists was the overthrow of "illegitimate" governments, principally those of Egypt and Saudi Arabia, and the re-establishment of an Islamic state. However, as the Salafist inspired leaders of al Qaeda realized they could not overthrow the "near enemy," because they were supported by the United States, the "far enemy," they changed course to focus on the far enemy (Sageman 2004b). In the meantime, the goal has grown to include the worldwide expansion of Islam under the leadership of a single caliph, or leader of an Islamic state. Working from a common ideological goal under the protection of the Taliban in Afghanistan, al Qaeda had operational and training bases from which they could manage the organization and prepare "spectacular" attacks on a global stage.

There is widespread debate surrounding the current state of the al Qaeda organization. In declassified sections of the National Intelligence Estimate (NIE), U.S. intelligence operatives assert that al Qaeda as an organization "will remain the most serious threat to the Homeland, while its central leadership continues to plan high-impact plots…" (National Intelligence Council, 2007). The assertion is based on evidence that al Qaeda is re-building operational capabilities in safe havens located within the Federally Administered Tribal Areas (FATA) of Pakistan. Other analysts suggest that consideration of al Qaeda as a structured organization in the post-Taliban era is misplaced. Internal al Qaeda documents revealed that even before 9/11, political infighting threatened the allegiance of cells to bin Laden and al Qaeda (Cullison, 2004). The subsequent invasion of Afghanistan further disrupted the structure of the organization. Al Qaeda's ability to communicate, raise money, train operatives, and direct a global "jihad" were hampered due to the lack of a home base. Counterterrorism experts point to this as an explanation for the lack of another "spectacular" attack in the United States (National Intelligence Council, 2007).

Al Qaeda as a "franchise" is comprised of jihadists from "disparate communities" who pledge allegiance to al Qaeda and collaborate with al Qaeda's central command, but maintain "semiautonomous" control of their own organization (Dabruzzi & Gartenstein-Ross, 2007). "Just as you can buy the franchise for, say, a Holiday Inn or an Intercontinental hotel, so you can adopt the principles of Osama bin Laden and set up your own deadly group, murdering those you identify as the enemies of the faith—and anyone else, of course, who happens to be passing at the time" (Simpson, 2005). Abu Musab al-Zarqawi represents an example of the al Qaeda franchise. His 2004 alliance between his Jama'at al-Tawhid wal-Jihad organization, which was conducting insurgent attacks in Iraq, and al Qaeda was the beginning of al Qaeda-Iraq. Dabruzzi and Gartenstein-Ross (2007) identified five other leaders who represent the al Qaeda franchise: Shaeikh Hassan Dahir Aweys in Somalia, Abu Ayyub al-Masri (al Zaraqawi's successor) in Iraq, Matiur Rehman and Faqir Mohammed in Pakistan, and Aris Sumarsono in Indonesia.

Al Qaeda as Social Movement

Sageman (2004a, 2004b) argues Islamic terrorism has become more like a social movement, not unlike supra-national NGOs, based on Muslim fundamentalist ideology. Corman and Schiefelbein (2006) refer to al Qaeda as an "ideal… replicated by relatively disconnected groups" (p. 4). Rather than "sleeper cells" these are groupings, with no formal names, consisting of unsatisfied Islamist elements, who easily advocated Jihadi doctrines and the broader strategy of global jihad" (Paz, 2005, p. 5). Particularly in the West, jihadi groups tend to be self-generating, with very little direct connection to al Qaeda outside of a shared rage and ideology. Sageman (2004b) says, "we often mistake the networked social movement for al Qaeda and vice versa" (p. 1).

Schofield (2007) and Knights (2005) outline three generations of jihadi terrorists: the first generation fought against the Soviets in Afghanistan; the second generation fought in the Caucasus, and Balkans; and the third generation is associated with the current al Qaeda cause. They explain that most current terrorists involved in the jihad against the West represent the third generation of recruits. There are multiple currents of explanation for the mobilization of young Arab's into jihad. Sageman (2004a, 2004b) performed social network analysis on the biographies of some 400 terrorists involved in the jihad against the United States, and discovered college-educated, professional men in their twenties, who have no criminal background, are not very religious, and are far removed from the fighting hotspots. Furthermore, many times the typical jihadi terrorist finds himself to be a social outcast in the society they are living in. This seems particularly true of displaced Muslims living in Europe.

Sageman traces the overwhelming cause of their entry into the jihadi movement back to loneliness (Telvick, 2005). "People want to believe that there are terror cells, awaiting awakening, all within a central terrorist organization, but the Islamic movement is simply people who want to belong..." (Schofield, 2007). Seeking friendship and a sense of community, they gravitate toward one of three connections to terrorism. These third generation terrorists are mobilized into the cause through relationships: they have a family member or friendship connection to the movement; they become involved with Mosques that teach radical Islam; and/or through the extensive use of new media. As Kalathil (2002) points out, new information technologies have "amplified the ideological power and cohesion of Diaspora communities" as they "project and reinforce traditional and nationalistic loyalties" (p. 348).

While bin Laden's direct control over the uprising may have diminished following the fall of the Taliban in Afghanistan, the supra-national network he helped bring to prominence is continuing to spread around the globe. The rapid spread of radical Islam is due in no small part to the emphasis he and other leaders of the movement placed on harnessing the power of communication technology. Thus, this latest incarnation of al Qaeda illustrates how contemporary global terrorism spreads through the creation of mediated-community among disaffected Muslims in the Diaspora. The mediated-community allows the marginalized to tap into the collective anti-Americanism in current international public opinion and express their particular grievances. As ICTs transform centralized organizations into franchises and then movements, these groups become dangerous and are no longer of use as client organizations.

INCREASINGLY SOPHISTICATED MEDIA STRATEGIES

We have already laid out our case that al Qaeda and the contemporary global terrorists are operating as networked social movements, rather than traditional insurgent/guerilla organizations of standing militants. These terrorist movements depend on and manipulate transnational media and information and communication technologies (Corman & Schiefelbein, 2006; Desanctis & Monge, 1999). These technologies of the information revolution—increasingly characterized as, inexpensive, ubiquitous, and asynchronous—are recognized by contemporary global terrorists as weapons of equal importance to guns and explosives (Coman & Schiefelbein, 2006; Hoffman, 2006). As Rheingold (2002) notes, the end-users of new technologies often utilize them "in ways often unimagined by inventors, vendors and regulators" (p. 3). This section identifies various new technologies and examines how groups bent on violence and terrorism are increasingly using them, both directly and indirectly, to accomplish their goals.

Satellite Television

Scholars who examine relationships between communication technologies and terrorism commonly refer to satellite television as "traditional" or "old" media (Hoffman, 2006), and relegate its influence on terrorists to a "second-class" status. The satellite TV networks' one-to-many delivery systems, content-controlling gatekeepers, and tendency to reflect rather than drive culture for the purpose of profit, are factors which limit satellite television's effectiveness for terrorists use, particularly in comparison with the relative media freedom allowed via the Internet.

However, many Westerners perceive Arab satellite TV to exercise influence over those who commit terrorist acts. As an example, since 9/11, the Al Jazeera Television Network—the flagship of pan-Arab satellite networks—has been continually denounced by U.S. government officials as a source of worldwide anti-Americanism, and occasionally, as a direct mouthpiece for terrorists. This sentiment now includes most pan-Arab TV networks. As Cal Thomas stated, the Bush team believes that the U.S. image abroad has "been distorted and the message concerning what America stands for is not getting out" (2005, p. A04) due to the actions of Arab satellite programmers. Thus, the Arab satellite networks are often blamed for the decline of U.S. status in the international marketplace of public opinion.

Various analysts argue that blaming the decline in U.S. public opinion status on Arab satellite television is misguided. Public opinion toward the U.S. has declined worldwide, including in Europe, where Arab satellite networks have limited reach and penetration (Rugh, 2006; Telhami, 2002b). In addition, analysts assert collective feelings of anger and mistrust are fueled by U.S. policies that are viewed as "empire building" and hypocritical. In particular, the Palestinian/Israeli issue and the U.S. presence in Iraq are cited as sources of "collective rage" that are reflected in Arab TV news (Telhami, 2002a, 2007).

Our purpose in this piece is not to advance arguments for either the powerful versus the limited effects of television. Rather, through example, we hope to illustrate how satellite networks can build cultural cohesion among disaffected and displaced groups in Diaspora. Due to the Western perspective described above, in addition to the much-publicized airing of bin Laden's messages by Al Jazeera television, this section focuses on Arab satellite television and its historical context.

Historically, Arab[2] media systems have been some of the most closed media systems in the world (Hafez, 2001). Therefore, press systems developed rather slowly compared to other regions. This can be partly explained by the oral nature of the Arab culture. Additionally, most Arab media was under state control. Media scholars use the label "authoritarian" to describe this type of press system.[3] Authoritarian press systems are defined as media systems that are "always subject to direct and implied control by the state or sovereign" (Hachten & Scotton, 2002, p. 149).

The oppressive political/media environment which operated in the region generated an atmosphere of media distrust (Wedeen, 1999). This is particularly true in nation states where the media follow a traditional government-controlled pattern, like Syria. According to Wedeen, in a cynical culture of "as-if" politics, people tend to have different ways of expressing doubts and disaffection, including jokes, conspiracies and espionage. Shared unbelief engenders a "mythical" public world in which these alternative conceptualizations of politics are communicated. Similar phenomena have been described in the repressed political cultures of pre-2003 Iraq and Saudi Arabia, as well as in less repressive societies like Egypt. Hence, patterns of press control have created discriminating media users. "A common viewing pattern is to flip between stations, comparing the coverage and perspectives, while keeping in mind the station's ideology" (Baylouny, 2005, p. 2). Furthermore, media accounts are weighed against the experience and opinion of family, religious and cultural influences. Therefore, cynicism and disbelief comprise a significant component of what is referred to as "Arab media culture."

However, Al Jazeera TV is largely viewed as the catalyst of significant media change in the Arab world. Launched in 1996 by the Emir of Qatar, Al Jazeera is an intended source of "uncensored" news from a pan-Arab perspective. With Al Jazeera's launch, an Arab news network freed from state controls was able to report the news from an Arab perspective across the bulk of the Middle East. In its wake, dozens of new networks were established in the region (some entirely devoted to news content, like Al Arabiya). According to Jamal Dajani (Museum of Television and Radio, 2007), there are at least 315 satellite networks operating in the Middle East. These networks reach increasingly larger Arab audiences due to the prevalence of inexpensive ($100 or less) satellite dishes and expansion of coverage into new territories. In so doing, these satellite networks blur borders and identity (Pintak, 2006b).

New satellite television media, Al Jazeera, Al Arabiya, Al Manar and others, no longer conform to a model of "authoritarian" press systems. However, Arab media is underpinned by increasingly varied combinations of state and private ownership structures, resulting in hybrid forms of authoritarian/commercial broadcasting (Rugh, 2004, 2007), and hybrid forms of censorship (Sakr, 2002). While it could be argued that these networks represent "revolutionary" media, the revolutionary press is really "a press of people who believe strongly that the government they live under does not serve their interests and should be overthrown. They believe they owe such a government no loyalty whatsoever" (Hacten & Scotten, 2002, p. 159). Although these media outlets are pushing previous boundaries of censorship and cultural "taboo," particularly Al Jazeera and Hezbollah's Al Manar, Arab media systems must still be situated within the cultural history of media censorship and "authoritarian" media systems within the Middle East.

Journalists within all media systems are culturally positioned (Pintak, 2006b). Culture or "standpoint" can lead to a subtle form of media self-censorship, or "likemindedness" among media producers. Likemindedness in the context of new Arab media manifests as a "pan-Arab" viewpoint concerned with Arab-related issues. Some scholars assert such a view dominates the mediated conversations on Arab satellite television. For instance, Hamzawy states that in the absence of true public opinion polls, Arab journalists with pan-Arabist and Islamist credos represent their own ideological views as those of the larger Arab culture (2005).

> Although it is debatable whether Al-Jazeera accurately conveys the opinion of the "Arab street" it has certainly been successful in casting itself as representative of that constituency's concerns and viewpoints, especially to mainstream U.S. audiences and policymakers (Kalathil, 2002, p. 352).

Two Al Jazeera programming studies assert there to be pan-Arab biases in the network's reporting. Ayish (2002) concluded that Al Jazeera's emphasis on the Palestinian question reveals a pan-Arab predisposition. Cherribi (2006), in his examination of Al Jazeera's news coverage and advertising during the height of the 2002 controversy over banning of headscarves (veils) in French public schools, concluded that Al Jazeera used the veil controversy to shape a "global Muslim identity, to mobilize a shared public opinion on this issue and construct an imagined Umma, a transnational Muslim community" (p. 121). Thus, through its promotion of cultural perspective and identity, Arab satellite television enables the necessary communal attachments to facilitate the formation of social movements (Sageman, 2004a, 2004b).

Instead of placing the pan-Arab television networks under the category of revolutionary press system, Ayish (2002) prefers to view them according to a liberal commercial pattern of political communication. He labels the distinguishing characteristics of this pattern as including an emphasis on professional journalism practices, sensationalism, and technically alluring formats in a commercial media business. While none of these networks are yet generating profits from advertising, most are still competing as commercial media, which requires garnering the largest audience possible. For pan-Arab networks, this means finding commonalities among Arabs, and programming to them (Telhami, 2004). Commercial pressures can result in hurried coverage and ethical dilemmas that arise in the hurry to be the first to cover breaking news and big events. Contemporary global terrorists can exploit this type of news environment, particularly if they are supplying the statements and footage of successful operations.

Al Jazeera English (originally Al Jazeera International), is the first English-language network based in the Middle East. Carried on more than 25 satellites, Al Jazeera English reaches into Europe, Asia, the Middle East, North America and Australia. However, the average U.S. viewer will have trouble finding the new network: there has been reluctance among major U.S. cable TV or direct broadcast satellite (DBS) providers to carry it. A majority of Americans do not believe the network should be available in the United States. A poll commissioned by Accuracy In Media (AIM) found that 53% of surveyed Americans opposed the launch of the new network (2006). While the network was originally conceived as a provider of "global perspectives" on the news, Pintak (2006a) claims that a management shakeup at the network brought about renewed emphasis in "Arab perspectives" and "non-Western" voices delivering the news.

Hence, political, religious, commercial, managerial and pan-Arab forces can result in programming which "resonates with [the audience's] pre-existing passions and opinions" (Telhami, 2004, p. 1). Pintak (2007, February) discussed this briefly when he explained the sudden spike in Al Manar's popularity during the 2006 Lebanon war (for the first time challenging Al Jazeera's viewership numbers) resulting in a shift in public opinion and "generating widespread support for Shiite Hizbullah among all Arabs, Sunni and Shia alike." We do not necessarily assert such opinions to be "wrong" or unjustified, or to, on their own, compel an individual toward terrorism. We merely seek to demonstrate the particular cultural framework for Arab satellite television in order to highlight how global media systems enable broadly-shared cultural perspectives and thus facilitate the diffusion of risk.

Such shared cultural resonance provides a channel for disaffection and political action, which sometimes turns violent. For instance, Al-Zawraa TV broadcasts the viewpoint of Sunni insurgents in Iraq. The station features video of insurgents training in camps, conducting operations against U.S. troops and Shia targets, and appeals for violence against Shia Iraqis and the Iraqi government. Some analysts suggest a link between the station and al Qaeda, although Al-Zawraa's creator Mishan al-Jabouri has denied any such links (Roggio, 2006). In the violent context of Baghdad, Al-Zawraa has "proved a hit with disaffected youth," (Howard, 2007, p. 1). As one young Iraqi said to a Western journalist, "I watch this channel every night…I don't like encouraging violence, but it is something unusual in the argument against the Americans." Hence satellite television can capitalize on shared grievances and exacerbate violent relations.

Cell Phones

The modern cell phone perpetuates risks of violence and terrorism. These new technology rich devices blur the lines between the traditional functions of phones, computers and media. The attractiveness of cellular telephones to terrorists is based on their potential use for clandestine communication, and as triggering devices (Knickerbocker, 2006). Cell phone use is shaped by both culture and economics (Castells Fernandez-Ardevol, Qui, & Sey, 2006), as demonstrated for instance by customs of "miss calling" in expensive cell phone markets; sectarian-based cellular provider-allegiance in Bosnia (Slatina, 2005); and suspicion of surveillance in the Middle East and among immigrants in the U.S. and U.K. Often culture and economics work in tandem to affect use, for instance, as familial allegiance drives heavy patterns of use among Latinos in the United States (Leonardi, 2003), providers have responded by offering special packages and pay-as-you-go options. In other markets, providers promote counter-surveillance devices.

Due to the accessibility and attractiveness of this technology, terrorists have turned to cell phones[4] and satellite phones for much of their internal and external communication functions. They utilize the technology to set up what Scarborough (2005) termed "mobile command-and-control centers." Although not impossible, it is difficult for authorities to track and locate terrorists through their use of wireless phone technology. Due to counter-surveillance technologies and practices, for instance removing the battery to avoid GPS detection, and/or changing SIM cards to deter tracing of calls, Knickerbocker (2006) asserted that wireless phones are the "tool of choice for staying ahead of government wiretappers."

In addition to voice communication, wireless phones are increasingly popular for text communication. SMS (Short Message Service) texting allows wireless phone users to send and receive short text messages via their phones. While not as popular in the United States, text messaging is extremely popular in many parts of the world including Europe, the Middle East and Southeast Asia. One reason for this popularity is the relatively inexpensive price of sending text messages relative to cellular phone calls. Another is the ease with which messages can be sent and forwarded to everyone in your handheld's phone book. Finally, with advancing cell phone technologies, cell phones are effectively being transformed into portable computers, data storage systems, and media production centers.

As an example of the social power of such technologies, Rheingold (2002) described how Filipinos protesting the Estrada Government were able to quickly mobilize crowds of demonstrators through text messages. In early 2001, Filipino protestors organized public demonstrations against President Estrada by using cell phones and text messages. After a few days of protests, the Estrada regime was toppled. Rheingold notes this is the "1st government in history to lose power to a smart mob" (p. 157).

Rheingold (2002) believed that the new third generation (3G) wireless phone technology has the potential to revolutionize social networking. 3G phones bring broadband Internet-like services, including audio/video, Web browsing, GPS (Global Positioning System) location tools, MMS text messaging (Multi-media Messaging Services), e-mail, paging, fax, videoconferencing and remote control capabilities to mobile users. The potential for these new wireless devices to be used in new imaginative ways is already being realized. As a result, Iran's telecommunication ministry announced it will attempt to filter SMS messages to prevent "immoral actions and social problems" (Reuters, 2007).

An even more direct and deadly use of cell phone technology is in improvised explosive devices (IED). The use of cell phones as a weapon may date as far back as 1996 when Israel's Shabak counter-intelligence service is believed to have assassinated Hamas bomb maker Yahya Ayyash with a cell phone bomb (Long, 2007). More recently, bomb makers have utilized cell phones as detonators on IEDs. Illustrating the speed at which terrorists can export their methods to a vast network of dispersed allies, the cell phone-detonated IED has been employed in attacks around the world. Cell phone detonated IEDs were used in terrorist bombings in London, Madrid, Bali, and in insurgent attacks on U.S. troops in Iraq. In one of the most highly coordinated and widespread terrorist attacks, a Bangladesh terrorist group set off more than 400 nearly-simultaneous explosions around the country on August 17, 2005. Debkafile (2006) reported that Jamaat el-Islami, a fundamentalist political group with links to al-Qaeda, carried out the attacks by triggering the IEDs via cell phones and the Internet. The June 2007, failed car bomb attacks in London also utilized cell phones as detonators. Journalists reported that the bombs made from propane tanks failed to detonate, although the phones had been called twice (Ross & Esposito, 2007).

Simultaneous to advancing technology and increased cell phone penetration rates, many U.S. cities are increasing the risk for cell phone attacks by expanding infrastructure for wireless phone capability in tunnels, transit systems and other "high-yield" targets. Adding more complexity to the wireless dilemma has been recent debate among telecommunication industry and public safety officials about shutting down wireless networks when there has been a terrorist attack or when officials feel that an attack is imminent (Searcey, 2005). "In ensuring that we have the ability to communicate in a crisis, we're ensuring that our adversary can do the same thing" (Savage, 2004, p. 1).

Computer-Mediated Communication

Computer-mediated communication (CMC) greatly facilitates the expansion of contemporary global terrorism as a risk system (Corman & Schiefelbein, 2006; Hoffman, 2006; Mishra, 2003;

Sageman, 2004a, 2004b; Weimann, 2004). The Internet provides a powerful communication system for building social moments, regardless of the geographic location of its members (Bollier, 2004). Sageman (2004a) thus asserts a single portrait of al Qaeda's Ramzi bin al-Shibh, in which bin al-Shibh is encircled by mobile phones and laptops in a Karachi hideout, summarizes the importance of communication technology to the terrorist movement. Thus, Hoffman (2006) described what he called a "global dialectic" being facilitated by the World Wide Web: "a situation in which awakening, awareness, activism, and radicalism can be stimulated at a local level and then mobilized into a wider process of dissent and protest" (Hoffman, 2006, p. 201).

Activist NGOs, organized crime and terrorist organizations are on the cutting edge of exploiting CMC to accomplish their aims. The first insurgent movement to utilize the Internet was the Zapatista National Liberation Army (EZLN) in Chiapas, Mexico in the early 1990s (Hoffman, 2006). Hoffman provides a detailed history of Internet growth among terrorist organizations. He argues that the U.S. invasion of Afghanistan, which forced al Qaeda to flee its operational bases, also forced the terrorists to depend more heavily on computer-mediated communication—so much so that the number of al Qaeda web sites grew from 1 to more than 50.

Researchers have identified multiple uses for ICTs by contemporary global terrorists. Mishra (2003) identifies five such purposes: command/control, perception management, intelligence gathering, financial support, and cyber terrorism. Weimann (2004) identified eight everyday uses of the Internet by terrorists: psychological warfare, publicity and propaganda, data mining, fundraising, recruitment and mobilization, networking, sharing information, and planning and coordination. These activities take place within high-tech web sites, chat rooms, message forums, weblogs, and social networking sites. Since many of the categories identified by Mishra and Weimann are overlapping, we categorize contemporary global terrorists' cyber presence in terms of (1) communication functions, which enhance the global social terrorist movement, including propaganda, recruiting, fundraising and public opinion formation; and (2) tactical functions, which directly increase the risk of violence and terrorism, such as training and instruction, operational planning, and cyber terrorism.

The video from the beheading of Nicholas Berg—posted across a range of web sites including some calling for and oriented toward terrorist attacks—provides a compelling example of how contemporary global terrorists use the Internet to intimidate their enemies and encourage their faithful. Labi (2006) stated that "with the slash of a knife, alZarqawi had pulled off the most successful online terrorist PR campaign ever" (p. 102). This is just one example of Internet-based publicity and propaganda by contemporary global terrorists. Research by Weimann (2004) indicated that modern terrorists rely on three rhetorical structures in their messages of propaganda: (1) the claim that violence is the only method available to an organization for advancing its agenda; (2) an attempt to discredit the legitimacy of the enemy, and (3) efforts at "image improvement" through an emphasis on the organization's nonviolent activities.

In addition to intimidating their enemies and improving their image, terrorist movements also work to propagate and legitimize their movements through the Internet (Corman & Schiefelbein, 2006). Describing the social value of the Internet for creating intimacy, Hamdy and Mobarak (2004) stated that the Internet is not only a newsroom, but it is also a living room-type of medium, where people can interact with others" (p. 249). Such online community building fosters contemporary global terrorism's shift from well-defined organizations into a decentralized social movement (Weimann, 2004). In the case of disaffected or marginalized migrants, virtual communities can fill a void stemming from lack of "local" or "physical" communities, lending appeal to terrorist ideologies or adoption of grievances via the web.

For the above reasons, terrorist organizations have become increasingly successful at propagating themselves as movement through ICTs. Online, for instance, Islamist-based terror groups draw numbers of disaffected Muslim youth, many from Europe or the United States, necessary to sustain a broad-based social movement (Labi, 2006). Terrorist movements do not really recruit, but rather they "mobilize" and "inspire" others to join. The following quotation describes how third generation "al Qaeda" terrorists are mobilized through Internet sites and chat rooms.

> Many may find it difficult to believe, but I was not very devout, though I did pray regularly. But enthusiasm and zeal filled the hearts of many young people, and unfortunately, I followed certain fatwas that were posted on the Internet. [These fatwas] call upon young people to wage jihad in certain regions. They tempt them [by describing' the great reward [they will receive], the status of the martyrs in Paradise and the virgins that await them [there]. These fatwas have great influence on young people who have no awareness or knowledge [that enables them] to examine them and verify their validity. (bin Hazam, 2006, p. 2)

In another example of the mobilization techniques found on Internet forums, a writer describes the joy of the volunteers that joined Abu Mus'ab al-Zarqawi, the commander of al Qaeda in Iraq. "I wish you could listen to what the returnees from Iraq say. Fighting the enemy became their best pleasures on earth… This notion became like a virus for them" (Paz, 2005). In addition to encouraging young Arabs to support the movement through physical action, many Internet sites also encourage visitors to support the movement through financial donations. The most obvious method is through the creation of links within the site for donating directly to the group.

While contemporary global terrorists have discovered the Internet's usefulness for communicating with both internal and external audiences, they have also discovered its significance for tactical operations. This use has grown more pronounced as contemporary global terrorism has become increasingly decentralized and as the ability to plan and train for operations in a training center, like those which existed in Afghanistan prior to the U.S. invasion, ebbs and flows.

ICT systems are neither inherently good nor bad, and besides the many productive uses to which they are put, these information technologies simultaneously facilitate the unsavory work as diverse groups such as gangsters, drug smugglers, and terrorists use these systems to gather intelligence for criminal and terrorist operations (Misrah 2003). This is particularly the case involving cyber terrorism, in which the Internet itself contains the bulk of information useful for those planning an attack (Kirk, 2003). The so-called "Manchester Manual" (n. d.), an al Qaeda training manual that circulated as early as the 1990s, encouraged within the organization intelligence gathering through public means stating that, "openly and without resorting to illegal means, it is possible to gather at least 80% of information about the enemy" (Information sources section, #1). The Internet facilitates these intelligence gathering operations, called "digital casing," while limiting the perpetrator's exposure to outsiders. Investigations by Internet security and counterterrorism experts have discovered numerous cases of digital casing in public sections of websites, as well as in private, secure areas of websites and computer networks. A highly publicized example of digital casing is "Moonlight Maze," the code name for an FBI investigation into data gathering intrusions into secure computer networks at the Pentagon, NASA and other government agencies (Kirk, 2003).

The Internet also is the primary means for communicating, planning, and coordinating attacks among members of highly dispersed decentralized networks. For instance, computer files discovered on al Qaeda computers revealed communication with operatives in Canada for gathering intelligence about Canadian and U.S. targets; as well as instructions sent to Richard Reid (the "shoe-bomber") for an intelligence gathering mission in Egypt and Israel (Cullison, 2004). Likewise, a foiled plot to attack Port Authority Trans-Hudson Corporation (PATH) trains under the Hudson River between New York and New Jersey revealed that those who planned the attack used the Internet to coordinate individuals located in Bosnia, Canada, Denmark and the United Arab Emirates (Nine/Eleven Finding Answers Foundation, 2007).

Tactical information on terrorist activities is distributed through a number of Internet methods, including forums, e-mail, and Internet file storage sites. According to Yehoshua (2007), Internet forums provide a much-used method for communicating among Islamist organizations, and with many existent examples of such activities. For instance, Labi (2006) describes how one second-generation Arab living in Europe and going by the Internet pseudonym "Irhabi007" used Internet forums to disseminate tactical information to the wider social movement. Web sites created by Irhabi007, including Muntada al-Ansar al-Islami (Forum of the Islamic Supporters), contained the Berg beheading video, and information on making explosives and becoming a sniper. In another well-known example, the document *Iraqi Jihad: Hopes and Risks*, which was distributed on Islamic web sites in 2004, outlined a plan for exporting terrorist operations to Europe (Paz, 2005). Within hours after the June 2007 failed attempts to detonate car bombs made from propane and butane bottles in London, ABC News posted links from web sites to a video that details how to construct bombs from propane and butane bottles. In a saturated media environment, there is no shortage of information on how to cause significant damage to life and property.

Many counterterrorism analysts emphasize the sustained risk of violence and terrorism through cyber terrorism or "electronic jihad" (the use of computer and Internet technology to attack electronic systems). Cyber attacks can range from the release of viruses that infect millions of personal computers, to direct attacks aimed at critical infrastructure targets. A February 27, 2002, letter, signed by 54 scientists and leaders, encouraged President George W. Bush to create a Cyber-Warfare defense program styled after the Manhattan Project: "Our nation is at grave risk of a cyber attack that could devastate the national psyche and economy more broadly than did the September 11th attack." The risk of cyber terrorism resonated at levels of political leadership, with the administration taking threats of cyber warfare more seriously when, according to Richard Clarke, former Director of Cyber Security at the White House, tactical information was discovered on al Qaeda computers recovered in Afghanistan. "What we found on Al Qaeda computers were that members of Al Qaeda were from outside the United States doing reconnaissance in the United States on our critical infrastructure" (Kirk, 2003). Critical infrastructure targets include energy, emergency services, banking and finance, transportation, water, defense and telecommunication. Subsequently, a White House report entitled The National Strategy To Secure Cyberspace gave the Department of Homeland Security a "central role" in securing the Internet (National Infrastructure Advisory Council, 2003).

Some experts on information systems and counter intelligence discount the potential effect of cyber terrorism, suggesting it is nothing more than a weapon of "mass annoyance." Those that support this position suggest that the Internet is more powerful in the hands of terrorists as an everyday tool for communication and virtual community building (Weimann, 2004; Becker, 2005).

EVOLVING AND CONGESTED MEDIA ENVIRONMENT

In addition to the hundreds of Arab satellite TV channels, radio stations, and Internet sites, international broadcasters contribute to the congested media environment of the Middle East. Historically, international broadcasting, both radio and TV, to the area has been intense and competitive. While accurate audience numbers for international broadcasters are difficult to locate, the BBC's Arabic-language radio service is widely recognized as the most listened to source of news produced by international broadcasters. Other popular services among Arabs have included French Arabic-language services through Radio France Internationale (RFI) and Radio Monte Carlo Moyen-Orient, and American radio services through Voice of America (VOA). There is also a trend of new satellite TV networks from international broadcasters into the Middle East. Germany's Deutsche Welle TV, France 24, and Russia TV Today are either commencing or increasing their Arabic language satellite television into the Middle East and Europe.

U.S. Public Diplomacy

Since 9/11, the Arab world has also become a "priority market" for American diplomacy. Public diplomacy is defined as

> the strategic planning and execution of informational, cultural and educational programming by an advocate country to create a public opinion environment in a target country or countries that will

> enable target country political leaders to make decisions that are supportive of advocate country's foreign policy objectives. (McClellan, 2004, p. 2)

Having been "chided" by the 9/11 commission for "ceding too much ground to Osama bin Laden in a 'war of ideas,'" the U.S. foreign policy establishment acquired a "new enthusiasm" for public diplomacy (Pein, 2005, p. 28). In an effort to stem the tide of distrust toward American actions and policies worldwide, and to improve what the U.S. administration perceives to be a "communication problem" surrounding its intentions and actions, President Bush pressed the Under-Secretary of State for Public Diplomacy and Public Affairs to improve U.S. public diplomacy efforts. This office takes responsibility for managing the U.S. image overseas, including in the Arab world. The task is a formidable one. As Deluca points out, the "challenge is to persuade a world cynical about spin that the U.S. is not just pushing good news stories but is being straightforward; and explaining policies many will not like" (2005, p. 17).

The Broadcasting Board of Governors (BBG), an independent, autonomous entity that reports to the State Department, bears responsibility for all international broadcasting on behalf of the U.S. government. The BBG, through its various organizations, broadcasts in more than 44 different languages to more than 100 markets. The BBG has in recent years prioritized reaching Arab markets with its message (see Table 32.1). A report from the Government Accountability Office (GAO)[5] on the public diplomacy initiatives of the U.S. State Department and Broadcasting Board of Governors highlights how U.S. public diplomacy resources are shifting toward Muslim-majority countries (2004). Reallocations of resources to Arab- and Muslim-targeted media began in early 2002, and include the Voice of America (VOA), Radio Sawa, Radio Farda and Alhurra TV.

David Jackson, Director of VOA, described the international broadcasting entity "as the world's oldest and largest" (Jackson, 2006). Currently, VOA broadcasts in 44 languages (down from more than 60 in the 1990s) to an estimated weekly audience of 120 million. In recent years, VOA has been "redefined" to maximize its reach into new high priority markets—President Bush's "war-on-terror" regions. Redefinition has included an emphasis in new languages, as for instance, broadcasts in Farsi into Iran have increased to four hours a day. VOA broadcasts in Afghanistan can now be heard in the native languages of Dari and Pashto.

Radio Sawa (Arabic for "together") began broadcasting to Arab audiences in 2002 as a 24-hour, 7-day-a-week Arabic radio network. Sawa can be heard on FM stations leased by the BBG from northwest Africa to Iraq. Programming on Radio Sawa is a mix of Arab and Western "pop" music meant to draw in listeners. Then, having acquired an audience, Radio Sawa also delivers information. Mouafac Harb, news director for sister television station Alhurra, which shares news content with Sawa, describes how Radio Sawa is a unique enterprise in the region: "We offer two news stops every hour, giving up-to-date, objective and accurate information. This is something new for our listeners—fast-paced, concise news bulletins that go straight to the point" (Silverman, 2002, p. 1).

TABLE 32.1
Matrix of U.S. Public Diplomacy Networks and Programming Content

	Alhurra	*Radio Sawa*	*Radio Farda*	*Voice of America*
Format	TV	Radio/Web	Radio/Web	Radio/TV/Web
Language(s)	Arabic	Arabic	Farsi	44 languages
Programming	News Entertainment Sports	Pop music News	Pop music News	News Information Music
Web content	Schedule	Schedule Streaming audio	Schedule Streaming audio	Information Schedule Audio/Video

Radio Farda (Persian for "tomorrow") began broadcasting into Iran on December 19, 2002. The station is a joint effort between Radio Free Europe/Radio Liberty and VOA. Like Sawa, Radio Farda targets a young Iranian audience. The station broadcasts 24-hours, 7-days-a-week using shortwave, AM, satellite and the Internet. Programming is a mix of pop music, news, and commentary in Farsi.

Alhurra Television beams Arabic language programming to the Middle East via satellite from the outskirts of the U.S. Capitol beltway, in Springfield, Virginia. Like Radio Sawa and Rado Farda, Alhurra targets a young (under 30 years of age) general audience. Besides news, programming includes programming on fitness, fashion, entertainment, science and technology, and sports. In April 2004, the BBG launched a second TV service, Alhurra-Iraq, with programming designed specifically for an Iraqi audience. "The Bush administration views satellite television as a so-called soft-power tool for building good will toward the United States" (Morgan, 2005). Thus, Alhurra was launched in order to counter the influence of pan-Arab satellite networks (al Jazerra and al Arabiaya).

Measuring Success

Before Radio Sawa, Radio Farda and Alhurra TV had even made their broadcasting debuts, widespread speculation circulated in the United States and overseas concerning the potential effectiveness of these public diplomacy efforts. Upon a few years of operation, the track record of this broadcast-oriented public diplomacy effort is widely recognized as leaving much to be desired. By most accounts, the BBG has failed to significantly improve public opinion toward the United States in the Middle East. Some critics go so far as to argue that BBG broadcasting efforts actually elicit the opposite effect, that they diminish goodwill toward the United States. Whether or not this is an overstatement, audience research indicates that these broadcasting efforts do little to improve public opinion and thus reduce the risk of violence and terrorism.

Officially, BBG officials proclaim that both Radio Sawa and Alhurra are success stories in international broadcasting. When asked about the stations, officials tend to focus on audience size (estimated to be 40 million to 50 million per week), the popularity of programming, and reliability of information. However, William Rugh, a former U.S. Foreign Service Officer and long-time analyst of Arab media, is one of the leading critics of the Broadcasting Board of Governors' public diplomacy efforts in the Middle East. Rugh asserts that the BBG data is "accurate, but misleading" (2005, p. 4), due to inaccurate research methodologies applied by the BBG to audience research. Rather than asking respondents if they have watched Alhurra in the last week, Rugh argues that the better question to ask is "which channel the audience prefers" (Wise, 2005, p. 15). While various claims are being made as to the accuracy and inaccuracy of poll numbers and whether they reflect penetration rates, little research has yet to address the seemingly more important question: does the programming result in opinion change among its Arab audience? According to a State Department report (Kessler, 2004), most of the research conducted on Radio Sawa and Alhurra TV has been focused on audience share, rather than on attitude change.

Critics also question the value of a "pop-agenda" in the programming of Sawa, Farda, and Alhurra. They argue that "pop" is actually a detriment to improving the U.S. image. Arab media analyst Ali Abunimah describes Radio Sawa's programming as "bland" and thus it reveals that "America doesn't have much to say in Arabic, and scarcely more respect for its audience" (2002, p. 3). Franke-Ruta (2005) argues that much of the cultural product found on the stations is precisely the type of material that is "likely to irritate Arab and Muslim traditionalists" (p. 16). Even BBG Chairman Tomlinson has expressed some concern with the "lite-programming" found on Radio Sawa and Alhurra TV.

News programming provides another area of contention concerning the stations. There is disagreement regarding the efficacy of standards of journalism at the BBG. BBG officials state that Radio Sawa and Alhurra TV were charged, from their inception, with being non-biased, journalistic enterprises. Yet,Ungar (2005) charged VOA's management with having pressured editors to develop "positive stories" that reflect favorably on the Bush administration and its foreign policy positions.

Ungar pointed out the removal of some photographs of abuses at the Abu Ghraib prison from the VOA web site as an example of this managerial, editorial pressure. This is a charge which VOA director David Jackson has flatly denied, claiming it would be a violation of his responsibilities under the International Broadcasting Act "to allow such political meddling" (Jackson, 2005, p. 1).

Regardless of intentionality or claims of non-bias, critics fear that U.S. government funding of Radio Sawa and Alhurra TV hinders any potential appearance of impartiality in news coverage. "This is a region where people are generally skeptical of the news and Alhurra smells to many people as the government spin from a government they don't particularly trust to begin with" (Wise, 2005, p. 2). Mamoun Fandy, a fellow at the James Baker institute, claimed that "Sawa comes across as propagandistic and lacking in professionalism" (Pein, 2005, p. 30), for instance in the failure of Radio Sawa to name reporters or sources during news stories—a violation of basic standards of journalism. Critics also levy the charge that Radio Sawa and Alhurra news programming relies too heavily on statements by American officials (Baylouny, 2005). Finally, critics see an Isreali bias in news coverage of the area. According to Pein (2005), "We hoped that Alhurra would emerge as the voice of reason and a source of information and investigative reports at the level of those produced by the US media. The last thing we expected was that the United States would try to sell us bad goods" (p. 30).

Further justification for these attitudes is based on the fact that neither Radio Sawa nor Alhurra cover "breaking" news stories. Critics point to the Sheikh Yassin assassination as an example. While Arab news networks reported live on Yassin's death, Alhurra continued to air a cooking show. Rugh (2005) asserts that such selective news coverage leads Arabs to compare Alhurra with their state TV networks, as lack of breaking news harks back to when the only Arabic news on television came from authoritarian state programming. In most Arab countries, state television never gave "direct, immediate visual access to political developments abroad, in other Arab countries, or even in their own countries" (Lynch, 2005, p. 4).

In a hostile environment of cynicism and distrust, perceptions by Arab audiences of partiality and non-professionalism among U.S. international broadcasters press upon a risk system already saddled by deep misgivings and mistrust. Not only do they deter audiences from tuning into the news broadcasts, or lead them to "turn down the volume" when "pop" formatting shifts to information, but they cause disbelief for and intellectual rejection of the information being provided. Ultimately, the notion that the United States is broadcasting propaganda over these networks merely raises the level of resentment toward the United States and chills any potential sense of political goodwill.

While proponents of BBG Arabic programming compare the current diplomatic broadcast agenda with Cold War VOA broadcasts transmitted behind the Iron Curtain, when Soviet-satellite teenagers huddled in "darkened rooms" to listen to VOA news and cultural programming (Ungar, 2005, p. 2), this is an erroneous comparison. Media such as Alhurra TV and Radio Sawa are competing in an extremely competitive media environment, saturated with Arabic, Asian and European programming. A majority of "news" competitors broadcasting in the area adhere to professional journalistic standards, unlike when VOA was the only source of professional, unbiased news into the Soviet Union.

Analysts argue whether BBG-based broadcasting inadequacies result from poor decision-making or merely poor organization. As shown, in Figure 32.1, the organizational structure of the BBG is convoluted with duplicated efforts and roles. Notably, the additional bureaucratic influence of the State Department increases the complexity of the public diplomacy apparatus. For instance, the General Accounting Office (GAO) report (2004) stated that the varied mix of governmental and grantee organizations working in public diplomacy posed serious challenges. GAO criticized the State Department for a lack of clear overall strategy for public diplomacy, and expressed concern that the BBG is "not effectively coordinating with other agencies with regard to program content" (p. 10). As in other domestic and foreign contexts of recent years, disorganization and lack of direct accountability is blamed for impeding the U.S. government's ability to respond to risk. As one critic writes:

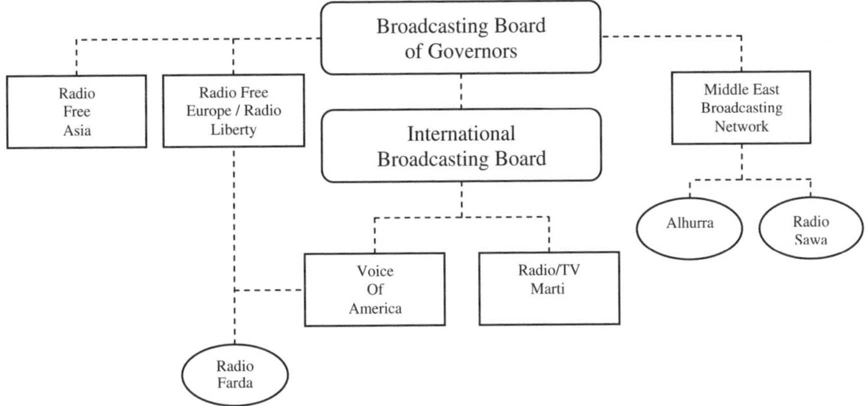

FIGURE 32.1 Organizational structure of BBG networks. *Note:* Adapted from 2005 Broadcasting Board of Governors' Annual Report.

> Alhurra and other new international broadcasters have developed under different legal frameworks and they work within a fragmented organizational structure. The problem is not merely a lack of cohesion between the different entities, but also the absence of a general, well-defined strategy regarding what our international broadcasting tries to achieve. (Dale, 2005, p. 1)

Subsequently, criticism of Radio Sawa, Radio Farda, Alhurra TV, and VOA programming is being voiced by policy makers and legislators. For instance, Congressman Tom Coburn (2007) argues that U.S. public diplomacy broadcasts may do more harm than good. Such critics seek more direct oversight of BBG broadcasts by the administration, with provision of English translations of the BBG public diplomacy broadcasts to overseers. However, whether such actions will lessen the Arab perception that BBG broadcasting constitutes U.S. government propaganda is questionable.

CONCLUSION

In either a stroke of genius, or simply by accident, Osama bin Laden avoided the "malignant narcissism" that often plagues the leaders of terrorist groups and allowed al Qaeda inspired terrorism to morph into a worldwide social movement (Sageman, 2004a, p. 172). Bin Laden and his counterparts have welcomed the change from terrorism based on local hierarchical organizations to a global social movement. We have highlighted bin Laden and Salafist terrorism as one example of contemporary global terrorism. Certainly, many other threats exist.

Communication technology is the driving force behind this expansion of contemporary global terrorism. In comparing media use by U.S. and other Western governments to that of terrorist organizations, a report by the Defense Science Board Task Force (2004) used the analogy of incumbent versus insurgent media. The report said insurgents are characterized by an "attitude of difference, move faster, and welcome change as opportunity. Their modus operandi: mobile and agile" (Defense Science Board [DSB], 2004, p. 49). Much like, Greenpeace and early NGOs, the new breed of contemporary global terrorists, guerrilla fighters and organized criminals are harnessing the power of insurgent media to propagate their cause. On the other hand, the DSB report referred to the U.S. government and its citizens as political and military incumbents, which are described as "bloated, slow, cautious, bureaucratic, change-resistant and more likely to play 'defense' than 'offense' to maintain power" (2004, p. 49). As our analysis reveals, so far, the U.S. government has operated from a defensive position in its attempts to use communication technology to counter the influence of terrorist movements. Furthermore, the examples provided in this chapter reveal that in the current age of instantaneous global communication, governments' attempts at controlling public opinion through mediated communication are severely hampered (Bauman, 1998). In the mean time, the likelihood, or risk, from violence and terrorism has increased as the threat has expanded from localized to global.

This chapter reveals some important implications for future research concerning the relationship between communication technology and the magnified risk of violence and terrorism due to contemporary global terrorism. Future research should continue exploring, through macro-level mass communication theories, the role of Arab media in forming international public opinion. Research should also explore the role of Arab media in "linking" the Arab Diaspora to a pan-Arab or pan-Islamic worldview. It may also examine the media choice and penetration among vulnerable groups. Rigorous social scientific research is also needed to examine the effectiveness of mediated public diplomacy initiatives in buffering anti-Americanism among Arabs. Research by Fullerton revealed that U.S. government sponsored advertising messages (Fullerton & Kendrick, 2006) and American entertainment programming (Fullerton, Hamilton, & Kendrick, 2007) had some positive impact on anti-Americanism. Further investigation of these studies using Arab respondents in the Middle East should be conducted. Finally, future research should examine the impact of coverage of human rights events and issues (AIDS, poverty, environment, health disparities, women's rights) as sources of intervention and prevention of contemporary global terrorism.

NOTES

1. According to Gladney (2004), "[McLuhan] explained that as everyone becomes involved in the affairs of all others (integral inclusiveness) or part of a simultaneous field of human affairs, the self-image of individuals and whole cultures and societies becomes threatened, inviting a mandate for war" (p. 21).
2. The terms Middle East and Arab are often used interchangeably to reference both people and location. However, George Hishmeh (2006), President of the Washington Association of Arab Journalists (WAAJ) argues that there is a distinct difference in these terms. He says that the term Middle East should refer to the geographical region that includes the Arab states, as well as, Turkey, Israel, and Iran. "The Arabs do not generally like to be referred to as Middle Easterners, but Arabs" (Hishmeh, 2006).
3. Normative press systems theories use categories or taxonomies to represent differing functions of media based on the political system and the historical development of the societies in which they operate (Hachten & Scotton, 2002). These various press systems include Libertarian, Western, Social Responsibility, Authoritarian, Communist, Revolutionary, Developmental, Transitional, and Liberal Commercial. See Rugh (1979) and Ayish (2002) for thorough discussion of typologies.
4. Textaully.org maintains news archives on cell phones used by terrorists at http://www.textually.org/textually/archives/cat_cell_phones_used_by_terrorists.htm.
5. The names General Accounting Office and Government Accountability Office refer to the same federal agency. We use the abbreviation GAO interchangeably. The current name, Government Accountability Office was established in July 2004.

BIBLIOGRAPHY

A letter from concerned scientists. (2002, February 27). Retrieved July 7, 2007, from http://www.pbs.org/wgbh/pages/frontline/shows/cyberwar/etc/letter.html.

Abunimah, A. (2002, August 20). Radio Sawa: All dressed up with nowhere to go. *The Electronic Intifada*. Retrieved December 14, 2005, from http://electronicintifada.net/v2/article494.shtml.

Accuracy in Media (2006, September 12). Executive summary and analysis: National omnibus survey. Retrieved March 27, 2007, from http://www.aim.org/pdf/AIM_Poll_on_Al-Jazeera_International.pdf.

Anderson, B. (1991). *Imagined communities: Reflections on the origin and spread of nationalism* (Rev. ed.). New York: Verso.

Ayish, M. (2002). Political communication on Arab world television: Evolving patterns. *Political Communication, 19,* 137–154.

Bauman, Z. (1999). *Culture as praxis*. London: Sage.

Bauman, Z. (1998). Europe of strangers. Retrieved September 15, 2007, from http://www.transcomm.ox.ac.uk/www.root/working_papers.htm

Baylouny, A. M. (2005, November). Alhurra, the free one: Assessing US satellite television in the Middle East. *Strategic Insights*, IV.

Beck, U. (1992). *Risk society: Towards a new modernity* (Mark Ritter, Trans.). London: Sage. (Original work published 1986)

Becker, A. (2005, January 25). Technology and terror: The new modus operandi. Frontline. Retrieved June 19, 2007, from http://www.pbs.org/wgbh/pages/frontline/shows/front/special/tech.html.

Bin Hazam, F. (2006, October 26). Online fatwas incite young Muslims to jihad. Al-Riyadh. Retrieved October 26, 2006, from http://www.memri.org/bin/opener_latest.cgi?ID=133506.

Bollier, D. (2004). *People/networks/power: Communications technology and the new international politics* (Report of the twelfth annual Roundtable on Information Technology). Washington, DC: Aspen Institute.

Broadcasting Board of Governors. (2005). Annual report. Washington, DC: Author. Retrieved July 7, 2007, from http://www.bbg.gov/reports/05anrprt.pdf.

Carey, J. (1988). *Communication as culture*. Boston, MA: Unwin Hyman.

Castells, M., Fernandez-Ardevol, M., Qui., J., & Sey, A. (2006). *Mobile communication and society. A global perspective*. Cambridge, MA: MIT.

Cherribi, S. (2006). From Baghdad to Paris; AL-Jazeera and the veil. *The Harvard International Journal of Press/Politics, 11*(2), 121–138.

Coburn, T. (2007, February 8). Letter to President George W. Bush. Retrieved May 24, 2007, from http:/coburn-senate.gov/ffm/index.cfm?FuseAction=Files,Views&FileStore_id=dc2fb01e-d537-4bdc-acca3d543741.

Corman, S. R., & Schiefelbein, J. S. (2006). *Communication and media strategy in the Jihadi war of ideas*. Arizona State University, Consortium for Strategic Communication.

Cullison, A. (2004, September). Inside Al-Qaeda's hard drive. *The Atlantic Monthly*. Retrieved January 21, 2007, from http://theatlantic.com/doc/print/200409/cullison.

Dabruzzi, K., & Gartenstein-Ross, D. (2007). Jihad's new leaders. *Middle East Quarterly*. XIV. Retrieved June 29, 2007, from http://www.meforum.org/article/1710.

Dale, H. C., (2005, November 18). Al-hurrah television and lessons for U.S. public diplomacy. The Heritage Foundation. Retrieved December 2, 2005, from http://www.heritage.org/Research/MiddleEast/Iraq/hl909.cfm.

Defense Science Board Task Force. (2004). *Report of the defense science board task force on strategic communication*. Washington, DC: Author.

Debkafile. (2006, October 1). Al Qaeda's novel death technique: Detonating hundreds of simultaneous explosions through cell phone and Internet. Retrieved February 10, 2007, from http://www.debka.com/headline.php?hid=3321.

DeFleur, M. L., & DeFleur, M. H. (2003). *Learning to hate Americans*. Spokane, WA: Marquette Books.

Deluca, N. (2005, September 16). US tries to paint a better picture. *PR Week*, 17.

DeSanctis, G. & Monge, P. (1999). Introduction to the special issue: Communication processes for virtual organizations. *Organization Science, 10*(6), 693–703.

Dominick, J. R. (1996). *The dynamics of mass communication*. New York: McGraw-Hill.

Downing, J., (2001). The Seattle IMC and the socialist anarchist tradition. Paper presented at Our Media, Not Theirs I, Washington, DC. Retrieved July 1, 2007, from http://www.ourmedianet.org/papers/om2001/Downing.om2001.pdf.

Franke-Ruta, G. (2005, September). Pop-agenda; A question for Karen Hughes: Why is the administration peddling the kind of schlock to the Arab world that it's always denouncing at home? *The American Prospect*, p. 16.

Fullerton, J., Hamilton, M., & Kendrick, A. (2007). U.S.-produced entertainment media and attitude toward Americans. *Mass Communication and Society, 10*, 171–187.

Fullerton, J., & Kendrick, A. (2006). *Advertising's war on terrorism: The story of the U.S. State Department's shared values campaign*. Spokane, WA: Marquette.

Gambill, G. (2003). Explaining the Arab democracy deficit: Part one. *Middle East Intelligence Bulletin, 5*(2), Retrieved August 6, 2007, from http://www.meib.org/articles/0302_me.htm.

Gartenstein-Ross, D., & Grace, N. (2006, December 15). Iraqi insurgents launch 24-hour television station. Politics Central. Retrieved May 23, 2007, from http://politicscentral.com/2006/12/15/iraqi_insurgents_launch_24hour.php

General Accounting Office. (2004, February). *U.S. Public Diplomacy: State Department and the Broadcasting Board of Governors expand efforts in the Middle East but face significant challenges* (GAO Publication No. GAO-04-435t). Washington, DC: Author.

Giddens, A. (1999). Risk and responsibility. *Modern Law Review, 62*(1), 1–10.

Gladney, G. A. (2004). Global village disconnected? In R. D. Berenger (Ed.), *Global media go to war: Role of news and entertainment media during the 2003 Iraq War* (pp. 15–27). Spokane, WA: Marquette.

Government Accountability Office. (2004, August). *U.S. Public Diplomacy: State Department and Broadcasting Board of Governors expand post-9/11 efforts but challenges remain* (GAO Publication No. GAO-04-1061T). Washington, DC: Author.

Hacten, W. A., & Scotton, J. F. (2002). *The world news prism: Global media in an era of terrorism* (6th ed.). Ames, IA: Iowa State Press.

Hafez, K. (2001). Mass media in the Middle East: Patterns of political and societal change. In K. Hafez (Ed.), *Mass media, politics & society in the middle east* (pp. 1–20). Cresskill, NJ: Hampton Press.

Hall, S. ([1973] 1980). 'Encoding/decoding.' In Centre for Contemporary Cultural Studies (Ed.), *Culture, media, language: Working papers in cultural studies, 1972–79* (pp. 128–138). London: Hutchinson.

Hamdy, N., & Mobarak, R. (2004). Iraq war ushers in Web-based era. In R. D. Berenger (Ed.), *Global media go to war: The role of news and entertainment media during the 2003 Iraq war* (pp. 245–254). Spokane, WA: Marquette Books.

Hamzawy, A. (2005, February 6). The real 'Arab street.' *The Washington Post*, p. B07.

Hass, R. N. (2004, January 19). Ending Islamic democracy deficit. *The Korea Herald*. Retrieved July 17, 2007, from http://www.cfr.org/publication/6670/ending_islamic_democracy_deficit.html.

Heil, A. L., Jr. (2007). Rate of Arabic language TV start-ups shows no sign of abating. *Arab Media & Society*. Retrieved July 1, 2007, from http://www.arabmediasociety.com/?article=180.

Hishmeh, G. S. (2006, March). Presented in The Middle East's America: The U.S. image abroad 2nd conference in the "U.S. Image Abroad" Series, Norman, OK.

Hoffman, B. (2006). *Inside terrorism*. New York: Columbia University Press.

Howard, M. (2007, January 15). Insurgent TV channel turns into Iraq's newest cult hit. *The Guardian*. Retrieved June 28, 2007, from http://www.guardian.co.uk/media/2007/jan/15/Iraqandthemedia.broadcasting.

Ikenberry, G. J. (2004, March/April). Illusions of Empire: Defining the new American order. *Foreign Affairs*. Retrieved July 3, 2007, from http://www.foreignaffairs.org/20040301fareviewessay83212a/g-john-ikenberry/illusions-of-empire-defining-the-new-american-order.html.

Innis, H. A. (1951). *The bias of communication*. Toronto: University of Toronto Press.

Innis, H. A. (1972). *Empire & communications*. Toronto: University of Toronto Press. (Original work published 1950)

Iyengar, S. (1990). The accessibility bias in politics: Television news and public opinion. *International Journal of Public Opinion Research, 2,* 1–15.

Iyengar, S. (1991). *Is anyone responsible? How television frames political issues*. Chicago, IL: University of Chicago Press.

Iyengar, S., & Simon, A. (1993). News coverage of the gulf crisis and public opinion: A study of agenda-setting, priming, and framing. *Communication Research, 20,* 365–383.

Jackson, D. (2005, July/August). His master's voice. *Foreign Affairs*. Retrieved July 8, 2007, from http://www.foreignaffairs.org/20050701/fareresponse84416/david-s-jackson/his-master-s-voice.html.

Jackson, D. (2006, April). Spreading democracy through the airwaves: A look at US efforts to broadcast abroad. Presented at the annual meeting of the Broadcast Education Association, Las Vegas, NV.

Junger, S. (2007, February). Blood oil. *Vanity Fair*. Retrieved January 26, 2007, from http://www.vanityfair.com/politics/features/2007/02/junger200702.

Kalathil, S. (2002). Community and communalism in the information age. *The Brown Journal of World Affairs, IX,* 347–354.

Kepel, G. (2002). *Jihad: The trail of political Islam*. Cambridge, MA: Belknap press of Harvard University Press.

Kessler, G. (2004, October 13). The role of Radio Sawa In Mideast questioned. *The Washington Post*, p. A12.

Kidd, D. (2002, July). Which would you rather: Seattle or Porto Alegre? Paper presented at Our Media, Not Theirs II, Barcelona, Spain. Retrieved July 1, 2007, from http://www.ourmedianet.org/papers/om2002/Kidd.om2002.pdf.

Kirk, M. (Writer & Director). (2003). Cyber War! [Television series episode]. In M. Kirk (Producer), Frontline. Boston: WGBH.

Knickerbocker, B. (2006, August 17). In terror war, phone sales raise alarm. *The Christian Science Monitor*. Retrieved March 6, 2007, from http://www.csmonitor.com/2006/0817/p02s01-usgn.html.

Knights, M. (2005). JTIC Briefing: Jeddah Attack Underscores Fall in Capabilities of Saudi Militants. Jane's Terrorism and Insurgency Center, Retrieved July 7, 2007, from http://www.janes.com/security/international_security/news/jtic/jtic050107_1_n.shtml.

Kramer, M. (2004). Nation and Assassination in the Middle East." *Middle East Quarterly,* 59–64.

Kramer, M. (2006, March 20). Islam's coming crusade. *Jerusalem Report,* 47.

Labi, N. (2006, July/August). Jihad 2.0. *The Atlantic Monthly,* 102–108.

Leonardi, P. M. (2003). Problematizing "new media": Culturally based perceptions of cell phones, computers, and the Internet among United States Latinos. *Critical Studies in Media Communication, 20,* 160–179.

Lerbinger, O. (1997). *The crisis manager: Facing risk and responsibility*. Mahwah, NJ: Erlbaum.

Levine, A. (2005, September 1). Voice-over America. *American Prospect*. Retrieved December 2, 2005, from http://www.prospect.org/weblid=10I09.

Lippman, W. (1956). *Public opinion* (15th printing). New York: MacMillan.

Long, T. (2007, January 10). Introducing the cell phone bomb. Wired News. Retrieved February 2, 2007, from http://www.wired.com/news/technology/0,72400-0.html?tw=rss.index.

Lynch, M. (2005, Spring). Assessing the democratizing power of satellite TV. Transnational Broadcasting Studies. 14. Retrieved December 2, 2005, from http://www.tbsjournal.com/Archives/Spring05/lynch.html.

Manchester Manual. (n.d.). Retrieved July 11, 2007, from http://www.usdoj.gov/ag/manualpart1_3.pdf.

Mathews, J. T. (1997, January/February). Power shift. *Foreign Affairs, 76,* 50–66.

McClellan, M. (2004, October 14). Public diplomacy in the context of traditional diplomacy. Paper presented at the Vienna Diplomatic Academy. Retrieved December 9, 2005, from http://www.publicdiplomacy.org/45.htm#head0.

McLuhan, M. (1962). *The Gutenberg galaxy.* London: Routledge & Kegan Paul.

McQuail, D. (2000). *McQuail's mass communication theory* (4th ed.). London: Sage.

Misra, S. (2003, July-September). Exploitation of information and communication technology by terrorist organizations. S*trategic Analysis*, XXVII. Retrieved January 30, 2007, from http://www.ciaonet.org.

Moore, J. F. (2003, March 31). The second superpower rears its beautiful head. Retrieved January 21, 2007, from the Berkman Center for Internet & Society Web site: http://cyber.law.harvard.edu/people/jmoore/secondsuperpower.pdf.

Morgan, D. (2005, February 28). U.S. to expand Arabic broadcasts. *The Boston Globe*. Retrieved November 16, 2007, from http://www.boston.com/news/nation/articles/2005/02/28/us_to_expand_arabic_broadcasts/.

Moy, P., & Pfau, M. (2000). *With malice toward all? The media and public confidence in democratic institutions.* Westport, CT: Praeger.

Museum of Television and Radio (Producer). (2007, April 16). The War of information in the Middle East [Television broadcast]. In MTR: News and views from the Middle East. New York: Producer.

National Infrastructure Advisory Council. (2003). The national strategy to secure cyberspace. Retrieved April 12, 2007, from http://www.whitehouse.gov/pcipb/.

National Intelligence Council. (2007). *The terrorist threat to the US homeland. National intelligence estimate.* Washington, DC: Author.

Nine/Eleven Finding Answers Foundation. (2007, June). The PATH tunnel plot. (Report #5 in Target: America series). Retrieved July 7, 2007, from http://www.nefafoundation.org/targetamerica.html.

Nisbet, E. C., Nisbet, M. C., Scheufele, D. A., & Shanahan, J. E. (2004). Public diplomacy, television news and Muslim opinion. *Press/Politics, 9*, 11–37.

O'Hair, D., Heath, R., & Ledlow, G. (Eds.). (2005). *Community preparedness and response to terrorism: Communication and the media.* Greenwood, CT: Praeger.

Pape, R. (2003). The strategic logic of suicide terrorism. *American Political Science Review, 97,* 343–361.

Paz, R. (2005, July 10). From Madrid to London: Al-Qaeda exports the war in Iraq to Europe. Retrieved June 19, 2007, from http://haganah.org.il/harchives/004469.html.

Pein, C. (2005, May/June). The new wave. *Columbia Journalism Review,* 28–30.

Perez-Lugo, M. (2004). Media uses in disaster situations: A new focus on the impact phase. *Sociological inquiry, 74*(2), 210–225.

Pew Research Center. (2006, June). America's image slips, but allies share U.S. concerns over Iran, Hamas. Retrieved April 1, 2007, from http://pewglobal.org/reports/display.php?ReportID=252.

Pintak, L. (2006a, September 16). A CNN for the developing world. Spiegel Online International. Retrieved May 5, 2007, from http://www.spiegel.de/international/0,1518,448830,00.html.

Pintak, L. (2006b, Spring). Arab Media: Not quite utopia. TBS Journal, 16. Retrieved May 5, 2007, from http://www.tbsjournal.com/letter.html.

Pintak, L. (2007, January 10). War of ideas: Insurgent channel coming to a satellite near you. Columbia Journalism Review. Retrieved July 1, 2007, from http://www.cjr.org/politics/insurgent_tv_coming_to_a_satel.php.

Pintak, L. (2007, February). Reporting a revolution: the changing Arab media landscape. *Arab Media & Society.* Retrieved July 31, 2007, from http://www.arabmediasociety.org/?article=23.

Postman, N. (1992). *Technopoly*. New York: Alfred A. Knopf.

Reuters (2007, April 28). *Iran to filter "immoral" mobil messages*. Retrieved May 2, 2007, from http://www.reuters.com/articlePrint?articleid=USDAH83913820070428.

Rheingold, H. (2002). *Smart mobs*. Cambridge, MA: Basic Books.

Roggio, B. (2006, December 25). Al-Zawraa responds to Muj TV. The Fourth Rail. Retrieved July 1, 2007, from http://billroggio.com/archives/2006/12/alzawraa_responds_to.php.

Ross, B. & Esposito, R. (2007, June 29). Officials: Car bomb plot bears Al Qaeda's Trademark. ABC News. Retrieved July 1, 2007, from http://blogs.abcnews.com/theblotter/2007/06/officials-car-b.html.

Rugh, W. A. (1979). *The Arab press: News media and political processes in the Arab world.* Syracuse, NY: Syracuse University Press.

Rugh, W. A. (2004). *Arab mass media: newspapers, radio, and television in Arab politics*. Westport, CT: Praeger.

Rugh, W. A. (2005, Spring). Broadcasting and American public diplomacy. *Transnational Broadcasting Studies, 14.* Retrieved November 25, 2006, from http://tbsjournal.com/rugh.html.

Rugh, W. A. (2006, Spring). Anti-Americanism on Arab television: Some outsider observations. TBS Journal, 15. Retrieved November 25, 2006, from http://www.tbsjournal.com/Archives/Fall05/Rugh.html.

Rugh, W. A. (2007, May). Do national political systems still influence Arab media? *Arab Media & Society*. Retrieved July 27, 2007, from http://www.arabmediasociety.com/articles/downloads/20070523081944_AMS2_William_A_Rugh.pdf.

Sageman, M. (2004a). *Understanding terror networks.* Philadelphia: University of Pennsylvania Press.

Sageman, M. (2004b, November 1). Understanding terror networks. E-Notes. Retrieved June 17, 2007, from http://www.fpri.org/enotes/20041101.middleeast.sageman.understandingterrornetworks.html.

Sakr, N. (2002). *Satellite realms: Transnational television, globalization and the Middle East.* London: Tauris.

Savage, C. (2004, August 28). Terror fears loom over subway cell phone service. The San Diego Union-Tribune. Retrieved March 6, 2007, from http://www.signonsandiego.com/uniontrib/20040828/news_1n28terror.html.

Scarborough, R. (2005, March 7). Cell-phone technology an explosive tool for insurgents. The Washington Times, Retrieved July 7, 2007, from http://www.washingtontimes.com/national/20050307-121323-4533r.htm.

Schofield, M. (2007, February 7). New generation of terrorists cyber-inspired, -trained. Real Cities. Retrieved February 12, 2007, from http://www.realcities.com/mld/krwashington/16645727.htm.

Schrum, L. J. (2001). Processing strategy moderates: The cultivation effect. *Human Communication Research, 27,* 94–120.

Searcey, D. (2005, August 12). Experts debate cell stoppages. *The Wall Street Journal,* p. A4.

Sheafer, T. (2007). How to evaluate it: The role of story-evaluative tone in agenda-setting and priming. *Journal of Communication, 57,* 21–39.

Silverman, V. (2002, April 29). Radio Sawa delivers Arab and American popular music. Retrieved October 12, 2005, from http://www.iwar.org.uk/psyops/resources/radio/sawa.htm.

Simpson, J. (2005, October 3). Battling the al-qaeda franchise. BBC News. Retrieved July 12, 2007, http://news.bbc.co.uk/2/hi/asia-pacific/4304516.stm.

Slatina, S. (2005, May/June). Brand war. Foreign Policy. Retrieved July 12, 2007, from http://www.foreign-policy.com/story/cms.php?story_id=2845.

Slevin, J. (2002). The Internet and forms of human association. In Denis McQuail (Ed.), *McQuail's reader in mass communication theory* (pp. 146–156). London: Sage.

Smith, G. D. (1998). Single issue terrorism. The Terrorism Research Center. Retrieved July 20, 2007, from http://www.terrorism.com/modules.php?op=modload&name=News&file=article&sid=5674.

Stivers, R. (1994). *The culture of cynicism: American morality in decline.* Cambridge, MA: Blackwell.

Sullivan, K. (2007, January 23). Views on U.S. drop sharply in worldwide opinion poll. *The Washington Post*, p. A14.

Telhami, S. (2002a, April 4). Why suicide terrorism takes root. *New York Times.* Retrieved July 8, 2007, from http://www.brookings.edu/views/op-ed/telhami/20020404.htm.

Telhami, S. (2002b, April 24). Public diplomacy. House committee on appropriations, subcommittee on the Departments of Commerce, Justice and State, the Judiciary and related agencies. Retrieved July 8, 2007, from http://www.brookings.edu/views/testimony/telhami/20020424.htm.

Telhami, S. (2004, April 29). Finding the right media for the message in the Middle East. Senate Foreign Relations Committee. Retrieved July 8, 2007, from http://www.brookings.edu/printme.wbs?page=/pagedefs/a4c8c784c7b4ff3d5713e9d50a1415cb.xml.

Telhami, S. (2007, February, 25). Poll takes the pulse of the Middle East. National Public Radio. Retrieved July 8, 2007, from http://www.brookings.edu/printme.wbs?page=/pagedefs/807dd254eb9aff4076faae1f0a1415cb.xml.

Telvick, M. (2005, January 25). Al Qaeda today: The new face of the global jihad. Frontline. Retrieved June 17, 2007, from http://www.pbs.org/wgbh/pages/frontline/shows/front/etc/today.html.

Terranova, T. (2004). *Network culture: Politics for the information age.* London: Pluto Press.

Thomas, C. (2005, September 14). The impossible job of Karen Hughes. *The Augusta Chronicle*, p. A04.

Tönnies, F. (2001). *Community and Civil Society* [*Gemeinschaft und Gesellschaft*]. (J. Harris & M. Hollis, Trans.). Cambridge: Cambridge University Press. (Original work published 1887).

Tuman, J. (2003). *Communicating terror: The rhetorical dimensions of terrorism.* Thousand Oaks, CA: Sage.

Ungar, S. J., (2005, May/June). Pitch imperfect. *Foreign Affairs.* Retrieved July 8, 2007, from http://www.foreignaffairs.org/20050501/facomment84302/sanford-j-ungar/pitch-imperfect.html.

Van Belle, D. A. (2000). *Press freedom and global politics.* Westport, CT: Praeger.

Van Ginneken, J. (2003). *Collective behavior and public opinion: Rapid shifts in opinion and communication.* Mahwah, NJ: Erlbaum.

Waiting for al-Qaeda's next bomb. (2007, May 3). *The Economist.* Retrieved July 31, 2007, from http://www.economist.com/world/displaystory.cfm?story_id=9111542&CFID=22687063&CFTOKEN=29017711.

Wedeen, L. (1999). *Ambiguities of domination: Politics, rhetoric, and symbols in contemporary.* Syria. Chicago: The University of Chicago Press.
Weimann, G. (2004, March). www.terror.net: How modern terrorism uses the Internet. Retrieved January 12, 2007, from United States Institute of Peace Web site: http://www.usip.org/pubs/specialreports/sr116.pdf.
Wise, L. (2005, Spring). A second look at Alhurra: US-funded channel comes of age on the front lines of the battle for hearts and minds. *TBS Journal*, 14. Retrieved December 2, 2005, from http://www.tbsjournal.com/Archives/Spring05/wise.htm.
Yehoshua, Y. (2007, February 21). Islamist websites as an integral part of jihad: A general overview. Retrieved February 21, 2007, from http://www.memri.org/bin/opener_latest.cgi?ID=IA32807.
Zogby International. (2007, March 2). Middle East opinion: Iran fears aren't hitting the Arab street. Retrieved May 5, 2007, from http://www.zogby.com/templates/printsb.cfm?id=14570.

33

Opportunity Knocks: Putting Communication Research into the Travel and Tourism Risk and Crisis Literature

Lynne M. Sallot
University of Georgia

Elizabeth Johnson Avery
University of Tennessee–Knoxville

Jeffrey K. Springston
University of Georgia

Our post-September 11, 2001, world—rife with war, terrorism, natural disasters, political uncertainties, health scares, economic and exchange rate fluctuations, ever-more costly oil-based fuels, and shrinking disposable income for many—inevitably has made travel more complex with enormous risk and crisis implications for global tourism.

Yet international tourist arrivals worldwide exceeded 842 million in 2006, a 4.5% increase over 2005, which broke all previous records after the 2001–2003 tourism slump, and exceeding long-term annual growth of 4.1% projected by the United Nations-affiliated World Tourism Organization (UNWTO Newsroom, 2007). By comparison, in 1956 when the WTO first published statistics, there were 50 million worldwide international arrivals (UNWTO Market Research, 2006).

While affecting destinations at local levels during specific periods, the disruptions listed above have not altered global or regional travel flows. Factors contributing to tourism growth include favorable economic conditions in key travel markets, continued consumer confidence, and the efforts of nations and other entities to develop and promote tourism (UNWTO *Barometer*, 2006).

GLOBAL TOURISM AND TRAVEL EQUALS BIG BUSINESS

The economic impact of tourism is huge, representing 6% of the total value of worldwide exports of goods and services. The WTO's 2005 estimates of worldwide receipts from international tourism, including passenger transport, exceeded US$800 billion, equivalent to the gross domestic products of Spain and the Republic of Korea, the world's ninth and tenth largest economies.

For many developing countries and island destinations, tourism is the biggest contributor to export earnings. The nine countries ranking at the top of separate lists for most tourism arrivals and for largest tourism receipts were France, United States, Spain, Italy, China, United Kingdom, Germany, Turkey, and Austria. Mexico was in the top 10 for arrivals and Australia ranks tenth for receipts (UNWTO *Barometer*, 2006). Domestic tourism around the globe generates substantial additional revenues within nations.

By 2020, the WTO projects there will be 1.56 billion international arrivals with Europe attracting 717 million tourists, East Asia and the Pacific attracting 397 million, and the Americas attracting 282 million. East Asia and the Pacific, South Asia, the Middle East, and Africa are forecasted to exceed 5% tourism growth each year while the more mature markets of Europe and the Americas are expected to grow more slowly (*Tourism 2020 Vision*, 2006).

THREATS TO TOURISM AND TRAVEL EVER PRESENT

Wars in the Middle East, Africa, and elsewhere. Suicide bombers, hijacked planes, bombs on trains and busses. Tsunamis, earthquakes, hurricanes, droughts, raging wildfires. Murders, kidnappings, thefts. Any crisis or catastrophe of potential threat to humans potentially threatens tourism and travel. Pandemics, such as SARS, HIV/AIDS and Avian influenza, and travel and tourism reciprocate risk and crises: while pandemics pose threats to travel and tourism, travel and tourism instigate and promulgate pandemics. These facts make risk and crisis preparedness essential—if not required by law—at every level of tourism and travel. Reminders to use the deadbolt security lock on the backs of doors in hotel guest rooms, spoken and written evacuation instructions prior to airplane takeoffs, and lifeboat drills on cruise ships are among common risk messages in the industry. In the United States, the ultimate travel risk message well might be the State Department's Travel Warning, which recommends Americans avoid certain countries based on press reports, information from embassies, officials from other U.S. agencies, host governments and other sources, and, to a lesser degree, "Public Announcements" advising would-be travelers about short-term, transnational terrorist threats such as coups, bombs, violence and anniversary dates (Goldstone, 2001). In an era of Code Red and other colored alerts, as never before, planning for and implementing risk communications to prevent or minimize crises, and planning for implementation of crisis response communications should be an integral part of risk and crisis preparedness in travel and tourism.

Public relations, the business of managing relationships (Pavlik, 1987), fills a wide variety of functions that may differ by industry. Almost invariably, however, two functions are the purview of public relations: media relations and crisis communications. Given the breadth and depth of its vulnerabilities to crises, travel and tourism can benefit greatly from expert public relations practice. Public relations scholarship benefits the practice; it follows that public relations scholarship can benefit the travel and tourism industry as well.

This chapter briefly considers how the tourism and travel industry is structured, vital to understanding its potential risks and crises. Then tourism literature on risk and crisis communication and management are briefly reviewed. Finally, the chapter examines how research in risk communication and crisis communication response from the public relations/communication literature might inform and improve management of risks and crises in the tourism and travel industry.

STRUCTURE LEAVES TOURISM AND TRAVEL INDUSTRY VULNERABLE TO RISKS AND CRISES

The travel and tourism industry involves a multilayered, overlapping, and interlocking distribution system of sellers and buyers of travel products. Travel suppliers—including destination tourism-and-convention entities; hotels, resorts, and others providing accommodations; transportation conveyors, such as cruise lines and ships, airlines, trains, and motor coach operators; sightseeing tour operators and other ground infrastructures, such as local car rental agencies, taxis, attractions, restaurants, duty-free shops, and souvenir retailers—are all travel sellers (Sallot, 2005). Travel sellers are mindful that travel is a highly perishable product with an extremely brief shelf life. When an airplane takes off with empty seats or a hotel's rooms aren't filled today, they cannot be sold tomorrow.

At the other end of the travel selling-buying continuum is the traveling public, the ultimate buyers and consumers of travel products. In between are travel wholesalers and consolidators, who buy and package travel products from suppliers and then sell travel packages to retail travel agents or directly to ultimate consumer travelers, and retail travel agents, who buy travel products either directly from suppliers or from travel wholesalers or consolidators and then sell the travel products to ultimate consumer travelers.

The growth of travel and tourism public relations mirrors the industry. Increasing numbers of professional communicators represent and act on behalf of any of the travel sellers—suppliers, wholesalers, or travel agents—with the goal of building relationships with any of the travel buyers—wholesalers, travel agents, or consumers—in a bid to generate awareness, disseminate information, and attract brand preference and loyalty for the travel products represented.

Travel sellers may have public relations representation "in house" or may contract for representation with an independent firm specializing in travel and tourism public relations; it is not uncommon for travel sellers to have both in-house and external independent public relations counsel simultaneously. Ideally, those charged with managing risk and crisis communications in travel and tourism are professionals qualified to counsel travel sellers about best practices in communicating risks in an ever-changing environment and responding to crisis challenges ranging from viral infections infecting cruise ship passengers to airplane crashes, from hijackings to terrorists bombing resorts, and any other risks or crises that may conceivably—or inconceivably—arise.

USING PUBLIC RELATIONS RISK AND CRISIS LITERATURE TO CAST A WIDER NET

Any review of the risk and crisis communication research literature from the public relations perspective will confirm the large extant and growing body of knowledge. In his essay on building theory in public relations, Glen Broom (2006) noted that public relations inquiry should not be limited to public relations literature. He challenged public relations scholars to resist drawing boundaries around our body of knowledge by taking an open-systems approach, "reaching beyond our limited literature and paradigms" (p. 142). By casting the widest nets possible for concepts and theoretical frameworks and attending more carefully to the "questions we ask, methods we employ, and the decisions we make about what gets published," we'll be more likely to give our best efforts to building theory that advances the scholarship and the practice of public relations and how it functions (pp. 141–142).

Broom's premise gave rise to the primary research question of this chapter, which is: have other scholarly disciplines cast a wide enough net to capture the public relations risk and crisis communication body of knowledge? Given the ubiquity of risks and crises in the industry, the travel and tourism scholarly literature seemed a good place to investigate the penetration of our knowledge into another discipline.

RISK COMMUNICATION LITERATURE CITATION ANALYSIS OMITS PR/ COMMUNICATION RESEARCH

Further prompting this chapter's research question was an analysis of scholarly articles on risk communication published in the environmental and technical domain between 1988 and 2000. Conducted by Gurabardhi, Gutteling, and Kuttschreuter (2004), the study investigated characteristics of the risk communication literature to identify trends in risk communication research. Keywords used in the search of selected online databases included risk, hazard, communications, warn, environment, industrial, technology, participation, and/or public involvement. Electronic databases searched included the ISI Social Sciences Citation Index, ISI Science Citation Index, and the ISI Arts and Humanities Citation Index, which together were reported to cover more than 6,000 scholarly journals in the social sciences, arts and humanities, and hard sciences (Gurabardhi, et al., 2004).

Of 349 journal articles Gurabardhi, et al. (2004) analyzed, 331 included the keyword "risk communication." Eleven authors who had published four or more articles were identified in the analysis as being "most productive." An analysis of *Public Relations Review* and *Journal of Public Relations Research* through 2000 had determined that Robert L. Heath was the most productive author of articles about risk communication, with many of his articles involving environmental and technical topics (Sallot, Lyon, Acosta-Alzuru, & Jones, 2003). Therefore, it seemed odd to us that Heath's name did not turn up in the findings of Gurabardhi, et al. (2004).[1] In fact, Heath had nine publications with "risk communication" as keywords during 1992–2000 (Heath, 2006), which should have placed Heath as third-most productive scholar in the Gurabardhi, et al. (2004) study.[2]

METHODS USED IN CITATION ANALYSIS OF TRAVEL AND TOURISM RISK CRISIS LITERATURE

Prompted by the omission of Heath in the Gurabardhi, et al. (2004) study, for this chapter a citation review was conducted to investigate whether and how public relations risk and crisis *communication* literature is cited in articles about risk and crisis management in the travel and tourism scholarly journals. A good starting point was a study assessing the role of tourism and hospitality journals in knowledge transfer that identified five of thirteen journals as being the most widely read by educator-trainer and researcher-consultant members of the Travel and Tourism Research Association and of the Travel Industry of America (Frechtling, 2004).[3] In order of popularity, they were: *Journal of Travel Research*, *Annals of Tourism Research*, *Journal of Travel and Tourism Marketing*, *Journal of Hospitality & Tourism Research*, and *Tourism Management.*

The online tables of contents of these five journals from 1999 through spring 2006 were reviewed to identify articles with "risk communication" or "crisis communication" in their titles or appearing in titles to address risks or crises in travel and tourism. The five journals and number of articles in them identified with risk or crisis communication were *Journal of Travel and Tourism Marketing*, 32 articles; *Annals of Tourism Research*, 15 articles; *Tourism Management*, 10 articles; *Journal of Travel Research*, 4 articles; and *Journal of Hospitality and Tourism Research*, 3 articles.

Forty-four of the 64 travel articles were downloaded.[4] Bibliographic references in each article were examined first for titles of any other prominent travel and tourism academic journals being cited. The five journals identified above seemed to predominate. Then a content analysis was conducted of the bibliographic references in each of the 44 articles for citations of research published in public relations and communications scholarly journals and professional journals; citations with "public relations" in the title; citations of books whose titles appeared to focus on crisis and/or risk communications; and citations of known public relations-communications scholars.

RESULTS OF CITATION ANALYSIS OF TRAVEL-TOURISM RISK CRISIS LITERATURE

Although 10 (22.7%) of the 44 articles in the top five travel and tourism academic journals analyzed had citations from the public relations risk and crisis communications literature, these citations accounted for only 46 (2.5%) of the 1,850 citations analyzed. (Table 33.1 summarizes the data and the Appendix further details findings and provides references for publications cited in this section of the chapter.)

Articles cited in public relations/communications journals were most frequently published in *Public Relations Review* with eight citations and in *Management Communication Quarterly* with two citations. Articles in *Communication Studies*, *International Journal for Mass Communication Studies*, *Journal of Business Communication*, and *Public Opinion Quarterly* were each cited once. Articles in PRSA's defunct trade magazine, *Public Relations Journal*, were cited three times. The

TABLE 33.1
Results of Analysis of Articles on Risk and Crisis Management in Travel and Tourism Journals for Public Relations and Communications Citations

Journal Name	*Total # of Articles Analyzed*	*# of Articles with PR Citations*	*Total # of Citations*	*# of PR Citations*
Journal of Travel and Tourism Marketing	12	5	605	32
Annals of Tourism Research	15	0	506	0
Tourism Management	10	4	445	11
Journal of Travel Research	4	0	208	0
Journal of Hospitality and Tourism Research	3	1	86	3
Totals	44	10	1,850	46

article titled "Marketing Crises in Tourism: Communication Strategies in the United States in Spain" by A. Gonzalez-Herrero and C. B. Pratt (1998) in *Public Relations Review* was cited four times; "Choosing the Right Words: The Development of Guidelines for the Selection of the 'Appropriate' Crisis-Response Strategies" by W. T. Coombs (1995) in *Management Communication Quarterly* was cited three times; and "When Fact and Fantasy Collide: Crisis Management in the Travel Industry" by C. K. Lehrman (1986) in *Public Relations Journal* was cited twice. No other article was cited more than once.

As for citations of risk and crisis public relations/communications books, *the Crisis Manager: Facing Risk and Responsibility* by Otto Lerbinger (1997) and *Strategic Communication in Crisis Management: Lessons from the Airline Industry* by Sally Ray (1999) were each cited twice. Books and book chapters cited once included *Accounts, Excuses and Apologies* by William Benoit (1995); *Responding to Crisis: A Rhetorical Approach to Crisis Communication* edited by Dan Millar and Robert Heath (2003), which included a chapter by J. E. Massey; *Crisis-response: Inside Stories on Managing Image Under Siege* by J. Gottschalk (1993); and *Ongoing Crisis Communication: Planning, Managing and Responding* by W. T. Coombs (1999).

Regarding citations of public relations-communications scholars, J. E. Massey was cited seven times (five were self citations) and L. T. Fall was cited six times (including five self citations). Authors each cited four times included W. T. Coombs, A. Gonzalez-Herrero, C. Pratt, and P. R. Ulmer. T. L. Sellnow was cited three times, and R. L. Heath, O. Lerbinger, and C. K. Lehrman were each cited twice.

CITATION ANALYSIS OF THREE TOURISM AND TRAVEL RISK CRISIS BOOKS CONDUCTED

Bibliographic references in three books, selected because "risk" and "crisis" appeared or were implied in their titles, were also reviewed for public relations/communication citations (findings are detailed in the Appendix). Dirk Glaesser's 2006 second edition of *Crisis Management in the Tourism Industry,* published in Oxford, England, cites a 1986 article on television coverage of natural disasters from *Journal of Communication*; a 1995 book titled *Public Relations* by Horst Avenarius published in Germany; the 2005 5th edition of *McQuail's Mass Communication Theory* book; a 1993 article published in German in *PR Magazin* [sic]; and a 2000 book titled *Advertising in Tourism and Leisure*. He also references a *Come back to Phuket!* press release issued by the Phuket Tourism Association a few weeks after the tragic tsunami hit Thailand's coast on Christmas Day 2004.

Patricia Goldstone's *Making the World Safe for Tourism*, published by Yale University Press in 2001, cites Bernays' *Biography of an Idea* memoir and his 1928 *Propaganda*; Ewen's *PR: A Social History of Spin*; David Finn's 1998 *The Way Forward: My First Fifty Years at Ruder Finn*, the eponymous New York-based PR firm which long has had numerous travel and tourism clients; Lippmann's classic *Public Opinion*, originally published in 1922; and *Jack O'Dwyer's Public Relations Newsletter*. Also cited are interviews conducted in 1999 with an assistant to the secretary-general of the United Nations, three travel and tourism industry executives, and three travel and tourism public relations practitioners.

Goldstone's book is a critical historical review of the politics of travel with damning but seemingly well-documented linkages motivated by profit among tourism, economic development in underdeveloped nations, the United Nations, the World Bank and the International Monetary Fund. These linkages may have had ethically and morally questionable consequences, such as the emergence of sex tourism in developing nations. The chapter titled "Have I Got a Country for You!" presents a litany of instances for which she justifiably castigates public relations for its dark-side deceptions and practices used to influence tourism policy and profits. Case studies of Cuba, Ireland, and the Middle East don't leave much room for citing public relations/communication risk and crisis scholarly research; this isn't that of kind of book. Still, chapter 4 makes an excellent cautionary tale for public relations scholars and practitioners.

David Beirman's 2003 *Restoring Tourism Destinations in Crisis: A Strategic Marketing Approach* did not cite any public relations or communications risk or crisis literature.

DISCUSSION

A scan of the Appendix suggests much of the travel and tourism scholarly literature makes sophisticated use of theory (such as Theory of Planned Behavior) and methods—from qualitative interviews, focus groups, historical and case study analyses to surveys and other quantitative methods; from descriptive statistics to more advanced statistics such as regression and path analyses. [See, for example, Hsu and Lin's (2005) article titled "Using Fuzzy Set Theoretic Techniques to Analyze Travel Risk: An Empirical Study" in *Tourism Management*, or Reisinger and Mavondo's (2005) article "Travel Anxiety and Intentions to Travel Internationally: Implications of Travel Risk Perception" in *Journal of Travel Research*.]

Results of the citation analysis conducted for this chapter suggest the *communication* component in the travel and tourism risk and crisis management literature from the public relations perspective is largely missing. Of the five travel and tourism journals analyzed, only three—*Journal of Travel and Tourism Marketing*, *Tourism Management*, and *Journal of Hospitality and Tourism Research*—used citations from public relations risk and crisis communications literature. However, several of the articles analyzed—and the readers of them—might have benefited greatly from inclusions of risk and crisis *communication* research.

Of the 10 articles analyzed with public relations risk and crisis literature citations, only one article cited the public relations literature to any extent, and it was authored by public relations scholars Lisa T. Fall, University of Tennessee Knoxville, and Joseph Eric Massey, then of California State University Fullerton. Many of the citations of the public relations literature in the other nine articles were dated, reaching back into the 1980s, and had a lag of three or more years between the time the articles with the cites were published and the articles cited were published.

More dismaying is the fact that the extensive risk and crisis research literature developed by public relations and communications scholars since 1995 is either nearly wholly unknown or ignored by the scholars conducting and publishing research about risk and crisis management in the travel and tourism literature. This neglect is surprising, since public relations practice seems to be playing an increasingly important role in the travel and tourism industry.

CRISIS MANAGEMENT VS. CRISIS COMMUNICATION

Fall and Massey (2005) made the point that crisis management and crisis communication "are two distinct fields. Crisis management is the strategic management activity that directs all technical and administrative activities during crisis, while crisis communication is the strategic management activity that directs all communication with internal and external stakeholders during crisis" (p. 80). The key word here may well be *management*. It is possible that the travel and tourism industry itself does not yet generally view public relations as a management function; this is an issue worthy of further investigation. Certainly, this analysis suggests that travel and tourism scholars do not recognize public relations as part of risk and crisis management.

Bill Faulkner's (2001) article, "Towards a Framework for Tourism Disaster Management" in *Tourism Management*, illustrates and typifies the point. Using chaos and complexity theoretical frames, Faulkner explicated "crisis" from the management literature; distinguished crises from disasters; reviewed responses and recovery strategies from a sociological perspective; explored measurement of effects on communities and communities' capacities to cope with crises and disasters; outlined stages of community response, impediments to disaster planning, and strategies to survive disasters; discussed several case studies; offered prerequisites for effective tourism disaster management planning; and presented a framework for managing disasters. However, Faulker only mentioned communication. He did not mention "public relations" at all, and he cited only the 1986 *Public Relations Journal* article, "When Fact and Fantasy Collide: Crisis Management in the Travel Industry," by Celia Lehrman, then assistant editor of the old PRSA trade magazine. In the article, Lehrman reported her interviews with editors of *Travel Weekly* and *Travel Agent* trade magazines and other industry sources about terrorism in the 1980s and other contemporary crises. Post-9/11, the article seems comparatively naïve, and, by 2000, presumably when Faulkner was writing his article, much more pertinent and comprehensive risk and crisis communication literature was available in the public relations and communications scholarly journals.

The 2006 second edition of *Crisis Management in the Tourism Industry* by Dirk Glaesser, Chief of Publications of the World Tourism Organization, published in Oxford, England, will likely be popular with the industry worldwide. It is disappointing, then, that the words "public relations" appear neither in the text nor the index. At least organizational charts in the chapter on crisis planning place corporate communications on the crisis management team, and responsibilities for the head of communications are outlined, including ensuring designation of the first and only official spokesperson, monitoring public opinion, preparing press conferences and releases, participating in meetings, responsibility for internal communications, etc.

In the chapter on "Crisis Management Instruments," the section about policy and recommended procedures for addressing risk and crisis communication comes last. None of the content is grounded in the public relations or communications literature, and some of it is simplistic: "Prepare a list with golden rules on how to handle clients in stressful situations (maximum two pages) so that they can be updated easily" (Glaesser, 2006, p. 219). In particular, the public relations literature could contribute useful guidelines for developing crisis messages. As it is, the only message suggestion in the book is a "first standby message" for media that "We are evaluating the situation" (Glaesser, 2006, p. 227).

IMPLICATIONS FOR PUBLIC RELATIONS SCHOLARS

What the results of this citation analysis mean for public relations scholars is that "opportunity knocks" with publication possibilities in the travel and tourism journals and books. Our body of knowledge holds great potential value for travel and tourism scholarship and practice, and it should be appreciated, particularly when presented in conjunction with case studies, used in more than half of the travel and tourism articles analyzed here. Conversely, having looked at some travel and tourism risk and crisis research, we can state unequivocally that literature could well inform our public relations scholarship.

Some public relations crisis communication research has used travel and tourism case studies published in public relations academic journals. One example is the case study comparison of crisis-response strategies used by marketing communications professionals in the United States and Spain by Gonzalez-Herrero and Pratt (1998), which this analysis found has been cited in the travel and tourism literature. Another example is Tilson and Stacks' (1997) study of the campaign strategies used in the late 1980s and early 1990s to counteract crimes against tourists in Miami-Dade County, Florida, which has not been cited in the travel and tourism literature, according to this analysis.

A third example is the study by Englehardt, Sallot, and Springston (2004) which tested the application of Coombs' (1995) crisis accident-decision flow chart with the case of the fatal crash of ValuJet's Flight 592 in the Florida Everglades on Mother's Day in 1996. Englehardt, et al. used Coombs' crisis response strategy theory and his accident-decision flow chart to develop expected strategic responses, such as "Our planes are safe" and "Our pilots are well-trained and experienced" to convey ingratiation, and "We've sent grief counselors to Miami and Atlanta to assist family and friends" and "We are sorry; our thoughts and prayers are with the victims' families" to express mortification (p. 136). A content analysis of 295 news items in two newspapers found that these kinds of corporate messages were issued by ValuJet and were covered by the press, primarily in the first week after the crash. The study successfully used a travel case to test the efficacy of crisis response messages and contributed to public relations crisis communication theory by concluding that the accident-decision flow chart lacked a necessary "compassion without blame" message strategy option. We can't speak for Professors Gonzalez-Herrero, Pratt, Tilson and Stacks, but Ms. Englehardt and the first and third authors of this chapter did not at the time consider submitting our research to a travel and tourism journal and, after this analysis, we think we should have.

The citation analysis reported in this chapter is obviously limited by covering only 12 of the 32 articles in the *Journal of Travel and Tourism Marketing* identified as addressing risk or crisis management or having "risk communication" or "crisis communication" in their titles, and only three travel and tourism books on risk and crisis management. Some also might argue that counting a citation such as Ashcroft's (1997) "Crisis Management: Public Relations" in *Journal of Managerial Psychology* is too liberal, skewing results, even though the article did itself heavily reference *PR Week* and *IPR Journal*.

CONCLUSION

Regardless of its limitations, this analysis strongly suggests public relations and travel and tourism academics are operating in what Broom (2006) terms closed scholarship systems and need more cross-fertilization. The travel and tourism risk and crisis literature would be better informed by referencing our public relations risk and crisis communication literature. Conversely, public relations risk and crisis communication scholars might well look to the travel and tourism industry for case studies for fertile testing grounds for publication of their research in public relations *and* travel and tourism academic journals, and public relations scholars can learn from the travel and tourism body of knowledge. Opportunity knocks. We just need to open the doors.

NOTES

1. Gurabardhi, et al. (2004) identified "nine most relevant" journals for risk communication which published five or more articles on the topic from 1988 to 2000. Of 104 journals which published the 349 articles analyzed, *Risk Analysis* published 42 articles. No public relations or communications journals appeared on the "most relevant" list.
2. P. Slovic published 11 articles to be "most productive" author and B. Fischoff published 10 articles as "second-most productive." Perhaps public relations and communications journals were not included as early as 1988 in the citation indices used by Gurabardhi, et al. (2004).
3. These five journals were also among the top six most widely read by marketing/sales and management/operations professionals in the two travel and tourism associations, who also read *International Journal of Tourism* Research. Three of these journals—*Annals of Tourism Research*, *Journal of Travel Research*, and *Tourism Management*—had been selected previously for analysis of statistical techniques used in tourism journals (Reid & Andereck, 1989).
4. Only 12 of the 32 articles in *Journal of Travel and Tourism Marketing* were available online, all from a special issue devoted to managing crisis response.

BIBLIOGRAPHY

Beirman, D. (2003). *Restoring tourism destinations in crisis: A strategic marketing approach.* Oxford, UK: CABI Publishing.

Benoit, W. L. (1995). *Accounts, excuses and apologies.* Albany, NY: State University of New York Press.

Broom, G. M. (2006). An open-system approach to building theory in public relations. *Journal of Public Relations Research, 18*(2), 141–150.

Burnett, J. J. (1998). A strategic approach to managing crises. *Public Relations Review, 24*(4), 475–488.

Coombs, W. T. (1995). Choosing the right words: The development of guidelines for the selection of the "appropriate" crisis-response strategies. *Management Communication Quarterly, 8*(4), 447–476.

Coombs, T. (1999). *Ongoing crisis communication: Planning, managing and responding.* Thousand Oaks, CA: Sage.

Englehardt, K. J., Sallot, L. M., & Springston, J. K. (2004). Compassion without blame: Testing the accident decision flow chart with the crash of ValuJet flight 592. *Journal of Public Relations Research, 16*(2), 127–157.

Fall, L. T., & Massey, J. E. (2005). The significance of crisis communication in the aftermath of 9/11: A national investigation of how tourism managers have re-tooled their promotional campaigns. *Journal of Travel and Tourism Marketing, 19*(2/3), 77–90.

Faulkner, B. (2001). Towards a framework for tourism disaster management. *Tourism Management, 22*(2), 135–147.

Frechtling, D. C. (2004). Assessment of tourism/hospitality journals' role in knowledge transfer: An exploratory study. *Journal of Travel Research, 43*(2), 100–107.

Glaesser, D. (2006). *Crisis management in the tourism industry* (2nd ed.). Oxford, UK: Elsevier.

Gonzalez-Herrero, A., & Pratt, C. B. (1998). Marketing crises in tourism: Communication strategies in the United State and Spain. *Public Relations Review, 24*(1), 83–97.

Goldstone, P. (2001). *Making the world safe for tourism.* New Haven, CT: Yale University Press.

Gottschalk, J. (1993). *Crisis-response: Inside stories on managing image under siege.* Detroit, MI: Gale Research.

Gurabardhi, Z., Gutteling, J. M., & Kuttschreuter, M. (2004). The development of risk communication: An empirical analysis of the literature in the field. *Science Communication, 25*(4), 323–349.

Heath, R. L. (2006, July 20). Personal communication and review of Heath's curriculum vitae.

Hsu, T.-H., & Lin, L.-Z. (2005). Using fuzzy set theoretic techniques to analyze travel risk: An empirical study. *Tourism Management*, listed online as *in press*.

Lehrman, C. K. (1986). When fact and fantasy collide: Crisis management in the travel industry. *Public Relations Journal*, 42(4), 25–28.

Lerbinger, O. (1997). *The crisis manager: Facing risk and responsibility.* Mahwah, NJ: Erlbaum.

Massey, J. E. (2003). Managing organizational images: Crisis response and legitimacy restoration. In D. P. Millar & R. L. Heath (Eds.) *Responding to crisis: A rhetorical approach to crisis communication* (pp. 233–246). Mahwah, NJ: Erlbaum.

Pavlik, J. (1987). *Public relations: What research tells us.* Newbury Park, CA: Sage.

Ray, S. (1999). *Strategic communication in crisis management: Lessons from the airline industry.* Westport, CT: Quorum Books.

Reid, L. J., & Anderek, K. L. (1989). Statistical analyses use in tourism research. *Journal of Travel Research, 27*(2), 21–24.

Reisinger, Y. & Mavondo, F. (2005). Travel anxiety and intentions to travel internationally: Implications of travel risk perception. *Journal of Travel Research, 43*(3), 212–225.

Sallot, L. M., Lyon, L. J., Acosta-Alzuru, C., & Jones, K. (2003). From aardvark to zebra: A new millennium analysis of theory development in public relations academic journals. *Journal of Public Relations Research, 15*(1), 27–90.

Sallot, L. M. (2005). Travel and tourism public relations. In R. L. Heath (Ed.), *Encyclopedia of Public Relations* (Vol. 2, pp. 861–863). Thousand Oaks, CA: Sage.

Tilson, D. J., & Stacks, D. W. (1997). To know us is to love us: The public relations campaign to sell a 'business-tourist-friendly' Miami. *Public Relations Review, 23*(2), 95–115.

Tourism 2020 Vision. (2006). World Tourism Organization, Madrid, Spain. Retrieved July 19, 2006, from http://www.world-tourism.org/facts/eng/vision.htm.

UNWTO World Tourism Barometer. (2006). *4*(2): World Tourism Organization, Madrid, Spain. Retrieved July 19, 2006, from http://www.world-tourism.org/publications.

UNWTO World Tourism Organization Market Research. (2006). Retrieved July 24, 2006, from http://www.world-tourism.org/market_research/facts/menu/html.

UNWTO World Tourism Organization Newsroom. (2007). World Tourism Organization, Madrid, Spain. Retrieved March 4, 2007, from http://www.world-tourism.org/newsroom/Releases/2007/january/recordyear.htm.

APPENDIX

The following articles were included in the citation analysis reported in this chapter. Citations from public relations or communications scholarly journals or books included in any article appear immediately after the article referenced.

From *Annals of Tourism Research*: 15 articles>506 citations>0 public relations-communications citations

Bhattarai, K., Conway, D., & Shrestha, N. (2005). Tourism, terrorism, and turmoil in Nepal. *Annals of Tourism Research, 32*(3), 669–688. 34 citations

Blake, A., & Sinclair, M. T. (2003). Tourism crisis management: US response to September 11. *Annals of Tourism Research, 30*(4), 813–832. 40 citations

De Albuquerque, K., McElroy, J. (1999). Tourism and crime in the Caribbean. *Annals of Tourism Research, 26*(4), 968–984. 41 citations

Floyd, M. F., & Pennington-Gray, L. (2004). Profiling risk perceptions of tourists. *Annals of Tourism Research, 31*(4), 1051–1054. 7 citations

Gonzalez, J. I., Morini, S., & Calatayud, F. P. (1999). How to cover risk in the hotel sector. *Annals of Tourism Research, 26*(3), 709–712. 8 citations

Harper, D. W. (2001). Comparing tourists crime victimization. *Annals of Tourism Research, 28*(4), 1053–1056. 9 citations

Herold, E., Garcia, R., & DeMoya, T. (2001). Female tourists and beach boys: Romance or sex tourism? *Annals of Tourism Research, 28*(4), 978–997. 18 citations

Hunter-Jones, P. (2005). Cancer and tourism. *Annals of Tourism Research, 32*(1), 70–92. 58 citations

Lepp, A., & Gibson, H. (2003). Tourist roles, perceived risk, and international tourism. *Annals of Tourism Research, 30*(3), 606–624. 84 citations

McKercher, B. (2004). The over-reaction to SARS and the collapse of Asian tourism. *Annals of Tourism Research, 31*(3), 716–719. 11 citations

Okumus, F., & Karamustafa, K. (2005). Impact of an economic crisis: Evidence from Turkey. *Annals of Tourism Research, 32*(4), 942–961. 33 citations

Oppermann, M. (1999). Sex tourism. *Annals of Tourism Research, 26*(2), 251–266. 60 citations

Page, S. J., Bentley, T., & Walker, L. (2005). Tourist safety in New Zealand and Scotland. *Annals of Tourism Research, 32*(1), 150–166. 35 citations

Soemodinoto, A., Wong, P. P., Saleh, M. (2001). Effects of prolonged political unrest on tourism. *Annals of Tourism Research, 28*(4), 1056–1060. 12 citations

Tzung-Cheng, H., Beaman, J., & Shelby, L. (2004). No-escape natural disaster: Mitigating impacts on tourism. *Annals of Tourism Research, 32*(2), 255–273. 56 citations

From *Journal of Hospitality and Tourism Research*: 3 articles>86 citations>3 public relations-communications citations

Hoffman, K. D., & Chung, B. G. (1999). Hospitality recovery strategies: Customer preference versus firm use. *Journal of Hospitality and Tourism Research 23*(1), 71–84. 27 citations

Milman, A., Jones, F., & Bach, S. (1999). The impact of security devices on tourists' perceived safety: The central Florida example. *Journal of Hospitality and Tourism Research 23*(4), 371–386. 22 citations

Reynolds, D, & Balinbin, W. M. (2003). Mad cow disease: An empirical investigation of restaurant strategies and consumer response. *Journal of Hospitality and Tourism Research 27*(3), 358–368. 37 citations

Sellnow, T. L., & Ulmer, R. R. (1995). Ambiguous argument as advocacy in organizational crisis communication. *Argumentation & Advocacy, 31*, 138–150.

Sparks, V. M., & Winter, J. P. (1980). Public interest in foreign news. *International Journal for Mass Communication Studies, 26*, 149.

Ulmer, R. R., & Sellnow, T. L. (2000). Consistent questions of ambiguity in organizational crisis communication: Jack in the Box as a case study. *Journal of Business Ethics, 25*, 143–155.

From *Journal of Travel Research*: 4 articles>208 citations>0 public relations-communications citations

Pizam, A., & Fleischer, A. (2002). Severity vs. frequency in acts of terrorism: Which has a larger impact on tourism demand? *Journal of Travel Research, 40*, 337–339. 16 citations

Reisinger, Y. & Mavondo, F. (2005). Travel anxiety and intentions to travel internationally: Implications of travel risk perception. *Journal of Travel Research, 43*(3), 212–225. 104 citations

Richter, L. K. (2003). International tourism and its global health consequences. *Journal of Travel Research, 41*(2), 340–347. 51 citations

Sonmez, S. F. (1999). Tourism in crisis: Managing the effects of terrorism. *Journal of Travel Research, 38*, 13–18. 37 citations

From *Journal of Travel and Tourism Marketing*: 12 articles>605 citations>32 public relations-communications citations

Cooper, M. (2005). Japanese Tourism and the SARS Epidemic of 2003. *Journal of Travel and Tourism Marketing, 19*(2/3), 117–131. 34 citations

Eugenio-Martin, J. L., Sinclair, M. T., & Yeoman, I. (2005). Quantifying the effects of tourism crises An application to Scotland. *Journal of Travel and Tourism Marketing, 19*(2/3), 21–34. 68 citations

Argenti, P. (2002). Crisis communication–lesson from 9/11. *Harvard Business Review*, 12, 103–109.

Coombs, W. T. (1995). The development of guidelines for the selection of the "appropriate" crisis response strategies. *Management Communication Quarterly, 4*, 447–476. [author's name was misspelled as "Coombes" and "Choosing the Right Words:" was omitted from the title]

Ray, S. (1999). *Strategic communication in crisis management: Lessons from the airline industry*. Westport, CT: Quorum Books.

Fall, L. T., & Massey, J. E. (2005). The Significance of Crisis Communication in the Aftermath of 9/11 A National Investigation of How Tourism Managers Have Re-Tooled Their Promotional Campaigns. *Journal of Travel and Tourism Marketing, 19*(2/3), 77–90. 51 citations

Allen, W. M., & Caillouet, R. H. (1994). Legitimation endeavors: Impression management strategies used by an organization in crisis. *Communication Monographs, 61*, 44–62.

Andereck, K., & Caldwell, L. (1993). The influence of tourists' characteristics on ratings of information sources for an attraction. In M. Uysal & D. Fesenmaier (Eds.), *Communication and channel systems in tourism marketing* (pp. 171–189). New York: The Haworth Press.

Benoit, W. L. (1995). *Accounts, excuses and apologies*. Albany, NY: State University of New York Press.

Caywood, C., & Stocker, K. P. (1993). The ultimate crisis plan. In J. Gottschalk (Ed.), *Crisis-response: Inside stories on managing image under siege*. Detroit: Gale Research.

Coombs, W. T. (1995). Choosing the right words: The development of guidelines for the selection of the "appropriate" crisis-response strategies. *Management Communication Quarterly, 8*(4), 447–476.

Coombs, W. T. (2002). Designing post-crisis messages: Lessons for crisis-response strategies. *Review of Business, 21*(3/4), 37–41.

DeFleur, M., & Ball-Rokeach, S. (1975). *Theories of mass communication*. New York: David McKay.

Fall, L. T. (1996). The crisis of Hurricane Hugo as it relates to public relations. In *Earth, wind, fire and water: Approaching natural disaster*. Lawrenceville, NJ: Open Door Publishers.

Fall, L. T. (2000a). An exploratory study of the relationship between human value and information sources within a tourism framework. *Journal of Hospitality & Leisure Marketing, 7*(1), 3–28.

Fall, L. T. (2000b). *Segmenting pleasure travelers on the basis of information source usefulness and personal value importance*. Unpublished doctoral dissertation. Michigan State University, Michigan.

Fall, L. T. (2004). A public relations segmentation study: Using Grunig's nested segmentation model and Yankelovich's generational influences model to distinguish vacation traveler publics. *Journal of Hospitality & Leisure Marketing, 11*(1), 5–30.

Hearit, K. M. (1995). "Mistakes were made": Organizations, apologia and crises of social legitimacy. *Communication Studies, 46*(1/2), 1–17.

Heath, R. L., Leth, S. A., & Nathan, K. (1994). Communicating service quality improvement: Another role for public relations. *Public Relations Review, 20*(1), 29–40.

Kinser, K., & Fall, L. T. (2005). Lions and tigers and bears, oh my! An examination of membership communication programs among our nation's zoos. *Journal of Hospitality & Leisure Marketing, 12*(1/2), 57–77.

Massey, J. E. (2001). Managing legitimacy: Communication strategies for organizations in crisis. *Journal of Business Communication, 38*(2), 153–183.

Massey, J. E. (2002). The airline industry in crisis. In J. Biberman & A. Alkhafaji (Eds.), *Business research yearbook, 9* (pp. 727–732). Saline, MI: McNaughton & Gunn.

Massey, J. E. (2003). Managing organizational images: Crisis response and legitimacy restoration. In D. Millar & R. L. Heath (Eds.), *Responding to crisis: A rhetorical approach to crisis communication* (pp. 233–246). Mahwah, NJ: Erlbaum.

Massey, J. E. (2005). The airline industry in crisis: Analyzing the response to the September 11th attacks on the U.S. *Journal of Hospitality & Leisure Marketing, 12*(1/2), 97–114.

Massey, J. E., & Larsen, J. (in press). Crisis management in real time: How to successfully plan for and respond to crisis. *Journal of Promotion Management*.

Massey, J. E., Simonson, K., Ward, D., & Campbell, A. (2004, June). United Airlines' image restoration strategies: A discourse of renewal. In *Conference on Corporate Communication, 2004 Proceedings* (pp. 249–258).

McCombs, M., & Shaw, D. L. (1972). The agenda-setting function of mass media. *Public Opinion Quarterly, 36*(2), 176–187.

Rise, A., & Rise, L. (2002). *The fall of advertising and the rise of PR*. New York: Harper Business.

Seeger, M. W., & Ulmer, P. R. (2001). Virtuous responses to organizational crisis: Aaron Feuerstein and Milt Cole. *Journal of Business Ethics, 31*, 369–376.

Stacks, D. W., & Carroll, T. B. (2005). Travel-tourism public relationships: One step forward, two steps back. *Journal of Hospitality & Leisure Marketing, 12*(1/2), 3–8.

Ulmer, P. R., & Sellnow, T. L. (2002). Crisis management and the discourse of renewal: Understanding the potential for positive outcomes of crisis. *Public Relations Review, 28*, 361–365.

Irvine, W., & Anderson, A. R. (2005). The impacts of Foot and Mouth Disease on a peripheral tourism area: The role and effect of crisis management. *Journal of Travel and Tourism Marketing, 19*(2/3), 47–60. 79 citations

Gonzalez-Herrero, A., & Pratt, C. B. (1998). Marketing crises in tourism: Communication strategies in the United State and Spain. *Public Relations Review, 24*(1), 83–97.

Lerbinger, O. (1997). *The crisis manager: Facing risk and responsibility*. Mahwah, NJ: Erlbaum.

Laws E., & Prideaux, B. (2005). Crisis management: A suggested typology. *Journal of Travel and Tourism Marketing, 19*(2/3), 1–8. 38 citations

Fall, L. T., & Massey, J. E. (2005). The significance of crisis communication in the aftermath of 9/11: A national investigation of how tourism managers have re-tooled their promotional campaigns. *Journal of Travel and Tourism Marketing*, Special issue: Crises, 2/3, 79–92.

Leslie, D., & Black, L. (2005). Tourism and the impact of the Foot and Mouth epidemic in the UK Reactions, Responses and realities with particular reference to Scotland. *Journal of Travel and Tourism Marketing, 19*(2/3), 35–46. 47 citations

McKercher, B., & Pine, R. (2005). Privation as a Stimulus to Travel Demand? *Journal of Travel and Tourism Marketing, 19*(2/3), 107 – 115. 44 citations

Peters, M., & Pikkemaat, B. (2005). Crisis management in Alpine winter sports resorts—The 1999 Avalanche Disaster in Tyrol. *Journal of Travel and Tourism Marketing, 19*(2/3), 9–20. 61 citations

Ross, G. F. (2005). Tourism industry employee workstress-A present and future crisis. *Journal of Travel and Tourism Marketing, 19*(2/3), 133–147. 101 citations

Scott, N., & Laws, E. (2005). Tourism crises and disasters enhancing understanding of system effects. *Journal of Travel and Tourism Marketing, 19*(2/3), 149–158. 43 citations

Smith, W. W., & Carmichael, B. A. (2005). Canadian seasonality and domestic travel patterns regularities and dislocations as a result of the events of 9/11. *Journal of Travel and Tourism Marketing, 19*(2/3), 61–76. 28 citations

Yu, L., Stafford, G., & Armoo, A. K. (2005). A study of crisis management strategies of hotel managers in the Washington, D.C. metro area. *Journal of Travel and Tourism Marketing, 19*(2/3), 91–105. 11 citations

Lerbinger, O. (1997). *The crisis manager: Facing risk and responsibility*. Mahwah, NJ: Erlbaum.

From *Tourism Management*: 10 articles>445 citations>11 public relations-communications citations

Callander, M., & Page, S. J. (2003). Managing risk in adventure tourism operations in New Zealand: A review of the legal case history and potential for litigation. *Tourism Management, 24*(1), 13–23. 35 citations

Incorrectly cites: Bovet, S. (1994). Safety concerns world travel market. *Public Relations Review, 50*(3), 8; probably meant to be *Public Relations Journal*.

Cater, C. I. (2006). Playing with Risk? Participant perceptions of risk and management implications in adventure tourism. *Tourism Management, 27*(2), 317–325. 43 citations

Faulkner, B. (2001). Towards a framework for tourism disaster management. *Tourism Management, 22*(2), 135–147. 56 citations

Cites: Gonzalez-Herrero, A., & Pratt, C. B. (1998). Marketing crises in tourism: Communication strategies in the United State and Spain. *Public Relations Review, 24*(1), 83–97.

Also cites: Lehrman, C. K. (1986). When fact and fantasy collide: Crisis management in the travel industry. *Public Relations Journal*, 42(4), 25–28.

Faulkner, B., & Vikulov, S. (2001). Katherine, washed out one day, back on track the next: A post-mortem of a tourism disaster. *Tourism Management, 22*(4), 331–344. 20 citations

Goodrich, J. N. (2002). September 11, 2001 attack on America: a record of the immediate impacts and reactions in the USA travel and tourism industry. *Tourism Management, 23*(6), 573–580. 28 citations

Henderson, J. C. (2003). Communicating in a crisis: Flight SQ 006. *Tourism Management, 24*(3), 279–287. 61 citations

Cites: Gonzalez-Herrero, A., & Pratt, C. B. (1998). Marketing crises in tourism: Communication strategies in the United State and Spain. *Public Relations Review, 24*(1), 83–97.

Ray, S. (1999). *Strategic communication in crisis management: Lessons from the airline industry*. Westport, CT: Quorum Books.

Also cites: Lehrman, C. K. (1986). When fact and fantasy collide: Crisis management in the travel industry. *Public Relations Journal*, 42(4), 25–28.

Hsu, T.-H., & Lin, L.-Z. (2005). Using fuzzy set theoretic techniques to analyze travel risk: An empirical study. *Tourism Management*, listed online as *in press*. 60 citations

Peattie, S., Clarke, P., & Peattie, K. (2005). Risk and responsibility in tourism: Promoting sun-safety. *Tourism Management, 26*(3), 399–408. 30 citations

Ritchie, B. W. (2004). Chaos, crises and disasters: A strategic approach to crisis management in the tourism industry. (2004). *Tourism Management, 25*(6), 669–683. 57 citations

Cites: Burnett, J. J. (1998). A strategic approach to managing crises. *Public Relations Review, 24*(4), 475–488.

Coombs, T. (1999). *Ongoing crisis communication: Planning, managing and responding*. Thousand Oaks, CA: Sage.

Gonzalez-Herrero, A., & Pratt, C. B. (1998). Marketing crises in tourism: Communication strategies in the United States and Spain. *Public Relations Review, 24*(1), 83–97.

Marra, F. (1998). Crisis communication plans: Poor predictors of excellent crisis public relations. *Public Relations Review, 24*(4), 461–474.

Also cited: Ashcroft, R. (1997). Crisis management: Public relations. *Journal of Managerial Psychology*, 12(5), 325–332.

Wilks, J., & Davis, R. J. (2000). Risk management for scuba diving operators on Australia's great barrier reef. *Tourism Management, 21*(6), 591–599. 55 citations

Books

Bibliographic references of the following books were analyzed for citations from public relations or communications scholarly journals or books. Citations found appear after the book.

Beirman, D. (2003). *Restoring tourism destinations in crisis: A strategic marketing approach.* Oxford, UK: CABI Publishing.

Glaesser, D. (2006). *Crisis management in the tourism industry*, 2nd ed. Oxford, UK: Elsevier.

Cites: Adams, W. (1986). "Whose lives count? TV coverage of natural disasters," *Journal of Communication*, 36(2), 113–122.

Avenarius, H. (1995). *Public Relations*. Wissenschaftliche Buchgesellschaft, Darmstadt.

Mathes, R., Gartner, H.-D., & Czaplicki, A. (1993). Krisenkommunikation Teil 1. *PR Magazin* (sic), *24*(11), 31–38.

McQuail, D. (2005). *McQuail's Mass Communication Theory*, 5th ed. London: Sage.

Morgan, N., & Pritchard, A. (2000). *Advertising in Tourism and Leisure*. Oxford, UK: Butterworth-Heinemann.

Come back to Phuket! (2005). Press release issued January 18, 2005. Phuket, Thailand: Phuket Tourism Association

Goldstone, P. (2001). *Making the world safe for tourism*. New Haven, CT: Yale University Press.

Cites: Bernays, E. (1965). *Biography of an idea: Memoirs of public relations counsel.* New York: Simon and Schuster.

Bernays, E. (1928). *Propaganda*. New York: H. Liveright.

Ewen, S. (1996). *PR: A social history of spin*. New York: Basic.

Finn, D. (1998). *The way forward: My first fifty years at Ruder Finn*. New York: Millwood.

Lippmann, W. (1922/1991). *Public opinion*. New Brunswick, NJ: Transaction Publishers.

O'Dwyer, J. (1998). *Jack O'Dwyer's Public Relations Newsletter*. New York.

Also cited are interviews conducted in 1999 with:

Gregg Anderson, then head of New Zealand Tourist Board 's North American office; Peggy Bendel, then senior vice president of travel for DCI, PR firm for the South African Tourist Board;

David Finn, a founding partner of Ruder Finn;

Cord Hansen-Sturm, then director of the Middle Eastern and Mediterranean Travel and Tourism Association and former American Express executive;

James Harff, then director of Washington-based Ruder Finn Global Public Affairs office;

John Ruggie, then assistant to the secretary-general, United Nations, then a pro bono client of Ruder Finn; and Nazli Weiss, of the Rebuild Dubrovnik Fund, then a pro bono client of Ruder Finn.

Index

Page numbers in italics refer to figures or tables.

T